P_c	Conversion price
P_f	Price of good in foreign country
P_h	Price of good in home country
P/E	Price/earnings ratio
PMT	Payment of an annuity
PPP	Purchasing power parity
PV	Present value
PVA_N	Present value of an annuity for N years
Q	Quantity produced or sold
Q_{BE}	Breakeven quantity
r	(1) A percentage discount rate, or cost of capital; also referred to as I
	(2) Nominal risk-adjusted required rate of return
$\bar{r}$	"r bar," historic, or realized, rate of return
$\hat{r}$	"r hat," an expected rate of return
r*	Real risk-free rate of return
r_d	Before-tax cost of debt
r_e	Cost of new common stock (outside equity)
r_f	Interest rate in foreign country
r_h	Interest rate in home country
r_i	Required return for an individual firm or security
r_M	Return for "the market," or an "average" stock
r_{NOM}	Nominal rate of interest; also referred to as I_{NOM}
r_p	(1) Cost of preferred stock
	(2) Portfolio's return
r_{PER}	Periodic rate of return
r_{RF}	Rate of return on a risk-free security
r_s	(1) Cost of retained earnings
	(2) Required return on common stock
ρ	Correlation coefficient; also denoted as R when using historical data
ROA	Return on assets
ROE	Return on equity
RP	Risk premium
RP_M	Market risk premium
RR	Retention rate
S	(1) Sales
	(2) Estimated standard deviation for sample data
SML	Security Market Line
Σ	Summation sign
σ	Standard deviation
σ^2	Variance
t	Time period
T	Marginal income tax rate
TV_N	A stock's horizon, or terminal, value
TIE	Times interest earned
V	Variable cost per unit
V_B	Bond value
V_p	Value of preferred stock
VC	Total variable costs
WACC	Weighted averaged cost of capital
X	Exercise price of option
YTC	Yield to call
YTM	Yield to maturity

DON'T THROW THIS CARD AWAY!
THIS MAY BE REQUIRED FOR YOUR COURSE!

THOMSON ONE | Business School Edition

Congratulations!

Your purchase of this NEW textbook includes complimentary access to THOMSON ONE – Business School Edition for Finance. THOMSON ONE – Business School Edition is a Web-based portal product that provides integrated access to Thomson Financial content for the purpose of financial analysis. This is an educational version of the same financial resources used by Wall Street analysts on a daily basis!

For hundreds of companies, this online resource provides seamless access to:

- **Current and Past Company Data:** Worldscope which includes company profiles, financials and accounting results, market per-share data, annual information, and monthly prices going back to 1980.

- **Financial Analyst Data and Forecasts:** I/B/E/S Consensus Estimates which provides consensus estimates, analyst-by-analyst earnings coverage, and analysts' forecasts.

- **SEC Disclosure Statements:** Disclosure SEC Database which includes company profiles, annual and quarterly company financials, pricing information, and earnings.

- **And More!**

Copyright ©2005 by South-Western, a division of Thomson Learning.
Thomson Learning is a trademark used herein under license.
ISBN-13: 978-0-3242-3596-8
ISBN-10: 0-324-23596-8

THOMSON
SOUTH-WESTERN

THOMSON ONE
Business School Edition

SERIAL NUMBER

PØGSP36PP3H55H

HOW TO REGISTER YOUR SERIAL NUMBER

1. Launch a web browser and go to **http://tobsefin.swlearning.com**

2. Click the "Register" button to enter your serial number.

3. Enter your serial number **exactly** as it appears here and create a unique User ID, or enter an existing User ID if you have previously registered for a different South-Western product via a serial number.

4. When prompted, create a password (or enter an existing password, if you have previously registered for a different product via a serial number.) Submit the necessary information when prompted. **Record your User ID and password in a secure location.**

5. Once registered, return to the URL above and select the "Enter" button; have your User ID and password handy.

For technical support, contact 1-800-423-0563 or email **tl.support@thomson.com**

Fundamentals of Financial Management

Eleventh Edition

Eugene F. Brigham
University of Florida

Joel F. Houston
University of Florida

THOMSON
SOUTH-WESTERN

Australia · Brazil · Canada · Mexico · Singapore · Spain · United Kingdom · United States

THOMSON

SOUTH-WESTERN

Fundamentals of Financial Management, Eleventh Edition
Eugene F. Brigham and Joel F. Houston

VP/Editorial Director:
Jack W. Calhoun

Editor-in-Chief:
Alex von Rosenberg

Executive Editor:
Michael R. Reynolds

Senior Developmental Editor:
Elizabeth R. Thomson

Senior Production Project Manager:
Deanna Quinn

Senior Marketing Communications Manager:
Jim Overly

Senior Media Technology Editor:
Vicky True

Senior Technology Project Editor:
Matthew McKinney

Web Site Coordinator:
Karen Schaffer

Senior Print Buyer:
Sandee Milewski

Production House:
Elm Street Publishing Services, Inc.

Compositor:
Lachina Publishing Services, Inc.

Printer:
R. R. Donnelley, Willard, OH

Art Director:
Bethany Casey

Internal Designer:
Stratton Design

Cover Designer:
Stratton Design

Cover Illustration:
Stratton Design

Photography Manager:
Deanna Ettinger

Photo Researcher:
Robin Samper

Library of Congress Control Number:
2005908954

For more information about our products, contact us at:

Thomson Learning
Academic Resource Center

1-800-432-0563

Thomson Higher Education
5191 Natorp Boulevard
Mason, OH 45040
USA

PREFACE

When the first edition of *Fundamentals* was published 28 years ago, we wanted to provide an introductory text that students would find interesting and understandable. *Fundamentals* immediately became the leading undergraduate finance text, and it has maintained that position ever since. Our goal with this edition has been to produce a book and ancillary package that will maintain its lead and set a new standard for finance textbooks.

Important changes in the financial environment have occurred since the last edition. New technology and increased globalization continue to transform practices and markets. Continued improvements in communications and transportation have made it easier for businesses to operate on a worldwide basis—a company can be headquartered in New York; develop products in India; manufacture them in China; and sell them in the United States, Europe, and the rest of the world. This has led to major changes in the labor market, especially to an increase in outsourcing, which has resulted in generally lower consumer prices, but it has caused job losses for some U.S. workers and gains for others. There have also been dramatic rises and falls in the stock market, and interest rates have plunged to record lows even as energy prices hit historic highs. Corporate scandals have led to the downfall of such giants as Enron, WorldCom, and AT&T, and this has led to important changes in the laws governing corporate management and financial reporting, as well as to equally important changes in managerial compensation. These issues are discussed in this edition of *Fundamentals*, where we analyze them from financial and ethical perspectives.

VALUATION FOCUS

The primary goal of financial management is to help managers maximize their firms' values. Therefore, the concept of valuation underlies everything in *Fundamentals*. In Chapter 1 we discuss the concept of valuation and explain its dependency on future cash flows and risk, and we show why value maximization is good for society in general. We also discuss the importance of ethical conduct and the consequences of unethical behavior, which include ruined businesses, financial losses for investors, and jail terms for guilty managers. We also explain how incentive compensation, along with the threat of takeovers, can be used to motivate managers to act in the interests of both stockholders and society at large.

The valuation theme is continued throughout the text. In Chapter 2, we take up the time value of money (TVM), a fundamental concept that underlies all of finance. The basic valuation equation as developed in Chapter 2 requires inputs—a set of cash flows in the numerator and a discount rate in the denominator. Therefore, in Chapters 3 and 4 we review basic accounting, including a discussion of cash flows and ways to analyze financial statements.

Of course, values are not established in a vacuum—stock and bond values are determined in the financial markets, so an understanding of those markets and the way they operate is essential to anyone working in finance. Therefore, in Chapter 5, we discuss the major types of financial markets, the returns that investors have historically earned in those markets, and the risks inherent in different securities. We then cover, in Chapter 6, interest rates and the factors that influence them—risk, inflation, liquidity, and the supply of and demand for capital. This leads directly into a discussion of bonds and bond valuation, in

Chapter 7. Next, in Chapter 8, we discuss risk and returns in the stock market, beginning with the risk of a stock held in isolation and then moving on to the risk of stocks held in portfolios. We then explain, in Chapter 9, how common stocks are valued.

With this background, in subsequent chapters we explain the financial tools and techniques managers use to help maximize their firms' values. Included are chapters on capital budgeting, the optimal capital structure, dividend policy, working capital, and financial forecasting. The final section of the book consists of four chapters that deal with derivatives, multinational finance, hybrid securities, and mergers.

Our organization has four important advantages:

Four important advantages of the Eleventh Edition's organization.

1. Covering TVM and valuation early helps students see how expected future cash flows, along with risk-adjusted discount rates, determine the value of the firm. Also, it takes time for students to digest TVM concepts and to learn how to do the required calculations, and providing this time is another benefit of early TVM coverage.
2. Structuring the book around markets and valuation enhances continuity and helps students see how the various topics are related to one another.
3. Most students—even those who do not plan to major in finance—are interested in stock and bond values, rates of return, and the like. Because the ability to learn is a function of individual interest and motivation, and because *Fundamentals* covers securities and security markets early, our organization is pedagogically sound.
4. Once the basic concepts have been established, it is easier for students to understand both how and why corporations make specific capital budgeting, financing, and working capital decisions.

SIGNIFICANT CHANGES IN THE ELEVENTH EDITION

A good working knowledge of finance is essential for success in business, regardless of one's specific job, because everything from marketing to human services is related to financial issues. This makes it important for anyone who plans to work in business to learn the fundamentals of finance. However, reading a finance text is different from reading a novel—one must focus on essential concepts and then work related problems to see how things tie together. For example, inflation affects interest rates, which affect stock and bond prices, which affect the feasibility of capital expenditures. To understand these relationships one must learn some basic principles and then work through problems to see how the various factors interact with one another.

Students sometimes find finance relatively abstract, and they don't see its relevance to them. This makes it difficult for professors to get students to do the work necessary to see just how interesting and relevant it really is. Based on our own and others' teaching experiences, in this edition we took a number of steps to alleviate this problem:

■ *Increased student interest.* Students learn a subject best if they find it interesting, so we need to get them excited about finance. To help here, we use examples that illustrate how successful corporations apply financial principles plus examples that show how firms sometimes go astray and fail. We also explain how financial concepts can help one make better personal decisions, ranging from choosing a job, to investing, to deciding whether to lease or buy a car.

- *Provided clear explanations.* Students justifiably become frustrated and lose interest if a subject is not explained clearly. We have always tried to provide a clear, well-written text, but in this edition we used computer technology to help us make significant improvements. First, the entire book was put on electronic files, which enabled us to edit and re-edit to get the writing as clear as possible. Second, we solved all of the numerical examples with *Excel*, and this helped us tweak the numbers to make the examples more clear and consistent. Third, we shifted sections around to improve the flow both within the chapters and from one chapter to the next. In total, these changes will help students learn more in less time, which will reduce their stress and thus increase their interest and comprehension.

- *Provided timely within-chapter self-tests.* Much of finance involves numerical problems, so students must learn a concept, then become familiar with formulas, and then learn how to apply the formulas to solve specific problems. In our earlier editions, we explained and illustrated the concepts within the chapters, then provided a set of end-of-chapter problems that students could use to practice and test their knowledge. Unfortunately, students learned the concepts and understood the examples when they read the text, but by the time they got to the end-of-chapter problems they had forgotten much and had to go back and re-read the text. With this edition, we provide questions and problems (with answers) immediately after each section, which permits students to work with the concepts while things are still fresh on their minds. Again, this facilitates the learning process.

- *Ranked end-of-chapter problems by difficulty.* In past editions we arranged the end-of-chapter problems by topic, not by difficulty level. Students would often start working the problems, hit a difficult one relatively quickly, become frustrated, and give up. In this edition we arranged the problems by difficulty, identifying the first set as "Easy" ones that most students should be able to work without too much trouble; then "Intermediate" problems that are a bit harder; and then "Challenging" problems that are longer, more complex, and will perhaps require some help from the instructor. This new setup again reduces students' stress and frustration.

- *Improved the* Test Bank. The *Test Bank* has been improved substantially, and many questions and problems that resemble the easy and intermediate end-of-chapter problems have been added. Moreover, as discussed later in this Preface, many of the problems can be algorithmically modified to create an almost infinite number of alternative versions, with different answers, for a given problem. Different instructors have different views on the way students should be tested, but the new *Test Bank* and related testing material can be used to provide students with a set of relatively straightforward problems that deal with all aspects of financial management to help them study for the exams. They will then see that if they work hard and learn how to solve the various types of problems, they will have a good grasp of finance and, consequently, should do well on exams that consist primarily of straightforward (easy and intermediate) problems. Most instructors also use a few "challenging" exam problems, where students must figure out how to apply finance concepts to deal with new and different situations they haven't seen before. The "challenging" end-of-chapter problems are representative of this type of exam problem, and a number of them are provided in the *Test Bank*.

- *Coordinated the text, problems, and* Test Bank. Students should be rewarded for their efforts, and they become frustrated if they study hard, learn how to answer most of the problems in the text, and then face an exam where the problems are different from what they have been studying. To alleviate this problem, we have consciously coordinated the text examples, within-chapter self-tests, end-of-chapter problems, and *Test Bank* questions and problems. If students read the text carefully and work the self-test problems, they should be able to work most of the easy end-of-chapter problems, which should prepare them for the intermediate problems, which should help with the challenging problems. Thus, students who work hard should do well on exams based on the *Test Bank*.

■ *Improved coverage of the time value of money.* As noted earlier, the time value of money is the most important concept in finance, as it underlies stock and bond valuation, capital budgeting, cost of capital, lease analysis, and other key topics. However, students often have trouble grasping the basics of TVM, and this makes it almost impossible to do well in the course. To help alleviate this problem, we have taken the following steps:

• We moved TVM forward, from Chapter 6 to Chapter 2. This gives students time to digest TVM concepts before they must use them in the bond, stock, and capital budgeting chapters.

• As noted earlier, we added self-test *problems*, with solutions, at the end of each section. This helps students check their understanding of each type of problem before moving on.

• We explain the basic TVM functions using a five-step procedure: We show a time line setup, go through a numerical step-by-step solution, explain a formula that simplifies the step-by-step approach, explain how the formula is programmed into a calculator and how the inputs can be entered to solve the problem very efficiently, and then (as an optional exercise) show how the problem can be worked using *Excel*. This procedure helps students see exactly what each function does, understand the mathematics of the solution process, and see how calculators (and *Excel*) can be used to solve TVM problems. This procedure helps avoid the "black box" problem, where students get answers with a calculator but don't really know what's happening and consequently can't work problems that deviate from those whose solutions they have memorized.

• We also developed revised calculator tutorials for the most popular TI and HP calculators. The tutorial illustrations are identical to our within-text examples, so when a student reads about, say, the future value in the text, he or she can simultaneously learn from the tutorial how to find the FV with a calculator. Students tell us that learning how to use their calculators as they learn TVM concepts is much more efficient than studying the two separately.

• The TVM chapter introduces concepts covered in the bond, stock, and capital budgeting chapters, and this makes coverage of those chapters more efficient. For example, we illustrate the present values in the TVM chapter with the same cash flows that are later used in the bond, stock, and capital budgeting chapters, so in those later chapters we can refer students back to TVM for a quick refresher on the concept and solution technique.

■ *Clarified capital budgeting.* This is another key concept, but again one that students have found difficult. In particular, they have trouble understanding the differences between ranking criteria such as the net present value and the internal rate of return methods. In this edition, we begin by discussing the NPV method, tie it back to the TVM chapter, explain why it's the best ranking criterion, and then explain how the other criteria supplement the NPV. This structure reduces confusion students had in the past and gives them a better understanding of capital budgeting.

■ *Reorganized the discussion of the financial environment.* Chapter 4 in the last edition was too long to be covered in a reasonable length of time. In this edition, we divided the chapter into two segments, one on financial markets and institutions and a second one that deals with interest rates and their determinants. The second chapter leads us into bond valuation.

- *Streamlined the discussion of working capital.* Current assets make up about half of the average firm's assets, and most students' first job after graduation is likely to deal with some aspect of working capital. However, this topic is often not covered in the introductory finance course, which means that nonfinance majors never cover it at all (and it may also be skipped in advanced finance courses). We concluded that our coverage was so long, detailed, and indeed boring that many instructors simply skipped it. We totally rewrote the working capital material and cover the key points in a logical and succinct manner. Reviewers unanimously agreed that the new chapter was considerably better than the two old ones, and two reviewers even said that they enjoyed reading the chapter!

RELATIONSHIP TO OTHER THOMSON/SOUTH-WESTERN BOOKS

The growing body of financial knowledge makes it impossible to include everything about financial management that one might desire in one textbook. This led Gene Brigham to coauthor two other texts that deal with materials that go beyond what can be covered in an introductory course. The first of these is a comprehensive book aimed primarily at MBAs, *Financial Management: Theory and Practice*, Eleventh Edition, coauthored with Michael C. Ehrhardt. The second is an upper-level undergraduate text, *Intermediate Financial Management*, Ninth Edition, coauthored with Phillip R. Daves. In addition, Brigham and Houston teamed up with Roy Crum to write a text focused on financial management in an international setting, *Fundamentals of International Finance*, published by Thomson in 2005.

Also, some time ago a survey of professors indicated that some preferred a smaller, more streamlined text than *Fundamentals*. With that in mind, we created *Fundamentals of Financial Management: Concise*, which is 20 percent shorter than *Fundamentals*. Most of *Concise*'s chapters are identical to the corresponding ones in *Fundamentals*, but *Fundamentals* includes an additional chapter on capital budgeting plus chapters on derivatives, hybrid securities, and mergers.

Although *Concise* has been well received, there are two significant advantages to a more complete book such as *Fundamentals*:

1. *Fundamentals* provides professors with more flexibility in designing their courses.
2. *Fundamentals* is a more complete reference book for students to use after completing the course. This is especially important for nonfinance majors, who will not otherwise have access to materials that are covered in *Fundamentals* but are omitted from *Concise*. In this regard, it should be noted that the chapters in *Fundamentals* are written in a modular, self-contained format that makes it easy for students to read them on their own.

INTENDED MARKET

Fundamentals is intended for use in an introductory finance course. The key chapters can be covered in one term, but if it is supplemented with cases and perhaps some outside readings, the book can also be used for a two-term course. When it is covered in one term, instructors generally assign only selected chapters, leaving the others for students to examine on their own or use for reference purposes in later courses and after graduation. Note also that the chapters are written in a flexible, modular format that helps instructors cover the material in whatever sequence they choose.

ThomsonNOW: A NEW WEB-BASED COURSE RESOURCE PLATFORM

ThomsonNOW is Thomson Publishing's new Web-based delivery system, and it contains items that were in the past provided on a CD. Since ThomsonNOW is Web based, it can be changed to reflect new developments and can also operate interactively to create an unlimited number of unique test questions. ThomsonNOW includes the following items, with more to be added over time:

Test Bank

The *Test Bank* for *Fundamentals* has been enhanced in several ways.

- Many new problems and questions have been added, and those new items are now contained in Part I of each *Test Bank* chapter, with Part II containing questions carried over from the old *Test Bank*.
- The problems and questions are categorized by difficulty, and more relatively short items suitable for quizzes and time-limited exams were added.
- Many of the problems are set up so that alternative versions can be algorithmically generated—one or more of the input parameters such as the interest rate or project cost is randomly changed and thus creates a similar problem but with a different answer. This feature enables an instructor to create unique exams and online quizzes ensure that each student does his or her own work.

Practice Problems

ThomsonNOW permits an instructor to generate sets of problems that can be used for

- Graded or ungraded homework
- Online or in-class quizzes.
- Practice sets for students to use as a study aid.

With the very large number of problems in the new *Test Bank* and the algorithmic feature, a virtually unlimited number of unique problems can be generated. Conscientious students can then work many problems and learn how to deal with most finance issues, but they can't memorize answers to specific problems because each problem's answer may be unique.

Excel Models

A set of new and improved models that go through the calculations in most chapters, plus additional models tied to the end-of-chapter integrated cases, are also provided on ThomsonNOW. These models are used to generate some of the text exhibits, including those used in the capital budgeting chapters. While we do not assume that students know *Excel*, we do set the models up so that those familiar with spreadsheets can get a better feel for how they are used in practice. We also provide, in the end-of-chapter materials for most chapters, an integrated spreadsheet problem with a model accessible from ThomsonNOW that does an analysis similar to that in the chapter, including data tables and graphs that give insights into the sensitivity of key outputs to input changes.

Thomson ONE—Business School Edition

I/B/E/S Consensus Estimates. Includes consensus estimates—averages, means, and medians; analyst-by-analyst earnings coverage; analysts' forecasts based on 15 industry standard measures; current and historic coverage for the selected 500 companies. Current history is five years forward and historic history is from 1976 for U.S. companies and 1987 for international companies; current data are updated daily, and historic are updated monthly.

Worldscope. Includes company profiles, financials, and accounting results and market per-share data for the selected 500 companies; annual information and monthly prices going back to 1980, all updated daily.

Disclosure SEC Database. Includes company profiles, annual and quarterly company financials, pricing information, and earnings estimates for selected U.S. and Canadian companies: annually from 1987, quarterly data rolling 10 years, and monthly pricing—all updated weekly.

DataStream Pricing. Daily international pricing, including share price (open, high, low, close, P/E), index, and exchange rate data. History is rolling 10 years.

ILX Systems Delayed Quotes. Includes 20-minute delayed quotes of equities and indices from U.S. and global tickers covering 130 exchanges in 25 developed countries.

Comtex Real-Time News. Includes current news releases.

SEC Edgar Filings and Global Image Source Filings. Includes regulatory and nonregulatory filings for both corporate and individual entities. Edgar filings are real-time and go back 10 years; image filings are updated daily and go back 7 years.

OTHER FEATURES OF THE ELEVENTH EDITION

Recent Financial Events

The past few years have witnessed great turmoil in the financial markets. We have seen an incredible rise and fall of the stock market and the stunning collapses of Enron, WorldCom, Arthur Andersen, and others. Some of these problems were caused by fraud and questionable accounting practices, which, in turn, stemmed largely from badly designed executive compensation programs. As we discuss in Chapter 1, the focus of many top executives shifted from maximizing their firms' long-run stock prices to maximizing prices on the day the executives' own stock options vested and could be sold. We consider the effects of this shift in focus, and ways to move the focus back to the long run and thus to benefit all parties, not just executives with stock options.

We also updated Chapters 6, 7, 8, and 9 to reflect the many changes that have occurred in the stock and bond markets since the last edition. We also restructured these chapters to improve the flow, and we streamlined the coverage of yield curves.

Revised Treatment of Financial Statements

In the wake of the corporate scandals, we have taken steps to enhance our discussion of financial statements and accounting-related issues. In Chapter 3, we continue our emphasis on cash flow, and we expanded our discussion of the differences between net income, net cash flow, and free cash flow. We also streamlined the discussion of taxes, focusing on the major tax issues facing investors and corporations but leaving many details for a Web Appendix, which can be found on ThomsonNOW.

Reworked Section on Market Efficiency and Behavioral Finance

The events surrounding the stock market bubble have led many to reevaluate the efficiency of financial markets, which, in turn, generated new academic research in the area of behavioral finance. While most authorities still believe that market efficiency is a cornerstone of finance, market efficiency does have limitations. Consequently, we discuss the evidence regarding the extent of stock market efficiency, along with the implications of behavioral finance.

Web Appendixes

To make room for important new materials and to streamline the book, we moved certain interesting but secondary material to appendixes available through ThomsonNOW. References to these appendixes are provided in the relevant text chapters.

Streamlined Discussion of the Time Value of Money

As noted earlier, we took several steps to increase the readability of this critically important chapter. First, we moved it from Chapter 6 to Chapter 2 to give students more time to digest it before using it in the bond, stock, and capital budgeting chapters. We also added end-of-section self-tests to ensure that students can work with the function that was just discussed before moving on to the next one, and we provide (on ThomsonNOW) tutorials on the most popular calculators to help in this regard. The new setup helps students *understand* the fundamental issues in TVM and work problems efficiently, but without falling into the "black box trap" of knowing how to work specific problems but not understanding concepts well enough to deal with problems that are structured somewhat differently.

Changes in the Working Capital Chapter

As noted earlier, we totally rewrote the working capital material, reducing it from two chapters to one to cover the key points in a logical and succinct manner. Reviewers unanimously agreed that the new chapter was considerably better than the two old ones. A quote from one reviewer summarizes their conclusions:

> I like the abbreviated one-chapter approach. I looked at the old Tenth Edition chapter again, and I like the new one much better—it is more readable than the original two chapters, and I actually enjoyed reading it. The two-chapter approach provided too much extraneous and confusing information. The new and more concise presentation gives introductory students exactly what they need. Also, the new chapter is so much better than the previous two that I could assign it to students to read and learn on their own. I would, however, cover the cash budget in class because that is a bit more complicated, but even cash budgeting is much better presented here.

Another reviewer stated that he has been skipping working capital in his class because, as it was presented, it would take too long to cover it, but that he planned to cover the chapter in its new format. We expect others to agree.

Analyzing Financial Decisions with Spreadsheets

We developed spreadsheet models for each chapter in the book except Chapters 1 and 5. Spreadsheet programs are ideally suited for analyzing many financial issues, and a knowledge of spreadsheets is rapidly becoming essential for people in business. Therefore, we indicate how spreadsheets are used to deal with the issues discussed in the text.

However, we recognize that students need to understand basic finance concepts before going into computer modeling. Therefore, in the text chapters, we discuss finance concepts, provide examples, and explain how the concepts are used in the decision process. Where the analysis involves arithmetic, we assume that students are using calculators. However, if the problem is one that could be solved more efficiently with a computer, we briefly describe how the computer would be used. These explanations are short, easy to follow, and can be skipped without loss of continuity. Thus, students get an idea of how they could go from calculators to spreadsheets, but they don't need to take that step. However, if an instructor wants to emphasize computers in the course, or if an individual student wants to learn more about spreadsheets on his or her own, the spreadsheet models available from ThomsonNOW make that relatively easy.

Also, we provide on ThomsonNOW an *Excel* tutorial that explains the functions and procedures used in the models. The tutorial has an index that makes it relatively easy to find information about each function and feature, and students can use the models and tutorial to learn *Excel* on their own.

CONTENTS

- Significantly revised and improved. New vignette, "Striking the Right Balance," discusses trade-off of maximizing shareholder value and making decisions that benefit society. Chapter emphasizes value orientation with discussion of relationship among shareholder value, intrinsic values, and stock prices. Enhanced and expanded discussion of business ethics. New boxes: "Is Shareholder Wealth Maximization a World-Wide Goal?"; "Protection for Whistle-Blowers."

- Improved! Moved from Chapter 6 to Chapter 2 to allow students more time to grasp the concepts. Discussion made clearer, takes less of a "black-box" approach; formulas are given. Added section, "Finding Annuity Payments, Periods, and Interest Rates." New boxes: "Simple versus Compound Interest"; "Hints on Using Financial Calculators."

- Improved! New Figure 3-1 diagrams a typical balance sheet to aid students with the discussion. Reorganized chapter so cash flow discussion immediately follows income statement and precedes cash flow statement discussions. "Uses and Limitations of Financial Statements" section moved so it precedes discussion on "Modifying Accounting Data for Investor and Managerial Decisions." MVA and EVA discussion shortened; not as computationally oriented. Updated tax discussion. New box: "Massaging the Cash Flow Statement."

- Updated vignette. Improved financial leverage discussion in "Debt Management Ratios" section. Updated Table 4-3. New box: "Global Perspectives: Global Accounting Standards: Can One Size Fit All?"

- Created from dividing Tenth Edition Chapter 4 into two separate chapters. New vignette: "A Strong Financial System Is Necessary for a Growing and Prosperous Economy." Reorganized to present overview of capital allocation process before discussing financial markets and institutions. Brought in discussions on "Market for Common Stock," "Stock Markets and Returns," and "Stock Market Efficiency" from old Stock chapter for better integration. Updated Tables 5-1, 5-2, and 5-3. Added discussion of hedge funds. Updated "Measuring the Market" box. New boxes: "Citigroup Built to Compete in a Changing Environment"; "The NYSE and Nasdaq Combine Forces with the Leading Online Trading Systems"; "A Closer Look at Behavioral Finance Theory."

- New chapter created from dividing Tenth Edition Chapter 4 into two separate chapters. Vignette highlights the discussion presented in chapter, "Low Interest Rates Encourage Investment and Stimulate Consumer Spending." All figures updated to show current economic situation. Rewrote and clarified section, "Using the Yield Curve to Estimate Future Interest Rates." Reorganized so that discussion of "Other Factors That Influence Interest Rate Levels" immediately follows the section on "Using the Yield Curve to Estimate Future Interest Rates." Updated boxes: "An Almost Riskless Treasury Security Bond" and "Global Perspectives: Measuring Country Risk." New box: "The Links between Expected Inflation and Interest Rates: A Closer Look."

- Improved! Reorganized chapter so that bond valuation and then bond yields are discussed before the section on "Changes in Bond Values over Time." Added Table 7-1 to clarify discussion of changes in bond values. Reduced discussion of bankruptcy and reorganization (which is in Web Appendix) and enhanced discussion of bond markets.

- Improved! Moved chapter to immediately precede chapter on stocks to help integrate concepts. Moved extensive footnote in prior edition on using historical data to measure risk into text. Updated box, "The Trade-Off between Risk and Return." Revised Figure 8-7 so partial correlation between stocks coincides with recent studies (0.35 vs. 0.67). Added new section, "Some Concluding Thoughts: Implications for Corporate Managers and Investors."

- Improved! New vignette, "Searching for the Right Stock." Moved market, returns, and efficient markets discussion to new Chapter 5 to allow for almost immediate discussion on stock valuation. Enhanced discussion of corporate valuation model.

- Improved! Enhanced discussion on the overview of the WACC along with new Figure 10-1, which is meant to improve students' understanding of different types of capital. WACC equation presented early in the chapter, followed by discussion of the individual cost components and their calculations. Added second-level headings in "Cost of New Common Stock" to clarify the discussion. Eliminated duplication of project risk discussion, which has now been moved to Chapter 12—where it fits better.

- Improved! New vignette, "Competition in the Aircraft Industry," details the chapter's concepts. Reorganized chapter discussion so NPV discussion appears early and is stressed as the best capital budgeting decision rule. Added discussion section, "Decision Criteria Used in Practice."

⟶ ■ Improved! Chapter begins with a fairly extensive capital budgeting illustration as an overview and lead-in to discussing capital budgeting concepts. Chapter then proceeds with other capital budgeting details, allowing professors to get the general idea of capital budgeting analysis across without having to cover the entire chapter (which was the case in the prior edition).

■ Improved! Reorganized to present real options discussion early. Mutually exclusive projects with unequal lives (both replacement chain and EAA approaches) then discussed.

■ Updated vignette on Kellogg Co. and Table 14-4. Clarified illustration and chapter discussion of concepts.

■ Improved! New vignette, "Microsoft Shifts Gears and Begins to Unload Part of Its Vast Cash Hoard," illustrates a recent event that ties in with chapter concepts. Improved discussion of dividend theories for recent tax changes. Enhanced discussion of investor preferences for dividends versus capital gains. Eliminated dividend stability section. Updated box, "Global Perspectives: Dividend Yields Around the World." New box: "Stock Repurchases Soar in 2004."

■ Improved! Combined two chapters into one. Presented overview of working capital management by discussing cash conversion cycle and current asset investment and financing policies. Chapter also discusses some of the more important accounts in greater detail, such as cash (including cash budgeting) and marketable securities, accounts receivable, accounts payable, bank loans, and accrued liabilities.

■ Improved! New vignette, "Forecasting Apple's Future." Rather than focusing on the "mechanics" of forecasting, the presentation stresses understanding the concepts involved. The AFN equation is presented earlier in the chapter to help students understand the concepts involved. Enhanced discussion with use of spreadsheets, regression analysis, and individual ratios in forecasting process.

■ Reconstructed Table 18-1 to use real numbers developed from data available on the Internet. Added Web address to tell students where to obtain call and put option data. Rewrote box, "Expensing Executive Stock Options," to incorporate the new stock option accounting rule. Reworked OPM illustration and Table 18-2 for a much lower, more current risk-free rate. Revised "Forward and Futures Contracts" section to incorporate hedging example with futures all within same section. "Other Types of Derivatives" section excludes forward and futures and includes only swaps, structured notes, and inverse floater. New box: "Credit Instruments Create New Opportunities and Risks."

■ Improved! Reorganized chapter to present discussion of international monetary system, terminology, and current monetary arrangements early. Exchange rates and cross rates are presented next. Enhanced discussion of international money and capital markets. Updated boxes: "Hungry for a Big Mac? Go to China!" and "Stock Market Indices Around the World."

■ Generally clarified sections for students.

■ Generally updated chapter for new mergers/acquisitions. New vignette about Procter & Gamble merger. Updated Table 21-2 for recent larger mergers. Reworked merger illustration for a lower, more current cost of equity number. Updated "Financial Reporting for Mergers" to exclude pooling method for mergers. New boxes: "Tempest in a Teapot"; "The Track Record of Recent Large Mergers."

THE INSTRUCTIONAL PACKAGE: AN INTEGRATED SYSTEM

Fundamentals offers an innovative, technologically advanced ancillary package to enhance students' learning and to make it easier for instructors to prepare for and conduct classes. The integrated package includes many outstanding resources, all of which have been revised and updated for the new Eleventh Edition.

Essential Course Management Tools for the Instructor

- **Spreadsheet Models for Integrated Cases**—The spreadsheet models were designed to illustrate spreadsheet applications to finance concepts using integrated case data. They can be found on the Instructor's Resource Web site on ThomsonNOW at **http://now.swlearning.com/brigham**.
- **Instructors' Resources CD-ROM**—The new instructor resource system includes electronic versions of the *Instructor's Manual,* a *Word* and electronic version of the *Test Bank*, spreadsheet models, solutions to spreadsheet problems, and *PowerPoint* presentations. It is laid out to maximize accessibility and minimize search time.
- ***Fundamentals of Financial Management* Online Course**—Delivered via the WebTutor platform, this integrated Web-based learning environment accompanies the textbook and ancillary package with the vast resources of the Internet and the convenience of anytime learning. Extremely user friendly, the powerful customization features of the WebTutor framework enable instructors to customize this online course to their own unique teaching styles and their students' individual needs. Course features include content keyed to the Eleventh Edition, self-tests and online exams, Internet activities and links to related resources, a suggested course syllabus, student and instructor materials, free technical support for instructors, and much more. Available for both Blackboard and WebCT platforms.
- *Instructor's Manual*—This comprehensive manual contains answers to all text questions and problems plus detailed solutions to the integrated cases. A computerized version in *Word* is also available on the Instructor's Resource Web site on ThomsonNOW at **http://now.swlearning.com/brigham**. This digital version of the *Instructor's Manual* is available for posting on a secure, instructor's password-protected Web site.
- *PowerPoint Lecture Presentation*—Prepared in *PowerPoint*, this slide show covers all the essential issues presented in each chapter. Graphs, tables, lists, and calculations are developed sequentially, much as one might develop them on a blackboard. The new and improved slides are even more crisp, colorful, and professor-friendly. Instructors can, of course, modify or delete our slides, or add some of their own. The *PowerPoint* slide can be found in the Instructor's Resource section of ThomsonNOW at **http://now .swlearning.com/brigham**.
- *Test Bank*—The revised and enhanced large *Test Bank* contains more than 1,500 class-tested questions and problems, is now broken into two parts, and is available both in print and electronic form. Part I has all new or substantially revised questions and problems, and Part II contains holdover items from the previous *Test Bank*. Many of the problems in Part I can be algorithmically modified in ThomsonNOW, which enables instructors to create an almost unlimited number of unique problems. Information regard-

ing the topics, degree of difficulty, and the correct answers, along with complete solutions for all numerical problems, is provided with each question. A version of the *Test Bank* in *Word* is also available to instructors for downloading.

- *ThomsonNOW*—ThomsonNOW has many features that make test preparation, scoring, and grade recording easy. In addition, questions can be altered to make different versions of a given test, and the software makes it easy to add to or edit the existing test items, or to compile a test that covers specific topics.

- *Technology Supplement*—The *Technology Supplement* contains tutorials for four commonly used financial calculators, for *Excel*, and for *PowerPoint* presentation software. The calculator tutorials cover everything a student needs to know about the calculator to work the problems in the text.

- **NewsWire: Finance in the News**—Adopters of *Fundamentals* will have access to a password-protected portion of the South-Western Finance Web site, where they will be provided with summaries of recent articles in *The Wall Street Journal*, *Business Week*, or other major business publications, along with discussion questions and references to the text. These summaries, written by Emery Trahan and Paul Bolster of Northeastern University, facilitate incorporating late-breaking news into classroom discussions.

Superior Student Ancillary Package

- ThomsonNOW—**http://now.swlearning.com/brigham**.
- ThomsonNOW is Thomson Publishing's new Web-based delivery system, and ThomsonNOW contains items that were in the past provided on a CD. Because ThomsonNOW is Web based, it can be changed to reflect new developments and also to operate interactively. ThomsonNOW provides students with the following robust set of additional online learning tools, with more to be added over time:

  - *PowerPoint Lecture Presentation*—The slide show covers all the essential issues presented in each chapter and follows the end-of-chapter Integrated Case.

  - **E-Lectures**—Difficult concepts from each chapter are explained and illustrated via streaming video and animated tutorials. These video clips and tutorials can be extremely helpful review and clarification tools if you have trouble understanding an in-class lecture or if you are more of a visual learner who sometimes has difficulty grasping concepts as they are presented in the text.

  - **Introductory Video and Ask the Author Video**—Introductory video pieces, as illustrated by text coauthor Eugene F. Brigham, set the tone for the study of each chapter. These streaming video clips provide context for the forthcoming reading and exercises. Upon finishing a chapter, they may be used as excellent review tools for summarizing key points and major concepts. In the Ask the Author video, difficult concepts and frequently asked questions from each chapter are explained and illustrated by the textbook coauthor, Joel F. Houston. These video clips can be extremely helpful review and clarification tools if you have trouble understanding an in-class lecture or if you are a visual learner.

  - **Online Homework and Additional Quizzing and Testing**—In addition to including online access to the end of chapter problem material, ThomsonNOW offers an opportunity to practice for midterms and finals by taking online quizzes that span multiple chapters.

- *The Problem Bank*—*The Problem Bank: Practice Problems for Financial Management* has been revised to fit specifically with this text and contains more than 400 multiple-choice finance problems with solutions, divided into seven major categories such as time value of money, capital budgeting, and risk and return. Solving these problems requires the use of a financial calculator (general calculator keystrokes also are provided) and is intended to supplement the text's end-of-chapter problems, thereby providing additional practice for students in their preparation of homework assignments and for exams.
- *Spreadsheet Models*—ThomsonNOW also contains spreadsheet models that illustrate how concepts covered in the text are implemented in the real world, giving students a significant advantage in the job market. The models include thorough explanations and serve both as an *Excel* tutorial and as a template for solving financial problems for each chapter of the book.

- **Thomson ONE—Business School Edition**—Use the Thomson ONE Academic online database to work a chapter's Thomson ONE—Business School Edition problem. Thomson ONE—Business School Edition, a product from Thomson Financial, combines a full range of fundamental financials, earnings estimates, market data, and source documents for hundreds of real-world companies. This is your opportunity to access and apply the industry's most reliable information to answer the discussion questions and work through group projects.
- *Study Guide*—This supplement lists the key learning objectives for each chapter, outlines the key sections, provides self-test questions, and provides a set of problems similar to those in the text and the *Test Bank*, but with fully worked-out solutions.
- **Spreadsheet Books**—Thomson/South-Western has published several books on spreadsheets, including *Financial Analysis with Microsoft Excel*, Third Edition.
- *Effective Use of a Financial Calculator*—Written by Pamela Hall, this handbook is designed to help increase students' understanding of both finance and financial calculators, enabling them to work problems more quickly and effectively.

ACKNOWLEDGMENTS

This textbook reflects the efforts of a great many people, both those who have worked on *Fundamentals* and our related books over a number of years, as well as those who worked specifically on this Eleventh Edition. First, we would like to thank Dana Aberwald Clark, who worked closely with us at every stage of the revision—her assistance was absolutely invaluable. Second, Christopher Buzzard did an outstanding job helping us develop the *Excel* models, the Web site, and the *PowerPoint* presentations.

Our colleagues Roy Crum, Andy Naranjo, M. Nimalendran, Jay Ritter, Mike Ryngaert, Craig Tapley, and Carolyn Takeda gave us many useful suggestions regarding the ancillaries and many parts of the book, including the integrated cases. Also, we benefited from the work of Mike Ehrhardt and Phillip Daves of the University of Tennessee, and Roy Crum of the University of Florida, who worked with us on companion books. Next, we would like to thank the following professors, who reviewed this edition in detail and provided many useful comments and suggestions:

Deb Bauer, *University of Oregon*
Mary R. Brown, *University of Illinois, Chicago*
Michael J. Highfield, *Louisiana Tech University*

James Keys, *Florida International University*
Shady Kholdy, *California State University, Pomona*
Karyl Leggio, *University of Missouri at Kansas City*
Adam Y. C. Lei, *Louisiana State University*
Rabih Moussawi, *The University of Texas–Dallas*
John Wald, *Rutgers University*
Mark D. Walker, *North Carolina State University*
Kenneth Williams, *Davenport University*
Michael Yest, *Tulane University*

We would also like to thank the following professors, whose reviews and comments on our earlier books have contributed to this edition:

Robert Adams, Mike Adler, Sharif Ahkam, Syed Ahmad, Ed Altman, Bruce Anderson, Ron Anderson, Tom Anderson, John Andrews, Bob Angell, Vince Apilado, Harvey Arbalaez, Kavous Ardalan, Henry Arnold, Bob Aubey, Gil Babcock, Peter Bacon, Kent Baker, Robert Balik, Tom Bankston, Babu Baradwaj, Les Barenbaum, Charles Barngrover, Sam Basu, Greg Bauer, Bill Beedles, Brian Belt, Moshe Ben-Horim, Gary Benesh, Bill Beranek, Tom Berry, Will Bertin, Scott Besley, Dan Best, Roger Bey, Gilbert W. Bickum, Dalton Bigbee, John Bildersee, Laurence E. Blose, Russ Boisjoly, Bob Boldin, Keith Boles, Michael Bond, Geof Booth, Waldo Born, Rick Boulware, Kenneth Boudreaux, Helen Bowers, Oswald Bowlin, Don Boyd, G. Michael Boyd, Pat Boyer, Joe Brandt, Elizabeth Brannigan, Mary Broske, David T. Brown, Christopher Brown, Kate Brown, Larry Brown, Bill Brueggeman, Paul Bursik, Bill Campsey, Bob Carlson, Severin Carlson, David Cary, Steve Celec, Mary Chaffin, Charles Chan, Don Chance, Antony Chang, Susan Chaplinsky, K. C. Chen, Jay Choi, S. K. Choudhary, Lal Chugh, Maclyn Clouse, Bruce Collins, Mitch Conover, Margaret Considine, Phil Cooley, Joe Copeland, David Cordell, Marsha Cornett, M. P. Corrigan, John Cotner, Charles Cox, David Crary, John Crockett, Jr., Brent Dalrymple, Bill Damon, Morris Danielson, Joel Dauten, Steve Dawson, Sankar De, Fred Dellva, Chad Denson, James Desreumaux, Bodie Dickerson, Bernard Dill, Gregg Dimkoff, Les Dlabay, James D'Mello, Mark Dorfman, Tom Downs, Frank Draper, Gene Drzycimski, Dean Dudley, David Durst, Ed Dyl, Fred J. Ebeid, Daniel Ebels, Richard Edelman, Charles Edwards, U. Elike, John Ellis, George Engler, Suzanne Erickson, Dave Ewert, John Ezzell, L. Franklin Fant, Richard J. Fendler, Michael Ferri, Jim Filkins, John Finnerty, Robert Fiore, Susan Fischer, Peggy Fletcher, Steven Flint, Russ Fogler, Jennifer Frazier, Dan French, Michael Garlington, David Garraty, Sharon Garrison, Jim Garven, Adam Gehr, Jr., Jim Gentry, Wafica Ghoul, Armand Gilinsky, Jr., Philip Glasgo, Rudyard Goode, Raymond Gorman, Walt Goulet, Bernie Grablowsky, Theoharry Grammatikos, Owen Gregory, Ed Grossnickle, John Groth, Alan Grunewald, Manak Gupta, Darryl Gurley, Sam Hadaway, Don Hakala, Gerald Hamsmith, William Hardin, John Harris, Paul Hastings, Bob Haugen, Steve Hawke, Stevenson Hawkey, Del Hawley, Eric M. Haye, Robert Hehre, Kath Henebry, David Heskel, George Hettenhouse, Hans Heymann, Kendall Hill, Roger Hill, Tom Hindelang, Linda Hittle, Ralph Hocking, J. Ronald Hoffmeister, Robert Hollinger, Jim Horrigan, John Houston, John Howe, Keith Howe, Steve Isberg, Jim Jackson, Vahan Janjigian, Narayanan Jayaraman, Zhenhn Jin, Kose John, Craig Johnson, Keith Johnson, Ramon Johnson, Ray Jones, Frank Jordan, Manuel Jose, Sally Joyner, Alfred Kahl, Gus Kalogeras, Rajiv Kalra, Ravi Kamath, John Kaminarides, Michael Keenan, Bill Kennedy, Peppi M. Kenny, Carol Kiefer, Joe Kiernan, Richard Kish, Robert Kleiman, Erich Knehans, Don Knight, Ladd Kochman, Dorothy Koehl, Jaroslaw Komarynsky, Duncan Kretovich, Harold Krogh, Charles Kroncke, Don Kummer, Robert A. Kunkel, Reinhold Lamb, Joan Lamm, Larry Lang, David Lange, P. Lange, Howard Lanser, Edward Lawrence, Martin Lawrence, Wayne Lee, Jim LePage, David E. LeTourneau, Jules Levine, John Lewis, Jason Lin, Chuck Linke, Bill Lloyd, Susan Long, Judy Maese, Bob Magee, Ileen Malitz, Bob Malko, Phil Malone, Abbas Mamoozadeh, Terry Maness, Chris Manning, Surendra Mansinghka, Timothy Manuel, Brian Maris, Terry Martell, David Martin, D. J. Masson, John Mathys, Ralph May, John McAlhany, Andy McCollough, Ambrose McCoy, Thomas McCue, Bill McDaniel, John McDowell, Charles McKinney, Robyn McLaughlin, James McNulty, Jeanette Medewitz-Diamond, Jamshid Mehran, Larry Merville, Rick Meyer, Jim Millar, Ed Miller, John Miller, John Mitchell, Carol Moerdyk, Bob Moore, Scott Moore, Barry Morris, Gene Morris, Dianne R. Morrison, Chris Muscarella, David Nachman, Tim Nantell, Don Nast, Edward Nelling, Bill Nelson, Bob Nelson, William Nelson, Bob Niendorf, Bruce Niendorf, Ben

Nonnally, Jr., Tom O'Brien, William O'Connell, Dennis O'Connor, John O'Donnell, Jim Olsen, Robert Olsen, Dean Olson, Jim Pappas, Stephen Parrish, Helen Pawlowski, Barron Peake, Michael Pescow, Glenn Petry, Jim Pettijohn, Rich Pettit, Dick Pettway, Aaron Phillips, Hugo Phillips, H. R. Pickett, John Pinkerton, Gerald Pogue, Eugene Poindexter, R. Potter, Franklin Potts, R. Powell, Dianna Preece, Chris Prestopino, John Primus, Jerry Prock, Howard Puckett, Herbert Quigley, George Racette, Bob Radcliffe, Allen Rappaport, Bill Rentz, Ken Riener, Charles Rini, John Ritchie, Bill Rives, Pietra Rivoli, Antonio Rodriguez, James Rosenfeld, Stuart Rosenstein, E. N. Roussakis, Dexter Rowell, Marjorie Rubash, Bob Ryan, Jim Sachlis, Abdul Sadik, Travis Sapp, Thomas Scampini, Kevin Scanlon, Frederick Schadeler, Patricia L. Schaeff, David Schalow, Mary Jane Scheuer, David Schirm, Robert Schwebach, Carol Schweser, John Settle, Alan Severn, James Sfiridis, Sol Shalit, Frederic Shipley, Dilip Shome, Ron Shrieves, Neil Sicherman, J. B. Silvers, Clay Singleton, Joe Sinkey, Stacy Sirmans, Jaye Smith, Patricia Smith, Patricia Matisz Smith, Don Sorensen, David Speairs, Ken Stanley, Ed Stendardi, Alan Stephens, Don Stevens, Jerry Stevens, Glen Strasburg, David Suk, Katherine Sullivan, Timothy Sullivan, Philip Swensen, Bruce Swenson, Ernest Swift, Paul Swink, Eugene Swinnerton, Gary Tallman, Dular Talukdar, Dennis Tanner, Russ Taussig, Richard Teweles, Ted Teweles, Madeline Thimmes, Francis D. Thomas, Andrew Thompson, John Thompson, Arlene Thurman, Dogan Tirtirogu, Janet Todd, Holland J. Toles, William Tozer, Emery Trahan, George Trivoli, George Tsetsekos, David Upton, Howard Van Auken, Pretorious Van den Dool, Pieter Vandenberg, Paul Vanderheiden, David Vang, JoAnn Vaughan, Jim Verbrugge, Patrick Vincent, Steve Vinson, Susan Visscher, John Wachowicz, Joe Walker, Mike Walker, Sam Weaver, Marsha Weber, Al Webster, Shelton Weeks, Kuo-Chiang Wei, Bill Welch, Fred Weston, Richard Whiston, Norm Williams, Tony Wingler, Ed Wolfe, Criss Woodruff, Don Woods, Robert Wyatt, Steve Wyatt, Michael Yonan, John Zietlow, Dennis Zocco, and Kent Zumwalt.

Special thanks are due to Chris Barry, Texas Christian University, and Shirley Love, Idaho State University, who wrote many of the boxes relating to small-business issues that are on the Web; to Steven Bouchard, Goldey Beacom College, who helped develop the Cyberproblems; to Emery Trahan and Paul Bolster, Northeastern University, who developed and wrote the summaries and questions for NewsWire; to Dilip Shome, Virginia Polytechnic Institute, who helped greatly with the capital structure chapter; to Dave Brown and Mike Ryngaert, University of Florida, who helped us with the bankruptcy and merger material; to Roy Crum, Andy Naranjo, and Subu Venkataraman, who worked with us on the international materials; to Scott Below, East Carolina University, who developed the Web site information and references; to Laurie and Stan Eakins of East Carolina, who developed the materials on *Excel* for the *Technology Supplement*; and to Larry Wolken, Texas A&M University, who offered his hard work and advice for the development of the *Lecture Presentation Software*. Susan Whitman typed the various manuscripts, and she and Allison Smith helped proof them. Finally, the South-Western and Elm Street Publishing Services staffs, especially Sue Nodine, Elizabeth Thomson, Mike Reynolds, Deanna Quinn, Vicky True, John Barans, Matthew McKinney, Karen Schaffer, Tom Grega, and Alex von Rosenberg, helped greatly with all phases of the textbook's development and production.

ERRORS IN THE TEXTBOOK

At this point, most authors make a statement like this: "We appreciate all the help we received from the people listed above, but any remaining errors are, of course, our own responsibility." And generally there are more than enough remaining errors! Having experienced difficulties with errors ourselves, both as students and instructors, we resolved to avoid this problem in *Fundamentals*. As a result of our detection procedures, we are convinced that this book is relatively free of significant errors, meaning those that either confuse or distract readers.

Partly because of our confidence that few such errors remain, but primarily because we want very much to detect any errors that may have slipped by to correct them in subsequent printings, we decided to offer a reward of $10 per error to the first person who reports it to us. For purpose of this reward, errors are defined as misspelled words, nonrounding numerical errors, incorrect statements, and any other error that inhibits comprehension. Typesetting problems such as irregular spacing and differences of opinion regarding grammatical or punctuation conventions do not qualify for this reward. Given the ever-changing nature of the World Wide Web, changes in Web addresses also do not qualify as errors, although we would like to learn about them. Finally, any qualifying error that has follow-through effects is counted as two errors only. Please report any errors to Joel Houston either through e-mail at **fundamentals@joelhouston.com** or by regular mail at the address below.

CONCLUSION

Finance is, in a real sense, the cornerstone of the enterprise system—good financial management is vitally important to the economic health of business firms, hence to the nation and the world. Because of its importance, finance should be widely and thoroughly understood, but this is easier said than done. The field is relatively complex, and it is undergoing constant change in response to shifts in economic conditions. All of this makes finance stimulating and exciting, but also challenging and sometimes perplexing. We sincerely hope that this Eleventh Edition of *Fundamentals* will meet its own challenge by contributing to a better understanding of our financial system.

EUGENE F. BRIGHAM
JOEL F. HOUSTON
4723 N.W. 53rd Ave., Suite A
Gainesville, Florida 32606-4399

December 2005

BRIEF CONTENTS

CONTENTS

Part 6
Working Capital and Financial Planning 511

Chapter 16
Working Capital Management 512

Best Buy Successfully Manages Its Working Capital **512**

PUTTING THINGS IN PERSPECTIVE 512

Chapter 17
Financial Planning and Forecasting 552

Forecasting Apple's Future **552**

PUTTING THINGS IN PERSPECTIVE 553

Part 7
Special Topics in Financial Management 577

Chapter 18
Derivatives and Risk Management 578
Using Derivatives to Manage Risk **578**

Chapter 19
Multinational Financial Management 615
U.S. Firms Look Overseas to Enhance Shareholder Value **615**

INTRODUCTION TO FINANCIAL MANAGEMENT

PART **1**

CHAPTER 1

AN OVERVIEW OF FINANCIAL MANAGEMENT

Striking the Right Balance

In 1776 Adam Smith described how an "invisible hand" guides companies striving to maximize profits so that they make decisions that also benefit society. Smith's insights led economists to reach two key conclusions: (1) Profit maximization is the proper goal for a business, and (2) the free enterprise system is best for society. However, the world has changed since 1776. Firms then were much smaller, they operated in one country, and they were generally managed by their owners. Firms today are much larger, operate across the globe, have thousands of employees, and are owned by millions of investors. Therefore, the "invisible hand" may no longer provide reliable guidance. If not, how should our giant corporations be managed, and what should their goals be? In particular, should companies try to maximize their owners' interests, or should they strike a balance between profits and actions designed specifically to benefit customers, employees, suppliers, and even society as a whole?

Most academics today subscribe to a slightly modified version of Adam Smith's theory: Maximize stockholder wealth, which amounts to maximizing the value of the stock. Stock price maximization requires firms to consider profits, but it also requires them to think about the riskiness of those profits and whether they are paid out as dividends or retained and reinvested in the business. Firms must develop desirable products, produce them efficiently, and sell them at competitive prices, all of which also benefit society. Obviously, some constraints are necessary—firms must not be allowed to pollute the air and water excessively, engage in unfair employment practices, or create monopolies that exploit consumers. *So, the view today is that management should try to maximize stock values, but subject to government-imposed constraints.* To paraphrase Charles Prince, chairman of Citigroup, in an interview with *Fortune*: We want to grow aggressively, but without breaking the law.[1] Citigroup had recently been fined hundreds of millions of dollars for breaking laws in the United States and abroad.

The constrained maximization theory does have critics. For example, General Electric (GE) chief executive officer (CEO) Jeffrey Immelt believes that alterations are needed. GE is the world's most valuable company, and it has an excellent reputation.[2] Immelt tells his management team that value and reputation go hand in glove—having a good reputation with customers, suppliers, employees, and regulators is essential if value is to be maximized. According to Immelt, "The reason people come to work for GE is that they want to be part of something that is bigger than themselves. They want to work hard, win promotions, and receive stock options. But they also want to work for a company that makes a difference, a company that's doing great things in the world. . . . It's up to GE to be a good citizen. Not only is it a nice thing to do, it's good for business."

This is a new position for GE. Immelt's predecessor, Jack Welch, focused on compliance—like Citigroup's Prince, Welch believed in obeying rules pertaining to the environment, employment practices, and the like, but his goal was to maximize shareholder value within those constraints. Immelt, on the other hand, thinks it's necessary to go further, doing some things because they benefit society, not just because they are profitable. But Immelt is not totally altruistic—he thinks that actions to improve world conditions will also enhance GE's reputation, helping it attract top workers and loyal customers, get better cooperation from suppliers, and obtain expedited regulatory approvals for new ventures, all of which would benefit GE's stock price. One could interpret all this as saying that the CEOs of both Citigroup and GE have stock price maximization as their top goal, but Citigroup's CEO focuses quite directly on that goal while GE's CEO takes a somewhat broader view.

Putting Things In Perspective

This chapter will give you an idea of what financial management is all about. We begin with a brief discussion of the different forms of business organization. For corporations, management's goal should be to maximize shareholder wealth, which means maximizing the value of the stock. When we say "maximizing the value of the stock," we mean the "true, long-run value," which may be different from the current stock price. Good managers understand the importance of ethics, and they recognize that maximizing long-run value is consistent with being socially responsible. We conclude the chapter by describing how finance is related to the overall business and how firms must provide the right incentives if they are to get managers to focus on long-run value maximization.

---

[1] "Tough Questions for Citigroup's CEO," *Fortune,* November 29, 2004, pp. 114–122.
[2] Marc Gunther, "Money and Morals at GE," *Fortune,* November 15, 2004, pp. 176–182.

1-1 FORMS OF BUSINESS ORGANIZATION

The key aspects of financial management are the same for all businesses, large or small, regardless of how they are organized. Still, its legal structure does affect some aspects of a firm's operations and thus must be recognized. There are three main forms of business organization: (1) sole proprietorships, (2) partnerships, and (3) corporations. In terms of numbers, about 80 percent of businesses are operated as sole proprietorships, while most of the remainder are divided equally between partnerships and corporations. However, based on the dollar value of sales, about 80 percent of all business is done by corporations, about 13 percent by sole proprietorships, and about 7 percent by partnerships. Because corporations conduct the most business, and because most successful proprietorships and partnerships eventually convert into corporations, we concentrate on them in this book. Still, it is important to understand the differences among the three types of firms.

Proprietorship
An unincorporated business owned by one individual.

A **proprietorship** is an unincorporated business owned by one individual. Going into business as a sole proprietor is easy—merely begin business operations. Proprietorships have three important advantages: (1) They are easily and inexpensively formed, (2) they are subject to few government regulations, and (3) they are subject to lower income taxes than corporations. However, proprietorships also have three important limitations: (1) Proprietors have unlimited personal liability for the business's debts, which can result in losses that exceed the money they have invested in the company; (2) it is difficult for proprietorships to obtain large sums of capital; and (3) the life of a business organized as a proprietorship is limited to the life of the individual who created it. For these reasons, sole proprietorships are used primarily for small businesses. However, businesses are frequently started as proprietorships and then converted to corporations when their growth causes the disadvantages of being a proprietorship to outweigh the advantages.

Partnership
An unincorporated business owned by two or more persons.

A **partnership** is a legal arrangement between two or more people who decide to do business together. Partnerships are similar to proprietorships in that they can be established easily and inexpensively, and they are not subject to the corporate income tax. They also have the disadvantages associated with proprietorships: unlimited personal liability, difficulty raising capital, and limited lives. The liability issue is especially important, because under partnership law, each partner is liable for the business's debts. Therefore, if any partner is unable to meet his or her pro rata liability and the partnership goes bankrupt, then the remaining partners are personally responsible for making good on the unsatisfied claims. The partners of a national accounting firm, Laventhol and Horvath, a huge partnership that went bankrupt as a result of suits filed by investors who relied on faulty audit statements, learned all about the perils of doing business as a partnership. Another major accounting firm, Arthur Andersen, suffered a similar fate because the partners who worked with Enron, WorldCom, and a few other clients broke the law and led to the firm's demise. Thus, a Texas partner who audits a business that goes under can bring ruin to a millionaire New York partner who never even went near the client company.[3]

---

[3] There are actually a number of types of partnerships, but we focus on "plain vanilla partnerships" and leave the variations to courses on business law. We note, though, that the variations are generally designed to limit the liabilities of some of the partners. For example, a "limited partnership" has a general partner, who has unlimited liability, and limited partners, whose liability is limited to their investment. This sounds great from the standpoint of the limited partners, but they have to cede sole and absolute authority to the general partner, which means that they have no say in the way the firm conducts its business. With a corporation, the owners (stockholders) have limited liability, but they also have the right to vote and thus influence management.

A **corporation** is a legal entity created by a state, and it is separate and distinct from its owners and managers. Corporations have unlimited lives, their owners are not subject to losses beyond the amount they have invested in the business, and it is easier to transfer one's ownership interest (stock) in a corporation than one's interest in a nonincorporated business. These three factors make it much easier for corporations to raise the capital necessary to operate large businesses. Thus, growth companies such as Hewlett-Packard and Microsoft generally begin life as proprietorships or partnerships, but at some point find it advantageous to convert to the corporate form.

The biggest drawback to incorporation is taxes: Corporate earnings are generally subject to double taxation—the earnings of the corporation are taxed at the corporate level, and then, when after-tax earnings are paid out as dividends, those earnings are taxed again as personal income to the stockholders. However, as an aid to small businesses Congress created **S corporations** and allowed them to be taxed as if they were proprietorships or partnerships and thus exempt from the corporate income tax. The S designation is based on the section of the Tax Code that deals with S corporations, though it could stand for "small." Larger corporations are known as C corporations. S corporations can have no more than 75 stockholders, which limits their use to relatively small, privately owned firms. The vast majority of small firms elect S status and retain that status until they decide to sell stock to the public and thus expand their ownership beyond 75 stockholders.

In deciding on a form of organization, firms must trade off the advantages of incorporation against a possibly higher tax burden. However, the value of any business other than a very small one will probably be maximized if it is organized as a corporation for the following three reasons:

1. Limited liability reduces the risks borne by investors, and, other things held constant, *the lower the firm's risk, the higher its value.*
2. A firm's value is dependent on its *growth opportunities*, which, in turn, are dependent on its ability to attract capital. Because corporations can attract capital more easily than can unincorporated businesses, they are better able to take advantage of growth opportunities.
3. The value of an asset also depends on its *liquidity*, which means the ease of selling the asset and converting it to cash at a "fair market value." Because an investment in the stock of a corporation is much easier to transfer to another investor than are proprietorship or partnership interests, a corporate investment is more liquid than a similar investment in a proprietorship or partnership, and this too enhances the value of a corporation.

As we just discussed, most firms are managed with value maximization in mind, and that, in turn, has caused most large businesses to be organized as corporations.

Corporation
A legal entity created by a state, separate and distinct from its owners and managers, having unlimited life, easy transferability of ownership, and limited liability.

S Corporation
A special designation that allows small businesses that meet qualifications to be taxed as if they were a proprietorship or partnership rather than as a corporation.

What are the key differences between sole proprietorships, partnerships, and corporations?

How do some firms get to enjoy the benefits of the corporate form of organization yet avoid corporate income taxes? Why don't all firms—for example, IBM or GE—do this?

Why is the value of a business other than a small one generally maximized if it is organized as a corporation?

1-2 STOCK PRICES AND SHAREHOLDER VALUE

At the outset, it is important to understand the chief goals of a business. As we will see, the goals of a sole proprietor may be different than the goals of a corporation. Consider first Larry Jackson, a sole proprietor who operates a sporting goods store on Main Street. Jackson is in business to make money, but he also likes to take time off to play golf on Fridays. Jackson also has a few employees who are no longer very productive, but he keeps them on the payroll out of friendship and loyalty. Jackson is clearly running the business in a way that is consistent with his own personal goals—which is perfectly reasonable given that he is a sole proprietor. Jackson knows that he would make more money if he didn't play golf or if he replaced some of his employees, but he is comfortable with the choices he has made, and since it is his business, he is free to make those choices.

By contrast, Linda Smith is CEO of a large corporation. Smith manages the company on a day-to-day basis, but she isn't the sole owner of the company. The company is owned primarily by shareholders who purchased its stock because they were looking for a financial return that would help them retire, send their kids to college, or pay for a long-anticipated trip. The shareholders elected a board of directors, who then selected Smith to run the company. Smith and the firm's other managers are working on behalf of the shareholders, and they were hired to pursue policies that enhance shareholder value. Throughout this book we focus primarily on publicly owned companies, hence we operate on the assumption that management's primary goal is **stockholder wealth maximization,** which translates into *maximizing the price of the firm's common stock.*

Stockholder Wealth Maximization
The primary goal for managerial decisions; considers the risk and timing associated with expected earnings per share in order to maximize the price of the firm's common stock.

If managers are to maximize shareholder wealth, they must know how that wealth is determined. Essentially, a company's shareholder wealth is simply the number of shares outstanding times the market price per share. If you own 100 shares of GE's stock and the price is $35 per share, then your wealth in GE is $3,500. The wealth of all its stockholders can be summed, and that is the value of GE, the item that management is supposed to maximize. The number of shares outstanding is for all intents and purposes a given, so what really determines shareholder wealth is the price of the stock. Therefore, a central issue is this: What determines the stock's price?

Throughout this book, we will see that the value of any asset is simply the present value of the cash flows it provides to its owners over time. We discuss stock valuation in depth in Chapter 9, where we will see that a stock's price at any given time depends on the cash flows an "average" investor expects to receive in the future if he or she bought the stock. To illustrate, suppose investors are aware that GE earned $1.58 per share in 2004 and paid out 51 percent of that amount, or $0.80 per share, in dividends. Suppose further that most investors expect earnings, dividends, and the stock price to all increase by about 6 percent per year. Management might run the company so that these expectations are met. However, management might make some wonderful decisions that cause profits to rise at a 12 percent rate, causing the dividends and stock price to increase at that same rate. Of course, management might make some big mistakes, profits might suffer, and the stock price might decline sharply rather than grow. Thus, investors are exposed to more risk if they buy GE stock than if they buy a new U.S. Treasury bond, which offers a guaranteed interest payment every six months plus repayment of the purchase price when the bond matures.

We see, then, that if GE's management makes good decisions, the stock price should increase, while if it makes enough bad decisions, the stock price will decrease. Management's goal is to make the set of decisions that leads to the maximum stock price, as that will maximize its shareholders' wealth. Note, though, that factors beyond management's control also affect stock prices. Thus, after the 9/11 terrorist attacks on the World Trade Center and Pentagon, the prices of virtually all stocks fell, no matter how effective their management was.

Firms have a number of different departments, including marketing, accounting, production, human resources, and finance. The finance department's principal task is to evaluate proposed decisions and judge how they will affect the stock price and therefore shareholder wealth. For example, suppose the production manager wants to replace some old equipment with new, automated machinery that will enable the firm to reduce labor costs. The finance staff will evaluate that proposal and determine if the savings are worth the cost. Similarly, if marketing wants to sign a contract with Tiger Woods that will cost $10 million per year for five years, the financial staff will evaluate the proposal, looking at the probable increased sales and other related factors, and reach a conclusion as to whether signing Tiger will lead to a higher stock price. Most significant decisions will be evaluated similarly.

Note too that stock prices change over time as conditions change and as investors obtain new information about companies' prospects. For example, Apple Computer's stock ranged from a low of $21.18 to $69.57 per share during 2004, rising and falling as good and bad news was released. GE, which is older, more diversified, and consequently more stable, had a narrower price range, from $28.88 to $37.75. Investors can predict future results for GE more accurately than for Apple, hence GE is less risky. Note too that the investment decisions firms make determine their future profits and investors' cash flows. Some corporate projects are relatively straightforward and easy to evaluate, hence not very risky. For example, if Wal-Mart were considering opening a new store, the expected revenues, costs, and profits for this project would be easier to estimate than an Apple Computer project for a new voice-activated computer. The success or lack of success of projects such as these will determine the future stock prices of Wal-Mart, Apple, and other companies.

Managers must estimate the probable effects of projects on profitability and thus on the stock price. Stockholders must forecast how successful companies will be, and current stock prices reflect investors' judgments as to that future success.

What is management's primary goal?

What do investors expect to receive when they buy a share of stock? Do investors know for sure what they will receive? Explain.

Based just on the name, which company would you regard as being riskier, General Foods or South Seas Oil Exploration Company? Explain.

When a company like Boeing decides to invest $5 billion in a new jet airliner, are its managers positive about the project's effect on Boeing's future profits and stock price? Explain.

Would Boeing's managers or its stockholders be better able to judge the effect of a new airliner on profits and the stock price? Explain.

Would all Boeing stockholders expect the same outcome from an airliner project, and how would these expectations affect the stock price? Explain.

1-3 INTRINSIC VALUES, STOCK PRICES, AND COMPENSATION PLANS

As noted in the preceding section, stock prices are based on cash flows expected in future years, not just in the current year. Thus, stock price maximization requires us to take a long-run view of operations. Academics have always assumed that managers adhere to this long-run focus, but the focus for many companies shifted to the short run during the latter part of the 20th century. To give managers an incentive to focus on stock prices, stockholders (acting through boards of directors) gave executives stock options that could be exercised on a specified future date. An executive could exercise the option on that date, receive stock, sell it immediately, and thereby earn a profit. That led many managers to try to maximize the stock price on the option exercise date, not over the long run. That, in turn, led to some horrible abuses. Projects that looked good in the long run were turned down because they would penalize profits in the short run and thus the stock price on the option exercise day. Even worse, some managers deliberately overstated profits, thus temporarily boosting the stock price. These executives then exercised their options, sold the inflated stock, and left outside stockholders holding the bag when the true situation was revealed. Enron, WorldCom, and Fannie Mae are examples of companies whose managers did this, but there were many others.

Many more companies use aggressive but legal accounting practices that boost current profits but will lower profits in future years. For example, management might truly think that an asset should be depreciated over 5 years but will then depreciate it over a 10-year life. This reduces reported costs and raises reported income for the next 5 years but will raise costs and lower income in the following 5 years. Many other legal but questionable accounting procedures were used, all in an effort to boost reported profits and the stock price on the options exercise day, and thus the executives' profits when they exercised their options. Obviously, all of this made it difficult for investors to decide how much stocks were really worth.

Figure 1-1 can be used to illustrate the situation. The top box indicates that managerial actions, combined with economic and political conditions, determine investors' returns. Remember too that we don't know for sure what those future returns will be—we can estimate them, but expected and realized returns are often quite different. Investors like high returns but dislike risk, so the larger the expected profits and the lower the perceived risk, the higher the stock price.

The second row of boxes differentiates between what we call "true expected returns" and "true risk" versus "perceived" returns and risk. By "true" we mean the returns and risk that most investors would expect if they had all the information that exists about the company. "Perceived" means what investors expect, given the limited information that they actually have. To illustrate, in early 2001 investors thought that Enron was highly profitable and would enjoy high and rising future profits. They also thought that actual results would be close to their expected levels, hence that Enron's risk was low. However, the best true estimates of Enron's profits, which were known by its executives but not the investing public, were negative, and Enron's true situation was extremely risky.

The third row of boxes shows that each stock has an **intrinsic value,** which is an estimate of its "true" value as calculated by a fully informed analyst based

Intrinsic Value
An estimate of a stock's "true" value based on accurate risk and return data. The intrinsic value can be estimated but not measured precisely.

FIGURE 1-1   *Determinants of Intrinsic Values and Stock Prices*

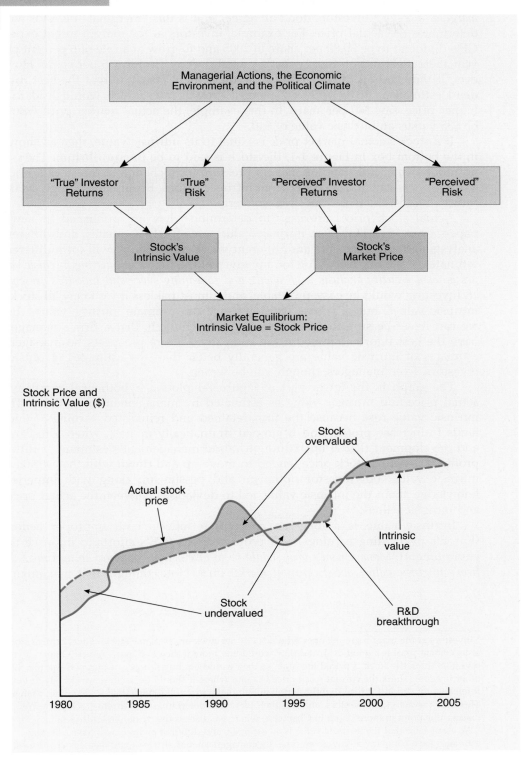

Market Price
The stock value based on perceived but possibly incorrect information as seen by the marginal investor.

Equilibrium
The situation in which the actual market price equals the intrinsic value, so investors are indifferent between buying or selling a stock.

on accurate risk and return data, and a **market price,** which is the value in the market based on perceived but possibly incorrect information as seen by the *marginal investor.*[4] Investors don't all agree, so it is this "marginal" investor who determines the actual price. For example, investors at the margin might expect GE's dividend to be $0.80 per share in 2005 and to grow at a rate of 6 percent per year thereafter, and on that basis they might set a price of $35 per share. However, if they had all the available facts, they might conclude that the best dividend estimate is $0.85 with a 7 percent growth rate, which would lead to a higher price, say, $40 per share. In this example, the actual market price would be $35 versus an intrinsic value of $40.

If a stock's actual market price is equal to its intrinsic value, then as shown in the bottom box in Figure 1-1, the stock is said to be in **equilibrium.** There is no fundamental imbalance, hence no pressure for a change in the stock's price. Market prices can and do differ from intrinsic values. Eventually, though, as the future unfolds, the two values will converge.

Actual stock prices are easy to determine—they are published in newspapers every day. However, intrinsic values are strictly estimates, and different analysts with different data and different views of the future will form different estimates of the intrinsic value for any given stock. *Indeed, estimating intrinsic values is what security analysis is all about, and something successful investors are good at.* Investing would be easy, profitable, and almost riskless if we knew all stocks' intrinsic values, but of course we don't—we can estimate intrinsic values, but we can never be sure that we are right. Note, though, that a firm's managers have the best information about the company's future prospects, so managers' estimates of intrinsic value are generally better than the estimates of outside investors. Even managers, though, can be wrong.

The graph in the lower part of Figure 1-1 plots a hypothetical company's actual price and intrinsic value as estimated by management over time.[5] The intrinsic value rose because the firm retained and reinvested earnings, which tends to increase profits, and it jumped dramatically in 1997, when a research and development (R&D) breakthrough raised management's estimate of future profits. The actual stock price tended to move up and down with the estimated intrinsic value, but investor optimism and pessimism, along with imperfect knowledge about the intrinsic value, led to deviations between the actual prices and intrinsic values.

Intrinsic value is a long-run concept. It reflects both improper actions (Enron's overstating earnings) and proper actions (GE's efforts to improve the environment). *Management's goal should be to take actions designed to maximize the firm's intrinsic value, not its current market price.* Note, though, that maximizing

---

[4] Investors at the margin are the ones who actually set stock prices. Some stockholders think a stock at its current price is a good deal, and they would buy more if they had more money. Other investors think the stock is priced too high, so they would not buy it unless it dropped sharply. Still other investors think the current stock price is about where it should be, so they would buy more if it fell slightly, sell it if it rose slightly, and maintain their current holdings unless something changes. These are the marginal investors, and it is their view that determines the current stock price. We discuss this point in more depth in Chapter 8, where we discuss the stock market in detail.

[5] We emphasize that the intrinsic value is an estimate, and different analysts will have different estimates for a company at any given time. Its managers should also estimate their firm's intrinsic value and then take actions to maximize that value. They should also try to help outside security analysts improve their intrinsic value estimates by providing accurate information about the company's financial position and operations, but without releasing information that would help its competitors. Enron, WorldCom, and a number of other companies tried successfully to deceive analysts and succeeded only too well.

the intrinsic value will maximize the *average* price over the long run but not necessarily the current price at each point in time. For example, management might make an investment that will lower profits for the current year but raise future profits substantially. If investors are not aware of the true situation, then the stock price might be held down by the low current profits even though the intrinsic value is actually increased. Management should provide information that helps investors make accurate estimates of the firm's "true" intrinsic value, which will keep the stock price closer to its equilibrium level over time, but there may be times when management cannot divulge the true situation because to do so would provide helpful information to its competitors.[6]

What's the difference between a stock's current market price and its intrinsic value?

Do stocks have a known and "provable" intrinsic value, or might different people reach different conclusions about intrinsic values? Explain.

Should a firm's managers estimate its intrinsic value or leave this estimation to outside security analysts? Explain.

If an action would maximize either the current market price or the intrinsic value, but not both, which one should stockholders (as a group) want managers to maximize? Explain.

Should its managers help investors improve their estimates of a firm's intrinsic value? Explain.

1-4 SOME IMPORTANT TRENDS

Three important trends should be noted. First, the points noted in the preceding section have led to profound changes in business practices. Executives at Enron, WorldCom, and other companies lied when they reported financial results, leading to huge stockholder losses. These companies' CEOs later claimed not to have been aware of what was happening. As a result, Congress passed legislation that requires the CEO and chief financial officer (CFO) to certify that their firm's financial statements are accurate, and these executives could be sent to jail if it later turns out that the statements did not meet the required standards. Consequently, published statements in the future are likely to be more accurate and dependable than those in the past.

A second trend is the increased globalization of business. Developments in communications technology have made it possible for firms like Wal-Mart to obtain real-time data on sales of hundreds of thousands of items in stores from China to Chicago, and to manage those stores from Bentonville, Arkansas. IBM, Microsoft, and other high-tech companies now have research labs and help desks in China, India, Romania, and the like, and the customers of Home Depot and other retailers have their telephone or e-mail questions answered by call-center operators in countries all around the globe. Moreover, many U.S. companies,

---

[6] As we discuss in Chapter 5, many academics believe that stock prices embody all publicly available information, hence that stock prices are typically reasonably close to their intrinsic values and thus at or close to an equilibrium. However, almost no one doubts that managers have better information than the public at large, that at times stock prices and equilibrium values diverge, and thus that stocks can be temporarily undervalued or overvalued, as we suggest in the graph in Figure 1-1.

Is Shareholder Wealth Maximization a Worldwide Goal?

Most academics agree that shareholder wealth maximization should be a firm's primary goal, at least in the United States; however, it's not clear that people really know how to implement it. Pricewaterhouse-Coopers (PWC), a global consulting firm, conducted a survey of 82 Singapore companies to test their understanding and implementation of shareholder value concepts. Ninety percent of the respondents said their firm's primary goal was to enhance shareholder value, but only 44 percent had taken steps to achieve this goal. Moreover, almost half of the respondents who had shareholder value programs in place said they were dissatisfied with the results achieved thus far. Even so, respondents who focused on shareholder value were more likely to believe that their stock was fairly valued than those with other focuses, and 50 percent of those without a specific program said they wanted to learn more and would probably adopt one eventually.

The study found that firms measure performance primarily with accounting-based measures such as the returns on assets, on equity, or on invested capital. These measures are easy to understand and thus to implement, even though they might not be the best conceptually. Compensation was tied to shareholder value, but only for mid-level managers and above.

It is unclear how closely these results correspond to U.S. firms, but firms from the United States and Singapore would certainly agree on one thing: It is easier to set the goal of shareholder wealth maximization than it is to figure out how to achieve it.

Source: Kalpana Rashiwala, "Low Adoption of Shareholder Value Concepts Here," *The Business Times (Singapore),* February 14, 2002.

including Coca-Cola, ExxonMobil, GE, and IBM, generate close to half their sales and income overseas. The trend toward globalization is likely to continue, and companies that resist it will have difficulty competing in the 21st century.

A third trend that's having a profound effect on financial management is ever-improving information technology (IT). These improvements are spurring globalization, and they are also changing financial management as it is practiced in the United States. Firms are collecting massive amounts of data and then using it to take much of the guesswork out of financial decisions. For example, when Wal-Mart is considering a potential site for a new store, it can draw on historical results from thousands of other stores to predict results at the proposed site, which lowers the risk of investing in the new store.

These trends are reflected in this book, and everyone involved in business should recognize the trends and their implications for decisions of all types.

 What are three trends that affect business management in general and financial management in particular?

1-5 BUSINESS ETHICS

As a result of the Enron and other recent scandals, there has been a strong push to improve *business ethics*. This is occurring on several fronts, from actions by New York Attorney General Elliot Spitzer and others who are suing companies for improper acts, to Congress, which has passed legislation imposing sanctions on executives who do bad things, to business schools trying to inform students about what's right and what's wrong, and about the consequences of their actions once they enter the business world.

As we discussed earlier, companies benefit from good reputations and are penalized by bad ones, and the same is true for individuals. Reputations reflect the extent to which firms and people are ethical. *Ethics* is defined in *Webster's Dictionary* as "standards of conduct or moral behavior." **Business ethics** can be thought of as a company's attitude and conduct toward its employees, customers, community, and stockholders. High standards of ethical behavior demand that a firm treat the parties that it deals with in a fair and honest manner. A firm's commitment to business ethics can be measured by the tendency of its employees, from the top down, to adhere to laws, regulations, and moral standards relating to product safety and quality, fair employment practices, fair marketing and selling practices, the use of confidential information for personal gain, community involvement, and illegal payments to obtain business.

Business Ethics
A company's attitude and conduct toward its employees, customers, community, and stockholders.

1-5a What Companies Are Doing

Most firms today have strong codes of ethical behavior, and they also conduct training programs to ensure that employees understand proper behavior in different situations. When conflicts arise between profits and ethics, ethical considerations sometimes are so obviously important that they clearly dominate. However, in many cases the right choice is not clear. For example, suppose Norfolk Southern's managers know that its coal trains are polluting the air, but the amount of pollution is within legal limits and further reduction would be costly. Are the managers ethically bound to reduce pollution? Similarly, some time ago Merck's own research indicated that its Vioxx pain medicine might be causing heart attacks, but the evidence was not overwhelmingly strong and the product was clearly helping some patients. Over time, additional tests produced stronger and stronger evidence that Vioxx did indeed pose a significant health risk. If the company released negative but still questionable information, this would hurt sales and possibly keep some patients who would benefit from using the product. If it delayed release, more and more patients might suffer irreversible harm. At what point should Merck make the potential problem known to the public? There are no obvious answers to questions such as these, but companies must deal with them, and a failure to handle them properly can lead to severe consequences.

1-5b Consequences of Unethical Behavior

Over the past few years ethical lapses have led to a number of bankruptcies. The recent collapses of Enron and WorldCom, as well as the accounting firm Arthur Andersen, dramatically illustrate how unethical behavior can lead to a firm's rapid decline. In all three cases, top executives came under fire for misleading accounting practices that led to overstated profits. Enron and WorldCom executives were busily selling their stock at the same time they were recommending the stock to employees and outside investors. Thus, senior executives reaped millions before the stock declined, while lower-level employees and outside investors were left holding the bag. Some of these executives are now in jail, and others will probably follow. Moreover, the financial institutions that facilitated these frauds, including Merrill Lynch and Citigroup, have been fined hundreds of millions of dollars, and more lawsuits are on the way.

These frauds also contributed to fatal wounds to other companies and even whole industries. For example, WorldCom understated its costs by some $11 billion. It used those artificially low costs when it set prices to its customers, and as a result its prices were the lowest in the industry. This allowed it to increase its market share and growth rate. Its earnings per share were badly overstated, and this caused its stock price to be way too high. Even though WorldCom's results were built on lies, they still had a tremendous effect on the industry. For example, AT&T's top executives, believing WorldCom's numbers, put pressure on their own managers to match WorldCom's costs and prices, but that was not possible without cheating. AT&T cut back on important projects, put far too much stress on its employees, and ended up ruining a wonderful 100-year-old company. A similar situation occurred in the energy industry as a result of Enron's cheating.

All of this caused many investors to lose faith in American business and to turn away from the stock market, which made it difficult for firms to raise the capital they needed to grow, create jobs, and stimulate our economy. So, unethical actions can have consequences far beyond the companies that perpetrate them.

This raises a question: Are *companies* unethical, or is it just some of their employees? That issue came up in the case of Arthur Andersen, the accounting firm that audited Enron, WorldCom, and several other companies that committed accounting fraud. Evidence showed that some Andersen accountants helped perpetrate the frauds. Its top managers argued that while some rogue employees did bad things, the firm's 85,000 other employees, and the firm itself, were innocent. The U.S. Justice Department disagreed, concluding that the firm itself was guilty because it fostered a climate where unethical behavior was permitted, and it built an incentive system that made such behavior profitable to both the perpetrators and the firm itself. As a result, Andersen was put out of business, its partners lost millions of dollars, and its 85,000 employees lost their jobs. In most other cases, individuals rather than firms were tried, and while the firms survived, they suffered reputational damage that greatly lowered their future profit potential and value.

1-5c How Should Employees Deal with Unethical Behavior?

Far too often the desire for stock options, bonuses, and promotions drives managers to take unethical actions, including fudging the books to make profits in the manager's division look good, holding back information about bad products that would depress sales, and failing to take costly but needed measures to protect the environment. Generally these acts don't rise to the level of an Enron or WorldCom, but they are still bad. If questionable things are going on, who should take action, and what should that action be? Obviously, in situations like Enron and WorldCom, where fraud was being perpetrated at or close to the top, senior managers knew about it. In other cases, the problem is caused by a mid-level manager trying to boost his unit's profits and thus his bonus. In all cases, though, at least some lower-level employees are aware of what's happening, and they may even be ordered to take fraudulent actions. Should the lower-level employees obey their boss's orders, refuse to obey those orders, or report the situation to a higher authority, such as the company's board of directors, its auditors, or a federal prosecutor?

In the WorldCom and Enron cases, it was clear to a number of employees that unethical and illegal acts were being committed, but in cases like Merck's Vioxx product, the situation is less clear. If early evidence that Vioxx led to heart attacks was quite weak but evidence of its pain reduction was strong, then it would probably not be appropriate to sound an alarm. However, as evidence accumulates, at some point the public should be given a strong warning, or the product should be taken off the market. But judgment comes into play when

Protection for Whistle-Blowers

As a result of the recent accounting and other frauds, Congress in 2002 passed the Sarbanes-Oxley Act, which codified certain rules pertaining to corporate behavior. One provision in the bill was designed to protect "whistle-blowers," or lower-level employees who sound an alarm over actions by their superiors. Employees who report improper actions are often fired or otherwise penalized, and this keeps many people from reporting things that should be investigated. The Sarbanes-Oxley provision was designed to alleviate this problem—if someone reports a corporate wrong-doing and is later penalized, he or she can ask the Occupational Safety and Health Administration (OSHA) to investigate the situation, and if the employee was improperly penalized, the company can be required to reinstate the person, along with back pay and a sizable penalty award. According to *The Wall Street Journal*, some big awards have been handed out, and a National Whistle-Blower Center has been established to help people sue companies.[a] It's still dangerous to blow a whistle, but less so than before the Sarbanes-Oxley Act was passed.

[a] Deborah Solomon and Kara Scannell, "SEC Is Urged to Enforce 'Whistle-Blower' Provision," *The Wall Street Journal*, November 15, 2004, p. A6.

deciding on what action to take and when to take it. If a lower-level employee thinks that the product should be pulled but his or her boss disagrees, what should the employee do? If an employee goes ahead and sounds the alarm, he or she might be in trouble regardless of the merits of the case. If the alarm is false, then the company will have been harmed and nothing will have been gained. In that case, the employee will probably lose his or her job. Even if the employee is correct, his or her career may still be ruined, because some companies, or at least some bosses, don't like "disloyal, troublemaking" employees.

Such situations arise frequently, and in contexts ranging from accounting fraud to product liability and environmental cases. Employees jeopardize their jobs if they come forward over their bosses' objections, but if they don't they can suffer emotional problems and also contribute to the downfall of their companies and the accompanying loss of jobs and savings. Moreover, if they obey orders that they know are illegal, they can end up going to jail. Indeed, in most of the scandals that have come to trial, the lower-level people who physically did the bad deeds have received longer jail sentences than the bosses who told them what to do. So, employees can be stuck between a rock and a hard place, that is, doing what they should do and possibly losing their jobs versus going along with the boss and possibly ending up in jail.

This discussion shows why ethics is such an important consideration in both business and business schools, and why we are concerned with it in this book.

How would you define "business ethics"?

Can a firm's incentive compensation plan lead to unethical behavior? Explain.

Unethical acts are generally committed by unethical people. What are some things companies can do to help ensure that their employees act ethically?

1-6 CONFLICTS BETWEEN MANAGERS AND STOCKHOLDERS[7]

It has long been recognized that managers' personal goals may compete with shareholder wealth maximization. In particular, managers might be more interested in maximizing their own wealth rather than their stockholders' wealth, hence pay themselves excessive salaries. For example, Disney paid its former president, Michael Ovitz, $140 million as a severance package after just 14 months on the job—$140 million to go away—because he and Disney CEO Michael Eisner were having disagreements. Eisner himself was also handsomely compensated the year Ovitz was fired—a $750,000 base salary, plus a $9.9 million bonus, plus a $565 million profit from stock options, for a total of just over $575 million. As another example of corporate excesses, Tyco CEO Dennis Kozlowski spent more than $1 million of the company's money on a birthday party for his wife.

Neither the Disney executives' pay nor Kozlowski's expenditures seem consistent with shareholder wealth maximization. Still, good executive compensation plans can motivate managers to act in their stockholders' best interests. Useful motivational tools include (1) reasonable compensation packages; (2) direct intervention by shareholders, including firing managers who don't perform well; and (3) the threat of a takeover.

The *compensation package* should be sufficient to attract and retain able managers but not go beyond what is needed. Also, compensation should be structured so that managers are rewarded on the basis of the stock's performance over the long run, not the stock's price on an option exercise date. This means that options (or direct stock awards) should be phased in over a number of years so managers will have an incentive to keep the stock price high over time. If the intrinsic value could be measured in an objective and verifiable manner, then performance pay could be based on changes in intrinsic value. However, because intrinsic value is not observable, compensation must be based on the stock's market price—but the price used should be an average over time rather than on a spot date.

Stockholders can intervene directly with managers. Years ago most stock was owned by individuals, but today the majority is owned by institutional investors such as insurance companies, pension funds, and mutual funds. These institutional money managers have the clout to exercise considerable influence over firms' operations. First, they can talk with managers and make suggestions about how the business should be run. In effect, institutional investors such as Calpers (California Public Employees Retirement System, with $165 billion of assets) and TIAA–CREF (a retirement plan originally set up for professors at private colleges that now has more than $300 billion of assets) act as lobbyists for the body of stockholders. When such large stockholders speak, companies listen. Second, any shareholder who has owned $2,000 of a company's stock for one year can sponsor a proposal that must be voted on at the annual stockholders' meeting, even if management opposes the proposal. Although shareholder-sponsored proposals are nonbinding, the results of such votes are clearly heard by top management.

Stockholder intervention can range from making suggestions for improving sales to threatening to fire the management team. Until recently, the probability of a large firm's management being ousted by its stockholders was so remote

---

[7] These conflicts are studied under the heading of *agency theory* in the finance literature. The classic work on agency theory is Michael C. Jensen and William H. Meckling, "Theory of the Firm, Managerial Behavior, Agency Costs, and Ownership Structure," *Journal of Financial Economics*, October 1976, pp. 305–360.

that it posed little threat. Most firms' shares were so widely distributed, and management had so much control over the voting mechanism, that it was virtually impossible for dissident stockholders to get the votes needed to overthrow a management team. However, that situation has changed. In recent years the top executives of AT&T, Coca-Cola, Fannie Mae, General Motors, IBM, and Xerox, to name a few, have been forced out. Also, Tyco's Kozlowski is gone and Disney's Eisner is under pressure and will soon be leaving. All of these departures were due to their firm's poor performance.

If a firm's stock is undervalued, then **corporate raiders** will see it to be a bargain and will attempt to capture the firm in a **hostile takeover.** If the raid is successful, the target's executives will almost certainly be fired. This situation gives managers a strong incentive to take actions to maximize their stock's price. In the words of one executive, "If you want to keep your job, never let your stock sell at a bargain price."

Again, note that the price managers should be trying to maximize is not the price on a specific day. Rather, it is the average price over the long run, which will be maximized if management focuses on the stock's intrinsic value. However, managers must communicate effectively with stockholders (without divulging information that would aid their competitors) in order to keep the actual price close to the intrinsic value. It's bad for both stockholders and managers for the intrinsic value to be high but the actual price low, because then a raider may swoop in, buy the company at a bargain price, and fire the managers. To repeat our earlier message: *Managers should try to maximize their stock's intrinsic value and then communicate effectively with stockholders. That will cause the intrinsic value to be high and the actual stock price to remain close to the intrinsic value over time.*

Because the intrinsic value cannot be observed, it is impossible to know if it is really being maximized. Still, as we will discuss in Chapter 9, there are procedures for estimating a stock's value. Managers can then use these valuation models to analyze alternative courses of action in terms of how they are likely to affect the estimated value. This type of value-based management is not as precise as we would like, but it is the best way to run a business.

Corporate Raider
An individual who targets a corporation for takeover because it is undervalued.

Hostile Takeover
The acquisition of a company over the opposition of its management.

What are three techniques stockholders can use to motivate managers to try to maximize their stock's long-run price?

Should managers focus directly on the actual stock price, on the stock's intrinsic value, or are both important? Explain.

1-7 THE ROLE OF FINANCE IN THE ORGANIZATION

The organizational structure of a typical corporation has the board of directors at the top, and the **chairman of the board** is the person most responsible for the firm's strategic policies. Under the chairman's guidance, the board sets policy, but implementing that policy is the responsibility of the firm's management. Note too that the boards of most publicly owned corporations have a **compensation committee** that consists of three outside (nonemployee) directors who set the compensation package for the senior officers. The compensation committee looks at factors such as the firm's stock price performance relative to the market as a whole and other firms in the same industry, the growth rate in earnings per share, and the compensation of executives in other similar firms. Obviously, this is a very important committee.

Chairman of the Board
The person most responsible for the firm's strategic policies.

Compensation Committee
A committee that consists of three outside (nonemployee) directors who set the compensation package for senior officers.

Chief Executive Officer (CEO)
Heads the management team, and ideally is separate from chairman of the board.

Chief Operating Officer (COO)
In charge of the firm's actual operations.

Chief Financial Officer (CFO)
Responsible for the accounting system, raising capital, and evaluating major investment decisions and the effectiveness of operations.

The management team is headed by the **chief executive officer (CEO).** Sometimes the chairman of the board is also the CEO, but corporate governance experts, including the New York Stock Exchange, think those two offices should be separated, and there is a clear trend toward separation. Directly below the CEO is the **chief operating officer (COO)** and the **chief financial officer (CFO).** The COO is in charge of actual operations, including producing and selling the firm's products. The CFO is responsible for the accounting system, for raising any capital the firm needs, for evaluating the effectiveness of operations in relation to other firms in the industry, and for evaluating all major investment decisions, including proposed new plants, stores, and the like. All of the CFO's duties are important if the firm is to maximize shareholder wealth. The accounting system must provide good information if the firm is to be run efficiently—management must know the true costs in order to make good decisions. Also, the accounting system must provide investors with accurate and timely information—if investors don't trust the reported numbers, they will avoid the stock and its value won't be maximized. We don't go deeply into accounting mechanics in this text, but we do explain how accounting numbers are used to make good internal decisions and by investors when they value securities. It is also important that the firm be financed in an optimal manner—it should use the value-maximizing mix of debt and equity. Finally, the financial staff must evaluate the various departments and divisions, including their proposed capital expenditures, to make sure the firm is operating efficiently and making investments that will enhance shareholders' wealth.

What are the principal responsibilities of the board of directors and the CEO?

What are the principal responsibilities of the CFO?

Tying It All Together

This chapter provides a broad overview of financial management. Management's goal should be to maximize the long-run value of the stock, which means the intrinsic value as measured by the average stock price over time. To maximize value, firms must develop products that consumers want, produce them efficiently, sell them at competitive prices, and observe laws relating to corporate behavior. If they are successful at maximizing the stock's value, they will also be contributing to social welfare and our citizens' well-being.

In the 1990s corporations tended to give executives stock options that could be exercised and then sold on a specific date. That led some managers to try to maximize the stock price on the option exercise day, not the long-run price that would be in their stockholders' best interests. This problem can be corrected by giving options that are phased in and can be exercised over time, which will cause managers to focus on the stock's long-run intrinsic value.

Businesses can be organized as proprietorships, partnerships, or corporations. The vast majority of all business is done by corporations, and the most successful firms end up as corporations. Therefore, we focus on corporations in the book. We also discussed some new developments that are affecting all businesses. The first is the focus on business ethics that resulted from a series of scandals in the late 1990s. The second is the trend toward globalization, which is changing the way companies do business. And the third is the continuing development of new technology, which is also changing the way business is done.

The primary tasks of the CFO are (1) to make sure that the accounting system provides "good" numbers for internal decisions and to investors, (2) to ensure that the firm is financed in the proper manner, (3) to evaluate the operating units to make sure they are performing in an optimal manner, and (4) to evaluate all proposed capital expenditures to make sure that they will increase the firm's value. In the balance of the book we discuss exactly how financial managers carry out these tasks.

SELF-TEST QUESTIONS AND PROBLEMS
(Solutions Appear in Appendix A)

ST-1 **Key terms** Define each of the following terms:
   a. Proprietorship; partnership; corporation; S corporation
   b. Stockholder wealth maximization
   c. Intrinsic value; market price
   d. Equilibrium; marginal investor
   e. Business ethics
   f. Corporate raider; hostile takeover
   g. Chairman of the board; compensation committee
   h. CEO; COO; CFO

QUESTIONS

1-1 If you bought a share of stock, what would you expect to receive, when would you expect to receive it, and would you be certain that your expectations would be met?

1-2 Are the stocks of different companies equally risky? If not, what are some factors that would cause a company's stock to be viewed as being relatively risky?

1-3 If most investors expect the same cash flows from Companies A and B but are more confident that A's cash flows will be close to their expected value, which should have the higher stock price? Explain.

1-4 Are all corporate projects equally risky, and if not, how do a firm's investment decisions affect the riskiness of its stock?

1-5 What is a firm's intrinsic value? Its current stock price? Is the stock's "true long-run value" more closely related to its intrinsic value or its current price?

1-6 When is a stock said to be in equilibrium? At any given time, would you guess that most stocks are in equilibrium as you defined it? Explain.

1-7 Suppose three *completely honest* individuals gave you their estimates of Stock X's intrinsic value. One is your current girlfriend or boyfriend, the second is a professional security analyst with an excellent reputation on Wall Street, and the third is Company X's CFO. If the three estimates differed, which one would you have the most confidence in? Why?

1-8 Is it better for a firm's actual stock price in the market to be under, over, or equal to its intrinsic value? Would your answer be the same from the standpoints of both stockholders in general and a CEO who is about to exercise a million dollars in options and then retire? Explain.

1-9 If a company's board of directors wants management to maximize shareholder wealth, should the CEO's compensation be set as a fixed dollar amount, or should it depend on how well the firm performs? If it is to be based on performance, how should performance be measured? Would it be *easier* to measure performance by the growth rate in reported profits or the growth rate in the stock's intrinsic value? Which would be the *better* performance measure? Why?

1-10 What are the three principal forms of business organization? What are the advantages and disadvantages of each?

1-11 Should stockholder wealth maximization be thought of as a long-term or a short-term goal—for example, if one action would probably increase the firm's stock price from a current level of $20 to $25 in 6 months and then to $30 in 5 years but another action would probably keep the stock at $20 for several years but then increase it to $40 in 5 years, which action would be better? Can you think of some specific corporate actions that might have these general tendencies?

1-12 What are some actions stockholders can take to ensure that management's and stockholders' interests are aligned?

1-13 The president of Southern Semiconductor Corporation (SSC) made this statement in the company's annual report: "SSC's primary goal is to increase the value of our common stockholders' equity." Later in the report, the following announcements were made:
a. The company contributed $1.5 million to the symphony orchestra in Birmingham, Alabama, its headquarters city.
b. The company is spending $500 million to open a new plant and expand operations in China. No profits will be produced by the Chinese operation for 4 years, so earnings will be depressed during this period versus what they would have been had the decision not been made to expand in that market.
c. The company holds about half of its assets in the form of U.S. Treasury bonds, and it keeps these funds available for use in emergencies. In the future, though, SSC plans to shift its emergency funds from Treasury bonds to common stocks.

Discuss how SSC's stockholders might view each of these actions, and how they might affect the stock price.

1-14 Investors generally can make one vote for each share of stock they hold. Teacher's Insurance and Annuity Association–College Retirement Equity Fund (TIAA–CREF) is the largest institutional shareholder in the United States, hence it holds many shares and has more votes than any other organization. Traditionally, this fund has acted as a passive investor, just going along with management. However, back in 1993 it mailed a notice to all 1,500 companies whose stocks it held that henceforth it planned to actively intervene if, in its opinion, management was not performing well. Its goal was to improve corporate performance so as to boost the prices of the stocks it held. It also wanted to encourage corporate boards to appoint a majority of independent (outside) directors, and it stated that it would vote against any directors of firms that "don't have an effective, independent board that can challenge the CEO."

In the past, TIAA–CREF responded to poor performance by "voting with its feet," which means selling stocks that were not doing well. However, by 1993 that position had become difficult for two reasons. First, the fund invested a large part of its assets in "index funds," which hold stocks in accordance with their percentage value in the broad stock market. Furthermore, TIAA–CREF owns such large blocks of stocks in many companies that if it tried to sell out, this would severely depress the prices of those stocks. Thus, TIAA–CREF is locked in to a large extent, and that led to its decision to become a more active investor.

a. Is TIAA–CREF an ordinary shareholder? Explain.
b. Due to its asset size, TIAA–CREF owns many shares in a number of companies. The fund's management plans to vote those shares. However, TIAA–CREF is itself owned by many thousands of investors. Should the fund's managers vote its shares, or should it pass those votes, on a pro rata basis, back to its own shareholders? Explain.

1-15 Edmund Enterprises recently made a large investment to upgrade its technology. While these improvements won't have much of an effect on performance in the short run, they are expected to reduce future costs significantly. What effect will this investment have on Edmund Enterprises' earnings per share this year? What effect might this investment have on the company's intrinsic value and stock price?

1-16 Suppose you were a member of Company X's board of directors and chairman of the company's compensation committee. What factors should your committee consider when setting the CEO's compensation? Should the compensation consist of a dollar salary, stock options that depend on the firm's performance, or a mix of the two? If "performance" is to be considered, how should it be measured? Think of both theoretical and practical (that is, measurement) considerations. If you were also a vice president of Company X, might your actions be different than if you were the CEO of some other company?

1-17 Suppose you are a director of an energy company that has three divisions—natural gas, oil, and retail (gas stations). These divisions operate independently from one another, but the division managers all report to the firm's CEO. If you were on the compensation committee as discussed in question 1-16 and your committee was asked to set the compensation for the three division managers, would you use the same criteria as you would use for the firm's CEO? Explain your reasoning.

cyberproblem

Please go to the ThomsonNOW Web site to access the Cyberproblems.

FUNDAMENTAL CONCEPTS IN FINANCIAL MANAGEMENT

P A R T **2**

TIME VALUE OF MONEY

Will You Be Able to Retire?

Your reaction to this question is probably, "First things first! I'm worried about getting a job, not about retiring!" However, understanding the retirement situation could help you land a job, because (1) this is an important issue today, (2) employers like to hire people who know what's happening in the real world, and (3) professors often test on the time value of money with problems related to saving for future purposes, including retirement.

A recent *Fortune* article began with some interesting facts: (1) The U.S. savings rate is the lowest of any industrial nation. (2) The ratio of U.S. workers to retirees, which was 17 to 1 in 1950, is now down to 3 to 1, and it will decline to less than 2 to 1 after 2020. (3) With so few people paying into the Social Security system and so many drawing funds out, Social Security is going to be in serious trouble. The article concluded that even people making $85,000 per year will have trouble maintaining a reasonable standard of living after they retire, and many of today's college students will have to support their parents.

This is an important issue for millions of Americans, but many don't know how to deal with it. When *Fortune* studied the retirement issue, using the tools and techniques described in this chapter, they concluded that most Americans have been putting their heads in the sand, ignoring what is almost certainly going to be a huge personal and social problem. However, if you study this chapter carefully, you can avoid the trap that is likely to catch so many people.

*Excellent retirement calculators are available at **http://www.ssa.gov** and **http://www .choosetosave.org/ calculators**. These calculators allow you to input hypothetical retirement savings information, and the program shows if current retirement savings will be sufficient to meet retirement needs.*

Putting Things In Perspective

Time value analysis has many applications, including planning for retirement, valuing stocks and bonds, setting up loan payment schedules, and making corporate decisions regarding investing in new plant and equipment. *In fact, of all financial concepts, time value of money is the single most important.*

Indeed, time value analysis is used throughout the book, so it is vital that you understand this chapter before continuing.

You need to understand basic time value concepts, but conceptual knowledge will do you little good if you can't do the required calculations. Therefore, this chapter is heavy on calculations. Also, most students studying finance have a financial or scientific calculator, and some also own or have access to a computer. Moreover, one of these tools is necessary to work many finance problems in a "reasonable" length of time. However, when they start on this chapter, many students don't know how to use the time value functions in their calculator or computer. If you are in that situation, you will find yourself simultaneously studying concepts and trying to learn to use your calculator, and you will need more time to cover this chapter than you might expect.[1]

2-1 TIME LINES

The first step in time value analysis is to set up a **time line,** which will help you visualize what's happening in a particular problem. To illustrate, consider the following diagram, where PV represents $100 that is on hand today and FV is the value that will be in the account on a future date:

Periods	0		1	2	3
		5%			
Cash	PV = $100				FV = ?

Time Line
An important tool used in time value analysis; it is a graphical representation used to show the timing of cash flows.

The intervals from 0 to 1, 1 to 2, and 2 to 3 are time periods such as years or months. Time 0 is today, and it is the beginning of Period 1; Time 1 is one period from today, and it is both the end of Period 1 and the beginning of Period 2; and so on. Although the periods are often years, periods can also be quarters or months or even days. Note that each tick mark corresponds to both the *end* of one period and the *beginning* of the next one. Thus, if the periods are years, the tick mark at Time 2 represents both the *end* of Year 2 and the *beginning* of Year 3.

Cash flows are shown directly below the tick marks, and the relevant interest rate is shown just above the time line. Unknown cash flows, which you are trying to find, are indicated by question marks. Here the interest rate is 5 percent; a single cash outflow, $100, is invested at Time 0; and the Time 3 value is an unknown inflow. In this example, cash flows occur only at Times 0 and 3, with no flows at Times 1 or 2. Note that in our example the interest rate is constant for all three years. That condition is generally true, but if it were not then we would show different interest rates for the different periods.

Time lines are essential when you are first learning time value concepts, but even experts use them to analyze complex finance problems, and we use them throughout the book. We begin each problem by setting up a time line to show what's happening, after which we provide an equation that must be solved to find the answer, and then we explain how to use a regular calculator, a financial calculator, and a spreadsheet to find the answer.

---

[1] Calculator manuals tend to be long and complicated, partly because they cover a number of topics that aren't required in the basic finance course. Therefore, we provide, on the ThomsonNOW Web site, tutorials for the most commonly used calculators. The tutorials are keyed to this chapter, and they show exactly how to do the required calculations. If you don't know how to use your calculator, go to the ThomsonNOW Web site, get the relevant tutorial, and go through it as you study the chapter.

Do time lines deal only with years or could other periods be used?

Set up a time line to illustrate the following situation: You currently have $2,000 in a three-year certificate of deposit (CD) that pays a guaranteed 4 percent annually.

2-2 FUTURE VALUES

Future Value (FV)
The amount to which a cash flow or series of cash flows will grow over a given period of time when compounded at a given interest rate.

Present Value (PV)
The value today of a future cash flow or series of cash flows.

Compounding
The arithmetic process of determining the final value of a cash flow or series of cash flows when compound interest is applied.

A dollar in hand today is worth more than a dollar to be received in the future because, if you had it now, you could invest it, earn interest, and end up with more than a dollar in the future. The process of going to **future values (FVs)** from **present values (PVs)** is called **compounding.** To illustrate, refer back to our three-year time line and assume that you plan to deposit $100 in a bank that pays a guaranteed 5 percent interest each year. How much would you have at the end of Year 3? We first define some terms, after which we set up a time line and show how the future value is calculated.

PV = Present value, or beginning amount. In our example, PV = $100.

FV_N = Future value, or ending amount, of your account after N periods. Whereas PV is the value now, or the *present value*, FV_N is the value N periods into the *future*, after the interest earned has been added to the account.

CF_t = Cash flow. Cash flows can be positive or negative. The cash flow for a particular period is often given a subscript, CF_t, where t is the period. Thus, CF_0 = PV = the cash flow at Time 0, whereas CF_3 would be the cash flow at the end of Period 3.

I = Interest rate earned per year. Sometimes a lowercase "i" is used. Interest earned is based on the balance at the beginning of each year, and we assume that it is paid at the end of the year. Here I = 5%, or, expressed as a decimal, 0.05. Throughout this chapter, we designate the interest rate as I because that symbol (or I/YR, for interest rate per year) is used on most financial calculators. Note, though, that in later chapters we use the symbol "r" to denote rates because r (for rate of return) is used more often in the finance literature. Note too that in this chapter we generally assume that interest payments are guaranteed by the U.S. government, hence they are certain. In later chapters we will consider risky investments, where the interest rate actually earned might differ from its expected level.

INT = Dollars of interest earned during the year = Beginning amount × I. In our example, INT = $100(0.05) = $5.

N = Number of periods involved in the analysis. In our example N = 3. Sometimes the number of periods is designated with a lowercase "n," so both N and n indicate number of periods.

We can use four different procedures to solve time value problems.[2] These methods are described in the following sections.

---

[2] A fifth procedure, using tables that show "interest factors," was used before financial calculators and computers became available. Now, though, calculators and spreadsheets such as *Excel* are programmed to calculate the specific factor needed for a given problem and then to use it to find the FV. This is much more efficient than using the tables. Moreover, calculators and spreadsheets can handle fractional periods and fractional interest rates, like the FV of $100 after 3.75 years when the interest rate is 5.375 percent, whereas tables provide numbers only for specific periods and rates. For these reasons, tables are not used in business today; hence we do not discuss them in the text.

Simple versus Compound Interest

As noted in the text, when interest is earned on the interest earned in prior periods, as was true in our example and is always true when we apply Equation 2-1, this is called **compound interest.** If interest is not earned on interest, then we have **simple interest.** The formula for FV with simple interest is FV = PV + PV(I)(N), so in our example FV would have been $100 + $100(0.05)(3) = $100 + $15 = $115 based on simple interest. Most financial contracts are based on compound interest, but in legal proceedings the law often specifies that simple interest must be used. For example, Maris Distributing, a company founded by home run king Roger Maris, won a lawsuit against Anheuser-Busch (A-B) because A-B had breached a contract and taken away Maris's franchise to sell Budweiser beer. The judge awarded Maris $50 million plus interest at 10 percent from 1997 (when A-B breached the contract) until the payment is actually made. The interest award was based on simple interest, which as of 2004 had raised the total from $50 million to $50 million + 0.10($50 million)(7 years) = $85 million. If the law had allowed compound interest, the award would have totaled ($50 million)(1.10)[7] = $97.44 million, or $12.44 million more. This legal procedure dates back to the days before we had calculators and computers. The law moves slowly!

2-2a Step-by-Step Approach

The time line used to find the FV of $100 compounded for three years at 5 percent, along with some calculations, is shown below:

Multiply the initial amount, and each succeeding amount, by (1 + I) = (1.05):

Time	0	5%	1	2	3

Amount at beginning of period $100.00 ----► $105.00 ----► $110.25 ----► $115.76

Compound Interest
Occurs when interest is earned on prior periods' interest.

Simple Interest
Occurs when interest is not earned on interest.

You start with $100 in the account—this is shown at t = 0:

- You earn $100(0.05) = $5 of interest during the first year, so the amount at the end of Year 1 (or t = 1) is $100 + $5 = $105.
- You begin the second year with $105, earn 0.05($105) = $5.25 on the now larger beginning-of-period amount, and end the year with $110.25. Interest during Year 2 is $5.25, and it is higher than the first year's interest, $5, because you earned $5(0.05) = $0.25 interest on the first year's interest. This is called "compounding," and when interest is earned on interest, this is called "compound interest."
- This process continues, and because the beginning balance is higher in each successive year, the interest earned each year increases.
- The total interest earned, $15.76, is reflected in the final balance, $115.76.

The step-by-step approach is useful because it shows exactly what is happening. However, this approach is time-consuming, especially if a number of years are involved, so streamlined procedures have been developed.

2-2b Formula Approach

In the step-by-step approach, we multiply the amount at the beginning of each period by (1 + I) = (1.05). If N = 3, then we multiply by (1 + I) three different times, which is the same as multiplying the beginning amount by $(1 + I)^3$. This concept can be extended, and the result is this key equation:

$$FV_N = PV(1 + I)^N \qquad \textbf{(2-1)}$$

We can apply Equation 2-1 to find the FV in our example:

$$FV_3 = \$100(1.05)^3 = \$115.76$$

Equation 2-1 can be used with any calculator that has an exponential function, making it easy to find FVs, no matter how many years are involved.

2-2c Financial Calculators

Financial calculators are extremely helpful when working time value problems. Their manuals explain calculators in detail, and we provide summaries of the features needed to work the problems in this book for several popular calculators on the ThomsonNOW Web site. Also, see the box entitled "Hints on Using Financial Calculators" for suggestions that will help you avoid some common mistakes. If you are not yet familiar with your calculator, we recommend that you go through our tutorial as you study this chapter.

First, note that financial calculators have five keys that correspond to the five variables in the basic time value equations. We show the inputs for our example above the keys and the output, the FV, below its key. Because there are no periodic payments, we enter 0 for PMT. We describe the keys in more detail below the diagram.

N = Number of periods. Some calculators use n rather than N.

I/YR = Interest rate per period. Some calculators use i or I rather than I/YR.

PV = Present value. In our example we begin by making a deposit, which is an outflow, so the PV should be entered with a negative sign. On most calculators you must enter the 100, then press the +/− key to switch from +100 to −100. If you enter −100 directly, this will subtract 100 from the last number in the calculator and give you an incorrect answer.

PMT = Payment. This key is used if we have a series of equal, or constant, payments. Because there are no such payments in our illustrative problem, we enter PMT = 0. We will use the PMT key when we discuss annuities later in this chapter.

FV = Future value. In this example, the FV is positive because we entered the PV as a negative number. If we had entered the 100 as a positive number, then the FV would have been negative.

As noted in our example, you first enter the known values (N, I/YR, PMT, and PV) and then press the FV key to get the answer, 115.76. Again, note that if you entered the PV as 100 without a minus sign, the FV would be given as a negative. The calculator *assumes* that either the PV or the FV is negative. This should not be confusing if you think about what you are doing.

2-2d Spreadsheets[3]

Students generally use calculators for homework and exam problems, but in business people generally use spreadsheets for problems that involve the time

---

[3] If you have never worked with spreadsheets, you might want to skip this section. However, you might want to go through it and refer to this chapter's *Excel* model to get an idea of how spreadsheets work.

Hints on Using Financial Calculators

When using a financial calculator, make sure your machine is set up as indicated below. Refer to your calculator manual or to our calculator tutorial on the ThomsonNOW Web site for information on setting up your calculator.

- **One payment per period.** Many calculators "come out of the box" assuming that 12 payments are made per year; that is, they assume monthly payments. However, in this book we generally deal with problems where only one payment is made each year. *Therefore, you should set your calculator at one payment per year and leave it there. See our tutorial or your calculator manual if you need assistance.*

- **End mode.** With most contracts, payments are made at the end of each period. However, some contracts call for payments at the beginning of each period. You can switch between "End Mode" and "Begin Mode," depending on the problem you are solving. *Because most of the problems in this book call for end-of-period payments, you should return your calculator to End Mode after you work a problem where payments are made at the beginning of periods.*

- **Negative sign for outflows.** *Outflows must be entered as negative numbers. This generally means typing the outflow as a positive number and then pressing the +/– key to convert from + to – before hitting the enter key.*

- **Decimal places.** With most calculators, you can specify from 0 to 11 decimal places. When working with dollars, we generally specify two decimal places. When dealing with interest rates, we generally specify two places if the rate is expressed as a percentage, like 5.25 percent, but we specify four places if the rate is expressed as a decimal, like 0.0525.

- **Interest rates.** *For arithmetic operations with a nonfinancial calculator, the 0.0525 must be used, but with a financial calculator you must enter 5.25, not .0525, because financial calculators assume that rates are stated as percentages.*

value of money (TVM). Spreadsheets show in detail what is happening, and they help us reduce both conceptual and data-entry errors. The spreadsheet discussion can be skipped without loss of continuity, but if you understand the basics of *Excel* and have access to a computer, we recommend that you go through this section. Even if you aren't familiar with spreadsheets, our discussion will still give you an idea of how they operate.

We used *Excel* to create Table 2-1, which summarizes the four methods for finding the FV and shows the spreadsheet formulas toward the bottom. Note that spreadsheets can be used to do calculations, but they can also be used like a word processor to create exhibits like Table 2-1, which includes text, drawings, and calculations. The letters across the top designate columns, the numbers to the left designate rows, and the rows and columns jointly designate cells. Thus, C14 is the cell where we specify the –$100 investment, C15 shows the interest rate, and C16 shows the number of periods. We then created a time line on Rows 17 to 19, and on Row 21 we have *Excel* go through the step-by-step calculations, multiplying the beginning-of-year values by (1 + I) to find the compounded value at the end of each period. Cell G21 shows the final result. Then, on Row 23, we illustrate the formula approach, using *Excel* to solve Equation 2-1 and find the FV, $115.76. Next, on Rows 25 to 27, we show a picture of the calculator solution. Finally, on Rows 29 and 30 we use *Excel*'s built-in FV function to find the answers given in Cells G29 and G30. The G29 answer is based on fixed inputs while the G30 answer is based on cell references, which makes it easy to change inputs and see the effects on the output.

Table 2-1 demonstrates that all four methods get the same result, but they use different calculating procedures. It also shows that with *Excel* all the inputs

TABLE 2-1 *Summary of Future Value Calculations*

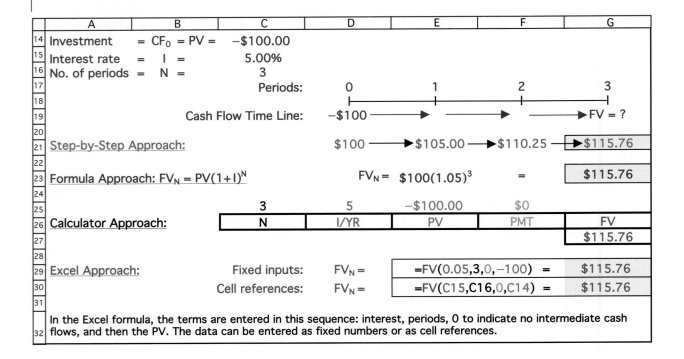

	A	B	C	D	E	F	G
14	Investment	$= CF_0 = PV =$	−$100.00				
15	Interest rate	$= I =$	5.00%				
16	No. of periods	$= N =$	3				
17			Periods:	0	1	2	3
18							
19		Cash Flow Time Line:	−$100 ⟶	⟶	⟶	⟶ FV = ?	
20							
21	Step-by-Step Approach:			$100 ⟶ $105.00 ⟶ $110.25 ⟶ $115.76			
22							
23	Formula Approach: $FV_N = PV(1+I)^N$			$FV_N =$ $100(1.05)^3$		=	$115.76
24							
25			3	5	−$100.00	$0	
26	Calculator Approach:		N	I/YR	PV	PMT	FV
27							$115.76
28							
29	Excel Approach:		Fixed inputs:	$FV_N =$	=FV(0.05,3,0,−100) =		$115.76
30			Cell references:	$FV_N =$	=FV(C15,C16,0,C14) =		$115.76
31							
32	In the Excel formula, the terms are entered in this sequence: interest, periods, 0 to indicate no intermediate cash flows, and then the PV. The data can be entered as fixed numbers or as cell references.						

are shown in one place, which makes checking data entries relatively easy. Finally, it shows that *Excel* can be used to create exhibits, which are quite important in the real world. In business, it's often as important to explain what you are doing as it is to "get the right answer," because if decision makers don't understand your analysis, they may well reject your recommendations.

2-2e Graphic View of the Compounding Process

Figure 2-1 shows how a $1 investment grows over time at different interest rates. We made the curves by solving Equation 2-1 with different values for N and I. The interest rate is a growth rate: If a sum is deposited and earns 5 percent interest per year, then the funds on deposit will grow by 5 percent per year. Note also that time value concepts can be applied to anything that grows—sales, population, earnings per share, or your future salary.

Explain why this statement is true: "A dollar in hand today is worth more than a dollar to be received next year."

What is compounding? What's the difference between simple interest and compound interest? What would the future value of $100 be after five years at 10 percent *compound* interest? At 10 percent *simple* interest? ($161.05; $150.00)

Suppose you currently have $2,000 and plan to purchase a three-year certificate of deposit (CD) that pays 4 percent interest compounded annually. How much will you have when the CD matures?

| FIGURE 2-1 | *Growth of $1 at Various Interest Rates and Time Periods* |

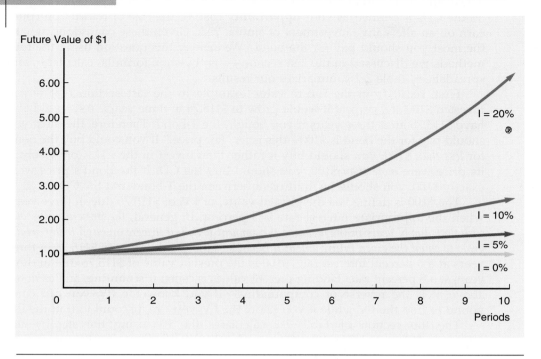

How would your answer change if the interest rate were 5 percent, or 6 percent, or 20 percent? ($2,249.73; $2,315.25; $2,382.03; $3,456.00) Hint: With a calculator, enter N = 3, I/YR = 4, PV = −2000, and PMT = 0, then press FV to get 2,249.73. Then, enter I/YR = 5 to override the 4 percent and press FV again to get the second answer. In general, you can change one input at a time to see how the output changes.

A company's sales in 2005 were $100 million. If sales grow at 8 percent, what will they be 10 years later, in 2015? ($215.89 million)

How much would $1, growing at 5 percent per year, be worth after 100 years? What would FV be if the growth rate were 10 percent? ($131.50; $13,780.61)

2-3 PRESENT VALUES

Finding a present value is the reverse of finding a future value. Indeed, we simply solve Equation 2-1, the formula for the future value, for the PV to produce the basic present value equation, 2-2:

$$\text{Future value} = FV_N = PV(1 + I)^N \qquad \textbf{(2-1)}$$

$$\text{Present value} = PV = \frac{FV_N}{(1 + I)^N} \qquad \textbf{(2-2)}$$

We illustrate PVs with the following example. A broker offers to sell you a Treasury bond that three years from now will pay $115.76. Banks are currently

Opportunity Cost
The rate of return you could earn on an alternative investment of similar risk.

offering a guaranteed 5 percent interest on three-year certificates of deposit (CDs), and if you don't buy the bond you will buy a CD. The 5 percent rate paid on the CDs is defined as your **opportunity cost,** or the rate of return you could earn on an alternative investment of similar risk. Given these conditions, what's the most you should pay for the bond? We answer this question using the four methods we discussed in the last section—step-by-step, formula, calculator, and spreadsheet. Table 2-2 summarizes our results.

First, recall from the future value example in the last section that if you invested $100 at 5 percent it would grow to $115.76 in three years. You would also have $115.76 after three years if you bought the T-bond. Therefore, the most you should pay for the bond is $100—this is its "fair price." If you could buy the bond for *less than* $100, you should buy it rather than invest in the CD. Conversely, if its price were *more than* $100, you should buy the CD. If the bond's price were exactly $100, you should be indifferent between the T-bond and the CD.

The $100 is defined as the present value, or PV, of $115.76 due in three years when the appropriate interest rate is 5 percent. In general, *the present value of a cash flow due N years in the future is the amount which, if it were on hand today, would grow to equal the given future amount.* Because $100 would grow to $115.76 in three years at a 5 percent interest rate, $100 is the present value of $115.76 due in three years at a 5 percent rate. Finding present values is called **discounting,** and as noted above, it is the reverse of compounding—if you know the PV, you can compound to find the FV, while if you know the FV, you can discount to find the PV.

Discounting
The process of finding the present value of a cash flow or a series of cash flows; discounting is the reverse of compounding.

The top section of Table 2-2 calculates the PV using the step-by-step approach. When we found the future value in the previous section, we worked from left to right, multiplying the initial amount and each subsequent amount

---

TABLE 2-2 *Summary of Present Value Calculations*

	A	B	C	D	E	F	G
64	Future payment = CF$_N$ = FV =		$115.76				
65	Interest rate = I =		5.00%				
66	No. of periods = N =		3				
67			Periods:	0	1	2	3
68							
69			Cash Flow Time Line:	PV = ? ←	←	←	$115.76
70							
71	Step-by-Step Approach:			$100.00 ← $105.00 ← $110.25 ← $115.76			
72							
73	Formula Approach: PV = FV$_N$ / (1 + I)^N			PV=$115.76/(1.05)^3	=		$100.00
74				3	5	$0	$115.76
75	Calculator Approach:			N	I/YR	PV	PMT	FV
76						−$100.00		
77								
78	Excel Approach:		Fixed inputs:	PV =	=PV(0.05,3,0,115.76) =	−$100.00	
79			Cell references:	PV =	=PV(C65,C66,0,C64) =	−$100.00	
80							
81							
82	In the Excel formula, 0 indicates that there are no intermediate cash flows.						

by $(1 + I)$. To find present values, we work backward, or from right to left, dividing the future value and each subsequent amount by $(1 + I)$. This procedure shows exactly what's happening, and that can be quite useful when you are working complex problems. However, it's inefficient, especially if you are dealing with a number of years.

With the formula approach we use Equation 2-2, simply dividing the future value by $(1 + I)^N$. This is more efficient than the step-by-step approach, and it gives the same result. Equation 2-2 is built into financial calculators, and as shown in Table 2-2, we can find the PV by entering values for N, I/YR, PMT, and FV, and then pressing the PV key. Finally, spreadsheets have a function that's essentially the same as the calculator, which also solves Equation 2-2.

The fundamental goal of financial management is to maximize the firm's value, and the value of a business (or any asset, including stocks and bonds) is the *present value* of its expected future cash flows. Because present value lies at the heart of the valuation process, we will have much more to say about it in the remainder of this chapter and throughout the book.

2-3a Graphic View of the Discounting Process

Figure 2-2 shows that the present value of a sum to be received in the future decreases and approaches zero as the payment date is extended further and further into the future and also that the present value falls faster the higher the interest rate. At relatively high rates, funds due in the future are worth very little today, and even at relatively low rates present values of sums due in the very distant future are quite small. For example, at a 20 percent discount rate, $1 million due in 100 years would be worth only $0.0121 today. This is because $0.0121 would grow to $1 million in 100 years when compounded at 20 percent.

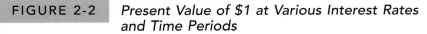

FIGURE 2-2   *Present Value of $1 at Various Interest Rates and Time Periods*

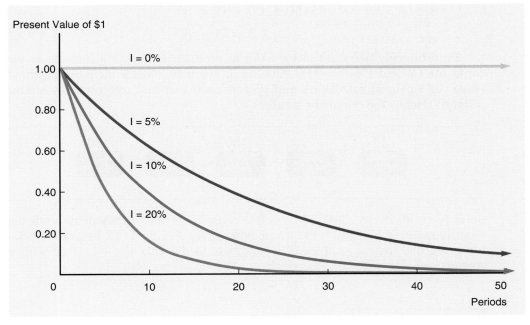

What is "discounting," and how is it related to compounding? How is the future value equation (2-1) related to the present value equation (2-2)?

How does the present value of a future payment change as the time to receipt is lengthened? As the interest rate increases?

Suppose a U.S. government bond promises to pay $2,249.73 three years from now. If the going interest rate on three-year government bonds is 4 percent, how much is the bond worth today? How would your answer change if the bond matured in five rather than three years? What if the interest rate on the five-year bond were 6 percent rather than 4 percent? ($2,000; $1,849.11; $1,681.13)

How much would $1,000,000 due in 100 years be worth today if the discount rate were 5 percent? If the discount rate were 20 percent? ($7,604.49; $0.0121)

2-4 FINDING THE INTEREST RATE, I

Thus far we have used Equations 2-1 and 2-2 to find future and present values. Those equations have four variables, and if we know three of them, we can solve for the fourth. Thus, if we know PV, I, and N, then we can solve 2-1 for FV, while if we know FV, I, and N we can solve 2-2 to find PV. That's what we did in the preceding two sections.

Now suppose we know PV, FV, and N, and we want to find I. For example, suppose we know that a given bond has a cost of $100 and that it will return $150 after 10 years. Thus, we know PV, FV, and N, and we want to find the rate of return we will earn if we buy the bond. Here's the situation:

$$FV = PV(1 + I)^N$$

$$\$150 = \$100(1 + I)^{10}$$

$$\$150/\$100 = (1 + I)^{10}$$

$$1.5 = (1 + I)^{10}$$

Unfortunately, we can't factor I out to produce as simple a formula as we could for FV and PV—we can solve for I, but it requires a bit more algebra.[4] However, financial calculators and spreadsheets can find interest rates almost instantly. Here's the calculator setup:

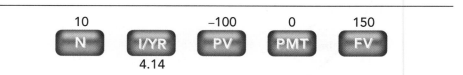

Enter N = 10, PV = −100, PMT = 0 because there are no payments until the security matures, and FV = 150. Then, when you press the I/YR key, the calculator gives the answer, 4.14 percent. You would get this same answer with a spreadsheet.

---

[4] Raise the left side of the equation, the 1.5, to the power $1/N = 1/10 = 0.1$, getting 1.0414. That number is 1 plus the interest rate, so the interest rate is 0.0414 = 4.14%.

The U.S. Treasury offers to sell you a bond for $585.43. No payments will be made until the bond matures 10 years from now, at which time it will be redeemed for $1,000. What interest rate would you earn if you bought this bond for $585.43? What rate would you earn if you could buy the bond for $550? For $600? (5.5%; 6.16%; 5.24%)

Microsoft earned $0.12 per share in 1994. Ten years later, in 2004, it earned $1.04. What was the growth rate in Microsoft's earnings per share (EPS) over the 10-year period? If EPS in 2004 had been $0.65 rather than $1.04, what would the growth rate have been? (24.1%; 18.41%)

2-5 FINDING THE NUMBER OF YEARS, N

We sometimes need to know how long it will take to accumulate a given sum of money, given our beginning funds and the rate we will earn on those funds. For example, suppose we believe that we could retire comfortably if we had $1 million, and we want to find how long it will take us to have $1 million, assuming we now have $500,000 invested at 4.5 percent. We cannot use a simple formula—the situation is like that with interest rates. We could set up a formula that uses logarithms, but calculators and spreadsheets can find N very quickly. Here's the calculator setup:

Enter I/YR = 4.5, PV = −500000, PMT = 0, and FV = 1000000. Then, when we press the N key, we get the answer, 15.7473 years. If you plug N = 15.7473 into the FV formula, you can prove that this is indeed the correct number of years:

$$FV = PV(1 + I)^N = \$500{,}000(1.045)^{15.7473} = \$1{,}000{,}000$$

We would also get N = 15.7473 with a spreadsheet.

How long would it take $1,000 to double if it were invested in a bank that pays 6 percent per year? How long would it take if the rate were 10 percent? (11.9 years; 7.27 years)

Microsoft's 2004 earnings per share were $1.04, and its growth rate during the prior 10 years was 24.1 percent per year. If that growth rate were maintained, how long would it take for Microsoft's EPS to double? (3.21 years)

2-6 ANNUITIES

Thus far we have dealt with single payments, or "lump sums." However, many assets provide a series of cash inflows over time, and many obligations like auto, student, and mortgage loans require a series of payments. If the payments are equal and are made at fixed intervals, then the series is an **annuity.** For example,

Annuity
A series of equal payments at fixed intervals for a specified number of periods.

Ordinary (Deferred) Annuity
An annuity whose payments occur at the end of each period.

Annuity Due
An annuity whose payments occur at the beginning of each period.

$100 paid at the end of each of the next three years is a three-year annuity. If the payments occur at the *end* of each year, then we have an **ordinary (or deferred) annuity.** If the payments are made at the *beginning* of each year, then we have an **annuity due.** Ordinary annuities are more common in finance, so when we use the term "annuity" in this book, assume that the payments occur at the ends of the periods unless otherwise noted.

Here are the time lines for a $100, three-year, 5 percent, ordinary annuity and for the same annuity on an annuity due basis. With the annuity due, each payment is shifted back to the left by one year. A $100 deposit will be made each year, so we show the payments with minus signs:

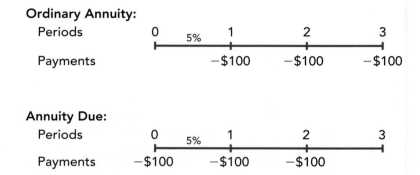

As we demonstrate in the following sections, we can find an annuity's future and present values, the interest rate built into annuity contracts, and how long it takes to reach a financial goal using an annuity. Keep in mind that annuities must have *constant payments* and a *fixed number of periods*. If these conditions don't hold, then we don't have an annuity.

What's the difference between an ordinary annuity and an annuity due?

Why should you rather receive an annuity due for $10,000 per year for 10 years than an otherwise similar ordinary annuity?

2-7 FUTURE VALUE OF AN ORDINARY ANNUITY

The future value of an annuity can be found using the step-by-step approach or with a formula, a financial calculator, or a spreadsheet. To illustrate, consider the ordinary annuity diagrammed earlier, where you deposit $100 at the end of each year for three years and earn 5 percent per year. How much will you have at the end of the third year? The answer, $315.25, is defined as the future value of the annuity, **FVA$_N$**, and it is shown in Table 2-3.

FVA$_N$
The future value of an annuity over N periods.

As shown in the step-by-step section of the table, we compound each payment out to Time 3, then sum those compounded values to find the annuity's FV, FVA$_3$ = $315.25. The first payment earns interest for two periods, the second for one period, and the third earns no interest at all because it is made at the end of the annuity's life. This approach is straightforward, but if the annuity extends out for many years, it is cumbersome and time-consuming.

As you can see from the time line diagram, with the step-by-step approach we apply the following equation, with N = 3 and I = 5%:

$$FVA_N = PMT(1 + I)^{N-1} + PMT(1 + I)^{N-2} + PMT(1 + I)^{N-3}$$
$$= \$100(1.05)^2 + \$100(1.05)^1 + \$100(1.05)^0$$
$$= \$315.25$$

We can generalize and streamline the equation as follows:

$$FVA_N = PMT(1 + I)^{N-1} + PMT(1 + I)^{N-2}$$
$$+ PMT(1 + I)^{N-3} + \cdots + PMT(1 + I)^0$$
$$= PMT \left[\frac{(1 + I)^N - 1}{I} \right] \qquad \text{(2-3)}$$

The first line shows the equation in its long form, and it can be transformed to the second form, which can be used to solve annuity problems with a non-financial calculator.[5] This equation is also built into financial calculators and

---

TABLE 2-3   *Summary: Future Value of an Ordinary Annuity*

	A	B	C	D	E	F	G
131	Payment amount	= PMT =	$100.00				
132	Interest rate	= I =	5.00%				
133	Number of periods	= N =	3				
134							
135		Periods:	0	1	2	3	
136							
137		Cash Flow Time Line:		−$100	−$100	−$100	
138							
139	Step-By-Step Approach.					−$100.00	
140	Multiply each payment by					−$105.00	
141	$(1+I)^{N-t}$ and sum these FVs to					−$110.25	
142	find FVA_N:					−$315.25	
143							
144	Formula Approach:						
145							
146		FVA_N =	$PMT \times \left(\dfrac{(1+I)^N - 1}{I} \right)$		=	$315.25	
147							
148							
149			3	5	$0	−$100.00	
150	Calculator Approach:		N	I/YR	PV	PMT	FV
151							$315.25
152							
153	Excel Function Approach:	Fixed inputs:	FVA_N =	=FV(0.05,3,−100,0)	=	= $315.25	
154		Cell references:	FVA_N =	=FV(C132,C133,−C131,0)=		$315.25	
155		Excel entries correspond with these calculator keys:		I/YR	N	PMT PV	FV

---

[5] The long form of the equation is a geometric progression that can be reduced to the second form.

spreadsheets. With an annuity, we have recurring payments, hence the PMT key is used. Here's the calculator setup for our illustrative annuity:

We enter PV = 0 because we start off with nothing, and we enter PMT = −100 because we plan to deposit this amount in the account at the end of each year. When we press the FV key we get the answer, $FVA_3 = 315.25$.

Because this is an ordinary annuity, with payments coming at the *end* of each year, we must set the calculator appropriately. As noted earlier, calculators "come out of the box" set to assume that payments occur at the end of each period, that is, to deal with ordinary annuities. However, there is a key that enables us to switch between ordinary annuities and annuities due. For ordinary annuities, the designation is "End Mode" or something similar, while for annuities due the designator is "Begin" or "Begin Mode" or "Due" or something similar. If you make a mistake and set your calculator on Begin Mode when working with an ordinary annuity, then each payment would earn interest for one extra year. That would cause the compounded amounts, and thus the FVA, to be too large.

The last approach in Table 2-3 shows the spreadsheet solution, using *Excel*'s built-in function. We could put in either fixed values for N, I, and PMT or set up an Input Section, where we assign values to those variables, and then to input values into the function as cell references. Using cell references makes it easy to change the inputs to see the effects of changes on the output.

For an ordinary annuity with five annual payments of $100 and a 10 percent interest rate, how many years will the first payment earn interest, and what will this payment's value be at the end? Answer this same question for the fifth payment. (4 years, $146.41; 0 years, $100)

Assume that you plan to buy a condo five years from now, and you estimate that you can save $2,500 per year. You plan to deposit the money in a bank that pays 4 percent interest, and you will make the first deposit at the end of the year. How much will you have after five years? How would your answer change if the interest rate were increased to 6 percent, or lowered to 3 percent? ($13,540.81; $14,092.73; $13,272.84)

2-8 FUTURE VALUE OF AN ANNUITY DUE

Because each payment occurs one period earlier with an annuity due, the payments will all earn interest for one additional period. Therefore, the FV of an annuity due will be greater than that of a similar ordinary annuity. If you went through the step-by-step procedure, you would see that our illustrative annuity due has an FV of $331.01 versus $315.25 for the ordinary annuity.

With the formula approach, we first use Equation 2-3, but since each payment occurs one period earlier, we multiply the Equation 2-3 result by $(1 + I)$:

$$FVA_{due} = FVA_{ordinary}(1 + I)$$

$$(2-4)$$

Thus, for the annuity due, $FVA_{due} = \$315.25(1.05) = \$331.01$, which is the same result as found using the period-by-period approach. With a calculator we input the variables just as we did with the ordinary annuity, but now we set the calculator to Begin Mode to get the answer, $331.01.

Why does an annuity due always have a higher future value than an ordinary annuity?

If you calculated the value of an ordinary annuity, how could you find the value of the corresponding annuity due?

Assume that you plan to buy a condo five years from now, and you need to save for a down payment. You plan to save $2,500 per year, with the first payment made *immediately*, and you will deposit the funds in a bank account that pays 4 percent. How much will you have after five years? How much would you have if you made the deposits at the end of each year? ($14,082.44; $13,540.81)

2-9 PRESENT VALUE OF AN ORDINARY ANNUITY

The present value of an annuity, **PVA$_N$**, can be found using the step-by-step, formula, calculator, or spreadsheet methods. Look back at Table 2-3. To find the FV of the annuity, we compounded the deposits. To find the PV, we discount them, dividing each payment by $(1 + I)$. The step-by-step procedure is diagrammed below:

PVA$_N$
The present value of an annuity of N periods.

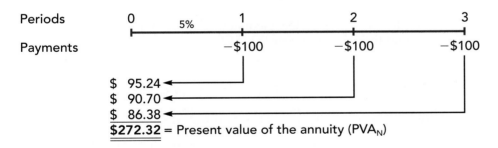

Equation 2-5 expresses the step-by-step procedure in a formula. The bracketed form of the equation can be used with a scientific calculator, and it is helpful if the annuity extends out for a number of years:

$$PVA_N = PMT/(1 + I)^1 + PMT/(1 + I)^2 + \cdots + PMT/(1 + I)^N$$

$$= PMT \left[\frac{1 - \dfrac{1}{(1 + I)^N}}{I} \right] \tag{2-5}$$

$$= \$100 \times [1 - 1/(1.05)^3]/0.05 = \$272.32$$

Calculators are programmed to solve Equation 2-5, so we merely input the variables and press the PV key, *being sure the calculator is set to End Mode*. The calculator setup is shown below for both an ordinary annuity and an annuity due. Note that the PV of the annuity due is larger because each payment is discounted back one less year. Note too that you could just find the PV of the ordinary annuity and then multiply by $(1 + I) = 1.05$, getting $272.32(1.05) = 285.94, the PV of the annuity due.

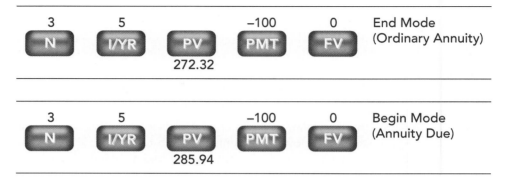

Why does an annuity due have a higher present value than an ordinary annuity?

If you know the present value of an ordinary annuity, how could you find the PV of the corresponding annuity due?

What is the PVA of an ordinary annuity with 10 payments of $100 if the appropriate interest rate is 10 percent? What would PVA be if the interest rate were 4 percent? What if the interest rate were 0 percent? How would the PVA values differ if we were dealing with annuities due? ($614.46; $811.09; $1,000.00; $675.90; $843.53; $1,000)

Assume that you are offered an annuity that pays $100 at the end of each year for 10 years. You could earn 8 percent on your money in other investments with equal risk. What is the most you should pay for the annuity? If the payments began immediately, how much would the annuity be worth? ($671.01; $724.69)

2-10 FINDING ANNUITY PAYMENTS, PERIODS, AND INTEREST RATES

We can find payments, periods, and interest rates for annuities. Here five variables come into play: N, I, PMT, FV, and PV. If we know any four, we can find the fifth.

2-10a Finding Annuity Payments, PMT

Suppose we need to accumulate $10,000 and have it available five years from now. Suppose further that we can earn a return of 6 percent on our savings, which are currently zero. Thus, we know that FV = 10,000, PV = 0, N = 5, and I/YR = 6. We can enter these values in a financial calculator and then press the PMT key to find how large our deposits must be. The answer will, of course, depend on whether we make deposits at the end of each year (ordinary annuity) or at the beginning (annuity due). Here are the results for each type of annuity:

5	6	0		10000	Begin Mode
N	**I/YR**	**PV**	**PMT**	**FV**	(Annuity Due)
			−1,673.55		

Thus, you must save $1,773.96 per year if you make payments at the *end* of each year, but only $1,673.55 if the payments begin *immediately*. Note that the required payment for the annuity due is the ordinary annuity payment divided by $(1 + I)$: $1,773.96/1.06 = $1,673.55. Spreadsheets can also be used to find annuity payments.

2-10b Finding the Number of Periods, N

Suppose you decide to make end-of-year deposits, but you can only save $1,200 per year. Again assuming that you would earn 6 percent, how long would it take you to reach your $10,000 goal? Here is the calculator setup:

	6	0	−1200	10000	End Mode
N	**I/YR**	**PV**	**PMT**	**FV**	
6.96					

With these smaller deposits, it would take 6.96 years to reach the $10,000 target. If you began the deposits immediately, then you would have an annuity due and N would be a bit less, 6.63 years.

2-10c Finding the Interest Rate, I

Now suppose you can only save $1,200 annually, but you still want to have the $10,000 in five years. What rate of return would enable you to achieve your goal? Here is the calculator setup:

5		0	−1200	10000	End Mode
N	**I/YR**	**PV**	**PMT**	**FV**	
	25.78				

You would need to earn a whopping 25.78 percent. About the only way to get such a high return would be to invest in speculative stocks or head to Las Vegas and the casino. Of course, speculative stocks and gambling aren't like making deposits in a bank with a guaranteed rate of return, so there's a good chance you'd end up with nothing. We'd recommend that you change your plans—save more, lower your $10,000 target, or extend your time horizon. It might be appropriate to seek a somewhat higher return, but trying to earn 25.78 percent in a 6 percent market would require taking on more risk than would be prudent.

It's easy to find rates of return with a financial calculator or a spreadsheet. However, without one of these tools you would have to go through a trial-and-error process, and that would be very time-consuming if many years were involved.

Suppose you inherited $100,000 and invested it at 7 percent per year. How much could you withdraw at the *end* of each of the next 10 years? How would your answer change if you made withdrawals at the *beginning* of each year? ($14,237.75; $13,306.31)

If you had $100,000 that was invested at 7 percent and you wanted to withdraw $10,000 at the end of each year, how long would your funds last? How long would they last if you earned 0 percent? How long would they last if you earned the 7 percent but limited your withdrawal to $7,000 per year? (17.8 years; 10 years; forever)

Your rich uncle named you as the beneficiary of his life insurance policy. The insurance company gives you a choice of $100,000 today or a 12-year annuity of $12,000 at the end of each year. What rate of return is the insurance company offering? (6.11%)

Assume that you just inherited an annuity that will pay you $10,000 per year for 10 years, with the first payment being made today. A friend of your mother offers to give you $60,000 for the annuity. If you sell it, what rate of return would your mother's friend earn on his investment? If you think a "fair" return would be 6 percent, how much should you ask for the annuity? (13.70%; $78,016.92)

2-11 PERPETUITIES

Consol
A perpetual bond issued by the British government to consolidate past debts; in general, any perpetual bond.

Perpetuity
A stream of equal payments at fixed intervals expected to continue forever.

In the last section we dealt with annuities whose payments continue for a specific number of periods—for example, $100 per year for 10 years. However, some securities promise to make payments forever. For example, in 1749 the British government issued some bonds whose proceeds were used to pay off other British bonds, and since this action consolidated the government's debt, the new bonds were called **consols**. Because consols promise to pay interest forever, they are "perpetuities." The interest rate on the consols was 2.5 percent, so a bond with a face value of $1,000 would pay $25 per year in perpetuity.[6]

A **perpetuity** is simply an annuity with an extended life. Because the payments go on forever, you couldn't apply the step-by-step approach. However, it's easy to find the PV of a perpetuity with a formula found by solving Equation 2-5 with N set at infinity:[7]

$$\text{PV of a perpetuity} = \frac{\text{PMT}}{\text{I}} \qquad \text{(2-6)}$$

Now we can use Equation 2-6 to find the value of a British consol with a face value of $1,000 that pays $25 per year in perpetuity. The answer depends on the interest rate. In 1888, the "going rate" as established in the financial marketplace was 2.5 percent, so at that time the consol's value was $1,000:

$$\text{Consol value}_{1888} = \$25/0.025 = \$1,000$$

In 2004, 116 years later, the annual payment was still $25, but the going interest rate had risen to 5.2 percent, causing the consol's value to fall to $480.77:

$$\text{Consol value}_{2004} = \$25/0.052 = \$480.77$$

Note, though, that if interest rates decline in the future, say, to 2 percent, the value of the consol will rise:

$$\text{Consol value if rates decline to 2\%} = \$25/0.02 = \$1,250.00$$

---

[6] The consols actually pay interest in pounds, but we discuss them in dollar terms for simplicity.
[7] Equation 2-6 was found by letting N in Equation 2-5 approach infinity. The result is Equation 2-6.

These examples demonstrate an important point: *When interest rates change, the prices of outstanding bonds also change. Bond prices decline if rates rise and increase if rates fall.* We will discuss this point in more detail in Chapter 7, where we cover bonds in depth.

Figure 2-3 gives a graphic picture of how much each payment contributes to the value of an annuity. Here we analyze an annuity that pays $100 per year when the market interest rate is 10 percent. We found the PV of each payment for the first 100 years and graphed those PVs. We also found the value of the annuity if it had a 25-year, 50-year, 100-year, and infinite life. Here are some points to note:

1. The value of an ordinary annuity is the sum of the present values of its payments.
2. We could construct graphs for annuities of any length—for 3 years, or 25 years, or 50 years, or any other period. The fewer the years, the fewer the bars in the graph.
3. As the years increase, the PV of each additional payment—which represents the amount the payment contributes to the annuity's value—decreases. This occurs because each payment is divided by $(1 + I)^t$, and that term increases exponentially with t. Indeed, in our graph the payments after 62 years are too small to be noticed.
4. The data below the graph show the value of a $100 annuity when the interest rate is 10 percent if the annuity lasts for 25, 50, and 100 years, and forever. The difference between these values shows how much the additional years contribute to the annuity's value. The payments for distant years are worth very little today, so the value of the annuity is determined largely by the

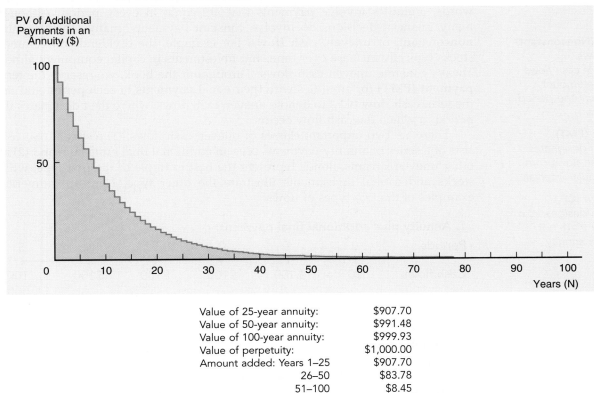

FIGURE 2-3 *Contribution of Payments to Value of $100 Annuity at 10% Interest Rate*

Value of 25-year annuity:	$907.70
Value of 50-year annuity:	$991.48
Value of 100-year annuity:	$999.93
Value of perpetuity:	$1,000.00
Amount added: Years 1–25	$907.70
26–50	$83.78
51–100	$8.45

payments to be received in the near term. Note, though, that the discount rate affects the values of distant cash flows and thus the graph. The higher the discount rate, the steeper the decline and thus the smaller the values of the distant flows.

Figure 2-3 highlights some important implications for financial issues. For example, if you win a "$10 million lottery" that actually pays $500,000 per year for 20 years, beginning immediately, the lottery is really worth a lot less than $10 million. Each cash flow must be discounted, and their sum is much less than $10 million. At a 10 percent discount rate, the "$10 million" is worth only $4,682,460, and that's before taxes. Not bad, but not $10 million.

What's the present value of a perpetuity that pays $1,000 per year, beginning one year from now, if the appropriate interest rate is 5 percent? What would the value be if the annuity began its payments immediately? ($20,000, $21,000. Hint: Just add the $1,000 to be received immediately to the value of the annuity.)

Would distant payments contribute more to the value of an annuity if interest rates were high or low? (Hint: When answering conceptual questions, it often helps to make up an example and use it to help formulate your answer. PV of $100 at 5 percent after 25 years = $29.53; PV at 20 percent = $1.05. So, distant payments contribute more at low rates.)

2-12 UNEVEN CASH FLOWS

Uneven (Nonconstant) Cash Flows
A series of cash flows where the amount varies from one period to the next.

Payment (PMT)
This term designates equal cash flows coming at regular intervals.

Cash Flow (CF$_t$)
This term designates a cash flow that's not part of an annuity.

The definition of an annuity includes the words *constant payment*—in other words, annuities involve payments that are equal in every period. Although many financial decisions do involve constant payments, many others involve **nonconstant,** or **uneven, cash flows.** For example, the dividends on common stocks typically increase over time, and investments in capital equipment almost always generate uneven cash flows. Throughout the book, we reserve the term **payment (PMT)** for annuities with their equal payments in each period and use the term **cash flow (CF$_t$)** to denote uneven cash flows, where the t designates the period in which the cash flow occurs.

There are two important classes of uneven cash flows: (1) a stream that consists of a series of annuity payments plus an additional final lump sum and (2) all other uneven streams. Bonds represent the best example of the first type, while stocks and capital investments illustrate the other type. Here are numerical examples of the two types of flows:

1. Annuity plus additional final payment:

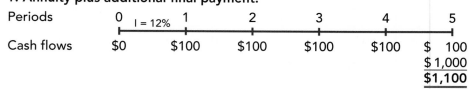

2. Irregular cash flows:

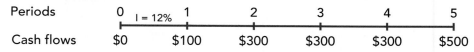

We can find the PV of either stream by using Equation 2-7 and following the step-by-step procedure, where we discount each cash flow and then sum them to find the PV of the stream:

$$PV = \frac{CF_1}{(1+I)^1} + \frac{CF_2}{(1+I)^2} + \cdots + \frac{CF_N}{(1+I)^N} = \sum_{t=1}^{N} \frac{CF_t}{(1+I)^t} \qquad \textbf{(2-7)}$$

If we did this, we would find the PV of Stream 1 to be $927.90 and the PV of Stream 2 to be $1,016.35.

The step-by-step procedure is straightforward, but if we have a large number of cash flows it is time-consuming. However, financial calculators speed up the process considerably. First, consider Stream 1, and notice that here we have a five-year, 12 percent, ordinary annuity plus a final payment of $1,000. We could find the PV of the annuity, then find the PV of the final payment, and then sum them to get the PV of the stream. Financial calculators do this in one simple step—use the five TVM keys, enter the data as shown below, and then press the PV key to get the answer, $927.90.

−927.90

The solution procedure is different for the second uneven stream. Here we must use the step-by-step approach as shown in Figure 2-4. Even calculators and spreadsheets solve the problem using the step-by-step procedure, but they do it quickly and efficiently. First, you enter all the cash flows and the interest rate, then the calculator or computer discounts each cash flow to find its present value and sums these PVs to produce the PV of the stream. You must enter the cash flows in the calculator's "cash flow register," then enter the interest rate, and then press the NPV key to find the PV of the stream. NPV stands for net present value. We cover the calculator mechanics in the tutorial, and we discuss the process in more detail in Chapters 9 and 11, where we use the NPV calculation to analyze stocks and proposed capital budgeting projects. If you don't

FIGURE 2-4   *PV of an Uneven Cash Flow Stream*

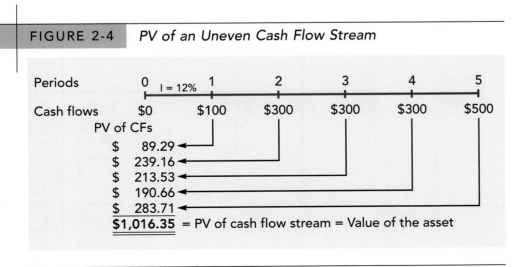

know how to do the calculation with your calculator, it would be worthwhile to go to our tutorial or your calculator manual, learn the steps, and be sure you can make this calculation. You will have to learn to do it eventually, and now is a good time.

Could you use Equation 2-2, once for each cash flow, to find the PV of an uneven stream of cash flows?

What's the present value of a five-year ordinary annuity of $100 plus an additional $500 at the end of Year 5 if the interest rate is 6 percent? What would the PV be if the $100 payments occurred in Years 1 through 10 and the $500 came at the end of Year 10? ($794.87; $1,015.21)

What's the present value of the following uneven cash flow stream: $0 at Time 0, $100 in Year 1 (or at Time 1), $200 in Year 2, $0 in Year 3, and $400 in Year 4 if the interest rate is 8 percent? ($558.07)

Would a typical common stock provide cash flows more like an annuity or more like an uneven cash flow stream? Explain.

2-13 FUTURE VALUE OF AN UNEVEN CASH FLOW STREAM

We find the future value of uneven cash flow streams by compounding rather than discounting. Consider Cash Flow Stream 2 in the preceding section. We discounted those cash flows to find the PV, but we would compound them to find the FV. Figure 2-5 illustrates the procedure for finding the FV of the stream, using the step-by-step approach.

The values of all financial assets—stocks, bonds, or business capital investments—are found as the present values of their expected future cash flows. Therefore, we need to calculate present values very often, far more often than future values. As a result, all financial calculators provide automated functions

FIGURE 2-5 *FV of an Uneven Cash Flow Stream*

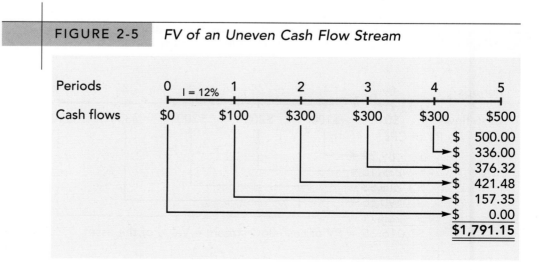

for finding PVs, but they generally do not provide automated FV functions. On the relatively few occasions when we need to find the FV of an uneven cash flow stream, we generally use the step-by-step procedure as shown in Figure 2-5. That approach works for any cash flow stream, even those where some cash flows are zero or negative.

 Why are we more likely to need to calculate the PV of cash flow streams than the FV of streams?

What is the future value of this cash flow stream: $100 at the end of one year, $150 due after two years, and $300 due after three years if the appropriate interest rate is 15 percent? ($604.75)

2-14 SOLVING FOR I WITH UNEVEN CASH FLOWS[8]

Before financial calculators and spreadsheets existed, it was *extremely difficult* to find I if the cash flows were uneven. With spreadsheets and financial calculators, though, it's relatively easy to find I. If you have an annuity plus a final lump sum, you can input values for N, PV, PMT, and FV into the calculator's TVM registers and then press the I/YR key. Here is the setup for Stream 1 from Section 2.12, assuming we must pay $927.90 to buy the asset. The rate of return on the $927.90 investment is 12 percent.

Finding the interest rate for an uneven cash flow stream such as Stream 2 is a bit more complicated. First, note that there is no simple procedure—finding the rate requires a trial-and-error process, which means that a financial calculator or a spreadsheet is needed. With a calculator, we would enter the CFs into the cash flow register and then press the IRR key to get the answer. IRR stands for "internal rate of return," and it is the rate of return the investment provides. The investment is the cash flow at Time 0, and it must be entered as a negative. To illustrate, consider the cash flows given below, where $CF_0 = -\$1,000$ is the cost of the asset:

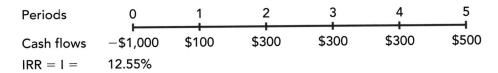

Periods	0	1	2	3	4	5
Cash flows	−$1,000	$100	$300	$300	$300	$500
IRR = I =	12.55%					

When we enter those cash flows in the calculator's cash flow register and press the IRR key, we get the rate of return on the $1,000 investment, 12.55 percent. You would get the same answer using *Excel*'s IRR function. The process is covered in our calculator tutorial, and it is also discussed in Chapter 11, where we study capital budgeting.

---

[8] This section is relatively technical. It can be deferred at this point, but the calculations will be required in Chapter 11.

An investment costs $465 and is expected to produce cash flows of $100 at the end of each of the next four years, then an extra lump sum payment of $200 at the end of the fourth year. What is the expected rate of return on this investment? (9.05%)

An investment costs $465 and is expected to produce cash flows of $100 at the end of Year 1, $200 at the end of Year 2, and $300 at the end of Year 3. What is the expected rate of return on this investment? (11.71%)

2-15 SEMIANNUAL AND OTHER COMPOUNDING PERIODS

Annual Compounding
The arithmetic process of determining the final value of a cash flow or series of cash flows when interest is added once a year.

Semiannual Compounding
The arithmetic process of determining the final value of a cash flow or series of cash flows when interest is added twice a year.

In all of our examples thus far we assumed that interest is compounded once a year, or annually. This is called **annual compounding.** Suppose, however, that you deposited $100 in a bank that pays a 5 percent annual interest rate but credits interest each six months, so in the second six-month period you earn interest on your original $100 plus interest on the interest earned during the first six months. This is called **semiannual compounding.** Note that banks generally pay interest more than once a year, virtually all bonds pay interest semiannually, and most mortgages, student loans, and auto loans require monthly payments. Therefore, it is important to understand how to deal with nonannual compounding.

To illustrate semiannual compounding, assume that we deposit $100 in an account that pays 5 percent and leave it there for 10 years. First, consider again what the future value would be under *annual* compounding:

$$FV_N = PV(1 + I)^N = \$100(1.05)^{10} = \$162.89$$

We would, of course, get this same answer using a financial calculator or a spreadsheet.

How would things change in this example if interest were paid semiannually rather than annually? First, whenever payments occur more than once a year, you must make two conversions: (1) Convert the stated interest rate into a "periodic rate," and (2) convert the number of years into "number of periods." The conversions are done as follows, where I is the stated annual rate, M is the number of compounding periods per year, and N is the number of years:

Periodic rate (I_{PER}) = Stated annual rate/Number of payments per year = I/M   **(2-8)**

With a stated annual rate of 5 percent, compounded semiannually, the periodic rate is 2.5 percent:

$$\text{Periodic rate} = 5\%/2 = 2.5\%$$

The number of compounding periods per year is found with Equation 2-9:

Number of periods = (Number of years)(Periods per year) = NM   **(2-9)**

With 10 years and semiannual compounding, there are 20 periods:

$$\text{Number of periods} = 10(2) = 20 \text{ periods}$$

Under semiannual compounding, our $100 investment will earn 2.5 percent every six months for 20 semiannual periods, not 5 percent per year for 10 years.

The periodic rate and number of periods, not the annual rate and number of years, must be shown on time lines and entered into the calculator or spreadsheet whenever you are working with nonannual compounding.[9]

With this background, we can find the value of $100 after 10 years if it is held in an account that pays a stated annual rate of 5.0 percent but with semiannual compounding. Here's the time line and the future value:

Periods	0		1		2		19		20
		$I = 2.5\%$				$\bullet\bullet\bullet$			
Cash flows	$-\$100$					$\longrightarrow PV (1 + I)^N = \$100(1.025)^{20} = FV = \$163.86$			

With a financial calculator, we would get the same result, using the periodic rate and number of periods:

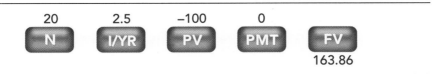

The future value under semiannual compounding, $163.86, exceeds the FV under annual compounding, $162.89, because interest starts accruing sooner and thus you earn more interest on interest.

How would things change in our example if interest were compounded quarterly, or monthly, or daily? With quarterly compounding, there would be NM = 10(4) = 40 periods, and the periodic rate would be I/M = 5%/4 = 1.25% per quarter. Using those values, we would find FV = $164.36. If we used monthly compounding, we would have 10(12) = 120 periods, the monthly rate would be 5%/12 = 0.416667%, and the FV would rise to $164.70. If we went to daily compounding, we would have 10(365) = 3,650 periods, the daily rate would be 5%/365 = 0.0136986% per day, and the FV would be $164.87, based on a 365-day year.

The same logic applies when we find present values under semiannual compounding. Again, we use Equation 2-8 to convert the stated annual rate to the periodic (semiannual) rate and Equation 2-9 to find the number of semiannual periods. We then use the periodic rate and number of periods in the calculations. For example, we can find the PV of $100 due after 10 years when the stated annual rate is 5 percent, with semiannual compounding:

$$\text{Periodic rate} = 5\%/2 = 2.5\% \text{ per period}$$

$$\text{Number of periods} = 10(2) = 20 \text{ periods}$$

$$\text{PV of } \$100 = \$100/(1.025)^{20} = \$61.03$$

We would get this same result with a financial calculator:

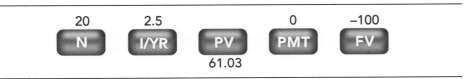

[9] With some financial calculators, you can enter the annual (nominal) rate and the number of compounding periods per year rather than make the conversions we recommend. We prefer the conversions because they must be used on time lines and also because it is easy to forget to reset your calculator after you change its settings, which may lead to an error on your next problem.

If we increased the number of compounding periods from 2 (semiannual) to 12 (monthly), the PV would decline to $60.72, and if we went to daily compounding, it would fall to $60.66.

Would you rather invest in an account that pays 7 percent with annual compounding or 7 percent with monthly compounding? Would you rather borrow at 7 percent and make annual or monthly payments? Why?

What's the *future value* of $100 after three years if the appropriate interest rate is 8 percent, compounded annually? Compounded monthly? ($125.97; $127.02)

What's the *present value* of $100 due in three years if the appropriate interest rate is 8 percent, compounded annually? Compounded monthly? ($79.38; $78.73)

2-16 COMPARING INTEREST RATES

Different compounding periods are used for different types of investments. For example, bank accounts generally pay interest daily; most bonds pay interest semiannually; stocks pay dividends quarterly; and mortgages, auto loans, and other instruments require monthly payments.[10] If we are to compare investments or loans with different compounding periods properly, we need to put them on a common basis. Here are some terms you need to understand:

Nominal (Quoted, or Stated) Interest Rate, I_{NOM}
The contracted, or quoted, or stated, interest rate.

Annual Percentage Rate (APR)
The periodic rate times the number of periods per year.

Effective (Equivalent) Annual Rate (EFF% or EAR)
The annual rate of interest actually being earned, as opposed to the quoted rate. Also called the "equivalent annual rate."

- The **nominal rate (I_{NOM})**, also called the **annual percentage rate** (or **APR**), or **stated,** or **quoted rate,** is the rate that banks, credit card companies, student loan officers, auto dealers, and so on, tell you they are charging on loans or paying on deposits. Note that if two banks offer loans with a stated rate of 8 percent but one requires monthly payments and the other quarterly payments, then they are not charging the same "true" rate—the one that requires monthly payments is really charging more than the one with quarterly payments because it will get your money sooner. So, to compare loans across lenders, or interest rates earned on different securities, you should calculate effective annual rates as described here.[11]

- The **effective annual rate,** abbreviated **EFF%,** is also called the **equivalent annual rate (EAR).** This is the rate that would produce the same future value under annual compounding as would more frequent compounding at a given nominal rate.

- If a loan or investment uses annual compounding, then its nominal rate is also its effective rate. However, if compounding occurs more than once a year, the EFF% is higher than I_{NOM}.

- To illustrate, a nominal rate of 10 percent, with semiannual compounding, is equivalent to a rate of 10.25 percent with annual compounding because both of those rates will cause $100 to grow to the same amount after one year.

---

[10] Some banks even pay interest compounded *continuously.* Continuous compounding is discussed in Web Appendix 2A.

[11] Note, though, if you are comparing two bonds that both pay interest semiannually, then it's OK to compare their nominal rates. Similarly, you can compare the nominal rates on two money funds that pay interest daily. But don't compare the nominal rate on a semiannual bond with the nominal rate on a money fund that compounds daily, because that will make the money fund look worse than it really is.

The top line in the following diagram shows that $100 will grow to $110.25 at a nominal rate of 10.25 percent. The lower line shows the situation if the nominal rate is 10 percent but semiannual compounding is used.

```
0   Nom = EFF% = 10.25%                                          1
├─────────────────────────────────────────────────────────────┤
$100.00 ─────────────────────────────────────────────────────→ $110.25
```

```
0   Nom = 10.00% semi; EFF% = 10.25%          1                 2
├───────────────────────────────────────────┼─────────────────┤
$100.00 ──────────────────────────────→ $105 ─────────────────→ $110.25
```

We can find the effective annual rate, given the nominal rate and the number of compounding periods per year, with this equation:

$$\text{Effective annual rate (EFF\%)} = \left(1 + \frac{I_{NOM}}{M}\right)^M - 1.0 \qquad \textbf{(2-10)}$$

Here I_{NOM} is the nominal rate expressed as a decimal and M is the number of compounding periods per year. In our example, the nominal rate is 10 percent but with semiannual compounding, hence $I_{NOM} = 10\% = 0.10$ and M = 2. This results in EFF% = 10.25%:[12]

$$\text{Effective annual rate (EFF\%)} = \left(1 + \frac{0.10}{2}\right)^2 - 1 = 0.1025 = 10.25\%$$

Thus, if one investment promises to pay 10 percent with semiannual compounding and an equally risky investment promises 10.25 percent with annual compounding, we would be indifferent between the two.

Define the terms "annual percentage rate, or APR," "effective annual rate, or EFF%," and "nominal interest rate, I_{NOM}."

A bank pays 5 percent with daily compounding on its savings accounts. Should it advertise the nominal or effective rate if it is seeking to attract new deposits?

Credit card issuers must by law print their annual percentage rate on their monthly statements. A common APR is 18 percent, with interest paid monthly. What is the EFF% on such a loan? [EFF% = $(1 + 0.18/12)^{12} - 1 = 0.1956 = 19.56\%$.]

Some years ago banks didn't have to reveal the rate they charged on credit cards. Then Congress passed a "truth in lending" law that required them to publish their APR. Is the APR really the "most truthful" rate, or would the EFF% be "more truthful"?

---

[12] Most financial calculators are programmed to find the EFF% or, given the EFF%, to find the nominal rate. This is called "interest rate conversion." You enter the nominal rate and the number of compounding periods per year and then press the EFF% key to find the effective annual rate. However, we generally use Equation 2-10 because it's as easy to use as the interest conversion feature is, and the equation reminds us of what we are really doing. If you use the interest rate conversion feature on your calculator, don't forget to reset your calculator settings. Interest conversion is discussed in the calculator tutorials.

2-17 FRACTIONAL TIME PERIODS

Thus far we have assumed that payments occur at either the beginning or the end of periods, but not *within* periods. However, we often encounter situations that require compounding or discounting over fractional periods. For example, suppose you deposited $100 in a bank that pays a nominal rate of 10 percent but adds interest daily, based on a 365-day year. How much would you have after 9 months? The answer is $107.79, found as follows:[13]

$$\text{Periodic rate} = I_{PER} = 0.10/365 = 0.000273973 \text{ per day}$$

$$\text{Number of days} = (9/12)(365) = 0.75(365) = 273.75 \text{ rounded to } 274$$

$$\text{Ending amount} = \$100(1.000273973)^{274} = \$107.79$$

Now suppose you borrow $100 from a bank whose nominal rate is 10 percent per year "simple interest," which means that interest is not earned on interest. If the loan is outstanding for 274 days, how much interest would you have to pay? Here we would calculate a daily interest rate, I_{PER}, as above, but multiply it by 274 rather than use the 274 as an exponent:

$$\text{Interest owed} = \$100(0.000273973)(274) = \$7.51$$

You would owe the bank a total of $107.51 after 274 days. This is the procedure most banks actually use to calculate interest on loans, except that they require borrowers to pay the interest on a monthly basis rather than after 274 days.

Suppose a company borrowed $1 million at a rate of 9 percent, simple interest, with interest paid at the end of each month. The bank uses a 360-day year. How much interest would the firm have to pay in a 30-day month? What would the interest be if the bank used a 365-day year? [(0.09/360)(30)($1,000,000) = $7,500 interest for the month. For the 365-day year, (0.09/365)(30)($1,000,000) = $7,397.26 of interest. The use of a 360-day year raises the interest cost by $102.74. That's why banks like to use it on loans.]

Suppose you deposited $1,000 in a credit union that pays 7 percent with daily compounding and a 365-day year. What is the EFF%, and how much could you withdraw after seven months, assuming this is seven-twelfths of a year? [EFF% = (1 + 0.07/365)^365 − 1 = 0.07250098 = 7.250098%. Thus, your account would grow from $1,000 to $1,000(1.07250098)^0.583333 = $1,041.67, and you could withdraw that amount.]

2-18 AMORTIZED LOANS[14]

Amortized Loan
A loan that is repaid in equal payments over its life.

An important application of compound interest involves loans that are paid off in installments over time. Included are automobile loans, home mortgage loans, student loans, and many business loans. A loan that is to be repaid in equal amounts on a monthly, quarterly, or annual basis is called an **amortized loan.**[15]

---

[13] Bank loan contracts specifically state whether they are based on a 360- or a 365-day year. If a 360-day year is used, then the daily rate is higher, so the effective rate is also higher. Here we assumed a 365-day year. Also, note that in real-world calculations, banks' computers have built-in calendars, so they can calculate the exact number of days, taking account of 30-day, 31-day, and 28- or 29-day months.

[14] Amortized loans are important, but this section can be omitted without loss of continuity.

[15] The word *amortized* comes from the Latin *mors*, meaning "death," so an amortized loan is one that is "killed off" over time.

Table 2-4 illustrates the amortization process. A homeowner borrows $100,000 on a mortgage loan, and the loan is to be repaid in five equal payments at the end of each of the next five years.[16] The lender charges 6 percent on the balance at the beginning of each year.

Our first task is to determine the payment the homeowner must make each year. Here's a picture of the situation:

The payments must be such that the sum of their PVs equals $100,000:

$$\$100,000 = \frac{PMT}{(1.06)^1} + \frac{PMT}{(1.06)^2} + \frac{PMT}{(1.06)^3} + \frac{PMT}{(1.06)^4} + \frac{PMT}{(1.06)^5} = \sum_{t=1}^{5} \frac{PMT}{(1.06)^t}$$

We could insert values into a calculator as shown below to get the required payments, $23,739.64:[17]

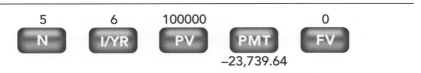

Therefore, the borrower must pay the lender $23,739.64 per year for the next five years.

TABLE 2-4   *Loan Amortization Schedule, $100,000 at 6% for 5 Years*

Amount borrowed: $100,000
Years: 5
Rate: 6%
PMT: −$23,739.64

Year	Beginning Amount (1)	Payment (2)	Interest[a] (3)	Repayment of Principal[b] (4)	Ending Balance (5)
1	$100,000.00	$23,739.64	$6,000.00	$17,739.64	$82,260.36
2	82,260.36	23,739.64	4,935.62	18,804.02	63,456.34
3	63,456.34	23,739.64	3,807.38	19,932.26	43,524.08
4	43,524.08	23,739.64	2,611.44	21,128.20	22,395.89
5	22,395.89	23,739.64	1,343.75	22,395.89	0.00

[a] Interest in each period is calculated by multiplying the loan balance at the beginning of the year by the interest rate. Therefore, interest in Year 1 is $100,000.00(0.06) = $6,000; in Year 2 it is $4,935.62; and so on.
[b] Repayment of principal is equal to the payment of $23,739.64 minus the interest charge for the year.

---

[16] Most mortgage loans call for monthly payments over 10 to 30 years, but we use a shorter period to reduce the calculations.
[17] You could also factor out the PMT term, find the value of the remaining summation term (it's 4.212364), and then divide it into the $100,000 to find the payment, $23,739.64.

Amortization Schedule
A table showing precisely how a loan will be repaid. It gives the required payment on each payment date and a breakdown of the payment, showing how much is interest and how much is repayment of principal.

Each payment will consist of two parts—interest and repayment of principal. This breakdown is shown on an **amortization schedule** such as the one in Table 2-4. The interest component is relatively high in the first year, but it declines as the loan balance decreases. For tax purposes, the borrower would deduct the interest component while the lender would report the same amount as taxable income.

Suppose you borrowed $30,000 on a student loan at a rate of 8 percent and now must repay it in three equal installments at the end of each of the next three years. How large would your payments be, how much of the first payment would represent interest, how much would be principal, and what would your ending balance be after the first year? (PMT = $11,641.01; Interest = $2,400; Principal = $9,241.01; Balance at end of Year 1 = $20,758.99)

Tying It All Together

In this chapter we worked with single payments, ordinary annuities, annuities due, perpetuities, and uneven cash flow streams. There is one fundamental equation, Equation 2-1, which is used to calculate the future value of a given amount. The equation can be transformed to Equation 2-2 and then used to find the present value of a given future amount. We used time lines to show when cash flows occur, and we saw that time value problems can be solved in a step-by-step manner where we work with individual cash flows, with formulas that streamline the approach, with financial calculators, and with spreadsheets.

As we noted at the outset, TVM is the single most important concept in finance, and the procedures developed in Chapter 2 are used throughout the book. Time value analysis is used to find the values of stocks, bonds, and capital budgeting projects. It is also used to analyze personal finance problems, like the retirement issue set forth in the opening vignette. You will become more familiar with time value analysis as you go through the book, but we *strongly recommend* that you get a good handle on Chapter 2 before you continue.

SELF-TEST QUESTIONS AND PROBLEMS
(Solutions Appear in Appendix A)

ST-1   **Key terms** Define each of the following terms:
a. Time line
b. FV_N; PV; I; INT; N; FVA_N; PMT; PVA_N
c. Compounding; discounting
d. Simple interest; compound interest

e. Opportunity cost
f. Annuity; ordinary (deferred) annuity; annuity due
g. Consol; perpetuity
h. Uneven cash flow; payment; cash flow (CF_t)
i. Annual compounding; semiannual compounding
j. Nominal (quoted) interest rate; annual percentage rate (APR); effective (equivalent) annual rate (EAR or EFF%)
k. Amortized loan; amortization schedule

ST-2 **Future value** It is now January 1, 2006. You will deposit $1,000 today into a savings account that pays 8 percent.

a. If the bank compounds interest annually, how much will you have in your account on January 1, 2009?
b. What would your January 1, 2009, balance be if the bank used quarterly compounding?
c. Suppose you deposit $1,000 in 3 payments of $333.333 each on January 1 of 2007, 2008, and 2009. How much would you have in your account on January 1, 2009, based on 8 percent annual compounding?
d. How much would be in your account if the 3 payments began on January 1, 2006?
e. Suppose you deposit 3 equal payments in your account on January 1 of 2007, 2008, and 2009. Assuming an 8 percent interest rate, how large must your payments be to have the same ending balance as in part a?

ST-3 **Time value of money** It is now January 1, 2006, and you will need $1,000 on January 1, 2010, in 4 years. Your bank compounds interest at an 8 percent annual rate.

a. How much must you deposit today to have a balance of $1,000 on January 1, 2010?
b. If you want to make 4 equal payments on each January 1 from 2007 through 2010 to accumulate the $1,000, how large must each payment be? (Note that the payments begin a year from today.)
c. If your father were to offer either to make the payments calculated in part b ($221.92) or to give you $750 on January 1, 2007 (a year from today), which would you choose? Explain.
d. If you have only $750 on January 1, 2007, what interest rate, compounded annually for 3 years, must you earn to have $1,000 on January 1, 2010?
e. Suppose you can deposit only $200 each January 1 from 2007 through 2010 (4 years). What interest rate, with annual compounding, must you earn to end up with $1,000 on January 1, 2010?
f. Your father offers to give you $400 on January 1, 2007. You will then make 6 additional equal payments each 6 months from July 2007 through January 2010. If your bank pays 8 percent, compounded semiannually, how large must each payment be for you to end up with $1,000 on January 1, 2010?
g. What is the EAR, or EFF%, earned on the bank account in part f? What is the APR earned on the account?

ST-4 **Effective annual rates** Bank A offers loans at an 8 percent nominal rate (its APR), but requires that interest be paid quarterly; that is, it uses quarterly compounding. Bank B wants to charge the same effective rate on its loans, but it wants to collect interest on a monthly basis, that is, use monthly compounding. What nominal rate must Bank B set?

QUESTIONS

2-1 What is an *opportunity cost*? How is this concept used in TVM analysis, and where is it shown on a time line? Is a single number used in all situations? Explain.

2-2 Explain whether the following statement is true or false: $100 a year for 10 years is an annuity, but $100 in Year 1, $200 in Year 2, and $400 in Years 3 through 10 does *not* constitute an annuity. However, the second series *contains* an annuity.

2-3 If a firm's earnings per share grew from $1 to $2 over a 10-year period, the *total growth* would be 100 percent, but the *annual growth rate* would be *less than* 10 percent. True or false? Explain. (Hint: If you aren't sure, plug in some numbers and check it out.)

2-4 Would you rather have a savings account that pays 5 percent interest compounded semiannually or one that pays 5 percent interest compounded daily? Explain.

2-5 To find the present value of an uneven series of cash flows, you must find the PVs of the individual cash flows and then sum them. Annuity procedures can never be of use, even if some of the cash flows constitute an annuity because the entire series is not an annuity. True or false? Explain.

2-6 The present value of a perpetuity is equal to the payment on the annuity, PMT, divided by the interest rate, I: PV = PMT/I. What is the *future value* of a perpetuity of PMT dollars per year? (Hint: The answer is infinity, but explain why.)

2-7 Banks and other lenders are required to disclose a rate called the APR. What is this rate? Why did Congress require that it be disclosed? Is it the same as the effective annual rate? If you were comparing the costs of loans from different lenders, could you use their APRs to determine the one with the lowest effective interest rate? Explain.

2-8 What is a loan amortization schedule, and what are some ways these schedules are used?

PROBLEMS

Easy
Problems 1–8

2-1 **Future value** If you deposit $10,000 in a bank account that pays 10 percent interest annually, how much would be in your account after 5 years?

2-2 **Present value** What is the present value of a security that will pay $5,000 in 20 years if securities of equal risk pay 7 percent annually?

2-3 **Finding the required interest rate** Your parents will retire in 18 years. They currently have $250,000, and they think they will need $1,000,000 at retirement. What annual interest rate must they earn to reach their goal, assuming they don't save any additional funds?

2-4 **Time for a lump sum to double** If you deposit money today in an account that pays 6.5 percent annual interest, how long will it take to double your money?

2-5 **Time to reach a financial goal** You have $42,180.53 in a brokerage account, and you plan to deposit an additional $5,000 at the end of every future year until your account totals $250,000. You expect to earn 12 percent annually on the account. How many years will it take to reach your goal?

2-6 **Future value: annuity versus annuity due** What's the future value of a 7 percent, 5-year ordinary annuity that pays $300 each year? If this were an annuity due, what would its future value be?

2-7 **Present and future values of a cash flow stream** An investment will pay $100 at the end of each of the next 3 years, $200 at the end of Year 4, $300 at the end of Year 5, and $500 at the end of Year 6. If other investments of equal risk earn 8 percent annually, what is its present value? Its future value?

2-8 **Loan amortization and EAR** You want to buy a car, and a local bank will lend you $20,000. The loan would be fully amortized over 5 years (60 months), and the nominal interest rate would be 12 percent, with interest paid monthly. What would be the monthly loan payment? What would be the loan's EAR?

Intermediate
Problems 9–26

2-9 **Present and future values for different periods** Find the following values, *using the equations* and then a financial calculator. Compounding/discounting occurs annually.

a. An initial $500 compounded for 1 year at 6 percent.
b. An initial $500 compounded for 2 years at 6 percent.
c. The present value of $500 due in 1 year at a discount rate of 6 percent.
d. The present value of $500 due in 2 years at a discount rate of 6 percent.

2-10 **Present and future values for different interest rates** Find the following values. Compounding/discounting occurs annually.

a. An initial $500 compounded for 10 years at 6 percent.
b. An initial $500 compounded for 10 years at 12 percent.
c. The present value of $500 due in 10 years at 6 percent.
d. The present value of $1,552.90 due in 10 years at 12 percent and also at 6 percent.
e. Define *present value*, and illustrate it using a time line with data from part d. How are present values affected by interest rates?

2-11 **Growth rates** Shalit Corporation's 2005 sales were $12 million. Its 2000 sales were $6 million.

    a. At what rate have sales been growing?

    b. Suppose someone made this statement: "Sales doubled in 5 years. This represents a growth of 100 percent in 5 years, so, dividing 100 percent by 5, we find the growth rate to be 20 percent per year." Is the statement correct?

2-12 **Effective rate of interest** Find the interest rates earned on each of the following:

    a. You *borrow* $700 and promise to pay back $749 at the end of 1 year.

    b. You *lend* $700 and the borrower promises to pay you $749 at the end of 1 year.

    c. You *borrow* $85,000 and promise to pay back $201,229 at the end of 10 years.

    d. You *borrow* $9,000 and promise to make payments of $2,684.80 at the end of each year for 5 years.

2-13 **Time for a lump sum to double** How long will it take $200 to double if it earns the following rates? Compounding occurs once a year.

    a. 7 percent.

    b. 10 percent.

    c. 18 percent.

    d. 100 percent.

2-14 **Future value of an annuity** Find the *future values* of these *ordinary annuities*. Compounding occurs once a year.

    a. $400 per year for 10 years at 10 percent.

    b. $200 per year for 5 years at 5 percent.

    c. $400 per year for 5 years at 0 percent.

    d. Rework parts a, b, and c assuming that they are *annuities due*.

2-15 **Present value of an annuity** Find the *present values* of these *ordinary annuities*. Discounting occurs once a year.

    a. $400 per year for 10 years at 10 percent.

    b. $200 per year for 5 years at 5 percent.

    c. $400 per year for 5 years at 0 percent.

    d. Rework parts a, b, and c assuming that they are *annuities due*.

2-16 **Present value of a perpetuity** What is the present value of a $100 perpetuity if the interest rate is 7 percent? If interest rates doubled to 14 percent, what would its present value be?

2-17 **Effective interest rate** You borrow $85,000; the annual loan payments are $8,273.59 for 30 years. What interest rate are you being charged?

2-18 **Uneven cash flow stream**

    a. Find the present values of the following cash flow streams at 8 percent, compounded annually.

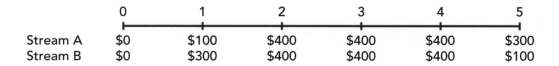

	0	1	2	3	4	5
Stream A	$0	$100	$400	$400	$400	$300
Stream B	$0	$300	$400	$400	$400	$100

    b. What are the PVs of the streams at 0 percent, compounded annually?

2-19 **Future value of an annuity** Your client is 40 years old, and she wants to begin saving for retirement, with the first payment to come one year from now. She can save $5,000 per year, and you advise her to invest it in the stock market, which you expect to provide an average return of 9 percent in the future.

    a. If she follows your advice, how much money would she have at 65?

    b. How much would she have at 70?

    c. If she expects to live for 20 years in retirement if she retires at 65 and for 15 years at 70, and her investments continue to earn the same rate, how much could she withdraw at the end of each year after retirement at each retirement age?

2-20 **PV of a cash flow stream** A rookie quarterback is negotiating his first NFL contract. His opportunity cost is 10 percent. He has been offered three possible 4-year contracts.

Payments are guaranteed, and they would be made at the end of each year. Terms of each contract are listed below:

	1	2	3	4
Contract 1	$3,000,000	$3,000,000	$3,000,000	$3,000,000
Contract 2	$2,000,000	$3,000,000	$4,000,000	$5,000,000
Contract 3	$7,000,000	$1,000,000	$1,000,000	$1,000,000

As his advisor, which would you recommend that he accept?

2-21 **Evaluating lump sums and annuities** Crissie just won the lottery, and she must choose between three award options. She can elect to receive a lump sum today of $61 million, to receive 10 end-of-year payments of $9.5 million, or 30 end-of-year payments of $5.5 million.

a. If she thinks she can earn 7 percent annually, which should she choose?
b. If she expects to earn 8 percent annually, which is the best choice?
c. If she expects to earn 9 percent annually, which would you recommend?
d. Explain how interest rates influence the optimal choice.

2-22 **Loan amortization** Jan sold her house on December 31 and took a $10,000 mortgage as part of the payment. The 10-year mortgage has a 10 percent nominal interest rate, but it calls for semiannual payments beginning next June 30. Next year, Jan must report on Schedule B of her IRS Form 1040 the amount of interest that was included in the 2 payments she received during the year.

a. What is the dollar amount of each payment Jan receives?
b. How much interest was included in the first payment? How much repayment of principal? How do these values change for the second payment?
c. How much interest must Jan report on Schedule B for the first year? Will her interest income be the same next year?
d. If the payments are constant, why does the amount of interest income change over time?

2-23 **Future value for various compounding periods** Find the amount to which $500 will grow under each of these conditions:

a. 12 percent compounded annually for 5 years.
b. 12 percent compounded semiannually for 5 years.
c. 12 percent compounded quarterly for 5 years.
d. 12 percent compounded monthly for 5 years.
e. 12 percent compounded daily for 5 years.
f. Why does the observed pattern of FVs occur?

2-24 **Present value for various compounding periods** Find the present value of $500 due in the future under each of these conditions:

a. 12 percent nominal rate, semiannual compounding, discounted back 5 years.
b. 12 percent nominal rate, quarterly compounding, discounted back 5 years.
c. 12 percent nominal rate, monthly compounding, discounted back 1 year.
d. Why do the differences in the PVs occur?

2-25 **Future value of an annuity** Find the future values of the following ordinary annuities:

a. FV of $400 paid each 6 months for 5 years at a nominal rate of 12 percent, compounded semiannually.
b. FV of $200 paid each 3 months for 5 years at a nominal rate of 12 percent, compounded quarterly.
c. These annuities receive the same amount of cash during the 5-year period and earn interest at the same nominal rate, yet the annuity in part b ends up larger than the one in part a. Why does this occur?

2-26 **PV and loan eligibility** You have saved $4,000 for a down payment on a new car. The largest monthly payment you can afford is $350. The loan would have a 12 percent APR based on end-of-month payments. What is the most expensive car you could afford if you finance it for 48 months? For 60 months?

Challenging
Problems 27–40

2-27 **Effective versus nominal interest rates** Bank A pays 4 percent interest, compounded annually, on deposits, while Bank B pays 3.5 percent, compounded daily.

a. Based on the EAR (or EFF%), which bank should you use?

b. Could your choice of banks be influenced by the fact that you might want to with-draw your funds during the year as opposed to at the end of the year? Assume that your funds must be left on deposit during an entire compounding period in order to receive any interest.

2-28 **Nominal interest rate and extending credit** As a jewelry store manager, you want to offer credit, with interest on outstanding balances paid monthly. To carry receivables, you must borrow funds from your bank at a nominal 6 percent, monthly compounding. To offset your overhead, you want to charge your customers an EAR (or EFF%) that is 2 percent more than the bank is charging you. What APR rate should you charge your customers?

2-29 **Building credit cost into prices** Your firm sells for cash only, but it is thinking of offering credit, allowing customers 90 days to pay. Customers understand the time value of money, so they would all wait and pay on the 90th day. To carry these receivables, you would have to borrow funds from your bank at a nominal 12 percent, daily compound-ing based on a 360-day year. You want to increase your base prices by exactly enough to offset your bank interest cost. To the closest whole percentage point, by how much should you raise your product prices?

2-30 **Reaching a financial goal** Erika and Kitty, who are twins, just received $30,000 each for their 25th birthdays. They both have aspirations to become millionaires. Each plans to make a $5,000 annual contribution to her "early retirement fund" on her birthday, begin-ning a year from today. Erika opened an account with the Safety First Bond Fund, a mutual fund that invests in high-quality bonds whose investors have earned 6 percent per year in the past. Kitty invested in the New Issue Bio-Tech Fund, which invests in small, newly issued bio-tech stocks and whose investors on average have earned 20 per-cent per year in the fund's relatively short history.

a. If the two women's funds earn the same returns in the future as in the past, how old will each be when she becomes a millionaire?

b. How large would Erika's annual contributions have to be for her to become a mil-lionaire at the same age as Kitty, assuming their expected returns are realized?

c. Is it rational or irrational for Erika to invest in the bond fund rather than in stocks?

2-31 **Required lump sum payment** You need $10,000 annually for 4 years to complete your education, starting next year. (One year from today you would withdraw the first $10,000.) Your uncle will deposit an amount *today* in a bank paying 5 percent annual interest, which would provide the needed $10,000 payments.

a. How large must the deposit be?

b. How much will be in the account immediately after you make the first withdrawal?

2-32 **Reaching a financial goal** Six years from today you need $10,000. You plan to deposit $1,500 annually, with the first payment to be made a year from today, in an account that pays an 8 percent effective annual rate. Your last deposit will be for less than $1,500 if less is needed to have the $10,000 in 6 years. How large will your last payment be?

2-33 **FV of uneven cash flow** You want to buy a house within 3 years, and you are currently saving for the down payment. You plan to save $5,000 at the end of the first year, and you anticipate that your annual savings will increase by 10 percent annually thereafter. Your expected annual return is 7 percent. How much would you have for a down pay-ment at the end of Year 3?

2-34 **Amortization schedule**

a. Set up an amortization schedule for a $25,000 loan to be repaid in equal installments at the end of each of the next 3 years. The interest rate is 10 percent, compounded annually.

b. What percentage of the payment represents interest and what percentage represents principal for each of the 3 years? Why do these percentages change over time?

2-35 **Amortization schedule with a balloon payment** You want to buy a house that costs $100,000. You have $10,000 for a down payment, but your credit is such that mortgage companies will not lend you the required $90,000. However, the realtor persuades the seller to take a $90,000 mortgage (called a seller take-back mortgage) at a rate of 7 per-cent, provided the loan is paid off in full in 3 years. You expect to inherit $100,000 in 3 years, but right now all you have is $10,000, and you can only afford to make payments of no more than $7,500 per year given your salary. (The loan would really call for monthly payments, but assume end-of-year annual payments to simplify things.)

a. If the loan were amortized over 3 years, how large would each annual payment be? Could you afford those payments?

b. If the loan were amortized over 30 years, what would each payment be, and could you afford those payments?

c. To satisfy the seller, the 30-year mortgage loan would be written as a "balloon note," which means that at the end of the 3rd year you would have to make the regular payment plus the remaining balance on the loan. What would the loan balance be at the end of Year 3, and what would the balloon payment be?

2-36 **Nonannual compounding**

a. You plan to make 5 deposits of $1,000 each, one every 6 months, with the first payment being made in 6 months. You will then make no more deposits. If the bank pays 4 percent nominal interest, compounded semiannually, how much would be in your account after 3 years?

b. One year from today you must make a payment of $10,000. To prepare for this payment, you plan to make 2 equal quarterly deposits, in 3 and 6 months, in a bank that pays 4 percent nominal interest, compounded quarterly. How large must each of the 2 payments be?

2-37 **Paying off credit cards** Simon recently received a credit card with an 18 percent nominal interest rate. With the card, he purchased a new stereo for $350.00. The minimum payment on the card is only $10 per month.

a. If he makes the minimum monthly payment and makes no other charges, how long will it be before he pays off the card? Round to the nearest month.

b. If he makes monthly payments of $30, how long will it take him to pay off the debt? Round to the nearest month.

c. How much more in total payments will he make under the $10-a-month plan than under the $30-a-month plan?

2-38 **PV and a lawsuit settlement** It is now December 31, 2005, and a jury just found in favor of a woman who sued the city for injuries sustained in a January 2004 accident. She requested recovery of lost wages, plus $100,000 for pain and suffering, plus $20,000 for her legal expenses. Her doctor testified that she has been unable to work since the accident and that she will not be able to work in the future. She is now 62, and the jury decided that she would have worked for another 3 years. She was scheduled to have earned $34,000 in 2004, and her employer testified that she would probably have received raises of 3 percent per year. The actual payment will be made on December 31, 2006. The judge stipulated that all dollar amounts are to be adjusted to a present value basis on December 31, 2006, using a 7 percent annual interest rate, using compound, not simple, interest. Furthermore, he stipulated that the pain and suffering and legal expenses should be based on a December, 31, 2005, date. How large a check must the city write on December 31, 2006?

2-39 **Required annuity payments** Your father is 50 years old and will retire in 10 years. He expects to live for 25 years after he retires, until he is 85. He wants a fixed retirement income that has the same purchasing power at the time he retires as $40,000 has today. (The real value of his retirement income will decline annually after he retires.) His *retirement income will begin the day he retires*, 10 years from today; and he will then receive 24 additional annual payments. Annual inflation is expected to be 5 percent. He currently has $100,000 saved, and he expects to earn 8 percent annually on his savings. How much must he save during each of the next 10 years (end-of-year deposits) to meet his retirement goal?

2-40 **Required annuity payments** A father is now planning a savings program to put his daughter through college. She is 13, she plans to enroll at the university in 5 years, and she should graduate in 4 years. Currently, the annual cost (for everything—food, clothing, tuition, books, transportation, and so forth) is $15,000, but these costs are expected to increase by 5 percent annually. The college requires that this amount be paid at the start of the year. She now has $7,500 in a college savings account that pays 6 percent annually. The father will make 6 equal annual deposits into her account; the 1st deposit today and the 6th on the day she starts college. How large must each of the 6 payments be? [Hint: Calculate the cost (inflated at 5 percent) for each year of college, then find the total present value of those costs, discounted at 6 percent, as of the day she enters college. Then find the compounded value of her initial $7,500 on that same day. The difference between the PV costs and the amount that would be in the savings account must be made up by the father's deposits, so find the 6 equal payments (starting immediately) that will compound to the required amount.]

COMPREHENSIVE/SPREADSHEET PROBLEM

2-41 **Time value of money** Answer the following questions:
- a. Find the FV of $1,000 after 5 years earning a rate of 10 percent annually.
- b. What would the investment's FV be at rates of 0 percent, 5 percent, and 20 percent after 0, 1, 2, 3, 4, and 5 years?
- c. Find the PV of $1,000 due in 5 years if the discount rate is 10 percent.
- d. What is the rate of return on a security that costs $1,000 and returns $2,000 after 5 years?
- e. Suppose California's population is 30 million people, and its population is expected to grow by 2 percent annually. How long would it take for the population to double?
- f. Find the PV of an ordinary annuity that pays $1,000 each of the next 5 years if the interest rate is 15 percent. What is the annuity's FV?
- g. How would the PV and FV of the above annuity change if it were an annuity due?
- h. What would the FV and the PV be for $1,000 due in 5 years if the interest rate were 10 percent, semiannual compounding?
- i. What would the annual payments be for an ordinary annuity for 10 years with a PV of $1,000 if the interest rate were 8 percent? What would the payments be if this were an annuity due?
- j. Find the PV and the FV of an investment that pays 8 percent annually and makes the following end-of-year payments:

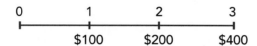

- k. Five banks offer nominal rates of 6 percent on deposits, but A pays interest annually, B pays semiannually, C quarterly, D monthly, and E daily.
  - (1) What effective annual rate does each bank pay? If you deposited $5,000 in each bank today, how much would you have at the end of 1 year? 2 years?
  - (2) If the banks were all insured by the government (the FDIC) and thus equally risky, would they be equally able to attract funds? If not, and the TVM were the only consideration, what *nominal rate* would cause all the banks to provide the same effective annual rate as Bank A?
  - (3) Suppose you don't have the $5,000 but need it at the end of 1 year. You plan to make a series of deposits, annually for A, semiannually for B, quarterly for C, monthly for D, and daily for E, with payments beginning today. How large must the payments be to each bank?
  - (4) Even if the 5 banks provided the same effective annual rate, would a rational investor be indifferent between the banks?
- l. Suppose you borrowed $15,000. The loan's annual interest rate is 8 percent, and it requires 4 equal end-of-year payments. Set up an amortization schedule that shows the annual payments, interest payments, principal repayments, and beginning and ending loan balances.

Integrated Case

First National Bank

2-42 **Time value of money analysis** You have applied for a job with a local bank. As part of its evaluation process, you must take an examination on time value of money analysis covering the following questions.

a. Draw time lines for (1) a $100 lump sum cash flow at the end of Year 2, (2) an ordinary annuity of $100 per year for 3 years, and (3) an uneven cash flow stream of −$50, $100, $75, and $50 at the end of Years 0 through 3.

b. (1) What's the future value of $100 after 3 years if it earns 10 percent, annual compounding?
(2) What's the present value of $100 to be received in 3 years if the interest rate is 10 percent, annual compounding?

c. What annual interest rate would cause $100 to grow to $125.97 in 3 years?

d. If a company's sales are growing at a rate of 20 percent annually, how long will it take sales to double?

e. What's the difference between an ordinary annuity and an annuity due? What type of annuity is shown here? How would you change it to the other type of annuity?

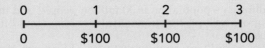

f. (1) What is the future value of a 3-year, $100 ordinary annuity if the annual interest rate is 10 percent?
(2) What is its present value?
(3) What would the future and present values be if it were an annuity due?

g. A 5-year $100 ordinary annuity has an annual interest rate of 10 percent.
(1) What is its present value?
(2) What would the present value be if it was a 10-year annuity?
(3) What would the present value be if it was a 25-year annuity?
(4) What would the present value be if this was a perpetuity?

h. A 20-year-old student wants to save $3 a day for her retirement. Every day she places $3 in a drawer. At the end of each year, she invests the accumulated savings ($1,095) in a brokerage account with an expected annual return of 12 percent.
(1) If she keeps saving in this manner, how much will she have accumulated at age 65?
(2) If a 40-year-old investor began saving in this manner, how much would he have at age 65?
(3) How much would the 40-year-old investor have to save each year to accumulate the same amount at 65 as the 20-year-old investor?

i. What is the present value of the following uneven cash flow stream? The annual interest rate is 10 percent.

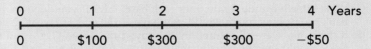

j. (1) Will the future value be larger or smaller if we compound an initial amount more often than annually, for example, *semiannually*, holding the stated (nominal) rate constant? Why?
(2) Define (a) the stated, or quoted, or nominal, rate, (b) the periodic rate, and (c) the effective annual rate (EAR or EFF%).
(3) What is the EAR corresponding to a nominal rate of 10 percent compounded semiannually? Compounded quarterly? Compounded daily?
(4) What is the future value of $100 after 3 years under 10 percent semiannual compounding? Quarterly compounding?

k. When will the EAR equal the nominal (quoted) rate?

l. (1) What is the value at the end of Year 3 of the following cash flow stream if interest is 10 percent, compounded semiannually? (Hint: You can use the EAR and treat the cash flows as an ordinary annuity or use the periodic rate and compound the cash flows individually.)

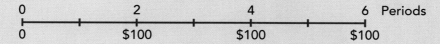

(2) What is the PV?

(3) What would be wrong with your answer to parts l(1) and l(2) if you used the nominal rate, 10 percent, rather than either the EAR or the periodic rate, $I_{NOM}/2 = 10\%/2 = 5\%$ to solve them?

m. (1) Construct an amortization schedule for a $1,000, 10 percent annual interest loan with 3 equal installments.

(2) What is the annual interest expense for the borrower, and the annual interest income for the lender, during Year 2?

cyberproblem

Please go to the ThomsonNOW Web site to access the Cyberproblems.

FINANCIAL STATEMENTS, CASH FLOW, AND TAXES

Doing Your Homework with Financial Statements

Suppose you are a small investor who knows a little about finance and accounting. Could you compete successfully against large institutional investors with armies of analysts, high-powered computers, and state-of-the-art trading strategies?

The answer, according to one Wall Street legend, is a resounding yes! Peter Lynch, who had an outstanding track record as manager of the $10 billion Fidelity Magellan fund and then went on to become the best-selling author of *One Up on Wall Street* and *Beating the Street*, has long argued that small investors can beat the market by using common sense and information available to all of us as we go about our day-to-day lives.

For example, a college student may be more adept at scouting out the new and interesting products that will become tomorrow's success stories than is an investment banker who works 75 hours a week in a New York office. Parents of young children are likely to know which baby foods will succeed or which diapers are best. Couch potatoes may have the best feel for which tortilla chips have the brightest future or whether a new remote control is worth its price.

The trick is to find a product that will boom, yet whose manufacturer's stock is undervalued. If this sounds too easy, you are right. Lynch argues that once you have discovered a good product, you still have a lot of homework to do. This involves combing through the vast amount of financial information that companies regularly provide. It also requires taking a closer and more critical look at how the company conducts its business—Lynch refers to this as "kicking the tires."

To illustrate his point, Lynch relates his experience with Dunkin' Donuts. As a consumer, Lynch was impressed with the quality of the product. This impression led him to take a closer look at the company's financial statements and operations. He liked what he saw, and Dunkin' Donuts became one of the best investments in his portfolio.

The next two chapters discuss what financial statements are and how they are analyzed. Once you have identified a good product as a possible investment, the principles discussed in these chapters will help you "kick the tires."

Putting Things In Perspective

A manager's primary goal is to maximize the value of his or her firm's stock. Value is based on the firm's future cash flows. But how does an investor estimate future cash flows, and how does a manager decide which actions are most likely to increase those flows? The answers to both questions lie in a study of the financial statements that publicly traded firms must provide to investors. Here "investors" include both institutions (banks, insurance companies, pension funds, and the like) and individuals like you.

This chapter begins with a discussion of what the basic financial statements are, how they are used, and what kinds of financial information users need. As we discussed in Chapter 1, the value of any business asset— whether it's a *financial asset* such as a stock or a bond, or a *real (physical) asset* such as land, buildings, and equipment—depends on the usable, after-tax cash flows the asset is expected to produce. Therefore, the chapter also explains the difference between accounting income and cash flow. Finally, because it is *after-tax* cash flow that is important, the chapter provides an overview of the federal income tax system.

Much of the material in the chapter deals with concepts covered in basic accounting courses. However, the information is important enough to warrant a review. Accounting is used to "keep score," and if a firm's managers do not know the score, they won't know if their actions are appropriate. If you took midterm exams but were not told how you were doing, you would have a difficult time improving your grades. The same thing holds in business. If a firm's managers—whether they are in marketing, personnel, production, or finance—do not understand financial statements, they will not be able to judge the effects of their actions, and that will make it hard for the firm to be successful. Only accountants need to know how to *make* financial statements, but everyone involved with business needs to know how to *interpret* and *use* them. Our focus is on interpretation and use.

3-1 A BRIEF HISTORY OF ACCOUNTING AND FINANCIAL STATEMENTS

Financial statements are pieces of paper with numbers written on them, but it is important to also think about the real assets behind those numbers. If you understand how and why accounting began, and how financial statements are used, you can better visualize what is going on and why accounting information is so important.

Thousands of years ago, individuals (or families) were self-contained, meaning that they gathered their own food, made their own clothes, and built their own shelters. Then specialization began—some people became good at making pots, others at making arrowheads, others at making clothing, and so on.

*Are you interested in learning more about the history of accounting? If so, take a tour through the "History of Accounting" organized by the Association of Chartered Accountants in the United States and located at **http://www.acaus.org/ acc_his.html**.*

As specialization began, so did trading, initially in the form of barter. At first, each artisan worked alone, and trade was strictly local. Eventually, though, master craftsmen set up small factories and employed workers, money (first in the form of clamshells and later gold) began to be used, and trade expanded beyond the local area. As these developments occurred, a primitive form of banking began, with wealthy merchants lending profits from past dealings to enterprising factory owners who needed capital to expand or to young traders who needed money to buy wagons, ships, and merchandise.

When the first loans were made, lenders could physically inspect borrowers' assets and judge the likelihood that the loans would be repaid. Eventually, though, things became more complex—borrowers were developing larger factories, traders were acquiring fleets of ships and wagons, and loans were being made to develop distant mines and trading posts. As this occurred, it became increasingly difficult for lenders to personally inspect the assets that backed their loans, so they needed a way to verify that borrowers actually had the assets they claimed to have. Also, some investments were made on a share-of-the-profits basis, and that meant that profits had to be determined. At the same time, factory owners and large merchants needed reports to see how effectively their managers were operating the businesses, and governments needed information for use in assessing taxes. For all these reasons, a need arose for financial statements, for accountants to prepare those statements, and for auditors to verify the accuracy of the accountants' work.

The economic system has grown enormously since its beginning, and accounting has become quite complex. However, the original reasons for financial statements still apply: Bankers and investors need accounting information to make intelligent decisions, managers need it to operate their businesses efficiently, and taxing authorities need it to assess taxes in a reasonable way.

It should be intuitively clear that it is not easy to translate physical assets into numbers, as accountants must do when they construct financial statements. The numbers shown in the assets section of a balance sheet generally represent the historical costs of the assets, less depreciation. However, inventories may be spoiled, obsolete, or even missing; fixed assets such as machinery and buildings may have higher or lower values than their depreciated historical costs; and accounts receivable may be uncollectible. On the liabilities side, some legitimate claims may not even appear on the balance sheet—obligations to pay retirees' medical costs are a good example. Similarly, some costs as reported on the income statement may be understated, as would be true if a plant with a useful life of 10 years were being depreciated over 40 years. When you examine a set of financial statements, you should keep in mind that a physical reality lies behind the numbers, and you should also realize that the translation from physical assets to "correct" numbers is far from precise.

As mentioned previously, it is important for accountants to be able to generate financial statements, while others involved in the business need to know how to interpret them. To be effective, both investors and general managers must have a working knowledge of financial statements and what they reveal. Providing this background is the purpose of this chapter.

Annual Report
A report issued annually by a corporation to its stockholders. It contains basic financial statements as well as management's analysis of the firm's past operations and future prospects.

3-2 FINANCIAL STATEMENTS AND REPORTS

The **annual report** is the most important report corporations issue to stockholders, and it contains two types of information. First, there is a verbal section, often presented as a letter from the chairman, that describes the firm's operating results during the past year and then discusses new developments that will affect future operations. Second, the report provides four basic financial statements—the *balance sheet*, the *income statement*, the *statement of cash flows*, and the *statement of retained earnings*. Taken together, these statements give an accounting picture of the firm's operations and financial position. Detailed data are provided for the two or three most recent years, along with historical summaries of key operating statistics for the past 5 or 10 years.[1]

The quantitative and verbal materials are equally important. The financial statements report *what has actually happened* to assets, earnings, and dividends over the past few years, whereas the verbal statements attempt to explain why things turned out the way they did and what might happen in the future.

For illustrative purposes, we use data for Allied Food Products, a processor and distributor of a wide variety of staple foods, to discuss the basic financial statements. Allied was formed in 1978, when several regional firms merged, and it has grown steadily while earning a reputation as one of the best firms in its industry. Allied's earnings dropped a bit in 2005, to $117.5 million versus $121.8 million in 2004. Management reported that the drop resulted from losses associated with a drought as well as increased costs due to a three-month strike. However, management then went on to paint a more optimistic picture for the future, stating that full operations had been resumed, that several unprofitable businesses had been eliminated, and that 2006 profits were expected to rise sharply. Of course, an increase in profitability may not occur, and analysts should compare management's past statements with subsequent results. In any event, *the information contained in an annual report can be used to help forecast future earnings and dividends*. Therefore, investors are very much interested in this report.

We should note that Allied's financial statements are relatively simple and straightforward. It finances with only debt and common stock—no preferred stock, convertibles, and no complex derivative securities. It has had no acquisitions that resulted in goodwill that must be carried on the balance sheet. And all of its assets are used in its basic business operations, hence no nonoperating assets must be stripped out to analyze its operating performance. We deliberately chose such a company because this is an introductory text, and as such we want to explain the basics of financial analysis, not wander into an arcane accounting discussion that is best left to accounting and security analysis courses. We point out some of the pitfalls that can be encountered when trying to interpret accounting statements, but we leave it to advanced courses to cover the intricacies of accounting.

For an excellent example of a corporate annual report, take a look at 3M's annual report, found at **http://www.3m.com/ index.jhtml**. *Then, click on investor relations at the bottom of the screen and then you can find 3M's most recent annual report in Adobe Acrobat format. A source for links to many companies' annual reports is* **http:// www.annualreportservice .com**.

What is the annual report, and what two types of information does it provide?

What four financial statements are typically included in the annual report?

Why is the annual report of great interest to investors?

---

[1] Firms also provide quarterly reports, but these are much less comprehensive. In addition, larger firms file even more detailed statements, giving breakdowns for each major division or subsidiary, with the Securities and Exchange Commission (SEC). These reports, called *10-K reports*, are made available to stockholders upon request to a company's corporate secretary. Finally, many larger firms also publish *statistical supplements*, which give financial statement data and key ratios for the last 10 to 20 years, and these reports are available on the World Wide Web.

3-3 THE BALANCE SHEET

Balance Sheet
A statement of the firm's financial position at a specific point in time.

The balance sheet represents a "snapshot" of the firm's position at a specific point in time. Figure 3-1 provides a simple illustration of a typical **balance sheet.** The left side of the statement shows the assets that the company owns. The right side shows the firm's liabilities and equity, which represent claims against the assets.

As Figure 3-1 indicates, assets are divided into two major categories: current and long term. Current assets include cash plus other items that should be converted to cash within one year, and they include cash and equivalents, accounts receivable, and inventory.[2] Long-term assets are those whose useful lives exceed one year, and they include physical assets such as plant and equipment and intellectual property such as patents and copyrights. Plant and equipment is generally reported net of accumulated depreciation. Allied's long-term assets consist entirely of net plant and equipment, and we often refer to them as "net fixed assets" for convenience.

The claims against assets are of two types—liabilities (or money the company owes creditors) and stockholders' equity, which represents ownership

---

FIGURE 3-1 *A Typical Balance Sheet*

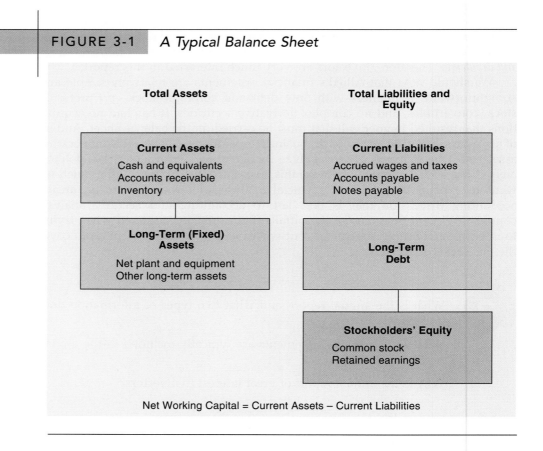

Net Working Capital = Current Assets − Current Liabilities

---

[2] Allied and most other companies hold some cash in bank checking accounts, and they also hold short-term, interest-bearing securities that can be sold and thus converted to cash immediately with a simple telephone call. Those securities are reported as "cash equivalents" and are included with checking account balances for financial reporting purposes. If a company has other marketable securities, they will be shown as "Marketable securities" in the Current Assets section if they mature in less than a year; otherwise, they will be shown in the Long-Term Assets section.

much like a homeowner's equity, which is the value of the house less the amount of any outstanding mortgage loan. Corporate liabilities are further divided into two major categories: current liabilities and long-term debt. Current liabilities are obligations that are due to be paid off within a year, and they include accounts payable, accruals (the total of accrued wages and accrued taxes), and notes payable that are due within one year. Long-term debt includes long-term loans and bonds that have maturities longer than a year.

Allied's stockholders' equity section is divided into two accounts—"common stock" and "retained earnings." The amount shown as common stock is, essentially, the amount of cash that stockholders paid to the company when it originally issued stock for use in acquiring assets. The **retained earnings** account is built up over time as the firm "saves" a part of its earnings rather than paying them all out as dividends. The breakdown of the stockholders' equity accounts is important for some purposes but not for others. For example, a potential stockholder might want to know whether the company actually earned the funds reported in its equity account or whether they came mainly from selling stock. A potential creditor, on the other hand, would be primarily interested in the total equity provided by the firm's owners and not with its source. We generally aggregate the two stockholders' equity accounts and call this sum **common equity,** or **net worth.**

Notice that the balance sheet items are listed in order of their "liquidity," or the length of time it takes to convert them to cash (current assets) or their expected useful lives (fixed assets). Similarly, the claims are listed in the order in which they must be paid: Accounts payable must generally be paid within 30 days, notes payable within 90 days, and so on, down to the stockholders' equity accounts, which represent ownership and need never be "paid off." A firm needs enough cash and other liquid assets to pay its bills as they come due, so its lenders, suppliers, and bond rating agencies keep an eye on its liquidity. **Net working capital,** which is defined as current assets minus current liabilities, is a frequently used measure of liquidity.

Table 3-1 shows Allied's year-end balance sheets for 2005 and 2004. From the 2005 statement we see that it had $2 billion of assets—half current and half long term. The $2 billion of assets were financed by $310 million of current liabilities, $750 million of long-term debt, and $940 million of common equity represented by 50 million shares outstanding. Its 2005 net working capital was $690 million (the $1 billion of current assets less the $310 million of current liabilities). Comparing the balance sheets for 2005 and 2004, we see that Allied's assets grew by $320 million, or slightly more than 19 percent.

Several additional points about the balance sheet are worth noting:

1. *Cash and equivalents versus other assets.* Although the assets are all stated in dollar terms, only the cash and equivalents account represents actual spendable money. Accounts receivable represent credit sales that have not yet been collected. Inventories show the investment in raw materials, work-in-process, and finished goods. Finally, net plant and equipment reflects the amount Allied paid for its fixed assets, less accumulated depreciation. Allied has $10 million of cash and equivalents, hence it can write checks totaling that amount (versus current liabilities of $310 million due within a year). The noncash assets should generate cash over time, but they do not represent cash in hand, and the cash they would bring if they were sold today could be higher or lower than their values as reported on the balance sheet.

2. *Inventory accounting.* Allied uses the FIFO (first-in, first-out) method to determine the inventory value shown on its balance sheet ($615 million), but it could have used LIFO (last-in, first-out) or an average cost method. During a period of rising prices, by assuming that old, low-cost inventory is sold first and new, high-cost items are kept in stock, FIFO results in a relatively high

Retained Earnings
That portion of the firm's earnings that has been saved rather than paid out as dividends.

Common Equity (Net Worth)
The capital supplied by common stockholders: common stock, paid-in capital, retained earnings, and, occasionally, certain reserves.

Net Working Capital
Defined as current assets minus current liabilities. It is a frequently used measure of liquidity.

TABLE 3-1	Allied Food Products: December 31 Balance Sheets (Millions of Dollars)		
		2005	**2004**
Assets			
Cash and equivalents		$ 10	$ 80
Accounts receivable		375	315
Inventories		615	415
Total current assets		$1,000	$ 810
Net plant and equipment		1,000	870
Total assets		$2,000	$1,680
Liabilities and Equity			
Accounts payable		$ 60	$ 30
Notes payable		110	60
Accruals		140	130
Total current liabilities		$ 310	$ 220
Long-term bonds		750	580
Total debt		$1,060	$ 800
Common stock (50,000,000 shares)		130	130
Retained earnings		810	750
Total common equity		$ 940	$ 880
Total liabilities and equity		$2,000	$1,680

Book value per share = $940/50 = $18.80

Notes:

1. The bonds have a sinking fund requirement of $20 million a year. Sinking funds are discussed in Chapter 7, but in brief, a sinking fund is used to help ensure the repayment of long-term debt. Thus, Allied was required to pay off $20 million of its mortgage bonds during 2005. We include the current portion of the long-term debt in notes payable, but in a more detailed balance sheet it would be shown as a separate item under current liabilities.

2. Also, note that a relatively few firms use preferred stock, which we discuss in Chapter 9. Preferred can take several different forms, but it is generally like debt in the sense that it pays a fixed amount each year. However, it is like common stock in the sense that a failure to pay the preferred dividend does not expose the firm to bankruptcy. If a firm does use preferred, it is shown on the balance sheet between Total debt and Common stock. There is no set rule on how preferred should be treated when financial ratios are calculated—it could be considered as debt or as equity—but as long as one is consistent in the treatment, either choice is appropriate.

balance sheet inventory value, a low cost of goods sold on the income statement, and thus relatively high reported profits. (This is strictly accounting; companies actually use older items first.) Allied uses FIFO, and because inflation is present, (a) its balance sheet inventories are higher than they would have been had it used LIFO, (b) its cost of goods sold is lower than it would have been under LIFO, and (c) its reported profits are higher. In Allied's case, if the company had used LIFO in 2005, its balance sheet figure for inventories would have been $585 million rather than $615 million, and its earnings (which will be discussed in the next section) would have been reduced by $18 million. Thus, the inventory valuation method can have a significant effect on financial statements. This is important when an analyst is comparing different companies, and the method used must be reported in the notes to the financial statements.

3. *Other sources of funds.* Most companies (including Allied) finance their assets with a combination of current liabilities, long-term debt, and common

equity. As we noted earlier, some companies also use hybrid (combination) securities such as preferred stock, convertible bonds, and long-term leases. Preferred stock is a hybrid between common stock and debt, while convertible bonds are debt securities that give the bondholder an option to exchange bonds for shares of common stock. In the event of bankruptcy, preferred stock ranks below debt but above common stock. When a firm has issued preferred stock, its total equity includes common equity plus preferred stock. Most firms do not use any preferred stock, and those that do generally do not use much of it. Therefore, when we use the term "equity," we mean "common equity" unless otherwise noted.

4. *Depreciation methods.* Most companies prepare two sets of financial statements—one for tax purposes and one for stockholder reporting. Generally, they use the most accelerated depreciation method permitted under the law for tax purposes but straight line for stockholder reporting. Accelerated depreciation results in high depreciation charges, thus low taxable income and therefore relatively low taxes, whereas straight-line depreciation results in lower depreciation charges and high reported profits.[3] Thus, accelerated depreciation results in lower taxes in the current year while straight line results in relatively high reported profits. However, Allied is a relatively conservative company, and it uses accelerated depreciation for both stockholder reporting and tax purposes. Had Allied elected to use straight-line depreciation for stockholder reporting, its 2005 depreciation expense would have been $25 million less, so the $1 billion shown for "net plant" on its balance sheet would have been $25 million higher. More importantly, its reported net income also would have been higher.

5. *Market values versus book values.* Companies use generally accepted accounting principles (GAAP) to determine the values reported on their balance sheets. In most cases, these accounting numbers (often referred to as *book values*) are different from the corresponding market values. For example, Allied purchased its headquarters building in Chicago in 1979. Under GAAP, the company must report the value of this asset at its historical cost (what it originally paid for the asset in 1979) less accumulated depreciation. Given that Chicago real estate prices have increased over the past 25 years, the current market value of the building is much higher than its book value. Other assets might also differ substantially from their values as based on historical costs.

The book and market values of liabilities are normally fairly close to one another, but this is not always true. When a company issues long-term debt, the balance sheet reflects its par value. As we demonstrate in Chapter 7, if interest rates change after debt was issued, its market value will be different from its book value.

Finally, the book value of the company's common equity is simply the reported book value of the assets minus the book value of the liabilities. Looking at Table 3-1, we see that the book value of Allied's common equity was $940 million in 2005. Because there were 50 million shares outstanding, the book value per share was $18.80. By contrast, the market value of the company's common stock is its current price, $23, multiplied by the number of shares outstanding, or $23 × 50 = $1,150 million. As is true for most companies in 2006, shareholders are willing to pay more than book value for the firm's stock in part because the values of its fixed assets have increased due

---

[3] Depreciation charges over an asset's life are equal to the asset's cost basis. Accelerated depreciation results in relatively high depreciation in the early years, hence low taxes, then lower depreciation and higher taxes later in the asset's life. This is advantageous due to the time value of money.

to inflation and in part because shareholders expect the company's future earnings to grow. Allied, like most other companies, has learned how to make investments that are expected to add to future profits. Apple Computer provides an excellent example of this "growth opportunity" phenomenon. When Apple first introduced the iPod, its balance sheet showed very little value for this product, but investors recognized that it was a great product and would lead to high profits in spite of its low book value. They then bid Apple's stock up well above its book value.

6. *The time dimension.* The balance sheet may be thought of as a snapshot of the firm's financial position *at a point in time*—for example, on December 31, 2005. Thus, we see that on December 31, 2004, Allied had $80 million of cash and equivalents, but that balance fell to $10 million by year-end 2005. The balance sheet changes every day as inventories are increased or decreased, as fixed assets are added or retired, as bank loans are increased or decreased, and so on. Companies whose business is seasonal experience especially large balance sheet changes over the year. For example, Allied's inventories are low just before the harvest season, but they are high just after the fall crops have been harvested and processed. Similarly, most retailers have large inventories just before Christmas but low inventories and high accounts receivable just after Christmas. Therefore, firms' balance sheets change during the year, depending on the date at which the statement is constructed.

What is the balance sheet, and what information does it provide?

How is the order of the items shown on the balance sheet determined?

A company has $2 million of cash and equivalents, $2 million of inventory, $3 million of accounts receivable, $3 million of accounts payable, $1 million of accruals, and $2 million of notes payable. What is its net working capital? ($1 million)

Why might Allied's December 31 balance sheet differ from its June 30 statement?

3-4 THE INCOME STATEMENT

Income Statement
A report summarizing the firm's revenues and expenses during an accounting period, generally a quarter or a year.

Table 3-2 gives Allied's 2005 and 2004 **income statements.** Net sales are shown at the top of the statement, after which operating costs, interest, and taxes are subtracted to obtain the net income available to common shareholders, which is generally referred to as "net income." Earnings and dividends per share are given at the bottom of the income statement. Earnings per share (EPS) is called "the bottom line," denoting that of all the items on the income statement, EPS is generally the most important to stockholders. Allied earned $2.35 per share in 2005, down from $2.44 in 2004, but it still increased the dividend from $1.06 to $1.15.[4]

Note that different firms have different financial structures, different tax situations, and different amounts of nonoperating assets. These differences can cause two companies with similar operations to report different levels of net income. For example, suppose two companies have identical operations—their sales, operating costs, and assets are identical. However, one finances with debt

---

[4] Companies must report "comprehensive income" as well as net income. Comprehensive income is equal to net income adjusted to include several additional items, such as unrealized gains or losses on marketable securities, classified as available for sale, when they are marked-to-market. For our purposes in this introductory text, we assume that there are no such items.

TABLE 3-2 *Allied Food Products: Income Statements for Years Ending December 31 (Millions of Dollars, Except for Per-Share Data)*

	2005	2004
Net sales	$3,000.0	$2,850.0
Operating costs except depreciation[a]	2,616.2	2,497.0
Earnings before interest, taxes, and depreciation (EBITDA)[b]	$ 383.8	$ 353.0
Depreciation	100.0	90.0
Earnings before interest and taxes (EBIT)	$ 283.8	$ 263.0
Less interest	88.0	60.0
Earnings before taxes (EBT)	$ 195.8	$ 203.0
Taxes	78.3	81.2
Net income	$ 117.5	$ 121.8
Common dividends	$ 57.5	$ 53.0
Addition to retained earnings	$ 60.0	$ 68.8
Per-share data:		
Common stock price	$ 23.00	$ 26.00
Earnings per share (EPS)[c]	$ 2.35	$ 2.44
Dividends per share (DPS)[c]	$ 1.15	$ 1.06
Book value per share (BVPS)[c]	$ 18.80	$ 17.60
Cash flow per share (CFPS)[c]	$ 4.35	$ 4.24

Notes:

[a] Operating costs include lease payments of $28 million.

[b] Allied has no amortization charges.

[c] Allied has 50 million shares of common stock outstanding. Note that EPS is based on net income available to common stockholders. Calculations of EPS, DPS, BVPS, and CFPS for 2005 are as follows:

$$\text{Earnings per share} = \text{EPS} = \frac{\text{Net income}}{\text{Common shares outstanding}} = \frac{\$117,500,000}{50,000,000} = \$2.35$$

$$\text{Dividends per share} = \text{DPS} = \frac{\text{Dividends paid to common stockholders}}{\text{Common shares outstanding}} = \frac{\$57,500,000}{50,000,000} = \$1.15$$

$$\text{Book value per share} = \text{BVPS} = \frac{\text{Total common equity}}{\text{Common shares outstanding}} = \frac{\$940,000,000}{50,000,000} = \$18.80$$

$$\text{Cash flow per share} = \text{CFPS} = \frac{\text{Net income} + \text{Depreciation} + \text{Amortization}}{\text{Common shares outstanding}} = \frac{\$217,500,000}{50,000,000} = \$4.35$$

If a firm has options or convertibles outstanding, or if it recently issued new common stock, then EPS calculations become a bit more complicated. See any financial accounting text for a discussion.

and the other uses only common equity. Despite the fact their operating performances are identical, the company with no debt (and therefore no interest expense) would report higher net income because no interest is deducted from its operating income. Consequently, if you want to compare companies' operating performances, it is essential to focus on their earnings before deducting taxes and interest payments. This is called *earnings before interest and taxes (EBIT)*, and it is often referred to as *operating income:*

$$\text{EBIT} = \text{Sales revenues} - \text{Operating costs} \qquad \text{(3-1)}$$

From Allied's income statement, we see that its operating income increased from $263.0 million in 2004 to $283.8 million in 2005, yet the company's 2005 net income declined. This discrepancy occurred because Allied increased its debt in 2005, and the increased interest expense reduced its net income despite its higher operating income.

Taking a closer look at the income statement, we see that depreciation and amortization are important components of operating costs.[5] Recall from accounting that **depreciation** is an annual charge against income that reflects the estimated dollar cost of the capital equipment and other **tangible assets** that were used up in the production process. **Amortization** amounts to the same thing, except represents the decline in value of **intangible assets** such as patents, copyrights, trademarks, and goodwill. Because they are so similar, depreciation and amortization are generally lumped together for purposes of financial analysis on the income statement and for other purposes. They both write off, or allocate, the costs of assets over their useful lives.

Even though depreciation and amortization are reported as costs on the income statements, they are not cash expenses—cash was spent in the past, when the assets being written off were acquired, but no cash is paid out to cover depreciation. Therefore, managers, security analysts, and bank loan officers who are concerned with the amount of cash a company is generating often calculate **EBITDA,** defined as earnings before interest, taxes, depreciation, and amortization. Allied has no amortization charges, so the depreciation and amortization on the income statement shown in Table 3-2 is all depreciation. In 2005, EBITDA was $383.8 million. Subtracting the $100 million of depreciation from EBITDA left the company with $283.8 million of operating income (EBIT). After subtracting $88 million in interest and $78.3 million in taxes, Allied had $117.5 million in net income.

While the balance sheet can be thought of as a snapshot in time, the income statement reports on operations *over a period of time*, for example, during the calendar year 2005. Allied's 2005 sales were $3 billion, and its net income was $117.5 million. Income statements can cover any period of time, but most companies prepare them monthly, quarterly, and annually. The quarterly and annual statements are released to investors, while the monthly statements are used internally for planning and control purposes, comparing actual results with forecasted (or "budgeted") results. If revenues drop below or costs rise above the forecasted levels, management should find out why and take corrective steps before the problem becomes serious.

Depreciation
The charge to reflect the cost of assets used up in the production process. Depreciation is not a cash outlay.

Tangible Assets
Physical assets such as plant and equipment.

Amortization
A noncash charge similar to depreciation except that it is used to write off the costs of intangible assets.

Intangible Assets
Assets such as patents, copyrights, trademarks, and goodwill.

EBITDA
Earnings before interest, taxes, depreciation, and amortization.

What is an income statement, and what information does it provide?

Why is earnings per share called "the bottom line"?

Differentiate between amortization and depreciation.

What are EBIT, operating income, and EBITDA?

Which is like a snapshot of the firm's operations—the balance sheet or the income statement—and which is more like a movie? Explain.

---

[5] Industrial companies like Allied generally have few intangible assets, hence little if any amortization. High-tech companies like Microsoft, which spend billions developing new products, and media companies, when they produce movies like *The Aviator*, do have sizable intangible assets, hence amortization is important for them. Actually, life would be simpler, and financial statements just as informative, if the accountants just applied the term "depreciation" to the periodic write-off of all assets, tangible and intangible alike. But until they change, we must continue using both terms.

We should note that prior to 2002 amortization was very important for companies that engaged in mergers. If a company pays more than book value when it acquires another firm, the excess is called "goodwill." Prior to 2002, firms were required to amortize goodwill, and the annual amortization charge reduced reported income by a like amount. After 2002, GAAP no longer required that goodwill be amortized, and that greatly reduced amortization charges for companies in general.

3-5 NET CASH FLOW

As we discussed in Chapter 1, management's goal should be to maximize the stock price. Because the value of any asset, including a share of stock, depends on the cash flows the asset is expected to produce, this means that managers should strive to maximize the cash flows available to investors over the long run. A business's **net cash flow** differs from its **accounting profit** because some of the revenues and expenses listed on the income statement are not paid in cash during the year.

Allied and many other companies have zero noncash revenues, and depreciation and amortization are the only noncash charges.[6] Under these conditions, the relationship between net cash flow and net income can be expressed as follows:

Net cash flow = Net income + Depreciation and amortization   **(3-2)**

We can illustrate Equation 3-2 with Allied's 2005 data from Table 3-2:

Net cash flow = $117.5 + $100.0 = $217.5 million

Depreciation is an important source of cash for Allied and most other companies, and it is important that you understand its financial implications. We discuss depreciation in more depth in Chapter 12, but for a quick illustration, suppose a machine with a life of five years and a zero salvage value was purchased in 2005 for $100,000 and placed in service in 2006. The $100,000 purchase price was paid in cash in 2005, but it does not show up as an expense in 2005; rather, a portion of it is charged as a cost of production over each year of the machine's life. If the $100,000 were taken as an expense in 2005, then profits in that year would be understated, but profits in each of the following five years would be overstated. So, under accrual accounting rules an annual depreciation charge is deducted from sales revenues when determining income in 2006 through 2010. However, the $100,000 cost of the machine was actually paid in cash in 2005, and the depreciation charged against income from 2006 through 2010 does not involve a cash payment. *Because depreciation is a noncash charge, it must be added back to net income to obtain net cash flow.* If we assume that all other noncash items sum to zero, Equation 3-2 will hold and net cash flows are equal to net income plus depreciation and amortization.

Net Cash Flow
The actual net cash, as opposed to accounting profit (net income), that a firm generates during a specified period.

Accounting Profit
A firm's net income as reported on its income statement.

How do we estimate net cash flow, and how does it differ from accounting profit?

In accounting, the emphasis is on net income. In finance, the primary emphasis is on cash flow. Why is this so?

3-6 STATEMENT OF CASH FLOWS

Its net cash flow represents the cash a business generates in a given year. However, the fact that a company generates a high cash flow does not necessarily mean that the cash reported on its balance sheet is also high. Cash flow is not

---

[6] Allied and most other companies have little if any noncash revenues, but this item can be important for construction companies that work on multiyear projects, report income on a percentage of completion basis, and then are paid only after the project is completed. Also, if a company has a substantial amount of deferred taxes, which means that taxes actually paid are less than that reported in the income statement, then this amount could also be added to net income when estimating the net cash flow. Other adjustments could also be made, but a discussion of these details would go beyond the scope of this text and is best left for advanced finance and accounting courses.

normally used just to build up the cash account. Rather, it is used in a variety of ways, including paying dividends, increasing inventories, financing accounts receivable, investing in fixed assets, retiring debt, and buying back common stock.

Here is a quick summary to the key factors that affect a company's cash balance:

1. *Cash flow.* Other things held constant, a positive net cash flow leads to more cash in the bank. However, other things are generally not held constant, and cash flow is used for other things.
2. *Changes in working capital.* Increases in working capital (inventories and receivables) are paid for with cash, so such increases decrease cash. On the other hand, decreases in working capital increase cash. For example, if inventories are to increase, the firm must use cash to purchase the additional inventory, whereas if inventories decrease, this generally means the firm is selling inventories and not replacing them, hence generating cash. Similarly, increases in current liabilities such as accounts payable increase cash, whereas decreases in payables reduce it. This occurs because, if payables increase, the firm has received additional credit from its suppliers, which saves cash, while if payables decrease, the firm has used cash to pay its suppliers.
3. *Fixed assets.* If a company invests in fixed assets, its cash position is reduced, whereas if it sells fixed assets, this increases cash.
4. *Security transactions and dividend payments.* If a company issues stock or bonds during the year, the funds raised will enhance its cash position. On the other hand, if it uses cash to pay off outstanding debt, to buy back some of its stock, or to pay dividends to shareholders, this will reduce cash.

Statement of Cash Flows
A statement reporting the impact of a firm's operating, investing, and financing activities on cash flows over an accounting period.

Each of these factors is reflected in the **statement of cash flows,** which summarizes the changes in a company's cash position. The statement separates activities into three categories:

1. *Operating activities*, which include net income, depreciation, and changes in working capital other than cash and short-term debt.
2. *Investing activities*, which include purchases or sales of fixed assets.
3. *Financing activities*, which include raising cash by issuing short-term debt, long-term debt, or stock, or using cash to pay dividends or to buy back outstanding stock or bonds.

Accounting texts explain how to prepare the statement of cash flows; however, in finance we're concerned with questions the statement can answer: Is the firm generating enough cash to acquire the assets needed to support its growth? Is it generating any extra cash that can be used to repay debt or to invest in new products? Will internally generated cash be sufficient, or will the company have to issue more common stock? This type of information is useful for both managers and investors, so the statement of cash flows is an important instrument. This statement, along with the cash budget, is used to help forecast a company's cash position.

Table 3-3 shows Allied's statement of cash flows as it would appear in the company's annual report. The top section is most important, as it shows the cash flows that were generated by and used in operations. Allied's operations *lost* cash flow—it was *minus* $2.5 million. This indicates that the company, in the normal course of business, was running a cash deficit. Its day-to-day operations brought in $257.5 million, but the increase in receivables and inventories more than offset this inflow, resulting in a *negative* $2.5 million cash flow from operations. Successful companies have large, positive cash flows from operations, as this is what gives them value. Allied clearly had an operating problem in 2005.

TABLE 3-3	*Allied Food Products: Statement of Cash Flows for 2005 (Millions of Dollars)*	

		2005
I. OPERATING ACTIVITIES		
Net Income before dividends		$117.5
Additions (Sources of Cash)		
Depreciation and amortization[a]		100.0
Increase in accounts payable		30.0
Increase in accruals		10.0
Subtractions (Uses of Cash)		
Increase in accounts receivable		(60.0)
Increase in inventories		(200.0)
Net cash provided by operating activities		($ 2.5)
II. LONG-TERM INVESTING ACTIVITIES		
Cash used to acquire fixed assets[b]		($230.0)
III. FINANCING ACTIVITIES		
Increase in notes payable		$ 50.0
Increase in bonds		170.0
Payment of dividends		(57.5)
Net cash provided by financing activities		$162.5
Net decrease in cash and equivalents		($ 70.0)
Cash and equivalents at beginning of the year		80.0
IV. CASH AND EQUIVALENTS AT END OF THE YEAR		$ 10.0

Notes:

[a] Depreciation and amortization are noncash charges, so they must be added back to net income to show the actual cash flow from operations.

[b] The net increase in fixed assets was $130 million, but this is a net amount after deducting the year's depreciation expense. Depreciation must be added to the $130 million to show the actual amount spent to purchase fixed assets. From the income statement, we see that the 2005 depreciation expense was $100 million, so we show expenditures on fixed assets as $230 million.

The second section shows Allied's long-term investing activities. The company purchased fixed assets totaling $230 million; this was the only long-term investment it made during 2005.

When we add the results of Sections I and II, we see that Allied had a cash deficit of $232.5 million in 2005. How was that deficit financed? This information is provided in Section III, Financing Activities. Here we see that Allied borrowed from banks (notes payable) and issued new bonds to bring in a total of $220 million, but it paid out $57.5 million in dividends to its stockholders, resulting in a net inflow of $162.5 million from financing activities.

Allied's deficit from operations and investment activities totaled $232.5 million, and it raised a net $162.5 million from financing activities, leaving a net deficit of $70 million. How was this $70 million shortfall covered? It was covered by drawing down the cash and equivalents account. The company started the year with $80 million of cash and cash equivalents (marketable securities), ended the year with only $10 million, hence used $70 million of its initial cash holdings to cover its operating deficit and fixed assets investments.

Allied's statement of cash flows should worry its managers and investors. It was able to cover the operating deficit and the investments by heavy borrowing and by drawing down its stockpile of cash and equivalents, but that obviously can't continue on into the future. In the long run, Section I should show good

Massaging the Cash Flow Statement

Profits as reported on the income statement can be "massaged" by changes in depreciation methods, inventory valuation procedures, and so on, but "cash is cash," so management can't mess with the cash flow statement, right? Nope—wrong. A recent article in *The Wall Street Journal* described how Ford, General Motors, and several other companies overstated their operating cash flows, the most interesting section of the cash flow statement. Indeed, GM reported more than twice as much cash from operations as it really had, $7.6 billion versus a true $3.5 billion. When GM sold cars to a dealer on credit, it created an account receivable, which should be shown in the "Operating Activities" section as a use of cash. However, GM classified these receivables as loans to dealers and reported them as a financing activity. That decision more than doubled the reported cash flow from operations. It didn't affect the end-of-year cash, but it made operations look stronger than they really were.

If Allied Foods, in Table 3-3, had done this, the $60 million increase in receivables, which is correctly shown as a use of cash, would have been shifted to the "Financing Activities" section, causing Allied's cash provided by operations to rise from −$2.5 million to +$57.5 million. That would have made Allied look better to investors and credit analysts, but it would have been just smoke, mirrors, and accounting.

GM's treatment was uncovered by Professor Charles Mulford of Georgia Tech. The SEC then sent GM a letter that basically required GM to change its procedures. The company issued a statement that it thought at the time it was acting in accordance with GAAP, but that it would reclassify its accounts in the future. GM's action was certainly not in the league of WorldCom's or Enron's, but it does show that companies sometimes do things to make their statements look better than they really are.

Source: Diya Gullapalli, "Little Campus Lab Shakes Big Firms," *The Wall Street Journal*, March 1, 2005, p. C3.

---

operating cash flows; Section II should show spending on fixed assets that is about equal to depreciation charges (to replace worn out fixed assets) plus a bit more to support growth; and Section III should show relatively little net borrowing along with a "reasonable" amount of dividends (for an average company, dividends amount to about 50 percent of net income). Finally, Section IV should show a reasonably stable cash and equivalents balance from year to year. These conditions obviously do not hold for Allied, so something should be done to right the ship. We will go into this more deeply in Chapter 4, when we move on to a more detailed financial analysis of the financial statements.

What is the statement of cash flows, and what are some questions it is designed to answer?

If a company has high cash flows, does this mean that its cash and equivalents will also be high? Explain.

Identify and briefly explain the three types of activities shown in the statement of cash flows.

Statement of Retained Earnings
A statement reporting how much of the firm's earnings were retained in the business rather than paid as dividends. The balance sheet number reported for retained earnings is the sum of the annual retained earnings for each year of the firm's history.

3-7 STATEMENT OF RETAINED EARNINGS

The change in retained earnings between balance sheet dates is reported in the **statement of retained earnings.** Table 3-4 shows that Allied earned $117.5 million during 2005, paid out $57.5 million in common dividends, and plowed $60

TABLE 3-4	*Allied Food Products: Statement of Retained Earnings for Year Ending December 31, 2005 (Millions of Dollars)*

	2005
Balance of Retained Earnings, December 31, 2004	$750.0
Add: Net Income, 2005	117.5
Less: Dividends to common stockholders	(57.5)[a]
Balance of Retained Earnings, December 31, 2005	$810.0

Note:
[a] Here, and throughout the book, parentheses are sometimes used to denote negative numbers.

million back into the business. Thus, the balance sheet item "Retained earnings" increased from $750 million at year-end 2004 to $810 million at year-end 2005.

Note that "retained earnings" represents a *claim against assets*, not assets per se. Moreover, firms retain earnings for reinvestment in the business, which means investing in plant and equipment, in inventories, and so on, *not* to pile up cash in a bank account. Changes in retained earnings occur because common stockholders allow management to reinvest funds that otherwise could be distributed as dividends. *Thus, the retained earnings account reported on the balance sheet does not represent cash and is not "available" for dividends or anything else.*[7]

What is the statement of retained earnings, and what information does it provide?

Why do changes in retained earnings occur?

Explain why the following statement is true: "The retained earnings account reported on the balance sheet does not represent cash and is not 'available' for dividend payments or anything else."

3-8 USES AND LIMITATIONS OF FINANCIAL STATEMENTS

The financial statements provide investors with a lot of useful information. You can look through the statements and answer a number of important questions such as these: How large is the company? Is it growing? Is it making or losing money? Does it have a high percentage of current assets versus fixed assets? To what extent does the firm use debt or equity to finance its assets? Does it rely more on short-term or long-term debt? Has it issued any new debt or equity in recent years? Has it made significant capital expenditures in recent years? Does it have a lot of cash on hand or is a shortage looming, and has the cash balance been rising or falling over time?

---

[7] The amount reported in the retained earnings account is *not* an indication of the cash the firm has. Cash (as of the balance sheet date) is found in the cash account, an asset account. A positive number in the retained earnings account indicates only that the firm has in the past earned some income and not paid out all of those earnings as dividends. Even though a company reports record earnings and shows an increase in retained earnings, it still may be short of cash.

The same situation holds for individuals. You might own a new BMW (no loan), lots of clothes, and an expensive stereo, hence have a high net worth, but if you had only 23 cents in your pocket plus $5 in your checking account, you would still be short of cash.

Financial Analysis on the Internet

A wide range of valuable financial information is available on the Internet. With just a couple of clicks, an investor can find the key financial statements for most publicly traded companies.

Suppose you are considering the purchase of Disney stock, and you want to analyze its recent performance. Here's a partial (but by no means a complete) list of places you could go to get started:

- One source is Yahoo!'s finance Web site, **finance .yahoo.com**.[a] Here you will find updated market information along with links to a variety of interesting research sites. Enter a stock's ticker symbol, click on Go, and you will see the stock's current price, along with recent news about the company. Click on Key Statistics and you will find a report on the company's key financial ratios. Links to the company's financials (income statement, balance sheet, and statement of cash flows) can also be found. The Yahoo! site also has a list of insider transactions, so you can tell if a company's CEO and other key insiders are buying or selling the company's stock. In addition, there is a message board where investors share opinions about the company, and there is a link to the company's filings with the Securities and Exchange Commission (SEC). Note also that, in most cases, a more complete listing of SEC filings can be found at **www.sec.gov** or at **www.edgar-online.com**.
- Another Web site with similar information is MSN Money (**moneycentral.msn.com**). After clicking the Investing and Stocks tabs, you enter the stock's ticker symbol. Then, you will see the current stock price and a list of recent news stories. Here you will also find links to the company's financial statements and key ratios (under Financial Results), as well as other information including analyst ratings, historical charts, earnings estimates, and a summary of insider transactions. Both MSN Money and Yahoo! Finance allow you to export the financial statements and historical prices to an *Excel* spreadsheet.

- Other sources for up-to-date market information are **money.cnn.com** and **www.marketwatch.com/ news/**. These sites also have areas where you can obtain stock quotes along with company financials, links to Wall Street research and SEC filings, company profiles, and charts of the firm's stock price plotted over time.

- After accumulating all of this information, you may be looking for sites that provide opinions regarding the direction of the overall market and views regarding the individual stock. Two popular sites in this category are The Motley Fool's Web site, **www.fool.com**, and the site for TheStreet.com, **www.thestreet.com**.

Keep in mind that this list is just a small subset of the information available online. You should also realize that sites come and go, and also change their content over time. New and interesting sites are constantly being added to the Internet.

[a] To avoid redundancy, we have intentionally left off **http://** in all Web addresses given here. A quick way to change an address is to highlight the portion of the address that is different and type in the appropriate letters of the new address. Once you're finished just press Enter.

At the same time, investors need to be cautious when they review financial statements. While companies are required to follow GAAP, managers still have quite a lot of discretion in deciding how and when to report certain transactions—see the box in Section 3.6 on GM's treatment of accounts receivable from its dealers. Consequently, two firms in exactly the same operating situation may report financial statements that convey different impressions about their financial strength. Some variations may stem from legitimate differences of opinion about the correct way to record transactions. In other cases, managers may choose to report numbers in a way that helps them present either higher earnings or more stable earnings over time. As long as they follow GAAP, such actions are not illegal, but these differences make it harder for investors to compare companies and gauge their true performances.

Unfortunately, as we noted in Chapter 1, there have also been cases where managers overstepped the bounds and reported fraudulent statements. Indeed, a number of high-profile executives have faced criminal charges because of their misleading accounting practices. For example, in June 2002 it was discovered that WorldCom (now called MCI) had committed the most massive accounting fraud of all time by recording more than $11 billion of ordinary operating costs as capital expenditures, thus overstating net income by the same amount.

WorldCom's published financial statements fooled most investors—investors bid the stock price up to $64.50, and banks and other lenders provided the company with more than $30 billion of loans. Arthur Andersen, the firm's auditor, was faulted for not detecting the fraud. Their defense was that WorldCom's management had lied. WorldCom's CFO pleaded guilty and was sentenced to 5 years in prison, while its CEO was sentenced to 25 years in prison. In the wake of this and other recent accounting scandals, regulators and accounting professionals are issuing new standards to make financial statements more transparent for investors and to create an environment where managers have strong incentives to report truthful numbers.

Also, keep in mind that even if investors are provided with accurate accounting data, it is really cash flow, not accounting income, that matters. Similarly, when managers decide on which projects to accept, their focus should be on cash flow. Therefore, when it comes to effective decision making, managers and investors generally need to modify even the most accurate and transparent financial statements to determine the relevant cash flows. We discuss this in the next section.

Can an investor have complete confidence that the financial statements of different companies are accurate and that the data reported by one company are truly comparable to the data provided by another?

Why might different companies account for similar transactions in different ways?

3-9 MODIFYING ACCOUNTING DATA FOR INVESTOR AND MANAGERIAL DECISIONS

Thus far in the chapter we have focused on financial statements as they are prepared by accountants and presented in the annual report. However, these statements are designed more for use by creditors and tax collectors than for managers and stock analysts. Therefore, certain modifications are helpful for corporate decision-making and stock valuation purposes.

Recall from Chapter 1 that the firm's primary financial objective is to maximize shareholder value. Investors provide companies with capital, and managers create value for shareholders by investing this capital in productive assets. In the following sections we discuss how financial managers and analysts use accounting data to measure and evaluate corporate performance.

3-9a Operating Assets and Operating Capital

Companies raise funds from a variety of sources. The primary source is investors, including stockholders, bondholders, and lenders such as banks. Investors must be paid for the use of their money, with payment coming as interest for bonds and other debt and as dividends plus capital gains for stock.

So, if a company obtains more assets than it actually needs, it will have raised too much capital and thus have unnecessarily high capital costs.

Not all of the capital used to acquire assets is provided by investors—some of the funds normally come from suppliers and are reported as accounts payable, while other funds as reported on the balance sheet come as accrued wages and accrued taxes, which amount to short-term loans from workers and tax authorities. Generally, both accounts payable and accruals are "free" because no explicit fee is charged for their use. These funds are commonly referred to as *spontaneously generated, non-interest-bearing current liabilities.* They are called "spontaneous" because they are generated spontaneously through normal business operations, not by a specific act such as going to a bank and borrowing money.

When evaluating a company's overall position and value, analysts often focus on **net operating working capital (NOWC),** defined as follows:[8]

Net Operating Working Capital (NOWC)

Operating working capital less accounts payable and accruals. It is the working capital acquired with investor-supplied funds.

$$\begin{matrix} \text{Net operating} \\ \text{working} \\ \text{capital} \end{matrix} = \text{NOWC} = \begin{matrix} \text{All current assets} \\ \text{required in} \\ \text{operations} \end{matrix} - \begin{matrix} \text{All non-interest-} \\ \text{bearing current} \\ \text{liabilities} \end{matrix} \quad \text{(3-3)}$$

Allied's net operating working capital for 2005 was

$$\text{NOWC} = \begin{matrix} \text{All current} \\ \text{assets required} \\ \text{in operations} \end{matrix} - \begin{matrix} \text{All non-interest-} \\ \text{bearing} \\ \text{current liabilities} \end{matrix}$$

$$= \left(\begin{matrix} \text{Cash and cash} \\ \text{equivalents} \end{matrix} + \begin{matrix} \text{Accounts} \\ \text{receivable} \end{matrix} + \text{Inventories} \right) - \left(\begin{matrix} \text{Accounts} \\ \text{payable} \end{matrix} + \text{Accruals} \right)$$

$$= (\$10 + \$375 + \$615) - (\$60 + \$140)$$

$$= \$800 \text{ million}$$

For 2004, Allied's net operating working capital (NOWC) was

$$\text{Net operating working capital} = (\$80 + \$315 + \$415) - (\$30 + \$130)$$
$$= \$650 \text{ million}$$

Thus, Allied's NOWC increased by $150 million during 2005.

Working capital is important for several reasons. First, all companies must carry some cash to "grease the wheels" of their operations. They continuously receive checks from customers and write checks to suppliers, employees, and so on. Because inflows and outflows do not coincide perfectly, firms must keep some cash (and cash equivalents) in their bank accounts to conduct operations without periodic disruptions. The same is true for most other current assets, such as inventory and accounts receivable.

Allied and most other companies try to hold only as much cash and marketable securities as is required under normal operations—they don't try to operate like a bank and hold excess amounts of these assets. However, in some

---

[8] Allied and many other companies have essentially zero nonoperating assets, but a number of companies do have significant amounts of nonoperating assets, often held as marketable securities, and report them on their balance sheets. Therefore, finance professionals typically differentiate operating from nonoperating assets and use the term NOWC as we do.

instances companies do accumulate more cash and marketable securities than are needed in operations. Perhaps these funds are on hand because the firm just sold a large bond issue and has not yet deployed the funds, or perhaps it is saving up funds for a specific purpose such as a merger or a major capital investment program. In these situations, the excess cash and marketable securities should not be viewed as part of operating working capital—it is nonoperating capital and is analyzed separately.

Also, as noted, accounts payable and accruals arise in the normal course of operations, and each dollar of these current liabilities is a dollar that the company does not have to raise from investors to fund its current assets. Therefore, we deduct these current liabilities from the operating current assets when calculating net operating working capital. However, those current liabilities that charge interest, such as notes payable to banks, are investor-supplied capital, and are not deducted when we calculate NOWC.

We see, then, that a company's assets can be divided into two groups, *operating assets (or operating capital)* and *nonoperating assets (or nonoperating capital)*. Operating capital includes those current and net fixed assets that are necessary to operate the business, while nonoperating assets include items like land held for future use, stock in other companies, and marketable securities in excess of those held for liquidity purposes.[9] Moreover, firm's holdings of nonoperating assets are always based on unique, special conditions, and decisions regarding them are similarly unique. Typically, the vast majority of assets are operating as opposed to nonoperating, and the firm's value is based on the cash flows that those operating assets provide. Therefore, our focus in the book is on operating, not on nonoperating, assets.

Companies typically use a combination of *investor-supplied capital* and *non-interest-bearing, spontaneous current liabilities* to finance their required operating assets. For example, when Allied opens a new plant, it needs to acquire fixed assets (land, building, and equipment) and current assets (inventory and receivables). However, the suppliers who ship materials to Allied generally expect to be paid 30 or so days later, so accounts payable, which are non-interest-bearing current liabilities, help finance the new operations. Accrued wages and taxes similarly reduce the amount of funds Allied's investors must provide to acquire the new operating assets. The amount of operating capital supplied by Allied's investors over the years, through December 31, 2005, is found as follows:

$$\begin{array}{c}\text{Total operating capital,} \\ 2005\end{array} = \begin{array}{c}\text{Net operating} \\ \text{working capital}\end{array} + \begin{array}{c}\text{Net fixed} \\ \text{assets}\end{array} \qquad \textbf{(3-4)}$$

$$= \$800 + \$1,000$$

$$= \$1,800 \text{ million}$$

In the prior year, 2004, Allied's total operating capital was

$$\text{Total operating capital, 2004} = \$650 + \$870$$

$$= \$1,520 \text{ million}$$

Therefore, Allied's operating capital increased from $1,520 to $1,800 million during 2005, or by $280 million.

---

[9] To value a firm, analysts typically use the techniques we describe in the text to value the firm's operations and then add to that value the value of the nonoperating assets. To keep things simple, we illustrate concepts with Allied Foods, which has only operating assets.

3-9b Operating Cash Flows

Financial managers create value by obtaining funds and investing them in operating assets, and the cash flow generated through operations determines the firm's value. These cash flows are found as follows:

$$\text{Operating cash flow} = \text{EBIT}(1 - \text{Tax rate}) + \frac{\text{Depreciation and}}{\text{amortization}} \quad \text{(3-5)}$$

Recall that EBIT is the firm's operating income—it is what remains after subtracting from sales all operating costs, including depreciation and amortization, but before subtracting taxes and interest. Investors are interested in after-tax cash flows, which are found by multiplying EBIT by one minus the tax rate. We add back depreciation and amortization when calculating the cash flow because they are noncash expenses.

Net Operating Profit After Taxes (NOPAT)
The profit a company would generate if it had no debt and held only operating assets.

EBIT(1 − Tax rate) is often referred to as **NOPAT,** or **net operating profit after taxes,** and it is the profit a company would generate if it had no debt and held only operating assets.[10] Thus, we can rewrite Equation 3-5 as follows:

$$\text{Operating cash flow} = \text{NOPAT} + \text{Depreciation and amortization} \quad \text{(3-5a)}$$

Using data from the income statement in Table 3-2, Allied's 2005 NOPAT was

$$\text{NOPAT} = \$283.8(1 - 0.4) = \$283.8(0.6) = \$170.3 \text{ million}$$

Because depreciation was the only noncash charge, Allied's 2005 operating cash flow was

$$\begin{aligned}
\text{Operating cash flow} &= \text{NOPAT} + \text{Depreciation and amortization} \\
&= \$170.3 + \$100 \\
&= \$270.3 \text{ million}
\end{aligned}$$

3-9c Free Cash Flow

Earlier in the chapter we defined net cash flow as being equal to net income plus noncash adjustments, typically net income plus depreciation. Note, though, that cash flows cannot be maintained over time unless depreciating fixed assets are replaced, and new products must also be developed. Therefore, management is not completely free to use the available cash flow however it pleases. Therefore, we now define another term, **free cash flow,** *which is the cash flow actually available for payments to investors (stockholders and debtholders) after the company has made the investments in fixed assets, new products, and working capital required to sustain ongoing operations.*

Free Cash Flow
The cash flow actually available for distribution to all investors (stockholders and debtholders) after the company has made all the investments in fixed assets, new products, and working capital necessary to sustain ongoing operations.

To be more specific, the value of a company's operations depends on its expected future free cash flows (FCF), defined as after-tax operating profit minus the investments in working capital and fixed assets necessary to sustain the business. Thus, free cash flow represents the cash that is actually available for payments to investors. Therefore, managers make their companies more valuable by increasing their free cash flow.

---

[10] For large, complex firms complications can arise. For additional information see Tim Koller, Marc Goedhart, and David Wessels, *Valuation: Measuring and Managing the Value of Companies,* 4th edition (New York: John Wiley & Sons, 2005); and G. Bennett Stewart III, *The Quest for Value,* 2nd edition (New York: HarperCollins Publishers, 1999).

The following equation can be used to calculate free cash flow:[11]

$$\text{FCF} = \left[\text{EBIT}(1 - T) + \begin{array}{c}\text{Depreciation} \\ \text{and amortization}\end{array}\right] - \left[\begin{array}{c}\text{Capital} \\ \text{expenditures}\end{array} + \begin{array}{c}\Delta \text{ Net} \\ \text{operating} \\ \text{working} \\ \text{capital}\end{array}\right]$$

$$= \quad \text{Operating cash flow} \quad - \text{ Investment in operating capital}$$

In 2005 Allied's EBIT was $283.8 million, and its depreciation and amortization was $100 million. Its fixed assets increased by $130 million after $100 million of depreciation, so its capital expenditures must have been $230 million. Finally, its net operating working capital (current assets less spontaneous current liabilities) rose by $150 million. Therefore, its free cash flow was −$109.7 million:

$$\text{FCF} = \text{Operating cash flow} - \text{Investment in operating capital} \quad \textbf{(3-6)}$$

$$= [\$283.8(1 - 0.4) + \$100] - (\$230 + \$150)$$

$$= \$270.3 - \$380$$

$$= -\$109.7 \text{ million}$$

Even though Allied's operating cash flow was positive, its very high investment in operating capital resulted in a negative free cash flow. Because free cash flow is what is available for distribution to investors, not only was there nothing for investors, but investors actually had to put in *more* money to keep the business going. Investors provided most of the needed funds as debt.

Is a negative free cash flow always bad? The answer is, Not necessarily; it depends on *why* the free cash flow was negative. If FCF was negative because NOPAT was negative, this is definitely bad, and it suggests that the company is experiencing operating problems. However, many high-growth companies have positive NOPAT but negative free cash flow because they must invest heavily in operating assets to support rapid growth. There is nothing wrong with a negative cash flow if it results from profitable growth.

What is net operating working capital?

What is total operating capital?

What is NOPAT?

What is free cash flow? Why is free cash flow the most important determinant of a firm's value?

A company has NOPAT of $30 million, and its depreciation and amortization expense is $10 million. During the year the company's gross capital expenditures (total purchases of fixed assets) were $20 million and its net operating working capital increased by $10 million. What is the company's operating cash flow? ($40 million) What is its free cash flow? ($10 million)

---

[11] In the finance literature, free cash flow is defined in two ways: (1) cash flow available to both stockholders and bondholders and (2) cash flow available to stockholders, that is, after interest payments. The first definition, which we prefer and incorporate into Equation 3-6, is the one most analysts use. FCF as found with Equation 3-6 can be discounted at the weighted average cost of capital (WACC) to find the value of the firm, whereas FCF after interest must be discounted at the cost of common stock to find the firm's value. This distinction is discussed at length in advanced finance courses, but the choice does not matter so long as the correct discount rate is used with each.

3-10 MVA AND EVA

Assets as reported on the financial statements reflect historical, in-the-past, values, not current market values, and there are often substantial differences between the two. Inflation results in differences, as do successful and unsuccessful operations. For example, it cost Microsoft very little to develop its first operating system, but that system turned out to be worth many billions that were not shown on its balance sheet. Of course, balance sheets must balance, so if the assets side of the statement totals to less than the market value of the firm's assets, then so will the liabilities and capital side. Debt values are fixed by contract, so it is the equity where the discrepancy between book and market values are concentrated.

To illustrate, consider the following situation. The firm was started with $1 million of assets at book value (historical cost), $500,000 of which was provided by bondholders, and $500,000 by stockholders (50,000 shares purchased at $10 per share). However, the firm was very successful, and its assets now produce $2 million of free cash flow per year. Investors discount that free cash flow at a 10 percent rate, resulting in a value of $20 million for the firm. After deducting the $500,000 of debt, the market value of the equity is found to be $19.5 million versus the $500,000 stockholders invested in the firm. The stock price is $19,500,000/ 50,000 = $390 per share, so the firm's managers have done a marvelous job for the stockholders.

The accounting statements do not reflect market values, so they are not sufficient for purposes of evaluating managers' performance. To help fill this void, financial analysts have developed two additional performance measures, the first of which is **MVA, or Market Value Added**.[12] MVA is simply the difference between the market value of a firm's equity and the book value as shown on the balance sheet, with market value found by multiplying the stock price by the number of shares outstanding. For our hypothetical firm, MVA is $19.5 million − $0.5 million = $19 million.

For Allied, which has 50 million shares outstanding and a $23 price, the market value of the equity is $1,150 million versus a book value as shown on the balance sheet in Table 3-1 of $940 million. Therefore, Allied's MVA is $1,150 − $940 = $210 million. This $210 million represents the difference between the money Allied's stockholders have invested in the corporation since its founding— including retained earnings—versus the cash they could get if they sold the business. The higher its MVA, the better the job management is doing for the firm's shareholders. Boards of directors often look at MVA when deciding on the compensation a firm's managers deserve. Note though, that just as all ships rise in a rising tide, most firms' stock prices rise in a rising stock market, so a positive MVA may not be entirely attributable to management.

A related concept, **Economic Value Added (EVA),** sometimes called "economic profit," is closely related to MVA and is found as follows:

Market Value Added (MVA)
The excess of the market value of equity over its book value.

Economic Value Added (EVA)
Excess of NOPAT over capital costs.

$$\text{EVA} = \begin{matrix} \text{Net operating} \\ \text{profit after taxes} \\ \text{(NOPAT)} \end{matrix} - \quad \text{Annual dollar cost of capital}$$

$$= \quad \text{EBIT}(1-T) \quad - \left(\begin{matrix} \text{Total} \\ \text{investor-supplied} \\ \text{operating capital} \end{matrix} \times \begin{matrix} \text{After-tax} \\ \text{percentage} \\ \text{cost of capital} \end{matrix} \right) \tag{3-7}$$

---

[12] The concepts of EVA and MVA were developed by Joel Stern and Bennett Stewart, co-founders of the consulting firm Stern Stewart & Company. Stern Stewart copyrighted the terms "MVA" and "EVA," so other consulting firms have given other names to these values. Still, MVA and EVA are the terms most commonly used in practice. For more on MVA and EVA, see Stewart, *The Quest for Value*.

EVA is an estimate of a business's true economic profit for a given year, and it differs sharply from accounting net income primarily in that accounting income has no deduction for the cost of equity whereas this cost is deducted when calculating EVA.

If EVA is positive, then after-tax operating income exceeds the cost of the capital needed to produce that income, and management's actions are adding value for stockholders. Positive EVA on a yearly basis will help ensure that MVA is also positive. Note that whereas MVA applies to the entire firm, EVA can be determined for divisions as well as for the company as a whole, so it is useful as a guide to "reasonable" compensation for divisional as well as top corporate managers.

Define the terms "Market Value Added (MVA)" and "Economic Value Added (EVA)."

How does EVA differ from accounting net income?

3-11 THE FEDERAL INCOME TAX SYSTEM

Corporations must pay out a significant portion of their income as taxes, and individuals are also taxed on their income. We summarize some important points about the U.S. tax system here, based on 2004 provisions. A more detailed discussion is provided in Web Appendix 3A accessed through the ThomsonNOW Web site.

3-11a Corporate Taxes

Corporate income is generally taxed by the federal government at rates that begin at 15 percent and go up to 35 percent on taxable income of $10 million or more.[13] Thus, the corporate tax structure is *progressive* in the sense that higher rates are imposed on companies with larger incomes. Most state governments also impose income taxes on corporations, with 5 percent being a typical rate. Therefore, larger companies generally pay a rate of about 40 percent on their income, and we typically use 40 percent in our examples. The tax system is incredibly complex, so we do not attempt to cover it in detail. However, as noted above, we do provide a bit more tax information on the ThomsonNOW Web site.

3-11b Personal Taxes

Individuals are taxed by the federal government at rates that begin at 10 percent and rise to 35 percent on incomes of $319,100 or more. Some states also impose a state income tax, with rates varying across states. Note that income on investments held in pension accounts is not taxed until the money is withdrawn, presumably after retirement. Thus, a person might be in the 35 percent tax bracket on his or her ordinary income, but the tax rate would be zero on income earned in a 401(k) or other retirement account (and certain college savings plans).

3-11c Interest Paid

Borrowers must pay interest on their debts. For a business, the interest payments are regarded as an expense, and they are deducted when calculating taxable income. Individuals also incur debts and pay interest, but generally individuals cannot deduct interest payments (the big exception is interest on home loans, which, within limits, is deductible).

A Web site of interest concerning federal tax law is **http://www.taxsites.com/ federal.html**. *From this home page one can visit other sites that provide summaries of recent tax legislation or current information on corporate and individual tax rates. The official government Web site is* **http://www.irs.gov**.

---

[13] Actually, the marginal corporate tax rate goes up to 38 percent for income between $15,000,000 and $18,333,333; however, it then declines to 35 percent for taxable income above $18,333,333.

3-11d Interest Earned

Most interest earned, whether by businesses or individuals, is taxable. An important exception is that interest on most state and local government debt is exempt from federal taxes. State and local bonds are often called "munis," and they are generally purchased by individuals in high tax brackets.

3-11e Dividends Paid

Corporations pay dividends, and dividends paid are generally not a deductible expense. Thus, corporations can deduct interest paid but they cannot deduct dividends. Thus, if a company had a combined federal-plus-state tax rate of 40 percent and $10 million of pre-tax cash income, it could pay out all $10 million as interest but only $6 million of dividends because it would have to pay $4 million of taxes.[14]

Note that if one company uses a lot of debt financing, whereas another with similar operations uses only common stock financing, the stock-financed company will have no interest, hence no interest tax deductions, hence a higher income tax bill. The company that uses debt can thus pass more of its operating income on to investors (stockholders and debtholders). For this reason, our tax system encourages debt financing, as we discuss at length in the chapter on capital structure.

3-11f Dividends Received

Dividends received by an individual are taxed at the same tax rate as capital gains, 15 percent.[15] Note that this creates a double tax on dividend income—the corporation that paid the dividend is first taxed, and then the individual who receives it is taxed again. For corporate recipients, the situation is somewhat different—the corporation that receives dividend income can exclude some of the dividends from its taxable income. This provision is in the Tax Code to minimize the amount of *triple taxation* that would otherwise occur—one corporation would pay dividends out of after-tax income, the second corporation would be taxed again on that income, and the person who received dividends from the second corporation would be taxed once more.

3-11g Tax Loss Carry-Back and Carry-Forward

Corporation income often fluctuates from year to year, so a firm might be taxed at a 40 percent rate one year and then have a large loss the following year, hence pay no taxes. The Tax Code allows firms to carry losses back to offset profits in prior years, and, if losses haven't been offset by past profits, to carry the remaining losses forward to offset future profits. The effect of this provision is to cause taxes to reflect average income over time.

3-11h Capital Gains

Capital gains are, generally speaking, defined as profits from the sale of assets that are not normally bought and sold in the course of business. For individuals, capital gains typically arise from the sale of stocks or bonds at a profit. Thus, if someone buys some Microsoft stock for $10,000 and later sells it for $15,000, then he or she will have a $5,000 capital gain. If the stock was held for less than a

---

[14] This calculation is not exact, because the tax bill on $10 million of income would actually be somewhat lower ($3.4 million) because some of the income would be taxed at lower rates.
[15] If an individual is in the 10 percent tax bracket, the applicable tax rate is only 5 percent.

year, the $5,000 gain is just added to ordinary income and taxed as such. If the stock had been held for more than a year, then the gain will be taxed at a lower rate. For someone in the top (35 percent) federal tax bracket, the long-term capital gains rate is generally 15 percent. Corporations face somewhat different rules, and individual tax rates also vary a bit.

3-11i Depreciation

When a business buys an asset with a life greater than one year, it depreciates the asset over the years in which it will be used. For stockholder reporting, the company generally estimates the actual likely years of use, divides the cost by the number of years, and charges the calculated value as a cost on the income statement each year. (This is called "straight-line depreciation.") However, for tax purposes Congress has specified different depreciation rates for different types of assets, and those rates generally result in higher depreciation charges than what the company uses for stockholder reporting. We discuss depreciation in greater detail in Chapter 12.

3-11j Small Businesses

If a business is a proprietorship or partnership, its income is allocated to its owners in proportion to their ownership interests. If the same business is operated as a corporation, there are two possibilities. First, if the firm meets certain requirements related to size and number of stockholders, then it can elect to be taxed as an S corporation. In this case, for tax purposes it is treated like a partnership. An S corporation can thus enjoy the advantages of the corporate form of organization yet still receive the tax advantages of a partnership. Most small business corporations are actually set up as S corporations. If the firm does not qualify for S corporation status, it is called a C corporation and is taxed at regular corporate tax rates.

Explain the statement, "Our tax rates are progressive."

What is a "muni" bond, and how are these bonds taxed?

What are long-term capital gains?

How does our tax system influence the use of debt financing by corporations?

Differentiate between S and C corporations.

Tying It All Together

The primary purposes of this chapter were to describe the basic financial statements, to present some background information on cash flows, to differentiate between net cash flow and accounting income, and to provide an overview of the federal income tax system. In the next chapter, we build on this information to analyze a firm's financial statements.

SELF-TEST QUESTIONS AND PROBLEMS
(Solutions Appear in Appendix A)

ST-1 **Key terms** Define each of the following terms:
   a. Annual report; balance sheet; income statement; statement of cash flows; statement of retained earnings
   b. Common stockholders' equity, or net worth; retained earnings; net working capital
   c. Depreciation; tangible assets; amortization; intangible assets; EBITDA
   d. Net cash flow; accounting profit
   e. Operating assets; nonoperating assets
   f. Total operating capital; net operating working capital
   g. Net operating profit after taxes (NOPAT); operating cash flow; free cash flow
   h. Market Value Added (MVA); Economic Value Added (EVA)
   i. Progressive tax
   j. Capital gain
   k. S corporation; C corporation

ST-2 **Net income and cash flow** Last year Rattner Robotics had $5 million in operating income (EBIT). Its depreciation expense was $1 million; its interest expense was $1 million; and its corporate tax rate was 40 percent. At year-end it had $14 million in current assets, $4 million in non-interest-bearing current liabilities, and $15 million in net plant and equipment. Assume that Rattner's only noncash item was depreciation.
   a. What was the company's net income?
   b. What was its net cash flow?
   c. What was its net operating profit after taxes (NOPAT)?
   d. What was its operating cash flow?
   e. What was its net operating working capital (NOWC)?
   f. If operating capital at the end of the previous year was $24 million, what was the company's free cash flow (FCF) for the year?
   g. If the firm had $4.5 million in retained earnings at the beginning of the year and paid out a total dividend of $1.2 million, what was its retained earnings at the end of the year?

QUESTIONS

3-1 What four financial statements are contained in most annual reports?

3-2 What do the numbers on financial statements actually represent?

3-3 Who are some of the basic users of financial statements, and how do they use them?

3-4 If a "typical" firm reports $20 million of retained earnings on its balance sheet, could its directors declare a $20 million cash dividend without any qualms whatsoever?

3-5 Explain the following statement: "While the balance sheet can be thought of as a snapshot of the firm's financial position *at a point in time*, the income statement reports on operations *over a period of time*."

3-6 Financial statements are based on generally accepted accounting principles (GAAP) and audited by CPA firms, so do investors need to worry about the validity of those statements?

3-7 Differentiate between accounting profit and net cash flow. Why do those two numbers differ?

3-8 Differentiate between operating cash flow and net cash flow. Why might those two numbers differ?

3-9 What's the difference between NOPAT and net income? How does debt affect the relationship between these two items?

3-10 What is free cash flow? If you were an investor, why might you be more interested in free cash flow than net income?

3-11 Would it be possible for a company to report *negative* free cash flow and still be highly valued by investors; that is, could a negative free cash flow ever be a good thing in the eyes of investors?

3-12 What does *double taxation of corporate income* mean? Could income ever be subject to *triple* taxation?

3-13 How does the deductibility of interest and dividends by the *paying corporation* affect the choice of financing (that is, the use of debt versus equity)?

PROBLEMS

Easy
Problems 1–4

3-1 **Income statement** Little Books Inc. recently reported $3 million of net income. Its EBIT was $6 million, and its tax rate was 40 percent. What was its interest expense? [Hint: Write out the headings for an income statement and then fill in the known values. Then divide $3 million of net income by $(1 - T) = 0.6$ to find the pre-tax income. The difference between EBIT and taxable income must be the interest expense. Use this same procedure to work some of the other problems.]

3-2 **Income statement** Pearson Brothers recently reported an EBITDA of $7.5 million and net income of $1.8 million. It had $2.0 million of interest expense, and its corporate tax rate was 40 percent. What was its charge for depreciation and amortization?

3-3 **Net cash flow** Kendall Corners Inc. recently reported net income of $3.1 million and depreciation of $500,000. What was its net cash flow? Assume it had no amortization expense.

3-4 **Statement of retained earnings** In its most recent financial statements, Newhouse Inc. reported $50 million of net income and $810 million of retained earnings. The previous retained earnings were $780 million. How much dividends were paid to shareholders during the year?

Intermediate
Problems 5–10

3-5 **Balance sheet** Which of the following actions are most likely to directly increase cash as shown on a firm's balance sheet? Explain, and state the assumptions that underlie your answer.
   a.   It issues $2 million of new common stock.
   b.   It buys new plant and equipment at a cost of $3 million.
   c.   It reports a large loss for the year.
   d.   It increases the dividends paid on its common stock.

3-6 **Statement of retained earnings** Computer World Inc. paid out $22.5 million in total common dividends and reported $278.9 million of retained earnings at year-end. The prior year's retained earnings were $212.3 million. What was the net income?

3-7 **Statement of cash flows** W.C. Cycling had $55,000 in cash at year-end 2004 and $25,000 in cash at year-end 2005. Cash flow from long-term investing activities totaled −$250,000, and cash flow from financing activities totaled +$170,000.
   a.   What was the cash flow from operating activities?
   b.   If accruals increased by $25,000, receivables and inventories increased by $100,000, and depreciation and amortization totaled $10,000, what was the firm's net income?

3-8 **Cash flow** The Klaven Corporation had operating income (EBIT) of $750,000 and depreciation expense of $200,000. It is 100 percent equity financed (no debt), and its corporate tax rate is 40 percent. The firm had no amortization expense. What are net income, net cash flow, and operating cash flow?

3-9   **MVA** Henderson Industries has $500 million of common equity; its stock price is $60 per share; and its Market Value Added (MVA) is $130 million. How many common shares are currently outstanding?

3-10   **Cash flow** Bailey Corporation's income statement (dollars are in thousands) is given here:

Sales	$14,000,000
Operating costs excluding depreciation	
and amortization	7,000,000
EBITDA	$ 7,000,000
Depreciation and amortization	3,000,000
EBIT	$ 4,000,000
Interest	1,500,000
EBT	$ 2,500,000
Taxes (40%)	1,000,000
Net income	$ 1,500,000

Its total operating capital is $20 billion, and its total after-tax dollar cost of operating capital is $2 billion. During the year, Bailey invested $1.3 billion in net operating capital.

a. What is its NOPAT?
b. What is its net cash flow?
c. What is its operating cash flow?
d. What is its free cash flow?

Challenging Problems 11–14

3-11   **Income statement** Hermann Industries is forecasting the following income statement:

Sales	$8,000,000
Operating costs excluding depreciation	
and amortization	4,400,000
EBITDA	$3,600,000
Depreciation and amortization	800,000
EBIT	$2,800,000
Interest	600,000
EBT	$2,200,000
Taxes (40%)	880,000
Net income	$1,320,000

The CEO would like to see higher sales and a forecasted net income of $2,500,000.

Assume that operating costs (excluding depreciation and amortization) are 55 percent of sales, and depreciation and amortization and interest expenses will increase by 10 percent. The tax rate, which is 40 percent, will remain the same. What level of sales would generate $2,500,000 in net income?

3-12   **Financial statements** The Davidson Corporation's balance sheet and income statement are given here:

Davidson Corporation: Balance Sheet as of December 31, 2005
(Millions of Dollars)

Assets			Liabilities and Equity	
Cash and equivalents	$ 15		Accounts payable	$ 120
Accounts receivable	515		Notes payable	220
Inventories	880		Accruals	280
Total current assets	$1,410		Total current liabilities	$ 620
Net plant and equipment	2,590		Long-term bonds	1,520
			Total debt	$2,140
			Common stock	
			(100 million shares)	260
			Retained earnings	1,600
			Common equity	$1,860
Total assets	$4,000		Total liabilities and equity	$4,000

Davidson Corporation: Income Statement for Year Ending December 31, 2005 (Millions of Dollars)

Sales	$6,250
Operating costs excluding depreciation and amortization	5,230
EBITDA	$1,020
Depreciation and amortization	220
EBIT	$ 800
Interest	180
EBT	$ 620
Taxes (40%)	248
Net income	$ 372
Common dividends paid	$ 146
Earnings per share	$ 3.72

a. All revenues were received in cash during the year and all costs except depreciation and amortization were paid in cash during the year. What was net cash flow? How was it different from reported accounting profit?
b. Construct the statement of retained earnings for December 31, 2005.
c. How much money has been reinvested in the firm over the years?
d. At the present time, how large a check could be written without it bouncing?
e. How much money must be paid to current creditors within the next year?

3-13   **Free cash flow** Financial information for Powell Panther Corporation is shown here:

Powell Panther Corporation: Income Statements for Year Ending December 31 (Millions of Dollars)

	2005	2004
Sales	$1,200.0	$1,000.0
Operating costs excluding depreciation and amortization	1,020.0	850.0
EBITDA	$ 180.0	$ 150.0
Depreciation and amortization	30.0	25.0
Earnings before interest and taxes	$ 150.0	$ 125.0
Interest	21.7	20.2
Earnings before taxes	$ 128.3	$ 104.8
Taxes (40%)	51.3	41.9
Net income	$ 77.0	$ 62.9
Common dividends	$ 60.5	$ 46.4

Powell Panther Corporation: Balance Sheets as of December 31 (Millions of Dollars)

	2005	2004
Assets		
Cash and equivalents	$ 12.0	$ 10.0
Accounts receivable	180.0	150.0
Inventories	180.0	200.0
Total current assets	$372.0	$360.0
Net plant and equipment	300.0	250.0
Total assets	$672.0	$610.0
Liabilities and Equity		
Accounts payable	$108.0	$ 90.0
Notes payable	67.0	51.5
Accruals	72.0	60.0
Total current liabilities	$247.0	$201.5
Long-term bonds	150.0	150.0
Total debt	$397.0	$351.5
Common stock (50 million shares)	50.0	50.0
Retained earnings	225.0	208.5
Common equity	$275.0	$258.5
Total liabilities and equity	$672.0	$610.0

a. What was the 2005 NOPAT?
b. What were the 2004 and 2005 net operating working capital?
c. What were the 2004 and 2005 total operating capital?
d. What was the 2005 free cash flow?
e. How would you explain the large increase in 2005 dividends?

3-14 **Income and cash flow analysis** The Menendez Corporation expects to have sales of $12 million in 2006. Costs other than depreciation and amortization are expected to be 75 percent of sales, and depreciation and amortization expenses are expected to be $1.5 million. All sales revenues will be collected in cash, and costs other than depreciation and amortization must be paid for during the year. The corporate tax rate is 40 percent.

a. Set up an income statement. What is the expected net cash flow?
b. Suppose Congress changed the tax laws so that depreciation and amortization expenses doubled and there were no changes in operations. What would happen to reported profit and net cash flow?
c. Now suppose that Congress reduced depreciation and amortization expenses by 50 percent. How would profit and net cash flow be affected?
d. Would you prefer that Congress double or halve depreciation and amortization expenses? Why?
e. Would a doubling of depreciation and amortization expenses possibly have an adverse effect on stock price and on the ability to borrow money? Explain.

COMPREHENSIVE/SPREADSHEET PROBLEM

3-15 **Financial statements, cash flow, and taxes** Laiho Industries' 2004 and 2005 balance sheets (in thousands of dollars) are shown below:

	2005	2004
Cash	$102,850	$ 89,725
Accounts receivable	103,365	85,527
Inventories	38,444	34,982
Total current assets	$244,659	$210,234
Net fixed assets	67,165	42,436
Total assets	$311,824	$252,670
Accounts payable	$ 30,761	$ 23,109
Accruals	30,477	22,656
Notes payable	16,717	14,217
Total current liabilities	$ 77,955	$ 59,982
Long-term debt	76,264	63,914
Total liabilities	$154,219	$123,896
Common stock	100,000	90,000
Retained earnings	57,605	38,774
Total common equity	$157,605	$128,774
Total liabilities and equity	$311,824	$252,670

a. Sales for 2005 were $455,150,000, and EBITDA was 15 percent of sales. Furthermore, depreciation was 11 percent of net fixed assets, interest was $8,575,000, the corporate tax rate was 40 percent, and Laiho pays 40 percent of its net income out in dividends. The firm has no amortization expense. Given this information, construct the 2005 income statement.
b. Construct the statement of retained earnings for the year ending December 31, 2005, and the 2005 statement of cash flows.
c. Calculate net working capital and net operating working capital. What are the differences in these two measures?

d. Calculate total operating capital, NOPAT, operating cash flow, and free cash flow for 2005.

e. Calculate the 2005 MVA. There were 10 million shares outstanding and the year-end closing price was $17.25 per share.

f. If Laiho increased its dividend payout ratio, what effect would this have on its corporate taxes paid? What effect would this have on the taxes paid by the company's shareholders?

Integrated Case

D'Leon Inc., Part I

3-16 **Financial statements and taxes** Donna Jamison, a 2000 graduate of the University of Florida with 4 years of banking experience, was recently brought in as assistant to the chairman of the board of D'Leon Inc., a small food producer that operates in north Florida and whose specialty is high-quality pecan and other nut products sold in the snack-foods market. D'Leon's president, Al Watkins, decided in 2004 to undertake a major expansion and to "go national" in competition with Frito-Lay, Eagle, and other major snack-food companies. Watkins felt that D'Leon's products were of a higher quality than the competition's; that this quality differential would enable it to charge a premium price; and that the end result would be greatly increased sales, profits, and stock price.

The company doubled its plant capacity, opened new sales offices outside its home territory, and launched an expensive advertising campaign. D'Leon's results were not satisfactory, to put it mildly. Its board of directors, which consisted of its president and vice president plus its major stockholders (who were all local businesspeople), was most upset when directors learned how the expansion was going. Suppliers were being paid late and were unhappy, and the bank was complaining about the deteriorating situation and threatening to cut off credit. As a result, Watkins was informed that changes would have to be made, and quickly, or he would be fired. Also, at the board's insistence Donna Jamison was brought in and given the job of assistant to Fred Campo, a retired banker who was D'Leon's chairman and largest stockholder. Campo agreed to give up a few of his golfing days and to help nurse the company back to health, with Jamison's help.

Jamison began by gathering the financial statements and other data given in Tables IC3-1, IC3-2, IC3-3, and IC3-4. Assume that you are Jamison's assistant, and you must help her answer the following questions for Campo. (Note: We will continue with this case in Chapter 4, and you will feel more comfortable with the analysis there, but answering these questions will help prepare you for Chapter 4. Provide clear explanations, not just yes or no answers!)

a. What effect did the expansion have on sales, NOPAT, net operating working capital (NOWC), total operating capital, and net income?

b. What effect did the company's expansion have on its net cash flow, operating cash flow, and free cash flow?

c. Looking at D'Leon's stock price today, would you conclude that the expansion increased or decreased MVA?

d. D'Leon purchases materials on 30-day terms, meaning that it is supposed to pay for purchases within 30 days of receipt. Judging from its 2005 balance sheet, do you think D'Leon pays suppliers on time? Explain. If not, what problems might this lead to?

e. D'Leon spends money for labor, materials, and fixed assets (depreciation) to make products, and still more money to sell those products. Then, it makes sales that result in receivables, which eventually result in cash inflows. Does it appear that D'Leon's sales price exceeds its costs per unit sold? How does this affect the cash balance?

f. Suppose D'Leon's sales manager told the sales staff to start offering 60-day credit terms rather than the 30-day terms now being offered. D'Leon's competitors react by offering similar terms, so sales remain constant. What effect would this have on the cash account? How would the cash account be affected if sales doubled as a result of the credit policy change?

g. Can you imagine a situation in which the sales price exceeds the cost of producing and selling a unit of output, yet a dramatic increase in sales volume causes the cash balance to decline?

h. Did D'Leon finance its expansion program with internally generated funds (additions to retained earnings plus depreciation) or with external capital? How does the choice of financing affect the company's financial strength?

i.   Refer to Tables IC3-2 and IC3-4. Suppose D'Leon broke even in 2005 in the sense that sales revenues equaled total operating costs plus interest charges. Would the asset expansion have caused the company to experience a cash shortage that required it to raise external capital?

j.   If D'Leon started depreciating fixed assets over 7 years rather than 10 years, would that affect (1) the physical stock of assets, (2) the balance sheet account for fixed assets, (3) the company's reported net income, and (4) its cash position? Assume the same depreciation method is used for stockholder reporting and for tax calculations, and the accounting change has no effect on assets' physical lives.

k.   Explain how earnings per share, dividends per share, and book value per share are calculated, and what they mean. Why does the market price per share *not* equal the book value per share?

l.   Explain briefly the tax treatment of (1) interest and dividends paid, (2) interest earned and dividends received, (3) capital gains, and (4) tax loss carry-back and carry-forward. How might each of these items affect D'Leon's taxes?

TABLE IC3-1   *Balance Sheets*

	2005	2004
Assets		
Cash	$ 7,282	$ 57,600
Accounts receivable	632,160	351,200
Inventories	1,287,360	715,200
Total current assets	$1,926,802	$1,124,000
Gross fixed assets	1,202,950	491,000
Less accumulated depreciation	263,160	146,200
Net fixed assets	$ 939,790	$ 344,800
Total assets	$2,866,592	$1,468,800
Liabilities and Equity		
Accounts payable	$ 524,160	$ 145,600
Notes payable	636,808	200,000
Accruals	489,600	136,000
Total current liabilities	$1,650,568	$ 481,600
Long-term debt	723,432	323,432
Common stock (100,000 shares)	460,000	460,000
Retained earnings	32,592	203,768
Total equity	$ 492,592	$ 663,768
Total liabilities and equity	$2,866,592	$1,468,800

TABLE IC3-2	*Income Statements*		
		2005	**2004**
Sales		$6,034,000	$3,432,000
Cost of goods sold		5,528,000	2,864,000
Other expenses		519,988	358,672
Total operating costs excluding depreciation and amortization		$6,047,988	$3,222,672
EBITDA		($ 13,988)	$ 209,328
Depreciation and amortization		116,960	18,900
EBIT		($ 130,948)	$ 190,428
Interest expense		136,012	43,828
EBT		($ 266,960)	$ 146,600
Taxes (40%)		(106,784)[a]	58,640
Net income		($ 160,176)	$ 87,960
EPS		($ 1.602)	$ 0.880
DPS		$ 0.110	$ 0.220
Book value per share		$ 4.926	$ 6.638
Stock price		$ 2.25	$ 8.50
Shares outstanding		100,000	100,000
Tax rate		40.00%	40.00%
Lease payments		40,000	40,000
Sinking fund payments		0	0

Note:
[a] The firm had sufficient taxable income in 2003 and 2004 to obtain its full tax refund in 2005.

TABLE IC3-3	*Statement of Retained Earnings, 2005*

Balance of retained earnings, 12/31/04	$203,768
Add: Net income, 2005	(160,176)
Less: Dividends paid	(11,000)
Balance of retained earnings, 12/31/05	$ 32,592

TABLE IC3-4 *Statement of Cash Flows, 2005*

OPERATING ACTIVITIES

Net income	($160,176)
Additions (Sources of Cash)	
Depreciation and amortization	116,960
Increase in accounts payable	378,560
Increase in accruals	353,600
Subtractions (Uses of Cash)	
Increase in accounts receivable	(280,960)
Increase in inventories	(572,160)
Net cash provided by operating activities	($164,176)

LONG-TERM INVESTING ACTIVITIES

Cash used to acquire fixed assets	($711,950)

FINANCING ACTIVITIES

Increase in notes payable	$436,808
Increase in long-term debt	400,000
Payment of cash dividends	(11,000)
Net cash provided by financing activities	$825,808
Sum: net decrease in cash	($ 50,318)
Plus: cash at beginning of year	57,600
Cash at end of year	$ 7,282

cyberproblem

Please go to the ThomsonNOW Web site to access the Cyberproblems.

THOMSON ONE | Business School Edition

Access the Thomson ONE problems through the ThomsonNOW Web site. Use the Thomson ONE—Business School Edition online database to work this chapter's questions.

Exploring Starbucks' Financial Statements

Over the past decade, Starbucks coffee shops have become an increasingly familiar part of the urban landscape. Currently, the company operates more than 6,000 coffee shops in all 50 states, the District of Columbia, and internationally, and in 2005 it had roughly 80,000 employees.

Thomson ONE can access a wealth of financial information for companies such as Starbucks. To find some background information, begin by entering the company's ticker symbol, SBUX, and then selecting "GO." On the opening screen, you will see a lot of useful information, including a summary of what Starbucks does, a chart of its recent stock price, EPS estimates, some recent news stories, and a list of key financial data and ratios.

In researching a company's operating performance, a good place to start is the recent stock price performance. At the top of the Stock Price Chart, click on the section labeled "Interactive Chart." From this point, we are able to obtain a chart of the company's stock price performance relative to the overall market, as measured by the S&P 500, between 1995 and 2005. To obtain a 10-year chart, go to "Time Frame," click on the down arrow, and select 10 years. Then, click on "Draw" and a 10-year price chart should appear.

As you can see, Starbucks has had its ups and downs, but the company's overall performance has been quite strong, and it has beat the overall market handily.

We can also find Starbucks' recent financial statements. Near the top of your screen, click on the "Financials" tab to find the company's balance sheet, income statement, and statement of cash flows for the past 5 years. Clicking on the Microsoft *Excel* icon downloads these statements directly to a spreadsheet.

Discussion Questions

1. Looking at the most recent year available, what is the amount of total assets on Starbucks' balance sheet? What percentage is fixed assets, such as plant and equipment, and what percentage is current assets? How much has the company grown over the years that are shown?
2. Does Starbucks have a lot of long-term debt? What are the chief ways in which Starbucks has financed assets?
3. Looking at the statement of cash flows, what factors can explain the change in the company's cash position over the last couple of years?
4. Looking at the income statement, what are the company's most recent sales and net income? Over the past several years, what has been the sales growth rate? What has been the growth rate in net income?
5. Over the past few years, has there been a strong correlation between stock price performance and reported earnings?

4

ANALYSIS OF FINANCIAL STATEMENTS[1]

Lessons Learned from Enron and WorldCom

In early 2001, Enron appeared to be on top of the world. The high-flying energy firm had a market capitalization of $60 billion, and its stock was trading at $80 a share. Wall Street analysts were touting its innovations and management success and strongly recommending the stock. Less than a year later, Enron had declared bankruptcy, its stock was basically worthless, and investors had lost billions of dollars. This dramatic and sudden collapse left many wondering how so much value could be destroyed in such a short period of time.

While Enron's stock fell steadily throughout the first part of 2001, most analysts voiced no concerns. The general consensus was that it was simply caught up in a sell-off that was affecting the entire stock market and that its long-run prospects remained strong. However, a hint of trouble came when Enron's CEO, Jeffrey Skilling, unexpectedly resigned in August 2001; he was replaced by its chairman and previous CEO, Ken Lay. By the end of August, its stock had fallen to $35 a share. Two months later, Enron stunned the financial markets by announcing a $638 million loss, along with a $1.2 billion write-down in its book value equity. The write-down, which turned out to be grossly inadequate, stemmed primarily from losses realized on a series of partnerships set up by its CFO, Andrew Fastow. Shortly thereafter, it was revealed that Enron had

---

[1] We have covered this chapter both early in the course and toward the end. Early coverage gives students an overview of how financial decisions affect financial statements and results, and thus of what financial management is all about. If it is covered later, after coverage of bond and stock valuation, risk analysis, capital budgeting, capital structure, and working capital management, students can better understand the logic of the ratios and see how they are used for different purposes. Depending on students' backgrounds, instructors may want to cover the chapter early or late.

© AP PHOTO/RON EDMONDS

guaranteed the partnerships' debt, so its true liabilities were far higher than the financial statements indicated. These revelations destroyed Enron's credibility, caused its customers to flee, and led directly to its bankruptcy.

Not surprisingly, Enron's investors and employees were enraged to learn that its senior executives had received $750 million in salaries, bonuses, and profits from stock options for good performance in the same year before the company went bankrupt. During that year, senior executives were bailing out of the stock as fast as they could, even as they put out misleading statements touting the stock to their employees and outside investors. Fastow has since pleaded guilty to fraud and is cooperating with authorities in the cases against his former bosses, Lay and Skilling, who have been indicted for their roles in Enron's collapse and await trial.

After Enron declared bankruptcy, critics turned their attention to the company's auditor, Arthur Andersen, and to certain Wall Street analysts who had blindly recommended the stock over the years. Critics contended that the auditors and analysts neglected their responsibilities because of conflicts of interest. Andersen partners looked the other way because they didn't want to compromise their lucrative consulting contracts with Enron, and the analysts kept recommending the stock because they wanted to help the investment banking side of their firms get more Enron business.

As if the Enron debacle was not enough, in June 2002 it was learned that WorldCom, an even larger company, had "cooked its books" and inflated its profits and cash flows by more than $11 billion. Shortly thereafter, WorldCom collapsed, with many more billions of investor losses and thousands unemployed. Enron had set up complicated partnerships to deceive investors, but WorldCom simply lied, reporting normal operating costs as capital expenditures and thus boosting its reported profits. Interestingly, Enron and WorldCom used the same auditing firm, Arthur Andersen, which was itself put out of business, causing about 70,000 employees to lose their jobs. It is also interesting to note that Citigroup's investment banking subsidiary, Salomon Smith Barney, earned many millions in fees from WorldCom, and that Salomon's lead telecom analyst, Jack Grubman, who helped bring in this business, did not downgrade World-Com to a sell until the very day the fraud was announced. At that point the stock was selling for less than a dollar, down from a high of $64.50.

The Enron and WorldCom collapses caused investors throughout the world to wonder if these companies' misdeeds were isolated situations or were symptomatic of undiscovered problems lurking in many other companies. Those fears led to a broad decline in stock prices, and President Bush expressed outrage at executives whose actions were imperiling our financial markets and economic system. In response to these and other abuses, Congress passed the Sarbanes-Oxley Act of 2002. One of its provisions requires the CEO and the CFO to sign a statement certifying that the "financial statements and disclosures fairly represent, in all material respects, the operations and financial condition" of the company. This will make it easier to haul off in handcuffs a CEO or CFO who has misled investors.

Financial statements have undoubtedly improved in the last few years, and they now provide a wealth of good information that can be used by managers, investors, lenders, customers, suppliers, and regulators. As you will see in this chapter, a careful analysis of a company's statements can highlight its strengths and shortcomings. Also, as you will see, financial analysis can be used to predict how such strategic decisions as the sale of a division, a change in credit or inventory policy, or a plant expansion will affect a firm's future performance.

Putting Things In Perspective

The primary goal of financial management is to maximize shareholders' wealth over the long run, not to maximize accounting measures such as net income or EPS. However, accounting data influence stock prices, and these data can be used to understand why a company is performing the way it is and to forecast where it is heading. Chapter 3 described the key financial statements and showed how they change as a firm's operations undergo change. Now, in Chapter 4, we show how the statements are used by managers to improve performance; by lenders to evaluate the likelihood of collecting on loans; and by stockholders to forecast earnings, dividends, and stock prices.

If management is to maximize a firm's value, it must take advantage of the firm's strengths and correct its weaknesses. Financial analysis involves (1) comparing the firm's performance to other firms, especially those in the same industry, and (2) evaluating trends in the firm's financial position over time. These studies help management identify deficiencies and then take corrective actions. We focus here on how financial managers and investors evaluate firms' financial positions. Then, in later chapters, we examine the types of actions management can take to improve future performance and thus increase the firm's stock price.

The most important ratio is the ROE, or return on equity, which is net income to common stockholders divided by total stockholders' equity. Stockholders obviously want to earn a high rate of return on their invested capital, and the ROE tells them the rate they are earning. If the ROE is high, then the stock price will also tend to be high, and actions that increase ROE are likely to increase the stock price. The other ratios provide information about how well such assets as inventory, accounts receivable, and fixed assets are managed, and about how the firm is financed. As we will see, these factors all affect the ROE, and management uses the other ratios primarily to help develop plans to improve the average ROE over the long run.

4-1 RATIO ANALYSIS

Financial statements report both a firm's position at a point in time and its operations over some past period. However, their real value lies in the fact that they can be used to help predict future earnings and dividends. From an investor's standpoint, *predicting the future is what financial statement analysis is all about,* while from management's standpoint, *financial statement analysis is useful both to help anticipate future conditions and, more important, as a starting point for planning actions that will improve future performance.*

Financial ratios are designed to help one evaluate a financial statement. For example, Firm A might have debt of $5,248,760 and interest charges of $419,900, while Firm B might have debt of $52,647,980 and interest charges of $3,948,600. Which company is stronger? The burden of these debts, and the companies' ability to repay them, can best be evaluated (1) by comparing each firm's debt to its assets and (2) by comparing the interest it must pay to the income it has available for payment of interest. Such comparisons involve *ratio analysis*.

In the paragraphs that follow, we will calculate Allied Food Products' financial ratios for 2005, using data from the balance sheets and income statements given in Tables 3-1 and 3-2. We will also evaluate the ratios relative to the industry averages.[2] Note that the dollar amounts in the ratio calculations are generally in millions.

4-2 LIQUIDITY RATIOS

A **liquid asset** is one that trades in an active market and hence can be quickly converted to cash at the going market price, and a firm's "liquidity position" deals with this question: Will the firm be able to pay off its debts as they come due in the coming year? As shown in Table 3-1 in Chapter 3, Allied has $310 million of debt that must be paid off within the coming year. Will it have trouble meeting those obligations? A full liquidity analysis requires the use of cash budgets, but by relating cash and other current assets to current liabilities, ratio analysis provides a quick, easy-to-use measure of liquidity. Two of the most commonly used **liquidity ratios** are discussed here.

4-2a Current Ratio

The primary liquidity ratio is the **current ratio,** which is calculated by dividing current assets by current liabilities:

$$\text{Current ratio} = \frac{\text{Current assets}}{\text{Current liabilities}}$$

$$= \frac{\$1,000}{\$310} = 3.2\times$$

$$\text{Industry average} = 4.2\times$$

Current assets include cash, marketable securities, accounts receivable, and inventories. Allied's current liabilities consist of accounts payable, short-term notes payable, current maturities of long-term debt, accrued taxes, and accrued wages.

If a company is getting into financial difficulty, it begins paying its bills (accounts payable) more slowly, borrowing from its bank, and so on, all of which increase current liabilities. If current liabilities are rising faster than current assets, the current ratio will fall, and this is a sign of possible trouble. Allied's current ratio of 3.2 is well below the industry average, 4.2, so its liquidity position is rather weak. Still, since its current assets are supposed to be converted to

Liquid Asset
An asset that can be converted to cash quickly without having to reduce the asset's price very much.

Liquidity Ratios
Ratios that show the relationship of a firm's cash and other current assets to its current liabilities.

Current Ratio
This ratio is calculated by dividing current assets by current liabilities. It indicates the extent to which current liabilities are covered by those assets expected to be converted to cash in the near future.

---

[2] In addition to the ratios discussed in this section, financial analysts sometimes employ a tool known as *common size analysis*. To form a common size balance sheet, simply divide each asset and liability item by total assets and then express the results as percentages. The resultant percentage statement can be compared with statements of larger or smaller firms, or with those of the same firm over time. To form a common size income statement, divide each income statement item by sales. With a spreadsheet, which most analysts use, this is trivially easy.

cash within a year, it is likely that they could be liquidated at close to their stated value. With a current ratio of 3.2, Allied could liquidate current assets at only 31 percent of book value and still pay off current creditors in full.[3]

Although industry average figures are discussed later in some detail, note that an industry average is not a magic number that all firms should strive to maintain—in fact, some very well-managed firms may be above the average while other good firms are below it. However, if a firm's ratios are far removed from the averages for its industry, an analyst should be concerned about why this variance occurs. Thus, a deviation from the industry average should signal the analyst (or management) to check further.

4-2b Quick, or Acid Test, Ratio

Quick (Acid Test) Ratio
This ratio is calculated by deducting inventories from current assets and then dividing the remainder by current liabilities.

The second most used liquidity ratio is the **quick, or acid test, ratio,** which is calculated by deducting inventories from current assets and then dividing the remainder by current liabilities:

$$\text{Quick, or acid test, ratio} = \frac{\text{Current assets} - \text{Inventories}}{\text{Current liabilities}}$$

$$= \frac{\$385}{\$310} = 1.2\times$$

$$\text{Industry average} = 2.2\times$$

Inventories are typically the least liquid of a firm's current assets, hence they are the assets on which losses are most likely to occur in the event of liquidation. Therefore, this measure of a firm's ability to pay off short-term obligations without relying on the sale of inventories is important.

The industry average quick ratio is 2.2, so Allied's 1.2 ratio is quite low in comparison with other firms in its industry. Still, if the accounts receivable can be collected, the company can pay off its current liabilities without having to liquidate its inventories.

What are some characteristics of a liquid asset? Give some examples.

What two ratios are used to analyze a firm's liquidity position? Write out their equations.

Why is the current ratio the most commonly used measure of short-term solvency?

Which current asset is typically the least liquid?

A company has current liabilities of $500 million, and its current ratio is 2.0. What is its level of current assets? ($1,000 million) If this firm's quick ratio is 1.6, how much inventory does it have? ($200 million)

Asset Management Ratios
A set of ratios that measure how effectively a firm is managing its assets.

4-3 ASSET MANAGEMENT RATIOS

A second group of ratios, the **asset management ratios,** measures how effectively the firm is managing its assets. These ratios answer this question: Does the amount of each type of asset seem reasonable, too high, or too low in view of

---

[3] $1/3.2 = 0.31$, or 31%. Note also that $0.31(\$1,000) = \$310$, the current liabilities balance.

current and projected sales? When they acquire assets, Allied and other companies must obtain capital from banks or other sources. If a firm has too many assets, its cost of capital will be too high and its profits will be depressed. On the other hand, if assets are too low, profitable sales will be lost. The asset management ratios described in this section are important.

4-3a Inventory Turnover Ratio

"Turnover ratios" are ratios where sales are divided by some asset, and as the name implies, they show how many times the item is "turned over" during the year. Thus, the **inventory turnover ratio** is defined as sales divided by inventories:

$$\text{Inventory turnover ratio} = \frac{\text{Sales}}{\text{Inventories}}$$

$$= \frac{\$3,000}{\$615} = 4.9\times$$

Industry average = 10.9×

Inventory Turnover Ratio
This ratio is calculated by dividing sales by inventories.

As a rough approximation, each item of Allied's inventory is sold out and restocked, or "turned over," 4.9 times per year. "Turnover" is a term that originated many years ago with the old Yankee peddler, who would load up his wagon with goods, then go off on his route to peddle his wares. The merchandise was called "working capital" because it was what he actually sold, or "turned over," to produce his profits, whereas his "turnover" was the number of trips he took each year. Annual sales divided by inventory equaled turnover, or trips per year. If he made 10 trips per year, stocked 100 pans, and made a gross profit of $5 per pan, his annual gross profit would be (100)($5)(10) = $5,000. If he went faster and made 20 trips per year, his gross profit would double, other things held constant. So, his turnover directly affected his profits.

Allied's turnover of 4.9 is much lower than the industry average of 10.9. This suggests that it is holding too much inventory. Excess inventory is, of course, unproductive and represents an investment with a low or zero rate of return. Allied's low inventory turnover ratio also makes us question the current ratio. With such a low turnover, the firm may be holding obsolete goods not worth their stated value.[4]

Note that sales occur over the entire year, whereas the inventory figure is for one point in time. For this reason, it might be better to use an average inventory measure.[5] If the business is highly seasonal, or if there has been a strong upward or downward sales trend during the year, it is especially useful to make an adjustment. To maintain comparability with industry averages, however, we did not use the average inventory figure.

---

[4] A problem arises when calculating and analyzing the inventory turnover ratio. Sales are stated at market prices, so if inventories are carried at cost, as they generally are, the calculated turnover overstates the true turnover ratio. Therefore, it might be more appropriate to use cost of goods sold in place of sales in the formula's numerator. However, some established compilers of financial ratio statistics such as Dun & Bradstreet use the ratio of sales to inventories carried at cost. To have a figure that can be compared with those published by Dun & Bradstreet and similar organizations, it is necessary to measure inventory turnover with sales in the numerator, as we do here.

[5] Preferably, the average inventory value should be calculated by summing the monthly figures during the year and dividing by 12. If monthly data are not available, the beginning and ending figures can be added and then divided by 2. Both methods adjust for growth but not for seasonal effects.

Days Sales Outstanding (DSO)
This ratio is calculated by dividing accounts receivable by average sales per day; it indicates the average length of time the firm must wait after making a sale before it receives cash.

4-3b Days Sales Outstanding

Days sales outstanding (DSO), also called the "average collection period" (ACP), is used to appraise accounts receivable, and it is calculated by dividing accounts receivable by average daily sales to find how many days' sales are tied up in receivables. Thus, the DSO represents the average length of time that the firm must wait after making a sale before receiving cash. Allied has 46 days sales outstanding, well above the 36-day industry average:

$$\text{DSO} = \frac{\text{Days sales outstanding}}{} = \frac{\text{Receivables}}{\text{Average sales per day}} = \frac{\text{Receivables}}{\text{Annual sales}/365}$$

$$= \frac{\$375}{\$3{,}000/365} = \frac{\$375}{\$8.2192} = 45.625 \text{ days} \approx 46 \text{ days}$$

$$\text{Industry average} = 36 \text{ days}$$

Note that in this calculation we used a 365-day year. Some analysts use a 360-day year; on this basis Allied's DSO would have been slightly lower, 45 days.[6]

The DSO can also be evaluated by comparing it with the terms on which the firm sells its goods. For example, Allied's sales terms call for payment within 30 days, so the fact that 46 days' sales, not 30 days', are outstanding indicates that customers, on the average, are not paying their bills on time. This deprives the company of funds that could be used to reduce bank loans or some other type of costly capital. Moreover, with a high average DSO, it is likely that a number of customers are paying very late, and those customers may well be in financial trouble, in which case Allied may never be able to collect the receivable.[7] Therefore, if the trend in DSO over the past few years has been rising, but the credit policy has not been changed, this would be strong evidence that steps should be taken to expedite the collection of accounts receivable.

4-3c Fixed Assets Turnover Ratio

Fixed Assets Turnover Ratio
The ratio of sales to net fixed assets.

The **fixed assets turnover ratio** measures how effectively the firm uses its plant and equipment. It is the ratio of sales to net fixed assets:

$$\text{Fixed assets turnover ratio} = \frac{\text{Sales}}{\text{Net fixed assets}}$$

$$= \frac{\$3{,}000}{\$1{,}000} = 3.0\times$$

$$\text{Industry average} = 2.8\times$$

---

[6] It would be somewhat better to use *average* receivables, either an average of the monthly figures or (Beginning receivables + Ending receivables)/2 = (\$315 + \$375)/2 = \$345 in the formula. Had average annual receivables been used, Allied's DSO on a 365-day basis would have been \$345/\$8.2192 = 41.975 days, or approximately 42 days. The 42-day figure is a more accurate one, but our interest is in comparisons, and because the industry average was based on year-end receivables, the 46-day number is better for our purposes. The DSO is discussed further in Part 6.

[7] For example, if further analysis along the lines suggested in Part 6 indicated that 85 percent of the customers pay in 30 days, then for the DSO to average 46 days, the remaining 15 percent must be paying on average in 136.67 days. Paying that late suggests financial difficulties. In Part 6 we also discuss refinements into this analysis, but a DSO of 46 days would alert a good analyst of the need to dig deeper.

Allied's ratio of 3.0 times is slightly above the 2.8 industry average, indicating that it is using its fixed assets at least as intensively as other firms in the industry. Therefore, Allied seems to have about the right amount of fixed assets relative to its sales.

Potential problems may arise when interpreting the fixed assets turnover ratio. Recall that fixed assets are shown on the balance sheet at their historical costs, less depreciation. Inflation has caused the value of many assets that were purchased in the past to be seriously understated. Therefore, if we compared an old firm that had acquired many of its fixed assets years ago at low prices with a new company with similar operations that had acquired its fixed assets only recently, we would probably find that the old firm had the higher fixed assets turnover ratio. However, this would be more reflective of when the assets were acquired than of inefficiency on the part of the new firm. The accounting profession is trying to develop procedures for making financial statements reflect current values rather than historical values, which would help us make better comparisons. However, at the moment the problem still exists, so financial analysts must recognize that a problem exists and deal with it judgmentally. In Allied's case, the issue is not serious because all firms in the industry have been expanding at about the same rate, hence the balance sheets of the comparison firms are reasonably comparable.[8]

4-3d Total Assets Turnover Ratio

The final asset management ratio, the **total assets turnover ratio,** measures the turnover of all the firm's assets, and it is calculated by dividing sales by total assets:

$$\text{Total assets turnover ratio} = \frac{\text{Sales}}{\text{Total assets}}$$

$$= \frac{\$3,000}{\$2,000} = 1.5\times$$

$$\text{Industry average} = 1.8\times$$

Total Assets Turnover Ratio
This ratio is calculated by dividing sales by total assets.

Allied's ratio is somewhat below the industry average, indicating that it is not generating enough sales given its total assets. Sales should be increased, some assets should be disposed of, or a combination of these steps should be taken.

Identify four ratios that are used to measure how effectively a firm manages its assets, and write out their equations.

If one firm is growing rapidly and another is not, how might this distort a comparison of their inventory turnover ratios?

If you wanted to evaluate a firm's DSO, with what would you compare it?

What potential problem might arise when comparing different firms' fixed assets turnover ratios?

A firm has annual sales of $100 million, $20 million of inventory, and $30 million of accounts receivable. What is its inventory turnover ratio? (5×) What is its DSO based on a 365-day year? (109.5 days)

---

[8] See FASB #89, *Financial Reporting and Changing Prices* (December 1986), for a discussion of the effects of inflation on financial statements. The report's age indicates how difficult the problem is.

4-4 DEBT MANAGEMENT RATIOS

Financial Leverage
The use of debt financing.

The extent to which a firm uses debt financing, or **financial leverage,** has three important implications: (1) By raising funds through debt, stockholders can control a firm with a limited amount of equity investment. (2) Creditors look to the equity, or owner-supplied funds, to provide a margin of safety, so the higher the proportion of the total capital provided by stockholders, the less the risk faced by creditors. (3) If the firm earns more on its assets than the interest rate it pays on debt, then using debt "leverages," or magnifies, the return on equity, ROE.

Table 4-1 illustrates both the potential benefits and risks resulting from the use of debt.[9] Here we analyze two companies that are identical except for how they are financed. Firm U (for "Unleveraged") has no debt and thus 100 percent common equity, whereas Firm L (for "Leveraged") is financed with half debt at a 10 percent interest rate and half equity. Both companies have $100 of assets. Their sales will range from $150 down to $75, depending on business conditions, with an expected level of $100. Some of their operating costs (rent, the president's salary, and so on) are fixed and will be there regardless of the level of sales, while other costs (some labor costs, materials, and so forth) will vary with sales.[10] When we deduct total operating costs from sales revenues, we are left with operating income, or earnings before interest and taxes (EBIT).

Notice in the table that everything is the same for the leveraged and unleveraged firms down through operating income—thus, they have the same EBIT under the three states of the economy. However, things then begin to differ. Firm U has no debt so it pays no interest, and its taxable income is the same as its operating income, and it then pays a 40 percent state and federal tax to get to its net income, which is $27 under good conditions and $0 under bad conditions. When net income is divided by common equity, we get the ROE, which ranges from 27 percent to 0 percent for Firm U.

Firm L has the same EBIT under each condition, but it uses $50 of debt with a 10 percent interest rate, so it has $5 of interest charges regardless of business conditions. This amount is deducted from EBIT to get to taxable income, taxes are then taken out, and the result is net income, which ranges from $24 to −$5, depending on conditions.[11] At first blush it looks like Firm U is better off under all conditions, but this is not correct—we need to consider how much the two firms' stockholders have invested. Firm L's stockholders have put up only $50, so when that investment is divided into net income, we see that their ROE under good conditions is a whopping 48 percent (versus 27 percent for U) and is 12 percent (versus 9 percent for U) under expected conditions. However, L's ROE falls to −10 percent under bad conditions, which means that it would go bankrupt if those conditions last for several years.

There are two reasons for the leveraging effect: (1) Because interest is deductible, the use of debt lowers the tax bill and leaves more of the firm's operating income available to its investors. (2) If operating income as a percentage of

---

[9] We discuss ROE in more depth later in the chapter, and we examine the effects of leverage in detail in the chapter on capital structure.

[10] The financial statements do not show the breakdown between fixed and variable operating costs, but companies can and do make this breakdown for internal purposes. Of course, the distinction is not always clear, because what's a fixed cost in the very short run can become a variable cost over a longer time horizon. It's interesting to note that companies are moving toward making more of their costs variable, using such techniques as increasing bonuses rather than base salaries, switching to profit-sharing plans rather than fixed-pension plans, and outsourcing various parts and materials.

[11] As we discussed in the last chapter, firms can carry losses back or forward for several years. Therefore, if Firm L had profits and thus paid taxes in recent prior years, it could carry its loss under bad conditions back and receive a credit (a check from the government). In Table 4-1 we assume that the firm cannot use the carry-back/carry-forward provision.

TABLE 4-1   *Effects of Financial Leverage on Stockholder Returns*

FIRM U [UNLEVERAGED (NO DEBT)]

Current assets	$ 50	Debt	$ 0
Fixed assets	50	Common equity	100
Total assets	$100	Total liabilities and equity	$100

	BUSINESS CONDITIONS		
	Good	**Expected**	**Bad**
Sales revenues	$150.0	$100.0	$75.0
Operating costs Fixed	45.0	45.0	45.0
Variable	60.0	40.0	30.0
Total operating costs	105.0	85.0	75.0
Operating income (EBIT)	$ 45.0	$ 15.0	$ 0.0
Interest (Rate = 10%)	0.0	0.0	0.0
Earnings before taxes (EBT)	$ 45.0	$ 15.0	$ 0.0
Taxes (Rate = 40%)	18.0	6.0	0.0
Net income (NI)	$ 27.0	$ 9.0	$ 0.0
ROE_U	27.0%	9.0%	0.0%

FIRM L [LEVERAGED (SOME DEBT)]

Current assets	$ 50	Debt	$ 50
Fixed assets	50	Common equity	50
Total assets	$100	Total liabilities and equity	$100

	BUSINESS CONDITIONS		
	Good	**Expected**	**Bad**
Sales revenues	$150.0	$100.0	$75.0
Operating costs Fixed	45.0	45.0	45.0
Variable	60.0	40.0	30.0
Total operating costs	105.0	85.0	75.0
Operating income (EBIT)	$ 45.0	$ 15.0	$ 0.0
Interest (Rate = 10%)	5.0	5.0	5.0
Earnings before taxes (EBT)	$ 40.0	$ 10.0	−$ 5.0
Taxes (Rate = 40%)	16.0	4.0	0.0
Net income (NI)	$ 24.0	$ 6.0	−$ 5.0
ROE_L	48.0%	12.0%	−10.0%

assets exceeds the interest rate on debt, as it generally is expected to do, then a company can use debt to acquire assets, pay the interest on the debt, and have something left over as a "bonus" for its stockholders. Under the expected conditions, our hypothetical firms expect to earn 15 percent on assets versus a 10 percent cost of debt, and this, combined with the tax benefit of debt, pushes Firm L's expected rate of return on equity up far above that of Firm U.

We see, then, that firms with relatively high debt ratios have higher expected returns when the economy is normal, but they are exposed to risk of loss when the economy enters a recession. Therefore, decisions about the use of debt require firms to balance higher expected returns against increased risk. Determining the optimal amount of debt is a complicated process, and we defer a discussion of that subject to a later chapter on capital structure. For now, we simply look at two procedures analysts use to examine the firm's debt: (1) They check the balance sheet to determine the proportion of total funds represented by debt, and (2) they review the income statement to see the extent to which fixed charges are covered by operating profits.

4-4a Total Debt to Total Assets

Debt Ratio
The ratio of total debt to total assets.

The ratio of total debt to total assets, generally called the **debt ratio,** measures the percentage of funds provided by creditors:

$$\text{Debt ratio} = \frac{\text{Total debt}}{\text{Total assets}}$$

$$= \frac{\$310 + \$750}{\$2,000} = \frac{\$1,060}{\$2,000} = 53.0\%$$

Industry average = 40.0%

Total debt includes all current liabilities and long-term debt. Creditors prefer low debt ratios because the lower the ratio, the greater the cushion against creditors' losses in the event of liquidation. Stockholders, on the other hand, may want more leverage because it can magnify expected earnings.

Allied's debt ratio is 53.0 percent, which means that its creditors have supplied more than half the total financing. As we will discuss in the capital structure chapter, a number of factors affect a company's optimal debt ratio. Nevertheless, the fact that Allied's debt ratio exceeds the industry average raises a red flag, and this will make it relatively costly for Allied to borrow additional funds without first raising more equity. Creditors will be reluctant to lend the firm more money, and management would probably be subjecting the firm to the risk of bankruptcy if it sought to borrow a substantial amount of additional funds.[12]

4-4b Times-Interest-Earned Ratio

Times-Interest-Earned (TIE) Ratio
The ratio of earnings before interest and taxes (EBIT) to interest charges; a measure of the firm's ability to meet its annual interest payments.

The **times-interest-earned (TIE)** ratio is determined by dividing earnings before interest and taxes (EBIT in Table 3-2) by the interest charges:

$$\text{Times-interest-earned (TIE) ratio} = \frac{\text{EBIT}}{\text{Interest charges}}$$

$$= \frac{\$283.8}{\$88} = 3.2\times$$

Industry average = 6.0×

The TIE ratio measures the extent to which operating income can decline before the firm is unable to meet its annual interest costs. Failure to pay interest will bring legal action by the firm's creditors and probably result in bankruptcy. Note that earnings before interest and taxes, rather than net income, is used in the numerator. Because interest is paid with pre-tax dollars, the firm's ability to pay current interest is not affected by taxes.

---

[12] The ratio of debt to equity is also used in financial analysis. The debt-to-assets (D/A) and debt-to-equity (D/E) ratios are simply transformations of each other:

$$\text{D/E} = \frac{\text{D/A}}{1 - \text{D/A}} \quad \text{and} \quad \text{D/A} = \frac{\text{D/E}}{1 + \text{D/E}}$$

Allied's interest is covered 3.2 times. The industry average is 6 times, so Allied is covering its interest charges by a relatively low margin of safety. Thus, the TIE ratio reinforces the primary conclusion from our analysis of the debt ratio, namely, that Allied would face difficulties if it attempted to borrow additional funds.

4-4c EBITDA Coverage Ratio

The TIE ratio is useful for assessing the ability to meet interest charges on debt, but it has two shortcomings: (1) Interest is not the only fixed financial charge—companies must also retire debt on a fixed schedule, and many firms also lease assets and thus must make lease payments. If they fail to repay debt or meet lease payments, they can be forced into bankruptcy. (2) EBIT does not represent all the cash flow available to service debt, especially if a firm has high depreciation and/or amortization charges. To account for these deficiencies, bankers and others also use the **EBITDA coverage ratio,** which shows all of the cash flow available for payments in the numerator and all of the required financial payments in the denominator. This ratio is defined as follows:[13]

EBITDA Coverage Ratio
A ratio whose numerator includes all cash flows available to meet fixed financial charges and whose denominator includes all fixed financial charges.

$$\text{EBITDA coverage ratio} = \frac{\text{EBITDA} + \text{Lease payments}}{\text{Interest} + \text{Principal payments} + \text{Lease payments}}$$

$$= \frac{\$383.8 + \$28}{\$88 + \$20 + \$28} = \frac{\$411.8}{\$136} = 3.0\times$$

$$\text{Industry average} = 4.3\times$$

Regarding the numerator, Allied had EBITDA of $383.8 million, consisting of $283.8 million of operating income (EBIT) and $100 million of depreciation. However, $28 million of lease payments were deducted when we calculated EBITDA, yet that $28 million was available to meet financial charges. Therefore, we must add it back to EBITDA, giving a total of $411.8 million that is available for fixed financial charges.[14] Fixed financial charges consisted of $88 million of interest, $20 million of sinking fund payments, and $28 million of lease payments, for a total of $136 million.[15] Therefore, Allied covered its fixed financial charges by 3.0 times. However, if operating income declines, the coverage will fall, and operating income certainly can decline. As Allied's ratio is well below the industry average, we again see that the company has a relatively high level of debt.

---

[13] Different analysts define the EBITDA coverage ratio in different ways. For example, some would omit the lease payment information, and others would "gross up" principal payments by dividing them by (1 − T) because these payments are not tax deductions, hence must be made with after-tax cash flows. We included lease payments because, for many firms, they are quite important, and failing to make them can lead to bankruptcy just as surely as can failure to make payments on "regular" debt. We did not gross up principal payments because, if a company is in financial difficulty, its tax rate will probably be zero, hence the gross up is not necessary whenever the ratio is really important.

[14] Lease payments are included in the numerator because, unlike interest, they were deducted when EBITDA was calculated. We want to find all the funds that were available to service fixed charges, so lease payments must be added to the EBIT and DA to find the funds that could be used to service debt and meet lease payments.

[15] A sinking fund is a required annual payment designed to reduce the balance of a bond or preferred stock issue. A sinking fund payment is like the principal repayment portion of the payment on an amortized loan, but sinking funds are used for publicly traded bond issues, whereas amortization payments are used for bank loans and other private loans.

The EBITDA coverage ratio is most useful for relatively short-term lenders such as banks, which rarely make loans (except real estate–backed loans) for longer than about five years. Over a relatively short period, depreciation-generated funds can be used to service debt. Over a longer time, those funds must be reinvested to maintain the plant and equipment or else the company cannot remain in business. Therefore, banks and other relatively short-term lenders focus on the EBITDA coverage ratio, whereas long-term bondholders focus on the TIE ratio.

What are three important implications of financial leverage?

How does the use of financial leverage affect stockholders' control position?

How does the U.S. tax structure influence a firm's willingness to finance with debt?

How does the decision to use debt involve a risk-versus-return trade-off?

Explain the following statement: "Analysts look at both balance sheet and income statement ratios when appraising a firm's financial condition."

Name three ratios that are used to measure financial leverage, and write out their equations.

A company has EBITDA of $500 million, interest payments of $50 million, lease payments of $40 million, and required principal payments (due this year) of $30 million. What is its EBITDA coverage ratio? (4.5×)

4-5 PROFITABILITY RATIOS

Accounting statements reflect things that happened in the past, but they also give us clues about what's really important—what's likely to happen in the future. The liquidity, asset management, and debt ratios covered thus far tell us something about the firm's policies and operations. Now we turn to the **profitability ratios,** which reflect the net result of all of the financing policies and operating decisions.

Profitability Ratios
A group of ratios that show the combined effects of liquidity, asset management, and debt on operating results.

Profit Margin on Sales
This ratio measures net income per dollar of sales; it is calculated by dividing net income by sales.

4-5a Profit Margin on Sales

The **profit margin on sales,** calculated by dividing net income by sales, gives the profit per dollar of sales:

$$\text{Profit margin on sales} = \frac{\text{Net income}}{\text{Sales}}$$

$$= \frac{\$117.5}{\$3,000} = 3.9\%$$

$$\text{Industry average} = 5.0\%$$

Allied's profit margin is below the industry average of 5 percent. This sub-par result occurs because costs are too high. High costs, in turn, generally occur because of inefficient operations. However, Allied's low profit margin is also a

GLOBAL PERSPECTIVES

Global Accounting Standards: Can One Size Fit All?

These days you must be a good financial detective to analyze financial statements, especially if the company operates overseas. Despite attempts to standardize accounting practices, there are still many differences in financial reporting in different countries that create headaches for investors making cross-border company comparisons. However, as businesses become more global and more foreign companies list on U.S. stock exchanges, accountants and regulators are realizing the need for a global convergence of accounting standards. As a result, the writing is on the wall regarding accounting standards, and differences are disappearing.

The effort to internationalize accounting standards began in 1973 with the formation of the International Accounting Standards Committee. However, in 1998 it became apparent that a full-time rule-making body with global representation was necessary, so the International Accounting Standards Board (IASB), with members representing nine major countries, was established. The IASB was charged with the responsibility for creating a set of International Financial Reporting Standards (IFRS) for European Union (EU) companies by January 1, 2005, when more than 7,000 publicly listed European companies were supposed to conform to these standards. In contrast, only 350 European companies were using international standards as of 2003. A number of other countries, including Australia and other Pacific Rim countries, South Africa, Canada, Russia, Japan, and China are interested in adopting IFRS.

A survey of senior executives from 85 financial institutions worldwide found that 92 percent of those responding favored a single set of international standards but only 55 percent thought universal adoption was achievable. Obviously, the globalization of accounting standards is a huge endeavor—one that will involve compromises between the IASB and FASB. Part of the problem is that U.S. GAAP takes a rules-based approach, while the IASB insists on using a principles-based approach. With a rules-based system, companies can tell whether or not they are in compliance, but they can also develop ways to get around a rule and thus subvert its intent. With a principles-based system, there is greater uncertainty about whether certain border-line procedures will be allowed, but such a system makes it easier to prosecute on the basis of intent.

A global accounting structure would enable investors and practitioners around the world to read and understand financial reports produced anywhere in the world. In addition, it would enhance all companies' access to all capital markets, which would improve investor diversification, reduce risk, and lower the cost of capital. However, it remains to be seen whether the IASB's lofty goal can be achieved.

Sources: "All Accountants Soon May Speak the Same Language," *The Wall Street Journal*, August 29, 1995, p. A15; Jim Cole, "Global Standards Loom for Accounting," *East Bay Business Times*, November 12, 2001; "Accountants Struggle to Reconcile Rules," *BestWire*, April 28, 2003; "For and Against; Standards Need Time to Work," *Accountancy Age*, June 5, 2003, p. 16; Larry Schlesinger, "Overview; Bringing about a New Dawn," *Accountancy Age*, September 4, 2003, p. 18; Cassell Bryan-Low, "Deals & Deal Makers: Accounting Changes Are in Store," *The Wall Street Journal*, September 10, 2003, p. C4; and Fay Hansen, "Get Ready for New Global Accounting Standards," January 2004, **www.BusinessFinanceMag.com**.

result of its heavy use of debt. Recall that net income is income *after interest*. Therefore, if two firms have identical operations in the sense that their sales, operating costs, and EBIT are the same, but if one firm uses more debt than the other, it will have higher interest charges. Those interest charges will pull net income down, and as sales are constant, the result will be a relatively low profit margin. In this situation, the low profit margin would indicate a difference in financing strategies, not an operating problem. Thus, the firm with the low profit margin might end up with a higher rate of return on its stockholders' investment due to its use of financial leverage.

Note too that while a high return on sales is good, other things held constant, other things may not be held constant—we must also be concerned with turnover. If a firm sets a very high price on its products, it may get a high return on each sale but not make many sales. That might result in a high profit margin but still not be optimal because total sales are low.

We will see exactly how profit margins, the use of debt, and turnover interact to affect overall stockholder returns shortly, when we examine the Du Pont equation.

4-5b Return on Total Assets

Return on Total Assets (ROA)
The ratio of the net income to total assets.

The ratio of net income to total assets measures the **return on total assets (ROA)** after interest and taxes:

$$\text{Return on total assets} = \text{ROA} = \frac{\text{Net income}}{\text{Total assets}}$$

$$= \frac{\$117.5}{\$2,000} = 5.9\%$$

$$\text{Industry average} = 9.0\%$$

Allied's 5.9 percent return is well below the 9 percent industry average. This is not good, but a low return on assets is not necessarily bad—it could result from a conscious decision to use a lot of debt, in which case high interest expenses will cause net income to be relatively low. Debt is part of the reason for Allied's low ROA. Never forget—you must look at a number of ratios, see what each suggests, and then look at the overall situation when you judge the performance of a company and try to figure out what it should do to improve.

4-5c Basic Earning Power (BEP) Ratio

Basic Earning Power (BEP) Ratio
This ratio indicates the ability of the firm's assets to generate operating income; calculated by dividing EBIT by total assets.

The **basic earning power (BEP) ratio** is calculated by dividing earnings before interest and taxes (EBIT) by total assets:

$$\text{Basic earning power (BEP) ratio} = \frac{\text{EBIT}}{\text{Total assets}}$$

$$= \frac{\$283.8}{\$2,000} = 14.2\%$$

$$\text{Industry average} = 18.0\%$$

This ratio shows the raw earning power of the firm's assets, before the influence of taxes and leverage, and it is useful when comparing firms with different degrees of financial leverage and tax situations. Because of its low turnover ratios and poor profit margin on sales, Allied is not earning as high a return on assets as the average food-processing company.[16]

---

[16] A related ratio is the return on investors' capital, defined as follows:

$$\text{Return on investors' capital} = \frac{\text{Net income} + \text{Interest}}{\text{Debt} + \text{Equity}}$$

The numerator shows the dollar returns to investors, the denominator shows the money investors have put up, and the ratio itself shows the rate of return on all investors' capital. This ratio is especially important in regulated industries such as electric utilities, where regulators are concerned about companies' using their monopoly power to earn excessive returns on investors' capital. In fact, regulators try to set electric rates at levels that will force the return on investors' capital to equal a company's cost of capital as defined in Chapter 10.

4-5d Return on Common Equity

The "bottom-line" accounting ratio is the **return on common equity (ROE)**, found as follows:

$$\text{Return on common equity} = \text{ROE} = \frac{\text{Net income}}{\text{Common equity}}$$

$$= \frac{\$117.5}{\$940} = 12.5\%$$

Industry average = 15.0%

Return on Common Equity (ROE)
The ratio of net income to common equity; measures the rate of return on common stockholders' investment.

Stockholders expect to earn a return on their money, and this ratio tells how well they are doing in an accounting sense. Allied's 12.5 percent return is below the 15 percent industry average, but not as far below as the return on total assets. This somewhat better ROE is due to the company's greater use of debt, a point that we discussed earlier in the chapter.

Identify four profitability ratios, and write out their equations.

Why is the basic earning power ratio useful?

Why does the use of debt lower the ROA?

What does ROE measure? Since interest expense lowers profits and thus the ROA, does using debt necessarily lower the ROE? Explain.

A company has $20 billion of sales and $1 billion of net income. Its total assets are $10 billion, financed half by debt and half by common equity. What is its profit margin? (5%) What is its ROA? (10%) What is its ROE? (20%) Would ROA increase if the firm used less leverage? (yes) Would ROE increase? (no)

4-6 MARKET VALUE RATIOS

The ROE reflects the effects of all the other ratios and is the best single measure of performance in an accounting sense. Investors obviously like to see a high ROE, and high ROEs are generally positively correlated with high stock prices. However, other things come into play. As we saw earlier, financial leverage generally increases the ROE but leverage also increases the firm's risk, which investors dislike. So, if a high ROE is achieved by the use of a very large amount of debt, the stock price might well be lower than it would be with less debt and a lower ROE. Similarly, investors are interested in growth, and if the current ROE was achieved by holding back on research and development costs, which will constrain future growth, this will not be regarded favorably.

This takes us to a final group of ratios, the **market value ratios,** which relate the firm's stock price to its earnings, cash flow, and book value per share. These ratios give management an indication of what investors think of the company's risk and future prospects. If the liquidity, asset management, debt management, and profitability ratios all look good, and if these conditions have been stable over time, then the market value ratios will be high, the stock price will probably be as high as can be expected, and management has been doing a good job and should be rewarded. Otherwise, changes might be needed.

Market Value Ratios
A set of ratios that relate the firm's stock price to its earnings, cash flow, and book value per share.

4-6a Price/Earnings Ratio

The **price/earnings (P/E) ratio** shows how much investors are willing to pay per dollar of reported profits. Allied's stock sells for $23, so with an EPS of $2.35 its P/E ratio is 9.8:

$$\text{Price/earnings (P/E) ratio} = \frac{\text{Price per share}}{\text{Earnings per share}}$$

$$= \frac{\$23.00}{\$2.35} = 9.8\times$$

Industry average $= 11.3\times$

As we will see in Chapter 9, P/E ratios are higher for firms with strong growth prospects and relatively little risk. Allied's P/E ratio is below the average for other food processors, so this suggests that the company is regarded as being somewhat riskier than most, as having poor growth prospects, or both.

4-6b Price/Cash Flow Ratio

In some industries, stock price is tied more closely to cash flow rather than net income. Consequently, investors often look at the **price/cash flow ratio**:

$$\text{Price/cash flow} = \frac{\text{Price per share}}{\text{Cash flow per share}}$$

$$= \frac{\$23.00}{\$4.35} = 5.3\times$$

Industry average $= 5.4\times$

The calculation for cash flow per share was discussed in Chapter 3, but to refresh your memory, it is equal to net income plus depreciation and amortization divided by common shares outstanding. Allied's price/cash flow ratio is slightly below the industry average, once again suggesting that its growth prospects are below average, its risk is above average, or both.

Note that for some purposes analysts look at multiples beyond just the price/earnings and the price/cash flow ratios. For example, depending on the industry, analysts may look at price/sales, price/customers, or price/(EBITDA per share). Ultimately, though, value depends on earnings and cash flows, so if these "exotic" ratios do not forecast future levels of EPS and cash flow, they may turn out to be misleading.[17]

4-6c Market/Book Ratio

The ratio of a stock's market price to its book value gives another indication of how investors regard the company. Companies that are well regarded by investors—which means companies with safe and growing earnings and cash

---

[17] During the "Internet bubble" of the late 1990s and early 2000s, some Internet companies were valued by multiplying the number of "hits" to a Web site times some sort of multiple. If those hits translated to sales and profits, this procedure would have made sense, but generally they did not, and the result was a vast overvaluation of stocks and a subsequent huge crash. Keep your eye on earnings and cash flows.

flows—sell at higher multiples of book value than those with low returns. First, we find Allied's book value per share:

$$\text{Book value per share} = \frac{\text{Common equity}}{\text{Shares outstanding}}$$

$$= \frac{\$940}{50} = \$18.80$$

Then we divide the market price per share by the book value per share to get the **market/book (M/B) ratio,** which for Allied is 1.2 times:

$$\text{Market/book ratio} = \text{M/B} = \frac{\text{Market price per share}}{\text{Book value per share}}$$

$$= \frac{\$23.00}{\$18.80} = 1.2\times$$

$$\text{Industry average} = 1.7\times$$

Market/Book (M/B) Ratio
The ratio of a stock's market price to its book value.

Investors are willing to pay less for a dollar of Allied's book value than for one of an average food-processing company. This is consistent with our other findings.

In today's market (September 2005), the average Standard & Poor's (S&P) 500 company had a market/book ratio of about 2.87.[18] Because M/B ratios typically exceed 1.0, this means that investors are willing to pay more for stocks than their accounting book values. This situation occurs primarily because asset values, as reported by accountants on corporate balance sheets, do not reflect either inflation or "goodwill." Thus, assets purchased years ago at preinflation prices are carried at their original costs, even though inflation might have caused their actual values to rise substantially, and successful going concerns have a value greater than their historical costs.

If a company earns a low rate of return on its assets, then its M/B ratio will be relatively low versus an average company. Some airlines, which have not fared well in recent years, sell at M/B ratios well below 1.0, while very successful firms such as Microsoft achieve high rates of return on their assets, resulting in market values far in excess of their book values. In September 2005 Microsoft's book value per share was about $4.49 versus a market price of $26.28, so its market/book ratio was $26.28/$4.49 = 5.9 times.

Describe three ratios that relate a firm's stock price to its earnings, cash flow, and book value per share, and write out their equations.

How do these market value ratios reflect investor's opinions about a stock's risk and expected future growth?

What does the price/earnings (P/E) ratio show? If one firm's P/E ratio is lower than that of another, what are some factors that might explain the difference?

How is book value per share calculated? Explain how inflation and "goodwill" built up over time could cause book values to deviate from market values.

---

[18] This was obtained from the key ratios section shown in **http://moneycentral.msn.com**.

4-7 TREND ANALYSIS

Trend Analysis
An analysis of a firm's financial ratios over time; used to estimate the likelihood of improvement or deterioration in its financial condition.

It is important to analyze trends in ratios as well as their absolute levels, for trends give clues as to whether a firm's financial condition is likely to improve or to deteriorate. To do a **trend analysis,** simply plot a ratio over time, as shown in Figure 4-1. This graph shows that Allied's rate of return on common equity has been declining since 2002, even though the industry average has been relatively stable. All the other ratios could be analyzed similarly.

How is a trend analysis done?

What important information does a trend analysis provide?

4-8 TYING THE RATIOS TOGETHER: THE DU PONT EQUATIONS

Basic Du Pont Equation
A formula that shows that the rate of return on assets can be found as the product of the profit margin times the total assets turnover.

Table 4-2 summarizes Allied's ratios. The profit margin times the total assets turnover is called the **basic Du Pont equation,** and it gives the rate of return on assets (ROA):

$$\text{ROA} = \text{Profit margin} \times \text{Total assets turnover}$$
$$= \frac{\text{Net income}}{\text{Sales}} \times \frac{\text{Sales}}{\text{Total assets}} \quad (4\text{-}1)$$
$$= 3.9\% \times 1.5 = 5.9\%$$

Allied made 3.9 percent, or 3.9 cents, on each dollar of sales, and assets were "turned over" 1.5 times during the year. Therefore, the company earned a return of 5.9 percent on its assets.

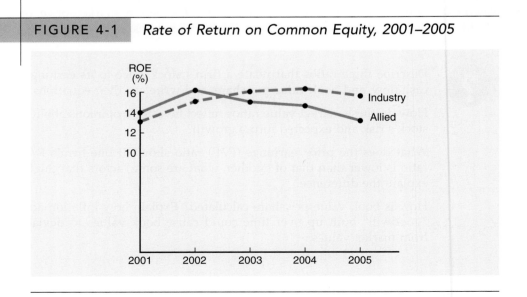

FIGURE 4-1 *Rate of Return on Common Equity, 2001–2005*

| TABLE 4-2 | Allied Food Products: Summary of Financial Ratios (Millions of Dollars) | | | | |

Ratio	Formula	Calculation	Ratio	Industry Average	Comment
Liquidity					
Current	$\dfrac{\text{Current assets}}{\text{Current liabilities}}$	$\dfrac{\$1,000}{\$310}$	$=3.2\times$	$4.2\times$	Poor
Quick	$\dfrac{\text{Current assets} - \text{Inventories}}{\text{Current liabilities}}$	$\dfrac{\$385}{\$310}$	$=1.2\times$	$2.2\times$	Poor
Asset Management					
Inventory turnover	$\dfrac{\text{Sales}}{\text{Inventories}}$	$\dfrac{\$3,000}{\$615}$	$=4.9\times$	$10.9\times$	Poor
Days sales outstanding (DSO)	$\dfrac{\text{Receivables}}{\text{Annual sales}/365}$	$\dfrac{\$375}{\$8.2192}$	$=46$ days	36 days	Poor
Fixed assets turnover	$\dfrac{\text{Sales}}{\text{Net fixed assets}}$	$\dfrac{\$3,000}{\$1,000}$	$=3.0\times$	$2.8\times$	OK
Total assets turnover	$\dfrac{\text{Sales}}{\text{Total assets}}$	$\dfrac{\$3,000}{\$2,000}$	$=1.5\times$	$1.8\times$	Somewhat low
Debt Management					
Total debt to total assets	$\dfrac{\text{Total debt}}{\text{Total assets}}$	$\dfrac{\$1,060}{\$2,000}$	$=53.0\%$	40.0%	High (risky)
Times-interest-earned (TIE)	$\dfrac{\text{Earnings before interest and taxes (EBIT)}}{\text{Interest charges}}$	$\dfrac{\$283.8}{\$88}$	$=3.2\times$	$6.0\times$	Low (risky)
EBITDA coverage	$\dfrac{\text{EBITDA} + \text{Lease payments}}{\text{Interest} + \text{Principal payments} + \text{Lease payments}}$	$\dfrac{\$411.8}{\$136}$	$=3.0\times$	$4.3\times$	Low (risky)
Profitability					
Profit margin on sales	$\dfrac{\text{Net income}}{\text{Sales}}$	$\dfrac{\$117.5}{\$3,000}$	$=3.9\%$	5.0%	Poor
Return on total assets (ROA)	$\dfrac{\text{Net income}}{\text{Total assets}}$	$\dfrac{\$117.5}{\$2,000}$	$=5.9\%$	9.0%	Poor
Basic earning power (BEP)	$\dfrac{\text{Earnings before interest and taxes (EBIT)}}{\text{Total assets}}$	$\dfrac{\$283.8}{\$2,000}$	$=14.2\%$	18.0%	Poor
Return on common equity (ROE)	$\dfrac{\text{Net income}}{\text{Common equity}}$	$\dfrac{\$117.5}{\$940}$	$=12.5\%$	15.0%	Poor
Market Value					
Price/earnings (P/E)	$\dfrac{\text{Price per share}}{\text{Earnings per share}}$	$\dfrac{\$23.00}{\$2.35}$	$=9.8\times$	$11.3\times$	Low
Price/cash flow	$\dfrac{\text{Price per share}}{\text{Cash flow per share}}$	$\dfrac{\$23.00}{\$4.35}$	$=5.3\times$	$5.4\times$	Low
Market/book (M/B)	$\dfrac{\text{Market price per share}}{\text{Book value per share}}$	$\dfrac{\$23.00}{\$18.80}$	$=1.2\times$	$1.7\times$	Low

If the company were financed only with common equity, the rate of return on assets (ROA) and the return on equity (ROE) would be the same because total assets would equal common equity:

$$ROA = \frac{Net\ income}{Total\ assets} = \frac{Net\ income}{Common\ equity} = ROE$$

This equality holds if and only if the company uses no debt. Allied does use debt, so its common equity is less than its total assets. Therefore, the return to the common stockholders (ROE) must be greater than the ROA of 5.9 percent. Specifically, to go from the rate of return on assets (ROA) to the return on equity (ROE) we multiply by the *equity multiplier*, which is the ratio of total assets to common equity:

$$Equity\ multiplier = \frac{Total\ assets}{Common\ equity}$$

Firms that use large amounts of debt (more leverage) will necessarily have a high equity multiplier—the greater the debt, the less the equity, hence the higher the equity multiplier. For example, if a firm has $1,000 of assets and finances with $800, or 80 percent debt, then its equity will be $200 and its equity multiplier will be $1,000/$200 = 5. Had it used only $200 of debt, its equity would have been $800, and its equity multiplier would have been only $1,000/$800 = 1.25.[19]

Allied's return on equity (ROE) depends on its ROA and its use of leverage:[20]

$$ROE = ROA \times Equity\ multiplier \qquad (4\text{-}2)$$

$$= \frac{Net\ income}{Total\ assets} \times \frac{Total\ assets}{Common\ equity}$$

$$= 5.9\% \times \$2,000/\$940$$

$$= 5.9\% \times 2.13$$

$$= 12.5\%$$

When they are combined, Equations 4-1 and 4-2 form the *extended Du Pont equation*, which shows how the profit margin, the total assets turnover ratio, and the equity multiplier combine to determine the ROE:

$$ROE = (Profit\ margin)(Total\ assets\ turnover)(Equity\ multiplier)$$

$$= \frac{Net\ income}{Sales} \times \frac{Sales}{Total\ assets} \times \frac{Total\ assets}{Common\ equity} \qquad (4\text{-}3)$$

---

[19] Expressed algebraically,

$$Debt\ ratio = \frac{D}{A} = \frac{A - E}{A} = \frac{A}{A} - \frac{E}{A} = 1 - \frac{1}{Equity\ multiplier}$$

Here D is debt, E is equity, A is total assets, and A/E is the equity multiplier. This equation ignores preferred stock.

[20] Note that we could also find the ROE by "grossing up" the ROA, that is, by dividing the ROA by the common equity fraction: ROE = ROA/Equity fraction = 5.9%/0.47 = 12.5%. The two procedures are algebraically equivalent.

For Allied, we have

$$ROE = (3.9\%)(1.5)(2.13)$$

$$= 12.5\%$$

The 12.5 percent rate of return could, of course, be calculated directly: both Sales and Total assets cancel, leaving Net income/Common equity = $117.5/$940 = 12.5%. However, the extended Du Pont equation shows how the profit margin, total assets turnover, and use of debt combine to determine the return on equity.

Allied's management can use the extended Du Pont equation to analyze ways of improving performance. Focusing on the profit margin, marketing people can study the effects of raising sales prices (or lowering them to increase volume), of moving into new products or markets with higher margins, and so on. Cost accountants can study various expense items and, working with engineers, purchasing agents, and other operating personnel, seek ways to hold down costs. Regarding the "turnover" term, the financial staff, working with both production and marketing people, can investigate ways to reduce the investment in various types of assets. Finance people can also analyze the effects of alternative financing strategies, seeking ways to hold down interest expense and the risk associated with debt while still using leverage to increase the return on equity.

As a result of such an analysis, Ellen Jackson, Allied's president, recently announced a series of moves that are expected to cut operating costs by more than 20 percent per year. Jackson and Allied's other executives have a strong incentive for improving its financial performance because their compensation is based to a large extent on how well the company does. Its executives receive a salary that is sufficient to cover their living costs, but their compensation package also includes stock options that will be awarded if and only if Allied meets or exceeds target levels for earnings and the stock price. These target levels are based on its performance relative to other food companies. So, if it does well, then Jackson and the other executives—and the stockholders—will also do well. But if things deteriorate, Jackson could be looking for a new job.

Write out the equation for the basic Du Pont equation.

What is the equity multiplier?

How can management use the extended Du Pont equation to analyze ways of improving the firm's performance?

4-9 COMPARATIVE RATIOS AND "BENCHMARKING"

Ratio analysis almost always involves comparisons—a company's ratios are compared with industry average figures. However, like most firms, Allied's managers go one step further—they also compare their ratios with those of leading food companies. This technique is called **benchmarking,** and the companies used for the comparison are called *benchmark companies*. Allied's management benchmarks against Campbell Soup, a leading manufacturer of canned soups; Dean Foods, a processor of canned and frozen vegetables; Del Monte Foods, a processor of fruits and vegetables; H. J. Heinz, which makes ketchup and other products; Flowers Industries, a producer of bakery and snack-food goods; Sara Lee, a manufacturer of baked goods; and Hershey Foods Corp., a producer of

A good site for comparative ratios is **http:// moneycentral.msn.com.** Here you can find stock quotes, detailed company reports, company ratios, and comparative ratios.

Benchmarking
The process of comparing a particular company with a group of "benchmark" companies.

chocolates, nonchocolate confectionary products, and pasta. Ratios are calculated for each company, then listed in descending order as shown below for the profit margin (the firms' latest 12 months' results reported by *Yahoo!Finance* as of September 15, 2005):

Company	Profit Margin
Hershey Foods	11.9%
Campbell Soup	9.4
H. J. Heinz	7.9
Allied Food Products	**3.9**
Del Monte Foods	3.9
Sara Lee	3.7
Flowers Industries	3.6
Dean Foods	2.6

TABLE 4-3   *Key Financial Ratios for Selected Industries[a]*

Industry Name	Current Ratio	Inventory Turnover[b]	Total Assets Turnover	Debt Ratio[c]	Days Sales Outstanding[d]	Profit Margin	Return on Assets	Return on Equity
Aerospace/defense	1.1	9.3	0.9	70.8%	49.3	2.8%	2.6%	8.9%
Apparel stores	2.5	4.4	1.6	44.2	12.7	5.0	8.2	14.7
Auto manufacturing—major	1.8	8.2	0.6	85.3	202.8	2.6	1.6	10.9
Beverage (soft drink)	1.0	7.8	0.8	65.0	39.7	10.6	8.5	24.3
Education and training services	1.4	59.4	1.1	40.8	38.4	9.8	10.0	16.9
Electronics—diversified	2.6	4.7	0.7	39.4	70.2	5.7	4.0	6.6
Food processing	2.0	4.6	1.1	52.6	36.1	4.4	4.6	9.7
Food wholesalers	1.2	16.1	3.6	64.1	18.1	2.0	7.1	19.8
Grocery stores	1.1	11.0	2.4	73.9	9.1	0.5	1.2	4.6
Health services—specialized	1.5	27.5	1.6	57.2	47.4	4.3	6.5	15.2
Lodging	1.0	49.4	0.7	56.8	35.1	6.0	4.1	9.5
Metals and minerals—industrial	1.6	4.8	0.6	58.3	42.9	8.4	5.0	12.0
Newspapers	1.1	10.9	0.5	53.4	57.0	9.9	5.4	11.6
Paper and paper products	1.3	6.1	0.7	69.0	71.6	2.7	1.8	5.8
Railroad	0.8	13.2	0.4	64.8	29.2	8.7	3.1	8.8
Restaurant	0.9	30.3	1.1	55.1	11.2	5.7	6.2	13.8
Retail—department stores	1.7	3.6	1.3	65.5	32.6	3.8	4.8	13.9
Scientific and technical instruments	2.6	3.2	0.8	41.1	76.0	5.4	4.3	7.3
Sporting goods	2.0	3.6	1.1	51.9	53.7	3.4	3.8	7.9
Steel and iron	1.7	5.2	1.0	61.9	46.2	3.9	3.7	9.7
Telecommunications equipment	2.2	7.7	0.7	50.0	86.9	0.2	0.2	0.4
Textile manufacturing	2.1	3.9	1.1	51.6	49.3	2.8	3.1	6.4
Tobacco (cigarettes)	1.1	3.4	0.8	77.6	32.3	6.2	5.0	22.3

Notes:

[a] The ratios presented are averages for each industry. Ratios for the individual companies are also available.

[b] The inventory turnover ratio in this table is calculated as the company's latest 12 months of cost of sales divided by the average of its inventory for the last quarter and the comparable year earlier quarter.

[c] The debt ratio in this table is calculated as 1 − (ROA/ROE).

[d] The days sales outstanding ratio in this table was calculated as 365/Receivable turnover. The receivable turnover is calculated as the company's latest 12 months of sales divided by the average of its receivables for the last quarter and the comparable year earlier quarter.

Source: Data obtained from the Key Ratios section, **http://moneycentral.msn.com**, February 25, 2005.

Looking for Warning Signs within the Financial Statements

Enron's decline spurred a renewed interest in financial accounting, and analysts now scour companies' financial statements to see if trouble is lurking. This renewed interest has led to a list of "red flags" to consider when reviewing a company's financial statements. For example, after conferring with New York University Accounting Professor Baruch Lev, *Fortune* magazine's Shawn Tully identified the following warning signs:

- Year after year, a company reports restructuring charges and/or write-downs. This practice raises concerns because companies can use write-downs to mask operating expenses and thus results in overstated earnings.
- A company's earnings have been propped up through a series of acquisitions. Acquisitions can increase earnings if the acquiring company has a higher P/E than the acquired firm, but such "growth" cannot be sustained over the long run.
- A company depreciates its assets more slowly than the industry average. Lower depreciation boosts current earnings, but again, this cannot be sustained because eventually depreciation must be recognized.
- A company routinely has high earnings but low cash flow. As Tully points out, this warning sign would have exposed Enron's problems. In the

second quarter of 2001 (a few months before its problems began to unfold), Enron reported earnings of $423 million versus a cash flow of minus $527 million.

Along similar lines, after consulting with various professionals, Ellen Simon of the *Newark Star Ledger* came up with her list of "red flags":

- You wouldn't buy the stock at today's price.
- You don't really understand the company's financial statements.
- The company is in a business that lends itself to "creative accounting."
- The company keeps taking nonrecurring charges.
- Accounts receivable and inventory are increasing faster than sales revenue.
- The company's insiders are selling their stock.
- The company is making aggressive acquisitions, especially in unrelated fields.

There is some overlap between these two lists. Also, none of these items automatically means there is something wrong with the company—instead, the items should be viewed as warning signs that cause you to take a closer look at the company's performance before making an investment.

The benchmarking setup makes it easy for Allied's management to see exactly where it stands relative to the competition. As the data show, Allied is in the middle of its benchmark group relative to its profit margin, so it has lots of room for improvement. Other ratios are analyzed similarly.

Comparative ratios are available from a number of sources, including the MSN Money Web site, **http://moneycentral.msn.com.** Table 4-3 presents a list of key ratios for a variety of industries covered by this site. Useful ratios are also compiled by *Value Line Investment Survey*, Dun and Bradstreet (D&B), and Robert Morris Associates, which is the national association of bank loan officers. Also, financial statement data for thousands of publicly owned corporations are available on other Internet sites, and as brokerage houses, banks, and other financial institutions have access to these data, security analysts can and do generate comparative ratios tailored to their specific needs.

Each of the data-supplying organizations uses a somewhat different set of ratios designed for its own purposes. For example, D&B deals mainly with small firms, many of which are proprietorships, and it sells its services primarily to banks and other lenders. Therefore, D&B is concerned largely with the creditor's viewpoint, and its ratios emphasize current assets and liabilities, not market value ratios. So, when you select a comparative data source, you should be sure that your emphasis is similar to that of the agency whose ratios you plan to use. Additionally, there are often definitional differences in the ratios presented by different sources, so before using a source, be sure to verify the exact definitions of the ratios to ensure consistency with your own work.

Why is it useful to do comparative ratio analyses?

Differentiate between trend and comparative analyses.

What is benchmarking?

4-10 USES AND LIMITATIONS OF RATIO ANALYSIS

To find quick information about a company, link to **http://www.investor .reuters.com**. *Here you can find company profiles and snapshots, stock price quotes and share information, key ratios, and comparative ratios.*

As noted earlier, ratio analysis is used by three main groups: (1) *managers*, who employ ratios to help analyze, control, and thus improve their firms' operations; (2) *credit analysts*, including bank loan officers and bond rating analysts, who analyze ratios to help judge a company's ability to pay its debts; and (3) *stock analysts*, who are interested in a company's efficiency, risk, and growth prospects. In later chapters we will look more closely at the basic factors that underlie each ratio, which will give you a better idea about how to interpret and use ratios. Note, though, that while ratio analysis can provide useful information concerning a company's operations and financial condition, it does have limitations that necessitate care and judgment. Some potential problems are listed here:

1. Many large firms operate different divisions in different industries, and for such companies it is difficult to develop a meaningful set of industry averages. Therefore, ratio analysis is more useful for small, narrowly focused firms than for large, multidivisional ones.
2. Most firms want to be better than average, so merely attaining average performance is not necessarily good. As a target for high-level performance, it is best to focus on the industry leaders' ratios. Benchmarking helps in this regard.
3. Inflation has badly distorted many firms' balance sheets—recorded values are often substantially different from "true" values. Further, because inflation affects both depreciation charges and inventory costs, profits are also affected. Thus, a ratio analysis for one firm over time, or a comparative analysis of firms of different ages, must be interpreted with judgment.
4. Seasonal factors can also distort a ratio analysis. For example, the inventory turnover ratio for a food processor will be radically different if the balance sheet figure used for inventory is the one just before versus just after the close of the canning season. This problem can be minimized by using monthly averages for inventory (and receivables) when calculating turnover ratios.
5. Firms can employ **"window dressing" techniques** to make their financial statements look stronger. To illustrate, a Chicago builder borrowed on a two-year basis on December 27, 2005, held the proceeds of the loan as cash for a few days, and then paid off the loan ahead of time on January 2, 2006. This improved his current and quick ratios, and made his year-end 2005 balance sheet look good. However, the improvement was strictly window dressing; a week later the balance sheet was back at the old level.
6. Different accounting practices can distort comparisons. As noted earlier, inventory valuation and depreciation methods can affect financial statements

"Window Dressing" Techniques
Techniques employed by firms to make their financial statements look better than they really are.

and thus distort comparisons among firms. Also, if one firm leases a substantial amount of its productive equipment, then its assets may appear low relative to sales because leased assets often do not appear on the balance sheet. At the same time, the liability associated with the lease obligation may not appear as debt. Therefore, leasing can artificially improve both the turnover and the debt ratios. However, the accounting profession has taken steps to reduce this problem.

7. It is difficult to generalize about whether a particular ratio is "good" or "bad." For example, a high current ratio may indicate a strong liquidity position, which is good, or excessive cash, which is bad (because excess cash in the bank is a nonearning asset). Similarly, a high fixed assets turnover ratio may indicate either that the firm uses its assets efficiently or that it is short of cash and cannot afford to make needed investments.

8. A firm may have some ratios that look "good" and others that look "bad," making it difficult to tell whether the company is, on balance, strong or weak. However, statistical procedures can be used to analyze the *net effects* of a set of ratios. Many banks and other lending organizations use such procedures to analyze firms' financial ratios, and then to classify them according to their probability of getting into financial trouble.[21]

Ratio analysis is useful, but analysts should be aware of these problems and make adjustments as necessary. Ratio analysis conducted in a mechanical, unthinking manner is dangerous, but used intelligently and with good judgment, it can provide useful insights into a firm's operations. Your judgment in interpreting a set of ratios is bound to be weak at this point, but it will improve as you read the remaining chapters of this book.

List three types of users of ratio analysis. Would the different users emphasize the same or different types of ratios? Explain.

List several potential problems with ratio analysis.

4-11 PROBLEMS WITH ROE

In Chapter 1 we said that managers should strive to maximize shareholder wealth. If a firm takes steps to improve its ROE, does it mean that shareholder wealth will also increase? Not necessarily, for despite its widespread use and the fact that ROE and shareholder wealth are often highly correlated, serious problems can arise if a firm uses ROE as its sole performance measure.

First, ROE does not consider risk. While shareholders clearly care about returns, they also care about risk. To illustrate this point, consider two divisions within the same firm. Division S has stable cash flows and a predictable 15 percent ROE. Division R, on the other hand, has a 16 percent expected ROE, but its cash flows are quite risky, so the expected ROE may not materialize. If managers were compensated solely on the basis of ROE, and if the expected ROEs were actually achieved, then Division R's manager would receive a higher bonus than S's, even though S might actually be creating more value for shareholders as a result of its lower risk. Also, as we discussed earlier, financial leverage can increase expected ROE but at the cost of higher risk, so raising ROE through greater use of leverage may not be good.

---

[21] The technique used is discriminant analysis. The seminal work on this subject was by Edward I. Altman, "Financial Ratios, Discriminant Analysis, and the Prediction of Corporate Bankruptcy," *Journal of Finance*, September 1968, pp. 589–609.

EVA and ROE

To better understand the idea behind EVA and how it is connected to ROE, let's look at Keller Electronics. Keller has $100,000 in investor-supplied operating capital, which, in turn, consists of $50,000 of long-term debt and $50,000 of common equity. The company has no preferred stock or notes payable. The long-term debt has a 10 percent interest rate. However, since the company is in the 40 percent tax bracket and interest expense is tax deductible, the after-tax cost of debt is only 6 percent. On the basis of their assessment of the company's risk, shareholders require a 14 percent return. This 14 percent return is what shareholders could expect to earn if they were to take their money elsewhere and invest in stocks that have the same risk as Keller. Keller's overall cost of capital is a weighted average of the cost of debt and equity, and it is 10 percent, found as 0.50(6%) + 0.50(14%) = 10%. The total dollar cost of capital per year is 0.10($100,000) = $10,000.

Now let's look at Keller's income statement. Its operating income, EBIT, is $20,000, and its interest expense is 0.10($50,000) = $5,000. Therefore, its taxable income is $20,000 − $5,000 = $15,000. Taxes equal 40 percent of taxable income, or 0.4($15,000) = $6,000, so the firm's net income is $9,000, and its return on equity, ROE, is $9,000/$50,000 = 18%.

Now what is Keller's EVA? The basic formula for EVA is

EVA = EBIT (1 − Corporate tax rate) − (Total investor-supplied operating capital) × (After-tax percentage cost of capital)

= $20,000(1 − 0.40) − ($100,000)(0.10)

= $2,000

This $2,000 EVA indicates that Keller provided its shareholders with $2,000 more than they could have earned elsewhere by investing in other stocks with the same risk as Keller's stock. To see where this $2,000 comes from, let's trace what happens to the money:

- The firm generates $20,000 in operating income.
- $6,000 goes to the government to pay taxes, leaving $14,000.
- $5,000 goes to the bondholders in the form of interest payments, thus leaving $9,000.
- $7,000 is what Keller's shareholders expected to earn: (0.14)($50,000) = $7,000. Note that this $7,000 payment is not a requirement to stay in business—companies can stay in business as long as they pay their bills and their taxes. However, this $7,000 is what shareholders *expected to earn*, and it is the amount the firm *must earn* if it is to avoid reducing shareholder wealth.

Second, ROE does not consider the amount of invested capital. To illustrate, consider a large company that has $100 invested in Project A, which has an ROE of 50 percent, and $1,000,000 invested in Project B, which has a 40 percent ROE. The projects are equally risky, and the two returns are both well above the company's cost of the capital invested in the projects. In this example, Project A has a higher ROE, but because it is so small, it does little to enhance shareholder wealth. Project B, on the other hand, has the lower ROE, but it adds much more to shareholder value.

Consider one last problem with ROE. Assume that you manage a division of a large firm. The firm uses ROE as the sole performance measure, and it determines bonuses on the basis of ROE. Toward the end of the year, your division's ROE is an impressive 45 percent. Now you have an opportunity to invest in a large, low-risk project that has an estimated ROE of 35 percent, which is well above the firm's cost of capital. Even though this project is profitable, you might be reluctant to make the investment because it would reduce your division's average ROE, and therefore reduce the size of your year-end bonus.

These three examples suggest that a project's return must be combined with its risk and size to determine its effect on shareholder value:

- What's left over, the $2,000, is EVA. In this case, Keller's management created wealth because it provided shareholders with a return greater than what they presumably would have earned on alternative investments with the same risk as Keller's stock.

Some Additional Points

- In practice, it is often necessary to make several adjustments in order to arrive at a "better" measure of EVA. The adjustments deal with leased assets, depreciation, and other accounting details.
- Shareholders may not immediately receive the $9,000 that Keller made for them this year (the $7,000 that shareholders expected plus the $2,000 of EVA). Keller can either pay its earnings out as dividends or keep them in the firm as retained earnings. In either event, the $9,000 is shareholders' money. The factors influencing the dividend payout decision are discussed in the chapter on dividend policy.

The Connection between ROE and EVA

EVA is different from the traditional accounting measure of profit because EVA explicitly considers not just the interest cost of debt but also the cost of equity. Indeed, using the simple example above, we could also express EVA as net income minus the dollar cost of equity:

$$\text{EVA} = \text{Net Income} - [(\text{Equity capital}) \times (\text{Cost of equity capital})]$$

$$= \$9,000 - [(\$50,000)(0.14)]$$

$$= \$2,000$$

Note that this is the same number we calculated before when we used the other formula for calculating EVA. Note also that the expression above could be rewritten as follows:

$$\text{EVA} = (\text{Equity capital})[\text{Net income}/\text{Equity capital} - \text{Cost of equity capital}]$$

or simply as

$$\text{EVA} = (\text{Equity capital})(\text{ROE} - \text{Cost of equity capital})$$

This last expression implies that EVA depends on three factors: rate of return, as reflected in ROE; risk, which affects the cost of equity; and size, which is measured by the equity employed. Recall that earlier in this chapter we said that shareholder value depends on risk, return, and capital invested. This final equation illustrates this point.

$$\text{Value} = f(\text{ROE, Risk, Size})$$

ROE is only one dimension of the value equation, and because actions that increase expected ROE may also affect the other two factors, steps designed to increase expected ROE may in some cases be inconsistent with increasing shareholder wealth. Note that we say "expected ROE," not simply ROE. All management decisions are designed to do something in the future, hence to affect *future* outcomes.

With all this in mind, academics, practitioners, and consultants have developed alternative measures that attempt to overcome ROE's potential problems when it is used to gauge performance. One such measure is Economic Value Added (EVA), which was mentioned in Chapter 3 where we calculated EVA. For a discussion of the connection between ROE and EVA, see the accompanying box, "EVA and ROE."

 If a firm takes steps that increase its expected future ROE, does this mean that shareholder wealth will also increase? Explain.

4-12 LOOKING BEYOND THE NUMBERS

Hopefully, working through this chapter has increased your ability to understand and interpret financial statements. This is critically important for anyone making business decisions, evaluating performance, or forecasting likely future developments. Moreover, sound financial analysis involves more than just calculating numbers—good analysis requires that certain qualitative factors be considered when evaluating a company. These factors, as summarized by the American Association of Individual Investors (AAII), include the following:

1. *Are the company's revenues tied to one key customer?* If so, the company's performance may decline dramatically if the customer goes elsewhere. On the other hand, if the relationship is firmly entrenched, this might actually stabilize sales.

2. *To what extent are the company's revenues tied to one key product?* Companies that focus on a single product may be more efficient, but this lack of diversification also increases risk. If revenues come from several different products, the overall bottom line will be less affected by an event that leads to a drop in the demand for one of the products.

3. *To what extent does the company rely on a single supplier?* Depending on a single supplier may lead to unanticipated shortages, which investors and potential creditors should consider.

4. *What percentage of the company's business is generated overseas?* Companies with a large percentage of overseas business are often able to realize higher growth and larger profit margins. However, firms with large overseas operations may be exposed to regional stability problems, and cash flows from their various operations also depend on the values of different currencies.

5. *Competition.* Increases in competition tend to lower prices and profit margins. In forecasting future performance, it is important to assess both the likely actions of the current competitors and the entry by new competitors.

6. *Future products.* Is it necessary for the company to invest heavily in research and development? If so, its future prospects will depend critically on the success of new products in the pipeline. For example, the market's assessment of Boeing's and Airbus's future profits depends on how their next generations of planes are shaping up. Likewise, investors in pharmaceutical companies are interested in knowing whether the company has a strong pipeline of potential blockbuster drugs, and that those products are doing well in the required tests.

7. *Legal and regulatory environment.* Changes in laws and regulations have important implications for many industries. For example, when forecasting the future of tobacco companies, it is crucial to factor in the effects of proposed regulations and pending or likely lawsuits. Likewise, when assessing banks, telecommunications firms, and electric utilities, analysts need to forecast both the extent to which these industries will be regulated in the future and the ability of individual firms to respond to changes in regulation.

What are some qualitative factors analysts should consider when evaluating a company's likely future financial performance?

The primary purpose of this chapter was to discuss techniques investors and managers use to analyze financial statements. The five main categories of ratios were discussed using data for Allied Foods, and we explained how trend analysis and benchmarking are used. It is important to realize ratio analysis is useful, but it must be done intelligently and with good judgment if it is to provide useful insights into firms' operations.

SELF-TEST QUESTIONS AND PROBLEMS
(Solutions Appear in Appendix A)

ST-1 **Key terms** Define each of the following terms:
   a. Liquidity ratios: current ratio; quick ratio
   b. Asset management ratios: inventory turnover ratio; days sales outstanding (DSO); fixed assets turnover ratio; total assets turnover ratio
   c. Financial leverage: debt ratio; times-interest-earned (TIE) ratio; EBITDA coverage ratio
   d. Profitability ratios: profit margin on sales; basic earning power (BEP) ratio; return on total assets (ROA); return on common equity (ROE)
   e. Market value ratios: price/earnings (P/E) ratio; price/cash flow ratio; market/book (M/B) ratio
   f. Trend analysis; comparative ratio analysis; benchmarking
   g. Basic and extended Du Pont equations; book value per share
   h. "Window dressing"; seasonal effects on ratios

ST-2 **Debt ratio** Last year, K. Billingsworth & Co. had earnings per share of $4 and dividends per share of $2. Total retained earnings increased by $12 million during the year, while book value per share at year-end was $40. Billingsworth has no preferred stock, and no new common stock was issued during the year. If its year-end total debt was $120 million, what was the company's year-end debt/assets ratio?

ST-3 **Ratio analysis** The following data apply to A.L. Kaiser & Company (millions of dollars):

Cash and equivalents	$100.00
Fixed assets	$283.50
Sales	$1,000.00
Net income	$50.00
Current liabilities	$105.50
Current ratio	3.0×
DSO[a]	40.55 days
ROE	12%

   [a] This calculation is based on a 365-day year.

Kaiser has no preferred stock—only common equity, current liabilities, and long-term debt.
   a. Find Kaiser's (1) accounts receivable, (2) current assets, (3) total assets, (4) ROA, (5) common equity, (6) quick ratio, and (7) long-term debt.

b. In part a, you should have found Kaiser's accounts receivable (A/R) = $111.1 million. If Kaiser could reduce its DSO from 40.55 days to 30.4 days while holding other things constant, how much cash would it generate? If this cash were used to buy back common stock (at book value), thus reducing common equity, how would this affect (1) the ROE, (2) the ROA, and (3) the total debt/total assets ratio?

QUESTIONS

4-1   Financial ratio analysis is conducted by four groups of analysts: short-term lenders, long-term lenders, stockholders, and managers. What is the primary emphasis of each group, and how would that affect the ratios they focus on?

4-2   Why would the inventory turnover ratio be more important for someone analyzing a grocery store chain than an insurance company?

4-3   Over the past year, M. D. Ryngaert & Co. had an increase in its current ratio and a decline in its total assets turnover ratio. However, the company's sales, cash and equivalents, DSO, and its fixed assets turnover ratio remained constant. What balance sheet accounts must have changed to produce the indicated changes?

4-4   Profit margins and turnover ratios vary from one industry to another. What differences would you expect to find between the turnover ratios, profit margins, and Du Pont equations for a grocery chain and a steel company?

4-5   How does inflation distort ratio analysis comparisons, both for one company over time (trend analysis) and when different companies are being compared? Are only balance sheet items or both balance sheet and income statement items affected?

4-6   If a firm's ROE is low and management wants to improve it, explain how using more debt might help.

4-7   Give some examples that illustrate how (a) seasonal factors and (b) different growth rates might distort a comparative ratio analysis. How might these problems be alleviated?

4-8   Why is it sometimes misleading to compare a company's financial ratios with those of other firms that operate in the same industry?

4-9   Suppose you were comparing a discount merchandiser with a high-end merchandiser. Suppose further that both companies had identical ROEs. If you applied the extended Du Pont equation to both firms, would you expect the three components to be the same for each company? If not, explain what balance sheet and income statement items might lead to the component differences.

4-10 Indicate the effects of the transactions listed in the following table on total current assets, current ratio, and net income. Use (+) to indicate an increase, (−) to indicate a decrease, and (0) to indicate either no effect or an indeterminate effect. Be prepared to state any necessary assumptions, and assume an initial current ratio of more than 1.0. (Note: A good accounting background is necessary to answer some of these questions; if yours is not strong, just answer the questions you can handle.)

	Total Current Assets	Current Ratio	Effect on Net Income
a. Cash is acquired through issuance of additional common stock.	_____	_____	_____
b. Merchandise is sold for cash.	_____	_____	_____
c. Federal income tax due for the previous year is paid.	_____	_____	_____
d. A fixed asset is sold for less than book value.	_____	_____	_____
e. A fixed asset is sold for more than book value.	_____	_____	_____
f. Merchandise is sold on credit.	_____	_____	_____
g. Payment is made to trade creditors for previous purchases.	_____	_____	_____
h. A cash dividend is declared and paid.	_____	_____	_____

	Total Current Assets	Current Ratio	Effect on Net Income
i. Cash is obtained through short-term bank loans.	____	____	____
j. Short-term notes receivable are sold at a discount.	____	____	____
k. Marketable securities are sold below cost.	____	____	____
l. Advances are made to employees.	____	____	____
m. Current operating expenses are paid.	____	____	____
n. Short-term promissory notes are issued to trade creditors in exchange for past due accounts payable.	____	____	____
o. Ten-year notes are issued to pay off accounts payable.	____	____	____
p. A fully depreciated asset is retired.	____	____	____
q. Accounts receivable are collected.	____	____	____
r. Equipment is purchased with short-term notes.	____	____	____
s. Merchandise is purchased on credit.	____	____	____
t. The estimated taxes payable are increased.	____	____	____

PROBLEMS

Easy Problems 1–6

4-1 **Days sales outstanding** Baker Brothers has a DSO of 40 days, and its annual sales are $7,300,000. What is its accounts receivable balance? Assume it uses a 365-day year.

4-2 **Debt ratio** Bartley Barstools has an equity multiplier of 2.4, and its assets are financed with some combination of long-term debt and common equity. What is its debt ratio?

4-3 **Du Pont analysis** Doublewide Dealers has an ROA of 10 percent, a 2 percent profit margin, and an ROE of 15 percent. What is its total assets turnover? What is its equity multiplier?

4-4 **Market/book ratio** Jaster Jets has $10 billion in total assets. Its balance sheet shows $1 billion in current liabilities, $3 billion in long-term debt, and $6 billion in common equity. It has 800 million shares of common stock outstanding, and its stock price is $32 per share. What is Jaster's market/book ratio?

4-5 **Price/earnings ratio** A company has an EPS of $2.00, a cash flow per share of $3.00, and a price/cash flow ratio of 8.0×. What is its P/E ratio?

4-6 **Du Pont and ROE** A firm has a profit margin of 2 percent and an equity multiplier of 2.0. Its sales are $100 million and it has total assets of $50 million. What is its ROE?

Intermediate Problems 7–19

4-7 **Du Pont and net income** Ebersoll Mining has $6 million in sales; its ROE is 12 percent; and its total assets turnover is 3.2×. The company is 50 percent equity financed. What is its net income?

4-8 **Basic earning power** Duval Manufacturing recently reported the following information:

Net income	$600,000
ROA	8%
Interest expense	$225,000

Its tax rate is 35 percent. What is its basic earning power (BEP)?

4-9 **M/B and share price** You are given the following information: Stockholders' equity = $3.75 billion; price/earnings ratio = 3.5; common shares outstanding = 50 million; and market/book ratio = 1.9. Calculate the price of a share of the company's common stock.

4-10 **Ratio calculations** Assume you are given the following relationships for the Brauer Corp.:

Sales/total assets	1.5×
Return on assets (ROA)	3%
Return on equity (ROE)	5%

Calculate Brauer's profit margin and debt ratio.

4-11 **EBITDA coverage ratio** Willis Publishing has $30 billion in total assets. Its basic earning power (BEP) ratio is 20 percent, and its times-interest-earned ratio is 8.0. Willis' depreciation and amortization expense totals $3.2 billion. It has $2 billion in lease payments, and

$1 billion must go toward principal payments on outstanding loans and long-term debt. What is Willis's EBITDA coverage ratio?

4-12 **Ratio calculations** Graser Trucking has $12 billion in assets, and its tax rate is 40 percent. Its basic earning power (BEP) ratio is 15 percent, and its return on assets (ROA) is 5 percent. What is its times-interest-earned (TIE) ratio?

4-13 **Times-interest-earned ratio** The H.R. Pickett Corp. has $500,000 of debt outstanding, and it pays an annual interest rate of 10 percent. Its annual sales are $2 million, its average tax rate is 30 percent, and its net profit margin on sales is 5 percent. What is its TIE ratio?

4-14 **Return on equity** Midwest Packaging's ROE last year was only 3 percent, but its management has developed a new operating plan that calls for a total debt ratio of 60 percent, which will result in annual interest charges of $300,000. Management projects an EBIT of $1,000,000 on sales of $10,000,000, and it expects to have a total assets turnover ratio of 2.0. Under these conditions, the tax rate will be 34 percent. If the changes are made, what will be its return on equity?

4-15 **Return on equity and quick ratio** Lloyd Inc. has sales of $200,000, a net income of $15,000, and the following balance sheet:

Cash	$ 10,000	Accounts payable	$ 30,000
Receivables	50,000	Other current liabilities	20,000
Inventories	150,000	Long-term debt	50,000
Net fixed assets	90,000	Common equity	200,000
Total assets	$300,000	Total liabilities and equity	$300,000

The new owner thinks that inventories are excessive and can be lowered to the point where the current ratio is equal to the industry average, 2.5×, without affecting either sales or net income. If inventories are sold off and not replaced thus reducing the current ratio to 2.5×, if the funds generated are used to reduce common equity (stock can be repurchased at book value), and if no other changes occur, by how much will the ROE change? What will be the firm's new quick ratio?

4-16 **Return on equity** Central City Construction (CCC) needs $1 million of assets to get started, and it expects to have a basic earning power ratio of 20 percent. CCC will own no securities, so all of its income will be operating income. If it chooses to, CCC can finance up to 50 percent of its assets with debt, which will have an 8 percent interest rate. Assuming a 40 percent tax rate on all taxable income, what is the *difference* between its expected ROE if CCC finances with 50 percent debt versus its expected ROE if it finances entirely with common stock?

4-17 **Conceptual: Return on equity** Which of the following statements is most correct? (Hint: Work Problem 4-16 before answering 4-17, and consider the solution setup for 4-16, as you think about 4-17.)

a. If a firm's expected basic earning power (BEP) is constant for all of its assets and exceeds the interest rate on its debt, then adding assets and financing them with debt will raise the firm's expected return on common equity (ROE).

b. The higher its tax rate, the lower a firm's BEP ratio will be, other things held constant.

c. The higher the interest rate on its debt, the lower a firm's BEP ratio will be, other things held constant.

d. The higher its debt ratio, the lower a firm's BEP ratio will be, other things held constant.

e. Statement a is false, but statements b, c, and d are all true.

4-18 **TIE ratio** AEI Incorporated has $5 billion in assets, and its tax rate is 40 percent. Its basic earning power (BEP) ratio is 10 percent, and its return on assets (ROA) is 5 percent. What is AEI's times-interest-earned (TIE) ratio?

4-19 **Current ratio** The Petry Company has $1,312,500 in current assets and $525,000 in current liabilities. Its initial inventory level is $375,000, and it will raise funds as additional notes payable and use them to increase inventory. How much can its short-term debt (notes payable) increase without pushing its current ratio below 2.0?

Challenging Problems 20–24

4-20 **DSO and accounts receivable** Harrelson Inc. currently has $750,000 in accounts receivable, and its days sales outstanding (DSO) is 55 days. It wants to reduce its DSO to 35 days by pressuring more of its customers to pay their bills on time. If this policy is adopted the company's average sales will fall by 15 percent. What will be the level of accounts receivable following the change? Assume a 365-day year.

4-21 **P/E and stock price** Fontaine Inc. recently reported net income of $2 million. It has 500,000 shares of common stock, which currently trades at $40 a share. Fontaine continues to expand and anticipates that 1 year from now its net income will be $3.25 million. Over the next year it also anticipates issuing an additional 150,000 shares of stock, so that 1 year from now it will have 650,000 shares of common stock. Assuming its price/earnings ratio remains at its current level, what will be its stock price 1 year from now?

4-22 **Balance sheet analysis** Complete the balance sheet and sales information that follows using the following financial data:

> Debt ratio: 50%
> Current ratio: 1.8×
> Total assets turnover: 1.5×
> Days sales outstanding: 36.5 days[a]
> Gross profit margin on sales: (Sales − Cost of goods sold)/Sales = 25%
> Inventory turnover ratio: 5×
>
> [a] Calculation is based on a 365-day year.

Balance Sheet

Cash	_____	Accounts payable	_____
Accounts receivable	_____	Long-term debt	60,000
Inventories	_____	Common stock	_____
Fixed assets	_____	Retained earnings	97,500
Total assets	$300,000	Total liabilities and equity	_____
Sales	_____	Cost of goods sold	_____

4-23 **Ratio analysis** Data for Barry Computer Co. and its industry averages follow.

a. Calculate the indicated ratios for Barry.
b. Construct the extended Du Pont equation for both Barry and the industry.
c. Outline Barry's strengths and weaknesses as revealed by your analysis.
d. Suppose Barry had doubled its sales as well as its inventories, accounts receivable, and common equity during 2005. How would that information affect the validity of your ratio analysis? (Hint: Think about averages and the effects of rapid growth on ratios if averages are not used. No calculations are needed.)

Barry Computer Company: Balance Sheet as of December 31, 2005 (In Thousands)

Cash	$ 77,500	Accounts payable	$129,000
Receivables	336,000	Notes payable	84,000
Inventories	241,500	Other current liabilities	117,000
Total current assets	$655,000	Total current liabilities	$330,000
		Long-term debt	256,500
Net fixed assets	292,500	Common equity	361,000
Total assets	$947,500	Total liabilities and equity	$947,500

Barry Computer Company: Income Statement for Year Ended December 31, 2005 (In Thousands)

Sales		$1,607,500
Cost of goods sold		
Materials	$717,000	
Labor	453,000	
Heat, light, and power	68,000	
Indirect labor	113,000	
Depreciation	41,500	1,392,500
Gross profit		$ 215,000
Selling expenses		115,000
General and administrative expenses		30,000
Earnings before interest and taxes (EBIT)		$ 70,000
Interest expense		24,500
Earnings before taxes (EBT)		$ 45,500
Federal and state income taxes (40 percent)		18,200
Net income		$ 27,300

Ratio	Barry	Industry Average
Current	_____	2.0×
Quick	_____	1.3×
Days sales outstanding[a]	_____	35 days
Inventory turnover	_____	6.7×
Total assets turnover	_____	3.0×
Net profit margin	_____	1.2%
ROA	_____	3.6%
ROE	_____	9.0%
Total debt/total assets	_____	60.0%

[a] Calculation is based on a 365-day year.

4-24 **Du Pont analysis** A firm has been experiencing low profitability in recent years. Perform an analysis of the firm's financial position using the extended Du Pont equation. The firm has no lease payments, but has a $2 million sinking fund payment on its debt. The most recent industry average ratios and the firm's financial statements are as follows:

Industry Average Ratios

Current ratio	2×	Fixed assets turnover	6×
Debt/total assets	30%	Total assets turnover	3×
Times interest earned	7×	Profit margin on sales	3%
EBITDA coverage	9×	Return on total assets	9%
Inventory turnover	10×	Return on common equity	12.9%
Days sales outstanding[a]	24 days		

[a] Calculation is based on a 365-day year.

Balance Sheet as of December 31, 2005 (Millions of Dollars)

Cash and equivalents	$ 78	Accounts payable	$ 45
Net receivables	66	Notes payable	45
Inventories	159	Other current liabilities	21
Total current assets	$303	Total current liabilities	$111
		Long-term debt	24
		Total liabilities	$135
Gross fixed assets	225		
Less depreciation	78	Common stock	114
Net fixed assets	$147	Retained earnings	201
		Total stockholders' equity	$315
Total assets	$450	Total liabilities and equity	$450

Income Statement for Year Ended December 31, 2005 (Millions of Dollars)

Net sales	$795.0
Cost of goods sold	660.0
Gross profit	$135.0
Selling expenses	73.5
EBITDA	$ 61.5
Depreciation expense	12.0
Earnings before interest and taxes (EBIT)	$ 49.5
Interest expense	4.5
Earnings before taxes (EBT)	$ 45.0
Taxes (40%)	18.0
Net income	$ 27.0

a. Calculate those ratios that you think would be useful in this analysis.
b. Construct an extended Du Pont equation, and compare the company's ratios to the industry average ratios.
c. Do the balance sheet accounts or the income statement figures seem to be primarily responsible for the low profits?
d. Which specific accounts seem to be most out of line relative to other firms in the industry?
e. If the firm had a pronounced seasonal sales pattern, or if it grew rapidly during the year, how might that affect the validity of your ratio analysis? How might you correct for such potential problems?

COMPREHENSIVE/SPREADSHEET PROBLEM

4-25 **Ratio analysis** The Corrigan Corporation's 2004 and 2005 financial statements follow, along with some industry average ratios.

a. Assess Corrigan's liquidity position, and determine how it compares with peers and how the liquidity position has changed over time.
b. Assess Corrigan's asset management position, and determine how it compares with peers and how its asset management efficiency has changed over time.
c. Assess Corrigan's debt management position, and determine how it compares with peers and how its debt management has changed over time.
d. Assess Corrigan's profitability ratios, and determine how they compare with peers and how the profitability position has changed over time.
e. Assess Corrigan's market value ratios, and determine how their valuation compares with peers and how it has changed over time.
f. Calculate Corrigan's ROE, as well as the industry average ROE, using the extended Du Pont equation. From this analysis, how does Corrigan's financial position compare with the industry average numbers?
g. What do you think would happen to its ratios if the company initiated cost-cutting measures that allowed it to hold lower levels of inventory and substantially decreased the cost of goods sold? No calculations are necessary. Think about which ratios would be affected by changes in these two accounts.

Corrigan Corporation: Balance Sheets as of December 31

	2005	2004
Cash	$ 72,000	$ 65,000
Accounts receivable	439,000	328,000
Inventories	894,000	813,000
Total current assets	$1,405,000	$1,206,000
Land and building	238,000	271,000
Machinery	132,000	133,000
Other fixed assets	61,000	57,000
Total assets	$1,836,000	$1,667,000
Accounts and notes payable	$ 432,000	$ 409,500
Accrued liabilities	170,000	162,000
Total current liabilities	$ 602,000	$ 571,500
Long-term debt	404,290	258,898
Common stock	575,000	575,000
Retained earnings	254,710	261,602
Total liabilities and equity	$1,836,000	$1,667,000

Corrigan Corporation: Income Statements for Years Ending December 31

	2005	2004
Sales	$4,240,000	$3,635,000
Cost of goods sold	3,680,000	2,980,000
Gross operating profit	$ 560,000	$ 655,000
General administrative and selling expenses	236,320	213,550
Depreciation	159,000	154,500
Miscellaneous	134,000	127,000
Earnings before taxes (EBT)	$ 30,680	$ 159,950
Taxes (40%)	12,272	63,980
Net income	$ 18,408	$ 95,970

Per-Share Data

	2005	2004
EPS	$0.80	$4.17
Cash dividends	$1.10	$0.95
Market price (average)	$12.34	$23.57
P/E ratio	15.4×	5.65×
Number of shares outstanding	23,000	23,000

Industry Financial Ratios[a]

Current ratio	2.7×
Inventory turnover[b]	7.0×
Days sales outstanding[c]	32 days
Fixed assets turnover[b]	13.0×
Total assets turnover[b]	2.6×
Return on assets	9.1%
Return on equity	18.2%
Debt ratio	50.0%
Profit margin on sales	3.5%
P/E ratio	6.0×
Price/cash flow ratio	3.5×

[a] Industry average ratios have been constant for the past 4 years.
[b] Based on year-end balance sheet figures.
[c] Calculation is based on a 365-day year.

Integrated Case

D'Leon Inc., Part II

4-26 **Financial statement analysis** Part I of this case, presented in Chapter 3, discussed the situation that D'Leon Inc., a regional snack-foods producer, was in after an expansion program. D'Leon had increased plant capacity and undertaken a major marketing campaign in an attempt to "go national." Thus far, sales have not been up to the forecasted level, costs have been higher than were projected, and a large loss occurred in 2005 rather than the expected profit. As a result, its managers, directors, and investors are concerned about the firm's survival.

Donna Jamison was brought in as assistant to Fred Campo, D'Leon's chairman, who had the task of getting the company back into a sound financial position. D'Leon's 2004 and 2005 balance sheets and income statements, together with projections for 2006, are given in Tables IC4-1 and IC4-2. In addition, Table IC4-3 gives the company's 2004 and 2005 financial ratios, together with industry average data. The 2006 projected financial statement data represent Jamison's and Campo's best guess for 2006 results, assuming that some new financing is arranged to get the company "over the hump."

Jamison examined monthly data for 2005 (not given in the case), and she detected an improving pattern during the year. Monthly sales were rising, costs were falling, and large losses in the early months had turned to a small profit by December. Thus, the annual data look somewhat worse than final monthly data. Also, it appears to be taking longer for the advertising program to get the message across, for the new sales offices to generate sales, and for the new manufacturing facilities to operate efficiently. In other words, the lags between spending money and deriving benefits were longer than D'Leon's managers had anticipated. For these reasons, Jamison and Campo see hope for the company—provided it can survive in the short run.

Jamison must prepare an analysis of where the company is now, what it must do to regain its financial health, and what actions should be taken. Your assignment is to help her answer the following questions. Provide clear explanations, not yes or no answers.

a. Why are ratios useful? What are the five major categories of ratios?

b. Calculate D'Leon's 2006 current and quick ratios based on the projected balance sheet and income statement data. What can you say about the company's liquidity positions in 2004, 2005, and as projected for 2006? We often think of ratios as being useful (1) to managers to help run the business, (2) to bankers for credit analysis, and (3) to stockholders for stock valuation. Would these different types of analysts have an equal interest in these liquidity ratios?

c. Calculate the 2006 inventory turnover, days sales outstanding (DSO), fixed assets turnover, and total assets turnover. How does D'Leon's utilization of assets stack up against other firms in its industry?

d. Calculate the 2006 debt, times-interest-earned, and EBITDA coverage ratios. How does D'Leon compare with the industry with respect to financial leverage? What can you conclude from these ratios?

e. Calculate the 2006 profit margin, basic earning power (BEP), return on assets (ROA), and return on equity (ROE). What can you say about these ratios?

f. Calculate the 2006 price/earnings ratio, price/cash flow ratio, and market/book ratio. Do these ratios indicate that investors are expected to have a high or low opinion of the company?

g. Use the extended Du Pont equation to provide a summary and overview of D'Leon's financial condition as projected for 2006. What are the firm's major strengths and weaknesses?

h. Use the following simplified 2006 balance sheet to show, in general terms, how an improvement in the DSO would tend to affect the stock price. For example, if the company could improve its collection procedures and thereby lower its DSO from 45.6 days to the 32-day industry average without affecting sales, how would that change "ripple through" the financial statements (shown in thousands below) and influence the stock price?

Accounts receivable	$ 878	Debt	$1,545
Other current assets	1,802		
Net fixed assets	817	Equity	1,952
Total assets	$3,497	Liabilities plus equity	$3,497

i. Does it appear that inventories could be adjusted, and, if so, how should that adjustment affect D'Leon's profitability and stock price?

j. In 2005, the company paid its suppliers much later than the due dates, and it was not maintaining financial ratios at levels called for in its bank loan agreements. Therefore, suppliers could cut the company off, and its bank could refuse to renew the loan when it comes due in 90 days. On the basis of data provided, would you, as a credit manager, continue to sell to D'Leon on credit? (You could demand cash on delivery—that is, sell on terms of COD—but that might cause D'Leon to stop buying from your company.) Similarly, if you were the bank loan officer, would you recommend renewing the loan or demand its repayment? Would your actions be influenced if, in early 2006, D'Leon showed you its 2006 projections plus proof that it was going to raise more than $1.2 million of new equity?

k. In hindsight, what should D'Leon have done back in 2004?

l. What are some potential problems and limitations of financial ratio analysis?

m. What are some qualitative factors analysts should consider when evaluating a company's likely future financial performance?

TABLE IC4-1   Balance Sheets

	2006E	2005	2004
Assets			
Cash	$ 85,632	$ 7,282	$ 57,600
Accounts receivable	878,000	632,160	351,200
Inventories	1,716,480	1,287,360	715,200
Total current assets	$2,680,112	$1,926,802	$1,124,000
Gross fixed assets	1,197,160	1,202,950	491,000
Less accumulated depreciation	380,120	263,160	146,200
Net fixed assets	$ 817,040	$ 939,790	$ 344,800
Total assets	$3,497,152	$2,866,592	$1,468,800
Liabilities and Equity			
Accounts payable	$ 436,800	$ 524,160	$ 145,600
Notes payable	300,000	636,808	200,000
Accruals	408,000	489,600	136,000
Total current liabilities	$1,144,800	$1,650,568	$ 481,600
Long-term debt	400,000	723,432	323,432
Common stock	1,721,176	460,000	460,000
Retained earnings	231,176	32,592	203,768
Total equity	$1,952,352	$ 492,592	$ 663,768
Total liabilities and equity	$3,497,152	$2,866,592	$1,468,800

Note: "E" indicates estimated. The 2006 data are forecasts.

TABLE IC4-2   Income Statements

	2006E	2005	2004
Sales	$7,035,600	$6,034,000	$3,432,000
Cost of goods sold	5,875,992	5,528,000	2,864,000
Other expenses	550,000	519,988	358,672
Total operating costs excluding depreciation	$6,425,992	$6,047,988	$3,222,672
EBITDA	$ 609,608	($ 13,988)	$ 209,328
Depreciation	116,960	116,960	18,900
EBIT	$ 492,648	($ 130,948)	$ 190,428
Interest expense	70,008	136,012	43,828
EBT	$ 422,640	($ 266,960)	$ 146,600
Taxes (40%)	169,056	(106,784)[a]	58,640
Net income	$ 253,584	($ 160,176)	$ 87,960
EPS	$1.014	($1.602)	$0.880
DPS	$0.220	$0.110	$0.220
Book value per share	$7.809	$4.926	$6.638
Stock price	$12.17	$2.25	$8.50
Shares outstanding	250,000	100,000	100,000
Tax rate	40.00%	40.00%	40.00%
Lease payments	40,000	40,000	40,000
Sinking fund payments	0	0	0

Note: "E" indicates estimated. The 2006 data are forecasts.
[a] The firm had sufficient taxable income in 2003 and 2004 to obtain its full tax refund in 2005.

TABLE IC4-3   *Ratio Analysis*

	2006E	2005	2004	Industry Average
Current		1.2×	2.3×	2.7×
Quick		0.4×	0.8×	1.0×
Inventory turnover		4.7×	4.8×	6.1×
Days sales outstanding (DSO)[a]		38.2	37.4	32.0
Fixed assets turnover		6.4×	10.0×	7.0×
Total assets turnover		2.1×	2.3×	2.6×
Debt ratio		82.8%	54.8%	50.0%
TIE		−1.0×	4.3×	6.2×
EBITDA coverage		0.1×	3.0×	8.0×
Profit margin		−2.7%	2.6%	3.5%
Basic earning power		−4.6%	13.0%	19.1%
ROA		−5.6%	6.0%	9.1%
ROE		−32.5%	13.3%	18.2%
Price/earnings		−1.4×	9.7×	14.2×
Price/cash flow		−5.2×	8.0×	11.0×
Market/book		0.5×	1.3×	2.4×
Book value per share		$4.93	$6.64	n.a.

Note: "E" indicates estimated. The 2006 data are forecasts.
[a] Calculation is based on a 365-day year.

cyberproblem

Please go to the ThomsonNOW Web site to access the Cyberproblems.

THOMSON ONE | Business School Edition

Access the Thomson ONE problems though the ThomsonNOW Web site. Use the Thomson ONE—Business School Edition online database to work this chapter's questions.

Conducting a Financial Ratio Analysis on Ford Motor Company

In Chapter 3, we took a look at Starbucks' financial statements. Now we use Thomson One to analyze Ford Motor Company.

Enter Ford's ticker symbol (F) and select "GO." If we select the tab at the top labeled "Financials," we can find Ford's key financial statements for the past several years. At the "Financials" screen on the second line of tabs, select the "Fundamental Ratios" tab. If you then select the SEC Database Ratios from the pull-down menu, you can select either annual or quarterly ratios.

Under annual ratios, there is an in-depth summary of Ford's various ratios over the past 3 years. This information enables you to evaluate Ford's performance over time for each of the ratio categories that we mention in the text (liquidity, asset management, debt management, profitability, and market-based ratios).

The text mentions that financial statement analysis has two major components: a trend analysis, where we evaluate changes in the key ratios over time, and a peer analysis, where we compare financial ratios with firms that are in the same industry and/or line of business. We have already used Thomson One to conduct a trend analysis—next we use this tool to conduct a peer analysis. If we click on the "Peers" tab (on the first line of tabs) near the top of the screen, some summary financial information for Ford and a few of its peers will be presented. If you click on the "Peer Sets" tab (second line of tabs), you can modify the list of peer firms. The default setup is "Peers set by SIC Code." To obtain a comparison of many of the key ratios presented in the text, just click on "Financials" (second line of tabs) and select "Key Financial Ratios" from the drop-down menu.

Discussion Questions

1. What has happened to Ford's liquidity position over the past 3 years? How does Ford's liquidity compare with its peers? (Hint: You may use both the peer key financial ratios and liquidity comparison to answer this question.)
2. Take a look at Ford's inventory turnover ratio. How does this ratio compare with its peers? Have there been any interesting changes over time in this measure? Do you consider Ford's inventory management to be a strength or a weakness?
3. Construct a simple Du Pont analysis for Ford and its peers. What are Ford's strengths and weaknesses relative to its competitors?

FINANCIAL MARKETS
AND INSTITUTIONS

A Strong Financial System Is Necessary for a Growing and Prosperous Economy

Financial managers and investors don't operate in a vacuum—they make decisions within a large and complex financial environment. This environment includes financial markets and institutions, tax and regulatory policies, and the state of the economy. The environment both determines the available financial alternatives and affects the outcomes of various decisions. Thus, it is crucial that investors and financial managers have a good understanding of the environment in which they operate.

History shows that a strong financial system is a necessary ingredient for a growing and prosperous economy. Companies raising capital to finance capital expenditures as well as investors saving to accumulate funds for future use require well-functioning financial markets and institutions.

Over the past few decades, changing technology and improving communications have increased cross-border transactions and expanded the scope and efficiency of the global financial system. Companies routinely raise funds throughout the world to finance projects all around the globe. Likewise, with the click of a mouse an individual investor in Nebraska can deposit funds in a European bank or purchase a mutual fund that invests in Chinese securities.

It is important to recognize that at the most fundamental level well-functioning markets and institutions are based heavily on trust. An investor who deposits money in a bank, buys stock through an online brokerage account, or contacts her broker to buy a mutual fund places her money and trust in the hands of the financial institutions that provide her with advice and transaction services. Similarly, when businesses approach commercial or investment banks to raise capital, they are relying on these institutions to provide them with funds under the best possible terms, and with sound, objective advice.

While changing technology and globalization have made it possible for more and more types of financial transactions to take place, a series of scandals in recent years have rocked the financial industry and have led many to question whether some of our institutions are serving their own or their clients' interests.

Many of these questionable practices have come to light because of the efforts of a single man: the Attorney General of New York, Eliot Spitzer. In 2001, Spitzer exposed conflicts of interest within investment banking firms regarding dealings between their underwriters, who help companies issue new securities, and their analysts, who make recommendations to individual investors to purchase these securities. Allegations were made that to attract the business of firms planning to issue new securities, investment banks leaned on their analysts to write glowing, overly optimistic research reports on these firms. While such practices helped produce large underwriting fees for the investment banks, they compromised their ability to provide the objective, independent research on which their clients depended. A few years later, Spitzer turned his attention to the mutual fund industry, where he exposed unethical fee structures and trading practices of some of the leading funds. More recently, Spitzer has questioned whether some insurance brokers have compromised their clients' interests in order to steer business toward insurers, who provide the broker with rebates of different types.[1]

While some have criticized Spitzer for being overly zealous and politically ambitious, his efforts have appropriately brought to light many questionable practices. Hopefully, this spotlight will put pressure on the institutions to establish practices that will restore the public's trust and lead to a better financial system in the long run.

Putting Things In Perspective

In earlier chapters, we discussed financial statements and showed how financial managers and others analyze them to evaluate a firm's operations and financial position—past, current, and future. To make good decisions, financial managers must understand the environment and markets within which businesses operate. Therefore, in this chapter we describe the markets where capital is raised, securities are traded, and stock prices are established, as well as the institutions that operate in these markets. Because the overall objective of financial managers is to maximize shareholder value, we also take a closer look at how the stock market operates, and we discuss the concept of market efficiency.

---

[1] For example, some insurance companies allowed brokers to keep premiums for as much as a year before remitting them to the insurance companies. The brokers invested these premiums and earned interest on them, and this gave them an incentive to steer business to these companies rather than to insurance companies whose policies might be better for the brokers' clients.

5-1 AN OVERVIEW OF THE CAPITAL ALLOCATION PROCESS

Businesses, individuals, and governments often need to raise capital. For example, suppose Carolina Power & Light (CP&L) forecasts an increase in the demand for electricity in North Carolina, and the company decides to build a new power plant. Because CP&L almost certainly will not have the $1 billion or so necessary to pay for the plant, the company will have to raise this capital in the financial markets. Or suppose Mr. Fong, the proprietor of a San Francisco hardware store, decides to expand into appliances. Where will he get the money to buy the initial inventory of TV sets, washers, and freezers? Similarly, if the Johnson family wants to buy a home that costs $200,000, but they have only $40,000 in savings, how can they raise the additional $160,000? And if the city of New York wants to borrow $200 million to finance a new sewer plant, or the federal government needs money to meet its needs, they too need access to the capital markets.

On the other hand, some individuals and firms have incomes that are greater than their current expenditures, so they have funds available to invest. For example, Carol Hawk has an income of $36,000, but her expenses are only $30,000, and as of December 31, 2004, Ford Motor Company had accumulated roughly $23.5 billion of cash and equivalents, which it has available for future investments.

People and organizations with surplus funds are saving today in order to accumulate funds for future use. A household might save to pay for future expenses such as their children's education or their retirement, while a business might save to fund future investments. Those with surplus funds expect to earn a positive return on their investments. People and organizations who need money today borrow to fund their current expenditures. They understand that there is a cost to this capital, and this cost is essentially the return that the investors with surplus funds expect to earn on those funds.

In a well-functioning economy, capital will flow efficiently from those who supply capital to those who demand it. This transfer of capital can take place in the three different ways described in Figure 5-1:

1. *Direct transfers* of money and securities, as shown in the top section, occur when a business sells its stocks or bonds directly to savers, without going through any type of financial institution. The business delivers its securities to savers, who in turn give the firm the money it needs.
2. As shown in the middle section, transfers may also go through an *investment banking house* such as Merrill Lynch, which *underwrites* the issue. An underwriter serves as a middleman and facilitates the issuance of securities. The company sells its stocks or bonds to the investment bank, which in turn sells these same securities to savers. The businesses' securities and the savers' money merely "pass through" the investment banking house. However, the investment bank does buy and hold the securities for a period of time, so it is taking a risk—it may not be able to resell them to savers for as much as it paid. Because new securities are involved and the corporation receives the proceeds of the sale, this is called a primary market transaction.
3. Transfers can also be made through a *financial intermediary* such as a bank or mutual fund. Here the intermediary obtains funds from savers in exchange for its own securities. The intermediary uses this money to buy and hold businesses' securities. For example, a saver might deposit dollars in a bank, receiving from it a certificate of deposit, and then the bank might lend the money to a small business as a mortgage loan. Thus, intermediaries literally create new forms of capital—in this case, certificates of deposit, which are both safer and more liquid than mortgages and thus are better for most

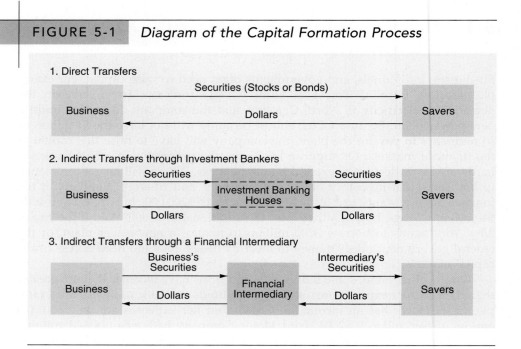

FIGURE 5-1   *Diagram of the Capital Formation Process*

savers to hold. The existence of intermediaries greatly increases the efficiency of money and capital markets.

Often the entity needing capital is a business, and specifically a corporation, but it is easy to visualize the demander of capital being a home purchaser, a small business, a government unit, and so on. For example, if your uncle lends you money to help fund a new business after you graduate, this would be a direct transfer of funds. Alternatively, if your family borrows money to purchase a home, you will probably raise the funds through a financial intermediary such as your local commercial bank or mortgage banker, which in turn may acquire its funds from a national institution, such as Fannie Mae.

In a global context, economic development is highly correlated with the level and efficiency of financial markets and institutions.[2] It is difficult, if not impossible, for an economy to reach its full potential if it doesn't have access to a well-functioning financial system. For this reason, policy makers often promote the globalization of financial markets.

In a well-developed economy like that of the United States, an extensive set of markets and institutions has evolved over time to facilitate the efficient allocation of capital. To raise capital efficiently, managers must understand how these markets and institutions work.

Identify three different ways capital is transferred between savers and borrowers.

Why do policy makers promote the globalization of financial markets?

---

[2] For a detailed review of the evidence linking financial development to economic growth, see Ross Levine, "Finance and Growth: Theory and Evidence," NBER Working Paper no. w10766, September 2004.

5-2 FINANCIAL MARKETS

People and organizations wanting to borrow money are brought together with those having surplus funds in the *financial markets*. Note that "markets" is plural; there are a great many different financial markets in a developed economy such as ours. We briefly describe the different types of financial markets and some recent trends in these markets.

5-2a Types of Markets

Different financial markets serve different types of customers or different parts of the country. Financial markets also vary depending on the maturity of the securities being traded and the types of assets used to back the securities. For these reasons it is often useful to classify markets along the following dimensions:

1. *Physical asset versus financial asset markets. Physical asset markets* (also called "tangible" or "real" asset markets) are those for products such as wheat, autos, real estate, computers, and machinery. *Financial asset markets*, on the other hand, deal with stocks, bonds, notes, mortgages, and other *claims on real assets*, as well as with *derivative securities* whose values are *derived* from changes in the prices of other assets. A share of Ford stock is a "pure financial asset," while an option to buy Ford shares is a derivative security whose value depends on the price of Ford stock.

2. *Spot versus futures markets.* **Spot markets** are markets in which assets are bought or sold for "on-the-spot" delivery (literally, within a few days). **Futures markets** are markets in which participants agree today to buy or sell an asset at some future date. For example, a farmer may enter into a futures contract in which he agrees today to sell 5,000 bushels of soybeans six months from now at a price of $5 a bushel. On the other side, an international food producer looking to buy soybeans in the future may enter into a futures contract in which it agrees to buy soybeans six months from now.

3. *Money versus capital markets.* **Money markets** are the markets for short-term, highly liquid debt securities. The New York, London, and Tokyo money markets are among the world's largest. **Capital markets** are the markets for intermediate- or long-term debt and corporate stocks. The New York Stock Exchange, where the stocks of the largest U.S. corporations are traded, is a prime example of a capital market. There is no hard and fast rule on this, but when describing debt markets, "short term" generally means less than 1 year, "intermediate term" means 1 to 10 years, and "long term" means more than 10 years.

4. *Primary versus secondary markets.* **Primary markets** are the markets in which corporations raise new capital. If GE were to sell a new issue of common stock to raise capital, this would be a primary market transaction. The corporation selling the newly created stock receives the proceeds from the sale in a primary market transaction. **Secondary markets** are markets in which existing, already outstanding, securities are traded among investors. Thus, if Jane Doe decided to buy 1,000 shares of GE stock, the purchase would occur in the secondary market. The New York Stock Exchange is a secondary market because it deals in outstanding, as opposed to newly issued, stocks and bonds. Secondary markets also exist for mortgages, various other types of loans, and other financial assets. The corporation whose securities are being traded is not involved in a secondary market transaction and, thus, does not receive any funds from such a sale.

Spot Markets
The markets in which assets are bought or sold for "on-the-spot" delivery.

Futures Markets
The markets in which participants agree today to buy or sell an asset at some future date.

Money Markets
The financial markets in which funds are borrowed or loaned for short periods (less than one year).

Capital Markets
The financial markets for stocks and for intermediate- or long-term debt (one year or longer).

Primary Markets
Markets in which corporations raise capital by issuing new securities.

Secondary Markets
Markets in which securities and other financial assets are traded among investors after they have been issued by corporations.

Private Markets
Markets in which transactions are worked out directly between two parties.

Public Markets
Markets in which standardized contracts are traded on organized exchanges.

5. *Private versus public markets.* **Private markets,** where transactions are negotiated directly between two parties, are differentiated from **public markets,** where standardized contracts are traded on organized exchanges. Bank loans and private debt placements with insurance companies are examples of private market transactions. Because these transactions are private, they may be structured in any manner that appeals to the two parties. By contrast, securities that are issued in public markets (for example, common stock and corporate bonds) are ultimately held by a large number of individuals. Public securities must have fairly standardized contractual features, both to appeal to a broad range of investors and also because public investors do not generally have the time and expertise to study unique, nonstandardized contracts. Their wide ownership also ensures that public securities are relatively liquid. Private market securities are, therefore, more tailor-made but less liquid, whereas publicly traded securities are more liquid but subject to greater standardization.

Other classifications could be made, but this breakdown is sufficient to show that there are many types of financial markets. Also, note that the distinctions among markets are often blurred and unimportant except as a general point of reference. For example, it makes little difference if a firm borrows for 11, 12, or 13 months, hence, whether we have a "money" or "capital" market transaction. You should be aware of the important differences among types of markets, but don't get hung up trying to distinguish them at the boundaries.

A healthy economy is dependent on efficient funds transfers from people who are net savers to firms and individuals who need capital. Without efficient transfers, the economy simply could not function: Carolina Power & Light could not raise capital, so Raleigh's citizens would have no electricity; the Johnson family would not have adequate housing; Carol Hawk would have no place to invest her savings; and so on. Obviously, the level of employment and productivity, hence our standard of living, would be much lower. Therefore, it is absolutely essential that our financial markets function efficiently—not only quickly, but also at a low cost.[3]

Table 5-1 (on pages 148–149) gives a listing of the most important instruments traded in the various financial markets. The instruments are arranged from top to bottom in ascending order of typical length of maturity. As we go through the book, we will look in more detail at many of the instruments listed in Table 5-1. For example, we will see that there are many varieties of corporate bonds, ranging from "plain vanilla" bonds to bonds that are convertible into common stocks to bonds whose interest payments vary depending on the inflation rate. Still, the table gives an idea of the characteristics and costs of the instruments traded in the major financial markets.

5-2b Recent Trends

Financial markets have experienced many changes during the last two decades. Technological advances in computers and telecommunications, along with the globalization of banking and commerce, have led to deregulation, and this has increased competition throughout the world. The result is a much more effi-

---

[3] As the countries of the former Soviet Union and other Eastern European nations move toward capitalism, just as much attention must be paid to the establishment of cost-efficient financial markets as to electrical power, transportation, communications, and other infrastructure systems. Economic efficiency is simply impossible without a good system for allocating capital within the economy.

cient, internationally linked market, but one that is far more complex than existed a few years ago. While these developments have been largely positive, they have also created problems for policy makers. At one conference, Federal Reserve Board Chairman Alan Greenspan stated that modern financial markets "expose national economies to shocks from new and unexpected sources and with little if any lag." He went on to say that central banks must develop new ways to evaluate and limit risks to the financial system. Large amounts of capital move quickly around the world in response to changes in interest and exchange rates, and these movements can disrupt local institutions and economies.

Globalization has exposed the need for greater cooperation among regulators at the international level. Various committees are currently working to improve coordination, but the task is not easy. Factors that complicate coordination include (1) the differing structures among nations' banking and securities industries, (2) the trend in Europe toward financial services conglomerates, and (3) reluctance on the part of individual countries to give up control over their national monetary policies. Still, regulators are unanimous about the need to close the gaps in the supervision of worldwide markets.

Another important trend in recent years has been the increased use of **derivatives.** A derivative is any security whose value is *derived* from the price of some other "underlying" asset. An option to buy IBM stock is a derivative, as is a contract to buy Japanese yen six months from now. The value of the IBM option depends on the price of IBM's stock, and the value of the Japanese yen "future" depends on the exchange rate between yen and dollars. The market for derivatives has grown faster than any other market in recent years, providing corporations with new opportunities but also exposing them to new risks.

Derivatives can be used either to reduce risks or to speculate. Suppose an importer's costs rise and its net income falls when the dollar falls relative to the yen. That company could reduce its risk by purchasing derivatives whose values increase when the dollar declines. This is a *hedging operation*, and its purpose is to reduce risk exposure. Speculation, on the other hand, is done in the hope of high returns, but it raises risk exposure. For example, several years ago Procter & Gamble disclosed that it lost $150 million on derivative investments, and Orange County (California) went bankrupt as a result of its treasurer's speculation in derivatives.

The size and complexity of derivatives transactions concern regulators, academics, and members of Congress. Fed Chairman Greenspan noted that, in theory, derivatives should allow companies to manage risk better, but that it is not clear whether recent innovations have "increased or decreased the inherent stability of the financial system."

Derivative
Any financial asset whose value is derived from the value of some other "underlying" asset.

Distinguish between physical asset and financial asset markets.

What's the difference between spot and futures markets?

Distinguish between money and capital markets.

What's the difference between primary and secondary markets?

Differentiate between private and public markets.

Why are financial markets essential for a healthy economy and economic growth?

What is a derivative, and how is its value related to that of an "underlying asset"?

TABLE 5-1   *Summary of Major Market Instruments, Market Participants, and Security Characteristics*

			SECURITY CHARACTERISTICS		
Instrument (1)	**Market** (2)	**Major Participants** (3)	**Riskiness** (4)	**Original Maturity** (5)	**Interest Rate on 2/1/05[a]** (6)
U.S. Treasury bills	Money	Sold by U.S. Treasury to finance federal expenditures	Default-free	91 days to 1 year	2.48%
Bankers' acceptances	Money	A firm's promise to pay, guaranteed by a bank	Low degree of risk if guaranteed by a strong bank	Up to 180 days	2.68
Dealer commercial paper	Money	Issued by financially secure firms to large investors	Low default risk	Up to 270 days	2.67
Negotiable certificates of deposit (CDs)	Money	Issued by major money-center commercial banks to large investors	Default risk depends on the strength of the issuing bank	Up to 1 year	2.70
Money market mutual funds	Money	Invest in Treasury bills, CDs, and commercial paper; held by individuals and businesses	Low degree of risk	No specific maturity (instant liquidity)	1.69
Eurodollar market time deposits	Money	Issued by banks outside U.S.	Default risk depends on the strength of the issuing bank	Up to 1 year	2.70
Consumer credit, including credit card debt	Money	Issued by banks/ credit unions/finance companies to individuals	Risk is variable	Variable	Variable, but goes up to 20% or more
U.S. Treasury notes and bonds	Capital	Issued by U.S. government	No default risk, but price will decline if interest rates rise	2 to 30 years	4.65

[a] The yields reported (except for corporate and municipal bonds) are from *The Wall Street Journal.* Money market rates assume a 3-month maturity. Corporate and municipal bond rates are for 30-year AAA-rated bonds; quotes are from *Federal Reserve Statistical Release.*

5-3 FINANCIAL INSTITUTIONS

Direct funds transfers are more common among individuals and small businesses, and in economies where financial markets and institutions are less developed. While businesses in more developed economies do occasionally rely on direct transfers, they generally find it more efficient to enlist the services of one or more financial institutions when it comes time to raise capital.

In the United States and other developed nations, a set of highly efficient financial intermediaries has evolved. Their original roles were generally quite specific, but many of them have diversified to the point where they serve

TABLE 5-1   *(Continued)*

Instrument (1)	Market (2)	Major Participants (3)	SECURITY CHARACTERISTICS		
			Riskiness (4)	Original Maturity (5)	Interest Rate on 2/1/05[a] (6)
Mortgages	Capital	Borrowings from commercial banks and S&Ls by individuals and businesses	Risk is variable	Up to 30 years	5.20
State and local government bonds	Capital	Issued by state and local governments to individuals and institutional investors	Riskier than U.S. government securities, but exempt from most taxes	Up to 30 years	4.40
Corporate bonds	Capital	Issued by corporations to individuals and institutional investors	Riskier than U.S. government securities, but less risky than preferred and common stocks; varying degree of risk within bonds depending on strength of issuer	Up to 40 years[b]	5.22
Leases	Capital	Similar to debt in that firms can lease assets rather than borrow and then buy the assets	Risk similar to corporate bonds	Generally 3 to 20 years	Similar to bond yields
Preferred stocks	Capital	Issued by corporations to individuals and institutional investors	Riskier than corporate bonds, but less risky than common stock	Unlimited	6 to 8%
Common stocks[c]	Capital	Issued by corporations to individuals and institutional investors	Risky	Unlimited	NA

[b] Just recently, a few corporations have issued 100-year bonds; however, the majority have issued bonds with maturities less than 40 years.

[c] While common stocks do not pay interest, they are expected to provide a "return" in the form of dividends and capital gains. As you will see in Chapter 8, historical stock returns have averaged between 10 and 15 percent a year. Of course, if you buy a stock, your actual return may be considerably higher or lower than these historical averages.

many different markets. As a result, the differences between institutions have tended to become blurred. Still, there remains a degree of institutional identity, and therefore it is useful to describe the major categories of financial institutions here:

Investment Banking House
An organization that underwrites and distributes new investment securities and helps businesses obtain financing.

1. **Investment banking houses** such as Merrill Lynch, Morgan Stanley, Goldman Sachs, or Credit Suisse Group provide a number of services to both investors and companies planning to raise capital. Such organizations (a) help

corporations design securities with features that are currently attractive to investors, (b) then buy these securities from the corporation, and (c) resell them to savers. Although the securities are sold twice, this process is really one primary market transaction, with the investment banker acting as a facilitator to help transfer capital from savers to businesses.

Commercial Bank
Traditional department store of finance serving a variety of savers and borrowers.

2. **Commercial banks,** such as Bank of America, Wells Fargo, Wachovia, and J. P. Morgan Chase, are the traditional "department stores of finance" because they serve a variety of savers and borrowers. Historically, commercial banks were the major institutions that handled checking accounts and through which the Federal Reserve System expanded or contracted the money supply. Today, however, several other institutions also provide checking services and significantly influence the money supply. Conversely, commercial banks are providing an ever-widening range of services, including stock brokerage services and insurance.

Financial Services Corporation
A firm that offers a wide range of financial services, including investment banking, brokerage operations, insurance, and commercial banking.

3. **Financial services corporations** are large conglomerates that combine many different financial institutions within a single corporation. Examples of financial services corporations, most of which started in one area but have now diversified to cover most of the financial spectrum, include Citigroup, American Express, Fidelity, and Prudential.

4. *Savings and loan associations (S&Ls)* traditionally served individual savers and residential and commercial mortgage borrowers, taking the funds of many small savers and then lending this money to home buyers and other types of borrowers. In the 1980s, the S&L industry experienced severe problems when (a) short-term interest rates paid on savings accounts rose well above the returns earned on the existing mortgages held by S&Ls and (b) commercial real estate suffered a severe slump, resulting in high mortgage default rates. Together, these events forced many S&Ls to merge with stronger institutions or close their doors.

5. *Mutual savings banks,* which are similar to S&Ls, operate primarily in the northeastern states, accepting savings primarily from individuals, and lending mainly on a long-term basis to home buyers and consumers.

6. *Credit unions* are cooperative associations whose members are supposed to have a common bond, such as being employees of the same firm. Members' savings are loaned only to other members, generally for auto purchases, home improvement loans, and home mortgages. Credit unions are often the cheapest source of funds available to individual borrowers.

7. *Pension funds* are retirement plans funded by corporations or government agencies for their workers and administered primarily by the trust departments of commercial banks or by life insurance companies. Pension funds invest primarily in bonds, stocks, mortgages, and real estate.

8. *Life insurance companies* take savings in the form of annual premiums; invest these funds in stocks, bonds, real estate, and mortgages; and finally make payments to the beneficiaries of the insured parties. In recent years, life insurance companies have also offered a variety of tax-deferred savings plans designed to provide benefits to the participants when they retire.

Mutual Funds
Organizations that pool investor funds to purchase financial instruments and thus reduce risks through diversification.

9. **Mutual funds** are corporations that accept money from savers and then use these funds to buy stocks, long-term bonds, or short-term debt instruments issued by businesses or government units. These organizations pool funds and thus reduce risks by diversification. They also achieve economies of scale in analyzing securities, managing portfolios, and buying and selling securities. Different funds are designed to meet the objectives of different types of savers. Hence, there are bond funds for those who desire safety, stock funds for savers who are willing to accept significant risks in the hope of higher returns, and still other funds that are used as interest-bearing

checking accounts (**money market funds**). There are literally thousands of different mutual funds with dozens of different goals and purposes.

Mutual funds have grown more rapidly than most other institutions in recent years, in large part because of a change in the way corporations provide for employees' retirement. Before the 1980s, most corporations said, in effect, "Come work for us, and when you retire, we will give you a retirement income based on the salary you were earning during the last five years before you retired." The company was then responsible for setting aside funds each year to make sure it had the money available to pay the agreed-upon retirement benefits. That situation is changing rapidly. Today, new employees are likely to be told, "Come work for us, and we will give you some money each payday that you can invest for your future retirement. You can't get the money until you retire (without paying a huge tax penalty), but if you invest wisely, you can retire in comfort." Most workers recognize that they don't know enough to invest wisely, so they turn their retirement funds over to a mutual fund. Hence, mutual funds are growing rapidly. Excellent information on the objectives and past performances of the various funds are provided in publications such as *Value Line Investment Survey* and *Morningstar Mutual Funds*, which are available in most libraries and on the Internet.

10. *Hedge funds* are similar to mutual funds because they accept money from savers and use the funds to buy various securities, but there are some important differences. While mutual funds are registered and regulated by the Securities and Exchange Commission (SEC), hedge funds are largely unregulated. This difference in regulation stems from the fact that mutual funds typically target small investors, whereas hedge funds typically have large minimum investments (often exceeding $1 million) that are effectively marketed to institutions and individuals with high net worths. Different hedge fund managers follow different strategies. For example, a hedge fund manager who believes that the spreads between corporate and Treasury bond yields are too large might simultaneously buy a portfolio of corporate bonds and sell a portfolio of Treasury bonds. In this case, the portfolio is "hedged" against overall movements in interest rates, but it will do well if the spread between these securities narrows. Likewise, hedge fund managers may take advantage of perceived incorrect valuations in the stock market, that is, where a stock's market and intrinsic values differ.

Hedge funds generally charge large fees, often a fixed amount plus 15 to 20 percent of the fund's capital gains. The average hedge fund has done quite well in recent years. In a recent report, Citigroup estimates that the average hedge fund has produced an annual return of 11.9 percent since 1990. Over the same time period, the average annual returns of the overall stock market were 10.5 percent, and the returns on mutual funds were even lower, 9.2 percent. Given the stock market's relatively lackluster performance in recent years, an increasing number of investors have flocked to hedge funds. Between 1999 and 2004, the money managed by them more than quadrupled to roughly $800 billion. However, the same article in *Business Week* that highlighted the strong growth and relative performance of these funds also suggested that their returns are showing signs of weakness and emphasized that they are certainly not without risk.[4]

Indeed, some hedge funds take on risks that are considerably higher than that of an average individual stock or mutual fund. Moreover, in recent years, some have also produced spectacular losses. For example, many

Money Market Funds
Mutual funds that invest in short-term, low-risk securities and allow investors to write checks against their accounts.

---

[4] See Anne Tergesen, "Time to Hedge on Hedge Funds? New Research Shows that Returns Are Sliding, and Some Don't Help You Diversify," *Business Week*, September 13, 2004, p. 104.

hedge fund investors suffered large losses in 1998 when the Russian economy collapsed. That same year, the Federal Reserve had to step in to help rescue Long Term Capital Management, a high-profile hedge fund whose managers included several well-respected practitioners as well as two Nobel Prize–winning professors who were experts in investment theory.[5]

As hedge funds have become more popular, many have begun to lower their minimum investment requirements. Perhaps not surprisingly, their rapid growth and shift toward smaller investors have also led to a call for more regulation.

With the notable exception of hedge funds, financial institutions have been heavily regulated to ensure the safety of these institutions and thus to protect investors. Historically, many of these regulations—which have included a prohibition on nationwide branch banking, restrictions on the types of assets the institutions could buy, ceilings on the interest rates they could pay, and limitations on the types of services they could provide—tended to impede the free flow of capital and thus hurt the efficiency of our capital markets. Recognizing this fact, policy makers took several steps during the 1980s and 1990s to deregulate financial services companies. For example, the barriers that restricted banks from expanding nationwide were eliminated. Likewise, regulations that once forced a strict separation of commercial and investment banking have been relaxed.

The result of the ongoing regulatory changes has been a blurring of the distinctions between the different types of institutions. Indeed, the trend in the United States today is toward huge financial services corporations, which own banks, S&Ls, investment banking houses, insurance companies, pension plan operations, and mutual funds, and which have branches across the country and around the world. For example, Citigroup combines one of the world's largest commercial banks (Citibank), a huge insurance company (Travelers), and a major investment bank (Smith Barney), along with numerous other subsidiaries that operate throughout the world. Citigroup's structure is similar to that of major institutions in Europe, Japan, and elsewhere around the globe.

Panel A of Table 5-2 lists the 10 largest U.S. bank and thrift holding companies, while Panel B shows the leading world banking companies. Among the world's 10 largest, only one (Citigroup) is based in the United States. While U.S. banks have grown dramatically as a result of recent mergers, they are still small by global standards. Panel C of the table lists the 10 leading underwriters in terms of dollar volume of new debt and equity issues. Six of the top underwriters are also major commercial banks or are part of bank holding companies, which confirms the continued blurring of distinctions among different types of financial institutions.

What is the difference between a pure commercial bank and a pure investment bank?

List the major types of financial institutions, and briefly describe the primary function of each.

What are some important differences between mutual and hedge funds? How are they similar?

---

[5] See Franklin Edwards, "Hedge Funds and the Collapse of Long Term Capital Management," *Journal of Economic Perspectives,* Vol. 13, no. 2 (Spring 1999), pp. 189–210, for a thoughtful review of the implications of Long Term Capital Management's collapse.

TABLE 5-2	*10 Largest U.S. Bank and Thrift Holding Companies and World Banking Companies and Top 10 Leading Underwriters*

Panel A U.S. Bank and Thrift Holding Companies[a]	Panel B World Banking Companies[b]	Panel C Leading Global Underwriters[c]
Citigroup Inc.	Mizuho Financial Group (Tokyo)	Citigroup Inc.
Bank of America Corp.	Citigroup Inc. (New York)	Morgan Stanley
J. P. Morgan Chase & Co.	Allianz AG (Munich)	J. P. Morgan
Wells Fargo & Co.	UBS AG (Zurich)	Merrill Lynch
Wachovia Corp.	HSBC Holdings PLC (London)	Lehman Brothers
MetLife Inc.	Deutsche Bank AG (Frankfurt)	Credit Suisse First Boston
Bank One	Credit Agricole (Paris)	Deutsche Bank AG
Washington Mutual Inc.	BNP Paribas (Paris)	UBS AG
U.S. Bancorp	ING Group NV (Amsterdam)	Goldman Sachs
SunTrust Banks Inc.	Sumitomo Mitsui Financial Group (Tokyo)	Banc of America Securities

Notes:
[a] Ranked by total assets as of June 30, 2004. *Source:* "Top 150 Bank and Thrift Holding Companies with the Most Assets," *AmericanBanker.com*, October 19, 2004.
[b] Ranked by total assets as of December 31, 2003. *Source:* "World's Largest Banking Companies by Assets," *AmericanBanker.com*, November 12, 2004.
[c] Ranked by dollar amount raised through new issues (stocks and bonds) in 2004. For this ranking, the lead underwriter (manager) is given credit for the entire issue. *Source:* Adapted from *The Wall Street Journal*, January 3, 2005, p. R17.

5-4 THE STOCK MARKET

As noted earlier, secondary markets are those in which outstanding, previously issued securities are traded. By far the most active secondary market, and the most important one to financial managers, is the *stock market*, where the prices of firms' stocks are established. Because the primary goal of financial managers is to maximize their firms' stock prices, knowledge of the stock market is important to anyone involved in managing a business.

While the two leading stock markets today are the New York Stock Exchange and the Nasdaq stock market, stocks are actually traded using a variety of market procedures. However, there are just two basic types of stock markets: (1) *physical location exchanges*, which include the New York Stock Exchange (NYSE), the American Stock Exchange (AMEX), and several regional stock exchanges, and (2) electronic dealer-based markets that include the Nasdaq stock market, the less formal over-the-counter market, and the recently developed electronic communications networks (ECNs). (See the box entitled, "The NYSE and Nasdaq Combine Forces with the Leading Online Trading Systems.") Because the physical location exchanges are easier to describe and understand, we consider them first.

Citigroup Built to Compete in a Changing Environment

The financial environment has been undergoing tremendous changes, including breakthroughs in technology, increased globalization, and shifts in the regulatory environment. All of these factors have presented financial managers and investors with opportunities, but those opportunities are accompanied by substantial risks.

Consider the case of Citigroup Inc., which was created in 1998 when Citicorp and Travelers Group (which included the investment firm Salomon Smith Barney) merged. Citigroup today operates in more than 100 countries, has roughly 200 million customers and 275,000 employees, and holds more than $1.4 trillion (that's over a thousand billion!) worth of assets.

Citigroup resulted from three important trends:

1. A regulatory change made it possible for U.S. corporations to engage in commercial banking, investment banking, and insurance.

2. Increased globalization made it desirable for financial institutions to follow their clients and operate in many countries.

3. Changing technology led to increased economies of scale and scope, both of which increase the relative efficiency of huge, diversified companies such as Citigroup.

The same forces that are transforming the financial services industry have affected other industries. In particular, the growth of the Internet has provided many companies with increased opportunities, but it has also created additional competition and risk. For example, it has altered the way millions of consumers purchase airline tickets, hotel rooms, books, and automobiles. Consequently, financial managers must understand today's technological environment and be ready to change operations as the environment evolves.

5-4a The Physical Location Stock Exchanges

Physical Location Exchanges
Formal organizations having tangible physical locations that conduct auction markets in designated ("listed") securities.

The **physical location exchanges** are tangible physical entities. Each of the larger ones occupies its own building, has a limited number of members, and has an elected governing body—its board of governors. Members are said to have "seats" on the exchange, although everybody stands up. These seats, which are bought and sold, give the holder the right to trade on the exchange. There are currently 1,366 seats on the New York Stock Exchange (this number has remained constant since 1953). In early 2005, a seat on the NYSE sold for $1.0 million, which was considerably lower than the record high of $2.65 million. Seat prices are at multiyear lows due to low trading volume, declines in commissions earned, and recent scandals that have rocked the NYSE.

Most of the larger investment banking houses operate *brokerage departments*, and they own seats on the exchanges and designate one or more of their officers as members. The exchanges are open on all normal working days, with the members meeting in a large room equipped with telephones and other electronic equipment that enable each member to communicate with his or her firm's offices throughout the country.

Like other markets, security exchanges facilitate communication between buyers and sellers. For example, Merrill Lynch (the fourth largest brokerage firm) might receive an order in its Atlanta office from a customer who wants to buy shares of GE stock. Simultaneously, the Denver office of Morgan Stanley (the second largest brokerage firm) might receive an order from a customer wishing to sell shares of GE. Each broker communicates electronically with the firm's representative on the NYSE. Other brokers throughout the country are

The NYSE and Nasdaq Combine Forces with the Leading Online Trading Systems

The forces that spurred consolidation in the financial services industry have also promoted online trading systems that bypass the traditional exchanges. These systems, which are known as electronic communications networks (ECNs), use electronic technology to bring buyers and sellers together. As of early 2005, the majority of these transactions were conducted by two firms: Instinet Group and Archipelago.

The rise of ECNs has accelerated the move toward 24-hour trading. Large clients who want to trade after other markets have closed may utilize an ECN, thus bypassing the NYSE and Nasdaq. The move toward faster, cheaper, and continuous trading obviously benefits investors, but it does present regulators, who try to ensure that all investors have access to a "level playing field," with a number of headaches.

Recognizing the new threat, the two leading exchanges have not been content to stand idly by. In April 2005, the NYSE announced plans to acquire Archipelago and to turn itself into a public company. If the deal goes through, the new company will be called NYSE Group Inc., and 70 percent of the combined company will be owned by those who currently hold seats on the NYSE. Archipelago

shareholders will own the remaining 30 percent. Two days after this stunning announcement, Nasdaq announced its own plans to purchase Instinet.

These announced mergers confirm the growing importance of electronic trading and have led many to conclude that the floor traders who buy and sell stock on the NYSE may soon become a thing of the past as an increasing number of transactions take place electronically. Others contend that there will remain a role for these floor traders for at least the foreseeable future. In any event, what is clear is that the financial landscape of stock trading will continue to undergo dramatic changes in the upcoming years.

Sources: Katrina Brooker, "Online Investing: It's Not Just for Geeks Anymore," *Fortune*, December 21, 1998, pp. 89–98; "Fidelity, Schwab Part of Deal to Create Nasdaq Challenger," *The Milwaukee Journal Sentinel*, July 22, 1999, p. 1; Aaron Lucchetti, Susanne Craig, and Dennis K. Berman, "NYSE to Acquire Electronic Trader and Go Public," *The Wall Street Journal*, April 21, 2005, p. A1; and "Nasdaq Agrees to Buy Instinet for $1.88 Billion," **www.wsj.com**, *Wall Street Online*, April 22, 2005.

also communicating with their own exchange members. The exchange members with *sell orders* offer the shares for sale, and they are bid for by the members with *buy orders*. Thus, the exchanges operate as *auction markets*.[6]

---

[6] The NYSE is actually a modified auction market, wherein people (through their brokers) bid for stocks. Originally—about 200 years ago—brokers would literally shout, "I have 100 shares of Erie for sale; how much am I offered?" and then sell to the highest bidder. If a broker had a buy order, he or she would shout, "I want to buy 100 shares of Erie; who'll sell at the best price?" The same general situation still exists, although the exchanges now have members known as *specialists* who facilitate the trading process by keeping an inventory of shares of the stocks in which they specialize. If a buy order comes in at a time when no sell order arrives, the specialist will sell off some inventory. Similarly, if a sell order comes in, the specialist will buy and add to inventory. The specialist sets a *bid price* (the price the specialist will pay for the stock) and an *asked price* (the price at which shares will be sold out of inventory). The bid and asked prices are set at levels designed to keep the inventory in balance. If many buy orders start coming in because of favorable developments or sell orders come in because of unfavorable events, the specialist will raise or lower prices to keep supply and demand in balance. Bid prices are somewhat lower than asked prices, with the difference, or *spread*, representing the specialist's profit margin.

Special facilities are available to help institutional investors such as mutual or pension funds sell large blocks of stock without depressing their prices. In essence, brokerage houses that cater to institutional clients will purchase blocks (defined as 10,000 or more shares) and then resell the stock to other institutions or individuals. Also, when a firm has a major announcement that is likely to cause its stock price to change sharply, it will ask the exchanges to halt trading in its stock until the announcement has been made and digested by investors.

5-4b The Over-the-Counter and the Nasdaq Stock Markets

Over-the-Counter (OTC) Market
A large collection of brokers and dealers, connected electronically by telephones and computers, that provides for trading in unlisted securities.

While the stocks of most large companies trade on the NYSE, a larger number of stocks trade off the exchange in what has traditionally been referred to as the **over-the-counter (OTC) market.** An explanation of the term "over-the-counter" will help clarify how this term arose. As noted earlier, the exchanges operate as auction markets—buy and sell orders come in more or less simultaneously, and exchange members match these orders. If a stock is traded infrequently, perhaps because the firm is new or small, few buy and sell orders come in, and matching them within a reasonable amount of time would be difficult. To avoid this problem, some brokerage firms maintain an inventory of such stocks and stand prepared to make a market for these stocks. These "dealers" buy when individual investors want to sell, and then sell part of their inventory when investors want to buy. At one time, the inventory of securities was kept in a safe, and the stocks, when bought and sold, were literally passed over the counter.

Dealer Market
Includes all facilities that are needed to conduct security transactions not conducted on the physical location exchanges.

Today, these markets are often referred to as **dealer markets.** A dealer market includes all facilities that are needed to conduct security transactions, but they are not made on the physical location exchanges. These facilities include (1) the relatively few *dealers* who hold inventories of these securities and who are said to "make a market" in these securities; (2) the thousands of brokers who act as *agents* in bringing the dealers together with investors; and (3) the computers, terminals, and electronic networks that provide a communication link between dealers and brokers. The dealers who make a market in a particular stock quote the price at which they will pay for the stock (the *bid price*) and the price at which they will sell shares (the *ask price*). Each dealer's prices, which are adjusted as supply and demand conditions change, can be read off computer screens all across the world. The *bid-ask spread*, which is the difference between bid and asked prices, represents the dealer's markup, or profit. The dealer's risk increases if the stock is more volatile, or if the stock trades infrequently. Generally, we would expect volatile, infrequently traded stocks to have wider spreads in order to compensate the dealers for assuming the risk of holding them in inventory.

Brokers and dealers who participate in the over-the-counter market are members of a self-regulatory body known as the *National Association of Securities Dealers (NASD)*, which licenses brokers and oversees trading practices. The computerized network used by the NASD is known as the NASD Automated Quotation System (Nasdaq).

Nasdaq started as just a quotation system, but it has grown to become an organized securities market with its own listing requirements. Over the past decade the competition between the NYSE and Nasdaq has become increasingly fierce. In an effort to become more competitive with the NYSE and with international markets, the Nasdaq and the AMEX merged in 1998 to form the Nasdaq-Amex Market Group. The merger turned out to be less than successful, and in early 2005 the AMEX members agreed to buy the exchange back from the NASD. Since most of the larger companies trade on the NYSE, the market capitalization of NYSE-traded stocks is much higher than for stocks traded on Nasdaq ($12.6 trillion compared with $3.7 trillion at year-end 2004). However, reported volume (number of shares traded) is often larger on Nasdaq, and more companies are listed on Nasdaq.[7]

Interestingly, many high-tech companies such as Microsoft and Intel have remained on Nasdaq even though they easily meet the listing requirements of the NYSE. At the same time, however, other high-tech companies such as Gateway, America Online, and Iomega have left Nasdaq for the NYSE. Despite these defec-

---

[7] One transaction on Nasdaq generally shows up as two separate trades (the buy and the sell). This "double counting" makes it difficult to compare the volume between stock markets.

tions, Nasdaq's growth over the past decade has been impressive. In the years ahead, competition between Nasdaq and the NYSE will no doubt remain fierce.

What are the differences between the physical location exchanges and the Nasdaq stock market?

What is the bid-ask spread?

5-5 THE MARKET FOR COMMON STOCK

Some companies are so small that their common stocks are not actively traded; they are owned by only a few people, usually the companies' managers. These firms are said to be *privately owned*, or **closely held, corporations,** and their stock is called *closely held stock*. In contrast, the stocks of most larger companies are owned by thousands of investors, most of whom are not active in management. These companies are called **publicly owned corporations,** and their stock is called *publicly held stock*.

A recent study found that institutional investors owned about 46 percent of all publicly held common stocks. Included are pension plans (26 percent), mutual funds (10 percent), foreign investors (6 percent), insurance companies (3 percent), and brokerage firms (1 percent). These institutions buy and sell relatively actively, however, so they account for about 75 percent of all transactions. Thus, institutional investors have a significant influence on the prices of individual stocks.

5-5a Types of Stock Market Transactions

We can classify stock market transactions into three distinct categories:

1. *Trading in the outstanding shares of established, publicly owned companies: the secondary market.* Allied Food Products, the company we analyzed in Chapters 3 and 4, has 50 million shares of stock outstanding. If the owner of 100 shares sells his or her stock, the trade is said to have occurred in the *secondary market*. Thus, the market for outstanding shares, or *used shares*, is the secondary market. The company receives no new money when sales occur in this market.
2. *Additional shares sold by established, publicly owned companies: the primary market.* If Allied decides to sell (or issue) an additional 1 million shares to raise new equity capital, this transaction is said to occur in the *primary market*.[8]
3. *Initial public offerings by privately held firms: the IPO market.* In the summer of 2004 Google sold shares to the public for the first time at $85 per share. By September 2005, the stock was selling for $303, so it had more than tripled. Several years ago, the Coors Brewing Company, which was owned by the Coors family at the time, decided to sell some stock to raise capital needed for a major expansion program.[9] These types of transactions are called

Closely Held Corporation
A corporation that is owned by a few individuals who are typically associated with the firm's management.

Publicly Owned Corporation
A corporation that is owned by a relatively large number of individuals who are not actively involved in its management.

---

[8] Allied has 60 million shares authorized but only 50 million outstanding; thus, it has 10 million authorized but unissued shares. If it had no authorized but unissued shares, management could increase the authorized shares by obtaining stockholders' approval, which would generally be granted without any arguments.

[9] The stock Coors offered to the public was designated Class B, and it was nonvoting. The Coors family retained the founders' shares, called Class A stock, which carried full voting privileges. The company was large enough to obtain an NYSE listing, but at that time the Exchange had a requirement that listed common stocks must have full voting rights, which precluded Coors from obtaining an NYSE listing.

Going Public
The act of selling stock to the public at large by a closely held corporation or its principal stockholders.

Initial Public Offering (IPO) Market
The market for stocks of companies that are in the process of going public.

going public—whenever stock in a closely held corporation is offered to the public for the first time, the company is said to be going public. The market for stock that is just being offered to the public is called the **initial public offering (IPO) market.**

IPOs have received a lot of attention in recent years, primarily because a number of "hot" issues have realized spectacular gains—often in the first few minutes of trading. Consider the 1999 IPO of Red Hat Inc., the open-source provider of software products and services. The company's underwriters set an offering price of $14 per share. However, because of intense demand for the issue, the stock's price rose more than 270 percent the first day of trading.

With the recent stock market decline, we have also seen a decline in the number of new IPOs. Table 5-3 lists the largest, the best performing, and the worst performing IPOs of 2004, and it shows how they performed from their offering dates through year-end 2004. As the table shows, not all IPOs are as well received as Red Hat's. Moreover, even if you are able to identify a "hot" issue, it is often difficult to purchase shares in the initial offering. These deals are generally *oversubscribed*, which means that the demand for shares at the offering price exceeds the number of shares issued. In such instances, investment bankers favor large institutional investors (who are their best customers), and small investors find it hard, if not impossible, to get in on the ground floor. They can buy the stock in the after-market, but evidence suggests that if you do not get in on the ground floor the average IPO underperforms the overall market over the long run.[10]

Indeed, the subsequent performance of Red Hat illustrates the risks that arise when investing in new issues. Figure 5-2 plots Red Hat's stock price from the time of its IPO in 1999 to early February 2005. After its dramatic first day run-up, Red Hat's stock closed just above $54 per share. Demand for the stock continued to surge, and the price reached a high of just over $300 in December 1999. Soon afterward, the company announced a two-for-one stock split. (Note that Figure 5-2 considers the stock split.) The split effectively cut the stock's price in half, but it doubled the number of shares held by each shareholder. After adjusting for the split, the stock's price stood at $132 per share in early January 2000. Soon thereafter, Red Hat's price tumbled—indeed, by mid-year 2001 its price was $3.50 per share, which was equivalent to $7.00 per share before the split. As Figure 5-2 shows, Red Hat's stock has slowly rebounded over the past few years, but its price still remains below its initial offering price of $14.

Amidst concerns about the allocation of IPO shares, Google Inc.'s highly publicized 2004 IPO attracted attention because of its size (Google raised $1.67 billion in stock) and the way it was conducted. Rather than having the offer price set by its investment bankers, Google conducted a Dutch auction in which individual investors directly placed bids for shares. In a *Dutch auction*, the actual transaction price is set at the highest price ("the clearing price") that causes all of the offered shares to be sold. Investors who set their bids at or above the clearing price receive all the shares they subscribed to at the offer price. While Google's IPO was in many ways precedent setting, it remains unclear whether other firms going public in the future will be able, or willing, to use the Dutch auction method to allocate shares in their IPOs.

It is important to recognize that firms can go public without raising any additional capital. For example, the Ford Motor Company was once owned

---

[10] See Jay R. Ritter, "The Long-Run Performance of Initial Public Offerings," *Journal of Finance,* Vol. 46, no. 1 (March 1991), pp. 3–27.

TABLE 5-3 *Initial Public Offerings in 2004*

Issuer	Issue Date	U.S. Proceeds (Billions)	PERCENT CHANGE FROM OFFER	
			First Day Trading	Through 12/31/04
The Biggest IPOs				
Genworth Financial	05/24/04	$2.86	unch.	+38.5%
Assurant	02/04/04	2.02	+12.3%	+38.9
Google	08/18/04	1.92	+18.0	+126.8
Semiconductor Manufacturing Intl.	03/11/04	1.80	−11.3	−38.5
Freescale Semiconductor	07/16/04	1.69	+7.9	+37.1
China Netcom	11/10/04	1.31	+14.1	+22.6
LG Philips	07/15/04	1.06	−6.3	+19.9
Navteq	08/06/04	1.01	+15.0	+110.7
Dex Media	07/21/04	1.01	+2.6	+31.4
Dreamworks Animation	10/27/04	0.93	+38.4	+34.0

Issuer	Issue Date	Offer Price	U.S. Proceeds (Millions)	PERCENT CHANGE FROM OFFER	
				First Day Trading	Through 12/31/04
The Best Performers					
Shanda Interactive Ent	05/12/04	$11.00	$169.0	+8.8%	+286.4%
51Job	09/28/04	14.00	84.5	+51.1	+271.2
Marchex	03/30/04	6.50	26.0	+35.4	+223.1
Volterra Semiconductor	07/28/04	8.00	36.5	+3.1	+177.0
eCOST.com	08/27/04	5.80	20.1	+3.5	+175.0
Cogent	09/23/04	12.00	248.4	+49.8	+175.0
Jed Oil	04/05/04	5.50	10.5	+103.6	+165.5
Syneron Medical	08/05/04	12.00	60.0	−10.4	+155.0
Kinetic Concepts	02/23/04	30.00	621.0	+34.7	+154.3
Kanbay International	07/22/04	13.00	106.9	+16.9	+140.8

Issuer	Issue Date	Offer Price	U.S. Proceeds (Millions)	PERCENT CHANGE FROM OFFER	
				First Day Trading	Through 12/31/04
The Worst Performers					
Xcyte Therapies	03/16/04	$ 8.00	$ 33.6	−8.6%	−65.5%
Staktek Holdings	02/05/04	13.00	145.5	+14.5	−64.3
AlphaSmart	02/06/04	6.00	26.4	+2.0	−50.8
Corgentech	02/12/04	16.00	110.4	+20.3	−48.3
Corcept Therapeutics	04/14/04	12.00	54.0	+1.9	−47.9
Daystar Technologies	02/05/04	5.00	10.6	−1.0	−43.0
Infosonics	06/16/04	6.00	12.0	−2.5	−40.3
Linktone	03/03/04	14.00	86.0	+24.4	−40.0
Semiconductor Manufacturing International	03/11/04	17.50	1,803.0	−11.3	−38.5
Cherokee International	02/19/04	14.50	110.1	+13.8	−33.7

Source: "Initial Public Offerings of Stock Bounce Back in 2004," *The Wall Street Journal*, January 3, 2005, p. R10.

FIGURE 5-2 *Red Hat Inc.'s Stock Price Performance from Its IPO to February 2005*

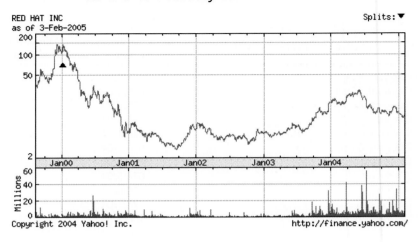

Source: **finance.yahoo.com**.

---

exclusively by the Ford family. When Henry Ford died, he left a substantial part of his stock to the Ford Foundation. When the Foundation later sold some of it to the general public, the Ford Motor Company went public, even though the company itself raised no capital in the transaction.

Differentiate between closely held and publicly owned corporations.

Differentiate between primary and secondary markets.

What is an IPO?

What is a Dutch auction? Why is it used?

5-6 STOCK MARKETS AND RETURNS

Anyone who has ever invested in the stock market knows that there can be, and generally are, large differences between *expected* and *realized* prices and returns. Figure 5-3 shows how total realized portfolio returns have varied from year to year. As logic would suggest (and as we demonstrate in Chapter 8), a stock's expected return as estimated by investors at the margin is always positive, for otherwise investors would not buy the stock. However, as Figure 5-3 shows, in some years actual returns are negative.

5-6a Stock Market Reporting

Up until a couple of years ago, the best source of stock quotations was the business section of a daily newspaper, such as *The Wall Street Journal*. One problem with newspapers, however, is that they report yesterday's prices. Now it is possible to obtain quotes all during the day from a wide variety of Internet sources.[11] One of the best is Yahoo!, and Figure 5-4 shows a detailed quote for GlaxoSmithKline PLC (GSK). As the heading shows, GlaxoSmithKline is traded on the New York Stock Exchange under the symbol GSK. (The NYSE is just one of many world markets on which the stock trades.) The first two rows of information show that GSK last traded at $45.55, and the stock traded thus far during the day from as low as $45.40 and as high as $45.65. (Note that the price is reported in decimals rather than fractions, reflecting a recent change in trading conventions.) The last trade was at 11:05 A.M. ET on February 4, 2005, and its price range during the past 52 weeks was from $38.80 to $47.59.

The next three lines show that GSK opened trading on February 4th at $45.42, that it closed on February 3rd at $44.65, and that its price rose by $0.90 (or a 2.02 percent increase) from the previous close to the current price. So far during the day, 401,700 shares had traded hands. GlaxoSmithKline's average daily trading volume (based on the past three months) was 1,349,318 shares, so trading was relatively light that day. The total value of all of GlaxoSmithKline's stock, called its market cap, was $130.09 billion.

The last three lines report other market information for GSK. If it were trading on Nasdaq rather than a listed exchange, the most recent bid and ask quotes from dealers would have been shown. However, because it trades on the NYSE, these data are not available. GSK's P/E ratio (price per share divided by the most recent 12 months' earnings) is 17.16, and its earnings per share for the most recent 12 months was $2.66. (Note that ttm stands for "trailing 12 months"—in other words, the most recent 12 months.) The mean of the analysts' one-year target price for GSK is $49.67. GSK's dividend is $1.46 per share, so the quarterly dividend is $0.365 per share, and the dividend yield, which is the annual dividend divided by the price, is 3.24 percent.

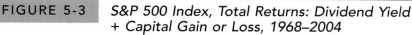

FIGURE 5-3 *S&P 500 Index, Total Returns: Dividend Yield + Capital Gain or Loss, 1968–2004*

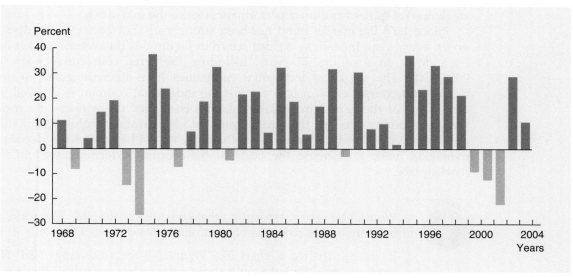

Source: Data taken from various issues of *The Wall Street Journal*, "Investment Scoreboard" section.

---

[11] Most free sources provide quotes that are delayed by 15 minutes. Real time quotes can be obtained for a fee.

| FIGURE 5-4 | *Stock Quote for GlaxoSmithKline, February 4, 2005* |

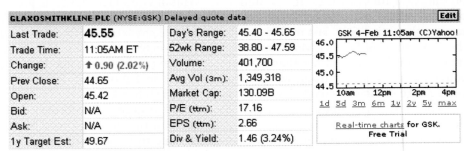

Source: **finance.yahoo.com**.

In Figure 5.4, the chart to the right plots the stock price during the day; however, the links below the chart allow you to pick different time intervals for plotting data. As you can see, Yahoo! provides a great deal of information in its detailed quote, and even more detail is available on the screen page below the basic quote information.

5-6b Stock Market Returns

In Chapters 8 and 9 we will discuss in detail how stock returns are calculated, the connection between stock market risk and returns, and the techniques that analysts use to value stocks. However, it is useful at this point for you to have a rough idea how stocks have performed in recent years. Figure 5-3 shows how the returns on large U.S. stocks have varied over the past years, and the box entitled "Measuring the Market" provides some information on the major U.S. stock market indices and their performances since the mid-1990s.

Since 1968 the market trend has been strongly up, but by no means does it go up every year. Indeed, as we can see from Figure 5-3, the overall market has been down in 9 of the 37 years, including the three consecutive years of 2000–2002. The stocks of individual companies have likewise gone up and down.[12] Of course, even in bad years some individual companies do well, so "the name of the game" in security analysis is to pick the winners. Financial managers attempt to put their companies into the winners' column, but they don't always succeed. In subsequent chapters, we will examine the decisions managers make to increase the odds of their firms performing well in the marketplace.

Would you expect a portfolio that consisted of the S&P 500 stocks to be more or less risky than a portfolio of Nasdaq stocks?

If we constructed a chart like Figure 5-3 for an average S&P 500 stock, do you think it would show more or less volatility? Explain.

---

[12] If we constructed a graph like Figure 5-3 for individual stocks rather than for the index, far greater variability would be shown. Also, if we constructed a graph like Figure 5-3 for bonds, it would have similar ups and downs, but the bars would be smaller, indicating that gains and losses on bonds are generally smaller than those on stocks. Above-average bond returns occur in years when interest rates decline, losses occur when interest rates rise sharply, but interest payments tend to stabilize bonds' total returns. We will discuss bonds in detail in Chapter 7.

5-7 STOCK MARKET EFFICIENCY

Figure 1-1 (presented back in Chapter 1) suggests that a stock's price is affected by its intrinsic value, which is determined by the true level and riskiness of the cash flows it is likely to provide, and investors' perceptions about the stock's intrinsic value. In a well-functioning market, investors' perceptions should be closely related to the stock's intrinsic value, in which case the stock price would be a reasonably accurate reflection of its true value.

A body of theory called the **efficient markets hypothesis (EMH)** holds (1) that stocks are always in equilibrium and (2) that it is impossible for an investor to consistently "beat the market." Essentially, those who believe in the EMH note that there are 100,000 or so full-time, highly trained, professional analysts and traders operating in the market, while there are fewer than 3,000 major stocks. Therefore, if each analyst followed 30 stocks (which is about right, as analysts tend to specialize in the stocks in a specific industry), there would on average be 1,000 analysts following each stock. Further, these analysts work for organizations such as Goldman Sachs, Merrill Lynch, Citigroup, Prudential, and the like, which have billions of dollars that can be used to take advantage of bargains. In addition, as a result of SEC disclosure requirements and electronic information networks, as new information about a stock becomes available, these 1,000 analysts generally receive and evaluate it at about the same time. Therefore, the price of a stock will adjust almost immediately to any new development. That makes it very difficult for anyone to consistently pick stocks that will beat the market.

Efficient Markets Hypothesis (EMH)
The hypothesis that securities are typically in equilibrium—that they are fairly priced in the sense that the price reflects all publicly available information on each security.

5-7a Levels of Market Efficiency

If markets are truly efficient, then stock prices will rapidly adjust to all relevant information as it becomes available. This raises an important question: What types of information are available to investors and, therefore, incorporated into stock prices? Financial theorists have discussed three forms, or levels, of market efficiency.

Weak-Form Efficiency

The *weak form* of the EMH states that all information contained in past stock price movements is fully reflected in current market prices. If this were true, then information about recent trends in stock prices would be of no use in selecting stocks—the fact that a stock has risen for the past three days, for example, would give us no useful clues as to what it will do today or tomorrow. People who believe that weak-form efficiency exists also believe that "tape watchers" and "chartists" are wasting their time.[13] For example, after studying the past history of the stock market, a chartist might "discover" the following pattern: If a stock falls three consecutive days, its price typically rises 10 percent the following day. The technician would then conclude that investors could make money by purchasing a stock whose price has fallen for three consecutive days.

But if this pattern truly existed, wouldn't other investors also discover it, and then why would anyone be willing to sell a stock after it had fallen three consecutive days if he or she knows the stock's price would likely increase by 10 percent the next day? In other words, if a stock were selling at $40 per share after falling three consecutive days, why would investors sell the stock at $40 if they expect it to rise to $44 per share the next day? Those who believe in weak-form efficiency argue that if the stock were really likely to rise to $44 per share

---

[13] Tape watchers are people who watch the NYSE tape, while chartists plot past patterns of stock price movements. Both are called "technicians," and both believe that they can tell if something is happening to the stock that will cause its price to move up or down in the near future.

Measuring the Market

Stock indexes are designed to show the performance of the stock market. The problem is that there are many stock indexes, and it is difficult to determine which index best reflects market actions. Some are designed to represent the whole equity market, some to track the returns of certain industry sectors, and others to track the returns of small-cap, mid-cap, or large-cap stocks. We discuss below three of the leading indexes.

Dow Jones Industrial Average

Unveiled in 1896 by Charles H. Dow, the Dow Jones Industrial Average (DJIA) provided a benchmark for comparing individual stocks with the overall market, for ascertaining the trend in stock prices over time, and for comparing the market with other economic indicators. The industrial average began with just 10 stocks, was expanded in 1916 to 20 stocks, and then to 30 in 1928. Also in 1928, *The Wall Street Journal* editors began adjusting the index for stock splits, and making substitutions. Today, the DJIA still includes 30 companies. They represent almost a fifth of the market value of all U.S. stocks, and all are both leading companies in their industries and widely held by individual and institutional investors. Visit **http://www.dowjones.com** to get more information about the DJIA. You can find out how it is calculated, the current divisor, the companies that make up the DJIA, more history about the DJIA, and other interesting facts. In addition, there is a DJIA time line annotated with historical events.

S&P 500 Index

Created in 1926, the S&P 500 Index is widely regarded as the standard for measuring large-cap U.S. stock market performance. The stocks in the S&P 500 are selected by the Standard & Poor's Index Committee as being the leading companies in the leading industries, and for accurately reflecting the U.S. stock market. It is value weighted, so the largest companies (in terms of value) have the greatest influence. The S&P 500 Index is used for benchmarking by 97 percent of all U.S. money managers and pension plan sponsors, and approximately $700 billion is managed so as to obtain the same performance as this index (that is, in indexed funds).

Nasdaq Composite Index

The Nasdaq Composite Index measures the performance of all common stocks listed on the Nasdaq stock market. Currently, it includes more than 5,000 companies, and because many of the technology-sector companies are traded on the computer-based Nasdaq exchange, this index is generally regarded as an economic indicator of the high-tech industry. Microsoft, Intel, and Cisco Systems are the three largest Nasdaq companies, and they comprise a high percentage of the index's value-weighted market capitalization. For this reason, substantial movements in the same direction by these three companies can move the entire index.

tomorrow, its price would actually rise to somewhere near $44 per share immediately, thereby eliminating the trading opportunity. Consequently, weak-form efficiency implies that any information that comes from an examination of past stock prices cannot be used to make money by predicting future stock prices.

Semistrong-Form Efficiency

The *semistrong form* of the EMH states that current market prices reflect all *publicly available* information. Therefore, if semistrong-form efficiency exists, it would do no good to pore over annual reports or yesterday's *Wall Street Journal* looking at sales and earnings trends and various types of ratios based on historical data because market prices would have adjusted to any good or bad news contained in such

Recent Performance

The accompanying figure plots the value that an investor would now have if he or she had invested $1.00 in each of the three indexes on January 1, 1995. The returns on the three indexes are compared with an investment strategy that only invests in T-bills. For the returns on T-bills, the one-year Treasury constant maturity rate is used. Over the past 10 years, each of these indexes performed quite well through 1999. However, for a couple years each index stumbled before beginning to rebound again in 2003. During the last 10 years the average annualized returns of these indexes ranged from 9.8 percent for the S&P 500 to 10.5 percent for the Nasdaq Composite Index. The Nasdaq experienced a huge bubble in 1999, reflecting overly optimistic valuations of technology companies. However, in 2000 the bubble burst and technology stock valuations spiraled downward, causing the Nasdaq Index to revert back to a level comparable to the S&P 500 and Dow Jones Industrial Average Index.

Growth of a $1 Investment Made on January 1, 1995

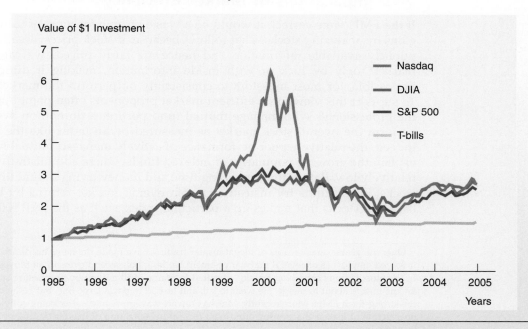

reports back when the news first came out over the Internet. With semistrong-form efficiency, investors should not expect to earn above-average returns except with good luck or information that is not publicly available.[14] However, insiders (for example, CEOs and CFOs) who have information that is not publicly available are able to earn above-average returns even under semistrong-form efficiency.

Another implication of semistrong-form efficiency is that whenever information is released to the public, stock prices will respond only if the information is different from what had been expected. If, for example, a company announces a

---

[14] Strictly speaking, these returns should be adjusted for risk. We discuss the relationship between risk and return in Chapter 8.

30 percent increase in earnings, and if that increase is about what analysts had been expecting, the announcement should have little or no effect on the company's stock price. On the other hand, the stock price would probably fall if analysts had expected earnings to increase by 50 percent, but it probably would rise if they had expected a 10 percent increase.

Strong-Form Efficiency

The *strong form* of the EMH states that current market prices reflect all pertinent information, whether publicly available or privately held. If this form holds, even insiders would find it impossible to earn abnormally high returns in the stock market.[15]

Many empirical studies have been conducted to test for the three forms of market efficiency. Most of these studies suggest that the stock market is indeed highly efficient in the weak form, reasonably efficient in the semistrong form (at least for the larger and more widely followed stocks), but not true for the strong form because abnormally large profits are often earned by those with inside information.

5-7b Implications of Market Efficiency

If the EMH were correct, it would be a waste of time for most of us to seek bargains by analyzing stocks. That follows because, if stock prices already reflect all publicly available information and hence are fairly priced, we can "beat the market" only by luck or with inside information, making it difficult, if not impossible, for most investors to consistently outperform the market averages. To support this viewpoint, efficient market proponents often point out that even the professionals who manage mutual fund portfolios do not, on average, outperform the overall stock market as measured by an index like the S&P 500.[16] Indeed, the relatively poor performance of actively managed mutual funds helps explain the growing popularity of indexed funds, where administrative costs are relatively low. Rather than spending time and money trying to find undervalued stocks, index funds try instead to match overall market returns by buying the basket of stocks that makes up a particular index, such as the S&P 500.[17]

---

[15] Over the years, several cases of illegal insider trading have made the news headlines. These cases involved employees of several major investment banking houses and even an employee of the SEC. In the most famous case, Ivan Boesky admitted to making $50 million by purchasing stocks of firms he knew were about to merge. He went to jail, and he had to pay a large fine, but he helped disprove the strong-form EMH. More recently, Martha Stewart was imprisoned after being convicted on obstruction of justice charges surrounding a federal investigation of insider trading of ImClone Systems Inc. shares.

[16] For a discussion of the recent performance of actively managed funds, see Jonathan Clements, "Resisting the Lure of Managed Funds," *The Wall Street Journal*, February 27, 2001, p. C1.

[17] We should also note that some Wall Street pros have consistently beaten the market over many years, which is inconsistent with the EMH. An interesting article in the April 3, 1995, issue of *Fortune* (Terence P. Paré, "Yes, You Can Beat the Market") argued strongly against the EMH. Paré suggested that each stock has a fundamental value, but when good or bad news about it is announced, most investors fail to interpret this news correctly. As a result, stocks are generally priced above or below their long-term values.

Think of Figure 1-1, which was illustrated in Chapter 1, with stock price on the vertical axis and years on the horizontal axis. A stock's fundamental value might be moving up steadily over time as it retains and reinvests earnings. However, its actual price might fluctuate about the intrinsic value line, overreacting to good or bad news and indicating departures from equilibrium. Successful value investors, according to Paré, use fundamental analysis to identify stocks' intrinsic values, and then they buy stocks that are undervalued and sell those that are overvalued.

Paré's argument implies that stocks are at times systematically out of equilibrium and that investors can act on this knowledge to beat the market. That position may turn out to be correct, but it may also be that the superior performance Paré noted simply demonstrates that some people are better at obtaining and interpreting information than others, or have been lucky in the past.

It is important to understand that market efficiency does not imply that all stocks are always priced correctly. With hindsight, it is apparent that at any point in time the situation shown in Figure 1-1 back in Chapter 1 tends to hold true, with some stocks overvalued and others undervalued. However, as the efficient markets hypothesis implies, it is hard to identify ahead of time the stocks in each category. To beat the market, you must have above-average information, above-average analytical skills, or above-average luck.

Finally, it is important to understand that even if markets are efficient and all stocks are fairly priced, an investor should still be careful when selecting stocks for his or her portfolio. To earn the greatest expected return with the least amount of risk, the portfolio should be diversified, with a mix of stocks from various industries. We will discuss diversification in greater detail in Chapter 8.

5-7c Is the Stock Market Efficient?

During the past 25 years, many empirical studies have been conducted to test the validity of the three forms of market efficiency. Until 10 years ago, most of these studies suggested that the stock market was highly efficient in the weak form and reasonably efficient in the semistrong form, at least for the larger and more widely followed stocks. However, the evidence also suggested that the strong form EMH did not hold, because those who possessed inside information could and did (illegally) make abnormal profits.

More recently, the empirical support for the EMH has been somewhat diminished. As we indicate in the **behavioral finance** box, skeptics point to the recent stock market bubble and suggest that at the height of the boom the prices of the stocks of many companies, particularly in the technology sector, vastly exceeded their intrinsic values. These skeptics suggest that investors are not simply machines that rationally process all available information—rather, a variety of psychological and perhaps irrational factors also come into play. Indeed, researchers have begun to incorporate elements of cognitive psychology in an effort to better understand how individuals and entire markets respond to different circumstances.[18]

Keep in mind that the EMH does not assume that all investors are rational. Rather, it assumes that whenever stock prices deviate from their intrinsic values due to the availability of new information, investors will quickly take advantage of these mispricings by buying undervalued stocks and selling overvalued stocks. Thus, investors' actions work to drive prices to their equilibrium level. Critics of the EMH stress, however, that the stock market is inherently risky and that rational investors trading in an irrational market can lose a lot of money even if they are ultimately proven to be correct. For example, a "rational" investor in mid-1999 might have concluded that the Nasdaq was overvalued when it was trading at 3,000. If that investor had acted on that assumption, he or she would have lost a lot of money the following year when the Nasdaq soared to over 5,000 as "irrational exuberance" pushed the prices of already overvalued stocks to even higher levels. Ultimately, if our "rational investor" had the courage and patience to hold on, he or she would have been vindicated, because the Nasdaq subsequently fell to about 1,300.

Behavioral Finance *Incorporates elements of cognitive psychology into finance in an effort to better understand how individuals and entire markets respond to different circumstances.*

---

[18] Three noteworthy sources for students interested in behavioral finance are Richard H. Thaler, Editor, *Advances in Behavioral Finance* (New York: Russell Sage Foundation, 1993); Andrei Shleifer, *Inefficient Markets: An Introduction to Behavioral Finance* (New York: Oxford University Press, 2000); and Nicholas Barberis and Richard Thaler, "A Survey of Behavioral Finance," Chapter 18, *Handbook of the Economics of Finance*, edited by George Constantinides, Milt Harris, and René Stulz, part of the *Handbooks in Economics Series* (New York: Elsevier/North-Holland, 2003). Students interested in learning more about the efficient markets hypothesis should consult Burton G. Malkiel, *A Random Walk Down Wall Street* (New York: W.W. Norton & Company, 1999).

A Closer Look at Behavioral Finance Theory

The efficient markets hypothesis (EMH) remains one of the cornerstones of modern finance theory. It implies that, on average, assets trade at prices equal to their intrinsic values. As we note in the text, the logic behind the EMH is straightforward. If a stock's price is "too low," rational traders will quickly take advantage of this opportunity and will buy the stock. Their actions will quickly push prices back to their equilibrium level. Likewise, if prices are "too high," rational traders will sell the stock, pushing the price down to its equilibrium level. Proponents of the EMH argue that prices cannot be systematically wrong unless you believe that market participants are unable or unwilling to take advantage of profitable trading opportunities.

While the logic behind the EMH is compelling, many events in the real world seem to be inconsistent with the EMH. This has spurred a growing field that is called *behavioral finance theory*. Rather than assuming that investors are rational, behavioral finance theorists borrow insights from psychology to better understand how irrational behavior can be sustained over time. Pioneers in this field include psychologists Daniel Kahneman and Amos Tversky and Richard Thaler, who is a professor of finance at the University of Chicago. Their work has encouraged a growing number of scholars to work in this promising area of research.

Professor Thaler and his colleague, Nicholas Barberis, have summarized much of this research in a recent article, which is cited below. They argue that behavioral finance theory's criticism of the EMH rests on two important building blocks. First, it is often difficult or risky for traders to take advantage of mispriced assets. For example, even if you know that a stock's price is too low because investors have overreacted to recent bad news, a trader with limited capital may be reluctant to buy the stock for fear that the same forces that pushed the price down may work to keep it artificially low for a long period of time. On the other side, during the recent stock market bubble, many traders who believed (correctly!) that stock prices were too high lost a lot of money selling stocks in the early stages of the bubble because stock prices went even higher before they eventually collapsed.

While the first building block explains why mispricings may persist, the second tries to understand how mispricings can occur in the first place. This component is where the insights from psychology come into play. For example, Kahneman and Tversky suggested that individuals view potential losses and potential gains very differently. If you ask an average person whether he or she would rather have $500 with certainty or flip a fair coin and receive $1,000 if a head comes up and nothing if it comes out tails, most would prefer the certain $500, which suggests an aversion to risk. However, if you ask the same person whether he or she would rather pay $500 with certainty or flip a coin and pay $1,000 if it's heads and nothing if it's tails, most indicate that they would prefer to flip the coin. Other studies suggest that people's willingness to take a gamble depends on recent performance. Gamblers who are ahead tend to take on more risks, whereas those who are behind tend to become more conservative.

These experiments suggest that investors and managers behave differently in down markets than they do in up markets, which might explain why those who made money early in the stock market bubble continued to keep investing in these stocks, even as their prices went higher. Other evidence suggests that individuals tend to overestimate their true abilities. For example, a large majority (upward of 90 percent in some studies) of us believe that we have above-average driving ability or above-average ability to get along with others. Barberis and Thaler point out that:

> Overconfidence may in part stem from two other biases, self-attribution bias and hindsight bias. Self-attribution bias refers to people's tendency to ascribe any success they have in some activity to their own talents, while blaming failure on bad luck, rather than on their ineptitude. Doing this repeatedly will lead people to the pleasing but erroneous conclusion that they are very talented. For example, investors might become overconfident after several quarters of investing success [Gervais and Odean (2001)]. Hindsight bias is the tendency of people to believe, after an event has occurred, that they predicted it before it happened. If people think they predicted the past better than they actually did, they may also believe that they can predict the future better than they actually can.

Recent research by Ulrike Malmendier of the Stanford Graduate School of Business and Geoffrey Tate of the Wharton School suggests that overconfidence leads managers to overestimate their ability and the quality of their projects. This result may explain why so many corporate projects fail to live up to their stated expectations.

Sources: Nicholas Barberis and Richard Thaler, "A Survey of Behavioral Finance," Chapter 18, *Handbook of the Economics of Finance*, edited by George Constantinides, Milt Harris, and René Stulz, part of the *Handbooks in Economics Series* (New York: Elsevier/North-Holland, 2003); and Ulrike Malmendier and Geoffrey Tate, "CEO Overconfidence and Corporate Investment," Stanford Graduate School of Business Research Paper #1799, June 2004.

The events of recent years, and the new ideas developed by researchers in behavioral finance, suggest that the stock market is not always efficient. Still, the logic behind the EMH is compelling, and most researchers believe that markets are generally efficient in the long run.

What is the efficient markets hypothesis (EMH)?

What are the differences among the three forms of the EMH: (1) weak form, (2) semistrong form, and (3) strong form?

What are the implications of the EMH for financial decisions?

What is behavioral finance? What do the new ideas in this area tell us about the stock market?

Tying It All Together

In this chapter we provided a brief overview of how capital is allocated and the financial markets, instruments, and institutions used in the allocation process. We discussed physical location exchanges and electronic markets for common stocks, stock price reporting, and stock indexes. We demonstrated that security prices are volatile—investors expect to make money, and over time they generally do, but losses can be large in any given year. Finally, we discussed the efficiency of the stock market and developments in behavioral finance. After reading this chapter, you should have a general understanding of the financial environment in which businesses and individuals operate, realize that actual returns are often different from expected returns, and be able to read stock market quotations from either business newspapers or various Internet sites. You should also recognize that the theory of financial markets is a "work in progress," and countless work remains to be done.

SELF-TEST QUESTIONS AND PROBLEMS

ST-1   **Key terms** Define each of the following terms:
   a.   Spot markets; futures markets
   b.   Money markets; capital markets
   c.   Primary markets; secondary markets
   d.   Private markets; public markets
   e.   Derivatives
   f.   Investment banking house; commercial banks; financial services corporations
   g.   Mutual funds; money market funds
   h.   Physical location exchanges; over-the-counter market (OTC); dealer market
   i.   Closely held corporation; publicly owned corporation
   j.   Going public; initial public offering (IPO) market
   k.   Efficient markets hypothesis (EMH)
   l.   Behavioral finance

QUESTIONS

5-1 How does a cost-efficient capital market help to reduce the prices of goods and services?

5-2 Describe the different ways in which capital can be transferred from suppliers of capital to those who are demanding capital.

5-3 Is an initial public offering an example of a primary or a secondary market transaction?

5-4 Indicate whether the following instruments are examples of money market or capital market securities.
  a. U.S. Treasury bills
  b. Long-term corporate bonds
  c. Common stocks
  d. Preferred stocks
  e. Dealer commercial paper

5-5 What would happen to the U.S. standard of living if people lost faith in the safety of our financial institutions? Why?

5-6 What types of changes have financial markets experienced during the last two decades? Have they been perceived as positive or negative changes? Explain.

5-7 Differentiate between dealer markets and stock markets that have a physical location.

5-8 Identify and briefly compare the two leading stock exchanges in the United States today.

5-9 Describe the three different forms of market efficiency.

5-10 Investors expect a company to announce a 10 percent increase in earnings, but instead the company announces a 1 percent increase. If the market is semistrong-form efficient, which of the following would you expect to happen?
  a. The stock's price increases slightly because the company had a slight increase in earnings.
  b. The stock's price falls because the earnings increase was less than expected.
  c. The stock's price stays the same because earnings announcements have no effect if the market is semistrong-form efficient.

5-11 Explain whether the following statements are true or false.
  a. Derivative transactions are designed to increase risk and are used almost exclusively by speculators who are looking to capture high returns.
  b. Hedge funds generally charge higher fees than mutual funds.
  c. Hedge funds have traditionally been highly regulated.
  d. The New York Stock Exchange is an example of a stock exchange that has a physical location.
  e. A larger bid-ask spread means that the dealer will realize a lower profit.
  f. The efficient market hypothesis assumes that all investors are rational.

Integrated Case

Smyth Barry & Company, Part I

5-1 **Financial markets and institutions** Assume that you recently graduated with a degree in finance and have just reported to work as an investment advisor at the brokerage firm of Smyth Barry & Co. Your first assignment is to explain the nature of the U.S. financial markets to Michelle Varga, a professional tennis player who has just come to the United States from Mexico. Varga is a highly ranked tennis player who expects to invest substantial amounts of money through Smyth Barry. She is also very bright, and, therefore, she would like to understand in general terms what will happen to her money. Your boss has developed the following set of questions that you must ask and answer to explain the U.S. financial system to Varga.

a.   Describe the three primary ways in which capital is transferred between savers and borrowers.
b.   What is a market? Differentiate between the following types of markets: physical asset versus financial markets, spot versus futures markets, money versus capital markets, primary versus secondary markets, and public versus private markets.
c.   Why are financial markets essential for a healthy economy and economic growth?
d.   What are derivatives? How can derivatives be used to reduce risk? Can derivatives be used to increase risk?
e.   Briefly describe each of the following financial institutions: commercial banks, investment banks, mutual funds, and hedge funds.
f.   What are the two leading stock markets? Describe the two basic types of stock markets.
g.   If Apple Computer decided to issue additional common stock, and Varga puchased 100 shares of this stock from Smyth Barry, the underwriter, would this transaction be a primary or a secondary market transaction? Would it make a difference if Varga purchased previously outstanding Apple stock in the dealer market? Explain.
h.   What is an initial public offering (IPO)?
i.   What is the efficient markets hypothesis (EMH), what are its three forms, and what are its implications?
j.   After the consultation with Michelle she asked you a few final questions:
   (1) While in the waiting room of your office, she overheard an analyst on a financial TV network say that a particular medical research company just received FDA approval for one of its products. On the basis of this "hot" information, Michelle wants to buy a lot of that company's stock. Assuming the stock market is semistrong-form efficient, what advice would you give her?
   (2) She has read a number of newspaper articles about a huge IPO being carried out by a leading technology company. She wants to get as many shares in the IPO as possible, and would even be willing to buy the shares in the open market right after the issue. What advice do you have for her?

cyberproblem

Please go to the ThomsonNOW Web site to access the Cyberproblems.

FINANCIAL ASSETS

PART **3**

CHAPTER

6

INTEREST RATES

Low Interest Rates Encourage Investment and Stimulate Consumer Spending

The U.S. economy has performed well since the early 1990s. Economic growth has been positive, unemployment fairly low, and inflation under control. One reason for the economy's steady performance has been the low level of interest rates over that period, especially the last few years. Since early 2001, the 10-year Treasury bond rate has generally been at or below 5 percent, a level not seen since the 1960s.

Low interest rates reduced the cost of capital for businesses, which has encouraged corporate investment, and they also stimulated consumer spending and the housing market. In the 1980s, 30-year fixed-rate mortgages cost 8 percent or more. At 8 percent, a homeowner who could afford a $1,000 monthly payment for 30 years could borrow $136,283. More recently, with mortgage rates at about 5.5 percent, the same homebuyer could handle a $176,122 loan and thus a lot more house. Or, if this individual borrowed the same $136,283, the monthly payment would decline from $1,000 to $773.80, leaving more funds available for other purchases. The drop in interest rates also led to a surge in mortgage refinancings, where high-rate loans are replaced with lower-rate and possibly larger loans, freeing up money for whatever the borrower chooses to spend it on.

The drop in interest rates was due to a number of factors—low inflation, foreign investors' purchases of U.S. securities (which drove their rates down), and effective management of the economy by the Federal Reserve and other government policy makers. While there are reasons for continued optimism, there are also reasons to think that low interest rates may not persist for much longer. Higher oil prices and a weakening dollar could lead to higher inflation, which, in turn, would push up interest rates. Likewise, the growing federal budget deficit and the weakening dollar could cause foreigners to sell U.S. bonds, which would also put upward pressure on rates. Because corporate treasurers—and individuals—are greatly affected by interest rates, this chapter takes a closer look at the major factors that determine rates in the market.

Putting Things In Perspective

Companies raise capital in two main forms: debt and equity. In a free economy, capital, like other items, is allocated through a market system, where funds are transferred and prices are established. The interest rate is the price lenders receive and borrowers pay for debt capital. Similarly, equity investors expect to receive dividends and capital gains, the sum of which represents the cost of equity. We will take up the cost of equity in later chapters, but our focus in this chapter is on the cost of debt. We begin by examining the factors that affect the supply of and demand for all investment capital, which, in turn, affects the overall cost of money. We will see that there is no one single interest rate—interest rates on different loans vary depending on the risk of the borrower, the use of the funds borrowed, the type of collateral used to back the loan, and the length of time the money is needed. In this chapter we concentrate mainly on how these various factors affect the cost of debt for individuals, but in later chapters we delve into the firm's cost of debt and its role in investment decisions. As you will see in Chapter 7, the cost of debt is a key determinant of bond prices, and it is also an important component of the cost of corporate capital, which we take up in Chapter 10.

6-1 THE COST OF MONEY

The four most fundamental factors affecting the cost of money are (1) **production opportunities,** (2) **time preferences for consumption,** (3) **risk,** and (4) **inflation.** To see how these factors operate, visualize an isolated island community where the people live on fish. They have a stock of fishing gear that permits them to survive reasonably well, but they would like to have more fish. Now suppose Mr. Crusoe had a bright idea for a new type of fishnet that would enable him to double his daily catch. However, it would take a year to perfect the design, build the net, and learn to use it efficiently, and Mr. Crusoe would probably starve before he could put his new net into operation. Therefore, he might suggest to Ms. Robinson, Mr. Friday, and several others that if they would give him one fish each day for a year, he would return two fish a day during all of the next year. If someone accepted the offer, then the fish that Ms. Robinson or one of the others gave to Mr. Crusoe would constitute *savings;* these savings would be *invested* in the fishnet; and the extra fish the net produced would constitute a *return on the investment.*

Obviously, the more productive Mr. Crusoe thought the new fishnet would be, the more he could afford to offer potential investors for their savings. In this example, we assume that Mr. Crusoe thought he would be able to pay, and thus he offered, a 100 percent rate of return—he offered to give back two fish for every one he received. He might have tried to attract savings for less—for example, he might have offered only 1.5 fish per day next year for every one he received this year, which would represent a 50 percent rate of return to Ms. Robinson and the other potential savers.

Production Opportunities
The investment opportunities in productive (cash-generating) assets.

Time Preferences for Consumption
The preferences of consumers for current consumption as opposed to saving for future consumption.

Risk
In a financial market context, the chance that an investment will provide a low or negative return.

Inflation
The amount by which prices increase over time.

How attractive Mr. Crusoe's offer appeared to a potential saver would depend in large part on the saver's *time preference for consumption*. For example, Ms. Robinson might be thinking of retirement, and she might be willing to trade fish today for fish in the future on a one-for-one basis. On the other hand, Mr. Friday might have a wife and several young children and need his current fish, so he might be unwilling to "lend" a fish today for anything less than three fish next year. Mr. Friday would be said to have a high time preference for current consumption and Ms. Robinson a low time preference. Note also that if the entire population were living right at the subsistence level, time preferences for current consumption would necessarily be high, aggregate savings would be low, interest rates would be high, and capital formation would be difficult.

The *risk* inherent in the fishnet project, and thus in Mr. Crusoe's ability to repay the loan, also affects the return investors require: the higher the perceived risk, the higher the required rate of return. Also, in a more complex society, there are many businesses like Mr. Crusoe's, many goods other than fish, and many savers like Ms. Robinson and Mr. Friday. Therefore, people use money as a medium of exchange rather than barter with fish. When money is used, its value in the future, which is affected by *inflation*, comes into play: the higher the expected rate of inflation, the larger the required dollar return. We discuss this point in detail later in the chapter.

Thus, we see that the interest rate paid to savers depends (1) on the rate of return producers expect to earn on invested capital, (2) on savers' time preferences for current versus future consumption, (3) on the riskiness of the loan, and (4) on the expected future rate of inflation. Producers' expected returns on their business investments set an upper limit to how much they can pay for savings, while consumers' time preferences for consumption establish how much consumption they are willing to defer, hence how much they will save at different interest rates.[1] Higher risk and higher inflation also lead to higher interest rates.

What is the price paid to borrow debt capital called?

What are the two items whose sum is the cost of equity?

What four fundamental factors affect the cost of money?

6-2 INTEREST RATE LEVELS

Borrowers bid for the available supply of debt capital using interest rates: The firms with the most profitable investment opportunities are willing and able to pay the most for capital, so they tend to attract it away from inefficient firms and firms whose products are not in demand. Of course, our economy is not completely free in the sense of being influenced only by market forces. For example, the federal government has agencies that help designated individuals or groups obtain credit on favorable terms. Among those eligible for this kind of assistance are small businesses, certain minorities, and firms willing to build plants in areas with high unemployment. Still, most capital in the United States is allocated through the price system, where interest is the price.

---

[1] The term "producers" is really too narrow. A better word might be "borrowers," which would include corporations, home purchasers, people borrowing to go to college, or even people borrowing to buy autos or to pay for vacations. Also, the wealth of a society and its demographics influence its people's ability to save and thus their time preferences for current versus future consumption.

| FIGURE 6-1 | *Interest Rates as a Function of Supply and Demand for Funds* |

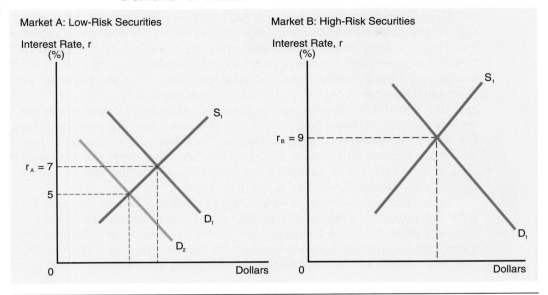

Figure 6-1 shows how supply and demand interact to determine interest rates in two capital markets. Markets A and B represent two of the many capital markets in existence. The going interest rate, designated as r, is initially 7 percent for the low-risk securities in Market A. Borrowers whose credit is strong enough to participate in this market can obtain funds at a cost of 7 percent, and investors who want to put their money to work without much risk can obtain a 7 percent return. Riskier borrowers must obtain higher-cost funds in Market B, where investors who are more willing to take risks expect to earn a 9 percent return but also realize that they might actually receive much less.

If the demand for funds declines, as it typically does during business recessions, the demand curves will shift to the left, as shown in curve D_2 in Market A. The market-clearing, or equilibrium, interest rate in this example declines to 5 percent. Similarly, you should be able to visualize what would happen if the Federal Reserve tightened credit: The supply curve, S_1, would shift to the left, and this would raise interest rates and lower the amount of borrowing in the economy.

Capital markets are interdependent. For example, if Markets A and B were in equilibrium before the demand shift to D_2 in Market A, then investors were willing to accept the higher risk in Market B in exchange for a *risk premium* of $9\% - 7\% = 2\%$. After the shift to D_2, the risk premium would initially increase to $9\% - 5\% = 4\%$. Immediately, though, this much larger premium would induce some of the lenders in Market A to shift to Market B, which would, in turn, cause the supply curve in Market A to shift to the left (or up) and that in Market B to shift to the right. The transfer of capital between markets would raise the interest rate in Market A and lower it in Market B, thus bringing the risk premium back closer to the original 2 percent.

There are many capital markets in the United States. U.S. firms also invest and raise capital throughout the world, and foreigners both borrow and lend in the United States. There are markets for home loans; farm loans; business loans; federal, state, and local government loans; and consumer loans. Within each category, there are regional markets as well as different types of submarkets. For example, in real estate there are separate markets for first and second mortgages and for loans on single-family homes, apartments, office buildings, shopping centers, vacant land, and so on. Within the business sector there are dozens of types of debt securities, and there are also several different markets for common stocks.

There is a price for each type of capital, and these prices change over time as supply and demand conditions change. Figure 6-2 shows how long- and short-term interest rates to business borrowers have varied since the early 1970s. Notice that short-term interest rates are especially volatile, rising rapidly during booms and falling equally rapidly during recessions. (The shaded areas of the chart indicate recessions.) When the economy is expanding, firms need capital, and this demand for capital pushes up rates. Also, inflationary pressures are strongest during business booms, and that also exerts upward pressure on rates. Conditions are reversed during recessions. Slack business reduces the demand for credit, the rate of inflation falls, and interest rates drop. Furthermore, the Federal Reserve tends to increase the supply of funds during recessions to help stimulate the economy, and that also lowers rates.

These tendencies do not hold exactly, as demonstrated in the period after 1984. Oil prices fell dramatically in 1985 and 1986, reducing inflationary pressures on other prices and easing fears of serious long-term inflation. Earlier, these fears had pushed interest rates to record levels. The economy from 1984 to 1987 was strong, but the declining fears of inflation more than offset the normal

---

FIGURE 6-2 *Long- and Short-Term Interest Rates, 1971–2005*

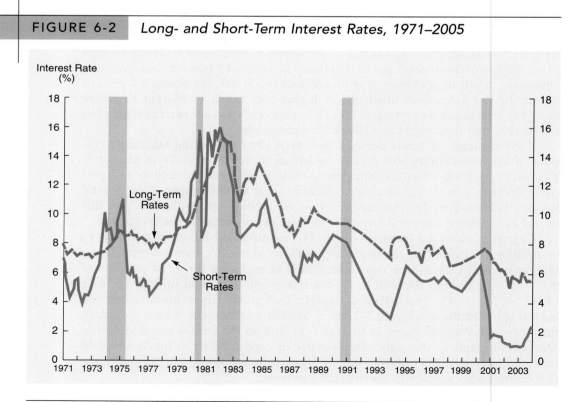

Notes:

a. The shaded areas designate business recessions.

b. Short-term rates are measured by 3- to 6-month loans to very large, strong corporations, and long-term rates are measured by AAA corporate bonds.

Source: St. Louis Federal Reserve Web site, FRED database, **http://research.stlouisfed.org/fred2**.

FIGURE 6-3	*Relationship between Annual Inflation Rates and Long-Term Interest Rates, 1971–2005*

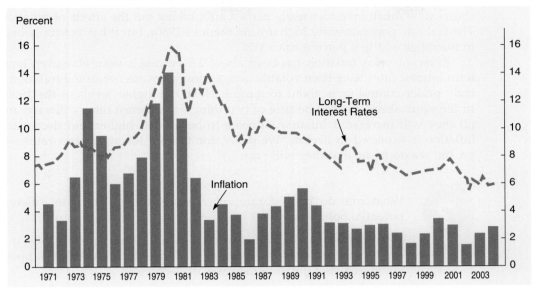

Notes:
a. Interest rates are those on AAA long-term corporate bonds.
b. Inflation is measured as the annual rate of change in the Consumer Price Index (CPI).
Source: St. Louis Federal Reserve Web site, FRED database, **http://research.stlouisfed.org/fred2**.

tendency for interest rates to rise during good economic times, and the net result was lower interest rates.[2]

The relationship between inflation and long-term interest rates is highlighted in Figure 6-3, which plots inflation over time along with long-term interest rates. In the early 1960s, inflation averaged 1 percent per year, and interest rates on high-quality, long-term bonds averaged 4 percent. Then the Vietnam War heated up, leading to an increase in inflation, and interest rates began an upward climb. When the war ended in the early 1970s, inflation dipped a bit, but then the 1973 Arab oil embargo led to rising oil prices, much higher inflation rates, and sharply higher interest rates.

Inflation peaked at about 13 percent in 1980, but interest rates continued to increase into 1981 and 1982, and they remained quite high until 1985, because people feared another increase in inflation. Thus, the "inflationary psychology" created during the 1970s persisted until the mid-1980s. People gradually realized that the Federal Reserve was serious about keeping inflation down, that global competition was keeping U.S. auto producers and other corporations from raising prices as they had in the past, and that constraints on corporate price increases were diminishing labor unions' ability to push through cost-increasing wage hikes. As these realizations set in, interest rates declined.

---

[2] Short-term rates are responsive to current economic conditions, whereas long-term rates primarily reflect long-run expectations for inflation. As a result, short-term rates are sometimes above and sometimes below long-term rates. The relationship between long-term and short-term rates is called the *term structure of interest rates,* and it is discussed later in this chapter.

The current interest rate minus the current inflation rate (which is also the gap between the inflation bars and the interest rate curve in Figure 6-3) is defined as the "current real rate of interest." It is called a "real rate" because it shows how much investors really earned after taking out the effects of inflation. The real rate was extremely high during the mid-1980s, but it has generally been in the range of 3 to 4 percent since 1987.

In recent years inflation has been about 2.5 percent a year. However, long-term interest rates have been volatile because investors are not sure if inflation is truly under control or is about to jump back to the higher levels of the 1980s. In the years ahead, we can be sure of two things: (1) interest rates will vary, and (2) they will increase if inflation appears to be headed higher and decrease if inflation is expected to decline. We really don't know where interest rates will go, but we do know that they will vary.

What role do interest rates play in allocating capital to different potential borrowers?

What happens to market-clearing, or equilibrium, interest rates in a capital market when the demand for funds declines? What happens when expected inflation increases or decreases?

How does the price of capital tend to change during a boom or a recession?

How does risk affect interest rates?

If inflation during the last 12 months was 2 percent and the interest rate during that period was 5 percent, what was the real rate of interest? If inflation is expected to average 4 percent during the next year and the real rate is 3 percent, what should the current rate of interest be? (3%; 7%)

6-3 THE DETERMINANTS OF MARKET INTEREST RATES

In general, the quoted (or nominal) interest rate on a debt security, r, is composed of a real risk-free rate of interest, r*, plus several premiums that reflect inflation, the security's risk, and its marketability (or liquidity). This relationship can be expressed as follows:

$$\text{Quoted interest rate} = r = r^* + IP + DRP + LP + MRP \qquad \textbf{(6-1)}$$

Here

> r = the quoted, or nominal, rate of interest on a given security.[3]
> r* = the real risk-free rate of interest. r* is pronounced "r-star," and it is the rate that would exist on a riskless security in a world with no inflation.

---

[3] The term *nominal* as it is used here means the *stated* rate as opposed to the *real* rate, which is adjusted to remove inflation's effects. If you had bought a 10-year Treasury bond in February 2005, the quoted, or nominal, rate would have been about 4.2 percent, but if inflation averages 2.5 percent over the next 10 years, the real rate would turn out to be about 4.2% − 2.5% = 1.7%.

Also, note that in later chapters, when we discuss both debt and equity, we use the subscripts d and s to designate returns on debt and stock, that is, r_d and r_s.

r_{RF} = r^* + IP, and it is the quoted rate on a risk-free security such as a U.S. Treasury bill, which is both very liquid and also free of most types of risk. Note that a premium for expected inflation, IP, is built into r_{RF}.

IP = inflation premium. IP is equal to the average expected inflation rate over the life of the security. The expected future inflation rate is not necessarily equal to the current inflation rate, so IP is not necessarily equal to current inflation, as shown back in Figure 6-3.

DRP = default risk premium. This premium reflects the possibility that the issuer will not pay interest or principal at the stated time and in the stated amount. DRP is zero for U.S. Treasury securities, but it rises as the riskiness of the issuer increases.

LP = liquidity (or marketability) premium. This is a premium charged by lenders to reflect the fact that some securities cannot be converted to cash on short notice at a "reasonable" price. LP is very low for Treasury securities and for securities issued by large, strong firms, but it is relatively high on securities issued by small, privately held firms.

MRP = maturity risk premium. As we will explain later, longer-term bonds, even Treasury bonds, are exposed to a significant risk of price declines due to increases in inflation and interest rates, and a maturity risk premium is charged by lenders to reflect this risk.

Because r_{RF} = r^* + IP, we can rewrite Equation 6-1 as follows:

$$\text{Nominal, or quoted, rate} = r = r_{RF} + DRP + LP + MRP$$

We discuss the components whose sum makes up the quoted, or nominal, rate on a given security in the following sections.

6-3a The Real Risk-Free Rate of Interest, r*

The **real risk-free rate of interest, r***, is the interest rate that would exist on a riskless security if no inflation were expected, and it may be thought of as the rate of interest on *short-term* U.S. Treasury securities in an inflation-free world. The real risk-free rate is not static—it changes over time depending on economic conditions, especially (1) on the rate of return corporations and other borrowers expect to earn on productive assets and (2) on people's time preferences for current versus future consumption. Borrowers' expected returns on real asset investments set an upper limit on how much they can afford to pay for borrowed funds, while savers' time preferences for consumption establish how much consumption they are willing to defer, hence the amount of funds they will lend at different interest rates. It is difficult to measure the real risk-free rate precisely, but most experts think that r^* has fluctuated in the range of 1 to 5 percent in recent years.[4] The best estimate of r^* is the rate of return on indexed Treasury bonds, which are discussed in a box later in the chapter.

Real Risk-Free Rate of Interest, r*
The rate of interest that would exist on default-free U.S. Treasury securities if no inflation were expected.

---

[4] The real rate of interest as discussed here is different from the *current* real rate as discussed in connection with Figure 6-3. The current real rate is the current interest rate minus the current (or latest past) inflation rate, while the real rate, without the word "current," is the current interest rate minus the *expected future* inflation rate over the life of the security. For example, suppose the current quoted rate for a one-year Treasury bill is 3 percent, inflation during the latest year was 2 percent, and inflation expected for the coming year is 2.5 percent. Then the *current* real rate would be 3% − 2% = 1%, but the *expected* real rate would be 3% − 2.5% = 0.5%. The rate on a 10-year bond would be related to the average expected inflation rate over the next 10 years, and so on. In the press, the term "real rate" generally means the current real rate, but in economics and finance, hence in this book unless otherwise noted, the real rate means the one based on *expected* inflation rates.

6-3b The Nominal, or Quoted, Risk-Free Rate of Interest, r_{RF}

Nominal (Quoted) Risk-Free Rate, r_{RF}
The rate of interest on a security that is free of all risk; r_{RF} is proxied by the T-bill rate or the T-bond rate. r_{RF} includes an inflation premium.

The **nominal,** or **quoted, risk-free rate,** r_{RF}, is the real risk-free rate plus a premium for expected inflation: $r_{RF} = r^* + IP$. To be strictly correct, the risk-free rate should mean the interest rate on a totally risk-free security—one that has no default risk, no maturity risk, no liquidity risk, no risk of loss if inflation increases, and no risk of any other type. There is no such security; hence, there is no observable truly risk-free rate. However, there is one security that is free of most risks—an indexed U.S. Treasury security. These securities are free of default, maturity, and liquidity risks, and also of risk due to changes in the general level of interest rates. However, they are not free of changes in the real rate.[5]

If the term "risk-free rate" is used without either the modifiers "real" or "nominal," people generally mean the quoted (nominal) rate, and we follow that convention in this book. Therefore, when we use the term risk-free rate, r_{RF}, we mean the nominal risk-free rate, which includes an inflation premium equal to the average expected inflation rate over the remaining life of the security. In general, we use the T-bill rate to approximate the short-term risk-free rate, and the T-bond rate to approximate the long-term risk-free rate. So, whenever you see the term "risk-free rate," assume that we are referring either to the quoted U.S. T-bill rate or to the quoted T-bond rate.

6-3c Inflation Premium (IP)

Inflation has a major impact on interest rates because it erodes the dollar's purchasing power and lowers real investment returns. To illustrate, suppose you saved $1,000 and invested it in a Treasury bill that pays a 3 percent interest rate and matures in one year. At the end of the year, you will receive $1,030—your original $1,000 plus $30 of interest. Now suppose the inflation rate during the year turned out to be 3.5 percent, and it affected all goods equally. If heating oil had cost $1 per gallon at the beginning of the year, it would cost $1.035 at the end of the year. Therefore, your $1,000 would have bought $1,000/$1 = 1,000 gallons at the beginning of the year, but only $1,030/$1.035 = 995 gallons at the end. In *real terms*, you would be worse off—you would receive $30 of interest, but it would not be sufficient to offset inflation. You would thus be better off buying 1,000 gallons of heating oil (or some other storable asset such as land, timber, apartment buildings, wheat, or gold) than buying the Treasury bill.

Inflation Premium (IP)
A premium equal to expected inflation that investors add to the real risk-free rate of return.

Investors are well aware of all this, so when they lend money, they build an **inflation premium (IP)** equal to the average expected inflation rate over the life of the security into the rate they charge. As discussed previously, the actual interest rate on a short-term, default-free U.S. Treasury bill, $r_{T\text{-bill}}$, would be the real risk-free rate, r^*, plus the inflation premium (IP):

$$r_{T\text{-bill}} = r_{RF} = r^* + IP$$

Therefore, if the real risk-free rate were $r^* = 1.7$ percent, and if inflation were expected to be 1.5 percent (and hence IP = 1.5%) during the next year, then the quoted rate of interest on one-year T-bills would be 1.7% + 1.5% = 3.2%.

It is important to note that the inflation rate built into interest rates is the *inflation rate expected in the future*, not the rate experienced in the past. Thus, the latest

---

[5] Indexed Treasury securities are the closest thing we have to a riskless security, but even they are not totally riskless, because r* itself can change and cause a decline in the prices of these securities. For example, between its issue date in March 1998 and December 2004, the price of one long-term indexed Treasury bond first declined from 100 to 89, or by almost 10 percent, but then rose to 131. The cause of the initial price decline was an *increase* in the real rate on long-term securities from 3.625 to 4.4 percent, and the cause of the more recent price increase was a *decline* in real rates to 1.93 percent.

reported figures might show an annual inflation rate of 3 percent over the past 12 months, but that is for the *past* year. If people on average expect a 4 percent inflation rate in the future, then 4 percent would be built into the current interest rate. Note also that the inflation rate reflected in the quoted interest rate on any security is the *average inflation rate expected over the security's life.* Thus, the inflation rate built into a 1-year bond is the expected inflation rate for the next year, but the inflation rate built into a 30-year bond is the average inflation rate expected over the next 30 years.[6]

Expectations for future inflation are closely, but not perfectly, correlated with rates experienced in the recent past. Therefore, if the inflation rate reported for last month increased, people would tend to raise their expectations for future inflation, and this change in expectations would cause an increase in current rates.

Note that Germany, Japan, and Switzerland have over the past several years had lower inflation rates than the United States, hence their interest rates have generally been lower than ours. Italy and most South American countries have experienced higher inflation, and so their rates have been higher than ours.

*Students should go to **www.bloomberg.com/ markets/rates** to find current interest rates in the United States, as well as those in Australia, Brazil, Germany, Japan, and Great Britain.*

6-3d Default Risk Premium (DRP)

The risk that a borrower will *default,* which means not make scheduled interest or principal payments, also affects the market interest rate on a bond: the greater the bond's risk of default, the higher the interest rate. Treasury securities have no default risk, hence they carry the lowest interest rates on taxable securities in the United States. For corporate bonds, the higher the bond's rating, the lower its default risk, and, consequently, the lower its interest rate.[7] Here are some representative interest rates on long-term bonds during February 2005:

	Rate	DRP
U.S. Treasury	4.65%	—
AAA	5.45	0.80
AA	5.60	0.95
A	5.78	1.13
BBB	6.34	1.69

The difference between the quoted interest rate on a T-bond and that on a corporate bond with similar maturity, liquidity, and other features is the **default risk premium (DRP)**. Therefore, if the bonds listed above have the same maturity, liquidity, etc., then the default risk premium would be DRP = 5.45% − 4.65% = 0.8 percentage point for AAA corporate bonds, 5.60% − 4.65% = 0.95 percentage point for AA, 5.78% − 4.65% = 1.13 percentage points for A corporate bonds, and so forth. Default risk premiums vary somewhat over time, but the February 2005 figures are representative of levels in recent years.

Default Risk Premium (DRP)
The difference between the interest rate on a U.S. Treasury bond and a corporate bond of equal maturity and marketability.

---

[6] To be theoretically precise, we should use a *geometric average.* Also, since millions of investors are active in the market, it is impossible to determine exactly the consensus expected inflation rate. Survey data are available, however, that give us a reasonably good idea of what investors expect over the next few years. For example, in 1980 the University of Michigan's Survey Research Center reported that people expected inflation during the next year to be 11.9 percent and that the average rate of inflation expected over the next 5 to 10 years was 10.5 percent. Those expectations led to record-high interest rates. However, the economy cooled thereafter and, as Figure 6-3 showed, actual inflation dropped sharply. This led to a gradual reduction in the *expected future* inflation rate, and as inflationary expectations dropped, so did quoted market interest rates.

[7] Bond ratings, and bonds' riskiness in general, are discussed in detail in Chapter 7. For now, merely note that bonds rated AAA are judged to have less default risk than bonds rated AA, while AA bonds are less risky than A bonds, and so on. Ratings are designated AAA or Aaa, AA or Aa, and so forth, depending on the rating agency. In this book, the designations are used interchangeably.

An Almost Riskless Treasury Bond

Investors who purchase bonds must constantly worry about inflation. If inflation turns out to be greater than expected, bonds will provide a lower-than-expected real return. To protect themselves against expected increases in inflation, investors build an inflation risk premium into their required rate of return. This raises borrowers' costs.

To provide investors with an inflation-protected bond, and also to reduce the cost of debt to the government, on January 29, 1997, the U.S. Treasury issued $7 billion of 10-year inflation-indexed bonds. These bonds pay an interest rate of 3.375 percent plus an additional amount that is just sufficient to offset inflation. At the end of each six-month period, the principal (originally set at par, or $1,000) is adjusted by the inflation rate. For example, during the first six-month interest period, inflation (as measured by the CPI) was 1.085 percent. The inflation-adjusted principal was then calculated as $1,000(1 + Inflation) = $1,000 \times 1.01085 = $1,010.85. So, on July 15, 1997, each bond paid interest of 0.03375/2 \times $1,010.85 = $17.06. Note that the interest rate is divided by two because interest on these (and most other) bonds is paid twice a year.

By January 15, 1998, a bit more inflation had occurred, and the inflation-adjusted principal was up to $1,019.69, so on January 15, 1998, each bond paid interest of 0.03375/2 \times $1,019.69 = $17.21. Thus, the total return during the first year consisted of $17.06 + $17.21 = $34.27 of interest and $1,019.69 - $1,000.00 = $19.69 of "capital gains," or $34.27 + $19.69 = $53.96 in total. Thus, the total return was $53.96/$1,000 = 5.396%.

This same adjustment process will continue each year until the bonds mature on January 15, 2007, at which time they will pay the adjusted maturity value. Thus, the cash income provided by the bonds rises by exactly enough to cover inflation, producing a real, inflation-adjusted rate of 3.375 percent. Further, since the principal also rises by the inflation rate, it too is protected from inflation. The accompanying table gives the inflation-adjusted principal and interest paid during the life of these 3⅜ percent coupon, 10-year, inflation-indexed bonds:

Date	Inflation-Adjusted Principal	Interest Paid
7/15/97	$1,010.85	$17.06
1/15/98	1,019.69	17.21
7/15/98	1,026.51	17.32
1/15/99	1,035.12	17.47
7/15/99	1,049.01	17.70
1/15/00	1,061.92	17.92
7/15/00	1,080.85	18.24
1/15/01	1,098.52	18.54
7/15/01	1,118.82	18.88
1/15/02	1,120.74	18.91
7/15/02	1,134.85	19.15
1/15/03	1,144.31	19.31
7/15/03	1,159.24	19.56
1/15/04	1,166.24	19.68
7/15/04	1,189.74	20.08
1/15/05	1,205.19	20.34

Source: Bureau of the Public Debt's Online, Historical Reference CPI Numbers and Daily Index Ratios for 3⅜ percent, 10-year note due January 15, 2007, **http://www.publicdebt.treas.gov/of/ofhiscpi.htm**.

The Treasury regularly conducts auctions to issue indexed bonds. The 3.375 percent rate was based on the relative supply and demand for the issue, and it will remain fixed over the life of the bond. However, new bonds are issued periodically, and their "coupon" real rates depend on the market at the time the bond is auctioned. In January 2005, 10-year indexed securities had a real rate of 1.625 percent.

Federal Reserve Board Chairman Greenspan lobbied in favor of the indexed bonds on the grounds that they would help him and the Fed make better estimates of investors' expectations about inflation. He did not explain his reasoning (to our knowledge), but it might have gone something like this:

- We know that interest rates in general are determined as follows:

$$r = r^* + IP + MRP + DRP + LP$$

- For Treasury bonds, DRP and LP are essentially zero, so for a 10-year bond the rate is

$$r_{RF} = r^* + IP + MRP$$

The reason the MRP is not zero is that if inflation increases, interest rates will rise and the price of the bonds will decline. Therefore, "regular" 10-year bonds are exposed to maturity risk, hence a maturity risk premium is built into their market interest rate.

- The indexed bonds are protected against inflation—if inflation increases, then so will their dollar returns, and as a result, their price will not decline in real terms. Therefore, indexed bonds should have no MRP, hence their market return is

$$r_{RF} = r^* + 0 + 0 = r^*$$

In other words, the market rate on an indexed bond is the real rate.

- The difference between the yield on a regular 10-year bond and that on an indexed bond is the sum of the 10-year bonds' IP and MRP. Regular 10-year bonds were yielding 6.80 percent when the first indexed bonds were issued in 1997 at a rate of 3.375 percent. The difference, 3.425 percent, was the average expected inflation rate over the next 10 years, plus an MRP for 10-year bonds.

- The 10-year MRP is about 1.0 percent, and it has been relatively stable in recent years. Therefore, the expected rate of inflation in January 1997 was 3.425% − 1.00% = 2.425%.

Both the annual interest received and the increase in principal are taxed each year as interest income, even though cash from the appreciation will not be received until the bond matures. Therefore, these bonds are not good for accounts subject to current income taxes but are excellent for individual retirement accounts [IRAs and 401(k) plans], which are not taxed until funds are withdrawn.

Keep in mind, though, that despite their protection against inflation, indexed bonds are not completely riskless. As we indicated earlier, the real rate can change, and if r* rises, the prices of indexed bonds will decline. This just confirms one more time that there is no such thing as a free lunch or a riskless security!

Sources: "Inflation Notes Will Offer Fed Forecast Tool," *The Wall Street Journal,* February 3, 1997, p. C1; and *The Wall Street Journal,* January 6, 2000, p. C21.

6-3e Liquidity Premium (LP)

A "liquid" asset can be converted to cash quickly at a "fair market value." Real assets are generally less liquid than financial assets, but different financial assets vary in their liquidity. Because liquidity is important, investors include a **liquidity premium (LP)** in the rates charged on different debt securities. Although it is difficult to accurately measure liquidity premiums, a differential of at least two and probably four or five percentage points exists between the least liquid and the most liquid financial assets of similar default risk and maturity.

6-3f Maturity Risk Premium (MRP)

U.S. Treasury securities are free of default risk in the sense that one can be virtually certain that the federal government will pay interest on its bonds and will also pay them off when they mature. Therefore, the default risk premium on Treasury securities is essentially zero. Further, active markets exist for Treasury securities, so their liquidity premiums are also close to zero. Thus, as a first approximation, the rate of interest on a Treasury security should be the risk-free rate, r_{RF}, which is equal to the real risk-free rate, r^*, plus an inflation premium, IP. However, the prices of long-term bonds decline whenever interest rates rise, and because interest rates can and do occasionally rise, all long-term bonds, even Treasury bonds, have an element of risk called **interest rate risk.** As a general rule, the bonds of any organization, from the U.S. government to Delta Airlines, have more interest rate risk the longer the maturity of the bond.[8] Therefore, a **maturity risk premium (MRP),** which is higher the greater the years to maturity, must be included in the required interest rate.

The effect of maturity risk premiums is to raise interest rates on long-term bonds relative to those on short-term bonds. This premium, like the others, is difficult to measure, but (1) it varies somewhat over time, rising when interest rates are more volatile and uncertain, then falling when interest rates are more stable, and (2) in recent years, the maturity risk premium on 20-year T-bonds has generally been in the range of one to two percentage points.[9]

We should also note that although long-term bonds are heavily exposed to interest rate risk, short-term bills are heavily exposed to **reinvestment rate risk.** When short-term bills mature and the principal must be reinvested, or "rolled over," a decline in interest rates would necessitate reinvestment at a lower rate, and this would result in a decline in interest income. To illustrate, suppose you had $100,000 invested in T-bills and you lived on the income. In 1981, short-term Treasury rates were about 15 percent, so your income would have been about $15,000. However, your income would have declined to about $9,000 by 1983, and to just $2,900 by February 2005. Had you invested your money in long-term T-bonds, your income (but not the value of the principal) would have been stable.[10] Thus, although "investing short" preserves one's principal, the interest income provided by short-term T-bills is less stable than the interest income on long-term bonds.

---

[8] For example, if someone had bought a 20-year Treasury bond for $1,000 in October 1998, when the long-term interest rate was 5.3 percent, and sold it in May 2002, when long-term T-bond rates were about 5.8 percent, the value of the bond would have declined to about $942. That would represent a loss of 5.8 percent, and it demonstrates that long-term bonds, even U.S. Treasury bonds, are not riskless. However, had the investor purchased short-term T-bills in 1998 and subsequently reinvested the principal each time the bills matured, he or she would still have had the original $1,000. This point is discussed in detail in Chapter 7.

[9] The MRP for long-term bonds has averaged 1.4 percent over the last 79 years. See *Stocks, Bonds, Bills, and Inflation: (Valuation Edition) 2005 Yearbook* (Chicago: Ibbotson Associates, 2005).

[10] Long-term bonds also have some reinvestment rate risk. If one is saving and investing for some future purpose, say, to buy a house or for retirement, then to actually earn the quoted rate on a

Write out an equation for the nominal interest rate on any security.

Distinguish between the *real* risk-free rate of interest, r*, and the *nominal*, or *quoted*, risk-free rate of interest, r$_{RF}$.

How do investors deal with inflation when they determine interest rates in the financial markets?

Does the interest rate on a T-bond include a default risk premium? Explain.

Distinguish between liquid and illiquid assets, and list some assets that are liquid and some that are illiquid.

Briefly explain the following statement: "Although long-term bonds are heavily exposed to interest rate risk, short-term T-bills are heavily exposed to reinvestment rate risk. The maturity risk premium reflects the net effects of these two opposing forces."

Assume that the real risk-free rate is r* = 2% and the average expected inflation rate is 3 percent for each future year. The DRP and LP for Bond X are each 1 percent, and the applicable MRP is 2 percent. What is Bond X's interest rate? Is Bond X (1) a Treasury bond or a corporate bond and (2) more likely to have a 3-month or a 20-year maturity? (9 percent, corporate, 20-year)

6-4 THE TERM STRUCTURE OF INTEREST RATES

The **term structure of interest rates** describes the relationship between long- and short-term rates. The term structure is important both to corporate treasurers deciding whether to borrow by issuing long- or short-term debt and to investors who are deciding whether to buy long- or short-term bonds. Therefore, both borrowers and lenders should understand (1) how long- and short-term rates relate to each other and (2) what causes shifts in their relative levels.

Interest rates for bonds with different maturities can be found in a variety of publications, including *The Wall Street Journal* and the *Federal Reserve Bulletin*, and on a number of Web sites, including Bloomberg, Yahoo!, CNN Financial, and the Federal Reserve Board. Using interest rate data from these sources, we can determine the term structure at any given point in time. For example, the tabular section below Figure 6-4 presents interest rates for different maturities on three different dates. The set of data for a given date, when plotted on a graph such as Figure 6-4, is called the **yield curve** for that date.

As the figure shows, the yield curve changes both in position and in slope over time. In March 1980, all rates were quite high because high inflation was expected. However, the rate of inflation was expected to decline, so short-term rates were higher than long-term rates and the yield curve was thus *downward sloping*. By February 2000, inflation had indeed declined and thus all rates were lower, and the yield curve had become *humped*—medium-term rates were higher

Term Structure of Interest Rates
The relationship between bond yields and maturities.

Yield Curve
A graph showing the relationship between bond yields and maturities.

(Footnote 10, continued)

long-term bond, the interest payments must be reinvested at the quoted rate. However, if interest rates fall, the interest payments must be reinvested at a lower rate; thus, the realized return would be less than the quoted rate. Note, though, that reinvestment rate risk is lower on a long-term bond than on a short-term bond because only the interest payments (rather than interest plus principal) on the long-term bond are exposed to reinvestment rate risk. Zero coupon bonds, which are discussed in Chapter 7, are completely free of reinvestment rate risk during their lifetime.

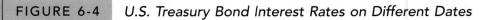

FIGURE 6-4   *U.S. Treasury Bond Interest Rates on Different Dates*

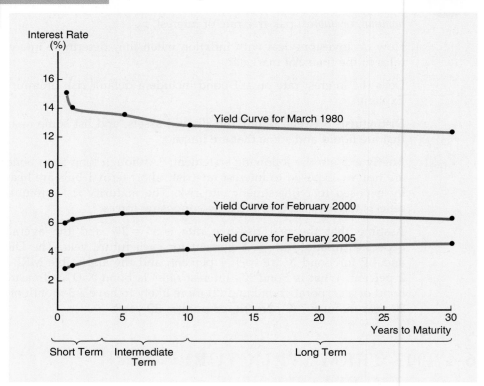

Term to Maturity	INTEREST RATE		
	March 1980	February 2000	February 2005
6 months	15.0%	6.0%	2.9%
1 year	14.0	6.2	3.1
5 years	13.5	6.7	3.8
10 years	12.8	6.7	4.2
30 years	12.3	6.3	4.6

than either short- or long-term rates. By February 2005, all rates had fallen below the 2000 levels, and because short-term rates had dropped below long-term rates, the yield curve was *upward sloping*.

Figure 6-4 shows yield curves for U.S. Treasury securities, but we could have constructed curves for bonds issued by GE, IBM, Delta Airlines, or any other company that borrows money over a range of maturities. Had we constructed such corporate yield curves and plotted them on Figure 6-4, they would have been above those for Treasury securities because corporate yields include default risk premiums and somewhat higher liquidity premiums than Treasury bonds. However, the corporate yield curves would have had the same general shape as the Treasury curves. Also, the riskier the corporation, the higher its yield curve, so Delta, which was flirting with bankruptcy, would have a higher yield curve than GE or IBM.

Historically, long-term rates are generally above short-term rates because of the maturity premium, so the yield curve usually slopes upward. For this reason, people often call an upward-sloping yield curve a **"normal" yield curve** and a yield curve that slopes downward an **inverted**, or **"abnormal" curve.**

"Normal" Yield Curve
An upward-sloping yield curve.

Inverted ("Abnormal") Yield Curve
A downward-sloping yield curve.

Thus, in Figure 6-4 the yield curve for March 1980 was inverted, while the yield curve in February 2005 was normal. However, the February 2000 curve was **humped,** which means that interest rates on medium-term maturities were higher than rates on both short- and long-term maturities. We explain in detail in the next section why an upward slope is the normal situation, but briefly, the reason is that short-term securities have less interest rate risk than longer-term securities, hence smaller MRPs. Therefore, short-term rates are normally lower than long-term rates.

Humped Yield Curve
A yield curve where interest rates on medium-term maturities are higher than rates on both short- and long-term maturities.

What is a yield curve, and what information would you need to draw this curve?

Distinguish among the shapes of a "normal" yield curve, an "abnormal" curve, and a "humped" curve.

If the interest rates on 1-, 5-, 10-, and 30-year bonds are 4, 5, 6, and 7 percent, respectively, how would you describe the yield curve? If the rates were reversed, how would you describe it?

6-5 WHAT DETERMINES THE SHAPE OF THE YIELD CURVE?

Because maturity risk premiums are positive, then if other things were held constant, long-term bonds would always have higher interest rates than short-term bonds. However, market interest rates also depend on expected inflation, default risk, and liquidity, and each of these factors can vary with maturity.

Expected inflation has an especially important effect on the yield curve's shape, especially the curve for U.S. Treasury securities. Treasuries have essentially no default or liquidity risk, so the yield on a Treasury bond that matures in t years can be expressed as follows:

$$\text{T-bond yield} = r^*_t + IP_t + MRP_t$$

While the real risk-free rate, r^*, varies somewhat over time because of changes in the economy and demographics, these changes are random rather than predictable, so the best forecast for the future value of r^* is its current value. However, the inflation premium, IP, does vary significantly over time, and in a somewhat predictable manner. Recall that the inflation premium is simply the average level of expected inflation over the life of the bond. Thus, if the market expects inflation to increase in the future, say, from 3 to 4 to 5 percent over the next three years, the inflation premium will be higher on a three-year bond than on a one-year bond. On the other hand, if the market expects inflation to decline in the future, long-term bonds will have a smaller inflation premium than short-term bonds. Finally, since investors consider long-term bonds to be riskier than short-term bonds because of interest rate risk, the maturity risk premium always increases with maturity.

Panel a of Figure 6-5 shows the yield curve when inflation is expected to increase. Here long-term bonds have higher yields for two reasons: (1) Inflation is expected to be higher in the future, and (2) there is a positive maturity risk premium. Panel b of the figure shows the yield curve when inflation is expected to decline. Such a downward sloping yield curve often foreshadows an economic

FIGURE 6-5	*Illustrative Treasury Yield Curves*

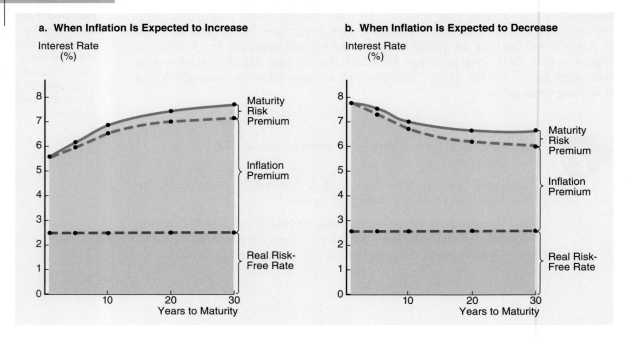

	WITH INFLATION EXPECTED TO INCREASE					WITH INFLATION EXPECTED TO DECREASE			
Maturity	r*	IP	MRP	Yield	Maturity	r*	IP	MRP	Yield
1 year	2.50%	3.00%	0.00%	**5.50%**	1 year	2.50%	5.00%	0.00%	**7.50%**
5 years	2.50	3.40	0.18	**6.08**	5 years	2.50	4.60	0.18	**7.28**
10 years	2.50	4.00	0.28	**6.78**	10 years	2.50	4.00	0.28	**6.78**
20 years	2.50	4.50	0.42	**7.42**	20 years	2.50	3.50	0.42	**6.42**
30 years	2.50	4.67	0.53	**7.70**	30 years	2.50	3.33	0.53	**6.36**

downturn, because weaker economic conditions generally lead to declining inflation, which, in turn, results in lower long-term rates.[11]

Now let's consider the yield curve for corporate bonds. Recall that corporate bonds include a default risk premium (DRP) and a liquidity premium (LP). Therefore, the yield on a corporate bond that matures in t years can be expressed as follows:

$$\text{Corporate bond yield} = r^*_t + IP_t + MRP_t + DRP_t + LP_t$$

Corporate bonds' default and liquidity risks are affected by their maturities. For example, the default risk on Coca-Cola's short-term debt is very small, since there is almost no chance that Coca-Cola will go bankrupt over the next few years. However, Coke has some bonds that have a maturity of almost 100 years, and while the odds of Coke defaulting on these bonds still might not be very

[11] Note that yield curves tend to rise or fall relatively sharply for 5 to 10 years, and then flatten out. One reason this occurs is that when forecasting future interest rates people often predict varying changes in inflation for the next 5 to 10 years after which they assume a long-run constant inflation rate. Consequently, the short end of the yield curve tends to have more volatility because there are more variations in the year-to-year interest rate forecasts. By contrast, the long end of the yield curve tends to be more stable because of the assumption of constant inflation rates.

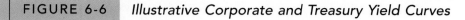

| FIGURE 6-6 | *Illustrative Corporate and Treasury Yield Curves* |

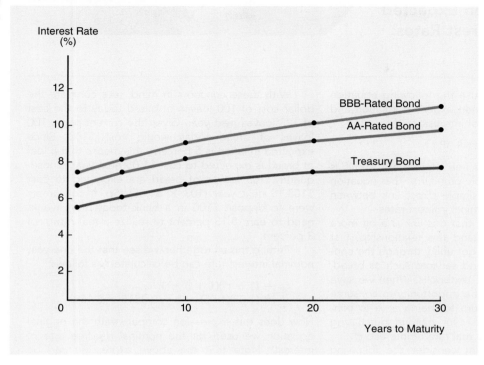

	INTEREST RATE		
Term to Maturity	**Treasury Bond**	**AA-Rated Bond**	**BBB-Rated Bond**
1 year	5.5%	6.7%	7.4%
5 years	6.1	7.4	8.1
10 years	6.8	8.2	9.1
20 years	7.4	9.2	10.2
30 years	7.7	9.8	11.1

high, there is still a higher probability of default risk on Coke's long-term bonds than on its short-term ones.

Longer-term corporate bonds are also less liquid than shorter-term bonds. Since short-term debt has less default risk, someone can buy a short-term bond without as much credit checking as would be necessary before buying a long-term bond. Thus, people can move in and out of short-term corporate debt more rapidly than long-term debt. As a result, a corporation's short-term bonds are more liquid and thus have lower liquidity premiums than its long-term bonds.

Figure 6-6 shows yield curves for two hypothetical corporate bonds, an AA-rated bond with minimal default risk and a BBB-rated bond with more default risk, along with the yield curve for Treasury securities as taken from Panel a of Figure 6-5. Here we assume that inflation is expected to increase, so the Treasury yield curve is upward sloping. Because of their additional default and liquidity risk, corporate bonds always yield more than Treasury bonds with the same maturity, and BBB-rated bonds yield more than AA-rated bonds. Finally, note that the yield spread between corporate bonds and Treasury bonds is larger the longer the maturity. This occurs because longer-term corporate bonds have more default and liquidity risk than shorter-term bonds, and both of these premiums are absent in Treasury bonds.

The Links between Expected Inflation and Interest Rates: A Closer Look

Throughout the text, we use the following equation to describe the link between expected inflation and the nominal risk-free rate of interest, r_{RF} :

$$r_{RF} = r* + IP$$

Recall that $r*$ is the real risk-free interest rate, and IP is the corresponding inflation premium. This equation suggests that there is a simple direct link between expected inflation and nominal interest rates.

It turns out, however, that this link is a bit more complex. To fully understand this relationship, first recognize that individuals get utility through the consumption of real goods and services such as bread, water, haircuts, pizza, and textbooks. When we save money we are giving up the opportunity to consume these goods today in return for being able to consume more in the future. Our gain in purchasing power is measured by the real rate of interest, $r*$.

To illustrate this point consider the following example. Assume that a loaf of bread costs $1.00 today. Also assume that the real rate of interest is 3 percent and that inflation is expected to be 5 percent over the next year. The 3 percent real rate indicates that the average consumer is willing to trade 100 loaves of bread today for 103 loaves next year. If there were a "bread bank," consumers who wanted to defer consumption until next year could deposit 100 loaves today and withdraw 103 loaves next year. In practice, most of us do not directly trade real goods such as bread—instead we purchase these goods with money because in a well-functioning economy it is much more efficient to exchange money than goods. However, when we lend money over time we worry that borrowers might pay us back with dollars that aren't worth as much due to inflation. To compensate for this risk, lenders build in a premium for expected inflation.

With these concerns in mind, let's compare the dollar cost of 100 loaves of bread today to the cost of 103 loaves next year. Given the current price, 100 loaves of bread today would cost $100. Since expected inflation is 5 percent, this means that a loaf of bread is expected to cost $1.05 next year. Consequently, 103 loaves of bread are expected to cost $108.15 next year (103 × $1.05). So, if consumers were to deposit $100 in a bank today, they would need to earn 8.15 percent to realize a real return of 3 percent.

Putting this all together, we see that the one-year nominal interest rate can be calculated as follows:

$$r_{RF} = (1 + r*)(1 + I) - 1$$
$$= (1.03)(1.05) - 1 = 0.0815 = 8.15\%$$

How does this expression compare with the original equation we used for the nominal risk-free rate of interest? Note that the above expression can be rewritten as

$$r_{RF} = r* + I + (r* \times I)$$

This equation is identical to our original expression for the nominal risk-free rate except it includes a "cross-term," $r* \times I$. When real interest rates and expected inflation are relatively low, the cross-term turns out to be quite small and thus it is often ignored. With this point in mind, in the text we will disregard the cross-term unless we state otherwise.

One last point—you should recognize that while it may be reasonable to ignore the cross-term when interest rates are low (as they are today), it is a mistake to do so when investing in a market where interest rates and inflation are quite high, as is often the case in many emerging markets. In these markets, the cross-term can be significant and thus should not be disregarded.

How do maturity risk premiums affect the yield curve?

If the inflation rate is expected to increase, would this increase or decrease the slope of the yield curve?

If the inflation rate is expected to remain constant at the current level in the future, would the yield curve slope up, down, or be horizontal? Consider all factors that affect the yield curve, not just inflation.

Explain why corporate bonds' default and liquidity premiums are likely to increase with their maturity.

Explain why corporate bonds always yield more than Treasury bonds and why BBB-rated bonds always yield more than AA-rated bonds.

6-6 USING THE YIELD CURVE TO ESTIMATE FUTURE INTEREST RATES[12]

In the last section we saw that the slope of the yield curve depends primarily on two factors: (1) expectations about future inflation and (2) the effects of maturity on bonds' risk. We also saw how to calculate the yield curve, given inflation and maturity-related risks. Note, though, that investors can reverse the process: They plot the yield curve and then use information embedded in it to estimate the market's expectations regarding future inflation and risk.

This process of using the yield curve to estimate future expected interest rates is straightforward, provided (1) we focus on Treasury bonds, and (2) we assume that all Treasury bonds have the same risk, that is, that there is no maturity risk premium. While this second assumption may not be reasonable, it enables us for the time being to take out the effects of risk and focus exclusively on how expectations about future interest rates affect the shape of the yield curve. Later on, we will show what happens when we once again assume that there is a maturity risk premium.

In fact, while most evidence suggests that there is a positive maturity risk premium, some academics and practitioners contend that this second assumption is reasonable, at least as an approximation. They argue that the market is dominated by large bond traders who buy and sell securities of different maturities each day, that these traders focus only on short-term returns, and that they are not concerned with maturity risk. According to this view, a bond trader is just as willing to buy a 20-year bond to pick up a short-term profit as he or she would be to buy a three-month security. Strict proponents of this view argue that the shape of the Treasury yield curve is therefore determined only by market expectations about future interest rates. This position has been called the *pure expectations theory* of the term structure of interest rates.

The **pure expectations theory** (often simply referred to as the "expectations theory") assumes that bond traders establish bond prices and interest rates strictly on the basis of expectations for future interest rates, and they are indifferent to maturity because they do not view long-term bonds as being riskier than short-term bonds. If this were true, then the maturity risk premium (MRP) would be zero, and long-term interest rates would simply be a weighted average of current and expected future short-term interest rates.

To illustrate this point, assume that one-year Treasury securities currently yield 5 percent, while two-year Treasury securities yield 5.5 percent. Investors with a two-year horizon have two primary options:

Option 1: *Buy a two-year security and hold it for two years.*
Option 2: *Buy a one-year security, hold it for one year, and then at the end of the year reinvest the proceeds in another one-year security.*

If they select Option 1, for every dollar they invest today, they will have accumulated $1.113025 by the end of Year 2:

$$\text{Funds at end of Year 2} = \$1 \times (1.055)^2 = \$1.113025$$

Pure Expectations Theory
A theory that states that the shape of the yield curve depends on investors' expectations about future interest rates.

---

[12] This section is relatively technical, but instructors can omit it without loss of continuity.

If they select Option 2, they should end up with the same amount, but this equation is used to find the ending amount:

$$\text{Funds at end of Year 2} = \$1 \times (1.05) \times (1 + X)$$

Here X is the expected interest rate on a one-year Treasury security one year from now.

If the expectations theory is correct, each option must provide the same amount of cash at the end of two years, which implies that

$$(1.05)(1 + X) = (1.055)^2$$

We can rearrange this equation and then solve for X:

$$1 + X = (1.055)^2/1.05$$
$$X = (1.055)^2/1.05 - 1 = 0.0600238 = 6.00238\%$$

Thus, if the expectations theory is correct, the current yield curve would indicate that the market expects the one-year rate to be 6.00238 percent one year from now.

We can use yield curve data to help predict future short-term interest rates. In the absence of maturity risk premiums, an upward sloping Treasury yield curve implies that the market expects future short-term rates to increase. Also, notice that the two-year rate of 5.5 percent is a geometric average of the current and expected one-year rates.[13] To understand the logic behind the averaging process, ask yourself what would happen if long-term yields were *not* an average of expected short-term yields. For example, suppose investors expected the one-year Treasury rate to be 6.00238 percent a year from now, but two-year bonds yielded only 5.25 percent. Bond traders would be able to earn a profit by adopting the following strategy:

1. Borrow money for two years at an annual cost of 5.25 percent.
2. Invest the money in a series of one-year securities. The annual expected return over the two-year period would be $[(1.05) \times (1.0600238)]^{1/2} - 1 = 5.5\%$.

Earning 5.5 percent when the cost is 5.25 percent is a good deal, so bond traders would rush to borrow money (demand funds) in the two-year market and invest (or supply funds) in the one-year market. Recall from Figure 6-1 that an increase in the demand for funds raises interest rates, whereas an increase in the supply of funds reduces interest rates. Therefore, bond traders would push up the two-year yield but reduce the yield on one-year bonds. The net effect would be a market equilibrium in which the two-year rate is a weighted average of expected future one-year rates.

The preceding analysis was based on the assumption that the maturity risk premium is zero, but most evidence suggests that there is a positive maturity risk premium. For example, assume once again that one- and two-year maturities yield 5.0 and 5.5 percent respectively, so we have a rising yield curve. However, now assume that the maturity risk premium on the two-year bond is

---

[13] The geometric average of the current and expected one-year rates can be expressed as: $[(1.05) \times (1.0600238)]^{1/2} - 1 = 0.055$ or 5.50%. The arithmetic average of the two rates is $(5\% + 6.00238\%)/2 = 5.50119\%$. The geometric average is theoretically superior, but the difference is only 0.00119%. With interest rates at the levels they have been in the United States and most other nations in recent years, the geometric and arithmetic averages are so close that many people simply use the arithmetic average, especially given the other assumptions that underlie the estimation of future one-year rates.

0.2 percent versus zero for the one-year bond. This premium means that in equilibrium the expected annual return on a two-year bond (5.5 percent) must be 0.2 percent higher than the expected return on a series of two one-year bonds (5 percent and X percent), so the expected return on the series must be 5.5% − 0.2% = 5.3%:

$$\text{Expected return on 2-year series} = \text{Rate on 2-year bond} - \text{MRP}$$

$$= 0.055 - 0.002 = 0.053 = 5.3\%$$

Now recall that the annual expected return from the series of two one-year securities can be expressed as follows, where X is the one-year rate next year:

$$(1.05)(1 + X) = (1 + \text{Expected return on 2-year series})^2 = (1.053)^2$$

$$1.05X = (1.053)^2 - 1.05$$

$$X = \frac{0.0588090}{1.05} = 0.0560086 = 5.60086\%$$

Therefore, in this scenario market participants must expect the one-year rate next year to be 5.60086 percent.

Note that the yield curve rises by 0.5 percent when the years to maturity increases from one to two: 5.5% − 5.0% = 0.5%. Of this 0.5 percent increase, 0.2 percent is attributable to the MRP and the remaining 0.3 percent is due to the increase in expected one-year rates next year.

Putting all this together, we see that we can use the yield curve to predict the short-term rates that will exist for next year, but to do this we must have an estimate of the maturity risk premium. If our estimate of the MRP is incorrect, then so will be our yield-curve-based interest-rate forecast. Thus, while the yield curve can be used to obtain insights into the direction of future interest rates, we cannot back out expected interest rates with precision unless either the pure expectations theory holds exactly or else we know with certainty the exact maturity risk premium. As neither of these conditions holds, forecasts of future interest rates are only approximations, though they may be good approximations.

What key assumption underlies the pure expectations theory?

Assuming that the pure expectations theory is correct, how are expected short-term rates used to calculate expected long-term rates?

According to the pure expectations theory, what would happen if long-term rates were *not* an average of expected short-term rates?

Most evidence suggests that a positive maturity risk premium exists. How would this affect your calculations when determining interest rates?

Assume the interest rate on a one-year T-bond is currently 7 percent and the rate on a two-year bond is 9 percent. If the maturity risk premium is zero, what is a reasonable forecast of the rate on a one-year bond next year? What would the forecast be if the maturity risk premium on the two-year bond were 0.5 percent and it was zero for the one-year bond? (11.04 percent; 10.02 percent)

6-7 OTHER FACTORS THAT INFLUENCE INTEREST RATE LEVELS

Four additional factors that influence both the general level of interest rates and the shape of the yield curve are (1) the Federal Reserve policy; (2) the federal budget deficit or surplus; (3) international factors, including the foreign trade balance and interest rates in other countries; and (4) the level of business activity.

6-7a Federal Reserve Policy

The home page for the Board of Governors of the Federal Reserve System can be found at http://www .federalreserve.gov/. You can access general information about the Federal Reserve, including press releases, speeches, and monetary policy.

As you probably learned in your economics courses, (1) the money supply has a significant effect on the level of economic activity, inflation rate, and interest rates, and (2) in the United States, the Federal Reserve Board controls the money supply. If the Fed wants to stimulate the economy, it increases growth in the money supply. The initial effect of this action is to cause interest rates to decline. However, a larger money supply may also lead to an increase in the expected inflation rate, which could push up interest rates in spite of the Fed's desire to lower them. The reverse holds if the Fed tightens the money supply.

To illustrate, in 1981 inflation was extremely high, so the Fed tightened the money supply. The Fed deals primarily in the short-term end of the market, so its tightening had the direct effect of pushing up short-term rates sharply. At the same time, the very fact that the Fed was taking strong action to reduce inflation led to a decline in expectations for long-run inflation, which caused long-term bond yields to decline even as short-term rates rose.

The situation in 1991 was just the reverse. To combat the recession, the Fed took actions that caused short-term rates to fall sharply. These lower rates benefited companies that used debt—lower rates helped companies finance capital expenditures, which stimulated the economy. At the same time, lower rates led to home mortgage refinancings, which lowered mortgage payments and thus put additional dollars into consumers' pockets, which also stimulated the economy. Savers, of course, lost out, but the net effect of lower interest rates was a stronger economy.

Lower rates also cause foreigners who hold U.S. bonds to sell those bonds. These investors are paid dollars, which they then sell in order to buy other currencies. The sale of dollars and the purchase of other currencies lowers the value of the dollar relative to other currencies, and that makes U.S. goods less expensive, which helps our manufacturers and thus lowers the trade deficit. Note, though, that during periods when the Fed is actively intervening in the markets, the yield curve may be temporarily distorted. Short-term rates may be driven below the equilibrium level if the Fed is easing credit and above equilibrium if it is tightening credit. Long-term rates are not affected as much by Fed intervention. During 2004, in order to bring interest rates back to levels more consistent with inflation, the Federal Reserve increased short-term interest rates five times, causing short-term rates to rise by 1.25 percentage points. However, long-term rates (as measured by the 10-year Treasury note) remained level.

6-7b Federal Budget Deficits or Surpluses

If the federal government spends more than it takes in from taxes, it runs a deficit, and that deficit must be covered by additional borrowing or by printing money. If the government borrows, this increases the demand for funds and thus pushes up interest rates. If it prints money, investors believe that with "more money chasing a given amount of goods," the result will be increased inflation, which will also increase interest rates. So, the larger the federal deficit, other things held constant, the higher the level of interest rates.

Over the past several decades, the federal government has usually run large budget deficits. There were some surpluses in the late 1990s, but the September 11, 2001, terrorist attacks, the subsequent recession, and the Iraq war all boosted government spending and caused the deficits to return.

6-7c International Factors

Businesses and individuals in the United States buy from and sell to people and firms all around the globe. If we buy more than we sell (that is, if we import more than we export), we are said to be running a **foreign trade deficit.** When trade deficits occur, they must be financed, and this generally means borrowing from nations with export surpluses. In other words, if we import $200 billion of goods but export only $100 billion, we run a trade deficit of $100 billion, while other countries would share in a $100 billion trade surplus. We would probably borrow the $100 billion from the surplus nations.[14] At any rate, the larger our trade deficit, the more we must borrow. Foreigners will hold U.S. debt if and only if the rates on U.S. securities are competitive with rates in other countries. So, our interest rates are highly dependent on rates in other parts of the world.

This interdependency limits the ability of the Federal Reserve to use monetary policy to control economic activity in the United States. For example, if the Fed attempts to lower U.S. interest rates in the United States, and this causes our rates to fall below rates abroad, then foreigners will begin selling U.S. bonds. Those sales will depress bond prices, and that will push up rates in the U.S. Thus, a large trade deficit hinders the Fed's ability to combat a recession by lowering interest rates.

For 25 or so years following World War II the United States ran large trade surpluses, and the rest of the world owed us many billions of dollars. However, the situation changed, and we have been running trade deficits since the mid-1970s. The cumulative effect of these deficits has been to change the United States from being the largest creditor nation to being the largest debtor nation of all time. As a result, our interest rates are very much influenced by interest rates in other countries—higher or lower rates abroad lead to higher or lower U.S. rates. Because of all this, U.S. corporate treasurers and everyone else who is affected by interest rates should keep up with developments in the world economy.

6-7d Business Activity

Figure 6-2, presented in Section 6.2, can be examined to see how business conditions influence interest rates. Here are the key points revealed by the graph:

1. Because inflation increased from 1971 to 1981, the general tendency during that period was toward higher interest rates. However, since the 1981 peak, the trend has generally been downward.
2. The shaded areas in the graph represent recessions, during which (a) both the demand for money and the rate of inflation tend to fall and (b) the Federal Reserve tends to increase the money supply in an effort to stimulate the economy. As a result, there is a tendency for interest rates to decline during recessions. For example, the economy began to slow down in 2000, and we entered a mild recession in 2001. In response to this economic weakness, the Federal Reserve cut interest rates. However, in 2004 the economy began to rebound, so the Fed began to raise rates.
3. During recessions, short-term rates decline more sharply than long-term rates. This occurs because (a) the Fed operates mainly in the short-term sector, so its

Foreign Trade Deficit
The situation that exists when a country imports more than it exports.

---

[14] The deficit could also be financed by selling assets, including gold, corporate stocks, entire companies, and real estate. The United States has financed its massive trade deficits by all of these means in recent years, but the primary method has been by borrowing from foreigners.

GLOBAL PERSPECTIVES

Measuring Country Risk

Various forecasting services measure the level of country risk in different countries and provide indexes that indicate factors such as each country's expected economic performance, access to world capital markets, political stability, and level of internal conflict. Country risk analysts use sophisticated models to measure risk, thus providing corporate managers and investors with a way to judge both the relative and absolute risk of investing in different countries. A sample of recent country risk estimates compiled by *Institutional Investor* is presented in the accompanying table. The higher the country's score, the lower its country risk. The maximum possible score is 100.

The countries with the least country risk all have strong, market-based economies, ready access to worldwide capital markets, relatively little social unrest, and a stable political climate. Switzerland's top ranking may surprise you, but that country's ranking is the result of its strong economic performance and political stability. You may also be surprised that the United States was ranked third, below both Switzerland and Luxembourg.

Arguably, there are fewer surprises when looking at the bottom five. Each of these countries has considerable social and political unrest and no market-based economic system. An investment in any of these countries is clearly a risky proposition.

Top Five Countries (Least Amount of Country Risk)

Rank	Country	Total Score (Maximum Possible = 100)
1	Switzerland	95.2
2	Luxembourg	93.9
3*	United States	93.7
4*	Norway	93.7
5	United Kingdom	93.6

Bottom Five Countries (Greatest Amount of Country Risk)

Rank	Country	Total Score (Minimum Possible = 0)
169	Afghanistan	11.0
170	Liberia	9.4
171	Sierra Leone	9.3
172	North Korea	8.9
173	Somalia	8.2

*Ranking was determined before rounding total score.

Source: "Country Ratings by Region," *Institutional Investor,* **www.institutionalinvestor.com**, September 2004.

intervention has the strongest effect there, and (b) long-term rates reflect the average expected inflation rate over the next 20 to 30 years, and this expectation generally does not change much, even when the current inflation rate is low because of a recession or high because of a boom. So, short-term rates are more volatile than long-term rates. Taking another look at Figure 6-2, we indeed see that short-term rates have declined much more than long-term rates.

Other than inflationary expectations, name some additional factors that influence interest rates, and explain the effects of each.

How does the Fed stimulate the economy? How does the Fed affect interest rates? Does the Fed have complete control over U.S. interest rates; that is, can it set rates at any level it chooses? Why or why not?

6-8 INVESTING OVERSEAS

Investors should consider additional risk factors if they invest overseas. First, there is **country risk,** which refers to the risk that is attributable to investing in a particular country. This risk depends on the country's economic, political, and social environment. Some countries provide a safer investment climate, and therefore less country risk, than others. Examples of country risk include the risk that property will be expropriated without adequate compensation plus risks associated with changes in tax rates, regulations, and currency repatriation. Country risk also includes changes in host-country requirements regarding local production and employment, as well as the danger of damage due to internal strife.

It is especially important to keep in mind when investing overseas that securities are often denominated in a currency other than the dollar, which means that returns on the investment will depend on what happens to exchange rates. This is known as **exchange rate risk.** For example, if a U.S. investor purchases a Japanese bond, interest will probably be paid in yen, which must then be converted into dollars before the investor can spend his or her money in the United States. If the yen weakens relative to the dollar, then it will buy fewer dollars, hence fewer dollars will be received when funds are repatriated. However, if the yen strengthens, this will increase the effective investment return. It therefore follows that returns on a foreign investment depend on both the performance of the foreign security and on changes in exchange rates.

Country Risk
The risk that arises from investing or doing business in a particular country.

Exchange Rate Risk
The risk that exchange rate changes will reduce the number of dollars provided by a given amount of a foreign currency.

What is country risk?

What is exchange rate risk?

On what two factors does the return on a foreign investment depend?

6-9 INTEREST RATES AND BUSINESS DECISIONS

The yield curve for February 2005, shown earlier in Figure 6-4 in Section 6.4, indicates how much the U.S. government had to pay in February 2005 to borrow money for 1 year, 5 years, 10 years, and so on. A business borrower would have had to pay somewhat more, but assume for the moment that it is February 2005 and that the yield curve shown for that year applies to your company. Now suppose your company has decided to build a new plant with a 30-year life that will cost $1 million, and to raise the $1 million by borrowing rather than by issuing new stock. If you borrowed in February 2005 on a short-term basis—say, for one year—your interest cost would be only 3.1 percent, or $31,000. On the other hand, if you used long-term financing, your cost would be 4.6 percent, or $46,000. Therefore, at first glance, it would seem that you should use short-term debt.

However, this could prove to be a horrible mistake. If you use short-term debt, you will have to renew your loan every year, and the rate charged on each new loan will reflect the then-current short-term rate. Interest rates could return to their previous highs, in which case you would be paying 14 percent, or

$140,000, per year. Those high interest payments would cut into and perhaps eliminate your profits. Your reduced profitability could increase your firm's risk to the point where your bond rating was lowered, causing lenders to increase the risk premium built into your interest rate. That would further increase your interest payments, which would further reduce your profitability, worry lenders still more, and make them reluctant to even renew your loan. If your lenders refused to renew the loan and demanded its repayment, as they would have every right to do, you might have to sell assets at a loss, which could result in bankruptcy.

On the other hand, if you used long-term financing in 2005, your interest costs would remain constant at $46,000 per year, so an increase in interest rates in the economy would not hurt you. You might even be able to acquire some of your bankrupt competitors at bargain prices—bankruptcies increase dramatically when interest rates rise, primarily because many firms do use so much short-term debt.

Does all this suggest that firms should always avoid short-term debt? Not at all. If inflation falls over the next few years, so will interest rates. If you had borrowed on a long-term basis for 4.6 percent in February 2005, your company would be at a disadvantage if it were locked into 4.6 percent debt while its competitors (who used short-term debt in 2005) had a borrowing cost of only 3 percent or so.

Financing decisions would be easy if we could make accurate forecasts of future interest rates. Unfortunately, predicting interest rates with consistent accuracy is nearly impossible. However, even if it is difficult to predict future interest rate *levels*, it is easy to predict that interest rates will *fluctuate*—they always have, and they always will. This being the case, sound financial policy calls for using a mix of long- and short-term debt, as well as equity, to position the firm so that it can survive in any interest rate environment. Further, the optimal financial policy depends in an important way on the nature of the firm's assets—the easier it is to sell off assets to generate cash, the more feasible it is to use more short-term debt. This makes it more feasible for a firm to finance current assets like inventories and receivables with short-term debt than fixed assets like buildings. We will return to this issue later in the book, when we discuss working capital policy.

Changes in interest rates also have implications for savers. For example, if you had a 401(k) plan—and someday most of you will—you would probably want to invest some of your money in a bond mutual fund. You could choose a fund that had an average maturity of 25 years, 20 years, on down to only a few months (a money market fund). How would your choice affect your investment results, hence your retirement income? First, your annual interest income would be affected. For example, if the yield curve were upward sloping, as it normally is, you would earn more interest if you chose a fund that held long-term bonds. Note, though, that if you chose a long-term fund and interest rates then rose, the market value of the bonds in the fund would decline. For example, as we will see in Chapter 7, if you had $100,000 in a fund whose average bond had a maturity of 25 years and a coupon rate of 6 percent, and if interest rates then rose from 6 to 10 percent, the market value of your fund would decline from $100,000 to about $64,000. On the other hand, if rates declined, your fund would increase in value. In any event, your choice of maturity would have a major effect on your investment performance, hence on your future income.

If short-term interest rates are lower than long-term rates, why might a borrower still choose to finance with long-term debt?

Explain the following statement: "The optimal financial policy depends in an important way on the nature of the firm's assets."

Tying It All Together

In this chapter, we discussed how interest rates are determined, the term structure of interest rates, and some of the ways interest rates affect business decisions. We saw that the interest rate on a given bond, r, is based on this equation:

$$r = r^* + IP + DRP + LP + MRP$$

where r^* is the real risk-free rate, IP is the premium for expected inflation, DRP is the premium for potential default risk, LP is the premium for lack of liquidity (or marketability), and MRP is the premium to compensate for the risk inherent in bonds with long maturities. Both r^* and the various premiums can and do change over time, depending on economic conditions, Federal Reserve actions, and the like. Since changes in these factors are difficult to predict, it is hard to forecast the future direction of interest rates.

The yield curve, which relates bonds' interest rates to their maturities, can slope up or down, and it changes in both slope and level over time. The main determinants of the slope of the curve are expectations for inflation in future years and the MRP. We can analyze yield curve data to estimate what market participants think future interest rates are likely to be.

We will use the insights gained from this chapter in later chapters, when we analyze the values of bonds and stocks and also when we examine various corporate investment and financing decisions.

SELF-TEST QUESTIONS AND PROBLEMS
(Solutions Appear in Appendix A)

ST-1 **Key terms** Define each of the following terms:
a. Production opportunities; time preferences for consumption; risk; inflation
b. Real risk-free rate of interest, r^*; nominal (quoted) risk-free rate of interest, r_{RF}
c. Inflation premium (IP)
d. Default risk premium (DRP)
e. Liquidity premium (LP); maturity risk premium (MRP)
f. Interest rate risk; reinvestment rate risk
g. Term structure of interest rates; yield curve
h. "Normal" yield curve; inverted ("abnormal") yield curve; humped yield curve
i. Pure expectations theory
j. Foreign trade deficit; country risk; exchange rate risk

ST-2 **Inflation and interest rates** The real risk-free rate of interest, r^*, is 3 percent, and it is expected to remain constant over time. Inflation is expected to be 2 percent per year for the next 3 years, and 4 percent per year for the next 5 years. The maturity risk premium is equal to $0.1(t - 1)\%$, where t = the bond's maturity. The default risk premium for a BBB-rated bond is 1.3 percent.
a. What is the average expected inflation rate over the next 4 years?
b. What is the yield on a 4-year Treasury bond?
c. What is the yield on a 4-year BBB-rated corporate bond with a liquidity premium of 0.5 percent?

d. What is the yield on an 8-year Treasury bond?

e. What is the yield on an 8-year BBB-rated corporate bond with a liquidity premium of 0.5 percent?

f. If the yield on a 9-year Treasury bond is 7.3 percent, what does that imply about expected inflation in 9 years?

ST-3 **Pure expectations theory** The yield on one-year Treasury securities is 6 percent, 2-year securities yield 6.2 percent, and three-year securities yield 6.3 percent. There is no maturity risk premium. Using expectations theory, forecast the yields on the following securities:

a. A 1-year security, 1 year from now?

b. A 1-year security, 2 years from now?

c. A 2-year security, 1 year from now?

QUESTIONS

6-1 Suppose interest rates on residential mortgages of equal risk were 5.5 percent in California and 7.0 percent in New York. Could this differential persist? What forces might tend to equalize rates? Would differentials in borrowing costs for businesses of equal risk located in California and New York be more or less likely to exist than differentials in residential mortgage rates? Would differentials in the cost of money for New York and California firms be more likely to exist if the firms being compared were very large or if they were very small? What are the implications of all this with respect to nationwide branching?

6-2 Which fluctuate more, long-term or short-term interest rates? Why?

6-3 Suppose you believe that the economy is just entering a recession. Your firm must raise capital immediately, and debt will be used. Should you borrow on a long-term or a short-term basis? Why?

6-4 Suppose the population of Area Y is relatively young while that of Area O is relatively old, but everything else about the two areas is equal.

a. Would interest rates likely be the same or different in the two areas? Explain.

b. Would a trend toward nationwide branching by banks and savings and loans, and the development of nationwide diversified financial corporations, affect your answer to part a?

6-5 Suppose a new process was developed that could be used to make oil out of seawater. The equipment required is quite expensive, but it would, in time, lead to very low prices for gasoline, electricity, and other types of energy. What effect would this have on interest rates?

6-6 Suppose a new and much more liberal Congress and administration were elected, and their first order of business was to take away the independence of the Federal Reserve System and to force the Fed to greatly expand the money supply. What effect would this have

a. On the level and slope of the yield curve immediately after the announcement?

b. On the level and slope of the yield curve that would exist two or three years in the future?

6-7 It is a fact that the federal government (1) encouraged the development of the savings and loan industry; (2) virtually forced the industry to make long-term, fixed-interest-rate mortgages; and (3) forced the savings and loans to obtain most of their capital as deposits that were withdrawable on demand.

a. Would the savings and loans have higher profits in a world with a "normal" or an inverted yield curve?

b. Would the savings and loan industry be better off if the individual institutions sold their mortgages to federal agencies and then collected servicing fees or if the institutions held the mortgages that they originated?

6-8 Suppose interest rates on Treasury bonds rose from 5 to 9 percent as a result of higher interest rates in Europe. What effect would this have on the price of an average company's common stock?

6-9 What does it mean when it is said that the United States is running a trade deficit? What impact will a trade deficit have on interest rates?

PROBLEMS

Easy
Problems 1–7

6-1 **Yield curves** The following yields on U.S. Treasury securities were taken from a recent financial publication:

Term	Rate
6 months	5.1%
1 year	5.5
2 years	5.6
3 years	5.7
4 years	5.8
5 years	6.0
10 years	6.1
20 years	6.5
30 years	6.3

a. Plot a yield curve based on these data.
b. What type of yield curve is shown?
c. What information does this graph tell you?
d. Based on this yield curve, if you needed to borrow money for longer than one year, would it make sense for you to borrow short term and renew the loan or borrow long term? Explain.

6-2 **Real risk-free rate** You read in *The Wall Street Journal* that 30-day T-bills are currently yielding 5.5 percent. Your brother-in-law, a broker at Safe and Sound Securities, has given you the following estimates of current interest rate premiums:

- Inflation premium = 3.25%
- Liquidity premium = 0.6%
- Maturity risk premium = 1.8%
- Default risk premium = 2.15%

On the basis of these data, what is the real risk-free rate of return?

6-3 **Expected interest rate** The real risk-free rate is 3 percent. Inflation is expected to be 2 percent this year and 4 percent during the next 2 years. Assume that the maturity risk premium is zero. What is the yield on 2-year Treasury securities? What is the yield on 3-year Treasury securities?

6-4 **Default risk premium** A Treasury bond that matures in 10 years has a yield of 6 percent. A 10-year corporate bond has a yield of 8 percent. Assume that the liquidity premium on the corporate bond is 0.5 percent. What is the default risk premium on the corporate bond?

6-5 **Maturity risk premium** The real risk-free rate is 3 percent, and inflation is expected to be 3 percent for the next 2 years. A 2-year Treasury security yields 6.2 percent. What is the maturity risk premium for the 2-year security?

6-6 **Inflation cross-product** An analyst is evaluating securities in a developing nation where the inflation rate is very high. As a result, the analyst has been warned not to ignore the cross-product between the real rate and inflation. If the real risk-free rate is 5 percent and inflation is expected to be 16 percent each of the next 4 years, what is the yield on a 4-year security with no maturity, default, or liquidity risk? (Hint: Refer to the box titled "The Links Between Expected Inflation and Interest Rates: A Closer Look.")

6-7 **Expectations theory** One-year Treasury securities yield 5 percent. The market anticipates that 1 year from now, 1-year Treasury securities will yield 6 percent. If the pure expectations theory is correct, what is the yield today for 2-year Treasury securities?

Intermediate
Problems 8–16

6-8 **Expectations theory** Interest rates on 4-year Treasury securities are currently 7 percent, while 6-year Treasury securities yield 7.5 percent. If the pure expectations theory is correct, what does the market believe that 2-year securities will be yielding 4 years from now?

6-9 **Expected interest rate** The real risk-free rate is 3 percent. Inflation is expected to be 3 percent this year, 4 percent next year, and then 3.5 percent thereafter. The maturity risk premium is estimated to be $0.05 \times (t - 1)\%$, where t = number of years to maturity. What is the yield on a 7-year Treasury note?

6-10 **Inflation** Due to a recession, expected inflation this year is only 3 percent. However, the inflation rate in Year 2 and thereafter is expected to be constant at some level above 3 percent. Assume that the expectations theory holds and the real risk-free rate is $r^* = 2\%$. If the yield on 3-year Treasury bonds equals the 1-year yield plus 2 percent, what inflation rate is expected after Year 1?

6-11 **Default risk premium** A company's 5-year bonds are yielding 7.75 percent per year. Treasury bonds with the same maturity are yielding 5.2 percent per year, and the real risk-free rate (r^*) is 2.3 percent. The average inflation premium is 2.5 percent, and the maturity risk premium is estimated to be $0.1 \times (t - 1)\%$, where t = number of years to maturity. If the liquidity premium is 1 percent, what is the default risk premium on the corporate bonds?

6-12 **Maturity risk premium** An investor in Treasury securities expects inflation to be 2.5 percent in Year 1, 3.2 percent in Year 2, and 3.6 percent each year thereafter. Assume that the real risk-free rate is 2.75 percent, and that this rate will remain constant. Three-year Treasury securities yield 6.25 percent, while 5-year Treasury securities yield 6.80 percent. What is the difference in the maturity risk premiums (MRPs) on the two securities; that is, what is $MRP_5 - MRP_3$?

6-13 **Default risk premium** The real risk-free rate, r^*, is 2.5 percent. Inflation is expected to average 2.8 percent a year for the next 4 years, after which time inflation is expected to average 3.75 percent a year. Assume that there is no maturity risk premium. An 8-year corporate bond has a yield of 8.3 percent, which includes a liquidity premium of 0.75 percent. What is its default risk premium?

6-14 **Expectations theory and inflation** Suppose 2-year Treasury bonds yield 4.5 percent, while 1-year bonds yield 3 percent. r^* is 1 percent, and the maturity risk premium is zero.

a. Using the expectations theory, what is the yield on a 1-year bond, 1 year from now?
b. What is the expected inflation rate in Year 1? Year 2?

6-15 **Expectations theory** Assume that the real risk-free rate is 2 percent and that the maturity risk premium is zero. If the 1-year bond yield is 5 percent and a 2-year bond (of similar risk) yields 7 percent, what is the 1-year interest rate that is expected for Year 2? What inflation rate is expected during Year 2? Comment on why the average interest rate during the 2-year period differs from the 1-year interest rate expected for Year 2.

6-16 **Inflation cross-product** An analyst is evaluating securities in a developing nation where the inflation rate is very high. As a result, the analyst has been warned not to ignore the cross-product between the real rate and inflation. A 6-year security with no maturity, default, or liquidity risk has a yield of 20.84 percent. If the real risk-free rate is 6 percent, what average rate of inflation is expected in this country over the next 6 years? (Hint: Refer to the box titled, "The Links Between Expected Inflation and Interest Rates: A Closer Look.")

Challenging
Problems 17–19

6-17 **Interest rate premiums** A 5-year Treasury bond has a 5.2 percent yield. A 10-year Treasury bond yields 6.4 percent, and a 10-year corporate bond yields 8.4 percent. The market expects that inflation will average 2.5 percent over the next 10 years ($IP_{10} = 2.5\%$). Assume that there is no maturity risk premium (MRP = 0), and that the annual real risk-free rate, r^*, will remain constant over the next 10 years. (Hint: Remember that the default risk premium and the liquidity premium are zero for Treasury securities: DRP = LP = 0.) A 5-year corporate bond has the same default risk premium and liquidity premium as the 10-year corporate bond described above. What is the yield on this 5-year corporate bond?

6-18 **Yield curves** Suppose the inflation rate is expected to be 7 percent next year, 5 percent the following year, and 3 percent thereafter. Assume that the real risk-free rate, r^*, will remain at 2 percent and that maturity risk premiums on Treasury securities rise from zero on very short-term bonds (those that mature in a few days) to 0.2 percent for 1-year securities. Furthermore, maturity risk premiums increase 0.2 percent for each year to maturity, up to a limit of 1.0 percent on 5-year or longer-term T-bonds.

a. Calculate the interest rate on 1-, 2-, 3-, 4-, 5-, 10-, and 20-year Treasury securities, and plot the yield curve.
b. Now suppose ExxonMobil, a AAA-rated company, had bonds with the same maturities as the Treasury bonds. As an approximation, plot an ExxonMobil yield curve on the same graph with the Treasury bond yield curve. (Hint: Think about the default risk premium on ExxonMobil's long-term versus its short-term bonds.)
c. Now plot the approximate yield curve of Exelon Corp., a risky nuclear utility.

6-19 **Inflation and interest rates** In late 1980, the U.S. Commerce Department released new data showing inflation was 15 percent. At the time, the prime rate of interest was 21 percent, a record high. However, many investors expected the new Reagan administration to be more effective in controlling inflation than the Carter administration had been. Moreover, many observers believed that the extremely high interest rates and generally tight credit, which resulted from the Federal Reserve System's attempts to curb the inflation rate, would lead to a recession, which, in turn, would lead to a decline in inflation and interest rates. Assume that at the beginning of 1981, the expected inflation rate for 1981 was 13 percent; for 1982, 9 percent; for 1983, 7 percent; and for 1984 and thereafter, 6 percent.

a. What was the average expected inflation rate over the 5-year period 1981–1985? (Use the arithmetic average.)

b. What average *nominal* interest rate would, over the 5-year period, be expected to produce a 2 percent real risk-free return on 5-year Treasury securities? Assume MRP = 0 here.

c. Assuming a real risk-free rate of 2 percent and a maturity risk premium that equals $0.1 \times (t)\%$, where t is the number of years to maturity, estimate the interest rate in January 1981 on bonds that mature in 1, 2, 5, 10, and 20 years, and draw a yield curve based on these data.

d. Describe the general economic conditions that could lead to an upward-sloping yield curve.

e. If investors in early 1981 expected the inflation rate for every future year was 10 percent (that is, $I_t = I_{t+1} = 10\%$ for t = 1 to ∞), what would the yield curve have looked like? Consider all the factors that are likely to affect the curve. Does your answer here make you question the yield curve you drew in part c?

COMPREHENSIVE/SPREADSHEET PROBLEM

6-20   **Interest rate determination and yield curves**

a. What effect would each of the following events likely have on the level of nominal interest rates?
(1) Households dramatically increase their savings rate.
(2) Corporations increase their demand for funds following an increase in investment opportunities.
(3) The government runs a larger than expected budget deficit.
(4) There is an increase in expected inflation.

b. Suppose you are considering two possible investment opportunities: a 12-year Treasury bond and a 7-year, A-rated corporate bond. The current real risk-free rate is 4 percent, and inflation is expected to be 2 percent for the next 2 years, 3 percent for the following 4 years, and 4 percent thereafter. The maturity risk premium is estimated by this formula: MRP = 0.1(t − 1)%. The liquidity premium for the corporate bond is estimated to be 0.7 percent. Finally, you may determine the default risk premium, given the company's bond rating, from the default risk premium table in the text. What yield would you predict for each of these two investments?

c. Given the following Treasury bond yield information from a recent financial publication, construct a graph of the yield curve.

Maturity	Yield
1 year	5.37%
2 years	5.47
3 years	5.65
4 years	5.71
5 years	5.64
10 years	5.75
20 years	6.33
30 years	5.94

d. Based on the information about the corporate bond that was given in part b, calculate yields and then construct a new yield curve graph that shows both the Treasury and the corporate bonds.

e. Which part of the yield curve (the left side or right side) is likely to be the most volatile over time?

f. Using the Treasury yield information above, calculate the following rates:
(1) The 1-year rate, 1 year from now.
(2) The 5-year rate, 5 years from now.
(3) The 10-year rate, 10 years from now.
(4) The 10-year rate, 20 years from now.

Integrated Case

Smyth Barry & Company, Part II

6-21 **Interest rate determination** In Part I of this case, presented in Chapter 5, you were asked to describe the U.S. financial system to Michelle Varga. Varga is a professional tennis player, and your firm (Smyth Barry) manages her money. Varga was impressed with your discussion and has asked you to give her more information about what determines the level of various interest rates. Once again, your boss has prepared some questions for you to consider.

a. What are the four most fundamental factors that affect the cost of money, or the general level of interest rates, in the economy?

b. What is the real risk-free rate of interest (r*) and the nominal risk-free rate (r_{RF})? How are these two rates measured?

c. Define the terms inflation premium (IP), default risk premium (DRP), liquidity premium (LP), and maturity risk premium (MRP). Which of these premiums is included when determining the interest rate on (1) short-term U.S. Treasury securities, (2) long-term U.S. Treasury securities, (3) short-term corporate securities, and (4) long-term corporate securities? Explain how the premiums would vary over time and among the different securities listed above.

d. What is the term structure of interest rates? What is a yield curve?

e. Suppose most investors expect the inflation rate to be 5 percent next year, 6 percent the following year, and 8 percent thereafter. The real risk-free rate is 3 percent. The maturity risk premium is zero for bonds that mature in 1 year or less, 0.1 percent for 2-year bonds, and then the MRP increases by 0.1 percent per year thereafter for 20 years, after which it is stable. What is the interest rate on 1-, 10-, and 20-year Treasury bonds? Draw a yield curve with these data. What factors can explain why this constructed yield curve is upward sloping?

f. At any given time, how would the yield curve facing a AAA-rated company compare with the yield curve for U.S. Treasury securities? At any given time, how would the yield curve facing a BB-rated company compare with the yield curve for U.S. Treasury securities? Draw a graph to illustrate your answer.

g. What is the pure expectations theory? What does the pure expectations theory imply about the term structure of interest rates?

h. Suppose that you observe the following term structure for Treasury securities:

Maturity	Yield
1 year	6.0%
2 years	6.2
3 years	6.4
4 years	6.5
5 years	6.5

Assume that the pure expectations theory of the term structure is correct. (This implies that you can use the yield curve given above to "back out" the market's expectations about future interest rates.) What does the market expect will be the interest rate on 1-year securities 1 year from now? What does the market expect will be the interest rate on 3-year securities 2 years from now?

i. Finally, Varga is also interested in investing in countries other than the United States. Describe the various types of risks that arise when investing overseas.

cyberproblem

Please go to the ThomsonNOW Web site to access the Cyberproblems.

CHAPTER 7

BONDS AND THEIR VALUATION

Sizing Up Risk in the Bond Market

Many investors view Treasury securities as a safe but lackluster place to invest their funds. Treasuries are among the safest investments; nevertheless, in any given year, changing interest rates can cause significant changes in bond values, particularly for long-term bonds. For example, long-term Treasuries lost nearly 9 percent in 1999. More recently, Treasury bonds have performed quite well—indeed, they outperformed stocks in three of the five years between 2000 and 2004.

All bonds don't move in the same direction. Because of call and default risks, corporate bonds have higher yields than Treasuries. The yield spread between high-grade corporate and Treasury bonds is fairly small, but it is quite wide for companies with lower credit ratings and thus higher default risk. Indeed, changes in a firm's credit situation can cause dramatic shifts in its yield spreads. For example, amidst concerns about WorldCom's long-term viability, the spread on its five-year bonds that once had been just 1.67 percent jumped to over 20 percent in mid-2002. These bonds subsequently defaulted, which is what the huge spread predicted.

When all is going well in the economy, corporate bonds generally return more to investors than Treasuries. However, when the economy weakens and concerns about defaults rise, corporate bonds do worse than Treasuries. For example, from the beginning of 2000 to the end of 2002, a sluggish economy and the string of accounting scandals led to some major corporate defaults, which worried investors. Corporate bond prices declined relative to Treasury prices, and the result was an increase in the average yield spread. Since the beginning of 2003, though, the spread has declined as the economy rebounded.

To deal with these various risks, a recent *BusinessWeek Online* article gave investors the following useful advice:

> Take the same diversified approach to bonds as you do with stocks. Blend in U.S. government, corporate—both high-quality and high-yield—and perhaps even some foreign government debt. If you're investing taxable dollars, consider tax-exempt municipal bonds. And it doesn't hurt to layer in some inflation-indexed bonds.

Sources: Susan Scherreik, "Getting the Most Bang Out of Your Bonds," *BusinessWeek Online*, November 12, 2001; and *Stocks, Bonds, Bills, and Inflation: 2005 Yearbook (Valuation Edition)*, (Chicago: Ibbotson Associates, 2005).

Putting Things In Perspective

Bonds are one of the most important securities. If you skim through *The Wall Street Journal*, you will see references to a wide variety of bonds. This variety may seem confusing, but in actuality only a few characteristics distinguish the various types of bonds. In this chapter, we discuss the types of bonds companies and governments issue, the terms built into bond contracts, the procedures for determining bond prices and rates of return, and the types of risk bond investors and issuers face.

7-1 WHO ISSUES BONDS?

Bond
A long-term debt instrument.

A **bond** is a long-term contract under which a borrower agrees to make payments of interest and principal, on specific dates, to the holders of the bond. For example, on January 3, 2006, Allied Food Products borrowed $50 million by issuing $50 million of bonds. For convenience, we assume that Allied sold 50,000 individual bonds for $1,000 each. Actually, it could have sold one $50 million bond, 10 bonds each with a $5 million face value, or any other combination that totals to $50 million. In any event, Allied received the $50 million, and in exchange it promised to make annual interest payments and to repay the $50 million on a specified maturity date.

Until the 1970s, most bonds were beautifully engraved pieces of paper, and their key terms, including their face values, were spelled out on the bonds themselves. Today, though, virtually all bonds are represented by electronic data stored in secure computers, much like the "money" in a bank checking account.[1]

---

[1] The Internal Revenue Service put pressure on corporations to move from paper bonds to "book entry" bonds for two reasons: (1) With paper bonds, there was no systematic record of who received interest payments, hence it was relatively easy for bondholders to cheat on their income taxes. (2) People could store unregistered paper bonds in safe-deposit boxes, and when they died, their heirs could simply remove them and thereby evade estate taxes. Book entry prevents these evasions.

Investors have many choices when investing in bonds, but bonds are classified into four main types: Treasury, corporate, municipal, and foreign. Each differs with respect to risk and consequently to its expected return.

Treasury bonds, generally called Treasuries and sometimes referred to as government bonds, are issued by the federal government.[2] It is reasonable to assume that the federal government will make good on its promised payments, so Treasuries have no default risk. However, these bonds' prices decline when interest rates rise, so they are not completely risk free.

Corporate bonds, as the name implies, are issued by corporations. Unlike Treasuries, corporate bonds are exposed to default risk—if the issuing company gets into trouble, it may be unable to make the promised interest and principal payments. Different corporate bonds have different levels of default risk, depending on the issuing company's characteristics and on the terms of the specific bond. Default risk is often referred to as "credit risk," and, as we saw in Chapter 6, the larger the default risk, the higher the interest rate investors demand.

Municipal bonds, or "munis," are issued by state and local governments. Like corporates, munis are exposed to some default risk. However, munis offer one major advantage over all other bonds: As we discussed in Chapter 3, the interest earned on most munis is exempt from federal taxes, and also from state taxes if the holder is a resident of the issuing state. Consequently, the interest rates on munis are considerably lower than on corporates of equivalent risk.

Foreign bonds are issued by foreign governments or foreign corporations. Foreign corporate bonds are, of course, exposed to default risk, and so are the bonds of some foreign governments. An additional risk exists if the bonds are denominated in a currency other than that of the investor's home currency. For example, if you purchase a corporate bond denominated in Japanese yen, even if the company does not default you still could lose money if the Japanese yen falls relative to the dollar.

Treasury Bonds
Bonds issued by the federal government, sometimes referred to as government bonds.

Corporate Bonds
Bonds issued by corporations.

Municipal Bonds
Bonds issued by state and local governments.

Foreign Bonds
Bonds issued by either foreign governments or foreign corporations.

What is a bond?

What are the four main types of bonds?

Why are U.S. Treasury bonds not completely riskless?

In addition to default risk, what key risk do investors in foreign bonds face?

7-2 KEY CHARACTERISTICS OF BONDS

Although all bonds have some common characteristics, different bonds also have some different contractual features. For example, most corporate bonds have provisions for early repayment (call features), but the specific call provisions can vary widely among different bonds. Similarly, some bonds are backed by specific assets that must be turned over to the bondholders if the issuer defaults, while other bonds have no such collateral backup. Differences in contractual provisions, and in the fundamental, underlying financial strength of the

---

[2] The U.S. Treasury actually calls its debt "bills," "notes," or "bonds." T-bills generally have maturities of 1 year or less at the time of issue, notes generally have original maturities of 2 to 7 years, and bonds mature in 8 to 30 years. There are technical differences between bills, notes, and bonds, but they are not important for our purposes, so we generally call all Treasury securities "bonds." Note too that a 30-year T-bond at the time of issue becomes a 29-year bond the next year, and it becomes a 1-year bond after 29 years.

companies backing the bonds, lead to differences in bonds' risks, prices, and expected returns. To understand bonds, it is essential that you understand the following terms.

7-2a Par Value

Par Value
The face value of a bond.

The **par value** is the stated face value of the bond; for illustrative purposes we generally assume a par value of $1,000, although any multiple of $1,000 (for example, $5,000 or $5 million) can be used. The par value generally represents the amount of money the firm borrows and promises to repay on the maturity date.

7-2b Coupon Interest Rate

Coupon Payment
The specified number of dollars of interest paid each year.

Coupon Interest Rate
The stated annual interest rate on a bond.

Allied Food Products' bonds require the company to pay a fixed number of dollars of interest each year. When this annual **coupon payment,** as it is called, is divided by the par value, the result is the **coupon interest rate.** For example, Allied's bonds have a $1,000 par value, and they pay $100 in interest each year. The bond's coupon payment is $100, so its coupon interest rate is $100/$1,000 = 10%. The $100 is the annual "rent" on the $1,000 loan. This payment, which is set at the time the bond is issued, remains in force during the bond's life.[3] Typically, at the time a bond is issued, its coupon payment is set at a level that will induce investors to buy the bond at or near its par value. Most of the examples and problems throughout this text will focus on bonds with fixed coupon rates.

Floating-Rate Bond
A bond whose interest rate fluctuates with shifts in the general level of interest rates.

In some cases, however, a bond's coupon payment will be allowed to vary over time. These **floating-rate bonds** work as follows. The coupon rate is set for an initial period, often six months, after which it is adjusted every six months based on some open market rate. For example, many corporate issues are tied to the 10-year Treasury bond rate. Other provisions can be included in these bonds. For example, some are convertible at the holders' option to fixed-rate debt, whereas others have upper and lower limits ("caps" and "floors") on how high or low the rate can go.

Zero Coupon Bond
A bond that pays no annual interest but is sold at a discount below par, thus providing compensation to investors in the form of capital appreciation.

Original Issue Discount (OID) Bond
Any bond originally offered at a price below its par value.

Some bonds pay no coupons at all, but are offered at a discount below their par values and hence provide capital appreciation rather than interest income. These securities are called **zero coupon bonds** (*zeros*). Other bonds pay some coupon interest, but not enough to allow them to be issued at par. In general, any bond originally offered at a price significantly below its par value is called an **original issue discount (OID) bond.** Some of the details associated with issuing or investing in zero coupon bonds are discussed more fully in Web Appendix 7A.

7-2c Maturity Date

Maturity Date
A specified date on which the par value of a bond must be repaid.

Bonds generally have a specified **maturity date** on which the par value must be repaid. Allied's bonds, which were issued on January 3, 2006, will mature on January 2, 2021; thus, they had a 15-year maturity at the time they were issued.

---

[3] Back when bonds were pieces of paper, the "main bond" had a number of small (1/2- by 2-inch), dated, coupons attached to them, and on each interest payment date, the owner would "clip the coupon" for that date, send it to the company's paying agent, and receive a check for the interest. A 30-year, semiannual bond would start with 60 coupons, whereas a 5-year, annual payment, bond would start with only 5 coupons. Today, no physical coupons are involved, and interest checks are mailed automatically to the bonds' registered owners. Even so, people continue to use the terms *coupon* and *coupon interest rate* when discussing bonds.

Most bonds have **original maturities** (the maturity at the time the bond is issued) ranging from 10 to 40 years, but any maturity is legally permissible.[4] Of course, the effective maturity of a bond declines each year after it has been issued. Thus, Allied's bonds had a 15-year original maturity, but in 2007, a year later, they will have a 14-year maturity, and so on.

7-2d Call Provisions

Most corporate and municipal bonds, but not Treasury bonds, contain a **call provision,** which gives the issuer the right to call the bonds for redemption.[5] The call provision generally states that the issuer must pay the bondholders an amount greater than the par value if they are called. The additional sum, which is termed a *call premium*, is often set equal to one year's interest. For example, the call premium on a 10-year bond with a 10 percent annual coupon and a par value of $1,000 would be $100, which means that the issuer would have to pay investors $1,100 (the par value plus the call premium) if they wanted to call the bonds. In most cases the provisions in the bond contract are set so that the call premium declines over time as the bonds approach maturity. Also, while some bonds are immediately callable, in most cases bonds are often not callable until several years (generally 5 to 10) after issue. This is known as a *deferred call*, and the bonds are said to have *call protection*.

Suppose a company sold bonds when interest rates were relatively high. Provided the issue is callable, the company could sell a new issue of low-yielding securities if and when interest rates drop, use the proceeds of the new issue to retire the high-rate issue, and thus reduce its interest expense. This process is called a *refunding operation*. Thus, the call privilege is valuable to the firm but detrimental to long-term investors, who will be forced to reinvest the amount they receive at the new and lower rates. Accordingly, the interest rate on new issues of callable bonds will exceed that on new noncallable bonds. For example, on August 30, 2005, Pacific Timber Company sold a bond issue yielding 8 percent; these bonds were callable immediately. On the same day, Northwest Milling Company sold an issue of similar risk and maturity that yielded only 7.5 percent; its bonds were noncallable for 10 years. Investors were willing to accept a 0.5 percent lower interest rate on Northwest's bonds for the assurance that the 7.5 percent interest rate would be earned for at least 10 years. Pacific, on the other hand, had to incur a 0.5 percent higher annual interest rate to obtain the option of calling the bonds in the event of a decline in rates.

7-2e Sinking Funds

Some bonds also include a **sinking fund provision** that facilitates the orderly retirement of the bond issue. Years ago, firms were required to deposit money with a trustee, which invested the funds and then used the accumulated sum to retire the bonds when they matured. Today, though, sinking fund provisions

Original Maturity
The number of years to maturity at the time a bond is issued.

Call Provision
A provision in a bond contract that gives the issuer the right to redeem the bonds under specified terms prior to the normal maturity date.

Sinking Fund Provision
A provision in a bond contract that requires the issuer to retire a portion of the bond issue each year.

---

[4] In July 1993, Walt Disney Co., attempting to lock in a low interest rate, issued the first 100-year bonds to be sold by any borrower in modern times. Soon after, Coca-Cola became the second company to stretch the meaning of "long-term bond" by selling $150 million worth of 100-year bonds.
[5] The number of new corporate issues with call provisions attached has declined somewhat in recent years. In the 1980s, nearly 80 percent of new issues contained call provisions; however, in recent years this number has fallen to about 35 percent. The use of call provisions also varies with credit quality. Roughly 25 percent of investment-grade bonds issued in recent years have call provisions. By contrast, about 75 percent of recent non-investment-grade bond issues include a call provision. For more information on the use of callable bonds, see Levent Güntay, N. R. Prabhala, and Haluk Unal, "Callable Bonds and Hedging," a Wharton Financial Institutions Center working paper.

require the issuer to buy back a specified percentage of the issue each year. A failure to meet the sinking fund requirement constitutes a default, which may throw the company into bankruptcy. Therefore, a sinking fund puts a significant cash drain on the firm.

In most cases, the issuer can handle the sinking fund in either of two ways:

1. The company can call in for redemption (at par value) a certain percentage of the bonds each year; for example, it might call 5 percent of the total original amount of the issue at a price of $1,000 per bond. The bonds are numbered serially, and those called for redemption are determined by a lottery administered by the trustee.
2. Alternatively, the company can buy the required bonds on the open market.

The firm will choose the least-cost method. If interest rates have risen since the bond was issued, then the bond will sell at a price below its par value, so the firm will buy bonds in the open market at a discount. On the other hand, if interest rates have fallen and the bond's price has risen above par, it will use the call option. Note that a call for sinking fund purposes is quite different from a refunding call—a sinking fund call requires no call premium, but only a small percentage of the issue is normally callable in a given year.[6]

Although sinking funds are designed to protect investors by ensuring that the bonds are retired in an orderly fashion, you should recognize that sinking funds can work to the detriment of bondholders. For example, suppose the bond carries a 10 percent interest rate, but yields on similar bonds have fallen to 7.5 percent. A sinking fund call at par would require a long-term investor to give up a bond that pays $100 of interest and then to reinvest in a bond that pays only $75 per year. This is an obvious disadvantage to those bondholders whose bonds are called. On balance, however, bonds that have a sinking fund are regarded as being safer than those without such a provision, so at the time they are issued sinking fund bonds have lower coupon rates than otherwise similar bonds without sinking funds.

7-2f Other Features

Convertible Bond
A bond that is exchangeable, at the option of the holder, for the issuing firm's common stock.

Warrant
A long-term option to buy a stated number of shares of common stock at a specified price.

Putable Bond
A bond with provisions that allow its investor to sell it back to the company prior to maturity at a pre-arranged price.

Income Bond
A bond that pays interest only if it is earned.

Several other types of bonds are used sufficiently often to warrant mention.[7] First, **convertible bonds** are bonds that are exchangeable into shares of common stock, at a fixed price, at the option of the bondholder. Convertibles have lower coupon rates than nonconvertible debt with similar credit risk, but they offer investors the chance for capital gains as compensation for the lower coupon rate. Bonds issued with **warrants** are similar to convertibles. Warrants are options that permit the holder to buy stock for a stated price, thereby providing a capital gain if the stock's price rises. Bonds issued with warrants, like convertibles, carry lower coupon rates than regular bonds.

Unlike callable bonds that give the issuer the option to buy back their debt prior to maturity, **putable bonds** allow investors to sell the bonds back to the company prior to maturity at a specified price. If interest rates rise, then investors will put these bonds back to the company and reinvest in higher coupon bonds. Another variation is the **income bond,** which pays interest only if the interest is earned. Thus, income bonds cannot bankrupt a company, but from an investor's standpoint they are riskier than "regular" bonds. Yet another bond

---

[6] Some sinking funds require the issuer to pay a call premium.

[7] A recent article by John D. Finnerty and Douglas R. Emery reviews new types of debt (and other) securities that have been created in recent years. See "Corporate Securities Innovations: An Update," *Journal of Applied Finance: Theory, Practice, Education*, Vol. 12, no. 1 (Spring/Summer 2002), pp. 21–47.

is the **indexed, or purchasing power, bond.** The interest rate is based on an inflation index such as the consumer price index, so the interest paid rises automatically when the inflation rate rises, thus protecting bondholders against inflation. The U.S. Treasury is the main issuer of indexed bonds, and today (2005) they generally pay from 1 to 2 percent, plus the rate of inflation during the past year.

Define floating-rate bonds, zero coupon bonds, putable bonds, income bonds, convertible bonds, and inflation indexed bonds.

How is the rate on a floating-rate bond determined? On an indexed bond?

What are the two ways sinking funds can be handled? Which alternative will be used if interest rates have risen? Which if interest rates have fallen?

> **Indexed (Purchasing Power) Bond**
> *A bond that has interest payments based on an inflation index so as to protect the holder from inflation.*

7-3 BOND VALUATION

The value of any financial asset—a stock, a bond, a lease, or even physical assets such as apartment buildings or pieces of machinery—is simply the present value of the cash flows the asset is expected to produce.

The cash flows for a standard coupon-bearing bond, like those of Allied Foods', consist of interest payments during the bond's 15-year life plus the amount borrowed (generally the par value) when the bond matures. In the case of a floating-rate bond, the interest payments vary over time. For zero coupon bonds, there are no interest payments, so the only cash flow is the face amount when the bond matures. For a "regular" bond with a fixed coupon rate, like Allied's, here is the situation:

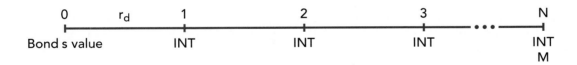

Here

> r_d = the bond's market rate of interest = 10 percent. This is the discount rate used to calculate the present value of the bond's cash flows, which is also its price. In Chapter 6 we discussed in detail the various factors that determine market interest rates. Note that r_d is *not* the coupon interest rate, and it is equal to the coupon rate if and only if (as in this case) the bond is selling at par.
>
> N = the number of years before the bond matures = 15. N declines each year after the bond has been issued, so a bond that had a maturity of 15 years when it was issued (original maturity = 15) will have N = 14 after one year, N = 13 after two years, and so on. At this point we assume that the bond pays interest once a year, or annually, so N is measured in years. Later on, we will analyze semiannual payment bonds, which pay interest each six months.
>
> INT = dollars of interest paid each year = Coupon rate × Par value = 0.10($1,000) = $100. In calculator terminology, INT = PMT = 100. If the

> bond had been a semiannual payment bond, the payment would have been $50 each six months. The payment would be zero if Allied had issued zero coupon bonds, and it would vary if the bond had been a "floater."
>
> M = the par, or maturity, value of the bond = $1,000. This amount must be paid at maturity.

We can now redraw the time line to show the numerical values for all variables except the bond's value, V_B:

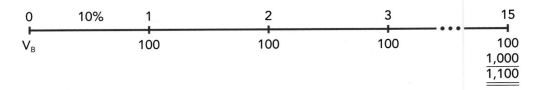

0	10%	1	2	3	15
V_B		100	100	100	100
					1,000
					1,100

The following general equation can be solved to find the value of any bond:

$$\text{Bond's value, } V_B = \frac{INT}{(1 + r_d)^1} + \frac{INT}{(1 + r_d)^2} + \cdots + \frac{INT}{(1 + r_d)^N} + \frac{M}{(1 + r_d)^N}$$

$$= \sum_{t=1}^{N} \frac{INT}{(1 + r_d)^t} + \frac{M}{(1 + r_d)^N}$$

(7-1)

Inserting values for our particular bond, we have

$$V_B = \sum_{t=1}^{15} \frac{\$100}{(1.10)^t} + \frac{\$1,000}{(1.10)^{15}}$$

The cash flows consist of an annuity of N years plus a lump sum payment at the end of Year N, and this fact is reflected in Equation 7-1.

We could simply discount each cash flow back to the present and sum these PVs to find the bond's value; see Figure 7-1 for an example. However, this procedure is not very efficient, especially if the bond has many years to maturity. Therefore, we use a financial calculator to solve the problem. Here is the setup:

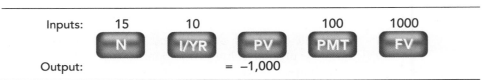

	Inputs:	15	10		100	1000
		N	I/YR	PV	PMT	FV
	Output:			= −1,000		

Simply input N = 15, r_d = I/YR = 10, INT = PMT = 100, M = FV = 1000, and then press the PV key to find the bond's value, $1,000.[8] Since the PV is an outflow to the investor, it is shown with a negative sign. The calculator is programmed to solve Equation 7-1: It finds the PV of an annuity of $100 per year for 15 years, discounted at 10 percent, then it finds the PV of the $1,000 maturity payment, and then it adds these two PVs to find the bond's value.

In this example the bond is selling at a price equal to its par value. Whenever the going rate of interest, r_d, is equal to the coupon rate, a *fixed-rate* bond

---

[8] Spreadsheets can also be used to solve for the bond's value, as we show in the *Excel* model for this chapter.

FIGURE 7-1 *Time Line for Allied Food Products' Bonds, 10% Interest Rate*

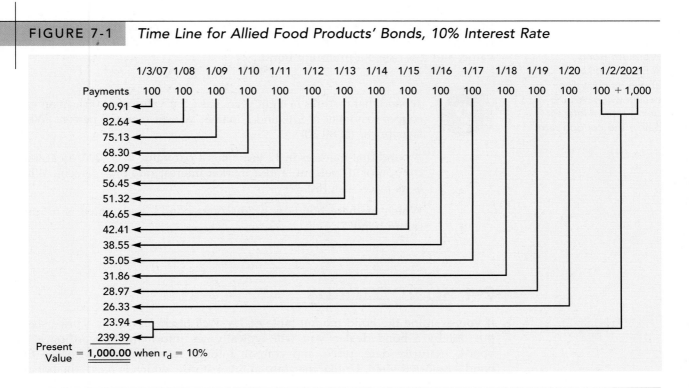

will sell at its par value. Normally, the coupon rate is set at the going rate when a bond is issued, causing it to sell at par initially.

The coupon rate remains fixed after the bond is issued, but interest rates in the market move up and down. Looking at Equation 7-1, we see that an *increase* in the market interest rate (r_d) will cause the price of an outstanding bond to *fall*, whereas a *decrease* in rates will cause the bond's price to *rise*. For example, if the market interest rate on Allied's bond increased to 15 percent immediately after it was issued, we would recalculate the price with the new market interest rate as follows:

The price would fall to $707.63. Notice that the bond would then sell at a price below its par value. Whenever the going rate of interest *rises above* the coupon rate, a fixed-rate bond's price will fall *below* its par value, and it is called a **discount bond.**

On the other hand, bond prices rise when market interest rates fall. For example, if the market interest rate on Allied's bond decreased to 5 percent, we would once again recalculate its price:

Discount Bond
A bond that sells below its par value; occurs whenever the going rate of interest is above the coupon rate.

In this case the price rises to $1,518.98. In general, whenever the going interest rate *falls below* the coupon rate, a fixed-rate bond's price will rise *above* its par value, and it is called a **premium bond.**

Premium Bond
A bond that sells above its par value; occurs whenever the going rate of interest is below the coupon rate.

A bond that matures in eight years has a par value of $1,000, an annual coupon payment of $70, and a market interest rate of 9 percent. What is its price? ($889.30)

A bond that matures in 12 years has a par value of $1,000, an annual coupon of 10 percent, and a market interest rate of 8 percent. What is its price? ($1,150.72)

Which of these bonds is a "discount bond," and which is a "premium bond"?

7-4 BOND YIELDS

If you examine the bond market table of *The Wall Street Journal* or a price sheet put out by a bond dealer, you will typically see information regarding each bond's maturity date, price, and coupon interest rate. You will also see the bond's reported yield. Unlike the coupon interest rate, which is fixed, the bond's reported yield varies from day to day depending on current market conditions. Moreover, the yield can be calculated in three different ways, as we explain in the following sections.

7-4a Yield to Maturity

Yield to Maturity (YTM)
The rate of return earned on a bond if it is held to maturity.

Suppose you were offered a 14-year, 10 percent annual coupon, $1,000 par value bond at a price of $1,494.93. What rate of interest would you earn on your investment if you bought the bond and held it to maturity? This rate is called the bond's **yield to maturity (YTM),** and it is the interest rate generally discussed by investors when they talk about rates of return and the rate reported by *The Wall Street Journal*. To find the YTM, all you need to do is solve Equation 7-1 for r_d:

$$V_B = \$1,494.93 = \frac{\$100}{(1 + r_d)^1} + \cdots + \frac{\$100}{(1 + r_d)^{14}} + \frac{\$1,000}{(1 + r_d)^{14}}$$

You could substitute values for r_d until you find a value that "works" and forces the sum of the PVs on the right side of the equation to equal $1,494.93. However, finding r_d = YTM by trial and error would be a tedious, time-consuming process that is, as you might guess, easy with a financial calculator.[9] Here is the setup:

---

[9] You could also find the YTM with a spreadsheet. In *Excel*, you would use the Rate function, inputting Nper = 14, Pmt = 100, Pv = −1494.93, Fv = 1000, 0 for Type, and leave Guess blank.

Simply enter N = 14, PV = −1494.93, PMT = 100, and FV = 1000, and then press the I/YR key. The answer, 5 percent, will then appear.

The yield to maturity can also be viewed as the bond's *promised rate of return*, which is the return that investors will receive if all the promised payments are made. However, the yield to maturity equals the *expected rate of return* only if (1) the probability of default is zero and (2) the bond cannot be called. If there is some default risk, or if the bond may be called, then there is some probability that the promised payments to maturity will not be received, in which case the calculated yield to maturity will differ from the expected return.

Note also that a bond's yield to maturity changes whenever interest rates in the economy change, and this is almost daily. An investor who purchases a bond and holds it until it matures will receive the YTM that existed on the purchase date, but the bond's calculated YTM will change frequently between the purchase date and the maturity date.

7-4b Yield to Call

If you purchased a bond that was callable and the company called it, you would not have the option of holding it until it matured. Therefore, the yield to maturity would not be earned. For example, if Allied's 10 percent coupon bonds were callable, and if interest rates fell from 10 to 5 percent, then the company could call in the 10 percent bonds, replace them with 5 percent bonds, and save $100 − $50 = $50 interest per bond per year. This would be beneficial to the company, but not to its bondholders.

If current interest rates are well below an outstanding bond's coupon rate, then a callable bond is likely to be called, and investors will estimate its expected rate of return as the **yield to call (YTC)** rather than as the yield to maturity. To calculate the YTC, solve this equation for r_d:

Yield to Call (YTC)
The rate of return earned on a bond if it is called before its maturity date.

$$\text{Price of callable bond} = \sum_{t=1}^{N} \frac{INT}{(1 + r_d)^t} + \frac{\text{Call price}}{(1 + r_d)^N} \qquad \textbf{(7-2)}$$

Here N is the number of years until the company can call the bond; call price is the price the company must pay in order to call the bond (it is often set equal to the par value plus one year's interest); and r_d is the YTC.

To illustrate, suppose Allied's bonds had a provision that permitted the company, if it desired, to call them 10 years after their issue date at a price of $1,100. Suppose further that interest rates had fallen, and one year after issuance the going interest rate had declined, causing their price to rise to $1,494.93. Here is the time line and the setup for finding the bonds' YTC with a financial calculator:

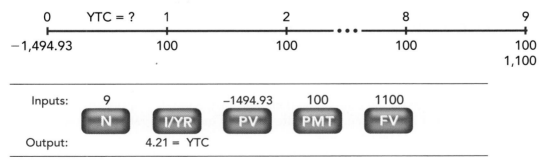

The YTC is 4.21 percent—this is the return you would earn if you bought an Allied bond at a price of $1,494.93 and it was called nine years from today. (It could not be called until 10 years after issuance, and 1 year has gone by, so there are 9 years left until the first call date.)

Do you think Allied *will* call its 10 percent bonds when they become callable? Allied's action will depend on what the going interest rate is when they become callable. If the going rate remains at $r_d = 5\%$, then Allied could save $10\% - 5\% = 5\%$, or $50 per bond per year, so it would call the 10 percent bonds and replace them with a new 5 percent issue. There would be some costs to the company to refund the bonds, but the interest savings would almost certainly be worth the cost, so Allied would almost certainly refund them. Therefore, you should expect to earn the YTC = 4.21% rather than the YTM = 5% if you bought the bond under the indicated conditions.

In the balance of this chapter, we assume that bonds are not callable unless otherwise noted, but some of the end-of-chapter problems deal with yield to call.

7-4c Current Yield

Current Yield
The annual interest payment on a bond divided by the bond's current price.

Brokerage house reports on bonds often refer to the **current yield,** which is defined as the annual interest payment divided by the bond's current price. For example, if Allied's 10 percent coupon bonds were currently selling for $985, the current yield would be $100/$985 = 10.15%.

Unlike the yield to maturity, the current yield *does not* represent the total return that investors should expect to receive from the bond because it does not take account of the capital gain or loss that will be realized if the bond is held until its maturity (or call). It does provide information regarding the amount of cash income that will be generated in a given year, but it does not provide an accurate measure of the total expected return. This point can be illustrated with a zero coupon bond. Because zeros pay no annual interest, they always have a zero current yield. However, zeros appreciate in value over time, so their total rate of return clearly exceeds zero.

Explain the difference between yield to maturity and yield to call.

Halley Enterprises' bonds currently sell for $975. They have a seven-year maturity, an annual coupon of $90, and a par value of $1,000. What is their yield to maturity? Their current yield? (9.51%; 9.23%)

The Henderson Company's bonds currently sell for $1,275. They pay a $120 annual coupon and have a 20-year maturity, but they can be called in 5 years at $1,120. What is their YTM and their YTC, and which is "more relevant" in the sense that investors should expect to earn it? (8.99%; 7.31%; YTC)

7-5 CHANGES IN BOND VALUES OVER TIME

When a coupon bond is issued, the coupon is generally set at a level that causes the bond's market price to equal its par value. If a lower coupon were set, investors would not be willing to pay $1,000 for the bond, while if a higher coupon were set, investors would clamor for it and bid its price up over $1,000. Investment bankers can judge quite precisely the coupon rate that causes a bond to sell at its $1,000 par value.

A bond that has just been issued is known as a *new issue*. Once it has been issued, it is an *outstanding bond*, also called a *seasoned issue*. Newly issued bonds generally sell at prices very close to par, but the prices of outstanding bonds can vary widely from par. Except for floating-rate bonds, coupon payments are constant, so when economic conditions change, a bond with a $100 coupon that sold at its $1,000 par value when it was issued will sell for more or less than $1,000 thereafter.

Among its outstanding bonds, Allied currently has three issues that will all mature in 15 years:

- As we have been discussing, Allied just issued 15-year bonds with a 10 percent coupon rate. These bonds were issued at par, which means that the market interest rate on the bonds was also 10 percent. Because the coupon rate equals the market interest rate, these bonds are trading at par, hence their price is $1,000.
- Five years ago, Allied issued 20-year bonds with a 7 percent coupon rate. These bonds currently have 15 years remaining until maturity. The bonds were originally issued at par, which means that 5 years ago when these bonds were issued, the market interest rate was 7 percent. For these bonds, the coupon rate is less than the market interest rate, so they sell at a discount. Using a financial calculator or spreadsheet, we can quickly find that they have a price of $771.82. (Set N = 15, I/YR = 10, PMT = 70, FV = 1000, and solve for the PV to get the price.)
- Ten years ago, Allied issued 25-year bonds with a 13 percent coupon rate. These bonds currently have 15 years remaining until maturity. They were originally issued at par, which means that 10 years ago the market interest rate must have been 13 percent. Because the coupon rate on these bonds is greater than the current market interest rate, they sell at a premium. Using a financial calculator or spreadsheet, we can find that their price is $1,228.18. (Set N = 15, I/YR = 10, PMT = 130, FV = 1000, and solve for the PV to get the price.)

Each of these three bonds has a 15-year maturity, each has the same credit risk, and thus each has the same market interest rate, 10 percent. However, the bonds have different prices because of their different coupon rates.

Now let's consider what would happen to the prices of these bonds over time, assuming that market interest rates remained constant at 10 percent and Allied does not default on its bonds. Table 7-1 demonstrates how the prices of each of these bonds will change over time if market interest rates remain at 10 percent. One year from now, each bond will have a maturity of 14 years—that is, N = 14. With a financial calculator, just override N = 15 with N = 14, press the PV key, and you find the value of each bond one year from now. Continuing, set N = 13, N = 12, and so forth, to see how the prices change over time.

Table 7-1 also shows the current yield, the capital gains yield, and the total return over time. For any given year, the *capital gains yield* is calculated as the bond's annual change in price divided by the beginning-of-year price. For example, if a bond were selling for $1,000 at the beginning of the year and $1,035 at the end of the year, its capital gains yield for the year would be $35/$1,000 = 3.5%. (If the bond were selling at a premium, then its price would decline over time, and the capital gains yield would be negative but offset by a high current yield.) A bond's total return is equal to the current yield plus the capital gains yield. In the absence of default risk, it is also equal to YTM and the market interest rate, which in our example is 10 percent.

Using the information from Table 7-1, Figure 7-2 plots the predicted changes in bond prices for the 7, 10, and 13 percent coupon bonds. Notice that the bonds have very different price paths over time, but at maturity all three bonds will sell at their par value of $1,000. Here are some points about the prices of the bonds over time:

- The price of the 10 percent coupon bond trading at par would remain at $1,000 if the market interest rate remains at 10 percent, so its current yield would remain at 10 percent and its capital gains yield would be zero each year.

TABLE 7-1 Calculation of Current Yields, Capital Gains Yields, and Total Returns for 7%, 10%, and 13% Coupon Bonds When the Market Rate Remains Constant at 10%

Number of Years until Maturity	7% COUPON BOND				10% COUPON BOND				13% COUPON BOND			
	Price[a]	Expected Current Yield[b]	Expected Capital Gains Yield[c]	Expected Total Return[d]	Price[a]	Expected Current Yield[b]	Expected Capital Gains Yield[c]	Expected Total Return[d]	Price[a]	Expected Current Yield[b]	Expected Capital Gains Yield[c]	Expected Total Return[d]
15	$ 771.82	9.1%	0.9%	10.0%	$1,000.00	10.0%	0.0%	10.0%	$1,228.18	10.6%	−0.6%	10.0%
14	779.00	9.0	1.0	10.0	1,000.00	10.0	0.0	10.0	1,221.00	10.6	−0.6	10.0
13	786.90	8.9	1.1	10.0	1,000.00	10.0	0.0	10.0	1,213.10	10.7	−0.7	10.0
12	795.59	8.8	1.2	10.0	1,000.00	10.0	0.0	10.0	1,204.41	10.8	−0.8	10.0
11	805.15	8.7	1.3	10.0	1,000.00	10.0	0.0	10.0	1,194.85	10.9	−0.9	10.0
10	815.66	8.6	1.4	10.0	1,000.00	10.0	0.0	10.0	1,184.34	11.0	−1.0	10.0
9	827.23	8.5	1.5	10.0	1,000.00	10.0	0.0	10.0	1,172.77	11.1	−1.1	10.0
8	839.95	8.3	1.7	10.0	1,000.00	10.0	0.0	10.0	1,160.05	11.2	−1.2	10.0
7	853.95	8.2	1.8	10.0	1,000.00	10.0	0.0	10.0	1,146.05	11.3	−1.3	10.0
6	869.34	8.1	1.9	10.0	1,000.00	10.0	0.0	10.0	1,130.66	11.5	−1.5	10.0
5	886.28	7.9	2.1	10.0	1,000.00	10.0	0.0	10.0	1,113.72	11.7	−1.7	10.0
4	904.90	7.7	2.3	10.0	1,000.00	10.0	0.0	10.0	1,095.10	11.9	−1.9	10.0
3	925.39	7.6	2.4	10.0	1,000.00	10.0	0.0	10.0	1,074.61	12.1	−2.1	10.0
2	947.93	7.4	2.6	10.0	1,000.00	10.0	0.0	10.0	1,052.07	12.4	−2.4	10.0
1	972.73	7.2	2.8	10.0	1,000.00	10.0	0.0	10.0	1,027.27	12.7	−2.7	10.0
0	1,000.00				1,000.00				1,000.00			

Notes:

[a] Using a financial calculator, the price of each bond is calculated by entering the data for N, I/YR, PMT, and FV, then solving for PV = the bond's value.

[b] The expected current yield is calculated as the annual interest divided by the price of the bond.

[c] The expected capital gains yield is calculated as the difference between the end-of-year bond price and the beginning-of-year bond price divided by the beginning-of-year price.

[d] The expected total return is the sum of the expected current yield and the expected capital gains yield.

FIGURE 7-2　*Time Paths of 7%, 10%, and 13% Coupon Bonds When the Market Rate Remains Constant at 10%*

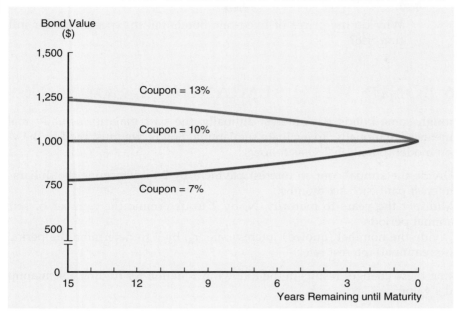

- The 7 percent bond trades at a discount, but its price must approach its par value as the maturity date approaches. At maturity it must sell for its par value, because that is the amount the company must give to its holders. So, its price must rise over time.
- The 13 percent coupon bond trades at a premium, but its price must be equal to its par value at maturity, so it must decline over time.

While the prices of the 7 and 13 percent coupon bonds move in opposite directions over time, each bond provides investors with the same total return, 10 percent, which is also the total return on the 10 percent coupon bond that sells at par. The discount bond has a lower coupon rate (and therefore a lower current yield), but it provides a capital gain each year. In contrast, the premium bond has a higher current yield, but it has an expected capital loss each year.[10]

What is meant by the terms "new issue" and "seasoned issue"?

Last year a firm issued 20-year, 8 percent annual coupon bonds at a par value of $1,000.

(1) Suppose that one year later the going rate had dropped to 6 percent. What is the new price of the bonds, assuming that they now have 19 years to maturity? ($1,223.16)

---

[10] In this example (and throughout the text) we ignore the tax effects associated with purchasing different types of bonds. For coupon bonds, under the current Tax Code, coupon payments are taxed as ordinary income, whereas capital gains are taxed at the capital gains tax rate. As we mentioned in Chapter 3, for most investors the capital gains tax rate is lower than the personal tax rate. Moreover, while coupon payments are taxed each year, capital gains taxes are deferred until the bond is sold or matures. Consequently, all else equal, investors would end up paying lower taxes on discount bonds, because a greater percentage of their total return comes in the form of capital gains. For details on the tax treatment of zero coupon bonds, see Web Appendix 7A.

(2) Suppose that one year after issue the going interest rate had been 10 percent (rather than 6 percent). What would the price have been? ($832.70)

Why do the prices of fixed-rate bonds fall if expectations for inflation rise?

7-6 BONDS WITH SEMIANNUAL COUPONS

Although some bonds pay interest annually, the vast majority actually make payments semiannually. To evaluate semiannual bonds, we must modify the valuation model (Equation 7-1) as follows:

1. Divide the annual coupon interest payment by 2 to determine the dollars of interest paid each six months.
2. Multiply the years to maturity, N, by 2 to determine the number of semiannual periods.
3. Divide the nominal (quoted) interest rate, r_d, by 2 to determine the periodic (semiannual) interest rate.

Making these changes results in the following equation for finding a semiannual bond's value:

$$V_B = \sum_{t=1}^{2N} \frac{INT/2}{(1 + r_d/2)^t} + \frac{M}{(1 + r_d/2)^{2N}} \qquad \textbf{(7-1a)}$$

To illustrate, now assume the Allied Food bonds discussed in Section 7.3 pay $50 of interest each six months rather than $100 at the end of each year. Thus, each interest payment is only half as large, but there are twice as many of them. The coupon rate is thus stated to be "10 percent with semiannual payments."[11]

When the going (nominal) rate of interest is r_d = 5% with semiannual compounding, the value of a 15-year, 10 percent semiannual coupon, bond that pays $50 interest every six months, is found as follows:

Inputs:	30	2.5		50	1000
	N	I/YR	PV	PMT	FV
Output:			=−1,523.26		

Enter N = 30, r_d = I/YR = 2.5, PMT = 50, FV = 1000, and then press the PV key to obtain the bond's value, $1,523.26. The value with semiannual interest payments is slightly larger than $1,518.98, the value when interest is paid annually

---

[11] In this situation, the coupon rate of "10 percent paid semiannually," is the rate that bond dealers, corporate treasurers, and investors generally would discuss. Of course, if this bond were issued at par, its *effective annual rate* would be higher than 10 percent:

$$EAR = EFF\% = \left(1 + \frac{r_{NOM}}{M}\right)^M - 1 = \left(1 + \frac{0.10}{2}\right)^2 - 1 = (1.05)^2 - 1 = 10.25\%$$

Since 10 percent with annual payments is quite different from 10 percent with semiannual payments, we have assumed a change in effective rates in this section from the situation in Section 7.3, where we assumed 10 percent with annual payments.

as we calculated in Section 7.3. This higher value occurs because each interest payment is received somewhat faster under semiannual compounding.

Describe how the annual payment bond valuation formula is changed to evaluate semiannual coupon bonds, and write out the revised formula.

Hartwell Corporation bonds have a 20-year maturity, an 8 percent semiannual coupon, and a face value of $1,000. The going interest rate (r_d) is 7 percent, based on semiannual compounding. What is the bond's price? ($1,106.78)

7-7 ASSESSING A BOND'S RISKINESS

7-7a Interest Rate Risk

As we saw in Chapter 6, interest rates fluctuate over time, and an increase in rates leads to a decline in the value of an outstanding bond. This risk of a decline in bond values due to an increase in interest rates is called **interest rate risk** (or **interest rate price risk**). To illustrate, refer back to Allied's bonds, assume once more that they have a 10 percent annual coupon, and assume that you bought one of these bonds at its par value, $1,000. Shortly after your purchase, the going interest rate rises from 10 to 15 percent.[12] As we saw in Section 7.3, this interest rate increase would cause the bond's price to fall from $1,000 to $707.63, so you would have a loss of $292.37 on the bond.[13] Interest rates can and do rise, and rising rates cause a loss of value for bondholders. Thus, people or firms who invest in bonds are exposed to risk from increasing interest rates.

Interest rate risk is higher on bonds with long maturities than on those maturing in the near future.[14] This follows because the longer the maturity, the longer before it is paid off and the bondholder can replace it with one with a higher coupon. This point can be demonstrated numerically by showing how the value of a 1-year bond with a 10 percent annual coupon fluctuates with changes in r_d, and then comparing these changes with those on a 15-year bond

Interest Rate (Price) Risk
The risk of a decline in a bond's price due to an increase in interest rates.

---

[12] An immediate increase in rates from 10 to 15 percent would be quite unusual, and it would occur only if something quite bad were revealed about the company or happened in the economy. Smaller but still significant rate increases that adversely affect bondholders do occur fairly often.

[13] You would have an accounting (and tax) loss only if you sold the bond; if you held it to maturity, you would not have such a loss. However, even if you did not sell, you would still have suffered a real economic loss in an opportunity cost sense because you would have lost the opportunity to invest at 15 percent and would be stuck with a 10 percent bond in a 15 percent market. In an economic sense, "paper losses" are just as bad as realized accounting losses.

[14] Actually, a bond's maturity and coupon rate both affect interest rate risk. Low coupons mean that most of the bond's return will come from repayment of principal, whereas on a high-coupon bond with the same maturity, more of the cash flows will come in during the early years due to the relatively large coupon payments. A measurement called "duration," which finds the average number of years the bond's PV of cash flows remain outstanding, has been developed to combine maturity and coupons. A zero coupon bond, which has no interest payments and whose payments all come at maturity, has a duration equal to its maturity. Coupon bonds all have durations that are shorter than maturity, and the higher the coupon rate, the shorter the duration. Bonds with longer duration are exposed to more interest rate risk. A discussion of duration would go beyond the scope of this book, but see any investments text for a discussion of the concept.

as calculated previously. The one-year bond's values at different interest rates are shown here:

Value of a one-year bond at

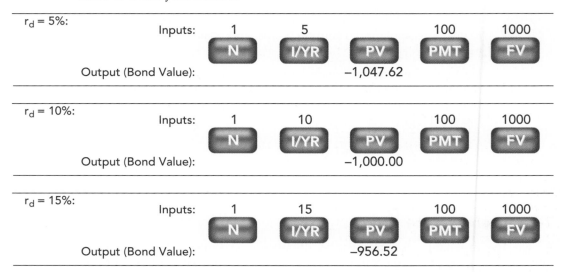

$r_d = 5\%$:

	Inputs:	1	5		100	1000
		N	I/YR	PV	PMT	FV
	Output (Bond Value):			−1,047.62		

$r_d = 10\%$:

	Inputs:	1	10		100	1000
		N	I/YR	PV	PMT	FV
	Output (Bond Value):			−1,000.00		

$r_d = 15\%$:

	Inputs:	1	15		100	1000
		N	I/YR	PV	PMT	FV
	Output (Bond Value):			−956.52		

You would obtain the first value with a financial calculator by entering N = 1, I/YR = 5, PMT = 100, and FV = 1000, and then pressing PV to get $1,047.62. With everything still in your calculator, enter I/YR = 10 to override the old I/YR = 5, and press PV to find the bond's value at a 10 percent market rate; it drops to $1,000. Then enter I/YR = 15 and press the PV key to find the last bond value, $956.52.

The effects of increasing rates on the 15-year bond as found earlier can be compared with the just-calculated effects for the 1-year bond. This comparison is shown in Figure 7-3, where we show bond prices at several rates and then plot those prices in the graph. Note how much more sensitive the price of the 15-year bond is to changes in interest rates. At a 10 percent interest rate, both the 15-year and the 1-year bonds are valued at $1,000. When rates rise to 15 percent, the 15-year bond falls to $707.63, but the 1-year bond only falls to $956.52. The price decline for the 1-year bond is only 4.35 percent, while that for the 15-year bond is 29.24 percent.

For bonds with similar coupons, this differential interest rate sensitivity always holds true—the longer its maturity, the more its price changes in response to a given change in interest rates. Thus, even if the risk of default on two bonds is exactly the same, the one with the longer maturity is typically exposed to more risk from a rise in interest rates.[15]

The logical explanation for this difference in interest rate risk is simple. Suppose you bought a 15-year bond that yielded 10 percent, or $100 a year. Now suppose interest rates on comparable-risk bonds rose to 15 percent. You would be stuck with only $100 of interest for the next 15 years. On the other hand, had you bought a 1-year bond, you would have a low return for only 1 year. At the

---

[15] If a 10-year bond were plotted in Figure 7-3, its curve would lie between those of the 15-year and the 1-year bonds. The curve of a one-month bond would be almost horizontal, indicating that its price would change very little in response to an interest rate change, but a 100-year bond would have a very steep slope, and the slope of a perpetuity would be even steeper. Also, a zero coupon bond's price is quite sensitive to interest rate changes, and the longer its maturity, the greater its price sensitivity. Therefore, a 30-year zero coupon bond would have a huge amount of interest rate risk.

FIGURE 7-3 *Values of Long- and Short-Term 10% Annual Coupon Bonds at Different Market Interest Rates*

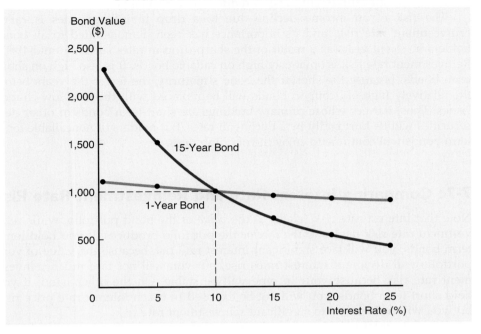

	VALUE OF	
Current Market Interest Rate, r_d	**1-Year Bond**	**15-Year Bond**
5%	$1,047.62	$1,518.98
10	1,000.00	1,000.00
15	956.52	707.63
20	916.67	532.45
25	880.00	421.11

Note: Bond values were calculated using a financial calculator assuming annual, or once-a-year, compounding.

end of the year, you would receive your $1,000 back, and you could then reinvest it and earn 15 percent, or $150 per year, for the next 14 years. Thus, interest rate risk reflects the length of time you are committed to a given investment.

7-7b Reinvestment Rate Risk

As we saw in the preceding section, an *increase* in interest rates will hurt bondholders because it will lead to a decline in the value of a bond portfolio. But can a *decrease* in interest rates also hurt bondholders? Actually, the answer is yes, because if interest rates fall, long-term bondholders will suffer a reduction in income. For example, consider a retiree who has a bond portfolio and lives off the income it produces. The bonds in the portfolio, on average, have coupon rates of 10 percent. Now suppose interest rates decline to 5 percent. Many of the bonds will be called, and as calls occur, the bondholder will have to replace

Reinvestment Rate Risk
The risk that a decline in interest rates will lead to a decline in income from a bond portfolio.

10 percent bonds with 5 percent bonds. Even bonds that are not callable will mature, and when they do, they too will have to be replaced with lower-yielding bonds. Thus, our retiree will suffer a reduction of income.

The risk of an income decline due to a drop in interest rates is called **reinvestment rate risk,** and its importance has been demonstrated to all bond-holders in recent years as a result of the sharp drop in rates since the mid-1980s. Reinvestment rate risk is obviously high on callable bonds. It is also high on short-term bonds, because the shorter the bond's maturity, the fewer the years before the relatively high old-coupon bonds will be replaced with the new low-coupon issues. Thus, retirees whose primary holdings are short-term bonds or other debt securities will be hurt badly by a decline in rates, but holders of noncallable long-term bonds will continue to enjoy the old high rates.

7-7c Comparing Interest Rate and Reinvestment Rate Risk

Note that interest rate risk relates to the *value* of the bond portfolio, while rein-vestment rate risk relates to the *income* the portfolio produces. If you hold long-term bonds, you will face significant interest rate risk because the value of your portfolio will decline if interest rates rise, but you will not face much reinvest-ment rate risk because your income will be stable. On the other hand, if you hold short-term bonds, you will not be exposed to much interest rate price risk, but you will be exposed to significant reinvestment rate risk.

Investment Horizon
The period of time an investor plans to hold a particular investment.

Which type of risk is "more relevant" to a given investor depends critically on how long the investor plans to hold the bonds—this is often referred to as the **investment horizon.** To illustrate, consider first an investor who has a relatively short, one-year investment horizon—say, the investor plans to go to graduate school a year from now and needs money for tuition and expenses. Reinvest-ment rate risk is of minimal concern to this investor, because there is little time for reinvestment. The investor could eliminate interest rate risk by buying a one-year Treasury security, since he or she would be assured of receiving the face value of the bond one year from now (the investment horizon). However, if this investor were to buy a long-term Treasury security, he or she would bear a con-siderable amount of interest rate risk because, as we have seen, long-term bond prices decline if interest rates rise. Consequently, investors with shorter invest-ment horizons should view long-term bonds as being especially risky.

By contrast, the reinvestment risk inherent in short-term bonds is especially relevant to investors with longer investment horizons. Consider a retiree who is living on income from his or her portfolio. If this investor buys one-year bonds, he or she will have to "roll them over" every year, and if rates fall, his or her income in subsequent years will likewise decline. A younger couple saving for something like their own retirement or their children's college costs would be affected similarly, because if they buy short-term bonds they too will have to roll their portfolio at possibly much lower rates. Since there is uncertainty today about the rates that will be earned on these reinvested cash flows, long-term investors should be especially concerned about the reinvestment rate risk inher-ent in short-term bonds.

One simple way to minimize both interest rate and reinvestment rate risk is to buy a zero coupon Treasury bond with a maturity that matches the investor's investment horizon. For example, assume your investment horizon is 10 years. If you buy a 10-year zero, you will receive a guaranteed payment in 10 years equal to the bond's face value, hence you face no interest rate price risk. More-over, as there are no coupons to reinvest, there is no reinvestment rate risk. This feature explains why investors with specific goals often invest in zero coupon bonds.[16]

Recall from Chapter 6 that maturity risk premiums are generally positive. Moreover, a positive maturity risk premium implies that investors on average regard longer-term bonds as being riskier than shorter-term bonds. That, in turn, suggests that the average investor is most concerned with interest rate price risk. Still, it is appropriate for each individual investor to consider his or her situation, to recognize the risks inherent in bonds with different maturities, and to construct a portfolio that deals best with the investor's most relevant risk.

Differentiate between interest rate risk and reinvestment rate risk.

To which type of risk are holders of long-term bonds more exposed? Short-term bondholders?

What type of security can be used to minimize both interest rate and reinvestment rate risk for an investor with a fixed investment horizon?

7-8 DEFAULT RISK

Potential default is another important risk faced by bondholders. If the issuer defaults, investors will receive less than the promised return. Recall from Chapter 6 that the quoted interest rate includes a default risk premium—the higher the probability of default, the higher the premium and thus the yield to maturity. Default risk on Treasuries is zero, but this risk is substantial for lower-grade corporate and municipal bonds.

To illustrate, suppose two bonds have the same promised cash flows—their coupon rates, maturities, liquidity, and inflation exposures are identical, but one has more default risk than the other. Investors will naturally pay more for the one with less chance of default. As a result, bonds with higher default risk will have higher market rates: $r_d = r^* + IP + DRP + LP + MRP$. If its default risk changes, this will affect r_d and thus the price. Thus, if the default risk on Allied's bonds increases, their price will fall and the yield to maturity (YTM = r_d) will increase.

In the next sections we consider some issues related to default risk. First, we show that corporations can influence default risk by changing the types of bonds they issue. Second, we discuss bond ratings, which are used to help judge default risk. Finally, we consider bankruptcy and reorganization, which affect how much an investor can expect to recover if a default occurs.

---

[16] Two words of caution about zeros are in order. First, as we show in Web Appendix 7A, investors in zeros must pay taxes each year on their accrued gain in value, even though the bonds don't pay any cash until they mature. Second, buying a zero coupon with a maturity equal to your investment horizon enables you to lock in nominal cash flow, but the value of that cash flow will still depend on what happens to inflation during your investment horizon. What we need is an inflation-indexed zero coupon Treasury bond, but to date no such bond exists.

Also, the fact that maturity risk premiums are positive suggests that most investors have relatively short investment horizons. See *Stocks, Bonds, Bills, and Inflation: (Valuation Edition) 2005 Yearbook* (Chicago: Ibbotson Associates, 2005), which finds that the maturity risk premium for long-term bonds has averaged 1.4 percent over the past 79 years.

7-8a Various Types of Corporate Bonds

Default risk is influenced by both the financial strength of the issuer and the terms of the bond contract, including whether or not collateral has been pledged to secure the bond. Some types of bonds are described in this section.

Mortgage Bonds

Mortgage Bond
A bond backed by fixed assets. First mortgage bonds are senior in priority to claims of second mortgage bonds.

Under a **mortgage bond,** the corporation pledges specific assets as security for the bond. To illustrate, in 2005, Billingham Corporation needed $10 million to build a regional distribution center. Bonds in the amount of $4 million, secured by a *first mortgage* on the property, were issued. (The remaining $6 million was financed with equity capital.) If Billingham defaults on the bonds, the bondholders can foreclose on the property and sell it to satisfy their claims.

If Billingham had chosen to, it could have issued *second mortgage bonds* secured by the same $10 million of assets. In the event of liquidation, the holders of the second mortgage bonds would have a claim against the property, but only after the first mortgage bondholders had been paid off in full. Thus, second mortgages are sometimes called *junior mortgages* because they are junior in priority to the claims of *senior mortgages*, or *first mortgage bonds*.

Indenture
A formal agreement between the issuer and the bondholders.

All mortgage bonds are subject to an **indenture,** which is a legal document that spells out in detail the rights of both the bondholders and the corporation. The indentures of many major corporations were written 20, 30, 40, or more years ago. These indentures are generally "open ended," meaning that new bonds can be issued from time to time under the same indenture. However, the amount of new bonds that can be issued is virtually always limited to a specified percentage of the firm's total "bondable property," which generally includes all land, plant, and equipment.

For example, in the past Savannah Electric Company had provisions in its bond indenture that allowed it to issue first mortgage bonds totaling up to 60 percent of its net fixed assets. If its fixed assets totaled $1 billion, and if it had $500 million of first mortgage bonds outstanding, it could, by the property test, issue another $100 million of bonds (60 percent of $1 billion = $600 million).

At times, Savannah Electric was unable to issue any new first mortgage bonds because of another indenture provision: its times-interest-earned (TIE) ratio was required to be greater than 2.5, and at times earnings declined to the point where the minimum was violated. Thus, although Savannah Electric passed the property test, it failed the coverage test, so it could not issue any more first mortgage bonds. Savannah Electric then had to finance with junior bonds. Since its first mortgage bonds carried lower interest rates than its junior long-term debt, this restriction was costly.

Savannah Electric's neighbor, Georgia Power Company, had more flexibility under its indenture—its interest coverage requirement was only 2.0. In hearings before the Georgia Public Service Commission, it was suggested that Savannah Electric should change its indenture coverage to 2.0 so it could issue more first mortgage bonds. However, this was simply not possible—the holders of the outstanding bonds would have to approve the change, and it is inconceivable that they would vote for a change that would seriously weaken their position.

Debentures

Debenture
A long-term bond that is not secured by a mortgage on specific property.

A **debenture** is an unsecured bond, and as such it provides no specific collateral as security for the obligation. Debenture holders are, therefore, general creditors whose claims are protected by property not otherwise pledged. In practice, the use of debentures depends both on the nature of the firm's assets and on its general credit strength. Extremely strong companies such as General Electric and

ExxonMobil can use debentures because they simply do not need to put up property as security for their debt. Debentures are also issued by weak companies that have already pledged most of their assets as collateral for mortgage loans. In this latter case, the debentures are quite risky, and that risk will be reflected in their interest rates.

Subordinated Debentures

The term *subordinate* means "below," or "inferior to," and, in the event of bankruptcy, subordinated debt has a claim on assets only after senior debt has been paid in full. **Subordinated debentures** may be subordinated either to designated notes payable (usually bank loans) or to all other debt. In the event of liquidation or reorganization, holders of subordinated debentures receive nothing until all senior debt, as named in the debentures' indenture, has been paid. Precisely how subordination works, and how it strengthens the position of senior debtholders, is explained in detail in Web Appendix 7B.

Subordinated Debenture
A bond having a claim on assets only after the senior debt has been paid off in the event of liquidation.

7-8b Bond Ratings

Since the early 1900s, bonds have been assigned quality ratings that reflect their probability of going into default. The three major rating agencies are Moody's Investors Service (Moody's), Standard & Poor's Corporation (S&P), and Fitch Investor's Service. Moody's and S&P's rating designations are shown in Table 7-2.[17] The triple- and double-A bonds are extremely safe. Single-A and triple-B bonds are also strong enough to be called **investment-grade bonds,** and they are the lowest-rated bonds that many banks and other institutional investors are permitted by law to hold. Double-B and lower bonds are speculative, or **junk, bonds,** and they have a significant probability of going into default.

Investment-Grade Bonds
Bonds rated triple-B or higher; many banks and other institutional investors are permitted by law to hold only investment-grade bonds.

Junk Bond
A high-risk, high-yield bond.

Bond Rating Criteria

Bond ratings are based on both qualitative and quantitative factors, some of which are listed below:

1. *Various ratios,* including the debt ratio and the times-interest-earned ratio. The better the ratios, the higher the rating.

TABLE 7-2   *Moody's and S&P Bond Ratings*

	INVESTMENT GRADE				JUNK BONDS			
Moody's	Aaa	Aa	A	Baa	Ba	B	Caa	C
S&P	AAA	AA	A	BBB	BB	B	CCC	C

Note: Both Moody's and S&P use "modifiers" for bonds rated below triple-A. S&P uses a plus and minus system; thus, A+ designates the strongest A-rated bonds and A− the weakest. Moody's uses a 1, 2, or 3 designation, with 1 denoting the strongest and 3 the weakest; thus, within the double-A category, Aa1 is the best, Aa2 is average, and Aa3 is the weakest.

---

[17] In the discussion to follow, reference to the S&P rating is intended to imply the Moody's and Fitch's ratings as well. Thus, triple-B bonds mean both BBB and Baa bonds; double-B bonds mean both BB and Ba bonds; and so on.

2. *Mortgage provisions:* Is the bond secured by a mortgage? If it is, and if the property has a high value relative to the amount of bonded debt, the rating is enhanced.

3. *Subordination provisions:* Is the bond subordinated to other debt? If so, it will be rated at least one notch below the rating it would have if it were not subordinated. Conversely, a bond with other debt subordinated to it will have a somewhat higher rating.

4. *Guarantee provisions:* Some bonds are guaranteed by other firms. If a weak company's debt is guaranteed by a strong company (usually the weak company's parent), the bond will be given the strong company's rating.

5. *Sinking fund:* Does the bond have a sinking fund to ensure systematic repayment? This feature is a plus factor to the rating agencies.

6. *Maturity:* Other things the same, a bond with a shorter maturity will be judged less risky than a longer-term bond, and this will be reflected in the ratings.

7. *Stability:* Are the issuer's sales and earnings stable?

8. *Regulation:* Is the issuer regulated, and could an adverse regulatory climate cause the company's economic position to decline? Regulation is especially important for utility, telephone, and insurance companies.

9. *Antitrust:* Are any antitrust actions pending against the firm that could erode its position?

10. *Overseas operations:* What percentage of the firm's sales, assets, and profits are from overseas operations, and what is the political climate in the host countries?

11. *Environmental factors:* Is the firm likely to face heavy expenditures for pollution remediation?

12. *Product liability:* Are the firm's products safe? The tobacco companies have for some time been under pressure, and so are their bond ratings.

13. *Pension liabilities:* Does the firm have unfunded pension and/or employee health insurance liabilities that could pose a future problem?

14. *Labor unrest:* Are there potential labor problems on the horizon that could weaken the firm's position? As we write this, a number of airlines face this problem, and it has caused their ratings to be lowered.

15. *Accounting policies:* If a firm's accounting policies, and thus its reported earnings, are questionable, this will have a negative effect on its bond ratings. As we were working on this chapter, the policies of American International Group (AIG) came into question, and its bonds were downgraded shortly after its problems were revealed.

Representatives of the rating agencies have consistently stated that no precise formula is used to set a firm's rating: all the factors listed, plus others, are taken into account, but not in a mathematically precise manner. Statistical studies have borne out this contention, for researchers who have tried to predict bond ratings on the basis of quantitative data have had only limited success, indicating that the agencies use subjective judgment when establishing a firm's rating.[18]

Nevertheless, as we see in Table 7-3, there is a strong correlation between bond ratings and many of the ratios that we described in Chapter 4. Not surprisingly, companies with lower debt ratios, higher free cash flow to debt, higher returns on invested capital, higher EBITDA coverage ratios, and higher TIE ratios typically have higher bond ratings.

Importance of Bond Ratings

Bond ratings are important both to firms and to investors. First, because a bond's rating is an indicator of its default risk, the rating has a direct, measurable

---

[18] See Amed Belkaoui, *Industrial Bonds and the Rating Process* (London: Quorum Books, 1983).

TABLE 7-3	*Bond Rating Criteria; Three-Year (1998–2000) Median Financial Ratios for Different Bond Rating Classifications of Industrial Companies*[a]

	AAA	AA	A	BBB	BB	B	CCC
Times-interest-earned (EBIT/Interest)	21.4×	10.1×	6.1×	3.7×	2.1×	0.8×	0.1×
EBITDA interest coverage (EBITDA/Interest)	26.5	12.9	9.1	5.8	3.4	1.8	1.3
Net cash flow/Total debt	128.8%	55.4%	43.2%	30.8%	18.8%	7.8%	1.6%
Free cash flow/Total debt	84.2	25.2	15.0	8.5	2.6	(3.2)	(12.9)
Return on capital	34.9	21.7	19.4	13.6	11.6	6.6	1.0
Operating income/Sales[b]	27.0	22.1	18.6	15.4	15.9	11.9	11.9
Long-term debt/Total capital	13.3	28.2	33.9	42.5	57.2	69.7	68.8
Total debt/Total capital	22.9	37.7	42.5	48.2	62.6	74.8	87.7

Notes:
[a] Somewhat different criteria are applied to firms in different industries, such as utilities and financial corporations. This table pertains to industrial companies, which include manufacturers, retailers, and service firms.
[b] Operating income here is defined as sales minus cost of goods manufactured (before depreciation and amortization), selling, general and administrative, and research and development costs.

Source: Adapted from "Adjusted Key Industrial Financial Ratios," *Standard & Poor's 2002 Corporate Ratings Criteria*, July 21, 2003, p. 54.

influence on the bond's interest rate and the firm's cost of debt. Second, most bonds are purchased by institutional investors rather than individuals, and many institutions are restricted to investment-grade securities. Thus, if a firm's bonds fall below BBB, it will have a difficult time selling new bonds because many potential purchasers will not be allowed to buy them.

As a result of their higher risk and more restricted market, lower-grade bonds have higher required rates of return, r_d, than high-grade bonds. Figure 7-4 illustrates this point. In each of the years shown on the graph, U.S. government bonds have had the lowest yields, AAA bonds have been next, and BBB bonds have had the highest yields. The figure also shows that the gaps between yields on the three types of bonds vary over time, indicating that the cost differentials, or yield spreads, fluctuate from year to year. This point is highlighted in Figure 7-5, which gives the yields on the three types of bonds and the yield spreads for AAA and BBB bonds over Treasuries in May 2002 and January 2005.[19] Note first from Figure 7-5 that the risk-free rate, or vertical axis intercept, was lower in early 2005 than it was in May 2002, primarily reflecting the decline in

---

[19] A yield spread is related to but not identical to risk premiums on corporate bonds. The true *risk premium* reflects only the difference in expected (and required) returns between two securities that results from differences in their risk. However, yield spreads reflect (1) a true risk premium; (2) a liquidity premium, which reflects the fact that U.S. Treasury bonds are more readily marketable than most corporate bonds; (3) a call premium, because most Treasury bonds are not callable whereas corporate bonds are; and (4) an expected loss differential, which reflects the probability of loss on the corporate bonds. As an example of the last point, suppose the yield to maturity on a BBB bond was 6.0 percent versus 4.8 percent on government bonds, but there was a 5 percent probability of total default loss on the corporate bond. In this case, the *expected* return on the BBB bond would be 0.95(6.0%) + 0.05(0%) = 5.7%, and the yield spread would be 0.9%, not the full 1.2 percentage points difference in "promised" yields to maturity.

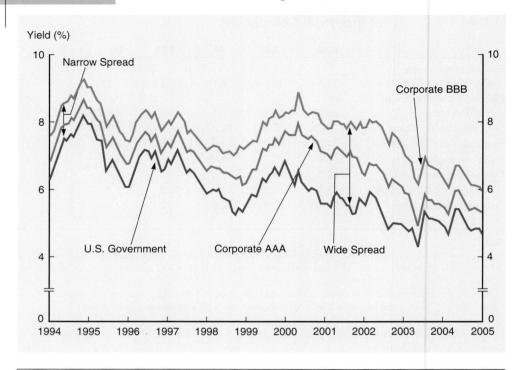

FIGURE 7-4   *Yields on Selected Long-Term Bonds, 1994–2005*

Source: *Federal Reserve Statistical Release*, Selected Interest Rates (Historical Data), **http://www .federalreserve.gov/releases/H15/data.htm**.

both real rates and expected inflation over the past few years. Second, the slope of the line has also decreased, indicating a decrease in investors' risk aversion. Thus, the penalty for having a low credit rating varies over time. Occasionally, as in 2002, the penalty is quite large, but at times like 1995 (shown in Figure 7-4) and in 2005 (shown in Figures 7-4 and 7-5) it is small. These spread differences reflect both investors' risk aversion and also their optimism or pessimism regarding the economy and corporate profits. In 2002, as more and more corporate scandals were being revealed, investors were both pessimistic and risk averse, so spreads were quite high.

Changes in Ratings

Changes in a firm's bond rating affect both the firm's ability to borrow funds capital and its cost of that capital. Rating agencies review outstanding bonds on a periodic basis, occasionally upgrading or downgrading a bond as a result of its issuer's changed circumstances. For example, the February 10, 2005, issue of *Standard & Poor's CreditWeek Focus* reported that Gap Inc.'s corporate credit rating was upgraded from BB+ to BBB−. The improved rating moved Gap's bonds into the investment-grade category. The rating upgrade reflected Gap's improved operating performance and its continued strong liquidity. On the other hand, a little more than a week later, *CreditWeek Focus* warned that it might have to downgrade the bonds of New York Times Co. The warning cited fears that the Times may have taken on too much debt to finance a recent acquisition. In the

FIGURE 7-5 *Relationship between Bond Ratings and Bond Yields, 2002 and 2005*

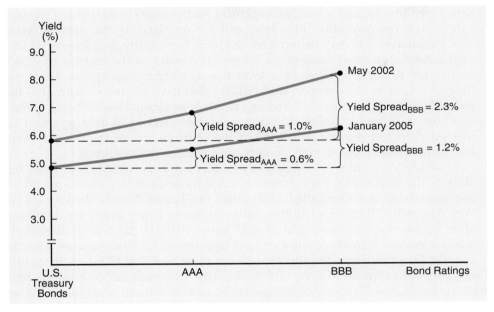

	Long-Term Government Bonds (Default-Free) (1)	AAA Corporate Bonds (2)	BBB Corporate Bonds (3)	YIELD SPREADS	
				AAA (4) = (2) − (1)	BBB (5) = (3) − (1)
May 2002	5.8%	6.8%	8.1%	1.0%	2.3%
January 2005	4.8	5.4	6.0	0.6	1.2

Source: Federal Reserve Statistical Release, Selected Interest Rates (Historical Data), **http://www.federalreserve.gov/releases/H15/data.htm**.

months that follow, the company may choose to strengthen its balance sheet in order to avoid a downgrade.

On balance, it is fair to say that ratings agencies generally do a good job of measuring the average credit risk of bonds, and that they do their best to change ratings whenever they perceive a change in credit quality. At the same time, it is important to understand that ratings do not adjust immediately to changes in credit quality, and in some cases there can be a considerable lag between a change in credit quality and a change in rating. For example, the rating agencies were caught off guard by Enron's rapid decline. Enron declared bankruptcy on a Sunday in December 2001, and the preceding Friday its bonds still carried an investment-grade rating.

7-8c Bankruptcy and Reorganization

When a business becomes *insolvent*, this means that it doesn't have enough cash to meet its interest and principal payments. A decision must then be made whether to dissolve the firm through *liquidation* or to permit it to *reorganize* and thus stay alive. These issues are addressed in Chapters 7 and 11 of the federal bankruptcy statutes, and the final decision is made by a federal bankruptcy court judge.

The decision to force a firm to liquidate versus permitting it to reorganize depends on whether the value of the reorganized firm is likely to be greater than the value of its assets if they were sold off piecemeal. In a reorganization, the firm's creditors negotiate with management on the terms of a potential reorganization. The reorganization plan may call for *restructuring* the debt, in which case the interest rate may be reduced, the term to maturity lengthened, or some of the debt may be exchanged for equity. The point of the restructuring is to reduce the financial charges to a level that is supportable by the firm's cash flows. Of course, the common stockholders also have to "take a haircut"—they generally see their position diluted as a result of additional shares being given to debtholders in exchange for accepting a reduced amount of debt principal and interest. A trustee may be appointed by the court to oversee the reorganization, but generally the existing management is allowed to retain control.

Liquidation occurs if the company is deemed to be worth more dead than alive. If the bankruptcy court orders a liquidation, assets are auctioned off and the cash obtained is distributed as specified in Chapter 7 of the Bankruptcy Act. Web Appendix 7B provides an illustration of how a firm's assets are distributed after liquidation. For now, you should know that (1) the federal bankruptcy statutes govern both reorganization and liquidation, (2) bankruptcies occur frequently, (3) a priority of the specified claims must be followed when distributing the assets of a liquidated firm, (4) bondholders' treatment depends on the terms of the bond, and (5) stockholders generally receive little in reorganizations and nothing in liquidations because the assets are generally worth less than the amount of debt outstanding.

Differentiate between mortgage bonds and debentures.

Name the major rating agencies, and list some factors that affect bond ratings.

Why are bond ratings important both to firms and to investors?

Do bond ratings adjust immediately to changes in credit quality? Explain.

Differentiate between Chapter 7 liquidations and Chapter 11 reorganizations. When should each be used?

7-9 BOND MARKETS

Corporate bonds are traded primarily in the over-the-counter market. Most bonds are owned by and traded among large financial institutions (for example, life insurance companies, mutual funds, and pension funds, all of which deal in very large blocks of securities), and it is relatively easy for the over-the-counter bond dealers to arrange the transfer of large blocks of bonds among the relatively few holders of the bonds. It would be much more difficult to conduct similar operations in the stock market among the literally millions of large and small stockholders, so a higher percentage of stock trades occur on the exchanges.

Information on bond trades in the over-the-counter market is not published, but a representative group of bonds is listed and traded on the bond division of the NYSE. Table 7-4 reprints the "Corporate Bonds" section from *The Wall Street Journal* that shows the 40 most active issues that traded on March 11, 2005, in descending order of sales volume.

TABLE 7-4 *The 40 Most Active Fixed-Coupon Corporate Bonds, March 11, 2005*

Corporate Bonds

Friday, March 11, 2005

Forty most active fixed-coupon corporate bonds

COMPANY (TICKER)	COUPON	MATURITY	LAST PRICE	LAST YIELD	*EST SPREAD	UST†	EST $ VOL (000's)
General Motors (GM)	8.375	Jul 15, 2033	94.965	8.861	405	30	207,068
Sprint Capital (FON)	8.750	Mar 15, 2032	132.794	6.226	141	30	156,583
General Motors Acceptance (GM)	6.750	Dec 01, 2014	94.652	7.534	300	10	145,696
Ford Motor Credit (F)	7.000	Oct 01, 2013	100.588	6.907	236	10	106,708
Pacific Gas and Electric (PCG)	6.050	Mar 01, 2034	104.102	5.757	95	30	85,516
General Motors Acceptance (GM)	8.000	Nov 01, 2031	96.463	8.331	352	30	84,803
Albertson's Inc (ABS)	8.000	May 01, 2031	121.594	6.303	149	30	84,000
Ford Motor Co (F)	7.450	Jul 16, 2031	93.804	8.017	320	30	78,926
Ford Motor Credit (F)	5.800	Jan 12, 2009	98.514	6.240	205	5	71,546
HSBC Bank USA (HSBC)	3.875	Sep 15, 2009	96.930	4.639	44	5	71,375
General Motors Acceptance (GM)	7.250	Mar 02, 2011	99.433	7.368	317	5	70,058
Morgan Stanley (MWD)	5.300	Mar 01, 2013	101.377	5.087	55	10	69,205
General Motors (GM)	8.250	Jul 15, 2023	95.261	8.772	396	30	68,514
Kinder Morgan Energy Partners, L.P. (KMP)	5.800	Mar 15, 2035	97.477	5.982	116	30	63,000
Kerr-McGee (KMG)	6.875	Sep 15, 2011	108.357	5.336	114	5	62,105
Time Warner (TWX)	5.625	May 01, 2005	100.295	3.239	n.a.	n.a.	61,500
Countrywide Home Loans (CFC)	4.125	Sep 15, 2009	97.255	4.811	61	5	61,470
JP Morgan Chase and Co (JPM)	4.000	Feb 01, 2008	99.081	4.342	42	3	61,410
Washington Mutual Bank, FA (WM)	5.125	Jan 15, 2015	98.566	5.311	77	10	59,725
Albertson's Inc (ABS)	7.450	Aug 01, 2029	114.438	6.284	147	30	57,484
Ford Motor Credit (F)	7.875	Jun 15, 2010	104.880	6.751	255	5	56,819
JP Morgan Chase and Co (JPM)	3.500	Mar 15, 2009	96.301	4.522	35	5	52,930
BellSouth Corp (BLS)	5.200	Sep 15, 2014	100.309	5.158	65	10	51,834
Consolidated Edison of New York Inc (ED)	5.300	Mar 01, 2035	97.175	5.493	68	30	50,500
GE Global Insurance Holding (GE)	7.500	Jun 15, 2010	110.655	5.154	97	5	50,000
Washington Mutual (WM)	5.625	Jan 15, 2007	102.678	4.088	38	2	48,055
General Motors Acceptance (GM)	6.875	Sep 15, 2011	97.625	7.341	314	5	47,654
General Motors Acceptance (GM)	6.125	Sep 15, 2006	101.448	5.108	140	2	47,287
General Motors Acceptance (GM)	6.125	Aug 28, 2007	100.993	5.683	197	2	46,932
Pulte Homes (PHM)	6.000	Feb 15, 2035	95.201	6.360	154	30	46,005
Wells Fargo (WFC)	4.125	Mar 10, 2008	99.370	4.352	43	3	45,120
Bear Stearns Companies (BSC)	5.700	Jan 15, 2007	102.767	4.112	39	2	44,251
Ford Motor Credit (F)	7.375	Feb 01, 2011	102.930	6.760	256	5	43,960
Kerr-McGee (KMG)	7.875	Sep 15, 2031	118.156	6.438	162	30	43,000
Markel Corp (MKL)	7.350	Aug 15, 2034	112.682	6.388	157	30	43,000
Credit Suisse First Boston (USA) (CRDSUI)	6.500	Jan 15, 2012	109.112	4.912	40	10	42,290
JP Morgan Chase and Co (JPM)	5.250	May 30, 2007	102.399	4.098	39	2	41,825
Merck (MRK)	4.750	Mar 01, 2015	96.769	5.168	65	10	41,265
Pitney Bowes Inc (PBI)	4.750	May 15, 2018	95.344	5.243	71	10	41,010
Boston Scientific Corp (BSX)	5.450	Jun 15, 2014	102.040	5.169	66	10	41,000
HSBC Finance Corp (HSBC)	4.125	Dec 15, 2008	98.602	4.533	62	3	40,912

Volume represents total volume for each issue; price/yield data are for trades of $1 million and greater. * Estimated spreads, in basis points (100 basis points is one percentage point), over the 2, 3, 5, 10 or 30-year hot run Treasury note/bond. 2-year: 3.375 02/07; 3-year: 3.375 02/08; 5-year: 3.500 02/10; 10-year: 4.000 02/15; 30-year: 5.375 02/31. †Comparable U.S. Treasury issue.

Source: MarketAxess Corporate BondTicker

Source: "Corporate Bonds," *The Wall Street Journal*, March 14, 2005, p. C12.

If you look at the first issue shown in Table 7-4, you will see that General Motors had the most actively traded issue on March 11, 2005. These bonds have an 8.375 percent coupon and will mature on July 15, 2033. On March 11, 2005, their price was 94.965 percent of par, or 0.94965 × $1,000 = $949.65, and their yield to maturity was 8.861 percent. (Thus, similarly rated bonds with a similar maturity would have required a coupon of roughly 8.86 percent on March 11 to sell at par.) Their estimated spread was 405 basis points over 30-year Treasuries. (If you looked at *The Wall Street Journal* for March 14, 2005, you would see that the 5.375 percent February 2031 Treasury issue's yield on March 11 was 4.81 percent, and 8.86% − 4.81% = 4.05%, which is the 405 basis points spread shown in Table 7-4.) The last column shows the estimated trading volume on March 11, which was $207,068,000.

If you examined the table closely, you would note that the GM bonds at the top of the list also have the highest yield and the largest yield spread over Treasuries. This reflects two things: First, the GM bonds at the top of the list have a very long maturity—2033—and when the yield curve is sharply upward sloping, long-term bonds have high yields. However, maturity doesn't explain the high yield spread over Treasuries—that is explained by the fact that GM is now (2005) in financial trouble, and its bonds were just downgraded to junk status. Seven other GM bonds are in the table, and they also have relatively high yields and yield spreads relative to their maturities. Ford also has several bonds in the table, and their yield spreads are second only to those of GM, reflecting its poor financial condition.

At the other end of the spectrum we see Time Warner, with a yield of only 3.239 percent and a yield spread so low that it is not even measurable. TW's bonds mature in only six weeks, and investors regard it as inconceivable that the company could go bankrupt in that short time. All the other data in the table have similar logical explanations.

As we noted earlier, coupon rates are generally set at levels that reflect the "going rate of interest" on the day the bonds are issued. If the rates were set lower, investors simply would not buy the bonds at the $1,000 par value, so the company could not borrow the money it needed. Thus, bonds generally sell at their par values on the day they are issued, but their prices fluctuate thereafter as interest rates change. Thus, the prices of the bonds in the table range from a low 93.804 (percent of par) for Ford to a high of 132.794 for Sprint, which issued bonds with a high yield but then gained strength (the opposite of GM) and saw its yields fall and its bond prices rise.

Why do most bond trades occur in the over-the-counter market?

If a bond issue is to be sold at par, at what rate must its coupon rate be set? Explain.

Tying It All Together

This chapter described the different types of bonds governments and corporations issue, explained how bond prices are established, and discussed how investors estimate the rates of return on bonds. It also discussed the various types of risks that investors face when they buy bonds.

It is important to remember that when an investor purchases a company's bonds, the investor is providing the company with capital. Therefore, when a firm issues bonds, *the return that investors require on the bonds represents the cost of debt capital to the firm*. This point is extended in

Chapter 10, where the ideas developed in this chapter are used to help determine a company's overall cost of capital, which is a basic component in the capital budgeting process.

In recent years many companies have used zero coupon bonds to raise billions of dollars, while bankruptcy is an important consideration for both companies that issue debt and investors. Therefore, these two related issues are discussed in detail in Web Appendixes 7A and 7B. Please go to the ThomsonNOW Web site to access these appendixes.

SELF-TEST QUESTIONS AND PROBLEMS
(Solutions Appear in Appendix A)

ST-1   **Key terms** Define each of the following terms:

     a.   Bond; treasury bond; corporate bond; municipal bond; foreign bond
     b.   Par value; maturity date; original maturity
     c.   Coupon payment; coupon interest rate
     d.   Floating-rate bond; zero coupon bond; original issue discount (OID) bond
     e.   Call provision; sinking fund provision; indenture
     f.   Convertible bond; warrant; putable bond; income bond; indexed, or purchasing power, bond
     g.   Discount bond; premium bond
     h.   Yield to maturity (YTM); yield to call (YTC); current yield; total return; yield spread
     i.   Interest rate risk; reinvestment rate risk; investment horizon
     j.   Default risk; credit risk
     k.   Mortgage bond; debenture; subordinated debenture
     l.   Investment-grade bond; junk bond

ST-2   **Bond valuation** The Pennington Corporation issued a new series of bonds on January 1, 1982. The bonds were sold at par ($1,000), had a 12 percent coupon, and matured in 30 years, on December 31, 2011. Coupon payments are made semiannually (on June 30 and December 31).

     a.   What was the YTM on January 1, 1982?
     b.   What was the price of the bonds on January 1, 1987, 5 years later, assuming that interest rates had fallen to 10 percent?
     c.   Find the current yield, capital gains yield, and total return on January 1, 1987, given the price as determined in part b.
     d.   On July 1, 2005, 6.5 years before maturity, Pennington's bonds sold for $916.42. What was the YTM, the current yield, the capital gains yield, and the total return at that time?
     e.   Now, assume that you plan to purchase an outstanding Pennington bond on March 1, 2005, when the going rate of interest given its risk was 15.5 percent. How large a check must you write to complete the transaction? This is a hard question.

ST-3   **Sinking fund** The Vancouver Development Company (VDC) is planning to sell a $100 million, 10-year, 12 percent, semiannual payment, bond issue. Provisions for a sinking fund to retire the issue over its life will be included in the indenture. Sinking fund payments will be made at the end of each year, and each payment must be sufficient to retire 10 percent of the original amount of the issue. The last sinking fund payment will retire the last of the bonds. The bonds to be retired each period can either be purchased on the open market or obtained by calling up to 5 percent of the original issue at par, at VDC's option.

a.   How large must each sinking fund payment be if the company (1) uses the option to call bonds at par or (2) decides to buy bonds on the open market? For part (2), you can only answer in words.

b.   What will happen to debt service requirements per year associated with this issue over its 10-year life?

c.   Now consider an alternative plan, where VDC sets up its sinking fund so that *equal annual amounts* are paid into a sinking fund trust held by a bank, with the proceeds being used to buy government bonds that are expected to pay 7 percent annual interest. The payments, plus accumulated interest, must total to $100 million at the end of 10 years, when the proceeds will be used to retire the issue. How large must the annual sinking fund payments be? Is this amount known with certainty, or might it be higher or lower?

d.   What are the annual cash requirements for covering bond service costs under the trusteeship arrangement described in part c? (Note: Interest must be paid on Vancouver's outstanding bonds but not on bonds that have been retired.) Assume level interest rates for purposes of answering this question.

e.   What would have to happen to interest rates to cause the company to buy bonds on the open market rather than call them under the plan where some bonds are retired each year?

QUESTIONS

7-1   A sinking fund can be set up in one of two ways:

a.   The corporation makes annual payments to the trustee, who invests the proceeds in securities (frequently government bonds) and uses the accumulated total to retire the bond issue at maturity.

b.   The trustee uses the annual payments to retire a portion of the issue each year, either calling a given percentage of the issue by a lottery and paying a specified price per bond or buying bonds on the open market, whichever is cheaper.

What are the advantages and disadvantages of each procedure from the viewpoint of (a) the firm and (b) the bondholders?

7-2   Is it true that the following equation can be used to find the value of a bond with N years to maturity that pays interest once a year? Assume that the bond was issued several years ago.

$$V_B = \sum_{t=1}^{N} \frac{\text{Annual interest}}{(1 + r_d)^t} + \frac{\text{Par value}}{(1 + r_d)^N}$$

7-3   "The values of outstanding bonds change whenever the going rate of interest changes. In general, short-term interest rates are more volatile than long-term interest rates. Therefore, short-term bond prices are more sensitive to interest rate changes than are long-term bond prices." Is this statement true or false? Explain. (Hint: Make up a "reasonable" example based on a 1-year and a 20-year bond to help answer the question.)

7-4   If interest rates rise after a bond issue, what will happen to the bond's price and YTM? Does the time to maturity affect the extent to which interest rate changes affect the bond's price? (Again, an example might help you answer this question.)

7-5 If you buy a *callable* bond and interest rates decline, will the value of your bond rise by as much as it would have risen if the bond had not been callable? Explain.

7-6 Assume that you have a short investment horizon (less than 1 year). You are considering two investments: a 1-year Treasury security and a 20-year Treasury security. Which of the two investments would you view as being more risky? Explain.

7-7 Indicate whether each of the following actions will increase or decrease a bond's yield to maturity:

   a. The bond's price increases.
   b. The bond is downgraded by the rating agencies.
   c. A change in the bankruptcy code makes it more difficult for bondholders to receive payments in the event the firm declares bankruptcy.
   d. The economy seems to be shifting from a boom to a recession. Discuss the effects of the firm's credit strength in your answer.
   e. Investors learn that these bonds are subordinated to another debt issue.

7-8 Why is a call provision advantageous to a bond issuer? When would the issuer be likely to initiate a refunding call?

7-9 Are securities that provide for a sinking fund more or less risky from the bondholder's perspective than those without this type of provision? Explain.

7-10 What's the difference between a call for sinking fund purposes and a refunding call?

7-11 Why are convertibles and bonds with warrants typically offered with lower coupons than similarly rated straight bonds?

7-12 Explain whether the following statement is true or false: "Only weak companies issue debentures."

7-13 Would the yield spread on a corporate bond over a Treasury bond with the same maturity tend to become wider or narrower if the economy appeared to be heading into a recession? Would the change in the spread for a given company be affected by the firm's credit strength?

7-14 A bond's expected return is sometimes estimated by its YTM and sometimes by its YTC. Under what conditions would the YTM provide a better estimate, and when would the YTC be better?

PROBLEMS

Easy
Problems 1–4

7-1 **Bond valuation** Callaghan Motors' bonds have 10 years remaining to maturity. Interest is paid annually; they have a $1,000 par value; the coupon interest rate is 8 percent; and the yield to maturity is 9 percent. What is the bond's current market price?

7-2 **Current yield and yield to maturity** A bond has a $1,000 par value, 10 years to maturity, a 7 percent annual coupon, and sells for $985.

   a. What is its current yield?
   b. What is its yield to maturity (YTM)?
   c. Assume that the yield to maturity remains constant for the next 3 years. What will the price be 3 years from today?

7-3 **Bond valuation** Nungesser Corporation's outstanding bonds have a $1,000 par value, a 9 percent semiannual coupon, 8 years to maturity, and an 8.5 percent YTM. What is the bond's price?

7-4 **Yield to maturity** A firm's bonds have a maturity of 10 years with a $1,000 face value, an 8 percent semiannual coupon, are callable in 5 years at $1,050, and currently sell at a price of $1,100. What are their nominal yield to maturity and their nominal yield to call? What return should investors expect to earn on this bond?

Intermediate
Problems 5–15

7-5 **Bond valuation** An investor has two bonds in his portfolio that both have a face value of $1,000 and pay a 10 percent annual coupon. Bond L matures in 15 years, while Bond S matures in 1 year.

    a. What will the value of each bond be if the going interest rate is 5 percent, 8 percent, and 12 percent? Assume that there is only one more interest payment to be made on Bond S, at its maturity, and 15 more payments on Bond L.

    b. Why does the longer-term bond's price vary more when interest rates change than does that of the shorter-term bond?

7-6 **Bond valuation** An investor has two bonds in his or her portfolio, Bond C and Bond Z. Each matures in 4 years, has a face value of $1,000, and has a yield to maturity of 9.6 percent. Bond C pays a 10 percent annual coupon, while Bond Z is a zero coupon bond.

    a. Assuming that the yield to maturity of each bond remains at 9.6 percent over the next 4 years, calculate the price of the bonds at the following years to maturity and fill in the following table:

Years to Maturity	Price of Bond C	Price of Bond Z
4	_____	_____
3	_____	_____
2	_____	_____
1	_____	_____
0	_____	_____

    b. Plot the time path of prices for each bond.

7-7 **Interest rate sensitivity** An investor purchased the following 5 bonds. Each of them had an 8 percent yield to maturity on the purchase day. Immediately after she purchased them, interest rates fell and each then had a new YTM of 7 percent. What is the percentage change in price for each bond after the decline in interest rates? Fill in the following table:

	Price @ 8%	Price @ 7%	Percentage Change
10-year, 10% annual coupon	_____	_____	_____
10-year zero	_____	_____	_____
5-year zero	_____	_____	_____
30-year zero	_____	_____	_____
$100 perpetuity	_____	_____	_____

7-8 **Yield to call** Six years ago, the Singleton Company issued 20-year bonds with a 14 percent annual coupon rate at their $1,000 par value. The bonds had a 9 percent call premium, with 5 years of call protection. Today, Singleton called the bonds. Compute the realized rate of return for an investor who purchased the bonds when they were issued and held them until they were called. Explain why the investor should or should not be happy that Singleton called them.

7-9 **Yield to maturity** Heymann Company bonds have 4 years left to maturity. Interest is paid annually, and the bonds have a $1,000 par value and a coupon rate of 9 percent.

    a. What is the yield to maturity at a current market price of (1) $829 or (2) $1,104?

    b. Would you pay $829 for each bond if you thought that a "fair" market interest rate for such bonds was 12 percent—that is, if r_d = 12 percent? Explain your answer.

7-10 **Current yield, capital gains yield, and yield to maturity** Hooper Printing Inc. has bonds outstanding with 9 years left to maturity. The bonds have an 8 percent annual coupon rate and were issued 1 year ago at their par value of $1,000, but due to changes in interest rates, the bond's market price has fallen to $901.40. The capital gains yield last year was −9.86 percent.

    a. What is the yield to maturity?

    b. For the coming year, what is the expected current yield and the expected capital gains yield?

    c. Will the actual realized yields be equal to the expected yields if interest rates change? If not, how will they differ?

7-11 **Bond yields** Last year, Clark Company issued a 10-year, 12 percent semiannual coupon bond at its par value of $1,000. Currently, the bond can be called in 4 years at a price of $1,060, and it sells for $1,100.

    a.   What are the bond's nominal yield to maturity and its nominal yield to call? Would an investor be more likely to actually earn the YTM or the YTC?

    b.   What is the current yield? Is this yield affected by whether or not the bond is likely to be called?

    c.   What is the expected capital gains (or loss) yield for the coming year? Is this yield dependent on whether or not the bond is expected to be called?

7-12   **Yield to call** It is now January 1, 2006, and you are considering the purchase of an outstanding bond that was issued on January 1, 2004. It has a 9.5 percent annual coupon and had a 30-year original maturity. (It matures on December 31, 2033.) There was 5 years of call protection (until December 31, 2008), after which time it can be called at 109 (that is, at 109 percent of par, or $1,090). Interest rates have declined since it was issued, and it is now selling at 116.575 percent of par, or $1,165.75.

    a.   What is the yield to maturity? What is the yield to call?

    b.   If you bought this bond, which return do you think you would actually earn? Explain your reasoning.

    c.   Suppose the bond had been selling at a discount rather than a premium. Would the yield to maturity then have been the most likely actual return, or would the yield to call have been most likely?

7-13   **Price and yield** An 8 percent semiannual coupon bond matures in 5 years. The bond has a face value of $1,000 and a current yield of 8.21 percent. What are the bond's price and YTM?

7-14   **Current yield** A semiannual coupon bond that matures in 7 years sells for $1,020. It has a face value of $1,000 and a yield to maturity of 10.5883 percent. What is its current yield?

7-15   **Expected interest rate** Lloyd Corporation's 14 percent coupon rate, semiannual payment, $1,000 par value bonds, which mature in 30 years, are callable 5 years from today at $1,050. They sell at a price of $1,353.54, and the yield curve is flat. Assume interest rates are expected to remain at their current level.

    a.   What is the best estimate of these bonds' remaining life?

    b.   If Lloyd plans to raise additional capital and wants to use debt financing, what coupon rate would it have to set in order to issue new bonds at par?

Challenging Problems 16–20

7-16   **Bond valuation** Bond X is noncallable, has 20 years to maturity, a 9 percent annual coupon, and a $1,000 par value. Your required return on Bond X is 10 percent, and if you buy it you plan to hold it for 5 years. You, and the market, have expectations that in 5 years the yield to maturity on a 15-year bond with similar risk will be 8.5 percent. How much should you be willing to pay for Bond X today? (Hint: You will need to know how much the bond will be worth at the end of 5 years.)

7-17   **Bond valuation** You are considering a 10-year, $1,000 par value bond. Its coupon rate is 9 percent, and interest is paid semiannually. If you require an "effective" annual interest rate (not a nominal rate) of 8.16 percent, then how much should you be willing to pay for the bond?

7-18   **Bond returns** Last year, Joan purchased a $1,000 face value corporate bond with an 11 percent annual coupon rate and a 10-year maturity. At the time of the purchase, it had an expected yield to maturity of 9.79 percent. If Joan sold the bond today for $1,060.49, what rate of return would she have earned for the past year?

7-19   **Bond reporting** Look back at Table 7-4, and examine the Albertson's and Ford Motor Co. bonds that mature in 2031.

    a.   If these companies were to sell new $1,000 par value long-term bonds, approximately what coupon interest rate would they have to set if they wanted to bring them out at par?

    b.   If you had $10,000 and wanted to invest in the Ford bonds, what return would you expect to earn? What about the Albertson's bonds? Just based on the data in the table, would you have more confidence about earning your expected rate of return if you bought the Ford or Albertson's bonds? Explain.

7-20   **Yield to maturity and yield to call** Kaufman Enterprises has bonds outstanding with a $1,000 face value and 10 years left until maturity. They have an 11 percent annual coupon payment and their current price is $1,175. The bonds may be called in 5 years at 109 percent of face value (Call price = $1,090).

a. What is the yield to maturity?
b. What is the yield to call, if they are called in 5 years?
c. Which yield might investors expect to earn on these bonds, and why?
d. The bond's indenture indicates that the call provision gives the firm the right to call them at the end of each year beginning in Year 5. In Year 5, they may be called at 109 percent of face value, but in each of the next 4 years the call percentage will decline by 1 percent. Thus, in Year 6 they may be called at 108 percent of face value, in Year 7 they may be called at 107 percent of face value, and so on. If the yield curve is horizontal and interest rates remain at their current level, when is the latest that investors might expect the firm to call the bonds?

COMPREHENSIVE/SPREADSHEET PROBLEM

7-21 **Bond valuation** Clifford Clark is a recent retiree who is interested in investing some of his savings in corporate bonds. His financial planner has suggested the following bonds:

- Bond A has a 7 percent annual coupon, matures in 12 years, and has a $1,000 face value.
- Bond B has a 9 percent annual coupon, matures in 12 years, and has a $1,000 face value.
- Bond C has an 11 percent annual coupon, matures in 12 years, and has a $1,000 face value.

Each bond has a yield to maturity of 9 percent.

a. Before calculating the prices of the bonds, indicate whether each bond is trading at a premium, discount, or at par.
b. Calculate the price of each of the three bonds.
c. Calculate the current yield for each of the three bonds.
d. If the yield to maturity for each bond remains at 9 percent, what will be the price of each bond 1 year from now? What is the expected capital gains yield for each bond? What is the expected total return for each bond?
e. Mr. Clark is considering another bond, Bond D. It has an 8 percent semiannual coupon and a $1,000 face value (that is, it pays a $40 coupon every 6 months). Bond D is scheduled to mature in 9 years and has a price of $1,150. It is also callable in 5 years at a call price of $1,040.
   (1) What is the bond's nominal yield to maturity?
   (2) What is the bond's nominal yield to call?
   (3) If Mr. Clark were to purchase this bond, would he be more likely to receive the yield to maturity or yield to call? Explain your answer.
f. Explain briefly the difference between interest rate (or price) risk and reinvestment rate risk. Which of the following bonds has the most interest rate risk?

   - A 5-year bond with a 9 percent annual coupon.
   - A 5-year bond with a zero coupon.
   - A 10-year bond with a 9 percent annual coupon.
   - A 10-year bond with a zero coupon.

g. Only do this part if you are using a spreadsheet. Calculate the price of each bond (A, B, and C) at the end of each year until maturity, assuming interest rates remain constant. Create a graph showing the time path of each bond's value similar to Figure 7-2.
   (1) What is the expected interest yield for each bond in each year?
   (2) What is the expected capital gains yield for each bond in each year?
   (3) What is the total return for each bond in each year?

Integrated Case

Western Money Management Inc.

7-22 **Bond valuation** Robert Black and Carol Alvarez are vice presidents of Western Money Management and co-directors of the company's pension fund management division. A major new client, the California League of Cities, has requested that Western present an investment seminar to the mayors of the represented cities, and Black and Alvarez, who will make the actual presentation, have asked you to help them by answering the following questions.

a. What are a bond's key features?

b. What are call provisions and sinking fund provisions? Do these provisions make bonds more or less risky?

c. How is the value of any asset whose value is based on expected future cash flows determined?

d. How is a bond's value determined? What is the value of a 10-year, $1,000 par value bond with a 10 percent annual coupon if its required return is 10 percent?

e. (1) What is the value of a 13 percent coupon bond that is otherwise identical to the bond described in part d? Would we now have a discount or a premium bond?

 (2) What is the value of a 7 percent coupon bond with these characteristics? Would we now have a discount or a premium bond?

 (3) What would happen to the values of the 7 percent, 10 percent, and 13 percent coupon bonds over time if the required return remained at 10 percent? [Hint: With a financial calculator, enter PMT, I/YR, FV, and N, and then change (override) N to see what happens to the PV as it approaches maturity.]

f. (1) What is the yield to maturity on a 10-year, 9 percent, annual coupon, $1,000 par value bond that sells for $887.00? That sells for $1,134.20? What does the fact that it sells at a discount or at a premium tell you about the relationship between r_d and the coupon rate?

 (2) What are the total return, the current yield, and the capital gains yield for the discount bond? (Assume it is held to maturity and the company does not default on it.)

g. What is *interest rate* (or *price*) *risk*? Which has more interest rate risk, an annual payment 1-year bond or a 10-year bond? Why?

h. What is *reinvestment rate risk*? Which has more reinvestment rate risk, a 1-year bond or a 10-year bond?

i. How does the equation for valuing a bond change if semiannual payments are made? Find the value of a 10-year, semiannual payment, 10 percent coupon bond if nominal $r_d = 13$ percent.

j. Suppose you could buy, for $1,000, either a 10 percent, 10-year, annual payment bond or a 10 percent, 10-year, semiannual payment bond. They are equally risky. Which would you prefer? If $1,000 is the proper price for the semiannual bond, what is the equilibrium price for the annual payment bond?

k. Suppose a 10-year, 10 percent, semiannual coupon bond with a par value of $1,000 is currently selling for $1,135.90, producing a nominal yield to maturity of 8 percent. However, it can be called after 4 years for $1,050.

 (1) What is the bond's *nominal yield to call (YTC)*?

 (2) If you bought this bond, do you think you would be more likely to earn the YTM or the YTC? Why?

l. Does the yield to maturity represent the promised or expected return on the bond? Explain.

m. These bonds were rated AA− by S&P. Would you consider them investment-grade or junk bonds?

n. What factors determine a company's bond rating?

o. If this firm were to default on the bonds, would the company be immediately liquidated? Would the bondholders be assured of receiving all of their promised payments? Explain.

cyberproblem

Please go to the ThomsonNOW Web site to access the Cyberproblems.

8

RISK AND RATES OF RETURN

No Pain No Gain

Throughout the 1990s, the market soared, and investors became accustomed to great stock market returns. In 2000, though, stocks began a sharp decline, leading to a reassessment of the risks inherent in the stock market. This point was underscored by a *Wall Street Journal* article shortly after the terrorist attacks of September 2001:

> Investing in the stock market can be risky, sometimes very risky. While that may seem obvious after the Dow Jones Industrial Average posted its worst weekly percentage loss in 61 years and its worst-ever weekly point loss, it wasn't something that most investors spent much time thinking about during the bull market of the 1990s.
>
> Now, with the Bush administration warning of a lengthy battle against terrorism, investment advisors say that the risks associated with owning stocks—as opposed to safer securities with more pre-dictable returns, such as bonds—are poised to rise. This is leading to an increase in what analysts call a "risk premium," and as it gets higher, investors require a greater return from stocks compared to bonds.
>
> For most analysts, it is not a question of whether stocks are riskier today than they have been in recent years. Rather, they are asking how much riskier? And for how long will this period of heightened risk continue?

It is also important to understand that some stocks are riskier than others. Moreover, even in years when the overall stock market goes up, many individual stocks go down, so there's less risk to holding a "basket" of stocks than just one stock. Indeed, according to a *BusinessWeek* article, the single best weapon against risk is diversification into stocks that are not highly correlated with one another: "By spreading your money around, you're not tied to the fickleness of a given market, stock, or industry. . . . Correlation, in portfolio-manager speak, helps you diversify properly because it describes how closely two investments

© DYNAMIC GRAPHICS/COMSTOCK/PICTUREQUEST

track each other. If they move in tandem, they're likely to suffer from the same bad news. So, you should combine assets with low correlations."

U.S. investors tend to think of "the stock market" as the U.S. stock market. However, U.S. stocks amount to only 35 percent of the value of all stocks. Foreign markets have been quite profitable, and they are not perfectly correlated with U.S. markets. Therefore, global diversification offers U.S. investors an opportunity to raise returns and at the same time reduce risk. However, foreign investing brings some risks of its own, most notably "exchange rate risk," which is the danger that exchange rate shifts will decrease the number of dollars a foreign currency will buy.

Although the central thrust of the *BusinessWeek* article was on measuring and then reducing risk, it also pointed out that some extremely risky instruments have been marketed to naive investors as having very little risk. For example, several mutual funds advertise that their portfolios "contain only securities backed by the U.S. government," but they failed to highlight that the funds themselves were using financial leverage, were investing in "derivatives," or were taking some other action that exposed investors to huge risks.

When you finish this chapter, you should understand what risk is, how it can be measured, and how to minimize it or at least be adequately compensated for bearing it.

Sources: "Figuring Risk: It's Not So Scary," *BusinessWeek,* November 1, 1993, pp. 154–155; "T-Bill Trauma and the Meaning of Risk," *The Wall Street Journal,* February 12, 1993, p. C1; and "Stock Risks Poised to Rise in Changed Postattack World," *The Wall Street Journal,* September 24, 2001, p. C1.

Putting Things In Perspective

We start this chapter from the basic premise that investors like returns and dislike risk and therefore will invest in risky assets only if those assets offer higher expected returns. We define precisely what the term *risk* means as it relates to investments, examine procedures that are used to measure risk, and discuss the relationship between risk and return. Investors should understand these concepts, as should managers as they develop the plans that will shape their firms' futures.

Risk can be measured in different ways, and different conclusions about an asset's riskiness can be reached depending on the measure used. Risk analysis can be confusing, but it will help if you keep the following points in mind:

1. All financial assets are expected to produce *cash flows,* and the riskiness of an asset is based on the riskiness of its cash flows.
2. An asset's risk can be considered in two ways: (a) on a *stand-alone basis,* where the asset's cash flows are analyzed by themselves, or (b) in a *portfolio context,* where the cash flows from a number of assets are combined and then the consolidated cash flows are analyzed.[1] There is an important difference between stand-alone and portfolio risk, and an

---

[1] A *portfolio* is a collection of investment securities. If you owned some General Motors stock, some ExxonMobil stock, and some IBM stock, you would be holding a three-stock portfolio. Because diversification lowers risk without sacrificing much if any expected return, most stocks are held in portfolios.

asset that has a great deal of risk if held by itself may be less risky if it is held as part of a larger portfolio.

3. In a portfolio context, an asset's risk can be divided into two components: (a) *diversifiable risk*, which can be diversified away and is thus of little concern to diversified investors, and (b) *market risk*, which reflects the risk of a general stock market decline and which cannot be eliminated by diversification, hence does concern investors. Only market risk is *relevant* to rational investors—diversifiable risk is *irrelevant* because it can and will be eliminated.

4. An asset with a high degree of relevant (market) risk must offer a relatively high expected rate of return to attract investors. Investors in general are *averse to risk*, so they will not buy risky assets unless those assets have high expected returns.

5. If investors on average think a security's expected return is too low to compensate for its risk, then the price of the security will decline, which will boost the expected return. Conversely, if the expected return is more than enough to compensate for the risk, then the security's market price will increase, thus lowering the expected return. The security will be in equilibrium when its expected return is just sufficient to compensate for its risk.

6. In this chapter, we focus on *financial assets* such as stocks and bonds, but the concepts discussed here also apply to *physical assets* such as computers, trucks, or even whole plants.

8-1 STAND-ALONE RISK

Risk
The chance that some unfavorable event will occur.

Risk is defined in *Webster's* as "a hazard; a peril; exposure to loss or injury." Thus, risk refers to the chance that some unfavorable event will occur. If you engage in skydiving, you are taking a chance with your life—skydiving is risky. If you bet on the horses, you are risking your money.

As we saw in previous chapters, both individuals and firms invest funds today with the expectation of receiving additional funds in the future. Bonds offer relatively low returns, but with relatively little risk—at least if you stick to Treasury bonds and high-grade corporates. Stocks offer the chance of higher returns, but, as we saw in Chapter 5, stocks are generally riskier than bonds. If you invest in speculative stocks (or, really, *any* stock), you are taking a significant risk in the hope of making an appreciable return.

Stand-Alone Risk
The risk an investor would face if he or she held only one asset.

An asset's risk can be analyzed in two ways: (1) on a stand-alone basis, where the asset is considered in isolation; and (2) on a portfolio basis, where the asset is held as one of a number of assets in a portfolio. Thus, an asset's **stand-alone risk** is the risk an investor would face if he or she held only this one asset. Obviously, most assets are held in portfolios, but it is necessary to understand stand-alone risk in order to understand risk in a portfolio context.

To illustrate stand-alone risk, suppose an investor buys $100,000 of short-term Treasury bills with an expected return of 5 percent. In this case, the investment's return, 5 percent, can be estimated quite precisely, and the investment is defined as being essentially *risk free*. This same investor could also invest the $100,000 in the stock of a company just being organized to prospect for oil in the mid-Atlantic. The returns on the stock would be much harder to predict. In the worst case the company would go bankrupt and the investor would lose all of her money, in which case the return would be −100 percent. In the best-case scenario, the company would discover large amounts of oil and the investor would receive huge positive returns. When evaluating this investment, the investor might analyze the situation and conclude that the *expected* rate of return, in a statistical sense, is 20 percent, but it should also be recognized that the *actual* rate of return could range from, say, +1,000 to −100 percent. Because there is a significant danger of actually earning much less than the expected return, such a stock would be relatively risky.

No investment would be undertaken unless the expected rate of return was high enough to compensate the investor for the perceived risk. In our example, it is clear that few, if any, investors would be willing to buy the oil exploration company's stock if its expected return were the same as that of the T-bill.

Risky assets rarely produce their expected rates of return—generally, risky assets earn either more or less than was originally expected. Indeed, if assets always produced their expected returns, they would not be risky. Investment risk, then, is related to the *probability* of actually earning a low or negative return—the greater the chance of a low or negative return, the riskier the investment. However, risk can be defined more precisely, as we demonstrate in the next section.

8-1a Probability Distributions

An event's *probability* is defined as the chance that the event will occur. For example, a weather forecaster might state, "There is a 40 percent chance of rain today and a 60 percent chance of no rain." If all possible events, or outcomes, are listed, and if a probability is assigned to each event, the listing is called a **probability distribution.** For our weather forecast, we could set up the following probability distribution:

Outcome (1)		Probability (2)	
Rain	0.4	=	40%
No rain	0.6	=	60
	1.0	=	100%

Probability Distribution
A listing of all possible outcomes, or events, with a probability (chance of occurrence) assigned to each outcome.

The possible outcomes are listed in Column 1, while the probabilities of these outcomes, expressed both as decimals and as percentages, are given in Column 2. Notice that the probabilities must sum to 1.0, or 100 percent.

Probabilities can also be assigned to the possible outcomes—in this case returns—from an investment. If you plan to buy a one-year bond and hold it for a year, you would expect to receive interest on the bond plus a return of your original investment, and those payments would provide you with a rate of return on your investment. The possible outcomes from this investment are (1) that the issuer will make the required payments or (2) that the issuer will default on the payments. The higher the probability of default, the riskier the bond, and the higher the risk, the higher the required rate of return. If you invest in a stock instead of buying a bond, you would again expect to earn a return on your money. A stock's return would come from dividends plus capital gains. Again, the riskier the stock—which means the higher the probability that the firm will fail to provide the dividends and capital gains you expect—the higher the expected return must be to induce you to invest in the stock.

With this in mind, consider the possible rates of return (dividend yield plus capital gain or loss) that you might earn next year on a $10,000 investment in the stock of either Martin Products Inc. or U.S. Water Company. Martin manufactures and distributes computer terminals and equipment for the rapidly growing data transmission industry. Because it faces intense competition, its new products may or may not be competitive in the marketplace, so its future earnings cannot be predicted very well. Indeed, some new company could develop better products and quickly bankrupt Martin. U.S. Water, on the other hand, supplies an essential service, and it has city franchises that protect it from competition. Therefore, its sales and profits are relatively stable and predictable.

The rate-of-return probability distributions for the two companies are shown in Table 8-1. There is a 30 percent chance of a strong economy and thus strong demand, in which case both companies will have high earnings, pay high dividends, and enjoy capital gains. There is a 40 percent probability of normal demand and moderate returns, and there is a 30 percent probability of weak demand, which will mean low earnings and dividends as well as capital losses. Notice, however, that Martin Products' rate of return could vary far more widely than that of U.S. Water. There is a fairly high probability that the value of Martin's stock will drop substantially, resulting in a 70 percent loss, while the worst that could happen to U.S. Water is a 10 percent return.[2]

8-1b Expected Rate of Return

If we multiply each possible outcome by its probability of occurrence and then sum these products, as in Table 8-2, we obtain a *weighted average* of outcomes. The weights are the probabilities, and the weighted average is the **expected rate of return, r̂,** called "r-hat."[3] The expected rates of return for both Martin Products and U.S. Water are shown in Table 8-2 to be 15 percent. This type of table is known as a *payoff matrix*.

Expected Rate of Return, r̂
The rate of return expected to be realized from an investment; the weighted average of the probability distribution of possible results.

TABLE 8-1	*Probability Distributions for Martin Products and U.S. Water*

		RATE OF RETURN ON STOCK IF THIS DEMAND OCCURS	
Demand for the Company's Products	Probability of this Demand Occurring	Martin Products	U.S. Water
Strong	0.3	100%	20%
Normal	0.4	15	15
Weak	0.3	(70)	10
	1.0		

---

[2] It is, of course, completely unrealistic to think that any stock has no chance of a loss. Only in hypothetical examples could this occur. To illustrate, the price of Columbia Gas's stock dropped from $34.50 to $20.00 in just three hours a few years ago. All investors were reminded that any stock is exposed to some risk of loss, and those investors who bought Columbia Gas learned that the hard way.

[3] In Chapters 7 and 9, we use r_d and r_s to signify the returns on bonds and stocks, respectively. However, this distinction is unnecessary in this chapter, so we just use the general term, r, to signify the expected return on an investment.

| TABLE 8-2 | *Calculation of Expected Rates of Return: Payoff Matrix* |

		MARTIN PRODUCTS		U.S. WATER	
Demand for the Company's Products (1)	Probability of This Demand Occurring (2)	Rate of Return If This Demand Occurs (3)	Product: (2) × (3) = (4)	Rate of Return If This Demand Occurs (5)	Product: (2) × (5) = (6)
Strong	0.3	100%	30%	20%	6%
Normal	0.4	15	6	15	6
Weak	0.3	(70)	(21)	10	3
	1.0		$\hat{r} = 15\%$		$\hat{r} = 15\%$

The expected rate of return can also be expressed as an equation that does the same thing as the payoff matrix table:[4]

$$\text{Expected rate of return} = \hat{r} = P_1r_1 + P_2r_2 + \cdots + P_Nr_N$$

$$= \sum_{i=1}^{N} P_i r_i \qquad \text{(8-1)}$$

Here r_i is the *i*th possible outcome, P_i is the probability of the *i*th outcome, and N is the number of possible outcomes. Thus, $\hat{r}$ is a weighted average of the possible outcomes (the r_i values), with each outcome's weight being its probability of occurrence. Using the data for Martin Products, we obtain its expected rate of return as follows:

$$\hat{r} = P_1(r_1) + P_2(r_2) + P_3(r_3)$$

$$= 0.3(100\%) + 0.4(15\%) + 0.3(-70\%)$$

$$= 15\%$$

U.S. Water's expected rate of return is also 15 percent:

$$\hat{r} = 0.3(20\%) + 0.4(15\%) + 0.3(10\%)$$

$$= 15\%$$

We can graph the rates of return to obtain a picture of the variability of possible outcomes; this is shown in the Figure 8-1 bar charts. The height of each bar signifies the probability that a given outcome will occur. The range of probable returns for Martin Products is from −70 to +100 percent, and the expected return is 15 percent. The expected return for U.S. Water is also 15 percent, but its possible range is much narrower.

---

[4] The second form of the equation is simply a shorthand expression in which sigma ($\sum$) means "sum up," or add the values of n factors. If i = 1, then $P_ir_i = P_1r_1$; if i = 2, then $P_ir_i = P_2r_2$; and so on until i = N, the last possible outcome. The symbol $\sum_{i=1}^{N}$ simply says, "Go through the following process: First, let i = 1 and find the first product; then i = 2 and find the second product; then continue until each individual product up to 1 = N has been found, and then add these individual products to find the expected rate of return."

FIGURE 8-1   *Probability Distributions of Martin Products'*
and U.S. Water's Rates of Return

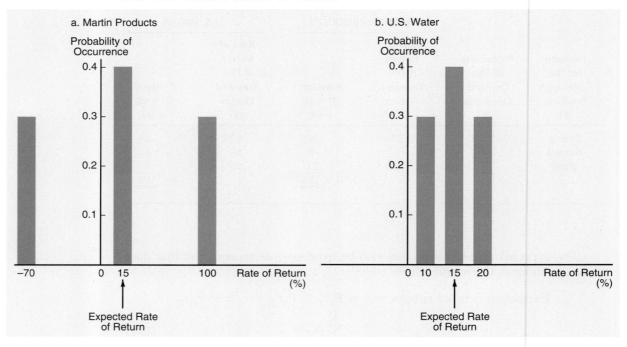

Thus far, we have assumed that only three outcomes could occur: strong, normal, and weak demand. Actually, of course, demand could range from a deep depression to a fantastic boom, and there are an unlimited number of possibilities in between. Suppose we had the time and patience to assign a probability to each possible level of demand (with the sum of the probabilities still equaling 1.0) and to assign a rate of return to each stock for each level of demand. We would have a table similar to Table 8-1, except that it would have many more entries in each column. This table could be used to calculate expected rates of return as shown previously, and the probabilities and outcomes could be represented by continuous curves such as those presented in Figure 8-2. Here we have changed the assumptions so that there is essentially a zero probability that Martin Products' return will be less than −70 percent or more than 100 percent, or that U.S. Water's return will be less than 10 percent or more than 20 percent. However, virtually any return within these limits is possible.

The tighter (or more peaked) the probability distribution, the more likely it is that the actual outcome will be close to the expected value, and, consequently, the less likely it is that the actual return will end up far below the expected return. Thus, the tighter the probability distribution, the lower the risk faced by the owners of a stock. Since U.S. Water has a relatively tight probability distribution, its *actual return* is likely to be closer to its 15 percent *expected return* than is that of Martin Products.

8-1c Measuring Stand-Alone Risk: The Standard Deviation

Risk is a difficult concept to grasp, and a great deal of controversy has surrounded attempts to define and measure it. However, a common definition, and one that is satisfactory for many purposes, is stated in terms of probability distributions such as those presented in Figure 8-2: *The tighter the probability distribution of expected future returns, the smaller the risk of a given investment.* According to this

FIGURE 8-2 *Continuous Probability Distributions of Martin Products' and U.S. Water's Rates of Returns*

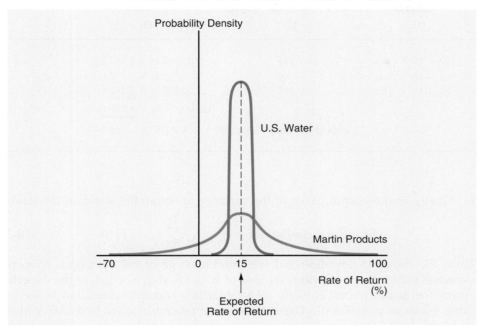

Note: The assumptions regarding the probabilities of various outcomes have been changed from those in Figure 8-1. There the probability of obtaining exactly 15 percent was 40 percent; here it is *much smaller* because there are many possible outcomes instead of just three. With continuous distributions, it is more appropriate to ask what the probability is of obtaining at least some specified rate of return than to ask what the probability is of obtaining exactly that rate. This topic is covered in detail in statistics courses.

definition, U.S. Water is less risky than Martin Products because there is a smaller chance that its actual return will end up far below its expected return.

To be most useful, our risk measure should have a definite value—we need to quantify the tightness of the probability distribution. One such measure is the **standard deviation,** whose symbol is σ, pronounced "sigma." The smaller the standard deviation, the tighter the probability distribution, and, accordingly, the lower the riskiness of the stock. To calculate the standard deviation, we proceed as shown in Table 8-3, taking the following steps:

Standard Deviation, σ
A statistical measure of the variability of a set of observations.

1. Calculate the expected rate of return:

$$\text{Expected rate of return} = \hat{r} = \sum_{i=1}^{N} P_i r_i$$

For Martin, we previously found $\hat{r} = 15\%$.

2. Subtract the expected rate of return ($\hat{r}$) from each possible outcome (r_i) to obtain a set of deviations about $\hat{r}$ as shown in Column 1 of Table 8-3:

$$\text{Deviation}_i = r_i - \hat{r}$$

3. Square each deviation, then multiply the result by its probability of occurrence, and then sum those products to obtain the **variance** of the probability distribution as shown in Columns 2 and 3 of the table:

Variance, σ²
The square of the standard deviation.

$$\text{Variance} = \sigma^2 = \sum_{i=1}^{N} (r_i - \hat{r})^2 P_i \qquad \textbf{(8-2)}$$

TABLE 8-3		*Calculating Martin Products' Standard Deviation*
$r_i - \hat{r}$ (1)	$(r_i - \hat{r})^2$ (2)	$(r_i - \hat{r})^2 P_i$ (3)
$100 - 15 = 85$	$7{,}225$	$(7{,}225)(0.3) = 2{,}167.5$
$15 - 15 = 0$	0	$(0)(0.4) = 0.0$
$-70 - 15 = -85$	$7{,}225$	$(7{,}225)(0.3) = \underline{2{,}167.5}$
		Variance $= \sigma^2 = \underline{4{,}335.0}$
		Standard deviation $= \sigma = \sqrt{\sigma^2} = \sqrt{4{,}335} = 65.84\%$

4. Finally, find the square root of the variance to obtain the standard deviation:

$$\text{Standard deviation} = \sigma = \sqrt{\sum_{i=1}^{N}(r_i - \hat{r})^2 P_i} \qquad \textbf{(8-3)}$$

Thus, the standard deviation is a weighted average of the deviations from the expected value, and it provides an idea of how far above or below the expected return the actual return is likely to be. Martin's standard deviation is seen in Table 8-3 to be $\sigma = 65.84\%$. Using these same procedures, we find U.S. Water's standard deviation to be 3.87 percent. Martin Products has a much larger standard deviation, which indicates a much greater variation of returns and thus a greater chance that the expected return will not be realized. Therefore, Martin Products is a riskier investment than U.S. Water when held alone.

If a probability distribution is "normal," the *actual* return will be within ±1 standard deviation around the *expected* return 68.26 percent of the time. Figure 8-3 illustrates this point, and it also shows the situation for ±2σ and ±3σ. For Martin Products, $\hat{r} = 15\%$ and $\sigma = 65.84\%$, whereas $\hat{r} = 15\%$ and $\sigma = 3.87\%$ for U.S. Water. Thus, if the two distributions were normal, there would be a 68.26% probability that Martin's actual return would be in the range of $15 \pm 65.84\%$, or from -50.84 to 80.84 percent. For U.S. Water, the 68.26 percent range is $15 \pm 3.87\%$, or from 11.13 to 18.87 percent. With such a small σ, there is only a small probability that U.S. Water's return would be much less than expected, so the stock is not very risky. For the average firm listed on the New York Stock Exchange, σ has generally been in the range of 35 to 40 percent in recent years.

8-1d Using Historical Data to Measure Risk

In the example just given, we described the procedure for finding the mean and standard deviation when the data are in the form of a probability distribution. If only sample returns data over some past period are available, the standard deviation of returns should be estimated using this formula:

$$\text{Estimated } \sigma = S = \sqrt{\dfrac{\sum_{t=1}^{N}(\bar{r}_t - \bar{r}_{Avg})^2}{N-1}} \qquad \textbf{(8-3a)}$$

Here $\bar{r}_t$ ("r bar t") denotes the past realized rate of return in Period t and $\bar{r}_{Avg}$ is the average annual return earned during the last N years. Here is an example:

Year	$\bar{r}_t$
2003	15%
2004	−5
2005	20

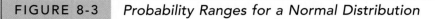

| FIGURE 8-3 | *Probability Ranges for a Normal Distribution* |

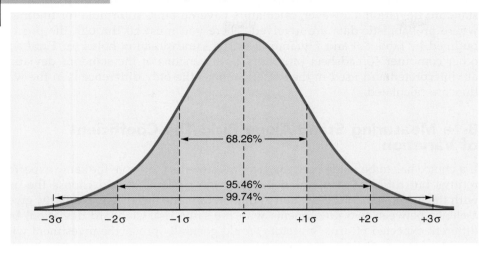

Notes:

a. The area under the normal curve always equals 1.0, or 100 percent. *Thus, the areas under any pair of normal curves drawn on the same scale, whether they are peaked or flat, must be equal.*

b. Half of the area under a normal curve is to the left of the mean, indicating that there is a 50 percent probability that the actual outcome will be less than the mean, and half is to the right of $\hat{r}$, indicating a 50 percent probability that it will be greater than the mean.

c. Of the area under the curve, 68.26 percent is within $\pm 1\sigma$ of the mean, indicating that the probability is 68.26 percent that the actual outcome will be within the range $\hat{r} - 1\sigma$ to $\hat{r} + 1\sigma$.

d. Procedures exist for finding the probability of other ranges. These procedures are covered in statistics courses.

e. For a normal distribution, the larger the value of σ, the greater the probability that the actual outcome will vary widely from, and hence perhaps be far below, the expected, or most likely, outcome. *Since the probability of having the actual result turn out to be far below the expected result is one definition of risk, and since σ measures this probability, we can use σ as a measure of risk. This definition may not be a good one, however, if we are dealing with an asset held in a diversified portfolio. This point is covered later in the chapter.*

$$\bar{r}_{Avg} = \frac{(15\% - 5\% + 20\%)}{3} = 10.0\%$$

$$\text{Estimated } \sigma \text{ (or S)} = \sqrt{\frac{(15\% - 10\%)^2 + (-5\% - 10\%)^2 + (20\% - 10\%)^2}{3 - 1}}$$

$$= \sqrt{\frac{350\%}{2}} = 13.2\%$$

The historical σ is often used as an estimate of the future σ. Much less often, and generally incorrectly, $\bar{r}_{Avg}$ for some past period is used as an estimate of $\hat{r}$, the expected future return. Because past variability is likely to be repeated, σ may be a good estimate of future risk. However, it is much less reasonable to expect that the average return during any particular past period is the best estimate of what investors think will happen in the future. For instance, from 2000 through 2002 the historical average return on the S&P 500 index was negative, but it is not reasonable to assume that investors expect returns to continue to be negative in the future. If they expected negative returns, they would obviously not have been willing to buy or hold stocks.

Equation 8-3a is built into all financial calculators, and it is easy to use.[5] We simply enter the rates of return and press the key marked S (or S_x) to obtain the standard deviation. However, calculators have no built-in formula for finding σ where probabilistic data are involved. There you must go through the process outlined in Table 8-3 and Equation 8-3. The same situation holds for *Excel* and other computer spreadsheet programs. Both versions of the standard deviation are interpreted and used in the same manner—the only difference is in the way they are calculated.

8-1e Measuring Stand-Alone Risk: The Coefficient of Variation

Coefficient of Variation (CV)
Standardized measure of the risk per unit of return; calculated as the standard deviation divided by the expected return.

If a choice has to be made between two investments that have the same expected returns but different standard deviations, most people would choose the one with the lower standard deviation and, therefore, the lower risk. Similarly, given a choice between two investments with the same risk (standard deviation) but different expected returns, investors would generally prefer the investment with the higher expected return. To most people, this is common sense—return is "good," risk is "bad," and, consequently, investors want as much return and as little risk as possible. But how do we choose between two investments if one has the higher expected return but the other the lower standard deviation? To help answer this question, we use another measure of risk, the **coefficient of variation (CV)**, which is the standard deviation divided by the expected return:

$$\text{Coefficient of variation} = \text{CV} = \frac{\sigma}{\hat{r}} \tag{8-4}$$

The coefficient of variation shows the risk per unit of return, and it provides a more meaningful risk measure when the expected returns on two alternatives are not the same. Since U.S. Water and Martin Products have the same expected return, the coefficient of variation is not necessary in this case. Here the firm with the larger standard deviation, Martin, must have the larger coefficient of variation. In fact, the coefficient of variation for Martin is 65.84/15 = 4.39 and that for U.S. Water is 3.87/15 = 0.26. Thus, Martin is almost 17 times riskier than U.S. Water on the basis of this criterion.

For a case where the coefficient of variation is actually necessary, consider Projects X and Y in Figure 8-4. These projects have different expected rates of return and different standard deviations. Project X has a 60 percent expected rate of return and a 15 percent standard deviation, while Y has an 8 percent expected return but only a 3 percent standard deviation. Is Project X riskier, on a relative basis, because it has the larger standard deviation? If we calculate the coefficients of variation for these two projects, we find that Project X has a coefficient of variation of 15/60 = 0.25, and Project Y has a coefficient of variation of 3/8 = 0.375. Thus, Project Y actually has more risk per unit of return than Project X, in spite of the fact that X's standard deviation is larger. Therefore, even though Project Y has the lower standard deviation, according to the coefficient of variation it is riskier than Project X.

Project Y has the smaller standard deviation, hence the more peaked probability distribution, but it is clear from the graph that the chances of a really low return are higher for Y than for X because X's expected return is so high. Because

---

[5] See our tutorials or your calculator manual for instructions on calculating historical standard deviations.

FIGURE 8-4	*Comparison of Probability Distributions and Rates of Return for Projects X and Y*

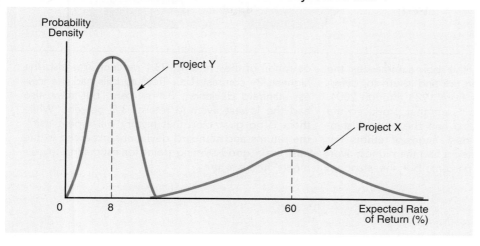

the coefficient of variation captures the effects of both risk and return, it is a better measure for evaluating risk in situations where investments have substantially different expected returns.

8-1f Risk Aversion and Required Returns

Suppose you have worked hard and saved $1 million, and you now plan to invest it and retire on the income it produces. You can buy a 5 percent U.S. Treasury bill, and at the end of one year you will have a sure $1.05 million, which is your original investment plus $50,000 in interest. Alternatively, you can buy stock in R&D Enterprises. If R&D's research programs are successful, your stock will increase in value to $2.1 million. However, if the research is a failure, the value of your stock will be zero, and you will be penniless. You regard R&D's chances of success or failure as being 50–50, so the expected value of the stock investment is 0.5($0) + 0.5($2,100,000) = $1,050,000. Subtracting the $1 million cost of the stock leaves an expected profit of $50,000, or an expected (but risky) 5 percent rate of return, the same as for the T-bill:

$$\text{Expected rate of return} = \frac{\text{Expected ending value} - \text{Cost}}{\text{Cost}}$$

$$= \frac{\$1,050,000 - \$1,000,000}{\$1,000,000}$$

$$= \frac{\$50,000}{\$1,000,000} = 5\%$$

Thus, you have a choice between a sure $50,000 profit (representing a 5 percent rate of return) on the Treasury bill and a risky expected $50,000 profit (also representing a 5 percent expected rate of return) on the R&D Enterprises stock. Which one would you choose? *If you choose the less risky investment, you are risk averse. Most investors are indeed risk averse, and certainly the average investor is risk averse with regard to his or her "serious money." Because this is a well-documented fact, we assume* **risk aversion** *in our discussions throughout the remainder of the book.*

Risk Aversion
Risk-averse investors dislike risk and require higher rates of return as an inducement to buy riskier securities.

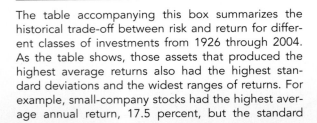

The Trade-Off between Risk and Return

The table accompanying this box summarizes the historical trade-off between risk and return for different classes of investments from 1926 through 2004. As the table shows, those assets that produced the highest average returns also had the highest standard deviations and the widest ranges of returns. For example, small-company stocks had the highest average annual return, 17.5 percent, but the standard deviation of their returns, 33.1 percent, was also the highest. By contrast, U.S. Treasury bills had the lowest standard deviation, 3.1 percent, but they also had the lowest average return, 3.8 percent. While there is no guarantee that history will repeat itself, the returns and standard deviations observed in the past are a good starting point for estimating investments' future returns.

What are the implications of risk aversion for security prices and rates of return? *The answer is that, other things held constant, the higher a security's risk the lower its price and the higher its required return.* To see how risk aversion affects security prices, look back at Figure 8-2 and consider again U.S. Water's and Martin Products' stocks. Suppose each stock sold for $100 per share and each had an expected rate of return of 15 percent. Investors are averse to risk, so under those conditions there would be a general preference for U.S. Water. People with money to invest would bid for U.S. Water rather than Martin stock, and Martin's stockholders would start selling their stock and using the money to buy U.S. Water. Buying pressure would drive up U.S. Water's stock, and selling pressure would simultaneously cause Martin's price to decline.

These price changes, in turn, would cause changes in the expected returns of the two securities. In general, if expected future cash flows remain the same, your expected return would be higher if you were able to purchase the stock at a lower price. Suppose, for example, that U.S. Water's stock price were bid up from $100 to $150, whereas Martin's stock price declined from $100 to $75. These price changes would cause U.S. Water's expected return to fall to 10 percent, and Martin's expected return to rise to 20 percent.[6] The difference in returns, 20% − 10% = 10%, would be a **risk premium, RP,** which represents the additional compensation investors require for bearing Martin's higher risk.

Risk Premium, RP
The difference between the expected rate of return on a given risky asset and that on a less risky asset.

This example demonstrates a very important principle: *In a market dominated by risk-averse investors, riskier securities must have higher expected returns as estimated by investors at the margin than less risky securities. If this situation does not exist, buying and selling will occur in the market until it does exist.* We will consider the question of how much higher the returns on risky securities must be later in the chapter, after we see how diversification affects the way risk should be measured.

---

[6] To understand how we might arrive at these numbers, assume that each stock is expected to pay shareholders $15 a year in perpetuity. The price of this perpetuity can be found by dividing the annual cash flow by the stock's return. Thus, in this example, if the stock's expected return is 15 percent, the price of the stock would be $15/0.15 = $100. Likewise, a 10 percent expected return would be consistent with a $150 stock price ($15/0.10), and a 20 percent expected return would be consistent with a $75 stock price ($15/0.20).

Selected Realized Returns, 1926–2004

	Average Return	Standard Deviation
Small-company stocks	17.5%	33.1%
Large-company stocks	12.4	20.3
Long-term corporate bonds	6.2	8.6
Long-term government bonds	5.8	9.3
U.S. Treasury bills	3.8	3.1

Source: Based on *Stocks, Bonds, Bills, and Inflation: (Valuation Edition) 2005 Yearbook* (Chicago: Ibbotson Associates, 2005), p. 28.

What does "investment risk" mean?

Set up an illustrative probability distribution table, or "payoff matrix," for an investment with probabilities for different conditions, returns under those conditions, and the expected return.

Which of the two stocks graphed in Figure 8-2 is less risky? Why?

How is the standard deviation calculated based on (1) a probability distribution of returns and (b) historical returns?

Which is a better measure of risk if assets have different expected returns: (1) the standard deviation or (2) the coefficient of variation? Why?

Explain why you agree or disagree with the following statement: "Most investors are risk averse."

How does risk aversion affect rates of return?

An investment has a 50 percent chance of producing a 20 percent return, a 25 percent chance of producing an 8 percent return, and a 25 percent chance of producing a −12 percent return. What is its expected return? (9%)

An investment has an expected return of 10 percent and a standard deviation of 30 percent. What is its coefficient of variation? (3.0)

8-2 RISK IN A PORTFOLIO CONTEXT

Thus far we have considered the riskiness of assets when they are held in isolation. Now we analyze the riskiness of assets held as a part of a portfolio. As we shall see, an asset held in a portfolio is less risky than the same asset held in isolation. Since investors dislike risk, and since risk can be reduced by holding portfolios—that is, by diversifying—most financial assets are indeed held in portfolios. Banks, pension funds, insurance companies, mutual funds, and other financial institutions are required by law to hold diversified portfolios. Even individual investors—at least those whose security holdings constitute a significant part of their total wealth—generally hold portfolios, not the stock of a single firm. Therefore, the fact that a particular stock goes up or down is not very important—*what is important is the return on the investor's portfolio, and the risk of that portfolio. Logically, then, the risk and return of an individual security should be analyzed in terms of how the security affects the risk and return of the portfolio in which it is held.*

To illustrate, Pay Up Inc. is a collection agency company that operates nationwide through 37 offices. The company is not well known, its stock is not very liquid, and its earnings have fluctuated quite a bit in the past. This suggests that Pay Up is risky and that its required rate of return, r, should be relatively high. However, Pay Up's required rate of return in 2005 (and all other years) was actually quite low in comparison to that of most other companies. This indicates that investors regard Pay Up as being a low-risk company in spite of its uncertain profits. The reason for this counterintuitive finding has to do with diversification and its effect on risk. Pay Up's earnings rise during recessions, whereas most other companies' earnings tend to decline when the economy slumps. Thus, Pay Up's stock is like fire insurance—it pays off when other things go bad. Therefore, adding Pay Up to a portfolio of "normal" stocks stabilizes returns on the portfolio, thus making the portfolio less risky.

8-2a Expected Portfolio Returns, $\hat{r}_p$

Expected Return on a Portfolio, $\hat{r}_p$
The weighted average of the expected returns on the assets held in the portfolio.

The **expected return on a portfolio, $\hat{r}_p$,** is simply the weighted average of the expected returns on the individual assets in the portfolio, with the weights being the percentage of the total portfolio invested in each asset:

$$\hat{r}_p = w_1\hat{r}_1 + w_2\hat{r}_2 + \cdots + w_N\hat{r}_N$$

$$= \sum_{i=1}^{N} w_i\hat{r}_i \qquad (8\text{-}5)$$

Here the $\hat{r}_i$'s are the expected returns on the individual stocks, the w_i's are the weights, and there are N stocks in the portfolio. Note that (1) w_i is the fraction of the portfolio's dollar value invested in Stock i (that is, the value of the investment in Stock i divided by the total value of the portfolio) and (2) the w_i's must sum to 1.0.

Assume that in March 2005, a security analyst estimated that the following returns could be expected on the stocks of four large companies:

	Expected Return, $\hat{r}$
Microsoft	12.0%
General Electric	11.5
Pfizer	10.0
Coca-Cola	9.5

Realized Rate of Return, $\bar{r}$
The return that was actually earned during some past period. The actual return ($\bar{r}$) usually turns out to be different from the expected return ($\hat{r}$) except for riskless assets.

If we formed a $100,000 portfolio, investing $25,000 in each stock, the portfolio's expected return would be 10.75 percent:

$$\hat{r}_p = w_1\hat{r}_1 + w_2\hat{r}_2 + w_3\hat{r}_3 + w_4\hat{r}_4$$

$$= 0.25(12\%) + 0.25(11.5\%) + 0.25(10\%) + 0.25(9.5\%)$$

$$= 10.75\%$$

Of course, after the fact and a year later, the actual **realized rates of return, $\bar{r}_i$,** on the individual stocks—the $\bar{r}_i$, or "r-bar," values—will almost certainly be different from their expected values, so $\bar{r}_p$ will be different from $\hat{r}_p = 10.75\%$. For example, Coca-Cola's price might double and thus provide a return of +100 percent, whereas Microsoft might have a terrible year, fall sharply, and have a return of −75 percent. Note, though, that those two events would be offsetting, so the portfolio's return might still be close to its expected return, even though the individual stocks' returns were far from their expected values.

8-2b Portfolio Risk

Although the expected return on a portfolio is simply the weighted average of the expected returns of the individual assets in the portfolio, the riskiness of the portfolio, σ_p, is *not* the weighted average of the individual assets' standard deviations. The portfolio's risk is generally *smaller* than the average of the assets' σ's.

To illustrate the effect of combining assets, consider the situation in Figure 8-5. The bottom section gives data on rates of return for Stocks W and M individually, and also for a portfolio invested 50 percent in each stock. The three top graphs show plots of the data in a time series format, and the lower graphs show the probability distributions of returns, assuming that the future is expected to be like the past. The two stocks would be quite risky if they were held in isolation, but when they are combined to form Portfolio WM, they are not risky at all. (Note: These stocks are called W and M because the graphs of their returns in Figure 8-5 resemble a W and an M.)

Stocks W and M can be combined to form a riskless portfolio because their returns move countercyclically to each other—when W's returns fall, those of M rise, and vice versa. The tendency of two variables to move together is called **correlation,** and the **correlation coefficient, ρ** (pronounced "rho"), measures this tendency.[7] In statistical terms, we say that the returns on Stocks W and M are *perfectly negatively correlated*, with $\rho = -1.0$.

The opposite of perfect negative correlation, with $\rho = -1.0$, is *perfect positive correlation*, with $\rho = +1.0$. Returns on two perfectly positively correlated stocks (M and M') would move up and down together, and a portfolio consisting of two such stocks would be exactly as risky as the individual stocks. This point is illustrated in Figure 8-6, where we see that the portfolio's standard deviation is equal to that of the individual stocks. *Thus, diversification does nothing to reduce risk if the portfolio consists of perfectly positively correlated stocks.*

Figures 8-5 and 8-6 demonstrate that when stocks are perfectly negatively correlated ($\rho = -1.0$), all risk can be diversified away, but when stocks are perfectly positively correlated ($\rho = +1.0$), diversification does no good whatever. In reality, virtually all stocks are positively correlated, but not perfectly so. Past studies have estimated that on average the correlation coefficient for the monthly returns on two randomly selected stocks is about 0.3.[8] *Under this condition, combining*

Correlation
The tendency of two variables to move together.

Correlation Coefficient, ρ
A measure of the degree of relationship between two variables.

---

[7] The correlation coefficient, ρ, can range from +1.0, denoting that the two variables move up and down in perfect synchronization, to −1.0, denoting that the variables always move in exactly opposite directions. A correlation coefficient of zero indicates that the two variables are not related to each other—that is, changes in one variable are independent of changes in the other. It is easy to calculate correlation coefficients with a financial calculator. Simply enter the returns on the two stocks and then press a key labeled "r." For W and M, $\rho = -1.0$. See our tutorial or your calculator manual for the exact steps. Also, note that the correlation coefficient is often denoted by the term "r." We use ρ here to avoid confusion with r as used to denote the rate of return.

[8] A recent study by Chan, Karceski, and Lakonishok (1999) estimated that the average correlation coefficient between two randomly selected stocks was 0.28, while the average correlation coefficient between two large-company stocks was 0.33. The time period of their sample was 1968 to 1998. See Louis K. C. Chan, Jason Karceski, and Josef Lakonishok, "On Portfolio Optimization: Forecasting Covariance and Choosing the Risk Model," *The Review of Financial Studies*, Vol. 12, no. 5 (Winter 1999), pp. 937–974.

FIGURE 8-5 *Rate of Return Distributions for Two Perfectly Negatively Correlated Stocks ($\rho = -1.0$) and for Portfolio WM*

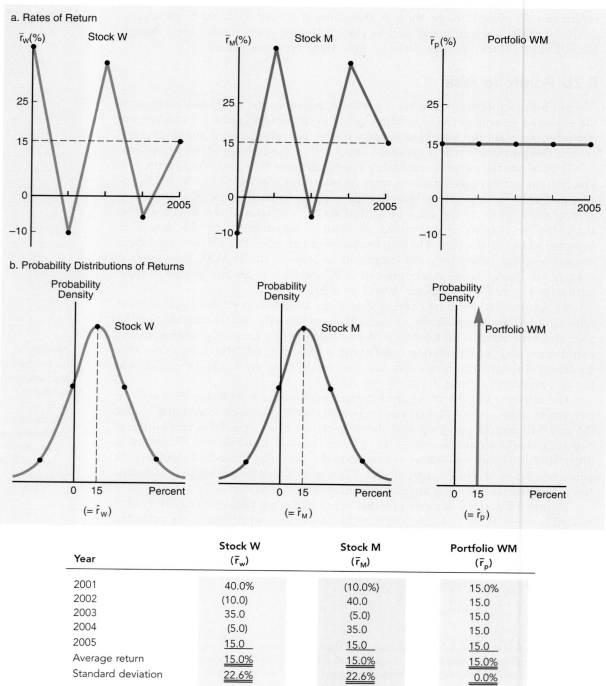

a. Rates of Return

b. Probability Distributions of Returns

Year	Stock W $(\bar{r}_W)$	Stock M $(\bar{r}_M)$	Portfolio WM $(\bar{r}_p)$
2001	40.0%	(10.0%)	15.0%
2002	(10.0)	40.0	15.0
2003	35.0	(5.0)	15.0
2004	(5.0)	35.0	15.0
2005	15.0	15.0	15.0
Average return	15.0%	15.0%	15.0%
Standard deviation	22.6%	22.6%	0.0%

stocks into portfolios reduces risk but does not completely eliminate it. Figure 8-7 illustrates this point with two stocks whose correlation coefficient is $\rho = +0.35$. The portfolio's average return is 15 percent, which is exactly the same as the average return for our other two illustrative portfolios, but its standard deviation is 18.6 percent, which is between the other two portfolios' standard deviations.

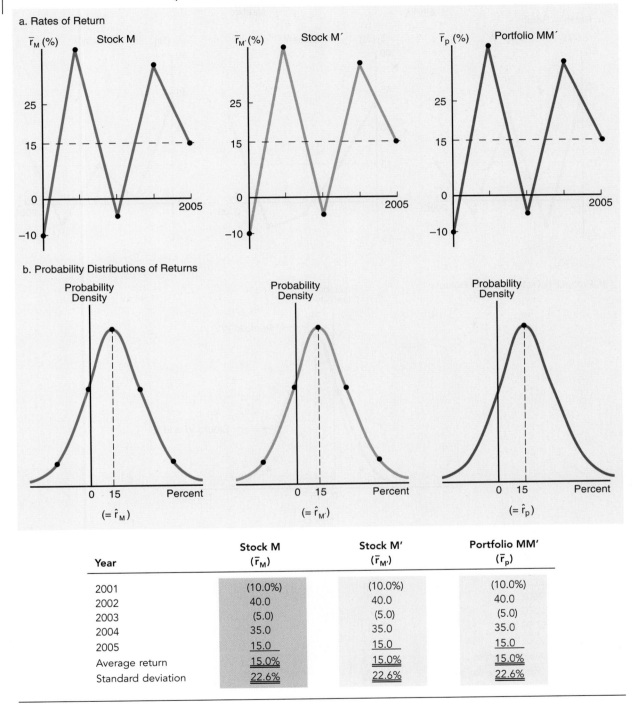

FIGURE 8-6 *Rate of Return Distributions for Two Perfectly Correlated Stocks ($\rho = +1.0$) and for Portfolio MM'*

a. Rates of Return

b. Probability Distributions of Returns

Year	Stock M $(\bar{r}_M)$	Stock M' $(\bar{r}_{M'})$	Portfolio MM' $(\bar{r}_p)$
2001	(10.0%)	(10.0%)	(10.0%)
2002	40.0	40.0	40.0
2003	(5.0)	(5.0)	(5.0)
2004	35.0	35.0	35.0
2005	15.0	15.0	15.0
Average return	15.0%	15.0%	15.0%
Standard deviation	22.6%	22.6%	22.6%

These examples demonstrate that in one extreme case ($\rho = -1.0$), risk can be completely eliminated, while in the other extreme case ($\rho = +1.0$), diversification does no good whatever. The real world lies between these extremes, so combining stocks into portfolios reduces, but does not eliminate, the risk inherent in the individual stocks. Also, we should note that in the real world, it is *impossible* to

FIGURE 8-7 *Rate of Return Distributions for Two Partially Correlated Stocks ($\rho = +0.35$) and for Portfolio WV*

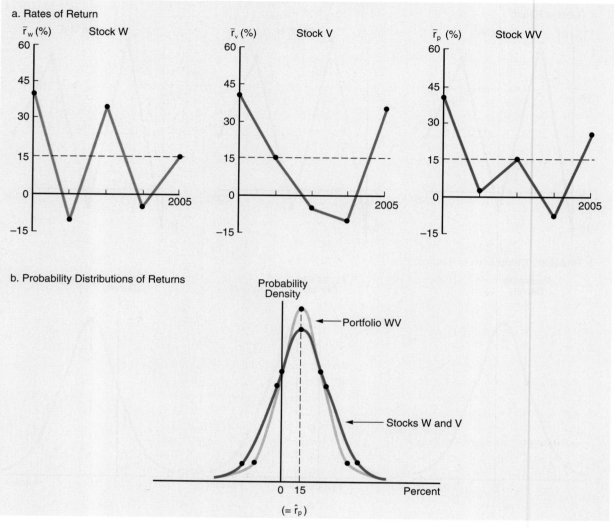

a. Rates of Return

b. Probability Distributions of Returns

Year	Stock W ($\bar{r}_w$)	Stock V ($\bar{r}_v$)	Portfolio WV ($\bar{r}_p$)
2001	40.0%	40.0%	40.0%
2002	(10.0)	15.0	2.5
2003	35.0	(5.0)	15.0
2004	(5.0)	(10.0)	(7.5)
2005	15.0	35.0	25.0
Average return	15.0%	15.0%	15.0%
Standard deviation	22.6%	22.6%	18.6%

find stocks like W and M, whose returns are expected to be perfectly negatively correlated. *Therefore, it is impossible to form completely riskless stock portfolios.* Diversification can reduce risk but not eliminate it, so the real world is similar to the situation depicted in Figure 8-7.

What would happen if we included more than two stocks in the portfolio? *As a rule, portfolio risk declines as the number of stocks in the portfolio increases.* If we

The Benefits of Diversification Are More Important Than Ever

Have stocks become riskier in recent years? Looking at what's happened to their individual portfolios, many investors may answer that question with a resounding yes. Furthermore, academic studies confirm this intuition—the average volatility of individual stocks has increased over time. However, studies have also found that volatility in the overall stock market has not increased. The reason for this apparent discrepancy is that the correlation between individual stocks has fallen in recent years, so declines in one stock are offset by gains in others, and this reduces overall market volatility. A study by Campbell, Lettau, Malkiel, and Xu found that the average correlation fell from around 0.35 in the late 1970s to less than 0.10 by the late 1990s.

What does this mean for the average investor? Individual stocks have become riskier, increasing the danger of putting all of your eggs in one basket, but at the same time, lower correlations between individual stocks mean that diversification is more useful than ever for reducing portfolio risk. Diversify, diversify, diversify!

Source: John Y. Campbell, Martin Lettau, Burton G. Malkiel, and Yexiao Xu, "Have Individual Stocks Become More Volatile? An Empirical Exploration of Idiosyncratic Risk," *Journal of Finance*, Vol. 56, no. 1 (February 2001), pp.1–43.

added enough partially correlated stocks, could we completely eliminate risk? In general, the answer is no, but here are two points worth noting:

1. The extent to which adding stocks to a portfolio reduces its risk depends on the *degree of correlation* among the stocks: The smaller the correlation coefficients, the lower the risk in a large portfolio. If we could find a set of stocks whose correlations were zero or negative, all risk could be eliminated. *However, in the real world, the correlations among the individual stocks are generally positive but less than +1.0, so some but not all risk can be eliminated.*

2. Some individual stocks are riskier than others, so some stocks will help more than others in terms of reducing the portfolio's risk. This point will be explored further in the next section, where we measure stocks' risks in a portfolio context.

To test your understanding up to this point, would you expect to find higher correlations between the returns on two companies in the same or in different industries? For example, is it likely that the correlation between Ford's and General Motors' stocks would be higher, or would the correlation be higher between either Ford or GM and Coke, and how would those correlations affect the risk of portfolios containing them?

Answer: Ford's and GM's returns are highly correlated with one another because both are affected by similar forces. These stocks are positively correlated with Coke, but the correlation is lower because stocks in different industries are subject to different factors. For example, people reduce auto purchases more than Coke consumption when interest rates rise.

Implications: A two-stock portfolio consisting of Ford and GM would be less well diversified than a two-stock portfolio consisting of Ford or GM, plus Coke. Thus, to minimize risk, portfolios should be diversified across industries.

8-2c Diversifiable Risk versus Market Risk

As noted earlier, it is difficult if not impossible to find stocks whose expected returns are negatively correlated to one another—most stocks tend to do well when the national economy is strong and badly when it is weak.[9] Thus, even very large portfolios end up with a substantial amount of risk, but not as much as if all the money were invested in only one stock.

To see more precisely how portfolio size affects portfolio risk, consider Figure 8-8, which shows how a portfolio's risk is affected by adding more and more randomly selected New York Stock Exchange (NYSE) stocks. Standard deviations are plotted for an average one-stock portfolio, a two-stock portfolio, and so on, up to a portfolio consisting of all 2,000-plus common stocks that were listed on the NYSE at the time the data were graphed. The graph illustrates that, in general, the riskiness of a portfolio consisting of large-company stocks tends to decline and to approach a minimum level as the size of the portfolio increases. According to data accumulated in recent years, σ_1, the standard deviation of a one-stock portfolio (or an average stock) is approximately 35 percent.

Market Portfolio
A portfolio consisting of all stocks.

A portfolio consisting of all stocks, which is called the **market portfolio,** would have a much lower standard deviation, σ_M, about 20 percent, as represented by the horizontal dashed line in Figure 8-8.

Thus, almost half of the riskiness inherent in an average individual stock can be eliminated if the stock is held in a reasonably well-diversified portfolio, which is one containing 40 or more stocks. Some risk will always remain, however, so it is virtually impossible to diversify away the effects of broad stock market movements that affect almost all stocks.

Diversifiable Risk
That part of a security's risk associated with random events; it can be eliminated by proper diversification.

The part of a stock's risk that *can* be eliminated is called **diversifiable risk,** while the part that *cannot* be eliminated is called **market risk.**[10] Diversifiable risk is caused by such random events as lawsuits, strikes, successful and unsuccessful marketing programs, winning or losing a major contract, and other events that are unique to a particular firm. Because these events are random, their effects on a portfolio can be eliminated by diversification—bad events in one firm will be offset by good events in another. Market risk, on the other hand, stems from factors that systematically affect most firms: war, inflation, recessions, and high interest rates. Because most stocks are negatively affected by these factors, market risk cannot be eliminated by diversification.

Market Risk
That part of a security's risk that cannot be eliminated by diversification.

We know that investors demand a premium for bearing risk; that is, the higher the riskiness of a security, the higher its expected return must be to induce investors to buy (or to hold) it. However, rational investors are primarily concerned with the riskiness of their *portfolios* rather than the riskiness of the individual securities in the portfolio, so the riskiness of an individual stock should be judged by its effect on the riskiness of the portfolio in which it is held. This type of risk is addressed by the **Capital Asset Pricing Model (CAPM),** which describes the relationship between risk and rates of return.[11] According to the CAPM, *the relevant riskiness of an individual stock is its contribution to the riski-*

Capital Asset Pricing Model (CAPM)
A model based on the proposition that any stock's required rate of return is equal to the risk-free rate of return plus a risk premium that reflects only the risk remaining after diversification.

---

[9] It is not too hard to find a few stocks that happened to have risen because of a particular set of circumstances in the past while most other stocks were declining, but it is much harder to find stocks that could logically be *expected* to increase in the future when other stocks are falling.

[10] Diversifiable risk is also known as *company-specific,* or *unsystematic,* risk. Market risk is also known as *nondiversifiable,* or *systematic,* or beta, risk; it is the risk that remains after diversification.

[11] Indeed, the 1990 Nobel Prize was awarded to the developers of the CAPM, Professors Harry Markowitz and William F. Sharpe. The CAPM is a relatively complex subject, and only its basic elements are presented in this text. For a more detailed discussion, see any standard investments textbook.

The basic concepts of the CAPM were developed specifically for common stocks, and, therefore, the theory is examined first in this context. However, it has become common practice to extend CAPM concepts to capital budgeting and to speak of firms having "portfolios of tangible assets and projects." Capital budgeting is discussed in Part 4.

| FIGURE 8-8 | *Effects of Portfolio Size on Portfolio Risk for Average Stocks* |

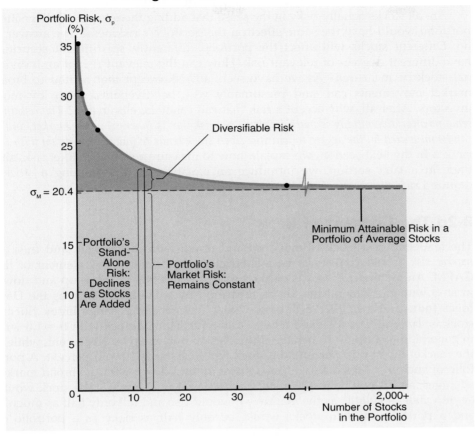

ness of a well-diversified portfolio. In other words, the riskiness of General Electric's stock to a doctor who has a portfolio of 40 stocks or to a trust officer managing a 150-stock portfolio is the contribution GE's stock makes to the portfolio's riskiness. The stock might be quite risky if held by itself, but if half of its risk can be eliminated by diversification, then its **relevant risk,** which is its *contribution to the portfolio's risk,* is much smaller than its stand-alone risk.

A simple example will help make this point clear. Suppose you are offered the chance to flip a coin once. If a head comes up, you win $20,000, but if a tail comes up, you lose $16,000. This is a good bet—the expected return is $0.5(\$20,000) + 0.5(-\$16,000) = \$2,000$. However, it is a highly risky proposition, because you have a 50 percent chance of losing $16,000. Thus, you might well refuse to make the bet. Alternatively, suppose you were offered the chance to flip a coin 100 times, and you would win $200 for each head but lose $160 for each tail. It is possible that you would flip all heads and win $20,000, and it is also possible that you would flip all tails and lose $16,000, but the chances are very high that you would actually flip about 50 heads and about 50 tails, winning a net of about $2,000. Although each individual flip is a risky bet, collectively you have a low-risk proposition because multiple flipping diversifies away most of the risk. This is the idea behind holding portfolios of stocks rather

Relevant Risk
The risk of a security that cannot be diversified away. This is the risk that affects portfolio risk and thus is relevant to a rational investor.

than just one stock, except that with stocks all of the risk cannot be eliminated by diversification—those risks that are related to broad, systematic changes in the stock market will remain even in a highly diversified portfolio.

Are all stocks equally risky in the sense that adding them to a well-diversified portfolio would have the same effect on the portfolio's riskiness? The answer is no. Different stocks will affect the portfolio differently, so different securities have different degrees of relevant risk. How can the relevant risk of an individual stock be measured? As we have seen, all risk except that related to broad market movements can, and presumably will, be diversified away by most investors. After all, why accept a risk that can easily be eliminated? *The risk that remains after diversifying is market risk, or the risk that is inherent in the market, and it can be measured by the degree to which a given stock tends to move up or down with the market.* In the next section, we explain how to measure a stock's market risk, and then, in a later section, we introduce an equation for determining a stock's required rate of return, given its market risk.

8-2d The Concept of Beta

Beta Coefficient, b
A metric that shows the extent to which a given stock's returns move up and down with the stock market. Beta thus measures market risk.

The tendency of a stock to move up and down with the market, and thus its *market risk,* is reflected in its **beta coefficient, b.** Beta is a key element of the CAPM. An *average-risk stock* is defined as one that tends to move up and down in step with the general market as measured by some index such as the Dow Jones Industrials, the S&P 500, or the New York Stock Exchange Index. Such a stock is, *by definition,* assigned a beta of b = 1.0. Thus, a stock with b = 1.0 will, in general, move up by 10 percent if the market moves up by 10 percent, while if the market falls by 10 percent, the stock will likewise fall by 10 percent. A portfolio of such b = 1.0 stocks will thus move up and down with the broad market averages, and it will be just as risky as the averages. If b = 0.5, the stock would be only half as volatile as the market—it would rise and fall only half as much— and a portfolio of such stocks would be only half as risky as a portfolio of b = 1.0 stocks. On the other hand, if b = 2.0, the stock would be twice as volatile as an average stock, so a portfolio of such stocks would be twice as risky as an average portfolio. The value of such a portfolio could double—or halve—in a short time, and if you held such a portfolio, you could quickly go from millionaire to pauper.

Figure 8-9 graphs the three stocks' returns to show their relative volatility. The illustrative data below the graph show that in Year 1, the "market," as defined by a portfolio containing all stocks, had a total return (dividend yield plus capital gains yield) of $r_M = 10\%$, and Stocks H, A, and L (for High, Average, and Low risk) also all had returns of 10 percent. In Year 2, the market went up sharply, and its return was $r_M = 20\%$. Returns on the three stocks were also high: H soared by 30 percent; A returned 20 percent, the same as the market; and L returned only 15 percent. In Year 3 the market dropped sharply, and its return was $\bar{r}_M = -10\%$. The three stocks' returns also fell, H plunging by −30 percent, A falling by −10 percent, and L returning $\bar{r}_L = 0\%$. Thus, the three stocks all moved in the same direction as the market, but H was by far the most volatile, A was exactly as volatile as the market, and L was less volatile.

Beta measures a given stock's volatility relative to an average stock, which by definition has b = 1.0, and the stock's beta can be calculated by plotting a line like those in Figure 8-9. The slopes of the lines show how each stock moves in response to a movement in the general market—indeed, *the slope coefficient of such a "regression line" is defined as the stock's beta coefficient.* (Procedures for calculating betas are described in Web Appendix 8A, which can be accessed through the ThomsonNOW Web site.) Betas for literally thousands of companies are calculated and published by Merrill Lynch, Value Line, and numerous other organiza-

FIGURE 8-9   *Relative Volatility of Stocks H, A, and L*

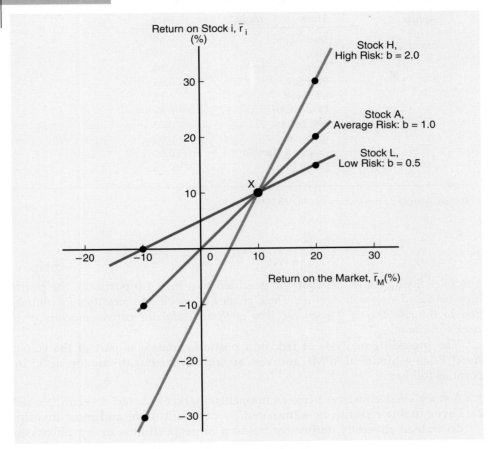

Year	$\bar{r}_H$	$\bar{r}_A$	$\bar{r}_L$	$\bar{r}_M$
1	10%	10%	10%	10%
2	30	20	15	20
3	(30)	(10)	0	(10)

Note: These three stocks plot exactly on their regression lines. This indicates that they are exposed only to market risk. Mutual funds that concentrate on stocks with betas of 2, 1, and 0.5 would have patterns similar to those shown in the graph.

tions, and the beta coefficients of some well-known companies are shown in Table 8-4. Most stocks have betas in the range of 0.50 to 1.50, and the average for all stocks is 1.0 by definition.

Theoretically, it would be possible for a stock to have a negative beta. In this case, the stock's returns would tend to rise whenever the returns on other stocks fall. However, we have never seen a negative beta as reported by one of the many organizations that publish betas for publicly held firms. Moreover, even though a stock may have a positive long-run beta, company-specific problems might cause its realized return to decline even when the general market is strong.

If a stock whose beta is greater than 1.0 is added to a $b_p = 1.0$ portfolio, then the portfolio's beta, and consequently its risk, will increase. Conversely, if

TABLE 8-4	*Illustrative List of Beta Coefficients*

Stock	Beta
Merrill Lynch	1.50
eBay	1.45
General Electric	1.30
Best Buy	1.25
Microsoft	1.15
ExxonMobil	0.80
FPL Group	0.70
Coca-Cola	0.60
Procter & Gamble	0.60
Heinz	0.55

Source: Adapted from *Value Line,* March 2005.

a stock whose beta is less than 1.0 is added to a $b_p = 1.0$ portfolio, the portfolio's beta and risk will decline. *Thus, because a stock's beta measures its contribution to the riskiness of a portfolio, beta is theoretically the correct measure of the stock's riskiness.*

The preceding analysis of risk in a portfolio context is part of the Capital Asset Pricing Model (CAPM), and we can summarize our discussion up to this point as follows:

1. A stock's risk consists of two components, market risk and diversifiable risk.
2. Diversifiable risk can be eliminated by diversification, and most investors do indeed diversify, either by holding large portfolios or by purchasing shares in a mutual fund. We are left, then, with market risk, which is caused by general movements in the stock market and which reflects the fact that most stocks are systematically affected by events like wars, recessions, and inflation. Market risk is the only relevant risk to a rational, diversified investor because such an investor would eliminate diversifiable risk.
3. Investors must be compensated for bearing risk—the greater the riskiness of a stock, the higher its required return. However, compensation is required only for risk that cannot be eliminated by diversification. If risk premiums existed on a stock due to its diversifiable risk, then that stock would be a bargain to well-diversified investors. They would start buying it and bidding up its price, and the stock's final (equilibrium) price would result in an expected return that reflected only its non-diversifiable market risk.

If this point is not clear, an example may help clarify it. Suppose half of Stock A's risk is market risk (it occurs because Stock A moves up and down with the market), while the other half of A's risk is diversifiable. You are thinking of buying Stock A and holding it as a one-stock portfolio, so if you buy it you will be exposed to all of its risk. As compensation for bearing so much risk, you want a risk premium of 8 percent over the 6 percent T-bond rate, so your required return is $r_A = 6\% + 8\% = 14\%$. But suppose other investors, including your professor, are well diversified; they are also looking at Stock A, but they would hold it in diversified portfolios, eliminate its diversifiable risk, and thus be exposed to only half as much risk as you. Therefore, their risk premium would be only half as large as yours, and their required rate of return would be $r_A = 6\% + 4\% = 10\%$.

If the stock were priced to yield the 14 percent you require, then diversified investors, including your professor, would rush to buy it. That would push its price up and its yield down; hence, you could not buy it at a price low enough to provide you with the 14 percent return. In the end, you would have to accept a 10 percent return or else keep your money in the bank. Thus, risk premiums in a market populated by rational, diversified investors can reflect only market risk.

4. The market risk of a stock is measured by its beta coefficient, which is an index of the stock's relative volatility. Some benchmark betas follow:

$b = 0.5$: Stock is only half as volatile, or risky, as an average stock.

$b = 1.0$: Stock is of average risk.

$b = 2.0$: Stock is twice as risky as an average stock.

5. A portfolio consisting of low-beta securities will itself have a low beta, because the beta of a portfolio is a weighted average of its individual securities' betas:

$$b_p = w_1 b_1 + w_2 b_2 + \cdots + w_N b_N$$

$$= \sum_{i=1}^{N} w_i b_i \qquad \text{(8-6)}$$

Here b_p is the beta of the portfolio, and it shows how volatile the portfolio is relative to the market; w_i is the fraction of the portfolio invested in the ith stock; and b_i is the beta coefficient of the ith stock. For example, if an investor holds a $100,000 portfolio consisting of $33,333.33 invested in each of three stocks, and if each of the stocks has a beta of 0.7, then the portfolio's beta will be $b_p = 0.7$:

$$b_p = 0.3333(0.7) + 0.3333(0.7) + 0.3333(0.7) = 0.7$$

Such a portfolio will be less risky than the market, so it should experience relatively narrow price swings and have relatively small rate-of-return fluctuations. In terms of Figure 8-9, the slope of its regression line would be 0.7, which is less than that for a portfolio of average stocks.

Now suppose one of the existing stocks is sold and replaced by a stock with $b_i = 2.0$. This action will increase the beta of the portfolio from $b_{p1} = 0.7$ to $b_{p2} = 1.13$:

$$b_{p2} = 0.333(0.7) + 0.3333(0.7) + 0.3333(2.0)$$

$$= 1.13$$

Had a stock with $b_i = 0.2$ been added, the portfolio's beta would have declined from 0.7 to 0.53. Adding a low-beta stock would therefore reduce the portfolio's riskiness. Consequently, changing the stocks in a portfolio can change the riskiness of that portfolio.

6. *Because a stock's beta coefficient determines how the stock affects the riskiness of a diversified portfolio, beta is the most relevant measure of any stock's risk.*

Explain the following statement: "An asset held as part of a portfolio is generally less risky than the same asset held in isolation."

What is meant by *perfect positive correlation, perfect negative correlation,* and *zero correlation?*

In general, can the riskiness of a portfolio be reduced to zero by increasing the number of stocks in the portfolio? Explain.

GLOBAL PERSPECTIVES

The Benefits of Diversifying Overseas

The increasing availability of international securities is making it possible to achieve a better risk-return trade-off than could be obtained by investing only in U.S. securities. So, investing overseas might result in a portfolio with less risk but a higher expected return. This result occurs because of low correlations between the returns on U.S. and international securities, along with potentially high returns on overseas stocks.

Figure 8-8, presented earlier, demonstrated that an investor can reduce the risk of his or her portfolio by holding a number of stocks. The figure accompanying this box suggests that investors may be able to reduce risk even further by holding a portfolio of stocks from all around the world, given the fact that the returns on domestic and international stocks are not perfectly correlated.

Even though foreign stocks represent roughly 60 percent of the worldwide equity market, and despite the apparent benefits from investing overseas, the typical U.S. investor still puts less than 10 percent of his or her money in foreign stocks. One possible explanation for this reluctance to invest overseas is that investors prefer domestic stocks because of lower transactions costs. However, this explanation is questionable because recent studies reveal that investors buy and sell overseas stocks more frequently than they trade their domestic stocks. Other explanations for the domestic bias include the additional risks from investing overseas (for example, exchange rate risk) and the fact that the typical U.S. investor is uninformed about international investments and/or thinks that international investments are extremely risky. It has been argued that world capital markets have become more integrated, causing the correlation of returns between different countries to increase, which reduces the benefits from international diversification. In addition U.S. corporations are investing more internationally, providing U.S. investors with international diversification even if they buy only U.S. stocks.

Whatever the reason for their relatively small holdings of international assets, our guess is that in the future U.S. investors will shift more of their assets to overseas investments.

Source: For further reading, see also Kenneth Kasa, "Measuring the Gains from International Portfolio Diversification," *Federal Reserve Bank of San Francisco Weekly Letter,* Number 94–14, April 8, 1994.

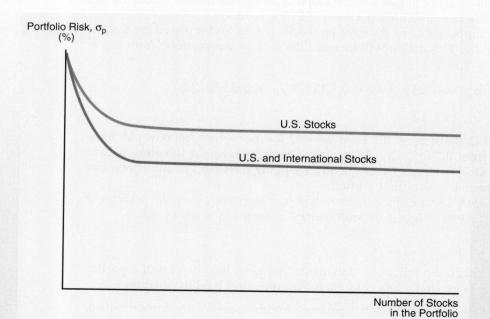

What is an average-risk stock? What is the beta of such a stock?

Why is it argued that beta is the best measure of a stock's risk?

If you plotted a particular stock's returns versus those on the Dow Jones Index over the past five years, what would the slope of the regression line indicate about the stock's risk?

An investor has a two-stock portfolio with $25,000 invested in Merrill Lynch and $50,000 invested in Coca-Cola. Merrill Lynch's beta is estimated to be 1.50 and Coca-Cola's beta is estimated to be 0.60. What is the estimated beta of the investor's portfolio? (0.90)

8-3 THE RELATIONSHIP BETWEEN RISK AND RATES OF RETURN

The preceding section demonstrated that under the CAPM theory, beta is the most appropriate measure of a stock's relevant risk. The next issue is this: For a given level of risk as measured by beta, what rate of return is required to compensate investors for bearing that risk? To begin, let us define the following terms:

$\hat{r}_i$ = *expected* rate of return on the *i*th stock.

r_i = *required* rate of return on the *i*th stock. Note that if $\hat{r}_i$ is less than r_i, the typical investor would not purchase this stock or would sell it if he or she owned it. If $\hat{r}_i$ were greater than r_i, the investor would buy the stock because it would look like a bargain. Investors would be indifferent if $\hat{r}_i = r_i$.

$\bar{r}$ = realized, after-the-fact return. One obviously does not know $\bar{r}$ at the time he or she is considering the purchase of a stock.

r_{RF} = risk-free rate of return. In this context, r_{RF} is generally measured by the return on long-term U.S. Treasury bonds.

b_i = beta coefficient of the *i*th stock. The beta of an average stock is $b_A = 1.0$.

r_M = required rate of return on a portfolio consisting of all stocks, which is called the *market portfolio*. r_M is also the required rate of return on an average ($b_A = 1.0$) stock.

$RP_M = (r_M - r_{RF})$ = risk premium on "the market," and also the premium on an average stock. This is the additional return over the risk-free rate required to compensate an average investor for assuming an average amount of risk. Average risk means a stock where $b_i = b_A = 1.0$.

$RP_i = (r_M - r_{RF})b_i = (RP_M)b_i$ = risk premium on the *i*th stock. A stock's risk premium will be less than, equal to, or greater than the premium on an average stock, RP_M, depending on whether its beta is less than, equal to, or greater than 1.0. If $b_i = b_A = 1.0$, then $RP_i = RP_M$.

The **market risk premium, RP_M,** shows the premium investors require for bearing the risk of an average stock. The size of this premium depends on how risky investors think the stock market is and on their degree of risk aversion. Let us assume that at the current time Treasury bonds yield $r_{RF} = 6\%$ and an average share of stock has a required rate of return of $r_M = 11\%$. Therefore, the market risk premium is 5 percent, calculated as follows:

$$RP_M = r_M - r_{RF} = 11\% - 6\% = 5\%$$

Market Risk Premium, RP_M
The additional return over the risk-free rate needed to compensate investors for assuming an average amount of risk.

Estimating the Market Risk Premium

The Capital Asset Pricing Model (CAPM) is more than a theory describing the trade-off between risk and return—it is also widely used in practice. As we will see later, investors use the CAPM to determine the discount rate for valuing stocks, and corporate managers use it to estimate the cost of equity capital.

The market risk premium is a key component of the CAPM, and it should be the difference between the *expected future return on the overall stock market* and the *expected future return on a riskless investment*. However, we cannot obtain investors' expectations, so instead academicians and practitioners often use a historical risk premium as a proxy for the expected risk premium. The historical premium is found by first taking the difference between the actual return on the overall stock market and the risk-free rate in a number of different years and then averaging the annual results. Ibbotson Associates, which provides perhaps the most comprehensive estimates of historical risk premiums, reports that the annual premiums have averaged 7.2 percent over the past 79 years.

However, there are three potential problems with historical risk premiums. First, what is the proper number of years over which to compute the average? Ibbotson goes back to 1926, when good data first became available, but that is a rather arbitrary choice, and the starting and ending points make a major difference in the calculated premium.

Second, historical premiums are likely to be misleading at times when the market risk premium is changing. To illustrate, the stock market was very strong from 1995 through 1999, *in part because investors were becoming less risk averse, which means that they applied a lower risk premium when*

they valued stocks. The strong market resulted in stock returns of about 30 percent per year, and when bond yields were subtracted the resulting annual risk premiums averaged 22.3 percent a year. When those high numbers were added to data from prior years, they caused the long-run historical risk premium as reported by Ibbotson to increase. Thus, a declining "true" risk premium led to very high stock returns, which, in turn, led to an increase in the calculated historical risk premium. That's a worrisome result, to say the least.

The third concern is that historical estimates may be biased upward because they only include the returns of firms that have survived—they do not reflect the losses incurred on investments in failed firms. Stephen Brown, William Goetzmann, and Stephen Ross discussed the implications of this "survivorship bias" in a 1995 *Journal of Finance* article. Putting these ideas into practice, Tim Koller, Marc Goedhart, and David Wessels recently suggested that "survivorship bias" increases historical returns by 1 to 2 percent a year. Therefore, they suggest that practitioners subtract 1 to 2 percent from the historical estimates to obtain a risk premium for use in the CAPM.

Sources: Stocks, Bonds, Bills, and Inflation: (Valuation Edition) 2005 Yearbook (Chicago: Ibbotson Associates, 2005); Stephen J. Brown, William N. Goetzmann, and Stephen A. Ross, "Survival," *Journal of Finance*, Vol. 50, no. 3 (July 1995), pp. 853–873; and Tim Koller, Marc Goedhart, and David Wessels, *Valuation: Measuring and Managing the Value of Companies*, 4th edition (New York: McKinsey & Company, 2005).

It should be noted that the risk premium of an average stock, $r_M - r_{RF}$, is actually hard to measure because it is impossible to obtain a precise estimate of the expected future return of the market, r_M.[12] Given the difficulty of estimating future market returns, analysts often look to historical data to estimate the market risk premium. Historical data suggest that the market risk premium varies somewhat from year to year due to changes in investors' risk aversion, but that it has generally ranged from 4 to 8 percent.

---

[12] This concept, as well as other aspects of the CAPM, is discussed in more detail in Chapter 3 of Eugene F. Brigham and Philip R. Daves, *Intermediate Financial Management*, 8th ed. (Mason, OH: Thomson/South-Western, 2004). That chapter also discusses the assumptions embodied in the CAPM framework. Some of those assumptions are unrealistic, and because of this the theory does not hold exactly.

While historical estimates might be a good starting point for estimating the market risk premium, those estimates would be misleading if investors' attitudes toward risk change considerably over time. (See the box entitled "Estimating the Market Risk Premium.") Indeed, many analysts have argued that the market risk premium has fallen in recent years. If this claim is correct, the market risk premium is considerably lower than one based on historical data.

The risk premium on individual stocks varies in a systematic manner from the market risk premium. For example, if one stock were twice as risky as another, its risk premium would be twice as high, while if its risk were only half as much, its risk premium would be half as large. Further, we can measure a stock's relative riskiness by its beta coefficient. If we know the market risk premium, RP_M, and the stock's risk as measured by its beta coefficient, b_i, we can find the stock's risk premium as the product $(RP_M)b_i$. For example, if $b_i = 0.5$ and $RP_M = 5\%$, then RP_i is 2.5 percent:

$$\text{Risk premium for Stock i} = RP_i = (RP_M)b_i \qquad \textbf{(8-7)}$$

$$= (5\%)(0.5)$$

$$= 2.5\%$$

As the discussion in Chapter 6 implied, the required return for any stock can be expressed in general terms as follows:

$$\begin{array}{c}\text{Required return} \\ \text{on a stock}\end{array} = \text{Risk-free return} + \begin{array}{c}\text{Premium} \\ \text{for the stock's} \\ \text{risk}\end{array}$$

Here the risk-free return includes a premium for expected inflation, and if we assume that the stocks under consideration have similar maturities and liquidity, then the required return on Stock i can be expressed by the **Security Market Line (SML) equation:**

SML Equation:

$$\begin{array}{c}\text{Required return} \\ \text{on Stock i}\end{array} = \begin{array}{c}\text{Risk-free} \\ \text{rate}\end{array} + \left(\begin{array}{c}\text{Market risk} \\ \text{premium}\end{array}\right)\left(\begin{array}{c}\text{Stock i's} \\ \text{beta}\end{array}\right)$$

$$r_i = r_{RF} + (r_M - r_{RF})b_i \qquad \textbf{(8-8)}$$

$$= r_{RF} + (RP_M)b_i$$

$$= 6\% + (11\% - 6\%)(0.5)$$

$$= 6\% + 5\%(0.5)$$

$$= 8.5\%$$

> **Security Market Line (SML) Equation**
> *An equation that shows the relationship between risk as measured by beta and the required rates of return on individual securities.*

If some other Stock j had $b_j = 2.0$ and thus was riskier than Stock i, then its required rate of return would be 16 percent:

$$r_j = 6\% + (5\%)2.0 = 16\%$$

An average stock, with $b = 1.0$, would have a required return of 11 percent, the same as the market return:

$$r_A = 6\% + (5\%)1.0 = 11\% = r_M$$

Security Market Line (SML)

The line on a graph that shows the relationship between risk as measured by beta and the required rate of return for individual securities.

When the SML equation is plotted on a graph, the resulting line is called the **Security Market Line (SML).** Figure 8-10 shows the SML situation when $r_{RF} = 6\%$ and $r_M = 11\%$. Note the following points:

1. Required rates of return are shown on the vertical axis, while risk as measured by beta is shown on the horizontal axis. This graph is quite different from the one shown in Figure 8-9, where the returns on individual stocks were plotted on the vertical axis and returns on the market index were shown on the horizontal axis. The slopes of the three lines in Figure 8–9 were used to calculate the three stocks' betas, and those betas were then plotted as points on the horizontal axis of Figure 8-10.

2. Riskless securities have $b_i = 0$; therefore, r_{RF} appears as the vertical axis intercept in Figure 8-10. If we could construct a portfolio that had a beta of zero, it would have an expected return equal to the risk-free rate.

3. The slope of the SML (5 percent in Figure 8-10) reflects the degree of risk aversion in the economy—the greater the average investor's risk aversion, then (a) the steeper the slope of the line, (b) the greater the risk premium for all stocks, and (c) the higher the required rate of return on all stocks.[13] These points are discussed further in a later section.

4. The values we worked out for stocks with $b_i = 0.5$, $b_i = 1.0$, and $b_i = 2.0$ agree with the values shown on the graph for r_{Low}, r_A, and r_{High}.

FIGURE 8-10 *The Security Market Line (SML)*

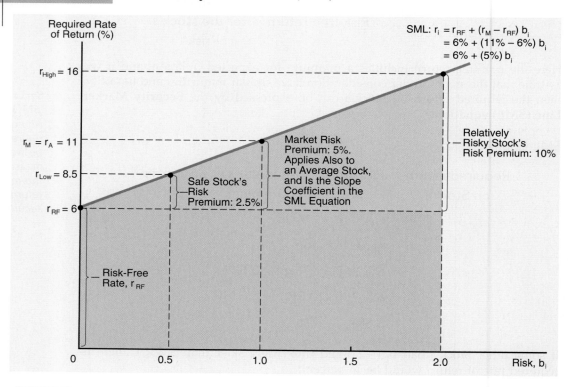

---

[13] Students sometimes confuse beta with the slope of the SML. This is a mistake. Consider Figure 8-10. The slope of any straight line is equal to the "rise" divided by the "run," or $(Y_1 - Y_0)/(X_1 - X_0)$. If we let $Y = r$ and $X = beta$, and we go from the origin to $b = 1.0$, we see that the slope is $(r_M - r_{RF})/(b_M - b_{RF}) = (11\% - 6\%)/(1 - 0) = 5\%$. Thus, the slope of the SML is equal to $(r_M - r_{RF})$, the market risk premium. In Figure 8-10, $r_i = 6\% + 5\%b_i$, so a doubling of beta from 1.0 to 2.0 would produce a 5 percentage point increase in r_i.

Both the Security Market Line and a company's position on it change over time due to changes in interest rates, investors' risk aversion, and individual companies' betas. Such changes are discussed in the following sections.

8-3a The Impact of Inflation

As we discussed in Chapter 6, interest amounts to "rent" on borrowed money, or the price of money. Thus, r_{RF} is the price of money to a riskless borrower. We also saw that the risk-free rate as measured by the rate on U.S. Treasury securities is called the *nominal*, or *quoted, rate*, and it consists of two elements: (1) a *real, inflation-free rate of return, r**, and (2) an *inflation premium, IP*, equal to the anticipated rate of inflation.[14] Thus, $r_{RF} = r^* + IP$. The real rate on long-term Treasury bonds has historically ranged from 2 to 4 percent, with a mean of about 3 percent. Therefore, if no inflation were expected, long-term Treasury bonds would yield about 3 percent. However, as the expected rate of inflation increases, a premium must be added to the real risk-free rate of return to compensate investors for the loss of purchasing power that results from inflation. Therefore, the 6 percent r_{RF} shown in Figure 8-10 might be thought of as consisting of a 3 percent real risk-free rate of return plus a 3 percent inflation premium: $r_{RF} = r^* + IP = 3\% + 3\% = 6\%$.

If the expected inflation rate rose by 2 percent, to $3\% + 2\% = 5\%$, this would cause r_{RF} to rise to 8 percent. Such a change is shown in Figure 8-11. Notice that under the CAPM, an increase in r_{RF} leads to an *equal* increase in the rate of return on all risky assets, because the same inflation premium is built into required rates of return on both riskless and risky assets.[15] Therefore, the rate of return on our illustrative average stock, r_M, increases from 11 to 13 percent. Other risky securities' returns also rise by two percentage points.

8-3b Changes in Risk Aversion

The slope of the Security Market Line reflects the extent to which investors are averse to risk—the steeper the slope of the line, the more the average investor requires as compensation for bearing risk, which denotes increased risk aversion. Suppose investors were indifferent to risk; that is, they were not at all risk averse. If r_{RF} were 6 percent, then risky assets would also have a required return of 6 percent, because if there were no risk aversion, there would be no risk premium. In that case, the SML would plot as a horizontal line. However, investors are risk averse, so there is a risk premium, and the greater the risk aversion, the steeper the slope of the SML.

Figure 8-12 illustrates an increase in risk aversion. The market risk premium rises from 5 to 7.5 percent, causing r_M to rise from $r_{M1} = 11\%$ to $r_{M2} = 13.5\%$. The returns on other risky assets also rise, and the effect of this shift in risk aversion is more pronounced on riskier securities. For example, the required return on a stock with $b_i = 0.5$ increases by only 1.25 percentage points, from 8.5 to 9.75 percent, whereas that on a stock with $b_i = 1.5$ increases by 3.75 percentage points, from 13.5 to 17.25 percent.

---

[14] Long-term Treasury bonds also contain a maturity risk premium, MRP. We include the MRP in r* to simplify the discussion.

[15] Recall that the inflation premium for any asset is the average expected rate of inflation over the asset's life. Thus, in this analysis we must assume either that all securities plotted on the SML graph have the same life or else that the expected rate of future inflation is constant.

It should also be noted that r_{RF} in a CAPM analysis can be proxied by either a long-term rate (the T-bond rate) or a short-term rate (the T-bill rate). Traditionally, the T-bill rate was used, but in recent years there has been a movement toward use of the T-bond rate because there is a closer relationship between T-bond yields and stocks than between T-bill yields and stocks. See *Stocks, Bonds, Bills, and Inflation: (Valuation Edition) 2005 Yearbook* (Chicago: Ibbotson Associates, 2005) for a discussion.

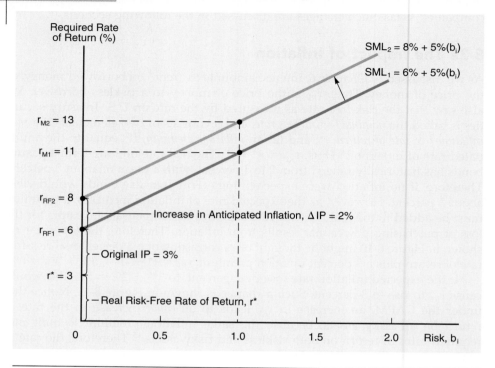

FIGURE 8-11   *Shift in the SML Caused by an Increase in Inflation*

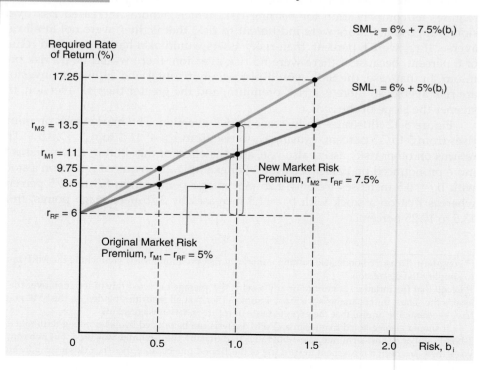

FIGURE 8-12   *Shift in the SML Caused by Increased Risk Aversion*

8-3c Changes in a Stock's Beta Coefficient

As we shall see later in the book, a firm can influence its market risk, hence its beta, through (1) changes in the composition of its assets and (2) changes in the amount of debt it uses. A company's beta can also change as a result of external factors such as increased competition in its industry, the expiration of basic patents, and the like. When such changes occur, the firm's required rate of return also changes, and, as we shall see in Chapter 9, this will affect the firm's stock price. For example, consider Allied Food Products, with a beta of 1.48. Now suppose some action occurred that caused Allied's beta to increase from 1.48 to 2.0. If the conditions depicted in Figure 8-10 held, Allied's required rate of return would increase from 13.4 to 16 percent:

$$r_1 = r_{RF} + (r_M - r_{RF})b_i$$
$$= 6\% + (11\% - 6\%)1.48$$
$$= 13.4\%$$

to

$$r_2 = 6\% + (11\% - 6\%)2.0$$
$$= 16\%$$

As we shall see in Chapter 9, this change would have a negative effect on Allied's stock price.

Differentiate among a stock's expected rate of return ($\hat{r}$), required rate of return (r), and realized, after-the-fact, historical return ($\bar{r}$). Which would have to be larger to induce you to buy the stock, $\hat{r}$ or r? At a given point in time, would $\hat{r}$, r, and $\bar{r}$ typically be the same or different? Explain.

What are the differences between the relative volatility graph (Figure 8-9), where "betas are made," and the SML graph (Figure 8-10), where "betas are used"? Explain how both graphs are constructed and the information they convey.

What would happen to the SML graph in Figure 8-10 if inflation increased or decreased?

What happens to the SML graph when risk aversion increases or decreases?

What would the SML look like if investors were indifferent to risk, that is, if they had zero risk aversion?

How can a firm influence the size of its beta?

A stock has a beta of 1.2. Assume that the risk-free rate is 4.5 percent and the market risk premium is 5 percent. What is the stock's required rate of return? (10.5%)

8-4 SOME CONCERNS ABOUT BETA AND THE CAPM

The Capital Asset Pricing Model (CAPM) is more than just an abstract theory described in textbooks—it has great intuitive appeal, and it is widely used by analysts, investors, and corporations. However, a number of recent studies have

Kenneth French's Web site, **http://mba.tuck .dartmouth.edu/pages/ faculty/ken.french/index .html** *is an excellent resource for data and information regarding factors related to stock returns.*

raised concerns about its validity. For example, a study by Eugene Fama of the University of Chicago and Kenneth French of Dartmouth found no historical relationship between stocks' returns and their market betas, confirming a position long held by some professors and stock market analysts.[16]

As an alternative to the traditional CAPM, researchers and practitioners are developing models with more explanatory variables than just beta. These multi-variable models represent an attractive generalization of the traditional CAPM model's insight that market risk—risk that cannot be diversified away—underlies the pricing of assets. In the multi-variable models, risk is assumed to be caused by a number of different factors, whereas the CAPM gauges risk only relative to returns on the market portfolio. These multi-variable models represent a potentially important step forward in finance theory; they also have some deficiencies when applied in practice. As a result, the basic CAPM is still the most widely used method for estimating required rates of return on stocks.

 Have there been any studies that question the validity of the CAPM? Explain.

8-5 SOME CONCLUDING THOUGHTS: IMPLICATIONS FOR CORPORATE MANAGERS AND INVESTORS

The connection between risk and return is an important concept, and it has numerous implications for both corporate managers and investors. As we will see in later chapters, corporate managers spend a great deal of time assessing the risk and returns on individual projects. Indeed, given their concerns about the risk of individual projects, it might be fair to ask why we spend so much time discussing the riskiness of stocks. Why not begin by looking at the riskiness of such business assets as plant and equipment? *The reason is that for a management whose primary goal is stock price maximization, the overriding consideration is the riskiness of the firm's stock, and the relevant risk of any physical asset must be measured in terms of its effect on the stock's risk as seen by investors.* For example, suppose Goodyear, the tire company, is considering a major investment in a new product, recapped tires. Sales of recaps, hence earnings on the new operation, are highly uncertain, so on a stand-alone basis the new venture appears to be quite risky. However, suppose returns in the recap business are negatively correlated with Goodyear's other operations—when times are good and people have plenty of money, they buy new cars with new tires, but when times are bad, they tend to keep their old cars and buy recaps for them. Therefore, returns would be high on regular operations and low on the recap division during good times, but the opposite would be true during recessions. The result might be a pattern like that shown earlier in Figure 8-5 for Stocks W and M. Thus, what appears to be a risky investment when viewed on a stand-alone basis might not be very risky when viewed within the context of the company as a whole.

---

[16] See Eugene F. Fama and Kenneth R. French, "The Cross-Section of Expected Stock Returns," *Journal of Finance*, Vol. 47 (1992), pp. 427–465; and Eugene F. Fama and Kenneth R. French, "Common Risk Factors in the Returns on Stocks and Bonds," *Journal of Financial Economics*, Vol. 33 (1993), pp. 3–56. They found that stock returns are related to firm size and market/book ratios—small firms, and those with low market/book ratios, had higher returns, but they found no relationship between returns and beta.

This analysis can be extended to the corporation's stockholders. Because Goodyear's stock is owned by diversified stockholders, the real issue each time management makes an investment decision is this: How will this investment affect the risk of our stockholders? Again, the stand-alone risk of an individual project may look quite high, but viewed in the context of the project's effect on stockholder risk, it may not be very large. We will address this issue again in Chapter 12, where we examine the effects of capital budgeting on companies' beta coefficients and thus on stockholders' risks.

While these concepts are obviously important for individual investors, they are also important for corporate managers. We summarize below some key ideas that all investors should consider.

1. There is a trade-off between risk and return. The average investor likes higher returns but dislikes risk. It follows that higher-risk investments need to offer investors higher expected returns. Put another way—if you are seeking higher returns, you must be willing to assume higher risks.
2. Diversification is crucial. By diversifying wisely, investors can dramatically reduce risk without reducing their expected returns. Don't put all of your money in one or two stocks, or one or two industries. A huge mistake many people make is to invest a high percentage of their funds in their employer's stock. If the company goes bankrupt, they not only lose their job but also their invested capital. While no stock is completely riskless, you can smooth out the bumps by holding a well-diversified portfolio.
3. Real returns are what matters. All investors should understand the difference between nominal and real returns. When assessing performance, the real return (what you have left over after inflation) is what really matters. It follows that as expected inflation increases, investors need to receive higher nominal returns.
4. The risk of an investment often depends on how long you plan to hold the investment. Common stocks, for example, can be extremely risky for short-term investors. However, over the long haul the bumps tend to even out, and thus, stocks are less risky when held as part of a long-term portfolio. Indeed, in his best-selling book *Stocks for the Long Run*, Jeremy Siegel of the University of Pennsylvania concludes that "The safest long-term investment for the preservation of purchasing power has clearly been stocks, not bonds."
5. While the past gives us insights into the risk and returns on various investments, there is no guarantee that the future will repeat the past. Stocks that have performed well in recent years might tumble, while stocks that have struggled may rebound. The same thing can hold true for the stock market as a whole. Even Jeremy Siegel, who has preached that stocks have historically been good long-term investments, has also argued that there is no assurance that returns in the future will be as strong as they have been in the past. More importantly, when purchasing a stock you always need to ask, "Is this stock fairly valued, or is it currently priced too high?" We discuss this issue more completely in the next chapter.

Explain the following statement: "The stand-alone risk of an individual corporate project may be quite high, but viewed in the context of its effect on stockholders' risk, the project's true risk may not be very large."

How does the correlation between returns on a project and returns on the firm's other assets affect the project's risk?

What are some important concepts for individual investors to consider when evaluating the risk and returns of various investments?

Tying It All Together

In this chapter, we described the relationship between risk and return. We discussed how to calculate risk and return for both individual assets and portfolios. In particular, we differentiated between stand-alone risk and risk in a portfolio context, and we explained the benefits of diversification. We also explained the CAPM, which describes how risk should be measured and how it affects rates of return. In the chapters that follow, we will give you the tools to estimate the required rates of return on a firm's common stock, and we will explain how that return and the yield on its bonds are used to develop the firm's cost of capital. As you will see, the cost of capital is a key element in the capital budgeting process.

SELF-TEST QUESTIONS AND PROBLEMS
(Solutions Appear in Appendix A)

ST-1 **Key terms** Define the following terms, using graphs or equations to illustrate your answers wherever feasible:
a. Risk; stand-alone risk; probability distribution
b. Expected rate of return, $\hat{r}$
c. Continuous probability distribution
d. Standard deviation, σ; variance, σ^2; coefficient of variation, CV
e. Risk aversion; realized rate of return, $\bar{r}$
f. Risk premium for Stock i, RP_i; market risk premium, RP_M
g. Expected return on a portfolio, $\hat{r}_p$; market portfolio
h. Correlation; correlation coefficient, ρ
i. Market risk; diversifiable risk; relevant risk
j. Capital Asset Pricing Model (CAPM)
k. Beta coefficient, b; average stock's beta, b_A
l. SML equation; Security Market Line (SML)

ST-2 **Realized rates of return** Stocks A and B have the following historical returns:

Year	Stock A's Returns, r_A	Stock B's Returns, r_B
2001	(24.25%)	5.50%
2002	18.50	26.73
2003	38.67	48.25
2004	14.33	(4.50)
2005	39.13	43.86

a. Calculate the average rate of return for each stock during the period 2001 through 2005. Assume that someone held a portfolio consisting of 50 percent of Stock A and 50 percent of Stock B. What would the realized rate of return on the portfolio have been in each year from 2001 through 2005? What would the average return on the portfolio have been during that period?
b. Now calculate the standard deviation of returns for each stock and for the portfolio. Use Equation 8-3a.
c. Looking at the annual returns on the two stocks, would you guess that the correlation coefficient between the two stocks is closer to +0.8 or to −0.8?
d. If more randomly selected stocks had been included in the portfolio, which of the following is the most accurate statement of what would have happened to σ_p?
(1) σ_p would have remained constant.
(2) σ_p would have been in the vicinity of 20 percent.
(3) σ_p would have declined to zero if enough stocks had been included.

ST-3 **Beta and the required rate of return** ECRI Corporation is a holding company with four main subsidiaries. The percentage of its capital invested in each of the subsidiaries, and their respective betas, are as follows:

Subsidiary	Percentage of Capital	Beta
Electric utility	60%	0.70
Cable company	25	0.90
Real estate development	10	1.30
International/special projects	5	1.50

a. What is the holding company's beta?

b. If the risk-free rate is 6 percent and the market risk premium is 5 percent, what is the holding company's required rate of return?

c. ECRI is considering a change in its strategic focus; it will reduce its reliance on the electric utility subsidiary, so the percentage of its capital in this subsidiary will be reduced to 50 percent. At the same time, it will increase its reliance on the international/special projects division, so the percentage of its capital in that subsidiary will rise to 15 percent. What will the company's required rate of return be after these changes?

QUESTIONS

8-1 Suppose you owned a portfolio consisting of $250,000 of long-term U.S. government bonds.

a. Would your portfolio be riskless? Explain.

b. Now suppose the portfolio consists of $250,000 of 30-day Treasury bills. Every 30 days your bills mature, and you will reinvest the principal ($250,000) in a new batch of bills. You plan to live on the investment income from your portfolio, and you want to maintain a constant standard of living. Is the T-bill portfolio truly riskless? Explain.

c. What is the least risky security you can think of? Explain.

8-2 The probability distribution of a less risky expected return is more peaked than that of a riskier return. What shape would the probability distribution have for (a) completely certain returns and (b) completely uncertain returns?

8-3 A life insurance policy is a financial asset, with the premiums paid representing the investment's cost.

a. How would you calculate the expected return on a 1-year life insurance policy?

b. Suppose the owner of a life insurance policy has no other financial assets—the person's only other asset is "human capital," or earnings capacity. What is the correlation coefficient between the return on the insurance policy and that on the human capital?

c. Life insurance companies must pay administrative costs and sales representatives' commissions, hence the expected rate of return on insurance premiums is generally low or even negative. Use portfolio concepts to explain why people buy life insurance in spite of low expected returns.

8-4 Is it possible to construct a portfolio of real-world stocks that has an expected return equal to the risk-free rate?

8-5 Stock A has an expected return of 7 percent, a standard deviation of expected returns of 35 percent, a correlation coefficient with the market of −0.3, and a beta coefficient of −0.5. Stock B has an expected return of 12 percent, a standard deviation of returns of 10 percent, a 0.7 correlation with the market, and a beta coefficient of 1.0. Which security is riskier? Why?

8-6 A stock had a 12 percent return last year, a year when the overall stock market declined. Does this mean that the stock has a negative beta and thus very little risk if held in a portfolio? Explain.

8-7 If investors' aversion to risk increased, would the risk premium on a high-beta stock increase by more or less than that on a low-beta stock? Explain.

8-8 If a company's beta were to double, would its required return also double?

8-9 In Chapter 7 we saw that if the market interest rate, r_d, for a given bond increased, then the price of the bond would decline. Applying this same logic to stocks, explain (a) how a decrease in risk aversion would affect stocks' prices and earned rates of return, (b) how this would affect risk premiums as measured by the historical difference between returns on stocks and returns on bonds, and (c) the implications of this for the use of historical risk premiums when applying the SML equation.

PROBLEMS

8-1 **Expected return** A stock's returns have the following distribution:

Demand for the Company's Products	Probability of This Demand Occurring	Rate of Return If This Demand Occurs
Weak	0.1	(50%)
Below average	0.2	(5)
Average	0.4	16
Above average	0.2	25
Strong	0.1	60
	1.0	

Calculate the stock's expected return, standard deviation, and coefficient of variation.

8-2 **Portfolio beta** An individual has $35,000 invested in a stock with a beta of 0.8 and another $40,000 invested in a stock with a beta of 1.4. If these are the only two investments in her portfolio, what is her portfolio's beta?

8-3 **Required rate of return** Assume that the risk-free rate is 6 percent and the expected return on the market is 13 percent. What is the required rate of return on a stock with a beta of 0.7?

8-4 **Expected and required rates of return** Assume that the risk-free rate is 5 percent and the market risk premium is 6 percent. What is the expected return for the overall stock market? What is the required rate of return on a stock with a beta of 1.2?

8-5 **Beta and required rate of return** A stock has a required return of 11 percent; the risk-free rate is 7 percent; and the market risk premium is 4 percent.
a. What is the stock's beta?
b. If the market risk premium increased to 6 percent, what would happen to the stock's required rate of return? Assume the risk-free rate and the beta remain unchanged.

8-6 **Expected returns** Stocks X and Y have the following probability distributions of expected future returns:

Probability	X	Y
0.1	(10%)	(35%)
0.2	2	0
0.4	12	20
0.2	20	25
0.1	38	45

a. Calculate the expected rate of return, $\hat{r}_Y$, for Stock Y. ($\hat{r}_X = 12\%$.)
b. Calculate the standard deviation of expected returns, σ_X for Stock X. ($\sigma_Y = 20.35\%$.) Now calculate the coefficient of variation for Stock Y. Is it possible that most investors might regard Stock Y as being *less* risky than Stock X? Explain.

8-7 **Portfolio required return** Suppose you are the money manager of a $4 million investment fund. The fund consists of 4 stocks with the following investments and betas:

Stock	Investment	Beta
A	$ 400,000	1.50
B	600,000	(0.50)
C	1,000,000	1.25
D	2,000,000	0.75

If the market's required rate of return is 14 percent and the risk-free rate is 6 percent, what is the fund's required rate of return?

8-8 **Beta coefficient** Given the following information, determine the beta coefficient for Stock J that is consistent with equilibrium: $\hat{r}_J = 12.5\%$; $r_{RF} = 4.5\%$; $r_M = 10.5\%$.

8-9 **Required rate of return** Stock R has a beta of 1.5, Stock S has a beta of 0.75, the expected rate of return on an average stock is 13 percent, and the risk-free rate of return is 7 percent. By how much does the required return on the riskier stock exceed the required return on the less risky stock?

8-10 **CAPM and required return** Bradford Manufacturing Company has a beta of 1.45, while Farley Industries has a beta of 0.85. The required return on an index fund that holds the entire stock market is 12.0 percent. The risk-free rate of interest is 5 percent. By how much does Bradford's required return exceed Farley's required return?

8-11 **CAPM and required return** Calculate the required rate of return for Manning Enterprises, assuming that investors expect a 3.5 percent rate of inflation in the future. The real risk-free rate is 2.5 percent and the market risk premium is 6.5 percent. Manning has a beta of 1.7, and its realized rate of return has averaged 13.5 percent over the past 5 years.

8-12 **CAPM and market risk premium** Consider the following information for three stocks, Stocks X, Y, and Z. The returns on the three stocks are positively correlated, but they are not perfectly correlated. (That is, each of the correlation coefficients is between 0 and 1.)

Stock	Expected Return	Standard Deviation	Beta
X	9.00%	15%	0.8
Y	10.75	15	1.2
Z	12.50	15	1.6

Fund P has half of its funds invested in Stock X and half invested in Stock Y. Fund Q has one-third of its funds invested in each of the three stocks. The risk-free rate is 5.5 percent, and the market is in equilibrium. (That is, required returns equal expected returns.) What is the market risk premium ($r_M - r_{RF}$)?

8-13 **Required rate of return** Suppose $r_{RF} = 9\%$, $r_M = 14\%$, and $b_i = 1.3$.
a. What is r_i, the required rate of return on Stock i?
b. Now suppose r_{RF} (1) increases to 10 percent or (2) decreases to 8 percent. The slope of the SML remains constant. How would this affect r_M and r_i?
c. Now assume r_{RF} remains at 9 percent but r_M (1) increases to 16 percent or (2) falls to 13 percent. The slope of the SML does not remain constant. How would these changes affect r_i?

Challenging Problems 14–21

8-14 **Portfolio beta** Suppose you held a diversified portfolio consisting of a $7,500 investment in each of 20 different common stocks. The portfolio's beta is 1.12. Now suppose you decided to sell one of the stocks in your portfolio with a beta of 1.0 for $7,500 and to use these proceeds to buy another stock with a beta of 1.75. What would your portfolio's new beta be?

8-15 **CAPM and required return** HR Industries (HRI) has a beta of 1.8, while LR Industries' (LRI) beta is 0.6. The risk-free rate is 6 percent, and the required rate of return on an average stock is 13 percent. Now the expected rate of inflation built into r_{RF} falls by 1.5 percentage points, the real risk-free rate remains constant, the required return on the market falls to 10.5 percent, and all betas remain constant. After all of these changes, what will be the difference in the required returns for HRI and LRI?

8-16 **CAPM and portfolio return** You have been managing a $5 million portfolio that has a beta of 1.25 and a required rate of return of 12 percent. The current risk-free rate is 5.25 percent. Assume that you receive another $500,000. If you invest the money in a stock with a beta of 0.75, what will be the required return on your $5.5 million portfolio?

8-17 **Portfolio beta** A mutual fund manager has a $20,000,000 portfolio with a beta of 1.5. The risk-free rate is 4.5 percent and the market risk premium is 5.5 percent. The manager expects to receive an additional $5,000,000, which she plans to invest in a number of stocks. After investing the additional funds, she wants the fund's required return to be 13 percent. What should be the average beta of the new stocks added to the portfolio?

8-18 **Expected returns** Suppose you won the lottery and had two options: (1) receiving $0.5 million or (2) a gamble in which you would receive $1 million if a head were flipped but zero if a tail came up.
a. What is the expected value of the gamble?
b. Would you take the sure $0.5 million or the gamble?
c. If you chose the sure $0.5 million, would that indicate that you are a risk averter or a risk seeker?
d. Suppose the payoff was actually $0.5 million—that was the only choice. You now face the choice of investing it in either a U.S. Treasury bond that will return $537,500

at the end of a year or a common stock that has a 50–50 chance of being either worthless or worth $1,150,000 at the end of the year.
  (1) The expected profit on the T-bond investment is $37,500. What is the expected dollar profit on the stock investment?
  (2) The expected rate of return on the T-bond investment is 7.5 percent. What is the expected rate of return on the stock investment?
  (3) Would you invest in the bond or the stock?
  (4) Exactly how large would the expected profit (or the expected rate of return) have to be on the stock investment to make *you* invest in the stock, given the 7.5 percent return on the bond?
  (5) How might your decision be affected if, rather than buying one stock for $0.5 million, you could construct a portfolio consisting of 100 stocks with $5,000 invested in each? Each of these stocks has the same return characteristics as the one stock—that is, a 50–50 chance of being worth either zero or $11,500 at year-end. Would the correlation between returns on these stocks matter?

8-19 **Evaluating risk and return** Stock X has a 10 percent expected return, a beta coefficient of 0.9, and a 35 percent standard deviation of expected returns. Stock Y has a 12.5 percent expected return, a beta coefficient of 1.2, and a 25 percent standard deviation. The risk-free rate is 6 percent, and the market risk premium is 5 percent.

  a. Calculate each stock's coefficient of variation.
  b. Which stock is riskier for a diversified investor?
  c. Calculate each stock's required rate of return.
  d. On the basis of the two stocks' expected and required returns, which stock would be more attractive to a diversified investor?
  e. Calculate the required return of a portfolio that has $7,500 invested in Stock X and $2,500 invested in Stock Y.
  f. If the market risk premium increased to 6 percent, which of the two stocks would have the larger increase in its required return?

8-20 **Realized rates of return** Stocks A and B have the following historical returns:

Year	Stock A's Returns, r_A	Stock B's Returns, r_B
2001	(18.00%)	(14.50%)
2002	33.00	21.80
2003	15.00	30.50
2004	(0.50)	(7.60)
2005	27.00	26.30

  a. Calculate the average rate of return for each stock during the period 2001 through 2005.
  b. Assume that someone held a portfolio consisting of 50 percent of Stock A and 50 percent of Stock B. What would the realized rate of return on the portfolio have been in each year? What would the average return on the portfolio have been during this period?
  c. Calculate the standard deviation of returns for each stock and for the portfolio.
  d. Calculate the coefficient of variation for each stock and for the portfolio.
  e. Assuming you are a risk-averse investor, would you prefer to hold Stock A, Stock B, or the portfolio? Why?

8-21 **Security Market Line** You plan to invest in the Kish Hedge Fund, which has total capital of $500 million invested in five stocks:

Stock	Investment	Stock's Beta Coefficient
A	$160 million	0.5
B	120 million	2.0
C	80 million	4.0
D	80 million	1.0
E	60 million	3.0

Kish's beta coefficient can be found as a weighted average of its stocks' betas. The risk-free rate is 6 percent, and you believe the following probability distribution for future market returns is realistic:

Probability	Market Return
0.1	7%
0.2	9
0.4	11
0.2	13
0.1	15

a. What is the equation for the Security Market Line (SML)? (Hint: First determine the expected market return.)
b. Calculate Kish's required rate of return.
c. Suppose Rick Kish, the president, receives a proposal from a company seeking new capital. The amount needed to take a position in the stock is $50 million, it has an expected return of 15 percent, and its estimated beta is 2.0. Should Kish invest in the new company? At what expected rate of return should Kish be indifferent to purchasing the stock?

COMPREHENSIVE/SPREADSHEET PROBLEM

8-22 **Evaluating risk and return** Bartman Industries' and Reynolds Inc.'s stock prices and dividends, along with the Winslow 5000 Index, are shown here for the period 2000–2005. The Winslow 5000 data are adjusted to include dividends.

	BARTMAN INDUSTRIES		REYNOLDS INC.		WINSLOW 5000
Year	Stock Price	Dividend	Stock Price	Dividend	Includes Dividends
2005	$17.250	$1.15	$48.750	$3.00	11,663.98
2004	14.750	1.06	52.300	2.90	8,785.70
2003	16.500	1.00	48.750	2.75	8,679.98
2002	10.750	0.95	57.250	2.50	6,434.03
2001	11.375	0.90	60.000	2.25	5,602.28
2000	7.625	0.85	55.750	2.00	4,705.97

a. Use the data to calculate annual rates of return for Bartman, Reynolds, and the Winslow 5000 Index, and then calculate each entity's average return over the 5-year period. (Hint: Remember, returns are calculated by subtracting the beginning price from the ending price to get the capital gain or loss, adding the dividend to the capital gain or loss, and dividing the result by the beginning price. Assume that dividends are already included in the index. Also, you cannot calculate the rate of return for 2000 because you do not have 1999 data.)
b. Calculate the standard deviations of the returns for Bartman, Reynolds, and the Winslow 5000. (Hint: Use the sample standard deviation formula, 8-3a, to this chapter, which corresponds to the STDEV function in *Excel*.)
c. Now calculate the coefficients of variation for Bartman, Reynolds, and the Winslow 5000.
d. Construct a scatter diagram that shows Bartman's and Reynolds's returns on the vertical axis and the Winslow Index's returns on the horizontal axis.
e. Estimate Bartman's and Reynolds's betas by running regressions of their returns against the index's returns. Are these betas consistent with your graph?
f. Assume that the risk-free rate on long-term Treasury bonds is 6.04 percent. Assume also that the average annual return on the Winslow 5000 is *not* a good estimate of the market's required return—it is too high, so use 11 percent as the expected return on the market. Now use the SML equation to calculate the two companies' required returns.
g. If you formed a portfolio that consisted of 50 percent Bartman and 50 percent Reynolds, what would the beta and the required return be?
h. Suppose an investor wants to include Bartman Industries' stock in his or her portfolio. Stocks A, B, and C are currently in the portfolio, and their betas are 0.769, 0.985, and 1.423, respectively. Calculate the new portfolio's required return if it consists of 25 percent of Bartman, 15 percent of Stock A, 40 percent of Stock B, and 20 percent of Stock C.

Integrated Case

Merrill Finch Inc.

8-23 **Risk and return** Assume that you recently graduated with a major in finance, and you just landed a job as a financial planner with Merrill Finch Inc., a large financial services corporation. Your first assignment is to invest $100,000 for a client. Because the funds are to be invested in a business at the end of 1 year, you have been instructed to plan for a 1-year holding period. Further, your boss has restricted you to the investment alternatives in the following table, shown with their probabilities and associated outcomes. (Disregard for now the items at the bottom of the data; you will fill in the blanks later.)

RETURNS ON ALTERNATIVE INVESTMENTS

ESTIMATED RATE OF RETURN

State of the Economy	Probability	T-Bills	High Tech	Collections	U.S. Rubber	Market Portfolio	2-Stock Portfolio
Recession	0.1	5.5%	(27.0%)	27.0%	6.0%[a]	(17.0%)	0.0%
Below average	0.2	5.5	(7.0)	13.0	(14.0)	(3.0)	
Average	0.4	5.5	15.0	0.0	3.0	10.0	7.5
Above average	0.2	5.5	30.0	(11.0)	41.0	25.0	
Boom	0.1	5.5	45.0	(21.0)	26.0	38.0	12.0
$\hat{r}$				1.0%	9.8%	10.5%	
σ		0.0		13.2	18.8	15.2	3.4
CV				13.2	1.9	1.4	0.5
b				−0.87	0.88		

[a] Note that the estimated returns of U.S. Rubber do not always move in the same direction as the overall economy. For example, when the economy is below average, consumers purchase fewer tires than they would if the economy was stronger. However, if the economy is in a flat-out recession, a large number of consumers who were planning to purchase a new car may choose to wait and instead purchase new tires for the car they currently own. Under these circumstances, we would expect U.S. Rubber's stock price to be higher if there is a recession than if the economy was just below average.

Merrill Finch's economic forecasting staff has developed probability estimates for the state of the economy, and its security analysts have developed a sophisticated computer program, which was used to estimate the rate of return on each alternative under each state of the economy. High Tech Inc. is an electronics firm; Collections Inc. collects past-due debts; and U.S. Rubber manufactures tires and various other rubber and plastics products. Merrill Finch also maintains a "market portfolio" that owns a market-weighted fraction of all publicly traded stocks; you can invest in that portfolio, and thus obtain average stock market results. Given the situation as described, answer the following questions.

a. (1) Why is the T-bill's return independent of the state of the economy? Do T-bills promise a completely risk-free return?
(2) Why are High Tech's returns expected to move with the economy whereas Collections' are expected to move counter to the economy?

b. Calculate the expected rate of return on each alternative and fill in the blanks on the row for $\hat{r}$ in the table above.

c. You should recognize that basing a decision solely on expected returns is only appropriate for risk-neutral individuals. Because your client, like virtually everyone, is risk averse, the riskiness of each alternative is an important aspect of the decision. One possible measure of risk is the standard deviation of returns.
(1) Calculate this value for each alternative, and fill in the blank on the row for σ in the table.
(2) What type of risk is measured by the standard deviation?
(3) Draw a graph that shows *roughly* the shape of the probability distributions for High Tech, U.S. Rubber, and T-bills.

d. Suppose you suddenly remembered that the coefficient of variation (CV) is generally regarded as being a better measure of stand-alone risk than the standard deviation when the alternatives being considered have widely differing expected returns. Calculate the missing CVs, and fill in the blanks on the row for CV in the table. Does the CV produce the same risk rankings as the standard deviation?

e. Suppose you created a 2-stock portfolio by investing $50,000 in High Tech and $50,000 in Collections.
(1) Calculate the expected return ($\hat{r}_p$), the standard deviation (σ_p), and the coefficient of variation (CV_p) for this portfolio and fill in the appropriate blanks in the table.
(2) How does the riskiness of this 2-stock portfolio compare with the riskiness of the individual stocks if they were held in isolation?

f.   Suppose an investor starts with a portfolio consisting of one randomly selected stock. What would happen (1) to the riskiness and (2) to the expected return of the portfolio as more and more randomly selected stocks were added to the portfolio? What is the implication for investors? Draw a graph of the 2 portfolios to illustrate your answer.

g.   (1) Should portfolio effects impact the way investors think about the riskiness of individual stocks? (2) If you decided to hold a 1-stock portfolio, and consequently were exposed to more risk than diversified investors, could you expect to be compensated for all of your risk; that is, could you earn a risk premium on that part of your risk that you could have eliminated by diversifying?

h.   The expected rates of return and the beta coefficients of the alternatives as supplied by Merrill Finch's computer program are as follows:

Security	Return (r̂)	Risk (Beta)
High Tech	12.4%	1.32
Market	10.5	1.00
U.S. Rubber	9.8	0.88
T-bills	5.5	0.00
Collections	1.0	(0.87)

(1) What is a beta coefficient, and how are betas used in risk analysis? (2) Do the expected returns appear to be related to each alternative's market risk? (3) Is it possible to choose among the alternatives on the basis of the information developed thus far? Use the data given at the start of the problem to construct a graph that shows how the T-bill's, High Tech's, and the market's beta coefficients are calculated. Then discuss what betas measure and how they are used in risk analysis.

i.   The yield curve is currently flat, that is, long-term Treasury bonds also have a 5.5 percent yield. Consequently, Merrill Finch assumes that the risk-free rate is 5.5 percent. (1) Write out the Security Market Line (SML) equation, use it to calculate the required rate of return on each alternative, and then graph the relationship between the expected and required rates of return. (2) How do the expected rates of return compare with the required rates of return? (3) Does the fact that Collections has an expected return that is less than the T-bill rate make any sense? (4) What would be the market risk and the required return of a 50–50 portfolio of High Tech and Collections? Of High Tech and U.S. Rubber?

j.   (1) Suppose investors raised their inflation expectations by 3 percentage points over current estimates as reflected in the 5.5 percent risk-free rate. What effect would higher inflation have on the SML and on the returns required on high- and low-risk securities? (2) Suppose instead that investors' risk aversion increased enough to cause the market risk premium to increase by 3 percentage points. (Inflation remains constant.) What effect would this have on the SML and on returns of high- and low-risk securities?

cyberproblem

Please go to the ThomsonNOW Web site to access the Cyberproblems.

THOMSON ONE | Business School Edition

Access the Thomson ONE problems though the ThomsonNOW Web site. Use the Thomson ONE—Business School Edition online database to work this chapter's questions.

Using Past Information to Estimate Required Returns

Chapter 8 discussed the basic trade-off between risk and return. In the Capital Asset Pricing Model (CAPM) discussion, beta is identified as the correct measure of risk for diversified shareholders. Recall that beta measures the extent to which the returns of a given stock move with the stock market. When using the CAPM to estimate required returns, we would ideally like to know how the stock will move with the market in the future, but since we don't have a crystal ball we generally use historical data to estimate this relationship with beta.

As mentioned in the Web Appendix for this chapter, beta can be estimated by regressing the individual stock's returns against the returns of the overall market. As an alternative to running our own regressions, we can instead rely on reported betas from a variety of sources. These published sources make it easy for us to readily obtain beta estimates for most large publicly traded corporations. However, a word of caution is in order. Beta estimates can often be quite sensitive to the time period in which the data are estimated, the market index used, and the frequency of the data used. Therefore, it is not uncommon to find a wide range of beta estimates among the various published sources. Indeed, Thomson One reports multiple beta estimates. These multiple estimates reflect the fact that Thomson One puts together data from a variety of different sources.

Discussion Questions

1. Begin by taking a look at the historical performance of the overall stock market. If you want to see, for example, the performance of the S&P 500, select INDICES and enter S&PCOMP. Click on PERFORMANCE and you will immediately see a quick summary of the market's performance in recent months and years. How has the market performed over the past year? The past 3 years? The past 5 years? The past 10 years?

2. Now let's take a closer look at the stocks of four companies: Colgate Palmolive (Ticker = CL), Gillette (G), Merrill Lynch (MER), and Microsoft (MSFT). Before looking at the data, which of these companies would you expect to have a relatively high beta (greater than 1.0), and which of these companies would you expect to have a relatively low beta (less than 1.0)?

3. Select one of the four stocks listed in question 2 by selecting COMPANIES, entering the company's ticker symbol, and clicking on GO. On the overview page, you should see a chart that summarizes how the stock has done relative to the S&P 500 over the past 6 months. Has the stock outperformed or underperformed the overall market during this time period?

4. Return to the overview page for the stock you selected. If you scroll down the page you should see an estimate of the company's beta. What is the company's beta? What was the source of the estimated beta?

5. Click on the tab labeled PRICES. What is the company's current dividend yield? What has been its total return to investors over the past 6 months? Over the past year? Over the past 3 years? (Remember that total return includes the dividend yield plus any capital gains or losses.)

6. What is the estimated beta on this page? What is the source of the estimated beta? Why might different sources produce different estimates of beta? [Note if you want to see even more beta estimates, click OVERVIEWS (on second line of tabs) and then select the SEC DATABASE MARKET DATA. Scroll through the STOCK OVERVIEW SECTION and you will see a range of different beta estimates.]

7. Select a beta estimate that you believe is best. (If you are not sure, you may want to consider an average of the given estimates.) Assume that the risk-free rate is 5 percent and the market risk premium is 6 percent. What is the required return on the company's stock?

8. Repeat the same exercise for each of the 3 remaining companies. Do the reported betas confirm your earlier intuition? In general, do you find that the higher-beta stocks tend to do better in up markets and worse in down markets? Explain.

CHAPTER 9

STOCKS AND THEIR VALUATION

Searching for the Right Stock

A recent study by the securities industry found that roughly half of all U.S. households have invested in common stocks. As noted in Chapter 8, the long-run performance of the U.S. stock market has been quite good. Indeed, during the past 75 years the market's average annual return has exceeded 12 percent. However, there is no guarantee that stocks will perform in the future as well as they have in the past. The stock market doesn't always go up, and investors can make or lose a lot of money in a short period of time. For example, in 2004, Apple Computer's stock more than tripled following sizzling sales of its iPod products. On the other hand, Merck's stock fell more than 30 percent in 2004, when it was forced to withdraw one of its best-selling drugs, Vioxx.

The broader market as represented by the Dow Jones Industrial Average declined 2.6 percent during the first quarter of 2005. The triggers here were concerns about rising interest rates, higher oil prices, and declining consumer confidence. During this quarter, several well-respected companies experienced much larger declines—for example, Microsoft fell 9.5 percent, Home Depot 10.5 percent, and General Motors 26.6 percent. This shows, first, that diversification is important, and second, that when it comes to picking stocks, it is not enough to simply pick a good company—the stock must also be "fairly" priced.

To determine if a stock is fairly priced, you first need to estimate the stock's true or "intrinsic value," a concept first discussed in Chapter 1. With this objective in mind, this chapter describes some models that analysts have used to estimate a stock's intrinsic value. As you will see, it is difficult to predict future stock prices, but we are not completely in the dark. After studying this chapter, you should have a reasonably good understanding of the factors that influence stock prices, and with that knowledge—plus a little luck—you should be able to successfully navigate the stock market's often treacherous ups and downs.

Source: Justin Lahart, "Last Year's Winners Had Little in Common," *The Wall Street Journal,* January 3, 2005, p. R8.

Key trends in the securities industry are listed and explained at http://www.sia.com/research/html/key_industry_trends_.html.

In Chapter 7 we examined bonds. We now turn to common and preferred stocks, beginning with some important background material that helps establish a framework for valuing these securities.

While it is generally easy to predict the cash flows received from bonds, forecasting the cash flows on common stocks is much more difficult. However, two fairly straightforward models can be used to help estimate the "true," or intrinsic, value of a common stock: (1) the dividend growth model and (2) the total corporate value model. A stock should be bought if its estimated intrinsic value exceeds its market price but sold if the price exceeds its intrinsic value. The same valuation concepts and models are also used in Chapter 10, where we estimate the cost of capital, a critical element in corporate investment decisions.

9-1 LEGAL RIGHTS AND PRIVILEGES OF COMMON STOCKHOLDERS

Its common stockholders are the *owners* of a corporation, and as such they have certain rights and privileges, as discussed in this section.

9-1a Control of the Firm

A firm's common stockholders have the right to elect its directors, who, in turn, elect the officers who manage the business. In a small firm, the major stockholder typically is also the president and chair of the board of directors. In large, publicly owned firms, the managers typically have some stock, but their personal holdings are generally insufficient to give them voting control. Thus, the managements of most publicly owned firms can be removed by the stockholders if the management team is not effective.

State and federal laws stipulate how stockholder control is to be exercised. First, corporations must hold elections of directors periodically, usually once a year, with the vote taken at the annual meeting. Frequently, one-third of the directors are elected each year for a three-year term. Each share of stock has one vote; thus, the owner of 1,000 shares has 1,000 votes for each director.[1] Stockholders can appear at the annual meeting and vote in person, but typically they transfer their right to vote to another person by means of a **proxy.** Management always solicits stockholders' proxies and usually gets them. However, if earnings are poor and stockholders are dissatisfied, an outside group may solicit the

Proxy
A document giving one person the authority to act for another, typically the power to vote shares of common stock.

---

[1] In the situation described, a 1,000-share stockholder could cast 1,000 votes for each of three directors if there were three contested seats on the board. An alternative procedure that may be prescribed in the corporate charter calls for cumulative voting. There the 1,000-share stockholder would get 3,000 votes if there were three vacancies, and he or she could cast all of them for one director. Cumulative voting helps small groups obtain representation on the board.

proxies in an effort to overthrow management and take control of the business. This is known as a **proxy fight.**

The question of control has become a central issue in finance in recent years. The frequency of proxy fights has increased, as have attempts by one corporation to take over another by purchasing a majority of the outstanding stock. These actions are called **takeovers.** Some well-known examples of takeover battles include KKR's acquisition of RJR Nabisco, Chevron's acquisition of Gulf Oil, and the QVC/Viacom fight to take over Paramount.

Managers without majority control (more than 50 percent of their firms' stock) are very much concerned about proxy fights and takeovers, and many of them have attempted to obtain stockholder approval for changes in their corporate charters that would make takeovers more difficult. For example, a number of companies have gotten their stockholders to agree (1) to elect only one-third of the directors each year (rather than electing all directors each year), (2) to require 75 percent of the stockholders (rather than 50 percent) to approve a merger, and (3) to vote in a "poison pill" provision that would allow the stockholders of a firm that is taken over by another firm to buy shares in the second firm at a reduced price. The poison pill makes the acquisition unattractive and, thus, wards off hostile takeover attempts. Managements seeking such changes generally cite a fear that the firm will be picked up at a bargain price, but it often appears that management's concern about its own position is an even more important consideration.

Management moves to make takeovers more difficult have been countered by stockholders, especially large institutional stockholders, who do not like barriers erected to protect incompetent managers. To illustrate, the California Public Employees Retirement System (Calpers), which is one of the largest institutional investors, has led proxy fights with several corporations whose financial performances were poor in Calpers' judgment. Calpers wants companies to give outside (nonmanagement) directors more clout and to force managers to be more responsive to stockholder complaints.

Prior to 1993, SEC rules prohibited large investors such as Calpers from getting together to force corporate managers to institute policy changes. However, the SEC changed its rules in 1993, and now large investors can work together to force management changes. This ruling has helped keep managers focused on stockholder concerns, which means the maximization of stock prices.

9-1b The Preemptive Right

Common stockholders often have the right, called the **preemptive right,** to purchase any additional shares sold by the firm. In some states, the preemptive right is automatically included in every corporate charter; in others, it must be specifically inserted into the charter.

The purpose of the preemptive right is twofold. First, it prevents the management of a corporation from issuing a large number of additional shares and purchasing these shares itself. Management could thereby seize control of the corporation and frustrate the will of the current stockholders. The second, and far more important, reason for the preemptive right is to protect stockholders against a dilution of value. For example, suppose 1,000 shares of common stock, each with a price of $100, were outstanding, making the total market value of the firm $100,000. If an additional 1,000 shares were sold at $50 a share, or for $50,000, this would raise the total market value to $150,000. When the new total market value is divided by new total shares outstanding, a value of $75 a share is obtained. The old stockholders would thus lose $25 per share, and the new stockholders would have an instant profit of $25 per share. Thus, selling common stock at a price below the market value would dilute its price and transfer

Proxy Fight
An attempt by a person or group to gain control of a firm by getting its stockholders to grant that person or group the authority to vote their shares to replace the current management.

Takeover
An action whereby a person or group succeeds in ousting a firm's management and taking control of the company.

Preemptive Right
A provision in the corporate charter or bylaws that gives common stockholders the right to purchase on a pro rata basis new issues of common stock (or convertible securities).

wealth from the present stockholders to those who were allowed to purchase the new shares. The preemptive right prevents this.

Identify some actions that companies have taken to make takeovers more difficult.

What is the preemptive right, and what are the two primary reasons for its existence?

9-2 TYPES OF COMMON STOCK

Classified Stock
Common stock that is given a special designation, such as Class A, Class B, and so forth, to meet special needs of the company.

Although most firms have only one type of common stock, in some instances **classified stock** is used to meet special needs. Generally, when special classifications are used, one type is designated *Class A*, another *Class B*, and so on. Small, new companies seeking funds from outside sources frequently use different types of common stock. For example, when Genetic Concepts went public recently, its Class A stock was sold to the public and paid a dividend, but this stock had no voting rights for five years. Its Class B stock, which was retained by the organizers of the company, had full voting rights for five years, but the legal terms stated that dividends could not be paid on the Class B stock until the company had established its earning power by building up retained earnings to a designated level. The use of classified stock thus enabled the public to take a position in a conservatively financed growth company without sacrificing income, while the founders retained absolute control during the crucial early stages of the firm's development. At the same time, outside investors were protected against excessive withdrawals of funds by the original owners. As is often the case in such situations, the Class B stock was also called **founders' shares.**

Founders' Shares
Stock owned by the firm's founders that has sole voting rights but restricted dividends for a specified number of years.

Note that "Class A," "Class B," and so on, have no standard meanings. Most firms have no classified shares, but a firm that does could designate its Class B shares as founders' shares and its Class A shares as those sold to the public, while another could reverse these designations. Still other firms could use stock classifications for entirely different purposes. For example, when General Motors acquired Hughes Aircraft for $5 billion, it paid in part with a new Class H common, GMH, which had limited voting rights and whose dividends were tied to Hughes's performance as a GM subsidiary. The reasons for the new stock were that (1) GM wanted to limit voting privileges on the new classified stock because of management's concern about a possible takeover and (2) Hughes employees wanted to be rewarded more directly on Hughes's own performance than would have been possible through regular GM stock. These Class H shares disappeared in 2003 when GM decided to sell off the Hughes unit.

What are some reasons why a company might use classified stock?

9-3 COMMON STOCK VALUATION

Common stock represents an ownership interest in a corporation, but to the typical investor, a share of common stock is simply a piece of paper characterized by two features:

1. It entitles its owner to dividends, but only if the company has earnings out of which dividends can be paid and management chooses to pay dividends rather than retaining and reinvesting all the earnings. Whereas a bond con-

tains a *promise* to pay interest, common stock provides no such promise—if you own a stock, you may *expect* a dividend, but your expectations may not in fact be met. To illustrate, Long Island Lighting Company (LILCO) had paid dividends on its common stock for more than 50 years, and people expected those dividends to continue. However, when the company encountered severe problems a few years ago, it stopped paying dividends. Note, though, that LILCO continued to pay interest on its bonds, because if it had not, then it would have been declared bankrupt and the bondholders could have taken over the company.

2. Stock can be sold, hopefully at a price greater than the purchase price. If the stock is actually sold at a price above its purchase price, the investor will receive a *capital gain*. Generally, when people buy common stock they expect to receive capital gains; otherwise, they would not buy the stock. However, after the fact, they can end up with capital losses rather than capital gains. LILCO's stock price dropped from $17.50 to $3.75 in one year, so the *expected* capital gain on that stock turned out to be a huge *actual* capital loss.

9-3a Definitions of Terms Used in Stock Valuation Models

Common stocks provide an expected future cash flow stream, and a stock's value is found as the present value of the expected future cash flows, which consist of two elements: (1) the dividends expected in each year and (2) the price investors expect to receive when they sell the stock. The final price includes the return of the original investment plus an expected capital gain.

We saw in Chapter 1 that managers should seek to maximize the value of their firms' stock. Therefore, managers need to know how alternative actions are likely to affect stock prices, and we develop some models to help show how the value of a share of stock is determined. We begin by defining the following terms:

D_t = dividend the stockholder *expects* to receive at the end of each Year t. D_0 is the most recent dividend, which has already been paid; D_1 is the first dividend expected, and it will be paid at the end of this year; D_2 is the dividend expected at the end of two years; and so forth. D_1 represents the first cash flow a new purchaser of the stock will receive. Note that D_0, the dividend that has just been paid, is known with certainty. However, all future dividends are *expected values*, those expectations differ somewhat from investor to investor, and those differences lead to differences in estimates of the stock's intrinsic value.[2]

P_0 = actual **market price** of the stock today.

$\hat{P}_t$ = expected price of the stock at the end of each Year t (pronounced "P hat t"). $\hat{P}_0$ is the **intrinsic value** of the stock today as seen by the particular investor doing the analysis; $\hat{P}_1$ is the price expected at the end of one year; and so on. Note that $\hat{P}_0$ is the intrinsic value of the stock today based on a particular investor's estimate of the stock's expected dividend stream and the riskiness of that stream. Hence, whereas the market price P_0 is fixed and

Market Price, P_0
The price at which a stock sells in the market.

Intrinsic Value, $\hat{P}_0$
The value of an asset that, in the mind of a particular investor, is justified by the facts; $\hat{P}_0$ may be different from the asset's current market price.

---

[2] Stocks generally pay dividends quarterly, so theoretically we should evaluate them on a quarterly basis. However, in stock valuation, most analysts work on an annual basis because the data generally are not precise enough to warrant refinement to a quarterly model. For additional information on the quarterly model, see Charles M. Linke and J. Kenton Zumwalt, "Estimation Biases in Discounted Cash Flow Analysis of Equity Capital Cost in Rate Regulation," *Financial Management*, Autumn 1984, pp. 15–21.

is identical for all investors, $\hat{P}_0$ could differ among investors, depending on how optimistic they are regarding the company. $\hat{P}_0$, the individual investor's estimate of the intrinsic value today, could be above or below P_0, the current stock price. An investor would buy the stock only if their estimate of $\hat{P}_0$ were equal to or greater than P_0.

As there are many investors in the market, there can be many values for $\hat{P}_0$. However, we can think of an "average," or "marginal," investor whose actions actually determine the market price. For the marginal investor, P_0 must equal $\hat{P}_0$; otherwise, a disequilibrium would exist, and buying and selling in the market would change P_0 until $P_0 = \hat{P}_0$ for the marginal investor.

Growth Rate, g
The expected rate of growth in dividends per share.

$g =$ expected **growth rate** in dividends as predicted by the marginal investor. If dividends are expected to grow at a constant rate, g is also equal to the expected rate of growth in earnings and in the stock's price. Different investors use different g's to evaluate a firm's stock, but the market price, P_0, is set on the basis of g as estimated by the marginal investor.

Required Rate of Return, r_s
The minimum rate of return on a common stock that a stockholder considers acceptable.

$r_s =$ minimum acceptable, or **required, rate of return** on the stock, considering both its riskiness and the returns available on other investments. Again, this term generally relates to the marginal investor. The determinants of r_s include the real rate of return, expected inflation, and risk as discussed in Chapter 8.

Expected Rate of Return, $\hat{r}_s$
The rate of return on a common stock that a stockholder expects to receive in the future.

$\hat{r}_s =$ **expected rate of return** that an investor who buys the stock expects to receive in the future. $\hat{r}_s$ (pronounced "r hat s") could be above or below r_s, but one would buy the stock only if $\hat{r}_s$ were equal to or greater than r_s.

Actual Realized Rate of Return, $\bar{r}_s$
The rate of return on a common stock actually received by stockholders in some past period. $\bar{r}_s$ may be greater or less than $\hat{r}_s$ and/or r_s.

$\bar{r}_s =$ **actual**, or **realized**, *after-the-fact* **rate of return**, pronounced "r bar s." You may *expect* to obtain a return of $\bar{r}_s = 10\%$ if you buy a stock today, but if the market goes down, you may end up next year with an actual realized return that is much lower, perhaps even negative.

Dividend Yield
The expected dividend divided by the current price of a share of stock.

$D_1/P_0 =$ expected **dividend yield** on the stock during the coming year. If the stock is expected to pay a dividend of $D_1 =$ \$1 during the next 12 months, and if its current price is $P_0 =$ \$20, then the expected dividend yield is \$1/\$20 = 0.05 = 5%.

Capital Gains Yield
The capital gain during a given year divided by the beginning price.

$\dfrac{\hat{P}_1 - P_0}{P_0} =$ expected **capital gains yield** on the stock during the coming year. If the stock sells for \$20 today, and if it is expected to rise to \$21.00 at the end of one year, then the expected capital gain is $\hat{P}_1 - P_0 =$ \$21.00 − \$20.00 = \$1.00, and the expected capital gains yield is \$1.00/\$20 = 0.05 = 5%.

Expected total return $= \hat{r}_s =$ expected dividend yield (D_1/P_0) plus expected capital gains yield $[(\hat{P}_1 - P_0)/P_0]$. In our example, the **expected total return** $= \hat{r}_s = 5\% + 5\% = 10\%$.

Expected Total Return
The sum of the expected dividend yield and the expected capital gains yield.

9-3b Expected Dividends as the Basis for Stock Values

In our discussion of bonds, we found the value of a bond as the present value of interest payments over the life of the bond plus the present value of the bond's maturity (or par) value:

$$V_B = \frac{INT}{(1 + r_d)^1} + \frac{INT}{(1 + r_d)^2} + \cdots + \frac{INT}{(1 + r_d)^N} + \frac{M}{(1 + r_d)^N}$$

Stock prices are likewise determined as the present value of a stream of cash flows, and the basic stock valuation equation is similar to the bond valuation equation. What are the cash flows that corporations provide to their stockholders? First, think of yourself as an investor who buys a stock with the intention of holding it (in your family) forever. In this case, all that you (and your heirs) would receive is a stream of dividends, and the value of the stock today is calculated as the present value of an infinite stream of dividends:

Value of stock $= \hat{P}_0 =$ PV of expected future dividends

$$= \frac{D_1}{(1 + r_s)^1} + \frac{D_2}{(1 + r_s)^2} + \cdots + \frac{D_\infty}{(1 + r_s)^\infty}$$

$$= \sum_{t=1}^{\infty} \frac{D_t}{(1 + r_s)^t} \qquad (9\text{-}1)$$

What about the more typical case, where you expect to hold the stock for a finite period and then sell it—what will be the value of $\hat{P}_0$ in this case? Unless the company is likely to be liquidated or sold and thus to disappear, *the value of the stock is again determined by Equation 9-1*. To see this, recognize that for any individual investor, the expected cash flows consist of expected dividends plus the expected sale price of the stock. However, the sale price the current investor receives will depend on the dividends some future investor expects. Therefore, for all present and future investors in total, expected cash flows must be based on expected future dividends. Put another way, unless a firm is liquidated or sold to another concern, the cash flows it provides to its stockholders will consist only of a stream of dividends; therefore, the value of a share of its stock must be established as the present value of that expected dividend stream.

The general validity of Equation 9-1 can also be confirmed by asking the following question: Suppose I buy a stock and expect to hold it for one year. I will receive dividends during the year plus the value $\hat{P}_1$ when I sell out at the end of the year. But what will determine the value of $\hat{P}_1$? The answer is that it will be determined as the present value of the dividends expected during Year 2 plus the stock price at the end of that year, which, in turn, will be determined as the present value of another set of future dividends and an even more distant stock price. This process can be continued ad infinitum, and the ultimate result is Equation 9-1.[3]

Explain the following statement: "Whereas a bond contains a promise to pay interest, a share of common stock typically provides an expectation of, but no promise of, dividends plus capital gains."

What are the two parts of most stocks' expected total return?

If $D_1 = \$2.00$, $g = 6\%$, and $P_0 = \$40$, what are the stock's expected dividend yield, capital gains yield, and total expected return for the coming year? (5%, 6%, 11%)

---

[3] We should note that investors periodically lose sight of the long-run nature of stocks as investments and forget that in order to sell a stock at a profit, one must find a buyer who will pay the higher price. If you analyze a stock's value in accordance with Equation 9-1, conclude that the stock's market price exceeds a reasonable value, and then buy the stock anyway, then you would be following the "bigger fool" theory of investment—you think you may be a fool to buy the stock at its excessive price, but you also think that when you get ready to sell it, you can find someone who is an even bigger fool. The bigger fool theory was widely followed in the summer of 1987, just before the stock market lost more than one-third of its value in the October 1987 crash.

9-4 CONSTANT GROWTH STOCKS

Equation 9-1 is a generalized stock valuation model in the sense that the time pattern of D_t can be anything: D_t can be rising, falling, fluctuating randomly, or it can even be zero for several years and Equation 9-1 will still hold. With a computer spreadsheet we can easily use this equation to find a stock's intrinsic value for any pattern of dividends. In practice, the hard part is obtaining an accurate forecast of the future dividends.

In many cases, the stream of dividends is expected to grow at a constant rate. If this is the case, Equation 9-1 may be rewritten as follows:

$$\hat{P}_0 = \frac{D_0(1+g)^1}{(1+r_s)^1} + \frac{D_0(1+g)^2}{(1+r_s)^2} + \cdots + \frac{D_0(1+g)^\infty}{(1+r_s)^\infty}$$

$$= \frac{D_0(1+g)}{r_s - g} = \frac{D_1}{r_s - g} \qquad \text{(9-2)}$$

Constant Growth (Gordon) Model
Used to find the value of a constant growth stock.

The last term of Equation 9-2 is called the **constant growth model,** or the **Gordon model,** after Myron J. Gordon, who did much to develop and popularize it.[4]

9-4a Illustration of a Constant Growth Stock

Assume that Allied Food Products just paid a dividend of $1.15 (that is, $D_0 = \$1.15$). Its stock has a required rate of return, r_s, of 13.4 percent, and investors expect the dividend to grow at a constant 8 percent rate in the future. The estimated dividend one year hence would be $D_1 = \$1.15(1.08) = \$1.24$; D_2 would be $1.34; and the estimated dividend five years hence would be $1.69:

$$D_5 = D_0(1+g)^5 = \$1.15(1.08)^5 = \$1.69$$

We could use this procedure to estimate all future dividends, then use Equation 9-1 to determine the current stock value, $\hat{P}_0$. In other words, we could find each expected future dividend, calculate its present value, and then sum all the present values to find the intrinsic value of the stock.

Such a process would be time consuming, but we can take a short cut—just insert the illustrative data into Equation 9-2 to find the stock's intrinsic value, $23:

$$\hat{P}_0 = \frac{\$1.15(1.08)}{0.134 - 0.08} = \frac{\$1.242}{0.054} = \$23.00$$

Note that a necessary condition for the derivation of Equation 9-2 is that the required rate of return, r_s, be greater than the long-run growth rate, g. *If the equation is used in situations where r_s is not greater than g, the results will be wrong, meaningless, and possibly misleading.*

The concept underlying the valuation process for a constant growth stock is graphed in Figure 9-1. Dividends are growing at the rate g = 8 percent, but because $r_s > g$, the present value of each future dividend is declining. For example, the dividend in Year 1 is $D_1 = D_0(1+g)^1 = \$1.15(1.08) = \$1.242$. However, the present value of this dividend, discounted at 13.4 percent, is $PV(D_1) = \$1.242/(1.134)^1 = \$1.095$. The dividend expected in Year 2 grows to $1.242 (1.08) = \$1.341$, but the present value of this dividend falls to $1.043. Continuing,

---

[4] The last term in Equation 9-2 is derived in the Web/CD Extension of Chapter 5 of Eugene F. Brigham and Phillip R. Daves, *Intermediate Financial Management*, 8th ed. (Mason, OH: Thomson/South-Western, 2004). In essence, Equation 9-2 is the sum of a geometric progression, and the final result is the solution value of the progression.

FIGURE 9-1   *Present Values of Dividends of a Constant Growth Stock where $D_0 = \$1.15$, $g = 8\%$, $r_s = 13.4\%$*

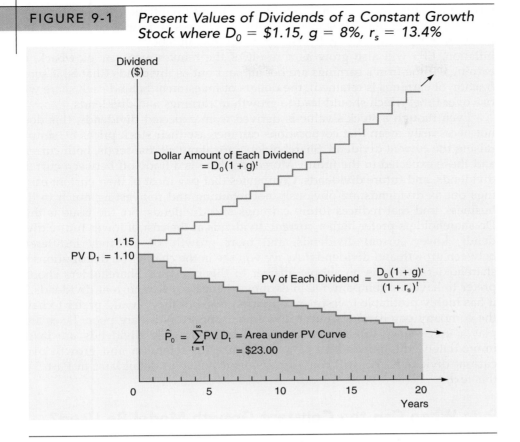

$D_3 = \$1.449$ and $PV(D_3) = \$0.993$, and so on. Thus, the expected dividends are growing, but the present value of each successive dividend is declining, because the dividend growth rate (8 percent) is less than the rate used for discounting the dividends to the present (13.4 percent).

If we summed the present values of each future dividend, this summation would be the value of the stock, $\hat{P}_0$. When g is a constant, this summation is equal to $D_1/(r_s - g)$, as shown in Equation 9-2. Therefore, if we extended the lower step-function curve in Figure 9-1 on out to infinity and added up the present values of each future dividend, the summation would be identical to the value given by Equation 9-2, $23.00.

Note that if the growth rate exceeded the required return, the PV of each future dividend would exceed that of the prior year. If this situation were graphed in Figure 9-1, both step-function curves would be increasing, suggesting an infinitely high stock price. Moreover, the stock price as calculated using Equation 9-2 would be *negative*. Obviously, stock prices can be neither infinite nor negative, and this illustrates why Equation 9-2 cannot be used unless $r_s > g$.

9-4b Dividend and Earnings Growth

Growth in dividends occurs primarily as a result of growth in *earnings per share (EPS)*. Earnings growth, in turn, results from a number of factors, including (1) the amount of earnings the company retains and reinvests, (2) the rate of return the company earns on its equity (ROE), and (3) inflation. Regarding inflation, if output (in units) is stable but both sales prices and input costs rise at the inflation rate, then EPS will also grow at the inflation rate. Even without inflation, EPS will also grow as a result of the reinvestment, or plowback, of earnings. If the firm's earnings are not all paid out as dividends (that is, if some fraction of earnings is retained), the dollars of investment behind each share will rise over time, which should lead to growth in earnings and dividends.

Even though a stock's value is derived from expected dividends, this does not necessarily mean that corporations can increase their stock prices by simply raising the current dividend. Shareholders care about *all* dividends, both current and those expected in the future. Moreover, there is a trade-off between current dividends, and future dividends. Companies that pay most of their current earnings out as dividends are obviously not retaining and reinvesting much in the business, and that reduces future earnings and dividends. So, the issue is this: Do shareholders prefer higher current dividends at the cost of lower future dividends, lower current dividends, and more growth, or are they indifferent between growth and dividends? As we will see in the chapter on distributions to shareholders, there is no simple answer to this question. Shareholders should prefer to have the company retain earnings, hence pay less current dividends, if it has highly profitable investment opportunities, but they should prefer to have the company pay earnings out if investment opportunities are poor. Taxes also play a role—since capital gains are tax deferred while dividends are taxed immediately, this might lead to a preference for retention and growth over current dividends. We will consider dividend policy in detail later in Part 5 of this text.

9-4c When Can the Constant Growth Model Be Used?

The constant growth model is most appropriate for mature companies with a stable history of growth and stable future expectations. Expected growth rates vary somewhat among companies, but dividends for mature firms are often expected to grow in the future at about the same rate as nominal gross domestic product (real GDP plus inflation). On this basis, one might expect the dividends of an average, or "normal," company to grow at a rate of 5 to 8 percent a year.

Note too that Equation 9-2 is sufficiently general to handle the case of a **zero growth stock,** where the dividend is expected to remain constant over time. If $g = 0$, Equation 9-2 reduces to Equation 9-3:

Zero Growth Stock
A common stock whose future dividends are not expected to grow at all; that is, $g = 0$.

$$\hat{P}_0 = \frac{D}{r_s} \qquad \text{(9-3)}$$

This is conceptually the same equation as the one we developed in Chapter 2 for a perpetuity, and it is simply the current dividend divided by the discount rate.

Write out and explain the valuation formula for a constant growth stock.

Explain how the formula for a zero growth stock is related to that for a constant growth stock.

A stock is expected to pay a dividend of $1 at the end of the year. The required rate of return is $r_s = 11\%$. What would the stock's price be if the growth rate were 5 percent? What would the price be if $g = 0\%$? ($16.67; $9.09)

9-5 EXPECTED RATE OF RETURN ON A CONSTANT GROWTH STOCK

We can solve Equation 9-2 for r_s, again using the hat to indicate that we are dealing with an expected rate of return:[5]

$$\text{Expected rate of return} = \text{Expected dividend yield} + \text{Expected growth rate, or capital gains yield}$$

$$\hat{r}_s = \frac{D_1}{P_0} + g \tag{9-4}$$

Thus, if you buy a stock for a price P_0 = $23, and if you expect the stock to pay a dividend D_1 = $1.242 one year from now and to grow at a constant rate g = 8% in the future, then your expected rate of return will be 13.4 percent:

$$\hat{r}_s = \frac{\$1.242}{\$23} + 8\% = 5.4\% + 8\% = 13.4\%$$

In this form, we see that $\hat{r}_s$ is the *expected total return* and that it consists of an *expected dividend yield*, D_1/P_0 = 5.4%, plus an *expected growth rate or capital gains yield*, g = 8%.

Suppose this analysis had been conducted on January 1, 2006, so P_0 = $23 is the January 1, 2006, stock price, and D_1 = $1.242 is the dividend expected at the end of 2006. What is the expected stock price at the end of 2006? We would again apply Equation 9-2, but this time we would use the year-end dividend, $D_2 = D_1(1 + g)$ = $1.242(1.08) = $1.3414:

$$\hat{P}_{12/31/06} = \frac{D_{2007}}{r_s - g} = \frac{\$1.3414}{0.134 - 0.08} = \$24.84$$

Notice that $24.84 is 8 percent greater than P_0, the $23 price on January 1, 2006:

$$\$23(1.08) = \$24.84$$

Thus, we would expect to make a capital gain of $24.84 − $23.00 = $1.84 during 2006, which would provide a capital gains yield of 8 percent:

$$\text{Capital gains yield}_{2006} = \frac{\text{Capital gain}}{\text{Beginning price}} = \frac{\$1.84}{\$23.00} = 0.08 = 8\%$$

We could extend the analysis on out, and in each future year the expected capital gains yield would always equal g, the expected dividend growth rate. For example, the dividend yield in 2007 could be estimated as follows:

$$\text{Dividend yield}_{2007} = \frac{D_{2007}}{\hat{P}_{12/31/06}} = \frac{\$1.3414}{\$24.84} = 0.054 = 5.4\%$$

The dividend yield for 2008 could also be calculated, and again it would be 5.4 percent. Thus, *for a constant growth stock*, the following conditions must hold:

1. The expected dividend yield is a constant.
2. The dividend is expected to grow forever at a constant rate, g.

The popular Motley Fool Web site, http://www.fool.com/school/introductiontovaluation.htm, provides a good description of some of the benefits and drawbacks of a few of the more commonly used valuation procedures.

---

[5] The r_s value in Equation 9-2 is a *required* rate of return, but when we transform to obtain Equation 9-4, we are finding an expected rate of return. Obviously, the transformation requires that $r_s = \hat{r}_s$. This equality holds if the stock market is in equilibrium, a condition that we discussed in Chapter 5.

3. The stock price is expected to grow at this same rate.
4. The expected capital gains yield is also a constant, and it is equal to g.

The term *expected* should be clarified—it means expected in a probabilistic sense, as the "statistically expected" outcome. Thus, when we say that the growth rate is expected to remain constant at 8 percent, we mean that the best prediction for the growth rate in any future year is 8 percent, not that we literally expect the growth rate to be exactly 8 percent in each future year. In this sense, the constant growth assumption is reasonable for many large, mature companies.

What conditions must hold if a stock is to be evaluated using the constant growth model?

What does the term "expected" mean when we say expected growth rate?

Suppose an analyst says that she values GE based on a forecasted growth rate of 6 percent for earnings, dividends, and the stock price. If the growth rate next year turns out to be 5 or 7 percent, would this mean that the analyst's forecast was faulty? Explain.

9-6 VALUING STOCKS EXPECTED TO GROW AT A NONCONSTANT RATE

For many companies, it is not appropriate to assume that dividends will grow at a constant rate because firms typically go through *life cycles* with different growth rates at different parts of the cycle. During their early years, they generally grow much faster than the economy as a whole; then they match the economy's growth; and finally they grow at a slower rate than the economy.[6] Automobile manufacturers in the 1920s, computer software firms such as Microsoft in the 1980s, and wireless firms in the early 2000s are examples of firms in the early part of the cycle; these firms are called **supernormal,** or **nonconstant, growth** firms. Figure 9-2 illustrates nonconstant growth and also compares it with normal growth, zero growth, and negative growth.[7]

Supernormal (Nonconstant) Growth
The part of the firm's life cycle in which it grows much faster than the economy as a whole.

---

[6] The concept of life cycles could be broadened to *product cycle*, which would include both small start-up companies and large companies like Microsoft and Procter & Gamble, which periodically introduce new products that give sales and earnings a boost. We should also mention *business cycles*, which alternately depress and boost sales and profits. The growth rate just after a major new product has been introduced, or just after a firm emerges from the depths of a recession, is likely to be much higher than the "expected long-run average growth rate," which is the proper number for DCF analysis.

[7] A negative growth rate indicates a declining company. A mining company whose profits are falling because of a declining ore body is an example. Someone buying such a company would expect its earnings, and consequently its dividends and stock price, to decline each year, and this would lead to capital losses rather than capital gains. Obviously, a declining company's stock price will be relatively low, and its dividend yield must be high enough to offset the expected capital loss and still produce a competitive total return. Students sometimes argue that they would never be willing to buy a stock whose price was expected to decline. However, if the present value of the expected dividends exceeds the stock price, the stock would still be a good investment that would provide a good return.

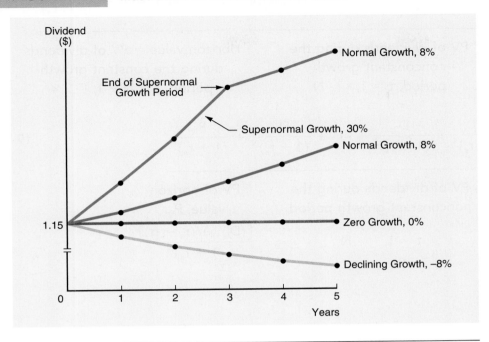

FIGURE 9-2   *Illustrative Dividend Growth Rates*

In the figure, the dividends of the supernormal growth firm are expected to grow at a 30 percent rate for three years, after which the growth rate is expected to fall to 8 percent, the assumed average for the economy. The value of this firm's stock, like any other asset, is the present value of its expected future dividends as determined by Equation 9-1. When D_t is growing at a constant rate, we can simplify Equation 9-1 to $\hat{P}_0 = D_1/(r_s - g)$. In the supernormal case, however, the expected growth rate is not a constant—it declines at the end of the period of supernormal growth.

Because Equation 9-2 requires a constant growth rate, we obviously cannot use it to value stocks that have nonconstant growth. However, assuming that a company currently enjoying supernormal growth will eventually slow down and become a constant growth stock, we can combine Equations 9-1 and 9-2 to form a new formula, Equation 9-5, for valuing it.

First, we assume that the dividend will grow at a nonconstant rate (generally a relatively high rate) for N periods, after which it will grow at a constant rate, g. N is often called the **terminal date,** or **horizon date.** Second, we can use the constant growth formula, Equation 9-2, to determine what the stock's **horizon,** or **terminal, value** will be N periods from today:

$$\text{Horizon value} = \hat{P}_N = \frac{D_{N+1}}{r_s - g}$$

The stock's intrinsic value today, $\hat{P}_0$, is the present value of the dividends during the nonconstant growth period plus the present value of the horizon value:

Terminal Date (Horizon Date)
The date when the growth rate becomes constant. At this date it is no longer necessary to forecast the individual dividends.

Horizon (Terminal) Value
The value at the horizon date of all dividends expected thereafter.

$$\hat{P}_0 = \frac{D_1}{(1 + r_s)^1} + \frac{D_2}{(1 + r_s)^2} + \cdots + \frac{D_N}{(1 + r_s)^N} + \frac{D_{N+1}}{(1 + r_s)^{N+1}} + \cdots + \frac{D_\infty}{(1 + r_s)^\infty}$$

PV of dividends during the
nonconstant growth
period, t = 1, · · · N

Horizon value = PV of dividends
during the constant growth
period, t = N + 1, · · · ∞

$$\hat{P}_0 = \frac{D_1}{(1 + r_s)^1} + \frac{D_2}{(1 + r_s)^2} + \cdots + \frac{D_N}{(1 + r_s)^N} + \frac{\hat{P}_N}{(1 + r_s)^N} \tag{9-5}$$

PV of dividends during the
nonconstant growth period

t = 1, · · · N

PV of horizon
value, $\hat{P}_N$:
$\dfrac{[(D_{N+1})/(r_s - g)]}{(1 + r_s)^N}$

To implement Equation 9-5, we go through the following three steps:

1. Find the PV of each dividend during the period of nonconstant growth and sum them.
2. Find the expected price of the stock at the end of the nonconstant growth period, at which point it has become a constant growth stock so it can be valued with the constant growth model, and discount this price back to the present.
3. Add these two components to find the intrinsic value of the stock, $\hat{P}_0$.

Figure 9-3 can be used to illustrate the process for valuing nonconstant growth stocks. Here we assume the following five facts exist:

> r_s = stockholders' required rate of return = 13.4%. This rate is used to discount the cash flows.
>
> N = years of nonconstant growth = 3.
>
> g_s = rate of growth in both earnings and dividends during the nonconstant growth period = 30%. This rate is shown directly on the time line. (Note: The growth rate during the nonconstant growth period could vary from year to year. Also, there could be several different nonconstant growth periods, for example, 30 percent for three years, then 20 percent for three years, and then a constant 8 percent.)
>
> g_n = rate of normal, constant growth after the nonconstant period = 8%. This rate is also shown on the time line, between Periods 3 and 4.
>
> D_0 = last dividend the company paid = $1.15.

The valuation process as diagrammed in Figure 9-3 is explained in the steps set forth below the time line. The value of the nonconstant growth stock is calculated to be $39.21.

Note that in this example we have assumed a relatively short three-year horizon to keep things simple. When evaluating stocks, most analysts would use a much longer horizon (for example, 10 years) to estimate intrinsic values. This

FIGURE 9-3 *Process for Finding the Value of a Nonconstant Growth Stock*

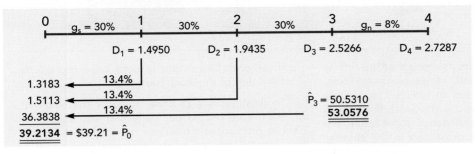

Notes to Figure 9-3:

Step 1. Calculate the dividends expected at the end of each year during the nonconstant growth period. Calculate the first dividend, $D_1 = D_0(1 + g_s) = \$1.15(1.30) = \$1.4950$. Here g_s is the growth rate during the three-year nonconstant growth period, 30 percent. Show the $1.4950 on the time line as the cash flow at Time 1. Then, calculate $D_2 = D_1(1 + g_s) = \$1.4950(1.30) = \$1.9435$, and then $D_3 = D_2(1 + g_s) = \$1.9435(1.30) = \$2.5266$. Show these values on the time line as the cash flows at Time 2 and Time 3. Note that D_0 is used only to calculate D_1.

Step 2. The price of the stock is the PV of dividends from Time 1 to infinity, so in theory we could project each future dividend, with the normal growth rate, $g_n = 8\%$, used to calculate D_4 and subsequent dividends. However, we know that after D_3 has been paid, which is at Time 3, the stock becomes a constant growth stock. Therefore, we can use the constant growth formula to find $\hat{P}_3$, which is the PV of the dividends from Time 4 to infinity as evaluated at Time 3.

First, we determine $D_4 = \$2.5266(1.08) = \$2.7287$ for use in the formula, and then we calculate $\hat{P}_3$ as follows:

$$\hat{P}_3 = \frac{D_4}{r_s - g_n} = \frac{\$2.7287}{0.134 - 0.08} = \$50.5310$$

We show this $50.5310 on the time line as a second cash flow at Time 3. The $50.5310 is a Time 3 cash flow in the sense that the stockholder could sell it for $50.5310 at Time 3 and also in the sense that $50.5310 is the present value of the dividend cash flows from Time 4 to infinity. Note that the total cash flow at Time 3 consists of the sum of $D_3 + \hat{P}_3 = \$2.5266 + \$50.5310 = \$53.0576$.

Step 3. Now that the cash flows have been placed on the time line, we can discount each cash flow at the required rate of return, $r_s = 13.4\%$. We could discount each cash flow by dividing by $(1.134)^t$, where $t = 1$ for Time 1, $t = 2$ for Time 2, and $t = 3$ for Time 3. This produces the PVs shown to the left below the time line, and the sum of the PVs is the value of the nonconstant growth stock, $39.21.

With a financial calculator, you can find the PV of the cash flows as shown on the time line with the cash flow (CFLO) register of your calculator. Enter 0 for CF_0 because you receive no cash flow at Time 0, $CF_1 = 1.495$, $CF_2 = 1.9435$, and $CF_3 = 2.5266 + 50.5310 = 53.0576$. Then enter I/YR = 13.4, and press the NPV key to find the value of the stock, $39.21.

requires a few more calculations, but analysts use spreadsheets so the arithmetic is not a problem. In practice, the real limitation is obtaining reliable forecasts for future growth.

Explain how one would find the value of a nonconstant growth stock.

Explain what is meant by "terminal (horizon) date" and "horizon (terminal) value."

Evaluating Stocks That Don't Pay Dividends

The dividend growth model assumes that the firm is currently paying a dividend. However, many firms, even highly profitable ones, including Cisco, Dell, and Apple, have never paid a dividend. If a firm is expected to begin paying dividends in the future, we can modify the equations presented in the chapter and use them to determine the value of the stock.

A new business often expects to have low sales during its first few years of operation as it develops its product. Then, if the product catches on, sales will grow rapidly for several years. Sales growth brings with it the need for additional assets—a firm cannot increase sales without also increasing its assets, and asset growth requires an increase in liability and/or equity accounts. Small firms can generally obtain some bank credit, but they must maintain a reasonable balance between debt and equity. Thus, additional bank borrowings require increases in equity, and getting the equity capital needed to support growth can be difficult for small firms. They have limited access to the capital markets, and, even when they can sell common stock, their owners are reluctant to do so for fear of losing voting control. Therefore, the best source of equity for most small businesses is retained earnings, and for this reason most small firms pay no dividends during their rapid growth years. Eventually, though, successful small firms do pay dividends, and those dividends generally grow rapidly at first but slow down to a sustainable constant rate once the firm reaches maturity.

If a firm currently pays no dividends but is expected to pay dividends in the future, the value of its stock can be found as follows:

1. Estimate when dividends will be paid, the amount of the first dividend, the growth rate during the supernormal growth period, the length of the supernormal period, the long-run (constant) growth rate, and the rate of return required by investors.
2. Use the constant growth model to determine the price of the stock after the firm reaches a stable growth situation.
3. Set out on a time line the cash flows (dividends during the supernormal growth period and the stock price once the constant growth state is reached), and then find the present value of

these cash flows. That present value represents the value of the stock today.

To illustrate this process, consider the situation for MarvelLure Inc., a company that was set up in 2004 to produce and market a new high-tech fishing lure. MarvelLure's sales are currently growing at a rate of 200 percent per year. The company expects to experience a high but declining rate of growth in sales and earnings during the next 10 years, after which analysts estimate that it will grow at a steady 10 percent per year. The firm's management has announced that it will pay no dividends for five years, but if earnings materialize as forecasted, it will pay a dividend of $0.20 per share at the end of Year 6, $0.30 in Year 7, $0.40 in Year 8, $0.45 in Year 9, and $0.50 in Year 10. After Year 10, current plans are to increase dividends by 10 percent per year.

MarvelLure's investment bankers estimate that investors require a 15 percent return on similar stocks. Therefore, we find the value of a share of MarvelLure's stock as follows:

$$P_0 = \frac{\$0}{(1.15)^1} + \cdots + \frac{\$0}{(1.15)^5} + \frac{\$0.20}{(1.15)^6}$$

$$+ \frac{\$0.30}{(1.15)^7} + \frac{\$0.40}{(1.15)^8}$$

$$+ \frac{\$0.45}{(1.15)^9} + \frac{\$0.50}{(1.15)^{10}}$$

$$+ \left(\frac{\$0.50(1.10)}{0.15 - 0.10} \right) \left(\frac{1}{(1.15)^{10}} \right)$$

$$= \$3.30$$

The last term finds the expected price of the stock in Year 10 and then finds the present value of that price. Thus, we see that the dividend growth model can be applied to firms that currently pay no dividends, provided we can estimate future dividends with a fair degree of confidence. However, in many cases we can have more confidence in the forecasts of free cash flows, and in these situations it is better to use the corporate valuation model as discussed in the next section.

9-7 VALUING THE ENTIRE CORPORATION[8]

Thus far we have discussed the discounted dividend approach to valuing a firm's common stock. This procedure is widely used, but it is based on the assumption that the analyst can forecast future dividends reasonably well. This is often true for mature companies that have a history of steady dividend payments. The model can be applied to firms that are not paying dividends, but as we show in the preceding box, this requires forecasting the time at which the firm will commence paying dividends, the amount of the initial dividend, and the growth rate of dividends once they commence. This suggests that a reliable dividend forecast must be based on forecasts of the firm's future sales, costs, and capital requirements.

An alternative approach, the **total company, or corporate valuation, model,** can be used to value firms in situations where future dividends are not easily predictable. Consider a start-up formed to develop and market a new product. Such companies generally expect to have low sales during their first few years as they develop and begin to market their products. Then, if the products catch on, sales will grow rapidly for several years. For example, eBay's sales were $48 million in 1998, the year it first went public, but in 1999 sales grew by nearly 400 percent and they hit $4.5 billion in 2005. Obviously, eBay has been more successful than most new businesses, but growth rates of 100, 500, or even 1,000 percent are not uncommon during a firm's early years.

Growing sales require additional assets—and eBay could not have grown without increasing its assets. Over the five-year period 1999–2004, its sales grew by 658 percent, and that growth required a 583 percent increase in assets. The increase in assets had to be financed, so eBay's liability and equity accounts also grew by 583 percent as was required to keep the balance sheet in balance.

Small firms can generally borrow some funds from their bank, but banks insist that the debt/equity ratio be kept at a reasonable level, which means that equity must also be raised. However, small firms have little or no access to the stock market, so they generally obtain new equity by retaining earnings, which means that they pay little or no dividends during their rapid growth years. Eventually, though, most successful firms do pay dividends, and those dividends grow rapidly at first but then slow down as the firm approaches maturity. It is difficult to forecast the future dividend stream of any firm that is expected to go through such a transition, and even in the case of large firms such as Cisco, Dell, and Apple that have never paid a dividend, it's hard to forecast when dividends will commence and how large they will be.

Another problem arises when it is necessary to find the value of a division as opposed to an entire firm. For example, in 2005 Kerr-McGee, a large oil and chemical company, decided to sell its chemical division. The parent company had been paying dividends for many years, so the discounted dividend model could be applied to it. However, the chemical division had no history of dividends, and it would likely be bought by another chemical company and folded into the purchaser's other operations. How could Kerr-McGee's chemical division be valued? The answer is, "Use the corporate valuation model as discussed in this section."

Total Company or Corporate Valuation Model
A valuation model used as an alternative to the dividend growth model to determine the value of a firm, especially one with no history of dividends or a division of a larger firm. This model first calculates the firm's free cash flows and then finds their present value to determine the firm's value.

---

[8] The corporate valuation model presented in this section is widely used by analysts, and it is in many respects superior to the discounted dividend model. However, it is rather involved as it requires the estimation of sales, costs, and cash flows on out into the future before beginning the discounting process. Therefore, some instructors may prefer to omit Section 9.7 and skip to Section 9.8 in the introductory course.

9-7a The Corporate Valuation Model

In Chapter 3 we explained that a firm's value is determined by its ability to generate cash flow, both now and in the future. Therefore, market value can be expressed as follows:

$$\text{Market value} = V_{\text{Company}} = \text{PV of expected future free cash flows of company}$$

$$= \frac{FCF_1}{(1 + WACC)^1} + \frac{FCF_2}{(1 + WACC)^2} + \cdots + \frac{FCF_\infty}{(1 + WACC)^\infty} \quad \textbf{(9-6)}$$

Here FCF_t is the free cash flow in Year t and WACC is the weighted average cost of the firm's capital.

Recall from Chapter 3 that free cash flow is the cash inflow during a given year less the cash needed to finance required asset additions. Inflows are equal to net after-tax operating income (also called NOPAT) plus noncash charges (depreciation and amortization), which were deducted when calculating NOPAT, while the required asset additions are the capital expenditures plus the net addition to working capital. This was discussed in Chapter 3, where we developed the following equation:

$$FCF = \left[EBIT(1 - T) + \begin{matrix} \text{Depreciation} \\ \text{and amortization} \end{matrix} \right] - \left[\begin{matrix} \text{Capital} \\ \text{expenditures} \end{matrix} + \begin{matrix} \Delta \text{ Net} \\ \text{operating} \\ \text{working} \\ \text{capital} \end{matrix} \right]$$

Depreciation and amortization can be shifted from the first bracketed term to the second term (and given a minus sign). Then the first term becomes EBIT(1 − T), also called *NOPAT*, and the second term becomes the *net (rather than gross) new investment in operating capital*. The result is Equation 9-7, which shows that free cash flow is equal to after-tax operating income (NOPAT) less the net new investment in operating capital:

$$FCF = NOPAT - \text{Net new investment in operating capital} \quad \textbf{(9-7)}$$

Turning to the discount rate, WACC, note first that free cash flow is the cash generated *before making any payments to any investors—the common stockholders, preferred stockholders, and bondholders—and that cash flow must provide a return to all these investors.* Each of these investor groups has a required rate of return that depends on the risk of the particular security, and as we discuss in Chapter 10, the average of those required returns is the WACC.

With this background, we can summarize the steps used to implement the corporate valuation model. This type of analysis is performed both internally by the firm's financial staff and also by external security analysts, who are generally experts on the industry and quite familiar with the firm's history and future plans. For illustrative purposes, we discuss an analysis conducted by Susan Buskirk, senior food analyst for the investment banking firm Morton Staley and Company. Her analysis is summarized in Table 9-1, which was reproduced from the chapter *Excel* model.

- Based on Allied's history and her knowledge of the firm's business plan, Susan estimated sales, costs, and cash flows on an annual basis for five years. Growth will vary during those years, but she assumes that things will stabilize and growth will be constant after the fifth year. She could have projected variability for more years if she thought it would take longer to reach a steady-state, constant growth situation.

| TABLE 9-1 | *Allied Food Products: Free Cash Flow Valuation* |

	A	B	C	D	E	F	G	H
133	Part 1. Key Inputs					**Forecasted Years**		
134				**2006**	**2007**	**2008**	**2009**	**2010**
135	Sales growth rate			10.0%	9.0%	9.0%	9.0%	8.0%
136	Operating costs as a % of sales			87.0%	87.0%	86.0%	85.0%	85.0%
137	Growth in operating capital			8.0%	8.0%	8.0%	8.0%	8.0%
138	Depr'n as a % of operating capital			6.0%	8.0%	7.0%	7.0%	7.0%
139	Tax rate			40%				
140	WACC			10%				
141	Long-run FCF growth, g_{LR}			6.0%				
142								
143	Part 2. Forecast of Cash Flows During Period of Nonconstant Growth							
144			**Historical**			**Forecasted Years**		
145			**2005**	**2006**	**2007**	**2008**	**2009**	**2010**
146								
147	Sales		$3,000.0	$3,300.0	$3,597.0	$3,920.7	$4,273.6	$4,615.5
148	Operating costs		2,616.2	2,871.0	3,129.4	3,371.8	3,632.6	3,923.2
149	Depreciation		100.0	116.6	168.0	158.7	171.4	185.1
150	EBIT		$283.8	$312.4	$299.6	$390.2	$469.6	$507.2
151	NOPAT = EBIT x (1-T)		$170.3	$187.4	$179.8	$234.1	$281.8	$304.3
152								
153	Total operating capital		$1,800.0	$1,944.0	$2,099.5	$2,267.5	$2,448.9	$2,644.8
154	Net new operating cap		280	144.0	155.5	168.0	181.4	195.9
155	Free Cash Flow, FCF		−$109.7	$43.4	$24.3	$66.1	$100.4	$108.4
156	PV of FCFs		N.A.	$39.5	$20.1	$49.7	$68.6	$67.3
157								
158	Part 3. Terminal Value and Intrinsic Value Estimation							
159	Estimated Value at the Horizon, 2010							
160	Free Cash Flow (2011)			$114.9		$FCF_{2010}(1+g_{LR})$		
161	Terminal Value at 2010, TV			$2,872.7		$TV_{2010} = \dfrac{FCF_{2011}}{WACC - g}$		
162	PV of the 2010 TV			$1,783.7		$TV / (1+WACC)^N$		
163								
164	Calculation of Firm's Intrinsic Value							
165	Sum of PVs of FCFs, 2006-2010			$245.1				
166	PV of 2010 TV			$1,783.7				
167	Total corporate value			$2,028.8				
168	Less: market value of debt and pfd			$860.0				
169	Intrinsic value of common equity			$1,168.8				
170	Shares outstanding (millions)			50.0				
171								
172	Intrinsic Value Per Share			$23.38				

- Susan next calculated the expected free cash flows (FCFs) for each of the five nonconstant growth years, and she found the PV of those cash flows, discounted at the WACC.
- After Year 5 she assumed that FCF growth would be constant, hence the constant growth model could be used to find Allied's total market value at Year 5. This "horizon, or terminal, value" is the sum of the PVs of the FCFs from Year 6 on out into the future, discounted back to Year 5 at the WACC.
- Next, she discounted the Year 5 terminal value back to the present to find its PV at Year 0.
- She then summed all the PVs, the annual cash flows during the nonconstant period plus the PV of the horizon value, to find the firm's estimated total market value.
- She then subtracted the value of the debt and preferred stock to find the value of the common equity.

Other Approaches to Valuing Common Stocks

While the dividend growth and the corporate value models presented in this chapter are the most widely used methods for valuing common stocks, they are by no means the only approaches. Analysts often use a number of different techniques to value stocks. Two of these alternative approaches are described here.

The P/E Multiple Approach

Investors have long looked for simple rules of thumb to determine whether a stock is fairly valued. One such approach is to look at the stock's price-to-earnings (P/E) ratio. Recall from Chapter 4 that a company's P/E ratio shows how much investors are willing to pay for each dollar of reported earnings. As a starting point, you might conclude that stocks with low P/E ratios are undervalued, since their price is "low" given current earnings, while stocks with high P/E ratios are overvalued.

Unfortunately, however, valuing stocks is not that simple. We should not expect all companies to have the same P/E ratio. P/E ratios are affected by risk—investors discount the earnings of riskier stocks at a higher rate. Thus, all else equal, riskier stocks should have lower P/E ratios. In addition, when you buy a stock, you not only have a claim on current earn-ings—you also have a claim on all future earnings. All else equal, companies with stronger growth opportunities will generate larger future earnings and thus should trade at higher P/E ratios. Therefore, eBay is not necessarily overvalued just because its P/E ratio is 52.8 at a time when the median firm has a P/E of 20.1. Investors believe that eBay's growth potential is well above average. Whether the stock's future prospects justify its P/E ratio remains to be seen, but in and of itself a high P/E ratio does not mean that a stock is overvalued.

Nevertheless, P/E ratios can provide a useful starting point in stock valuation. If a stock's P/E ratio is well above its industry average, and if the stock's growth potential and risk are similar to other firms in the industry, this may indicate that the stock's price is too high. Likewise, if a company's P/E ratio falls well below its historical average, this may signal that the stock is undervalued—particularly if the company's growth prospects and risk are unchanged, and if the overall P/E for the market has remained constant or increased.

One obvious drawback of the P/E approach is that it depends on reported accounting earnings. For this reason, some analysts choose to rely on other multiples to value stocks. For example, some analysts

- Finally, she divided the equity value by the number of shares outstanding, and the result was her estimate of Allied's intrinsic value per share. This value was quite close to the stock's market price, so she concluded that Allied's stock is priced at its equilibrium level. Consequently, she issued a "Hold" rec-ommendation on the stock. If the estimated intrinsic value had been signifi-cantly below the market price, she would have issued a "Sell" recommenda-tion, and had it been well above, she would have called the stock a "Buy."

9-7b Comparing the Total Company and Dividend Growth Models

Analysts use both the discounted dividend model and the corporate model when valuing mature, dividend-paying firms, and they generally use the corpo-rate model when valuing firms that do not pay dividends and divisions. In prin-ciple, we should find the same intrinsic value using either model, but differences are often observed. When a conflict exists, then the assumptions embedded in the corporate model can be reexamined, and once the analyst is convinced they are reasonable, then the results of that model are used. In our Allied example, the estimates were extremely close—the dividend growth model predicted a price of $23.00 per share versus $23.38 using the total company model, and both are essentially equal to Allied's actual $23 price.

look at a company's price-to-cash-flow ratio, while others look at the price-to-sales ratio.

The EVA Approach

In recent years, analysts have looked for more rigorous alternatives to the dividend growth model. More than a quarter of all stocks listed on the NYSE pay no dividends. This proportion is even higher on Nasdaq. While the dividend growth model can still be used for these stocks (see box, "Evaluating Stocks That Don't Pay Dividends"), this approach requires that analysts forecast when the stock will begin paying dividends, what the dividend will be once it is established, and the future dividend growth rate. In many cases, these forecasts contain considerable errors.

An alternative approach is based on the concept of Economic Value Added (EVA), which we discussed back in Chapter 3. Also, recall from the box in Chapter 4 entitled, "EVA and ROE" that EVA can be written as

$$\text{(Equity capital)(ROE} - \text{Cost of equity capital)}$$

This equation suggests that companies can increase their EVA by investing in projects that provide shareholders with returns that are above their cost of capital, which is the return they could expect to earn on alternative investments with the same level of risk. When you buy stock in a company, you receive more than just the book value of equity—you also receive a claim on all future value that is created by the firm's managers (the present value of all future EVAs). It follows that a company's market value of equity can be written as

$$\begin{array}{ccc} \text{Market value} \\ \text{of equity} \end{array} = \begin{array}{c} \text{Book} \\ \text{value} \end{array} + \begin{array}{c} \text{PV of all} \\ \text{future EVAs} \end{array}$$

We can find the "fundamental" value of the stock, P_0, by simply dividing the above expression by the number of shares outstanding.

As is the case with the dividend growth model, we can simplify the above expression by assuming that at some point in time annual EVA becomes a perpetuity, or grows at some constant rate over time.[a]

[a] What we have presented here is a simplified version of what is often referred to as the Edwards-Bell-Ohlson (EBO) model. For a more complete description of this technique and an excellent summary of how it can be used in practice, take a look at the article "Measuring Wealth," by Charles M. C. Lee, in *CA Magazine*, April 1996, pp. 32–37.

In practice, intrinsic value estimates based on the two models normally deviate both from one another and from actual stock prices, leading different analysts to reach different conclusions about the attractiveness of a given stock. The better the analyst, the more often his or her valuations will turn out to be correct, but no one can make perfect predictions because too many things can change randomly and unpredictably in the future. Given all this, does it matter whether you use the total company model or the dividend growth model to value stocks? We would argue that it does. If we had to value, say, 100 mature companies whose dividends were expected to grow steadily in the future, we would probably use the dividend growth model. Here we would only need to estimate the growth rate in dividends, not the entire set of pro forma financial statements, hence it would be more feasible to use the dividend model.

However, if we were studying just one or a few companies, especially companies still in the high-growth stage of their life cycles, we would want to project future financial statements before estimating future dividends. Then, because we would already have projected future financial statements, we would go ahead and apply the total company model. Intel, which pays a quarterly dividend of 8 cents versus quarterly earnings of about $1.24, is an example of a company where either model could be used, but we think the corporate model would be better.

Now suppose you were trying to estimate the value of a company that has never paid a dividend, such as eBay, or a new firm that is about to go public, or

Kerr-McGee's chemical division that it plans to sell. In all of these situations, you would be much better off using the corporate valuation model. Actually, even if a company is paying steady dividends, much can be learned from the corporate valuation model, so analysts today use it for all types of valuations. The process of projecting future financial statements can reveal a great deal about the company's operations and financing needs. Also, such an analysis can provide insights into actions that might be taken to increase the company's value, and for this reason it is integral to the planning and forecasting process, as we discuss in a later chapter.

Write out the equation for free cash flows, and explain it.

Why might someone use the corporate valuation model even for companies that have a history of paying dividends?

What steps are taken to find a stock price as based on the firm's total value?

Why might the calculated intrinsic stock value differ from the stock's current market price? Which would be "correct," and what does "correct" mean?

9-8 STOCK MARKET EQUILIBRIUM

Recall that r_X, the required return on Stock X, can be found using the Security Market Line (SML) equation from the Capital Asset Pricing Model (CAPM) as discussed back in Chapter 8:

$$r_X = r_{RF} + (r_M - r_{RF})b_X = r_{RF} + (RP_M)b_X$$

If the risk-free rate is 6 percent, the market risk premium is 5 percent, and Stock X has a beta of 2, then the marginal investor would require a return of 16 percent on the stock:

$$r_X = 6\% + (5\%)2.0$$
$$= 16\%$$

This 16 percent required return is shown as the point on the SML in Figure 9-4 associated with beta = 2.0.

Marginal Investor
A representative investor whose actions reflect the beliefs of those people who are currently trading a stock. It is the marginal investor who determines a stock's price.

A **marginal investor** will buy Stock X if its expected return is more than 16 percent, will sell it if the expected return is less than 16 percent, and will be indifferent, hence will hold but not buy or sell, if the expected return is exactly 16 percent. Now suppose the investor's portfolio contains Stock X, and he or she analyzes its prospects and concludes that its earnings, dividends, and price can be expected to grow at a constant rate of 5 percent per year. The last dividend was $D_0 = \$2.8571$, so the next expected dividend is

$$D_1 = \$2.8571(1.05) = \$3$$

The investor observes that the present price of the stock, P_0, is $30. Should he or she buy more of Stock X, sell the stock, or maintain the present position?

The investor can calculate Stock X's *expected rate of return* as follows:

$$\hat{r}_X = \frac{D_1}{P_0} + g = \frac{\$3}{\$30} + 5\% = 15\%$$

FIGURE 9-4   *Expected and Required Returns on Stock X*

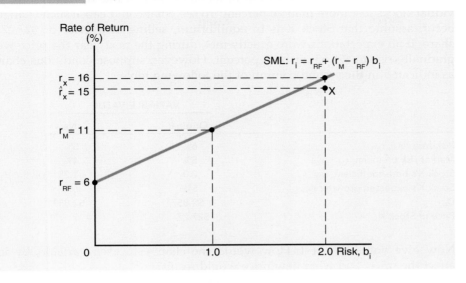

Equilibrium
The condition under which the expected return on a security is just equal to its required return, r̂ = r. Also, P̂ = P₀, and the price is stable.

This value is plotted on Figure 9-4 as Point X, which is below the SML. Because the expected rate of return is less than the required return, he or she, and many other investors, would want to sell the stock. However, few people would want to buy at the $30 price, so the present owners would be unable to find buyers unless they cut the price of the stock. Thus, the price would decline, and the decline would continue until the price hit $27.27. At that point the stock would be in **equilibrium,** defined as the price at which the expected rate of return, 16 percent, is equal to the required rate of return:

$$\hat{r}_X = \frac{\$3}{\$27.27} + 5\% = 11\% + 5\% = 16\% = r_X$$

Had the stock initially sold for less than $27.27, say, $25, events would have been reversed. Investors would have wanted to purchase the stock because its expected rate of return would have exceeded its required rate of return, buy orders would have come in, and the stock's price would be driven up to $27.27.

To summarize, in equilibrium two related conditions must hold:

1. A stock's expected rate of return as seen by the marginal investor must equal its required rate of return: $\hat{r}_i = r_i$.
2. The actual market price of the stock must equal its intrinsic value as estimated by the marginal investor: $P_0 = \hat{P}_0$.

Of course, some individual investors may believe that $\hat{r}_i > r_i$ and $\hat{P}_0 > P_0$, hence they would invest most of their funds in the stock, while other investors might have an opposite view and thus sell all of their shares. However, investors at the margin establish the actual market price, and for these investors, we must have $\hat{r}_i = r_i$ and $\hat{P}_0 = P_0$. If these conditions do not hold, trading will occur until they do.

9-8a Changes in Equilibrium Stock Prices

Stock prices are not constant—they undergo violent changes at times. For example, on October 27, 1997, the Dow Jones Industrials fell 554 points, a 7.18 percent drop in value. Even worse, on October 19, 1987, the Dow lost 508 points, causing an average stock to lose 23 percent of its value on that one day, and some individual stocks lost more than 70 percent. To see what could cause such changes to occur, assume that Stock X is in equilibrium, selling at a price of $27.27 per share. If all expectations were exactly met, during the next year the price would gradually rise to $28.63, or by 5 percent. However, suppose conditions changed as indicated in the second column of the following table:

	VARIABLE VALUE	
	Original	New
Risk-free rate, r_{RF}	6%	5%
Market risk premium, $r_M - r_{RF}$	5%	4%
Stock X's beta coefficient, b_X	2.0	1.25
Stock X's expected growth rate, g_X	5%	6%
D_0	$2.8571	$2.8571
Price of Stock X	$27.27	?

Now give yourself a test: How would the change in each variable, by itself, affect the price, and what new price would result?

Every change, taken alone, would lead to an *increase* in the price. The first three changes together all lower r_X, which declines from 16 to 10 percent:

$$\text{Original } r_X = 6\% + 5\%(2.0) = 16\%$$

$$\text{New } r_X = 5\% + 4\%(1.25) = 10\%$$

Using these values, together with the new g, we find that $\hat{P}_0$ rises from $27.27 to $75.71, or by 178 percent:[9]

$$\text{Original } \hat{P}_0 = \frac{\$2.8571(1.05)}{0.16 - 0.05} = \frac{\$3}{0.11} = \$27.27$$

$$\text{New } \hat{P}_0 = \frac{\$2.8571(1.06)}{0.10 - 0.06} = \frac{\$3.0285}{0.04} = \$75.71$$

Note too that at the new price, the expected and required rates of return will be equal:[10]

$$\hat{r}_X = \frac{\$3.0285}{\$75.71} + 6\% = 10\% = r_X$$

Evidence suggests that stocks, especially those of large companies, adjust rapidly when their fundamental positions change. Such stocks are followed closely by a number of security analysts, so as soon as things change, so does the stock price. Consequently, equilibrium ordinarily exists for any given stock, and required and expected returns are generally close to equal. Stock prices certainly

---

[9] A price change of this magnitude is by no means rare. The prices of *many* stocks double or halve during a year. For example, during 2004, Starbucks Corporation, which operates a chain of retail stores that sell whole bean coffees, increased in value by 88.1 percent. Novellus Systems, a semiconductor equipment manufacturer, fell by 33.3 percent.

[10] It should be obvious by now that *actual realized* rates of return are not necessarily equal to expected and required returns. Thus, an investor might have expected to receive a return of 15 percent if he or she had bought Novellus or Starbucks stock in 2004, but, after the fact, the realized return on Starbucks was far above 15 percent, whereas that on Novellus was far below.

change, sometimes violently and rapidly, but this simply reflects changing conditions and expectations. There are, of course, times when a stock will continue to react for several months to unfolding favorable or unfavorable developments. However, this does not signify a long adjustment period; rather, it simply indicates that as more new information about the situation becomes available, the market adjusts to it.

For a stock to be in equilibrium, what two conditions must hold?

If a stock is not in equilibrium, explain how financial markets adjust to bring it into equilibrium.

9-9 INVESTING IN INTERNATIONAL STOCKS

As noted in Chapter 8, the U.S. stock market amounts to only 40 percent of the world stock market, and as a result many U.S. investors hold at least some foreign stock. Analysts have long touted the benefits of investing overseas, arguing that foreign stocks both improve diversification and provide good growth opportunities. For example, after the U.S. stock market rose an average of 17.5 percent a year during the 1980s, many analysts thought that the U.S. market in the 1990s was due for a correction, and they suggested that investors should increase their holdings of foreign stocks.

To the surprise of many, however, U.S. stocks outperformed foreign stocks in the 1990s—they gained about 15 percent a year versus only 3 percent for foreign stocks. However, the Dow Jones STOXX Index (which tracks 600 European companies) outperformed the S&P 500 from 2002 through 2004. Table 9-2 shows how stocks in different countries performed in 2004. Column 2 indicates how stocks in each country performed in terms of the U.S. dollar, while Column 3 shows how the country's stocks performed in terms of its local currency. For example, in 2004 Brazilian stocks rose by 25.12 percent, but the Brazilian real increased 8.87 percent versus the U.S. dollar. Therefore, if U.S. investors had bought Brazilian stocks, they would have made 25.12 percent in Brazilian real terms, but those Brazilian reals would have bought 8.87 percent more U.S. dollars, so the effective return would have been 36.22 percent. Thus, the results of foreign investments depend in part on what happens to the exchange rate. Indeed, when you invest overseas, you are making two bets: (1) that foreign stocks will increase in their local markets, and (2) that the currencies in which you will be paid will rise relative to the dollar. For Brazil and most of the other countries shown in Table 9-2, both of these situations occurred during 2004.

Although U.S. stocks have generally outperformed foreign stocks in recent years, this by no means suggests that investors should avoid foreign stocks. Holding some foreign investments still improves diversification, and it is inevitable that there will be years when foreign stocks outperform domestic stocks, such as the period from 2002–2004. When this occurs, U.S. investors will be glad they put some of their money into overseas markets.

What are the key benefits of adding foreign stocks to a portfolio?

When a U.S. investor purchases foreign stocks, what two things is he or she hoping will happen?

TABLE 9-2	*Dow Jones Global Stock Indexes in 2004 (Ranked by Performance in U.S.-Dollar Terms)*	

Country	U.S. Dollars	Local Currency
Austria	+67.96%	+55.61%
South Africa	+52.17	+28.12
Mexico	+46.53	+45.45
Norway	+46.47	+32.96
Belgium	+43.07	+32.55
Greece	+40.02	+29.72
Ireland	+37.91	+27.77
Brazil	+36.22	+25.12
Sweden	+33.50	+23.15
Indonesia	+31.84	+45.30
Philippines	+30.09	+31.46
New Zealand	+30.03	+17.87
Denmark	+28.75	+19.01
Australia	+28.69	+23.38
Italy	+27.59	+18.21
Spain	+26.07	+16.80
Chile	+25.59	+17.68
South Korea	+23.99	+7.63
Canada	+21.98	+12.61
Portugal	+21.24	+12.32
Singapore	+19.09	+14.49
Hong Kong	+17.99	+18.13
France	+17.07	+8.47
United Kingdom	+16.93	+8.92
Japan	+16.62	+11.27
Germany	+14.29	+5.89
Switzerland	+14.18	+4.78
Netherlands	+11.84	+3.62
Malaysia	+11.11	+11.12
United States	+10.16	+10.16
Taiwan	+10.03	+2.68
Finland	+5.84	−1.94
Thailand	−8.77	−10.55
Venezuela	−18.83	+31.12
World	+14.47	—
World ex. U.S.	+19.23	—

Source: Craig Karmin, "Currency Effect Enhances Overseas Returns," *The Wall Street Journal,* January 3, 2005, p. R6.

9-10 PREFERRED STOCK

Preferred stock is a *hybrid*—it is similar to bonds in some respects and to common stock in others. This hybrid nature becomes apparent when we try to classify preferred in relation to bonds and common stock. Like bonds, preferred stock has a par value and a fixed dividend that must be paid before dividends can be paid on the common stock. However, the directors can omit (or "pass") the preferred dividend without throwing the company into bankruptcy. So, although preferred stock calls for a fixed payment like bonds, not making the payment will not lead to bankruptcy.

As noted earlier, a preferred stock entitles its owners to regular, fixed dividend payments. If the payments last forever, the issue is a *perpetuity* whose value, V_p, is found as follows:

$$V_p = \frac{D_p}{r_p} \qquad (9\text{-}8)$$

V_p is the value of the preferred stock, D_p is the preferred dividend, and r_p is the required rate of return on the preferred. Allied Food has no preferred outstanding, but suppose it did, and this stock paid a dividend of $10 per year. If its required return were 10.3 percent, then the preferred's value would be $97.09, found as follows:

$$V_p = \frac{\$10.00}{0.103} = \$97.09$$

In equilibrium, the expected return, $\hat{r}_p$, must be equal to the required return, r_p. Thus, if we know the preferred's current price and dividend, we can solve for the expected rate of return as follows:

$$\hat{r}_p = \frac{D_p}{V_p} \qquad (9\text{-}8a)$$

Some preferreds have a stated maturity, often 50 years. Assume that our illustrative preferred matured in 50 years, paid a $10 annual dividend, and had a required return of 8 percent. We could then find its price as follows: Enter N = 50, I/YR = 8, PMT = 10, and FV = 100. Then press PV to find the price, V_p = $124.47. If r_p = 10 percent, change I/YR to 10, in which case V_p = PV = $100. If you know the price of a share of preferred stock, you can solve for I/YR to find the expected rate of return, $\hat{r}_p$.

Explain the following statement: "Preferred stock is a hybrid security."

Is the equation used to value preferred stock more like the one used to evaluate a bond or the one used to evaluate a "normal," constant growth common stock? Explain.

GLOBAL PERSPECTIVES

Investing in Emerging Markets

Given the possibilities of better diversification and higher returns, U.S. investors have been putting more and more money into foreign stocks. While most investors limit their foreign holdings to developed countries such as Japan, Germany, Canada, and the United Kingdom, some have broadened their portfolios to include emerging markets such as South Korea, Mexico, Singapore, Taiwan, and Russia.

Emerging markets provide opportunities for larger returns, but they also entail greater risks. For example, Russian stocks rose more than 150 percent in the first half of 1996, as it became apparent that Boris Yeltsin would be reelected president. By contrast, if you had invested in Taiwanese stocks, you would have lost 30 percent in 1995—a year in which most stock markets performed extremely well. Rapidly declining currency values caused many Asian markets to fall by more than 30 percent in 1997; however, more recently most Asian markets have recovered, and they ended 2004 on a positive note. Factors that helped these markets rise included peaceful elections, inflows of foreign capital, economic growth, and the positive expectations for China's economy. During 2004, only Thai and Chinese stocks in the Asian region posted negative returns.

Stocks in emerging markets are intriguing for two reasons. First, developing nations have the greatest potential for growth. Second, while stock returns in developed countries often move in sync with one another, stocks in emerging markets generally march to their own drummers. Therefore, the correlations between U.S. stocks and those in emerging markets are generally lower than between U.S. stocks and those of other developed countries. Thus, correlations suggest that emerging markets improve the diversification of U.S. investors' portfolios. (Recall from Chapter 8 that the lower the correlation, the greater the benefit of diversification.)

On the other hand, stocks in emerging markets are often extremely risky, illiquid, and involve higher transactions costs, and most U.S. investors do not have ready access to information on the companies involved. To reduce these problems, mutual funds focused on specific countries have been created—they are called "country funds." Country funds help investors avoid the problem of picking individual stocks, but they do little to protect you when entire regions decline.

Sources: "World Stock Markets Gamble—and Win," *The Wall Street Journal*, January 3, 2005, p. R6; and Mary Kissel, "Asian Markets Post Gains on Solid Economic Growth: China IPOs May Be '05 Hit," *The Wall Street Journal*, January 3, 2005, p. R6.

Tying It All Together

Corporate decisions should be analyzed in terms of how alternative courses of action are likely to affect a firm's value. However, it is necessary to know how stock prices are established before attempting to measure how a given decision will affect a specific firm's value. This chapter discussed the rights and privileges of common stockholders, showed how stock values are determined, and explained how investors estimate stocks' intrinsic values and expected rates of return.

Two types of stock valuation models were discussed: the discounted dividend model and the corporate valuation model. The dividend model is useful for mature, stable companies, and it is easier to use, but the corporate model is more flexible and better for use with companies that do not pay dividends or whose dividends would be especially hard to predict.

We also discussed preferred stock, which is a hybrid security that has some characteristics of a common stock and some of a bond. Preferreds are valued using models similar to those for perpetual and "regular" bonds.

We also discussed market equilibrium, noting that for a stock to be in equilibrium its price must be equal to its intrinsic value as estimated by a marginal investor, and its expected and required returns as seen by such investors must also be equal. Finally, we noted that stocks are traded worldwide, that U.S. markets account for less than half of the value of all stocks, that U.S. investors can benefit from global diversification, but also that international investing can be risky and for most individuals should be done through mutual funds whose managers have specialized knowledge of foreign markets.

SELF-TEST QUESTIONS AND PROBLEMS (Solutions Appear in Appendix A)

ST-1   **Key terms** Define each of the following terms:
   a.   Proxy; proxy fight; takeover
   b.   Preemptive right
   c.   Classified stock; founders' shares
   d.   Intrinsic value $(\hat{P}_0)$; market price (P_0)
   e.   Required rate of return, r_s; expected rate of return, $\hat{r}_s$; actual, or realized, rate of return, $\bar{r}_s$
   f.   Capital gains yield; dividend yield; expected total return; growth rate, g
   g.   Zero growth stock
   h.   Normal, or constant, growth; supernormal (nonconstant) growth
   i.   Total company (corporate valuation) model
   j.   Terminal (horizon) date; horizon (terminal) value
   k.   Marginal investor
   l.   Equilibrium
   m.   Preferred stock

ST-2   **Stock growth rates and valuation** You are considering buying the stocks of two companies that operate in the same industry. They have very similar characteristics except for their dividend payout policies. Both companies are expected to earn $3 per share this year, but Company D (for "dividend") is expected to pay out all of its earnings as dividends, while Company G (for "growth") is expected to pay out only one-third of its earnings, or $1 per share. D's stock price is $25. G and D are equally risky. Which of the following statements is most likely to be true?
   a.   Company G will have a faster growth rate than Company D. Therefore, G's stock price should be greater than $25.
   b.   Although G's growth rate should exceed D's, D's current dividend exceeds that of G, and this should cause D's price to exceed G's.
   c.   A long-term investor in Stock D will get his or her money back faster because D pays out more of its earnings as dividends. Thus, in a sense, D is like a short-term bond, and G is like a long-term bond. Therefore, if economic shifts cause r_d and r_s to increase, and if the expected streams of dividends from D and G remain constant, both Stocks D and G will decline, but D's price should decline further.
   d.   D's expected and required rate of return is $\hat{r}_s = r_s = 12\%$. G's expected return will be higher because of its higher expected growth rate.
   e.   If we observe that G's price is also $25, the best estimate of G's growth rate is 8 percent.

ST-3 **Constant growth stock valuation** Fletcher Company's current stock price is $36, its last dividend was $2.40, and its required rate of return is 12 percent. If dividends are expected to grow at a constant rate, g, in the future, and if r_s is expected to remain at 12 percent, what is Fletcher's expected stock price 5 years from now?

ST-4 **Nonconstant growth stock valuation** Snyder Computers Inc. is experiencing rapid growth. Earnings and dividends are expected to grow at a rate of 15 percent during the next 2 years, 13 percent the following year, and at a constant rate of 6 percent during Year 4 and thereafter. Its last dividend was $1.15, and its required rate of return is 12 percent.

    a. Calculate the value of the stock today.
    b. Calculate $\hat{P}_1$ and $\hat{P}_2$.
    c. Calculate the dividend and capital gains yields for Years 1, 2, and 3.

QUESTIONS

9-1 It is frequently stated that the one purpose of the preemptive right is to allow individuals to maintain their proportionate share of the ownership and control of a corporation.

    a. How important do you suppose control is for the average stockholder of a firm whose shares are traded on the New York Stock Exchange?
    b. Is the control issue likely to be of more importance to stockholders of publicly owned or closely held (private) firms? Explain.

9-2 Is the following the correct equation for finding the value of a constant growth stock? Explain.

$$\hat{P}_0 = \frac{D_0}{r_s + g}$$

9-3 If you bought a share of common stock, you would probably expect to receive dividends plus an eventual capital gain. Would the distribution between the dividend yield and the capital gain yield be influenced by the firm's decision to pay more dividends rather than to retain and reinvest more of its earnings? Explain.

9-4 Two investors are evaluating GE's stock for possible purchase. They agree on the expected value of D_1 and also on the expected future dividend growth rate. Further, they agree on the riskiness of the stock. However, one investor normally holds stocks for 2 years, while the other holds stocks for 10 years. On the basis of the type of analysis done in this chapter, should they both be willing to pay the same price for GE's stock? Explain.

9-5 A bond that pays interest forever and has no maturity is a perpetual bond. In what respect is a perpetual bond similar to a no-growth common stock? Are there preferred stocks that are evaluated similarly to perpetual bonds and other preferred stocks that are more like bonds with finite lives? Explain.

PROBLEMS

Easy
Problems 1–6

9-1 **DPS calculation** Warr Corporation just paid a dividend of $1.50 a share (that is, $D_0 = \$1.50$). The dividend is expected to grow 7 percent a year for the next 3 years and then at 5 percent a year thereafter. What is the expected dividend per share for each of the next 5 years?

9-2 **Constant growth valuation** Thomas Brothers is expected to pay a $0.50 per share dividend at the end of the year (that is, $D_1 = \$0.50$). The dividend is expected to grow at a constant rate of 7 percent a year. The required rate of return on the stock, r_s, is 15 percent. What is the stock's value per share?

9-3 **Constant growth valuation** Harrison Clothiers' stock currently sells for $20 a share. It just paid a dividend of $1.00 a share (that is, $D_0 = \$1.00$). The dividend is expected to grow at a constant rate of 6 percent a year. What stock price is expected 1 year from now? What is the required rate of return?

9-4 **Nonconstant growth valuation** Hart Enterprises recently paid a dividend, D_0, of $1.25. It expects to have nonconstant growth of 20 percent for 2 years followed by a constant rate of 5 percent thereafter. The firm's required return is 10 percent.

a. How far away is the terminal, or horizon, date?
b. What is the firm's horizon, or terminal, value?
c. What is the firm's intrinsic value today, $\hat{P}_0$?

9-5 **Corporate value model** Smith Technologies is expected to generate $150 million in free cash flow next year, and FCF is expected to grow at a constant rate of 5 percent per year indefinitely. Smith has no debt or preferred stock, and its WACC is 10 percent. If Smith has 50 million shares of stock outstanding, what is the stock's value per share?

9-6 **Preferred stock valuation** Fee Founders has perpetual preferred stock outstanding that sells for $60 a share and pays a dividend of $5 at the end of each year. What is the required rate of return?

Intermediate
Problems 7–17

9-7 **Preferred stock rate of return** What will be the nominal rate of return on a perpetual preferred stock with a $100 par value, a stated dividend of 8 percent of par, and a current market price of (a) $60, (b) $80, (c) $100, and (d) $140?

9-8 **Preferred stock valuation** Ezzell Corporation issued perpetual preferred stock with a 10 percent annual dividend. The stock currently yields 8 percent, and its par value is $100.

a. What is the stock's value?
b. Suppose interest rates rise and pull the preferred stock's yield up to 12 percent. What would be its new market value?

9-9 **Preferred stock returns** Bruner Aeronautics has perpetual preferred stock outstanding with a par value of $100. The stock pays a quarterly dividend of $2, and its current price is $80.

a. What is its nominal annual rate of return?
b. What is its effective annual rate of return?

9-10 **Valuation of a declining growth stock** Martell Mining Company's ore reserves are being depleted, so its sales are falling. Also, its pit is getting deeper each year, so its costs are rising. As a result, the company's earnings and dividends are declining at the constant rate of 5 percent per year. If $D_0 = \$5$ and $r_s = 15\%$, what is the value of Martell Mining's stock?

9-11 **Valuation of a constant growth stock** A stock is expected to pay a dividend of $0.50 at the end of the year (that is, $D_1 = 0.50$), and it should continue to grow at a constant rate of 7 percent a year. If its required return is 12 percent, what is the stock's expected price 4 years from today?

9-12 **Valuation of a constant growth stock** Investors require a 15 percent rate of return on Levine Company's stock (that is, $r_s = 15\%$).

a. What is its value if the previous dividend was $D_0 = \$2$ and investors expect dividends to grow at a constant annual rate of (1) −5 percent, (2) 0 percent, (3) 5 percent, or (4) 10 percent?
b. Using data from part a, what would the Gordon (constant growth) model value be if the required rate of return were 15 percent and the expected growth rate were (1) 15 percent or (2) 20 percent? Are these reasonable results? Explain.
c. Is it reasonable to think that a constant growth stock could have $g > r_s$?

9-13 **Rates of return and equilibrium** Stock C's beta coefficient is $b_C = 0.4$, while Stock D's is $b_D = -0.5$. (Stock D's beta is negative, indicating that its return rises when returns on most other stocks fall. There are very few negative beta stocks, although collection agency stocks are sometimes cited as an example.)

a. If the risk-free rate is 7 percent and the expected rate of return on an average stock is 11 percent, what are the required rates of return on Stocks C and D?
b. For Stock C, suppose the current price, P_0, is $25; the next expected dividend, D_1, is $1.50; and the stock's expected constant growth rate is 4 percent. Is the stock in equilibrium? Explain, and describe what would happen if the stock is not in equilibrium.

9-14 **Constant growth** You are considering an investment in Keller Corp's stock, which is expected to pay a dividend of $2 a share at the end of the year ($D_1 = \$2.00$) and has a beta of 0.9. The risk-free rate is 5.6 percent, and the market risk premium is 6 percent. Keller currently sells for $25 a share, and its dividend is expected to grow at some constant rate g. Assuming the market is in equilibrium, what does the market believe will be the stock price at the end of 3 years? (That is, what is $\hat{P}_3$?)

9-15 **Equilibrium stock price** The risk-free rate of return, r_{RF}, is 6 percent; the required rate of return on the market, r_M, is 10 percent; and Upton Company's stock has a beta coefficient of 1.5.

 a. If the dividend expected during the coming year, D_1, is $2.25, and if g = a constant 5 percent, at what price should Upton's stock sell?

 b. Now, suppose the Federal Reserve Board increases the money supply, causing the risk-free rate to drop to 5 percent and r_M to fall to 9 percent. What would happen to Upton's price?

 c. In addition to the change in part b, suppose investors' risk aversion declines, and this, combined with the decline in r_{RF}, causes r_M to fall to 8 percent. Now, what is Upton's price?

 d. Now suppose Upton has a change in management. The new group institutes policies that increase the expected constant growth rate from 5 to 6 percent. Also, the new management smooths out fluctuations in sales and profits, causing beta to decline from 1.5 to 1.3. Assume that r_{RF} and r_M are equal to the values in part c. After all these changes, what is its new equilibrium price? (Note: D_1 is now $2.27.)

9-16 **Nonconstant growth** Microtech Corporation is expanding rapidly and currently needs to retain all of its earnings, hence it does not pay dividends. However, investors expect Microtech to begin paying dividends, beginning with a dividend of $1.00 coming 3 years from today. The dividend should grow rapidly—at a rate of 50 percent per year—during Years 4 and 5, but after Year 5 growth should be a constant 8 percent per year. If the required return on Microtech is 15 percent, what is the value of the stock today?

9-17 **Corporate valuation** Dozier Corporation is a fast-growing supplier of office products. Analysts project the following free cash flows (FCFs) during the next 3 years, after which FCF is expected to grow at a constant 7 percent rate. Dozier's WACC is 13 percent.

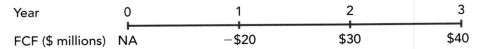

Year	0	1	2	3
FCF ($ millions)	NA	−$20	$30	$40

 a. What is Dozier's terminal, or horizon, value? (Hint: Find the value of all free cash flows beyond Year 3 discounted back to Year 3.)

 b. What is the firm's value today?

 c. Suppose Dozier has $100 million of debt and 10 million shares of stock outstanding. What is your estimate of the price per share?

Challenging Problems 18-24

9-18 **Nonconstant growth** Mitts Cosmetics Co.'s stock price is $58.88, and it recently paid a $2 dividend. This dividend is expected to grow by 25 percent for the next 3 years, and then grow forever at a constant rate, g, and r_s = 12%. At what constant rate is the stock expected to grow after Year 3?

9-19 **Constant growth** Your broker offers to sell you some shares of Bahnsen & Co. common stock that paid a dividend of $2 *yesterday*. Bahnsen's dividend is expected to grow at 5 percent per year for the next 3 years, and, if you buy the stock, you plan to hold it for 3 years and then sell it. The appropriate discount rate is 12 percent.

 a. Find the expected dividend for each of the next 3 years; that is, calculate D_1, D_2, and D_3. Note that D_0 = $2.00.

 b. Given that the first dividend payment will occur 1 year from now, find the present value of the dividend stream; that is, calculate the PV of D_1, D_2, and D_3, and then sum these PVs.

 c. You expect the price of the stock 3 years from now to be $34.73; that is, you expect $\hat{P}_3$ to equal $34.73. Discounted at a 12 percent rate, what is the present value of this expected future stock price? In other words, calculate the PV of $34.73.

 d. If you plan to buy the stock, hold it for 3 years, and then sell it for $34.73, what is the most you should pay for it today?

 e. Use Equation 9-2 to calculate the present value of this stock. Assume that g = 5%, and it is constant.

 f. Is the value of this stock dependent upon how long you plan to hold it? In other words, if your planned holding period were 2 years or 5 years rather than 3 years, would this affect the value of the stock today, $\hat{P}_0$? Explain.

9-20 **Nonconstant growth stock valuation** Taussig Technologies Corporation (TTC) has been growing at a rate of 20 percent per year in recent years. This same growth rate is expected to last for another 2 years, then to decline to g_n = 6%.

a.   If $D_0 = \$1.60$ and $r_s = 10\%$, what is TTC's stock worth today? What are its expected dividend and capital gains yields at this time, that is, during Year 1?

b.   Now assume that TTC's period of supernormal growth is to last for 5 years rather than 2 years. How would this affect the price, dividend yield, and capital gains yield? Answer in words only.

c.   What will TTC's dividend and capital gains yields be once its period of supernormal growth ends? (Hint: These values will be the same regardless of whether you examine the case of 2 or 5 years of supernormal growth; the calculations are very easy.)

d.   Of what interest to investors is the changing relationship between dividend and capital gains yields over time?

9-21   **Corporate value model** Barrett Industries invests a lot of money in R&D, and as a result it retains and reinvests all of its earnings. In other words, Barrett does not pay any dividends, and it has no plans to pay dividends in the near future. A major pension fund is interested in purchasing Barrett's stock. The pension fund manager has estimated Barrett's free cash flows for the next 4 years as follows: $3 million, $6 million, $10 million, and $15 million. After the 4th year, free cash flow is projected to grow at a constant 7 percent. Barrett's WACC is 12 percent, its debt and preferred stock total to $60 million, and it has 10 million shares of common stock outstanding.

a.   What is the present value of the free cash flows projected during the next 4 years?
b.   What is the firm's terminal value?
c.   What is the firm's total value today?
d.   What is an estimate of Barrett's price per share?

9-22   **Corporate value model** Assume that today is December 31, 2005, and the following information applies to Vermeil Airlines:

- After-tax operating income [EBIT(1 − T), also called NOPAT] for 2006 is expected to be $500 million.
- The depreciation expense for 2006 is expected to be $100 million.
- The capital expenditures for 2006 are expected to be $200 million.
- No change is expected in net operating working capital.
- The free cash flow is expected to grow at a constant rate of 6 percent per year.
- The required return on equity is 14 percent.
- The WACC is 10 percent.
- The market value of the company's debt is $3 billion.
- 200 million shares of stock are outstanding.

Using the free cash flow approach, what should the company's stock price be today?

9-23   **Beta coefficients** Suppose Chance Chemical Company's management conducted a study and concluded that if it expands its consumer products division (which is less risky than its primary business, industrial chemicals), its beta would decline from 1.2 to 0.9. However, consumer products have a somewhat lower profit margin, and this would cause its constant growth rate in earnings and dividends to fall from 6 percent to 4 percent. The following also apply: $r_M = 9\%$; $r_{RF} = 6\%$; and $D_0 = \$2.00$.

a.   Should management expand the consumer products division?
b.   Assume all the facts as given above except the change in the beta coefficient. How low would the beta have to fall to cause the expansion to be a good one? (Hint: Set $\hat{P}_0$ under the new policy equal to $\hat{P}_0$ under the old one, and find the new beta that will produce this equality.)

9-24   **Nonconstant growth** Assume that it is now January 1, 2006. Wayne-Martin Electric Inc. (WME) has just developed a solar panel capable of generating 200 percent more electricity than any solar panel currently on the market. As a result, WME is expected to experience a 15 percent annual growth rate for the next 5 years. By the end of 5 years, other firms will have developed comparable technology, and WME's growth rate will slow to 5 percent per year indefinitely. Stockholders require a return of 12 percent on WME's stock. The most recent annual dividend (D_0), which was paid yesterday, was $1.75 per share.

a.   Calculate WME's expected dividends for 2006, 2007, 2008, 2009, and 2010.
b.   Calculate the value of the stock today, $\hat{P}_0$. Proceed by finding the present value of the dividends expected at the end of 2006, 2007, 2008, 2009, and 2010 plus the present value of the stock price that should exist at the end of 2010. The year-end 2010 stock price can be found by using the constant growth equation. Notice that to find the December 31, 2010, price, you must use the dividend expected in 2011, which is 5 percent greater than the 2010 dividend.
c.   Calculate the expected dividend yield, D_1/P_0, capital gains yield, and total return (dividend yield plus capital gains yield) expected for 2006. (Assume that $\hat{P}_0 = P_0$, and

recognize that the capital gains yield is equal to the total return minus the dividend yield.) Then calculate these same three yields for 2011.

d. How might an investor's tax situation affect his or her decision to purchase stocks of companies in the early stages of their lives, when they are growing rapidly, versus stocks of older, more mature firms? When does WME's stock become "mature" for purposes of this question?

e. Suppose your boss tells you she believes that WME's annual growth rate will be only 12 percent during the next 5 years and that the firm's long-run growth rate will be only 4 percent. Without doing any calculations, what general effect would these growth-rate changes have on the price of WME's stock?

f. Suppose your boss also tells you that she regards WME as being quite risky and that she believes the required rate of return should be 14 percent, not 12 percent. Without doing any calculations, how would the higher required rate of return affect the price of the stock, the capital gains yield, and the dividend yield? Again, assume that the long-run growth rate is 4 percent.

COMPREHENSIVE/SPREADSHEET PROBLEM

9-25 **Nonconstant growth and corporate valuation** Rework Problem 9-20, parts a, b, and c, using a spreadsheet model. For part b, calculate the price, dividend yield, and capital gains yield as called for in the problem. After completing parts a through c, answer the following additional question using the spreadsheet model.

d. TTC recently introduced a new line of products that has been wildly successful. On the basis of this success and anticipated future success, the following free cash flows were projected:

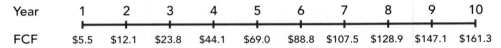

Year	1	2	3	4	5	6	7	8	9	10
FCF	$5.5	$12.1	$23.8	$44.1	$69.0	$88.8	$107.5	$128.9	$147.1	$161.3

After the 10th year, TTC's financial planners anticipate that its free cash flow will grow at a constant rate of 6 percent. Also, the firm concluded that the new product caused the WACC to fall to 9 percent. The market value of TTC's debt is $1,200 million, it uses no preferred stock, and there are 20 million shares of common stock outstanding. Use the free cash flow method to value the stock.

Integrated Case

Mutual of Chicago Insurance Company

9-26 **Stock valuation** Robert Balik and Carol Kiefer are senior vice presidents of the Mutual of Chicago Insurance Company. They are co-directors of the company's pension fund management division, with Balik having responsibility for fixed income securities (primarily bonds) and Kiefer being responsible for equity investments. A major new client, the California League of Cities, has requested that Mutual of Chicago present an investment seminar to the mayors of the represented cities, and Balik and Kiefer, who will make the actual presentation, have asked you to help them.

To illustrate the common stock valuation process, Balik and Kiefer have asked you to analyze the Bon Temps Company, an employment agency that supplies word-processor operators and computer programmers to businesses with temporarily heavy workloads. You are to answer the following questions:

a. Describe briefly the legal rights and privileges of common stockholders.
b. (1) Write out a formula that can be used to value any stock, regardless of its dividend pattern.
    (2) What is a constant growth stock? How are constant growth stocks valued?
    (3) What are the implications if a company forecasts a constant g that exceeds its r_s? Will many stocks have expected $g > r_s$ in the short run (that is, for the next few years)? In the long run (that is, forever)?
c. Assume that Bon Temps has a beta coefficient of 1.2, that the risk-free rate (the yield on T-bonds) is 7 percent, and that the required rate of return on the market is 12 percent. What is Bon Temps' required rate of return?
d. Assume that Bon Temps is a constant growth company whose last dividend (D_0, which was paid yesterday) was $2.00 and whose dividend is expected to grow indefinitely at a 6 percent rate.
    (1) What is the firm's expected dividend stream over the next 3 years?
    (2) What is its current stock price?
    (3) What is the stock's expected value 1 year from now?
    (4) What are the expected dividend yield, capital gains yield, and total return during the first year?
e. Now assume that the stock is currently selling at $30.29. What is its expected rate of return?
f. What would the stock price be if its dividends were expected to have zero growth?
g. Now assume that Bon Temps is expected to experience nonconstant growth of 30 percent for the next 3 years, then to return to its long-run constant growth rate of 6 percent. What is the stock's value under these conditions? What are its expected dividend and capital gains yields in Year 1? Year 4?
h. Suppose Bon Temps is expected to experience zero growth during the first 3 years and then to resume its steady-state growth of 6 percent in the fourth year. What would its value be then? What would its expected dividend and capital gains yields be in Year 1? In Year 4?
i. Finally, assume that Bon Temps' earnings and dividends are expected to decline at a constant rate of 6 percent per year, that is, g = −6%. Why would anyone be willing to buy such a stock, and at what price should it sell? What would be its dividend and capital gains yields in each year?
j. Suppose Bon Temps embarked on an aggressive expansion that requires additional capital. Management decided to finance the expansion by borrowing $40 million and by halting dividend payments to increase retained earnings. Its WACC is now 10 percent, and the projected free cash flows for the next 3 years are −$5 million, $10 million, and $20 million. After Year 3, free cash flow is projected to grow at a constant 6 percent. What is Bon Temps' total value? If it has 10 million shares of stock and $40 million of total debt, what is the price per share?
k. For Bon Temps' stock to be in equilibrium, what relationship must exist between its estimated intrinsic value and its current stock price and between its expected and required rates of return? Are the equilibrium intrinsic value and expected rate of return the values that management estimates or values as estimated by some other entity? Explain.
l. If equilibrium does not exist, how will it be established?
m. Suppose Bon Temps decided to issue preferred stock that would pay an annual dividend of $5, and the issue price was $50 per share. What would the expected return be on this stock? Would the expected rate of return be the same if the preferred was a perpetual issue or if it had a 20-year maturity?

cyberproblem

Please go to the ThomsonNOW Web site to access the Cyberproblems.

THOMSON ONE | Business School Edition

Access the Thomson ONE problems though the ThomsonNOW Web site. Use the Thomson ONE—Business School Edition online database to work this chapter's questions.

Estimating ExxonMobil's Intrinsic Stock Value

In this chapter we described the various factors that influence stock prices and the approaches that analysts use to estimate a stock's intrinsic value. By comparing these intrinsic value estimates to the current price, an investor can assess whether it makes sense to buy or sell a particular stock. Stocks trading at a price far below their estimated intrinsic values may be good candidates for purchase, whereas stocks trading at prices far in excess of their intrinsic value may be good stocks to avoid or sell.

While estimating a stock's intrinsic value is a complex exercise that requires reliable data and good judgment, we can use the data available in Thomson One to arrive at a quick "back of the envelope" calculation of intrinsic value.

Discussion Questions

1. For purposes of this exercise, let's take a closer look at the stock of ExxonMobil Corporation (XOM). Looking at the COMPANY OVERVIEW we can immediately see the company's current stock price and its performance relative to the overall market in recent months. What is ExxonMobil's current stock price? How has the stock performed relative to the market over the past few months?

2. Click on the "NEWS" tab to see the recent news stories for the company. Have there been any recent events impacting the company's stock price, or have things been relatively quiet?

3. To provide a starting point for gauging a company's relative valuation, analysts often look at a company's price-to-earnings (P/E) ratio. Returning to the COMPANY OVERVIEW page, you can see XOM's current P/E ratio. To put this number in perspective, it is useful to compare this ratio with other companies in the same industry and to take a look at how this ratio has changed over time. If you want to see how XOM's P/E ratio stacks up to its peers, click on the tab labeled PEERS. Click on FINANCIALS on the next row of tabs and then select KEY FINANCIAL RATIOS. Toward the bottom of the table you should see information on the P/E ratio in the section titled Market Value Ratios. Toward the top, you should see an item where it says CLICK HERE TO SELECT NEW PEER SET—do this if you want to compare XOM to a different set of firms. For the most part, is XOM's P/E ratio above or below that of its peers? In Chapter 4, we discussed the various factors that may influence P/E ratios. Off the top of your head, can these factors explain why XOM's P/E ratio differs from its peers?

4. Now to see how XOM's P/E ratio has varied over time—return back to the COMPANY OVERVIEW page. Next click FINANCIALS—GROWTH RATIOS and then select WORLDSCOPE—INCOME STATEMENT RATIOS. Is XOM's current P/E ratio well above or well below its historical average? If so, do you have any explanation for why the current P/E deviates from its historical trend? On the basis of this information, does XOM's current P/E suggest that the stock is undervalued or overvalued? Explain.

5. In the text, we discussed using the dividend growth model to estimate a stock's intrinsic value. To keep things as simple as possible, let's assume at first that XOM's dividend is expected to grow at some constant rate over time. If so, the intrinsic value equals $D_1/(r_s - g)$, where D_1 is the expected annual dividend 1 year from now, r_s is the stock's required rate of return, and g is the dividend's constant growth rate. To estimate the dividend growth rate, it's first helpful to look at XOM's dividend history.

Staying on the current Web page (WORLDSCOPE—INCOME STATEMENT RATIOS) you should immediately find the company's annual dividend over the past several years. On the basis of this information, what has been the average annual dividend growth rate? Another way to get estimates of dividend growth rates is to look at analysts' forecasts for future dividends, which can be found on the ESTIMATES tab. Scrolling down the page you should see an area marked "Consensus Estimates" and a tab under "Available Measures." Here you click on the down arrow key and select Dividends Per Share (DPS). What is the median year-end dividend forecast? You can use this as an estimate of D_1 in your measure of intrinsic value. You can also use this forecast along with the historical data to arrive at a measure of the forecasted dividend growth rate, g.

6. The required return on equity, r_s, is the final input needed to estimate intrinsic value. For our purposes you can either assume a number (say, 8 or 9 percent), or you can use the CAPM to calculate an estimate of the cost of equity using the data available in Thomson One. (For more details take a look at the Thomson One exercise for Chapter 8). Having decided on your best estimates for D_1, r_s, and g, you can calculate XOM's intrinsic value. How does this estimate compare with the current stock price? Does your preliminary analysis suggest that XOM is undervalued or overvalued? Explain.

7. It is often useful to perform a sensitivity analysis, where you show how your estimate of intrinsic value varies according to different estimates of D_1, r_s, and g. To do so, recalculate your intrinsic value estimate for a range of different estimates for each of these key inputs. One convenient way to do this is to set up a simple data table in *Excel*. Refer to the *Excel* tutorial accessed through the ThomsonNOW Web site for instructions on data tables. On the basis of this analysis, what inputs justify the current stock price?

8. On the basis of the dividend history you uncovered in question 5 and your assessment of XOM's future dividend payout policies, do you think it is reasonable to assume that the constant growth model is a good proxy for intrinsic value? If not, how would you use the available data in Thomson One to estimate intrinsic value using the nonconstant growth model?

9. Finally, you can also use the information in Thomson One to value the entire corporation. This approach requires that you estimate XOM's annual free cash flows. Once you estimate the value of the entire corporation, you subtract the value of debt and preferred stock to arrive at an estimate of the company's equity value. Divide this number by the number of shares of common stock outstanding, and you calculate an alternative estimate of the stock's intrinsic value. While this approach may take some more time and involves more judgment concerning forecasts of future free cash flows, you can use the financial statements and growth forecasts in Thomson One as useful starting points. Go to Worldscope's Cash Flow Ratios Report (which you find by clicking on FINANCIALS, FUNDAMENTAL RATIOS, and WORLDSCOPE RATIOS) and you will find an estimate of "free cash flow per share." While this number is useful, Worldscope's definition of free cash flow subtracts out dividends per share; therefore, to make it comparable to the measure in this text, you must add back dividends. To see Worldscope's definition of free cash flow (or any term), click on SEARCH FOR COMPANIES from the left toolbar, and select the ADVANCED SEARCH tab. In the middle of your screen, on the right-hand side, you will see a dialog box with terms. Use the down arrow to scroll through the terms, highlighting the term for which you would like to see a definition. Then, click on the DEFINITION button immediately below the dialog box.

INVESTING IN LONG-TERM ASSETS: CAPITAL BUDGETING

P A R T **4**

10

THE COST OF CAPITAL

Creating Value at GE

General Electric is one of the world's best-managed companies, and as such it has rewarded its shareholders with outstanding returns. GE creates shareholder value by investing in projects that earn more than the cost of the capital invested in them. For example, if a project earns 20 percent but the capital invested in it costs only 10 percent, then taking on the project will increase the stock price.

Capital is obtained in three primary forms: debt, preferred stock, and common equity, with equity coming from issuing new stock and by retaining earnings. The investors who provide that capital do so expecting to earn at least their required rate of return on that capital, and the required return represents the cost of capital to the firm.[1] A variety of factors influence the cost of capital. Some—including interest rates, state and federal tax policies, and the regulatory environment—are outside the firm's control. However, financing and investment policies, especially choices related to the types of capital the firm uses and the riskiness of the projects it undertakes, have a profound effect on its cost of capital.

Estimating the cost of capital for a company like GE is conceptually straightforward. GE's capital comes largely from debt and equity obtained by retaining earnings, so its cost of capital depends largely on the level of interest rates in the economy and the marginal stockholder's required rate of return on equity. However, GE operates many different divisions throughout the world, so it is similar to a portfolio that contains a number of different stocks, each with a different risk. Recall that the risk of the portfolio is a weighted average of the

---

[1] Recall from earlier chapters that expected and required returns as seen by the marginal investor must be equal for a security to be in equilibrium, and buying and selling forces this equality to hold, except for short periods immediately following the release of new information. As expected and required returns are normally equal, we use the two terms interchangeably.

relevant risks of the different stocks in the portfolio. Similarly, each of GE's divisions has its own level of risk, hence its own cost of capital, and GE's overall cost of capital is an average of its divisions' costs. For example, GE's NBC subsidiary probably has a different cost of capital than its aircraft engine division, and even within divisions, some projects are riskier than others. Moreover, overseas projects may have different risks and thus different costs of capital than otherwise similar domestic projects.

As we will see in this chapter, estimating projects' costs of capital is an essential element in the capital budgeting process, and managing this process effectively is essential to maximizing the firm's intrinsic stock price.

Putting Things In Perspective

In the last three chapters, we explained how risk influences the prices and required rates of return on bonds and stocks. The firm's primary objective is to maximize shareholder value, and a company can increase this value by investing in projects that earn more than the cost of capital. Capital is necessary to take on those projects, and like all factors of production, it has a cost that is equal to the marginal investor's required return. For this reason, the cost of capital is referred to as a *hurdle rate*—for a project to be accepted its expected return must exceed its hurdle rate.

Most of the formulas used in this chapter were developed in earlier chapters, where we examined the required rates of return on bonds and stocks. Indeed, the rates of return that marginal investors require on securities represent the costs of those securities to the firm. As we shall see, companies estimate the required returns on their securities, obtain a weighted average of the costs of the different types of securities they use, and then use this average in their capital budgeting analyses.

10-1 AN OVERVIEW OF THE WEIGHTED AVERAGE COST OF CAPITAL

Figure 10-1 shows the types of capital firms use. Debt is typically raised by issuing bonds or borrowing money from a financial institution such as a bank.[2] Some companies also finance with preferred stock. The third type of capital,

---

[2] As we saw in Chapter 7, there are actually many different types of debt, and each type typically has a somewhat different cost. For the purpose of this chapter, assume that the firm's cost of debt is an average of the costs of its different types of debt.

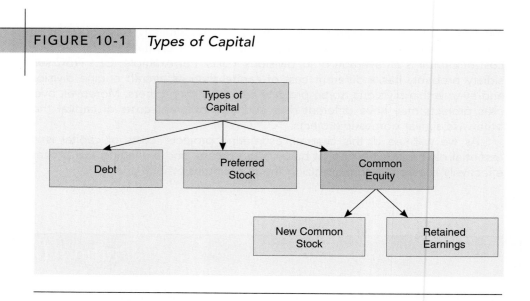

FIGURE 10-1   *Types of Capital*

common equity, is provided by the company's common stockholders, and it is raised in two ways: (1) by issuing new common stock and (2) by retaining earnings (that is, by not paying out all of their earnings as dividends). Equity raised by selling newly issued stock is called *external equity*, while retained earnings are called *internal equity*. As we will discuss later, all equity has a cost, whether it is raised internally or externally, but the cost of newly issued shares exceeds the cost of retained earnings because of fees that must be paid to investment bankers for helping sell the new shares.

A firm's overall cost of capital is an average of the costs of the various types of funds it uses. Consider Allied Food Products, the firm we've been following throughout the text. Allied uses debt with a 10 percent cost, no preferred stock, and common equity whose cost is 13.4 percent, which is the return that stockholders require on the stock. Now assume that Allied has made the decision to finance next year's projects with debt. The argument is sometimes made that the cost of capital for these projects will be 10 percent because only debt will be used to finance them. However, this position is incorrect. If Allied finances a particular set of projects with debt, it will be using up some of its future capacity for borrowing. As expansion occurs in subsequent years, it will at some point have to raise more equity to prevent the debt ratio from getting too high.

To illustrate, suppose Allied borrows heavily at 10 percent during 2006, using up its debt capacity in the process, to finance projects yielding 11.5 percent. In 2007, it has new projects available that yield 13 percent, well above the return on 2006 projects, but it could not accept them because they would have to be financed with 13.4 percent equity. *To avoid this problem, Allied and other firms take a long-run view, and the cost of capital is calculated as a weighted average, or composite, of the various types of funds used over time, regardless of the specific financing used to fund projects in a given year.*

Why should the cost of capital be calculated as a weighted average of the various types of funds a firm generally uses, not the cost of the specific financing used during a given year?

10-2 BASIC DEFINITIONS

The items on the right side of a firm's balance sheet—various types of debt, preferred stock, and common equity—are called **capital components.** Any increase in total assets must be financed by an increase in one or more of these capital components. The cost of each component is called the *component cost* of that particular type of capital; for example, if Allied can borrow money at 10 percent, its component cost of debt is 10 percent.[3] Throughout this chapter, we concentrate on the three major capital components—debt, preferred stock, and common equity—and the following symbols identify the cost of each:

Capital Component
One of the types of capital used by firms to raise funds.

r_d = interest rate on the firm's new debt = before-tax component cost of debt.

$r_d(1 - T)$ = after-tax component cost of debt, where T is the firm's marginal tax rate. $r_d(1 - T)$ is the debt cost used to calculate the weighted average cost of capital. The after-tax cost of debt is lower than the before-tax cost because interest is deductible for tax purposes.

r_p = component cost of preferred stock. Preferred dividends are not deductible, hence the before and after-tax costs of preferred are equal.

r_s = component cost of common equity raised by retaining earnings, or *internal equity*. It is identical to the r_s developed in Chapters 8 and 9 and defined there as the rate of return investors require on a firm's common stock. Most firms, once they have become established, obtain all of their new equity in the form of retained earnings, hence r_s is their cost of equity.

r_e = component cost of *external equity*, or common equity raised by issuing new stock. As we will see, r_e is equal to r_s plus a factor that reflects the cost of issuing new stock. Note, though, that established firms like Allied Foods rarely issue new stock, hence r_e is rarely a relevant consideration except for very young firms.

As we shall see in the chapter on capital structure, each firm has an optimal capital structure, defined as the mix of debt, preferred, and common equity that causes its stock price to be maximized. Therefore, a value-maximizing firm will estimate its **optimal capital structure,** use it as a **target,** and then raise new capital in a manner designed to keep the actual capital structure on target over time. In this chapter, we assume that the firm has identified its optimal capital structure, that it uses this optimum as the target, and that it finances so as to remain on target.

Target (Optimal) Capital Structure
The percentages of debt, preferred stock, and common equity that will maximize the firm's stock price.

Weighted Average Cost of Capital (WACC)
A weighted average of the component costs of debt, preferred stock, and common equity.

The target proportions of debt (w_d), preferred stock (w_p), and common equity (w_c), along with the costs of those components, are used to calculate the firm's **weighted average cost of capital, WACC.** We assume at this point that all new common equity is raised as retained earnings, as is true for most companies, hence the cost of common equity is r_s.

$$
\text{WACC} = \begin{pmatrix} \% \\ \text{of} \\ \text{debt} \end{pmatrix} \begin{pmatrix} \text{After-tax} \\ \text{cost of} \\ \text{debt} \end{pmatrix} + \begin{pmatrix} \% \text{ of} \\ \text{preferred} \\ \text{stock} \end{pmatrix} \begin{pmatrix} \text{Cost of} \\ \text{preferred} \\ \text{stock} \end{pmatrix} + \begin{pmatrix} \% \text{ of} \\ \text{common} \\ \text{equity} \end{pmatrix} \begin{pmatrix} \text{Cost of} \\ \text{common} \\ \text{equity} \end{pmatrix}
$$

$$
= \quad w_d r_d(1 - T) \quad + \quad w_p r_p \quad + \quad w_c r_s \qquad \textbf{(10-1)}
$$

---

[3] We will see shortly that there is both a before-tax and an after-tax cost of debt; for now, it is sufficient to know that 10 percent is the before-tax component cost of debt.

These definitions and concepts are discussed in the remainder of the chapter, using Allied Foods for illustrative purposes. Later, in the capital structure chapter, we extend the discussion to the mix of securities that minimizes the firm's cost of capital and maximizes its value.

Identify the firm's three major capital structure components, and give their respective component cost symbols.

Why might there be two different component costs for common equity? Which is the one that is generally relevant, and for what type of firm is the second one likely to be relevant?

10-3 COST OF DEBT, $r_d(1 - T)$

After-Tax Cost of Debt, $r_d(1 - T)$
The relevant cost of new debt, taking into account the tax deductibility of interest; used to calculate the WACC.

The **after-tax cost of debt, $r_d(1 - T)$,** is used to calculate the weighted average cost of capital, and it is the interest rate on debt, r_d, less the tax savings that result because interest is deductible.[4]

$$\text{After-tax cost of debt} = \text{Interest rate} - \text{Tax savings}$$
$$= r_d - r_d T$$
$$= r_d(1 - T) \tag{10-2}$$

In effect, the government pays part of the cost of debt because interest is deductible. Therefore, if Allied can borrow at an interest rate of 10 percent and its marginal federal-plus-state tax rate is 40 percent, then its after-tax cost of debt will be 6 percent:

$$\text{After-tax cost of debt} = r_d(1 - T) = 10\%(1.0 - 0.4)$$
$$= 10\%(0.6)$$
$$= 6.0\%$$

We use the after-tax cost of debt in calculating the WACC because we are interested in maximizing the value of the firm's stock, and the stock price depends on *after-tax* cash flows. Because we are concerned with after-tax cash flows, and because cash flows and rates of return should be calculated on a comparable basis, we adjust the interest rate downward to take account of debt's preferential tax treatment.[5]

---

[4] The federal tax rate for most large corporations is 35 percent. However, most corporations are also subject to state income taxes, so the marginal tax rate on most corporate income is about 40 percent. For illustrative purposes, we assume that the effective federal-plus-state tax rate on marginal income is 40 percent. Also, note that the cost of debt is considered in isolation. The effect of debt on the cost of equity, as well as the cost of future increments of debt, is ignored when the weighted cost of a combination of debt and equity is derived in this chapter. However, this will be addressed in the capital structure chapter.

[5] The tax rate is *zero* for a firm with losses. Therefore, for a company that does not pay taxes, the cost of debt is not reduced; that is, in Equation 10-2, the tax rate equals zero, so the after-tax cost of debt is equal to the interest rate.

Strictly speaking, the after-tax cost of debt should reflect the *expected* cost of debt. While Allied's bonds have a promised return of 10 percent, there is some chance of default, so its bondholders' expected return (and consequently Allied's cost) is a bit less than 10 percent. For a relatively strong company such as Allied, this difference is quite small. As we discuss later in the chapter, Allied must also incur flotation costs when it issues debt, but like the difference between the

Note that the cost of debt is the interest rate on *new* debt, not that on already outstanding debt. We are interested in the cost of new debt because our primary concern with the cost of capital is to use it for capital budgeting decisions. For example, would a new machine earn a return greater than the cost of the capital needed to acquire the machine? The rate at which the firm has borrowed in the past is irrelevant when answering this question—we need to know the cost of *new capital*.

Why is the after-tax cost of debt rather than the before-tax cost used to calculate the WACC?

Why is the relevant cost of debt the interest rate on *new* debt, not that on already outstanding, or *old*, debt?

A company has outstanding long-term bonds with a face value of $1,000, an 11 percent coupon, and an 8 percent yield to maturity. If the company were to issue new debt, what would be a reasonable estimate of the interest rate on that debt? If the company's tax rate is 40 percent, what would its after-tax cost of debt be? (8.0%; 4.8%)

10-4 COST OF PREFERRED STOCK, r_p

The component **cost of preferred stock** used to calculate the weighted average cost of capital, r_p, is the preferred dividend, D_p, divided by the current price of the preferred stock, P_p.

$$\text{Component cost of preferred stock} = r_p = \frac{D_p}{P_p} \qquad \textbf{(10-3)}$$

Allied does not have any preferred stock outstanding, but suppose the company plans to issue some preferred in the future and therefore has included it in its target capital structure. Allied would sell this stock to a few large pension funds, the stock would have a $10 dividend per share, and it would be priced at $97.50 a share. Therefore, Allied's cost of preferred stock would be 10.3 percent:[6]

$$r_p = \$10/\$97.50 = 10.3\%$$

As we can see from Equation 10-3, calculating the cost of preferred stock is generally quite simple. This is particularly true for traditional, "plain vanilla" preferred that pays a fixed dividend in perpetuity. However, in Chapter 9 we noted that some preferred issues have a specified maturity date, and we described how to calculate the expected return on these issues. Also, preferred stock may include an option to convert to common stock, and that adds another layer of complexity to calculating the cost of preferred stock. We will leave these more

> **Cost of Preferred Stock, r_p**
> The rate of return investors require on the firm's preferred stock. r_p is calculated as the preferred dividend, D_p, divided by the current price, P_p.

(Footnote 5 continued)
promised and the expected rates of return, flotation costs for debt are generally small. Finally, note that these two factors tend to offset one another—not including the possibility of default leads to an overstatement of the cost of debt, but not including flotation costs leads to an understatement. For all these reasons, r_d is generally a good approximation of the before-tax cost of debt capital and $r_d(1 - T)$ of the after-tax cost.

[6] This preferred stock would be sold directly to a group of pension funds, so no flotation costs would be incurred. If significant flotation costs were involved, then the cost of the preferred would have to be adjusted upward like new common equity issues, as we explain in a later section.

Funny-Named Preferred-Like Securities

Wall Street's "financial engineers" are constantly developing new securities that will appeal to issuers and investors. One such new security is a special type of preferred stock created by Goldman Sachs in the mid-1990s. These securities trade under a variety of colorful names, including MIPS (modified income preferred securities), QUIPS (quarterly income preferred securities), and QUIDS (quarterly income debt securities). The corporation that wants to raise capital (the "parent") establishes a trust, which issues fixed-dividend preferred stock. The parent then sells bonds (or debt of some type) to the trust, and the trust pays for the bonds with cash raised by selling preferred stock. At that point, the parent has the cash it needs, the trust holds debt issued by the parent, and the investing public holds preferred stock issued by the trust. The parent then makes interest payments to the trust, and the trust uses that income to make the preferred dividend payments. Because the parent company has issued debt, its interest payments are tax deductible.

If the dividends could be excluded from taxable income by corporate investors, this preferred would really be a great deal—the issuer could deduct the interest, corporate investors could exclude most of the dividends, and the IRS would be the loser. The corporate parent can deduct the interest paid to the trust, but IRS regulations do not allow the dividends on these securities to be excluded from the recipient's taxable income.

Because there is only one deduction, why are these new securities attractive? The answer is as follows:

(1) Since the parent company gets to take the deduction, its cost of funds from the preferred is $r_p(1 - T)$, just as it would be if it used debt. (2) The parent generates a tax savings, and it can thus afford to pay a relatively high rate on trust-related preferred; that is, it can pass on some of its tax savings to investors to induce them to buy the new securities. (3) The primary purchasers of the preferred are low-tax-bracket individuals and tax-exempt institutions such as pension funds. For such purchasers, not being able to exclude the dividend from taxable income is not important. (4) Due to the differential tax rates, the arrangement results in a net tax savings. Competition in capital markets results in a sharing of the savings between investors and corporations.

A recent *SmartMoney Online* article argued that these hybrid securities are a good deal for individual investors in low tax brackets for the reasons set forth here and also because they are sold in small increments—often as small as $25. However, these securities are complex, which increases their risk and makes them hard to value. There is also risk to the issuing corporations, because the IRS has expressed concerns about these securities, and if at some point the IRS decides to disallow interest paid to the trusts, that would have a profound negative effect on the issuing corporations.

Sources: Kerry Capell, "High Yields, Low Cost, Funny Names," *BusinessWeek*, September 9, 1996, p. 122; and Leslie Haggin, "SmartMoney Online: MIPS, QUIDS, and QUIPS," *SmartMoney Interactive*, April 6, 1999.

complicated cases for advanced classes and deal only with "plain vanilla" preferred issues.

No tax adjustments are made when calculating r_p because preferred dividends, unlike interest on debt, are *not* deductible. Therefore, no tax savings are associated with the use of preferred stock. However, as we discuss in the accompanying box, "Funny-Named Preferred-Like Securities," some companies have devised ways to issue securities that are similar to preferred stock but are structured in ways that enable them to deduct the payments made on these securities.

Is a tax adjustment made to the cost of preferred stock? Why or why not?

A company's preferred stock currently trades at $80 per share and pays a $6 annual dividend per share. If the company were to sell a new preferred issue, what would the cost of that capital be? Ignore flotation costs. (7.50%)

10-5 COST OF RETAINED EARNINGS, r_s

The costs of debt and preferred stock are based on the returns investors require on these securities. Similarly, the cost of common equity is based on the rate of return investors require on the company's common stock. Note, though, that new common equity is raised in two ways: (1) by retaining some of the current year's earnings and (2) by issuing new common stock. Equity raised by issuing stock has a somewhat higher cost than equity raised as retained earnings due to the flotation costs involved with new stock issues. Therefore, once they get beyond the startup stage, firms normally obtain all of their new equity by retaining earnings. We use the symbol r_s to designate the **cost of retained earnings** and r_e to designate the **cost of new stock,** or external equity.[7]

We might think that retained earnings are "free" because they represent money that is "left over" after paying dividends. While it is true that no direct costs are associated with capital raised as retained earnings, this capital still has a cost. The reasoning here involves the *opportunity cost principle.* The firm's after-tax earnings belong to its stockholders. Bondholders are compensated by interest payments and preferred stockholders by preferred dividends. All earnings remaining after interest and preferred dividends belong to the common stockholders, and these earnings serve to compensate stockholders for the use of their capital. Management can either pay out earnings in the form of dividends or retain earnings for reinvestment in the business. If management decides to retain earnings, there is an *opportunity cost* involved—stockholders could have received the earnings as dividends and invested this money in other stocks, in bonds, in real estate, or in anything else. *Thus, the firm needs to earn on its retained earnings at least as much as the stockholders themselves could earn on alternative investments of comparable risk.*

What rate of return can stockholders expect to earn on equivalent-risk investments? First, recall from Chapter 9 that stocks are normally in equilibrium, with expected and required rates of return being equal: $\hat{r}_s = r_s$. Thus, Allied's stockholders can expect to be able to earn r_s on their money. *Therefore, if the firm cannot invest retained earnings and earn at least r_s, it should pay those funds to its stockholders and let them invest directly in assets that do provide that return.*

Whereas debt and preferred stocks are contractual obligations whose costs are clearly stated on the contracts themselves, stocks have no comparable stated cost rate. That makes it difficult to measure r_s. However, we can employ techniques developed in Chapters 8 and 9 to produce reasonably good estimates of the cost of equity. To begin, recall that if a stock is in equilibrium, its required rate of return, r_s, must be equal to its expected rate of return, $\hat{r}_s$. Further, its *required* return is equal to a risk-free rate, r_{RF}, plus a risk premium, RP, whereas the *expected* return on the stock is its dividend yield, D_1/P_0, plus its expected growth rate, g. Thus, we can write out the following equation and then estimate r_s using the left or the right term, or both:

$$\text{Required rate of return} = \text{Expected rate of return}$$

$$r_s = r_{RF} + RP \quad = \quad D_1/P_0 + g = \hat{r}_s \qquad \textbf{(10-4)}$$

In other words, we can estimate r_s as $r_s = r_{RF} + RP$ or as $\hat{r}_s = D_1/P_0 + g$.

Cost of Retained Earnings, r_s
The rate of return required by stockholders on a firm's common stock.

Cost of New Common Stock, r_e
The cost of external equity; based on the cost of retained earnings, but increased for flotation costs.

---

[7] The term *retained earnings* can be interpreted to mean either the balance sheet item "retained earnings," consisting of all the earnings retained in the business throughout its history, or the income statement item "addition to retained earnings." The income statement item is used in this chapter; for our purpose, *retained earnings* refers to that part of the current year's earnings not paid as dividends, hence available for reinvestment in the business this year.

10-5a The CAPM Approach

The most widely used approach to the cost of common equity is the Capital Asset Pricing Model (CAPM) as developed in Chapter 8, following these steps:

Step 1: Estimate the risk-free rate, r_{RF}. Many analysts use the 10-year Treasury bond rate as a measure of the risk-free rate. Others use a short-term Treasury bill rate.

Step 2: Estimate the stock's beta coefficient, b_i, and use it as an index of the stock's risk. The i signifies the *i*th company's beta.

Step 3: Estimate the expected market risk premium. Recall that the market risk premium is the difference between the return that investors require to hold an average stock and the risk-free rate.[8]

Step 4: Substitute the preceding values into the CAPM equation to estimate the required rate of return on the stock in question:

$$r_s = r_{RF} + (RP_M)b_i$$
$$= r_{RF} + (r_M - r_{RF})b_i \qquad \textbf{(10-5)}$$

Equation 10-5 shows that the CAPM estimate of r_s is equal to the risk-free rate, r_{RF}, plus a risk premium that is equal to the risk premium on an average stock, $r_M - r_{RF}$, scaled up or down to reflect the particular stock's risk exposure as measured by its beta coefficient.

Assume that in today's market, $r_{RF} = 6\%$ and the market risk premium $RP_M = (r_M - r_{RF}) = 5\%$, and Allied's beta is 1.48. Using the CAPM approach, Allied's cost of equity is estimated as follows:

$$r_s = 6\% + (5\%)(1.48)$$
$$= 13.4\%$$

Although the CAPM appears to yield an accurate, precise estimate of r_s, several potential problems exist. First, as we saw in Chapter 8, if a firm's stockholders are not well diversified, they may be concerned with *stand-alone risk* rather than just market risk. In that case, the firm's true investment risk would not be measured by its beta, and the CAPM estimate would understate the correct value of r_s. Further, even if the CAPM method is valid, it is hard to obtain accurate estimates of the required inputs because (1) there is controversy about whether to use long-term or short-term Treasury yields for r_{RF}, (2) it is hard to estimate the beta that investors expect the company to have in the future, and (3) it is difficult to estimate the proper market risk premium. As we indicated earlier, the CAPM approach is used most often, but because of the just-noted problems, analysts also estimate the cost of equity using other approaches.

10-5b Dividend-Yield-plus-Growth-Rate, or Discounted Cash Flow (DCF), Approach

In Chapter 9, we saw that both the price and the expected rate of return on a share of common stock depend, ultimately, on the stock's expected cash flows. For companies that are expected to go on indefinitely, the cash flows are the dividends, while if investors expect the firm to be acquired by some other firm or to

---

[8] Note that your estimate of the market risk premium (RP_M, or $r_M - r_{RF}$) depends on the measure used for the risk-free rate. In the common situation where the yield curve is upward sloping, the 10-year Treasury bond rate will exceed the short-term Treasury bill rate—and it follows that you will have a lower estimate of the market risk premium if you select the higher longer-term rate as the risk-free rate.

be liquidated, then the cash flows would be dividends for some time plus a terminal price when the firm is acquired or liquidated. For simplicity, we assume that the firm is expected to go on indefinitely, in which case the following equation applies:

$$P_0 = \frac{D_1}{(1 + r_s)^1} + \frac{D_2}{(1 + r_s)^2} + \cdots + \frac{D_\infty}{(1 + r_s)^\infty}$$

$$= \sum_{t=1}^{\infty} \frac{D_t}{(1 + r_s)^t} \tag{10-6}$$

Here P_0 is the current price of the stock; D_t is the dividend expected to be paid at the end of Year t; and r_s is the required rate of return. If dividends are expected to grow at a constant rate, then, as we saw in Chapter 9, Equation 10-6 reduces to this important formula:[9]

$$P_0 = \frac{D_1}{r_s - g} \tag{10-7}$$

We can solve for r_s to obtain the required rate of return on common equity, which for the marginal investor is also equal to the expected rate of return:

$$r_s = \hat{r}_s = \frac{D_1}{P_0} + \text{Expected g} \tag{10-8}$$

Thus, investors expect to receive a dividend yield, D_1/P_0, plus a capital gain, g, for a total expected return of $\hat{r}_s$, and in equilibrium this expected return is also equal to the required return, r_s. This method of estimating the cost of equity is called the *discounted cash flow, or DCF, method*. Henceforth, we will assume that equilibrium exists, and we will use the terms r_s and $\hat{r}_s$ interchangeably.

It is easy to determine the dividend yield, but it is difficult to establish the proper growth rate. If past growth rates in earnings and dividends have been relatively stable, and if investors appear to be projecting a continuation of past trends, then g may be based on the firm's historic growth rate. *However, if the company's past growth has been abnormally high or low, either because of its own unique situation or because of general economic fluctuations, then investors will not project the past growth rate into the future.* In this case, g must be estimated in some other manner.

Security analysts regularly make earnings and dividend growth forecasts, looking at such factors as projected sales, profit margins, and competition. For example, *Value Line*, which is available in most libraries, provides growth rate forecasts for 1,700 companies, and Merrill Lynch, Smith Barney, and other organizations make similar forecasts. Therefore, someone estimating a firm's cost of equity can obtain several analysts' forecasts, average them, use the average as a proxy for the growth expectations of investors in general, and then combine this g with the current dividend yield to estimate $\hat{r}_s$ as follows:

$$\hat{r}_s = \frac{D_1}{P_0} + \text{Growth rate as projected by security analysts}$$

---

[9] If the growth rate is not expected to be constant, the DCF procedure can still be used to estimate r_s, but in this case it is necessary to calculate an average growth rate using the procedures described in this chapter's *Excel* model.

Again, note that this estimate of $\hat{r}_s$ is based on the assumption that g is expected to remain constant in the future or else we must use an average of expected future rates.[10]

Another method for estimating g involves first forecasting the firm's average future dividend payout ratio and its complement, the *retention rate*, and then multiplying the retention rate by the company's average expected future rate of return on equity (ROE):

$$g = (\text{Retention rate})(\text{ROE}) = (1.0 - \text{Payout rate})(\text{ROE}) \quad \textbf{(10-9)}$$

Intuitively, we know that profitable firms that retain a larger portion of their earnings for reinvestment will tend to have higher growth rates than firms that are less profitable or else pay out a higher percentage of their earnings as dividends. Security analysts often use Equation 10-9 when they estimate growth rates. For example, suppose a company is expected to have a constant ROE of 13.4 percent, and it is expected to pay out 40 percent of its earnings and to retain 60 percent. In this case, its forecasted growth rate would be g = (0.60)(13.4%) = 8.0%.

To illustrate the DCF approach, suppose Allied's stock sells for $23; its next expected dividend is $1.24; and its expected growth rate is 8 percent. Allied's expected and required rate of return, hence its cost of retained earnings, would then be 13.4 percent:

$$\hat{r}_s = r_s = \frac{\$1.24}{\$23} + 8.0\%$$

$$= 5.4\% + 8.0\%$$

$$= 13.4\%$$

This 13.4 percent is the minimum rate of return that management should expect to earn on retained earnings to justify plowing earnings back in the business rather than paying them out to stockholders as dividends. Put another way, since investors have an *opportunity* to earn 13.4 percent if earnings are paid to them as dividends, then the *opportunity cost* of equity from retained earnings is 13.4 percent.

In this example, Allied's estimated cost of equity, 13.4 percent, is the same using both the CAPM and DCF approaches. Consequently, we would use 13.4 percent as Allied's estimated cost of equity from retained earnings. In most cases, however, these two approaches will not produce exactly the same estimate, which requires managers to use judgment when deciding on the proper value for r_s. In some cases, an average of the two estimates will be used, while in other cases managers will rely solely on the approach they believe is most appropriate. For example, if a company doesn't pay a dividend, it will probably rely on the CAPM approach, while if it does pay steady dividends but has a beta that appears to be out of line with other firms in its industry, it may rely primarily on the DCF approach.[11]

---

[10] Analysts' growth rate forecasts are usually for five years into the future, and the rates provided represent the average growth rate over that five-year horizon. Studies have shown that analysts' forecasts represent the best source of growth rate data for DCF cost of capital estimates. See Robert Harris, "Using Analysts' Growth Rate Forecasts to Estimate Shareholder Required Rates of Return," *Financial Management*, Spring 1986.

Two organizations—IBES and Zacks—collect the forecasts of leading analysts for most larger companies, average these forecasts, and then publish the averages. The IBES and Zacks data are available over the Internet through online computer data services.

[11] A recent survey by John Graham and Campbell Harvey indicates that the CAPM approach is most often used to estimate the cost of equity. More than 70 percent of the surveyed firms used the CAPM approach, whereas only about 15 percent used the DCF approach. For more details, see John R. Graham and Campbell R. Harvey, "The Theory and Practice of Corporate Finance: Evidence from the Field," *Journal of Financial Economics*, Vol. 60, nos. 2 and 3 (May-June 2001), pp. 187–243.

People experienced in estimating the cost of equity recognize that both careful analysis and sound judgment are required. It would be nice to pretend that judgment is unnecessary and to specify an easy, precise way of determining the cost of equity. Unfortunately, this is not possible—finance is in large part a matter of judgment, and we simply must face that fact.

10-5c Bond-Yield-plus-Risk-Premium Approach

In situations where reliable inputs for neither the CAPM nor the DCF approaches are available, analysts often use a somewhat more subjective procedure to estimate the cost of equity. Both surveys of portfolio managers and empirical studies suggest that the risk premium on a firm's stock over its own bonds generally ranges from 3 to 5 percentage points.[12] Based on this evidence, the analysts simply add a judgmental risk premium of 3 to 5 percent to the interest rate on the firm's own long-term debt to estimate its cost of equity. Firms with risky, low-rated, and consequently high-interest-rate debt also have risky, high-cost equity, and the procedure of basing the cost of equity on the firm's readily observable debt cost utilizes this logic. For example, given that Allied's bonds yield 10 percent, its cost of equity might be estimated as follows:

$$r_s = \text{Bond yield} + \text{Risk premium} = 10\% + 4\% = 14\%$$

The bonds of a riskier company might yield 12 percent, in which case its estimated cost of equity would be 16 percent:

$$r_s = 12\% + 4\% = 16\%$$

Because the 4 percent risk premium is a judgmental estimate, the estimated value of r_s is also judgmental. Therefore, an analyst might use a range of 3 to 5 percent for the risk premium and obtain a range of 13 to 15 percent for Allied. While this method does not produce a precise cost of equity, it should "get us into the right ballpark."

Why must a cost be assigned to retained earnings?

What three approaches are used to estimate the cost of common equity?

Identify some problems with the CAPM approach.

Which of the two components of the DCF formula, the dividend yield or the growth rate, is more difficult to estimate? Why?

What's the logic behind the bond-yield-plus-risk-premium approach?

Suppose you are an analyst with the following data: $r_{RF} = 5.5\%$; $r_M - r_{RF} = 6\%$; $b = 0.8$; $D_1 = \$1.00$; $P_0 = \$25.00$; $g = 6\%$; r_d = firm's bond yield = 6.5%. What is this firm's cost of equity using the CAPM, DCF, and bond-yield-plus-risk-premium approaches? Use the mid-range of the judgmental risk premium for the bond-yield-plus-risk-premium approach. (CAPM = 10.3%; DCF = 10%; Bond yield + RP = 10.5%)

---

[12] Some security analysts send out questionnaires to portfolio managers asking this question: "If a given firm's bonds yield 8 percent, what is the minimum rate of return you would have to earn on its equity in order to induce you to buy its common stock?" The answers are generally in the 3 to 5 percent range. The reports that we have seen were proprietary, so the studies are not generally available. Also, analysts have calculated the historical returns on common stocks and on corporate bonds and then used the differential as an estimate of the equity risk premium over a firm's own bonds. The best known of these studies is by Ibbotson Associates. The historical results vary from year to year, but again, a range of 3 to 5 percent is quite common.

How Much Does It Cost to Raise External Capital?

A study by four professors provides some insights into how much it costs U.S. corporations to raise external capital. Using information from the Securities Data Company, they found the average flotation cost for equity and debt as presented here.

The common stock flotation costs are for established firms, not for firms raising funds in IPOs. Costs associated with IPOs are much higher—flotation costs are about 17 percent of gross proceeds for common equity if the amount raised in the IPO is less than $10 million and about 6 percent if more than $500 million is raised. The data shown include both utility and nonutility companies. If utilities were excluded, flotation costs would be somewhat higher. Also, the debt costs are for debt raised using investment bankers. Most debt is actually obtained from banks and other creditors, and there flotation costs are generally quite small or nonexistent.

Amount of Capital Raised (Millions of Dollars)	Average Flotation Cost for Common Stock (% of Total Capital Raised)	Average Flotation Cost for New Debt (% of Total Capital Raised)
2–9.99	13.28	4.39
10–19.99	8.72	2.76
20–39.99	6.93	2.42
40–59.99	5.87	1.32
60–79.99	5.18	2.34
80–99.99	4.73	2.16
100–199.99	4.22	2.31
200–499.99	3.47	2.19
500 and up	3.15	1.64

Source: Inmoo Lee, Scott Lochhead, Jay Ritter, and Quanshui Zhao, "The Costs of Raising Capital," *The Journal of Financial Research*, Vol. XIX, no. 1 (Spring 1996), pp. 59–74. Reprinted with permission.

10-6 COST OF NEW COMMON STOCK, r_e[13]

Companies generally use an investment banker when they issue common or preferred stock, and sometimes when they issue bonds. In return for a fee, the investment banker helps the company structure the terms and set a price for the issue, then sells the issue to investors. The banker's fees are called *flotation costs*, and the total cost of the capital raised reflects the investors' required return plus the flotation costs.

For most firms at most times, flotation costs are not high enough to worry about because (1) most equity comes from retained earnings, (2) most debt is raised from banks and in private placements and hence involves no flotation costs, and (3) preferred stock is rarely used. Therefore, in our discussion thus far we have simply ignored flotation costs. However, as you can see in the

---

[13] This section is relatively technical, but it can be omitted without loss of continuity if time pressures necessitate.

accompanying box, flotation costs can be substantial, and they vary depending on the size of the issue and the type of capital raised. We now describe two approaches that can be used to account for these flotation costs when firms use investment bankers to raise capital.[14]

10-6a Add Flotation Costs to a Project's Cost

With the first approach we add the estimated dollar amount of flotation costs for each project to the project's up-front cost. In the next chapter, we will see that capital budgeting projects typically involve an initial cash outlay followed by a series of cash inflows. We can add any required flotation costs, found as the sum of the flotation costs for the debt, preferred, and common stock used to finance the project, to the initial investment cost. Because of the now-higher investment cost, the project's expected rate of return and NPV will be decreased. For example, consider a one-year project with an up-front cost (not including flotation costs) of $100 million. After one year, the project is expected to produce an inflow of $115 million. Therefore, its expected return is $115/$100 − 1 = 0.15 = 15.0%. However, if the project requires the company to raise $100 million of new capital with an estimated $2 million of flotation costs, the total up-front cost will rise to $102 million and the expected rate of return will fall to $115/$102 − 1 = 0.1275 = 12.75%.

10-6b Increase the Cost of Capital

The second approach involves adjusting the cost of capital rather than increasing the project's cost. If the firm plans to continue using the capital in the future, as is generally true for equity, then this second approach is theoretically better. The adjustment process is based on the following logic. If there are flotation costs, the issuing company receives only a portion of the capital provided by investors, with the remainder going to the underwriter. To provide investors with their required rate of return, given that less money is available to the company than the amount the investors put up, then each dollar received must "work harder," that is, it must earn a higher rate of return than the investors required on the funds they put up. For example, suppose investors require a 10 percent return on their investment, but the firm actually gets to keep and invest only 90 percent of the amount investors put up. In that case, the firm would have to earn about 11 percent on the available funds in order to provide investors with a 10 percent return on their investment. This higher rate of return is the flotation-adjusted cost of equity.

The DCF approach can be adapted to account for flotation costs, using the following equation for the *cost of new common stock*, r_e:[15]

$$\text{Cost of equity from new stock issues} = r_e = \frac{D_1}{P_0(1 - F)} + g \quad \text{(10-10)}$$

Here **F** is the percentage **flotation cost** required to sell the new stock, so $P_0(1 - F)$ is the net price per share received by the company.

Flotation Cost, F
The percentage cost of issuing new common stock.

---

[14] A more complete discussion of flotation cost adjustments can be found in Brigham and Daves, *Intermediate Financial Management*, and other advanced texts.
[15] Equation 10-10 is derived in Brigham and Daves, *Intermediate Financial Management*, 8th ed., p. 319.

Assuming that Allied has a flotation cost of 10 percent, its cost of new common equity, r_e, is computed as follows:

$$r_e = \frac{\$1.24}{\$23(1 - 0.10)} + 8.0\%$$

$$= \frac{\$1.24}{\$20.70} + 8.0\%$$

$$= 6.0\% + 8.0\% = 14.0\%$$

Investors require a return of $r_s = 13.4\%$ on the stock. However, because of flotation costs the company must earn *more* than 13.4 percent on the net funds it receives in order to give investors a 13.4 percent return on their money. Specifically, if the firm earns 14 percent on funds obtained by issuing new stock, then earnings per share will remain at the previously expected level, the firm's expected dividend can be maintained, and the stock price will not decline. If the firm earns less than 14 percent, then earnings, dividends, and growth will fall below expectations and the stock price will decline. If the firm earns more than 14 percent, the stock price will rise.

10-6c When Must External Equity Be Used?

Because of flotation costs, dollars raised by selling new stock must "work harder" than dollars raised by retaining earnings. Moreover, because no flotation costs are involved, retained earnings cost less than new stock. Therefore, firms should utilize retained earnings to the extent possible. However, if a firm has more good investment opportunities than can be financed with retained earnings plus debt supported by those retained earnings, it may need to issue new common stock. The total amount of capital raised beyond which new stock must be issued is defined as the **retained earnings breakpoint,** and it can be calculated as follows:

Retained Earnings Breakpoint
The amount of capital raised beyond which new common stock must be issued.

$$\text{Retained earnings breakpoint} = \frac{\text{Addition to retained earnings}}{\text{Equity fraction}} \quad \textbf{(10-11)}$$

Allied's addition to retained earnings in 2006 is expected to be $68 million, and its target capital structure consists of 45 percent debt, 2 percent preferred, and 53 percent equity. Therefore, its retained earnings breakpoint is

$$\text{Retained earnings breakpoint} = \$68/0.53 = \$128 \text{ million}$$

If Allied's capital budget called for spending any amount up to $128 million, then 0.45($128) = $57.6 million would be financed with debt, 0.02($128) = $2.6 million with preferred stock, and 0.53($128) = $67.8 million with equity raised from retained earnings. However, if the capital budget exceeded $128 million, the company would have to obtain equity by issuing new, high-cost common stock.[16]

---

[16] It's important to recognize that this breakpoint is only suggestive—it is not written in stone. For example, rather than issuing new common stock, the company could use more debt (hence increasing its debt ratio), or it might increase its additions to retained earnings by reducing its dividend payout ratio. Both actions would change the retained earnings breakpoint. Also, breakpoints could occur due to increases in the costs of debt and preferred. Indeed, all manner of changes could occur, and the end result would be a large number of breakpoints. All of this is discussed in more detail in Brigham and Daves, *Intermediate Financial Management*, 8th ed., Chapter 9.

Explain briefly the two approaches that can be used to adjust for flotation costs.

Would firms that have many good investment opportunities be likely to have higher or lower dividend payout ratios than firms with few good investment opportunities? Explain.

A firm has common stock with $D_1 = \$1.50$; $P_0 = \$30$; $g = 5\%$; and $F = 4\%$. If the firm must issue new stock, what is its cost of issuing new external equity? (10.21%)

10-7 COMPOSITE, OR WEIGHTED AVERAGE, COST OF CAPITAL, WACC

Allied's target capital structure calls for 45 percent debt, 2 percent preferred stock, and 53 percent common equity. Earlier we saw that Allied's before-tax cost of debt is 10 percent; its after-tax cost of debt is $r_d(1 - T) = 10\%(0.6) = 6.0\%$; its cost of preferred stock is 10.3 percent; its cost of common equity from retained earnings is 13.4 percent; and its marginal tax rate is 40 percent. Equation 10-1, presented earlier, can be used to calculate the WACC when all of the new common equity comes from retained earnings:

$$\text{WACC} = w_d r_d (1 - T) + w_p r_p + w_c r_s$$
$$= 0.45(10\%)(0.6) + 0.02(10.3\%) + 0.53(13.4\%)$$
$$= 10.0\%$$

Under these conditions, every dollar of new capital that Allied raises would consist of 45 cents of debt with an after-tax cost of 6 percent, 2 cents of preferred stock with a cost of 10.3 percent, and 53 cents of common equity (all from additions to retained earnings) with a cost of 13.4 percent. The average cost of each whole dollar, or the WACC, would be 10 percent.[17]

As long as Allied keeps its capital structure on target, its debt has an after-tax cost of 6 percent, its preferred stock has a cost of 10.3 percent, and its common equity comes from retained earnings at a cost of 13.4 percent, then its WACC will be 10 percent. Each dollar raised will consist of some debt, some preferred stock, and some common equity, and the cost of the whole dollar will be 10 percent.

Our estimate of Allied's WACC assumed that Allied's common equity comes exclusively from retained earnings. If Allied were to instead issue new common stock its WACC would be slightly higher because of the additional flotation costs. In the Web Appendix 10A we discuss in more detail the connection between the WACC and the costs of issuing new common stock.

---

[17] The WACC is the cost of investor-supplied capital used to finance new projects. The debt component of the target capital structure includes only interest-bearing, investor-supplied debt—long-term bonds and bank notes payable. It does not include accounts payable and accruals because those items are not provided by investors.

Write out the equation for the WACC.

Is short-term debt included in the capital structure used to calculate WACC? Why or why not?

Why does the WACC at every amount of capital raised represent the marginal cost of that capital?

A firm has the following data: Target capital structure of 46 percent debt, 3 percent preferred, and 51 percent common equity; Tax rate = 40%; r_d = 7%; r_p = 7.5%; and r_s = 11.5%. Assume the firm will not be issuing new stock. What is this firm's WACC? (8.02% ≈ 8%)

10-8 FACTORS THAT AFFECT THE WACC

The cost of capital is affected by a number of factors. Some are beyond a firm's control, but others are influenced by its financing and investment decisions.

10-8a Factors the Firm Cannot Control

The two most important factors that are beyond a firm's direct control are *interest rates* and *tax rates*. If interest rates in the economy rise, the cost of debt increases because firms will have to pay bondholders more when they borrow. Also, recall from our discussion of the CAPM that higher interest rates increase the costs of common and preferred equity. In recent years inflation, and consequently, interest rates, have been trending down. This has reduced the costs of capital for all firms, and that has encouraged corporate investment.

Tax rates are used in the calculation of the component cost of debt and thus they have an important effect on the cost of capital. Taxes also affect the cost of capital in other less apparent ways. For example, the recent lowering of tax rates on dividends and capital gains relative to rates on interest income makes stocks relatively attractive, and that reduces the relative cost of equity and thus the WACC. Also, as we will see in the capital structure chapter, lower dividend and capital gains taxes have led to a change in the optimal capital structure—toward less debt and more equity.

10-8b Factors the Firm Can Control

A firm can directly affect its cost of capital in three primary ways: (1) by changing its *capital structure*, (2) by changing its *dividend payout*, and (3) by *altering its capital budgeting decision rules* to accept projects with more or less risk than in the past.

Regarding capital structure, we have assumed that firms have given target capital structures, and we used those target weights to calculate their WACCs. However, if a firm changes its target capital structure, then the weights used to calculate the WACC will change. Because the after-tax cost of debt is lower than the cost of equity, an increase in the target debt ratio will tend to lower the WACC, and vice versa if the debt ratio is lowered. However, an increase in the use of debt will increase the riskiness of both the debt and the equity, and these increases in component costs might offset the effects of the change in the weights and leave the WACC unchanged or even higher. In the capital structure chapter, we will discuss these effects in more detail.

Dividend policy affects the amount of retained earnings available to the firm, and thus the possible need to sell new stock and thus incur flotation costs. This suggests that the higher the dividend payout ratio, the smaller the addition to retained earnings and thus the higher the cost of equity and therefore the WACC. However, investors may want the firm to pay out more dividends, and thus a reduction in the payout ratio might lead to an increase in the required rate of return on equity. As we will see in the chapter on dividends, the optimal dividend policy is a complicated issue but one with a potentially important effect on the cost of capital.

The firm's capital budgeting decisions can also affect its cost of capital. When we estimate the cost of capital, we use as the starting point the required rates of return on the firm's outstanding stock and bonds. Those cost rates reflect the riskiness of the firm's existing assets. Therefore, we have been implicitly assuming that new capital will be invested in the same types of assets and with the same degrees of risk as the existing assets. This assumption is generally correct, as most firms do invest in assets similar to those they currently operate. However, if the firm decides to invest in an entirely new and risky line of business, then its component costs of debt and equity, and thus the WACC, will increase. To illustrate, ITT Corporation recently sold off its finance company and purchased Caesar's World, which operates gambling casinos. This dramatic shift in corporate focus almost certainly affected ITT's cost of capital. The effect of investment decisions on capital costs is discussed in detail in the next section.

What two factors that affect the cost of capital are generally beyond the firm's control?

What are three factors under the firm's control that can affect its cost of capital?

Suppose interest rates in the economy increase. How would such a change affect each component of the WACC?

10-9 ADJUSTING THE COST OF CAPITAL FOR RISK

As you will see in the chapters on capital budgeting that follow, the cost of capital is a key element in the capital budgeting process. Projects should be accepted if and only if their estimated returns exceed their costs of capital. Thus, the cost of capital is a "hurdle rate"—a project's expected rate of return must "jump the hurdle" for it to be accepted. Moreover, investors require higher returns on riskier investments. Consequently, companies that are raising capital to take on risky projects will have higher costs of capital than companies that are investing in safer projects.

Figure 10-2 illustrates the trade-off between risk and the cost of capital. Firm L is in a low-risk business and has a WACC of 8 percent, whereas Firm H's business is exposed to greater risk and consequently it has a WACC of 12 percent. Thus, Firm L will accept a typical project if its expected return is above 8 percent, whereas the corresponding hurdle rate for Firm H is 12 percent.

It is important to remember that the costs of capital at points L and H in Figure 10-2 represent the overall, or composite, WACCs for the two firms, and thus apply to only "typical" projects for each firm. However, different projects often have different risks, even for a given firm. Therefore, each project's hurdle rate should reflect the risk of the project itself, not the risk associated with the firm's average project as reflected in its composite WACC. For example, assume that Firms L and H are both considering Project A. This project has more risk than a typical Firm L project, but less risk than a typical Firm H project. As shown in Figure 10-2, Project A has a 10.5 percent expected return. At first, we might be

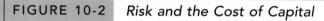

FIGURE 10-2 *Risk and the Cost of Capital*

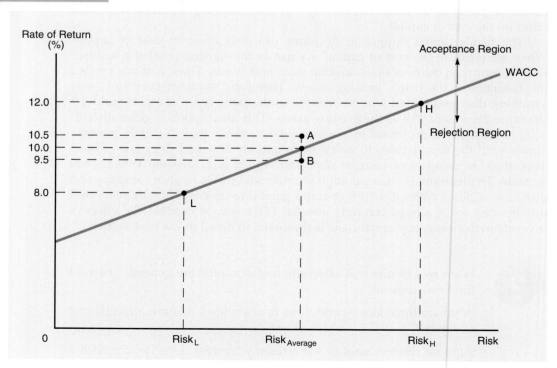

tempted to conclude that Firm L should accept Project A because its 10.5 percent return is above L's 8 percent WACC, while H should turn the project down because its return is less than H's 12 percent WACC. However, this would be wrong. The relevant hurdle rate is the *project's WACC*, which is 10 percent, as read from the WACC line in Figure 10-2. Since the project's return exceeds its 10 percent cost, it should be acceptable to *both* Firms L and H.

Next, consider Project B. It has the same risk as Project A, but its expected return is 9.5 percent versus its 10 percent hurdle rate. Both firms should reject Project B because its return is not high enough to justify its risk.

We see, then, that the hurdle rate applied to each project should reflect the project's own risk, not necessarily the firm's overall risk as reflected in its WACC. Empirical studies do indicate that firms take account of individual projects' risks, but they also indicate that most firms regard most projects as having about the same risk as the firm's average existing assets. Therefore, the WACC is used to evaluate most projects, but if a project has an especially high or low risk, then the WACC will be adjusted up or down to account for this difference. We will discuss this point in more detail in Chapter 12.

These same arguments apply to the cost of capital for multidivisional firms. Consider Firm A in Figure 10-3. It has two divisions, L and H. Division L has relatively little risk, and if it were operated as a separate firm, its WACC would be 7 percent. Division H has higher risk, and its divisional cost of capital is 13 percent. If the two divisions were of equal size, Firm A's composite WACC would be 0.50(7%) + 0.50(13%) = 10.0%. However, it would be a mistake to use this 10 percent WACC for either division. To see this point, assume that Division L is considering a relatively low-risk project with an expected return of 9 percent, while Division H is considering a higher-risk project with an expected return of

---

FIGURE 10-3   *Divisional Cost of Capital*

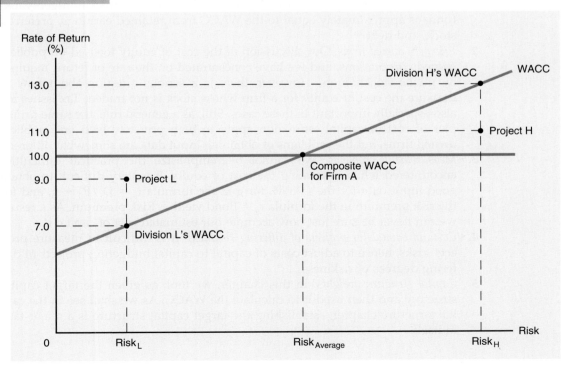

11 percent. As shown in Figure 10-3, Division L's project should be accepted because its return is above its risk-based cost of capital, whereas Division H's project should be rejected. If the 10 percent corporate WACC were used by each division, the decision would be reversed: Division H would incorrectly accept its project, and Division L would incorrectly reject its project. In general, failing to adjust for differences in risk would lead the firm to accept too many risky projects and reject too many safe ones. Over time, the firm would become more risky, its WACC would increase, and its shareholder value would suffer. Actually measuring project risk and then deciding exactly how to account for it is discussed in Chapter 12.

Why is the cost of capital sometimes referred to as a "hurdle rate"?

How should firms evaluate projects with different risks?

Should divisions within the same firm all use the firm's composite WACC when considering capital budgeting projects? Explain.

10-10 SOME OTHER PROBLEMS WITH COST OF CAPITAL ESTIMATES

A number of issues relating to the cost of capital either have not been mentioned or were glossed over in this chapter. These topics are covered in advanced finance courses, but they deserve mention now both to alert you to potential dangers and to provide a preview of some matters covered in advanced courses.

1. *Depreciation-generated funds.* The largest single source of capital for many firms is depreciation, yet we have not discussed the cost of funds from this source. In brief, depreciation cash flows can either be reinvested or returned to investors (stockholders *and* creditors). The cost of depreciation-generated funds is approximately equal to the WACC from retained earnings, preferred stock, and debt.[18]
2. *Privately owned firms.* Our discussion of the cost of equity focused on publicly owned corporations, and we have concentrated on the rate of return required by public stockholders. However, there is a serious question about how to measure the cost of equity for a firm whose stock is not traded. Tax issues are also especially important in these cases. Still, as a general rule, the same principles of cost of capital estimation apply to both privately held and publicly owned firms, but the problems of obtaining input data are somewhat different.
3. *Measurement problems.* We cannot overemphasize the practical difficulties encountered when estimating the cost of equity. It is very difficult to obtain good input data for the CAPM, for g in the formula $\hat{r}_s = D_1/P_0 + g$, and for the risk premium in the formula $r_s = $ Bond yield + Risk premium. As a result, we can never be sure just how accurate our estimated cost of capital is.
4. *Costs of capital for projects of differing riskiness.* It is difficult to measure projects' risks, hence to adjust costs of capital to capital budgeting projects of differing degrees of riskiness.
5. *Capital structure weights.* In this chapter, we took as given the target capital structure and then used it to calculate the WACC. As we shall see in the capital structure chapter, establishing the target capital structure is a major task in itself.

[18] See Brigham and Daves, *Intermediate Financial Management*, 8th ed., Chapter 9, for a discussion.

Although this list of problems may appear formidable, the state of the art in cost of capital estimation is really not in bad shape. The procedures outlined in this chapter can be used to obtain cost of capital estimates that are sufficiently accurate for practical purposes, and the problems listed here merely indicate the desirability of refinements. The refinements are not unimportant, but the problems we have listed do not invalidate the usefulness of the procedures outlined in the chapter.

Identify some problem areas in cost of capital analysis. Do these problems invalidate the cost of capital procedures discussed in the chapter?

Tying It All Together

We began this chapter by discussing the concept of the weighted average cost of capital. We then discussed the three capital components (debt, preferred stock, and common equity) and procedures used to estimate their component costs. Next, we calculated the WACC, which is a key element in capital budgeting. We assumed that the target capital structure has been specified, and we used the given target weights to calculate the WACC. However, changes in the target capital structure can affect the WACC, so we discuss capital structure in detail in a later chapter.

We also noted that the corporate WACC is based on the riskiness of the entire firm, and it should be used as the hurdle rate in capital budgeting if and only if the project under consideration has about the same risk as the firm's existing assets. If the project is judged to be more risky than average, the WACC should be increased, and vice versa if the project has less than average risk. The amount by which to increase or decrease the WACC to adjust for differential project risk is somewhat subjective, but as we discuss in Chapter 12, techniques are available that help us measure a project's risk.

SELF-TEST QUESTIONS AND PROBLEMS
(Solutions Appear in Appendix A)

ST-1 **Key terms** Define each of the following terms:
a. Capital components
b. After-tax cost of debt, $r_d(1 - T)$
c. Cost of preferred stock, r_p
d. Cost of retained earnings, r_s; cost of new common stock, r_e
e. Target (optimal) capital structure; target weights (w_d, w_p, w_c)
f. Weighted average cost of capital, WACC
g. Flotation cost, F; retained earnings breakpoint

ST-2 **WACC** Lancaster Engineering Inc. (LEI) has the following capital structure, which it considers to be optimal:

Debt	25%
Preferred stock	15
Common equity	60
	100%

LEI's expected net income this year is $34,285.72, its established dividend payout ratio is 30 percent, its federal-plus-state tax rate is 40 percent, and investors expect earnings and dividends to grow at a constant rate of 9 percent in the future. LEI paid a dividend of $3.60 per share last year, and its stock currently sells for $54 per share.

LEI can obtain new capital in the following ways:

- *Preferred*: New preferred stock with a dividend of $11 can be sold to the public at a price of $95 per share.
- *Debt*: Debt can be sold at an interest rate of 12 percent.

a. Determine the cost of each capital component.
b. Calculate the WACC.
c. LEI has the following investment opportunities that are average-risk projects for the firm:

Project	Cost at t = 0	Rate of Return
A	$10,000	17.4%
B	20,000	16.0
C	10,000	14.2
D	20,000	13.7
E	10,000	12.0

Which projects should LEI accept? Why?

QUESTIONS

10-1 How would each of the following affect a firm's cost of debt, $r_d(1 - T)$; its cost of equity, r_s; and its WACC? Indicate by a plus (+), a minus (−), or a zero (0) if the factor would raise, lower, or have an indeterminate effect on the item in question. Assume for each answer that other things are held constant, even though in some instances this would probably not be true. Be prepared to justify your answer, but recognize that several of the parts have no single correct answer; these questions are designed to stimulate thought and discussion.

		EFFECT ON		
		$r_d(1 - T)$	r_s	WACC
a.	The corporate tax rate is lowered.	_____	_____	_____
b.	The Federal Reserve tightens credit.	_____	_____	_____
c.	The firm uses more debt; that is, it increases its debt/assets ratio.	_____	_____	_____
d.	The dividend payout ratio is increased.	_____	_____	_____
e.	The firm doubles the amount of capital it raises during the year.	_____	_____	_____
f.	The firm expands into a risky new area.	_____	_____	_____
g.	The firm merges with another firm whose earnings are countercyclical both to those of the first firm and to the stock market.	_____	_____	_____
h.	The stock market falls drastically, and the firm's stock price falls along with the rest.	_____	_____	_____
i.	Investors become more risk averse.	_____	_____	_____

	EFFECT ON		
	$r_d(1 - T)$	r_s	WACC

j. The firm is an electric utility with a
    large investment in nuclear plants.
    Several states are considering a ban on
    nuclear power generation. _____ _____ _____

10-2 Assume that the risk-free rate increases. What impact would this have on the cost of debt? What impact would it have on the cost of equity?

10-3 How should the capital structure weights used to calculate the WACC be determined?

10-4 Suppose a firm estimates its WACC to be 10 percent. Should the WACC be used to evaluate all of its potential projects, even if they vary in risk? If not, what might be "reasonable" costs of capital for average-, high-, and low-risk projects?

10-5 The WACC is a weighted average of the costs of debt, preferred stock, and common equity. Would the WACC be different if the equity for the coming year will all come in the form of retained earnings versus some equity from the sale of new common stock? Would the calculated WACC depend in any way on the size of the capital budget? How might dividend policy affect the WACC?

PROBLEMS

Easy
Problems 1–5

10-1 **After-tax cost of debt** The Heuser Company's currently outstanding bonds have a 10 percent coupon and a 12 percent yield to maturity. Heuser believes it could issue new bonds at par that would provide a similar yield to maturity. If its marginal tax rate is 35 percent, what is Heuser's after-tax cost of debt?

10-2 **Cost of preferred stock** Tunney Industries can issue perpetual preferred stock at a price of $47.50 a share. The stock would pay a constant annual dividend of $3.80 a share. What is the company's cost of preferred stock, r_p?

10-3 **Cost of common equity** Percy Motors has a target capital structure of 40 percent debt and 60 percent common equity, with no preferred stock. The yield to maturity on the company's outstanding bonds is 9 percent, and its tax rate is 40 percent. Percy's CFO estimates that the company's WACC is 9.96 percent. What is Percy's cost of common equity?

10-4 **Cost of equity with and without flotation** Javits & Sons' common stock currently trades at $30 a share. It is expected to pay an annual dividend of $3.00 a share at the end of the year (D_1 = $3.00), and the constant growth rate is 5 percent a year.
   a. What is the company's cost of common equity if all of its equity comes from retained earnings?
   b. If the company were to issue new stock, it would incur a 10 percent flotation cost. What would the cost of equity from new stock be?

10-5 **Project selection** Midwest Water Works estimates that its WACC is 10.5 percent. The company is considering the following capital budgeting projects:

Project	Size	Rate of Return
A	$1 million	12.0%
B	2 million	11.5
C	2 million	11.2
D	2 million	11.0
E	1 million	10.7
F	1 million	10.3
G	1 million	10.2

Assume that each of these projects is just as risky as the firm's existing assets, and the firm may accept all the projects or only some of them. Which set of projects should be accepted? Explain.

Intermediate
Problems 6–13

10-6 **Cost of common equity** The earnings, dividends, and common stock price of Carpetto Technologies Inc. are expected to grow at 11 percent per year in the future. Carpetto's common stock sells for $23 per share, its last dividend was $2.00, and it will pay a dividend of $2.14 at the end of the current year.

a. Using the DCF approach, what is its cost of common equity?
b. If the firm's beta is 1.6, the risk-free rate is 9 percent, and the average return on the market is 13 percent, what will be the firm's cost of common equity using the CAPM approach?
c. If the firm's bonds earn a return of 12 percent, what will r_s be based on the bond-yield-plus-risk-premium approach, using the midpoint of the risk premium range?
d. Assuming you have equal confidence in the inputs used for the three approaches, what is your estimate of Carpetto's cost of common equity?

10-7 **Cost of common equity with and without flotation** The Evanec Company's next expected dividend, D_1, is $3.18; its growth rate is 6 percent; and its common stock now sells for $36. New stock (external equity) can be sold to net $32.40 per share.

a. What is Evanec's cost of retained earnings, r_s?
b. What is Evanec's percentage flotation cost, F?
c. What is Evanec's cost of new common stock, r_e?

10-8 **Cost of common equity and WACC** Patton Paints Corporation has a target capital structure of 40 percent debt and 60 percent common equity, with no preferred stock. Its before-tax cost of debt is 12 percent, and its marginal tax rate is 40 percent. The current stock price is $P_0 = 22.50. The last dividend was $D_0 = 2.00, and it is expected to grow at a constant rate of 7 percent. What is its cost of common equity and its WACC?

10-9 **WACC** The Patrick Company's cost of common equity is 16 percent, its before-tax cost of debt is 13 percent, and its marginal tax rate is 40 percent. The stock sells at book value. Using the following balance sheet, calculate Patrick's WACC.

Assets		Liabilities and Equity	
Cash	$ 120		
Accounts receivable	240		
Inventories	360	Long-term debt	$1,152
Plant and equipment, net	2,160	Common equity	1,728
Total assets	$2,880	Total liabilities and equity	$2,880

10-10 **WACC** Klose Outfitters Inc. believes that its optimal capital structure consists of 60 percent common equity and 40 percent debt, and its tax rate is 40 percent. Klose must raise additional capital to fund its upcoming expansion. The firm will have $2 million of new retained earnings with a cost of $r_s = 12\%$. New common stock in an amount up to $6 million would have a cost of $r_e = 15\%$. Furthermore, Klose can raise up to $3 million of debt at an interest rate of $r_d = 10\%$, and an additional $4 million of debt at $r_d = 12\%$. The CFO estimates that a proposed expansion would require an investment of $5.9 million. What is the WACC for the last dollar raised to complete the expansion?

10-11 **WACC and percentage of debt financing** Hook Industries' capital structure consists solely of debt and common equity. It can issue debt at $r_d = 11\%$, and its common stock currently pays a $2 dividend per share ($D_0 = 2). The stock's price is currently $24.75; its dividend is expected to grow at a constant rate of 7 percent per year; its tax rate is 35 percent; and its WACC is 13.95 percent. What percentage of the company's capital structure consists of debt?

10-12 **WACC** Midwest Electric Company (MEC) uses only debt and common equity. It can borrow unlimited amounts at an interest rate of $r_d = 10\%$ as long as it finances at its target capital structure, which calls for 45 percent debt and 55 percent common equity. Its last dividend was $2, its expected constant growth rate is 4 percent, and its common stock sells for $20. MEC's tax rate is 40 percent. Two projects are available: Project A has a rate of return of 13 percent, while Project B's return is 10 percent. These two projects are equally risky and also about as risky as the firm's existing assets.

a. What is its cost of common equity?
b. What is the WACC?
c. Which projects should Midwest accept?

10-13 **Cost of common equity with flotation** Ballack Co.'s common stock currently sells for $46.75 per share. The growth rate is a constant 12 percent, and the company has an expected dividend yield of 5 percent. The expected long-run dividend payout ratio is 25 percent, and the expected return on equity (ROE) is 16 percent. New stock can be sold to the public at the current price, but a flotation cost of 5 percent would be incurred. What would the cost of new equity be?

Challenging
Problems 14–20 **10-14** **Cost of preferred stock including flotation** Trivoli Industries plans to issue perpetual preferred stock with an $11 dividend. It is currently selling for $97.00,

but flotation costs will be 5 percent of the market price, so the net price will be $92.15 per share. What is the cost of the preferred stock, including flotation?

10-15 **WACC and cost of common equity** Kahn Inc. has a target capital structure of 60 percent common equity and 40 percent debt to fund its $10 billion in operating assets. Furthermore, Kahn Inc. has a WACC of 13 percent, a before-tax cost of debt of 10 percent, and a tax rate of 40 percent. The company's retained earnings are adequate to provide the common equity portion of its capital budget. Its expected dividend next year (D_1) is $3 and the current stock price is $35.

  a. What is the company's expected growth rate?
  b. If the firm's net income is expected to be $1.1 billion, what portion of its net income is the firm expected to pay out as dividends? (Hint: Use Equation 10-9.)

10-16 **Cost of common equity** The Bouchard Company's EPS was $6.50 in 2005, up from $4.42 in 2000. The company pays out 40 percent of its earnings as dividends, and its common stock sells for $36.

  a. Calculate the past growth rate in earnings. (Hint: This is a 5-year growth period.)
  b. The last dividend was $D_0 = 0.4(\$6.50) = \$2.60$. Calculate the *next* expected dividend, D_1, assuming that the past growth rate continues.
  c. What is Bouchard's cost of retained earnings, r_s?

10-17 **Calculation of g and EPS** Sidman Products' common stock currently sells for $60 a share. The firm is expected to earn $5.40 per share this year and to pay a year-end dividend of $3.60, and it finances only with common equity.

  a. If investors require a 9 percent return, what is the expected growth rate?
  b. If Sidman reinvests retained earnings in projects whose average return is equal to the stock's expected rate of return, what will be next year's EPS? [Hint: $g = (1 - \text{Payout rate})(\text{ROE})$.]

10-18 **WACC and optimal capital budget** Adams Corporation is considering four average-risk projects with the following costs and rates of return:

Project	Cost	Expected Rate of Return
1	$2,000	16.00%
2	3,000	15.00
3	5,000	13.75
4	2,000	12.50

The company estimates that it can issue debt at a rate of $r_d = 10\%$, and its tax rate is 30 percent. It can issue preferred stock that pays a constant dividend of $5 per year at $49 per share. Also, its common stock currently sells for $36 per share; the next expected dividend, D_1, is $3.50, and the dividend is expected to grow at a constant rate of 6 percent per year. The target capital structure consists of 75 percent common stock, 15 percent debt, and 10 percent preferred stock.

  a. What is the cost of each of the capital components?
  b. What is Adams's WACC?
  c. Which projects should Adams accept?

10-19 **Adjusting cost of capital for risk** Ziege Systems is considering the following independent projects for the coming year.

Project	Required Investment	Rate of Return	Risk
A	$4 million	14.0%	High
B	5 million	11.5	High
C	3 million	9.5	Low
D	2 million	9.0	Average
E	6 million	12.5	High
F	5 million	12.5	Average
G	6 million	7.0	Low
H	3 million	11.5	Low

Ziege's WACC is 10 percent, but it adjusts for risk by adding 2 percent to the WACC for high-risk projects and subtracting 2 percent for low-risk projects.

  a. Which projects should Ziege accept if it faces no capital constraints?
  b. If Ziege can only invest a total of $13 million, which projects should it accept, and what would the dollar size of its capital budget be?

c. Suppose that Ziege can raise additional funds beyond the $13 million, but each new increment (or partial increment) of $5 million of new capital will cause the WACC to increase by 1 percent. Assuming Ziege uses the same method of risk adjustment, which projects should it now accept, and what would be the dollar size of its capital budget?

10-20 WACC The following table gives Foust Company's earnings per share for the last 10 years. The common stock, 7.8 million shares outstanding, is now (1/1/06) selling for $65 per share, and the expected dividend at the end of the current year (12/31/06) is 55 percent of the 2005 EPS. Because investors expect past trends to continue, g may be based on the historical earnings growth rate. (Note that 9 years of growth are reflected in the 10 years of data.)

Year	EPS	Year	EPS
1996	$3.90	2001	$5.73
1997	4.21	2002	6.19
1998	4.55	2003	6.68
1999	4.91	2004	7.22
2000	5.31	2005	7.80

The current interest rate on new debt is 9 percent, Foust's marginal tax rate is 40 percent, and its capital structure, considered to be optimal, is as follows:

Debt	$104,000,000
Common equity	156,000,000
Total liabilities and equity	$260,000,000

a. Calculate Foust's after-tax cost of debt and common equity. Calculate the cost of equity as $r_s = D_1/P_0 + g$.
b. Find Foust's WACC.

COMPREHENSIVE/SPREADSHEET PROBLEM

10-21 Calculating the WACC Here is the condensed 2005 balance sheet for Skye Computer Company (in thousands of dollars):

	2005
Current assets	$2,000
Net fixed assets	3,000
Total assets	$5,000
Current liabilities	$ 900
Long-term debt	1,200
Preferred stock	250
Common stock	1,300
Retained earnings	1,350
Total common equity	$2,650
Total liabilities and equity	$5,000

Skye's earnings per share last year were $3.20, the common stock sells for $55, last year's dividend was $2.10, and a flotation cost of 10 percent would be required to sell new common stock. Security analysts are projecting that the common dividend will grow at a rate of 9 percent per year. Skye's preferred stock pays a dividend of $3.30 per share, and new preferred could be sold at a price to net the company $30 per share. The firm can issue long-term debt at an interest rate (or before-tax cost) of 10 percent, and its marginal tax rate is 35 percent. The market risk premium is 5 percent, the risk-free rate is 6 percent, and Skye's beta is 1.516. In its cost of capital calculations, the company considers only long-term capital, hence it disregards current liabilities.

a. Calculate the cost of each capital component, that is, the after-tax cost of debt, the cost of preferred stock, the cost of equity from retained earnings, and the cost of newly issued common stock. Use the DCF method to find the cost of common equity.
b. Now calculate the cost of common equity from retained earnings using the CAPM method.
c. What is the cost of new common stock, based on the CAPM? (Hint: Find the difference between r_e and r_s as determined by the DCF method, and add that differential to the CAPM value for r_s.)

d.   If Skye continues to use the same capital structure, what is the firm's WACC assuming (1) that it uses only retained earnings for equity and (2) that it expands so rapidly that it must issue new common stock?

Integrated Case

Coleman Technologies Inc.

10-22 **Cost of capital** Coleman Technologies is considering a major expansion program that has been proposed by the company's information technology group. Before proceeding with the expansion, the company must estimate its cost of capital. Assume that you are an assistant to Jerry Lehman, the financial vice president. Your first task is to estimate Coleman's cost of capital. Lehman has provided you with the following data, which he believes may be relevant to your task.

(1)   The firm's tax rate is 40 percent.
(2)   The current price of Coleman's 12 percent coupon, semiannual payment, noncallable bonds with 15 years remaining to maturity is $1,153.72. Coleman does not use short-term interest-bearing debt on a permanent basis. New bonds would be privately placed with no flotation cost.
(3)   The current price of the firm's 10 percent, $100 par value, quarterly dividend, perpetual preferred stock is $111.10.
(4)   Coleman's common stock is currently selling for $50 per share. Its last dividend (D_0) was $4.19, and dividends are expected to grow at a constant rate of 5 percent in the foreseeable future. Coleman's beta is 1.2, the yield on T-bonds is 7 percent, and the market risk premium is estimated to be 6 percent. For the bond-yield-plus-risk-premium approach, the firm uses a risk premium of 4 percent.
(5)   Coleman's target capital structure is 30 percent debt, 10 percent preferred stock, and 60 percent common equity.

To structure the task somewhat, Lehman has asked you to answer the following questions.

a.   (1) What sources of capital should be included when you estimate Coleman's WACC?
     (2) Should the component costs be figured on a before-tax or an after-tax basis?
     (3) Should the costs be historical (embedded) costs or new (marginal) costs?
b.   What is the market interest rate on Coleman's debt and its component cost of debt?
c.   (1) What is the firm's cost of preferred stock?
     (2) Coleman's preferred stock is riskier to investors than its debt, yet the preferred's yield to investors is lower than the yield to maturity on the debt. Does this suggest that you have made a mistake? (Hint: Think about taxes.)
d.   (1) Why is there a cost associated with retained earnings?
     (2) What is Coleman's estimated cost of common equity using the CAPM approach?
e.   What is the estimated cost of common equity using the DCF approach?
f.   What is the bond-yield-plus-risk-premium estimate for Coleman's cost of common equity?
g.   What is your final estimate for r_s?
h.   Explain in words why new common stock has a higher cost than retained earnings.
i.   (1) What are two approaches that can be used to adjust for flotation costs?
     (2) Coleman estimates that if it issues new common stock, the flotation cost will be 15 percent. Coleman incorporates the flotation costs into the DCF approach. What is the estimated cost of newly issued common stock, considering the flotation cost?
j.   What is Coleman's overall, or weighted average, cost of capital (WACC)? Ignore flotation costs.
k.   What factors influence Coleman's composite WACC?
l.   Should the company use the composite WACC as the hurdle rate for each of its projects? Explain.

cyberproblem

Please go to the ThomsonNOW Web site to access the Cyberproblems.

THOMSON ONE | Business School Edition

Access the Thomson ONE problems though the ThomsonNOW Web site. Use the Thomson ONE—Business School Edition online database to work this chapter's questions.

Calculating 3M's Cost of Capital

In this chapter we described how to estimate a company's WACC, which is the weighted average of its costs of debt, preferred stock, and common equity. Most of the data we need to do this can be found in Thomson One. Here, we walk through the steps used to calculate Minnesota Mining & Manufacturing's (MMM) WACC.

Discussion Questions

1. As a first step we need to estimate what percentage of MMM's capital comes from long-term debt, preferred stock, and common equity. If we click on FINANCIALS, we can see immediately from the balance sheet the amount of MMM's long-term debt and common equity (as of mid-2004, MMM had no preferred stock). Alternatively, you can click on FUNDAMENTAL RATIOS in the next row of tabs below and then select WORLDSCOPE'S BALANCE SHEET RATIOS. Here, you will also find a recent measure of long-term debt as a percentage of total capital. Recall that the weights used in the WACC are based on the company's target capital structure. If we assume that the company wants to maintain the same mix of capital that it currently has on its balance sheet, what weights should you use to estimate the WACC for MMM? (In the Capital Structure and Leverage chapter, we will see that we might arrive at different estimates for these weights if we instead assume that MMM bases its target capital structure on the market values of debt and equity, rather than the book values.)

2. Once again, we can use the CAPM to estimate MMM's cost of equity. Thomson One provides various estimates of beta—select the measure that you believe is best and combine this with your estimates of the risk-free rate and the market risk premium to obtain an estimate of its cost of equity. (See the Thomson One exercise for Chapter 8 for more details.) What is your estimate for the cost of equity? Why might it not make much sense to use the DCF approach to estimate MMM's cost of equity?

3. Next, we need to calculate MMM's cost of debt. Unfortunately, Thomson One doesn't provide a direct measure of the cost of debt. However, we can use different approaches to estimate it. One approach is to take the company's long-term interest expense and divide it by the amount of long-term debt. This approach only works if the historical cost of debt equals the yield to maturity in today's market (that is, if MMM's outstanding bonds are trading at close to par). This approach may produce misleading estimates in years in which MMM issues a significant amount of new debt. For example, if a company issues a lot of debt at the end of the year, the full amount of debt will appear on the year-end balance sheet, yet we still may not see a sharp increase in interest expense on the annual income statement because the debt was outstanding for only a small portion of the entire year. When this situation occurs, the estimated cost of debt will likely understate the true cost of debt. Another approach is to try to find this number in the notes to the company's annual report by accessing the company's home page and its Investor Relations section. Alternatively, you can go to other external sources, such as **www.bondsonline.com**, for corporate bond spreads, which can be used to find estimates of the cost of debt. Remember that you need the after-tax cost of debt to calculate a firm's WACC, so you will need MMM's tax rate (which has averaged about 37 percent in recent years). What is your estimate of MMM's after-tax cost of debt?

4. Putting all this information together, what is your estimate of MMM's WACC? How confident are you in this estimate? Explain your answer.

CHAPTER 11

THE BASICS OF CAPITAL BUDGETING

Competition in the Aircraft Industry

In early 2005 Boeing was involved in a titanic struggle with European consortium Airbus SAS for dominance of the commercial aircraft industry.[1] Airbus first committed to spend $16 billion to develop the A380, the largest plane ever built. Boeing countered by announcing that it would spend $6 billion on a super efficient new plane, the 7E7 Dreamliner. Airbus then announced plans to spend another $6 billion on the A350, a competitor to the 7E7. Many detailed calculations went into these multi-billion-dollar investment decisions—development costs were estimated, the cost of each plane was forecasted, a sales price per plane was established, and the number of planes that would be sold through 2025 was predicted.

> **Airbus, Boeing**

Both companies projected negative cash flows for 5 or 6 years, then positive cash flows for the following 20 years. Given their forecasted cash flows, both managements decided that taking on the projects would increase their company's intrinsic value. Because the planes will compete with one another, either Boeing's or Airbus's forecast is probably incorrect. One will probably be a winner and the other a loser, and one set of stockholders is likely to be happy and the other unhappy.

Projects like the A350, A380, and 7E7 receive a lot of attention, but Boeing, Airbus, and other companies make a great many more routine investment

---

[1] Airbus SAS is owned by European Aeronautics Defense & Space Company (EADS), which, in turn, is owned by the French government and several large European companies. Airbus was formed because the Europeans wanted to create an organization large enough to raise the huge amounts of capital needed to compete with Boeing.

decisions every year, ranging from buying new trucks or machinery to spending millions on computer software to optimize inventory holdings. The techniques described in this chapter are required to analyze all types and sizes of projects.

Sources: Daniel Michaels, "EADS and BAE Systems Approve Launch of Airbus's A350 Plane," *The Wall Street Journal*, December 13, 2004, p. A6; and Carol Matlack, "Is Airbus Caught in a Down-draft?" *BusinessWeek*, December 27, 2004, p. 64.

Putting Things In Perspective

Capital Budgeting
The process of planning expenditures on assets whose cash flows are expected to extend beyond one year.

In the last chapter, we discussed the cost of capital. Now we turn to investment decisions involving fixed assets, or *capital budgeting*. Here *capital* refers to long-term assets used in production, while a *budget* is a plan that details projected expenditures during some future period. Thus, the *capital budget* is an outline of planned investments in long-term assets, and **capital budgeting** is the whole process of analyzing projects and deciding which ones to include in the capital budget. Boeing, Airbus, and other companies use the techniques in this chapter when deciding to accept or reject proposed capital expenditures.

11-1 GENERATING IDEAS FOR CAPITAL PROJECTS

The same general concepts that are used in security valuation are also used in capital budgeting, but there are two major differences. First, stocks and bonds exist in the security markets and investors select from the available set, whereas firms create capital budgeting projects. Second, most investors in the security markets have no influence on the cash flows produced by their investments, whereas corporations have a major influence on their projects' results. Still, in both security valuation and capital budgeting, we first forecast a set of cash flows, then find the present value of those flows, and make the investment only if the PV of the inflows exceeds the investment's cost.

A firm's growth, and even its ability to remain competitive and to survive, depends on a constant flow of ideas relating to new products, actions to improve existing products, and ways to operate more efficiently. Accordingly, well-managed firms go to great lengths to develop good capital budgeting proposals. For example, the executive vice president of one successful corporation told us that his company takes the following steps to generate projects:

> Our R&D department constantly searches for new products and ways to improve existing products. In addition, our Executive Committee, which consists of senior executives in marketing, production, and finance, identifies the products and markets in which our company should compete, and the Committee sets long-run targets for each divi-

sion. These targets, which are spelled out in the corporation's **strategic business plan,** provide a general guide to the operating executives who must meet them. The operating executives then seek new products, set expansion plans for existing products, and look for ways to reduce production and distribution costs. Since bonuses and promotions are based on each unit's ability to meet or exceed its targets, these economic incentives encourage our operating executives to seek out profitable investment opportunities.

> While our senior executives are judged and rewarded on the basis of how well their units perform, people further down the line are given bonuses and stock options for suggestions that lead to profitable investments. Additionally, a percentage of our corporate profit is set aside for distribution to nonexecutive employees, and we have an Employees' Stock Ownership Plan (ESOP) to provide further incentives. Our objective is to encourage employees at all levels to keep an eye out for good ideas, especially those that lead to capital investments.

If a firm has capable and imaginative executives and employees, and if its incentive system is working properly, many ideas for capital investment will be advanced. Some ideas will be good ones, but others will not. Therefore, procedures must be established for screening projects, the primary topic of this chapter.

Strategic Business Plan

A long-run plan that outlines in broad terms the firm's basic strategy for the next 5 to 10 years.

 How is capital budgeting similar to security valuation? How is it different?

What are some ways firms generate ideas for capital projects?

11-2 PROJECT CLASSIFICATIONS

Analyzing capital expenditure proposals is not a costless operation—benefits can be gained, but analysis does have a cost. For certain types of projects, a relatively detailed analysis may be warranted; for others, simpler procedures should be used. Accordingly, firms generally categorize projects and then analyze those in each category somewhat differently:

1. *Replacement: needed to continue current operations.* One category consists of expenditures to replace worn-out or damaged equipment required in the production of profitable products. The only questions here are should the operation be continued, and if so, should the firm continue to use the same production processes? If the answers are yes, then the project will be approved without going through an elaborate decision process.
2. *Replacement: cost reduction.* This category includes expenditures to replace serviceable but obsolete equipment and thereby lower costs. These decisions are discretionary, and a fairly detailed analysis is generally required.
3. *Expansion of existing products or markets.* These are expenditures to increase output of existing products or to expand retail outlets or distribution facilities in markets now being served. Expansion decisions are more complex because they require an explicit forecast of growth in demand, so a more detailed analysis is required. The go/no-go decision is generally made at a higher level within the firm.
4. *Expansion into new products or markets.* These investments relate to new products or geographic areas, and they involve strategic decisions that could change the fundamental nature of the business. Invariably, a detailed analysis is required, and the final decision is generally made at the very top level of management.

5. *Safety and/or environmental projects.* Expenditures necessary to comply with government orders, labor agreements, or insurance policy terms fall into this category. How these projects are handled depends on their size, with small ones being treated much like the Category 1 projects.

6. *Other.* This catch-all includes items such as office buildings, parking lots, and executive aircraft. How they are handled varies among companies.

In general, relatively simple calculations, and only a few supporting documents, are required for replacement decisions, especially maintenance investments in profitable plants. More detailed analyses are required for cost-reduction projects, for expansion of existing product lines, and especially for investments in new products or areas. Also, within each category projects are grouped by their dollar costs: Larger investments require increasingly detailed analysis and approval at higher levels. Thus, a plant manager might be authorized to approve maintenance expenditures up to $10,000 using a relatively unsophisticated analysis, but the full board of directors might have to approve decisions that involve either amounts greater than $1 million or expansions into new products or markets.

Note that the term "investments" encompasses more than buildings and equipment. Computer software used to manage inventories and costs related to major marketing programs are examples. These are "intangible" assets, but decisions to invest in them are analyzed in the same way as decisions related to buildings, equipment, and other tangible assets. In the following sections we examine the specific techniques used to evaluate proposed capital budgeting projects.

Identify the major project classification categories, and explain why and how they are used.

11-3 THE NET PRESENT VALUE (NPV) CRITERION

Net Present Value (NPV) Method
A method of ranking investment proposals using the NPV, which is equal to the present value of future net cash flows, discounted at the cost of capital.

The **net present value (NPV) method,** which estimates how much a potential project will contribute to shareholder wealth, is the primary capital budgeting decision criterion. In this section we use the cash flow data for Projects S and L as shown in Figure 11-1 to explain how the NPV is calculated. The S stands for *short* and the L for *long:* Project S is a short-term project in the sense that most of its cash inflows come in sooner than L's. We assume that the projects are equally risky and that the cash flows have been adjusted to reflect taxes, depreciation, and salvage values. Further, because many projects require an investment in both fixed assets and working capital, the investment outlays shown as CF_0 include any necessary investment in working capital.[2] Finally, we assume that all cash flows occur at the end of the year.

The NPV is a direct measure of the projects' contribution to shareholder wealth, and as such it is the primary criterion. It is found as follows:

1. Find the present value of each cash flow, including the cost, discounted at the project's cost of capital.

2. The sum of these discounted cash flows is defined as the project's NPV.

---

[2] The most difficult aspect of capital budgeting is estimating the relevant cash flows. For simplicity, the net cash flows are treated as a given in this chapter, which allows us to focus on the capital budgeting decision rules. However, in Chapter 12 we will discuss cash flow estimation in detail. Also, note that *net operating working capital* is defined as the increase in current assets associated with the project minus the associated increases in payables and accruals. Thus, in capital budgeting, investment in working capital means the net amount that must be financed by investors.

FIGURE 11-1   *Net Cash Flows for Projects S and L*

	EXPECTED AFTER-TAX NET CASH FLOWS, CF$_t$		
Year (t)	Project S	Project L	
0	−$1,000	−$1,000	(Initial cost in Year 1)
1	500	100	
2	400	300	
3	300	400	
4	100	675	

Project S	0	1	2	3	4
	├────────┼────────┼────────┼────────┤				
	−$1,000	$500	$400	$300	$100

Project L	0	1	2	3	4
	├────────┼────────┼────────┼────────┤				
	−$1,000	$100	$300	$400	$675

The equation for the NPV is as follows:

$$NPV = CF_0 + \frac{CF_1}{(1 + r)^1} + \frac{CF_2}{(1 + r)^2} + \cdots + \frac{CF_N}{(1 + r)^N}$$

$$= \sum_{t=0}^{N} \frac{CF_t}{(1 + r)^t} \tag{11-1}$$

Here CF_t is the expected net cash flow at Time t, r is the project's cost of capital (or WACC), and N is its life. Cash outflows (for example, developing the product, buying production equipment, building a factory, and stocking inventory) are *negative* cash flows. For Projects S and L, only CF_0 is negative, but for large projects such as Boeing's 7E7, outflows occur for several years before cash inflows begin.

At a 10 percent cost of capital, Project S's NPV is $78.82:

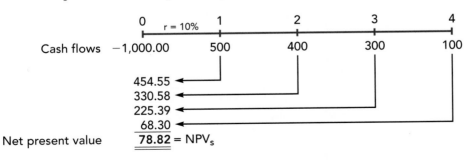

```
              0    r = 10%    1        2        3        4
              ├──────────────┼────────┼────────┼────────┤
Cash flows  −1,000.00        500      400      300      100
            454.55 ◄─────────┘         │        │        │
            330.58 ◄──────────────────┘         │        │
            225.39 ◄───────────────────────────┘         │
             68.30 ◄────────────────────────────────────┘
Net present value  78.82 = NPVₛ
```

By a similar process, we find NPV_L = $100.40.

If the projects were *mutually exclusive*, the one with the higher NPV should be accepted and the other rejected. L would be ranked over S and thus accepted because L has the higher NPV. **Mutually exclusive** means that if one project is taken on, the other must be rejected. For example, a conveyor-belt system to move goods in a warehouse and a fleet of forklifts for the same purpose illustrates

Mutually Exclusive Projects
A set of projects where only one can be accepted.

Independent Projects
Projects whose cash flows are not affected by the acceptance or nonacceptance of other projects.

mutually exclusive projects—accepting one implies rejecting the other. **Independent projects** are those whose cash flows are independent of one another. If Wal-Mart were considering a new store in Boise and another in Atlanta, those projects would be independent of one another. If our Projects S and L were independent, then both should be accepted because both have a positive NPV and thus add value to the firm. If they were mutually exclusive, then L should be chosen because it has the higher NPV.

It is not hard to calculate the NPV as shown in the time line by using Equation 11-1 and a regular calculator. However, it is more efficient to use a financial calculator. Different calculators are set up somewhat differently, but as we discussed in Chapter 2, they all have a "cash flow register" that can be used to evaluate uneven cash flows such as those in Projects S and L. Equation 11-1 is programmed into the calculators, and all you have to do is enter the cash flows (observe the correct signs), along with r = I/YR (the cost of capital). Once the entries have been made using data for Project S, this equation is in the calculator:

$$NPV_S = -1,000 + \frac{500}{(1.10)^1} + \frac{400}{(1.10)^2} + \frac{300}{(1.10)^3} + \frac{100}{(1.10)^4}$$

There is one unknown, NPV, and when you press the NPV key the answer, 78.82, will appear on the screen.[3]

The rationale for the NPV method is straightforward: If NPV exceeds zero, then the project increases the firm's value, and if it is negative, the project reduces shareholders' wealth. In our example, Project L would increase shareholders' wealth by $100.40 and S would increase it by $78.82:

$$NPV_L = \$100.40$$
$$NPV_S = \$78.82$$

Viewed in this manner, it is easy to see the logic of the NPV approach, and it is also easy to see why both projects should be accepted if they are independent and why L should be chosen if they are mutually exclusive.

Why is the NPV regarded as being the primary capital budgeting decision criterion?

What's the difference between "independent" and "mutually exclusive" projects?

What are the NPVs of Projects SS and LL if both have a 10 percent cost of capital and the indicated cash flows? ($NPV_{SS} = \$77.61$; $NPV_{LL} = \$89.63$)

	END-OF-YEAR CASH FLOWS				
	0	1	2	3	WACC = r = 10%
SS	−$700	$500	$300	$100	
LL	−700	100	300	600	

Which project or projects would you recommend if they are (a) independent or (b) mutually exclusive?

---

[3] The keystrokes for finding the NPV are shown for several calculators in the calculator tutorials provided on the ThomsonNOW Web site. Since many projects last for more than four years and a number of calculations are required to develop their estimated cash flows, financial analysts often use spreadsheets when analyzing real world capital budgeting projects. We demonstrate this usage in Chapter 12.

11-4 INTERNAL RATE OF RETURN (IRR)

When deciding on a potential investment, it is useful to know the investment's most likely rate of return. In Chapter 7 we discussed the yield to maturity on a bond—if you invest in a bond and hold it to maturity, you will earn the YTM on the money you invest. The YTM is defined as the discount rate that causes the PV of the cash inflows to equal the price paid for the bond. The same procedure is used in capital budgeting when we calculate the **internal rate of return, or IRR.** The IRR is defined as the discount rate that forces the project's NPV to equal zero. We simply take Equation 11-1 for the NPV and transform it to Equation 11-2 for the IRR by replacing r in the denominator with IRR and specifying that the NPV must equal zero. We then find the rate that forces NPV to equal zero, and that is the IRR:

Internal Rate of Return (IRR)
The discount rate that forces a project's NPV to equal zero.

$$NPV = CF_0 + \frac{CF_1}{(1 + IRR)^1} + \frac{CF_2}{(1 + IRR)^2} + \cdots + \frac{CF_N}{(1 + IRR)^N} = 0$$

$$= \sum_{t=0}^{N} \frac{CF_t}{(1 + IRR)^t} = 0 \qquad \textbf{(11-2)}$$

Note that for a project like Boeing's 7E7 jetliner, costs are incurred for several years before cash inflows begin, but that does not invalidate the equation. That simply means that we have more than one negative cash flow.

For our Project S, here's a picture of the process:

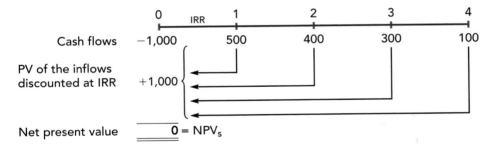

We have an equation with one unknown, IRR, and we can solve it to find the IRR. Without a calculator, we would have to solve Equation 11-2 by trial-and-error—try some discount rate, see if the equation solves to zero, if it does not, try a different discount rate, and continue until we find the rate that forces the equation to equal zero. That rate is the IRR. For a project with a fairly long life, the trial-and-error calculations would be time-consuming, but with a financial calculator we can find IRR quickly. Simply enter the cash flows into the calculator's cash flow register as we did to find the NPV and then press the button labeled "IRR." Here are the IRRs for Projects S and L:[4]

$$IRR_S = 14.49\%$$

$$IRR_L = 13.55\%$$

Why is the discount rate that equates a project's cost to the present value of its inflows so special? The reason is straightforward: The IRR is the project's expected rate of return. If this return exceeds the cost of the funds used to

---

[4] See our calculator tutorial on the ThomsonNOW Web site. Note that once the cash flows have been entered in the cash flow register, you can immediately find both the NPV and the IRR. To find the NPV, enter the interest rate (I/YR) and then press the NPV key. Then, with no further entries, press the IRR key to find the IRR. Thus, once you set up the calculator to find the NPV, it is trivially easy to find the IRR. This is one reason most companies calculate both the NPV and the IRR—if you calculate one, it is easy to also calculate the other, and both provide information that decision makers find useful.

finance the project, then the excess goes to the firm's stockholders. On the other hand, if the internal rate of return were less than the cost of capital, then stockholders would have to make up the shortfall, which would cause the stock price to decline. It is this "breakeven" characteristic that makes the IRR useful.

Again, note that the internal rate of return formula, Equation 11-2, is simply the NPV formula, Equation 11-1, solved for the particular discount rate that forces the NPV to zero. Thus, the same basic equation is used for both methods, but with the NPV method the discount rate is given and we find the NPV, whereas with the IRR method the NPV is set equal to zero and the interest rate that produces this equality is calculated.

In what sense is the IRR on a project related to the YTM on a bond?

The cash flows for projects SS and LL are shown below. What are the projects' IRRs, and which one would the IRR method select if the firm has a 10 percent cost of capital and the projects are (a) independent or (b) mutually exclusive? (IRR_{SS} = 18.0%; IRR_{LL} = 15.6%)

| | **END-OF-YEAR CASH FLOWS** | | | | |
	0	**1**	**2**	**3**	**WACC = r = 10%**
SS	−$700	$500	$300	$100	
LL	−700	100	300	600	

11-5 COMPARISON OF THE NPV AND IRR METHODS

In many respects the NPV method is better than IRR, so it is tempting to simply explain NPV, state that it should be used to select projects, and go on to the next topic. However, the IRR is familiar to many corporate executives, it is widely entrenched in industry, and it is useful to know the rate of return a project is likely to produce. Also, the NPV and IRR methods can provide conflicting recommendations when used to evaluate mutually exclusive projects. Therefore, it is important that you understand the IRR method, know how it is related to the NPV, and know why it is sometimes better to choose a project with a relatively low IRR over a mutually exclusive alternative with a higher IRR.

11-5a NPV Profiles

Net Present Value Profile
A graph showing the relationship between a project's NPV and the firm's cost of capital.

A graph that plots a project's NPV against the discount rates used to calculate the NPV is defined as the project's **net present value profile,** and the profile for Project S is shown in Figure 11-2. To construct the profile, we used the data on Project S in Figure 11-1, calculated NPVs at the discount rates shown in the data below the graph, and then plotted those values on the graph. Note that at a zero cost of capital the NPV is simply the total of the undiscounted cash flows, or $300. This value is plotted as the vertical axis intercept. Also, recall that the IRR is the discount rate that causes the NPV to equal zero. Therefore, the discount rate at which the profile line crosses the horizontal axis is the project's IRR. When we connect the data points, we have the net present value profile.[5] These profiles are quite useful, and we refer to them often in the remainder of the chapter.

---

[5] Notice that the NPV profiles are curved—they are *not* straight lines. NPV approaches CF_0, that is, the cost of the project, as the discount rate increases without limit. The reason is that, at an infinitely

FIGURE 11-2 *NPV Profile for Project S*

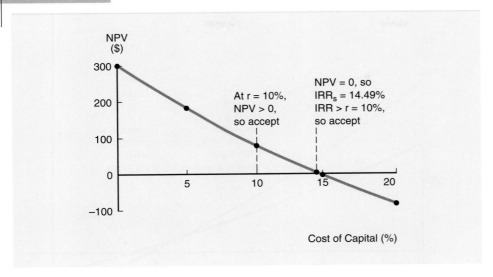

	Cost of Capital	NPV_S
	0%	$300.00
	5	180.42
	10	78.82
IRR_S =	14.49	0.00
	15	−8.33
	20	−83.72

11-5b NPV Rankings Depend on the Cost of Capital

Now consider Figure 11-3, which shows the NPV profiles for both S and L. Notice that the IRRs are fixed and that S has the higher IRR regardless of the level of the cost of capital. However, the NPV varies depending on the level of the cost of capital, and the project with the higher NPV depends on the actual cost of capital. Specifically, L has the higher NPV if the cost of capital is below 11.97 percent, but S has the higher NPV if the cost of capital is above that rate. The discount rate at which the profile lines cross, 11.97 percent, is called the **crossover rate.**[6]

Notice also that L's profile has the steeper slope, indicating that increases in the cost of capital lead to larger declines in its NPV. To see why L has the greater sensitivity, recall first that L's cash flows come in later than those of S. Therefore,

Crossover Rate
The cost of capital at which the NPV profiles of two projects cross and, thus, at which the projects' NPVs are equal.

(Footnote 5 continued)
high cost of capital, the PVs of the inflows would all be zero, so NPV at $r = \infty$ is simply CF_0, which in our example is −$1,000. We should also note that under certain conditions the NPV profiles can cross the horizontal axis several times, or never cross it. This point is discussed later in Section 11.6.
[6] For an explanation of how to calculate the crossover rate, see Eugene F. Brigham and Phillip R. Daves, *Intermediate Financial Management*, 8th edition (Mason, OH: Thomson/South-Western, 2004), footnote 6, p. 385.

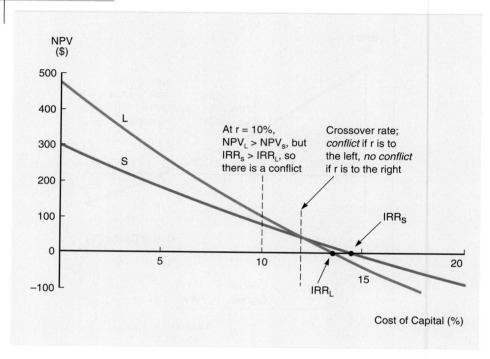

FIGURE 11-3 *NPV Profiles for Projects S and L*

	Cost of Capital	NPV$_S$	NPV$_L$
	0 %	$300.00	$475.00
	5	180.42	268.21
	10	78.82	100.40
Crossover =	11.97	42.84	42.84
IRR$_L$ =	13.55	15.64	0.00
IRR$_S$ =	14.49	0.00	−24.37
	15	−8.33	−37.26
	20	−83.72	−151.33

L is a long-term project, while S is a short-term project. Next, recall the equation for the NPV:

$$NPV = CF_0 + \frac{CF_1}{(1 + r)^1} + \frac{CF_2}{(1 + r)^2} + \cdots + \frac{CF_N}{(1 + r)^N}$$

The impact of an increase in the cost of capital is much greater on distant than on near-term cash flows as is demonstrated in the following examples:

$$PV \text{ of } \$100 \text{ due in 1 year @ } r = 5\%: \frac{\$100}{(1.05)^1} = \$95.24$$

$$PV \text{ of } \$100 \text{ due in 1 year @ } r = 10\%: \frac{\$100}{(1.10)^1} = \$90.91$$

$$\text{Percentage decline due to higher } r = \frac{\$95.24 - \$90.91}{\$95.24} = 4.5\%$$

$$\text{PV of \$100 due in 20 years @ r} = 5\%: \frac{\$100}{(1.05)^{20}} = \$37.69$$

$$\text{PV of \$100 due in 20 years @ r} = 10\%: \frac{\$100}{(1.10)^{20}} = \$14.86$$

$$\text{Percentage decline due to higher r} = \frac{\$37.69 - \$14.86}{\$37.69} = 60.6\%$$

Thus, a doubling of the discount rate causes only a 4.5 percent decline in the PV of a Year 1 cash flow, but the same discount rate doubling causes the PV of a Year 20 cash flow to fall by more than 60 percent. Therefore, if a project has most of its cash flows coming in the early years, its NPV will not decline very much if the cost of capital increases, but a project whose cash flows come later will be severely penalized by high capital costs. Most of Project L's cash flows come in the later years, so L is hurt badly if the cost of capital is high, but S is not affected as much by high capital costs. Therefore, Project L's NPV profile has the steeper slope.

11-5c Independent Projects

If an *independent* project with normal cash flows is being evaluated, then the NPV and IRR criteria always lead to the same accept/reject decision: if NPV says accept, IRR also says accept. To see why this is so, look back at Figure 11-2 and notice (1) that the IRR criterion for acceptance is that the project's cost of capital is less than (or to the left of) the IRR and (2) that if the cost of capital is less than the IRR, then the NPV will be positive. Thus, at any cost of capital less than 14.49 percent, Project S will be acceptable by both the NPV and the IRR criteria, while both methods reject the project if the cost of capital is greater than 14.49 percent. A similar graph could be used for Project L or any other normal project, and we would reach the same conclusion. *Thus, for normal projects it always turns out that if the IRR says accept, then so will the NPV.*

11-5d Mutually Exclusive Projects[7]

Now assume that Projects S and L are *mutually exclusive* rather than independent. That is, we can choose either S or L, or we can reject both, but we can't accept both. Now look at Figure 11-3 and note that as long as the cost of capital is *greater than* the crossover rate of 11.97 percent, both methods recommend Project S: $NPV_S > NPV_L$ and $IRR_S > IRR_L$. Therefore, if r is *greater* than the crossover rate, no conflict occurs because both methods choose S. However, if the cost of capital is *less than* the crossover rate, a conflict arises: NPV ranks L higher but IRR chooses S.

Two basic conditions cause NPV profiles to cross and thus lead to conflicts:[8]

1. *Timing differences* exist, where most of the cash flows from one project come in early while most of those from the other project come in later, as occurred with our Projects S and L.

---

[7] This section is relatively technical and can be omitted without loss of continuity.
[8] Of course, mutually exclusive projects can differ with respect to both scale and timing. Also, if mutually exclusive projects have different lives (as opposed to different cash flow patterns over a common life), this introduces further complications, and for meaningful comparisons, some mutually exclusive projects must be evaluated over a common life. This point is discussed later in the text or on the ThomsonNOW Web site.

2. *Project size (or scale) differences* exist, where the amount invested in one project is larger than the other.

When either size or timing differences occur, the firm will have different amounts of funds to invest in the various years, depending on which of the two mutually exclusive projects it chooses. For example, if the firm chooses Project S, then it will have more funds to invest in Year 1 because S has a higher cash flow in that year than L. Similarly, if one project costs more than the other, then the firm will have more money at t = 0 to invest elsewhere if it selects the smaller project. *Given this situation, the rate of return at which differential cash flows can be reinvested is a critical issue.*

The key to resolving conflicts between mutually exclusive projects is this: At what rate of return can the firm invest the differential cash flows it would receive if it chooses the shorter or smaller project; that is, at what rate can they be reinvested? *The NPV method implicitly assumes that the **reinvestment rate** is the cost of capital, whereas the IRR method assumes that the reinvestment rate is the IRR itself.* To see why this is so, think back to Chapter 2, where we discussed the time value of money. There we started with $100 and assumed that it would be invested at the rate I% for N years. We also assumed that the interest earned during each year would itself earn I% in the following years. Thus, we were assuming that earnings would be reinvested and would earn I%, and we then compounded by (1 + I) to find the future value. Then, when we found present values, we reversed the process, discounting at the rate I% to find the present value of a given future value. That leads to this conclusion: *When we calculate present values, we are implicitly assuming that cash flows can be reinvested and that they will earn the specified interest rate, I%.*[9]

That leads to another very important conclusion: *When we find the NPV, we use the WACC as the discount rate, which means that the NPV method automatically assumes that cash flows can be reinvested at the WACC. However, when we find the IRR, we are discounting at the rate that causes the NPV to be zero, which means that the IRR method assumes that cash flows can be reinvested at the IRR itself.*

Which assumption is more realistic? For most firms, reinvestment at the WACC is more realistic because, if a firm has access to the capital markets, it can raise additional capital at the going rate, which in our examples is 10 percent. Since it can obtain capital at 10 percent, if it has investment opportunities that return more than 10 percent, it can take them on using external capital at a 10 percent cost. If it chooses to use internally generated cash flows from past projects rather than external capital, it will save the 10 percent cost of capital, which implies reinvestment at the 10 percent cost of capital.[10]

If the firm does not have good access to external capital and also has a lot of projects with high IRRs, then it would be reasonable to assume that project cash flows would be reinvested at rates close to their IRRs. However, this situation rarely exists because firms with good investment opportunities generally do have access to debt and equity markets. *Therefore, the fundamental assumption built into the NPV method is generally more valid than the assumption built into the IRR method.*

We should reiterate that, when projects are independent, the NPV and IRR methods both lead to exactly the same accept/reject decision. However, *when evaluating mutually exclusive projects, especially those that differ in size or timing, the NPV method is generally superior.*

Reinvestment Rate Assumption
The assumption that cash flows from a project can be reinvested (1) at the cost of capital, if using the NPV method, or (2) at the internal rate of return, if using the IRR method.

---

[9] It's not critical that cash flows actually be reinvested at the specified interest rate. What's critical is that cash flows *could be* reinvested at that rate.

[10] The 10 percent is also called the *opportunity cost rate*, which is the return on the next best alternative. The opportunity cost for reinvested cash flows for firms with access to capital markets is the cost of capital.

Describe in words how a project's NPV profile is constructed. What is the Y-axis intercept equal to?

Do the NPV and IRR criteria lead to conflicting recommendations for normal independent projects? For mutually exclusive projects?

What is the "crossover rate," and how does it interact with the cost of capital to determine whether or not a conflict exists between NPV and IRR?

What two characteristics can lead to conflicts between the NPV and the IRR when evaluating mutually exclusive projects?

What reinvestment rate assumptions are built into the NPV and IRR? Which assumption is better for firms (a) with good access to external capital or (b) with no access to external capital?

11-6 MULTIPLE IRRs[11]

A project has *normal* cash flows if it has one or more cash outflows (costs) followed by a series of cash inflows. If, however, a cash *outflow* occurs sometime after the inflows have commenced, meaning that the signs of the cash flows change more than once, then the project is said to have *nonnormal* cash flows. Examples:

Normal:	−	+	+	+	+	+	or	−	−	−	+	+	+	+	+
Nonnormal:	−	+	+	+	+	−	or	−	+	+	+	−	+	+	+

If a project has nonnormal cash flows, it can have two or more IRRs, that is, **multiple IRRs.** This occurs because, when we solve Equation 11-2 to find the IRR for such a project, it is possible to obtain more than one solution value for IRR.[12]

To illustrate this problem, suppose a firm is considering the development of a strip mine (Project M). The mine will cost $1.6 million, then it will produce a cash flow of $10 million at the end of Year 1, and then, at the end of Year 2, the firm must spend $10 million to restore the land to its original condition. Therefore, the project's expected net cash flows are as follows (in millions):

Multiple IRRs
The situation where a project has two or more IRRs.

EXPECTED NET CASH FLOWS

Year 0	End of Year 1	End of Year 2
−$1.6	+$10	−$10

We can substitute these values into Equation 11-2 and then solve for the IRR:

$$\text{NPV} = \frac{-\$1.6 \text{ million}}{(1 + \text{IRR})^0} + \frac{\$10 \text{ million}}{(1 + \text{IRR})^1} + \frac{-\$10 \text{ million}}{(1 + \text{IRR})^2} = 0$$

---

[11] This section is relatively technical and can be omitted without loss of continuity.

[12] Equation 11-2 is a polynomial of degree n, so it has n different roots, or solutions. All except one of the roots is an imaginary number when investments have normal cash flows (one or more cash outflows followed by cash inflows), so in the normal case, only one value of IRR appears. However, the possibility of multiple real roots, hence multiple IRRs, arises when negative net cash flows occur during some year after the project has been placed in operation.

NPV equals 0 when IRR = 25% and also when IRR = 400%.[13] Therefore, Project M has an IRR of 25 percent and another of 400 percent, and we don't know which one to use. This relationship is depicted graphically in the NPV profile shown in Figure 11-4.[14] The graph is constructed by plotting the project's NPV at different discount rates. Note that no dilemma would arise if the NPV method were used; we would simply use Equation 11-1, find the NPV, and use this to evaluate the project. If Project M's cost of capital were 10 percent, then its NPV would be −$0.77 million, and the project should be rejected. If r were between 25 and 400 percent, NPV would be positive.

Another example of multiple internal rates of return occurred when a major California bank borrowed funds from an insurance company and then used these funds (plus an initial investment of its own) to buy a number of jet engines, which it then leased to a major airline. The bank expected to receive

---

FIGURE 11-4 *NPV Profile for Project M*

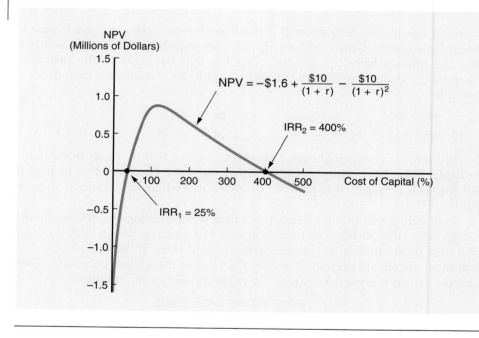

$$NPV = -\$1.6 + \frac{\$10}{(1 + r)} - \frac{\$10}{(1 + r)^2}$$

---

[13] If you attempt to find Project M's IRR with an HP calculator, you will get an error message, while TI calculators give only the IRR that's closest to zero. When you encounter either situation, you can find the approximate IRRs by first calculating NPVs using several different values for r = I/YR and then plotting the NPV profile. The intersections with the X-axis give a rough idea of the IRR values. With an HP calculator, you can actually find both IRRs by entering guesses as we explain in the tutorial. We are not aware of a corresponding feature for TI calculators.

[14] Does Figure 11-4 suggest that the firm should try to *raise* its cost of capital to about 100 percent in order to maximize the NPV of the project? Certainly not. The firm should seek to *minimize* its cost of capital; this will cause its stock price to be maximized. Actions taken to raise the cost of capital might make this particular project look good, but those actions would be terribly harmful to the firm's more numerous projects with normal cash flows. Only if the firm's cost of capital is high in spite of efforts to keep it down will the illustrative project have a positive NPV.

positive net cash flows (lease payments minus interest on the insurance company loan) for a number of years, then several large negative cash flows as it repaid the insurance company loan, and, finally, a large inflow from the sale of the engines when the lease expired. The bank discovered two IRRs and wondered which was correct. It could not ignore the IRR and just use the NPV method because the bank's senior loan committee, as well as Federal Reserve bank examiners, wanted to know the return on the lease. The bank's solution called for calculating and then using the "modified internal rate of return," which is discussed in the next section.

What characteristic must a project's cash flow stream have for more than one IRR to exist?

Project MM has the cash flows shown below. Calculate MM's NPV at discount rates of 0, 10, 12.2258, 25, 122.1470, and 150 percent. What are MM's IRRs? If the cost of capital were 10 percent, should the project be accepted or rejected? (NPVs range from −$350 to +$164 and back to −$94; the IRRs are 12.23 and 122.15 percent)

END-OF-YEAR CASH FLOWS

0	1	2	3
−$1,000	$2,000	$2,000	−$3,350

11-7 MODIFIED INTERNAL RATE OF RETURN (MIRR)[15]

Managers like to know the rates of return projects are expected to provide. The regular IRR assumes that cash flows will be reinvested at the IRR, but that may not be correct. In addition, projects can have more than one IRR. Given these problems, can we find a percentage evaluator that is better than the regular IRR? The answer is yes—we can modify the IRR and make it both a better indicator of relative profitability and also free of the multiple IRR problem. The new measure is called the **modified IRR,** or **MIRR,** and it is defined as follows:

$$\text{PV costs} = \text{PV terminal value}$$

$$\sum_{t=0}^{N} \frac{\text{COF}_t}{(1+r)^t} = \frac{\sum_{t=0}^{N} \text{CIF}_t(1+r)^{N-t}}{(1+\text{MIRR})^N}$$

$$\text{PV costs} = \frac{\text{TV}}{(1+\text{MIRR})^N} \qquad \textbf{(11-2a)}$$

Here COF refers to cash outflows (negative numbers, or costs associated with the project) and CIF refers to cash inflows (positive numbers). The left term is simply the PV of the investment outlays when discounted at the cost of capital, and the numerator of the right term is the compounded value of the inflows, *assuming that the cash inflows are reinvested at the cost of capital.* The compounded value of the cash inflows is also called the *terminal value,* or *TV.* The discount

Modified IRR (MIRR)
The discount rate at which the present value of a project's cost is equal to the present value of its terminal value, where the terminal value is found as the sum of the future values of the cash inflows, compounded at the firm's cost of capital.

---

[15] Again, this section is relatively technical, but it can be omitted without loss of continuity.

rate that forces the PV of the TV to equal the PV of the costs is defined as the MIRR.[16]

If the investment costs are all incurred at $t = 0$, and if the first operating inflow occurs at $t = 1$, as is true for our illustrative Projects S and L as presented in Figure 11-1, then this equation can be used:

$$\text{Cost} = \frac{\text{TV}}{(1 + \text{MIRR})^N} = \frac{\sum_{t=1}^{N} \text{CIF}_t(1 + r)^{N-t}}{(1 + \text{MIRR})^N} \qquad \textbf{(11-2b)}$$

We can illustrate the calculation with Project S:

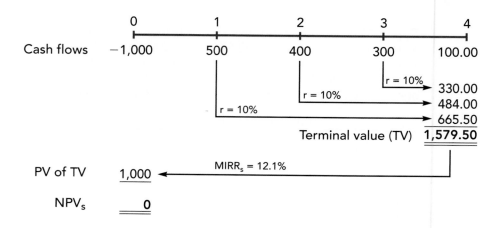

Using the cash flows as set out on the time line, first find the terminal value by compounding each cash inflow at the 10 percent cost of capital. Then enter $N = 4$, $PV = -1000$, $PMT = 0$, $FV = 1579.5$, and then press the I/YR button to find $\text{MIRR}_S = 12.1\%$. Similarly, we find $\text{MIRR}_L = 12.7\%$.[17]

The MIRR has two significant advantages over the regular IRR. First, whereas the regular IRR assumes that the cash flows from each project are reinvested at the IRR itself, the MIRR assumes that cash flows are reinvested at the cost of capital.[18] As we discussed earlier, reinvestment at the cost of capital is generally more correct, so the MIRR is a better indicator of a project's true profitability than the IRR. Also, the MIRR solves the multiple IRR problem—there can never be more than one MIRR, and it can be compared with the cost of capital when deciding to accept or reject projects.

Is MIRR as good as NPV for choosing between mutually exclusive projects? In general, the answer is no. If projects differ in size or length of life, conflicts

---

[16] There are several alternative definitions for the MIRR. The differences relate to whether negative cash flows after the positive cash flows begin should be compounded and treated as part of the TV or discounted and treated as a cost. A related issue is whether negative and positive flows in a given year should be netted or treated separately. For a complete discussion, see William R. McDaniel, Daniel E. McCarty, and Kenneth A. Jessell, "Discounted Cash Flow with Explicit Reinvestment Rates: Tutorial and Extension," *The Financial Review*, August 1988, pp. 369–385; and David M. Shull, "Interpreting Rates of Return: A Modified Rate of Return Approach," *Financial Practice and Education*, Fall 1993, pp. 67–71.

[17] It is easy to calculate the MIRR in practice. Some calculators, including the HP-17B and the TI BAII+ Professional, can do the MIRR calculations, and *Excel* has a MIRR function that makes the calculation trivially easy.

[18] This statement is not completely true. With *Excel*, the reinvestment rate can be specified to be a rate other than either the IRR or the WACC if the most likely reinvestment rate is known.

can arise, and in such cases the NPV is better because it leads to the choice that maximizes value.

Our conclusion is that the MIRR is superior to the regular IRR as an indicator of a project's "true" rate of return. However, NPV is still best for choosing among competing projects because it provides the best indication of how much each project will add to the value of the firm.

What is the primary difference between the MIRR and the regular IRR?

What advantages does the MIRR have over the regular IRR?

What conditions can cause MIRR and NPV to produce conflicting rankings?

Projects S and L have the following cash flows, and their cost of capital is 10 percent. What are the projects' IRRs, MIRRs, and NPVs? Which project would each method select? (IRR$_S$ = 23.1%, IRR$_L$ = 19.1%, MIRR$_S$ = 16.8%, MIRR$_L$ = 18.7%, NPV$_S$ = $128.10, NPV$_L$ = $165.29)

	0	1	2
S	−$1,000	$1,150	$ 100
L	−1,000	100	1,300

11-8 PAYBACK PERIOD

The NPV and IRR are the most used methods today, but the earliest selection criterion was the **payback period,** defined as the number of years required to recover a project's cost from operating cash flows. Equation 11-3 is used for the calculation, and the process is diagrammed in Figure 11-5. We start with the project's cost, then add the cash inflow for each year until the cumulative cash flow turns positive. The payback year is the year prior to full recovery plus a fraction equal to the shortfall at the end of that year divided by the cash flow during the full recovery year:[19]

Payback Period
The length of time required for an investment's net revenues to cover its cost.

$$\text{Payback} = \begin{array}{c}\text{Number of}\\\text{years prior to}\\\text{full recovery}\end{array} + \dfrac{\begin{array}{c}\text{Unrecovered cost}\\\text{at start of year}\end{array}}{\begin{array}{c}\text{Cash flow during}\\\text{full recovery year}\end{array}} \qquad \textbf{(11-3)}$$

The shorter the payback, the better. Therefore, if the firm requires a payback of three years or less, S would be accepted but L would be rejected. If the projects were mutually exclusive, S would be ranked over L because of its shorter payback.

The payback has three main flaws: (1) Dollars received in different years are all given the same weight—a dollar in Year 4 is assumed to be just as valuable as a dollar in Year 1. (2) Cash flows beyond the payback year are given no consideration whatever, regardless of how large they might be. (3) Unlike the NPV, which tells us by how much the project should increase shareholder wealth, and

---

[19] Equation 11-3 assumes that cash flows come in uniformly during the year and the cash flow during the full recovery year is positive.

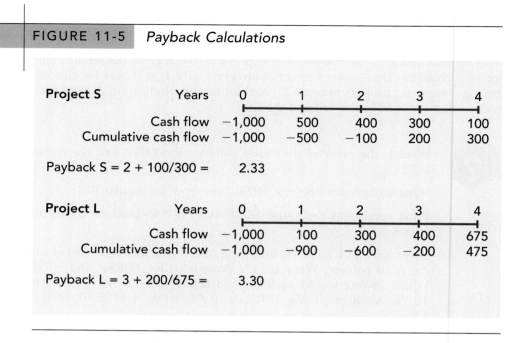

FIGURE 11-5 *Payback Calculations*

Project S	Years	0	1	2	3	4
Cash flow		−1,000	500	400	300	100
Cumulative cash flow		−1,000	−500	−100	200	300

Payback S = 2 + 100/300 = 2.33

Project L	Years	0	1	2	3	4
Cash flow		−1,000	100	300	400	675
Cumulative cash flow		−1,000	−900	−600	−200	475

Payback L = 3 + 200/675 = 3.30

Discounted Payback
The length of time required for an investment's cash flows, discounted at the investment's cost of capital, to cover its cost.

the IRR, which tells us how much a project yields over the cost of capital, the payback merely tells us when we get our investment back. There is no necessary relationship between a given payback and investor wealth maximization, so we don't know how to set the "right" payback. The two years, three years, or whatever is used as the cutoff is essentially arbitrary.

To counter the first criticism, analysts developed the **discounted payback,** where cash flows are first discounted at the WACC and then used to find the payback year. Thus, the discounted payback period is defined as the number of years required to recover the investment's cost from *discounted* cash flows. Figure 11-6 calculates the discounted paybacks for S and L, assuming both have a 10 percent cost of capital. Each cash inflow is divided by $(1 + r)^t = (1.10)^t$, where t is the year in which the cash flow occurs and r is the project's cost of capital, and those PVs are used to find the payback. Project S's discounted payback is just under three years, while L's is almost four years.

Note that the payback is a "breakeven" calculation in the sense that if cash flows come in at the expected rate until the payback year, then the project will break even. However, since the regular payback doesn't consider the cost of capital, it doesn't really specify the breakeven year. The discounted payback does consider capital costs, but it still disregards cash flows beyond the payback year, which is a serious flaw. Further, there is no way of telling how low the paybacks must be to maximize shareholder wealth.

Although both payback methods have faults as ranking criteria, they do provide information on how long funds will be tied up in a project. The shorter the payback, other things held constant, the greater the project's *liquidity*. This factor is often important for smaller firms that don't have ready access to the capital markets. Also, cash flows expected in the distant future are generally riskier than near-term cash flows, so the payback can be used as a risk indicator.

What two pieces of information does the payback convey that are absent from the other capital budgeting decision methods?

FIGURE 11-6	*Discounted Payback Calculations at 10% Cost of Capital*

Project S

	Years	0	1	2	3	4
Cash flow		−1,000	500	400	300	100
Discounted cash flow		−1,000	455	331	225	68
Cumulative discounted CF		−1,000	−545	−215	11	79

Discounted payback S = 2 + 215/225 =   2.95

Project L

	Years	0	1	2	3	4
Cash flow		−1,000	100	300	400	675
Discounted cash flow		−1,000	91	248	301	461
Cumulative discounted CF		−1,000	−909	−661	−361	100

Discounted payback L = 3 + 361/461 =   3.78

What three flaws does the regular payback have? Does the discounted payback correct these flaws?

Project P has a cost of $1,000 and cash flows of $300 per year for three years plus another $1,000 in Year 4. The project's cost of capital is 15 percent. What are P's regular and discounted paybacks? (3.10, 3.55) If the company requires a payback of three years or less, would the project be accepted? Would this be a good accept/reject decision, considering the NPV and/or the IRR? (NPV = $256.72, IRR = 24.78%)

11-9 CONCLUSIONS ON CAPITAL BUDGETING METHODS

We have discussed five capital budgeting decision criteria—NPV, IRR, MIRR, payback, and discounted payback. We compared these methods with one another and highlighted their strengths and weaknesses. In the process, we may have created the impression that "sophisticated" firms should use only one method in the decision process, NPV. However, virtually all capital budgeting decisions are analyzed by computer, so it is easy to calculate all five of the decision criteria. In making the accept/reject decision, large, sophisticated firms such as GE, Boeing, and Airbus generally calculate and consider all five measures, because each provides a somewhat different piece of information.

NPV is important because it gives a direct measure of the dollar benefit of the project to shareholders, so we regard it as the best measure of profitability. IRR and MIRR also measure profitability, but expressed as a percentage rate of return, which is interesting to decision makers. Further, IRR and MIRR contain information concerning a project's "safety margin." To illustrate, consider two projects, Project SS (for small), which costs $10,000 and is expected to return $16,500 at the end of one year, and Project LL (for large), which costs $100,000 and has an expected payoff of $115,550 after one year. SS has a huge IRR and MIRR, 65 percent, while LL's IRR and MIRR are a more modest 15.6 percent. The NPV paints a somewhat different picture—at a 10 percent cost of capital, SS's NPV is $5,000 while LL's is $5,045. By the NPV rule we would choose LL. However, SS's IRR and MIRR indicate that it has a much larger margin for error: Even if its realized cash flow fell by 39 percent from the $16,500 forecast, the firm would still recover its $10,000 investment. On the other hand, if LL's inflows fell by only 13.5 percent from its forecasted $115,550, the firm would not recover its investment. Further, if neither project generated any cash flows at all, the firm would lose only $10,000 on SS but $100,000 if it took on LL.

The modified IRR has all the virtues of the IRR, but it incorporates a better reinvestment rate assumption, and it also avoids the multiple rate of return problem. Thus, if decision makers want to know projects' rates of return, the MIRR is a better indicator than the regular IRR.

Payback and discounted payback provide indications of a project's *liquidity* and *risk*. A long payback means that investment dollars will be locked up for many years, hence the project is relatively illiquid, and also that cash flows must be forecasted far out into the future, hence the project is probably riskier than if it had a shorter payback. A good analogy for this is bond valuation. An investor should never compare the yields to maturity on two bonds without also considering their terms to maturity because a bond's riskiness is significantly influenced by its maturity. The same holds true for capital projects.

In summary, the different measures provide different types of information. Since it is easy to calculate all of them, all should be considered when making capital budgeting decisions. For most decisions, the greatest weight should be given to the NPV, but it would be foolish to ignore the information provided by the other criteria.

Describe the advantages and disadvantages of the five capital budgeting methods discussed in this chapter.

Should capital budgeting decisions be made solely on the basis of a project's NPV?

11-10 DECISION CRITERIA USED IN PRACTICE

Surveys designed to find out which of the criteria managers actually use have been taken over the years. Surveys taken prior to 1999 asked companies to indicate their primary criterion (the method they gave the most weight to), while the most recent one, in 1999, asked what method or methods managers calculated and used. The summary of the results as shown in Table 11-1 reveals some interesting trends.

First, the NPV criterion was not used significantly before the 1980s, but by 1999 it was close to the top in usage. Moreover, informal discussions with companies suggest that if 2005 data were available, NPV would have moved to the top. Second, the IRR method is widely used, but its recent growth is much less dramatic than that of NPV. Third, payback was the most important criterion 40 years ago, but its use as the primary criterion had fallen drastically by

TABLE 11-1	*Capital Budgeting Methods Used in Practice*			
	PRIMARY CRITERION			**CALCULATE AND USE**
	1960	**1970**	**1980**	**1999**
NPV	0%	0%	15%	75%
IRR	20	60	65	76
Payback	35	15	5	57
Discounted Payback	NA	NA	NA	29
Other	45	25	15	NA
Totals	100%	100%	100%	

Sources: The 1999 data are from John R. Graham and Campbell R. Harvey, "The Theory and Practice of Corporate Finance: Evidence from the Field," *Journal of Financial Economics*, 2001, pp. 187–244. Data from prior years are our estimates based on averaging data from these studies: J. S. Moore and A. K. Reichert, "An Analysis of the Financial Management Techniques Currently Employed by Large U.S. Corporations," *Journal of Business Finance and Accounting*, Winter 1983, pp. 623–645; and M. T. Stanley and S. R. Block, "A Survey of Multinational Capital Budgeting," *The Financial Review*, March 1984, pp. 36–51.

1980. Companies still use payback because it is easy to calculate and it does provide some information, but it is rarely used today as the primary criterion. Fourth, "other methods," which are generally offshoots of NPV and/or IRR, have been fading as a primary criterion due to the increased use of IRR and especially NPV.

These trends are consistent with our evaluation of the various methods. NPV is the best single criterion, but all of the methods provide useful information, all are easy to calculate, and thus all are used, along with judgment and common sense. We will have more to say about all this when we discuss cash flow.

What trends in capital budgeting methodology can be seen from Table 11-1?

11-11 USING CAPITAL BUDGETING TECHNIQUES IN OTHER CONTEXTS

The techniques developed in this chapter are also used to help managers make other types of decisions. One example is the analysis relating to a corporate merger. Companies frequently decide to acquire other firms to obtain low-cost production facilities, to increase capacity, or to expand into new markets, and the analysis related to such mergers is similar to that used in capital budgeting. Thus, when the bank that is now Bank of America began to expand out of its North Carolina base, it often had the choice of building new facilities from the ground up or acquiring existing banks. It frequently chose to acquire other banks, and its managers used the same techniques we employ in capital budgeting when making this choice.

Managers also use similar techniques when deciding whether to downsize operations or to sell off particular assets or divisions. Like capital budgeting, such an analysis requires an assessment of how the action will affect the firm's cash flows. In a downsizing, companies typically spend money (that is, invest) in severance payments to employees who will be laid off, but the companies then receive benefits in the form of lower future wage costs. Regarding asset sales, the pattern of cash flows is reversed from those in a typical capital budgeting decision—positive cash flows are realized at the outset, but the firm is sacrificing future cash flows that it would have received if it had continued to use the asset. So, when deciding whether it makes sense to shed assets, managers compare the cash received with the present value of the lost inflows. If the net present value is positive, selling the asset would increase shareholder value.

 Give some examples of other types of decisions that can be analyzed with the capital budgeting techniques developed in this chapter.

11-12 THE POST-AUDIT

Post-Audit

A comparison of actual versus expected results for a given capital project.

An important aspect of the capital budgeting process is the **post-audit,** which involves (1) comparing actual results with those predicted by the project's sponsors and (2) explaining why any differences occurred. For example, many firms require that the operating divisions send a monthly report for the first six months after a project goes into operation, and a quarterly report thereafter, until the project's results are up to expectations. From then on, reports on the operation are reviewed on a regular basis like those of other operations.

The post-audit has two main purposes:

1. *Improve forecasts.* When decision makers are forced to compare their projections with actual outcomes, there is a tendency for estimates to improve. Conscious or unconscious biases are observed and eliminated; new forecasting methods are sought as the need for them becomes apparent; and people simply tend to do everything better, including forecasting, if they know that their actions are being monitored. How hard and how effectively would you study if you never had to take a test?

2. *Improve operations.* Businesses are run by people, and people can perform at higher or lower levels of efficiency. When a divisional team has made a forecast about an investment, the team members are, in a sense, putting their reputations on the line. Accordingly, if costs are above predicted levels, sales are below expectations, and so on, then executives in production, marketing, and other areas will strive to improve operations and to bring results into line with forecasts. In a discussion related to this point, one executive made this statement: "You academicians only worry about making good decisions. In business, we also worry about making decisions good."

The post-audit is not a simple process, and a number of factors can cause complications. First, we must recognize that each element of the cash flow forecast is subject to uncertainty, so a percentage of all projects undertaken by any reasonably aggressive firm will necessarily go awry. This fact must be considered when appraising the performances of the operating executives who submit capital expenditure requests. Second, projects sometimes fail to meet expectations for reasons beyond the control of the operating executives and for reasons that no one could realistically be expected to anticipate. For example, the unanticipated run-up in oil prices in 2005 adversely affected many projects. Third, it is often difficult to separate the operating results of one investment from those of a larger system. Although some projects stand alone and permit ready identification of costs and revenues, the cost savings that result from assets like new computers may be very hard to measure. Fourth, it is often hard to hand out blame or praise because the executives who were responsible for launching a given investment have moved on by the time the results are known.

Because of these difficulties, some firms tend to play down the importance of the post-audit. However, observations of both businesses and governmental units suggest that the best-run and most successful organizations are the ones that put the greatest emphasis on post-audits. Accordingly, we regard the post-audit as an important element in a good capital budgeting system.

What is done in the post-audit?

Identify several benefits of the post-audit.

What are some factors that complicate the post-audit process?

Tying It All Together

In this chapter we described five techniques—NPV, IRR, MIRR, payback, and discounted payback—that are used to evaluate proposed capital budgeting projects. The NPV is the best single measure and is gaining in usage. However, the other approaches provide useful information, and in this age of computers, it is easy to calculate all of them. Therefore, managers generally look at all five criteria when deciding to accept or reject projects and when choosing among mutually exclusive projects.

We simplified things greatly in this chapter. In particular, you were given a set of cash flows and a risk-adjusted cost of capital, and you were then asked to evaluate the projects. The hardest part of capital budgeting, however, is estimating the cash flows and risk. We address these issues later when we discuss cash flow.

SELF-TEST QUESTIONS AND PROBLEMS
(Solutions Appear in Appendix A)

ST-1 **Key terms** Define each of the following terms:
   a. Capital budget; capital budgeting; strategic business plan
   b. Net present value (NPV) method
   c. Internal rate of return (IRR)
   d. NPV profile; crossover rate
   e. Reinvestment rate assumption
   f. Mutually exclusive projects; independent projects
   g. Nonnormal cash flows; normal cash flows; multiple IRRs
   h. Modified internal rate of return (MIRR)
   i. Payback period; discounted payback
   j. Post-audit

ST-2 **Capital budgeting criteria** You must analyze two projects, X and Y. Each project costs $10,000, and the firm's WACC is 12 percent. The expected net cash flows are

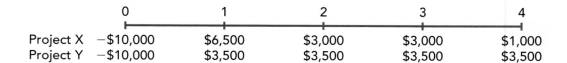

	0	1	2	3	4
Project X	−$10,000	$6,500	$3,000	$3,000	$1,000
Project Y	−$10,000	$3,500	$3,500	$3,500	$3,500

   a. Calculate each project's NPV, IRR, MIRR, payback, and discounted payback.
   b. Which project(s) should be accepted if they are independent?
   c. Which project should be accepted if they are mutually exclusive?
   d. How might a change in the WACC produce a conflict between the NPV and IRR rankings of these two projects? Would there be a conflict if WACC were 5 percent? (Hint: Plot the NPV profiles. The crossover rate is 6.21875 percent.)
   e. Why does the conflict exist?

QUESTIONS

11-1 How are project classifications used in the capital budgeting process?

11-2 What are three potential flaws with the regular payback method? Does the discounted payback method correct all three flaws?

11-3 Why is the NPV of a relatively long-term project (one for which a high percentage of its cash flows occur in the distant future) more sensitive to changes in the WACC than that of a short-term project?

11-4 What is a mutually exclusive project? How should managers rank mutually exclusive projects?

11-5 If two mutually exclusive projects were being compared, would a high cost of capital favor the longer-term or the shorter-term project? Why? If the cost of capital declined, would that lead firms to invest more in longer-term projects or shorter-term projects? Would a decline (or an increase) in the WACC cause changes in the IRR ranking of mutually exclusive projects?

11-6 Discuss the following statement: "If a firm has only independent projects, a constant WACC, and projects with normal cash flows, then the NPV and IRR methods will always lead to identical capital budgeting decisions." What does this imply about the choice between IRR and NPV? If each of the assumptions above were changed (one by one), how would your answer change?

11-7 Why might it be rational for a small firm that does not have access to the capital markets to use the payback method rather than the NPV method?

11-8 Project X is very risky and has an NPV of $3 million. Project Y is very safe and has an NPV of $2.5 million. They are mutually exclusive, and project risk has been properly considered in the NPV analyses. Which project should be chosen? Explain.

11-9 What reinvestment rate assumptions are built into the NPV, IRR, and MIRR methods? Give an explanation (other than "because the text says so") for your answer.

11-10 A firm has a $100 million capital budget. It is considering two projects that each cost $100 million. Project A has an IRR of 20 percent, an NPV of $9 million, and will be terminated after 1 year at a profit of $20 million, resulting in an immediate increase in EPS. Project B, which cannot be postponed, has an IRR of 30 percent and an NPV of $50 million. However, the firm's short-run EPS will be reduced if it accepts Project B, because no revenues will be generated for several years.

    a.   Should the short-run effects on EPS influence the choice between the two projects?
    b.   How might situations like this influence a firm's decision to use payback?

PROBLEMS

Easy Problems 1–6

11-1 **NPV** Project K costs $52,125, its expected net cash inflows are $12,000 per year for 8 years, and its WACC is 12 percent. What is the project's NPV?

11-2 **IRR** Refer to problem 11-1. What is the project's IRR?

11-3 **MIRR** Refer to problem 11-1. What is the project's MIRR?

11-4 **Payback period** Refer to problem 11-1. What is the project's payback?

11-5 **Discounted payback** Refer to problem 11-1. What is the project's discounted payback?

11-6 **NPV** Your division is considering two projects with the following net cash flows (in millions):

	0	1	2	3
Project A	−$25	$5	$10	$17
Project B	−$20	$10	$9	$6

    a.   What are the projects' NPVs, assuming the WACC is 5 percent? 10 percent? 15 percent?
    b.   What are the projects' IRRs at each of these WACCs?
    c.   If the WACC were 5 percent and A and B were mutually exclusive, which would you choose? What if the WACC were 10 percent? 15 percent? (Hint: The crossover rate is 7.81 percent.)

Intermediate Problems 7–13

11-7 **Capital budgeting criteria** A firm with a 14 percent WACC is evaluating two projects for this year's capital budget. After-tax cash flows, including depreciation, are as follows:

	0	1	2	3	4	5
Project A	−$6,000	$2,000	$2,000	$2,000	$2,000	$2,000
Project B	−$18,000	$5,600	$5,600	$5,600	$5,600	$5,600

    a.   Calculate NPV, IRR, MIRR, payback, and discounted payback for each project.
    b.   Assuming the projects are independent, which one or ones would you recommend?
    c.   If the projects are mutually exclusive, which would you recommend?
    d.   Notice that the projects have the same cash flow timing pattern. Why is there a conflict between NPV and IRR?

11-8 **Capital budgeting criteria: ethical considerations** A mining company is considering a new project. It has received a permit, so the mine would be legal, but it would cause significant harm to a nearby river. The firm could spend an additional $10 million at Year 0 to mitigate the environmental problem, but it would not be required to do so.

Developing the mine (without mitigation) would cost $60 million, and the expected net cash inflows would be $20 million per year for 5 years. If the firm does invest in mitigation, the annual inflows would be $21 million. The risk-adjusted WACC is 12 percent.

a. Calculate the NPV and IRR with and without mitigation.
b. How should the environmental effects be dealt with when evaluating this project?
c. Should this project be undertaken? If so, should the firm do the mitigation?

11-9 **Capital budgeting criteria: ethical considerations** An electric utility is considering a new power plant in northern Arizona. Power from the plant would be sold in the Phoenix area, where it is badly needed. The firm has received a permit, so the plant would be legal, but it would cause some air pollution near the plant. The company could spend an additional $40 million at Year 0 to mitigate the environmental problem, but it would not be required to do so. The plant without mitigation would cost $240 million, and the expected net cash inflows would be $80 million per year for 5 years. If the firm does invest in mitigation, the annual inflows would be $84 million. Unemployment in the area where the plant would be built is high, and the plant would provide about 350 good jobs. The risk-adjusted WACC is 17 percent.

a. Calculate the NPV and IRR with and without mitigation.
b. How should the environmental effects be dealt with when evaluating this project?
c. Should this project be undertaken? If so, should the firm do the mitigation?

11-10 **Capital budgeting criteria: mutually exclusive projects** A firm with a WACC of 10 percent is considering the following mutually exclusive projects:

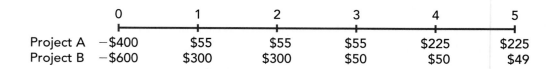

	0	1	2	3	4	5
Project A	−$400	$55	$55	$55	$225	$225
Project B	−$600	$300	$300	$50	$50	$49

Which project would you recommend? Explain.

11-11 **Capital budgeting criteria: mutually exclusive projects** Project S costs $15,000, and its expected cash flows would be $4,500 per year for 5 years. Mutually exclusive Project L costs $37,500, and its expected cash flows would be $11,100 per year for 5 years. If both projects have a WACC of 14 percent, which project would you recommend? Explain.

11-12 **IRR and NPV** A company is analyzing two mutually exclusive projects, S and L, with the following cash flows:

	0	1	2	3	4
Project S	−$1,000	$900	$250	$10	$10
Project L	−$1,000	$0	$250	$400	$800

The company's WACC is 10 percent. What is the IRR of the *better* project? (Hint: Note that the better project may or may not be the one with the higher IRR.)

11-13 **MIRR** A firm is considering two mutually exclusive projects, X and Y, with the following cash flows:

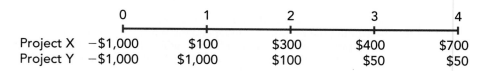

	0	1	2	3	4
Project X	−$1,000	$100	$300	$400	$700
Project Y	−$1,000	$1,000	$100	$50	$50

The projects are equally risky, and their WACC is 12 percent. What is the MIRR of the better project?

Challenging
Problems 14–22

11-14 **Choosing mandatory projects on the basis of least cost** K. Kim Inc. must install a new air conditioning unit in its main plant. Kim absolutely must install one or the other of the units because otherwise the highly profitable plant would have to shut down. Two units are available, HCC and LCC (for high and low capital costs). HCC has a high capital cost but relatively low operating costs, while LCC has a low capital cost but higher operating costs because it uses more electricity. The units' costs are shown below. Kim's WACC is 7 percent.

	0	1	2	3	4	5
HCC	−$600,000	−$50,000	−$50,000	−$50,000	−$50,000	−$50,000
LCC	−$100,000	−$175,000	−$175,000	−$175,000	−$175,000	−$175,000

a. Which unit would you recommend? Explain.
b. If Kim's controller wanted to know the IRRs of the two projects, what would you tell him?
c. If the WACC rose to 15 percent would this affect your recommendation? Explain your answer and why this result occurred.

11-15 **NPV profiles: timing differences** An oil drilling company must choose between two mutually exclusive extraction projects, and each costs $12 million. Under Plan A, all the oil would be extracted in 1 year, producing a cash flow at t = 1 of $14.4 million. Under Plan B, cash flows would be $2.1 million per year for 20 years. The firm's WACC is 12 percent.

a. Construct NPV profiles for Plans A and B, identify each project's IRR, and show the approximate crossover rate.
b. Is it logical to assume that the firm would take on all available independent, average-risk projects with returns greater than 12 percent? If all available projects with returns greater than 12 percent have been undertaken, would this mean that cash flows from past investments would have an opportunity cost of only 12 percent, because all it could do with these cash flows would be to replace money that has a cost of 12 percent? Does this imply that the WACC is the correct reinvestment rate assumption for a project's cash flows?

11-16 **NPV profiles: scale differences** A company is considering two mutually exclusive expansion plans. Plan A requires a $40 million expenditure on a large-scale, integrated plant that would provide expected cash flows of $6.4 million per year for 20 years. Plan B requires a $12 million expenditure to build a somewhat less efficient, more labor-intensive plant with an expected cash flow of $2.72 million per year for 20 years. The firm's WACC is 10 percent.

a. Calculate each project's NPV and IRR.
b. Graph the NPV profiles for Plan A and Plan B and approximate the crossover rate.
c. Why is NPV better than IRR for making capital budgeting decisions that add to shareholder value?

11-17 **Capital budgeting criteria** A company has a 12 percent WACC and is considering two mutually exclusive investments (that cannot be repeated) with the following net cash flows:

	0	1	2	3	4	5	6	7
Project A	−$300	−$387	−$193	−$100	$600	$600	$850	−$180
Project B	−$405	$134	$134	$134	$134	$134	$134	$0

a. What is each project's NPV?
b. What is each project's IRR?
c. What is each project's MIRR? (Hint: Consider Period 7 as the end of Project B's life.)
d. From your answers to parts a, b, and c, which project would be selected? If the WACC were 18 percent, which project would be selected?
e. Construct NPV profiles for Projects A and B.
f. What is each project's MIRR at a WACC of 18 percent?

11-18 **NPV and IRR** A store has 5 years remaining on its lease in a mall. Rent is $2,000 per month, 60 payments remain, and the next payment is due in 1 month. The mall's owner plans to sell the property in a year and wants rent at that time to be high so the property will appear more valuable. Therefore, the store has been offered a "great deal" (owner's words) on a new 5-year lease. The new lease calls for no rent for 9 months, then payments of $2,600 per month for the next 51 months. The lease cannot be broken, and the store's WACC is 12 percent (or 1 percent per month).

a. Should the new lease be accepted? (Hint: Be sure to use 1 percent per month.)
b. If the storeowner decided to bargain with the mall's owner over the new lease payment, what new lease payment would make the storeowner indifferent between the new and old leases? (Hint: Find FV of the old lease's original cost at t = 9, then treat this as the PV of a 51-period annuity whose payments represent the rent during months 10 to 60.)
c. The storeowner is not sure of the 12 percent WACC—it could be higher or lower. At what *nominal* WACC would the storeowner be indifferent between the two leases? (Hint: Calculate the differences between the two payment streams, and then find its IRR.)

11-19 **Multiple IRRs and MIRR** A mining company is deciding whether to open a strip mine, which costs $2 million. Net cash inflows of $13 million would occur at the end of Year 1. The land must be returned to its natural state at a cost of $12 million, payable at the end of Year 2.

a. Plot the project's NPV profile.
b. Should the project be accepted if WACC = 10%? If WACC = 20%? Explain your reasoning.
c. Can you think of some other capital budgeting situations in which negative cash flows during or at the end of the project's life might lead to multiple IRRs?
d. What is the project's MIRR at WACC = 10%? At WACC = 20%? Does MIRR lead to the same accept/reject decision for this project as the NPV method? Does the MIRR method *always* lead to the same accept/reject decision as NPV? (Hint: Consider mutually exclusive projects that differ in size.)

11-20 **NPV** A project has annual cash flows of $7,500 for the next 10 years and then $10,000 each year for the following 10 years. The IRR of this 20-year project is 10.98 percent. If the firm's WACC is 9 percent, what is the project's NPV?

11-21 **MIRR** Project X costs $1,000, and its cash flows are the same in Years 1 through 10. Its IRR is 12 percent, and its WACC is 10 percent. What is the project's MIRR?

11-22 **MIRR** A project has the following cash flows:

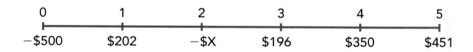

This project requires two outflows at Years 0 and 2, but the remaining cash flows are positive. Its WACC is 10 percent, and its MIRR is 14.14 percent. What is the Year 2 cash outflow?

COMPREHENSIVE/SPREADSHEET PROBLEM

11-23 **Capital budgeting criteria** Your division is considering two projects. Its WACC is 10 percent, and the projects' after-tax cash flows (in millions of dollars) would be:

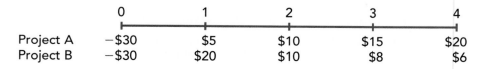

a. Calculate the projects' NPVs, IRRs, MIRRs, regular paybacks, and discounted paybacks.
b. If the two projects are independent, which project(s) should be chosen?
c. If the two projects are mutually exclusive and the WACC is 10 percent, which project should be chosen?
d. Plot NPV profiles for the two projects. Identify the projects' IRRs on the graph.
e. If the WACC were 5 percent, would this change your recommendation if the projects were mutually exclusive? If the WACC were 15 percent, would this change your recommendation? Explain your answers.
f. The "crossover rate" is 13.5252 percent. Explain in words what this rate is and how it affects the choice between mutually exclusive projects.
g. Is it possible for conflicts to exist between the NPV and the IRR when *independent* projects are being evaluated? Explain your answer.
h. Now, just look at the regular and discounted paybacks. Which project looks better when judged by the paybacks?
i. If the payback were the only method a firm used to accept or reject projects, what payback should it choose as the cutoff point, that is, reject projects if their payouts are not below the chosen cutoff? Is your selected cutoff based on some economic criteria or is it more or less arbitrary? Are the cutoff criteria equally arbitrary when firms use the NPV and/or the IRR as the criteria?
j. Define the MIRR. What's the difference between the IRR and the MIRR, and which generally gives a better idea of the rate of return on the investment in a project?
k. Why do most academics and financial executives regard the NPV as being the single best criterion, and better than the IRR? Why do companies still calculate IRRs?

Integrated Case

Allied Components Company

11-24 **Basics of capital budgeting** You recently went to work for Allied Components Company, a supplier of auto repair parts used in the after-market with products from DaimlerChrysler, Ford, and other auto makers. Your boss, the chief financial officer (CFO), has just handed you the estimated cash flows for two proposed projects. Project L involves adding a new item to the firm's ignition system line; it would take some time to build up the market for this product, so the cash inflows would increase over time. Project S involves an add-on to an existing line, and its cash flows would decrease over time. Both projects have 3-year lives, because Allied is planning to introduce entirely new models after 3 years.

Here are the projects' net cash flows (in thousands of dollars):

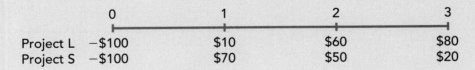

	0	1	2	3
Project L	−$100	$10	$60	$80
Project S	−$100	$70	$50	$20

Depreciation, salvage values, net operating working capital requirements, and tax effects are all included in these cash flows.

The CFO also made subjective risk assessments of each project, and he concluded that both projects have risk characteristics that are similar to the firm's average project. Allied's WACC is 10 percent. You must now determine whether one or both of the projects should be accepted.

a. What is capital budgeting? Are there any similarities between a firm's capital budgeting decisions and an individual's investment decisions?
b. What is the difference between independent and mutually exclusive projects? Between projects with normal and nonnormal cash flows?

c. (1) Define the term *net present value (NPV)*. What is each project's NPV?
    (2) What is the rationale behind the NPV method? According to NPV, which project or projects should be accepted if they are independent? Mutually exclusive?
    (3) Would the NPVs change if the WACC changed?
d. (1) Define the term *internal rate of return (IRR)*. What is each project's IRR?
    (2) How is the IRR on a project related to the YTM on a bond?
    (3) What is the logic behind the IRR method? According to IRR, which projects should be accepted if they are independent? Mutually exclusive?
    (4) Would the projects' IRRs change if the WACC changed?
e. (1) Draw NPV profiles for Projects L and S. At what discount rate do the profiles cross?
    (2) Look at your NPV profile graph without referring to the actual NPVs and IRRs. Which project or projects should be accepted if they are independent? Mutually exclusive? Explain. Are your answers correct at any WACC less than 23.6 percent?
f. (1) What is the underlying cause of ranking conflicts between NPV and IRR?
    (2) What is the "reinvestment rate assumption," and how does it affect the NPV versus IRR conflict?
    (3) Which method is the best? Why?
g. (1) Define the term *modified IRR (MIRR)*. Find the MIRRs for Projects L and S.
    (2) What are the MIRR's advantages and disadvantages vis-à-vis the NPV?
h. (1) What is the payback period? Find the paybacks for Projects L and S.
    (2) What is the rationale for the payback method? According to the payback criterion, which project or projects should be accepted if the firm's maximum acceptable payback is 2 years, and if Projects L and S are independent? If they are mutually exclusive?
    (3) What is the difference between the regular and discounted payback methods?
    (4) What are the two main disadvantages of discounted payback? Is the payback method of any real usefulness in capital budgeting decisions?
i. As a separate project (Project P), the firm is considering sponsoring a pavilion at the upcoming World's Fair. The pavilion would cost $800,000, and it is expected to result in $5 million of incremental cash inflows during its 1 year of operation. However, it would then take another year, and $5 million of costs, to demolish the site and return it to its original condition. Thus, Project P's expected net cash flows look like this (in millions of dollars):

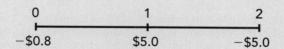

The project is estimated to be of average risk, so its WACC is 10 percent.
    (1) What is Project P's NPV? What is its IRR? Its MIRR?
    (2) Draw Project P's NPV profile. Does Project P have normal or nonnormal cash flows? Should this project be accepted? Explain.

cyberproblem

Please go to the ThomsonNOW Web site to access the Cyberproblems.

CHAPTER
12
HD

CASH FLOW ESTIMATION
AND RISK ANALYSIS

Home Depot Keeps Growing

Home Depot Inc. (HD) has grown phenomenally since 1990, and it shows no signs of slowing down. At the beginning of 1990, it had 118 stores with annual sales of $2.8 billion. By early 2005, it had 1,866 stores and annual sales of $65 billion. Stockholders have benefited mightily from this growth, as the stock's price has increased from a split-adjusted $1.87 in 1990 to $32.35 in early 2005, or by 1,630 percent.

Despite concerns that the economy might be slowing, the company expects to open another 175 stores in 2005. It costs, on average, over $20 million to purchase land, construct a new store, and stock it with inventory. (The required inventory investment is $7 million, but suppliers provide $4 million in the form of accounts payable.) Each new store involves a capital expenditure of about $17 million, so the company must perform a financial analysis to determine if a potential store's expected cash flows will cover its costs.

Home Depot uses information from its existing stores to forecast new stores' expected cash flows. Thus far, its forecasts have been outstanding, but there are always risks. First, a store's sales might be less than projected if the economy weakens. Second, some of HD's customers might in the future bypass it altogether and buy directly from manufacturers through the Internet. Third, its new stores could "cannibalize," that is, take sales away from, its existing stores. This happens when large, multi-store retailers oversaturate a given market area. The companies first pick the "low-hanging fruit," that is, enter the most attractive markets.

To avoid cannibalization by opening new stores too close to older ones while still generating substantial growth, HD has been developing complementary formats. For example, it rolled out its Expo Design Center chain, which offers one-stop sales and service for kitchen and bath and other remodeling and renovation work.

Home Depot

Rational expansion decisions require detailed assessments of the forecasted cash flows, along with a measure of the risk that forecasted sales might not be realized. That information can then be used to determine the risk-adjusted NPV associated with each potential project. In this chapter, we describe techniques for estimating projects' cash flows and the associated risk. Companies such as Home Depot use these techniques on a regular basis when making capital budgeting decisions.

Putting Things In Perspective

The basic principles of capital budgeting were covered in Chapter 11. Given a project's expected cash flows, it is easy to calculate the primary decision criterion, the NPV, as well as the supplemental criteria, IRR, MIRR, payback, and discounted payback. However, in the real world cash flows are not just provided as they were in the last chapter—rather, they must be estimated based on information from various sources. Moreover, uncertainty surrounds the cash flow estimates, and some projects are less certain and thus riskier than others. In this chapter, we go through an example that illustrates how project cash flows are estimated and discuss techniques for measuring and then dealing with risk.

Also, recall that in Chapter 9 we discussed how a firm's value is fundamentally dependent on its free cash flows. We will see in this chapter that there is a direct relationship between capital budgeting, the firm's free cash flows, and therefore the value of its stock. Indeed, since capital budgeting is the primary source of cash flows, one could argue that it is the primary determinant of stock prices.

12-1 BACKGROUND ON THE PROJECT

In Chapter 11 we saw that the NPV method, generally supplemented by the IRR and several other criteria, is used when deciding whether or not to accept potential projects. Conceptually, the decision is straightforward: A potential project creates value for the firm's shareholders, if and only if, its NPV is positive, so firms should accept positive NPV projects and reject those with negative NPVs. This is easy enough in theory, but in practice estimating the cash flows can be difficult, and it requires care and judgment. However, if we adhere to the principles discussed in this chapter, reasonable cash flow estimates and thus reliable NPVs can be obtained.

We illustrate the capital budgeting process with a new project being considered by Brandt-Quigley Corporation (BQC), an Atlanta-based technology company. BQC's research and development department has used its expertise in microprocessor technology to develop a small computer designed to control home appliances. The computer automatically controls the heating and air-conditioning system as well as the security system, hot water heater, oven, and even small appliances such as a coffee maker. By increasing a home's energy efficiency, the computer can cut the average homeowner's costs enough to pay for itself within three years. Developments have now reached the stage where a decision must be made about whether to go forward with full-scale production. BQC currently has a profitable division that produces mechanical (as opposed to computerized) controls that do some of the things the new system would do. However, the new system would be far superior to the existing product and thus would enable BQC to increase its share of the home controls market.

Also, the idea for the new computer actually came as a by-product from work the company was doing on other projects. The R&D manager saw its potential and authorized the expenditure of $500,000 to look into the feasibility of the new controls computer. This cost was incurred in 2005, charged to general corporate R&D, and expensed in 2005 for tax purposes.

BQC's marketing vice president believes that 20,000 units could be sold per year if they were priced at $3,000 each, so annual sales revenues are estimated at $60 million. The firm would need additional manufacturing capability, and BQC has an option to purchase an existing building at a cost of $12 million to meet this need. The building would be paid for on December 31, 2006, and for tax purposes it would be depreciated under MACRS with a 39-year life. BQC has an unused building that could be used for the new project, but the project manager decided that the building under option would work out better.

The necessary equipment would be purchased and installed late in 2006 and paid for on December 31, 2006. The equipment would fall into the MACRS 5-year class, and it would cost $8 million, including transportation and installation.

The project would also require an investment of $6 million in net working capital, which would also be made on December 31, 2006.[1] This investment would be recovered at the end of the project's life.

Operations would commence in January 2007, and the project's estimated economic life would be 4 years, from 2007 through 2010. At the end of 2010, the building should have a market value of $7.5 million versus a book value of $10.91 million, while the equipment should have a market value of $2 million versus a book value of $1.36 million.

Variable manufacturing costs are estimated at $2,100 per unit, and fixed overhead costs, excluding depreciation, would be $8 million a year. Depreciation expenses as shown in Table 12-1, Part 2, were determined as shown in Appendix 12A, which explains Internal Revenue Service allowed procedures.

BQC's marginal federal-plus-state tax rate is 40 percent; its corporate WACC is 12 percent; and, for capital budgeting purposes, the company assumes that operating cash flows occur at the end of each year. Because the plant would begin operations on January 1, 2007, the first operating cash flows would occur on December 31, 2007.

Several other points should be noted: (1) BQC is a relatively large corporation, with sales of more than $4 billion, and it takes on many investments each year. Thus, if the computer control project does not work out, it will not bankrupt the company—this is not a "bet-the-company project." (2) If the project is accepted, the company will be contractually obligated (to component suppliers) to operate it for the full four-year life. However, the company might be able to negotiate a release from this restriction. (3) The project's returns would be positively correlated with returns on other BQC projects and also with the stock

---

[1] Inventories and receivables would increase by $8 million while payables and accruals would increase by $2 million, so net operating working capital would increase by $6 million. This amount would have to be financed by investors, and it would be part of the project's capital requirements.

market—this project would do well if other parts of the firm were doing well, which would happen if the general economy were strong.

Assume that you are on the company's financial staff, and you must conduct the capital budgeting analysis. For now, assume that the project is about as risky as an average BQC project, so use the corporate WACC, 12 percent.

12-2 PROJECT ANALYSIS

Capital budgeting projects can be analyzed using a calculator or with a spreadsheet such as *Excel*. Either way, one must conduct the analysis as shown in Parts 1 through 5 of Table 12-1. For exam purposes, you will probably have to work with a calculator. However, for reasons that will become obvious as we go through the analysis, spreadsheets are much more efficient and are virtually always used in practice. Even so, the setup and the analysis are exactly the same for both the calculator and computer approaches.

Table 12-1 is a printout from the chapter model, divided into five parts:

1. Input Data.
2. Depreciation Schedule.
3. Salvage Value Calculations.
4. Projected Cash Flows.
5. Appraisal of the Proposed Project.[2]

The table shows row and column headers, and cells in the table can be identified by cell references such as "D17," which is the cell for the building cost, found in "Part 1. Input Data." If we deleted the row and column headers, the table would look like the setup for a calculator analysis, and a calculator would indeed give you exactly the same answers.

12-2a Input Data, Part 1

The Input Data section provides the basic data used in the analysis. The inputs are really *assumptions*—thus, in the analysis we *assume* that 20,000 units can be sold at a price of $3,000 per unit.[3] Some of the inputs are known with near certainty—for example, the 40 percent tax rate is not likely to change. Others are more speculative—units sold and the variable costs are in this category. Obviously, if sales or costs are different from the assumed levels, then profits and cash flows, hence NPV and the other outputs, will differ from their calculated levels. Later in the chapter we demonstrate how changes in the inputs can affect the results.

12-2b Depreciation Schedule, Part 2

Here we calculate depreciation over the project's four-year life. Rows 28 through 31 give data on the building. Row 28 shows the MACRS rates. Row 29 shows the dollar depreciation charge, which is the rate times the asset's depreciable basis, which in this example is the initial cost. Row 30 shows the cumulative depreciation taken through the year, and Row 31 shows the book value at the end of each year, found by subtracting the accumulated depreciation from the original depreciable basis. This same information is provided for the equipment on Rows 32 through 35.

---

[2] If you have access to a computer, you might want to look at the model, *12 Chapter Model.xls*.
[3] The sales price is $3,000, but for convenience we show dollars in thousands in the model and thus in the table.

TABLE 12-1   *Parts 1 and 2: Input Data and Depreciation (Thousands of Dollars)*

	A	B	C	D	E	F	G	H	I
15	**Part 1. Input Data**								
16									
17	Building cost (= Depr'n basis)			$12,000					
18	Equipment cost (= Depr'n basis)			$8,000		Market value of building in 2010			$7,500
19	Net Operating WC			$6,000		Market value of equip. in 2010			$2,000
20	First year sales (in units)			20,000		Tax rate			40%
21	Growth rate in units sold			0.0%		WACC			12%
22	Sales price per unit			$3.00		Inflation: growth in sales price			0.0%
23	Variable cost per unit			$2.10		Inflation: growth in VC per unit			0.0%
24	Fixed costs			$8,000		Inflation: growth in fixed costs			0.0%
25									
26	**Part 2. Depreciation Schedule**[a]					Years			
27					2007	2008	2009	2010	
28	Building Depr'n Rate				1.3%	2.6%	2.6%	2.6%	
29	Building Depr'n Expense				$156	$312	$312	$312	
30	Cumulative Depr'n				$156	$468	$780	$1,092	
31	Ending Book Value: Cost − Cum. Depr'n				$11,844	$11,532	$11,220	$10,908	
32	Equipment Depr'n Rate				20.0%	32.0%	19.0%	12.0%	
33	Equipment Depr'n Expense				$1,600	$2,560	$1,520	$960	
34	Cumulative Depr'n				$1,600	$4,160	$5,680	$6,640	
35	Ending Book Value: Cost − Cum. Depr'n				$6,400	$3,840	$2,320	$1,360	
36	[a] The indicated percentages are multiplied by the depreciable basis ($12,000 for the building and $8,000 for								
37	the equipment) to determine the depreciation expense for the year.								

12-2c Salvage Value Calculations, Part 3

Here we show the estimated cash flows the firm will realize when it disposes of the building and equipment. Row 42 shows the expected market (salvage) value when it sells each asset 4 years hence. Row 43 shows the book values at the end of Year 4 as calculated in Part 2. Row 44 shows the expected gain or loss, defined as the difference between the market and book values.

Gains and losses are treated as ordinary income, not capital gains or losses.[4] Gains result in tax liabilities while losses produce tax credits. These are equal to the gain or loss times the 40 percent tax rate, and they are shown on Row 45. Finally, Row 46 shows the after-tax cash flow the company expects to receive when it disposes of the asset, found as the salvage value minus the tax liability or plus the credit. Thus, BQC expects to net $8.863 million from the sale of the building and $1.744 million from the equipment, for a total of $10.607 million.

---

[4] If an asset is sold for exactly its book value, there will be no gain or loss, hence no tax liability or credit. However, if an asset is sold for other than its book value, a gain or loss will be created. For example, BQC's building will have a book value of $10,908, but the company expects to realize only $7,500 when it is sold. This would result in a loss of $3,408. This indicates that the building should have been depreciated at a faster rate—only if accumulated depreciation had been $3,408 larger would the book and salvage values have been equal. So, the Tax Code stipulates that losses on the sale of operating assets can be used to reduce ordinary income, just as depreciation reduces income. On the other hand, if an asset is sold for *more* than its book value, as is the case for the equipment, then this signifies that the depreciation rates were too high, so the gain is called "depreciation recapture" and is taxed as ordinary income.

TABLE 12-1	*Part 3: Salvage Value Calculations (Thousands of Dollars)*

	A	B	C	D	E	F	G	H	I
40	**Part 3. Salvage Value Calculations**								
41					Building	Equipment	Total		
42	Estimated Market Value in 2010				$7,500	$2,000			
43	Book Value in 2010[b]				10,908	1,360			
44	Expected Gain or Loss[c]				−3,408	640			
45	Tax liability or credit				−1,363	256			
46	Net cash flow from salvage[d]				$8,863	$1,744	$10,607		
47									
48	[b] Book value equals depreciable basis (initial cost in this case) minus accumulated MACRS depreciation.								
49	For the building, accumulated depreciation is $1,092, so book value is $12,000 − $1,092 = $10,908. For the								
50	equipment, accumulated depreciation is $6,640, so book value is $8,000 − $6,640 = $1,360.								
51									
52	[c] Building: $7,500 market value − $10,908 book value = −$3,408, a loss. Thus there's a shortfall in depreciation								
53	taken versus "true" depreciation, and it is treated as an operating expense for 2010. Equipment: $2,000								
54	market value − $1,360 book value = $640 profit. Here the depreciation charge exceeds the "true"								
55	depreciation, and the difference is called "depreciation recapture." It is taxed as ordinary income in 2010.								
56									
57	[d] Net cash flow from salvage equals salvage (market) value minus taxes. For the building, the loss results								
58	in a tax credit, so net salvage value = $7,500 − (−$1,363) = $8,863.								

12-2d Projected Cash Flows, Part 4

We use the information developed in Parts 1, 2, and 3 to find the project's forecasted stream of cash flows. Five periods are shown, from Year 0 (2006) to Year 4 (2010). The cash outlays required at Year 0 are the negative numbers in Column E, and their sum, −$26 million, is shown on Row 88. We calculate the operating cash flows in the next four columns. We begin with units sold (20,000 per year), then show the sales price, and then the sales revenues, found as the product of units sold times the sales price.[5] Next, we subtract variable costs, found by multiplying the 20,000 units times the $2,100 cost per unit. Fixed operating costs and depreciation on the building and equipment are then deducted to find operating earnings before interest and taxes, or EBIT. No interest is deducted because it is accounted for by discounting the cash flows.[6] Taxes (at a 40 percent rate) must be subtracted, leaving us with net operating profit after taxes, or NOPAT.

Note that we are seeking *cash flows*, not accounting income. BQC requires payment upon delivery, and both taxes and all expenses other than depreciation must be paid in cash. Therefore, each item in the "Operating Cash Flows" section of Part 4 represents cash with one exception—*depreciation*, which is a noncash charge. Because depreciation is not a cash charge, it is added back (on Row 80) to obtain the operating cash flow, which is shown on Row 81.

When the project's life ends at the end of Year 4, the company will receive the "Terminal Year Cash Flows" as shown on Rows 84, 85, and 86. As shown on Row 66, BQC must invest $6 million in working capital—inventories and

---

[5] Notice in Part 1, Input Data, that we show a growth rate in unit sales and inflation rates for the sales price, variable costs, and fixed costs. BQC anticipates that unit sales, the sales price, and costs will be stable for the project's life, so these variables are all set at zero. However, nonzero values could be inserted in the input section to determine the effects of growth and inflation. The inflation figures are all specific for this particular project—they do not reflect inflation as measured by the CPI. The expected CPI inflation rate as seen by marginal investors is built into the WACC, and neither it nor WACC is expected to change over the forecast period.

[6] If we deducted interest when finding the cash flows, then discounted those cash flows, this would double count interest.

TABLE 12-1	*Part 4: Projected Cash Flows (Thousands of Dollars)*

	A	B	C	D	E	F	G	H	I
60	**Part 4. Projected Cash Flows**				\multicolumn{5}{c}{**Years**}				
61					0	1	2	3	4
62					2006	2007	2008	2009	2010
63	*Investment Outlays at Time Zero*								
64	Building				−$12,000				
65	Equipment				−8,000				
66	Increase in Net Working Capital				−6,000				
67									
68	*Operating Cash Flows over the Project's Life*								
69	Units sold					20,000	20,000	20,000	20,000
70	Sales price					$3.00	$3.00	$3.00	$3.00
71									
72	Sales revenue					$60,000	$60,000	$60,000	$60,000
73	Variable costs					42,000	42,000	42,000	42,000
74	Fixed operating costs					8,000	8,000	8,000	8,000
75	Depreciation (building)					156	312	312	312
76	Depreciation (equipment)					1,600	2,560	1,520	960
77	EBIT					$8,244	$7,128	$8,168	$8,728
78	Taxes on operating income (40%)					3,298	2,851	3,267	3,491
79	NOPAT					$4,946	$4,277	$4,901	$5,237
80	Add back depreciation					1,756	2,872	1,832	1,272
81	Operating cash flow					$6,702	$7,149	$6,733	$6,509
82									
83	*Terminal Year Cash Flows*								
84	Return of net operating working capital[e]								$6,000
85	Net salvage value								10,607
86	Total termination cash flows								$16,607
87									
88	Projected Cash Flows (CF time line)				−$26,000	$6,702	$7,149	$6,733	$23,116
89									
90	[e] Net working capital will be recovered at the end of the project's operating life, at year-end 2010, as								
91	inventories are sold off and receivables are collected.								

accounts receivable less payables and accruals—at Year 0. However, as operations wind down in Year 4, inventories would be sold and not replaced, and accounts receivable would be collected and not replaced, and both of these actions would provide cash. The end result is that the firm would recover its $6 million investment in working capital during the project's last year. In addition, when the company disposes of the building and equipment at the end of Year 4, it would receive the $10.607 million net salvage value as estimated in Part 3 of the table. Thus, total terminal year cash flows total $16.607 million as shown on Row 86. When we sum the columns in Part 4, we obtain the projected cash flows on Row 88. Those cash flows constitute a *cash flow time line*, just like the cash flow time lines we analyzed in Chapter 11, and they are evaluated in Part 5.

12-2e Appraisal of the Proposed Project, Part 5

In Part 5 of the table we calculate the key decision criteria—NPV, IRR, MIRR, and payback—based on the cash flows on Row 88. BQC focuses primarily on the NPV, and since it is positive, the project appears to be acceptable. The other outputs all support this conclusion—the IRR and MIRR both exceed the 12 percent WACC, and the payback indicates that the project would return the invested funds in 3.23 years. Therefore, on the basis of the analysis thus far, it appears that the project should be accepted. However, we have assumed thus far that the

TABLE 12-1 *Part 5: Appraisal of the Proposed Project*

	A	B	C	D	E	F	G	H	I
93	**Part 5. Appraisal of the Proposed Project**								
94									
95	NPV (at 12%)			$5,166					
96	IRR			19.33%					
97	MIRR			17.19%					
98	Payback (Excel function)			3.23					

project is about as risky as an average project. If the project is later judged to be riskier than average, it would be necessary to increase the WACC, which in turn might cause the NPV to become negative and the IRR and MIRR to drop below the then-higher WACC. Therefore, we cannot make a final go/no-go decision until we evaluate the project's risk, the topic of Section 12.4.

Refer to Table 12-1 and answer these questions:

(1) If the WACC increased to 15 percent, what would the new NPV be? ($2,877)

(2) Look at Part 1, Input Data. In what direction would NPV be changed by an *increase* in each input variable?

(3) If the equipment had to be depreciated over a 10-year life rather than a 5-year life, but other aspects of the project were unchanged, would the NPV increase or decrease? Why?

(4) It is relatively easy to determine the effect of an increase in the WACC. Would it be equally easy to quantify the effects of changes in the other variables if (a) you were working with a calculator or (b) you were working with an *Excel* spreadsheet? Why?

12-3 OTHER POINTS ON CASH FLOW ANALYSIS

We can use the BQC case to illustrate several other important points related to determining the cash flows that are relevant in a capital budgeting analysis.

12-3a Cash Flow versus Accounting Income

We calculated the BQC project's expected cash flows, not its net income. Net income would be based on the depreciation rate the firm's accountants chose to use, not necessarily the depreciation rates allowed by the IRS. Also, net income would represent the income that belongs to the stockholders, not that available to all investors, so interest charges would be deducted. Moreover, the investment in working capital would not be deducted, nor would its later recovery be taken into account. For these and other reasons, net income is generally different from cash flow. Each has a role in financial management, *but for capital budgeting purposes it is the project's cash flow, not its net accounting income, that is relevant.*

12-3b Timing of Cash Flows

Accounting income statements are for periods such as years or months, so they do not reflect the exact timing of when cash revenues and expenses occur. Because of the time value of money, capital budgeting analyses should in theory deal with cash flows exactly as they occur. Daily cash flows would be theoretically best, but they would be costly to estimate and probably no more accurate than annual estimates because we simply cannot forecast accurately at a daily level. Therefore, in most cases we simply assume that all cash flows occur at the end of the year. However, for some projects it might be useful to assume that cash flows occur at mid-year, or even quarterly or monthly.

12-3c Incremental Cash Flows

A project's **incremental cash flow** is defined as one that will occur *if and only if* the firm takes on the project. All of the cash flows in Table 12-1 are obviously incremental—BQC would not make the investments in buildings, equipment, and working capital if the project were not accepted, nor would it receive the operating cash flows shown in the table. However, some items are not so obvious, as we discuss next.

Incremental Cash Flow
A cash flow that will occur if and only if the firm takes on a project.

12-3d Replacement Projects

The BQC analysis related to a completely new project, where a new product will be produced. The analysis is somewhat different if a **replacement analysis** is involved, where the project calls for replacing machinery used to produce an existing product. Here the benefits are generally cost savings, although the new machinery may also permit additional output. The data for replacement analysis are generally easier to obtain than for new products, but the analysis itself is somewhat more complicated because almost all of the cash flows are incremental, found by subtracting the new cost numbers from the old numbers. Thus, a more efficient new machine might require labor of $100,000 per year versus $175,000 with the old machine. The difference, a savings of $75,000, would be built into the analysis. Similarly, we would need to find the difference in depreciation and any other factor that affects cash flows. We do not discuss replacement decisions further in the text, but we do explain and illustrate the process on a tab in the chapter model and in Web Appendix 12B.

Replacement Analysis
The situation where old and less efficient equipment is replaced by newer and more efficient equipment.

12-3e Sunk Costs

A **sunk cost** is an outlay that was incurred in the past and cannot be recovered regardless of whether or not the project under consideration is accepted. In capital budgeting, we are concerned with *future incremental cash flows*—we want to know if the new investment will justify enough incremental cash flow to justify the incremental investment. Because sunk costs were incurred in the past and will not be changed regardless of whether or not the project under consideration is accepted or rejected, they are not relevant in the capital budgeting analysis. The $500,000 BQC spent in 2005 on R&D related to the computer project is a sunk cost. That cash flow was incurred in the past—the money is gone, and it won't come back regardless of whether or not BQC decides to accept the new project.

The project's expected NPV as calculated in Table 12-1, Part 5, was $5,166,000. The R&D expenditure was $500,000. Therefore, even if this expenditure were incorrectly charged to the project, the NPV would still be positive, so the mistake would not change the decision. But suppose the R&D had been $6,000,000. If that amount were taken as a cost of the project, then the NPV

Sunk Cost
A cash outlay that has already been incurred and that cannot be recovered regardless of whether the project is accepted or rejected.

would be negative and the project would be rejected. *However, that would be a bad decision*: The real issue is whether or not the *incremental* cash inflows as shown in Table 12-1 exceed the *incremental* cash outflow by enough to cause the NPV to be positive, and the analysis in the table indicates that they do. So, including sunk costs could lead to an incorrect decision.

12-3f Opportunity Costs

Opportunity Costs
The return on the best alternative use of an asset, or the highest return that will not be earned if funds are invested in a particular project.

Another issue relates to **opportunity costs,** which are cash flows that could be generated from an asset the firm already owns, provided the asset is not used for the project in question. Recall from the background section that BQC owns a building that could be used for the computer project. Management decided to buy a new building rather than use the one it owns, but for illustrative purposes suppose it had decided to use the existing building. The company already owns the building, so it would not incur the $12 million cash outlay to buy a new building. Would this mean that we should delete the $12 million expenditure from the analysis, which would obviously raise the estimated NPV above the $5.166 million we found in Table 12-1?

The answer is that we should remove the cash flows related to the new building, but we should include the *opportunity cost* associated with the existing building as a cash cost. For example, if the building had a market value, after taxes and brokerage expenses, of $13 million, then BQC would be giving up $13 million if it used the building for the computer project. Therefore, we should charge the $13 million that would be foregone to the project as an opportunity cost.

12-3g Externalities

Externality
An effect on the firm or the environment that is not reflected in the project's cash flows.

Cannibalization Effect
The situation when a new project reduces cash flows that the firm would otherwise have had.

Another potential problem involves **externalities,** which are the effects a project has on other parts of the firm or on the environment. As was noted in the background section, BQC currently makes mechanical controls that are profitable, and the new computerized controls would take away some of that business. Thus, while the new project would generate positive cash flows, it would also reduce some of the company's current cash flows. This type of externality is called a **cannibalization effect,** because the new business would eat into the company's existing business. The lost cash flows should be charged to the new project. However, it often turns out that if the one company does not produce a new product, some other company will, so the old cash flows would be lost anyway. In this case, no charge should be assessed against the new project. All this makes determining the cannibalization effect difficult, because it requires estimates of changes in sales and costs, and also the timing of when those changes would occur. Still, cannibalization can be important, so its potential effects should be considered.

Note that externalities can be positive as well as negative. For example, suppose BQC also produces high-priced convection ovens, and the new control units would make the ovens more efficient and easier to use. In that case, the control project might lead to higher oven sales, in which case some of the incremental cash flows in the stove division should be attributed to the control project. It often turns out that a project's direct cash flows are insufficient to produce a positive NPV, but when indirect effects are considered, the project is deemed to be a good one.

Firms must also be concerned with *environmental externalities*. For example, it might be that manufacturing the new computers would give off noxious fumes that, while not bad enough to trigger governmental actions, would still cause ill feelings in the plant's neighborhood. Those ill feelings might not show up in the cash flow analysis, but they should still be considered. Perhaps a relatively small expenditure could correct the problem and keep the firm from suffering future ill will which might be costly in some hard-to-measure way.

Why should companies use project cash flow rather than accounting income when finding the NPV of a project?

Explain the following terms: incremental cash flow, sunk cost, opportunity cost, externality, and cannibalization.

Give an example of a "good" externality, that is, one that makes a project look better.

12-4 ESTIMATING PROJECT RISK

Although it is clear that riskier projects should be assigned a higher cost of capital, it is often difficult to estimate project risk. First, note that three separate and distinct types of risk can be identified:

1. **Stand-alone risk,** which is the project's risk disregarding the facts (a) that it is but one asset within the firm's portfolio of assets and (b) that the firm is but one stock in a typical investor's portfolio of stocks. Stand-alone risk is measured by the variability of the project's expected returns.
2. **Corporate, or within-firm, risk,** which is the project's risk to the corporation, giving consideration to the fact that the project represents only one of the firm's portfolio of assets, hence that some of its risk will be eliminated by diversification within the firm. Corporate risk is measured by the project's impact on uncertainty about the firm's future earnings.
3. **Market, or beta, risk,** which is the riskiness of the project as seen by well-diversified stockholders who recognize that the project is only one of the firm's assets and that the firm's stock is but one small part of their total portfolios. Market risk is measured by the project's effect on the firm's beta coefficient.

Taking on a project with a high degree of either stand-alone or corporate risk will not necessarily affect the firm's beta. However, if the project has highly uncertain returns, and if those returns are highly correlated with returns on the firm's other assets and with most other firms in the economy, the project will have a high degree of all types of risk. For example, suppose General Motors decides to undertake a major expansion to build commuter airplanes. GM is not sure how its technology will work on a mass production basis, so there are great risks in the venture—its stand-alone risk is high. Management also estimates that the project will do best if the economy is strong, for then people will have more money to spend on the new planes. This means that the project will tend to do well if GM's other divisions do well and do badly if other divisions do badly. This being the case, the project will also have a high corporate risk. Finally, since GM's profits are highly correlated with those of most other firms, the project's beta will also be high. Thus, this project will be risky under all three definitions of risk.

Of the three measures, market risk is theoretically the most relevant because it is the one reflected in stock prices. Unfortunately, market risk is also the most difficult to estimate, because projects don't have "market prices" that can be related to stock market returns. For this reason, most decision makers consider all three risk measures in a judgmental manner and then classify projects into subjective risk categories. Then, using the composite WACC as a starting point,

Stand-Alone Risk
The risk an asset would have if it were a firm's only asset and if investors owned only one stock. It is measured by the variability of the asset's expected returns.

Corporate, or Within-Firm, Risk
Risk not considering the effects of stockholders' diversification; it is measured by a project's effect on uncertainty about the firm's future earnings.

Market, or Beta, Risk
That part of a project's risk that cannot be eliminated by diversification; it is measured by the project's beta coefficient.

Risk-Adjusted Cost of Capital
The cost of capital appropriate for a given project, given the riskiness of that project. The greater the risk, the higher the cost of capital.

risk-adjusted costs of capital are developed for each category. For example, a firm might establish three risk classes, then assign the corporate WACC to average-risk projects, use a somewhat higher cost rate for higher-risk projects, and a somewhat lower rate for lower-risk projects. Thus, if a company's composite WACC estimate were 10 percent, its managers might use 10 percent to evaluate average-risk projects, 12 percent for high-risk projects, and 8 percent for low-risk projects. While this approach is probably better than not making any risk adjustments, these adjustments are subjective and often arbitrary. Unfortunately, there's no perfect way to specify how much higher or lower we should go in setting risk-adjusted costs of capital.[7]

What are the three types of project risk?

Which type of project risk is theoretically the most relevant? Why?

Explain the classification scheme many firms use when developing *subjective* risk-adjusted costs of capital.

12-5 MEASURING STAND-ALONE RISK

A project's stand-alone risk is determined by the uncertainty inherent in its cash flows. Most of the key inputs shown in Part 1 of Table 12-1 for BQC's appliance control computer project are subject to uncertainty. Sales were projected at 20,000 units to be sold at a price of $3,000 per unit. However, actual unit sales would almost certainly be somewhat higher or lower than 20,000, and the price would probably turn out to be different from the projected $3,000 per unit. Similarly, the other variables would probably differ from their indicated values. *Indeed, all the inputs are expected values of probability distributions, and as such they could vary from their expected values.*

Three techniques are used to assess risk: (1) sensitivity analysis, (2) scenario analysis, and (3) Monte Carlo simulation. We discuss them in the following sections.

12-5a Sensitivity Analysis

Sensitivity Analysis
A risk analysis technique in which key variables are changed one at a time and the resulting changes in the NPV are observed.

Base-Case NPV
The NPV when sales and other input variables are set equal to their most likely (or base-case) values.

Intuitively, we know that the input variables could turn out to be different from the values used in the analysis. We also know that a change in a key input variable such as units sold would cause the NPV to change. **Sensitivity analysis** measures the percentage change in NPV that results from a given percentage change in an input variable, other things held constant.

Sensitivity analysis begins with a *base-case* situation, where the *expected value* is used for each input variable. The input data in Part 1 of Table 12-1 are the *most likely, or base-case, values*, and the resulting $5.166 million NPV shown in Part 5 of the table is the **base-case NPV.**

When senior managers review capital budgeting studies, they are interested in the base-case NPV, but they generally go ask a series of "what if" questions: "What if unit sales turn out to be 15 percent below the most likely level?" "What if the sales price per unit is actually $2,500, not $3,000?" "What if variable costs are $2,500 per unit rather than the expected $2,100?" Sensitivity analysis is designed

---

[7] We should note that the CAPM approach can be used for projects provided there are specialized publicly-traded firms in the same business as that of the project under consideration. For further information on estimating the risk-adjusted cost of capital see Web Appendix 12D, and for more information on measuring market (or beta) risk see Web Appendix 12E.

to provide answers to such questions. Each variable is increased or decreased by several percentage points from its expected value, holding all other variables constant. Then NPVs are calculated using each of these values. Finally, the resulting set of NPVs is plotted to show how sensitive NPV is to changes in each variable.

Figure 12-1 shows the computer project's sensitivity graph for the six most important input variables.[8] The table below the graph gives the NPVs based on different values of the inputs, and those NPVs were then plotted to make the graph. The ranges shown at the bottom of the table, and the slopes of the lines in the graph, indicate how sensitive NPV is to changes in each input: *The larger the range and the steeper the slope, the more sensitive the NPV is to a change in the variable.* We see that NPV is very sensitive to changes in the sales price and variable cost, fairly sensitive to changes in the growth rate and units sold, and not very sensitive to changes in fixed cost or the WACC.

FIGURE 12-1 *Evaluating Risk: Sensitivity Analysis (Dollars in Thousands)*

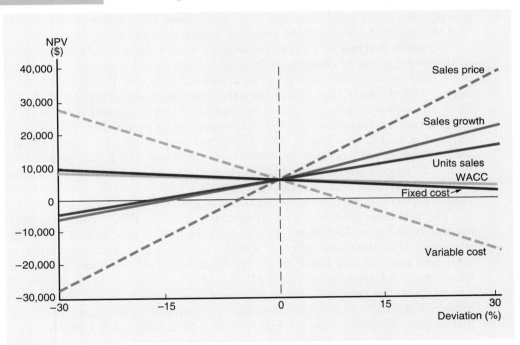

Deviation from Base	NPV AT DIFFERENT DEVIATIONS FROM BASE					
	Sales Price	Variable Cost/Unit	Sales Growth	Year 1 Units Sold	Fixed Cost	WACC
−30%	($27,637)	$28,129	($ 5,847)	($ 4,675)	$9,540	$8,294
−15	(11,236)	16,647	(907)	246	7,353	6,674
0	5,166	5,166	5,166	5,166	5,166	5,166
15	21,568	(6,315)	12,512	10,087	2,979	3,761
30	37,970	(17,796)	21,269	15,007	792	2,450
Range	$65,607	$45,925	$27,116	$19,682	$8,748	$5,844

---

[8] "Important" here means that a relatively small change in an input leads to a large change in the output.

If we were comparing two projects, the one with the steeper sensitivity lines would be riskier, other things held constant, because that would indicate that relatively small errors in estimating the input variables would produce large errors in the NPV. Thus, sensitivity analysis provides useful insights into a project's risk.

Sensitivity analysis is easy with a computer spreadsheet model. We used the chapter model, which first calculated the NPVs and then drew the graph. To conduct such an analysis by hand would be very time consuming, and if the basic data were changed even slightly—say, the cost of the equipment was increased slightly—all of the calculations would have to be redone. With a spreadsheet, we would simply replace the old input with the new one, and presto, the analysis would be revised.

12-5b Scenario Analysis

In sensitivity analysis as described earlier we change one variable at a time. However, it is often useful to know what would happen to NPV if all of the inputs turn out to be either better or worse than expected. Also, if we can assign probabilities to the good, bad, and most likely (base-case) scenarios, then we can find the expected value and the standard deviation of the NPV.

Scenario analysis is a technique that allows for these extensions—it brings in the probabilities of changes in the key variables, and it allows us to change more than one variable at a time. In a scenario analysis, the financial analyst begins with the **base case,** which uses the most likely set of input values. Then he or she asks marketing, engineering, and other operating managers to specify a **worst-case scenario** (low unit sales, low sales price, high variable costs, and so on) and a **best-case scenario.** Often, the best and worst cases are defined as where there is a 25 percent probability of conditions being that good or bad, with a 50 percent probability of the base-case conditions. Obviously, conditions could actually take on other values, but such a scenario setup is useful to help people focus on the central issues in risk analysis.

The best-case, base-case, and worst-case values for BQC's computer project are shown in Figure 12-2, along with plots of the data. If the product were highly successful, then the combination of a high sales price, low production costs, and high unit sales would result in a very high NPV, $87.5 million. However, if things turn out badly, then the NPV would be a negative $43.7 million. The graphs show the very wide range of possibilities, suggesting that this is a risky project. If the bad conditions materialize, this will not bankrupt the company—this is just one project for a large company. Still, losing $43.7 million would certainly hurt the stock price.

If we multiply each scenario's probability by the NPV under that scenario and then sum the products, we calculate the project's expected NPV, $13.531 million as shown in the data below Figure 12-2. We can also calculate the standard deviation of that NPV; it is $47.139 million. When we divide the standard deviation by the expected NPV we get the coefficient of variation, 3.48.[9] BQC's average project has a coefficient of variation of about 2.0, so the 3.48 indicates that this project is riskier than most of the firm's other projects.

BQC's WACC is 12 percent, so that rate should be used to find the NPV of an average-risk project. The computer project is riskier than average, so a higher discount rate should be used to find its NPV. There is no way to determine the "correct" discount rate—this is a judgment call. However, BQC's management generally adds 3 percent to the corporate WACC when it evaluates projects

---

[9] The coefficient of variation (CV) only makes sense when it is a positive number. A negative CV implies that the project's expected NPV is negative—which means the project would not be accepted.

Scenario Analysis
A risk analysis technique in which "bad" and "good" sets of financial circumstances are compared with a most likely, or base-case, situation.

Base-Case Scenario
An analysis in which all of the input variables are set at their most likely values.

Worst-Case Scenario
An analysis in which all of the input variables are set at their worst reasonably forecasted values.

Best-Case Scenario
An analysis in which all of the input variables are set at their best reasonably forecasted values.

FIGURE 12-2 *Scenario Analysis (Dollars in Thousands)*

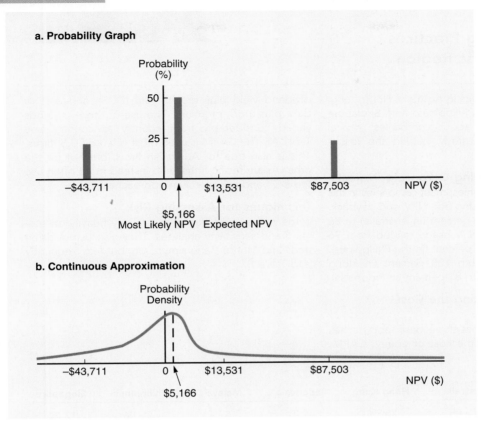

Scenario	Probability	Unit Sales	Sales Price	Variable Costs	NPV
Best case	25%	26,000	$3.90	$1.47	$87,503
Base case	50	20,000	3.00	2.10	5,166
Worst case	25	14,000	2.10	2.73	(43,711)
			Expected NPV = Sum, probability times NPV		$13,531
			Standard deviation (calculated in *Excel* model)		$47,139
			Coefficient of variation = Standard deviation/Expected NPV		3.48

deemed to be risky. When the NPV was recalculated using a 15 percent WACC, the base-case NPV fell from $5.166 to $2.877 million and the expected NPV dropped from $13.531 to $10.740 million, so the project was still acceptable by the NPV criterion.[10]

12-5c Monte Carlo Simulation

Monte Carlo simulation, so named because this type of analysis grew out of work on the mathematics of casino gambling, is a version of scenario analysis, where the project is analyzed under a very large number of scenarios, or "runs." In each run, the computer picks at random a value for each variable—units sold,

---

[10] Note that both the risk and expected return can change when real options are considered. Indeed, as we demonstrate in Chapter 13, this happens for BQC's computer project.

Monte Carlo Simulation
A risk analysis technique in which probable future events are simulated on a computer, generating estimated rates of return and risk indexes.

GLOBAL PERSPECTIVES

Capital Budgeting Practices in the Asian/Pacific Region

A recent survey of executives in Australia, Hong Kong, Indonesia, Malaysia, the Philippines, and Singapore asked several questions about companies' capital budgeting practices. The study yielded the results summarized here.

Techniques for Evaluating Corporate Projects
Consistent with U.S. companies, most companies in this region evaluate projects using IRR, NPV, and payback. IRR usage ranged from 96 percent (in Australia) to 86 percent (in Hong Kong). NPV usage ranged from 96 percent (in Australia) to 81 percent (in the Philippines). Payback usage ranged from 100 percent (in Hong Kong and the Philippines) to 81 percent (in Indonesia).

Techniques for Estimating the Cost of Equity Capital
Recall from Chapter 10 that three basic approaches can be used to estimate the cost of equity: CAPM,

dividend yield plus growth rate (DCF), and cost of debt plus a risk premium. The use of these methods varied considerably from country to country (see Table A). The CAPM is used most often by U.S. firms. This is also true for Australian firms, but not for the other Asian/Pacific firms, who instead more often use the DCF and risk premium approaches.

Techniques for Assessing Risk
Firms in the Asian/Pacific region rely heavily on scenario and sensitivity analyses. They also use decision trees and Monte Carlo simulation, but less frequently (see Table B).

TABLE A

Method	Australia	Hong Kong	Indonesia	Malaysia	Philippines	Singapore
CAPM	72.7%	26.9%	0.0%	6.2%	24.1%	17.0%
Dividend yield plus growth rate	16.4	53.8	33.3	50.0	34.5	42.6
Cost of debt plus risk premium	10.9	23.1	53.4	37.5	58.6	42.6

TABLE B

Risk Assessment Technique	Australia	Hong Kong	Indonesia	Malaysia	Philippines	Singapore
Scenario analysis	96%	100%	94%	80%	97%	90%
Sensitivity analysis	100	100	88	83	94	79
Decision tree analysis	44	58	50	37	33	46
Monte Carlo simulation	38	35	25	9	24	35

Source: Adapted from George W. Kester et al., "Capital Budgeting Practices in the Asia-Pacific Region: Australia, Hong Kong, Indonesia, Malaysia, Philippines, and Singapore," *Financial Practice and Education*, Vol. 9, no. 1 (Spring/Summer 1999), pp. 25–33.

sales price, variable costs per unit, and so on. Those values are then used to calculate the project's NPV, and that NPV is stored in the computer's memory. Next, a second set of input values is selected at random, and a second NPV is calculated. This process is repeated perhaps 1,000 times, generating 1,000 NPVs. The mean and standard deviation of the set of NPVs are determined. The mean, or average value, is used as a measure of the project's expected profitability, and the standard deviation (or perhaps the coefficient of variation) of the NPV is used as a measure of the project's risk.

Monte Carlo simulation is considerably more complex than scenario analysis, but simulation software packages make the process manageable. These packages may be used as add-ons to spreadsheet programs. Simulation is useful, but because of its complexity a detailed discussion is best left for advanced finance courses.[11]

Explain briefly how one does a sensitivity analysis, and what the analysis is designed to show.

What is a scenario analysis, what is it designed to show, and how does it differ from a sensitivity analysis?

What is Monte Carlo simulation? How does a simulation analysis differ from a simple scenario analysis?

12-6 DIFFERENT CAPITAL STRUCTURES

The discount rate used in capital budgeting decisions is a weighted average of the costs of debt and equity, so if the mix of debt and equity changes, then so might the WACC. Generally, firms raise capital based on their optimal capital structures as described in Chapter 14, and they generally assume that the same structure applies to all capital budgeting projects. However, if a firm finances different assets in different ways, this should be taken into account in the capital budgeting process. For example, a kitchen equipment manufacturer might have a retail division that operates stores in malls and "outlets." This division might invest heavily in real estate that is used as collateral for loans, while the manufacturing division might have most of its capital tied up in specialized machinery, which is not good collateral. As a result, the retail division might finance with far more debt than the manufacturing division. In that case, the financial staff should calculate different WACCs for the two divisions, and those WACCs should be used for capital budgeting.[12]

How might capital structure issues affect capital budgeting decisions?

12-7 INCORPORATING RISK INTO CAPITAL BUDGETING

Capital budgeting affects a firm's market and corporate risk, but it is extremely difficult to quantify these effects. Although we may be able to conclude that one project is riskier than another, it is difficult to *quantify* the difference. This makes it necessary to incorporate risk into capital budgeting decisions in a subjective

---

[11] To use Monte Carlo simulation, one needs both probability distributions for the inputs and correlation coefficients between each pair of inputs so that if the particular run has a low value for unit sales, the sales price will also be low (assuming positive correlation). It is often difficult to obtain "reasonable" values for the correlations, especially for new projects where no historical data are available. This has limited the use of simulation analysis.

[12] We will say more about the optimal capital structure and debt capacity in Chapter 14.

manner. Still, it is useful not only to build risk into the analysis, but also to recognize that conclusions should be used with caution and judgment.

Two primary methods are used to incorporate project risk into capital budgeting: (1) the certainty equivalent approach and (2) the risk-adjusted discount rate approach. When using the *certainty equivalent* approach we translate all cash inflows that are not known with certainty into their **certainty equivalents,** which means the certain (guaranteed) amounts that the decision maker would accept in lieu of the risky expected amounts. For example, an investor might be willing to exchange a risky expected cash flow of $100,000 for a sure $75,000, in which case $75,000 would be the investor's certainty equivalent for the risky $100,000. The riskier the flow, the lower its certainty equivalent. In capital budgeting, a project's most likely cash flows would be estimated as discussed earlier in the chapter, then the certainty equivalent of each cash flow would be determined, and then those certainty equivalent cash flows would be discounted at the risk-free rate to find the project's NPV. The main problem with this approach is that we have no way of estimating the certainty equivalents of the firm's stockholders, and those are the certainty equivalents that should be used in the analysis.

The other method, which is generally the one used in practice, is the **risk-adjusted discount rate** approach. Here the discount rate is increased when evaluating riskier projects—the greater the risk, the higher the discount rate used in the analysis. Average-risk projects are discounted at the firm's WACC, higher-risk projects are discounted at a rate above the WACC, and lower-risk projects are discounted at a rate below the firm's WACC. Unfortunately, there is no precise way of specifying exactly how much higher or lower these discount rates should be. Risk adjustments are necessarily judgmental and somewhat arbitrary. Still, as noted earlier, most analysts are more comfortable estimating risk-adjusted discount rates than certainty equivalents, hence the risk-adjusted discount rate is the approach that is most often used in practice.

Certainty Equivalent
The amount that would be paid with certainty that is equivalent to a risky cash flow.

Risk-Adjusted Discount Rate
The discount rate that applies to a particular risky cash flow stream; the riskier the project's cash flow stream, the higher the discount rate.

What are *certainty equivalents* and *risk-adjusted discount rates?* How is each used to incorporate project risk into the capital budgeting decision process? Which is used most often in practice? Why?

Tying It All Together

The value of any asset depends on the amount, timing, and riskiness of the cash flows it is expected to produce. Therefore, to evaluate a proposed capital budgeting project we must estimate the project's cash flows and risk. First, cash flows are different from net income, and our focus must be on cash flows. Second, we need to focus on *incremental cash flows*, which are the *new* flows that will be added if the project is accepted. Some costs associated with the project may be *sunk costs*, which have already been expended and thus should be ignored. Third, *depreciation* is not a cash expense, hence it must be added back to estimate the incremental cash flow. Fourth, *externalities* must be considered when determining a project's cash flows. *Cannibalization*, which occurs if a new project takes sales and profits from an existing project, is an important externality. And fifth, the investment in *net operating working capital* must be recognized as an initial cost, and the recovery of this working capital is a cash inflow at the end of the project's life.

Given the projected cash flows, we can calculate the NPV, IRR, MIRR, and payback. However, the cash flows, hence the NPV and other profitability measures, are not certain, so we must do a *risk analysis* before deciding to accept or reject the given project. *Sensitivity analysis, scenario analysis,* and *Monte Carlo simulation* are methods used to evaluate projects' risks. In theory, only *market risk* is relevant, but in practice *stand-alone* and *corporate risks* are also considered. If a project's risk is deemed to be higher or lower than average, then a *risk-adjusted WACC* should be used in the analysis. Note too that if different types of projects are financed with different mixes of debt and equity, this should be recognized, and different WACCs should be used when finding projects' NPVs.

SELF-TEST QUESTIONS AND PROBLEMS
(Solutions Appear in Appendix A)

ST-1   **Key terms** Define each of the following terms:
   a.   Change in net operating working capital
   b.   Incremental cash flow; sunk cost; opportunity cost; externality; cannibalization effect
   c.   Replacement analysis
   d.   Stand-alone risk; corporate (within-firm) risk; market (beta) risk
   e.   Risk-adjusted cost of capital
   f.   Sensitivity analysis; base-case NPV
   g.   Scenario analysis; base-case scenario; worst-case scenario; best-case scenario
   h.   Monte Carlo simulation
   i.   Certainty equivalent; risk-adjusted discount rate

ST-2   **Project and risk analysis** As a financial analyst, you must evaluate a proposed project to produce printer cartridges. The equipment would cost $55,000, plus $10,000 for installation. Annual sales would be 4,000 units at a price of $50 per cartridge, and the project's life would be 3 years. Current assets would increase by $5,000 and payables by $3,000. At the end of 3 years the equipment could be sold for $10,000. Depreciation would be based on the MACRS 3-year class, so the applicable rates would be 33, 45, 15, and 7 percent. Variable costs would be 70 percent of sales revenues, fixed costs excluding depreciation would be $30,000 per year, the marginal tax rate is 40 percent, and the corporate WACC is 11 percent.
   a.   What is the required investment, that is, the Year 0 project cash flow?
   b.   What are the annual depreciation charges?
   c.   What is the terminal cash flow?
   d.   What are the net operating cash flows in Years 1, 2, and 3?
   e.   What are the annual project cash flows?
   f.   If the project is of average risk, what is its NPV, and should it be accepted?
   g.   Suppose management is uncertain about the exact unit sales. What would the project's NPV be if unit sales turned out to be 20 percent below forecast, but other inputs were as forecasted? Would this change the decision?
   h.   The CFO asks you to do a scenario analysis using these inputs:

	Probability	Unit Sales	VC%
Best case	25%	4,800	65%
Base case	50	4,000	70
Worst case	25	3,200	75

Other variables are unchanged. What are the expected NPV, its standard deviation, and the coefficient of variation? [Hint: To do the scenario analysis, you must change unit sales and VC% to the values specified for each scenario, get the scenario cash flows, and then find each scenario's NPV. Then you must calculate the project's expected NPV, standard deviation (SD), and coefficient of variation (CV). This is not difficult, but it would require a lot of calculations. You might want to look at the answer, but make sure you understand how it was developed.]

i. The firm's project CVs generally range from 1.0 to 1.5. A 3 percent risk premium is added to the WACC if the initial CV exceeds 1.5, and the WACC is reduced by 0.5 percent if the CV is 0.75 or less. Then a revised NPV is calculated. What WACC should be used for this project? What are the revised values for the NPV, standard deviation, and coefficient of variation? Would you recommend that the project be accepted?

QUESTIONS

12-1 Operating cash flows rather than accounting profits are listed in Table 12-1. Why do we focus on cash flows as opposed to net income in capital budgeting?

12-2 Explain why sunk costs should not be included in a capital budgeting analysis, but opportunity costs and externalities should be included. Give an example of each.

12-3 Explain why working capital is included in a capital budgeting analysis and how it is recovered at the end of a project's life.

12-4 Why are interest charges not deducted when a project's cash flows for use in a capital budgeting analysis are calculated?

12-5 Most firms generate cash inflows every day, not just once at the end of the year. In capital budgeting, should we recognize this fact by estimating daily project cash flows and then using them in the analysis? If we do not, are our results biased, and if so, would the NPV be biased up or down? Explain.

12-6 What are some differences in the analysis for a replacement project versus that for a new expansion project?

12-7 Distinguish among beta (or market) risk, within-firm (or corporate) risk, and stand-alone risk for a project being considered for inclusion in the capital budget.

12-8 In theory, market risk should be the only "relevant" risk. However, companies focus as much on stand-alone risk as on market risk. What are the reasons for the focus on stand-alone risk?

12-9 Define (a) sensitivity analysis, (b) scenario analysis, and (c) simulation analysis. If GE were considering two projects, one for $500 million to develop a satellite communications system and the other for $30,000 for a new truck, on which would the company be more likely to use a simulation analysis?

12-10 If you were the CFO of a company that had to decide on hundreds of potential projects every year, would you want to use sensitivity analysis and scenario analysis as described in the chapter, or would the amount of arithmetic required take too much time and thus not be cost effective? What involvement would nonfinancial people such as those in marketing, accounting, and production have in the analysis?

PROBLEMS

Easy
Problems 1–3

12-1 **Required investment** Truman Industries is considering an expansion. The necessary equipment would be purchased for $9 million, and it would also require an additional $3 million investment in working capital. The tax rate is 40 percent.
a. What is the initial investment outlay?
b. The company spent and expensed $50,000 on research related to the project last year. Would this change your answer? Explain.
c. The company plans to use a building it owns but is not now using to house the project. The building could be sold for $1 million after taxes and real estate commissions. How would that affect your answer?

12-2 **Operating cash flow** Eisenhower Communications is trying to estimate the first-year net operating cash flow (at Year 1) for a proposed project. The financial staff has collected the following information on the project:

Sales revenues	$10 million
Operating costs (excluding depreciation)	7 million
Depreciation	2 million
Interest expense	2 million

The company has a 40 percent tax rate, and its WACC is 10 percent.

a. What is the project's operating cash flow for the first year (t = 1)?

b. If this project would cannibalize other projects by $1 million of cash flow before taxes per year, how would this change your answer to part a?

c. Ignore part b. If the tax rate dropped to 30 percent, how would that change your answer to part a?

12-3 **Net salvage value** Kennedy Air Services is now in the final year of a project. The equipment originally cost $20 million, of which 80 percent has been depreciated. Kennedy can sell the used equipment today for $5 million, and its tax rate is 40 percent. What is the equipment's after-tax net salvage value?

Intermediate
Problems 4–8

12-4 **Depreciation methods** Kristin is evaluating a capital budgeting project that should last for 4 years. The project requires $800,000 of equipment. She is unsure what depreciation method to use in her analysis, straight-line or the 3-year MACRS accelerated method. Under straight-line depreciation, the cost of the equipment would be depreciated evenly over its 4-year life (ignore the half-year convention for the straight-line method). The applicable MACRS depreciation rates are 33, 45, 15, and 7 percent as discussed in Appendix 12A. The company's WACC is 10 percent, and its tax rate is 40 percent.

a. What would the depreciation expense be each year under each method?

b. Which depreciation method would produce the higher NPV, and how much higher would it be?

12-5 **Scenario analysis** Huang Industries is considering a proposed project whose estimated NPV is $12 million. This estimate assumes that economic conditions will be "average." However, the CFO realizes that conditions could be better or worse, so she performed a scenario analysis and obtained these results:

Economic Scenario	Probability of Outcome	NPV
Recession	0.05	($70 million)
Below average	0.20	(25 million)
Average	0.50	12 million
Above average	0.20	20 million
Boom	0.05	30 million

Calculate the project's expected NPV, standard deviation, and coefficient of variation.

12-6 **New project analysis** You must evaluate a proposed spectrometer for the R&D department. The base price is $140,000, and it would cost another $30,000 to modify the equipment for special use by the firm. The equipment falls into the MACRS 3-year class and would be sold after 3 years for $60,000. The applicable depreciation rates are 33, 45, 15, and 7 percent as discussed in Appendix 12A. The equipment would require an $8,000 increase in working capital (spare parts inventory). The project would have no effect on revenues, but it should save the firm $50,000 per year before-tax labor costs. The firm's marginal federal-plus-state tax rate is 40 percent.

a. What is the net cost of the spectrometer, that is, what is the Year 0 project cash flow?

b. What are the net operating cash flows in Years 1, 2, and 3?

c. What is the terminal cash flow?

d. If the WACC is 12 percent, should the spectrometer be purchased?

12-7 **New project analysis** You must evaluate a proposal to buy a new milling machine. The base price is $108,000, and shipping and installation costs would add another $12,500. The machine falls into the MACRS 3-year class, and it would be sold after 3 years for $65,000. The applicable depreciation rates are 33, 45, 15, and 7 percent as discussed in Appendix 12A. The machine would require a $5,500 increase in working capital (increased inventory less increased accounts payable). There would be no effect on revenues, but pre-tax labor costs would decline by $44,000 per year. The marginal tax rate is 35 percent, and the WACC is 12 percent. Also, the firm spent $5,000 last year investigating the feasibility of using the machine.

a. How should the $5,000 spent last year be handled?

b. What is the net cost of the machine for capital budgeting purposes, that is, the Year 0 project cash flow?

c. What are the net operating cash flows during Years 1, 2, and 3?

    d.   What is the terminal year cash flow?

    e.   Should the machine be purchased? Explain your answer.

12-8 **Project risk analysis** The Butler-Perkins Company (BPC) must decide between two mutually exclusive projects. Each costs $6,750 and has an expected life of 3 years. Annual project cash flows begin 1 year after the initial investment, and are subject to the following probability distributions:

PROJECT A		PROJECT B	
Probability	Cash Flows	Probability	Cash Flows
0.2	$6,000	0.2	$ 0
0.6	6,750	0.6	6,750
0.2	7,500	0.2	18,000

BPC has decided to evaluate the riskier project at 12 percent and the less-risky project at 10 percent.

    a.   What is each project's expected annual cash flow? Project B's standard deviation (σ_B) is $5,798 and its coefficient of variation (CV_B) is 0.76. What are the values of σ_A and CV_A?

    b.   Based on their risk-adjusted NPVs, which project should BPC choose?

    c.   If you knew that Project B's cash flows were negatively correlated with the firm's other cash flow, whereas Project A's flows were positively correlated, how might this affect the decision? If Project B's cash flows were negatively correlated with gross domestic product (GDP), while A's flows were positively correlated, would that influence your risk assessment?

Challenging Problems 9–10

12-9 **Scenario analysis** Your firm, Agrico Products, is considering a tractor that would have a net cost of $36,000, would increase pre-tax operating cash flows before taking account of depreciation by $12,000 per year, and would be depreciated on a straight-line basis to zero over 5 years at the rate of $7,200 per year, beginning the first year. (Thus annual cash flows would be $12,000, before taxes, plus the tax savings that result from $7,200 of depreciation.) The managers are having a heated debate about whether the tractor would actually last 5 years. The controller insists that she knows of tractors that have lasted only 4 years. The treasurer agrees with the controller, but he argues that most tractors actually do give 5 years of service. The service manager then states that some actually last for as long as 8 years.

Given this discussion, the CFO asks you to prepare a scenario analysis to determine the importance of the tractor's life on the NPV. Use a 40 percent marginal federal-plus-state tax rate, a zero salvage value, and a WACC of 10 percent. Assuming each of the indicated lives has the same probability of occurring (probability = 1/3), what is the tractor's expected NPV? (Hint: Here straight-line depreciation is based on the MACRS class life of the tractor and is not affected by the actual life. Also, ignore the half-year convention for this problem.)

12-10 **New project analysis** Holmes Manufacturing is considering a new machine that costs $250,000 and would reduce pre-tax manufacturing costs by $90,000 annually. Holmes would use the 3-year MACRS method to depreciate the machine, and management thinks the machine would have a value of $23,000 at the end of its 5-year operating life. The applicable depreciation rates are 33, 45, 15, and 7 percent as discussed in Appendix 12A. Working capital would increase by $25,000 initially, but it would be recovered at the end of the project's 5-year life. Holmes's marginal tax rate is 40 percent, and a 10 percent WACC is appropriate for the project.

    a.   Calculate the project's NPV, IRR, MIRR, and payback.

    b.   Assume management is unsure about the $90,000 cost savings—this figure could deviate by as much as plus or minus 20 percent. What would the NPV be under each of these situations?

    c.   Suppose the CFO wants you to do a scenario analysis with different values for the cost savings, the machine's salvage value, and the working capital (WC) requirement. She asks you to use the following probabilities and values in the scenario analysis:

Scenario	Probability	Cost Savings	Salvage Value	WC
Worst case	0.35	$ 72,000	$18,000	$30,000
Base case	0.35	90,000	23,000	25,000
Best case	0.30	108,000	28,000	20,000

Calculate the project's expected NPV, its standard deviation, and its coefficient of variation. Would you recommend that the project be accepted?

COMPREHENSIVE/SPREADSHEET PROBLEM

12-11 **New project analysis** You must analyze a potential new product—a caulking compound that Cory Materials' R&D people developed for use in the residential construction industry. Cory's marketing manager thinks they can sell 115,000 tubes per year at a price of $3.25 each for 3 years, after which the product will be obsolete. The required equipment would cost $150,000, plus another $25,000 for shipping and installation. Current assets (receivables and inventories) would increase by $35,000, while current liabilities (accounts payable and accruals) would rise by $15,000. Variable costs would be 60 percent of sales revenues, fixed costs (exclusive of depreciation) would be $70,000 per year, and the fixed assets would be depreciated under MACRS with a 3-year life. (Refer to Appendix 12A for MACRS depreciation rates.) When production ceases after 3 years, the equipment should have a market value of $15,000. Cory's tax rate is 40 percent, and it uses a 10 percent WACC for average-risk projects.

a. Find the required Year 0 investment, the annual after-tax operating cash flows, and the terminal year cash flow, and then calculate the project's NPV, IRR, MIRR, and payback. Assume at this point that the project is of average risk.

b. Suppose you now learn that R&D costs for the new product were $30,000, and those costs were incurred and expensed for tax purposes last year. How would this affect your estimate of NPV and the other profitability measures?

c. If the new project would reduce cash flows from Cory's other projects, and if the new project were to be housed in an empty building that Cory owns and could sell if it chose to, how would those factors affect the project's NPV?

d. Are this project's cash flows likely to be positively or negatively correlated with returns on Cory's other projects and with the economy, and should this matter in your analysis? Explain.

e. **Spreadsheet assignment: at instructor's option** Construct a spreadsheet that calculates the cash flows, NPV, IRR, payback, and MIRR.

f. The CEO expressed concern that some of the base-case inputs might be too optimistic or too pessimistic, and he wants to know how the NPV would be affected if these 6 variables were all 20 percent better or 20 percent worse than the base-case level: unit sales, sales price, variable costs, fixed costs, WACC, and equipment cost. Hold other things constant when you consider each variable, and construct a sensitivity graph to illustrate your results.

g. Do a scenario analysis based on the assumption that there is a 25 percent probability that each of the 6 variables itemized in part f would turn out to have their best-case values as calculated in part f, a 50 percent probability that all will have their base-case values, and a 25 percent probability that all will have their worst-case values. The other variables remain at base-case levels. Calculate the expected NPV, the standard deviation of NPV, and the coefficient of variation.

h. Does Cory's management use the risk-adjusted discount rate or the certainty equivalent method to adjust for project risk? Explain what it does and how it would use the alternative method.

Integrated Case

Allied Food Products

12-12 **Capital budgeting and cash flow estimation** Allied Food Products is considering expanding into the fruit juice business with a new fresh lemon juice product. Assume that you were recently hired as assistant to the director of capital budgeting, and you must evaluate the new project.

The lemon juice would be produced in an unused building adjacent to Allied's Fort Myers plant; Allied owns the building, which is fully depreciated. The required equipment would cost $200,000, plus an additional $40,000 for shipping and installation. In addition, inventories would rise by $25,000, while accounts payable would increase by $5,000. All of these costs would be incurred at t = 0. By a special ruling, the machinery could be depreciated under the MACRS system as 3-year property. The applicable depreciation rates are 33, 45, 15, and 7 percent.

The project is expected to operate for 4 years, at which time it will be terminated. The cash inflows are assumed to begin 1 year after the project is undertaken, or at t = 1, and to continue out to t = 4. At the end of the project's life (t = 4), the equipment is expected to have a salvage value of $25,000.

Unit sales are expected to total 100,000 units per year, and the expected sales price is $2.00 per unit. Cash operating costs for the project (total operating costs less depreciation) are expected to total 60 percent of dollar sales. Allied's tax rate is 40 percent, and its WACC is 10 percent. Tentatively, the lemon juice project is assumed to be of equal risk to Allied's other assets.

You have been asked to evaluate the project and to make a recommendation as to whether it should be accepted or rejected. To guide you in your analysis, your boss gave you the following set of questions:

a. Allied has a standard form that is used in the capital budgeting process; see Table IC12-1. Part of the table has been completed, but you must replace the blanks with the missing numbers. Complete the table in the following steps:
    (1) Fill in the blanks under Year 0 for the initial investment outlay.
    (2) Complete the table for unit sales, sales price, total revenues, and operating costs excluding depreciation.
    (3) Complete the depreciation data.
    (4) Now complete the table down to NOPAT, and then down to operating cash flows.
    (5) Now fill in the blanks under Year 4 for the terminal cash flows, and complete the project cash flow line. Discuss working capital. What would have happened if the machinery were sold for less than its book value?

b. (1) Allied uses debt in its capital structure, so some of the money used to finance the project will be debt. Given this fact, should the projected cash flows be revised to show projected interest charges? Explain.
    (2) Suppose you learned that Allied had spent $50,000 to renovate the building last year, expensing these costs. Should this cost be reflected in the analysis? Explain.
    (3) Now suppose you learned that Allied could lease its building to another party and earn $25,000 per year. Should that fact be reflected in the analysis? If so, how?
    (4) Now assume that the lemon juice project would take away profitable sales from Allied's fresh orange juice business. Should that fact be reflected in your analysis? If so, how?

c. Disregard all the assumptions made in part b, and assume there was no alternative use for the building over the next 4 years. Now calculate the project's NPV, IRR, MIRR, and payback. Do these indicators suggest that the project should be accepted?

d. If this project had been a replacement rather than an expansion project, how would the analysis have changed? Think about the changes that would have to occur in the cash flow table.

e. (1) What are the three levels, or types, of project risk that are normally considered?
    (2) Which type is most relevant?
    (3) Which type is easiest to measure?
    (4) Are the three types of risk generally highly correlated?

f. (1) What is sensitivity analysis?
    (2) How would one perform a sensitivity analysis on the unit sales, salvage value, and WACC for the project? Assume that each of these variables deviates from its base-case, or expected, value by plus and minus 10, 20, and 30 percent. Explain how you would calculate the NPV, IRR, MIRR, and payback for each case, but don't do the analysis unless your instructor asks you to.
    (3) What is the primary weakness of sensitivity analysis? What are its primary advantages?

Work out quantitative answers to the remaining questions only if your instructor asks you to. Also, note that it would take a *long time* to do the calculations unless you are using an *Excel* model.

g. Assume that inflation is expected to average 5 percent over the next 4 years, and this expectation is reflected in the WACC. Moreover, inflation is expected to increase revenues and variable costs by this same 5 percent. Does it appear that inflation has been dealt with properly in the initial analysis to this point? If not, what should be done, and how would the required adjustment affect the decision?

h. The expected cash flows, considering inflation (in thousands of dollars), are given in Table IC12-2. Allied's WACC is 10 percent. Assume that you are confident about the estimates of all the variables that affect the cash flows except unit sales. If product acceptance is poor, sales would be only 75,000 units a year, while a strong consumer response would produce sales of 125,000 units. In either case, cash costs would still amount to 60 percent of revenues. You believe that there is a 25 percent chance of poor acceptance, a 25 percent chance of excellent acceptance, and a 50 percent chance of average acceptance (the base case). Provide numbers only if you are using a computer model.
    (1) What is the worst-case NPV? The best-case NPV?
    (2) Use the worst, most likely (or base), and best-case NPVs, with their probabilities of occurrence, to find the project's expected NPV, standard deviation, and coefficient of variation.

i. Assume that Allied's average project has a coefficient of variation (CV) in the range of 1.25 to 1.75. Would the lemon juice project be classified as high risk, average risk, or low risk? What type of risk is being measured here?

j. Based on common sense, how highly correlated do you think the project would be with the firm's other assets? (Give a correlation coefficient or range of coefficients, based on your judgment.)

k. How would the correlation coefficient and the previously calculated σ combine to affect the project's contribution to corporate, or within-firm, risk? Explain.

l. Based on your judgment, what do you think the project's correlation coefficient would be with respect to the general economy and thus with returns on "the market"? How would correlation with the economy affect the project's market risk?

m. Allied typically adds or subtracts 3 percent to its WACC to adjust for risk. After adjusting for risk, should the lemon juice project be accepted? Should any subjective risk factors be considered before the final decision is made? Explain.

TABLE IC12-1 *Allied's Lemon Juice Project (Total Cost in Thousands)*

End of Year:	0	1	2	3	4
I. INVESTMENT OUTLAY					
Equipment cost					
Installation					
Increase in inventory					
Increase in accounts payable	_____				
Total net investment	_____				
II. OPERATING CASH FLOWS					
Unit sales (thousands)			100		
Price/unit		$ 2.00	$ 2.00		
Total revenues		_____	_____	_____	$200.0
Operating costs excluding depreciation			$120.0		
Depreciation				36.0	16.8
Total costs		$199.2	$228.0	_____	_____
Operating income before taxes (EBIT)				$44.0	
Taxes on operating income		0.3	_____	_____	25.3
Operating income after taxes (NOPAT)				$26.4	
Depreciation		79.2	_____	36.0	_____
Operating cash flow	$ 0.0	$ 79.7	_____	_____	$ 54.7
III. TERMINAL YEAR CASH FLOWS					
Return of net operating working capital					
Salvage value					
Tax on salvage value					
Total termination cash flows					_____
IV. PROJECT CASH FLOWS					
Project cash flow	($260.0)	_____	_____	_____	$ 89.7
V. RESULTS					
NPV =					
IRR =					
MIRR =					
Payback =					

TABLE IC12-2 *Allied's Lemon Juice Project Considering 5 Percent Inflation (in Thousands)*

		YEAR			
	0	1	2	3	4
Investment in:					
Fixed assets	($240)				
Net operating working capital	(20)				
Unit sales (thousands)		100	100	100	100
Sales price (dollars)		$2.100	$2.205	$2.315	$2.431
Total revenues		$210.0	$220.5	$231.5	$243.1
Cash operating costs (60%)		126.0	132.3	138.9	145.9
Depreciation		79.2	108.0	36.0	16.8
Operating income before taxes (EBIT)		$ 4.8	($ 19.8)	$ 56.6	$ 80.4
Taxes on operating income (40%)		1.9	(7.9)	22.6	32.1
Operating income after taxes (NOPAT)		$ 2.9	($ 11.9)	$ 34.0	$ 48.3
Plus depreciation		79.2	108.0	36.0	16.8
Operating cash flow		$ 82.1	$ 96.1	$ 70.0	$ 65.1
Salvage value					25.0
Tax on SV (40%)					(10.0)
Recovery of NOWC					20.0
Project cash flow	($260)	$ 82.1	$ 96.1	$ 70.0	$100.1
Cumulative cash flows for payback:	(260.0)	(177.9)	(81.8)	(11.8)	88.3
Compounded inflows for MIRR:		109.2	116.3	77.0	100.1
Terminal value of inflows:					402.6
NPV	= $15.0				
IRR	= 12.6%				
MIRR	= 11.6%				

cyberproblem

Please go to the ThomsonNOW Web site to access the Cyberproblems.

APPENDIX 12A

Tax Depreciation

Depreciation is covered in detail in accounting courses, so we provide here only some basic information that is needed for capital budgeting. First, note that accountants generally calculate each asset's depreciation in two ways—they generally use straight line to figure the depreciation used for reporting profits to investors, but they use depreciation rates provided by the Internal Revenue Service (IRS) and called MACRS (Modified Accelerated Cost Recovery System) rates when they calculate depreciation for tax purposes. In capital budgeting, we are concerned with tax depreciation, so the relevant rates are the MACRS rates.

Under MACRS, each type of fixed asset is assigned to a "class" and is then depreciated over the asset's **class life**. Table 12A-1 provides class lives for different types of assets as they existed in 2005. Next, as we show in Table 12A-2, MACRS specifies **annual depreciation rates** for assets in each class life. Real properties (buildings) are depreciated on a straight-line basis over 27.5 or 39 years, but all other assets are depreciated over shorter periods and on an accelerated basis, with high depreciation charges in the early years and less depreciation in the later years. The IRS tables are based on the **half-year convention,** where it is assumed that the asset is placed in service halfway through the first year and is taken out of service halfway through the year after its class life.

In the following example, we calculate depreciation on the equipment that BQC would use for the computer project discussed in Chapter 12. That equipment would be classified as a 5-year asset with a cost of $8 million. In developing the tables, the IRS assumes that the machinery would be used for only six months of the year in which it is acquired, for 12 months in each of the next four years, and then for six months of the sixth year. Here are the depreciation charges, in thousands, that could be deducted for tax purposes based on MACRS:

Year	1	2	3	4	5	6
Rate	20%	32%	19%	12%	11%	6%
Depreciation	$1,600	$2,560	$1,520	$960	$880	$480

Class Life
The specified life of assets under the MACRS system.

Annual Depreciation Rates
The annual expense accountants charge against income for "wear and tear" of an asset. For tax purposes, the IRS provides that appropriate MACRS rates be used that are dependent on an asset's class life.

Half-Year Convention
Assumes assets are used for half of the first year and half of the last year.

The total of the annual depreciation charges equals the $8 million cost of the asset, but it would be taken over six years and thus would affect cash flows over those six years.

Of course, BQC only plans to use the equipment for four years, so the allowable depreciation shown above for Years 5 and 6 will not enter into BQC's capital budgeting analysis.

TABLE 12A-1   *Major Classes and Asset Lives for MACRS*

Class	Type of Property
3-year	Certain special manufacturing tools
5-year	Automobiles, light-duty trucks, computers, and certain special manufacturing equipment
7-year	Most industrial equipment, office furniture, and fixtures
10-year	Certain longer-lived types of equipment
27.5-year	Residential rental real property such as apartment buildings
39-year	All nonresidential real property, including commercial and industrial buildings

---

TABLE 12A-2   *Recovery Allowance Percentage for Personal Property*

	CLASS OF INVESTMENT			
Ownership Year	3-Year	5-Year	7-Year	10-Year
1	33%	20%	14%	10%
2	45	32	25	18
3	15	19	17	14
4	7	12	13	12
5		11	9	9
6		6	9	7
7			9	7
8			4	7
9				7
10				6
11				3
	100%	100%	100%	100%

Notes:

a. We developed these recovery allowance percentages based on the 200 percent declining balance method prescribed by MACRS, with a switch to straight-line depreciation at some point in the asset's life. For example, consider the 5-year recovery allowance percentages. The straight-line percentage would be 20 percent per year, so the 200 percent declining balance multiplier is 2.0(20%) = 40% = 0.4. However, because the half-year convention applies, the MACRS percentage for Year 1 is 20 percent. For Year 2, there is 80 percent of the depreciable basis remaining to be depreciated, so the recovery allowance percentage is 0.40(80%) = 32%. In Year 3, 20% + 32% = 52% of the depreciation has been taken, leaving 48 percent, so the percentage is 0.4(48%) = 19%. In Year 4, the percentage is 0.4(29%) = 12%. After 4 years, straight-line depreciation exceeds the declining balance depreciation, so a switch is made to straight-line (this is permitted under the law). However, the half-year convention must also be applied at the end of the class life, and the remaining 17 percent of depreciation must be taken (amortized) over 1.5 years. Thus, the percentage in Year 5 is 17%/1.5 ≈ 11%, and in Year 6, 17% − 11% = 6%. Although the tax tables carry the allowance percentages out to two decimal places, we have rounded to the nearest whole number for ease of illustration.

b. Residential rental property (apartments) is depreciated over a 27.5-year life, whereas commercial and industrial structures are depreciated over 39 years. In both cases, straight-line depreciation must be used. The depreciation allowance for the first year is based, pro rata, on the month the asset was placed in service, with the remainder of the first year's depreciation being taken in the 28th or 40th year.

REAL OPTIONS AND OTHER TOPICS IN CAPITAL BUDGETING

Keeping Your Options Open

The last two chapters described the basic procedures used in capital budgeting, including cash flow estimation and adjusting for project risk. Those procedures assume that the expected cash flows are locked in once the project has been accepted. However, the resulting NPV may be misleading if managers are able to modify operations in reaction to changing circumstances, thereby altering the initially forecasted cash flow stream. For example, if demand turns out to be stronger than anticipated, it might be possible to expand the plant, increase output, and thus increase the NPV.

In this chapter, we describe *real option analysis*, which incorporates the possibility of mid-course corrections into the traditional NPV analysis. The possible corrections are called *embedded real options*, or choices. For example, the initial analysis might indicate that a project has a negative NPV, but if the operation could be expanded if demand turns out to be stronger than was anticipated, this might change the expected NPV from negative to positive. Other types of real options include changing a plant's output (say, from sedans to SUVs if the auto market changes), abandoning a project that is generating lower than anticipated cash flows, or waiting to see how the market is developing before making the final go/no-go decision. As we will demonstrate, all of these possibilities can lead to increases in the expected NPV and thus to a change in the accept/reject decision.

A recent article in the *Journal of Applied Corporate Finance* reported that companies like Intel, Texaco, and Genentech use real option analysis extensively in capital budgeting. While the analysis can be quite complex, the basic principles are straightforward and can be described in simple terms. After reading this chapter, you should see why real option analysis is important in capital budgeting.

Source: Alex Triantis and Adam Borison, "Real Options: State of the Practice," *Journal of Applied Corporate Finance*, Vol. 14, no. 2 (Summer 2001), pp. 8–24.

Chapters 11 and 12 covered the basic principles of capital budgeting. Now we examine three important extensions. First, we discuss real options and present some examples to demonstrate their importance. Next, we discuss mutually exclusive projects that have unequal lives. As we shall see, if such projects can be repeated, the analysis must be extended out into the future to make a valid comparison and thus make the right choice between the alternatives. Finally, we discuss the relationship between the size of the capital budget and the WACC. The WACC tends to increase as the firm raises larger and larger amounts of capital, creating a feedback relationship between the size of the capital budget and the WACC.

13-1 INTRODUCTION TO REAL OPTIONS[1]

Traditional discounted cash flow (DCF) analysis—where cash flows are estimated and then discounted to obtain the expected NPV—has been the cornerstone for capital budgeting since the 1950s. However, in recent years it has been demonstrated that DCF techniques do not always lead to proper capital budgeting decisions.[2]

DCF techniques were originally developed to value securities such as stocks and bonds. Those securities are passive investments—once they have been purchased, most investors have no influence over the cash flows they produce.[3] However, real assets are not passive investments—managers can often take actions to alter the cash flow stream. Such opportunities are called **real options**—"real" to distinguish them from financial options like an option to buy shares of GE stock, and options because they provide the right but not the obligation to take some future action that can increase cash flows. Real options are valuable, and as this value is not captured by conventional NPV analysis, it must be considered separately.

There are several types of real options, including (1) *abandonment*, where the project can be shut down if its cash flows are low; (2) *timing*, where a project can

Real Option
The right but not the obligation to take some action in the future.

---

[1] Real option analysis is relatively technical, and the topic is covered in depth in advanced corporate finance courses. However, since many students do not take additional finance courses, and since this is an important topic, we provide this introduction. However, Sections 13.1 through 13.5 may be omitted without loss of continuity if there is insufficient time to cover it.

[2] For an early but excellent discussion of the problems inherent in discounted cash flow valuation techniques as applied to capital budgeting, see Avinash K. Dixit and Robert S. Pindyck, "The Options Approach to Capital Investment," *Harvard Business Review*, May–June 1995, pp. 105–115. For more information on the option value inherent in investment timing decisions, see Stephen A. Ross, "Uses, Abuses, and Alternatives to the Net-Present-Value Rule," *Financial Management*, Autumn 1995, pp. 96–101. Also, the Summer 2001 issue of the *Journal of Applied Corporate Finance* contains several interesting articles on the use of option concepts in capital budgeting.

[3] Large investors such as Warren Buffett and some hedge fund operators can buy stock in companies and then influence the firms' operations and cash flows. However, the average stockholder does not have such influence.

be delayed until more information about demand and/or costs can be obtained; (3) *expansion*, where the project can be expanded if demand turns out to be stronger than expected; (4) *output flexibility*, where the output can be changed if market conditions change; and (5) *input flexibility*, where the inputs used in the production process (say, coal versus oil for generating electricity) can be changed if input prices and/or availability change.

Why might DCF techniques not always lead to proper capital budgeting decisions?

What is a real option?

Why might recognizing a real option raise but not lower a project's NPV as found in a traditional analysis?

What are the five types of real options? Briefly explain each one.

13-2 ABANDONMENT/SHUTDOWN OPTIONS

In capital budgeting we generally assume that a project will be operated for its full physical life. However, this is not always the best course of action. If the firm has the **option to abandon** a project during its operating life, this can lower its risk and increase its expected profitability.

Recall from Chapter 12 that due to contractual obligations to component suppliers, BQC's computer control project could not be terminated before the end of its four-year life. Under that constraint, we evaluated the best-case, base-case, and worst-case scenarios. The earlier analysis is reproduced in the decision tree given in Situation 1 of Table 13-1, "Cannot Abandon." In Column B we see the probabilities for each scenario. In Column C, which is Time 0, we see that the firm must invest $26 million. Columns D through G show the annual cash flows under each scenario, and in Column H we show the NPV under each scenario when the cash flows are discounted at a 12 percent WACC. The sum of the products obtained by multiplying each probability times each branch NPV is the expected NPV, which is $13.531 million. The standard deviation and the coefficient of variation are also calculated to provide an idea of the project's risk. This project has a positive expected NPV based on the 12 percent WACC, but management might choose to reject it because if things turn out badly the company would be seriously damaged (as illustrated in Row 20 of Table 13-1).

Now suppose the constraint against closing the operation could be relaxed, and the company could make a second decision, at t = 1, to abandon (or shut down) the project if things turn out badly. To see what would happen then, we add another branch to the tree, as shown in Situation 2 of Table 13-1. Here we assume that the company *can abandon* the project at the end of Year 1, when information about the actual production costs and demand conditions become available. If things were going well, the project would be continued. However, if things were going badly, BQC would sell the related assets at their $18.244 million book value and realize this cash flow at the end of Year 2. (There would be no tax consequences, as a sale at book value produces neither a gain nor a loss.) Thus, the Year 2 cash flow would be a positive $18.244 million rather than the loss of $8.943 million if the operation were continued. Of course, if the project were abandoned, the cash flows in Years 3 and 4 would become zero. With these changes, we recalculate the NPV for the bottom (or "Can Abandon") branch. It is still negative, but

Abandonment Option
The option of abandoning a project if operating cash flows turn out to be lower than expected. This option can both raise expected profitability and lower project risk.

TABLE 13-1	Decision Trees without and with the Abandonment Option (Dollars in Thousands)

	A	B	C	D	E	F	G	H	I
15	Situation 1: Cannot Abandon				WACC =	12%			
16				End-of-Period Cash Flows:				NPV @	
17		Prob:	0	1	2	3	4	12%	
18	Best Case	25%	−26,000	33,810	34,257	33,841	50,224	$87,503	
19	Base Case	50%	−26,000	6,702	7,149	6,733	23,116	5,166	
20	Worst Case	25%	−26,000	−9,390	−8,943	−9,359	7,024	−43,711	
21							Expected NPV	$13,531	
22							Standard Deviation (SD)	$47,139	
23							Coefficient of Variation (CV)	3.48	
24									
25	Situation 2: Can Abandon				WACC =	12%			
26				End-of-Period Cash Flows:				NPV @	
27		Prob.	0	1	2	3	4	12%	
28	Best Case	25%	−26,000	33,810	34,257	33,841	50,224	$87,503	
29	Base Case	50%	−26,000	6,702	7,149	6,733	23,116	5,166	
30	Worst #1	0%	−26,000	−9,390	−8,943	−9,359	7,024	−43,711	Disregard
31	Worst #2	25%	−26,000	−9,390	18,244	0	0	−19,840	Choose
32							Expected NPV	$19,499	
33							Standard Deviation (SD)	$40,567	
34							Coefficient of Variation (CV)	2.08	
35									
36			Abandonment Option Value						
37			Expected NPV w/ Abandonment					$19,499	
38			Expected NPV w/o Abandonment					13,531	
39			Difference = Abandonment Option Value					$ 5,968	

considerably less negative than in the worst-case scenario before considering abandonment.[4]

The option to abandon raises the expected NPV from $13.531 million to $19.499 million, and it also lowers the standard deviation. Those changes combine to lower the coefficient of variation. The coefficient of variation is 2.08, which is close to the company's average of 2.0, which indicates that the project is of average risk once abandonment is factored in. Therefore, the 12 percent WACC is appropriate. Also, note that the difference between the expected NPVs with and without abandonment represents the **value of the option** to abandon. As shown in the lower part of Table 13-1, the option is worth $5.968 million.

In this case, the ability to abandon makes the NPV look better, but it does not reverse the accept/reject decision. However, it often turns out that if we fail to consider abandonment, the bad case is so bad that the expected NPV is negative, but when abandonment is considered, the expected NPV becomes positive. Clearly, abandonment must be considered to obtain valid assessments for different projects, and the opportunity to abandon is an important way to limit downside losses.

Note too that it might be necessary for the firm to arrange things so that it has the possibility of abandonment when it is making the initial decision. This

Option Value
The difference between the expected NPVs with and without the relevant option. It is the value that is not accounted for in a traditional NPV analysis. A positive option value expands the firm's opportunities.

---

[4] In Situation 2, where the company has the option to abandon if the worst-case scenario occurs, it would abandon the project as that action would minimize its losses. Thus, we show a zero probability of continuing to operate under the worst-case scenario.

might require contractual arrangements with suppliers, customers, and its union, and there might be some costs to obtaining the advance permissions. Any such costs could be compared with the value of the option as we calculated it, and this could enter into the initial decision.

Would you expect an abandonment option to increase or decrease a project's NPV and risk as measured by the coefficient of variation? Why?

How could the value of the abandonment option be estimated?

13-3 INVESTMENT TIMING OPTIONS

A conventional NPV analysis assumes that projects will either be accepted or rejected, which implies that they will be undertaken now or never. However, in practice companies sometimes have a third choice—delay the decision until later, when more information becomes available. Such **investment timing options** can affect a project's estimated profitability and risk.

To illustrate timing options, assume that Williams Inc. is considering a project that requires an initial investment of $5 million at the beginning of 2006 (or t = 0). The project will generate positive net cash flows at the end of each of the next four years (t = 1, 2, 3, and 4). However, the size of each annual cash flow will depend on what happens to future market conditions. Table 13-2 shows two decision trees that illustrate the problem. As shown in the top section, there is a 50 percent probability that market conditions will be strong, in which case the project will generate cash flows of $2.5 million at the end of each of the next four years. There is also a 50 percent probability that demand for the product will be weak, in which case the annual cash flows will be only $1.2 million.

Note that each branch of the decision tree is equivalent to a time line. Thus, the top line, which describes the payoffs under good conditions, shows a cost of $5.0 million in 2006 and cash inflows of $2.5 million for 2007 through 2010. Williams considers the project to have average risk, hence it will be evaluated using a 10 percent WACC. The NPV, if the market is strong, will turn out to be $2.92 million. On the other hand, if product demand is weak, the NPV will turn out to be −$1.20 million, so it will be a money loser.

The expected value is found as a weighted average of the NPVs of the two possible outcomes, with each outcome's weight being its 50 percent probability. The expected NPV, if the project is undertaken today, is $0.864 million. The project has a positive NPV, so it appears that the company should proceed with it, even though there is some risk, and there is a 50–50 chance that it will actually turn out to be a loser.

However, suppose Williams can delay the project until next year, when more information will be available about market conditions, before making the decision. If conditions are good, the firm will proceed, but if they are bad, it will not make the investment, hence the NPV will be zero. The probability of each outcome is 50 percent, and the expected NPV is $1.462 million, almost twice that as if we go ahead right now and possibly have the low cash flows under the bad conditions. Note, though, that if the firm waits, the expected NPV will come a year later. Therefore, we discount the expected NPV under the delay option at the WACC to get an adjusted NPV of $1.329 million. Since this exceeds the NPV under the proceed immediately decision, Williams should delay the project for a year.

When making go-versus-wait decisions, financial managers need to consider several other factors. First, if a firm decides to wait, it may lose strategic advantages

Investment Timing Option
An option as to when to begin a project. Often, if a firm can delay a decision, it can increase a project's expected NPV.

TABLE 13-2	*Illustration of a Timing Option (Dollars in Millions)*

Proceed Immediately: Invest Now

Conditions	Probability	END-OF-PERIOD CASH FLOWS:					NPV @ 10%
		2006	2007	2008	2009	2010	
Good	50%	(5.0)	2.5	2.5	2.5	2.5	$2.92
Bad	50%	(5.0)	1.2	1.2	1.2	1.2	(1.20)

Expected NPV	$0.864
Standard deviation	$2.060
Coefficient of variation	2.38

Delay Decision: Invest Only If Conditions Are Good

Conditions	Probability	END-OF-PERIOD CASH FLOWS:						NPV @ 10%
		2006	2007	2008	2009	2010	2011	
Good	50%	Delay	(5.0)	2.5	2.5	2.5	2.5	$2.92
Bad but irrelevant	50%	Delay	0.0	0.0	0.0	0.0	0.0	0.00

Expected NPV	$1.462
Standard deviation	$1.462
Coefficient of variation	1.00
Discount expected NPV 1 year to make it comparable to "Invest Now" NPV	$1.329
Expected NPV with the timing option	$1.329
Expected NPV without the timing option	0.864
Difference = Timing option value	$0.465

---

associated with being the first supplier in a new line of business, and this could reduce the cash flows. On the other hand, as we saw in the preceding example, waiting may enable the company to avoid a costly mistake. In general, the more uncertainty there is about future market conditions, the more attractive it becomes to wait, but this risk reduction may be offset by the loss of the "first mover advantage." Again, any such first mover advantage can be compared with the value of the option.

Briefly describe what investment timing options are and why they are valuable.

Explain why the following statement is true: "In general, the more uncertainty there is about future market conditions, the more attractive it is to delay the decision."

Growth Option
If an investment creates the opportunity to make other potentially profitable investments that would not otherwise be possible, then the investment is said to contain a growth option.

13-4 GROWTH OPTIONS

We can illustrate **growth options** with a distribution center in mainland China being considered by the Crum Corporation. An investment of $3 million would be required at t = 0. Under good conditions the project would generate cash flows of $1.5 million during each of the next 3 years (t = 1, 2, and 3), but under

TABLE 13-3	*Analysis of a Growth Option (Dollars in Millions)*

Project without the Growth Option

		END-OF-PERIOD CASH FLOWS:				
		0	1	2	3	NPV @ 12%
Good	50%	(3.00)	1.50	1.50	1.50	$0.603
Bad	50%	(3.00)	0.75	0.75	0.75	(1.199)
					Expected NPV	($0.298)

Project with the Growth Option

			END-OF-PERIOD CASH FLOWS:				
			0	1	2	3	NPV @ 12%
Good	Distribution Center	50%	(3.00)	1.50	1.50	1.50	
	New Investment				(10.00)	20.00	
			(3.00)	1.50	(8.50)	21.50	$6.866
Bad	Distribution Center	50%	(3.00)	0.75	0.75	0.75	(1.199)
					Total expected NPV		$2.834

Expected NPV with growth	$2.834
Expected NPV without growth	(0.298)
Difference = Growth option value	$3.132

bad conditions its cash flows would be only $0.75 million. There is a 50 percent probability of each outcome. Crum uses a WACC of 12 percent for international investments.

As shown in the top section of Table 13-3, the distribution center's NPV is −$0.298 million, so under a traditional analysis it would be rejected. However, Crum believes that if it invests in the distribution center and conditions are good, it will gain experience that will give it the opportunity to make another investment in China. The new venture would cost $10 million at t = 2, and it could be sold for cash one year after it is completed, at t = 3, for $20 million.

As we show in the top section of the table, taken alone the distribution center does not appear to be a good investment. However, when the growth opportunity is considered, the project has a positive NPV and thus should be accepted.

 If a firm fails to consider growth options, would this cause it to underestimate or overestimate projects' NPVs? Explain.

13-5 FLEXIBILITY OPTIONS

Many projects offer **flexibility options** that permit the firm to alter operations depending on how conditions change during the project's life. Typically, inputs, outputs, or both can be changed. BMW's Spartanburg, South Carolina, auto assembly plant provides a good example of a flexibility option. BMW needed

Flexibility Option
An investment that permits operations to be altered depending on how conditions change during a project's life.

the plant to produce sports coupes. If it built the plant configured optimally to produce these vehicles, the construction cost would be minimized. However, the company thought that later on it might want to switch production to some other type of vehicle, and that would be difficult if the plant were designed just for coupes. Therefore, BMW decided to spend additional funds to construct a more flexible plant, one that could produce several different models should demand patterns shift. Sure enough, things did change. The demand for coupes dropped, while the demand for sports utility vehicles soared. But BMW was ready, and the Spartanburg plant is now spewing out hot-selling SUVs. The plant's cash flows are much higher than they would have been without the flexibility option that BMW "bought" by building a more flexible plant.

Electric utilities provide a good example of building input flexibility into capital budgeting projects. Utilities can build plants that generate electricity by burning coal, oil, or natural gas. The prices of those fuels change over time depending on developments such as actions in Iraq or Iran, changing environmental policies, and weather conditions. Some years ago, virtually all power plants were designed to burn one type of fuel because this resulted in the lowest construction cost. However, as fuel cost volatility increased, power companies began to build higher-cost but more flexible plants, especially ones that could switch from oil to gas and back again, depending on relative fuel prices.

Flexibility options tend to reduce the risk of a bad outcome, and this increases the expected NPV and reduces risk. Of course, flexibility options do have costs, but those costs can be compared with the benefits of the options as we have demonstrated in the examples presented earlier.

What are "input flexibility options" and "output flexibility options?"

How do flexibility options affect projects' NPVs and risk?

13-6 COMPARING MUTUALLY EXCLUSIVE PROJECTS WITH UNEQUAL LIVES

If a company is choosing between two mutually exclusive projects with significantly different lives, an adjustment may be necessary. For example, suppose BQC is planning to modernize a distribution center, and it is choosing between a conveyor system (Project C) and a fleet of forklift trucks (Project F). Figure 13-1, Part I, shows the traditional analysis that might be used to analyze the two projects. We see that Project C, when discounted at a 12 percent WACC, has the higher NPV and thus it appears to be the better project.

However, the traditional analysis is incomplete, and the decision to choose Project C is actually incorrect. If we choose Project F, we will have an opportunity (a real option) to make a similar investment in three years, and if cost and revenue conditions remain at the Part I levels, this second investment will also be profitable. If we choose Project C, we will not have the option to make this second investment. Therefore, to make a proper comparison between C and F we must make an adjustment. There are two methods for making the adjustment and we discuss them in the remainder of this section.

13-6a Replacement Chains

First, we could apply the **replacement chain (common life) approach** as shown in Part II of Figure 13-1. This involves finding the NPV of Project F over six years, which is the life of Project C, and then comparing this extended NPV with

Replacement Chain (Common Life) Approach
A method of comparing projects with unequal lives that assumes that each project can be repeated as many times as necessary to reach a common life span; the NPVs over this life span are then compared, and the project with the higher common-life NPV is chosen.

| FIGURE 13-1 | *Analysis of Mutually Exclusive Projects with Unequal Lives* |

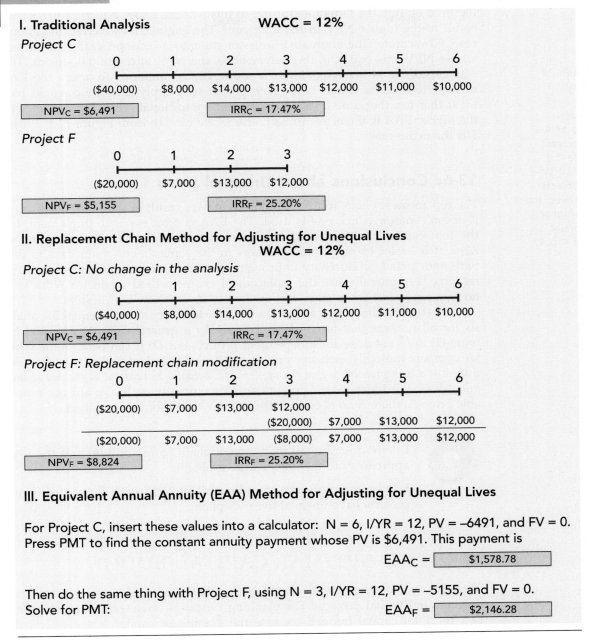

I. Traditional Analysis WACC = 12%

Project C

0	1	2	3	4	5	6
($40,000)	$8,000	$14,000	$13,000	$12,000	$11,000	$10,000

NPV$_C$ = $6,491   IRR$_C$ = 17.47%

Project F

0	1	2	3
($20,000)	$7,000	$13,000	$12,000

NPV$_F$ = $5,155   IRR$_F$ = 25.20%

II. Replacement Chain Method for Adjusting for Unequal Lives
WACC = 12%

Project C: No change in the analysis

0	1	2	3	4	5	6
($40,000)	$8,000	$14,000	$13,000	$12,000	$11,000	$10,000

NPV$_C$ = $6,491   IRR$_C$ = 17.47%

Project F: Replacement chain modification

0	1	2	3	4	5	6
($20,000)	$7,000	$13,000	$12,000			
			($20,000)	$7,000	$13,000	$12,000
($20,000)	$7,000	$13,000	($8,000)	$7,000	$13,000	$12,000

NPV$_F$ = $8,824   IRR$_F$ = 25.20%

III. Equivalent Annual Annuity (EAA) Method for Adjusting for Unequal Lives

For Project C, insert these values into a calculator: N = 6, I/YR = 12, PV = –6491, and FV = 0. Press PMT to find the constant annuity payment whose PV is $6,491. This payment is

EAA$_C$ = $1,578.78

Then do the same thing with Project F, using N = 3, I/YR = 12, PV = –5155, and FV = 0. Solve for PMT:

EAA$_F$ = $2,146.28

the NPV of Project C over the same six years. We see that on a common life basis F turns out to be the better project.[5]

13-6b Equivalent Annual Annuities (EAA)

Electrical engineers designing power plants and distribution lines were the first to encounter the unequal life problem. They could use transformers and other

---

[5] In this case, we only need to extend F's life out for one replacement. However, if C had a life of seven years and F had a life of three years it would have been necessary to go out to Year 21, using three replacements for C and seven for F, in order to reach a common life span.

equipment that had relatively low initial costs but short lives, or they could use equipment that had higher initial costs but longer lives. The services would be required on into the indefinite future, so this was the issue: Which choice would result in the higher NPV in the long run? The engineers converted the annual cash flows under the alternative investments into a constant cash flow stream whose NPV was equal to, or equivalent to, the NPV of the initial stream. This was called the **equivalent annual annuity (EAA) method.** To apply the EAA method to Projects C and F, for each project we simply find the constant payment that has the same NPV as the project's traditional NPV. The project with the higher EAA is the better project, and as we can see from Figure 13-1, Project F is the better one.

Equivalent Annual Annuity (EAA) Method
A method that calculates the annual payments a project would provide if it were an annuity. When comparing projects with unequal lives, the one with the higher equivalent annual annuity (EAA) should be chosen.

13-6c Conclusions about Unequal Lives

The replacement chain and EAA methods always result in the same decision, so it doesn't matter which one is used. The EAA is a bit easier to implement, but the replacement chain method is often easier to explain to senior managers. Also, it is easier to make modifications to the replacement chain data to deal with anticipated productivity improvements and asset price changes. For these reasons, we generally use the replacement chain method when we work with nonengineers, but when engineers are involved, we show both results.

Another question often arises: Do we have to worry about unequal life analysis for all projects that have unequal lives? As a general rule, the unequal life issue (1) does not arise for independent projects but (2) it can be an issue when we compare mutually exclusive projects with significantly different lives, but *only if there is a high probability that the projects will actually be repeated at the end of their initial lives.* For independent projects and for mutually exclusive but not repeatable projects, there is no need to make an adjustment for unequal lives.

Briefly describe the replacement chain (common life) and the EAA approaches to the unequal life problem.

Is it always necessary to adjust all projects' cash flows if different projects have unequal lives? Explain.

13-7 THE OPTIMAL CAPITAL BUDGET

Thus far we have described various factors that managers consider when they evaluate individual projects. For planning purposes, managers must also forecast the total capital budget, because the amount of capital raised affects the WACC and thus influences projects' NPVs. We use Automotive Products Inc. (API), a manufacturer and distributor of auto parts, to illustrate how this process works in practice.

Step 1. The treasurer obtains an estimate of the firm's overall composite WACC. As we discussed in Chapter 10, this composite WACC is based on market conditions, the firm's capital structure, and the riskiness of its assets. API's projects are roughly similar from year to year in terms of their risks.

Step 2. The corporate WACC is scaled up or down for each of the firm's divisions to reflect the division's capital structure and risk characteristics.

API, for example, assigns a factor of 0.9 to its stable, low-risk replacement battery division, but a factor of 1.1 to its auto frame division, which sells to new car manufacturers and whose business is extremely competitive. Therefore, if the corporate cost of capital is determined to be 10.50 percent, the cost of capital for the battery division is 0.9(10.50%) = 9.45%, while that for the frame division is 1.1(10.50%) = 11.55%.

Step 3. Financial managers within each of the firm's divisions estimate the relevant cash flows and risks of each of their potential projects. The estimated cash flows should explicitly consider any embedded real options, which include opportunities to repeat the projects at a later date. Then, within each division, projects are classified into one of three groups—high risk, average risk, and low risk—and the same 0.9 and 1.1 factors are used to adjust the divisional cost of capital estimates. (A factor of 1 would be used for an average-risk project.) For example, a low-risk project in the battery division would be assigned a cost of capital of 0.9(9.45%) = 8.51%, while a high-risk project in the frame division would have a cost of 1.1(11.55%) = 12.71%.

Step 4. Each project's NPV is then determined, using its risk-adjusted cost of capital. The optimal capital budget consists of all independent projects with positive NPVs plus those mutually exclusive projects with the highest positive NPVs.

In estimating its **optimal capital budget**, we assumed that API will be able to obtain financing for all of its profitable projects. This assumption is reasonable for large, mature firms with good track records. However, smaller firms, new firms, and firms with dubious track records may have difficulties raising capital, even for projects that the firm concludes would have highly positive NPVs. In such circumstances, the size of the firm's capital budget may be constrained, a situation called **capital rationing.** In such situations capital is limited, so it should be used in the most efficient way possible. Procedures have been explored for allocating capital so as to maximize the firm's aggregate NPV subject to the constraint that the capital rationing ceiling is not exceeded. However, these procedures are extremely complicated, so they are best left for advanced finance courses.

The procedures discussed in this section cannot be implemented with much precision. However, they do force the firm to think carefully about each division's relative risk, about the risk of each project within the divisions, and about the relationship between the total amount of capital raised and the cost of that capital. Further, the process forces the firm to adjust its capital budget to reflect capital market conditions. If the costs of debt and equity rise, this fact will be reflected in the cost of capital used to evaluate projects, and projects that would be marginally acceptable when capital costs were low would (correctly) be ruled unacceptable when capital costs become high.

Optimal Capital Budget
The annual investment in long-term assets that maximizes the firm's value.

Capital Rationing
The situation in which a firm can raise only a specified, limited amount of capital regardless of how many good projects it has.

Explain how a financial manager might estimate his or her firm's optimal capital budget.

What is capital rationing?

What factors must be considered when a firm is developing its optimal capital budget?

How does a firm's annual capital budget reflect market conditions?

Tying It All Together

This chapter and the previous three focused on capital budgeting. Chapter 10 described how a company estimates its cost of capital. Then, Chapter 11 described several methods used to evaluate projects. We concluded that NPV is the best single method, but IRR, MIRR, and payback all provide information that managers find useful. Next, Chapter 12 described techniques for estimating project cash flows and risk. Finally, here in Chapter 13 we discussed some topics that go beyond the simple capital budgeting framework, including the analysis of projects with real options and mutually exclusive projects with unequal lives. Chapter 13 also discussed the optimal capital budget, the relationship between the total capital budget and WACCs for individual projects, and capital rationing. We go on, in the following chapters, to discuss how the optimal capital structure is determined and the effect of this capital structure on the firm's cost of capital, on its optimal capital budget, and consequently, on its dividend policy.

SELF-TEST QUESTIONS AND PROBLEMS
(Solutions Appear in Appendix A)

ST-1 **Key terms** Define each of the following terms:
a. Real option; option value
b. Abandonment option; investment timing option
c. Growth option; flexibility option
d. Replacement chain (common life)
e. Equivalent annual annuity (EAA)
f. Optimal capital budget
g. Capital rationing

ST-2 **Abandonment option** Your firm is considering a project with the following cash flows:

		PREDICTED CASH FLOW FOR EACH YEAR			
		0	1	2	3
Best case	25%	($25,000)	$18,000	$18,000	$18,000
Base case	50%	(25,000)	12,000	12,000	12,000
Worst case	25%	(25,000)	(8,000)	(8,000)	(8,000)

You learn that the firm can abandon the project, if it so chooses, after one year of operation, in which case it can sell the asset and receive $15,000 in cash at the end of Year 2. Assume that all cash flows are after-tax amounts. The WACC is 12 percent.
a. What is the project's NPV if the abandonment option is not considered?
b. What is the NPV considering abandonment?
c. What is the value of the abandonment option?

ST-3 **Projects with unequal lives** Wisconsin Dairy Co. is currently deciding on its capital budget for the upcoming year. Among the projects being considered are 2 machines, W and WW. W costs $500,000 and will produce expected after-tax cash flows of $300,000 during the next 2 years. WW also costs $500,000, but it will produce after-tax cash flows of $165,000 during the next 4 years. Both projects have a 10 percent WACC.

a. If the projects are independent and not repeatable, which project or projects should the company accept?

b. If the projects are mutually exclusive but not repeatable, which project should the company accept?

c. Assume the projects are mutually exclusive and can be repeated indefinitely.
   (1) Use the replacement chain method to determine the NPV of the project selected.
   (2) Use the equivalent annual annuity method to determine the annuity of the project selected.

d. Could a replacement chain analysis be modified for use where the project's cash flows are different each time it is repeated? Explain.

QUESTIONS

13-1 Explain in general terms what each of the following real options is and how it could change projects' NPVs, relative to what would have been estimated if the options were not considered, and their corresponding risk.

a. Abandonment.
b. Timing.
c. Growth.
d Flexibility.

13-2 Would a failure to recognize growth options cause a firm's actual capital budget to be above or below the optimal level? Would your answer be the same for abandonment, timing, and flexibility options? Explain.

13-3 Companies often have to increase their investment costs to obtain real options. Why might this be so, and how could a firm decide if it was worth the cost to obtain a given real option?

13-4 What's a "replacement chain?" When and how are replacement chains used in capital budgeting?

13-5 What's an "equivalent annual annuity (EAA)?" When and how are EAAs used in capital budgeting?

13-6 Suppose a firm is considering two mutually exclusive projects. One has a life of 6 years and the other a life of 10 years. Both projects can be repeated at the end of their lives. Might the failure to employ a replacement chain or EAA analysis bias the decision toward one of the projects? If so, which one, and why?

13-7 How might the corporate WACC be affected by the size of a firm's capital budget?

13-8 What is capital rationing?

PROBLEMS

Easy
Problems 1–5

13-1 **Growth option** Martin Development Co. is deciding whether to proceed with Project X. The cost would be $9 million in Year 0. There is a 50 percent chance that X would be hugely successful and would generate annual after-tax cash flows of $6 million per year during Years 1, 2, and 3. However, there is a 50 percent chance that X would be less successful and would generate only $1 million per year for the 3 years. If Project X is hugely successful, it would open the door to another investment, Project Y, that would require a $10 million outlay at the end of Year 2. Project Y would then be sold to another company at a price of $20 million at the end of Year 3. Martin's WACC is 11 percent.

a. If the company does not consider real options, what is Project X's NPV?
b. What is X's NPV considering the growth option?
c. How valuable is the growth option?

13-2 **Projects with unequal lives** Haley's Graphic Designs Inc. is considering two mutually exclusive projects. Both require an initial investment of $10,000, and their risks are average for the firm. Project A has an expected life of 2 years with after-tax cash inflows of $6,000 and $8,000 at the end of Years 1 and 2, respectively. Project B has an expected life of 4 years with after-tax cash inflows of $4,000 at the end of each of the next 4 years. The firm's WACC is 10 percent.

    a.   If the projects cannot be repeated, which project should be selected if Haley uses NPV as its criterion for project selection?

    b.   Assume the projects can be repeated and that there are no anticipated changes in the cash flows. Use the replacement chain analysis to determine the NPV of the project selected.

    c.   Make the same assumptions in part b. Use the equivalent annual method to determine the annuity of the project selected.

13-3 **Replacement chain** Cotner Clothes Inc. is considering the replacement of its old, fully depreciated knitting machine. Two new models are available: Machine 190-3, which has a cost of $190,000, a 3-year expected life, and after-tax cash flows (labor savings and depreciation) of $87,000 per year; and Machine 360-6, which has a cost of $360,000, a 6-year life, and after-tax cash flows of $98,300 per year. Assume that both projects can be repeated. Knitting machine prices are not expected to rise, because inflation will be offset by cheaper components (microprocessors) used in the machines. Assume that Cotner's WACC is 14 percent. Should the firm replace its old knitting machine, and, if so, which new machine should it use?

13-4 **Equivalent annual annuity** Corcoran Consulting is deciding which of two computer systems to purchase. They can purchase state-of-the-art equipment (System A) for $20,000, which will generate cash flows of $6,000 at the end of each of the next 6 years. Alternatively, they can spend $12,000 for equipment that can be used for 3 years and generates cash flows of $6,000 at the end of each year (System B). If the company's WACC is 10 percent and both "projects" can be repeated indefinitely, which system should be chosen and what is its EAA?

13-5 **Optimal capital budget** Marble Construction estimates that its WACC is 10 percent if equity comes from retained earnings. However, if the company issues new stock to raise new equity, it estimates that its WACC will rise to 10.8 percent. The company believes that it will exhaust its retained earnings at $2,500,000 of capital due to the number of highly profitable projects available to the firm and its limited earnings. The company is considering the following seven investment projects:

Project	Size	IRR
A	$ 650,000	14.0%
B	1,050,000	13.5
C	1,000,000	11.2
D	1,200,000	11.0
E	500,000	10.7
F	650,000	10.3
G	700,000	10.2

Assume that each of these projects is independent and that each is just as risky as the firm's existing assets. Which set of projects should be accepted, and what is the firm's optimal capital budget?

Intermediate Problems 6–9

13-6 **Replacement chain** Zappe Airlines is considering two alternative planes. Plane A has an expected life of 5 years, will cost $100 million, and will produce net cash flows of $30 million per year. Plane B has a life of 10 years, will cost $132 million, and will produce net cash flows of $25 million per year. Zappe plans to serve the route for 10 years. The company's WACC is 12 percent. If Zappe needs to purchase a new Plane A, the cost will be $105 million, but cash inflows will remain the same. Should Zappe acquire Plane A or Plane B? Explain your answer.

13-7 **Replacement chain** The Fernandez Company has the opportunity to invest in one of two mutually exclusive machines that will produce a product it will need for the next 8 years. Machine A costs $10 million but would provide after-tax inflows of $4 million per year for 4 years. If Machine A were replaced, its cost would be $12 million due to inflation, and its cash inflows would increase to $4.2 million due to production efficiencies.

Machine B costs $15 million and would provide after-tax inflows of $3.5 million per year for 8 years. If the WACC is 10 percent, which machine should be acquired?

13-8 **Equivalent annual annuity** A firm has two mutually exclusive investment projects to evaluate. The projects have the following cash flows:

Time	Project X	Project Y
0	($100,000)	($70,000)
1	30,000	30,000
2	50,000	30,000
3	70,000	30,000
4	—	30,000
5	—	10,000

Projects X and Y are equally risky and may be repeated indefinitely. If the firm's WACC is 12 percent, what is the EAA of the project that adds the most value to the firm? (Round your final answer to the nearest whole dollar.)

13-9 **Investment timing option** Digital Inc. is considering production of a new cell phone. The project would require an investment of $20 million. If the phone were well received, then the project would produce cash flows of $10 million a year for 3 years, but if the market did not like the product, then the cash flows would be only $5 million per year. There is a 50 percent probability of both good and bad market conditions. Digital could delay the project for a year while it conducts a test to determine if demand would be strong or weak. The delay would not affect either the project's cost or its cash flows. Digital's WACC is 10 percent. What action would you recommend?

Challenging Problems 10–13

13-10 **Abandonment option** The Scampini Supplies Company recently purchased a new delivery truck. The new truck costs $22,500, and it is expected to generate after-tax cash flows, including depreciation, of $6,250 per year. The truck has a 5-year expected life. The expected year-end abandonment values (salvage values after tax adjustments) for the truck are given here. The company's WACC is 10 percent.

Year	Annual After-Tax Cash Flow	Abandonment Value
0	($22,500)	—
1	6,250	$17,500
2	6,250	14,000
3	6,250	11,000
4	6,250	5,000
5	6,250	0

a. Should the firm operate the truck until the end of its 5-year physical life; if not, what is its optimal economic life?

b. Would the introduction of abandonment values, in addition to operating cash flows, ever *reduce* the expected NPV and/or IRR of a project? Explain.

13-11 **Optimal capital budget** Hampton Manufacturing estimates that its WACC is 12 percent if equity comes from retained earnings. However, if the company issues new stock to raise new equity, it estimates that its WACC will rise to 12.5 percent. The company believes that it will exhaust its retained earnings at $3,250,000 of capital due to the number of highly profitable projects available to the firm and its limited earnings. The company is considering the following 7 investment projects:

Project	Size	IRR
A	$ 750,000	14.0%
B	1,250,000	13.5
C	1,250,000	13.2
D	1,250,000	13.0
E	750,000	12.7
F	750,000	12.3
G	750,000	12.2

a. Assume that each of these projects is independent and that each is just as risky as the firm's existing assets. Which set of projects should be accepted, and what is the firm's optimal capital budget?

b. Now, assume that Projects C and D are mutually exclusive. Project D has an NPV of $400,000, whereas Project C has an NPV of $350,000. Which set of projects should be accepted, and what is the firm's optimal capital budget?

c. Ignore part b, and now assume that each of the projects is independent but that management decides to incorporate project risk differentials. Management judges Projects B, C, D, and E to have average risk, Project A to have high risk, and Projects F and G to have low risk. The company adds 2 percent to the WACC of those projects that are significantly more risky than average, and it subtracts 2 percent from the WACC for those that are substantially less risky than average. Which set of projects should be accepted, and what is the firm's optimal capital budget?

13-12 Investment timing option The Bush Oil Company is deciding whether to drill for oil on a tract of land that the company owns. The company estimates that the project would cost $8 million today. Bush estimates that once drilled, the oil will generate positive net cash flows of $4 million a year at the end of each of the next 4 years. While the company is fairly confident about its cash flow forecast, it recognizes that if it waits 2 years, it would have more information about the local geology as well as the price of oil. Bush estimates that if it waits 2 years, the project would cost $9 million. Moreover, if it waits 2 years, there is a 90 percent chance that the net cash flows would be $4.2 million a year for 4 years, and there is a 10 percent chance that the cash flows would be $2.2 million a year for 4 years. Assume that all cash flows are discounted at 10 percent.

a. If the company chooses to drill today, what is the project's net present value?
b. Would it make sense to wait 2 years before deciding whether to drill? Explain.
c. What is the value of the investment timing option?
d. What disadvantages might arise from delaying a project like this drilling project?

13-13 Real options Nevada Enterprises is considering buying a vacant lot that sells for $1.2 million. If the property is purchased, the company's plan is to spend another $5 million today (t = 0) to build a hotel on the property. The after-tax cash flows from the hotel will depend critically on whether the state imposes a tourism tax in this year's legislative session. If the tax is imposed, the hotel is expected to produce after-tax cash inflows of $600,000 at the end of each of the next 15 years. If the tax is not imposed, the hotel is expected to produce after-tax cash inflows of $1,200,000 at the end of each of the next 15 years. The project has a 12 percent WACC. Assume at the outset that the company does not have the option to delay the project.

a. What is the project's expected NPV if the tax is imposed?
b. What is the project's expected NPV if the tax is not imposed?
c. Given that there is a 50 percent chance that the tax will be imposed, what is the project's expected NPV if they proceed with it today?
d. While the company does not have an option to delay construction, it does have the option to abandon the project 1 year from now if the tax is imposed. If it abandons the project, it would sell the complete property 1 year from now at an expected price of $6 million. Once the project is abandoned the company would no longer receive any cash inflows from it. Assuming that all cash flows are discounted at 12 percent, would the existence of this abandonment option affect the company's decision to proceed with the project today? Explain.
e. Finally, assume that there is no option to abandon or delay the project, but that the company has an option to purchase an adjacent property in 1 year at a price of $1.5 million. If the tourism tax is imposed, the net present value of developing this property (as of t = 1) is only $300,000 (so it wouldn't make sense to purchase the property for $1.5 million). However, if the tax is not imposed, the net present value of the future opportunities from developing the property would be $4 million (as of t = 1). Thus, under this scenario it would make sense to purchase the property for $1.5 million. Assume that these cash flows are discounted at 12 percent and the probability that the tax will be imposed is still 50 percent. How much would the company pay today for the option to purchase this property 1 year from now for $1.5 million?

COMPREHENSIVE/SPREADSHEET PROBLEMS

13-14 Real options Use a spreadsheet model to evaluate the project analyzed in Problem 13-13.

13-15 Real options Bankers' Services Inc. (BSI) is considering a project that has a cost of $10 million and an expected life of 3 years. There is a 30 percent probability of good conditions, in which case the project will provide a cash flow of $9 million at the end of each year for 3 years. There is a 40 percent probability of average conditions, in which case the annual cash flows will be $4.5 million, and there is a 30 percent probability of bad conditions and a cash flow of −$1.5 million per year. BSI can, if it chooses, close down the project at the end of any year and sell the related assets for 90 percent of the book value. The asset sale price will be received at the end of the year the project is shut down. The related assets will be depreciated by the straight-line method over 3 years, and the value at the end of Year 3 is zero. (Don't worry about IRS regulations for this problem.) BSI uses a 12 percent WACC to evaluate projects like this.

a. Find the project's expected NPV with and without the abandonment option.

b. How sensitive is the NPV to changes in the company's WACC? To the percentage of book value at which the asset can be sold?

c. Now assume that the project cannot be shut down. However, expertise gained by taking it on will lead to an opportunity at the end of Year 3 to undertake a venture that would have the same cost as the original project, and would be undertaken if the best-case scenario developed. If the project is wildly successful (the good conditions), the firm will go ahead with the project, but it will not go ahead if the other two scenarios occur (because consumer demand will still be considered too difficult to determine). As a result, the new project would generate the same cash flows as the original project in the best-case scenario. In other words, there would be a second $10 million cost at the end of Year 3, and then cash flows of $9 million for the following 3 years. This new project could also not be abandoned if it is under-taken. How does this new information affect the original project's expected NPV? At what WACC would the project break even in the sense that NPV = $0?

d. Now suppose the original (no abandonment) project could be delayed a year. All the cash flows would remain unchanged, but information obtained during that year would tell the company exactly which set of demand conditions existed. How does this option to delay the project affect its NPV?

Integrated Case

21st Century Educational Products

13-16 Other topics in capital budgeting 21st Century Educational Products is a rapidly growing software company, and, consistent with its growth, it has a relatively large capital budget. While most of the company's projects are fairly easy to evaluate, a handful of projects involve more complex evaluations.

John Keller, a senior member of the company's finance staff, coordinates the evaluation of these more complex projects. His group brings their recommendations directly to the company's CFO and CEO, Kristin Riley and Bob Stevens, respectively.

a. In recent months, Keller's group has begun to focus on real option analysis.
  (1) What is real option analysis?
  (2) What are some examples of projects with embedded real options?

b. Considering real options, one of Keller's colleagues, Barbara Hudson, has suggested that instead of investing in Project X today, it might make sense to wait a year because 21st Century would learn a lot more about market conditions and would be better able to forecast the project's cash flows. Right now, 21st Century forecasts that Project X, which will last 4 years, will generate expected annual net cash flows of $33,500. However, if the company waits a year, it will learn more about market conditions. There is a 50 percent chance that the market will be strong and a 50 percent chance it will be weak. If the market is strong, the annual cash flows will be $43,500. If the market is weak, the annual cash flows will be only $23,500. If 21st Century chooses to wait a year, the initial investment will remain $100,000. Assume that all cash flows are discounted at 10 percent. Should 21st Century invest in Project X today, or should it wait a year before deciding whether to invest in the project?

c. Now let's assume that there is more uncertainty about the future cash flows. More specifically, assume that the annual cash flows are now $53,500 if the market is strong and $13,500 if the market is weak. Assume that the up-front cost is still $100,000 and that the WACC is still 10 percent. Will this increased uncertainty make the firm more or less willing to invest in the project today?

d.   21st Century is considering another project, Project Y. Project Y has an up-front cost of $200,000 and an economic life of 3 years. If the company develops the project, its after-tax operating costs will be $100,000 a year; however, the project is expected to produce after-tax cash inflows of $180,000 a year. Thus, the project's estimated cash flows are as follows:

Year	Cash Outflows	Cash Inflows	Net Cash Flows
0	($200,000)	$ 0	($200,000)
1	(100,000)	180,000	80,000
2	(100,000)	180,000	80,000
3	(100,000)	180,000	80,000

(1) The project has an estimated WACC of 10 percent. What is the project's NPV?

(2) While the project's operating costs are fairly certain at $100,000 per year, the estimated cash inflows depend critically on whether 21st Century's largest customer uses the product. Keller estimates that there is a 60 percent chance the customer will use the product, in which case the project will produce after-tax cash inflows of $250,000. Thus, its net cash flows would be $150,000 per year. However, there is a 40 percent chance the customer will not use the product, in which case the project will produce after-tax cash inflows of only $75,000. Thus, its net cash flows would be −$25,000. Write out the estimated cash flows, and calculate the project's NPV under each of the two scenarios.

(3) While 21st Century does not have the option to delay the project, it will know 1 year from now if the key customer has selected the product. If the customer chooses not to adopt the product, 21st Century has the option to abandon the project. If it abandons the project, it will not receive any cash flows after Year 1, and it will not incur any operating costs after Year 1. Thus, if the company chooses to abandon the project, its estimated cash flows are as follows:

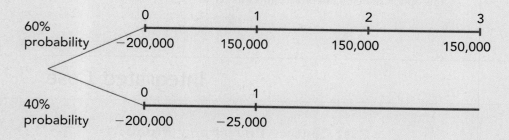

Again, assuming a WACC of 10 percent, what is the project's expected NPV if it abandons the project? Should 21st Century invest in Project Y today, realizing it has the option to abandon the project at t = 1?

(4) Up until now we have assumed that the abandonment option has not affected the project's WACC. Is this assumption reasonable? How might the abandonment option affect the WACC?

e.   21st Century is also considering Project Z. Project Z has an up-front cost of $500,000, and it is expected to produce after-tax cash inflows of $100,000 at the end of each of the next 5 years (t = 1, 2, 3, 4, and 5). Because Project Z has a WACC of 12 percent, it clearly has a negative NPV. However, Keller and his group recognize that if 21st Century goes ahead with Project Z today, there is a 10 percent chance that this will lead to subsequent opportunities that have a net present value at t = 5 equal to $3,000,000. At the same time, there is a 90 percent chance that the subsequent opportunities will have a negative net present value (−$1,000,000) at t = 5. On the basis of their knowledge of real options, Keller and his group understand that the company will choose to develop these subsequent opportunities only if they appear to be profitable at t = 5. Given this information, should 21st Century invest in Project Z today?

f. Keller's group is looking at a variety of other interesting projects. For example, the group has been asked to choose between the following two mutually exclusive projects:

	EXPECTED NET CASH FLOWS	
Year	Project S	Project L
0	($100,000)	($100,000)
1	59,000	33,500
2	59,000	33,500
3	—	33,500
4	—	33,500

Both projects may be repeated and both are of average risk, so they should be evaluated at the firm's WACC, 10 percent. Using both the replacement chain and equivalent annual annuity methods, which project should be chosen?

cyberproblem

Please go to the ThomsonNOW Web site to access the Cyberproblems.

PART 5

CAPITAL STRUCTURE AND DIVIDEND POLICY

CAPITAL STRUCTURE AND LEVERAGE

Debt: Rocket Booster or Anchor?

If it is to grow, a firm needs capital, and that capital can come in the form of debt or equity. Debt financing has two important advantages: (1) Interest paid on debt is tax deductible, whereas dividends paid on stock are not deductible. This lowers debt's relative cost. (2) The return on debt is fixed, so stockholders do not have to share the firm's profits if it is extremely successful.

However, debt also has disadvantages: (1) Using more debt increases the firm's risk, which raises the costs of both debt and equity. (2) If the company falls on hard times and its operating income is not sufficient to cover interest charges, the stockholders will have to make up the shortfall; if they cannot, the firm will go bankrupt. Good times may be just around the corner, but too much debt can keep the company from getting there and thus can wipe out the stockholders' equity.

Because of these factors, companies with volatile earnings and operating cash flows tend to limit their use of debt. On the other hand, companies with less business risk and more stable operating cash flows can take on more debt. Kellogg Co., the world's largest cereal manufacturer, is a good example of a company that uses a lot of debt financing. Indeed, just after its acquisition of Keebler Food Co., Kellogg's capital structure consisted of 86 percent debt and 14 percent equity. An 86 percent debt ratio is quite high, though, and Kellogg's management was well aware that high debt can push an otherwise well-regarded company into bankruptcy. Aware of this possibility, Kellogg's management began to pay down its debt and restore its balance sheet to a more "reasonable" level, so by mid-2005 its debt ratio had stabilized at about 60 percent.

For many companies, a 60 percent debt ratio would still be considered quite high. However, because its business is so stable, this ratio is not too bad for

Kellogg. After all, the consumption of Frosted Flakes and Pop Tarts has remained stable even during economic downturns. Moreover, if we examine Kellogg's capital structure in more detail, it soon becomes apparent that there is more here than meets the eye. According to its balance sheet, Kellogg has about $4.8 billion of total debt versus stockholders' equity of about $2.8 billion. But in June 2005, the market capitalization of Kellogg's equity (which is simply the stock price times the number of shares outstanding) was approximately $17.7 billion. From a market value perspective, Kellogg's capital structure ($4.8 billion of debt and $17.7 billion of equity) is much more conservative, which helps explain why the company has a relatively strong BBB+ level bond rating.

Kellogg and other companies can finance with either debt or equity. Is one better than the other? If so, should firms be financed either with all debt or all equity? If the best solution is some mix of debt and equity, what is the optimal mix? As you read the chapter, think about these questions and consider how you would answer them.

Putting Things In Perspective

When we calculated the weighted average cost of capital (WACC) in Chapter 10 we assumed that the firm had a specific target capital structure. However, the target capital structure may change over time, such a change will affect the risk and cost of each type of capital, and all this can change the WACC. Moreover, a change in the WACC can affect capital budgeting decisions and, ultimately, the firm's stock price.

Many factors influence capital structure decisions, and, as we will see, determining the optimal capital structure is not an exact science. Therefore, even firms in the same industry often have dramatically different capital structures. In this chapter we consider the effects of debt on risk and thus on the optimal capital structure.

*Two video clips of Steve Walsh, Assistant Treasurer at JCPenney, talking about capital structure are available at **http://fisher.osu.edu/fin/clips.htm**. The first clip on capital structure discusses the cost of capital and debt, while the second clip discusses the optimal capital structure as seen by JCPenney relative to the capital structure theory as seen by Modigliani/Miller.*

14-1 THE TARGET CAPITAL STRUCTURE

A firm's **optimal capital structure** is defined as the structure that would maximize its stock price. It is useful to analyze the situation and seek to determine the optimal structure, but in practice it is difficult to estimate it with much confidence. As a result, in practice we tend to think of the optimal capital structure more as a range, say, from 40 to 50 percent debt, rather than as a precise number, say, 45 percent. Firms generally study the situation, reach a conclusion as to the optimal structure, and then set a **target capital structure**, perhaps a fixed number such as 45 percent debt. Then, if the actual debt ratio is below the target

Optimal Capital Structure
The firm's capital structure that maximizes its stock price.

Target Capital Structure
The mix of debt, preferred stock, and common equity with which the firm plans to raise capital.

level, they would raise capital by issuing debt, whereas if the debt ratio is above the target, equity would be used. The target may change over time as conditions change, but at any given moment, management generally has a specific structure in mind.

Setting the capital structure involves a trade-off between risk and return:

- Using more debt will raise the risk borne by stockholders.
- However, using more debt generally increases the expected return on equity.

The higher risk associated with more debt tends to lower the stock's price, but the higher debt-induced expected rate of return raises it. *Therefore, we seek to find the capital structure that strikes a balance between risk and return so as to maximize the stock price.*

Four primary factors influence capital structure decisions:

1. *Business risk*, or the riskiness inherent in the firm's operations if it used no debt. The greater the firm's business risk, the lower its optimal debt ratio.
2. The firm's *tax position*. A major reason for using debt is that interest is tax deductible, which lowers the effective cost of debt. However, if most of a firm's income is already sheltered from taxes by depreciation tax shields, interest on currently outstanding debt, or tax loss carry-forwards, its tax rate will be low, hence additional debt would not be as advantageous as it would be to a firm with a higher effective tax rate.
3. *Financial flexibility*, or the ability to raise capital on reasonable terms under adverse conditions. Corporate treasurers know that a steady supply of capital is necessary for stable operations, which is vital for long-run success. They also know that when money is tight in the economy, or when a firm is experiencing operating difficulties, it is easier to raise debt than equity capital, and lenders are more willing to accommodate companies with strong balance sheets. Therefore, the potential future need for funds and the consequences of a funds shortage influence the target capital structure—the greater the probability that capital will be needed, and the worse the consequences of not being able to obtain it, the less debt the firm should have on its balance sheet.
4. *Managerial conservatism or aggressiveness*. Some managers are more aggressive than others, hence they are more willing to use debt in an effort to boost profits. This factor does not affect the true optimal, or value-maximizing, capital structure, but it does influence the firm's target capital structure.

These four points largely determine the target capital structure, but operating conditions can cause the actual capital structure to vary from the target. For example, a company's actual stock price might for some reason be well below the intrinsic value as seen by management. In this case, management would be reluctant to issue new stock to raise capital, so it might use debt financing even though this caused the debt ratio to rise above the target level. Presumably, though, the company would take steps to return the capital structure to its target level as soon as the stock price approached its intrinsic value.

Define optimal capital structure and differentiate it from target capital structure.

What four factors influence the target capital structure?

In what sense does setting the target capital structure involve a trade-off between risk and return?

Why might market conditions cause a firm's actual capital structure to vary from its target?

14-2 BUSINESS AND FINANCIAL RISK

In Chapter 8, we examined risk from the viewpoint of an individual investor, and we distinguished between *risk on a stand-alone basis*, where an asset's cash flows are analyzed by themselves, and *risk in a portfolio context*, where the cash flows from a number of assets are combined and then the consolidated cash flows are analyzed. In a portfolio context, we saw that an asset's risk can be divided into two components: *diversifiable risk*, which can be diversified away and hence is of little concern to most investors, and *market risk*, which is measured by the beta coefficient and which reflects broad market movements that cannot be eliminated by diversification and therefore is of concern to all investors. Then, in Chapter 12, we examined risk from the viewpoint of the corporation, and we considered how capital budgeting decisions affect the firm's riskiness.

Now we introduce two new dimensions of risk:

1. *Business risk*, which is the riskiness of the firm's assets if it uses no debt.
2. *Financial risk*, which is the additional risk placed on the common stockholders as a result of using debt.

14-2a Business Risk

Business risk is perhaps the single most important determinant of capital structure. For firms with no debt, business risk can be measured by the variability in the projected return on assets (ROAs). Consider Bigbee Electronics Company, a *debt-free (unlevered)* firm. Because the company has no debt, its ROE is equal to its ROA, and either can be used to estimate business risk. Figure 14-1 gives some clues about the company's business risk. The top graph shows the trend in ROE from 1995 through 2005; this graph gives both security analysts and Bigbee's management an idea of the degree to which ROE has varied in the past and might vary in the future. The lower graph shows the beginning-of-year subjectively estimated probability distribution of Bigbee's ROE for 2005, based on the trend line in the top section of Figure 14-1. As the graphs indicate, Bigbee's actual ROE in 2005 (8 percent) fell below the expected value (12 percent).

Bigbee's past fluctuations in ROE were caused by many factors—booms and recessions in the national economy, successful new products introduced both by Bigbee and by its competitors, labor strikes, a fire in Bigbee's main plant, and so on. Similar events will doubtless occur in the future, and when they do, the realized ROE will be higher or lower than the projected level. Further, there is always the possibility that a long-term disaster will strike, permanently depressing the company's earning power. For example, a competitor might introduce a new product that would make Bigbee's products totally obsolete and put the company out of business. The more uncertainty there is about Bigbee's future ROE, the greater the company's *business risk*. Bigbee uses no debt, so its stockholders bear all of this risk.

Business risk varies from industry to industry and also among firms in a given industry. Further, business risk can change over time. For example, the electric utilities were for many years regarded as having little business risk, but a combination of events in recent years altered the utilities' situation, producing sharp declines in their ROEs and greatly increasing the industry's risk. Today, food processors and health care firms are frequently given as examples of industries with low business risk, while cyclical manufacturing industries such as autos and steel, as well as many small startup companies, are regarded as having especially high business risks.[1]

Business Risk
The riskiness inherent in the firm's operations if it uses no debt.

---

[1] We have avoided any discussion of market versus company-specific risk in this section. We note now (1) that any action that increases business risk in the stand-alone risk sense will generally also increase a firm's beta coefficient and (2) that a part of business risk as we define it will generally be company specific, hence subject to elimination by diversification by the firm's stockholders.

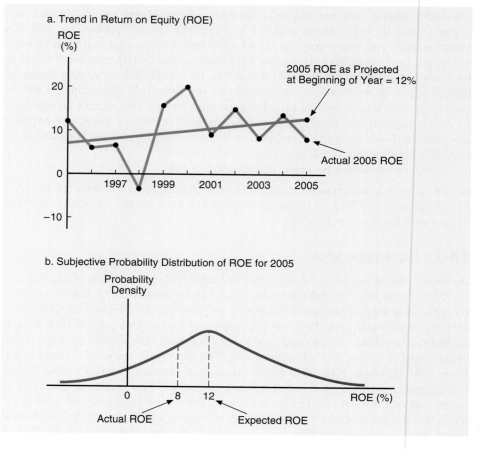

FIGURE 14-1 *Bigbee Electronics: Trend in ROE, 1995–2005, and Estimated Probability Distribution of ROE, 2005*

Business risk depends on a number of factors, the more important of which are listed here:

1. *Demand variability.* The more stable the demand for a firm's products, other things held constant, the lower its business risk.
2. *Sales price variability.* Firms whose products are sold in highly volatile markets are exposed to more business risk than similar firms whose output prices are more stable.
3. *Input cost variability.* Firms whose input costs are highly uncertain are exposed to a high degree of business risk.
4. *Ability to adjust output prices for changes in input costs.* Some firms are better able than others to raise their own output prices when input costs rise. The greater the ability to adjust output prices to reflect cost conditions, the lower the degree of business risk.
5. *Ability to develop new products in a timely, cost-effective manner.* Firms in such high-tech industries as drugs and computers depend on a constant stream of new products. The faster its products become obsolete, the greater a firm's business risk.
6. *Foreign risk exposure.* Firms that generate a high percentage of their earnings overseas are subject to earnings declines due to exchange rate fluctuations.

Also, if a firm operates in a politically unstable area, it may be subject to political risk.

7. *The extent to which costs are fixed: operating leverage.* If a high percentage of its costs are fixed, hence do not decline when demand falls, then the firm is exposed to a relatively high degree of business risk. This factor is called *operating leverage*, and it is discussed at length in the next section.

Each of these factors is determined partly by the firm's industry characteristics, but each of them is also controllable to some extent by management. For example, most firms can, through their marketing policies, take actions to stabilize both unit sales and sales prices. However, this stabilization may require spending a great deal on advertising and/or price concessions to obtain commitments from customers to purchase fixed quantities at fixed prices in the future. Similarly, firms such as Bigbee Electronics can reduce the volatility of future input costs by negotiating long-term labor and materials supply contracts, but they may have to pay prices above the current spot price to obtain these contracts. Many firms are also using hedging techniques to reduce business risk, as we discuss in Chapter 18.

14-2b Operating Leverage

As noted earlier, business risk depends in part on the extent to which a firm builds fixed costs into its operations—if fixed costs are high, even a small decline in sales can lead to a large decline in ROE. So, other things held constant, the higher a firm's fixed costs, the greater its business risk. Higher fixed costs are generally associated with more highly automated, capital intensive firms and industries. However, businesses that employ highly skilled workers who must be retained and paid even during recessions also have relatively high fixed costs, as do firms with high product development costs, because the amortization of development costs is an element of fixed costs.

If a high percentage of total costs are fixed, then the firm is said to have a high degree of **operating leverage.** In physics, leverage implies the use of a lever to raise a heavy object with a small force. In politics, if people have leverage, their smallest word or action can accomplish a lot. *In business terminology, a high degree of operating leverage, other factors held constant, implies that a relatively small change in sales results in a large change in ROE.*

Figure 14-2 illustrates the concept of operating leverage by comparing the results that Bigbee could expect if it used different degrees of operating leverage. Plan A calls for a relatively small amount of fixed costs, $20,000. Here the firm would not have much automated equipment, so its depreciation, maintenance, property taxes, and so on would be low. However, the total operating costs line has a relatively steep slope, indicating that variable costs per unit are higher than they would be if the firm used more operating leverage. Plan B calls for a higher level of fixed costs, $60,000. Here the firm uses automated equipment (with which one operator can turn out a few or many units at the same labor cost) to a much larger extent. The breakeven point is higher under Plan B—breakeven occurs at 60,000 units under Plan B versus only 40,000 units under Plan A.

We can calculate the breakeven quantity by recognizing that **operating breakeven** occurs when ROE = 0, hence when earnings before interest and taxes (EBIT) = 0:[2]

$$EBIT = PQ - VQ - F = 0 \qquad (14\text{-}1)$$

Operating Leverage
The extent to which fixed costs are used in a firm's operations.

Operating Breakeven
The output quantity at which EBIT = 0.

---

[2] This definition of breakeven does not include any fixed financial costs because Bigbee is an unlevered firm. If there were fixed financial costs, the firm would suffer an accounting loss at the operating breakeven point. We will introduce financial costs shortly.

FIGURE 14-2	*Illustration of Operating Leverage*

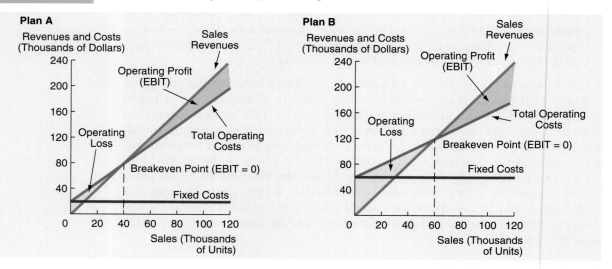

	Plan A	Plan B
Price	$2.00	$2.00
Variable costs	$1.50	$1.00
Fixed costs	$20,000	$60,000
Assets	$200,000	$200,000
Tax rate	40%	40%

				PLAN A				PLAN B			
Demand	Proba-bility	Units Sold	Dollar Sales	Oper-ating Costs	Operating Profits (EBIT)	Net Income	ROE	Oper-ating Costs	Operating Profits (EBIT)	Net Income	ROE
Terrible	0.05	0	$ 0	$ 20,000	($20,000)	($12,000)	(6.00)%	$ 60,000	($ 60,000)	($36,000)	(18.00)%
Poor	0.20	40,000	80,000	80,000	0	0	0.00	100,000	(20,000)	(12,000)	(6.00)
Normal	0.50	100,000	200,000	170,000	30,000	18,000	9.00	160,000	40,000	24,000	12.00
Good	0.20	160,000	320,000	260,000	60,000	36,000	18.00	220,000	100,000	60,000	30.00
Wonderful	0.05	200,000	400,000	320,000	80,000	48,000	24.00	260,000	140,000	84,000	42.00
Expected value:		100,000	$200,000	$170,000	$30,000	$18,000	9.00%	$160,000	$ 40,000	$24,000	12.00%
Standard deviation:					$24,698		7.41%		$ 49,396		14.82%
Coefficient of variation:					0.82		0.82		1.23		1.23

Notes: a. Operating costs = Variable costs + Fixed costs.

b. The federal-plus-state tax rate is 40 percent, so NI = EBIT(1 − Tax rate) = EBIT(0.6).

c. ROE = NI/Equity. The firm has no debt, so Assets = Equity = $200,000.

d. The breakeven sales level for Plan B is not shown in the table, but it is 60,000 units or $120,000.

e. The expected values, standard deviations, and coefficients of variation were found using the procedures discussed in Chapter 8.

Here P is average sales price per unit of output, Q is units of output, V is variable cost per unit, and F is fixed operating costs. If we solve for the breakeven quantity, Q_{BE}, we get this expression:

$$Q_{BE} = \frac{F}{P - V}$$

(14-1a)

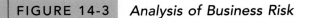

FIGURE 14-3   *Analysis of Business Risk*

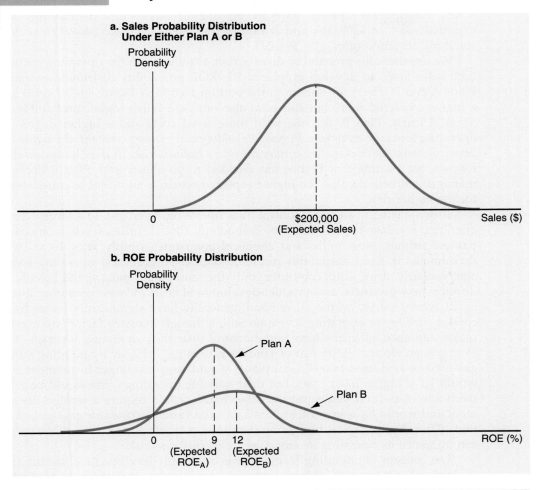

Note: We are using continuous distributions to approximate the discrete distributions contained in Figure 14-2.

Thus for Plan A,

$$Q_{BE} = \frac{\$20,000}{\$2.00 - \$1.50} = 40,000 \text{ units}$$

and for Plan B,

$$Q_{BE} = \frac{\$60,000}{\$2.00 - \$1.00} = 60,000 \text{ units}$$

How does operating leverage affect business risk? *Other things held constant, the higher a firm's operating leverage, the higher its business risk.* This point is demonstrated in Figure 14-3, where we develop probability distributions for ROE under Plans A and B.

The top section of Figure 14-3 graphs the probability distribution of sales that was presented in tabular form in Figure 14-2. The sales probability distribution depends on how demand for the product varies, not on whether the product is manufactured by Plan A or by Plan B. Therefore, the same sales probability distribution applies to both production plans; this distribution has expected sales of $200,000, and it ranges from zero to about $400,000, with a standard deviation of $\sigma_{Sales} = \$98,793$.

We use the sales probability distribution, together with the operating costs at each sales level, to develop graphs of the ROE probability distributions under Plans A and B. These are shown in the bottom section of Figure 14-3. Plan B has a higher expected ROE, but this plan also entails a much higher probability of losses. Clearly, Plan B, the one with more fixed costs and a higher degree of operating leverage, is riskier. *In general, holding other factors constant, the higher the degree of operating leverage, the greater the firm's business risk.* In the discussion that follows, we assume that Bigbee has decided to go ahead with Plan B because management believes that the higher expected return is sufficient to compensate for the higher risk.

To what extent can firms control their operating leverage? To a large extent, operating leverage is determined by technology. Electric utilities, telephone companies, airlines, steel mills, and chemical companies simply *must* have large investments in fixed assets; this results in high fixed costs and operating leverage. Similarly, drug, auto, computer, and other companies must spend heavily to develop new products, and product-development costs increase operating leverage. Grocery stores, on the other hand, generally have significantly lower fixed costs, hence lower operating leverage. Still, although industry factors do exert a major influence, all firms have some control over their operating leverage. For example, an electric utility can expand its generating capacity by building either gas-fired or coal-fired plants. Coal plants would require a larger investment and would have higher fixed costs, but their variable operating costs would be relatively low. Gas-fired plants, on the other hand, would require a smaller investment and would have lower fixed costs, but the variable costs (for gas) would be high. Thus, by its capital budgeting decisions, a utility (or any other company) can influence its operating leverage, hence its business risk.

The concept of operating leverage was originally developed for use in capital budgeting. Mutually exclusive projects that involve alternative methods for producing a given product often have different degrees of operating leverage, hence different breakeven points and different degrees of risk. Bigbee Electronics and many other companies regularly undertake a type of breakeven analysis (the sensitivity analysis discussed in Chapter 12) for each proposed project as a part of their regular capital budgeting process. Still, once a corporation's operating leverage has been established, this factor exerts a major influence on its capital structure decision.

14-2c Financial Risk

Financial Risk
An increase in stockholders' risk, over and above the firm's basic business risk, resulting from the use of financial leverage.

Financial risk is the additional risk placed on the common stockholders as a result of the decision to finance with debt. Conceptually, stockholders face a certain amount of risk that is inherent in the firm's operations—this is its business risk, defined as the uncertainty inherent in projections of future operating income. If a firm uses debt (financial leverage), this concentrates the business risk on common stockholders. To illustrate, suppose 10 people decide to form a corporation to build houses. There is a certain amount of business risk in the operation. If the firm is capitalized only with common equity, and if each person buys 10 percent of the stock, then each investor shares equally in the business risk. However, suppose the firm is capitalized with 50 percent debt and 50 percent equity, with five of the investors putting up their capital as debt and the other five putting up their money as equity. The debtholders will receive a fixed payment, and it will come before the stockholders receive anything. Also, if the firm goes bankrupt, the debtholders must be paid off before the stockholders get anything. In this case, the five investors who put up the equity will have to bear all of the business risk, so the common stock will be twice as risky as it would have been had the firm been financed only with equity. Thus, the use of debt, or **financial leverage,** concentrates the firm's business risk on the stockholders. (In Web Appendix 14A, we describe in more detail the interaction between operating leverage and financial leverage.)

To illustrate the business risk concentration, we can extend the Bigbee Electronics example. To date, the company has never used debt, but the treasurer is now considering a possible change in its capital structure. Changes in the use of debt would cause changes in earnings per share (EPS) as well as changes in risk—both of which would affect the stock price. To understand the relationship between financial leverage and EPS, first consider Table 14-1, which shows how Bigbee's cost of debt would vary if it used different amounts of debt to finance a fixed amount of assets. The higher the percentage of debt in the capital structure, the riskier the debt, hence the higher the interest rate lenders will charge.

For now, assume that only two financing choices are being considered—remain at 100 percent equity, or shift to 50 percent debt and 50 percent equity. We also assume that with no debt Bigbee has 10,000 shares of common stock outstanding and, if it decides to change its capital structure, common stock can be repurchased at the $20 current stock price. Now consider Table 14-2, which shows how the financing choice will affect Bigbee's profitability and risk.

First, focus on Section I, which assumes that Bigbee uses no debt. Because debt is zero, interest is also zero, hence pre-tax income is equal to EBIT. Taxes at 40 percent are deducted to obtain net income, which is then divided by the $200,000 of equity to calculate ROE. Note that Bigbee receives a tax credit if net income is negative (when demand is terrible or poor). Here we assume that Bigbee's losses can be carried back to offset income earned in the prior year. The ROE at each sales level is then multiplied by the probability of that sales level to calculate the 12 percent expected ROE. Note that this 12 percent is the same as we found in Figure 14-2 for Plan B.

Section I of the table also calculates Bigbee's earnings per share (EPS) for each scenario under the assumption that the company continues to use no debt. Net income is divided by the 10,000 common shares outstanding to obtain EPS. If demand is terrible, the EPS will be −$3.60, but if demand is wonderful, the EPS will rise to $8.40. The EPS at each sales level is then multiplied by the probability of that level to calculate the expected EPS, which is $2.40 if Bigbee uses

Financial Leverage *The extent to which fixed-income securities (debt and preferred stock) are used in a firm's capital structure.*

TABLE 14-1 *Interest Rates for Bigbee with Different Debt/Assets Ratios*

Amount Borrowed[a]	Debt/Assets Ratio	Interest Rate, r_d, on All Debt
$20,000	10%	8.0%
40,000	20	8.3
60,000	30	9.0
80,000	40	10.0
100,000	50	12.0
120,000	60	15.0

[a] We assume that the firm must borrow in increments of $20,000. We also assume that Bigbee is unable to borrow more than $120,000, which is 60 percent of its $200,000 of assets, due to restrictions in its corporate charter.

TABLE 14-2	*Effects of Financial Leverage: Bigbee Electronics Financed with Zero Debt or 50 Percent Debt*

SECTION I. ZERO DEBT

Debt ratio	0%
Assets	$200,000
Debt	$ 0
Equity	$200,000
Shares outstanding	10,000

Demand for Product (1)	Probability (2)	EBIT (3)	Interest (4)	Pre-Tax Income (5)	Taxes (40%) (6)	Net Income (7)	ROE (8)	EPSa (9)
Terrible	0.05	($ 60,000)	$0	($ 60,000)	($24,000)	($36,000)	(18.00)%	($3.60)
Poor	0.20	(20,000)	0	(20,000)	(8,000)	(12,000)	(6.00)	(1.20)
Normal	0.50	40,000	0	40,000	16,000	24,000	12.00	2.40
Good	0.20	100,000	0	100,000	40,000	60,000	30.00	6.00
Wonderful	0.05	140,000	0	140,000	56,000	84,000	42.00	8.40
Expected value:		$ 40,000	$0	$ 40,000	$16,000	$24,000	12.00%	$2.40
Standard deviation:							14.82%	$2.96
Coefficient of variation:							1.23	1.23

Assumptions:
1. In terms of its operating leverage, Bigbee has chosen Plan B. The probability distribution and EBIT are obtained from Figure 14-2.
2. Sales and operating costs, hence EBIT, are not affected by the financing decision. Therefore, EBIT under both financing plans is identical, and it is taken from the EBIT column for Plan B in Figure 14-2.
3. All losses can be carried back to offset income in the prior year.

a The EPS figures can also be obtained using the following formula, in which the numerator amounts to an income statement at a given sales level laid out horizontally:

$$\text{EPS} = \frac{(\text{Sales} - \text{Fixed costs} - \text{Variable costs} - \text{Interest})(1 - \text{Tax rate})}{\text{Shares outstanding}} = \frac{(\text{EBIT} - \text{I})(1 - \text{T})}{\text{Shares outstanding}}$$

(note continued)

no debt. We also calculate the standard deviation of EPS and the coefficient of variation as indicators of the firm's risk at a zero debt ratio: $\sigma_{\text{EPS}} = \$2.96$, and $\text{CV}_{\text{EPS}} = 1.23$.

Now look at the situation if Bigbee decides to use 50 percent debt financing, shown in Section II, with the interest rate on debt at 12 percent. Sales will not be affected, nor will operating costs, hence the EBIT columns are the same for the zero debt and 50 percent debt cases. However, the company will now have $100,000 of debt with a cost of 12 percent, hence its interest expense will be $12,000. This interest must be paid regardless of the state of the economy—if it is not paid, the company will be forced into bankruptcy, and stockholders will probably be wiped out. Therefore, we show a $12,000 cost in Column 4 as a fixed number for all sales levels. Column 5 shows pre-tax income, Column 6 the applicable taxes, and Column 7 the resulting net income. When the net income figures are divided by the equity investment—which now will be only $100,000 because $100,000 of the $200,000 total requirement was obtained as debt—we find the ROE under each demand state. If demand is terrible and sales are zero, then a very large loss will be incurred, and the ROE will be −43.2 percent. However, if demand is wonderful, then ROE will be 76.8 percent. The expected ROE is the probability-weighted average, which is 16.8 percent if the company uses 50 percent debt.

TABLE 14-2 *continued*

SECTION II. 50% DEBT

Debt ratio	50.00%	
Assets	$200,000	
Debt	$100,000	
Interest rate	12.00%	
Equity	$100,000	
Shares outstanding	5,000	

Demand for Product (1)	Probability (2)	EBIT (3)	Interest (4)	Pre-Tax Income (5)	Taxes (40%) (6)	Net Income (7)	ROE (8)	EPSª (9)
Terrible	0.05	($ 60,000)	$12,000	($ 72,000)	($28,800)	($43,200)	(43.20)%	($ 8.64)
Poor	0.20	(20,000)	12,000	(32,000)	(12,800)	(19,200)	(19.20)	(3.84)
Normal	0.50	40,000	12,000	28,000	11,200	16,800	16.80	3.36
Good	0.20	100,000	12,000	88,000	35,200	52,800	52.80	10.56
Wonderful	0.05	140,000	12,000	128,000	51,200	76,800	76.80	15.36
Expected value:		$ 40,000	$12,000	$ 28,000	$11,200	$16,800	16.80%	$ 3.36
Standard deviation:							29.64%	5.93
Coefficient of variation:							1.76	1.76

For example, with zero debt and Sales = $200,000, EPS is $2.40:

$$\text{EPS}_{D/A=0} = \frac{(\$200,000 - \$60,000 - \$100,000 - 0)(0.6)}{10,000} = \$2.40$$

With 50% percent debt and Sales = $200,000, EPS is $3.36:

$$\text{EPS}_{D/A=0.5} = \frac{(\$200,000 - \$60,000 - \$100,000 - \$12,000)(0.6)}{5,000} = \$3.36$$

Refer to the tabular data given in Figure 14-2 to arrive at sales, fixed costs, and variable costs that are used in these equations.

Typically, financing with debt increases the expected rate of return for an investment, but debt also increases risk to the firm's owners, its common stockholders. This situation holds with our example—financial leverage raises the expected ROE from 12 to 16.8 percent, but it also increases the risk of the investment as measured by the coefficient of variation from 1.23 to 1.76.

Figure 14-4 graphs the data in Table 14-2. It shows in another way that using financial leverage increases the expected ROE but that leverage also flattens out the probability distribution, increases the probability of a large loss, and thus increases the risk borne by stockholders.

We can also calculate Bigbee's EPS if it is financed with 50 percent debt. With Debt = $0, there would be 10,000 shares outstanding, but if half of the equity were replaced by debt (Debt = $100,000), there would be only 5,000 shares outstanding. We must therefore determine the EPS that would result at each of the possible demand levels under the different capital structures.[3] With no debt, EPS would

---

[3] We assume in this example that the firm could change its capital structure by repurchasing common stock at its book value of $100,000/5,000 shares = $20 per share. However, the firm may actually have to pay a higher price to repurchase its stock on the open market. If Bigbee had to pay $22 per share, then it could repurchase only $100,000/$22 = 4,545 shares, and, in this case, expected EPS would be only $16,800/(10,000 − 4,545) = $16,800/5,455 = $3.08 rather than $3.36.

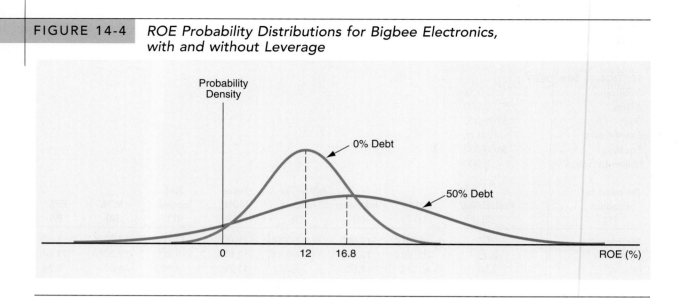

FIGURE 14-4 *ROE Probability Distributions for Bigbee Electronics, with and without Leverage*

be −$3.60 if demand were terrible; $2.40 if demand were normal; and $8.40 if demand were wonderful. With 50 percent debt, EPS would be −$8.64 if demand were terrible; $3.36 if demand were normal; and $15.36 if demand were wonderful. Expected EPS would be $2.40 with no debt but $3.36 with 50 percent financial leverage.

The EPS distributions under the two financial structures are graphed in Figure 14-5, where we use continuous distributions rather than the discrete distributions contained in Table 14-2. Although expected EPS would be much higher if financial leverage were employed, the graph makes it clear that the risk of low, or even negative, EPS would also be higher if debt were used.

FIGURE 14-5 *Probability Distributions of EPS with Different Amounts of Financial Leverage*

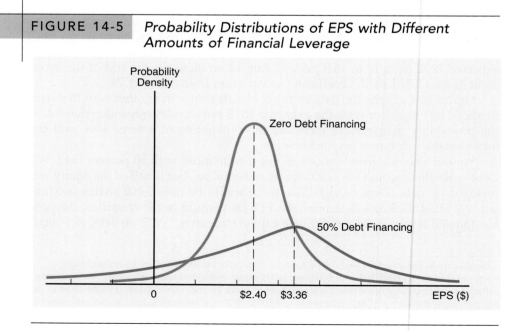

Another view of the relationships among expected EPS, risk, and financial leverage is presented in Figure 14-6. The tabular data in the lower section were calculated in the manner set forth in Table 14-2, and the graphs plot these data. Here we see that expected EPS rises until the firm is financed with 50 percent debt. Interest charges rise, but this effect is more than offset by the declining number of shares outstanding as debt is substituted for equity. However, EPS peaks at a debt ratio of 50 percent, beyond which interest rates rise so rapidly that EPS falls in spite of the falling number of shares outstanding.

The right panel of Figure 14-6 shows that risk, as measured by the coefficient of variation of EPS, rises continuously, and at an increasing rate, as debt is substituted for equity.

FIGURE 14-6 *Relationships among Expected EPS, Risk, and Financial Leverage*

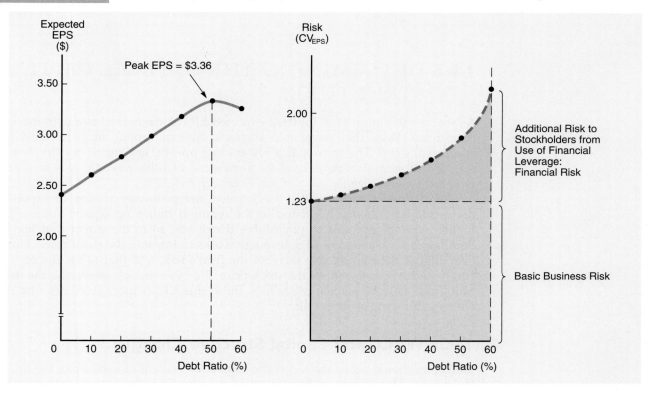

Debt Ratio	Expected EPS	Standard Deviation of EPS	Coefficient of Variation
0%[a]	$2.40[a]	$2.96[a]	1.23[a]
10	2.56	3.29	1.29
20	2.75	3.70	1.35
30	2.97	4.23	1.43
40	3.20	4.94	1.54
50[a]	3.36[a]	5.93[a]	1.76[a]
60	3.30	7.41	2.25

[a] Values for debt ratios = 0% and 50% are taken from Table 14-2. Values at other debt ratios were calculated similarly.

These examples make it clear that using leverage has both positive and negative effects: higher leverage increases expected EPS (in this example, until the debt ratio equals 50 percent), but it also increases risk. When determining its optimal capital structure, Bigbee needs to balance these positive and negative effects of leverage. This issue is discussed in the following sections.

What is business risk, and how can it be measured?

What are some determinants of business risk?

Why does business risk vary from industry to industry?

What is operating leverage?

How does operating leverage affect business risk?

What is financial risk, and how does it arise?

Explain this statement: "Using leverage has both good and bad effects."

14-3 DETERMINING THE OPTIMAL CAPITAL STRUCTURE

As we saw in Figure 14-6, Bigbee's expected EPS is maximized at a debt ratio of 50 percent. Does that mean that Bigbee's optimal capital structure calls for 50 percent debt? The answer is a resounding no—*the optimal capital structure is the one that maximizes the price of the firm's stock, and this generally calls for a debt ratio that is lower than the one that maximizes expected EPS.*

Recall from Chapter 9 that stock prices are positively related to expected dividends but negatively related to the required return on equity. Firms with higher earnings are able to pay higher dividends, so to the extent that higher debt levels raise expected EPS, leverage works to increase the stock price. However, higher debt levels also increase the firm's risk, and that raises the cost of equity and works to reduce the stock price. So, even though increasing the debt ratio from 40 to 50 percent raises EPS, the higher EPS is more than offset by the corresponding increase in risk.

14-3a WACC and Capital Structure Changes

Managers should set as the target the capital structure that maximizes the firm's stock price. However, it is difficult to estimate how a given change in the capital structure will affect the stock price. As it turns out, the capital structure that maximizes the stock price also minimizes the WACC, and at times it is easier to predict how a capital structure change will affect the WACC than the stock price. Therefore, many managers use the estimated relationship between capital structure and the WACC to guide their capital structure decisions.

Recall from Chapter 10 that when there is no preferred stock in a firm's capital structure, the WACC is defined as follows:

$$\text{WACC} = w_d(r_d)(1 - T) + w_c(r_s)$$
$$= (D/A)(r_d)(1 - T) + (E/A)(r_s)$$

In this expression, D/A and E/A represent the debt-to-assets and equity-to-assets ratios, and they sum to 1.0.

TABLE 14-3	*Bigbee's Stock Price and WACC Estimates with Different Debt/Assets Ratios*

Debt/ Assets (1)	Debt/ Equity[a] (2)	AT r_d (3)	Expected EPS (and DPS)[b] (4)	Estimated Beta[c] (5)	$r_s = [r_{RF} + (RP_M)b]$[d] (6)	Estimated Price[e] (7)	Resulting P/E Ratio (8)	WACC[f] (9)
0%	0.00%	4.8%	$2.40	1.50	12.0%	$20.00	8.33×	12.00%
10	11.11	4.8	2.56	1.60	12.4	20.65	8.06	11.64
20	25.00	5.0	2.75	1.73	12.9	21.33	7.75	11.32
30	42.86	5.4	2.97	1.89	13.5	21.90	7.38	11.10
40	**66.67**	**6.0**	**3.20**	**2.10**	**14.4**	**22.22**	**6.94**	**11.04**
50	100.00	7.2	3.36	2.40	15.6	21.54	6.41	11.40
60	150.00	9.0	3.30	2.85	17.4	18.97	5.75	12.36

[a] $D/E = \dfrac{D/A}{1 - D/A}$

[b] Bigbee pays all of its earnings out as dividends, so EPS = DPS.

[c] The firm's unlevered beta, b_U, is 1.5. The remaining betas were calculated using the Hamada equation, given the unlevered beta, tax rate, and D/E ratio as inputs.

[d] We assume that $r_{RF} = 6\%$ and $RP_M = 4\%$. Therefore, at D/A = 0, $r_s = 6\% + (4\%)1.5 = 12\%$. Other values of r_s are calculated similarly.

[e] Since all earnings are paid out as dividends, no retained earnings will be plowed back into the business, and growth in EPS and DPS will be zero. Hence, the zero growth stock price model developed in Chapter 9 can be used to estimate the price of Bigbee's stock. For example, at D/A = 0,

$$P_0 = \frac{DPS}{r_s} = \frac{\$2.40}{0.12} = \$20$$

Other prices were calculated similarly.

[f] Column 9 is found by use of the WACC equation developed in Chapter 10:

$$WACC = w_d r_d (1 - T) + w_c r_s$$
$$= (D/A)(r_d)(1 - T) + (1 - D/A)r_s$$

For example, at D/A = 40%,

$$WACC = 0.4(10\%)(0.6) + 0.6(14.4\%) = 11.04\%$$

We use book weights here, but market value weights would be theoretically better. See Eugene F. Brigham and Phillip R. Daves, *Intermediate Financial Management,* 8th ed. (Mason, OH: Thomson/South-Western, 2004), Chapter 9, for a discussion of this point.

Note that in Table 14-3 an increase in the debt ratio raises the costs of both debt and equity. [The cost of debt, r_d, is taken from Table 14-1, but multiplied by $(1 - T)$ to put it on an after-tax basis.] Bondholders recognize that if a firm has a higher debt ratio, this increases the risk of financial distress, and this increase in risk leads to higher interest rates.

In practice, financial managers use financial statement forecasting models to determine how changes in the debt ratio will affect the current ratio, times-interest-earned ratio, and EBITDA coverage ratio.[4] They then discuss their pro forma financial statements with bankers and bond rating agencies, who ask probing questions and may make their own adjustments to the firm's forecasts. The bankers and rating agencies then compare the firm's ratios with those of other firms in its industry, and arrive at a "what if" rating and corresponding

---

[4] We discuss financial statement forecasts in Chapter 17.

interest rate. Moreover, if the company plans to issue bonds to the public, the SEC requires that it inform investors what the coverages will be after the new bonds have been sold. Recognizing all this, sophisticated financial managers use their forecasted ratios to predict how bankers and other lenders will judge their firms' risks and thus determine their costs of debt. Thus, they can judge quite accurately the effects of capital structure on the cost of debt.

14-3b The Hamada Equation

Increasing the debt ratio increases the risks faced by bondholders and thus increases the cost of debt. More debt also raises the risk borne by stockholders, and that raises the cost of equity, r_s. It is harder to quantify leverage's effects on the cost of equity, but a theoretical formula can help measure the effect.

To begin, recall from Chapter 8 that a stock's beta is the relevant measure of risk for a diversified investor. Moreover, beta increases with financial leverage, and Robert Hamada formulated the following equation to quantify this effect.[5]

$$b_L = b_U[1 + (1 - T)(D/E)] \qquad \text{(14-2)}$$

Here b_L is the firm's actual, current beta, which presumably is based on the existence of some financial leverage, and b_U is the beta the firm would have if it were debt free, or unlevered. If the firm were debt free, then beta would depend entirely on business risk and thus be a measure of the firm's "basic business risk." D/E is the measure of financial leverage as used in the Hamada equation, and T is the corporate tax rate.[6]

Now recall the CAPM version of the cost of equity:

$$r_s = r_{RF} + (RP_M)b_i$$

Note that beta is the only variable in the equity cost equation that is under management's control—the other two variables, r_{RF} and RP_M, are determined by market forces that are beyond the firm's control, but b_L is determined by the firm's operating decisions as discussed earlier in the chapter, which affect its basic business risk, and by the firm's capital structure decisions as reflected in its D/A (or D/E) ratio.

We can solve Equation 14-2 to find the **unlevered beta, b_U**, obtaining Equation 14-2a:

$$b_U = b_L/[1 + (1 - T)(D/E)] \qquad \text{(14-2a)}$$

Unlevered Beta, b_U
The firm's beta coefficient if it has no debt.

---

[5] See Robert S. Hamada, "Portfolio Analysis, Market Equilibrium, and Corporation Finance," *Journal of Finance*, March 1969, pp. 13–31. See Eugene F. Brigham and Phillip R. Daves, *Intermediate Financial Management*, 8th ed. (Mason, OH: Thomson/South-Western, 2004), Chapter 14, for further discussion of the Hamada equation.

[6] Recall from Chapter 4 that the debt/equity ratio, D/E, is directly related to the D/A ratio:

$$\frac{D}{E} = \frac{D/A}{1 - D/A}$$

For example, if the firm has $40 of debt and $60 of equity, then D/A = 0.4, E/A = 0.6, and

$$\frac{D}{E} = \frac{0.4}{1 - 0.4} = 0.4/0.6 = 0.6667$$

Thus any D/A ratio can be directly translated into a D/E ratio. Note also that Hamada's equation assumes that assets are reported at market values rather than accounting book values. This point is discussed at length in Brigham and Daves, *Intermediate Financial Management*, where the feedbacks among capital structure, stock prices, and capital costs are examined.

The current (levered) beta is known, as are the tax rate and the debt/equity ratio, so we can insert values for these known variables to find the unlevered beta. The unlevered beta can then be used in Equation 14-2, with different debt levels, to find the levered betas that would exist with different debt levels. Those betas can then be used to find the cost of equity with different amounts of debt.

We can illustrate the procedure with Bigbee Electronics. First, assume that the risk-free rate of return, r_{RF}, is 6 percent, and that the market risk premium, RP_M, is 4 percent. Next, we need the unlevered beta, b_U. Because Bigbee has no debt, its $D/E = 0$. Therefore, its current 1.5 beta is also its unlevered beta, hence $b_U = 1.5$. With b_U, r_{RF}, and RP_M specified, we can use Equation 14-2 to estimate Bigbee's betas at different degrees of financial leverage, and then its cost of equity at those debt ratios.

Bigbee's betas at different debt/equity ratios are shown in Column 5 of Table 14-3. The current cost of equity is 12 percent as shown at the top of Column 6:

$$r_s = r_{RF} + \text{Risk premium}$$
$$= 6\% + (4\%)(1.5)$$
$$= 6\% + 6\% = 12\%$$

The first 6 percent is the risk-free rate, the second is the firm's risk premium. Because Bigbee currently uses no debt, it has no financial risk. Therefore, the 6 percent risk premium is entirely attributable to business risk.

If Bigbee changes its capital structure by adding debt, this would increase the risk stockholders would have to bear. That, in turn, would result in a higher risk premium. Conceptually, this situation would exist:

$$r_s = r_{RF} + \text{Premium for business risk} + \text{Premium for financial risk}$$

Figure 14-7, which is based on data shown in Column 6 of Table 14-3, graphs Bigbee's cost of equity at different debt ratios. As the figure shows, r_s consists of the 6 percent risk-free rate, a constant 6 percent premium for business risk, and a premium for financial risk that starts at zero but rises at an increasing rate as the debt ratio increases.

14-3c The Optimal Capital Structure

Column 9 of Table 14-3 also shows Bigbee's WACC at different capital structures. Currently, it has no debt, so its debt ratio is zero, and at this point WACC = r_s = 12%. As Bigbee begins to use lower-cost debt, its WACC declines. However, as the debt ratio rises, the costs of both debt and equity rise, at first slowly but then at a faster and faster rate. Eventually, the increasing costs of the two components offset the fact that more low-cost debt is being used. Thus, at 40 percent debt, the WACC hits a minimum of 11.04 percent, and after that it rises with further increases in the debt ratio.

Note too that even though the component cost of equity is higher than that of debt, using only lower-cost debt would not maximize value because of the feedback effects of debt on the costs of debt and equity. For example, if Bigbee used more than 40 percent debt, say, 50 percent, it would have more of the cheaper capital, but this benefit would be more than offset by the fact that using more debt would raise the costs of both debt and equity.

These thoughts were echoed in a statement made by the Georgia-Pacific Corporation:

On a market-value basis, our debt-to-capital ratio is 47 percent. By employing this capital structure, we believe that our weighted average cost of capital is

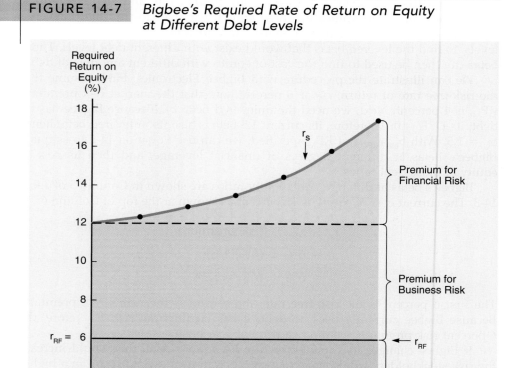

FIGURE 14-7 — *Bigbee's Required Rate of Return on Equity at Different Debt Levels*

minimized, at approximately 10 percent. Although reducing debt would reduce our marginal cost of debt, this action would likely increase our weighted average cost of capital because we would then have to use more higher-cost equity.

Finally, and very importantly, recall that the capital structure that minimizes the WACC is also the capital structure that maximizes the firm's stock price. Bigbee pays out all of its earnings as dividends, so it plows zero earnings back into the business, and this leads to an expected growth rate in earnings and dividends of zero. Thus, in Bigbee's case we can use the zero growth stock price model developed in Chapter 9 to estimate the stock price at each different capital structure. These estimates are shown in Column 7 of Table 14-3. Here we see that the stock price first rises with financial leverage, hits a peak of $22.22 at a debt ratio of 40 percent, and then begins to decline. *Thus, Bigbee's optimal capital structure occurs at a debt ratio of 40 percent, and that debt ratio both maximizes its stock price and minimizes its WACC.*[7]

---

[7] We could also estimate the price of the stock if some earnings were retained and the expected growth rate was positive. However, this would complicate the analysis, and it is another reason we generally analyze the optimal capital structure decision using the WACC rather than the stock price.

The EPS, cost of capital, and stock price data shown in Table 14-3 are plotted in Figure 14-8. As the graph shows, the debt ratio that maximizes Bigbee's expected EPS is 50 percent. However, the expected stock price is maximized, and the WACC is minimized, at a 40 percent debt ratio. Thus, Bigbee's optimal capital structure calls for 40 percent debt and 60 percent equity. Management should set its target capital structure at these ratios, and if the existing ratios are off target, it should move toward the target when new securities are issued.

FIGURE 14-8   *Effects of Capital Structure on EPS, Cost of Capital, and Stock Price*

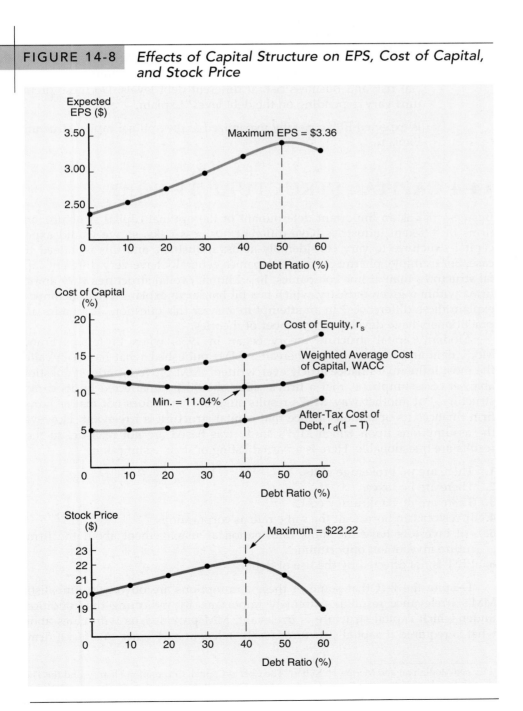

What happens to the component costs of debt and equity when the debt ratio is increased? Why does this occur?

Using the Hamada equation, explain the effects of financial leverage on beta.

What is the equation for calculating a firm's unlevered beta?

Use the Hamada equation to calculate the unlevered beta for Firm X with the following data: $b_L = 1.25$; $T = 40\%$; Debt/Assets $= 0.42$; Equity/Assets $= 0.58$. ($b_U = 0.8714$)

What would the cost of equity be for Firm X at Equity/Assets ratios of 1.0 (no debt) and 0.58, assuming that $r_{RF} = 5\%$ and $RP_M = 4\%$? (8.49%, 10%)

Using a graph and illustrative data, discuss the premiums for financial risk and business risk at different debt levels. Do these premiums vary depending on the debt level? Explain.

Is expected EPS generally maximized at the optimal capital structure? Explain.

14-4 CAPITAL STRUCTURE THEORY

Business risk is an important determinant of the optimal capital structure, and firms in different industries have different business risks, so we would expect capital structures to vary considerably across industries, and this is indeed the case. For example, pharmaceutical companies generally have very different capital structures than airline companies. In addition, capital structures vary among firms within a given industry, which is a bit harder to explain. What factors can explain these differences? In an attempt to answer this question, academics and practitioners have developed a number of theories.

Modern capital structure theory began in 1958, when Professors Franco Modigliani and Merton Miller (hereafter MM) published what has been called the most influential finance article ever written.[8] MM proved, under a questionable set of assumptions, that a firm's value should be unaffected by its capital structure. Put another way, MM's results suggest that it does not matter how a firm finances its operations, hence that capital structure is irrelevant. However, the assumptions upon which MM's study was based are not realistic, so their results are questionable. Here is a partial listing of their assumptions:

1. There are no brokerage costs.
2. There are no taxes.
3. There are no bankruptcy costs.
4. Investors can borrow at the same rate as corporations.
5. All investors have the same information as management about the firm's future investment opportunities.
6. EBIT is not affected by the use of debt.

Despite the fact that some of these assumptions are obviously unrealistic, MM's irrelevance result is extremely important. By indicating the conditions under which capital structure is irrelevant, MM provided us with clues about what is required if capital structure is to be relevant and hence to affect a firm's

---

[8] Franco Modigliani and Merton H. Miller, "The Cost of Capital, Corporation Finance, and the Theory of Investment," *American Economic Review*, June 1958. Both Modigliani and Miller won Nobel Prizes for their work.

Yogi Berra on the M&M Proposition

When a waitress asked Yogi Berra (Baseball Hall of Fame catcher for the New York Yankees) whether he wanted his pizza cut into four pieces or eight, Yogi replied: "Better make it four. I don't think I can eat eight."[a]

Yogi's quip helps convey the basic insight of Modigliani and Miller. The firm's choice of leverage "slices" the distribution of future cash flows in a way that is like slicing a pizza. MM recognized that if you fix a company's investment activities, it's like fixing the size of the pizza; no information costs means that everyone sees the same pizza; no taxes means the IRS gets none of the pie; and no "contracting" costs means nothing sticks to the knife.

So, just as the substance of Yogi's meal is unaffected by whether the pizza is sliced into four pieces or eight, the economic substance of the firm is unaffected by whether the liability side of the balance sheet is sliced to include more or less debt under the MM assumptions. Note, though, that whereas the IRS may get none of Yogi's pizza, it is very likely to get some of the firm's income. Yogi's assumptions are a lot more realistic than MM's.

[a] Lee Green, *Sportswit* (New York: Fawcett Crest, 1984), p. 228.

Source: "Yogi Berra on the M&M Proposition," *Journal of Applied Corporate Finance*, Vol. 7, no. 4 (Winter 1995), p. 6. Used by permission.

value. MM's work marked the beginning of modern capital structure research, and subsequent research has focused on relaxing the MM assumptions in order to develop a more realistic theory of capital structure. Research in this area is quite extensive, but the highlights are summarized in the following sections.

14-4a The Effect of Taxes[9]

MM's original paper was criticized harshly, so they published a follow-up paper in 1963 in which they relaxed the assumption that there are no corporate taxes.[10] Here they recognized that the Tax Code allows corporations to deduct interest payments as an expense, but dividend payments to stockholders are not deductible. This differential treatment encourages corporations to use debt in their capital structures. Indeed, MM demonstrated that if all their other assumptions hold, this differential treatment leads to an optimal capital structure with 100 percent debt.

MM's 1963 work was modified several years later by Merton Miller (this time without Modigliani), when he brought in the effects of personal taxes.[11] Miller noted that bonds pay interest, which is taxed as personal income at rates going up to 35 percent, while income from stocks comes partly from dividends and partly from capital gains. Further, long-term capital gains are taxed at a maximum rate of 15 percent, and this tax can be deferred until the stock is sold and the gain realized. If a stock is held until the owner dies, no capital gains tax whatever must be paid. So, on balance, returns on common stocks are taxed at lower effective rates than returns on debt.[12]

---

[9] This section is relatively technical, and it can be omitted without loss of continuity.
[10] Franco Modigliani and Merton H. Miller, "Corporate Income Taxes and the Cost of Capital: A Correction," *American Economic Review*, Vol. 53 (June 1963), pp. 433–443.
[11] Merton H. Miller, "Debt and Taxes," *Journal of Finance*, Vol. 32 (May 1977), pp. 261–275.
[12] When Miller wrote his article, dividends were taxed at a maximum rate of 70 percent and capital gains at a much lower rate. Today (2005), dividends and capital gains are both taxed at a maximum rate of 15 percent, but interest is taxed at a maximum rate of 35 percent. These tax law changes would not affect Miller's final conclusion.

Because of the tax situation, Miller argued that investors are willing to accept relatively low before-tax returns on stocks as compared to the before-tax returns on bonds. For example, an investor in the 35 percent tax bracket might require a 10 percent pre-tax return on Bigbee's bonds, which would result in a $10\% (1 - T) = 10\%(0.65) = 6.5\%$ after-tax return. Bigbee's stock is riskier than its bonds, so the investor would require a higher after-tax return, say, 8.5 percent, on the stock. Because the stock's returns (either dividends or capital gains) would be taxed at only 15 percent, a pre-tax return of $8.5\%/(1 - T) = 8.5\%/0.85 = 10.0\%$ would provide the required 8.5 percent after-tax return. In this example, the interest rate on the bonds would be 10 percent, the same as the required return on the stock, r_s. Thus, the more favorable treatment of income on the stock would cause investors to accept the same before-tax returns on the stock and the bond.[13]

As Miller pointed out, (1) the *deductibility of interest* favors the use of debt financing, but (2) the *more favorable tax treatment of income from stocks* lowers the required rates of return on stocks and thus favors the use of equity financing. It is difficult to specify the net effect of these two factors. However, most observers believe that interest deductibility has the stronger effect, hence that our tax system favors the corporate use of debt. Still, that effect is certainly reduced by the lower taxes on stock income.

Duke University professor John Graham estimated the overall tax benefits of debt financing.[14] He concluded that the tax benefits associated with debt financing represent about 7 percent of the average firm's value, so if a leverage-free firm decided to use an average amount of debt, its value would rise by 7 percent.

We can observe changes in corporate financing patterns following major changes in tax rates. For example, in 1993 the top personal tax rate on interest and dividends was raised sharply, but the capital gains tax rate was not increased. This resulted in greater reliance on equity financing, especially through retained earnings. Subsequent reductions in the tax rate on both dividends and capital gains further benefited equity over debt, which continued the trend toward a greater reliance on equity financing.

14-4b The Effect of Potential Bankruptcy

MM's irrelevance results also depend on the assumption that firms don't go bankrupt, hence that bankruptcy costs are irrelevant. However, in practice bankruptcy exists, and it can be quite costly. Firms in bankruptcy have very high legal and accounting expenses, and they also have a hard time retaining customers, suppliers, and employees. Moreover, bankruptcy often forces a firm to liquidate assets for less than they would be worth if the firm continued to operate. Assets such as plant and equipment are often illiquid because they are configured to a company's individual needs and also because they are difficult to disassemble and move.

Note too that the *threat of bankruptcy*, not just bankruptcy per se, brings about these problems. If they become concerned about the firm's future, key employees start jumping ship, suppliers start refusing to grant credit, customers begin seeking more stable suppliers, and lenders start demanding higher interest rates and imposing more restrictive loan covenants.

---

[13] The situation here is similar to that with tax-exempt municipal bonds versus taxable bonds as discussed in Chapter 7.

[14] John R. Graham, "How Big Are the Tax Benefits of Debt?" *Journal of Finance*, Vol. 55 (2000), pp. 1901–1941; and "Estimating the Tax Benefits of Debt," *Journal of Applied Corporate Finance*, Vol. 14, no. 1 (Spring 2001), pp. 42–54.

Bankruptcy-related problems are likely to increase the more debt a firm has in its capital structure. Therefore, bankruptcy costs discourage firms from pushing their use of debt to excessive levels. Note too that bankruptcy-related costs have two components: (1) the probability of their occurrence and (2) the costs that would be incurred if financial distress arises. A firm whose earnings are relatively volatile, all else equal, faces a greater chance of bankruptcy and thus should use less debt than a more stable firm. This is consistent with our earlier point that firms with high operating leverage, and thus greater business risk, should limit their use of financial leverage. Likewise, firms whose assets are illiquid and thus would have to be sold at "fire sale" prices should limit their use of debt financing.

14-4c Trade-Off Theory

The preceding arguments led to the development of what is called "the trade-off theory of leverage," in which firms trade off the tax benefits of debt financing against problems caused by potential bankruptcy. A summary of the **trade-off theory** is expressed graphically in Figure 14-9. Here are some observations about the figure:

1. The fact that interest paid is a deductible expense makes debt less expensive than common or preferred stock. In effect, the government pays part of the cost of debt, or, to put it another way, debt provides *tax shelter benefits*. As a result, using more debt reduces taxes and thus allows more of the firm's operating income (EBIT) to flow through to investors. This factor, on which MM focused, tends to raise the stock's price. Indeed, under the assumptions

Trade-Off Theory
The capital structure theory that states firms trade off the tax benefits of debt financing against problems caused by potential bankruptcy.

FIGURE 14-9   *Effect of Leverage on the Value of Bigbee's Stock*

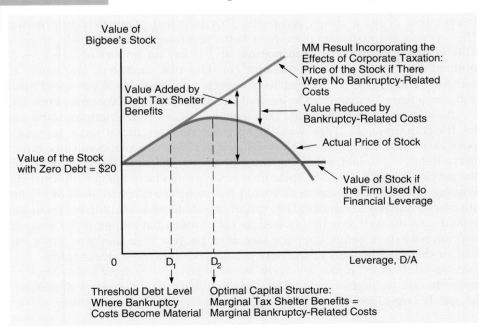

of their original paper, the stock price would be maximized at 100 percent debt. The line labeled "MM Result Incorporating the Effects of Corporate Taxation" in Figure 14-9 expresses the relationship between stock prices and debt under their assumptions.

2. In the real world, firms have target debt ratios that call for less than 100 percent debt, and the reason is to hold down the adverse effects of potential bankruptcy.

3. There is some threshold level of debt, labeled D_1 in Figure 14-9, below which the probability of bankruptcy is so low as to be immaterial. Beyond D_1, however, bankruptcy-related costs become increasingly important, and they begin to offset the tax benefits of debt. In the range from D_1 to D_2, bankruptcy-related costs reduce but do not completely offset the tax benefits of debt, so the firm's stock price continues to rise (but at a decreasing rate) as its debt ratio increases. However, beyond D_2, bankruptcy-related costs exceed the tax benefits, so from this point on increasing the debt ratio lowers the stock price. Therefore, D_2 is the optimal capital structure, the one where the stock price is maximized. Of course, D_1 and D_2 vary from firm to firm, depending on their business risk and bankruptcy costs.

4. While theoretical and empirical work supports the general shape of the curves in Figures 14-8 and 14-9, these graphs must be taken as approximations, not as precisely defined functions. The numbers in Figure 14-8 are shown out to two decimal places, but that is merely for illustrative purposes—the numbers are not nearly that accurate in view of the fact that the graph is based on judgmental estimates.

5. Another disturbing aspect of capital structure theory as expressed in Figure 14-9 is the fact that many large, successful firms such as Intel and Microsoft use far less debt than the theory suggests. This point led to the development of signaling theory, which is discussed next.

14-4d Signaling Theory

Symmetric Information
The situation in which investors and managers have identical information about firms' prospects.

Asymmetric Information
The situation in which managers have different (better) information about firms' prospects than do investors.

MM assumed that everyone—investors and managers alike—have the same information about a firm's prospects. This is called **symmetric information.** However, in fact managers often have better information than outside investors. This is called **asymmetric information,** and it has an important effect on the optimal capital structure. To see why, consider two situations, one where the company's managers know that its prospects are extremely favorable (Firm F) and one where the managers know that the future looks unfavorable (Firm U).

Now suppose Firm F's R&D labs have just discovered a nonpatentable cure for the common cold. They want to keep the new product a secret as long as possible to delay competitors' entry into the market. New plants must be built to make the new product, so capital must be raised, but how should Firm F raise the needed capital? If it sells stock, then when profits from the new product start flowing in, the price of the stock would rise sharply and purchasers of the new stock would make a bonanza. The current stockholders (including the managers) would also do well, but not as well as they would have done if the company had not sold stock before the price increased, because then they would not have had to share the benefits of the new product with the new stockholders. *Therefore, we would expect a firm with very favorable prospects to avoid selling stock and, rather, to raise required new capital by using new debt even if this moved the debt ratio beyond the target level.*[15]

---

[15] It would be illegal for Firm F's managers to personally purchase more shares on the basis of their inside knowledge of the new product. They could be sent to jail if they did.

Now consider Firm U. Suppose its managers have information that new orders are off sharply because a competitor has installed new technology that improved its products' quality. Firm U must upgrade its own facilities, at a high cost, just to maintain its current sales. As a result, its return on investment will fall (but not by as much as if it took no action, which would lead to a 100 percent loss through bankruptcy). How should Firm U raise the needed capital? Here the situation is just the reverse of that facing Firm F—it will want to sell stock so that some of the adverse consequences will be borne by new investors. *Therefore, a firm with unfavorable prospects would want to finance with stock, which would mean bringing in new investors to share the losses.*[16]

The conclusion from all this is that firms with extremely bright prospects prefer not to finance through new stock offerings, whereas firms with poor prospects do like to finance with outside equity. How should you, as an investor, react to this conclusion? You ought to say, "If I see that a company plans to issue new stock, this should worry me because I know that management would not want to issue stock if future prospects looked good. However, management would want to issue stock if things looked bad. Therefore, I should lower my estimate of the firm's value, other things held constant, if it plans to issue new stock."

If you gave this answer, your views are consistent with those of sophisticated portfolio managers. *In a nutshell, the announcement of a stock offering is generally taken as a* **signal** *that the firm's prospects as seen by its management are not bright.* This, in turn, suggests that when a firm announces a new stock offering, more often than not, the price of its stock will decline.[17] Empirical studies have shown that this situation does indeed exist.[18]

What are the implications of all this for capital structure decisions? Issuing stock emits a negative signal and thus tends to depress the stock price, so even if the company's prospects are bright, a firm should, in normal times, maintain a **reserve borrowing capacity** that can be used in the event that some especially good investment opportunity comes along. *This means that firms should, in normal times, use more equity and less debt than is suggested by the tax benefit/bankruptcy cost trade-off model illustrated in Figure 14-9.*

14-4e Using Debt Financing to Constrain Managers

In Chapter 1 we stated that conflicts of interest may arise if managers and shareholders have different objectives. Such conflicts are particularly likely when the firm has more cash than is needed to support its core operations. Managers often use excess cash to finance their pet projects or for perquisites such as plush offices, corporate jets, and sky boxes at sports arenas, all of which may do little to benefit stock prices.[19] By contrast, managers with more limited free cash flow are less able to make wasteful expenditures.

Firms can reduce excess cash flow in a variety of ways. One way is to funnel some of it back to shareholders through higher dividends or stock repurchases.

Signal
An action taken by a firm's management that provides clues to investors about how management views the firm's prospects.

Reserve Borrowing Capacity
The ability to borrow money at a reasonable cost when good investment opportunities arise. Firms often use less debt than specified by the MM optimal capital structure in "normal" times to ensure that they can obtain debt capital later if necessary.

---

[16] Of course, Firm U would have to make certain disclosures when it offered new shares to the public, but it might be able to meet the legal requirements without fully disclosing management's worst fears.

[17] Stock issues are more of a negative signal for mature companies than for new, rapidly growing ones, where investors expect rapid growth to require additional equity.

[18] See Paul Asquith and David W. Mullins, Jr., "The Impact of Initiating Dividend Payments on Shareholders' Wealth," *Journal of Business*, January 1983, pp. 77–96.

[19] If you don't believe corporate managers can waste money, read Bryan Burrough, *Barbarians at the Gate* (New York: Harper & Row, 1990), the story of the takeover of RJR-Nabisco.

Another alternative is to tilt the target capital structure toward more debt in the hope that higher debt service requirements will force managers to become more disciplined. If debt is not serviced as required, the firm will be forced into bankruptcy, in which case its managers would lose their jobs. Therefore, a manager is less likely to buy an expensive new corporate jet if the firm has large debt service requirements.

A leveraged buyout (LBO) is a good way to reduce excess cash flow. In an LBO debt is used to finance the purchase of a high percentage of the company's shares. Indeed, the projected savings from reducing frivolous waste has motivated quite a few leveraged buyouts. As noted, high debt payments after the LBO force managers to conserve cash by eliminating unnecessary expenditures.

Of course, increasing debt and reducing free cash flow has its downside: It increases the risk of bankruptcy. A former professor (who is the newly appointed Federal Reserve Chairman) has argued that adding debt to a firm's capital structure is like putting a dagger into the steering wheel of a car.[20] The dagger—which points toward your stomach—motivates you to drive more carefully, but you may get stabbed if someone runs into you, even if you are being careful. The analogy applies to corporations in the following sense: Higher debt forces managers to be more careful with shareholders' money, but even well-run firms could face bankruptcy (get stabbed) if some event beyond their control such as a war, an earthquake, a strike, or a recession occurs. To complete the analogy, the capital structure decision comes down to deciding how big a dagger stockholders should use to keep managers in line.

If you find our discussion of capital structure theory imprecise and somewhat confusing, you're not alone. In truth, no one knows how to identify a firm's precise optimal capital structure or how to measure the effects of capital structure changes on stock prices and the cost of capital. In practice, capital structure decisions must be made using a combination of judgment and numerical analysis. Still, an understanding of the theoretical issues presented here can help you make better judgments on capital structure issues.

Why does MM's theory with taxes lead to 100 percent debt?

How would an increase in corporate taxes tend to affect firms' capital structures? What about personal taxes?

Explain what asymmetric information means, and how signals affect capital structure decisions.

What is meant by reserve borrowing capacity, and why is it important to firms?

How can the use of debt serve to discipline managers?

14-5 CHECKLIST FOR CAPITAL STRUCTURE DECISIONS

In addition to the types of analysis discussed previously, firms generally consider the following factors when making capital structure decisions:

---

[20] Ben Bernanke, "Is There Too Much Corporate Debt?" Federal Reserve Bank of Philadelphia *Business Review*, September/October 1989, pp. 3–13.

1. *Sales stability.* A firm whose sales are relatively stable can safely take on more debt and incur higher fixed charges than a company with unstable sales. Utility companies, because of their stable demand, have historically been able to use more financial leverage than industrial firms.

2. *Asset structure.* Firms whose assets are suitable as security for loans tend to use debt rather heavily. General-purpose assets that can be used by many businesses make good collateral, whereas special-purpose assets do not. Thus, real estate companies are usually highly leveraged, whereas companies involved in technological research are not.

3. *Operating leverage.* Other things the same, a firm with less operating leverage is better able to employ financial leverage because it will have less business risk.

4. *Growth rate.* Other things the same, faster growing firms must rely more heavily on external capital. Further, the flotation costs involved in selling common stock exceed those incurred when selling debt, which encourages rapidly growing firms to rely more heavily on debt. At the same time, however, those firms often face higher uncertainty, which tends to reduce their willingness to use debt.

5. *Profitability.* It is often observed that firms with very high rates of return on investment use relatively little debt. Although there is no theoretical justification for this fact, one practical explanation is that very profitable firms such as Intel, Microsoft, and Coca-Cola simply do not need to do much debt financing. Their high rates of return enable them to do most of their financing with internally generated funds.

6. *Taxes.* Interest is a deductible expense, and deductions are most valuable to firms with high tax rates. Therefore, the higher a firm's tax rate, the greater the advantage of debt.

7. *Control.* The effect of debt versus stock on a management's control position can influence capital structure. If management currently has voting control (more than 50 percent of the stock) but is not in a position to buy any more stock, it may choose debt for new financings. On the other hand, management may decide to use equity if the firm's financial situation is so weak that the use of debt might subject it to serious risk of default, because if the firm goes into default, the managers will probably lose their jobs. However, if too little debt is used, management runs the risk of a takeover. Thus, control considerations could lead to the use of either debt or equity because the type of capital that best protects management will vary from situation to situation. In any event, if management is at all insecure, it will consider the control situation.

8. *Management attitudes.* No one can prove that one capital structure will lead to higher stock prices than another. Management, then, can exercise its own judgment about the proper capital structure. Some managements tend to be more conservative than others, and thus use less debt than an average firm in their industry, whereas aggressive managements use more debt in their quest for higher profits.

9. *Lender and rating agency attitudes.* Regardless of managers' own analyses of the proper leverage factors for their firms, lenders' and rating agencies' attitudes frequently influence financial structure decisions. Corporations often discuss their capital structures with lenders and rating agencies and give much weight to their advice. For example, one large utility was recently told by Moody's and Standard & Poor's that its bonds would be downgraded if it issued more bonds. This influenced its decision, and it financed its expansion with common equity.

10. *Market conditions.* Conditions in the stock and bond markets undergo both long- and short-run changes that can have an important bearing on a firm's optimal capital structure. For example, during a recent credit crunch, the junk bond market dried up, and there was simply no market at a "reasonable" interest rate for any new long-term bonds rated below BBB. Therefore, low-rated companies in need of capital were forced to go to the stock market or to the short-term debt market, regardless of their target capital structures. When conditions eased, however, these companies sold long-term bonds to get their capital structures back on target.

11. *The firm's internal condition.* A firm's own internal condition can also have a bearing on its target capital structure. For example, suppose a firm has just successfully completed an R&D program, and it forecasts higher earnings in the immediate future. However, the new earnings are not yet anticipated by investors, hence are not reflected in the stock price. This company would not want to issue stock—it would prefer to finance with debt until the higher earnings materialize and are reflected in the stock price. Then it could sell an issue of common stock, use the proceeds to retire the debt, and return to its target capital structure. This point was discussed earlier in connection with asymmetric information and signaling.

12. *Financial flexibility.* An astute corporate treasurer made this statement to the authors:

> Our company can earn a lot more money from good capital budgeting and operating decisions than from good financing decisions. Indeed, we are not sure exactly how financing decisions affect our stock price, but we know for sure that having to turn down promising ventures because funds are not available will reduce our long-run profitability. For this reason, my primary goal as treasurer is to always be in a position to raise the capital needed to support operations.
>
> We also know that when times are good, we can raise capital with either stocks or bonds, but when times are bad, suppliers of capital are much more willing to make funds available if we give them a stronger position, and this means debt. Further, when we sell a new issue of stock, this sends a negative "signal" to investors, so stock sales by a mature company such as ours are not desirable.

Putting all these thoughts together gives rise to the goal of maintaining financial flexibility, which, from an operational viewpoint, means maintaining adequate "reserve borrowing capacity." Determining the "adequate" reserve is judgmental, but it clearly depends on the factors discussed in the chapter, including the firm's forecasted need for funds, predicted capital market conditions, management's confidence in its forecasts, and the consequences of a capital shortage.

How does sales stability affect the target capital structure?

How do the types of assets used affect a firm's capital structure?

How do taxes affect the target capital structure?

How do lender and rating agency attitudes affect capital structure?

How does the firm's internal condition affect its actual capital structure?

What is financial flexibility, and is it increased or decreased by a high debt ratio?

GLOBAL PERSPECTIVES

Taking a Look at Global Capital Structures

To what extent does capital structure vary across different countries? The following table, which is taken from a recent study by Raghuram Rajan and Luigi Zingales, both of the University of Chicago, shows the median debt ratios of firms in the largest industrial countries.

Rajan and Zingales show that there is considerable variation in capital structure among firms within each of the seven countries. They also show that capital structures for the firms in each country are generally determined by a similar set of factors: firm size, profitability, market-to-book ratio, and the ratio of fixed assets to total assets. All in all, the Rajan-Zingales study suggests that the points developed in this chapter apply to firms all around the world.

Source: Raghuram G. Rajan and Luigi Zingales, "What Do We Know about Capital Structure? Some Evidence from International Data," *Journal of Finance*, Vol. 50, no. 5 (December 1995), pp. 1421–1460. Used with permission.

MEDIAN PERCENTAGE OF DEBT TO TOTAL ASSETS IN DIFFERENT COUNTRIES

Country	Book Value Debt Ratio
United Kingdom	10%
Germany	11
France	18
Italy	21
Japan	21
United States	25
Canada	32

14-6 VARIATIONS IN CAPITAL STRUCTURES

As might be expected, wide variations in the use of financial leverage occur both across industries and among the individual firms in each industry. Table 14-4 illustrates differences for selected industries; the ranking is in descending order of the common equity ratio, as shown in Column 1.[21]

Pharmaceutical and computer companies use relatively little debt because their industries tend to be cyclical, oriented toward research, or subject to huge product liability suits. Utility companies, on the other hand, use debt relatively heavily because their fixed assets make good security for mortgage bonds and also because their relatively stable sales make it safe to carry more than average debt.

The times-interest-earned (TIE) ratio gives an indication of how vulnerable the company is to financial distress. This ratio depends on three factors: (1) the percentage of debt, (2) the interest rate on the debt, and (3) the company's profitability. Generally, low-leveraged industries such as computers and pharmaceuticals have high coverage ratios, whereas industries such as utilities, which finance heavily with debt, have low coverages.

Wide variations also exist among firms within given industries. For example, although the average ratio of common equity to total capital in 2005 for the pharmaceutical industry was about 81 percent, GlaxoSmithKline had a ratio of only 57.5 percent. Thus, factors unique to individual firms, including managerial attitudes, play an important role in setting target capital structures.

---

[21] Information on capital structures and financial strength is available from a multitude of sources. We used the *MSN Money* Web site to develop Table 14-4, but published sources include *The Value Line Investment Survey, Robert Morris Association Annual Studies*, and *Dun & Bradstreet Key Business Ratios*.

	TABLE 14-4	*Capital Structure Percentages, 2005: Six Industries Ranked by Common Equity Ratios*[a]			

Industry	Common Equity Ratio[b] (1)	Long-Term Debt Ratio (2)	Times-Interest-Earned Ratio (3)	Return on Equity (4)
Pharmaceuticals	80.65%	19.35%	31.6	22.00%
Computers	76.34	23.66	61.6	15.90
Steel	67.57	32.43	10.4	39.30
Aerospace	64.10	35.90	4.7	11.60
Railroads	59.17	40.83	3.8	9.80
Utilities	40.65	59.35	2.2	10.10

Notes:

[a] Capital structure ratios are calculated as a percentage of total capital, where total capital is defined as long-term debt plus equity, with both measured at book value.

[b] These ratios are based on accounting (or book) values. Stated on a market-value basis, the equity percentages would rise because most stocks sell at prices that are much higher than their book values.

Source: MSN Money; **http://moneycentral.msn.com**; June 24, 2005.

Why do wide variations in the use of financial leverage occur both across industries and among individual firms in each industry?

Tying It All Together

When we studied the cost of capital in Chapter 10, we took the firm's financing choice as given and then calculated the cost of capital based on that capital structure. Then, in Chapters 11, 12, and 13, we described capital budgeting techniques, which use the cost of capital as input. Capital budgeting decisions determine the types of projects that the firm accepts, which affect the nature of the firm's assets and its business risk. In this chapter we reverse the process, taking the firm's assets and business risk as given and then seeking to determine the best way to finance those assets. More specifically, in this chapter we examined the effects of financial leverage on stock prices, earnings per share, and the cost of capital, and we discussed various theories of capital structure.

The different theories lead to different conclusions about the optimal capital structure, and no one has been able to prove that one theory is better than the others. Therefore, we cannot estimate the optimal capital structure with much precision. Accordingly, financial executives generally treat the optimal capital structure as a range—for example, 40 to 50 percent debt—rather than as a precise point, such as 45 percent. The concepts discussed in this chapter are used as a guide, and they help managers understand the factors that should be considered when setting their target capital structures.

SELF-TEST QUESTIONS AND PROBLEMS
(Solutions Appear in Appendix A)

ST-1 **Key terms** Define each of the following terms:
a. Optimal capital structure; target capital structure
b. Business risk; financial risk
c. Financial leverage; operating leverage; operating breakeven
d. Hamada equation; unlevered beta
e. Symmetric information; asymmetric information
f. Modigliani-Miller theories
g. Trade-off theory; signaling theory
h. Reserve borrowing capacity

ST-2 **Operating leverage and breakeven analysis** Olinde Electronics Inc. produces stereo components that sell at P = $100 per unit. Olinde's fixed costs are $200,000; variable costs are $50 per unit; 5,000 components are produced and sold each year; EBIT is currently $50,000; and Olinde's assets (all equity financed) are $500,000. Olinde can change its production process by adding $400,000 to assets and $50,000 to fixed operating costs. This change would (1) reduce variable costs per unit by $10 and (2) increase output by 2,000 units, but (3) the sales price on all units would have to be lowered to $95 to permit sales of the additional output. Olinde has tax loss carry-forwards that cause its tax rate to be zero, it uses no debt, and its average cost of capital is 10 percent.
a. Should Olinde make the change?
b. Would Olinde's breakeven point increase or decrease if it made the change?
c. Suppose Olinde were unable to raise additional equity financing and had to borrow the $400,000 at an interest rate of 10 percent to make the investment. Use the Du Pont equation to find the expected ROA of the investment. Should Olinde make the change if debt financing must be used?

ST-3 **Financial leverage** Gentry Motors Inc., a producer of turbine generators, is in this situation: EBIT = $4 million; tax rate = T = 35%; debt outstanding = D = $2 million; r_d = 10%; r_s = 15%; shares of stock outstanding = N_0 = 600,000; and book value per share = $10. Because Gentry's product market is stable and the company expects no growth, all earnings are paid out as dividends. The debt consists of perpetual bonds.
a. What are Gentry's earnings per share (EPS) and its price per share (P_0)?
b. What is Gentry's weighted average cost of capital (WACC)?
c. Gentry can increase its debt by $8 million, to a total of $10 million, using the new debt to buy back and retire some of its shares at the current price. Its interest rate on debt will be 12 percent (it will have to call and refund the old debt), and its cost of equity will rise from 15 to 17 percent. EBIT will remain constant. Should Gentry change its capital structure?
d. If Gentry did not have to refund the $2 million of old debt, how would this affect things? Assume that the new and the still outstanding debt are equally risky, with r_d = 12%, but that the coupon rate on the old debt is 10 percent.
e. What is Gentry's TIE coverage ratio under the original situation and under the conditions in part c of this question?

QUESTIONS

14-1 Changes in sales cause changes in profits. Would the profit change associated with sales changes be larger or smaller if a firm increased its operating leverage? Explain your answer.

14-2 Would each of the following increase, decrease, or have an indeterminant effect on a firm's breakeven point (unit sales)?
a. An increase in the sales price with no change in unit costs.
b. An increase in fixed costs accompanied by a decrease in variable costs.
c. A new firm decides to use MACRS depreciation for both book and tax purposes rather than the straight-line depreciation method.
d. Variable labor costs decline; other things are held constant.

14-3 Discuss the following statement: "All else equal, firms with relatively stable sales are able to carry relatively high debt ratios." Is the statement true or false? Why?

14-4 If Congress increased the personal tax rate on dividends and capital gains but simultaneously reduced the rate on corporate income, what effect would this have on the average company's capital structure?

14-5 Which of the following would likely encourage a firm to increase the debt in its capital structure?

    a. The corporate tax rate increases.
    b. The personal tax rate increases.
    c. Due to market changes, the firm's assets become less liquid.
    d. Changes in the bankruptcy code make bankruptcy less costly to the firm.
    e. The firm's sales and earnings become more volatile.

14-6 Why do public utilities generally use different capital structures than drug companies?

14-7 Why is EBIT generally considered to be independent of financial leverage? Why might EBIT actually be affected by financial leverage at high debt levels?

14-8 Is the debt level that maximizes a firm's expected EPS the same as the one that maximizes its stock price? Explain.

14-9 If a firm goes from zero debt to successively higher levels of debt, why would you expect its stock price to first rise, then hit a peak, and then begin to decline?

14-10 When the Bell System was originally broken up, the old AT&T was split into a new AT&T plus 7 regional telephone companies. The specific reason for forcing the breakup was to increase the degree of competition in the telephone industry. AT&T had a monopoly on local service, long distance, and the manufacture of all the equipment used by telephone companies, and the breakup was expected to open most of these markets to competition. In the court order that set the terms of the breakup, the capital structures of the surviving companies were specified, and much attention was given to the increased competition telephone companies could expect in the future. Do you think the optimal capital structure after the breakup was the same as the pre-breakup optimal capital structure? Explain your position.

14-11 A firm is about to double its assets to serve its rapidly growing market. It must choose between a highly automated production process and a less automated one, and it must also choose a capital structure for financing the expansion. Should the asset investment and financing decisions be jointly determined, or should each decision be made separately? How would these decisions affect one another? How could the leverage concept be used to help management analyze the situation?

PROBLEMS

**Easy
Problems 1–5**

14-1 **Breakeven analysis** A company's fixed operating costs are $500,000, its variable costs are $3.00 per unit, and the product's sales price is $4.00. What is the company's breakeven point; that is, at what unit sales volume would its income equal its costs?

14-2 **Optimal capital structure** Jackson Trucking Company is in the process of setting its target capital structure. The CFO believes the optimal debt ratio is somewhere between 20 and 50 percent, and her staff has compiled the following projections for EPS and the stock price at various debt levels:

Debt Ratio	Projected EPS	Projected Stock Price
20%	$3.20	$35.00
30	3.45	36.50
40	3.75	36.25
50	3.50	35.50

Assuming that the firm uses only debt and common equity, what is Jackson's optimal capital structure? At what debt ratio is the company's WACC minimized?

14-3 **Risk analysis**

a. Given the following information, calculate the expected value for Firm C's EPS. Data for Firms A and B are as follows: $E(EPS_A) = \$5.10$, and $\sigma_A = \$3.61$; $E(EPS_B) = \$4.20$, and $\sigma_B = \$2.96$.

	PROBABILITY				
	0.1	**0.2**	**0.4**	**0.2**	**0.1**
Firm A: EPS_A	($1.50)	$1.80	$5.10	$8.40	$11.70
Firm B: EPS_B	(1.20)	1.50	4.20	6.90	9.60
Firm C: EPS_C	(2.40)	1.35	5.10	8.85	12.60

b. You are given that $\sigma_C = \$4.11$. Discuss the relative riskiness of the three firms' earnings.

14-4 **Unlevered beta** Harley Motors has $10 million in assets, which were financed with $2 million of debt and $8 million in equity. Harley's beta is currently 1.2 and its tax rate is 40 percent. Use the Hamada equation to find Harley's unlevered beta, b_U.

14-5 **Financial leverage effects** Firms HL and LL are identical except for their leverage ratios and the interest rates they pay on debt. Each has $20 million in assets, $4 million of EBIT, and is in the 40 percent federal-plus-state tax bracket. Firm HL, however, has a debt ratio (D/A) of 50 percent and pays 12 percent interest on its debt, whereas LL has a 30 percent debt ratio and pays only 10 percent interest on its debt.

a. Calculate the rate of return on equity (ROE) for each firm.
b. Observing that HL has a higher ROE, LL's treasurer is thinking of raising the debt ratio from 30 to 60 percent, even though that would increase LL's interest rate on all debt to 15 percent. Calculate the new ROE for LL.

Intermediate
Problems 6–9

14-6 **Breakeven analysis** The Weaver Watch Company sells watches for $25; the fixed costs are $140,000; and variable costs are $15 per watch.

a. What is the firm's gain or loss at sales of 8,000 watches? At 18,000 watches?
b. What is the breakeven point? Illustrate by means of a chart.
c. What would happen to the breakeven point if the selling price were raised to $31? What is the significance of this analysis?
d. What would happen to the breakeven point if the selling price were raised to $31 but variable costs rose to $23 a unit?

14-7 **Financial leverage effects** The Neal Company wants to estimate next year's return on equity (ROE) under different leverage ratios. Neal's total assets are $14 million, it currently uses only common equity, and its federal-plus-state tax rate is 40 percent. The CFO has estimated next year's EBIT for 3 possible states of the world: $4.2 million with a 0.2 probability, $2.8 million with a 0.5 probability, and $700,000 with a 0.3 probability. Calculate Neal's expected ROE, standard deviation, and coefficient of variation for each of the following debt ratios, and evaluate the results:

Debt Ratio	Interest Rate
0%	—
10	9%
50	11
60	14

14-8 **Hamada equation** Cyclone Software Co. is trying to establish its optimal capital structure. Its current capital structure consists of 25 percent debt and 75 percent equity; however, the CEO believes the firm should use more debt. The risk-free rate, r_{RF}, is 5 percent, the market risk premium, RP_M, is 6 percent, and the firm's tax rate is 40 percent. Currently, Cyclone's cost of equity is 14 percent, which is determined by the CAPM. What would be Cyclone's estimated cost of equity if it changed its capital structure to 50 percent debt and 50 percent equity?

14-9 **Recapitalization** Tapley Inc. currently has assets of $5 million, zero debt, is in the 40 percent federal-plus-state tax bracket, has a net income of $1 million, and pays out 40 percent of its earnings as dividends. Net income is expected to grow at a constant rate of 5 percent per year, 200,000 shares of stock are outstanding, and the current WACC is 13.40 percent.

The company is considering a recapitalization where it will issue $1 million in debt and use the proceeds to repurchase stock. Investment bankers have estimated that if the company goes through with the recapitalization, its before-tax cost of debt will be 11 percent, and its cost of equity will rise to 14.5 percent.

a. What is the stock's current price per share (before the recapitalization)?
b. Assuming that the company maintains the same payout ratio, what will be its stock price following the recapitalization?

Challenging
Problems 10–13

14-10 **Breakeven and operating leverage**

a. Given the graphs shown below, calculate the total fixed costs, variable costs per unit, and sales price for Firm A. Firm B's fixed costs are $120,000, its variable costs per unit are $4, and its sales price is $8 per unit.
b. Which firm has the higher operating leverage at any given level of sales? Explain.
c. At what sales level, in units, do both firms earn the same operating profit?

BREAKEVEN CHARTS FOR PROBLEM 14-10

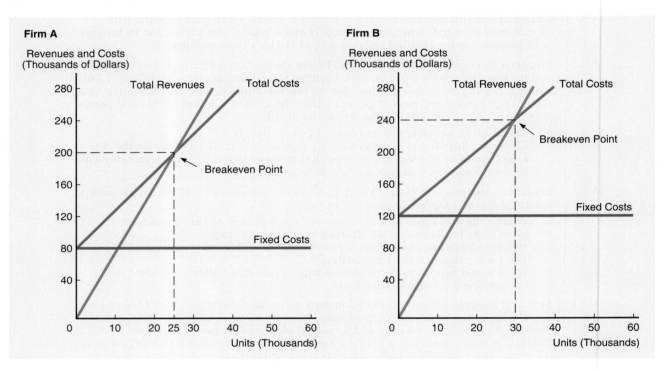

14-11 **Recapitalization** Currently, Bloom Flowers Inc. has a capital structure consisting of 20 percent debt and 80 percent equity. Bloom's debt currently has an 8 percent yield to maturity. The risk-free rate (r_{RF}) is 5 percent, and the market risk premium ($r_M - r_{RF}$) is 6 percent. Using the CAPM, Bloom estimates that its cost of equity is currently 12.5 percent. The company has a 40 percent tax rate.

a. What is Bloom's current WACC?
b. What is the current beta on Bloom's common stock?
c. What would Bloom's beta be if the company had no debt in its capital structure? (That is, what is Bloom's unlevered beta, b_U?)

Bloom's financial staff is considering changing its capital structure to 40 percent debt and 60 percent equity. If the company went ahead with the proposed change, the yield to maturity on the company's bonds would rise to 9.5 percent. The proposed change will have no effect on the company's tax rate.

d. What would be the company's new cost of equity if it adopted the proposed change in capital structure?
e. What would be the company's new WACC if it adopted the proposed change in capital structure?
f. Based on your answer to part e, would you advise Bloom to adopt the proposed change in capital structure? Explain.

14-12 **Breakeven and leverage** Wingler Communications Corporation (WCC) produces premium stereo headphones that sell for $28.80 per set, and this year's sales are expected to be 450,000 units. Variable production costs for the expected sales under present production methods are estimated at $10,200,000, and fixed production (operating) costs at present are $1,560,000. WCC has $4,800,000 of debt outstanding at an interest rate of 8 percent. There are 240,000 shares of common stock outstanding, and there is no preferred stock. The dividend payout ratio is 70 percent, and WCC is in the 40 percent federal-plus-state tax bracket.

The company is considering investing $7,200,000 in new equipment. Sales would not increase, but variable costs per unit would decline by 20 percent. Also, fixed operating costs would increase from $1,560,000 to $1,800,000. WCC could raise the required capital by borrowing $7,200,000 at 10 percent or by selling 240,000 additional shares at $30 per share.

a. What would be WCC's EPS (1) under the old production process, (2) under the new process if it uses debt, and (3) under the new process if it uses common stock?

b. At what unit sales level would WCC have the same EPS, assuming it undertakes the investment and finances it with debt or with stock? {Hint: V = variable cost per unit = $8,160,000/450,000, and EPS = $[(PQ - VQ - F - I)(1 - T)]/N$. Set $EPS_{Stock} = EPS_{Debt}$ and solve for Q.}

c. At what unit sales level would EPS = 0 under the three production/financing setups—that is, under the old plan, the new plan with debt financing, and the new plan with stock financing? (Hint: Note that $V_{Old} = $10,200,000/450,000$, and use the hints for part b, setting the EPS equation equal to zero.)

d. On the basis of the analysis in parts a through c, and given that operating leverage is lower under the new setup, which plan is the riskiest, which has the highest expected EPS, and which would you recommend? Assume here that there is a fairly high probability of sales falling as low as 250,000 units, and determine EPS_{Debt} and EPS_{Stock} at that sales level to help assess the riskiness of the two financing plans.

14-13 **Financing alternatives** The Severn Company plans to raise a net amount of $270 million to finance new equipment and working capital in early 2006. Two alternatives are being considered: Common stock may be sold to net $60 per share, or bonds yielding 12 percent may be issued. The balance sheet and income statement of the Severn Company prior to financing are as follows:

The Severn Company: Balance Sheet as of December 31, 2005 (Millions of Dollars)

Current assets	$ 900.00	Accounts payable	$ 172.50
		Notes payable to bank	255.00
		Other current liabilities	225.00
		Total current liabilities	$ 652.50
Net fixed assets	450.00	Long-term debt (10%)	300.00
		Common stock, $3 par	60.00
		Retained earnings	337.50
Total assets	$1,350.00	Total liabilities and equity	$1,350.00

The Severn Company: Income Statement for Year Ended December 31, 2005 (Millions of Dollars)

Sales	$2,475.00
Operating costs	2,227.50
Earnings before interest and taxes (10%)	$ 247.50
Interest on short-term debt	15.00
Interest on long-term debt	30.00
Earnings before taxes	$ 202.50
Federal-plus-state taxes (40%)	81.00
Net income	$ 121.50

The probability distribution for annual sales is as follows:

Probability	Annual Sales (Millions of Dollars)
0.30	$2,250
0.40	2,700
0.30	3,150

Assuming that EBIT equals 10 percent of sales, calculate earnings per share (EPS) under both the debt financing and the stock financing alternatives at each possible level of sales. Then calculate expected EPS and σ_{EPS} under both debt and stock financing alternatives. Also, calculate the debt ratio and the times-interest-earned (TIE) ratio at the expected sales level under each alternative. The old debt will remain outstanding. Which financing method do you recommend?

COMPREHENSIVE/SPREADSHEET PROBLEM

14-14 **WACC and optimal capital structure** Elliott Athletics is trying to determine its optimal capital structure, which now consists of only debt and common equity. The firm does not currently use preferred stock in its capital structure, and it does not plan to do so in the future. Its treasury staff has consulted with investment bankers and, on the basis of those discussions, has created the following table showing its debt cost at different levels:

Debt-to-Assets Ratio (w_d)	Equity-to-Assets Ratio (w_c)	Debt-to-Equity Ratio (D/E)	Bond Rating	Before-Tax Cost of Debt (r_d)
0.0	1.0	0.00	A	7.0%
0.2	0.8	0.25	BBB	8.0
0.4	0.6	0.67	BB	10.0
0.6	0.4	1.50	C	12.0
0.8	0.2	4.00	D	15.0

Elliott uses the CAPM to estimate its cost of common equity, r_s, and estimates that the risk-free rate is 5 percent, the market risk premium is 6 percent, and its tax rate is 40 percent. Elliott estimates that if it had no debt, its "unlevered" beta, b_U, would be 1.2.

a. What is the firm's optimal capital structure, and what would be its WACC at the optimal capital structure?

b. If Elliott's managers anticipate that the company's business risk will increase in the future, what effect would this increase likely have on its target capital structure?

c. If Congress were to dramatically increase the corporate tax rate, what effect would this increase likely have on Elliott's target capital structure?

d. Plot a graph of the after-tax cost of debt, the cost of equity, and the WACC versus (1) the debt/assets ratio and (2) the debt/equity ratio.

Integrated Case

Campus Deli Inc.

14-15 **Optimal capital structure** Assume that you have just been hired as business manager of Campus Deli (CD), which is located adjacent to the campus. Sales were $1,100,000 last year; variable costs were 60 percent of sales; and fixed costs were $40,000. Therefore, EBIT totaled $400,000. Because the university's enrollment is capped, EBIT is expected to be constant over time. Because no expansion capital is required, CD pays out all earnings as dividends. Assets are $2 million, and 80,000 shares are outstanding. The management group owns about 50 percent of the stock, which is traded in the over-the-counter market.

CD currently has no debt—it is an all-equity firm—and its 80,000 shares outstanding sell at a price of $25 per share, which is also the book value. The firm's federal-plus-state tax rate is 40 percent. On the basis of statements made in your finance text, you believe that CD's shareholders would be better off if some debt financing were used. When you suggested this to your new boss, she encouraged you to pursue the idea, but to provide support for the suggestion.

In today's market, the risk-free rate, r_{RF}, is 6 percent and the market risk premium, RP_M, is 6 percent. CD's unlevered beta, b_U, is 1.0. CD currently has no debt, so its cost of equity (and WACC) is 12 percent.

If the firm were recapitalized, debt would be issued, and the borrowed funds would be used to repurchase stock. Stockholders, in turn, would use funds provided by the repurchase to buy equities in other fast-food companies similar to CD. You plan to complete your report by asking and then answering the following questions.

a. (1) What is business risk? What factors influence a firm's business risk?
    (2) What is operating leverage, and how does it affect a firm's business risk?
b. (1) What is meant by the terms "financial leverage" and "financial risk"?
    (2) How does financial risk differ from business risk?
c. Now, to develop an example that can be presented to CD's management as an illustration, consider two hypothetical firms, Firm U, with zero debt financing, and Firm L, with $10,000 of 12 percent debt. Both firms have $20,000 in total assets and a 40 percent federal-plus-state tax rate, and they have the following EBIT probability distribution for next year:

Probability	EBIT
0.25	$2,000
0.50	3,000
0.25	4,000

(1) Complete the partial income statements and the firms' ratios in Table IC14-1.
(2) Be prepared to discuss each entry in the table and to explain how this example illustrates the effect of financial leverage on expected rate of return and risk.
d. After speaking with a local investment banker, you obtain the following estimates of the cost of debt at different debt levels (in thousands of dollars):

Amount Borrowed	D/A Ratio	D/E Ratio	Bond Rating	r_d
$ 0	0	0	—	—
250	0.125	0.1429	AA	8.0%
500	0.250	0.3333	A	9.0
750	0.375	0.6000	BBB	11.5
1,000	0.500	1.0000	BB	14.0

Now consider the optimal capital structure for CD.

(1) To begin, define the terms "optimal capital structure" and "target capital structure."
(2) Why does CD's bond rating and cost of debt depend on the amount of money borrowed?
(3) Assume that shares could be repurchased at the current market price of $25 per share. Calculate CD's expected EPS and TIE at debt levels of $0, $250,000, $500,000, $750,000, and $1,000,000. How many shares would remain after recapitalization under each scenario?
(4) Using the Hamada equation, what is the cost of equity if CD recapitalizes with $250,000 of debt? $500,000? $750,000? $1,000,000?
(5) Considering only the levels of debt discussed, what is the capital structure that minimizes CD's WACC?
(6) What would be the new stock price if CD recapitalizes with $250,000 of debt? $500,000? $750,000? $1,000,000? Recall that the payout ratio is 100 percent, so g = 0.
(7) Is EPS maximized at the debt level that maximizes share price? Why or why not?

(8) Considering only the levels of debt discussed, what is CD's optimal capital structure?

(9) What is the WACC at the optimal capital structure?

e. Suppose you discovered that CD had more business risk than you originally estimated. Describe how this would affect the analysis. What if the firm had less business risk than originally estimated?

f. What are some factors a manager should consider when establishing his or her firm's target capital structure?

g. Put labels on Figure IC14-1, and then discuss the graph as you might use it to explain to your boss why CD might want to use some debt.

h. How does the existence of asymmetric information and signaling affect capital structure?

TABLE IC14-1 *Income Statements and Ratios*

	Firm U			Firm L		
Assets	$20,000	$20,000	$20,000	$20,000	$20,000	$20,000
Equity	$20,000	$20,000	$20,000	$10,000	$10,000	$10,000
Probability	0.25	0.50	0.25	0.25	0.50	0.25
Sales	$ 6,000	$ 9,000	$12,000	$ 6,000	$ 9,000	$12,000
Operating costs	4,000	6,000	8,000	4,000	6,000	8,000
Earnings before interest and taxes	$ 2,000	$ 3,000	$ 4,000	$ 2,000	$ 3,000	$ 4,000
Interest (12%)	0	0	0	1,200		1,200
Earnings before taxes	$ 2,000	$ 3,000	$ 4,000	$ 800	$	$ 2,800
Taxes (40%)	800	1,200	1,600	320		1,120
Net income	$ 1,200	$ 1,800	$ 2,400	$ 480	$	$ 1,680
Basic earning power						
(BEP = EBIT/Assets)	10.0%	15.0%	20.0%	10.0%	%	20.0%
ROE	6.0%	9.0%	12.0%	4.8%	%	16.8%
TIE	∞	∞	∞	1.7×	×	3.3×
Expected basic earning power		15.0%			%	
Expected ROE		9.0%			10.8%	
Expected TIE		∞			2.5×	
σ_{BEP}		3.5%			%	
σ_{ROE}		2.1%			4.2%	
σ_{TIE}		0			0.6×	

FIGURE IC14-1 *Relationship between Capital Structure and Stock Price*

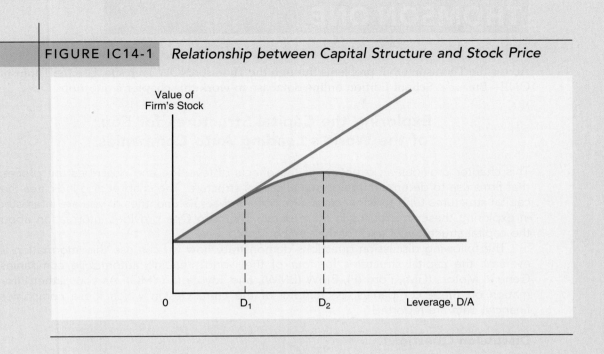

cyberproblem

Please go to the ThomsonNOW Web site to access the Cyberproblems.

THOMSON ONE | Business School Edition

Access the Thomson ONE problems through the ThomsonNOW Web site. Use the Thomson ONE—Business School Edition online database to work this chapter's questions.

Exploring the Capital Structures for Four of the World's Leading Auto Companies

This chapter provides an overview of the effects of leverage and describes the process that firms use to determine their optimal capital structure. The chapter also indicates that capital structures tend to vary across industries and across countries. If you are interested in exploring these differences in more detail, Thomson One provides information about the capital structures of each of the companies it follows.

The following discussion questions demonstrate how we can use this information to evaluate the capital structures for four of the world's leading automobile companies: General Motors (GM), Ford (F), BMW (BMW), and Toyota (J:TYMO). As you gather information on these companies, be mindful of the currencies in which these companies' financial data are reported.

Discussion Questions

1. To get an overall picture of each company's capital structure it is helpful to see a chart that summarizes the company's capital structure over the past decade. To obtain this chart, choose a company to start with and select FINANCIALS. Next, select MORE>THOMSON REPORTS & CHARTS>CAPITAL STRUCTURE. This should generate a chart that plots the company's long-term debt, common equity, and total current liabilities over the past decade. What, if any, are the major trends that emerge from looking at these charts? Do these companies tend to have relatively high or relatively low levels of debt? Do these companies have significant levels of current liabilities? Have their capital structures changed over time? (Note an alternative chart can be found by selecting FINANCIALS>FUNDAMENTAL RATIOS> WORLDSCOPE RATIOS>DEBT TO ASSETS & EQUITY RATIOS.)

2. To get more details about the companies' capital structures over the past five years, select FINANCIALS>FUNDAMENTAL RATIOS>THOMSON RATIOS. From here you can select ANNUAL RATIOS and/or 5 YEAR AVERAGE RATIOS REPORT. In each case, you can scroll down and look for "Leverage Ratios." Here you will find a variety of leverage ratios for the past 5 years. (Notice that these 2 pages offer different information. The ANNUAL RATIOS page offers year-end leverage ratios, while the 5 YEAR AVERAGE RATIOS REPORT offers the average ratio over the previous 5 years for each calendar date. In other words, the 5 YEAR AVERAGE RATIOS REPORT smooths the changes in capital structure over the reporting period.) Do these ratios suggest that the company has significantly changed its capital structure over the past 5 years? If so, what factors could possibly explain this shift? (Financial statements might be useful to detect any shifts that may have led to the company's changing capital structure. You may also consult the company's annual report to see if there is any discussion and/or explanation for these changes. Both the historical financial statements and annual report information can be found via Thomson One.)

3. Repeat this procedure for the other 3 auto companies. Do you find similar capital structures for each of the 4 companies? Do you find that the capital structures have moved in the same direction over the past 5 years, or have the different companies changed their capital structures in different ways over the past 5 years?

4. The financial ratios investigated thus far are based on book values of debt and equity. Determine whether using the market value of equity (market capitalization

found on the OVERVIEW page) makes a significant difference in the most recent year's "LT Debt Pct Common Equity" and "Total Debt Pct Total Assets." (Note: "LT Debt" is defined by Thomson One as the "Long Term Debt" listed on the balance sheet, while "Total Debt" is defined as "Long Term Debt" plus "ST Debt & Current Portion Due LT Debt.") Are there big differences between the capital structures measured on a book or market basis?

5. You can also use Thomson One to search for companies with either very large or very small debt ratios. For example, if you want to find the top 50 companies with the highest debt ratio select: SEARCH FOR COMPANIES, ADVANCED SEARCH, ALL COMPANIES, THOMSON FINANCIAL, RATIOS, and LEVERAGE. From here, let's select "LT Debt Pct Total Cap 5 Yr. Avg." (This will focus in on the average capital structure over the past 5 years, which should give us perhaps a better indication of the company's long-run target capital structure.) Once you click on SELECT, you should see the "Search Expression Builder" screen. From here, you go to "Rank" and select the top 50 by typing 50 in the box below rank, and click on ADD. You can easily change this to also select the bottom 50 (or perhaps the bottom 5 or 10 percent). Take a close look at the resulting firms by clicking on SEARCH. Do you observe any differences between the types of firms that have high debt levels and the types of firms that have low debt levels? Are these patterns similar to what you expect after reading the chapter? (As a quick review, you may want to look at the average capital structures for different industries, which is summarized in the text). *Note: The searches are cumulative, so that if you ask for the top 10 percent of the database, and follow that by asking for the bottom 5 percent, you will be shown the bottom 5 percent of the top 10 percent. In other words, you would only see a small subset of the firms you are asking for. Hence, when beginning a new search, clear all existing searches first.*

6. From the submenu just above the list of firms, you may choose a number of options. "List" displays a list of the firms and allows you to access a firm report. "Profiles" provides key information about the firms, such as ticker, country, exchange, and industry code. "Financials" gives a couple of key financial figures (expressed in US dollars) from the firms' balance sheets and income statements. "Market Data" includes the firms' market capitalization, current price, P/E ratio, EPS, etc. "Report Writer" allows you to create customized company reports.

CHAPTER 15

DISTRIBUTIONS TO SHAREHOLDERS: DIVIDENDS AND SHARE REPURCHASES

Microsoft Shifts Gears and Begins to Unload Part of Its Vast Cash Hoard

Profitable companies regularly face three important questions: (1) How much of their free cash flow should they pass on to shareholders? (2) Should they provide this cash to stockholders by raising the dividend or by repurchasing stock? (3) Should they maintain a stable, consistent payment policy, or should they let the payments vary as conditions change?

In this chapter we discuss many of the issues that affect firms' cash distribution policies. As we will see, mature companies with stable cash flows and limited growth opportunities tend to return more of their cash to shareholders, either by paying dividends or by using the cash to repurchase common stock. By contrast, rapidly growing companies with good investment opportunities are prone to invest most of their available cash in new projects and thus are less likely to pay dividends or repurchase stock. Microsoft, which has long been regarded as the epitome of a growth company, illustrates this tendency. Its sales grew from $786 *million* in 1989 to a projected $39.7 *billion* in 2005, which translates to an annual rate of nearly 28 percent. Much of this growth came from large, long-term investments in new products and technology, and, given its emphasis on growth, it paid no dividends.

However, over time this quintessential growth company has begun to evolve into a mature "cash-cow." Its Windows and Office products have saturated the market, and they help the company regularly produce $1 billion worth of free cash flow each month. As a result, the company reported a staggering $37.6 billion in cash on its balance sheet as of March 31, 2005.

Then Microsoft shifted gears and began paying a significant portion of that cash to shareholders. First, in 2003 it initiated a regular quarterly dividend of 8 cents a share. That regular dividend was doubled in 2004 and doubled again in 2005. More dramatically, in mid-2004 it announced plans to pay a one-time special dividend of $3 a share. All told, in 2004 the company returned $32.62 billion in cash to its shareholders. In addition, it announced plans to repurchase up to $30 billion worth of stock in the open market. These repurchases would return cash to shareholders and also tend to drive up the stock price.

Microsoft's decision to pay dividends coincided with a change in the Tax Code that lowered the tax rate on dividends from 35 to 15 percent for most investors. This change obviously made dividends even more attractive to investors, and as we will see in the chapter, it is causing many companies, in addition to Microsoft, to rethink their dividend policies.

Putting Things In Perspective

Successful companies earn income. That income can then be reinvested in operating assets, used to retire debt, or distributed to stockholders. If the decision is made to distribute income to stockholders, three key issues arise: (1) How much should be distributed? (2) Should the distribution be in the form of dividends or should the cash be passed on to shareholders by buying back stock? (3) How stable should the distribution be; that is, should the funds paid out from year to year be stable and dependable, which stockholders like, or be allowed to vary with the firms' cash flows and investment requirements, which might be better from the firm's standpoint? These three issues are the primary focus of this chapter.

15-1 DIVIDENDS VERSUS CAPITAL GAINS: WHAT DO INVESTORS PREFER?

When deciding how much cash to distribute, financial managers must keep in mind that the firm's objective is to maximize shareholder value. Consequently, the **target payout ratio**—defined as the percentage of net income to be paid out as cash dividends—should be based in large part on investors' preferences for dividends versus capital gains: Do investors prefer to receive dividends or to have the firm plow the cash back into the business, which presumably will produce capital gains? This preference can be considered in terms of the constant growth stock valuation model.

Target Payout Ratio
The target percentage of net income paid out as cash dividends.

$$\hat{P}_0 = \frac{D_1}{r_s - g}$$

If the company increases the payout ratio, this raises D_1. This increase in the numerator, taken alone, would cause the stock price to rise. However, if D_1 is raised, then less money will be available for reinvestment, which will cause the expected growth rate to decline and thus lower the stock's price. Therefore, any

Optimal Dividend Policy
The dividend policy that strikes a balance between current dividends and future growth and maximizes the firm's stock price.

Dividend Irrelevance Theory
The theory advanced by Professors Merton Miller and Franco Modigliani which stated that a firm's dividend policy has no effect on either its value or its cost of capital.

change in the payout policy will have two opposing effects, so the **optimal dividend policy** must strike the particular balance between current dividends and future growth that maximizes the stock price. In the following sections we discuss the major theories that have been advanced to explain how investors regard current dividends versus future growth.

15-1a Dividend Irrelevance Theory

Professors Merton Miller and Franco Modigliani (MM) advanced the theory that dividend policy has no effect on either the price of a firm's stock or its cost of capital; that is, dividend policy is **irrelevant**.[1] MM developed their theory under a stringent set of assumptions, and under those assumptions, they proved that a firm's value is determined only by its basic earning power and its business risk. In other words, the value of the firm depends only on the income produced by its assets, not on how this income is split between dividends and retained earnings. Note, though, MM assumed, among other things, that no taxes are paid on dividends, that stocks can be bought and sold with no transactions costs, and that everyone—investors and managers alike—has the same information regarding firms' future earnings.

Given their assumptions, MM argued that any shareholder can construct his or her own dividend policy. For example, if a firm does not pay dividends, a shareholder who wants a 5 percent dividend can "create" it by selling 5 percent of his or her stock. Conversely, if a company pays a higher dividend than an investor desires, the investor can use the unwanted dividends to buy additional shares of the company's stock. Note, though, that in the real world individual investors who want additional dividends would have to incur transactions costs to sell shares, and investors who do not want dividends would have to first pay taxes on the unwanted dividends and then incur transactions costs to purchase shares with the after-tax dividends. Because taxes and transactions costs certainly exist, dividend policy may well be relevant and investors may prefer policies that help them reduce taxes and transactions costs.

In defense of their theory, MM noted that many stocks are owned by institutional investors who pay no taxes and who can buy and sell stocks with very low transactions costs. For such investors, dividend policy might well be irrelevant, and if these investors dominate the market and represent the "marginal investor," then MM's theory could be valid in spite of its unrealistic assumptions. Note too that for tax-paying investors, the taxes and transactions costs depend on the individual investor's income and how long he or she plans to hold the stock. As a result—when it comes to investors' preferences for dividends, one size doesn't fit all. Next we discuss why some investors prefer dividends whereas others may prefer capital gains.

15-1b Reasons Some Investors Prefer Dividends

The principal conclusion of MM's dividend irrelevance theory is that dividend policy does not affect stock prices and thus the required rate of return on equity, r_s. Early critics of MM's theory suggested that investors preferred a sure dividend today to an uncertain future capital gain. In particular, Myron Gordon and John Lintner argued that r_s decreases as the dividend payout is increased because investors are less certain of receiving the capital gains that are supposed to result from retaining earnings than they are of receiving dividend payments.[2]

---

[1] Merton H. Miller and Franco Modigliani, "Dividend Policy, Growth, and the Valuation of Shares," *Journal of Business*, October 1961, pp. 411–433.

[2] Myron J. Gordon, "Optimal Investment and Financing Policy," *Journal of Finance*, May 1963, pp. 264–272; and John Lintner, "Dividends, Earnings, Leverage, Stock Prices, and the Supply of Capital to Corporations," *Review of Economics and Statistics*, August 1962, pp. 243–269.

MM disagreed. They argued that r_s is independent of dividend policy, which implies that investors are indifferent between dividends and capital gains, that is, between D_1/P_0 and g. MM called the Gordon-Lintner argument the **bird-in-the-hand** fallacy because, in MM's view, most investors plan to reinvest their dividends in the stock of the same or similar firms, and, in any event, the riskiness of the firm's cash flows to investors in the long run is determined by the riskiness of operating cash flows, not by dividend payout policy.

Keep in mind, however, that MM's theory relied on the assumption that there are no taxes and transactions costs, which means that investors who prefer dividends could simply create their own dividend policy by selling a percentage of their stock each year. In reality, most investors face transactions costs when they sell stock, so investors who are looking for a steady stream of income would logically prefer that companies pay regular dividends. For example, retirees who have accumulated wealth over time and now want yearly income from their investments should prefer dividend-paying stocks.

Bird-in-the-Hand Theory
MM's name for the theory that a firm's value will be maximized by setting a high dividend payout ratio.

15-1c Reasons Some Investors May Prefer Capital Gains

While dividends reduce transactions costs for investors who are looking for steady income from their investments, dividends would increase transactions costs for other investors who are less interested in income and more interested in saving money for the long-term future. These long-term investors would want to reinvest their dividends, and that would create transactions costs. Given this concern, a number of companies have established dividend reinvestment plans that help investors automatically reinvest their dividends. (We discuss dividend reinvestment plans in Section 15.4 of this chapter.)

In addition, and perhaps more importantly, the Tax Code encourages many individual investors to prefer capital gains to dividends. Prior to 2003, dividends were taxed at the ordinary income tax rate, which went up to 38 percent versus a rate of 20 percent on capital gains. Since 2003, the maximum tax rate on dividends and long-term capital gains has been set at 15 percent. This change lowered the tax disadvantage of dividends, but reinvestment and the accompanying capital gains still have two tax advantages over dividends. First, taxes must be paid on dividends the year they are received, whereas taxes on capital gains are not paid until the stock is sold. Due to time value effects, a dollar of taxes paid in the future has a lower effective cost than a dollar of taxes paid today. Moreover, if a stock is held by someone until he or she dies, there is no capital gains tax at all—the beneficiaries who receive the stock can use the stock's value on the death day as their cost basis, which permits them to completely escape the capital gains tax.

Because of these tax advantages, some investors probably prefer to have companies retain most of their earnings, and those investors might be willing to pay more for low-payout companies than for otherwise similar high-payout companies.

Explain briefly the ideas behind the dividend irrelevance theory.

What did Modigliani and Miller assume about taxes and brokerage costs when they developed their dividend irrelevance theory?

Why did MM refer to the Gordon-Lintner dividend argument as the bird-in-the-hand fallacy?

Why do some investors prefer high-dividend-paying stocks?

Why might other investors prefer low-dividend-paying stocks?

15-2 OTHER DIVIDEND POLICY ISSUES

Before we discuss how dividend policy is set in practice, we need to examine two other issues that affect dividend policy: (1) the *information content*, or *signaling, hypothesis* and (2) the *clientele effect*.

15-2a Information Content, or Signaling, Hypothesis

It has been observed that an increase in the dividend is often accompanied by an increase in the stock price, while a dividend cut generally leads to a stock price decline. This observation was used to refute MM's irrelevance theory—their opponents argued that stock price actions after changes in dividend payouts demonstrate that investors prefer dividends to capital gains. However, MM argued differently. They noted that corporations are reluctant to cut dividends, hence that they do not raise dividends unless they anticipate earning more in the future to support the higher dividends. Thus, MM argued that a higher-than-expected dividend increase is a **signal** to investors that the firm's management forecasts good future earnings.[3] Conversely, a dividend reduction, or a smaller-than-expected increase, is a signal that management forecasts poor future earnings. If the MM position is correct, then stock price changes after dividend increases or decreases do not demonstrate a preference for dividends over retained earnings. Rather, price changes simply indicate that dividend announcements have **information,** or **signaling, content** about future earnings.

Managers often do have better information about future prospects for dividends than public stockholders, so there is clearly some information content in dividend announcements. However, it is difficult to tell whether the stock price changes that follow increases or decreases in dividends reflect only signaling effects (as MM argue) or both signaling and dividend preference. Still, signaling effects should definitely be considered when a firm is contemplating a change in dividend policy. For example, if a firm has good long-term prospects but also a need for cash to fund current investments, it might be tempted to cut the dividend to increase funds available for investment. However, this action might cause the stock price to decline because the dividend reduction was taken as a signal that management thought future earnings were going to decline, when just the reverse was true. So, managers should consider signaling effects when they set dividend policy.

15-2b Clientele Effect

As we indicated earlier, different groups, or **clienteles,** of stockholders prefer different dividend payout policies. For example, retired individuals, pension funds, and university endowment funds generally prefer cash income, so they often want the firm to pay out a high percentage of its earnings. Such investors are frequently in low or even zero tax brackets, so taxes are of little concern. On the other hand, stockholders in their peak-earning years might prefer reinvestment, because they

Signal
An action taken by a firm's management that provides clues to investors about how management views the firm's prospects.

Information Content (Signaling) Hypothesis
The theory that investors regard dividend changes as signals of management's earnings forecasts.

Clienteles
Different groups of stockholders who prefer different dividend payout policies.

---

[3] Stephen Ross has suggested that managers can use capital structure as well as dividends to give signals concerning firm's future prospects. For example, a firm with good earnings prospects can carry more debt than a similar firm with poor earnings prospects. This theory, called *incentive signaling*, rests on the premise that signals with cash-based variables (either debt interest or dividends) cannot be mimicked by unsuccessful firms because such firms do not have the future cash-generating power to maintain the announced interest or dividend payment. Thus, investors are more likely to believe a glowing verbal report when it is accompanied by a dividend increase or a debt-financed expansion program. See Stephen A. Ross, "The Determination of Financial Structure: The Incentive-Signaling Approach," *The Bell Journal of Economics*, Spring 1977, pp. 23–40.

have less need for current investment income and would simply reinvest dividends received, after incurring both income taxes and brokerage costs.

If a firm retains and reinvests income rather than paying dividends, those stockholders who need current income would be disadvantaged. The value of their stock might increase, but they would be forced to go to the trouble and expense of selling off some of their shares to obtain cash. Also, some institutional investors (or trustees for individuals) would be legally precluded from selling stock and then "spending capital." On the other hand, stockholders who are saving rather than spending dividends would favor the low dividend policy: The less the firm pays out in dividends, the less these stockholders would have to pay in current taxes, and the less trouble and expense they would have to go through to reinvest their after-tax dividends. Therefore, investors who want current investment income should own shares in high-dividend-payout firms, while investors with no need for current investment income should own shares in low-dividend-payout firms. For example, investors seeking high cash income might invest in electric utilities, which had an average payout of 61 percent in 2004, while those favoring growth could invest in the software industry, which paid out only 5 percent that same year.

All of this suggests that a **clientele effect** exists, which means that firms have different clienteles, that the clienteles have different preferences, and hence that a dividend policy change might upset the dominant clientele and thus have a negative effect on the stock's price.[4] This suggests that companies should stabilize their dividend policy so as to avoid disrupting their clienteles.

Clientele Effect
The tendency of a firm to attract a set of investors who like its dividend policy.

Define (1) information content and (2) the clientele effect, and explain how they affect dividend policy.

15-3 ESTABLISHING THE DIVIDEND POLICY IN PRACTICE

Investors may or may not prefer dividends to capital gains; however, they almost certainly prefer *predictable* dividends. Given this situation, how should firms set their basic dividend policies? In particular, how should a company establish the specific percentage of earnings it will distribute, the form of this distribution, and the stability of its distributions over time? In this section, we describe how most firms answer these questions.

15-3a Setting the Target Payout Ratio: The Residual Dividend Model[5]

When deciding how much cash to distribute to stockholders, two points should be kept in mind: (1) The overriding objective is to maximize shareholder value, and (2) the firm's cash flows really belong to its shareholders, so management

---

[4] For example, see R. Richardson Pettit, "Taxes, Transactions Costs and the Clientele Effect of Dividends," *The Journal of Financial Economics*, December 1977, pp. 419–436.

[5] The term "payout ratio" can be interpreted in two ways: (1) the conventional way, where the payout ratio means the percentage of net income paid out as cash dividends, or (2) the percentage of net income distributed to stockholders through both dividends and share repurchases. In this section, we assume that no repurchases occur. Increasingly, though, firms are using the residual model to determine "distributions to shareholders" and then making a separate decision as to the form of those distributions. Further, over time an increasing percentage of the distribution has been in the form of share repurchases.

should not retain income unless they can reinvest those earnings at higher rates of return than shareholders could earn themselves. On the other hand, recall from Chapter 10 that internal equity (retained earnings) is cheaper than external equity (new common stock), so if good investments are available, it is better to finance them with retained earnings than with new stock.

When establishing a dividend policy, one size does not fit all. Some firms produce a lot of cash but have limited investment opportunities—this is true for firms in profitable but mature industries where few growth opportunities exist. Such firms typically distribute a large percentage of their cash to shareholders, thereby attracting investor clienteles who prefer high dividends. Other firms generate little or no excess cash but have many good investment opportunities. Such firms generally distribute little or no cash but enjoy rising earnings and stock prices, thereby attracting investors who prefer capital gains.

Over the past few decades, there have been increasing numbers of young, high-growth firms trading on the stock exchanges. A recent study by Eugene Fama and Kenneth French shows that the proportion of firms paying dividends has fallen sharply over this time period. In 1978, 66.5 percent of firms on the major stock exchanges paid dividends. By 1999, that proportion had fallen to 20.8 percent. Fama and French's analysis suggested that part of this decline was due to the changing composition of firms on the exchanges. Their analysis also indicates that this decline is due to the fact that firms of all types have become less likely to pay dividends.[6]

As a result of the 2003 tax changes, which lowered the tax rate on dividends to that on capital gains, many companies initiated or increased their dividend payments. Previously, these companies would have been more inclined to buy back shares. In 2002, only 113 companies raised or initiated dividends; however, in 2003 that number doubled, to 229. As of 2004, 2,000 domestic U.S. companies paid dividends and 356 of the 500 companies in the S&P 500 index paid dividends.[7]

As Table 15-1 suggests, dividend payouts and dividend yields for large corporations vary considerably. Generally, firms in stable, cash-producing industries such as utilities, food, and tobacco pay relatively high dividends, whereas companies in rapidly growing industries such as computer software and biotechnology tend to pay lower dividends. Average dividends also differ significantly across countries. Higher payout ratios in some countries can be partially explained by lower tax rates on earnings distributed as cash dividends relative to applicable rates on reinvested income. This biases the dividend policy toward higher payouts.

For a given firm, the optimal payout ratio is a function of four factors: (1) management's opinion about its investors' preferences for dividends versus capital gains, (2) the firm's investment opportunities, (3) its target capital structure, and (4) the availability and cost of external capital. The last three elements are combined in what we call the **residual dividend model.** Under this model a firm follows these four steps when establishing its target payout ratio: (1) It determines the optimal capital budget; (2) it determines the amount of equity needed to finance that budget, given its target capital structure; (3) it uses retained earnings to meet equity requirements to the extent possible; and (4) it pays dividends only if more earnings are available than are needed to support

Residual Dividend Model

A model in which the dividend paid is set equal to net income minus the amount of retained earnings necessary to finance the firm's optimal capital budget.

---

[6] Eugene F. Fama and Kenneth R. French, "Disappearing Dividends: Changing Firm Characteristics or Lower Propensity to Pay?" *Journal of Applied Corporate Finance*, Vol. 14, no. 1 (Spring 2001), pp. 67–79; and "Disappearing Dividends: Changing Firm Characteristics or Lower Propensity to Pay?" *Journal of Financial Economics*, Vol. 60 (April 2001), pp. 3–43. The last citation is a longer and more technical version of the first paper cited.

[7] Carla Pasternak, "Get the Most Out of Dividend-Paying Stocks," *High-Yield Investing*, March 8, 2004.

TABLE 15-1	*Dividend Payouts in 2005*		

Company	Industry	Dividend Payout	Dividend Yield
I. COMPANIES THAT PAY HIGH DIVIDENDS			
General Motors Corporation	Auto manufacturing	266.67%	5.40%
The Southern Company	Electric utilities	73.04	4.20
Merck & Co. Inc.	Pharmaceuticals	60.56	4.80
Verizon Communications	Telecommunications	54.18	4.70
Bank of America Corporation	Banking	51.15	4.30
II. COMPANIES THAT PAY LITTLE OR NO DIVIDENDS			
Wal-Mart Stores Inc.	Discount retail	24.10%	1.20%
Marriott International Inc.	Lodging	15.97	0.60
Texas Instruments Incorporated	Semiconductor	9.17	0.30
Dell Inc.	Personal computing	0.00	0.00
eBay Inc.	Internet software and services	0.00	0.00
Genentech Inc.	Biotechnology	0.00	0.00

Source: MSN Money Web site, **http://moneycentral.msn.com,** July 18, 2005.

the optimal capital budget. The word *residual* implies "leftover," and the residual policy implies that dividends are paid out of "leftover" earnings.

If a firm rigidly follows the residual dividend policy, then dividends paid in any given year can be expressed in the following equation:

$$\text{Dividends} = \text{Net income} - \text{Retained earnings required to help finance new investments}$$

$$= \text{Net income} - [(\text{Target equity ratio})(\text{Total capital budget})]$$

For example, suppose the company has $100 million of earnings, a target equity ratio of 60 percent, and it plans to spend $50 million on capital projects. In that case, it would need $50(0.6) = $30 million of common equity plus $20 million of new debt to finance the capital budget. That would leave $100 − $30 = $70 million available for dividends, which would result in a 70 percent payout ratio.

Note that the amount of equity needed to finance the capital budget might exceed the net income; in the preceding example, if the capital budget were $100/0.6 = $166.67 million or more, no dividends would be paid, and the company would have to issue new common stock in order to maintain its target capital structure.

Most firms have a target capital structure that calls for at least some debt, so new financing is done partly with debt and partly with equity. As long as a firm finances with the optimal mix of debt and equity, and assuming it uses only internally generated equity (retained earnings), then the marginal cost of each new dollar of capital will be minimized. Internally generated equity is available for financing a certain amount of new investment, but beyond that amount, the firm must turn to more expensive new common stock. At the point where new stock must be sold, the cost of equity, and consequently the marginal cost of capital, rises.

To illustrate these points, consider the case of Texas and Western (T&W) Transport Company. T&W's overall composite cost of capital is 10 percent. However, this cost assumes that all new equity comes from retained earnings. If the company must issue new stock, its cost of capital will be higher. T&W has $60 million of net income and a target capital structure of 60 percent equity and 40 percent debt. Provided it does not pay any cash dividends, T&W could make net investments (investments in addition to asset replacements from depreciation) of $100 million, consisting of $60 million from retained earnings plus $40 million of new debt supported by the retained earnings, at a 10 percent marginal cost of capital. If the capital budget exceeded $100 million, the required equity component would exceed net income, which is of course the maximum amount of retained earnings. In this case, T&W would have to issue new common stock, thereby pushing its cost of capital above 10 percent.[8]

At the beginning of its planning period, T&W's financial staff considers all proposed projects for the upcoming period. Any independent project is accepted if its estimated IRR exceeds its risk-adjusted cost of capital. In choosing among mutually exclusive projects, the project with the highest positive NPV is accepted. The capital budget represents the amount of capital that is required to finance all accepted projects. If T&W follows a strict residual dividend policy, we can see from Table 15-2 that the estimated capital budget will have a profound effect on its dividend payout ratio. If investment opportunities are poor, the capital budget will be only $40 million. To maintain the target capital structure, 0.6($40) = $24 million must be equity, with the remaining $16 million coming as debt. If T&W followed a strict residual policy, it would therefore pay out $60 − $24 = $36 million as dividends, hence its payout ratio would be $36/$60 = 0.6 = 60%.

If the company's investment opportunities were average, its capital budget would be $70 million. This would require $42 million of equity, so dividends would be $60 − $42 = $18 million, for a payout of $18/$60 = 30%. Finally, if investment opportunities were good, the capital budget would be $150 million, and 0.6($150) = $90 million of equity would be required. Therefore, all of the net income would be retained, dividends would be zero, and the company would have to issue new common stock to maintain the target capital structure.

We see, then, that under the residual model dividends and the payout ratio would vary with investment opportunities. Similar dividend variations would result from fluctuations in earnings. Because investment opportunities and earnings will surely vary from year to year, strict adherence to the residual dividend policy would result in highly unstable dividends. One year the firm might pay zero dividends because it needed the money to finance good investment opportunities, but the next year it might pay a large dividend because investment opportunities were poor and it therefore did not need to retain much. Similarly, fluctuating earnings would also lead to variable dividends, even if investment opportunities were stable. Therefore, following the residual dividend policy would almost certainly lead to fluctuating, unstable dividends. This would not be bad if investors were not bothered by fluctuating dividends, but since investors do prefer stable, dependable dividends, it would not be optimal to follow the residual model in a strict sense. Therefore, firms should

1. Estimate earnings and investment opportunities, on average, over the next five or so years.
2. Use this forecasted information to find the average residual model amount of dividends, and the payout ratio, during the planning period.
3. Then set a target payout policy based on the projected data.

---

[8] If T&W does not retain all of its earnings, its cost of capital will rise above 10% before its capital budget reaches $100 million. For example, if T&W chose to retain $36 million, its cost of capital would increase once the capital budget exceeded $36/0.6 = $60 million. To see this point, note that a capital budget of $60 million would require $36 million of equity—if the capital budget rose above $60 million, the company's required equity capital would exceed its retained earnings, thereby requiring it to issue new common stock.

TABLE 15-2	*T&W's Dividend Payout Ratio with $60 Million of Net Income When Faced with Different Investment Opportunities (Dollars in Millions)*		
		INVESTMENT OPPORTUNITIES	
	Poor	Average	Good
Capital budget	$40	$70	$150
Net income (NI)	60	60	60
Required equity (0.6 × Capital budget)	24	42	90
Dividends paid (NI − Required equity)	$36	$18	($ 30)[a]
Dividend payout ratio (Dividends/NI)	60%	30%	0%

[a] With a $150 million capital budget, T&W would retain all of its earnings and also issue $30 million of new stock.

Thus, firms should use the residual policy to help set their long-run target payout ratios, but not as a guide to the payout in any one year.

Most larger companies use the residual dividend model in a conceptual sense, then implement it with a computerized financial forecasting model. Information on projected capital expenditures and working capital requirements is entered into the model, along with sales forecasts, profit margins, depreciation, and the other elements required to forecast cash flows. The target capital structure is also specified, and the model then generates the amount of debt and equity that will be required to meet the capital budgeting requirements while maintaining the target capital structure.

Then dividend payments are introduced, and the higher the payout ratio, the greater the required external equity. Most companies use the model to find a dividend payout over the forecast period (generally five years) that will provide sufficient equity to support the capital budget without having to sell new common stock or move the capital structure ratios outside the optimal range. This chapter's *Excel* model includes an illustration of this. In addition, Web Appendix 15A discusses this approach in more detail. The end result might be a memo like the following from the CFO to the chairman of the board:

> We forecasted the total market demand for our products, what our share of the market is likely to be, and our required investments in capital assets and working capital. Using this information, we developed projected balance sheets and income statements for the period 2006–2010.
>
> Our 2005 dividends totaled $50 million, or $2 per share. On the basis of projected earnings, cash flows, and capital requirements, we can increase the dividend by 6 percent per year. This would be consistent with a payout ratio of 42 percent, on average, over the forecast period. Any faster dividend growth rate would require us to sell common stock, cut the capital budget, or raise the debt ratio. Any slower growth rate would lead to increases in the common equity ratio. Therefore, I recommend that the Board increase the dividend for 2006 by 6 percent, to $2.12, and that it plan for similar increases in the future.
>
> Events over the next five years will undoubtedly lead to differences between our forecasts and actual results. If and when such events occur, we would want to reexamine our position. However, I am confident that we can meet random cash shortfalls by increasing our borrowings—we have unused debt capacity that gives us flexibility in this regard.
>
> We ran the corporate model under several scenarios. If the economy totally collapses, our earnings will not cover the dividend. However, in all

GLOBAL PERSPECTIVES

Dividend Yields Around the World

Average dividend yields have varied over time, and they also vary considerably in different countries around the world. The accompanying graph, obtained from a recent study by Elroy Dimson, Paul Marsh, and Mike Staunton of the London Business School, shows how the average dividend yield for 16 different countries has changed over the past century. In both 1900 and 1950, dividend yields varied from nation to nation, but the average around the world was about 5 percent. However, by 2004, the yield in most countries had declined significantly, and the average had fallen to about 3 percent. For the United States, the average dividend yield was 4.3 percent in 1900, 7.2 percent in 1950, and 1.7 percent in 2004. Thus, U.S. stocks went from having one of the highest yields in 1900 to the second lowest in 2004.

DIVIDEND YIELDS AROUND THE WORLD: 1900, 1950, AND 2004

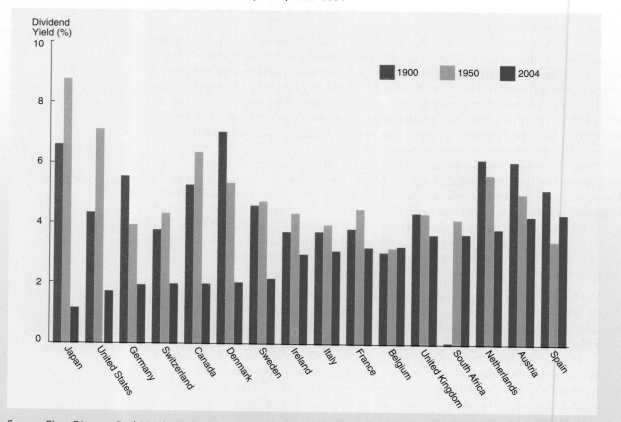

Source: Elroy Dimson, Paul Marsh, and Mike Staunton, "Forecasting the Market," London Business School, Working Paper Draft 1, March 10, 2004.

likely scenarios our cash flows would cover the recommended dividend. I know the Board does not want to push the dividend up to a level where we would have to cut it under bad conditions. Our model runs indicate, though, that the $2.12 dividend could be maintained under any reasonable set of forecasts. Only if we increased the dividend to over $3 would we be seriously exposed to the danger of having to reduce it.

I might also note that most analysts' reports are forecasting that our dividends will grow in the 5 to 6 percent range. Thus, if we go to $2.12, we will be at the high end of the range, which should give our stock a boost. With takeover rumors so widespread, getting the stock up a bit would make us all breathe a little easier.

Finally, we considered distributing cash to shareholders through a stock repurchase program. Here we would reduce the dividend payout ratio and use the funds so generated to buy our stock on the open market. Such a program has several advantages, but it would also have drawbacks. I do not recommend that we institute a stock repurchase program at this time. However, if our free cash flows exceed our forecasts, I would recommend that we use these surpluses to buy back stock. Also, I plan to continue looking into a regular repurchase program, and I may recommend such a program in the future.

This company has very stable operations, so it can plan its dividends with a fairly high degree of confidence. Other companies, especially those in cyclical industries, have difficulty maintaining a dividend in bad times that is really too low in good times. Such companies often set a very low "regular" dividend and then supplement it with an "extra" dividend when times are good. General Motors, Ford, and other auto companies have followed such a **low-regular-dividend-plus-extras** policy in the past. Each company announced a low regular dividend that it was confident it could maintain "through hell or high water," one that stockholders could count on under all conditions. Then, when times were good and profits and cash flows were high, the company would pay a clearly designated extra dividend. Investors recognized that the extras might not be maintained in the future, so they did not interpret them as a signal that the companies' earnings were permanently higher, nor did they take the elimination of the extra as a negative signal.

Low-Regular-Dividend-Plus-Extras
The policy of announcing a low, regular dividend that can be maintained no matter what and then, when times are good, paying a designated "extra" dividend.

15-3b Earnings, Cash Flows, and Dividends

We normally think of earnings as being the primary determinant of dividends, but in reality cash flows are more important. This situation is revealed in Figure 15-1, which gives data for Chevron Corporation from 1979 through 2004. Chevron's dividends increased steadily from 1979 to 1981; during that period both earnings and cash flows were rising, as was the price of oil. After 1981, oil prices declined sharply, pulling earnings down. Cash flows per share (CFPS), though, remained well above the dividend requirement.

Chevron acquired Gulf Oil in 1984, and it borrowed more than $10 billion to finance the acquisition. Interest on the debt hurt earnings immediately after the merger, as did certain write-offs connected with the merger. Further, Chevron's management wanted to pay off new debt as fast as possible. All of this influenced the company's decision to hold the dividend constant from 1982 through 1987. Earnings improved dramatically in 1988, and the dividend has increased more or less steadily since then. Note that the dividend was increased in 1991 in spite of the weak earnings and cash flow resulting from the Persian Gulf War. Then, in October 2001, Chevron acquired Texaco. Earnings in 2001 and 2002 declined due to the decline in crude oil and natural gas prices. On April 13, 2005, Chevron announced plans to acquire Unocal (Union Oil Company of California). The merger is expected to be completed in late 2005. Although the merger appears to be a good fit for Chevron, earnings will still fall over the next couple of years if oil prices decline from their recent highs.

Now look at Columns 4 and 6, which show payout ratios based on earnings and on cash flows. The earnings payout is quite volatile—dividends ranged from 25 to 260 percent of earnings. The cash flow payout, on the other hand, is

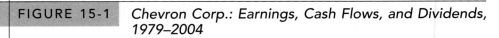

FIGURE 15-1 *Chevron Corp.: Earnings, Cash Flows, and Dividends, 1979–2004*

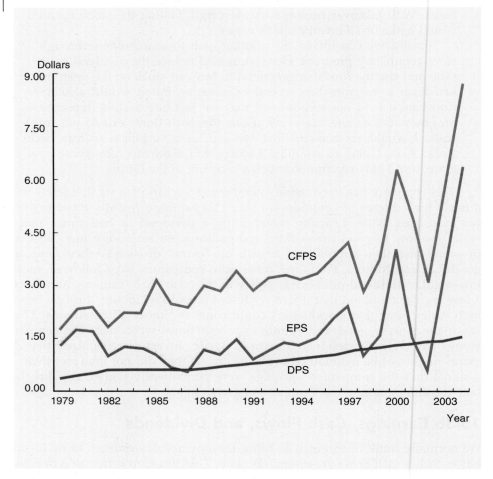

much more stable—it ranged from 18 to 47 percent. Further, the correlation between dividends and cash flows was 0.78 versus 0.46 between dividends and earnings. Thus, dividends clearly depend more on cash flows, which reflect the company's ability to pay cash dividends, than on current earnings, which are heavily influenced by accounting practices and which do not necessarily reflect the firm's cash position.

15-3c Payment Procedures

Dividends are normally paid quarterly, and, if conditions permit, the dividend is increased once each year. For example, Katz Corporation paid $0.50 per quarter in 2005, or at an annual rate of $2.00. In common financial parlance, we say that in 2005 Katz's *regular quarterly dividend* was $0.50, and its *annual dividend* was $2.00. In late 2005, Katz's board of directors met, reviewed projections for 2006, and decided to keep the 2006 dividend at $2.00. The directors announced the $2 rate, so stockholders could count on receiving it unless the company experienced unanticipated operating problems.

The actual payment procedure is as follows:

Declaration Date
The date on which a firm's directors issue a statement declaring a dividend.

1. *Declaration date.* On the **declaration date**—say, November 8—the directors meet and declare the regular dividend, issuing a statement similar to the fol-

| | FIGURE 15-1 | *continued* | | | |

Year (1)	Dividends per Share (2)	Earnings per Share (3)	Earnings Payout (4)	Cash Flow per Share (5)	Cash Flow Payout (6)
1979	$0.36	$1.31	27.78%	$1.82	19.92%
1980	0.45	1.76	25.64	2.32	19.40
1981	0.50	1.74	28.74	2.40	20.83
1982	0.60	1.01	59.55	1.84	32.61
1983	0.60	1.29	46.60	2.23	26.91
1984	0.60	1.24	48.58	2.25	26.67
1985	0.60	1.05	57.28	3.19	18.81
1986	0.60	0.66	91.25	2.47	24.29
1987	0.60	0.53	112.68	2.37	25.32
1988	0.64	1.22	52.47	2.99	21.32
1989	0.70	1.04	67.31	2.83	24.73
1990	0.74	1.51	49.01	3.44	21.51
1991	0.81	0.92	88.04	2.82	28.72
1992	0.83	1.18	70.34	3.22	25.78
1993	0.88	1.40	62.86	3.28	26.83
1994	0.93	1.30	71.54	3.16	29.43
1995	0.96	1.51	63.58	3.34	28.74
1996	1.04	2.03	51.23	3.73	27.88
1997	1.14	2.43	46.91	4.18	27.27
1998	1.22	1.02	119.61	2.80	43.57
1999	1.24	1.57	78.98	3.76	32.98
2000	1.30	3.99	32.58	6.26	20.77
2001	1.33	1.55	85.81	4.88	27.25
2002	1.40	0.54	259.26	2.98	46.98
2003	1.43	3.48	41.09	5.90	24.24
2004	1.54	6.28	24.52	8.67	17.76

Note: For consistency, data have been adjusted for two-for-one splits in 1994 and 2004.

Source: Adapted from *Value Line Investment Survey*, various issues.

lowing: "On November 8, 2005, the directors of Katz Corporation met and declared the regular quarterly dividend of 50 cents per share, payable to holders of record at the close of business on December 8, payment to be made on January 3, 2006." For accounting purposes, the declared dividend becomes an actual liability on the declaration date. If a balance sheet were constructed, the amount ($0.50) × (Number of shares outstanding) would appear as a current liability, and retained earnings would be reduced by a like amount.

2. *Holder-of-record date.* At the close of business on the **holder-of-record date,** December 8, the company closes its stock transfer books and makes up a list of shareholders as of that date. If Katz Corporation is notified of the sale before 5 p.m. on December 8, then the new owner receives the dividend. However, if notification is received on or after December 9, the previous owner receives the dividend check.

3. *Ex-dividend date.* Suppose Jean Buyer buys 100 shares of stock from John Seller on December 5. Will the company be notified of the transfer in time to list Buyer as the new owner and thus pay the dividend to her? To avoid conflict, the securities industry has set up a convention under which the right to the dividend remains with the stock until two business days prior to the holder-of-record date; on the second day before that date, the right to the dividend no longer goes with the shares. The date when the right to the dividend leaves

Holder-of-Record Date
If the company lists the stockholder as an owner on this date, then the stockholder receives the dividend.

Ex-Dividend Date

The date on which the right to the current dividend no longer accompanies a stock; it is usually two business days prior to the holder-of-record date.

the stock is called the **ex-dividend date.** In this case, the ex-dividend date is two days prior to December 8, or December 6:

Dividend goes with stock if it is bought on or before	December 5
Ex-dividend date. Buyer does not receive the dividend	December 6
Buyer does not receive the dividend	December 7
Holder-of-record date; not normally of concern to stockholder	December 8

Therefore, if Buyer is to receive the dividend, she must buy the stock on or before December 5. If she buys it on December 6 or later, Seller will receive the dividend because he will be the official holder of record.

Katz's dividend amounts to $0.50, so the ex-dividend date is important. Barring fluctuations in the stock market, we would normally expect the price of a stock to drop by approximately the amount of the dividend on the ex-dividend date. Thus, if Katz closed at $30.50 on December 5, it would probably open at about $30 on December 6.[9]

4. *Payment date.* The company actually mails the checks to the holders of record on January 3, the **payment date.**

Payment Date

The date on which a firm actually mails dividend checks.

Explain the logic of the residual dividend model, the steps a firm would take to implement it, and why it is more likely to be used to establish a long-run payout target than to set the actual year-by-year payout ratio.

How do firms use long-run planning models to help set dividend policy?

Which are more critical to the dividend decision, earnings or cash flow? Explain.

Explain the procedures used to actually pay the dividend.

Why is the ex-dividend date important to investors?

A firm has a capital budget of $30 million, net income of $35 million, and a target capital structure of 45 percent debt and 55 percent equity. If the residual dividend policy were used, what would its dividend payout ratio be? (52.86%)

---

[9] Tax effects cause the price decline on average to be less than the full amount of the dividend. If you bought Katz's stock on December 5, you would receive the dividend, but you would almost immediately pay 15% of it out in taxes. Thus, you would want to wait until December 6 to buy the stock if you thought you could get it for $0.50 less per share. Your reaction, and that of others, would influence stock prices around dividend payment dates. Here is what would happen:

1. Other things held constant, a stock's price should rise during the quarter, with the daily price increase (for Katz) equal to $0.50/90 = $0.005556. Therefore, if the price started at $30 just after its last ex-dividend date, it would rise to $30.50 on December 5.
2. In the absence of taxes, the stock's price would fall to $30 on December 6 and then start up as the next dividend accrual period began. Thus, over time, if everything else were held constant, the stock's price would follow a sawtooth pattern if it were plotted on a graph.
3. Because of taxes, the stock's price would neither rise by the full amount of the dividend nor fall by the full dividend amount when it goes ex-dividend.
4. The amount of the rise and subsequent fall would be the Dividend $\times$ (1 − T), where generally T = 15%, the tax rate on individual dividends.

See Edwin J. Elton and Martin J. Gruber, "Marginal Stockholder Tax Rates and the Clientele Effect," *Review of Economics and Statistics,* February 1970, pp. 68–74, for an interesting discussion of the subject.

15-4 DIVIDEND REINVESTMENT PLANS

During the 1970s, most large companies instituted **dividend reinvestment plans (DRIPs),** whereby stockholders can automatically reinvest their dividends in the stock of the paying corporation.[10] Today most larger companies offer DRIPs, and participation rates vary considerably. More than 1,000 companies offer DRIPS, and this number keeps increasing. There are two types of DRIPs: (1) plans that involve only "old stock" that is already outstanding and (2) plans that involve newly issued stock. In either case, the stockholder must pay taxes on the amount of the dividends, even though stock rather than cash is received.

Under both types of DRIPs, stockholders choose between continuing to receive dividend checks versus having the company use the dividends to buy more stock in the corporation for the investor. Under an "old stock" plan, the company gives the money that stockholders who elect to use the DRIP would have received to a bank, which acts as a trustee. The bank then uses the money to purchase the corporation's stock on the open market and allocates the shares purchased to the participating stockholders' accounts on a pro rata basis. The transaction costs of buying shares (brokerage costs) are low because of volume purchases, so these plans benefit small stockholders who do not need cash dividends for current consumption.

A "new stock" DRIP invests the dividends in newly issued stock, hence these plans raise new capital for the firm. AT&T, Xerox, and many other companies have used new stock plans to raise substantial amounts of equity capital. No fees are charged to stockholders, and some companies have offered stock at discounts of 2 to 5 percent below the actual market price. The companies offer discounts as a trade-off against flotation costs that would have been incurred if the new stock had been issued through investment bankers.

One interesting aspect of DRIPs is that they are forcing corporations to re-examine their basic dividend policies. A high participation rate in a DRIP suggests that stockholders might be better served if the firm simply reduced cash dividends, which would save stockholders some personal income taxes. Quite a few firms are surveying their stockholders to learn more about their preferences and to find out how they would react to a change in dividend policy. A more rational approach to basic dividend policy decisions may emerge from this research. Companies switch from old stock to new stock DRIPs depending on their need for equity capital.

About 40 percent of the companies offering DRIPs have expanded their programs by moving to "open enrollment," whereby anyone can purchase the firm's stock directly and thus bypass brokers' commissions. ExxonMobil not only allows investors to buy their initial shares at no fee but also lets them pick up additional shares through automatic bank account withdrawals. Several plans, including ExxonMobil's, offer dividend reinvestment for individual retirement accounts, and some, such as U.S. West, allow participants to invest weekly or monthly rather than on the quarterly dividend schedule. With all of these plans, and many others, stockholders can invest more than the dividends they are forgoing—they simply send a check to the company and buy shares without a brokerage commission. According to First Chicago Trust, which handles the paperwork for 13 million shareholder DRIP accounts, at least half of all DRIPs will offer open enrollment, extra purchases, and other expanded services within the next few years.

Dividend Reinvestment Plan (DRIP)
A plan that enables a stockholder to automatically reinvest dividends received back into the stock of the paying firm.

---

[10] See Richard H. Pettway and R. Phil Malone, "Automatic Dividend Reinvestment Plans," *Financial Management*, Winter 1973, pp. 11–18, for an old but still excellent discussion of the subject.

What are dividend reinvestment plans?

What are their advantages and disadvantages from both the stockholders' and the firm's perspectives?

15-5 SUMMARY OF FACTORS INFLUENCING DIVIDEND POLICY

In earlier sections we described the theories of investor preference for dividends and the potential effects of dividend policy on the value of a firm. We also discussed the residual dividend model for setting a firm's long-run target payout ratio. In this section, we discuss several other factors that affect the dividend decision. These factors may be grouped into four broad categories: (1) constraints on dividend payments, (2) investment opportunities, (3) availability and cost of alternative sources of capital, and (4) effects of dividend policy on r_s. We discuss these factors next.

15-5a Constraints

1. *Bond indentures.* Debt contracts often limit dividend payments to earnings generated after the loan was granted. Also, debt contracts often stipulate that no dividends can be paid unless the current ratio, times-interest-earned ratio, and other safety ratios exceed stated minimums.
2. *Preferred stock restrictions.* Typically, common dividends cannot be paid if the company has omitted its preferred dividend. The preferred arrearages must be satisfied before common dividends can be resumed.
3. *Impairment of capital rule.* Dividend payments cannot exceed the balance sheet item "retained earnings." This legal restriction, known as the impairment of capital rule, is designed to protect creditors. Without the rule, a company that is in trouble might distribute most of its assets to stockholders and leave its debtholders out in the cold. (Liquidating dividends can be paid out of capital, but they must be indicated as such, and they must not reduce capital below the limits stated in debt contracts.)
4. *Availability of cash.* Cash dividends can be paid only with cash. Thus, a shortage of cash in the bank can restrict dividend payments. However, the ability to borrow can offset this factor.
5. *Penalty tax on improperly accumulated earnings.* To prevent wealthy individuals from using corporations to avoid personal taxes, the Tax Code provides for a special surtax on improperly accumulated income. Thus, if the IRS can demonstrate that a firm's dividend payout ratio is being deliberately held down to help its stockholders avoid personal taxes, the firm is subject to heavy penalties. This factor is relevant primarily to privately owned firms.

15-5b Investment Opportunities

1. *Number of profitable investment opportunities.* As we saw in our discussion of the residual model, if a firm has a large number of profitable investment opportunities, this will tend to produce a low target payout ratio, and vice versa if the firm has few profitable investment opportunities.
2. *Possibility of accelerating or delaying projects.* The ability to accelerate or postpone projects will permit a firm to adhere more closely to a stable dividend policy.

15-5c Alternative Sources of Capital

1. *Cost of selling new stock.* If a firm needs to finance a given level of investment, it can obtain equity by retaining earnings or by issuing new common stock. If flotation costs (including any negative signaling effects of a stock offering) are high, r_e will be well above r_s, making it better to set a low payout ratio and to finance through retention rather than through sale of new common stock. On the other hand, a high dividend payout ratio is more feasible for a firm whose flotation costs are low. Flotation costs differ among firms—for example, the flotation percentage is especially high for small firms, so they tend to set low payout ratios.

2. *Ability to substitute debt for equity.* A firm can finance a given level of investment with either debt or equity. As noted, low stock flotation costs permit a more flexible dividend policy because equity can be raised either by retaining earnings or by selling new stock. A similar situation holds for debt policy: If the firm can adjust its debt ratio without raising its WACC sharply, it can pay the expected dividend, even if earnings fluctuate, by increasing its debt ratio.

3. *Control.* If management is concerned about maintaining control, it may be reluctant to sell new stock, hence the company may retain more earnings than it otherwise would. However, if stockholders want higher dividends and a proxy fight looms, then the dividend will be increased.

15-5d Effects of Dividend Policy on r_s

The effects of dividend policy on r_s may be considered in terms of four factors: (1) stockholders' desire for current versus future income, (2) the perceived riskiness of dividends versus capital gains, (3) the tax advantage of capital gains over dividends, and (4) the information content of dividends (signaling). We discussed each of these factors earlier, so we only note here that the importance of each factor varies from firm to firm depending on the makeup of its current and possible future stockholders.

It should be apparent that dividend policy decisions are based more on informed judgment than quantitative analysis. Even so, to make rational dividend decisions, financial managers must take account of all the points discussed in the preceding sections.

Identify the four broad sets of factors that affect dividend policy.

What constraints affect dividend policy?

How do investment opportunities affect dividend policy?

How do the availability and cost of outside capital affect dividend policy?

15-6 STOCK DIVIDENDS AND STOCK SPLITS

Stock dividends were originally used by firms that were short of cash in lieu of regular cash dividends. Today, though, their primary purpose is to increase the number of shares outstanding and thus to lower the stock's price in the market. Stock splits have a similar purpose.

Up-to-date information about changes in stock splits and stock repurchases is now just a few clicks away. A good place to get started is The Online Investor at **http://www.investhelp .com**. The Online Investor's home page includes recent stock repurchase and stock split announcements at "Buybacks" and "Splits Center."

Stock dividends and splits can best be explained through an example, and we use Porter Electronic Controls Inc., a $700 million electronic components manufacturer, for this purpose. Since its inception, Porter's markets have been expanding, and the company has enjoyed growth in sales and earnings. Some of its earnings have been paid out in dividends, but some were also retained each year, causing its earnings per share and the stock price to grow. The company began its life with only a few thousand shares outstanding, and, after some years of growth, each of Porter's shares had a very high EPS and DPS. When a "normal" P/E ratio was applied, the resulting market price was so high that few people could afford to buy a "round lot" of 100 shares. This limited demand for the stock and thus kept the firm's total market value below what it would have been if more shares, at a lower price, had been outstanding. To correct this situation, Porter "split its stock," as described in the next section.

15-6a Stock Splits

Stock Split

An action taken by a firm to increase the number of shares outstanding, such as doubling the number of shares outstanding by giving each stockholder two new shares for each one formerly held.

Although there is little empirical evidence to support the contention, there is nevertheless a widespread belief in financial circles that *an optimal price range* exists for stocks. "Optimal" means that if the price is within this range, the price/earnings ratio, hence the firm's value, will be maximized. Many observers, including Porter's management, believe that the best range for most stocks is from $20 to $80 per share. Accordingly, if the price of Porter's stock rose to $80, management would probably declare a two-for-one **stock split,** thus doubling the number of shares outstanding, halving the earnings and dividends per share, and thereby lowering the stock price. Each stockholder would have more shares, but each share would be worth less. If the post-split price were $40, Porter's stockholders would be exactly as well off as they were before the split. However, if the stock price were to stabilize above $40, stockholders would be better off. Stock splits can be of any size—for example, the stock could be split two-for-one, three-for-one, one-and-a-half-for-one, or in any other way.[11]

15-6b Stock Dividends

Stock Dividend

A dividend paid in the form of additional shares of stock rather than in cash.

Stock dividends are similar to stock splits in that they "divide the pie into smaller slices" without affecting the fundamental position of the current stockholders. On a 5 percent stock dividend, the holder of 100 shares would receive an additional 5 shares (without cost); on a 20 percent stock dividend, the same holder would receive 20 new shares; and so on. Again, the total number of shares is increased, so earnings, dividends, and price per share all decline.

If a firm wants to reduce the price of its stock, should it use a stock split or a stock dividend? Stock splits are generally used after a sharp price run-up to produce a large price reduction. Stock dividends used on a regular annual basis will keep the stock price more or less constrained. For example, if a firm's earnings and dividends were growing at about 10 percent per year, its stock price would tend to increase at about that same rate, and it would soon be outside the desired trading range. A 10 percent annual stock dividend would maintain the stock price within the optimal trading range. Note, though, that small stock div-

---

[11] *Reverse splits,* which reduce the shares outstanding, can also be used. For example, a company whose stock sells for $5 might employ a one-for-five reverse split, exchanging one new share for five old ones and raising the value of the shares to about $25, which is within the optimal price range. LTV Corporation did this after several years of losses had driven its stock price below the optimal range.

idends create bookkeeping problems and unnecessary expenses, so firms use stock splits far more often than stock dividends.[12]

15-6c Effect on Stock Prices

If a company splits its stock or declares a stock dividend, will this increase the market value of its stock? Several empirical studies have addressed this question. Here is a summary of their findings.[13]

1. On average, the price of a company's stock rises shortly after it announces a stock split or dividend.
2. One reason that stock splits and stock dividends may lead to higher prices is that investors often take stock splits/dividends as signals of higher future earnings. Because only companies whose managements think things look good tend to split their stocks, the announcement of a stock split is taken as a signal that earnings and cash dividends are likely to rise. Thus, the price increases associated with stock splits/dividends may be the result of a favorable signal for earnings and dividends.
3. If a company announces a stock split or dividend, its price will tend to rise. However, if during the next few months it does not announce an increase in earnings and dividends, then its stock price will drop back to the earlier level. This supports the signaling effect discussed earlier.
4. By creating more shares and lowering the stock price, stock splits may also increase the stock's liquidity. This would tend to increase the firm's value.
5. There is also evidence that stock splits change the mix of shareholders. The proportion of trades made by individual investors tends to increase after a stock split, whereas the proportion of trades made by institutional investors tends to fall. We are not sure how this would affect the stock's value.

What do we conclude from all this? From a pure economic standpoint, stock dividends and splits are just additional pieces of paper. However, they provide management with a relatively low-cost way of signaling that the firm's prospects look good. Further, we should note that since few large, publicly owned stocks sell at prices above several hundred dollars, we simply do not know what the effect would be if Chevron, Microsoft, Xerox, Hewlett-Packard, and other highly successful firms had never split their stocks, and consequently sold at prices in the thousands or even tens of thousands of dollars.[14]

---

[12] Accountants treat stock splits and stock dividends somewhat differently. For example, in a two-for-one stock split, the number of shares outstanding is doubled and the par value is halved, and that is about all there is to it. With a stock dividend, a bookkeeping entry is made transferring "retained earnings" to "common stock." For example, if a firm had 1,000,000 shares outstanding, if the stock price was $10, and if it wanted to pay a 10 percent stock dividend, then (1) each stockholder would be given one new share of stock for each 10 shares held, and (2) the accounting entries would involve showing 100,000 more shares outstanding and transferring 100,000($10) = $1,000,000 from "retained earnings" to "common stock." The retained earnings transfer limits the size of stock dividends, but that is not important because companies can always split their stock in any way they choose.

[13] See Eugene F. Fama, Lawrence Fisher, Michael C. Jensen, and Richard Roll, "The Adjustment of Stock Prices to New Information," *International Economic Review*, February 1969, pp. 1–21; Mark S. Grinblatt, Ronald M. Masulis, and Sheridan Titman, "The Valuation Effects of Stock Splits and Stock Dividends," *Journal of Financial Economics*, December 1984, pp. 461–490; Ravi Dahr, William N. Goetzmann, Shane Shepherd, and Ning Zhu, "The Impact of Clientele Changes: Evidence from Stock Splits," Working Paper Draft, March 2004; and Thomas E. Copeland, "Liquidity Changes Following Stock Splits," *Journal of Finance*, March 1979, pp. 115–141.

[14] It is interesting to note that Berkshire Hathaway, which is controlled by billionaire Warren Buffett, one of the most successful financiers of the 20th century, has never had a stock split, and its stock sold on the NYSE for $84,400 per share in July 2005. But, in response to investment trusts that were being formed to sell fractional units of the stock, and thus, in effect, split it, Buffett himself created a new class of Berkshire Hathaway stock (Class B) worth about 1/30 of a Class A (regular) share.

What are stock dividends and stock splits?

How do stock dividends and splits affect stock prices?

In what situation should a firm pay a stock dividend?

In what situation should a firm split its stock?

Suppose you have 100 common shares of Tillman Industries. The EPS is $4.00, the DPS is $2.00, and the stock sells for $60 per share. Now Tillman announces a two-for-one split. Immediately after the split, how many shares will you have, what will the adjusted EPS and DPS be, and what would you expect the stock price to be? (200 shares; $2.00; $1.00; probably a little over $30)

15-7 STOCK REPURCHASES

Several years ago, a *Fortune* article entitled "Beating the Market by Buying Back Stock" discussed the fact that during a one-year period, more than 600 major corporations repurchased significant amounts of their own stocks. It also gave illustrations of some specific companies' repurchase programs and the effects of these programs on stock prices. The article's conclusion was that "buybacks have made a mint for shareholders who stay with the companies carrying them out."

More recently, as we noted in the opening vignette, Microsoft announced plans to establish a dividend and to repurchase shares of its common stock. As we see in the box entitled, "Stock Repurchases Soar in 2004," Microsoft's recent actions are part of a larger trend in which many leading companies have repurchased stock. How do stock repurchase programs work, and why have they become so prevalent over the past several years? We discuss these questions in the remainder of this section.

Stock Repurchase

A transaction in which a firm buys back shares of its own stock, thereby decreasing shares outstanding, increasing EPS, and, often, increasing the stock price.

There are three principal types of **stock repurchases**: (1) situations where the firm has cash available for distribution to its stockholders, and it distributes this cash by repurchasing shares rather than by paying cash dividends; (2) situations where the firm concludes that its capital structure is too heavily weighted with equity, and it then sells debt and uses the proceeds to buy back its stock; and (3) situations where the firm has issued options to employees and it then uses open market repurchases to obtain stock for use when the options are exercised.

Stock that has been repurchased by a firm is called *treasury stock*. If some of the outstanding stock is repurchased, fewer shares will remain outstanding. Assuming that the repurchase does not adversely affect the firm's future earnings, the earnings per share on the remaining shares will increase, resulting in a higher market price per share. As a result, capital gains will have been substituted for dividends.

15-7a The Effects of Stock Repurchases

Many companies have been repurchasing their stock in recent years. Until the 1980s, most repurchases amounted to a few million dollars, but in 1985, Phillips Petroleum announced plans for the largest repurchase on record at that time—81 million of its shares with a market value of $4.1 billion. Even more dramatic, in 2004, Microsoft announced plans for a $30 billion stock repurchase that will take place over a number of years. Other large repurchases have been made by Procter & Gamble, Dell, Home Depot, Texas Instruments, IBM, Coca-Cola, Tele-

Stock Repurchases Soar in 2004

During 2004, companies announced plans to repurchase $233 billion of common stock. The amount repurchased was more than double the $101 billion repurchased in 2003, and reversed a several year decline in the number of stock buybacks. Over the same time period, there was also a steady increase in corporate dividend payments. Analysts attributed the accelerated activity to the recent surge in corporate cash holdings and increased confidence concerning the health of the economy and financial markets.

The accompanying graph summarizes the recent trends in repurchase activity. Looking ahead, it will be interesting to see if the increased activity in 2004 was a one-year phenomenon or part of a larger trend where companies are directing more of their cash back into the hands of shareholders. In the first quarter of 2005, $61 billion has been allocated to buybacks of shares for S&P 500 companies such as Procter & Gamble, Dell, and Home Depot.

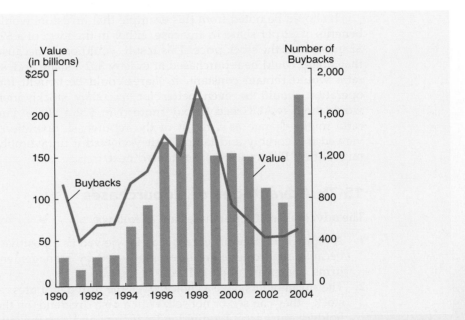

Note: Data include stock repurchases and self-tenders, in which companies buy back shares at a specified price.

Source: Thomson Financial.

Sources: Steven D. Jones, "Moving the Market—Tracking the Numbers, Street Sleuth: Firms Share the Wealth More Often These Days—Share Buyback Programs and Dividend Payments Increased from Last Year," *The Wall Street Journal*, December 31, 2004, p. C3; and "Share Repurchases Surge Among S&P 500 Members; But Buybacks Don't Often Help Shareholders," *SNL IR Advisor*, July 2005.

dyne, Atlantic Richfield, Goodyear, and Xerox. Indeed, since 1985, more shares have been repurchased than issued.

The effects of a repurchase can be illustrated with data on American Development Corporation (ADC). The company expects to earn $4.4 million in 2006, and 50 percent of this amount, or $2.2 million, has been allocated for distribution to common shareholders. There are 1.1 million shares outstanding, and the market price is $20 a share. ADC believes that it can either use the $2.2 million to repurchase 100,000 of its shares through a tender offer at $22 a share or else pay a cash dividend of $2 a share.[15]

The effect of the repurchase on the EPS and market price per share of the remaining stock can be analyzed in the following way:

1. Current EPS $= \dfrac{\text{Total earnings}}{\text{Number of shares}} = \dfrac{\$4.4 \text{ million}}{1.1 \text{ million}} = \$4$ per share

2. P/E ratio $= \dfrac{\$20}{\$4} = 5\times$

3. EPS after repurchasing 100,000 shares $= \dfrac{\$4.4 \text{ million}}{1 \text{ million}}$

   $= \$4.40$ per share

4. Expected market price after repurchase $= (\text{P/E})(\text{EPS}) = (5)(\$4.40)$

   $= \$22$ per share

It should be noted from this example that investors would receive before-tax benefits of $2 per share in any case, either in the form of a $2 cash dividend or a $2 increase in the stock price. This result would occur because we assumed, first, that shares could be repurchased at exactly $22 a share and, second, that the P/E ratio would remain constant. If shares could be bought for less than $22, the operation would be even better for *remaining* stockholders, but the reverse would hold if ADC had to pay more than $22 a share. Furthermore, the P/E ratio might change as a result of the repurchase operation, rising if investors viewed it favorably and falling if they viewed it unfavorably. Some factors that might affect P/E ratios are considered next.

15-7b Advantages of Repurchases

The advantages of repurchases are as follows:

1. A repurchase announcement may be viewed as a positive signal by investors because repurchases are often motivated by managements' belief that their firms' shares are undervalued.
2. The stockholders have a choice when the firm distributes cash by repurchasing stock—they can sell or not sell. With a cash dividend, on the other hand, stockholders must accept a dividend payment and pay the tax. Thus, those stockholders who need cash can sell back some of their shares, while those who do not want additional cash can simply retain their stock. From a tax standpoint, a repurchase permits both types of stockholders to get what they want.
3. A repurchase can remove a large block of stock that is "overhanging" the market and keeping the price per share down.

---

[15] Stock repurchases are generally made in one of three ways: (1) A publicly owned firm can simply buy its own stock through a broker on the open market. (2) It can make a *tender offer*, under which it permits stockholders to send in (that is, "tender") their shares to the firm in exchange for a specified price per share. In this case, it generally indicates that it will buy up to a specified number of shares within a particular time period (usually about two weeks); if more shares are tendered than the company wishes to purchase, purchases are made on a pro rata basis. (3) The firm can purchase a block of shares from one large holder on a negotiated basis. If a negotiated purchase is employed, care must be taken to ensure that this one stockholder does not receive preferential treatment over other stockholders or that any preference given can be justified by "sound business reasons." A number of years ago, Texaco's management was sued by stockholders who were unhappy over the company's repurchase of about $600 million of stock from the Bass Brothers at a substantial premium over the market price. The suit charged that Texaco's management, afraid the Bass Brothers would attempt a takeover, used the buyback to get them off its back. Such payments have been dubbed "greenmail."

4. Dividends are "sticky" in the short run because managements are reluctant to raise the dividend if the increase cannot be maintained in the future—managements dislike cutting cash dividends because of the negative signal a cut gives. Hence, if the excess cash flow is expected to be temporary, management may prefer to make the distribution as a share repurchase rather than to declare an increased cash dividend that cannot be maintained.

5. Companies can use the residual model to set a target cash distribution level, then divide the distribution into a *dividend component* and a *repurchase component*. The dividend payout ratio will be relatively low, but the dividend itself will be relatively secure, and it will grow as a result of the declining number of shares outstanding. This gives the company more flexibility in adjusting the total distribution than if the entire distribution were in the form of cash dividends, because repurchases can be varied from year to year without giving off adverse signals. This procedure has much to recommend it, and it is an important reason for the dramatic increase in the volume of share repurchases.

6. Repurchases can be used to produce large-scale changes in capital structure. For example, a number of years ago Consolidated Edison decided that its debt ratio was too low to minimize its WACC. It then borrowed $400 million and used the funds to repurchase shares of its common stock. This resulted in an immediate shift from a nonoptimal to an optimal capital structure.

7. Companies that use stock options as an important component of employee compensation can repurchase shares and then use those shares when employees exercise their options. This avoids having to issue new shares and the resulting dilution of earnings. Microsoft and other high-tech companies have used this procedure in recent years.

15-7c Disadvantages of Repurchases

Disadvantages of repurchases include the following:

1. Stockholders may not be indifferent between dividends and capital gains, and the price of the stock might benefit more from cash dividends than from repurchases. Cash dividends are generally dependable, but repurchases are not.

2. The *selling* stockholders may not be fully aware of all the implications of a repurchase, or they may not have all the pertinent information about the corporation's present and future activities. This is especially true in situations where management has good reason to believe that the stock price is well below its intrinsic value. However, firms generally announce repurchase programs before embarking on them to avoid potential stockholder suits.

3. The corporation may pay too high a price for the repurchased stock, to the disadvantage of remaining stockholders. If its shares are not actively traded, and if the firm seeks to acquire a relatively large amount of its stock, then the price may be bid above its intrinsic value and then fall after the firm ceases its repurchase operations.

15-7d Conclusions on Stock Repurchases

When all the pros and cons on stock repurchases have been totaled, where do we stand? Our conclusions may be summarized as follows:

1. Because of the deferred tax on capital gains, repurchases have a tax advantage over dividends as a way to distribute income to stockholders. This advantage

is reinforced by the fact that repurchases provide cash to stockholders who want cash but allow those who do not need current cash to delay its receipt. On the other hand, dividends are more dependable and are thus better suited for those who need a steady source of income.

2. Because of signaling effects, companies should not pay fluctuating dividends—that would lower investors' confidence in the company and adversely affect its cost of equity and its stock price. However, cash flows vary over time, as do investment opportunities, so the "proper" dividend in the residual model sense varies. To get around this problem, a company can set its dividend at a level low enough to keep dividend payments from constraining operations and then use repurchases on a more or less regular basis to distribute excess cash. Such a procedure would provide regular, dependable dividends plus additional cash flows to those stockholders who want it.

3. Repurchases are also useful when a firm wants to make a large, rapid shift in its capital structure, wants to distribute cash from a one-time event such as the sale of a division, or wants to obtain shares for use in an employee stock option plan.

In an earlier edition of this book, we argued that companies ought to be doing more repurchasing and paying out less cash as dividends than they were. Increases in the size and frequency of repurchases in recent years suggest that companies have finally reached this same conclusion.

Explain how repurchases can (1) help stockholders hold down taxes and (2) help firms change their capital structures.

What is treasury stock?

What are the three procedures a firm can use to repurchase its stock?

What are some advantages and disadvantages of stock repurchases?

How can stock repurchases help a company operate in accordance with the residual dividend model?

Tying It All Together

Once a company becomes profitable, it must decide what to do with the cash it generates. It may choose to retain cash and use it to purchase additional assets or to repay outstanding debt. Alternatively, it may choose to return cash to shareholders. Keep in mind that every dollar that management chooses to retain is a dollar that shareholders could have received and invested elsewhere. Therefore, managers should retain earnings if and only if they can invest the money within the firm and earn more than stockholders could earn outside the firm. Consequently, high-growth companies with many good projects will tend to retain a high percentage of earnings, whereas mature companies with lots of cash but limited investment opportunities will tend to have generous cash distribution policies.

SELF-TEST QUESTIONS AND PROBLEMS
(Solutions Appear in Appendix A)

ST-1 **Key terms** Define each of the following terms:
  a. Target payout ratio; optimal dividend policy
  b. Dividend irrelevance theory; bird-in-the-hand theory
  c. Information content, or signaling, hypothesis; clientele effect; signal; clienteles
  d. Residual dividend model
  e. Low-regular-dividend-plus-extras policy
  f. Declaration date; holder-of-record date; ex-dividend date; payment date
  g. Dividend reinvestment plan (DRIP)
  h. Stock split; stock dividend
  i. Stock repurchase

ST-2 **Alternative dividend policies** Components Manufacturing Corporation (CMC) has an all-common-equity capital structure. It has 200,000 shares of $2 par value common stock outstanding. When CMC's founder, who was also its research director and most successful inventor, retired unexpectedly to the South Pacific in late 2005, CMC was left suddenly and permanently with materially lower growth expectations and relatively few attractive new investment opportunities. Unfortunately, there was no way to replace the founder's contributions to the firm. Previously, CMC found it necessary to plow back most of its earnings to finance growth, which averaged 12 percent per year. Future growth at a 5 percent rate is considered realistic, but that level would call for an increase in the dividend payout. Further, it now appears that new investment projects with at least the 14 percent rate of return required by CMC's stockholders (r_s = 14%) would amount to only $800,000 for 2006 in comparison to a projected $2,000,000 of net income. If the existing 20 percent dividend payout were continued, retained earnings would be $1.6 million in 2006, but, as noted, investments that yield the 14 percent cost of capital would amount to only $800,000.

  The one encouraging point is that the high earnings from existing assets are expected to continue, and net income of $2 million is still expected for 2006. Given the dramatically changed circumstances, CMC's management is reviewing the firm's dividend policy.

  a. Assuming that the acceptable 2006 investment projects would be financed entirely by earnings retained during the year, calculate DPS in 2006, assuming that CMC uses the residual dividend model.
  b. What payout ratio does your answer to part a imply for 2006?
  c. If a 60 percent payout ratio is maintained for the foreseeable future, what is your estimate of the present market price of the common stock? How does this compare with the market price that should have prevailed under the assumptions existing just before the news about the founder's retirement? If the two values of P_0 are different, comment on why.
  d. What would happen to the price of the stock if the old 20 percent payout were continued? Assume that if this payout is maintained, the average rate of return on the retained earnings will fall to 7.5 percent and the new growth rate will be

$$g = (1.0 - \text{Payout ratio})(\text{ROE})$$

$$= (1.0 - 0.2)(7.5\%)$$

$$= (0.8)(7.5\%) = 6.0\%$$

QUESTIONS

15-1 Discuss the pros and cons of having the directors formally announce what a firm's dividend policy will be in the future.

15-2 "The cost of retained earnings is less than the cost of new outside equity capital. Consequently, it is totally irrational for a firm to sell a new issue of stock and to pay dividends during the same year." Discuss this statement.

15-3 Would it ever be rational for a firm to borrow money in order to pay dividends? Explain.

15-4 Modigliani and Miller (MM) on the one hand and Gordon and Lintner (GL) on the other have expressed strong views regarding the effect of dividend policy on a firm's cost of capital and value.

   a. In essence, what are the MM and GL views regarding the effect of dividend policy on the cost of capital and stock prices?
   b. How could MM use the information content, or signaling, hypothesis to counter their opponents' arguments? If you were debating MM, how would you counter them?
   c. How could MM use the clientele effect concept to counter their opponents' arguments? If you were debating MM, how would you counter them?

15-5 How would each of the following changes tend to affect aggregate (that is, the average for all corporations) payout ratios, other things held constant? Explain your answers.

   a. An increase in the personal income tax rate.
   b. A liberalization of depreciation for federal income tax purposes—that is, faster tax write-offs.
   c. A rise in interest rates.
   d. An increase in corporate profits.
   e. A decline in investment opportunities.
   f. Permission for corporations to deduct dividends for tax purposes as they now do interest charges.
   g. A change in the Tax Code so that both realized and unrealized capital gains in any year were taxed at the same rate as dividends.

15-6 One position expressed in the financial literature is that firms set their dividends as a residual after using income to support new investment.

   a. Explain what a residual dividend policy implies, illustrating your answer with a table showing how different investment opportunities could lead to different dividend payout ratios.
   b. Think back to Chapter 14, where we considered the relationship between capital structure and the cost of capital. If the WACC-versus-debt-ratio plot were shaped like a sharp V, would this have a different implication for the importance of setting dividends according to the residual policy than if the plot were shaped like a shallow bowl (or a flattened U)?

15-7 "Executive salaries have been shown to be more closely correlated to the size of the firm than to its profitability. If a firm's board of directors is controlled by management instead of by outside directors, this might result in the firm's retaining more earnings than can be justified from the stockholders' point of view." Discuss the statement, being sure (a) to discuss the interrelationships among cost of capital, investment opportunities, and new investment and (b) to explain the implied relationship between dividend policy and stock prices.

15-8 What is the difference between a stock dividend and a stock split? As a stockholder, would you prefer to see your company declare a 100 percent stock dividend or a two-for-one split? Assume that either action is feasible.

15-9 Most firms would like to have their stock selling at a high P/E ratio, and they would also like to have extensive public ownership (many different shareholders). Explain how stock dividends or stock splits may help achieve these goals.

15-10 Indicate whether the following statements are true or false. If the statement is false, explain why.

   a. If a firm repurchases its stock in the open market, the shareholders who tender the stock are subject to capital gains taxes.
   b. If you own 100 shares in a company's stock and the company's stock splits 2-for-1, you will own 200 shares in the company following the split.
   c. Some dividend reinvestment plans increase the amount of equity capital available to the firm.
   d. The Tax Code encourages companies to pay a large percentage of their net income in the form of dividends.

e. If your company has established a clientele of investors who prefer large dividends, the company is unlikely to adopt a residual dividend policy.

f. If a firm follows a residual dividend policy, holding all else constant, its dividend payout will tend to rise whenever the firm's investment opportunities improve.

PROBLEMS

Easy
Problems 1–3

15-1 **Residual dividend model** Axel Telecommunications has a target capital structure that consists of 70 percent debt and 30 percent equity. The company anticipates that its capital budget for the upcoming year will be $3,000,000. If Axel reports net income of $2,000,000 and it follows a residual dividend payout policy, what will be its dividend payout ratio?

15-2 **Stock split** Gamma Medical's stock trades at $90 a share. The company is contemplating a 3-for-2 stock split. Assuming that the stock split will have no effect on the market value of its equity, what will be the company's stock price following the stock split?

15-3 **Stock repurchases** Beta Industries has net income of $2,000,000 and it has 1,000,000 shares of common stock outstanding. The company's stock currently trades at $32 a share. Beta is considering a plan in which it will use available cash to repurchase 20 percent of its shares in the open market. The repurchase is expected to have no effect on either net income or the company's P/E ratio. What will be its stock price following the stock repurchase?

Intermediate
Problems 4–6

15-4 **Stock split** After a 5-for-1 stock split, the Strasburg Company paid a dividend of $0.75 per new share, which represents a 9 percent increase over last year's pre-split dividend. What was last year's dividend per share?

15-5 **External equity financing** Northern Pacific Heating and Cooling Inc. has a 6-month backlog of orders for its patented solar heating system. To meet this demand, management plans to expand production capacity by 40 percent with a $10 million investment in plant and machinery. The firm wants to maintain a 40 percent debt-to-total-assets ratio in its capital structure; it also wants to maintain its past dividend policy of distributing 45 percent of last year's net income. In 2005, net income was $5 million. How much external equity must Northern Pacific seek at the beginning of 2006 to expand capacity as desired? Assume the firm uses only debt and common equity in its capital structure.

15-6 **Residual dividend model** The Welch Company is considering three independent projects, each of which requires a $5 million investment. The estimated internal rate of return (IRR) and cost of capital for these projects are presented here:

> Project H (high risk):   Cost of capital = 16%;   IRR = 20%
> Project M (medium risk): Cost of capital = 12%;   IRR = 10%
> Project L (low risk):   Cost of capital = 8%;   IRR = 9%

Note that the projects' costs of capital vary because the projects have different levels of risk. The company's optimal capital structure calls for 50 percent debt and 50 percent common equity. Welch expects to have net income of $7,287,500. If Welch establishes its dividends from the residual model, what will be its payout ratio?

Challenging
Problems 7–9

15-7 **Dividends** Bowles Sporting Inc. is prepared to report the following income statement (shown in thousands of dollars) for the year 2006.

Sales	$15,200
Operating costs including depreciation	11,900
EBIT	$ 3,300
Interest	300
EBT	$ 3,000
Taxes (40 percent)	1,200
Net income	$ 1,800

Prior to reporting this income statement, the company wants to determine its annual dividend. The company has 500,000 shares of stock outstanding and its stock trades at $48 per share.

a. The company had a 40 percent dividend payout ratio in 2005. If Bowles wants to maintain this payout ratio in 2006, what will be its per-share dividend in 2006?

b. If the company maintains this 40 percent payout ratio, what will be the current dividend yield on the company's stock?

c. The company reported net income of $1.5 million in 2005. Assume that the number of shares outstanding has remained constant. What was the company's per-share dividend in 2005?

d. As an alternative to maintaining the same dividend payout ratio, Bowles is considering maintaining the same per-share dividend in 2006 that it paid in 2005. If it chooses this policy, what will be the company's dividend payout ratio in 2006?

e. Assume that the company is interested in dramatically expanding its operations and that this expansion will require significant amounts of capital. The company would like to avoid transactions costs involved in issuing new equity. Given this scenario, would it make more sense for the company to maintain a constant dividend payout ratio or to maintain the same per-share dividend?

15-8 **Alternative dividend policies** Rubenstein Bros. Clothing is expecting to pay an annual dividend per share of $0.75 out of annual earnings per share of $2.25. Currently, Rubenstein Bros.' stock is selling for $12.50 per share. Adhering to the company's target capital structure, the firm has $10 million in assets, of which 40 percent is funded by debt. Assume that the firm's book value of equity equals its market value. In past years, the firm has earned a return on equity (ROE) of 18 percent, which is expected to continue this year and into the foreseeable future.

a. Based on this information, what long-run growth rate can the firm be expected to maintain? (Hint: g = Retention rate × ROE.)

b. What is the stock's required return?

c. If the firm were to change its dividend policy and pay an annual dividend of $1.50 per share, financial analysts predict that the change in policy will have no effect on the firm's stock price or ROE. Therefore, what must the firm's new expected long-run growth rate and required return be?

d. Suppose instead that the firm has decided to proceed with its original plan of disbursing $0.75 per share to shareholders, but the firm intends to do so in the form of a stock dividend rather than a cash dividend. The firm will allot new shares based on the current stock price of $12.50. In other words, for every $12.50 in dividends due to shareholders, a share of stock will be issued. How large will the stock dividend be relative to the firm's current market capitalization? (Hint: Remember market capitalization = P_0 × number of shares outstanding.)

e. If the plan in part d is implemented, how many new shares of stock will be issued, and by how much will the company's earnings per share be diluted?

15-9 **Alternative dividend policies** In 2005 the Keenan Company paid dividends totaling $3,600,000 on net income of $10.8 million. Note that 2005 was a normal year, and for the past 10 years, earnings have grown at a constant rate of 10 percent. However, in 2006, earnings are expected to jump to $14.4 million, and the firm expects to have profitable investment opportunities of $8.4 million. It is predicted that Keenan will not be able to maintain the 2006 level of earnings growth—the high 2006 earnings level is attributable to an exceptionally profitable new-product line introduced that year—and the company will return to its previous 10 percent growth rate. Keenan's target capital structure is 40 percent debt and 60 percent equity.

a. Calculate Keenan's total dividends for 2006 if it follows each of the following policies:

(1) Its 2006 dividend payment is set to force dividends to grow at the long-run growth rate in earnings.

(2) It continues the 2005 dividend payout ratio.

(3) It uses a pure residual dividend policy (40 percent of the $8.4 million investment is financed with debt and 60 percent with common equity).

(4) It employs a regular-dividend-plus-extras policy, with the regular dividend being based on the long-run growth rate and the extra dividend being set according to the residual policy.

b. Which of the preceding policies would you recommend? Restrict your choices to the ones listed, but justify your answer.

c. Assume that investors expect Keenan to pay total dividends of $9,000,000 in 2006 and to have the dividend grow at 10 percent after 2006. The stock's total market value is $180 million. What is the company's cost of equity?

d. What is Keenan's long-run average return on equity? [Hint: g = Retention rate × ROE = (1.0 − Payout rate)(ROE).]

e. Does a 2006 dividend of $9,000,000 seem reasonable in view of your answers to parts c and d? If not, should the dividend be higher or lower?

COMPREHENSIVE/SPREADSHEET PROBLEM

15-10 **Residual dividend model** Buena Terra Corporation is reviewing its capital budget for the upcoming year. It has paid a $3.00 dividend per share (DPS) for the past several years, and its shareholders expect the dividend to remain constant for the next several years. The company's target capital structure is 60 percent equity and 40 percent debt; it has 1,000,000 shares of common equity outstanding; and its net income is $8 million. The company forecasts that it would require $10 million to fund all of its profitable (that is, positive NPV) projects for the upcoming year.

a. If Buena Terra follows the residual dividend model, how much retained earnings will it need to fund its capital budget?

b. If Buena Terra follows the residual dividend model, what will be the company's dividend per share and payout ratio for the upcoming year?

c. If Buena Terra maintains its current $3.00 DPS for next year, how much retained earnings will be available for the firm's capital budget?

d. Can the company maintain its current capital structure, maintain the $3.00 DPS, and maintain a $10 million capital budget without having to raise new common stock?

e. Suppose that Buena Terra's management is firmly opposed to cutting the dividend; that is, it wishes to maintain the $3.00 dividend for the next year. Also, assume that the company was committed to funding all profitable projects and was willing to issue more debt (along with the available retained earnings) to help finance the company's capital budget. Assume that the resulting change in capital structure has a minimal effect on the company's composite cost of capital, so that the capital budget remains at $10 million. What portion of this year's capital budget would have to be financed with debt?

f. Suppose once again that Buena Terra's management wants to maintain the $3.00 DPS. In addition, the company wants to maintain its target capital structure (60 percent equity and 40 percent debt) and maintain its $10 million capital budget. What is the minimum dollar amount of new common stock that the company would have to issue in order to meet each of its objectives?

g. Now consider the case where Buena Terra's management wants to maintain the $3.00 DPS and its target capital structure, but it wants to avoid issuing new common stock. The company is willing to cut its capital budget in order to meet its other objectives. Assuming that the company's projects are divisible, what will be the company's capital budget for the next year?

h. What actions can a firm that follows the residual dividend policy take when its forecasted retained earnings are less than the retained earnings required to fund its capital budget?

Integrated Case

Southeastern Steel Company

15-11 **Dividend policy** Southeastern Steel Company (SSC) was formed 5 years ago to exploit a new continuous-casting process. SSC's founders, Donald Brown and Margo Valencia, had been employed in the research department of a major integrated-steel company, but when that company decided against using the new process (which Brown and Valencia had developed), they decided to strike out on their own. One advantage of the new process was that it required relatively little capital in comparison with the typical steel company, so Brown and Valencia have been able to avoid issuing new stock, and thus they own all of the shares. However, SSC has now reached the stage in which outside equity capital is necessary if the firm is to achieve its growth targets yet still maintain its target capital structure of 60 percent equity and 40 percent debt. Therefore, Brown and Valencia have decided to take the company public. Until now, Brown and Valencia have paid themselves reasonable salaries but routinely reinvested all after-tax earnings in the firm, so dividend policy has not been an issue. However, before talking with potential outside investors, they must decide on a dividend policy.

Assume that you were recently hired by Arthur Adamson & Company (AA), a national consulting firm, which has been asked to help SSC prepare for its public offering. Martha Millon, the senior AA consultant in your group, has asked you to make a presentation to Brown and Valencia in which you review the theory of dividend policy and discuss the following questions.

a. (1) What is meant by the term "dividend policy"?

   (2) Explain briefly the dividend irrelevance theory that was put forward by Modigliani and Miller. What were the key assumptions underlying their theory?

   (3) Discuss why some investors may prefer high-dividend-paying stocks, while other investors prefer stocks that pay low or nonexistent dividends.

b. Discuss (1) the information content, or signaling, hypothesis, (2) the clientele effect, and (3) their effects on dividend policy.

c. (1) Assume that SSC has an $800,000 capital budget planned for the coming year. You have determined that its present capital structure (60 percent equity and 40 percent debt) is optimal, and its net income is forecasted at $600,000. Use the residual dividend model approach to determine SSC's total dollar dividend and payout ratio. In the process, explain what the residual dividend model is. Then, explain what would happen if net income were forecasted at $400,000, or at $800,000.

   (2) In general terms, how would a change in investment opportunities affect the payout ratio under the residual payment policy?

   (3) What are the advantages and disadvantages of the residual policy? (Hint: Don't neglect signaling and clientele effects.)

d. What is a dividend reinvestment plan (DRIP), and how does it work?

e. Describe the series of steps that most firms take in setting dividend policy in practice.

f. What are stock repurchases? Discuss the advantages and disadvantages of a firm's repurchasing its own shares.

g. What are stock dividends and stock splits? What are the advantages and disadvantages of stock dividends and stock splits?

cyberproblem

Please go to the ThomsonNOW Web site to access the Cyberproblems.

THOMSON ONE | Business School Edition

Access the Thomson ONE problems through the ThomsonNOW Web site. Use the Thomson ONE—Business School Edition online database to work this chapter's questions.

Microsoft's Dividend Policy

In this chapter's opening vignette, we discuss Microsoft's decision to establish a dividend payout policy in 2003. Let's find out what has happened to Microsoft's (MSFT) dividend policy since the time of this announcement. We can address this issue by relying on the data that are provided to you in Thomson One.

Discussion Questions

1. To get information about MSFT's dividend policy, enter its ticker and select OVERVIEW>FULL REPORTS>WORLDSCOPE FULL REPORTS>FULL COMPANY REPORT. Click on STOCK & EARNINGS DATA and scroll down to the "Annual Historical Data" section. What has happened to MSFT's dividend per share, dividend yield, and dividend payout over the past 5 years? Do you have any explanations?

2. Compare this with other firms in the same industry. To see how MSFT stacks up against its peers, select PEERS>OVERVIEWS>PER SHARE DATA to get MSFT's peers' last annual dividends. Accessing PEER>OVERVIEWS>ABSOLUTE RANKINGS will give their dividend yields. You can also get this information from the VALUATION COMPARISON in this same section. Has MSFT behaved differently from its peers or have there been industrywide shifts?

3. Refer back to the FULL COMPANY REPORT used in Question 1. Manually, plot earnings and dividends over time. In the text we point out that dividends are often much more stable than earnings. Do you see a similar pattern for MSFT?

4. In the "Interim Financial Data" section of the FULL COMPANY REPORT, identify the dividend declared date, ex date, and pay date. Explain the significance of these dates. Go back to "Overview," and access the "Interactive Price Chart." Can you observe price shifts around these dates? Explain what price shifts you might expect to see.

5. Investors are more concerned with future dividends than historical dividends, so go to ESTIMATES and scroll down to the "Consensus Estimates" section. Click on the "Available Measures" menu to toggle between earnings per share and dividends per share. How do analysts expect MSFT's payout policy to behave in the future?

6. Refer back to the FULL COMPANY REPORT and scroll down to the "5 Yr Annual Balance Sheet" section. Does it appear that MSFT has been repurchasing any stock, or has it been issuing new stock?

WORKING CAPITAL AND FINANCIAL PLANNING

P A R T **6**

WORKING CAPITAL MANAGEMENT

Best Buy Successfully Manages Its Working Capital

Best Buy Company, North America's largest consumer electronics retailer, operates Best Buy and Musicland stores. Its stock price sold for $67 in June 2005, up from $20 three years earlier.[1] This success stemmed from sound financial and operating practices, especially its working capital management, the focus of this chapter.

Working capital management involves finding the optimal levels for cash, marketable securities, accounts receivable, and inventory and then financing those assets in the least-cost manner. Most of Best Buy's customers use credit cards, so neither in-store cash nor accounts receivable is significant. Therefore, Best Buy's working capital policy focuses on its inventories. To maintain sales, stores must be well stocked with the goods customers are seeking at the time. This involves determining what new products are coming out, where they can be obtained at the lowest cost, and then delivering them to stores in a timely manner.

Dramatic improvements in communications and computer technology have transformed the way Best Buy manages its inventories. It now collects real-time data from each store on how each product is selling, and its computers place orders automatically to keep the shelves full. Moreover, if sales of an item are slipping, prices are lowered to reduce stocks of that item before the situation gets out of hand and steeper price cuts become necessary. After studying this chapter, you should have a good understanding of how working capital management affects profits and stock prices.

Putting Things In Perspective

About 60 percent of a typical financial manager's time is devoted to working capital, and many students' first jobs focus on working capital. This is particularly true in smaller businesses, where most new jobs in the United States are being created.

---

[1] Later in 2005, Best Buy announced a two-for-one stock split.

Working capital policy involves two basic questions: (1) What is the optimal amount of each type of current asset for the firm to carry and (2) how should current asset holdings be financed? This chapter addresses these issues.

16-1 WORKING CAPITAL TERMINOLOGY

The term *working capital* originated with the old Yankee peddler, who would load up his wagon and then go off to peddle his wares. The merchandise was called "working capital" because it was what he actually sold, or "turned over," to produce his profits. The wagon and horse were his fixed assets. He generally owned the horse and wagon, so they were financed with "equity" capital, but he bought his merchandise on credit (that is, by borrowing from his supplier) or with money borrowed from a bank. Those loans were called *working capital loans*, and they had to be repaid after each trip to demonstrate to the lender that the credit was sound. Once the peddler repaid the loan, he could take out another loan, and lenders that followed this procedure were said to be employing "sound lending practices." Obviously, the more trips the peddler took per year, the faster his working capital turnover and the greater his profits.

This concept can be applied to modern businesses, as we demonstrate here. We begin our discussion with a review of some basic definitions and concepts:

1. **Working capital,** sometimes called *gross working capital*, simply refers to current assets used in operations.
2. **Net working capital** is defined as current assets minus *all* current liabilities.
3. **Net *operating* working capital** is defined as current assets minus non-interest-bearing current liabilities (accounts payable and accruals).[2]
4. The **cash conversion cycle (CCC)** is the length of time funds are tied up in working capital, or the length of time between paying for working capital and collecting cash from the sale of the working capital. We discuss the CCC in the next section.

How did the term working capital originate?

Differentiate between net working capital and net operating working capital.

16-2 THE CASH CONVERSION CYCLE

All firms follow a "working capital cycle" in which they purchase or produce inventory, hold it for a time, and eventually sell it and receive cash. This process is similar to the Yankee peddler's trips, and it is known as the *cash conversion cycle (CCC)*.

Working Capital
All short-term, or current, assets—cash, marketable securities, inventories, and accounts receivable.

Net Working Capital
Current assets minus all current liabilities.

Net Operating Working Capital
Current assets minus non-interest-bearing current liabilities.

Cash Conversion Cycle
The length of time funds are tied up in working capital, or the length of time between paying for working capital and collecting cash from the sale of the working capital.

---

[2] This definition assumes that cash and marketable securities on the balance sheet are at their normal long-run target levels and that the company is not holding any excess cash. Excess holdings of cash and marketable securities are generally not included as part of net operating working capital.

16-2a Calculating the Targeted CCC

Great Fashions Inc. (GFI) is just starting in business, buying ladies golf outfits from a manufacturer in China and selling them through pro shops at high-end golf clubs. Its business plan calls for it to purchase $100,000 of merchandise at the start of each month and have it sold after 60 days. The company will have 40 days to pay its suppliers, and it will give its customers 60 days to pay for their purchases. GFI also expects monthly sales of $100,000, which means that it will just break even during its first few years. Any funds required to support operations will be obtained from the bank, and those loans must be repaid as soon as cash is available.

This information can be used to calculate GFI's cash conversion cycle, which nets out the three time periods described here:[3]

Inventory Conversion Period
The average time required to convert raw materials into finished goods and then to sell them.

Average Collection Period (ACP)
The average length of time required to convert the firm's receivables into cash, that is, to collect cash following a sale.

Payables Deferral Period
The average length of time between the purchase of materials and labor and the payment of cash for them.

1. **Inventory conversion period.** For GFI, this is the 60 days it takes to sell the merchandise.[4]
2. **Average collection period (ACP).** This is the length of time customers are given to pay for goods following a sale. The ACP is also called the days' sales outstanding (DSO). GFI's business plan calls for an ACP of 60 days, which is consistent with its 60-day credit terms.
3. **Payables deferral period.** This is the length of time GFI's suppliers give it to pay for its purchases, 40 days in our example.

On Day 1 GFI buys merchandise, and it expects to sell the goods and thus convert them to accounts receivable in 60 days. It should take another 60 days to collect the receivables, making a total of 120 days between receiving merchandise and collecting cash. However, GFI is able to defer its own payments for 40 days.

We combine these three periods to find the planned cash conversion cycle, shown below as an equation and in Figure 16-1 as a picture.

$$\begin{matrix} \text{Inventory} \\ \text{conversion} \\ \text{period} \end{matrix} + \begin{matrix} \text{Average} \\ \text{collection} \\ \text{period} \end{matrix} - \begin{matrix} \text{Payables} \\ \text{deferral} \\ \text{period} \end{matrix} = \begin{matrix} \text{Cash} \\ \text{conversion} \\ \text{cycle} \end{matrix} \quad \textbf{(16-1)}$$

$$60 \quad + \quad 60 \quad - \quad 40 \quad = \quad 80 \text{ days}$$

FIGURE 16-1 *The Cash Conversion Cycle*

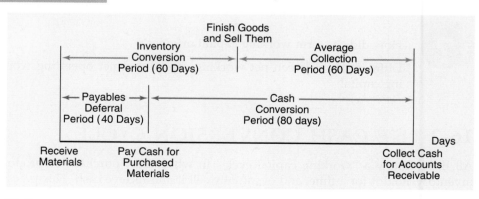

---

[3] See Verlyn D. Richards and Eugene J. Laughlin, "A Cash Conversion Cycle Approach to Liquidity Analysis," *Financial Management*, Spring 1980, pp. 32–38.

[4] If GFI were a manufacturer, the inventory conversion period would be the time required to convert raw materials into finished goods and then to sell those goods.

Although GFI must pay $100,000 to its suppliers after 40 days, it will not receive any cash until $60 + 60 = 120$ days into the cycle. Therefore, it will have to borrow the $100,000 cost of the merchandise from its bank on Day 40, and it will not be able to repay the loan until it collects on Day 120. Thus, for $120 - 40 = 80$ days—which is the CCC—it will owe the bank $100,000 and will be paying interest on this debt. The shorter the cash conversion cycle the better because that will lower interest charges.

Note that if GFI could sell goods faster, collect receivables faster, or defer its payables longer without hurting sales or increasing operating costs, then its CCC would decline, its interest charges would be reduced, and its profits and stock price would be improved.

16-2b Calculating the Actual CCC

The preceding section illustrates the CCC concept, but in practice we would actually calculate the CCC based on the firm's financial statements. Moreover, the actual CCC would almost certainly differ from the theoretically forecasted value because of such real-world complexities as shipping delays, sales slow-downs, and customer delays in making payments. Moreover, a firm such as GFI would start new cycles before the earlier ones ended, and this too would muddy the waters.

To see how the CCC is calculated in practice, assume that GFI has been in business for several years and is now in a stable position—placing orders, making sales, getting collections, and making payments on a recurring basis. The following data were taken from its latest financial statements:

Annual sales	$1,216,666
Cost of goods sold	1,013,889
Inventories	250,000
Accounts receivable	300,000
Accounts payable	150,000

We begin with the inventory conversion period, and show its calculation for GFI:

$$\text{Inventory conversion period} = \frac{\text{Inventory}}{\text{Cost of goods sold per day}} \quad \textbf{(16-2)}$$

$$= \frac{\$250,000}{\$1,013,889/365} = 90 \text{ days}$$

Thus, it takes GFI an average of 90 days to sell its merchandise, not the 60 days called for in the business plan. Note also that inventory is carried at cost, so the denominator of the equation should be the cost of goods sold, not sales.

The average collection period (or days sales outstanding) for GFI is calculated next:

$$\text{Average collection period} = \text{ACP (or DSO)} = \frac{\text{Receivables}}{\text{Sales}/365} \quad \textbf{(16-3)}$$

$$= \frac{\$300,000}{\$1,216,666/365} = 90 \text{ days}$$

Thus, it takes GFI 90 days after a sale to receive cash, not the 60 days called for in the business plan. Because receivables are recorded at the sales price, we use sales rather than the cost of goods sold in the denominator.

Some Firms Operate with Negative Working Capital!

Some firms are able to operate with zero or even negative net working capital. Dell Computer and Amazon .com are examples. When customers order computers from Dell's Web site or books from Amazon, they must provide a credit card number. Dell and Amazon then receive next-day cash, even before the product is shipped and even before they have paid their own suppliers. This results in a negative CCC, which means that working capital provides cash, not uses it.

To grow, most companies need cash for working capital. However, if the CCC is negative, then (again) growth in sales *provides* cash rather than *uses* it. This cash can be invested in plant and equipment as well as research and development, thus further increasing growth and leading to even more cash generation. Analysts recognize this point when they value Dell and Amazon, and it benefits their stock prices.

The payables deferral period is found as follows, again using cost of goods sold in the denominator because payables are recorded at cost:

$$\begin{array}{l} \text{Payables} \\ \text{deferral} \\ \text{period} \end{array} = \frac{\text{Payables}}{\text{Purchases per day}} = \frac{\text{Payables}}{\text{Cost of goods sold}/365} \quad \textbf{(16-4)}$$

$$= \frac{\$150,000}{\$1,013,889/365}$$

$$= 54 \text{ days}$$

GFI is supposed to pay its suppliers after 40 days, but it is actually a slow payer, delaying payment until Day 54.

We can combine the three periods to calculate GFI's actual cash conversion cycle:

Cash conversion cycle (CCC) = 90 days + 90 days − 54 days = 126 days

GFI's actual 126-day CCC is quite different from the planned 80 days. It takes longer than planned to sell merchandise, customers don't pay as fast as they should, and GFI itself pays suppliers slower than it should. The end result is a CCC of 126 days versus the planned 80 days.

If the planned 80-day CCC is "reasonable," then the actual 126 days is way too high. The CFO should push the sales and credit personnel to speed up sales and collections. Also, the purchasing department should seek longer payment terms. If GFI could take these steps without hurting sales and operating costs, this would help its profits and the stock price.

Two professors, Hyun-Han Shin and Luc Soenen, studied more than 2,900 companies over a 20-year period, and they found that shortening the cash conversion cycle results in higher profits and better stock price performances.[5] This demonstrates that good working capital management is important.

---

[5] See Hyun-Han Shin and Luc Soenen, "Efficiency of Working Capital Management and Corporate Profitability," *Financial Practice and Education*, Fall/Winter 1998, pp. 37–45.

Define the following terms: inventory conversion period, average collection period, and payables deferral period. Explain how these terms are used to form the cash conversion cycle.

How would a reduction in the cash conversion cycle increase profitability?

What are some actions a firm can take to shorten its cash conversion cycle?

16-3 ALTERNATIVE CURRENT ASSET INVESTMENT POLICIES

The cash conversion cycle highlights the strengths and weaknesses of the company's working capital policy. In this section, we explain how the amount of current assets held affects profitability. To begin, Figure 16-2 shows three alternative policies regarding the size of current asset holdings. The top line has the steepest slope and shows that the firm holds a lot of cash, marketable securities, and inventories relative to its sales, and it has a liberal credit policy that results in a

---

FIGURE 16-2 *Alternative Current Asset Investment Policies (Millions of Dollars)*

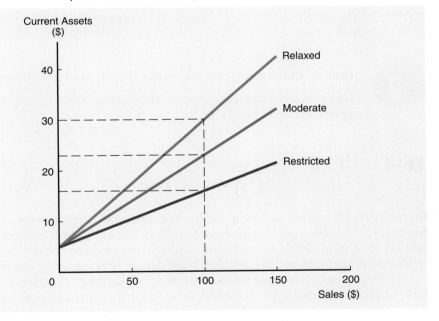

Policy	Current Assets Per $100 of Sales	Turnover of Current Assets: Sales/CA
Relaxed	$30	3.3×
Moderate	23	4.3
Restricted	16	6.3

Note: The sales/current assets relationship is shown here as being linear, but the relationship could be curvilinear.

Relaxed Current Asset Investment Policy
Relatively large amounts of cash, marketable securities, and inventories are carried, and a liberal credit policy results in a high level of receivables.

Restricted Current Asset Policy
Holdings of cash, marketable securities, inventories, and receivables are constrained.

Moderate Current Asset Policy
Between the relaxed and restricted policies.

high level of accounts receivable. This is a **relaxed** (or "fat cat") **policy.** On the other hand, with a **restricted** (or "lean-and-mean") **policy,** holdings of current assets are minimized. The **moderate policy** lies between the two extremes.

We can use the Du Pont equation to evaluate working capital management's effects on ROE.

$$\text{ROE} = \text{Profit margin} \times \text{Total asset turnover} \times \text{Leverage factor}$$

$$= \frac{\text{Net income}}{\text{Sales}} \times \frac{\text{Sales}}{\text{Assets}} \times \frac{\text{Assets}}{\text{Equity}}$$

A restricted, lean-and-mean policy means a low level of assets, hence a high total asset turnover ratio, which results in a high expected ROE. However, this policy also exposes the firm to risks, because shortages can lead to work stoppages, unhappy customers, and serious long-run problems. The relaxed policy minimizes operating problems but results in a low turnover, which lowers ROE. The moderate policy falls between the two extremes. The optimal strategy is the one that maximizes the stock's intrinsic value.

Note that changing technologies can lead to changes in the optimal policy. For example, if a new technology makes it possible for a manufacturer to produce a given product in 5 rather than 10 days, then work-in-progress inventories can be cut in half. Similarly, retailers such as Wal-Mart and Home Depot have installed systems under which bar codes on all merchandise are read at the cash register. This information is transmitted electronically to a computer that records the stock of each item, and the computer automatically places an order with the supplier's computer when the stock falls to a prescribed level. This process lowers the "safety stocks" that would otherwise be necessary to avoid running out of stock, which lowers inventories to optimal, profit-maximizing levels.

Identify and explain three alternative current asset investment policies.

Use the Du Pont equation to show how working capital policy affects the expected ROE.

16-4 ALTERNATIVE CURRENT ASSET FINANCING POLICIES

Permanent Current Assets
Current assets that a firm must carry even at the trough of its cycles.

Temporary Current Assets
Current assets that fluctuate with seasonal or cyclical variations in sales.

Current Asset Financing Policy
The way current assets are financed.

Investments in current assets must be financed, and the primary sources of funds include bank loans, credit from suppliers (accounts payable), accrued liabilities, long-term debt, and common equity. Each of these sources has advantages and disadvantages, so each firm must decide which sources are best for it.

To begin our discussion, note that most businesses experience seasonal and/or cyclical fluctuations. For example, construction firms tend to peak in the summer, retailers peak around Christmas, and the manufacturers who supply both construction companies and retailers follow related patterns. Similarly, the sales of virtually all businesses increase when the economy is strong, hence they build up current assets at those times but let inventories and receivables fall when the economy slackens. Note, though, that current assets rarely drop to zero—companies maintain some **permanent current assets,** which are the current assets needed at the low point of the cycle. Then, as sales increase during the upswing, current assets are increased, and these extra current assets are defined as **temporary current assets.** The way these current assets are financed is called the firm's **current asset financing policy.**

16-4a Maturity Matching, or "Self-Liquidating," Approach

The **maturity matching, or "self-liquidating," approach** calls for matching asset and liability maturities as shown in Panel a of Figure 16-3. All of the fixed assets plus the permanent current assets are financed with long-term capital, but temporary current assets are financed with short-term debt. Inventory expected to be sold in 30 days would be financed with a 30-day bank loan; a machine expected to last for 5 years would be financed with a 5-year loan; a 20-year building would be financed with a 20-year mortgage bond; and so on. Actually, two factors prevent an exact maturity matching: (1) There is uncertainty about the lives of assets. For example, a firm might finance inventories with a 30-day bank loan, expecting to sell the inventories and then use the cash to retire the loan. But if sales are slow, then the cash would not be forthcoming and the firm might not be able to pay off the loan when it matures. (2) Some common equity must be used, and common equity has no maturity. Still, if a firm attempts to match asset and liability maturities, this is defined as a *moderate current asset financing policy.*

> **Maturity Matching, or "Self-Liquidating," Approach**
> *A financing policy that matches asset and liability maturities. This is a moderate policy.*

16-4b Aggressive Approach

Panel b of Figure 16-3 illustrates the situation for a more aggressive firm that finances some of its permanent assets with short-term debt. Note that we used the term "relatively" in the title for Panel b because there can be different *degrees* of aggressiveness. For example, the dashed line in Panel b could have been drawn *below* the line designating fixed assets, indicating that all of the current assets—both permanent and temporary—and part of the fixed assets were financed with short-term credit. This would be a highly aggressive, extremely nonconservative position, and the firm would be very much subject to dangers from loan renewal as well as rising interest rate problems. However, short-term interest rates are generally lower than long-term rates, and some firms are willing to sacrifice safety for the chance of higher profits.

The reason for adopting the aggressive policy is to take advantage of the fact that the yield curve is generally upward sloping, hence short-term rates are generally lower than long-term rates. However, a strategy of financing long-term assets with short-term debt is really quite risky. To illustrate, suppose a company borrows $1 million on a one-year basis and uses the funds to buy machinery that will lower labor costs by $200,000 per year for 10 years. Cash flows from the equipment would not be sufficient to pay off the loan at the end of only one year, so the loan would have to be renewed. If the company encountered temporary financial problems, the lender might refuse to renew the loan, and that could lead to bankruptcy. Had the firm matched maturities and financed the plant with a 10-year loan, the required loan payments would have been better matched with the cash flows, and the renewal problem would not have arisen.

16-4c Conservative Approach

Panel c of the figure shows the dashed line *above* the line designating permanent current assets, indicating that long-term capital is used to finance all the permanent assets and also to meet some of the seasonal needs. In this situation, the firm uses a small amount of short-term credit to meet its peak requirements, but it also meets a part of its seasonal needs by "storing liquidity" in the form of marketable securities. The humps above the dashed line represent short-term financing, while the troughs below the dashed line represent short-term security holdings. This is a very safe, conservative financing policy.

FIGURE 16-3   *Alternative Current Asset Financing Policies*

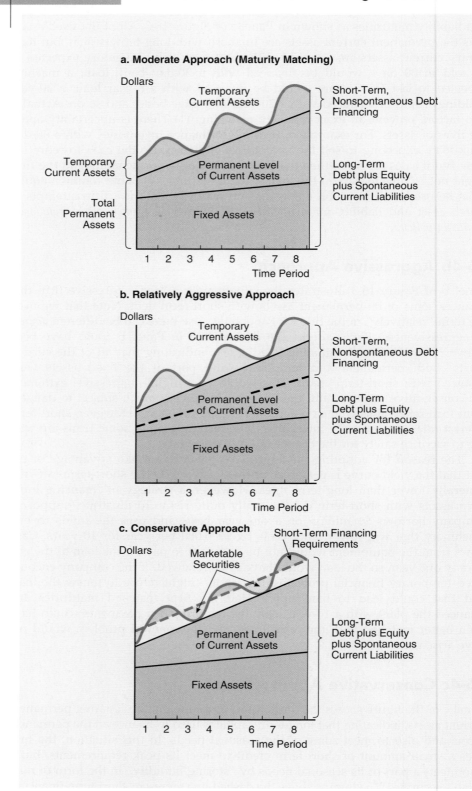

16-4d Choosing between the Approaches

Because the yield curve is normally upward-sloping, the *cost of short-term debt is generally lower than that of long-term debt*. However, *short-term debt is riskier to the borrowing firm* for two reasons: (1) If a firm borrows on a long-term basis, its interest costs will be relatively stable over time, but if it uses short-term credit, its interest expense can fluctuate widely, perhaps going so high that profits are extinguished. (2) If a firm borrows heavily on a short-term basis, a temporary recession may adversely affect its financial ratios and render it unable to repay this debt. Recognizing this point, if the borrower's financial position is weak, the lender may not renew the loan, which could force the borrower into bankruptcy.

Note too that *short-term loans can generally be negotiated much faster* than long-term loans. Lenders need to make a more thorough financial examination before extending long-term credit, and the loan agreement must be spelled out in great detail because a lot can happen during the life of a 10- to 20-year loan.

Finally, *short-term debt may offer greater flexibility*. If the firm thinks that interest rates are abnormally high, it may prefer short-term credit to gain flexibility in changing the debt contract. Also, if its needs for funds are seasonal or cyclical, it may not want to commit itself to long-term debt because, while provisions for repaying long-term debt can be built into the contract, prepayment penalties are generally built into long-term debt contracts to permit the lender to recover its setup costs. Finally, long-term loan agreements generally contain provisions, or covenants, that constrain the firm's future actions in order to protect the lender, whereas short-term credit agreements generally have fewer restrictions.

All things considered, it is not possible to state that either long-term or short-term financing is better than the other. The firm's specific conditions will affect the choice, as will the preferences of managers. Optimistic and/or aggressive managers will probably lean more toward short-term credit to gain an interest cost advantage, while more conservative managers will lean toward long-term financing to avoid potential renewal problems. The factors discussed here should be considered, but the final decision will reflect managers' personal preferences and judgments.

Up until this point, we have provided a brief overview of how companies may go about establishing their working capital policy. Next, we discuss how companies can manage their various current assets and current liabilities in a way that is consistent with their overall policy. We begin by showing how to put together a simple cash budget, after which we discuss briefly the management of each of the major components of current assets and current liabilities.

Differentiate between permanent current assets and temporary current assets.

What does maturity matching mean, and what is the advantage of this policy?

What are advantages and disadvantages of short-term versus long-term debt?

16-5 THE CASH BUDGET

Firms need to forecast their cash flows. If they will need additional cash, they should line up funds well in advance, while if they will generate surplus cash, they should plan for its productive use. The primary forecasting tool is the

Cash Budget
A table that shows cash receipts, disbursements, and balances over some period.

cash budget, illustrated in Table 16-1, which is a printout from the chapter's *Excel* model.[6]

Cash budgets can be of any length, but firms typically develop a monthly cash budget like Table 16-1 for the coming year and a daily cash budget at the start of each month. The monthly budget is good for long-range planning, while the daily budget gives a more precise picture of the actual cash flows.

The monthly cash budget begins with a forecast of sales for each month and a projection of when collections will occur. Then comes a forecast of materials purchases, followed by forecasted payments for materials, labor, leases, new equipment, taxes, and other expenses. When the forecasted payments are subtracted from the forecasted collections, the result is the expected net cash gain or loss for each month. This gain or loss is added to or subtracted from the beginning cash balance, and the result is the amount of cash the firm would have on hand at the end of the month if it neither borrowed nor invested.

We use Allied Foods to illustrate cash budgets. To shorten the example, we only deal with the last half of 2006. Allied sells mainly to grocery chains, and its projected 2006 sales are $3,300 million. As Table 16-1 shows, sales increase during the summer, peak in September, and then decline during the fall. All sales are on terms of 2/10, net 30, meaning that a 2 percent discount is allowed if payment is made within 10 days but if the discount is not taken, the full amount is due in 30 days. However, like most companies, Allied finds that some customers pay late. Experience shows that 20 percent of customers pay during the month of the sale—these are the discount customers, 70 percent pay during the month immediately following the sale, and 10 percent are late, paying in the second month after the sale.[7]

The costs to Allied of foodstuffs, spices, preservatives, and packaging materials average 70 percent of sales revenues. Purchases are generally made one month before the firm expects to sell the finished products, but Allied's suppliers allow it to delay payments for 30 days. July sales are forecasted at $300 million, so purchases during June should amount to $210 million, and this amount must be paid in July.

Wages and lease payments are also built into the cash budget, as are Allied's estimated tax payments, $30 million due September 15 and $20 million due December 15. Also, a $100 million payment for a new plant must be made in October, and miscellaneous other required payments are shown in the budget.

Target Cash Balance
The desired cash balance that a firm plans to maintain in order to conduct business.

Allied's **target cash balance** is $10 million, and it plans either to borrow to achieve this target or to invest it if it generates more cash than is needed.

We use this information in Table 16-1 to forecast monthly cash surpluses or shortfalls for the period from July through December, along with the amount Allied will need to borrow or will have to invest so as to keep the end-of-month cash balance at the target level.

Inputs used in the forecast—which are really assumptions that may not be correct—are given on Rows 6 through 16. These values are used in the calculations shown here. Row 19 gives the sales forecast for the period May through

---

[6] For a better understanding of working capital management, go through the *Excel* chapter model while reading through the text to see how spreadsheets can streamline the working capital analysis process.

[7] A negligible percentage of sales results in bad debts. The low bad debt losses result from Allied's careful screening of customers and its generally tight credit policies. However, the cash budget model can show the effects of bad debts, so Allied's CFO could show top management how cash flows would be affected if the firm relaxed its credit policy in order to stimulate sales.

TABLE 16-1 *Allied Food Products: 2006 Cash Budget (Millions of Dollars)*

	A–F	G	H
6	**Selected Input Data**		
7	Collections during month of sale	20%	Assumed constant. Don't change.
8	Collections during 1st month after sale	70%	Assumed constant. Don't change.
9	Collections during 2nd month after sale	10%	Fixed at 10% less bad debt %
10	Percent bad debts	0%	Can change to see effects
11	Discount on first month collections	2%	Can change to see effects
12	Purchases as a % of next month's sales	70%	Can change to see effects
13	Lease payments per month	$15	Can change to see effects
14	Construction cost for new plant (Oct)	$100	Can change to see effects
15	Target cash balance	$10	Will borrow this amount at start
16	Sales adjustment factor	0%	(% increase or decrease from base)

		May	June	July	August	Sept	Oct	Nov	Dec
19	*Sales (gross)*	$200	$250	$300	$400	$500	$350	$250	$200
20	**Collections**								
21	During month of sale: 0.2(Sales)(0.98)			$59	$78	$98	$69	$49	$39
22	During 1st month after sale: 0.7(prior month's sales)			175	210	280	350	245	175
23	During 2nd month after sale: 0.1(sales 2 months ago)			20	25	30	40	50	35
24	Total collections			$254	$313	$408	$459	$344	$249
25	**Payments**								
26	Purchases: 70% of next month's sales		$210	$280	$350	$245	$175	$140	
27	Payment for materials: Last month's purchases			$210	$280	$350	$245	$175	$140
28	Wages and salaries			30	40	50	40	30	30
29	Lease payments			15	15	15	15	15	15
30	Other expenses			10	15	20	15	10	10
31	Taxes					30			20
32	Payment for plant construction						$100		
33	Total payments			$265	$350	$465	$415	$230	$215
34	**Net cash flows**								
35	Net cash inflow (NCF) for month: Row 24 minus Row 33			($11)	($37)	($57)	$44	$114	$34
36	Cumulative NCF: Month's NCF plus prior month's cumulative NCF			($11)	($48)	($105)	($61)	$53	$87
37	**Cash surplus (or loan requirement)**								
38	Target cash balance			$10	$10	$10	$10	$10	$10
39	Surplus cash (or loan needed): Row 36 - Row 38			($21)	($58)	($115)	($71)	$43	$77
40	Maximum required loan (shown as a negative)	($115)							
41	Maximum available for investment	$77							

Notes:
a. Although the budget period is July through December, sales and purchases data for May and June are needed to determine collections and payments during July and August.
b. Firms can both borrow and pay off commercial loans on a daily basis, so the $21 million borrowed during July would likely be taken down on a daily basis, as needed, and during October the $115 million loan that existed at the beginning of the month would be reduced daily to the $71 million ending balance, which, in turn, would be completely paid off sometime during November.

December. May and June sales are needed to determine collections for July and August. Rows 20 through 24 relate to collections. Row 21 shows that 20 percent of the sales during any given month are collected during that month. However, customers who pay in the first month take the discount, so collections for that month are reduced by 2 percent. For example, collections for July are calculated as 20 percent of the $300 million sales for that month, minus the 2 percent discount, or 0.2($300) − 0.2($300)(0.02) = $58.8 million, rounded to $59 million. Row 22 shows the collections for the previous month's sales. For example, in July, 70 percent of the $250 million June sales, or $175 million, should be collected. Row 23 shows collections from sales two months earlier. Thus, in July collections for May sales should be (0.10)($200) = $20 million. The collections during each month are summed and shown on Row 24. Thus, the July collections include 20 percent of July sales (minus the discount), 70 percent of June sales, plus 10 percent of May sales, or $254 million in total.

Raw material costs, which are 70 percent of the following month's sales, are shown on Row 26. July sales are forecasted at $300 million, so June purchases are 0.7($300) = $210 million. The $210 million must be paid in July, so that amount is shown on Row 27. Continuing, forecasted sales for August are $400 million, so Allied must purchase 0.7($400) = $280 million of materials in July, and that amount must be paid in August. Other required payments are shown on Rows 28 through 32, and the total of all payments is shown on Row 33.

Next, on Row 35, we show the net cash flow (NCF) for each month, calculated as collections on Row 24 minus total payments on Row 33. The NCF for July is −$11 million, and cash flows remain negative until October, when positive cash flows begin.

The monthly cash flows are then used to calculate the cumulative net cash flows as shown on Row 36. Here we add the NCF for each month to the cumulative NCF from the prior month. Since there was no prior cumulative NCF at the beginning of July, the cumulative NCF for July is simply the NCF for that month, −$11 million. For August, we add the NCF for that month, −$37 million, to the prior cumulative NCF, the −$11 million at the end of July, to get the −$48 million cumulative NCF at the end of August. There is another negative cash flow during September, so the cumulative NCF rises to −$105 million. However, in October the NCF is positive, so the cumulative figure declines to −$61 million, and it continues to decline in November and December.

Allied's target cash balance is $10 million—it wants to maintain that balance at all times. We assume that it borrows the $10 million at the start of the analysis, and we show that amount on Row 38. Because there is a projected cash loss of $11 million during July, and because it borrowed $10 million at the start of the month, at the end of July Allied's loan outstanding will total to $21 million as shown on Row 39.[8] It will incur additional cash shortfalls in August and September, and the required loan will continue to increase, peaking at $115 million at the end of September. However, positive cash flows begin in October, and they will be used to reduce the loan, which will be completely paid off by the end of November, at which time the company will actually have funds to invest. Indeed, by the end of December Allied should have no loans outstanding and $77 million available for investment.

Row 40 shows the maximum required loan, $115 million, and Row 41 shows the maximum projected surplus, $77 million. Allied's treasurer will need to arrange a line of credit so that the firm can borrow up to $115 million, increasing the loan over time as funds are needed and repaying it later when cash flows become positive.

The treasurer would show the cash budget to the bankers when negotiating for the line of credit. Lenders would want to know how much Allied expects to need, when the funds will be needed, and when the loan will be repaid. The

---

[8] If Allied had begun with a positive cash balance, that amount would have been deducted from the initial loan needed. Note too that our cash budget is simplified because it does not show interest expense for the loan or interest income on investments. These items could be added quite easily.

lenders—and Allied's top executives—would question the treasurer about the budget, and they would want to know how the forecasts would be affected if sales were higher or lower than were projected, how changes when customers pay would affect the forecasts, and the like. The central issues of the questioning are these: *How accurate is the forecast likely to be, and what would be the effects of significant errors?*

Note that if cash inflows and outflows do not occur uniformly during each month, then the actual funds needed might be quite different from the indicated amounts. For example, the data in Table 16-1 show the situation on the last day of each month, and we see that the maximum projected loan is $115 million. However, if all payments had to be made on the 1st but most collections came on the 30th, Allied would have to make $465 million of payments in September before it received the $408 inflow from collections. In that case, the firm would need to borrow about $500 million, not the $115 million shown in Table 16-1. A daily cash budget would reveal that situation.

Table 16-1 was prepared using a spreadsheet, which makes it easy to change the assumptions. Therefore, we could examine the cash flow effects of changing sales, the target cash balance, when customers pay, and so forth. Also, the effects of changes in the credit policy and inventory management could be examined through the cash budget.

How could the cash budget be used when negotiating the terms of a bank loan?

Suppose a firm's cash flows do not occur uniformly throughout the month. What effect would this have on the accuracy of the forecasted borrowing requirements based on a monthly cash budget? How could the firm deal with this problem?

16-6 CASH AND MARKETABLE SECURITIES

When most of us use the term *cash*, we mean currency (paper money and coins) plus bank demand deposits. However, when corporate treasurers use the term, they often mean currency and demand deposits *plus very safe, highly liquid marketable securities that can be sold quickly at a predictable price and thus be converted to bank deposits.*[9] Therefore, "cash" as reported on balance sheets generally includes short-term securities, which are also called "cash equivalents."

Note, though, that a firm's marketable security holdings can be divided into two categories: (1) *Operating short-term securities*, which are held primarily to provide liquidity and which are bought and sold as needed to provide funds for operations. These are a component of operating working capital. (2) *Other short-term securities*, which are holdings in excess of the amount needed to support normal operations. Highly profitable firms such as Microsoft often hold far more securities than are needed for liquidity purposes. Those securities will eventually be liquidated and the cash will be used for such things as paying a large one-time dividend, repurchasing stock, retiring debt, acquiring other firms, or

---

[9] The reason corporate treasurers think of cash as they do is that, from their perspective, there is little difference between demand deposits and liquid marketable securities—they can call a dealer, sell securities, and have the proceeds deposited in the firm's bank account in an hour or so. Also, note that many types of short-term securities are available. Treasury bills are an obvious example, but as we discussed in Chapter 5, there are many other safe, liquid, short-term, marketable securities.

financing major expansions. This breakdown is not reported on the balance sheet, but financial managers know how much of their securities will be needed for operating versus other purposes. In our discussion of working capital, the focus is on securities held to provide operating liquidity.

16-6a Currency

Retailers, casinos, hotels, movie theaters, and a few other businesses hold substantial amounts of currency, but the importance of currency has decreased over time due to the rise of credit cards, debit cards, and other payment mechanisms. Companies such as McDonald's need to hold enough currency to support operations, but more would raise capital costs and tempt robbers. Each firm decides its own optimal level, but even for retailers, currency generally represents a small part of total cash holdings.[10]

16-6b Demand Deposits

Demand (or checking) deposits are far more important than currency for most businesses. These deposits are used for *transactions*—paying for labor and raw materials, buying fixed assets, paying taxes, servicing debt, paying dividends, and so on. However, commercial demand deposits typically earn no interest, so firms try to minimize their holdings while still ensuring that they are able to pay suppliers promptly, take trade discounts, and take advantage of bargain purchases. The following techniques are used to optimize demand deposit holdings:

1. *Hold marketable securities rather than demand deposits to provide liquidity.* If the firm holds marketable securities, this reduces the need for demand deposits. For example, if a large bill requiring immediate payment comes in unexpectedly, the treasurer can simply call a securities dealer, sell some securities, and have funds deposited into the firm's checking account that same day. Securities pay interest whereas demand deposits do not, so holding securities in lieu of demand deposits increases profits.

2. *Borrow on short notice.* Firms can establish lines of credit under which they can borrow with just a telephone call if and when they need extra cash. Note, though, that they may have to pay fees for these commitments, and the cost of those fees must be considered when deciding to use borrowing capacity rather than securities to provide liquidity.

3. *Forecast payments and receipts better.* The better the firm can forecast its cash inflows and outflows, the smaller its needs for funds to meet unexpected requirements. Therefore, improving inflow/outflow forecasts lessens the need to hold liquid assets and thus reduces the required amount of working capital. The cash budget is the key tool used to improve cash forecasts.

4. *Speed up payments.* Firms can take actions to speed up their cash receipts. For example, they can use **lockboxes,** which are post office boxes operated by banks. Suppose a New York firm sells to customers all across the country. If it sends out bills and has customers make payments to its New York headquarters, time would be lost in the mail, in opening envelopes, in depositing checks in the bank, and in waiting for the bank to clear the checks to make sure they are good. To speed up this process, the firm can direct customers to send payments to a post office box in the customer's local area, then have a bank empty the box several times each day and get the collection process

Lockbox
A post office box operated by a bank to which payments are sent. Used to speed up effective receipt of cash.

---

[10] In the "olden days," currency was held as a store of value, for use during emergencies, to make bargain purchases, and the like. That is true today only in undeveloped parts of the world.

started. If a firm's receipts average $1 million per day, and if the use of lock-boxes can reduce the delay in getting usable cash from five days to one day, then the firm will receive an effective cash infusion of $4 million. This will be a one-time benefit, but the firm will gain additional benefits as it grows.[11]

5. *Use credit cards, debit cards, wire transfers, and direct deposits.* If a firm switches from selling on credit to accepting credit or debit cards, it will receive next-day cash and thus the same cash flow benefits as were described earlier. Similarly, if it requires customers to pay via wire deposits, this too will speed up collections, increase free cash flows, and reduce required cash holdings.

6. *Synchronize cash flows.* If a firm can synchronize its cash inflows and out-flows, this can reduce its need for cash balances. For example, utilities, oil companies, department stores, and the like generally use "billing cycles" under which different customers are billed on different days, causing cash to flow in evenly during the month. These firms can then set up their own pay-ment schedules to match their inflows. This reduces average cash balances, just as your personal average monthly balance could be reduced if your income came in at the same time as your required payments.

Banks have experts who can help firms optimize their cash management proce-dures. They charge a fee for this service, but the benefits of a good cash manage-ment system are well worth the cost.

16-6c Marketable Securities

Marketable securities held for operations are managed in conjunction with demand deposits—the management of one requires coordination with the other. Firms also purchase marketable securities as cash builds up from operations and then sell those securities when they need cash. Microsoft is a good example. It had accumulated more than $60 billion of cash (mostly marketable securities) by the end of 2004. It needed to hold some of those securities for liquidity purposes, but mainly the funds just built up because Microsoft generated more cash from operations than it needed. Investors agitated for management to either use this "cash" in a more productive manner or else pay it out as dividends so stock-holders could invest it themselves. Partly because of this pressure, in the fall of 2004 Microsoft announced a one-time dividend of $30 billion, and it also stepped up its stock repurchase program. Microsoft's holdings of nonoperating mar-ketable securities were the largest on record, but many other firms have large holdings and periodically go through similar self-evaluations.

Given the size and importance of marketable securities holdings, how they are managed can obviously have a significant effect on profits. A trade-off between risk and return is involved—the firm wants to earn high returns, but since marketable securities are held primarily to provide liquidity, treasurers want to hold securities that can be sold very quickly and at a known price. That means high-quality, short-term instruments. Long-term Treasury bonds are safe, but they are not well-suited for the marketable security portfolio because their prices will decline if interest rates rise. Similarly, short-term securities issued by

---

[11] We should mention the term *float*, as it often comes up in connection with cash management. If you write a check and it takes five days for the recipient to receive and deposit the check, and for it to be deducted from your account, then you have five days of float, or the use of the money for five days before you have to deposit funds in your account. That's "payment float." On the other hand, if someone sends you a check and it takes six days for you to receive and deposit it, and for the bank to clear the funds, then that's six days of "collection float." Your "net float" would be minus one day. Positive net float is good, negative net float is bad from the standpoint of minimizing required cash holdings.

Delta Airlines and other risky companies are not suitable because their prices will decline if the issuers' problems grow worse. Treasury bills, commercial paper (discussed in Section 16.11), bank certificates of deposit, and money market funds are suitable holdings.

A firm's relationship with its bank—especially its ability to borrow on short notice—has a significant effect on its need for demand deposits and marketable securities. If it has a firmly committed line of credit under which it can obtain funds with a simple telephone call, then it won't need much in the way of liquidity reserves.

Finally, note too that larger corporations shop for securities all around the world, buying wherever risk-adjusted rates are highest. This shopping tends to equalize worldwide rates—if interest rates in Europe are higher than rates in the United States for equally risky securities, then companies will buy European securities, driving their prices up and their yields down, until an equilibrium has been established. We truly live in a global economy.[12]

What two definitions of cash are commonly encountered?

Differentiate between marketable securities held for operating (transactions) purposes and securities held for other reasons.

How has the development of credit and debit cards affected firms' currency holdings?

How would the use of credit cards affect a firm's cash conversion cycle, assuming it previously allowed customers 30 days to pay for their purchases?

How does a firm's ability to borrow affect its optimal holdings of cash and securities?

Common stocks that are traded on the NYSE are liquid in the sense that they can be sold and converted to cash on short notice. Are stocks a good choice for a firm's marketable securities portfolio? Explain.

16-7 INVENTORIES

Inventories, which can include (1) *supplies*, (2) *raw materials*, (3) *work-in-process*, and (4) *finished goods*, are an essential part of virtually all business operations. Optimal inventory levels depend on sales, so sales must be forecasted before target inventories can be established. Moreover, because errors in setting inventory levels lead to lost sales or excessive carrying costs, inventory management is quite important. Therefore, firms use sophisticated computer systems to monitor their inventory holdings.

As we mentioned in the opening vignette to this chapter, retailers such as Best Buy, Wal-Mart, and Home Depot use computers to keep track of each inventory item by size, shape, and color, and the bar code information collected at checkout updates inventory records. When the inventory stock as indicated in

---

[12] Companies can also buy securities that are denominated in different currencies. Thus, if a firm's treasurer thinks that the euro is likely to appreciate against the dollar, then he or she might purchase securities denominated in euros, and if things work out as expected, the firm will earn interest and also enjoy an additional gain from the change in exchange rates. Again, these actions help to keep world financial markets in equilibrium.

Supply Chain Management

Herman Miller Inc. manufactures a wide variety of office furniture, and a typical order from a single customer might require work at five different plants. Each plant uses components from different suppliers, and each plant works on orders for many customers. Imagine all the coordination that's required. The sales force generates the order, the purchasing department orders components from suppliers, and the suppliers must order materials from their own suppliers. Then, the suppliers ship the components to the appropriate Herman Miller plant, the plants build the products, the different products are gathered together to complete the order, and then the order is shipped to the customer. If one part of that process malfunctions, then the order will be delayed, inventory will pile up, extra costs to expedite the order will be incurred, and the company's reputation will be damaged, hurting future sales growth.

To prevent such consequences, Herman Miller turned to a process called supply chain management (SCM). The key element in SCM is sharing information all the way from the point-of-sale at the retailer to suppliers, and even back to suppliers' suppliers. SCM requires special software, but even more important, it requires cooperation among the different companies and departments in the supply chain. A new culture of open communication is required, and this is often difficult for many companies because they are reluctant to divulge operating information. Many of Herman Miller's suppliers were initially wary of these new relationships. However, SCM has been a win-win situation, with increases in value for Herman Miller and its suppliers.

SCM enabled Herman Miller to sharply reduce its inventory and also to cut two weeks off delivery times to customers, in addition to operating its plants at a 20 percent higher volume without further capital expenditures. The bottom line result was higher earnings, cash flows, and stock prices.

Sources: Elaine L. Appleton, "Supply Chain Brain," *CFO*, July 1997, pp. 51–54; and Kris Frieswick, "Up Close and Virtual," *CFO*, April 1998, pp. 87–91.

---

the computer declines to a set level, the computer sends an order to the supplier's computer, specifying exactly what is needed. The computer also reports how fast items are moving, and if an item is moving too slowly it suggests a price cut to lower the inventory stock before the item becomes obsolete. Manufacturers like GE use similar systems to keep track of items and to place orders as they are needed.

Although inventory management is important, it is more of an issue for production managers and marketing people than financial managers. Still, financial managers are involved in several ways. First, it is expensive to install and maintain the computer systems used to track inventories, and a capital budgeting analysis as discussed in Part 4 of this text must be used to determine which system is best. Second, if the firm decides to increase its inventory holdings, then the financial manager must raise the capital needed to acquire the additional inventory. And third, the financial manager is responsible for identifying factors that affect the firm's overall profitability, using ratios and other procedures for comparing the firm with its benchmark companies. Therefore, the CFO will compare the firm's inventory-to-sales ratio with those of its benchmarks to see if things look "reasonable."

As inventory management is outside the mainstream of finance, we cover it in Web Appendix 16A rather than in the text chapter. We do, however, provide the box entitled "Supply Chain Management" to illustrate how inventories are managed by modern corporations.

What are the three primary tasks of the financial manager regarding inventory management?

16-8 ACCOUNTS RECEIVABLE

Although retail sales are often made for cash, sales of expensive items such as autos and appliances are generally on credit. Furthermore, most business-to-business sales are on credit. Thus, in the typical situation goods are shipped, inventories are reduced, and an **account receivable** is created.[13] Eventually, the customer pays, the firm receives cash, and its receivables decline. Since the firm's credit policy is the primary determinant of accounts receivable, we begin by discussing credit policy.

Account Receivable
A balance due from a customer.

16-8a Credit Policy

Credit policy consists of these four variables:

Credit Policy
A set of rules that include the firm's credit period, discounts, credit standards, and collection procedures offered.

Credit Period
The length of time customers have to pay for purchases.

Discounts
Price reductions given for early payment.

1. **Credit period** is the length of time buyers are given to pay for their purchases. For example, the credit period might be 30 days. Customers prefer longer credit periods, so lengthening the period will stimulate sales. However, long credit periods lengthen the cash conversion cycle, hence ties up more capital in receivables, and that is costly. Also, the longer a receivable is outstanding, the higher the probability that the customer will default and the account will end up as a bad debt.

2. **Discounts** are price reductions given for early payment. The discount specifies the percentage reduction and how rapidly payment must be made to be eligible for the discount. For example, a 2 percent discount might be given if the customer pays within 10 days. Offering discounts has two benefits. First, the discount amounts to a price reduction, and lower prices stimulate sales. Second, discounts will cause some customers to pay earlier than they otherwise would, which will shorten the cash conversion cycle. However, discounts mean lower prices, hence lower revenues unless the quantity sold increases by enough to offset the price reduction. The benefits and costs of discounts must be balanced if a rational decision about them is to be made.

Credit Standards
The financial strength customers must exhibit to qualify for credit.

3. **Credit standards** refer to the required financial strength of acceptable credit customers. Factors considered here would be ratios like the customer's debt and interest coverage ratios, credit history (has the customer paid on time in the past, or tended to be delinquent), and the like. In essence, what is the likelihood that the customer will be willing and able to pay off the receivable on schedule? Note that if standards are set too low bad debt losses will be high, while if standards are set too high the firm will lose sales and thus profits. Thus, a balance must be struck between the costs and benefits of tighter credit standards.

Collection Policy
Degree of toughness in enforcing the credit terms.

4. **Collection policy** refers to the procedures used to collect past due accounts, including the toughness or laxity used in the process. At one extreme, the firm might write a series of polite letters after a fairly long delay, while at the other extreme delinquent accounts would be turned over to a collection agency relatively quickly. Some firmness should be used, but excessive pressure can lead basically good customers to take their business elsewhere. Again, a balance must be struck between the costs and benefits of different collection policies.

---

[13] Whenever goods are sold on credit, two accounts are created—an asset item entitled *accounts receivable* appears on the books of the selling firm, and a liability item called *accounts payable* appears on the books of the purchaser. At this point, we are analyzing the transaction from the viewpoint of the seller, so we are concentrating on the variables under its control, in this case, the receivables. We will examine the transaction from the viewpoint of the purchaser in Section 16.9, when we discuss accounts payable as a source of funds and consider their cost relative to the cost of funds obtained from other sources.

Firms generally publish their **credit terms,** defined as a statement of their credit period and discounts policy. Thus, Allied Foods might have stated credit terms of 2/10, net 30, which means that a 2 percent discount is allowed if payment is received within 10 days of the purchase, and if the discount is not taken then the full amount is due in 30 days. Credit standards and collection policy are relatively subjective, so they are not generally discussed in the published credit terms.

Credit Terms
Statement of the credit period and any discount offered.

16-8b Setting and Implementing the Credit Policy

Credit policy is important for three main reasons: (1) It has a significant effect on sales, (2) it influences the amount of funds tied up in receivables, and (3) it affects the bad debt losses. Because of its importance, the firm's executive committee, which normally consists of the president plus the vice presidents of finance, marketing, and production, has the final say on setting the credit policy. Once the policy has been established, the credit manager, who typically works under the treasurer, must carry it out and monitor its effects. Managing a credit department requires fast, accurate, and up-to-date information. Several organizations, including Dun & Bradstreet, Equifax, and TransUnion, use computer-based networks to collect, store, and distribute credit information. A typical business credit report would include the following:

1. A summary balance sheet and income statement.
2. A number of key ratios, with trend information.
3. Information obtained from the firm's suppliers telling whether it pays promptly or slowly, and whether it has recently failed to make any payments.
4. A verbal description of the physical condition of the firm's operations.
5. A verbal description of the backgrounds of the firm's owners, including any previous bankruptcies, lawsuits, divorce settlement problems, and the like.
6. A summary rating, ranging from A for the best credit risks down to F for those that are deemed likely to default.

Credit scores, which are numerical scores from 0 to 10 that are based on a statistical analysis, provide a summary assessment of the likelihood that a potential customer will default on a required payment. 10 is very good, 1 is very bad. Computerized analytical systems assist in making better credit decisions, but in the final analysis, most credit decisions are really exercises in informed judgment.[14]

Credit Score
A numerical score from 1 to 10 that indicates the likelihood that a person or business will pay on time.

We have emphasized the costs of granting credit. *However, if it is possible to sell on credit and also to impose a carrying charge on the receivables that are outstanding, then credit sales can actually be more profitable than cash sales.* This is especially true for consumer durables (autos, appliances, and so on), but it is also true for certain types of industrial equipment. Thus, GM's General Motors Acceptance Corporation (GMAC) unit, which finances automobiles, is highly profitable, as

---

[14] Credit analysts use procedures ranging from highly sophisticated, computerized "credit-scoring" systems, which actually calculate the statistical probability that a given customer will default, to informal procedures, which involve going through a checklist of factors that should be considered when processing a credit application. The credit-scoring systems use various financial ratios, such as the current ratio and the debt ratio (for businesses), and income, years with the same employer, and the like (for individuals), to determine the statistical probability of default. Credit is then granted to those with low default probabilities. The informal procedures often involve examining the "5 C's of Credit": character, capacity, capital, collateral, and conditions. Character is obvious; capacity is a subjective estimate of ability to repay; capital means how much net worth the borrower has; collateral means assets pledged to secure the loan; and conditions refers to business conditions, which affect ability to repay.

are other companies' credit subsidiaries.[15] Some encyclopedia companies even lose money on cash sales but more than make up these losses from the carrying charges on their credit sales. Obviously, such companies would rather sell on credit than for cash!

The carrying charges on outstanding credit are generally about 18 percent on a nominal basis: 1.5 percent per month, so $1.5\% \times 12 = 18\%$. This is equivalent to an effective annual rate of $(1.015)^{12} - 1.0 = 19.6\%$. Having receivables outstanding that earn more than 18 percent is highly profitable unless there are too many bad debt losses.

Legal considerations must also be taken into account when setting credit policy. It is illegal, under the Robinson-Patman Act, for a firm to charge prices that discriminate between customers unless the different prices are cost-justified. The same holds true for credit—it is illegal to offer more favorable credit terms to one customer or class of customers than another unless the differences are cost-justified.

16-8c Monitoring Accounts Receivable

The total amount of accounts receivable outstanding at any given time is determined by the volume of credit sales and the average length of time between sales and collections. For example, suppose Boston Lumber Company (BLC), a wholesale distributor of lumber products, has credit sales of $1,000 per day, requires payment after 10 days, and has no bad debts or slow-paying customers. Under these conditions, it must have the capital to carry $10,000 of receivables:

$$\frac{\text{Accounts}}{\text{receivable}} = \frac{\text{Credit sales}}{\text{per day}} \times \frac{\text{Length of}}{\text{collection period}} \qquad \textbf{(16-5)}$$

$$= \$1,000 \times 10 \text{ days} = \$10,000$$

If either credit sales or the collection period changes, so will accounts receivable. For example, if sales doubled to $2,000/day, then receivables would also double, and the firm would need an additional $10,000 of capital to finance this increase. Similarly, if the collection period lengthened to 20 days, this too would double the receivables and require additional capital.

If management is not careful the collection period will creep up, as good customers take longer to pay and as sales are made to weaker customers, who tend to pay slowly or not at all, and thus accounts will become bad debts. So, it is important for the CFO to monitor receivables. Two monitoring techniques—days sales outstanding (DSO) and the aging schedule—are discussed next.

Days Sales Outstanding (DSO)

Suppose Super Sets Inc., a television manufacturer, sells 200,000 television sets a year at a price of $198 each. All sales are on credit, with terms of 2/10, net 30, which means that if payment is made within 10 days, customers receive a 2 percent discount; otherwise the full amount is due within 30 days. Also, 70 percent of the customers take discounts and pay on Day 10, while the other 30 percent pay on Day 30.

Super Sets' *days sales outstanding (DSO)*, also known as the average collection period (ACP), is 16 days.

$$\text{DSO} = \text{ACP} = 0.7(10 \text{ days}) + 0.3(30 \text{ days}) = 16 \text{ days}$$

---

[15] Companies that do a large volume of sales financing typically set up subsidiary companies called *captive finance companies* to do the actual financing. Thus, General Motors, DaimlerChrysler, and Ford all have captive finance companies, as do Sears, IBM, and General Electric.

Its average daily sales (ADS) is $108,493:[16]

$$\text{ADS} = \frac{(\text{Units sold})(\text{Sales price})}{365} = \frac{\text{Annual sales}}{365} \qquad \textbf{(16-6)}$$

$$= \frac{200,000(\$198)}{365} = \frac{\$39,600,000}{365} = \$108,493$$

Super Sets' accounts receivable, assuming a constant rate of sales throughout the year, will at all times be $1,735,888:

$$\text{Receivables} = (\text{ADS})(\text{DSO})$$

$$= (\$108,493)(16) = \$1,735,888$$

The DSO, or average collection period, is a measure of the average length of time it takes customers to pay for their credit purchases, and it can be compared with the industry average. For example, if all television manufacturers sell on the same credit terms, and if the industry average DSO is 25 days versus Super Sets' 16 days, then Super Sets either has a higher percentage of discount customers or a very good credit department. Finally, note that if you know the annual sales and the receivables balance, you can calculate DSO:

$$\text{DSO} = \frac{\text{Receivables}}{\text{Annual sales}/365} = \frac{\$1,735,888}{\$108,493} = 16 \text{ days}$$

The DSO can also be compared with the firm's own credit terms. For example, suppose Super Sets' DSO had been 35 days. In this case, some customers would obviously be taking more than 30 days to pay their bills. In fact, if many customers were paying within 10 days to take advantage of the discount, then others must, on average, be taking much longer than 35 days. One way to check this possibility is to use an aging schedule, which we describe next.

Aging Schedules

An **aging schedule** breaks down the receivables by age of account. Table 16-2 contains the December 31, 2005, aging schedules of Super Sets and another television manufacturer, Wonder Vision. Both firms offer the same credit terms, and both have the same total receivables. However, Super Sets' aging schedule indicates that all of its customers pay on time—70 percent pay on Day 10 while 30 percent pay on Day 30. Wonder Vision's schedule, which is more typical, shows that many of its customers are not abiding by its credit terms—some 27 percent of its receivables are more than 30 days past due, even though its credit terms call for full payment by Day 30.

Aging schedules cannot be constructed from the data reported in financial statements; they must be developed from the firm's accounts receivable ledger. However, well-run firms have computerized accounts receivable records, so it is easy to determine the age of each invoice, to sort electronically by age, and thus to generate an aging schedule.

Management should constantly monitor both the DSO and the aging schedule to detect developing trends and to see how actual collection experience compares with its credit terms and with those of other firms in the industry. If the DSO starts to lengthen, or if the aging schedule shows a high percentage of

Aging Schedule
A report showing how long accounts receivable have been outstanding.

---

[16] Note that the full sales price, not the price less the discount, is used in the equation. Discounts are treated as a reduction from sales, but the full sales price is used to calculate the accounts receivable.

TABLE 16-2 Aging Schedules

Age of Account (Days)	SUPER SETS		WONDER VISION	
	Value of Account	Percentage of Total Value	Value of Account	Percentage of Total Value
0–10 (discount customers)	$1,215,122	70%	$ 815,867	47%
11–30 (pay on time)	520,766	30	451,331	26
31–45 (late)	0	0	260,383	15
46–60 (later)	0	0	173,589	10
60+ (very late or bad debts)	0	0	34,718	2
Total receivables	$1,735,888	100%	$1,735,888	100%

past-due accounts, as Wonder Vision's does, then the credit policy may need to be tightened.[17]

What are credit terms?

What are the four credit policy variables?

Define days sales outstanding (DSO). What can be learned from it, and how is it affected by seasonal sales fluctuations?

What is an aging schedule? What can be learned from it? How is it affected by sales fluctuations?

What is credit quality, and how is it assessed?

How does collection policy influence sales, the collection period, and the bad debt loss percentage?

How can cash discounts be used to influence sales volume and the DSO?

How do legal considerations affect a firm's credit policy?

16-9 ACCOUNTS PAYABLE (TRADE CREDIT)

Trade Credit
Debt arising from credit sales and recorded as an account receivable by the seller and as an account payable by the buyer.

Firms generally make purchases from other firms on credit and record the debt as an *account payable*. Accounts payable, or **trade credit,** is the largest single category of short-term debt, representing about 40 percent of the average corporation's current liabilities. This credit is a spontaneous source of financing in the sense that *it arises spontaneously from ordinary business transactions.* For example, suppose a firm makes a purchase of $1,000 on terms of net 30, meaning that it must pay for goods 30 days after the invoice date. This instantly and spontaneously provides it with $1,000 of credit for 30 days. If it purchases $1,000 of goods each day,

---

[17] Seasonal sales can make monitoring of receivables a bit more complicated. See Eugene F. Brigham and Phillip R. Daves, *Intermediate Financial Management*, 8th ed. (Mason, OH: Thomson/South-Western, 2004), Chapter 21, for a more complete discussion of the problems with the DSO and aging schedule and ways to correct for them.

then on average, it will be receiving 30 times $1,000, or $30,000, of credit from its suppliers. If sales, and consequently purchases, double, then its accounts payable would also double, to $60,000. So, simply by growing, the firm spontaneously generates another $30,000 of financing. Similarly, if the terms under which it bought were extended from 30 to 40 days, its accounts payable would expand from $30,000 to $40,000. Thus, both expanding sales and lengthening the credit period generate additional financing.

Trade credit can either be free or costly. If the seller does not offer discounts, then it is free in the sense that there is no cost for using this credit. However, if discounts are available, a complication arises. To illustrate, suppose PCC Inc. buys 20 microchips each day with a list price of $100 per chip on terms of 2/10, net 30. Under these terms, the "true" price of the chips is 0.98($100) = $98, because the chips can be purchased for only $98 by paying within 10 days. Thus, the $100 list price has two components:

$$\text{List price} = \$98 \text{ "true" price} + \$2 \text{ finance charge}$$

If PCC decides to take the discount, it will pay at the end of Day 10 and show $19,600 of accounts payables:[18]

$$\text{Accounts payable}_{\text{(Take discounts)}} = (10 \text{ days})(20 \text{ chips}) (\$98 \text{ per chip})$$
$$= \$19,600$$

If it decides to delay payment until the 30th day, then its trade credit will be $58,800:

$$\text{Accounts payable}_{\text{(No discounts)}} = (30 \text{ days})(20 \text{ chips})(\$98 \text{ per chip})$$
$$= \$58,800$$

By not taking discounts, PCC can obtain an additional $39,200 of trade credit, *but this $39,200 is costly credit because the firm must give up the discounts to get it.* Therefore, PCC must answer this question: Could we obtain the additional $39,200 at a lower cost from some other source, say, a bank?

To illustrate the situation, assume that PCC operates 365 days per year and buys 20 chips per day at a "true" price of $98 per chip. Therefore, its total chip purchases are 20($98)(365) = $715,400 per year. If it does not take discounts, then its chips would cost 20($100)(365) = $730,000, or an additional $14,600. *This $14,600 is the annual cost of the $39,200 of extra credit.* Dividing the $14,600 cost by the $39,200 additional credit yields the nominal annual cost rate of the additional trade credit, 37.2 percent:

$$\text{Nominal annual cost of trade credit} = \frac{\$14,600}{\$39,200} = 37.24\%$$

If PCC can borrow from its bank or some other source for less than 37.24 percent, it should take the discount and use only $19,600 of trade credit.

---

[18] A question arises here: Should accounts payable reflect gross purchases or purchases net of discounts? Generally accepted accounting principles permit either treatment if the difference is not material, but if the discount is material, then the account payable must be recorded net of discounts, or at "true" prices. Then, the cost of not taking discounts is reported as an additional expense called "discounts lost." This procedure highlights the often very high cost of not taking discounts. In PCC's case, it would record payables of 20($98) = $1,960, not $2,000, per day, and if it did not take the discount and had to pay the full $2,000, then it would show the $40 discount lost per day as an expense.

The same result can be obtained with the following equation:

$$\frac{\text{Nominal annual cost}}{\text{of trade credit}} = \frac{\text{Discount \%}}{100 - \text{Discount \%}} \times \frac{365}{\text{Days credit is} - \text{Discount}} \quad \text{(16-7)}$$
$$\text{outstanding} \quad \text{period}$$

$$= \frac{2}{98} \times \frac{365}{20} = 2.04\% \times 18.25 = 37.24\%$$

The numerator of the first term, Discount %, is the cost per dollar of credit, while the denominator, 100 − Discount %, represents the funds made available by not taking the discount. Thus, the first term, 2.04 percent, is the cost per period for the trade credit. The denominator of the second term is the number of days of extra credit obtained by not taking the discount, so the entire second term shows how many times per year the cost is incurred, 18.25 times in this example.[19]

With this background, we can define two types of trade credit, free and costly:

Free Trade Credit
Credit received during the discount period.

1. **Free trade credit** is the trade credit that is obtained without a cost, and it consists of all trade credit that is available without giving up discounts. In PCC's case, where it buys on terms of 2/10, net 30, the first 10 days of purchases, or $19,600, are free.

Costly Trade Credit
Credit taken in excess of free trade credit, whose cost is equal to the discount lost.

2. **Costly trade credit** is any trade credit over and above the free trade credit. For PCC, the additional 20 days, or $39,200, are not free because getting them means giving up the discount.

Firms should always use the free component, but they should use the costly component only if they cannot obtain funds at a lower cost from another source.

Note that the cost of trade credit can be reduced by paying late. If PCC could get away with paying in 60 days rather than the specified 30 days, then the effective credit period would become 60 − 10 = 50 days, the number of times the discount would be lost would fall to 365/50 = 7.3, and the nominal cost would drop from 37.2 percent to 2.04% × 7.3 = 14.9%.

Stretching Accounts Payable
The practice of deliberately paying late.

In periods of excess capacity, firms may be able to get away with deliberately paying late, or **stretching accounts payable**. However, this will subject them to a variety of problems associated with being a "slow payer."

The costs of the extra trade credit from not taking discounts under different credit terms, assuming payments are made on time, are shown here:

Credit Terms	COST OF ADDITIONAL CREDIT IF THE CASH DISCOUNT IS NOT TAKEN	
	Nominal Cost	Effective Cost
1/10, net 20	36.9%	44.3%
1/10, net 30	18.4	20.1
2/10, net 20	74.5	109.0
3/15, net 45	37.6	44.9

---

[19] The nominal annual cost formula does not take account of compounding, and in effective annual interest terms, the cost of trade credit is even higher. The discount amounts to interest, and with terms of 2/10, net 30, the firm gains use of the funds for 30 − 10 = 20 days, so there are 365/20 = 18.25 "interest periods" per year. Remember that the first term in Equation 16-7, (Discount %)/(100 − Discount %) = 0.02/0.98 = 0.0204, is the periodic interest rate. That rate is paid 18.25 times each year, so the effective annual cost of trade credit is 44.6 percent, as shown:

$$\text{Effective annual rate} = (1.0204)^{18.25} - 1.0 = 1.4459 - 1.0 = 44.6\%$$

Thus, the 37.2 percent nominal cost calculated with Equation 16-7 understates the true cost.

As these data show, the cost of not taking discounts can be substantial. Incidentally, throughout the chapter, we assume that payments are made on either the *last day* for taking discounts or on the *last day* of the credit period unless otherwise noted. It would be foolish to pay on the 9th day or earlier, or on the 29th day or earlier, if the credit terms are 2/10, net 30.

What is trade credit?

What is the difference between free trade credit and costly trade credit?

What is the formula for finding the nominal annual cost of trade credit? What is the formula for the effective annual cost of trade credit?

How is the cost of trade credit affected by "stretching" accounts payable?

How does the cost of costly trade credit generally compare with the cost of short-term bank loans?

16-10 BANK LOANS

The key features of bank loans, another important source of short-term financing, are discussed in this section.

16-10a Promissory Note

The terms of a bank loan are spelled out in a **promissory note.** Here are some key features contained in most promissory notes:[20]

1. *Amount.* The amount borrowed is indicated.
2. *Maturity.* Although banks do make longer-term loans, *the bulk of their lending is on a short-term basis*—about two-thirds of all bank loans mature in a year or less. Long-term loans always have a specific maturity date, while a short-term loan may or may not have a specified maturity. For example, a loan may mature in 30 days, 90 days, 6 months, or 1 year, or it may call for payment "on demand," in which case the loan can remain outstanding as long as the borrower wants to continue using the funds and the bank agrees. Bank loans to businesses are frequently written as 90-day notes, so the loan must be repaid or renewed at the end of 90 days. It is often expected that the loan will be renewed, but if the borrower's financial position deteriorates, the bank can refuse to renew it. This can lead to bankruptcy. Because banks virtually never demand payment unless the borrower's creditworthiness has deteriorated, some "short-term loans" remain outstanding for years, with the interest rate floating with rates in the economy.
3. *Interest rate.* The interest rate can be either *fixed* or *floating.* For larger loans it is typically indexed to the bank's prime rate, to the T-bill rate, or to the London Inter-Bank Offer Rate (LIBOR). The note will also indicate whether the

Promissory Note
A document specifying the terms and conditions of a loan, including the amount, interest rate, and repayment schedule.

---

[20] Sometimes the note will also specify that the firm must maintain a "compensating balance" equal to from 10 to 20 percent of the face amount of the loan. This balance generally has the effect of increasing the true cost of the loan. Recent surveys indicate that compensating balances are much less common today than they were a few years ago.

bank uses a *360- or 365-day year* for purposes of calculating interest. The indicated rate is a *nominal rate*, and the effective annual rate is generally higher.

4. *Interest only versus amortized.* Loans are either *interest only*, meaning that only interest is paid during the life of the loan, with the principal being repaid when the loan matures, or *amortized*, meaning that some of the principal is repaid on each payment date. Amortized loans are also called *installment loans*.

5. *Frequency of interest payments.* If the note is on an interest-only basis, it will indicate *how frequently interest must be paid*. Interest is typically calculated daily but paid monthly.

6. *Discount interest.* Most loans call for interest to be paid after it has been earned, but banks also lend on a *discount basis*, where interest is paid in advance. On a discount loan, the borrower actually receives less than the face amount of the loan, and this increases its effective cost. We discuss discount loans in Web Appendix 16B.

7. *Add-on loans.* Auto loans and other consumer installment loans are generally set up on an "add-on basis," which means that interest charges over the life of the loan are calculated and then added to the face amount of the loan. Thus, the borrower signs a note calling for payment of the funds received plus all interest that must be paid over the life of the loan. The add-on feature raises the effective cost of a loan.

8. *Collateral.* If a loan is secured by equipment, buildings, accounts receivable, or inventories, this fact is indicated in the note. Security for loans is discussed in more detail in Section 16.13.

9. *Restrictive covenants.* The note may also specify that the borrower must maintain its current ratio, interest coverage ratio, and so on, at prescribed levels, and it spells out what happens if the borrower defaults on those covenants. Default provisions often allow the lender to demand immediate payment of the entire loan balance, or to increase the interest rate until the default is corrected.

10. *Loan guarantees.* If the borrower is a small corporation, the bank may insist that the larger stockholders *personally guarantee* the loan. Troubled companies' owners have been known to divert assets from the company to relatives or other entities they own, so banks protect themselves by obtaining personal guarantees.

16-10b Line of Credit

Line of Credit
An arrangement in which a bank agrees to lend up to a specified maximum amount of funds during a designated period.

A **line of credit** is an agreement between a bank and a borrower indicating the maximum amount of credit the bank will extend to the borrower. For example, in December, a bank loan officer might indicate to a financial manager that the bank regards the firm as being "good for" up to $80,000 during the coming year, provided the borrower's financial condition does not deteriorate. If on January 10 the financial manager signs a promissory note for $15,000 for 90 days, this would be called "taking down" $15,000 of the credit line. The $15,000 would be credited to the firm's checking account, and before it was repaid the firm could borrow an additional $65,000 for a total of $80,000. Such a line of credit would be informal and nonbinding, but formal and binding lines are available as discussed next.

16-10c Revolving Credit Agreement

Revolving Credit Agreement
A formal, committed line of credit extended by a bank or other lending institution.

A **revolving credit agreement** is a formal line of credit. To illustrate, in 2005 a Texas petroleum company negotiated a revolving credit agreement for $100 million with a group of banks. The banks were formally committed for four years to lend the firm up to $100 million if the funds were needed. The company, in turn, paid an annual commitment fee of one-fourth of 1 percent on the unused balance of the commitment to compensate the banks for making the commitment. Thus, if the firm did not take down any of the $100 million commitment during a year, it would still be required to pay a $250,000 annual fee, normally in monthly installments of $20,833.33. If it borrowed $50 million on the first day of the agreement, the unused portion of the line of credit would fall to $50 million, and the annual fee would fall to $125,000. Of course, interest would also have to be paid on the money the firm actually borrowed. In this case, the interest rate on the "revolver" was pegged to the banks' prime rate, being set at prime minus 0.5 percentage point, so the cost of the loan will vary over time as interest rates change.[21]

Note that a revolving credit agreement is similar to an informal line of credit, but with an important difference: The bank has a *legal obligation* to honor a revolving credit agreement, and it receives a commitment fee. Neither the legal obligation nor the fee exists under the informal line of credit.

16-10d Costs of Bank Loans

The costs of bank loans vary for different types of borrowers at any given point in time and for all borrowers over time. Interest rates are higher for riskier borrowers, and rates are also higher on smaller loans because of the fixed costs involved in making and servicing loans. If a firm can qualify as a "prime credit" because of its size and financial strength, it can borrow at the **prime rate,** which at one time was the lowest rate banks charged. Rates on other loans are generally scaled up from the prime rate, but loans to large, strong customers are made at rates below prime. Thus, loans to smaller, riskier borrowers are generally stated to carry an interest rate of "prime *plus* some number of percentage points," but loans to larger borrowers like the Texas oil company may have a rate stated as "prime *minus* some percentage points."

Prime Rate
A published interest rate charged by commercial banks to large, strong borrowers.

Bank rates vary widely over time depending on economic conditions and Federal Reserve policy. When the economy is weak, loan demand is usually slack, inflation is low, and the Fed also makes plenty of money available to the system. As a result, rates on all types of loans are relatively low. Conversely, when the economy is booming, loan demand is typically strong, the Fed restricts the money supply, and the result is high interest rates. As an indication of the kinds of fluctuations that can occur, the prime rate during 1980 rose from 11 to 21 percent in just four months, and it rose from 6 to 9 percent during 1994. The prime rate currently (August 2005) is 6.25 percent.

Calculating Banks' Interest Charges: Regular or "Simple" Interest

Banks calculate interest in several different ways. In this section we explain the procedure used for most business loans. We discuss procedures used for consumer and small business loans in Web Appendix 16B. For illustrative purposes, we assume a loan of $10,000 at the prime rate, currently 6.25 percent, with a 365-day year. Interest must be paid monthly, and the principal is payable "on demand" if and when the bank wants to end the loan. Such a loan is called a **regular,** or **simple, interest,** loan.

Regular, or Simple, Interest
The situation when interest only is paid monthly.

---

[21] Each bank sets its own prime rate, but, because of competitive forces, most banks' prime rates are identical. Further, most banks follow the rate set by the large New York City banks.

In recent years many banks have been lending to large, strong companies at rates below the prime rate. As we discuss in Section 16.11, larger firms have ready access to the commercial paper market, and if banks want to do business with these companies, they must match, or at least come close to, the commercial paper rate.

We begin by dividing the nominal interest rate, 6.25 percent in this case, by 365 to get the rate per day. The rate is expressed as a *decimal fraction*, not as a percentage:

$$\text{Simple interest rate per day} = \frac{\text{Nominal rate}}{\text{Days in year}}$$

$$= 0.0625/365 = 0.000171233$$

To find the monthly interest payment, the daily rate is multiplied by the amount of the loan, and then by the number of days during the payment period. For our illustrative loan, the daily interest charge would be $1.71233, and the total for January would be $53.08:

$$\text{Interest charge for month} = (\text{Rate per day})(\text{Amount of loan})(\text{Days in month})$$

$$= (0.000171233)(\$10,000)(31 \text{ days}) = \$53.08$$

If interest were payable quarterly, and if there were 90 days in the particular quarter, then the interest payment would be $154.11. The annual interest would be $0.000171233 \times \$10,000 \times 365 = \$625.00$.

The *effective interest rate* on a loan depends on how frequently interest must be paid—the more frequently, the higher the effective rate. If interest is paid once per year, then the nominal rate is also the effective rate. However, if interest must be paid monthly, then the effective rate is $(1 + 0.0625/12)^{12} - 1 = 6.4322\%$.

Calculating Banks' Interest Charges: Add-On Interest

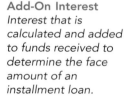

Add-On Interest
Interest that is calculated and added to funds received to determine the face amount of an installment loan.

Banks and other lenders typically use **add-on interest** for automobiles and other types of installment loans. The term *add-on* means that the interest is calculated and then added to the amount borrowed to determine the loan's face value. To illustrate, suppose you borrow $10,000 on an *add-on* basis at a nominal rate of 6.25 percent to buy a car, with the loan to be repaid in 12 monthly installments. At a 6.25 percent add-on rate, you would pay total interest charges of $10,000(0.0625) = $625. However, since the loan is paid off in monthly installments, you would have the use of the full $10,000 for only the first month, and the outstanding balance would decline until, during the last month, only 1/12 of the original loan was still outstanding. Thus, you would be paying $625 for the use of only about half the loan's face amount, as the average usable funds would be only about $5,000. Therefore, we can calculate the approximate annual rate as 12.5 percent:

$$\text{Approximate annual rate}_{\text{Add-on}} = \frac{\text{Interest paid}}{(\text{Amount received})/2} \qquad \textbf{(16-8)}$$

$$= \frac{\$625}{\$10,000/2} = 12.5\%$$

To determine the effective rate of an add-on loan, we proceed as follows:

1. The total amount to be repaid is $10,000 of principal plus $625 of interest, or $10,625.
2. The monthly payment is $10,625/12 = $885.42.
3. You are thus paying off a 12-period annuity of $885.42 to receive $10,000 today. $10,000 is the present value of the annuity, and here is the time line:

4. With a financial calculator, enter N = 12, PV = 10000, PMT = −885.42, FV = 0, and then press I/YR to obtain 0.945298 percent.
5. However, this is a *monthly* rate. The annual percentage rate (APR), which by law the bank is required to state in bold print on all "consumer loan" agreements, would be 11.34 percent:

$$\text{APR} = (\text{Periods per year})(\text{Rate per period})$$
$$= 12(0.945298\%) = 11.343576\% \text{ rounded to } 11.34\%$$

Prior to the passage of the truth in lending laws in the 1970s, most banks would have simply told borrowers that they were paying 6.25 percent. Now, though, they must highlight the 11.34 percent APR.
6. The effective annual rate is found as follows. Note that the monthly percentage rate, 0.945298 percent, must be divided by 100 to get a decimal fraction, $r_d = 0.00945298$, for use in this formula:[22]

$$\text{Effective annual rate}_{\text{Add-on}} = (1 + r_d)^N - 1.0 \qquad \textbf{(16-9)}$$
$$= (1 + 0.00945298)^{12} - 1.0$$
$$= 1.1195 - 1.0 = 11.95\%$$

Other features of bank financing are discussed in Web Appendix 16B to this chapter.

What is a promissory note, and what are some terms that are normally included in such notes?

What is a line of credit? A revolving credit agreement?

What's the difference between simple interest and add-on interest as bankers use these terms?

If a firm borrowed $500,000 at a rate of 10 percent, simple interest, with monthly interest payments and a 365-day year, what would the required interest payment be for a 30-day month? What would the effective annual rate be? ($4,109.59; 10.47%)

If this loan had been on a 10 percent add-on basis, payable in 12 end-of-month installments, what would the monthly payments be, and the APR and effective rates? ($45,833.33; 17.97% 19.52%)

16-11 COMMERCIAL PAPER

Commercial paper is a short-term promissory note issued by large, strong firms and sold primarily to other business firms, insurance companies, pension funds, money market mutual funds, and banks. Commercial paper is issued in denominations of at least $100,000. It is generally unsecured, but "asset-backed paper" secured by credit card debt and other small, short-term loans, has also been issued. The amount of commercial paper outstanding is slightly larger than the amount of bank loans outstanding, so the paper market is huge and very important. A large majority of the commercial paper outstanding is issued by

Commercial Paper
Unsecured, short-term promissory notes of large firms, usually issued in denominations of $100,000 or more and having an interest rate somewhat below the prime rate.

---

[22] Note that if an installment loan is paid off ahead of schedule, additional complications arise. For the classic discussion of this point, see Dick Bonker, "The Rule of 78," *Journal of Finance*, June 1976, pp. 877–888.

financial institutions. A likely reason for why this market is dominated by large financial institutions is that banks and other financial institutions are more likely to need large and varying amounts of short-term funds, and they tend to have among the highest credit ratings, which makes it easier for them to raise unsecured debt. Nonfinancial companies still tend to rely more heavily on bank loans for short-term funding. For example, in the first quarter of 2005, the Federal Reserve reported that commercial paper issued by nonfinancial firms totaled slightly more than $115 billion—that same quarter nonfinancial firms had more than a trillion dollars of bank loans outstanding.

What is commercial paper?

What types of companies can use commercial paper to meet their short-term financing needs?

16-12 ACCRUALS (ACCRUED LIABILITIES)

Firms generally pay employees on a weekly, biweekly, or monthly basis, so the balance sheet will typically show some accrued wages. Similarly, the firm's own estimated income taxes, Social Security and income taxes withheld from employee payrolls, and sales taxes collected are generally paid on a weekly, monthly, or quarterly basis. Therefore, the balance sheet will typically show some accrued wages and taxes, which we refer to as **accruals.**

Accruals arise automatically, or spontaneously, from a firm's operations, hence they are **spontaneous funds.** For example, if sales grow by 50 percent, then accrued wages and taxes should also grow by about 50 percent. Accruals are "free" in the sense that no interest is paid on them. However, firms cannot generally control their amounts because the timing of wage payments is set by industry custom and tax payments are set by law. Thus, firms use all the accruals they can, but they have little control over their levels.

Note too that trade credit is also a spontaneous source of funds to support growth, because as the firm grows, so does its purchases and thus its accounts payable. However, the firm has more control over accounts payable because it can either take or not take discounts, and also delay payments to a certain extent. It does not have the same flexibility to delay payments for labor and taxes.

Accruals
Continually recurring short-term liabilities, especially accrued wages and accrued taxes.

Spontaneous Funds
Funds that are generated spontaneously as the firm expands.

What types of short-term credit are classified as accrued liabilities?

What is the cost of accrued liabilities?

If accruals have such a low cost, why don't firms use them even more?

16-13 USE OF SECURITY IN SHORT-TERM FINANCING

Loans can be secured by specific assets or they can be unsecured. Commercial paper is generally not secured, but other types of loans can be secured if this is deemed necessary or if it will result in a lower interest rate. Other things held constant, it is better to borrow on an unsecured basis because the bookkeeping costs associated with **secured loans** are often high. However, firms may find that they can borrow only if they put up collateral to protect the lender or that securing the loan enables them to borrow at a lower rate.

Secured Loan
A loan backed by collateral, often inventories or accounts receivable.

Stocks and bonds, land and buildings, equipment, inventory, and accounts receivable can all be used as collateral. However, few firms that need loans also hold portfolios of stocks and bonds. Similarly, land, buildings, and equipment are good forms of collateral, but they are generally used as security for long-term loans rather than short-term working capital loans. Therefore, most secured short-term business borrowing uses accounts receivable and inventories as collateral.

To understand the use of security, consider the case of a Chicago hardware dealer who wanted to modernize and expand his store. He requested a $200,000 loan. After examining the financial statements, the bank indicated that it would lend him a maximum of $100,000 on an unsecured basis, and that the interest rate would be 10 percent. However, the company had about $300,000 of accounts receivable that could be used as collateral, and with the receivables as security the bank agreed to lend the full $200,000, and at the prime rate of 6.25 percent. Processing costs for administering the loan were fairly high, but even so the secured loan was less expensive than an unsecured loan would have been.[23]

If the collateral securing a loan is to be kept on the borrower's premises, then a form called a *UCC-1* (Uniform Commercial Code-1) is filed with the secretary of the state in which the collateral is located, along with a *Security Agreement* (also part of the Uniform Commercial Code) that describes the nature of the agreement. The UCC-1 prevents the borrower from using the same collateral to secure loans from different lenders, and the security agreement spells out conditions under which the lender can seize the collateral.

What are the advantages and disadvantages of securing a loan from the borrower's standpoint?

What are two types of current assets that are frequently used as security for short-term loans?

How does the filed UCC-1 protect a secured lender?

Tying It All Together

This chapter discussed the management of current assets, including cash, marketable securities, inventory, and receivables. Current assets are essential, but there are costs associated with holding them, so if a company can reduce its current assets without hurting sales, this will increase its profitability. The investment in current assets must be financed, and this financing can be in the form of long-term debt, common equity, and/or short-term credit. Firms typically use trade credit and accruals, and they may also use bank debt or commercial paper.

Although current assets and procedures for financing them can be analyzed as we did in this chapter, decisions are normally made within the context of the firm's overall financial plan. We take up financial planning in the next chapter, hence we continue our discussion of working capital there.

---

[23] The term *asset-based financing* is often used as a synonym for *secured financing*. In recent years, accounts receivable have been used as security for long-term bonds, and this has permitted corporations to borrow from lenders such as pension funds rather than being restricted to banks and other traditional short-term lenders.

SELF-TEST QUESTIONS AND PROBLEMS
(Solutions Appear in Appendix A)

ST-1 **Key terms** Define each of the following terms:
   a. Working capital; net working capital; net operating working capital
   b. Cash conversion cycle; inventory conversion period; average collection period; payables deferral period
   c. Relaxed current asset policy; restricted current asset policy; moderate current asset policy
   d. Permanent current assets; temporary current assets
   e. Current asset financing policies; maturity matching (self-liquidating) approach to financing working capital
   f. Cash budget; target cash balance; currency; demand deposits
   g. Lockbox; synchronized cash flows
   h. Marketable securities held to provide operating liquidity
   i. Account receivable; days sales outstanding; aging schedule; credit score
   j. Credit policy; credit period; discounts; credit standards; collection policy; credit terms
   k. Trade credit; free versus costly trade credit
   l. Promissory note; covenants
   m. Line of credit; revolving credit agreement
   n. Prime rate; "simple interest" versus add-on interest
   o. Commercial paper
   p. Accruals; spontaneous funds
   q. Secured loan; UCC-1; security agreement

ST-2 **Working capital policy** The Calgary Company is thinking of modifying its working capital assets policy. Fixed assets are $600,000, sales are projected at $3 million, the EBIT/sales ratio is projected at 15 percent, the interest rate is 10 percent on all debt, the federal-plus-state tax rate is 40 percent, and Calgary plans to maintain a 50 percent debt-to-assets ratio. Three alternative current asset policies are under consideration: 40, 50, and 60 percent of projected sales. What is the expected return on equity under each alternative?

ST-3 **Current asset financing** Vanderheiden Press Inc. and the Herrenhouse Publishing Company had the following balance sheets as of December 31, 2005 (thousands of dollars):

	Vanderheiden Press	**Herrenhouse Publishing**
Current assets	$100,000	$ 80,000
Fixed assets (net)	100,000	120,000
Total assets	$200,000	$200,000
Current liabilities	$ 20,000	$ 80,000
Long-term debt	80,000	20,000
Common stock	50,000	50,000
Retained earnings	50,000	50,000
Total liabilities and equity	$200,000	$200,000

Earnings before interest and taxes for both firms are $30 million, and the effective federal-plus-state tax rate is 40 percent.

   a. What is the return on equity for each firm if the interest rate on current liabilities is 10 percent and the rate on long-term debt is 13 percent?
   b. Assume that the short-term rate rises to 20 percent. While the rate on new long-term debt rises to 16 percent, the rate on existing long-term debt remains unchanged. What would be the returns on equity for Vanderheiden Press and Herrenhouse Publishing under these conditions?
   c. Which company is in a riskier position? Why?

QUESTIONS

16-1 Define cash conversion cycle (CCC), and explain why, holding other things constant, a firm's profitability would increase if it lowered its CCC.

16-2   What are some pros and cons of holding high levels of current assets in relation to sales? Use the Du Pont equation to help explain your answer.

16-3   What are the two definitions of cash, and why do corporate treasurers often use the second definition?

16-4   What is a cash budget and how can this statement be used to help reduce the amount of cash that a firm needs to carry? What are the advantages and disadvantages of daily over monthly cash budgets, and how might a cash budget be used when a firm is negotiating a loan from its bank?

16-5   What are the four key factors in a firm's credit policy? How would an easy policy differ from a tight policy? Give examples of how the four factors might differ between the two policies. How would the easy versus the tight policy affect sales? Profits?

16-6   What are two techniques that are used to help monitor accounts receivable? How would an easy versus a tight credit policy affect the results of these two monitoring techniques?

16-7   What does it mean to adopt a maturity matching approach to financing assets, including current assets? How would a more aggressive or a more conservative approach differ from the maturity matching approach, and how would each affect expected profits and risk? In general, is one approach better than the others?

16-8   Why is some trade credit called free while other credit is called costly? If a firm buys on terms of 2/10, net 30, pays at the end of the 30th day, and typically shows $300,000 of accounts payable on its balance sheet, would the entire $300,000 be free credit, would it be costly credit, or would some be free and some costly? Explain your answer. No calculations are necessary.

16-9   Define each of the following loan terms, and explain how they are related to one another: the prime rate, the rate on commercial paper, the simple interest rate on a bank loan calling for interest to be paid monthly, and the rate on an installment loan based on add-on interest. If the stated rate on each of these loans was 6 percent, would they all have equal effective annual rates? Explain.

16-10   Why are accruals called spontaneous sources of funds, what are their costs, and why don't firms use more of them?

16-11   Indicate by a (+), (−), or (0) whether each of the following events would probably cause accounts receivable (A/R), sales, and profits to increase, decrease, or be affected in an indeterminate manner:

	A/R	Sales	Profits
The firm tightens its credit standards.	_____	_____	_____
The terms of trade are changed from 2/10, net 30, to 3/10, net 30.	_____	_____	_____
The terms are changed from 2/10, net 30, to 3/10, net 40.	_____	_____	_____
The credit manager gets tough with past-due accounts.	_____	_____	_____

PROBLEMS

Easy
Problems 1–3

16-1   **Cash conversion cycle** Primrose Corp has $15 million of sales, $2 million of inventories, $3 million of receivables, and $1 million of payables. Its cost of goods sold is 80 percent of sales, and it finances working capital with bank loans at an 8 percent rate. What is Primrose's cash conversion cycle (CCC)? If Primrose could *lower* its inventories and receivables by 10 percent each and *increase* its payables by 10 percent, all without affecting either sales or cost of goods sold, what would the new CCC be, how much cash would be freed up, and how would that affect pre-tax profits?

16-2   **Receivables investment** Lamar Lumber Company has sales of $10 million per year, all on credit terms calling for payment within 30 days, and its accounts receivable are $2 million. What is Lamar's DSO, what would it be if all customers paid on time, and how much capital would be released if Lamar could take actions that led to on-time payments?

16-3   **Cost of trade credit and bank loan** Lamar Lumber buys $8 million of materials (net of discounts) on terms of 3/5, net 60, and it currently pays after 5 days and takes discounts.

Lamar plans to expand, and this will require additional financing. If Lamar decides to forego discounts, how much additional credit could it get, and what would the nominal and effective cost of that credit be? If it could get the funds from a bank at a rate of 10 percent, interest paid monthly, based on a 365-day year, what would be the effective cost of the bank loan, and should Lamar use bank debt or additional trade credit? Explain.

Intermediate Problems 4–6

16-4 **Cash conversion cycle** The Zocco Corporation has an inventory conversion period of 75 days, an average collection period of 38 days, and a payables deferral period of 30 days.
  a. What is the length of the cash conversion cycle?
  b. If Zocco's annual sales are $3,421,875 and all sales are on credit, what is the investment in accounts receivable?
  c. How many times per year does Zocco turn over its inventory?

16-5 **Receivables investment** McDowell Industries sells on terms of 3/10, net 30. Total sales for the year are $912,500; 40 percent of the customers pay on the 10th day and take discounts, while the other 60 percent pay, on average, 40 days after their purchases.
  a. What is the days' sales outstanding?
  b. What is the average amount of receivables?
  c. What is the percentage cost of trade credit to customers who take the discount and to those who do not take it?
  d. What would happen to its accounts receivable if McDowell toughened up on its collection policy with the result that all nondiscount customers paid on the 30th day?

16-6 **Working capital investment** The Prestopino Corporation produces motorcycle batteries. Prestopino turns out 1,500 batteries a day at a cost of $6 per battery for materials and labor. It takes the firm 22 days to convert raw materials into a battery. Prestopino allows its customers 40 days in which to pay for the batteries, and the firm generally pays its suppliers in 30 days.
  a. What is the length of Prestopino's cash conversion cycle?
  b. At a steady state in which Prestopino produces 1,500 batteries a day, what amount of working capital must it finance?
  c. By what amount could Prestopino reduce its working capital financing needs if it was able to stretch its payables deferral period to 35 days?
  d. Prestopino's management is trying to analyze the effect of a proposed new production process on its working capital investment. The new production process would allow Prestopino to decrease its inventory conversion period to 20 days and to increase its daily production to 1,800 batteries. However, the new process would cause the cost of materials and labor to increase to $7. Assuming the change does not affect the average collection period (40 days) or the payables deferral period (30 days), what will be the length of its cash conversion cycle and its working capital financing requirement if the new production process is implemented?

Challenging Problems 7–10

16-7 **Working capital cash flow cycle** The Christie Corporation is trying to determine the effect of its inventory turnover ratio and days sales outstanding (DSO) on its cash flow cycle. Christie's 2005 sales (all on credit) were $150,000, and it earned a net profit of 6 percent, or $9,000. It turned over its inventory 6 times during the year, and its DSO was 36.5 days. The firm had fixed assets totaling $35,000. Christie's payables deferral period is 40 days.
  a. Calculate Christie's cash conversion cycle.
  b. Assuming Christie holds negligible amounts of cash and marketable securities, calculate its total assets turnover and ROA.
  c. Suppose Christie's managers believe that the inventory turnover can be raised to 7.3 times. What would Christie's cash conversion cycle, total assets turnover, and ROA have been if the inventory turnover had been 7.3 for 2005?

16-8 **Working capital policy** The Rentz Corporation is investigating the optimal level of current assets for the coming year. Management expects sales to increase to approximately $2 million as a result of an asset expansion presently being undertaken. Fixed assets total $1 million, and the firm plans to maintain a 60 percent debt ratio. Rentz's interest rate is currently 8 percent on both short-term and longer-term debt (which the firm uses in its permanent structure). Three alternatives regarding the projected current asset level are under consideration: (1) a tight policy where current assets would be only 45 percent of projected sales, (2) a moderate policy where current assets would be 50 percent of sales, and (3) a relaxed policy where current assets would be 60 percent of sales. Earnings before interest and taxes should be 12 percent of total sales, and the federal-plus-state tax rate is 40 percent.

a. What is the expected return on equity under each current asset level?
b. In this problem, we assume that expected sales are independent of the current asset policy. Is this a valid assumption?
c. How would the firm's risk be affected by the different policies?

16-9 **Lockbox system** The Hardin-Gehr Corporation (HGC) began operations 5 years ago as a small firm serving customers in the Detroit area. However, its reputation and market area grew quickly, and today HGC has customers all over the United States. Despite its broad customer base, HGC has maintained its headquarters in Detroit, and it keeps its central billing system there. On average, it takes 5 days from the time customers mail in payments until HGC can receive, process, and deposit them. HGC would like to set up a lockbox collection system, which it estimates would reduce the time lag from customer mailing to deposit by 3 days—bringing it down to 2 days. HGC receives an average of $1,400,000 in payments per day.

a. How much free cash would HGC generate if it implemented the lockbox system? Would this be a one-time cash flow or a recurring one, assuming the company ceases to grow? How would growth affect your answer?
b. If HGC has an opportunity cost of 10 percent, how much is the lockbox system worth on an annual basis?
c. What is the maximum monthly charge HGC should pay for the lockbox system?

16-10 **Cash budgeting** Helen Bowers, owner of Helen's Fashion Designs, is planning to request a line of credit from her bank. She has estimated the following sales forecasts for the firm for parts of 2006 and 2007:

May 2006	$180,000
June	180,000
July	360,000
August	540,000
September	720,000
October	360,000
November	360,000
December	90,000
January 2007	180,000

Estimates regarding payments obtained from the credit department are as follows: collected within the month of sale, 10 percent; collected the month following the sale, 75 percent; collected the second month following the sale, 15 percent. Payments for labor and raw materials are made the month after these services were provided. Here are the estimated costs of labor plus raw materials:

May 2006	$ 90,000
June	90,000
July	126,000
August	882,000
September	306,000
October	234,000
November	162,000
December	90,000

General and administrative salaries are approximately $27,000 a month; lease payments under long-term leases are $9,000 a month; depreciation charges are $36,000 a month; miscellaneous expenses are $2,700 a month; income tax payments of $63,000 are due in both September and December; and a progress payment of $180,000 on a new design studio must be paid in October. Cash on hand on July 1 will be $132,000, and a minimum cash balance of $90,000 should be maintained throughout the cash budget period.

a. Prepare a monthly cash budget for the last 6 months of 2006.
b. Prepare monthly estimates of the required financing or excess funds—that is, the amount of money Bowers will need to borrow or will have available to invest.
c. Now suppose receipts from sales come in uniformly during the month (that is, cash receipts come in at the rate of $1/30$ each day), but all outflows must be paid on the 5th. Will this affect the cash budget; that is, will the cash budget you prepared be

valid under these assumptions? If not, what could be done to make a valid estimate of the peak financing requirements? No calculations are required, although if you want to, you can use calculations to illustrate the effects.

d. Bowers sales are seasonal, and it produces on a seasonal basis, just ahead of sales. Without making any calculations, discuss how the company's current and debt ratios would vary during the year if all financial requirements are met with short-term bank loans. Could changes in these ratios affect the firm's ability to obtain bank credit?

COMPREHENSIVE/SPREADSHEET PROBLEM

16-11   **Cash budgeting** Rework Problem 16-10 using a spreadsheet model. After completing parts a through d, answer the following related question.

e. If its customers began to pay late, this would slow down collections and thus increase the required loan amount. If sales declined this would also have an effect on the required loan. Do a sensitivity analysis that shows the effects of these two factors on the maximum loan requirement.

Integrated Case

Ski Equipment Inc.

16-12   **Managing current assets** Dan Barnes, financial manager of Ski Equipment Inc. (SKI), is excited, but apprehensive. The company's founder recently sold his 51 percent controlling block of stock to Kent Koren, who is a big fan of EVA (Economic Value Added). EVA is found by taking the after-tax operating profit and then subtracting the dollar cost of all the capital the firm uses:

$$EVA = EBIT(1 - T) - \text{Capital costs}$$
$$= EBIT(1 - T) - WACC(\text{Capital employed})$$

If EVA is positive, then the firm is creating value. On the other hand, if EVA is negative, the firm is not covering its cost of capital, and stockholders' value is being eroded. Koren rewards managers handsomely if they create value, but those whose operations produce negative EVAs are soon looking for work. Koren frequently points out that if a company can generate its current level of sales with less assets, it would need less capital. That would, other things held constant, lower capital costs and increase its EVA.

Shortly after he took control of SKI, Koren met with SKI's senior executives to tell them of his plans for the company. First, he presented some EVA data that convinced everyone that SKI had not been creating value in recent years. He then stated, in no uncertain terms, that this situation must change. He noted that SKI's designs of skis, boots, and clothing are acclaimed throughout the industry, but something is seriously amiss elsewhere in the company. Costs are too high, prices are too low, or the company employs too much capital, and he wants SKI's managers to correct the problem or else.

Barnes has long felt that SKI's working capital situation should be studied—the company may have the optimal amounts of cash, securities, receivables, and inventories, but it may also have too much or too little of these items. In the past, the production manager resisted Barnes's efforts to question his holdings of raw materials inventories, the marketing manager resisted questions about finished goods, the sales staff resisted questions about credit policy (which affects accounts receivable), and the treasurer did not want to talk about her cash and securities balances. Koren's speech made it clear that such resistance would no longer be tolerated.

Barnes also knows that decisions about working capital cannot be made in a vacuum. For example, if inventories could be lowered without adversely affecting operations, then less capital would be required, the dollar cost of capital would decline, and EVA would increase. However, lower raw materials inventories might lead to production slowdowns and higher costs, while lower finished goods inventories might lead to the loss of profitable sales. So, before inventories are changed, it will be necessary to study operating as well as financial effects. The situation is the same with regard to cash and receivables.

a. Barnes plans to use the ratios in Table IC16-1 as the starting point for discussions with SKI's operating executives. He wants everyone to think about the pros and cons of changing each type of current asset and how changes would interact to affect profits and EVA. Based on the Table IC16-1 data, does SKI seem to be following a relaxed, moderate, or restricted working capital policy?

b. How can we distinguish between a relaxed but rational working capital policy and a situation where a firm simply has a lot of current assets because it is inefficient? Does SKI's working capital policy seem appropriate?

c. SKI tries to match the maturity of its assets and liabilities. Describe how SKI could adopt either a more aggressive or more conservative financing policy.

d. Assume that SKI's payables deferral period is 30 days. Now, calculate the firm's cash conversion cycle.

e. What might SKI do to reduce its cash and securities without harming operations?

In an attempt to better understand SKI's cash position, Barnes developed a cash budget. Data for the first 2 months of the year are shown in Table IC16-2. (Note that Barnes's preliminary cash budget does not account for interest income or interest expense.) He has the figures for the other months, but they are not shown in Table IC16-2.

f. In his preliminary cash budget, Barnes has assumed that all sales are collected and, thus, that SKI has no bad debts. Is this realistic? If not, how would bad debts be dealt with in a cash budgeting sense? (Hint: Bad debts will affect collections but not purchases.)

g. Barnes's cash budget for the entire year, although not given here, is based heavily on his forecast for monthly sales. Sales are expected to be extremely low between May and September but then increase dramatically in the fall and winter. November is typically the firm's best month, when SKI ships equipment to retailers for the holiday season. Interestingly, Barnes's forecasted cash budget indicates that the company's cash holdings will exceed the targeted cash balance every month except for October and November, when shipments will be high but collections will not be coming in until later. Based on the ratios in Table IC16-1, does it appear that SKI's target cash balance is appropriate? In addition to possibly lowering the target cash balance, what actions might SKI take to better improve its cash management policies, and how might that affect its EVA?

h. Is there any reason to think that SKI may be holding too much inventory? If so, how would that affect EVA and ROE?

i. If the company reduces its inventory without adversely affecting sales, what effect should this have on the company's cash position (1) in the short run and (2) in the long run? Explain in terms of the cash budget and the balance sheet.

j. Barnes knows that SKI sells on the same credit terms as other firms in its industry. Use the ratios presented in Table IC16-1 to explain whether SKI's customers pay more or less promptly than those of its competitors. If there are differences, does that suggest that SKI should tighten or loosen its credit policy? What four variables make up a firm's credit policy, and in what direction should each be changed by SKI?

k. Does SKI face any risks if it tightens its credit policy?

l. If the company reduces its DSO without seriously affecting sales, what effect would this have on its cash position (1) in the short run and (2) in the long run? Answer in terms of the cash budget and the balance sheet. What effect should this have on EVA in the long run?

m. Assume that SKI buys on terms of 1/10, net 30, but that it can get away with paying on the 40th day if it chooses not to take discounts. Also, assume that it purchases $3 million of components per year, net of discounts. How much free trade credit can the company get, how much costly trade credit can it get, and what is the percentage cost of the costly credit? Should SKI take discounts?

n. Suppose SKI decided to raise an additional $100,000 as a 1-year loan from its bank, for which it was quoted a rate of 8 percent. What is the effective annual cost rate assuming simple interest and add-on interest on a 12-month installment loan?

TABLE IC16-1 *Selected Ratios: SKI and Industry Average*

	SKI	Industry
Current	1.75	2.25
Debt/assets	58.76%	50.00%
Turnover of cash and securities	16.67	22.22
Days sales outstanding (365-day basis)	45.63	32.00
Inventory turnover	4.82	7.00
Fixed assets turnover	11.35	12.00
Total assets turnover	2.08	3.00
Profit margin on sales	2.07%	3.50%
Return on equity (ROE)	10.45%	21.00%

TABLE IC16-2 *SKI's Cash Budget for January and February*

	Nov	Dec	Jan	Feb	Mar	Apr
I. COLLECTIONS AND PURCHASES WORKSHEET						
(1) Sales (gross)	$71,218	$68,212	$65,213	$52,475	$42,909	$30,524
Collections						
(2) During month of sale (0.2)(0.98) (month's sales)			12,781.75	10,285.10		
(3) During first month after sale (0.7)(previous month's sales)			47,748.40	45,649.10		
(4) During second month after sale (0.1) (sales 2 months ago)			7,121.80	6,821.20		
(5) Total collections (Lines 2+3+4)			$67,651.95	$62,755.40		
Purchases						
(6) (0.85) (forecasted sales 2 months from now)		$44,603.75	$36,472.65	$25,945.40		
(7) Payments (1-month lag)			44,603.75	36,472.65		
II. CASH GAIN OR LOSS FOR MONTH						
(8) Collections (from Section I)			$67,651.95	$62,755.40		
(9) Payments for purchases (from Section I)			44,603.75	36,472.65		
(10) Wages and Salaries			6,690.56	5,470.90		
(11) Rent			2,500.00	2,500.00		
(12) Taxes						
(13) Total payments			$53,794.31	$44,443.55		
(14) Net cash gain (loss) during month (Line 8−Line 13)			$13,857.64	$18,311.85		

TABLE IC16-2 *continued*

	Nov	Dec	Jan	Feb	Mar	Apr
III. CASH SURPLUS OR LOAN REQUIREMENT						
(15) Cash at beginning of month if no borrowing is done			$ 3,000.00	$16,857.64		
(16) Cumulative cash [cash at start + gain or − loss = (Line 14 + Line 15)]			$16,857.64	$35,169.49		
(17) Target cash balance			1,500.00	1,500.00		
(18) Cumulative surplus cash or loans outstanding to maintain $1,500 target cash balance (Line 16 − Line 17)			$15,357.64	$33,669.49		

cyberproblem

Please go to the ThomsonNOW Web site to access the Cyberproblems.

FINANCIAL PLANNING AND FORECASTING

Forecasting Apple's Future

In early 2005, corporations were reporting 2004 earnings and giving security analysts "guidance" to help them forecast earnings for 2005 and beyond. If analysts forecast earnings properly, then there will be fewer of the "negative surprises" that cause stock prices to plummet, so corporate executives try to help analysts forecast more accurately. Providing good guidance obviously requires that firms accurately forecast their own results.

Apple Computer illustrates the link between earnings forecasts and stock prices. Back in 1998 the company appeared to be in serious trouble, and its stock fell to $5. However, new products that were being developed came to fruition in 2000, leading to improved earnings and a stock price increase to $35. But then profits declined again in 2002 and 2003, and its price again plunged, this time to $7. Nevertheless, the iPod was under development, and when it came out it produced high sales and profits, plus a "halo effect" that boosted Apple's reputation and thus its computer sales. The stock price roared up from $7 to $45.

In early 2005, the central issue was this: Would iPod's sales continue to be strong and help the company's computer sales, or would they pull back due to a saturated market and new competitive products? In July 2005 part of the answer was revealed—Apple announced blockbuster earnings, up five-fold from the previous year, and both iPod and computer sales remained extremely strong. The company had forecasted quarterly EPS of $0.28, but the actual figure was $0.37, more than 30 percent higher. Moreover, about the time the earnings results were released, reports came out that Apple was planning a new version of the iPod, one designed to handle movies as well as music.

Stock price volatility is not desirable. It creates great uncertainty, which investors dislike, so if Apple's management could provide better guidance and thus reduce volatility, the stock price would benefit. Of course, good guidance depends on good management forecasts, and no guidance at all is better than one based on bad forecasts. Our task in this chapter is to explain how financial forecasts are made and then used by management, both to provide guidance to analysts and, more importantly, to help judge the results of alternative operating decisions, which are really the key determinants of a stock's long-run value.

Putting Things In Perspective

Managers make **pro forma**, or **projected, financial statements** and then use them in five ways: (1) Pro forma statements can be used to help estimate the effect of proposed operating changes, as with Apple's decision to go ahead with the video iPod. If the pro forma results look good, charge ahead, but if they look bad, hold back. (2) As noted, the projected statements can help managers provide better guidance to security analysts and thus reduce stock price volatility. (3) The forecasts can be used to help top management establish reasonable targets for the operating managers. Serious problems are created if managers' bonuses are based on targets that are unrealistically high, and good forecasts can help avoid this problem. (4) Pro forma statements are used to anticipate the firm's future financing needs. How much money will be needed for planned investments; how much of those funds will be generated internally; and, consequently, how much cash must the company plan to raise or how much will be available for dividends, stock repurchases, or other investments? (5) The pro forma results can be analyzed, individual problem areas can be identified, and then corrective actions can be taken. With these issues in mind, we explain how to create and use forecasted financial statements.

Pro Forma (Projected) Financial Statements
Financial statements that forecast the company's financial position and performance over a period of years.

17-1 STRATEGIC PLANNING

Financial planning should be done within the context of a well-articulated strategic plan that contains a number of elements. First, the plan should begin with a *mission statement*. For example, the first sentence of PepsiCo's mission statement says that its goal is to "increase the value of our shareholders' investment" but also to consider the effects of its actions on customers and the environment. This corporate focus on creating wealth for stockholders is common in the United States and in developed countries around the world.

The second key element in the strategic plan is a statement of the firm's *corporate scope*, which means the lines of business it plans to pursue and the geographic areas in which it will operate. Studies show that investors generally value focused firms more highly than diversified ones.[1] However, if a firm is successful in combining a group of diversified businesses so that they help one another, as GE has done, this can produce synergistic effects that raise the value of the overall enterprise.[2] In any event, the stated corporate scope should make good business sense and be consistent with the firm's capabilities.

---

[1] See, for example, Philip G. Berger and Eli Ofek, "Diversification's Effect on Firm Value," *Journal of Financial Economics*, Vol. 37, no. 1 (1995), pp. 39–66; and Larry Lang and René Stulz, "Tobin's Q, Corporate Diversification, and Firm Performance," *Journal of Political Economy*, Vol. 102, Issue 6 (1994), pp. 1248–1280.

[2] Synergy means a situation where the whole is greater than the sum of the parts, and it's sometimes called the 2 + 2 = 5 effect. GE has 11 diverse business units, ranging from jet engines to financial services to its Universal-NBC entertainment unit. This diversification provides stability

A third key element in the corporate plan is the *statement of corporate objectives*, which sets forth the specific goals that operating managers are expected to meet. Most firms have both qualitative and quantitative objectives. For example, a firm might have as its objectives a sales growth rate of 8 percent, the maintenance of an A or better bond rating, an ROE in the upper quartile of its industry, and shareholder returns in the top quarter of the S&P 500 companies. In its latest annual report, GE indicated that it had a number of such goals, including the goal of generating $20 billion of operating cash flow per year, which would be used for dividends, stock repurchases, and investments to grow the business. Each of GE's 11 business units has a profitability goal and a cash flow goal, and executive compensation is based on achieving these objectives. GE's stockholders will, of course, also benefit if the executives meet their goals.

A set of *corporate strategies* that spell out how the firm plans to achieve its goals is the fourth element in the corporate plan. For example, Nucor Corporation, which is now the U.S. steel company with the highest market value, had as its corporate strategy a plan to build electric furnaces to make steel products from scrap rather than from iron ore as the other steel companies did. Nucor's strategy led to a huge stock price increase at a time when the old-guard steel companies were going down the tube. Southwest Airlines had a strategy of providing one class of efficient, low-cost service between major metropolitan areas, with nonunion labor, which was a very different approach from that of most other airlines. Southwest has flourished while most other airlines have either gone bankrupt or are teetering on the brink of bankruptcy. These examples demonstrate the importance of a good strategic plan.

A detailed *operating plan* for each unit is the fifth component of the overall corporate plan. Here each unit's management is given detailed implementation guidance, based on the corporate strategy, to help it achieve the corporate objectives. Operating plans can be developed for any time horizon, but most companies use a five-year horizon. The plan explains in considerable detail who is responsible for each particular function, when specific tasks are to be accomplished, what the sales and profit targets are, and the like.

The *financial plan* is the final element of the overall corporate plan. A separate plan is set forth for each unit, and those plans are then consolidated to show the projected results for the entire corporation. The heart of the financial plan is a set of projected financial statements, with a number of ratios based on those statements, for the separate units and the consolidated firm. The base-case projections show the results that are expected if all the forecast assumptions are exactly right. However, things rarely go exactly according to plan, so results under alternative scenarios are provided. For example, the firm's base-case assumptions might call for a strong economy, but another 9/11-type terrorist attack, or $100-a-barrel oil, could change circumstances substantially. Therefore, the financial plan should be designed to give management an indication of what would happen if another such event should occur.

The financial statements are also used to examine the effects of alternative strategies and operating plans. A company such as Southwest Airlines can use its financial model to simulate results with different strategies under different economic conditions. Southwest concluded that high jet-fuel costs were a distinct possibility and that a run-up would have a tremendous adverse effect on costs and profits. Based on these forecasts, it decided to hedge its fuel costs (that

---

Footnote 2 continued

that has resulted in a triple-A bond rating and a relatively low cost of capital, which apparently benefits all the businesses. A number of academic studies dispute this conclusion, but in spite of that criticism, GE's stockholders have enjoyed remarkable results over the years, probably because their management has done such an exceptionally good job of running the corporation.

is, in effect buy fuel ahead of time) and also to invest in the most fuel-efficient aircraft that were available. Those strategies turned out to be exactly right, and effective financial planning and forecasting helped management make the right decisions.

In what five ways do managers use pro forma financial statements?

Briefly describe each of these corporate planning terms: (1) mission statement, (2) corporate scope, (3) corporate objectives, and (4) corporate strategies.

How can the financial plan be used to help formulate corporate strategies?

17-2 THE SALES FORECAST

Financial planning requires us to forecast and then analyze a set of financial statements. We begin with the *sales forecast*, which starts with a review of sales during the past 5 to 10 years, shown as a graph such as that in Figure 17-1 for Allied Foods, our illustrative company. These numbers are based on Allied's financial statements, which were first presented in Chapter 3. You may also refer to this chapter's *Excel* model. The data below the graph show five years of historical sales, which Allied thinks are most relevant for planning purposes.

FIGURE 17-1 *Allied Food Products: 2006 Sales Projection (Millions of Dollars)*

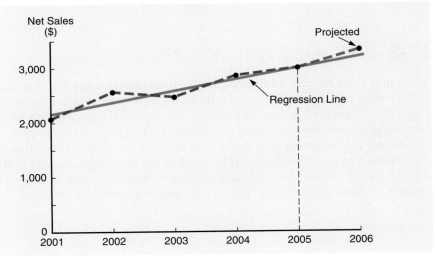

Year	Sales
2001	$2,058
2002	2,534
2003	2,472
2004	2,850
2005	3,000
2006	3,300 (Projected)

Allied had its ups and downs during the period from 2001 to 2005. In 2003, poor weather in California's fruit-producing regions resulted in low production, which caused 2003 sales to fall below the 2002 level. Then a bumper crop in 2004 pushed sales up by 15 percent, an unusually high growth rate for a mature food processor. As shown in the chapter *Excel* model, the compound annual growth rate over the four-year period was 9.88 percent. However, due to planned new-product introductions, the firm's production and distribution capacity, its competitors' capacities and new-product introductions, pricing strategies, inflation, advertising campaigns, credit terms, and the like, management projects that the growth rate will increase to 10 percent in 2006, so sales should rise from $3,000 million to $3,300 million.

Forecasts are made for each of its three divisions, both in the aggregate and on an individual product basis. The individual product sales forecasts are summed, and this sum is compared with the aggregated division forecasts. Differences are reconciled, and the end result is a sales forecast for the company as a whole but with breakdowns by the three divisions and by individual products.

If the sales forecast is off, the consequences can be serious. First, if the market expands by *more* than Allied expects, it will not be able to meet demand. Its customers will end up buying competitors' products, and it will lose market share. On the other hand, if its projections are overly optimistic, it could end up with too much plant, equipment, and inventory. This would mean low turnover ratios, high costs for depreciation and storage, and write-offs of spoiled inventory. All of this would result in low profits, a low ROE, and a depressed stock price. If Allied finances its capacity expansion with debt, high interest charges would compound its problems.[3]

Why is an accurate sales forecast critical for financing planning?

17-3 THE AFN EQUATION

AFN
Additional funds needed, that is, the amount of external capital that will be needed to acquire the needed assets.

Increasing sales require additional assets, these assets must be financed, and it may or may not be possible to obtain all the funds needed for the firm's business plan. Therefore, a key element in the financial forecasting process is to determine the external financing requirements. The most accurate procedure for forecasting requirements is to develop a detailed forecast of the future financial statements, but Equation 17-1 can be used to get an approximation of the funds needed. **AFN** stands for "additional funds needed," and it represents the amount of external capital the firm must raise to support its growth.[4]

---

[3] A sales forecast is actually the *expected value of a probability distribution*, so there are many possible levels of sales. Because any sales forecast is subject to uncertainty, financial planners are just as interested in the degree of uncertainty inherent in the sales forecast, as measured by the standard deviation, as in the expected level of sales.

[4] In this chapter we do a lot of calculating, using calculators and *Excel*, which carry decimal places out to eight or so places. However, we round to show our results. You should disregard minor discrepancies because they are probably due to rounding. In forecasting, it's really silly to carry things out to very many decimal places, as the final results are bound to be off far more than any rounding differences.

$$
\begin{array}{ccccc}
\text{Additional} & & \text{Projected} & & \text{Spontaneous} & & \text{Increase in} \\
\text{funds} & = & \text{increase} & - & \text{increase in} & - & \text{retained} & \quad\quad \textbf{(17-1)} \\
\text{needed} & & \text{in assets} & & \text{liabilities} & & \text{earnings} \\
\text{AFN} & = & (A^*/S_0)\Delta S & - & (L^*/S_0)\Delta S & - & MS_1(RR)
\end{array}
$$

Here

AFN = additional funds needed.

A^* = assets that are tied directly to sales and that must increase if sales are to increase. Note that A designates total assets and A^* designates those assets that must increase if sales are to increase. When the firm is operating at full capacity, as is the case here, $A^* = A$. Often, though, A^* and A are not equal, and then the equation must be modified.

S_0 = sales during the past year.

A^*/S_0 = percentage of required assets to sales, which also shows the required dollar increase in assets per $1 increase in sales. For Allied, as shown in its financial statements in Chapter 3, A^*/S_0 = \$2,000/\$3,000 = 0.6667, so for every $1 increase in sales, assets must increase by about 66.67 cents.

L^* = liabilities that increase spontaneously with sales. Spontaneous liabilities include accounts payable and accruals, but not bank loans and bonds. Therefore, L^* is normally less than total liabilities.

L^*/S_0 = percentage of spontaneous liabilities to sales, which is also the spontaneously generated financing per $1 increase in sales. For Allied, L^*/S_0 = (\$60 + \$140)/\$3,000 = 0.06667, so every $1 increase in sales generates 6.667 cents of spontaneous financing as accounts payable and accruals.

S_1 = total sales projected for the coming year. Note that S_0 designates last year's sales, while S_1 is the forecasted sales, which for Allied is \$3,300 million.

ΔS = change in sales = $S_1 - S_0$ = \$3,300 - \$3,000 = \$300 million for Allied.

M = profit margin, or profit per $1 of sales. M = \$117.5/\$3,000 = 0.03917 for Allied, so Allied earns 3.917 cents on each dollar of sales.

RR = retention ratio, which is the percentage of net income that is retained during the last year. In 2005 Allied earned \$117.5 million and paid out \$57.5 million in dividends, so its retained earnings were \$60 million. Therefore, RR = \$60/\$117.5 = 0.51064.

Inserting Allied's numbers (dollars in millions) into Equation 17-1, we find that Allied's additional funds needed equal $114 million:

$$
\begin{array}{ccccc}
& \text{Required} & & \text{Spontaneous} & & \text{Increase} \\
\text{AFN} = & \text{asset} & - & \text{liability} & - & \text{in retained} \\
& \text{increase} & & \text{increase} & & \text{earnings}
\end{array}
$$

$$= 0.6667(\Delta S) - 0.06667(\Delta S) - 0.03917(S_1)(0.51064)$$

$$= 0.6667(\$300) - 0.06667(\$300) - 0.03917(\$3,300)(0.51064)$$

$$= \$200 - \$20 - \$66$$

$$= \$114 \text{ million}$$

To increase sales by $300 million, Allied must increase assets by $200 million, where $20 million will come from spontaneous increases in payables and accruals, while another $66 million will come from retained earnings. The remaining $114 million must be raised from external sources. Note, though, that the AFN equation assumes that the key ratios in 2005 will be maintained in 2006. If economic conditions change and cause the ratios to change, then the forecasted $114 million AFN will not be correct.

17-3a Key Determinants of External Funds Requirements

Note that the need for external financing depends on five key factors:

- *Sales growth (ΔS).* Rapidly growing companies require large increases in assets, other things held constant.
- *Capital intensity* (A^*/S_0). The amount of assets required per dollar of sales, A^*/S_0 in Equation 17-1, is called the **capital intensity ratio,** and it has a major effect on capital requirements. Companies with high assets-to-sales ratios require more assets for a given increase in sales, hence have a greater need for external financing. Electric utilities, with their expensive power plants and distribution systems, are very capital intensive, whereas grocery stores, whose high inventory turnover results in relatively little assets in relation to sales, are not capital intensive.
- *Spontaneous liabilities-to-sales ratio* (L^*/S_0). Companies that spontaneously generate a large amount of funds from accounts payable and accruals have a reduced need for external financing.
- *Profit margin (M).* The higher the profit margin, the larger the net income available to support increases in assets, hence the lower the need for external financing.
- *Retention ratio (RR).* Companies that retain a high percentage of their earnings rather than paying them out as dividends generate more retained earnings and thus need less external financing.

> **Capital Intensity Ratio**
> *The amount of assets required per dollar of sales (A^*/S_0).*

Based on the AFN equation, we forecasted that Allied will require $114 million of external funds to carry out its business plan for 2006. Note, though, that changes in any of the key determinants could result in a situation where the AFN is *negative,* which would indicate that surplus funds would be generated and available for investment. In Allied's case, as we demonstrate in the chapter's *Excel* model, AFN would be zero at a sales growth rate of 3.447 percent, and at any lower growth rate surplus funds would be generated. Also, as we discuss here and later in Section 17.4, changes in the other determinants would also alter the calculated AFN.

17-3b Excess Capacity Adjustments

The AFN equation assumes that the ratio A^*/S_0 = $2,000/$3,000 = 0.6667 is a constant. However, note that A* consists of all the firm's assets, and $1,000 of that total was fixed assets. Thus, $1,000/$3,000 = 0.3333 of the 0.6667 is attributable to fixed assets. We then forecasted that Allied would need 0.6667(ΔS) = 0.6667($300 million) = $200 million of new assets, and $100 million of that total would be for fixed assets.

Now suppose that excess capacity in fixed assets existed in the base year. For example, suppose Allied was using its fixed assets in 2005 at only 96 percent of capacity. This means that if fixed assets had been used to full capacity, 2005 sales could have been as high as $3,125 million versus the $3,000 million of actual sales:

$$\begin{array}{l}\text{Full} \\ \text{capacity} \\ \text{sales}\end{array} = \dfrac{\text{Actual sales}}{\begin{array}{c}\text{Percentage of capacity} \\ \text{at which fixed assets} \\ \text{were operated}\end{array}} = \$3{,}000/0.96 = \$3{,}125 \text{ million}$$

This indicates that Allied's target fixed assets/sales ratio should be 32.0 percent rather than 33.3 percent:

$$\text{Target fixed assets/Sales} = \dfrac{\text{Actual fixed assets}}{\text{Full capacity sales}}$$

$$= \$1{,}000/\$3{,}125 = 0.32 = 32\%$$

Therefore, sales could increase to $3,125 million with no increase in fixed assets, and a sales increase to $3,300 million would require only $1,056 million of fixed assets:

$$\begin{array}{l}\text{Required level} \\ \text{of fixed assets}\end{array} = (\text{Target fixed assets/Sales})(\text{Projected sales})$$

$$= 0.32(\$3{,}300) = \$1{,}056 \text{ million}$$

Our earlier estimate of AFN assumed that fixed assets would have to increase at the same rate as sales, 10 percent, from $1,000 million to $1,100 million, or by $100 million. Now we see that the actual required increase is only from $1,000 million to $1,056 million, or by $56 million, a decline of $44 million. This lowers the required AFN by $44 million, from $114 million to $70 million.

The same situation could occur with respect to inventories, cash, or other assets. Moreover, the L^*/S_0 ratio might be too low because the firm is underutilizing supplier credit and accruals. Because of all this, it is useful to go beyond the AFN equation and on to projected financial statements, as we do in the next section.

If the key ratios are expected to remain constant, the AFN equation can be used to forecast the need for external funds. Write out the equation and explain its logic.

How do the following factors affect the AFN, or the requirements for external capital?

(1) Retention ratio.
(2) Capital intensity.
(3) Profit margin.
(4) Dividend payout ratio.
(5) Sales growth.

Is it possible for the AFN to be negative? What would that indicate?

If excess capacity exists, how will that affect the AFN?

17-4 FORECASTED FINANCIAL STATEMENTS

The AFN equation provides useful insights into the forecasting process, but, as we noted earlier, the basic equation assumes that all of the company's key ratios remain constant, a condition that is not likely to hold true. Therefore, it is useful to forecast the firm's financial statements. We begin with a forecast based on the same assumption that underlies the AFN equation—namely, that most assets and many liabilities increase at the same rate as sales—after which we modify the assumptions to make the forecast more reflective of likely future conditions. The modified financial forecasts, and ratios based on the forecasted statements, are especially useful for comparing predicted results with target results as called for in the firm's strategic plan. If the predicted results deviate from the target results, then either the targets should be changed or the plan should be modified to help operating managers meet their targets.

Forecasting financial statements requires a lot of number crunching. It can be done with a calculator, but realistically it is necessary to use a spreadsheet like *Excel*. Therefore, in the text we discuss the concepts involved and the results generated with our model. If you want to learn about the details of the calculation, you should access the chapter model and go through it. This would be quite useful if you need to make a forecast for an actual company, but it is not necessary to understand the general ideas behind financial forecasting and to see how such forecasts are used.

17-4a Initial Forecast: "Business as Usual"

Allied, like most companies, begins by forecasting its financial statements on the assumption that things in the future go pretty much like they did in the recent past. This means that assets and spontaneous liabilities will grow at the same rate as sales, the profit margin will remain fairly constant, the capital structure will not be changed materially, and dividend policy will not be altered substantially. Sales for the coming year are then forecasted, and, based on the sales forecast, the expected future income statement and balance sheet are forecasted. The forecast actually proceeds (within the computer) in stages. A "first-pass" income statement and balance sheet are forecasted, holding constant the relationship between sales and most of the items on those statements. Here assets and those liabilities that increase spontaneously with sales are forecasted, but notes payable, long-term debt, and common stock are held constant at their prior level. Retained earnings in the first-pass balance sheet are set equal to the prior retained earnings plus the addition to retained earnings as found in the first-pass income statement. Typically, the first-pass balance sheet will not balance—the forecasted assets exceed the forecasted liabilities and equity, with the difference equal to an initial estimate of the AFN.

Tables 17-1 and 17-2 show Allied's forecasted income statements and balance sheets. The first column shows 2005 data. Then, in the second column, we show the first-pass statements. Note that the first-pass balance sheet does not balance, and the $108.7 million of AFN must be financed. The first-pass AFN means that notes payable, long-term debt, and common stock must be increased by a total of $108.7 million, and that will lead to a second-pass balance sheet (shown in the chapter model but not here) where those items are increased. When debt is increased in the second-pass balance sheet, this

TABLE 17-1   *Actual 2005 and Forecasted 2006 Income Statements*

		2006 FORECAST		
	Actual 2005	**1st Pass**	**4th Pass**	**Modified**
Sales	$3,000.0	$3,300.0	$3,300.0	$3,300.0
Costs except depreciation	2,616.2	2,877.8	2,877.8	2,854.5
Depreciation	100.0	110.0	110.0	105.0
Total operating costs	$2,716.2	$2,987.8	$2,987.8	$2,959.5
EBIT	$ 283.8	$ 312.2	$ 312.2	$ 340.5
Less interest	88.0	88.0	94.3	86.2
EBT	$ 195.8	$ 224.2	$ 217.9	$ 254.3
Taxes (40%)	78.3	89.7	87.2	101.7
Net income	$ 117.5	$ 134.5	$ 130.7	$ 152.6
Common dividends	$ 57.5	$ 63.3	$ 63.3	$ 63.3
Addition to RE	$ 60.0	$ 71.3	$ 67.5	$ 89.3

Note: Table 17-1 is an excerpt of this chapter's *Excel* model.

TABLE 17-2   *Actual 2005 and Forecasted 2006 Balance Sheets*

		2006 FORECAST		
Assets	**Actual 2005**	**1st Pass**	**4th Pass**	**Modified**
Cash	$ 10.0	$ 11.0	$ 11.0	$ 75.0
Accounts receivable	375.0	412.5	412.5	381.2
Inventories	615.0	676.5	676.5	578.2
Total current assets	$1,000.0	$1,100.0	$1,100.0	$1,034.4
Net plant and equipment	1,000.0	1,100.0	1,100.0	1,056.0
Total assets	$2,000.0	$2,200.0	$2,200.0	$2,090.4
Liabilities and Equity				
Accounts payable	$ 60.0	$ 66.0	$ 66.0	$ 66.0
Notes payable	110.0	110.0	117.9	91.1
Accruals	140.0	154.0	154.0	154.0
Total current liabilities	$ 310.0	$ 330.0	$ 337.9	$ 311.1
Long-term bonds	750.0	750.0	801.7	750.0
Total debt	$1,060.0	$1,080.0	$1,139.6	$1,061.1
Common stock	130.0	130.0	182.9	130.0
Retained earnings	810.0	881.3	877.5	899.3
Total common equity	$ 940.0	$1,011.3	$1,060.4	$1,029.3
Total liabilities and equity	$2,000.0	$2,091.3	$2,200.0	$2,090.4
Additional funds needed (AFN)		$ 108.7	$ 0.01	$ 0.0
Cumulative AFN		$ 108.7	$ 112.50	−$ 18.9

Note: Table 17-2 is an excerpt of this chapter's *Excel* model.

causes interest charges to increase, and that changes the second-pass income statement. Because of the higher interest charges, net income and thus the addition to retained earnings are lowered in the second pass, and that leads to a further increase in the calculated AFN, which leads to further changes in the statements.

The change in the AFN declines with each pass, or iteration, and after four passes the balance sheet is in balance out to one decimal place. In the text tables we show only the statements for the first and fourth passes, but the model itself shows results for the second and third passes, along with a detailed explanation of how the adjustments are made. Tables 17-1 and 17-2 also show, in the final column, some "Modified" results that we will discuss shortly.

Table 17-3 shows a set of ratios based on the calculated financial statements. Note that Allied's ROE for 2005 is below the industry average ROE of 15 percent, as is the fourth-pass ROE, which assumes no significant change in operations. (The forecasted ROE is slightly less than the 2005 figure because, in the forecast, the debt ratio declines very slightly.) Management looked at the ratios to try to determine why Allied has been performing worse than the industry average. They immediately saw that the inventory turnover was only half that of an average firm in its industry, meaning that Allied had almost twice as much inventory for its level of sales as an average firm in its industry does. Similarly, Allied's DSO was much higher than average, indicating an excessive investment in accounts receivable. These excessive investments in inventories and receivables involved carrying costs, which caused the operating costs/sales ratio to be high, and that reduced profits and the profit margin, which obviously hurt the ROE.

The Du Pont equation in the lower part of the table shows that under its current operating plan Allied's profit margin is relatively low and its asset turnover is also below average. On the other hand, Allied has an above average equity multiplier, which raises its ROE, but at the cost of a very high debt ratio and high interest costs. When we put these three factors together, the result is a relatively low ROE.

Allied's managers reviewed the actual 2005 results and the forecast for 2006 and noted that the company was performing below the industry average. They also saw that the unmodified 2006 forecast would require $112.5 of external capital, with much of it coming from debt. However, in view of the company's high debt ratio and low TIE ratio, there were questions about whether lenders would actually provide Allied the required funds, and what the cost of those funds would be. After this review, management developed an operating plan designed to improve performance in 2006. Results under the proposed plan are shown in the tables under the column heading labeled "Modified." The plan calls for increasing the inventory turnover, lowering the DSO, and lowering the operating costs-to-sales ratio. As we also show in Table 17-3, Allied had a negative free cash flow in 2005, and under current conditions this key number would be only +$7.3 million. However, under the modified forecast FCF would rise to $313.9 million, largely because of reductions in inventories, accounts receivable, and fixed assets, plus an increase in net income. The FCF would be used to build the cash account, reduce long-term debt, and finance the assets needed to support the sales increase.

The bottom line is this: If management can indeed implement the proposed modifications, this would result in significantly higher profits and cash flows and a 14.8 percent ROE, which is close to the industry average. Those results would certainly improve the firm's stock price, which is management's ultimate goal.

TABLE 17-3	*Actual 2005 and Forecasted 2006 Ratios and Free Cash Flow*

	A	B	C	D	E	F
				4th Pass	**Modified**	**Industry**
129			**2005**	**2006**	**2006**	**Average**
130	Current Ratio		3.2	3.3	3.3	4.2
131	Inventory Turnover		4.9	4.9	5.7	9.0
132	Days sales outstanding		45.6	45.6	42.2	36.0
133	Total assets turnover		1.5	1.5	1.6	1.8
134	Debt ratio		53.0%	51.8%	50.8%	40.0%
135	Assets/Equity (multiplier)		2.13	2.07	2.03	1.67
136	TIE		3.23	3.31	3.95	6.0
137	Operating costs/Sales		90.5%	90.5%	89.7%	87.0%
138	Profit Margin		3.9%	4.0%	4.6%	5.0%
139	Return on Assets		5.9%	5.9%	7.3%	9.0%
140	Return on Equity		12.5%	12.3%	14.8%	15.0%
141						
142				**Total Asset**	**Equity**	
143			**Profit Margin**	**Turnover**	**Multiplier**	**ROE**
144	Du Pont ROE, 2005	=	3.92%	1.50	2.13	12.50%
145	Du Pont ROE, 4th pass	=	3.96%	1.50	2.07	12.33%
146	Du Pont ROE, modified	=	4.62%	1.58	2.03	14.82%
147	Industry	=	5.00%	1.80	1.67	15.03%
148						
149				**4th**	**Modified**	
150			**2005**	**2006**	**2006**	
151	Free Cash Flow		($109.7)	$7.3	$313.9	

What advantages does the forecasted financial statement method have over the AFN equation for forecasting financial requirements?

Using the AFN equation, we forecasted that Allied would need $114 million of external funds, while the fourth-pass (final) AFN forecast based on financial statements was $112.5 million. However, the AFN forecast under the modified statement approach was *negative*. What caused the huge change in AFN?

17-5 USING REGRESSION TO IMPROVE FINANCIAL FORECASTS

In our financial statement forecasts, we assumed that the various assets would increase at the same rate as sales. However, that is not necessarily the case. We noted in our discussion of the AFN equation that excess capacity might exist, in which case assets would increase less rapidly than sales. Similarly, economies of scale might exist, and if this condition holds, then again assets will not have to grow as fast as sales. Other conditions might also exist to invalidate the lock-step tie between sales and specific asset categories, even if the firm plans no major change in operations (like a change in credit policy or in inventory management procedures). We can use regression techniques to investigate such situations and thus improve the financial forecasts.

To illustrate regression analysis for use in forecasting, consider Figure 17-2, which shows Allied's sales, inventories, and receivables during the last five years, and a scatter diagram plot of inventories and receivables versus sales. Estimated regression equations, determined using a financial calculator or a spreadsheet, can also be developed. For example, the estimated relationship between inventories and sales (in millions of dollars) is shown here:

$$\text{Inventories} = -\$35.7 + 0.186(\text{Sales})$$

The plotted points are not very close to the regression line, which indicates that changes in inventory are affected by factors other than changes in sales. In fact, the correlation coefficient between inventories and sales is only 0.71, indicating that there is only a moderate linear relationship between these two variables. Still, the regression relationship is strong enough to help us consider a revision in the target inventory level, as described in Figure 17-2.

We can use the regression equation to estimate a "better" 2006 inventory level. As 2006 sales are projected at $3,300 million, then according to the regression, 2006 inventories should be $578 million:

$$\text{Inventories} = -\$35.7 + 0.186(\$3,300) = \$578 \text{ million}$$

This is $99 million less than the fourth-pass forecast based on the projected financial statements. The difference occurs because the projected financial statement method assumed that the ratio of inventories to sales will remain constant,

---

FIGURE 17-2 *Allied Food Products: Regression Models (Millions of Dollars)*

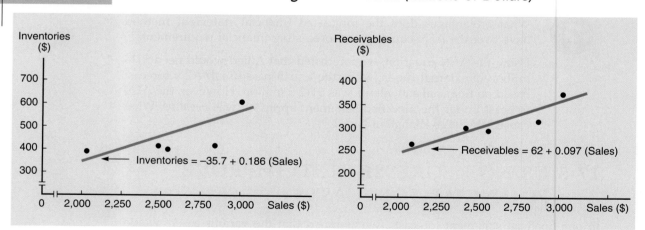

Year	Sales	Inventories	Accounts Receivable
2001	$2,058	$387	$268
2002	2,534	398	297
2003	2,472	409	304
2004	2,850	415	315
2005	3,000	615	375

whereas under the regression method it is forecasted to decline. Note also that although our graphs show linear relationships, we could have easily used a nonlinear regression model had we felt that such a relationship was more appropriate.

After analyzing the regression results, Allied's managers decided that a new forecast of AFN should be developed assuming a lower days sales outstanding (DSO) and a higher inventory turnover ratio. Management recognized that the 2005 levels of these accounts were above the industry averages, hence that the preliminary results projected for 2006 in Table 17-2 were unnecessarily high. When simple linear regression was used to forecast the receivables and inventory accounts, this caused the 2006 levels to reflect both the average relationships of these accounts to sales over the five-year period, as well as the trend in the variables' values. In contrast, the projected financial statement method assumed that the (nonoptimal) 2005 relationships would remain constant in 2006 and beyond. These new assumptions about DSO and inventory turnover contributed to the modified forecasts shown in the projected statements.

Examine the following statement: "Using regression to predict items like inventories is better than basing such predictions on the latest inventory/sales ratio because regression helps smooth out the effects of random fluctuations." Do you agree or disagree? Explain.

17-6 USING INDIVIDUAL RATIOS IN THE FORECASTING PROCESS

Thus far we have seen how financial statements can be forecasted assuming that there are no material changes in operations and that most things increase with sales, how ratios based on the projected statements can be calculated, and then how the initial forecasts can be modified so that the projected results will produce an improved set of ratios. Under this approach, a number of items can be changed, and the combined results can be observed.

17-6a Modifying Accounts Receivable

We can also look at the effects of modifying individual asset forecasts, such as inventories, receivables, and fixed assets. For example, consider accounts receivable. We saw in Table 17-3 that Allied's DSO is projected to be 45.6 days versus an industry average of 36 days. The 45.6 days is based on sales of $3,300 million and a receivables balance of $412.5 million as shown in Tables 17-1 and 17-2:

$$\text{DSO} = \frac{\text{Receivables}}{\text{Sales}/365} = \frac{\$412.5}{\$3,300/365} = \frac{\$412.5}{\$9.04} = 45.63 \text{ days}$$

We can then solve this equation for receivables:

$$\text{Receivables} = \$9.04(45.63) = \$412.5$$

Now we can use this expression to find the receivables Allied would have if it could change its credit operations so as to achieve the industry average DSO, 36 days:

$$\text{Modified receivables} = \$9.04(36.0) = \$325.4$$

Thus, Allied could generate a $412.5 − $325.4 = $87.1 million one-time addition to its free cash flow, plus smaller improvements in FCF as it grows in later years, by improving its credit operations. The CFO could use this type of analysis to help motivate the credit manager to change his or her operations.

17-6b Modifying Inventories

Inventories can be analyzed is a similar manner. First, note in Table 17-3 that Allied's fourth-pass forecasted inventory turnover is 4.9 times versus 9.0 times for the industry. Moreover, in Table 17-2 Allied's forecasted inventory number is $676.5 million against sales of $3,300 million. Given these data, we can determine Allied's situation if it were able to lower inventories sufficiently to achieve the industry average turnover:

Allied's inventory turnover = Sales/Inventories = $3,300/$676.5 = 4.878

We can then solve this equation for Allied's inventory balance:

Inventories = $3,300/4.878 = $676.5

Now substitute the industry average inventory turnover, 9.0, into the expression for 4.878, and we calculate $366.7 as the target inventory number. This indicates the potential for generating a one-time addition to FCF of $676.5 − $366.7 = $309.8 million, plus additional savings as the company grows. Again, the CFO could use this example in a discussion with Allied's inventory manager.

17-6c Other "Special Studies"

Once a firm has developed a model to forecast its financial statements, it can do all types of special "what if" studies. For example, Allied could use its model to estimate the effects of changing the dividend policy both on the statements and on the required AFN. Indeed, the AFN equation itself could be modified to obtain a "quick and dirty" estimate of the effects of dividends on the AFN. As we saw earlier in Section 17.3 in the discussion of the AFN, Allied has a retention ratio of RR = 0.51064, and when that number was used in the AFN equation (dollars in millions), an AFN of $114 million resulted:

$$\text{AFN} = 0.6667(\Delta S) - 0.06667(\Delta S) - 0.03917(S_1)(0.51064)$$
$$= 0.6667(\$300) - 0.06667(\$300) - 0.03917(\$3,300)(0.51064)$$
$$= \$200 - \$20 - \$66$$
$$= \$114 \text{ million}$$

The RR of approximately 0.51 implies a dividend payout of roughly 1.0 − 0.51 = 0.49, or 49 percent. Assume that Allied would really have to raise $114 million to carry out its business plan, that is, disregard the modifications we have suggested. Then, if the CFO anticipated a problem raising these funds, he or she might suggest to the directors that they consider lowering the dividend payout ratio to, say, 25 percent, which would result in RR = 0.75. With that RR, the AFN would decline by about $31 million, to $83 million. Of course, as we saw in the dividend chapter, lowering the dividend creates problems of its own, but at times such an action is necessary to maximize the firm's intrinsic value and long-run stock price.

Tying It All Together

This chapter described techniques for forecasting financial statements, which is a crucial part of the financial planning process. Both investors and corporations regularly use forecasting techniques to help value a company's stock; to estimate the benefits of potential projects; and to estimate how changes in capital structure, dividend policy, and working capital policy would influence shareholder value.

The type of forecasting described in this chapter is important for several reasons. First, if the projected operating results are unsatisfactory, management can "go back to the drawing board," reformulate its plans, and develop more reasonable targets for the coming year. Second, it is possible that the funds required to meet the sales forecast simply cannot be obtained. If so, it is obviously better to know this in advance and to scale back the projected level of operations than to suddenly run out of cash and have operations grind to a halt. And third, even if the required funds can be raised, it is desirable to plan for their acquisition well in advance of when the funds would be needed.

SELF-TEST QUESTIONS AND PROBLEMS
(Solutions Appear in Appendix A)

ST-1 **Key terms** Define each of the following terms:
a. Pro forma (projected) financial statements
b. Additional funds needed (AFN); AFN equation
c. Capital intensity ratio
d. Spontaneously generated funds; retention ratio
e. Excess capacity adjustments
f. Regression analysis for forecasting
g. Use of ratios in forecasting

ST-2 **Growth rate** Weatherford Industries Inc. has the following ratios: $A^*/S_0 = 1.6$; $L^*/S_0 = 0.4$; profit margin = 0.10; and retention ratio = 0.55, or 55 percent. Sales last year were $100 million. Assuming that these ratios will remain constant, use the AFN equation to determine the maximum growth rate Weatherford can achieve without having to employ nonspontaneous external funds.

ST-3 **Additional funds needed** Suppose Weatherford's financial consultants report (1) that the inventory turnover ratio is sales/inventory = 3 times versus an industry average of 4 times and (2) that Weatherford could reduce inventories and thus raise its turnover to 4 without affecting sales, the profit margin, or the other asset turnover ratios. Under these conditions, use the AFN equation to determine the amount of additional funds Weatherford would require next year if sales grow by 20 percent.

QUESTIONS

17-1 What are the 5 key factors on which external financing depends, as indicated in the AFN equation?

17-2   Assume that an average firm in the office supply business has a 6 percent after-tax profit margin, a 40 percent debt/assets ratio, a total assets turnover of 2 times, and a dividend payout ratio of 40 percent. Is it true that if such a firm is to have *any* sales growth (g > 0), it will be forced either to borrow or to sell common stock (that is, it will need some nonspontaneous, external capital even if g is very small)?

17-3   Would you agree that computerized corporate planning models were a fad during the 1990s but, because of a need for flexibility in corporate planning, they are no longer used by most firms?

17-4   Certain liability and net worth items generally increase spontaneously with increases in sales. Put a check (✓) by those items that typically increase spontaneously:

Accounts payable	_____
Notes payable to banks	_____
Accrued wages	_____
Accrued taxes	_____
Mortgage bonds	_____
Common stock	_____
Retained earnings	_____

17-5   Suppose a firm makes the following policy changes. If the change means that external, nonspontaneous financial requirements (AFN) will increase, indicate this by a (+); indicate a decrease by a (−); and indicate an indeterminate or negligible effect by a (0). Think in terms of the immediate, short-run effect on funds requirements.

a.   The dividend payout ratio is increased.   _____
b.   A computer company decides to produce computers for sale
     only after an order has been received rather than produce
     them in advance.   _____
c.   The firm decides to pay all suppliers on delivery, rather than
     after a 30-day delay, to take advantage of discounts for
     rapid payment.   _____
d.   The firm begins to sell on credit (previously all sales had been
     on a cash basis).   _____
e.   The firm's profit margin is eroded by increased competition;
     sales are steady.   _____
f.   Advertising expenditures are stepped up.   _____
g.   A decision is made to substitute long-term mortgage bonds for
     short-term bank loans.   _____
h.   The firm begins to pay employees on a weekly basis
     (previously it had paid employees at the end of each month).   _____

PROBLEMS

Easy
Problems 1–6

17-1   **AFN equation**   Carter Corporation's sales are expected to increase from $5 million in 2005 to $6 million in 2006, or by 20 percent. Its assets totaled $3 million at the end of 2005. Carter is at full capacity, so its assets must grow in proportion to projected sales. At the end of 2005, current liabilities are $1 million, consisting of $250,000 of accounts payable, $500,000 of notes payable, and $250,000 of accrued liabilities. The after-tax profit margin is forecasted to be 5 percent, and the forecasted retention ratio is 30 percent. Use the AFN equation to forecast Carter's additional funds needed for the coming year.

17-2   **AFN equation**   Refer to Problem 17-1. What would the additional funds needed be if the company's year-end 2005 assets had been $4 million? Assume that all other numbers are the same. Why is this AFN different from the one you found in Problem 17-1? Is the company's "capital intensity" the same or different? Explain.

17-3   **AFN equation**   Refer to Problem 17-1 and assume that the company had $3 million in assets at the end of 2005. However, now assume that the company pays no dividends. Under these assumptions, what would be the additional funds needed for the coming year? Why is this AFN different from the one you found in Problem 17-1?

17-4 **Pro forma income statement** Austin Grocers recently reported the following 2005 income statement (in millions of dollars):

Sales	$700
Operating costs including depreciation	500
EBIT	$200
Interest	40
EBT	$160
Taxes (40%)	64
Net income	$ 96
Dividends	$ 32
Addition to retained earnings	$ 64

This year the company is forecasting a 25 percent increase in sales, and it expects that its year-end operating costs including depreciation will equal 70 percent of sales. Austin's tax rate, interest expense, and dividend payout ratio are all expected to remain constant.

a. What is Austin's projected 2006 net income?
b. What is the expected growth rate in Austin's dividends?

17-5 **Excess capacity** Walter Industries has $5 billion in sales and $1.7 billion in fixed assets. Currently, the company's fixed assets are operating at 90 percent of capacity.

a. What level of sales could Walter Industries have obtained if it had been operating at full capacity?
b. What is Walter's target fixed assets/sales ratio?
c. If Walter's sales increase 12 percent, how large of an increase in fixed assets would the company need in order to meet its target fixed assets/sales ratio?

17-6 **Regression and inventories** Jasper Furnishings has $300 million in sales. The company expects that its sales will increase 12 percent this year. Jasper's CFO uses a simple linear regression to forecast the company's inventory level for a given level of projected sales. On the basis of recent history, the estimated relationship between inventories and sales (in millions of dollars) is

$$\text{Inventories} = \$25 + 0.125(\text{Sales})$$

Given the estimated sales forecast and the estimated relationship between inventories and sales, what are your forecasts of the company's year-end inventory level and the inventory turnover ratio?

Intermediate Problems 7–12

17-7 **Pro forma income statement** At the end of last year, Roberts Inc. reported the following income statement (in millions of dollars):

Sales	$3,000
Operating costs excluding depreciation	2,450
EBITDA	$ 550
Depreciation	250
EBIT	$ 300
Interest	125
EBT	$ 175
Taxes (40%)	70
Net income	$ 105

Looking ahead to the following year, the company's CFO has assembled the following information:

- Year-end sales are expected to be 10 percent higher than the $3 billion in sales generated last year.
- Year-end operating costs, excluding depreciation, are expected to equal 80 percent of year-end sales.
- Depreciation is expected to increase at the same rate as sales.
- Interest costs are expected to remain unchanged.
- The tax rate is expected to remain at 40 percent.

On the basis of this information, what will be the forecast for Roberts' year-end net income?

17-8 **Long-term financing needed** At year-end 2005, total assets for Ambrose Inc. were $1.2 million and accounts payable were $375,000. Sales, which in 2005 were $2.5 million, are expected to increase by 25 percent in 2006. Total assets and accounts payable are proportional to sales, and that relationship will be maintained; that is, they will grow at the same rate as sales. Ambrose typically uses no current liabilities other than accounts payable. Common stock amounted to $425,000 in 2005, and retained earnings were $295,000. Ambrose plans to sell new common stock in the amount of $75,000. The firm's profit margin on sales is 6 percent; 60 percent of earnings will be retained.

a. What was Ambrose's total debt in 2005?
b. How much new, long-term debt financing will be needed in 2006?
(Hint: AFN − New stock = New long-term debt.)

17-9 **Sales increase** Pierce Furnishings generated $2.0 million in sales during 2005, and its year-end total assets were $1.5 million. Also, at year-end 2005, current liabilities were $500,000, consisting of $200,000 of notes payable, $200,000 of accounts payable, and $100,000 of accrued liabilities. Looking ahead to 2006, the company estimates that its assets must increase by 75 cents for every $1 increase in sales. Pierce's profit margin is 5 percent, and its retention ratio is 40 percent. How large a sales increase can the company achieve without having to raise funds externally?

17-10 **Regression and receivables** Edwards Industries has $320 million in sales. The company expects that its sales will increase 12 percent this year. Edwards's CFO uses a simple linear regression to forecast the company's receivables level for a given level of projected sales. On the basis of recent history, the estimated relationship between receivables and sales (in millions of dollars) is

$$\text{Receivables} = \$9.25 + 0.07(\text{Sales})$$

Given the estimated sales forecast and the estimated relationship between receivables and sales, what are your forecasts of the company's year-end balance for receivables and its year-end days sales outstanding (DSO) ratio? Assume that DSO is calculated on the basis of a 365-day year.

17-11 **Regression and inventories** Charlie's Cycles Inc. has $110 million in sales. The company expects that its sales will increase 5 percent this year. Charlie's CFO uses a simple linear regression to forecast the company's inventory level for a given level of projected sales. On the basis of recent history, the estimated relationship between inventories and sales (in millions of dollars) is

$$\text{Inventories} = \$9 + 0.0875(\text{Sales})$$

Given the estimated sales forecast and the estimated relationship between inventories and sales, what are your forecasts of the company's year-end inventory level and its inventory turnover ratio?

17-12 **Excess capacity** Edney Manufacturing Company has $2 billion in sales and $0.6 billion in fixed assets. Currently, the company's fixed assets are operating at 80 percent of capacity.

a. What level of sales could Edney have obtained if it had been operating at full capacity?
b. What is Edney's target fixed assets/sales ratio?
c. If Edney's sales increase 30 percent, how large of an increase in fixed assets would the company need in order to meet its target fixed assets/sales ratio?

Challenging Problems 13–14

17-13 **Additional funds needed** Morrissey Technologies Inc.'s 2005 financial statements are shown here.

Morrissey Technologies Inc.: Balance Sheet as of December 31, 2005

Cash	$ 180,000	Accounts payable	$ 360,000
Receivables	360,000	Notes payable	156,000
Inventories	720,000	Accrued liabilities	180,000
Total current assets	$1,260,000	Total current liabilities	$ 696,000
Fixed assets	1,440,000	Common stock	1,800,000
		Retained earnings	204,000
Total assets	$2,700,000	Total liabilities and equity	$2,700,000

Morrissey Technologies Inc.: Income Statement for December 31, 2005

Sales	$3,600,000
Operating costs	3,279,720
EBIT	$ 320,280
Interest	20,280
EBT	$ 300,000
Taxes (40%)	120,000
Net Income	$ 180,000

Per Share Data:

Common stock price	$24.00
Earnings per share (EPS)	$ 1.80
Dividends per share (DPS)	$ 1.08

a. Suppose that in 2006 sales increase by 10 percent over 2005 sales and that 2006 DPS will increase to $1.12. Construct the pro forma financial statements using the projected financial statement method. Use AFN to balance the pro forma balance sheet. How much additional capital will be required? Assume the firm operated at full capacity in 2005.

b. If the profit margin were to remain at 5 percent and the dividend payout rate were to remain at 60 percent, at what growth rate in sales would the additional financing requirements be exactly zero? (Hint: Set AFN equal to zero and solve for g.)

17-14 **Excess capacity** Krogh Lumber's 2005 financial statements are shown here.

Krogh Lumber: Balance Sheet as of December 31, 2005 (Thousands of Dollars)

Cash	$ 1,800	Accounts payable	$ 7,200
Receivables	10,800	Notes payable	3,472
Inventories	12,600	Accrued liabilities	2,520
Total current assets	$25,200	Total current liabilities	$13,192
		Mortgage bonds	5,000
		Common stock	2,000
Net fixed assets	21,600	Retained earnings	26,608
Total assets	$46,800	Total liabilities and equity	$46,800

Krogh Lumber: Income Statement for December 31, 2005 (Thousands of Dollars)

Sales	$36,000
Operating costs	30,783
Earnings before interest and taxes	$ 5,217
Interest	1,017
Earnings before taxes	$ 4,200
Taxes (40%)	1,680
Net income	$ 2,520
Dividends (60%)	$ 1,512
Addition to retained earnings	$ 1,008

a. Assume that the company was operating at full capacity in 2005 with regard to all items *except* fixed assets; fixed assets in 2005 were being utilized to only 75 percent of capacity. By what percentage could 2006 sales increase over 2005 sales without the need for an increase in fixed assets?

b. Now suppose 2006 sales increase by 25 percent over 2005 sales. How much additional external capital will be required? Assume that Krogh cannot sell any fixed assets. (Hint: Use the projected financial statement method to develop a pro forma income statement and balance sheet as in Tables 17-1 and 17-2.) Assume that any required financing is borrowed as notes payable. Use a pro forma income statement to determine the addition to retained earnings. (Another hint: Notes payable = $6,021.)

COMPREHENSIVE/SPREADSHEET PROBLEM

17-15 **Forecasting financial statements** Use a spreadsheet model to forecast the financial statements in Problems 17-13 and 17-14.

Integrated Case

New World Chemicals Inc.

17-16 **Financial forecasting** Sue Wilson, the new financial manager of New World Chemicals (NWC), a California producer of specialized chemicals for use in fruit orchards, must prepare a formal financial forecast for 2006. NWC's 2005 sales were $2 billion, and the marketing department is forecasting a 25 percent increase for 2006. Wilson thinks the company was operating at full capacity in 2005, but she is not sure about this. The first step in her forecast was to assume that key ratios would remain unchanged and that it would be "business as usual" at NWC. The 2005 financial statements, the 2006 initial forecast, and a ratio analysis for 2005 and the 2006 initial forecast are given in Table IC17-1.

TABLE IC17-1 *Financial Statements and Other Data on NWC (Millions of Dollars)*

A. BALANCE SHEETS

	2005	2006E
Cash and equivalents	$ 20	$ 25
Accounts receivable	240	300
Inventories	240	300
Total current assets	$ 500	$ 625
Net fixed assets	500	625
Total assets	$1,000	$1,250
Accounts payable and accrued liabilities	$ 100	$ 125
Notes payable	100	190
Total current liabilities	$ 200	$ 315
Long-term debt	100	190
Common stock	500	500
Retained earnings	200	245
Total liabilities and equity	$1,000	$1,250

TABLE IC17-1 *continued*

B. INCOME STATEMENT

	2005	2006E
Sales	$2,000.00	$2,500.00
Less: Variable costs	1,200.00	1,500.00
Fixed costs	700.00	875.00
Earnings before interest and taxes (EBIT)	$ 100.00	$ 125.00
Interest	16.00	16.00
Earnings before taxes (EBT)	$ 84.00	$ 109.00
Taxes (40%)	33.60	43.60
Net income	$ 50.40	$ 65.40
Dividends (30%)	$ 15.12	$ 19.62
Addition to retained earnings	$ 35.28	$ 45.78

C. KEY RATIOS

	NWC(2005)	NWC(2006E)	Industry	Comment
Basic earning power	10.00%	10.00%	20.00%	
Profit margin	2.52	2.62	4.00	
Return on equity	7.20	8.77	15.60	
Days sales outstanding (365 days)	43.80 days	43.80 days	32.00 days	
Inventory turnover	8.33×	8.33×	11.00×	
Fixed assets turnover	4.00	4.00	5.00	
Total assets turnover	2.00	2.00	2.50	
Debt/assets	30.00%	40.34%	36.00%	
Times interest earned	6.25×	7.81×	9.40×	
Current ratio	2.50	1.99	3.00	
Payout ratio	30.00%	30.00%	30.00%	

Assume that you were recently hired as Wilson's assistant, and your first major task is to help her develop the formal financial forecast. She asked you to begin by answering the following set of questions.

a. Assume (1) that NWC was operating at full capacity in 2005 with respect to all assets, (2) that all assets must grow at the same rate as sales, (3) that accounts payable and accrued liabilities will also grow at the same rate as sales, and (4) that the 2005 profit margin and dividend payout will be maintained. Under these conditions, what would the AFN equation predict the company's financial requirements to be for the coming year?

b. Consultations with several key managers within NWC, including production, inventory, and receivable managers, have yielded some very useful information.

   (1) NWC's high DSO is largely due to one significant customer who battled through some hardships over the past 2 years but who appears to be financially healthy again and is generating strong cash flow. As a result, NWC's accounts receivable manager expects the firm to lower receivables enough to make the DSO equal to 34 days, without adversely affecting sales.

   (2) NWC was operating a little below capacity, but its forecasted growth will require a new facility, which is expected to increase NWC's net fixed assets to $700 million.

   (3) A relatively new inventory management system (installed last year) has taken some time to catch on and operate efficiently. NWC's inventory turnover improved slightly last year, but this year NWC expects even more improvement as inventories decrease and inventory turnover is expected to rise to 10×.

Incorporate this information into the 2006 initial forecast results, as these adjustments to the initial forecast represent the final forecast for 2006.

c. Calculate NWC's forecasted ratios based on its final forecast, and compare them with the company's 2005 historical ratios, the 2006 initial forecast ratios, and with the industry averages. How does NWC compare with the average firm in its industry, and is the company's financial position expected to improve during the coming year?

d. Based on the final forecast, calculate NWC's free cash flow for 2006. How does this FCF differ from the FCF forecasted by NWC's initial, "business as usual" forecast?

e. Initially, some NWC managers questioned whether the new facility expansion was necessary, especially since it results in increasing net fixed assets from $500 million to $700 million (a 40 percent increase). However, after extensive discussions about NWC needing to position itself for future growth and being flexible and competitive in today's marketplace, NWC's top managers agreed the expansion was necessary. Among the issues raised by opponents was that NWC's fixed assets were being operated at only 85 percent of capacity. Assuming that its fixed assets were operating at only 85 percent of capacity, by how much could sales have increased, both in dollar terms and in percentage terms, before NWC reached full capacity?

f. How would changes in these items affect the AFN? (1) The dividend payout ratio, (2) the profit margin, (3) the capital intensity ratio, and (4) if NWC begins buying from its suppliers on terms that permit it to pay after 60 days rather than after 30 days. (Consider each item separately and hold all other things constant.)

cyberproblem

Please go to the ThomsonNOW Web site to access the Cyberproblems.

THOMSON ONE | Business School Edition

Access the Thomson ONE problems through the ThomsonNOW Web site. Use the Thomson ONE—Business School Edition online database to work this chapter's questions.

Forecasting the Future Performance of Abercrombie & Fitch

Clothing retailer Abercrombie & Fitch enjoyed phenomenal success in the late 1990s. Between 1996 and 2000, its sales grew almost fourfold, from $335 million to more than $1.2 billion, and its stock price soared by more than 500 percent. More recently, however, the growth rate has begun to slow down, and Abercrombie has had a hard time meeting its quarterly earnings targets. As a result, the stock price in late 2002 was about half of what it was 3 years earlier. Abercrombie's struggles resulted from increased competition, a sluggish economy, and the challenges of staying ahead of the fashion curve. Since 2002, the company's stock has rebounded strongly but questions always remain about the firm's long-term growth prospects.

Given the questions about Abercrombie's future growth rate, analysts have focused on the company's earnings reports. Thomson One provides a convenient and detailed summary of the company's recent earnings history, along with a summary of analysts' earnings forecasts.

To access this information, we begin by entering the company's ticker symbol, ANF, on Thomson One's main screen and then selecting "GO." This takes us to an overview of the company's recent performance. After checking out the overview, you should click on the tab labeled "Estimates," near the top of your screen. Here you will find a wide range of information about the company's past and projected earnings.

Discussion Questions

1. What are the mean and median forecasts for Abercrombie's earnings per share over the next fiscal year?
2. Based on analysts' forecasts, what is the expected long-term growth rate in earnings?
3. Have analysts made any significant changes to their forecasted earnings for Abercrombie & Fitch in the past few months?
4. Historically, have Abercrombie's reported earnings generally met, exceeded, or fallen short of analysts' forecasted earnings?
5. How has Abercrombie's stock performed this year relative to the S&P 500?

SPECIAL TOPICS IN FINANCIAL MANAGEMENT

PART 7

© JOHN ZICH/BLOOMBERG NEWS/LANDOV

CHAPTER

18

DERIVATIVES AND RISK MANAGEMENT

Using Derivatives to Manage Risk

Consumer-products giant Procter & Gamble (P&G) has more than 5 billion customers in 160 countries. Its products include such well-known brands as Crest, Tide, Pampers, Folgers, and Charmin. Its products are consumed regularly, and its sales and earnings are fairly immune to changes in the economic cycle, making it a relatively low-risk company. Indeed, *Value Line* estimates that P&G's beta is 0.55, which suggests that its risk is 45 percent below that of an average stock.

Low risk does not mean no risk, and P&G's managers devote considerable time and effort to managing the risks it does face. For example, in a recent annual report management described in detail how the company deals with risks resulting from changes in interest rates, exchange rates, and commodity prices. In each instance, P&G first examines its net exposure to the risk factor, and then it uses derivatives such as options, futures, and swaps to hedge and thus reduce those risks. Here is its statement:

> Derivative positions are monitored using techniques including market value, sensitivity analysis, and value-at-risk modeling. The tests for interest rate and currency rate exposures are based on a Monte Carlo simulation value-at-risk model using a one-year horizon and a 95 percent confidence level. The model incorporates the impact of correlation (exposures that tend to move in tandem over time) and diversification from holding multiple currency and interest rate instruments and assumes that financial returns are normally distributed.

It is clear from its annual report that P&G spends a lot of time and energy managing its various risks. However, nothing is completely riskless, and in some instances the steps taken to control risk have actually backfired. Indeed, P&G incurred huge losses in the 1990s on derivative transactions that were supposedly undertaken to reduce risk.

This chapter first discusses the various types of risks that companies face. Then it provides an overview of options, futures, and swaps and describes how companies use these instruments to help minimize their risks.

Source: Procter & Gamble's 2004 Annual Report, p. 42.

Putting Things In Perspective

In this chapter, we discuss risk management, a topic of increasing importance to financial managers. The term *risk management* can mean many things, but in business it involves identifying events that could have adverse financial consequences and then taking actions to prevent and/or minimize the damage caused by these events. Years ago, corporate risk managers dealt primarily with insurance—they made sure the firm was adequately insured against fire, theft, and other casualties and that it had adequate liability coverage. More recently, the scope of risk management has been broadened to include such things as controlling the costs of key inputs like petroleum by purchasing oil futures or protecting against changes in interest rates or exchange rates through dealings in the interest rate or foreign exchange markets. In addition, risk managers try to ensure that actions designed to hedge against risk are not actually increasing risk.

18-1 REASONS TO MANAGE RISK

We know that investors dislike risk. We also know that most investors hold well-diversified portfolios, so at least in theory the only "relevant risk" is systematic risk. Therefore, if you asked corporate executives what type of risk they were concerned about, you might expect the answer to be, "beta." However, this is almost certainly not the answer you would get. The most likely answer, if you asked a CEO to define risk, is something like this: "Risk is the possibility that our future earnings and free cash flows will be significantly lower than we expect." For example, consider Plastics Inc., which manufactures dashboards, interior door panels, and other plastic components used by auto companies. Petroleum is the key feedstock for plastic and thus makes up a large percentage of its costs. Plastics has a three-year contract with an auto company to deliver 500,000 door panels each year, at a price of $60 each. When the company signed this contract, oil sold for $59 per barrel, and oil was expected to stay at that level for the next three years. If oil prices fall, Plastics will have higher than expected profits and free cash flows, but if oil prices rise, profits will fall. Plastics' value depends on its profits and free cash flows, so a change in the price of oil will cause stockholders to earn either more or less than they anticipated.

Now suppose Plastics announces that it plans to lock in a three-year supply of oil at a guaranteed price of $59 per barrel, and the cost of the guarantee is zero. Would that cause its stock price to rise? At first glance, it seems that the answer should be yes, but maybe that's not correct. Recall that the long-run value of a stock depends on the present value of its expected future free cash flows, discounted at the weighted average cost of capital (WACC). Locking in the cost of oil will cause an increase in Plastics' stock price if and only if (1) it causes the expected future free cash flows to increase or (2) it causes the WACC to decline.

Consider first the free cash flows. Before the announcement of guaranteed oil costs, investors had formed an estimate of the expected future free cash flows, based on an expected oil price of $59 per barrel. Therefore, while locking in the cost of oil at $59 per barrel will lower the riskiness of the expected future free cash flows, it will not change the *size* of these cash flows because investors already expected a price of $59 per barrel.

Now what about the WACC? It will change only if locking in the cost of oil causes a change in the cost of debt or equity or the target capital structure. Assuming the foreseeable increases in the price of oil were not enough to cause bankruptcy, Plastics' cost of debt should not change, and neither should its target capital structure. Regarding the cost of equity, recall from Chapter 8 that most investors hold well-diversified portfolios, which means that the cost of equity should depend only on systematic risk. Moreover, even though an increase in oil prices would have a negative effect on Plastics' stock price, it would not have a negative effect on all stocks. Indeed, oil producers should have higher than expected returns and stock prices. Assuming that Plastics' investors hold well-diversified portfolios, including stocks of oil-producing companies, there would not appear to be much reason to expect its cost of equity to decrease. The bottom line is this: If Plastics' expected future cash flows and WACC will not change significantly due to an elimination of the risk of oil price increases, then neither should the value of its stock.

We discuss futures contracts and hedging in detail in the next section, but for now let's assume that Plastics has *not* locked in oil prices. Therefore, if oil prices increase, its stock price will fall. However, its stockholders know this, so they can build portfolios that contain oil futures whose values will rise or fall with oil prices and thus offset changes in the price of Plastics' stock. By choosing the correct amount of futures contracts, investors can thus "hedge" their portfolios and completely eliminate the risk due to changes in oil prices. There will be a cost to hedging, but that cost to large, sophisticated investors should be about the same as the cost to Plastics. If stockholders can hedge away oil price risk themselves, why should they pay a higher price for Plastics' stock just because the company itself hedged away the risk?

This discussion suggests that unless something else is going on, it doesn't make sense for firms to hedge risk. At the same time, a 1995 survey reported that 59 percent of firms with market values greater than $250 million engage in risk management, and that percentage is surely much higher today.[1] One explanation is that corporate managers frequently hedge risk even though it does little to increase corporate value. The other (perhaps more likely) explanation is that hedging creates other benefits that ultimately lead to either higher cash flows and/or a lower WACC. Here are some of the reasons that have been suggested for why it might make sense for companies to manage risks:

1. *Debt capacity.* Risk management can reduce the volatility of cash flows, and this decreases the probability of bankruptcy. As we discussed in Chapter 14,

---

[1] See Gordon M. Bodnar, Gregory S. Hayt, and Richard C. Marston, "1995 Wharton Survey of Derivative Usage by U.S. Non-Financial Firms," *Financial Management*, Winter 1996, pp. 113–133.

firms with lower operating risks can use more debt, and this can lead to higher stock prices due to the interest tax savings.

2. *Maintaining the optimal capital budget over time.* Recall from Chapters 10, 13, and 14 that firms are reluctant to raise external equity due to high flotation costs and market pressure. This means that the capital budget must generally be financed with debt plus internally generated funds, mainly retained earnings and depreciation. In years when internal cash flows are low, they may be too small to support the optimal capital budget, causing firms to either slow investment below the optimal rate or else incur the high costs associated with external equity. By smoothing out the cash flows, risk management can alleviate this problem.

3. *Financial distress.* Financial distress—which can range from worrying stockholders to higher interest rates on debt to customer defections to bankruptcy—is associated with having cash flows fall below expected levels. Risk management can reduce the likelihood of low cash flows, hence of financial distress.

4. *Comparative advantages in hedging.* Many investors cannot implement a home-made hedging program as efficiently as can a company. First, firms generally have lower transactions costs due to a larger volume of hedging activities. Second, there is the problem of asymmetric information—managers know more about the firm's risk exposure than outside investors, hence managers can create more effective hedges. And third, effective risk management requires specialized skills and knowledge that firms are more likely to have.

5. *Borrowing costs.* As discussed later in the chapter, firms can sometimes reduce input costs, especially the interest rate on debt, through the use of derivative instruments called "swaps." Any such cost reduction adds value to the firm.

6. *Tax effects.* Companies with volatile earnings pay more taxes than more stable companies due to the treatment of tax credits and the rules governing corporate loss carry-forwards and carry-backs. Moreover, if volatile earnings lead to bankruptcy, then tax loss carry-forwards are generally lost. Therefore, our tax system encourages risk management to stabilize earnings.[2]

7. *Compensation systems.* Many compensation systems establish "floors" and "ceilings" on bonuses or else reward managers for meeting targets. To illustrate, suppose a firm's compensation system calls for a manager to receive no bonus if net income is below $1 million, a bonus of $10,000 if income is between $1 million and $2 million, and one of $20,000 if income is $2 million or more. Moreover, the manager will receive an additional $10,000 if actual income is at least 90 percent of the forecasted level, which is $1 million. Now consider the following two situations. First, if income is stable at $2 million each year, the manager receives a $30,000 bonus each year, for a two-year total of $60,000. However, if income is zero the first year and $4 million the second, the manager receives no bonus the first year and $30,000 the second, for a two-year total of $30,000. So, even though the company has the same total income ($4 million) over the two years, the manager's bonus is higher if earnings are stable. So, even if hedging does not add much value for stockholders, it may still be beneficial to managers.

Perhaps the most important aspect of risk management involves derivative securities. The next section explains **derivatives**, which are securities whose values are determined by the market price of some other asset. Derivatives include *options*, whose values depend on the price of some underlying asset; *interest rate*

Derivatives
Securities whose values are determined by the market price or interest rate of some other asset.

---

[2] See Clifford W. Smith and René Stulz, "The Determinants of Firms' Hedging Policies," *The Journal of Financial and Quantitative Analysis*, December 1985, pp. 395–406.

and exchange rate futures and swaps, whose values depend on interest rate and exchange rate levels; and *commodity futures*, whose values depend on commodity prices.

Explain why finance theory, combined with well-diversified investors and "homemade hedging," might suggest that risk management should not add much value to a company.

List and explain some reasons companies might actually employ risk management techniques.

18-2 BACKGROUND ON DERIVATIVES

The Chicago Board of Trade has an excellent Web site at **http://www .cbot.com**. Make sure to check out the wealth of information on the history and operations of the exchange by clicking on "About CBOT."

A historical perspective is useful when studying derivatives. One of the first formal markets for derivatives was the futures market for wheat. Farmers were concerned about the price they would receive for their wheat when they sold it in the fall, and millers were concerned about the price they would have to pay. The risks faced by both parties could be reduced if they could establish a price earlier in the year. Accordingly, mill agents would go out to the wheat belt and make contracts with farmers that called for the farmers to deliver grain at a predetermined price. Both parties benefited from the transaction in the sense that their risks were reduced. The farmers could concentrate on growing their crop without worrying about the price of grain, and the millers could concentrate on their milling operations. Thus, *hedging with futures* lowered aggregate risk in the economy.

These early futures dealings were between two parties who arranged transactions between themselves. Soon, though, middlemen came into the picture, and trading in futures was established. The Chicago Board of Trade was an early marketplace for this dealing, and *futures dealers* helped make a market in futures contracts. Thus, farmers could sell futures on the exchange, and millers could buy them there. This improved the efficiency and lowered the cost of hedging operations.

Quickly, a third group—*speculators*—entered the scene. As we will see in the next section, most derivatives, including futures, are highly leveraged, meaning that a small change in the value of the underlying asset will produce a large change in the price of the derivative. This leverage appealed to speculators. At first blush, one might think that the appearance of speculators would increase risk, but this is not true. Speculators add capital and players to the market, and this tends to stabilize the market. Of course, derivatives markets are inherently volatile due to the leverage involved, hence risk to the speculators themselves is high. Still, their bearing that risk makes the derivatives markets more stable for the hedgers.

Natural Hedges
Situations in which aggregate risk can be reduced by derivatives transactions between two parties known as counterparties.

Natural hedges, defined as situations in which aggregate risk can be reduced by derivatives transactions between two parties (called *counterparties*), exist for many commodities, foreign currencies, interest rates on securities with different maturities, and even common stocks where portfolio managers want to "hedge their bets." Natural hedges occur when futures are traded between cotton farmers and cotton mills, copper mines and copper fabricators, importers and foreign manufacturers for currency exchange rates, electric utilities and coal miners, and oil producers and oil users. In all such situations, hedging reduces aggregate risk and thus benefits the economy.

Hedging can also be done in situations where no natural hedge exists. Here one party wants to reduce some type of risk, and another party agrees to sell a

GLOBAL PERSPECTIVES

Barings and Sumitomo Suffer Large Losses in the Derivatives Market

Barings, a conservative English bank with a long, impressive history dating back to its financing of the Louisiana Purchase in the 19th century, collapsed in 1995 when one of its traders lost $1.4 billion in derivatives trades. Nicholas Leeson, a 28-year-old trader in Barings' Singapore office, had speculated in Japanese stock index and interest rate futures without his superiors' knowledge. A lack of internal controls at the bank allowed him to accumulate large losses without being detected. Leeson's losses caught many by surprise, and they provided ammunition to those who argue that trading in derivatives should be more highly regulated if not sharply curtailed.

Most argue that the blame goes beyond Leeson—that both the bank and the exchanges were at fault for failing to provide sufficient oversight. For misreporting his trades, Leeson was sentenced to a 6½-year term in a Singapore prison. What remained of Barings was ultimately sold to a Dutch banking concern.

Many analysts, including those who argued that the Barings episode was just an unsettling but isolated incident, were startled by a similar case a year and a half after the Barings debacle. In June 1996, Japan's Sumitomo Corporation disclosed that its well-respected chief copper trader, Yasuo Hamanaka, had been conducting unauthorized speculative trades for more than a decade. The cumulative loss on these trades was $2.6 billion.

These two events illustrate both the dangers of derivatives and the importance of internal controls. While it is unsettling to learn that the actions of a single, relatively low-level employee can suddenly cripple a giant corporation, these losses should be placed in perspective. The overwhelming majority of firms that use derivatives have been successful in enhancing performance and/or reducing risk. For this reason, most analysts argue that it would be a huge mistake to use the rare instances where fraud occurred to limit a market that has, for the most part, been a resounding success. However, given the volume of business in this market, we can in the future expect to see other problems similar to those encountered by Barings and Sumitomo.

---

contract that protects the first party from that specific event or situation. Insurance is an obvious example of this type of hedge. Note, though, that with nonsymmetric hedges, risks are generally *transferred* rather than *eliminated*. Even here, though, insurance companies can reduce certain types of risk through diversification.

The derivatives markets have grown more rapidly than any other major market in recent years, for a number of reasons. First, analytical techniques such as the Black-Scholes Option Pricing Model, which is discussed in Section 18.5, have been developed to help establish "fair" prices, and having a better basis for pricing hedges makes the counterparties more comfortable with deals. Second, computers and electronic communications make it much easier for counterparties to deal with one another. Third, globalization has greatly increased the importance of currency markets and the need for reducing the exchange rate risks brought on by global trade. Recent trends and developments are sure to continue if not accelerate, so the use of derivatives for risk management is bound to grow.

Note, though, that derivatives do have a potential downside. These instruments are highly leveraged, so small miscalculations can lead to huge losses. Also, they are complicated, hence not well understood by most people. This makes mistakes more likely than with less complex instruments, and it makes it harder for a firm's top management to exercise proper control over derivatives transactions. One 28-year-old, relatively low-level employee, operating in the Far East, entered into transactions that led to the bankruptcy of Britain's oldest bank (Barings Bank), the institution that held the accounts of the Queen of England. (See the Global Perspectives box entitled "Barings and Sumitomo Suffer Large

Losses in the Derivatives Market.") Just prior to the problems at Barings, Orange County, California, went bankrupt due to its treasurer's speculation in derivatives, and Procter & Gamble got into a nasty fight with Bankers Trust over derivative-related losses. A few years later in 1998, the high-profile hedge fund, Long Term Capital Management LP, nearly collapsed because of bad bets made in the derivatives market. More recently, it has been argued that extensive derivative positions enabled Enron to hide some of its losses and to hide debt that had been incurred on some of its unprofitable businesses.

The P&G, Orange County, Barings Bank, Long Term Capital Management, and Enron affairs make the headlines, causing some people to argue that derivatives should be regulated out of existence to "protect the public." However, derivatives are used far more often to hedge risks than in harmful speculations, but these beneficial transactions never make the headlines. So, while the horror stories point out the need for top managers to exercise control over the personnel who deal with derivatives, they certainly do not justify the elimination of derivatives. In the balance of this chapter, we discuss how firms can manage risks, and how derivatives are used in risk management.

What is a "natural hedge"? Give some examples of natural hedges.

How does a nonsymmetric hedge differ from a natural hedge? Name an example of a nonsymmetric hedge.

List three reasons the derivatives markets have grown more rapidly than any other major market in recent years.

18-3 OPTIONS

Option
A contract that gives its holder the right to buy (or sell) an asset at a predetermined price within a specified period of time.

An **option** is a contract that gives its holder the right to buy (or sell) an asset at some predetermined price within a specified period of time. Financial managers should understand option theory both for risk management and also because such an understanding will help them structure warrant and convertible financings, discussed in Chapter 20.

18-3a Option Types and Markets

Strike (Exercise) Price
The price that must be paid for a share of common stock when an option is exercised.

Call Option
An option to buy, or "call," a share of stock at a certain price within a specified period.

There are many types of options and option markets.[3] To illustrate how options work, suppose you owned 100 shares of IBM, which on Wednesday, August 24, 2005, sold for $81.84 per share. You could sell to someone the right to buy your 100 shares at any time during the next five months at a price of, say, $85 per share. The $85 is called the **strike**, or **exercise, price**. Such options exist, and they are traded on a number of exchanges, with the Chicago Board Options Exchange (CBOE) being the oldest and the largest. This type of option is defined as a **call option**, because the purchaser has a "call" on 100 shares of stock. The seller of an option is called the option *writer*. An investor who "writes" call options against stock held in his or her portfolio is said to be selling *covered options*. Options sold without the stock to back them up are called *naked options*. When the exercise price exceeds the current stock price, a call option is said to be *out-of-the-money*. When the exercise price is below the current price of the stock, the option is *in-the-money*.

---

[3] For an in-depth treatment of options, see Don M. Chance, *An Introduction to Derivatives and Risk Management* (Mason, OH: Thomson/South-Western, 2004).

Table 18-1 is a listing of selected options quotations (calls and puts) for IBM obtained from the *MSN Money Web site* on August 24, 2005. As we see in the first column, IBM's closing stock price was $81.84. This implies that the first two call options listed were selling in-the-money, while the third option with an $85 strike price was trading out-of-the-money. Taking a closer look, we see that IBM's September $85 call option sold at the end of the day for $0.30. Thus, for $0.30(100) = $30 you could buy options that would give you the right to purchase 100 shares of IBM stock at a price of $85 per share until September 17, 2005.[4] If the stock price stayed below $85 during that period, you would lose your $30, but if it rose to $95, your $30 investment would increase in value to ($95 − $85)(100) = $1,000 in less than 30 days. That translates into a very healthy annualized return. Incidentally, if the stock price did go up, you would not actually exercise your options and buy the stock—rather, you would sell the options, which would then have a value of $1,000 versus the $30 you paid, to another option buyer or back to the original seller.

You can also buy an option that gives you the right to *sell* a stock at a specified price within some future period—this is called a **put option.** For example, suppose you think IBM's stock price is likely to decline from its current level of $81.84 sometime during the next five months. Table 18-1 provides data on IBM's put options. You could buy a five-month put option (the January put option) for $110.00 ($1.10 × 100) that would give you the right to sell 100 shares (that you would not necessarily own) at a price of $75 per share ($75 is the strike price). Suppose you bought this 100-share contract for $110.00 and then IBM's stock fell to $70. You could buy a share of stock for $70 and exercise your put option by selling the stock for $75. Your profit from exercising the option would be ($75 − $70)(100) = $500. After subtracting the $110.00 you paid for the option, your profit (before taxes and commissions) would be $390.00.

In addition to options on individual stocks, options are also available on several stock indexes such as the NYSE Index, Dow Jones Industrials, the S&P 100, and the S&P 500—just to name a few. Index options permit one to hedge (or bet) on a rise or fall in the general market as well as on individual stocks.

Option trading is one of the hottest financial activities in the United States. The leverage involved makes it possible for speculators with just a few dollars to make a fortune almost overnight. Also, investors with sizable portfolios can sell options against their stocks and earn the value of the option (less brokerage commissions), even if the stock's price remains constant. Most importantly,

*You can obtain information for a specific company's call and put options at **http://moneycentral.msn.com/investor/options**. Just type the firm's ticker symbol and select go. Shaded options are "in-the-money."*

Put Option
An option to sell a share of stock at a certain price within a specified period.

TABLE 18-1   *Selected IBM Options Quotations, August 24, 2005*

Closing Price	Strike Price	CALLS—LAST QUOTE			PUTS—LAST QUOTE		
		Sept.	Oct.	Jan.	Sept.	Oct.	Jan.
81.84	75	7.30	8.20	9.00	0.10	0.40	1.10
81.84	80	2.70	4.00	5.50	0.50	1.30	2.40
81.84	85	0.30	1.15	2.75	3.40	3.80	4.80

Note: Table created from data for August 24, 2005, from *MSN Money Web site,* **http://moneycentral.msn.com/investor/options**.

---

[4] Actually, the *expiration date,* which is the last date that the option can be exercised, is the Friday before the third Saturday of the exercise month. Also, note that option contracts are generally written in 100-share multiples.

though, options can be used to create *hedges* that protect the value of an individual stock or portfolio. We will discuss hedging strategies in more detail later in the chapter.[5]

Conventional options are generally written for six months or less, but another type of option called a **Long-term Equity AnticiPation Security (LEAPS)** is also traded. Like conventional options, LEAPS are listed on exchanges and are tied both to individual stocks and to stock indexes. The major difference is that LEAPS are long-term options, having maturities of up to 2½ years. One-year LEAPS cost about twice as much as the matching three-month option, but because of their much longer time to expiration, LEAPS provide buyers with more potential for gains and offer better long-term protection for a portfolio.

Corporations on whose stocks options are written have nothing to do with the option market. Corporations do not raise money in the option market, nor do they have any direct transactions in it. Moreover, option holders do not vote for corporate directors or receive dividends. There have been studies by the SEC and others as to whether option trading stabilizes or destabilizes the stock market, and whether this activity helps or hinders corporations seeking to raise new capital. The studies have not been conclusive, but option trading is here to stay, and many regard it as the most exciting game in town.

Long-term Equity AnticiPation Security (LEAPS)
A long-term option that is listed on the exchanges and tied to both individual stocks and to stock indexes.

18-3b Factors That Affect the Value of a Call Option

A study of Table 18-1 provides some insights into call option valuation. First, we see that there are at least three factors that affect a call option's value: (1) The higher the stock's market price in relation to the strike price, the higher will be the call option price. Thus, IBM's $85 September call option sells for $0.30, whereas IBM's $75 September option sells for $7.30. This difference arises because IBM's current stock price is $81.84. (2) The higher the strike price, the lower the call option price. Thus, all of IBM's call options shown, regardless of exercise month, decline as the strike price increases. (3) The longer the option period, the higher the option price. This occurs because the longer the time before expiration, the greater the chance that the stock price will climb substantially above the exercise price. Thus, option prices increase as the expiration date is lengthened. As shown in Table 18-1, the January 2006 options are all higher in price than either the September or October options. Other factors that affect option values, especially the volatility of the underlying stock, are discussed in later sections.

18-3c Exercise Value versus Option Price

How is the actual price of a call option determined in the market? In Section 18.5, we present a widely used model (the Black-Scholes model) for pricing call options, but first it is useful to establish some basic concepts. To begin, we define a call option's exercise value as follows:

$$\text{Exercise value} = \text{Current price of the stock} - \text{Strike price} \quad \textbf{(18-1)}$$

[5] It should be noted that insiders who trade illegally generally buy options rather than stock because the leverage inherent in options increases the profit potential. Note, though, that it is illegal to use insider information for personal gain, and an insider using such information would be taking advantage of the option seller. Insider trading, in addition to being unfair and essentially equivalent to stealing, hurts the economy: Investors lose confidence in the capital markets and raise their required returns because of an increased element of risk, and this raises the cost of capital and thus reduces the level of real investment.

The exercise value is what the option would be worth if you had to exercise it immediately. For example, if a stock sells for $50 and its option has a strike price of $20, then you could buy the stock for $20 by exercising the option. You would own a stock worth $50, but you would have to pay only $20. Therefore, the option would be worth $30 if you had to exercise it immediately. Note that the calculated exercise value of a call option could be negative, but realistically the minimum "true" value of an option is zero, because no one would exercise an out-of-the-money option. Note also that an option's exercise value is only a first approximation value—it merely provides a starting point for finding the actual value of the option.

Now consider Figure 18-1, which presents some data on Space Technology Inc. (STI), a company that recently went public and whose stock price has fluctuated widely during its short history. The third column in the tabular data shows the exercise values for STI's call option when the stock was selling at different prices; the fourth column gives the actual market prices for the option; and the

FIGURE 18-1 *Space Technology Inc.: Option Price and Exercise Value*

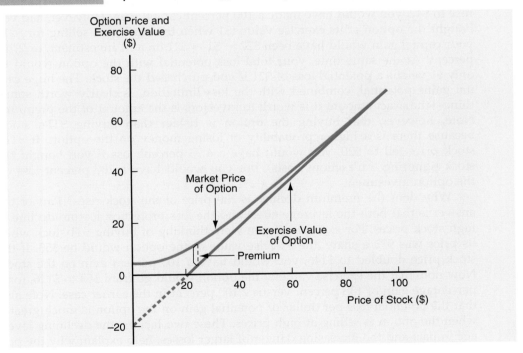

Price of Stock (1)	Strike Price (2)	Exercise Value of Option (1) − (2) = (3)	Market Price of Option (4)	Premium (4) − (3) = (5)
$20.00	$20.00	$ 0.00	$ 9.00	$9.00
21.00	20.00	1.00	9.75	8.75
22.00	20.00	2.00	10.50	8.50
35.00	20.00	15.00	21.00	6.00
42.00	20.00	22.00	26.00	4.00
50.00	20.00	30.00	32.00	2.00
73.00	20.00	53.00	54.00	1.00
98.00	20.00	78.00	78.50	0.50

fifth column shows the premium of the actual option price over its exercise value. At any stock price below $20, the exercise value is set at zero, but above $20, each $1 increase in the price of the stock brings with it a $1 increase in the option's exercise value. Note, however, that the actual market price of the call option lies above the exercise value at each price of the common stock, although the premium declines as the price of the stock increases above the strike price. For example, when the stock sold for $20 and the option had a zero exercise value, its actual price, and the premium, was $9. Then, as the price of the stock rose, the *exercise value's increase* matched the stock's increase dollar for dollar, but the *market price* of the option climbed less rapidly, causing the premium to decline. The premium was $9 when the stock sold for $20 a share, but it had declined to $1 by the time the stock price had risen to $73 a share. Beyond that point, the premium virtually disappeared.

Why does this pattern exist? Why should a call option ever sell for more than its exercise value, and why does the premium decline as the price of the stock increases? The answer lies in part in the speculative appeal of options—they enable someone to gain a high degree of personal leverage when buying securities. To illustrate, suppose STI's option sold for exactly its exercise value. Now suppose you were thinking of investing in the company's common stock at a time when it was selling for $21 a share. If you bought a share and the price rose to $42, you would have made a 100 percent capital gain. However, had you bought the option at its exercise value ($1 when the stock was selling for $21), your capital gain would have been $22 − $1 = $21 on a $1 investment, or 2,100 percent! At the same time, your total loss potential with the option would be only $1 versus a potential loss of $21 if you purchased the stock. The huge capital gains potential, combined with the loss limitation, is clearly worth something—the exact amount it is worth to investors is the amount of the premium. Note, however, that buying the option is riskier than buying STI's stock, because there is a higher probability of losing money on the option. If STI's stock price fell to $20, you would have a 4.76 percent loss if you bought the stock (ignoring transactions costs), but you would have a 100 percent loss on the option investment.

Why does the premium decline as the price of the stock rises? Part of the answer is that both the leverage effect and the loss protection feature decline at high stock prices. For example, if you were thinking of buying STI stock when its price was $73 a share, the exercise value of the option would be $53. If the stock price doubled to $146, you would have a 100 percent gain on the stock. Now note that the exercise value of the option would go from $53 to $126, for a percentage gain of 138 percent versus 2,100 percent in the earlier case. Note also that the potential loss per dollar of potential gain on the option is much greater when the option is selling at high prices. These two factors, the declining leverage impact and the increasing danger of larger losses, help explain why the premium diminishes as the price of the common stock rises.

In addition to the stock price and the exercise price, the price of an option depends on three other factors: (1) the option's term to maturity, (2) the variability of the stock price, and (3) the risk-free rate. We will explain precisely how these factors affect call option prices later, but for now, note these points:

1. The longer a call option has to run, the greater its value and the larger its premium. If an option expires at 4 p.m. today, there is not much chance that the stock price will go up very much, so the option must sell at close to its exercise value, and its premium must be small. On the other hand, if the expiration date is a year away, the stock price could rise sharply, pulling the option's value up with it.

2. An option on an extremely volatile stock is worth more than one on a very stable stock. If the stock price rarely moves, then there is only a small chance of a large gain. However, if the stock price is highly volatile, the option could easily become very valuable. At the same time, losses on options are limited—you can make an unlimited amount, but you can only lose what you paid for the option. Therefore, a large decline in a stock's price does not have a corresponding bad effect on option holders. As a result of the unlimited upside but limited downside, the more volatile a stock, the higher the value of its options.

3. The effect of the risk-free rate on a call option isn't as obvious. The expected growth rate of a firm's stock price increases as interest rates increase, but the present value of future cash flows decreases. The first effect tends to increase the call option's price, while the second tends to decrease it. As it turns out, the first effect dominates the second one, so the price of a call option always increases as the risk-free rate increases. We illustrate this fact later in Table 18-2 in Section 18.5.

Because of Points 1 and 2, in a graph such as Figure 18-1 the longer an option's life, the higher its market price line would be above the exercise value line. Similarly, the more volatile the price of the underlying stock, the higher is the market price line. We will see precisely how these factors, and also the discount rate, affect option values when we discuss the Black-Scholes option pricing model.

What is an option? A call option? A put option?

Define a call option's exercise value. Why is the actual market price of a call option usually above its exercise value?

What are some factors that affect a call option's value?

Underwater Technology stock is currently trading at $30 a share. A call option on the stock with a $25 strike price currently sells for $12. What are the exercise value and the premium of the call option? ($5.00; $7.00)

18-4 INTRODUCTION TO OPTION PRICING MODELS[6]

In the next section, we discuss a widely used but complex option pricing model, the Black-Scholes model. First, though, we go through a simple example to illustrate basic principles. To begin, note that all option pricing models are based on the concept of a **riskless hedge.** Here an investor buys a stock and simultaneously sells a call option on that stock. If the stock's price goes up, the investor will earn a profit on the stock, but the holder of the option will exercise it, and that will cost the investor money. Conversely, if the stock goes down, the investor will lose on his or her investment in the stock, but gain from the option (which will expire worthless if the stock price declines). As we demonstrate, it is possible to set things up such that the investor will end up with a riskless position—regardless of what the stock does, the value of the investor's portfolio will remain constant. Thus, a riskless investment will have been created.

Riskless Hedge
A hedge in which an investor buys a stock and simultaneously sells a call option on that stock and ends up with a riskless position.

---

[6] This section and the following one on the Black-Scholes model are relatively technical, and they can be omitted without loss of continuity.

Expensing Executive Stock Options

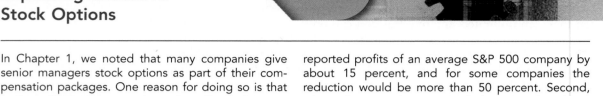

In Chapter 1, we noted that many companies give senior managers stock options as part of their compensation packages. One reason for doing so is that options give managers a strong incentive to increase their companies' stock prices. Another benefit is that options are a substitute for salaries, which reduces cash requirements. Reducing the need for cash payments is particularly important for young, startup companies where cash for salaries is generally in short supply. However, options are not free to the issuing company—they have a very real cost because they lead to an increase in the number of shares outstanding, which in turn reduces the company's earnings per share.

In the past, there was another important reason companies liked to issue stock options. Cash paid as salaries must be reported as salary expense on the income statement, thus lowering reported profits. By contrast, until recently, stock options, even though they may have a true value in the millions of dollars, did not have to be reported on the income statement, and thus did not reduce reported profits.[a] While some companies such as Microsoft, Cisco, Citigroup, and GE took steps to voluntarily expense their executive stock options, many other companies resisted.

Companies had been reluctant to expense options for two reasons. First, managers generally dislike any action that reduces reported profits because their own salaries, bonuses, and future options are generally based on reported profits. Recent studies indicate that expensing options would reduce the reported profits of an average S&P 500 company by about 15 percent, and for some companies the reduction would be more than 50 percent. Second, companies weren't sure exactly how to value them. The Black-Scholes model is used most frequently, but it has limitations. In particular, some executive stock options are worth less than the valuations implied by Black-Scholes because grantees must wait several years before they can exercise their options.

Despite their reluctance, accountants and corporate managers faced intense pressure from investors who argued that it is better to be approximately correct than exactly wrong (that is, expense options using Black-Scholes for an approximate valuation rather than not expensing them and getting an obviously incorrect result). Responding to this pressure, the Financial Accounting Standards Board (FASB) recently put in place new guidelines that require public companies to deduct as an expense the value of their stock options granted each year. Some critics have complained that the new guidelines still give companies too much discretion in deciding how to value these options, but many contend that this is at least a step in the right direction.

[a] Although options were not reported as an expense on firms' income statements, they had to be reported in the notes to the financial statements.

Sources: Elizabeth MacDonald, "A Volatile Brew: Easing the Impact of Strict New Stock Option Rules," *Forbes*, August 15, 2005, pp. 70–71; and Anthony Bianco, "The Angry Market," *BusinessWeek*, July 29, 2002, pp. 32–51.

If an investment is riskless, it must, in equilibrium, yield the risk-free rate. If it offered a higher return, arbitrageurs would buy it and in the process push the return down, and vice versa if it offered less than the risk-free rate.

Given the price of the stock, its potential volatility, the option's exercise price, the life of the option, and the risk-free rate, there is but one price for the option if it is to meet the equilibrium condition, namely, that a portfolio that consists of the stock and the call option will earn the risk-free rate. We value an illustrative option below, and then we use the Black-Scholes model to value options under more realistic conditions.

1. *Assumptions of the example.* The stock of Western Cellular, a manufacturer of cell phones, sells for $40 per share. Options exist that permit the holder to buy one share of Western at an exercise price of $35. These options will expire at the end of one year, at which time Western's stock will be selling at one of two prices, either $30 or $50. Also, the risk-free rate is 8 percent. Based on these assumptions, we must find the value of the options.

2. *Find the range of values at expiration.* When the option expires at the end of the year, Western's stock will sell for either $30 or $50, and here is the situation with regard to the value of the options:

Ending Stock Price	−	Strike Price Value	=	Ending Option Value	
$30.00	−	$35.00	=	$ 0.00	(The option will be worthless. It cannot have a negative value.)
50.00	−	35.00	=	15.00	
Range $20.00				$15.00	

3. *Equalize the range of payoffs for the stock and the option.* As shown above, the ranges of payoffs for the stock and the option are $20 and $15. To construct the riskless portfolio, we need to equalize these ranges. We do so by buying 0.75 share and selling one option (or 75 shares and 100 options) to produce the following situation, where the range for both the stock and the option is $15:

Ending Stock Price	×	0.75	=	Ending Value of Stock	Ending Value of Option
$30.00	×	0.75	=	$22.50	$ 0.00
50.00	×	0.75	=	37.50	15.00
Range $20.00				$15.00	$15.00

4. *Create a riskless hedged investment.* We can now create a riskless investment portfolio by buying 0.75 share of Western's stock and selling one call option. Here is the situation:

Ending Stock Price	×	0.75	=	Ending Value of Stock in the Portfolio	+	Ending Value of Option in the Portfolio	=	Ending Total Value of the Portfolio
$30.00	×	0.75	=	$22.50	+	$ 0.00	=	$22.50
50.00	×	0.75	=	37.50	+	−15.00	=	22.50

The stock in the portfolio will have a value of either $22.50 or $37.50, depending on what happens to the price of the stock. The call option that was sold will have no effect on the value of the portfolio if Western's price falls to $30, because it will then not be exercised—it will expire worthless. However, if the stock price ends at $50, the holder of the option will exercise it, paying the $35 exercise price for stock that would cost $50 on the open market, so in that case, the option would have a cost of $15 to the holder of the portfolio.

Now note that the value of the portfolio is $22.50 regardless of whether Western's stock goes up or down. So, the portfolio is riskless. A hedge has been created that protects against both increases or decreases in the price of the stock.

5. *Pricing the call option.* To this point, we have not mentioned the price of the call option that was sold to create the riskless hedge. How much should it sell for? Obviously, the seller would like to get a high price, but the buyer would want a low price. What is the *fair*, or *equilibrium*, price? To find this price, we proceed as follows:

   a. The value of the portfolio will be $22.50 at the end of the year, regardless of what happens to the price of the stock. This $22.50 is riskless.

   b. The risk-free rate is 8 percent, so the present value of the riskless $22.50 year-end value is shown below.

$$PV = \$22.50/1.08 = \$20.83$$

c. Because Western's stock is currently selling for $40, and because the portfolio contains 0.75 share, the cost of the stock in the portfolio is shown below.

$$0.75(\$40) = \$30.00$$

d. If you paid $30 for the stock, and if the present value of the portfolio is $20.83, the option would have to sell for at least $9.17.

$$\text{Price of option} = \text{Cost of stock} - \text{PV of portfolio}$$
$$= \$30 - \$20.83 = \$9.17$$

If this option sold at a price higher than $9.17, other investors could create riskless portfolios as described above and earn more than the risk-free rate. Investors would create such portfolios—and options—until their price fell to $9.17, at which point the market would be in equilibrium. Conversely, if the options sold for less than $9.17, investors would refuse to create them, and the resulting supply shortage would drive the price up to $9.17. Thus, investors (or arbitrageurs) would buy and sell in the market until the options were priced at their equilibrium level.

Clearly, this example is overly simplistic—Western's stock price could be almost anything after one year, and you could not purchase 0.75 share of stock (but you could do so in effect by buying 75 shares and selling 100 options). Still, the example does illustrate that investors can, in principle, create riskless portfolios by buying stocks and selling call options against those stocks, and the return on such portfolios should be the risk-free rate. If call options are not priced to reflect this condition, arbitrageurs will actively trade stocks and options until option prices reflect equilibrium conditions. In the next section, we discuss the Black-Scholes Option Pricing Model, which is based on the general premise we developed here—the creation of a riskless portfolio—but which is applicable to "real-world" option pricing because it allows for a complete range of ending stock prices.

Describe how a risk-free portfolio can be created using stocks and options.

How can such a portfolio be used to help estimate a call option's value?

18-5 THE BLACK-SCHOLES OPTION PRICING MODEL (OPM)

The *Black-Scholes Option Pricing Model (OPM)*, developed in 1973, helped give rise to the rapid growth in options trading.[7] This model, which has even been programmed into the permanent memories of some hand-held calculators, is widely used by option traders.

18-5a OPM Assumptions and Equations

In deriving their option pricing model, Fischer Black and Myron Scholes made the following assumptions:

---

[7] See Fischer Black and Myron Scholes, "The Pricing of Options and Corporate Liabilities," *Journal of Political Economy*, May/June 1973, pp. 637–659.

1. The stock underlying the call option provides no dividends or other distributions during the life of the option.
2. There are no transactions costs for buying or selling either the stock or the option.
3. The short-term, risk-free interest rate is known and is constant during the life of the option.
4. Any purchaser of a security may borrow any fraction of the purchase price at the short-term, risk-free interest rate.
5. Short selling is permitted, and the short seller will receive immediately the full cash proceeds of today's price for a security sold short.[8]
6. The call option can be exercised only on its expiration date.
7. Trading in all securities takes place continuously, and the stock price moves randomly.

The derivation of the Black-Scholes model rests on the concept of a riskless hedge such as the one we set up in the last section. By buying shares of a stock and simultaneously selling call options on that stock, an investor can create a risk-free investment position, where gains on the stock will exactly offset losses on the option. This riskless hedged position must earn a rate of return equal to the risk-free rate. Otherwise, an arbitrage opportunity would exist, and people trying to take advantage of this opportunity would drive the price of the option to the equilibrium level as specified by the Black-Scholes model.

The Black-Scholes model consists of the following three equations.

$$V = P[N(d_1)] - Xe^{-r_{RF}t}[N(d_2)] \tag{18-2}$$

$$d_1 = \frac{\ln(P/X) + [r_{RF} + (\sigma^2/2)]t}{\sigma\sqrt{t}} \tag{18-3}$$

$$d_2 = d_1 - \sigma\sqrt{t} \tag{18-4}$$

Here

V = current value of the call option.
P = current price of the underlying stock.
$N(d_i)$ = probability that a deviation less than d_i will occur in a standard normal distribution. Thus, $N(d_1)$ and $N(d_2)$ represent areas under a standard normal distribution function.
X = exercise, or strike, price of the option.
$e \approx 2.7183$.
r_{RF} = risk-free interest rate.
t = time until the option expires (the option period).
$\ln(P/X)$ = natural logarithm of P/X.
σ^2 = variance of the rate of return on the stock.

Note that the value of the option is a function of the variables we discussed earlier: (1) P, the stock's price; (2) t, the option's time to expiration; (3) X, the strike price; (4) σ^2, the variance of the underlying stock; and (5) r_{RF}, the risk-free rate.

---

[8] Suppose an investor (or speculator) does not now own any IBM stock. If the investor anticipates a rise in the stock price and consequently buys IBM stock, he or she is said to have *gone long* in IBM. On the other hand, if the investor thinks IBM's stock is likely to fall, he or she could *go short*, or *sell IBM short*. Since the short seller has no IBM stock, he or she would have to borrow the shares sold short from a broker. If the stock price falls, the short seller could, later on, buy shares on the open market and pay back the ones borrowed from the broker. The short seller's profit, before commissions and taxes, would be the difference between the price received from the short sale and the price paid later to purchase the replacement stock.

We do not derive the Black-Scholes model—the derivation involves some extremely complicated mathematics that go far beyond the scope of this text. However, it is not difficult to use the model. Under the assumptions set forth previously, if the option price is different from the one found by Equation 18-2, this would provide the opportunity for arbitrage profits, which would force the option price back to the value indicated by the model.[9] As we noted earlier, the Black-Scholes model is widely used by traders, so actual option prices conform reasonably well to values derived from the model.

In essence, the first term of Equation 18-2, $P[N(d_1)]$, can be thought of as the expected present value of the terminal stock price, while the second term, $Xe^{-r_{RF}t}$ $[N(d_2)]$, can be thought of as the present value of the exercise price. However, rather than try to figure out exactly what the equations mean, it is more productive to insert some numbers to see how changes in the inputs affect the value of an option.

18-5b OPM Illustration

Robert's Online Option Pricer can be accessed at http://www.intrepid .com/~robertl/ option-pricer1.html. The site is designed to provide a financial service over the Internet to small investors for option pricing, giving anyone a means to price option trades without having to buy expensive software and hardware.

The current stock price, P, the exercise price, X, and the time to maturity, t, can be obtained from a newspaper such as *The Wall Street Journal* or on leading financial Web sites such as *Yahoo! Finance* or *MSN Money*. The risk-free rate, r_{RF}, is the yield on a Treasury bill with a maturity equal to the option expiration date. The annualized variance of stock returns, σ^2, can be estimated by multiplying the variance of the percentage change in daily stock prices for the past year [that is, the variance of $(P_t - P_{t-1})/P_{t-1}$] by 365 days.

Assume that the following information has been obtained:

$$
\begin{aligned}
P &= \$21. \\
X &= \$21. \\
t &= 0.36 \text{ year.} \\
r_{RF} &= 5\% = 0.05. \\
\sigma^2 &= 0.09. \text{ Note that } \sigma^2 = 0.09, \text{ then } \sigma = \sqrt{0.09} = 0.3.
\end{aligned}
$$

Given this information, we can now use the OPM by solving Equations 18-2, 18-3, and 18-4. Since d_1 and d_2 are required inputs for Equation 18-2, we solve Equations 18-3 and 18-4 first:

$$
\begin{aligned}
d_1 &= \frac{\ln(\$21/\$21) + [0.05 + (0.09/2)](0.36)}{0.3(0.6)} \\
&= \frac{0 + 0.0342}{0.18} = 0.19 \\
d_2 &= d_1 - 0.3\sqrt{0.36} = 0.19 - 0.18 = 0.01
\end{aligned}
$$

Note that $N(d_1) = N(0.19)$ and $N(d_2) = N(0.01)$ represent areas under a standard normal distribution function. From Appendix C at the end of the book, we see that the value $d_1 = 0.19$ implies a probability of $0.0753 + 0.5000 = 0.5753$, so $N(d_1) = 0.5753$. Similarly, $N(d_2) = 0.504$. We can use those values to solve Equation 18-2:

$$
\begin{aligned}
V &= \$21[N(d_1)] - \$21e^{-(0.05)(0.36)}[N(d_2)] \\
&= \$21[N(0.19)] - \$21(0.98216)[N(0.01)] \\
&= \$21(0.5753) - \$20.625(0.504) \\
&= \$12.081 - \$10.395 = \$1.686
\end{aligned}
$$

---

[9] *Programmed trading*, in which stocks are bought and options are sold, or vice versa, is an example of arbitrage between stocks and options.

TABLE 18-2   *Effects of OPM Factors on the Value of a Call Option*

| | INPUT FACTORS | | | | | OUTPUT |
Case	P	X	t	r_{RF}	σ^2	V
Base case	$21	$21	0.36	5%	0.09	$1.686
Increase P by $4	**25**	21	0.36	5	0.09	4.672
Increase X by $4	21	**25**	0.36	5	0.09	0.434
Increase t to 0.5	21	21	**0.50**	5	0.09	2.023
Increase r_{RF} to 8%	21	21	0.36	**8**	0.09	1.802
Increase σ^2 to 0.16	21	21	0.36	5	**0.16**	2.181

Thus, the value of the option, under the assumed conditions, is $1.686. Suppose the actual option price were $2.25. Arbitrageurs could simultaneously sell the option, buy the underlying stock, and earn a riskless profit. Such trading would occur until the price of the option was driven down to $1.686. The reverse would occur if the option sold for less than $1.686. Thus, investors would be unwilling to pay more than $1.686 for the option, and they could not buy it for less, so $1.686 is the *equilibrium value* of the option.

To see how the five OPM factors affect the value of the option, consider Table 18-2. Here the top row shows the base-case input values that were used above to illustrate the OPM and the resulting option value, V = $1.686. In each of the subsequent rows, the boldfaced factor is increased, while the other four are held constant at their base-case levels. The resulting value of the call option is given in the last column. Now let's consider the effects of the changes:

1. *Current stock price.* If the current stock price, P, increases from $21 to $25, the option value increases from $1.686 to $4.672. Thus, the value of the option increases as the stock price increases, but by less than the stock price increase, $2.986 versus $4.00. Note, though, that the percentage increase in the option value, ($4.672 − $1.686)/$1.686 = 177%, far exceeds the percentage increase in the stock price, ($25 − $21)/$21 = 19%.

2. *Exercise price.* If the exercise price, X, increases from $21 to $25, the value of the option declines. Again, the decrease in the option value is less than the exercise price increase, but the percentage change in the option value (in absolute value terms), ($0.434 − $1.686)/$1.686 = −74%, exceeds the percentage change in the exercise price, ($25 − $21)/$21 = 19%.

3. *Option period.* As the time to expiration increases from t = 0.36 year to t = 0.50 year, the value of the option increases from $1.686 to $2.023. This occurs because the value of the option depends on the chances for an increase in the price of the underlying stock, and the longer the option has before its expiration, the higher the stock price may climb.

4. *Risk-free rate.* As the risk-free rate increases from 5 to 8 percent, the value of the option increases slightly, from $1.686 to $1.802. Equations 18-2, 18-3, and 18-4 suggest that the principal effect of an increase in r_{RF} is to reduce the present value of the exercise price, $Xe^{-r_{RF}t}$, hence to increase the current value of the option.[10] The risk-free rate also plays a role in determining the

---

[10] At this point, you may be wondering why the first term in Equation 18-2, $P[N(d_1)]$, is not discounted. In fact, it has been, because the current stock price, P, already represents the present value of the expected stock price at expiration. In other words, P is a discounted value, and the discount rate used in the market to determine today's stock price includes the risk-free rate. Thus, Equation 18-2 can be thought of as the present value of the end-of-option-period spread between the stock price and the strike price, adjusted for the probability that the stock price will be higher than the strike price.

values of the normal distribution functions $N(d_1)$ and $N(d_2)$, but this effect is of secondary importance. Indeed, option prices in general are not very sensitive to interest rate changes, at least not to changes within the ranges normally encountered.

5. *Variance.* As the variance increases from the base case 0.09 to 0.16, the value of the option increases from $1.686 to $2.181. Therefore, the riskier the underlying security, the more valuable the option. This result is logical. First, if you bought an option to buy a stock that sells at its exercise price, and if $\sigma^2 = 0$, then there would be a zero probability of the stock increasing, hence a zero probability of making money on the option. On the other hand, if you bought an option on a high-variance stock, there would be a fairly high probability that the stock price would go way up, hence that you would make a large profit on the option. Of course, a high-variance stock could go way down, but as an option holder, your losses would be limited to the price paid for the option—only the right-hand side of the stock's probability distribution counts. Put another way, an increase in the price of the stock helps option holders more than a decrease hurts them, so the greater the variance, the greater is the value of the option. This makes options on risky stocks more valuable than those on safer, low-variance stocks.

Myron Scholes and Robert Merton were awarded the 1997 Nobel Prize in Economics, and Fischer Black would have been a co-recipient had he still been living.[11] Their work provided analytical tools and methodologies that are widely used to solve many types of financial problems, not just option pricing. Indeed, the entire field of modern risk management is based primarily on their contributions. This concludes our discussion of options and option pricing theory. The next section discusses some other types of derivative securities.

What is the purpose of the Black-Scholes Option Pricing Model?

Explain what a "riskless hedge" is and how the riskless hedge concept is used in the Black-Scholes OPM.

Describe the effect of a change in each of the following factors on the value of a call option:

(1) Stock price.
(2) Exercise price.
(3) Option life.
(4) Risk-free rate.
(5) Stock price variance; that is, riskiness of stock.

What is the value of a call option with these data: $P = \$25$; $X = \$25$; $r_{RF} = 8\%$; $t = 0.5$ (6 months); $\sigma^2 = 0.09$; $N(d_1) = 0.61586$; and $N(d_2) = 0.53287$? ($2.60)

Forward Contract
A contract under which one party agrees to buy a commodity at a specific price on a specific future date and the other party agrees to make the sale. Physical delivery occurs.

18-6 FORWARD AND FUTURES CONTRACTS

Forward contracts are agreements where one party agrees to buy a commodity at a specific price on a specific future date and the other party agrees to make the sale. *Goods are actually delivered under forward contracts.* Unless both parties

---

[11] See Robert C. Merton, "Theory of Rational Option Pricing," *Bell Journal of Economics and Management Science*, Vol. 4 (1973), pp. 141–183.

are financially strong, there is a danger that one party will default on the contract, especially if the price of the commodity changes markedly after the agreement is reached.

A **futures contract** is similar to a forward contract, but with three key differences: (1) Futures contracts are "marked to market" on a daily basis, meaning that gains and losses are noted and money must be put up to cover losses. This greatly reduces the risk of default that exists with forward contracts. (2) With futures, physical delivery of the underlying asset is virtually never taken—the two parties simply settle up with cash for the difference between the contracted price and the actual price on the expiration date. (3) Futures contracts are generally standardized instruments that are traded on exchanges, whereas forward contracts are generally tailor-made, are negotiated between two parties, and are not traded after they have been signed.

Futures and forward contracts were originally used for commodities such as wheat, where farmers would sell forward contracts to millers, enabling both parties to lock in prices and thus reduce their risk exposure. Commodities contracts are still important, but today more trading is done in foreign exchange and interest rate futures. To illustrate how foreign exchange contracts are used, suppose GE arranges to buy electric motors from a German manufacturer on terms that call for GE to pay 1 million euros in 180 days. GE would not want to give up the free trade credit, but if the euro appreciated against the dollar during the next six months, the dollar cost of the million euros would rise. GE could hedge the transaction by buying a forward contract under which it agreed to buy the million euros in 180 days at a fixed dollar price. This would lock in the dollar cost of the motors. This transaction would probably be conducted through a money center bank, which would try to find a German company (a "counterparty") that needed dollars in six months. Alternatively, GE could buy a futures contract on an exchange.

Interest rate futures represent another huge and growing market. For example, suppose Simonset Corporation decides to build a new plant at a cost of $20 million. It plans to finance the project with 15-year bonds that would carry an 8 percent interest rate if they were issued today. However, the company will not need the money for about six months. Simonset could go ahead and sell 15-year bonds now, locking in the 8 percent rate, but it would have the money before it was needed, so it would have to invest in short-term securities that would yield less than 8 percent. However, if Simonset waits six months to sell the bond issue, interest rates might be higher than they are today, in which case the firm would have to pay higher interest costs on the bonds, perhaps to the point of making it unprofitable to build the plant.

One solution to Simonset's dilemma involves *interest rate futures*, which are based on a hypothetical 15-year Treasury bond with a 6 percent semiannual coupon. If interest rates in the economy rise, the value of the hypothetical T-bond will fall, and vice versa. In our example, Simonset is worried about an increase in interest rates. Should rates rise, the hypothetical Treasury bond's value would decline. Therefore, Simonset could sell T-bond futures for delivery in six months to hedge its position. If interest rates rise, Simonset will have to pay more when it issues its own bonds. However, it will make a profit on its futures position because it will have pre-sold the bonds at a higher price than it will have to pay to cover (repurchase) them. Of course, if interest rates decline, Simonset will lose on its futures position, but this will be offset by the fact that it will get to pay a lower interest rate when it issues its bonds.

In 2005, futures contracts were available on more than 30 real and financial assets traded on 14 U.S. exchanges, the largest of which are the Chicago Board of Trade (CBOT) and the Chicago Mercantile Exchange (CME). Futures contracts are divided into two classes, **commodity futures** and **financial futures.** Commodity

Futures Contract
Standardized contracts that are traded on exchanges and are "marked to market" daily, but where physical delivery of the underlying asset is virtually never taken.

Commodity Futures
A contract that is used to hedge against price changes for input materials.

Financial Futures
A contract that is used to hedge against fluctuating interest rates, stock prices, and exchange rates.

TABLE 18-3 *Interest Rate Futures*

TREASURY BONDS (CBT)—$100,000; PTS. 32nds OF 100%

Delivery Month (1)	Open (2)	High (3)	Low (4)	Settle (5)	Change (6)	LIFETIME High (7)	LIFETIME Low (8)	Open Interest (9)
Sept	116-07	116-24	116-00	116-17	9	119-23	108-15	563,857
Dec	115-28	116-12	115-22	116-05	9	119-07	108-23	55,147
Mar06	115-30	115-30	115-28	115-29	9	118-19	113-03	207
June	115-21	115-21	115-21	115-25	9	115-21	115-05	2

Est vol 242,706; vol Mon 271,374; open int 619,213, +3,204.
Source: The Wall Street Journal, August 24, 2005, p. B9.

futures, which cover oil, various grains, oilseeds, livestock, meats, fibers, metals, and wood, were first traded in the United States in the mid-1800s. Financial futures, which were first traded in 1975, include Treasury bills, notes, bonds, certificates of deposit, eurodollar deposits, foreign currencies, and stock indexes.

To illustrate how futures contracts work, consider the CBOT's contract on Treasury bonds. The basic contract is for $100,000 of a hypothetical 6 percent coupon, semiannual payment Treasury bond with 15 years to maturity. Table 18-3 shows an extract from the Treasury bond futures table that appeared in the August 24, 2005, issue of *The Wall Street Journal.*

The first column gives the delivery month; the next three columns give the opening, high, and low prices for that contract on that day. The opening price for the September future, 116-07, means 116 plus $7/32$, or 116.21875 percent of par. Column 5 gives the settlement price, which is typically the price at the close of trading. Column 6 reports the change in the settlement price from the preceding day—the September contract rose $9/32$. Columns 7 and 8 give the lifetime-of-contract highs and lows. Finally, Column 9 shows the "open interest," which is the number of contracts outstanding.

To illustrate, we focus on the Treasury bonds for December delivery. The settlement price was 116-05, or 116 plus $5/32$ percent of the $100,000 contract value. Thus, the price at which one could buy $100,000 face value of 6 percent, 15-year Treasury bonds to be delivered in December was 116.15625 percent of par, or 1.1615625($100,000) = $116,156.25. The contract price increased by $9/32$ of 1 percent of $100,000, or by $281.25, from the previous day, so if you had bought the contract yesterday, you would have gained $281.25. Over its life, the contract's price has ranged from 108.71875 to 119.21875 percent of par, and there were 55,147 contracts outstanding, representing a total value of about $6.41 billion.

Note that the contract increased by $9/32$ of a percent on this particular day. Why would the value of the bond futures contract increase? Since bond prices increase when interest rates fall, we know that interest rates fell on that day. Moreover, we can calculate the implied rates inherent in the futures contracts. (*The Wall Street Journal* formerly provided the implied yields, but now we must calculate them.) Recall that the contract relates to a hypothetical 15-year, semiannual payment, 6 percent coupon bond. The closing price (settlement price) was $116^5/_{32}$, or 116.15625 percent of par. Using a financial calculator, we can solve for r_d in the following equation:

$$\sum_{t=1}^{30} \frac{\$30}{(1 + r_d/2)^t} + \frac{\$1,000}{(1 + r_d/2)^{30}} = \$1,161.5625$$

The solution value for the six-month rate is 2.25326 percent, which is equivalent to a nominal annual rate of 4.50652 percent, or 4.51 percent. Because the price of the bond rose by $\frac{9}{32}$ that day, we could find the previous day's closing (settlement) price and its implied interest rate, which would turn out to be 4.53 percent. Therefore, interest rates fell by 2 basis points, which was enough to increase the value of the contract by $281.25.

Thus, the futures contract for December delivery of this hypothetical bond sold for $116,156.25 for 100 bonds with a par value of $100,000, which translates to a yield to maturity of about 4.5 percent. This yield reflects investors' beliefs about what the interest rate level will be in December. The spot yield on T-bonds was about 4.4 percent at the time, so the marginal trader in the futures market was predicting about a 10-basis-point increase in yields over the next four months. That prediction could, of course, turn out to be incorrect.

Now suppose that two months later interest rates in the futures market had fallen from the earlier levels, say, from 4.5 to 4.0 percent. Falling interest rates mean rising bond prices, and we could calculate that the December contract would then be worth about $122,396.46. Thus, the contract's value would have increased by $122,396.46 − $116,156.25 = $6,240.21.

When futures contracts are purchased, the purchaser does not have to put up the full amount of the purchase price; rather, the purchaser is required to post an initial *margin*, which for CBT Treasury bond contracts is $1,553 per $100,000 contract. However, investors are required to maintain a certain value in the margin account, called a *maintenance margin*. The maintenance margin for CBT Treasury bond contracts is $1,150 per $100,000 contract. If the value of the contract declines, then the owner may be required to add additional funds to the margin account, and the more the contract value falls, the more money must be added. The value of the contract is checked at the end of every working day, and margin account adjustments are made at that time. This is called "marking to market." If an investor purchased our illustrative contract and then sold it later for $122,396.46, he or she would have made a profit of $6,240.21 on a $1,553 investment, or a return of about 402 percent in only two months. It is clear, therefore, that futures contracts offer a considerable amount of leverage. Of course, if interest rates had risen, then the value of the contract would have declined, and the investor could easily have lost his or her $1,553, or more. Futures contracts are never settled by delivery of the securities involved. Rather, the transaction is completed by reversing the trade, which amounts to selling the contract back to the original seller.[12] The actual gains and losses on the contract are realized when the futures contract is closed.

Our examples show that forward contracts and futures can be used to hedge, or reduce, risks. Later on, in Section 18.9, we describe in more detail how futures can be used to hedge various types of risk. It has been estimated that more than 95 percent of all futures transactions are indeed designed as hedges, with banks and futures dealers serving as middlemen between hedging counterparties. Interest rate and exchange rate futures can, of course, be used for speculative as well as hedging purposes. We can buy a T-bond contract on $100,000 of bonds with only $1,553 down, in which case a small change in interest rates will result in a very large gain or loss. Still, the primary motivation behind the vast majority of these transactions is to hedge risks, not to create them.

---

[12] The buyers and sellers of most financial futures contracts do not actually trade with one another—each trader's contractual obligation is with a futures exchange. This feature helps to guarantee the fiscal integrity of the trade. Incidentally, commodities futures traded on the exchanges are settled in the same way as financial futures, but in the case of commodities much of the contracting is done off the exchange, between farmers and processors, as *forward contracts*, in which case actual deliveries occur.

Futures contracts and options are similar to one another—so similar that people often confuse the two. Therefore, it is useful to compare the two instruments. A *futures contract* is a definite agreement on the part of one party to buy something on a specific date and at a specific price, and the other party agrees to sell on the same terms. No matter how low or how high the price goes, the two parties must settle the contract at the agreed-upon price. An *option*, on the other hand, gives someone the right to buy (call) or sell (put) an asset, but the holder of the option does not have to complete the transaction. Note also that options exist both for individual stocks and for "bundles" of stocks such as those in the S&P and *Value Line* indexes, but generally not for commodities. Futures, on the other hand, are used for commodities, debt securities, and stock indexes. The two types of instruments can be used for the same purposes. One is not necessarily better or worse than another—they are simply different.

What is a forward contract?

What is a futures contract? What are the key differences between forward and futures contracts?

What is the difference between the initial margin and the maintenance margin on a futures contract?

Suppose you buy a March futures contract on a hypothetical 15-year, 6 percent semiannual coupon bond with a settlement price today of $109^9/_{32}$. You post the initial margin required for this transaction ($1,553 per $100,000 contract). What nominal yield to maturity is implied by the settlement price? If interest rates fall to 4.5 percent, what return would you earn on one futures contract? If interest rates rose to 5.5 percent, what is the return on one futures contract? (5.11%, 448%, −271.66%)

18-7 OTHER TYPES OF DERIVATIVES

Options, forwards, and futures are among the most important classes of derivative securities, but there are other types of derivatives, including swaps, structured notes, inverse floaters, and a host of other "exotic" contracts.

18-7a Swaps

Swap
Two parties agree to exchange obligations to make specified payment streams.

A **swap** is just what the name implies—two parties agree to swap something, generally obligations to make specified payment streams. Most swaps today involve either interest payments or currencies. To illustrate an interest rate swap, suppose Company S has a 20-year, $100 million floating-rate bond outstanding, while Company F has a $100 million, 20-year, fixed-rate issue outstanding. Thus, each company has an obligation to make a stream of interest payments, but one payment stream is fixed while the other will vary as interest rates change in the future.

Now suppose Company S has stable cash flows, and it wants to lock in its cost of debt. Company F has cash flows that fluctuate with the economy, rising when the economy is strong and falling when it is weak. Recognizing that interest rates also move up and down with the economy, Company F has concluded that it would be better off with variable rate debt. If the companies swapped their payment obligations, an *interest rate swap* would occur. Company S would now have to make fixed payments, which is consistent with its stable cash inflows, and Company F would have a floating stream, which for it is less risky.

Note, though, that swaps can involve *side payments*. For example, if interest rates had fallen sharply since Company F issued its bonds, then its old payment obligations would be relatively high, and it would have to make a side payment to get S to agree to the swap. Similarly, if the credit risk of one company was higher than that of the other, the stronger company would be concerned about the ability of its weaker "counterparty" to make the required payments. This too would lead to the need for a side payment.

Currency swaps are similar to interest rate swaps. To illustrate, suppose Company A, an American firm, had issued $100 million of dollar-denominated bonds in the United States to fund an investment in Germany. Meanwhile, Company G, a German firm, had issued $100 million of euro-denominated bonds in Germany to make an investment in the United States. Company A would earn euros but be required to make payments in dollars, and Company G would be in a reverse situation. Thus, both companies would be exposed to exchange rate risk. However, both companies' risks would be eliminated if they swapped payment obligations. As with interest rate swaps, differences in interest rates or credit risks would require side payments.

Originally, swaps were arranged between companies by money center banks, which would match up counterparties. Such matching still occurs, but today most swaps are between companies and banks, with the banks then taking steps to ensure that their own risks are hedged. For example, Citibank might arrange a swap with Company A, which would agree to make specified payments in euros to the bank, and the bank would make the dollar payments Company A would otherwise owe. Citibank would charge a fee for setting up the swap, and these charges would reflect the creditworthiness of Company A. To protect itself against exchange rate movements, the bank would hedge its position, either by lining up a German company that needed to make dollar payments or else by using currency futures.

18-7b Structured Notes

The term **structured note** often means a debt obligation that is derived from some other debt obligation. For example, in the early 1980s, investment bankers began buying large blocks of 30-year, noncallable Treasury bonds and then *stripping* them to create a series of zero coupon bonds. The zero with the shortest maturity was backed by the first interest payment on the T-bond issue, the second shortest zero was backed by the next interest payment, and so forth, on out to a 30-year zero backed by the last interest payment plus the maturity value of the T-bond. Zeros formed by stripping T-bonds were one of the first types of structured notes.

Another important type of structured note is backed by the interest and principal payments on mortgages. In the 1970s, Wall Street firms began to buy large packages of mortgages backed by federal agencies and then place these packages, or "pools," with a trustee. Then bonds called *collateralized mortgage obligations (CMOs)*, backed by the mortgage pool held in trust, were sold to pension funds, individuals for their IRA accounts, and other investors who were willing to invest in CMOs but who would not have purchased individual mortgages. This *securitization* of mortgages made billions of dollars of new capital available to home buyers.

CMOs are more difficult to evaluate than straight bonds for several reasons. First, the underlying mortgages can be prepaid at any time, and when this occurs the prepayment proceeds are used to retire part of the CMO debt itself.

Structured Note
A debt obligation derived from another debt obligation.

Therefore, the holder of a CMO is never sure when his or her bond will be called. This situation is further complicated by the fact that when interest rates decline, this causes bond prices to rise. However, declining rates also lead to mortgage prepayments, which cause the CMOs to be called especially rapidly.

It should also be noted that a variety of structured notes can be created, ranging from notes whose cash flows can be predicted with virtual certainty to other notes whose payment streams are highly uncertain. For example, investment bankers can (and do) create notes called *IOs* (for *interest only*), which provide cash flows from the interest component of the mortgage amortization payments, and *POs* (for *principal only*), which are paid from the principal repayment stream. In each case, the value of the note is found as the PV of an expected payment stream, but the length and size of the stream are uncertain. Suppose, for example, that you are offered an IO that you expect to provide payments of $100 for 10 years (you expect the mortgages to be refinanced after 10 years, at which time your payments will cease). Suppose further that you discount the expected payment stream at a rate of 10 percent and determine that the value is $614.46. You have $614.46 to invest, so you buy the IO, expecting to earn 10 percent on your money.

Now suppose interest rates decline. If rates fall, the discount rate would drop, and that would normally imply an increase in the IO's value. However, if rates decline sharply, this would lead to a rash of mortgage refinancings, in which case your payments, which come from interest only, would cease (or be greatly reduced), and the value of your IO would fall sharply. On the other hand, a sharp increase in interest rates would reduce refinancings, lengthen your expected payment stream, and probably increase the value of your IO.

Investment bankers can slice and dice a pool of mortgages into a bewildering array of structured notes, ranging from "plain vanilla" ones with highly predictable cash flows to "exotic" ones (sometimes called "toxic waste") whose risks are almost incalculable but are surely large.

Securitizing mortgages through CMOs serves a useful economic function—it provides an investment outlet for pension funds and others with money to invest, and it makes more money available to homeowners at a reasonable cost. Also, some investors want relatively safe investments, while others are willing to buy more speculative securities for the higher expected returns they provide. Structured notes permit a partitioning of risks to give investors what they want. There are dangers, though. The "toxic waste" is often bought by naive officials managing money for local governments like Orange County, California, when they really ought to be holding only safe securities.

More recently, Wall Street firms have put together a similar set of instruments called *collateralized debt obligations (CDOs)*. CDOs are similar to CMOs but instead of assembling a portfolio of mortgages, the issuing firm assembles a portfolio of debt instruments. Once again the overall risk is partitioned into several classes. If you are holding the senior class you are first in line to receive cash flows from the portfolio, and as a result, your risk may not be all that great. On the other hand, if you buy one of the riskier classes that have lower priority, you can expect higher returns but a lot more risk.

18-7c Inverse Floaters

A floating-rate note has an interest rate that rises and falls with some interest rate index. For example, the interest rate on a $100,000 note at prime plus 1 percent would be 7.50 percent when the prime rate is 6.50 percent, and the note's rate would move up and down with the prime rate. Because both the cash flows associated with the note and the discount rate used to value it rise and fall together, the market value of the note would be relatively stable.

Credit Instruments Create New Opportunities and Risks

While market participants have traditionally used derivatives to hedge interest rate risk and currency risk, they still often faced credit risk. Perhaps not surprisingly, a new set of derivative instruments has evolved to help market participants manage this credit risk.

One example of a credit derivative is a credit swap (sometimes called a credit default swap). In its simplest form, one party agrees to bear the credit risk of another party in exchange for an ongoing payment. For example, let's say that Company Z agrees to sell a credit swap to Bank A who recently made a loan to Company L. Under the terms of the agreement, Bank A agrees to make regular payments to Company Z. In return, Company Z agrees to compensate Bank A if Company L defaults on the loan. In effect, the seller of the swap is providing a form of insurance to Bank A by agreeing to bear all or part of the loan's credit risk.

Credit derivatives provide value to the extent that they increase market liquidity and help financial institutions manage risk. On the other hand, the value of these positions can change dramatically in a short period of time. Moreover, there are concerns where a sudden loss could create a chain reaction. For example, if a hedge fund loses big money on its credit derivative positions, this could have a negative effect on the banks who have lent money to the hedge fund.

Trying to put this in perspective, a Wall Street veteran quoted in a recent issue of *BusinessWeek* compared credit derivatives to fertilizer: "It can help your garden grow or can be made into bombs."

Source: Mara Der Hovanesian, Chester Dawson, and Kerry Capell, "Taking Risk to Extremes: Will Derivatives Cause a Major Blowup in the World's Credit Markets?" *Business-Week*, May 23, 2005, p. 96.

With an **inverse floater,** the rate paid on the note moves counter to market rates. Thus, if interest rates in the economy rose, the interest rate paid on an inverse floater would fall, lowering its cash interest payments. At the same time, the discount rate used to value the inverse floater's cash flows would rise along with other rates. The combined effect of lower cash flows and a higher discount rate would lead to a very large decline in the value of the inverse floater. Thus, inverse floaters are exceptionally vulnerable to increases in interest rates. Of course, if interest rates fall, the value of an inverse floater will soar.

We have discussed the most important types of derivative securities, but certainly not all types. This discussion should, though, give you a good idea of how and why derivatives are created, and how they can be used and misused.

Inverse Floater
A note in which the interest rate paid moves counter to market rates.

Briefly describe the following types of derivative securities:

(1) Swaps.
(2) Structured notes.
(3) Inverse floaters.

18-8 RISK MANAGEMENT

As businesses become increasingly complex, it is becoming more and more difficult for CEOs and directors to know what problems might lie in wait. Therefore, companies need to have someone systematically look for potential problems and design safeguards to minimize potential damage. With this in mind, most larger firms have designated "risk managers" who report to the chief financial officer, while the CFOs of smaller firms personally assume risk management responsibilities. In any event, **risk management** is becoming increasingly important, and it is something finance students should understand. Therefore, in the remainder of this chapter we discuss the basics of risk management, with particular emphasis on how derivatives can be used to hedge financial risks.

It is useful to begin our discussion of risk management by defining some commonly used terms that describe different risks. Some of these risks can be mitigated, or managed, and that is what risk management is all about.

1. *Pure risks* are risks that offer only the prospect of a loss. Examples include the risk that a plant will be destroyed by fire or that a product liability suit will result in a large judgment against the firm.
2. *Speculative risks* are situations that offer the chance of a gain but might result in a loss. Thus, investments in new projects and marketable securities involve speculative risks.
3. *Demand risks* are associated with the demand for a firm's products or services. Because sales are essential to all businesses, demand risk is one of the most significant risks that firms face.
4. *Input risks* are risks associated with input costs, including both labor and materials. Thus, a company that uses copper as a raw material in its manufacturing process faces the risk that the cost of copper will increase and that it will not be able to pass this increase on to its customers.
5. *Financial risks* are risks that result from financial transactions. As we have seen, if a firm plans to issue new bonds, it faces the risk that interest rates will rise before the bonds can be brought to market. Similarly, if the firm enters into contracts with foreign customers or suppliers, it faces the risk that fluctuations in exchange rates will result in unanticipated losses.
6. *Property risks* are associated with destruction of productive assets. Thus, the threat of fire, floods, and riots imposes property risks on a firm.
7. *Personnel risks* are risks that result from employees' actions. Examples include the risks associated with employee fraud or embezzlement, or suits based on charges of age or sex discrimination.
8. *Environmental risks* include risks associated with polluting the environment. Public awareness in recent years, coupled with the huge costs of environmental cleanup, has increased the importance of this risk.
9. *Liability risks* are associated with product, service, or employee actions. Examples include the very large judgments assessed against asbestos manufacturers and some health care providers as well as costs incurred as a result of improper actions of employees, such as driving corporate vehicles in a reckless manner.
10. *Insurable risks* are risks that can be covered by insurance. In general, property, personnel, environmental, and liability risks can be transferred to insurance companies. Note, though, that the *ability* to insure a risk does not necessarily mean that the risk *should* be insured. Indeed, a major function of risk management involves evaluating all alternatives for managing a particular risk, including self-insurance, and then choosing the optimal alternative.

Note that the risk classifications we used are somewhat arbitrary, and different classifications are commonly used in different industries. However, the list does give an idea of the wide variety of risks to which a firm can be exposed.

18-8a An Approach to Risk Management

Firms often use the following process for managing risks.

1. *Identify the risks faced by the firm.* Here the risk manager identifies the potential risks faced by his or her firm. (See the box entitled "Microsoft's Goal: Manage Every Risk!")
2. *Measure the potential effect of each risk.* Some risks are so small as to be immaterial, whereas others have the potential for dooming the company. It is useful to segregate risks by potential effect and then to focus on the most serious threats.
3. *Decide how each relevant risk should be handled.* In most situations, risk exposure can be reduced through one of the following techniques:

   a. *Transfer the risk to an insurance company.* Often, it is advantageous to insure against, hence transfer, a risk. However, insurability does not necessarily mean that a risk should be covered by insurance. In many instances, it might be better for the company to *self-insure*, which means bearing the risk directly rather than paying another party to bear it.

   b. *Transfer the function that produces the risk to a third party.* For example, suppose a furniture manufacturer is concerned about potential liabilities arising from its ownership of a fleet of trucks used to transfer products from its manufacturing plant to various points across the country. One way to eliminate this risk would be to contract with a trucking company to do the shipping, thus passing the risks to a third party.

   c. *Purchase derivative contracts to reduce risk.* As we indicated earlier, firms use derivatives to hedge risks. Commodity derivatives can be used to reduce input risks. For example, a cereal company may use corn or wheat futures to hedge against increases in grain prices. Similarly, financial derivatives can be used to reduce risks that arise from changes in interest rates and exchange rates.

   d. *Reduce the probability of occurrence of an adverse event.* The expected loss arising from any risk is a function of both the probability of occurrence and the dollar loss if the adverse event occurs. In some instances, it is possible to reduce the probability that an adverse event will occur. For example, the probability that a fire will occur can be reduced by instituting a fire-prevention program, by replacing old electrical wiring, and by using fire-resistant materials in areas with the greatest fire potential.

   e. *Reduce the magnitude of the loss associated with an adverse event.* Continuing with the fire risk example, the dollar cost associated with a fire can be reduced by such actions as installing sprinkler systems, designing facilities with self-contained fire zones, and locating facilities close to a fire station.

   f. *Totally avoid the activity that gives rise to the risk.* For example, a company might discontinue a product or service line because the risks outweigh the rewards, as with the decision by Dow-Corning to discontinue its manufacture of silicon breast implants.

Note that risk management decisions, like all corporate decisions, should be based on a cost/benefit analysis for each feasible alternative. For example, suppose it would cost $50,000 per year to conduct a comprehensive fire safety training program for all personnel in a high-risk plant. Presumably, this program would reduce the expected value of future fire losses. An alternative to the training program would be to place $50,000 annually in a reserve fund set aside to cover future fire losses. Both alternatives involve expected cash flows, and from an economic standpoint the choice should be made on the basis of the lowest present value of future costs. Thus, the same financial management techniques

Microsoft's Goal: Manage Every Risk!

Twenty years ago, risk management meant buying insurance against fire, theft, and liability losses. Today, though, due to globalization, volatile markets, and a host of lawyers looking for someone to sue, a multitude of risks can adversely affect companies. Microsoft addressed these risks by creating a virtual consulting practice, called Microsoft Risk Co., to help manage the risks faced by its sales, operations, and product groups.

In an article in *CFO*, Scott Lange, who was head of Microsoft Risk at the time the article appeared, identified these 12 major sources of risk:

1. *Business partners* (interdependency, confidentiality, cultural conflict, contractual risks).
2. *Competition* (market share, price wars, industrial espionage, antitrust allegations, etc.).
3. *Customers* (product liability, credit risk, poor market timing, inadequate customer support).
4. *Distribution systems* (transportation, service availability, cost, dependence on distributors).
5. *Financial* (foreign exchange, portfolio, cash, interest rate, stock market).
6. *Operations* (facilities, contractual risks, natural hazards, internal processes and control).
7. *People* (employees, independent contractors, training, staffing inadequacy).
8. *Political* (civil unrest, war, terrorism, enforcement of intellectual property rights, change in leadership, revised economic policies).
9. *Regulatory and legislative* (antitrust, export licensing, jurisdiction, reporting and compliance, environmental).
10. *Reputations* (corporate image, brands, reputations of key employees).
11. *Strategic* (mergers and acquisitions, joint ventures and alliances, resource allocation and planning, organizational agility).
12. *Technological* (complexity, obsolescence, workforce skill-sets).

According to Lange, it is important to resist the idea that risk should be categorized by how the insurance industry views it. Insurance coverage lines are a tiny subset of the risks a modern enterprise faces in the pursuit of its business objectives. He also defined the role of finance in risk management: The role of finance is to put on paper all the risks that can be identified and to try to quantify them. When possible, use a number—one number, perhaps, or a probability distribution. For example, what is the probability of losing $1 million on a product, or $10 million? At Microsoft, the finance department works with the product groups to determine the exposure. "We try to use common sense," Lange says.

In many ways risk management mirrors the quality movement of the 1980s and 1990s. The goal of the quality movement was to take the responsibility for quality out of a separate Quality Control Department and to make all managers and employees responsible for quality. Lange had a similar goal for Microsoft—to have risk management permeate the thinking of all Microsoft managers and employees.

Source: Edward Teach, "Microsoft's Universe of Risk," *CFO,* March 1997, pp. 69–72.

---

applied to other corporate decisions can also be applied to risk management decisions. Note, though, that if a fire occurs and a life is lost, the trade-off between fire prevention and expected losses may not sit well with a jury. The same thing holds true for product liability, as Ford, GM, and others have learned.

Define the following terms:

(1) Pure risks.
(2) Speculative risks.
(3) Demand risks.
(4) Input risks.
(5) Financial risks.
(6) Property risks.

(7) Personnel risks.

(8) Environmental risks.

(9) Liability risks.

(10) Insurable risks.

(11) Self-insurance.

Should a firm insure itself against all of the insurable risks it faces? Explain.

18-9 USING DERIVATIVES TO REDUCE RISKS

Firms are subject to numerous risks related to interest rate, stock price, and exchange rate fluctuations in the financial markets. For an investor, one of the most obvious ways to reduce financial risks is to hold a broadly diversified portfolio of stocks and debt securities, including international securities and debt of varying maturities. However, derivatives can also be used to reduce the risks associated with financial and commodity markets.[13]

18-9a Security Price Exposure

Firms are obviously exposed to losses due to changes in security prices when securities are held in investment portfolios, and they are also exposed during times when securities are being issued. In addition, firms are exposed to risk if they use floating-rate debt to finance an investment that produces a fixed income stream. Risks such as these can often be mitigated by using derivatives. As we discussed earlier, derivatives are securities whose values stem, or are derived, from the values of other assets. Thus, options and futures contracts are derivatives because their values depend on the prices of some underlying assets. Now we will explore further the use of two types of derivatives, futures and swaps, to help manage certain types of risk.

Futures

Futures are used for both speculation and hedging. **Speculation** involves betting on future price movements, and futures are used because of the leverage inherent in the contract. **Hedging,** on the other hand, is done by a firm or individual to protect against a price change that would otherwise negatively affect profits. For example, rising interest rates and commodity (raw material) prices can hurt profits, as can adverse currency fluctuations. If two parties have mirror-image risks, then they can enter into a transaction that eliminates, as opposed to transfers, risks. This is a "natural hedge." Of course, one party to a futures contract could be a speculator, the other a hedger. Thus, to the extent that speculators broaden the market and make hedging possible, they help decrease risk to those who seek to avoid it.

There are two basic types of hedges: (1) **long hedges,** in which futures contracts are *bought* in anticipation of (or to guard against) price increases, and (2) **short hedges,** where a firm or individual *sells* futures contracts to guard against price declines. Recall that rising interest rates lower bond prices and thus

Speculation
With futures, it involves betting on future price movements.

Hedging
Using transactions to lower risk.

Long Hedges
Futures contracts are bought in anticipation of (or to guard against) price increases.

Short Hedges
Futures contracts are sold to guard against price declines.

---

[13] In Chapter 19, we discuss both the risks involved with holding foreign currencies and procedures for reducing such risks.

decrease the value of bond futures contracts. Therefore, if a firm or individual needs to guard against an *increase* in interest rates, a futures contract that makes money if rates rise should be used. That means selling, or going short, on a futures contract. To illustrate, assume that in August Carson Foods is considering a plan to issue $10,000,000 of 15-year bonds in December to finance a capital expenditure program. The interest rate would be 7 percent if the bonds were issued today, and at that rate the project would have a positive NPV. However, interest rates may rise over the next four months, and when the issue is actually sold, the interest rate might be substantially above 7 percent, which would make the project a bad investment. Carson can protect itself against a rise in rates by hedging in the futures market.

In this situation, Carson would be hurt by an increase in interest rates, so it would use a short hedge. It would choose a futures contract on that security most similar to the one it plans to issue, long-term bonds. In this case, Carson would probably hedge with Treasury bond futures. Since it plans to issue $10,000,000 of bonds, it would sell $10,000,000/$100,000 = 100 Treasury bond contracts for delivery in December. Carson would have to put up 100($1,553) = $155,300 in margin money and also pay brokerage commissions. For illustrative purposes we use the numbers in Table 18-3. We can see from Table 18-3 that each December contract has a value of 116 plus $5/32$ percent, so the total value of the 100 contracts is 1.1615625($100,000)(100) = $11,615,625. Now suppose renewed fears of inflation push the interest rate on Carson's debt up by 100 basis points, to 8 percent, over the next four months. If Carson issued 7 percent coupon bonds, they would bring only $913.54 per bond, because investors now require an 8 percent return. Thus, Carson would lose $86.46 per bond times 10,000 bonds, or $864,602, as a result of delaying the financing. However, the increase in interest rates would also bring about a change in the value of Carson's short position in the futures market. Interest rates have increased, so the value of the futures contract would fall, and if the interest rate on the futures contract also increased by the same full percentage point, from 4.5 to 5.5 percent, the contract value would fall to $10,506,233. Carson would then close its position in the futures market by repurchasing for $10,506,233 the contracts which it earlier sold short for $11,615,625, giving it a profit of $1,109,392, less commissions.

Thus, Carson would, if we ignore commissions and the opportunity cost of the margin money, offset the loss on the bond issue. In fact, in our example Carson more than offsets the loss, pocketing an additional $244,790. Of course, if interest rates had fallen, Carson would have lost on its futures position, but this loss would have been offset by the fact that Carson could now sell its bonds with a lower coupon.

If futures contracts existed on Carson's own debt, and interest rates moved identically in the spot and futures markets, then the firm could construct a **perfect hedge,** in which gains on the futures contract would exactly offset losses on the bonds. In reality, it is virtually impossible to construct perfect hedges, because in most cases the underlying asset is not identical to the futures asset, and even when they are, prices (and interest rates) may not move exactly together in the spot and futures markets.

Note too that if Carson had been planning an equity offering, and if its stock tended to move fairly closely with one of the stock indexes, the company could have hedged against falling stock prices by selling short the index future. Even better, if options on Carson's stock were traded in the option market, then it could use options rather than futures to hedge against falling stock prices.

The futures and options markets permit flexibility in the timing of financial transactions, because the firm can be protected, at least partially, against changes that occur between the time a decision is reached and the time when

Perfect Hedge
Occurs when the gain or loss on the hedged transaction exactly offsets the loss or gain on the unhedged position.

the transaction will be completed. However, this protection has a cost—the firm must pay commissions. Whether or not the protection is worth the cost is a matter of judgment. The decision to hedge also depends on management's risk aversion as well as the company's strength and ability to assume the risk in question. In theory, the reduction in risk resulting from a hedge transaction should have a value exactly equal to the cost of the hedge. Thus, a firm should be indifferent to hedging. However, many firms believe that hedging is worthwhile. Trammell Crow, a large Texas real estate developer, has used T-bill futures to lock in interest costs on floating-rate construction loans, while Dart & Kraft has used eurodollar futures to protect its marketable securities portfolio. Merrill Lynch, Salomon Smith Barney, and the other investment banking houses hedge in the futures and options markets to protect themselves when they are engaged in major underwritings.

Swaps

A *swap* is another method for reducing financial risks. As we noted earlier, a swap is an exchange.[14] In finance, it is an exchange of cash payment obligations, in which each party to the swap prefers the payment type or pattern of the other party. In other words, swaps occur because the counterparties prefer the terms of the other's debt contract, and the swap enables each party to obtain a preferred payment obligation. Generally, one party has a fixed-rate obligation and the other a floating-rate obligation, or one has an obligation denominated in one currency and the other in another currency.

Major changes have occurred over time in the swaps market. First, standardized contracts have been developed for the most common types of swaps, and this has had two effects: (1) Standardized contracts lower the time and effort involved in arranging swaps, and thus lower transactions costs. (2) The development of standardized contracts has led to a secondary market for swaps, which has increased the liquidity and efficiency of the swaps market. A number of international banks now make markets in swaps and offer quotes on several standard types. Also, as noted above, the banks now take counterparty positions in swaps, so it is not necessary to find another firm with mirror-image needs before a swap transaction can be completed. The bank would generally find a final counterparty for the swap at a later date, so its positioning helps make the swap market more operationally efficient.

To further illustrate a swap transaction, consider the following situation. An electric utility currently has outstanding a five-year floating-rate note tied to the prime rate. The prime rate could rise significantly over the period, so the note carries a high degree of interest rate risk. The utility could, however, enter into a swap with a counterparty, say, Citibank, wherein the utility would pay Citibank a fixed series of interest payments over the five-year period and Citibank would make the company's required floating-rate payments. As a result, the utility would have converted a floating-rate loan to a fixed-rate loan, and the risk of rising interest rates would have been passed from the utility to Citibank. Such a transaction can lower both parties' risks—because banks' revenues rise as interest rates rise, Citibank's risk would actually be lower if it had floating-rate obligations.

Longer-term swaps can also be made. Recently, Citibank entered into a 17-year swap in an electricity cogeneration project financing deal. The project's sponsors were unable to obtain fixed-rate financing on reasonable terms, and

[14] For more information on swaps, see Clifford W. Smith, Jr., Charles W. Smithson, and Lee Macdonald Wakeman, "The Evolving Market for Swaps," *Midland Corporate Finance Journal*, Winter 1986, pp. 20–32; and Mary E. Ruth and Steve R. Vinson, "Managing Interest Rate Uncertainty Amidst Change," *Public Utilities Fortnightly*, December 22, 1988, pp. 28–31.

they were afraid that interest rates would increase and make the project unprofitable. The project's sponsors were, however, able to borrow from local banks on a floating-rate basis and then arrange a simultaneous swap with Citibank for a fixed-rate obligation.

18-9b Commodity Price Exposure

An excellent source to find information on physical commodities is from the New York Mercantile Exchange's Web site, http://www.nymex.com/index.aspx. NYMEX is the world's largest physical commodity futures exchange.

As we noted earlier, futures markets were established for many commodities long before they began to be used for financial instruments. We can use Porter Electronics, which uses large quantities of copper as well as several precious metals, to illustrate inventory hedging. Suppose that in August 2005, Porter foresaw a need for 100,000 pounds of copper in June 2006 for use in fulfilling a fixed-price contract to supply solar power cells to the U.S. government. Porter's managers are concerned that a strike by Chilean copper miners will occur, which could raise the price of copper in world markets and possibly turn the expected profit on the solar cells into a loss.

Porter could, of course, go ahead and buy the copper that it will need to fulfill the contract, but if it does it will incur substantial carrying costs. As an alternative, the company could hedge against increasing copper prices in the futures market. The New York Commodity Exchange trades standard copper futures contracts of 25,000 pounds each. Thus, Porter could buy four contracts (go long) for delivery in June 2006. Assume that these contracts were trading in August for about $1.47 per pound, and that the spot price at that date was about $1.74 per pound. If copper prices continue to rise appreciably over the next 10 months, the value of Porter's long position in copper futures would increase, thus offsetting some of the price increase in the commodity itself. Of course, if copper prices fall, Porter would lose money on its futures contract, but the company would be buying the copper on the spot market at a cheaper price, so it would make a higher-than-anticipated profit on its sale of solar cells. Thus, hedging in the copper futures market locks in the cost of raw materials and removes some risk to which the firm would otherwise be exposed.

Eastman Kodak uses silver futures to hedge against short-term increases in the price of silver, which is the primary ingredient in black-and-white film. Many other manufacturers, such as Alcoa with aluminum and Archer Daniels Midland with grains, routinely use the futures markets to reduce the risks associated with input price volatility.

18-9c The Use and Misuse of Derivatives

Most of the news stories about derivatives are related to financial disasters. Much less is heard about the benefits of derivatives. However, because of these benefits, more than 90 percent of large U.S. companies use derivatives on a regular basis. In today's market, sophisticated investors and analysts are demanding that firms use derivatives to hedge certain risks. For example, Compaq Computer was sued by a shareholder group for failing to properly hedge its foreign exchange exposure. The shareholders lost the suit, but Compaq got the message and now uses currency futures to hedge its international operations. In another example, Prudential Securities reduced its earnings estimate for Cone Mills, a North Carolina textile company, because Cone did not sufficiently hedge its exposure to changing cotton prices. These examples lead to one conclusion: If a company can safely and inexpensively hedge its risks, it should do so.

There can, however, be a downside to the use of derivatives. Hedging is invariably cited by authorities as a "good" use of derivatives, whereas speculating with derivatives is often cited as a "bad" use. Some people and organizations can afford to bear the risks involved in speculating with derivatives, but others are either not sufficiently knowledgeable about the risks they are taking or else should not be taking those risks in the first place. Most would agree that the typical corporation should use derivatives only to hedge risks, not to speculate in an effort to increase profits. Hedging allows managers to concentrate on running their core businesses without having to worry about interest rate, currency, and commodity price variability. However, problems can arise quickly when hedges are improperly constructed or when a corporate treasurer, eager to report relatively high returns, uses derivatives for speculative purposes.

Explain how a company can use the futures market to hedge against rising interest rates.

What is a swap? Describe the mechanics of a fixed-rate to floating-rate swap.

Explain how a company can use the futures market to hedge against rising raw materials prices.

How should derivatives be used in risk management? What problems can occur?

Tying It All Together

Companies face a variety of risks every day, for it is hard to succeed without taking some chances. Back in Chapter 8, we discussed the trade-off between risk and return. If some action can lower risk without lowering returns too much, then the action can enhance value. With this in mind, in this chapter we described the various types of risks that companies face and the basic principles of corporate risk management. One important tool for managing risk is the derivatives market, and this chapter provided an introduction to derivative securities.

SELF-TEST QUESTIONS AND PROBLEMS
(Solutions Appear in Appendix A)

ST-1   **Key terms** Define each of the following terms:
   a.   Derivative
   b.   Option; call option; put option
   c.   Exercise value; strike price
   d.   Black-Scholes Option Pricing Model; riskless hedge
   e.   Risk management
   f.   Futures contract; forward contract
   g.   Hedging; natural hedge; long hedges; short hedges; perfect hedge
   h.   Swap; structured note
   i.   Commodity futures; financial futures
   j.   Long-term Equity AnticiPation Security (LEAPS)
   k.   Inverse floater
   l.   Speculation

ST-2 **Black-Scholes model** An analyst is interested in using the Black-Scholes model to value call options on the stock of Ledbetter Inc. The analyst has accumulated the following information:
- The price of the stock is $33.
- The strike price is $33.
- The option matures in 6 months (t = 0.50).
- The standard deviation of the stock's returns is 0.30 and the variance is 0.09.
- The risk-free rate is 10 percent.

Given this information, the analyst is then able to calculate some other necessary components of the Black-Scholes model:
- $d_1 = 0.34177$.
- $d_2 = 0.12964$.
- $N(d_1) = 0.63369$.
- $N(d_2) = 0.55155$.

$N(d_1)$ and $N(d_2)$ represent areas under a standard normal distribution function. Using the Black-Scholes model, what is the value of the call option?

QUESTIONS

18-1 List seven reasons risk management might increase the value of a firm.

18-2 Why do options typically sell at prices higher than their exercise values?

18-3 Discuss some of the techniques available to reduce risk exposure.

18-4 Explain how the futures markets can be used to reduce interest rate and input price risk.

18-5 How can swaps be used to reduce the risks associated with debt contracts?

18-6 Give two reasons stockholders might be indifferent between owning the stock of a firm with volatile cash flows and that of a firm with stable cash flows.

PROBLEMS

Easy
Problems 1–3

18-1 **Options** A call option on Bedrock Boulders stock has a market price of $7. The stock sells for $30 a share, and the option has an exercise price of $25 a share.

a. What is the exercise value of the call option?
b. What is the premium on the option?

18-2 **Options** The exercise price on one of Flanagan Company's options is $15, its exercise value is $22, and its premium is $5. What are the option's market value and the price of the stock?

18-3 **Options** Which of the following events are likely to increase the market value of a call option on a common stock? Explain.

a. An increase in the stock's price.
b. An increase in the volatility of the stock price.
c. An increase in the risk-free rate.
d. A decrease in the time until the option expires.

Intermediate
Problems 4–5

18-4 **Black-Scholes model** Assume you have been given the following information on Purcell Industries:

Current stock price = $15	Exercise price of option = $15
Time to maturity of option = 6 months	Risk-free rate = 10%
Variance of stock price = 0.12	$d_1 = 0.32660$
$d_2 = 0.08165$	$N(d_1) = 0.62795$
$N(d_2) = 0.53252$	

Using the Black-Scholes Option Pricing Model, what would be the value of the option?

18-5 **Futures** What is the implied interest rate on a Treasury bond ($100,000) futures contract that settled at 100-16? If interest rates increased by 1 percent, what would be the contract's new value?

Challenging Problems 6–7

18-6 **Hedging** The Zinn Company plans to issue $20,000,000 of 10-year bonds in December to help finance a new research and development laboratory. It is now August, and the current cost of debt to the high-risk biotech company is 11 percent. However, the firm's financial manager is concerned that interest rates will climb even higher in coming months.

    a.   Use data in Table 18-3 to create a hedge against rising interest rates.
    b.   Assume that interest rates in general increase by 200 basis points. How well did your hedge perform?
    c.   What is a perfect hedge? Are most real-world hedges perfect? Explain.

18-7 **Options** Audrey is considering an investment in Morgan Communications, whose stock currently sells for $60. A put option on Morgan's stock, with an exercise price of $55, has a market value of $3.06. Meanwhile, a call option on the stock with the same exercise price and time to maturity has a market value of $9.29. The market believes that at the expiration of the options the stock price will be either $70 or $50, with equal probability.

    a.   What is the premium associated with the put option? The call option?
    b.   If Morgan's stock price increases to $70, what would be the return to an investor who bought a share of the stock? If the investor bought a call option on the stock? If the investor bought a put option on the stock?
    c.   If Morgan's stock price decreases to $50, what would be the return to an investor who bought a share of the stock? If the investor bought a call option on the stock? If the investor bought a put option on the stock?
    d.   If Audrey buys 0.6 share of Morgan Communications and sells one call option on the stock, has she created a riskless hedged investment? What is the total value of her portfolio under each scenario?
    e.   If Audrey buys 0.75 share of Morgan Communications and sells one call option on the stock, has she created a riskless hedged investment? What is the total value of her portfolio under each scenario?

COMPREHENSIVE/SPREADSHEET PROBLEM

18-8 **Black-Scholes model** Rework Problem 18-4 using the spreadsheet model. Then work the next two parts of this problem given below.

    a.   Construct data tables for the intrinsic value and Black-Scholes exercise value for this option, and graph this relationship. Include possible stock price values ranging up to $30.00.
    b.   Suppose this call option is purchased today. Draw the profit diagram of this option position at expiration.

Integrated Case

Tropical Sweets Inc.

18-9 **Derivatives and corporate risk management** Assume that you have just been hired as a financial analyst by Tropical Sweets Inc., a mid-sized California company that specializes in creating exotic candies from tropical fruits such as mangoes, papayas, and dates. The firm's CEO, George Yamaguchi, recently returned from an industry corporate executive conference in San Francisco, and one of the sessions he attended was on the pressing need for smaller companies to institute corporate risk management programs. As no one at Tropical Sweets is familiar with the basics of derivatives and corporate risk management, Yamaguchi has asked you to prepare a brief report that the firm's executives could use to gain at least a cursory understanding of the topics.

To begin, you gathered some outside materials on derivatives and corporate risk management and used these materials to draft a list of pertinent questions that need to be answered. In fact, one possible approach to the paper is to use a question-and-answer format. Now that the questions have been drafted, you have to develop the answers.

a. Why might stockholders be indifferent to whether or not a firm reduces the volatility of its cash flows?
b. What are seven reasons risk management might increase the value of a corporation?
c. What is an option? What is the single most important characteristic of an option?
d. Options have a unique set of terminology. Define the following terms:
   (1) Call option.
   (2) Put option.
   (3) Exercise price.
   (4) Striking, or strike, price.
   (5) Option price.
   (6) Expiration date.
   (7) Exercise value.
   (8) Covered option.
   (9) Naked option.
   (10) In-the-money call.
   (11) Out-of-the-money call.
   (12) LEAPS.
e. Consider Tropical Sweets' call option with a $25 strike price. The following table contains historical values for this option at different stock prices:

Stock Price	Call Option Price
$25	$ 3.00
30	7.50
35	12.00
40	16.50
45	21.00
50	25.50

   (1) Create a table that shows (a) stock price, (b) strike price, (c) exercise value, (d) option price, and (e) the premium of option price over exercise value.
   (2) What happens to the premium of option price over exercise value as the stock price rises? Why?
f. In 1973, Fischer Black and Myron Scholes developed the Black-Scholes Option Pricing Model (OPM).
   (1) What assumptions underlie the OPM?
   (2) Write out the three equations that constitute the model.
   (3) What is the value of the following call option according to the OPM?

   Stock price = $27.00

   Exercise price = $25.00

   Time to expiration = 6 months

   Risk-free rate = 6.0%

   Stock return variance = 0.11

g. What effect does each of the following call option parameters have on the value of a call option?
   (1) Current stock price.
   (2) Exercise price.
   (3) Option's term to maturity.
   (4) Risk-free rate.
   (5) Variability of the stock price.
h. What are the differences between forward and futures contracts?
i. Explain briefly how swaps work.
j. Explain briefly how a firm can use futures and swaps to hedge risk.
k. What is corporate risk management? Why is it important to all firms?

cyberproblem

Please go to the ThomsonNOW Web site to access the Cyberproblems.

C H A P T E R

19

MULTINATIONAL FINANCIAL MANAGEMENT[1]

U.S. Firms Look Overseas to Enhance Shareholder Value

From the end of World War II until the 1970s, the United States dominated the world economy. However, that situation no longer exists. Raw materials, finished goods, services, and money flow freely across most national boundaries, as do innovative ideas and new technologies. World-class U.S. companies are making breakthroughs in foreign labs, obtaining capital from foreign investors, and putting foreign employees on the fast track to the top. Dozens of top U.S. manufacturers, including Dow Chemical, Colgate-Palmolive, Hewlett-Packard, and Xerox, sell more of their products outside the United States than they do at home. Service firms are not far behind, as Citigroup, Merrill Lynch, McDonald's, and AFLAC all receive more than 20 percent of their revenues from foreign sales.

The trend is even more pronounced in profits. In recent years, Coca-Cola and many other companies have made more money in the Pacific Rim and western Europe than in the United States. All told, Coke now reports that more than 75 percent of its operating profits come from outside of North America. As a result, economic events around the globe and changing exchange rates now have a profound effect on Coke's bottom line.

Successful global companies such as Coca-Cola must conduct business in different economies, and they must be sensitive to the many subtleties of different cultures and political systems. Accordingly, they find it useful to blend into the foreign landscape to help win product acceptance and avoid political problems. At the same time, foreign-based multinationals are arriving on American shores in ever greater numbers. Sweden's ABB, the Netherlands's Philips, France's Thomson, and Japan's Fujitsu and Honda are all waging campaigns to be

---

[1] This chapter was coauthored with Professor Roy Crum of the University of Florida.

identified as American companies that employ Americans, transfer technology to America, and help the U.S. trade balance. Few Americans know or care that Thomson owns the RCA and General Electric names in consumer electronics, or that Philips owns Magnavox.

The emergence of "world companies" raises a host of questions for governments. For example, should domestic firms be favored, or does it make no difference what a company's nationality is as long as it provides domestic jobs? Should a company make an effort to keep jobs in its home country, or should it produce where total production costs are lowest? What nation controls the technology developed by a multinational corporation, particularly if the technology can be used in military applications? Must a multinational company adhere to rules imposed in its home country with respect to its operations outside the home country? And if a U.S. firm such as Xerox produces copiers in Japan and then ships them to the United States, should they be reflected in the trade deficit in the same way as Toshiba copiers imported from Japan? Keep these questions in mind as you read this chapter. When you finish it, you should have a better appreciation of both the problems facing governments and the difficult but profitable opportunities facing managers of multinational companies.

Putting Things In Perspective

Managers of multinational companies must deal with a wide range of issues that are not present when a company operates in a single country. In this chapter, we highlight the key differences between multinational and domestic corporations, and we discuss the impact these differences have on the financial management of multinational businesses.

19-1 MULTINATIONAL OR GLOBAL CORPORATIONS

Multinational, or Global, Corporation
A firm that operates in an integrated fashion in a number of countries.

The term **multinational,** or **global, corporation** is used to describe a firm that operates in an integrated fashion in a number of countries. During the past 20 years, a new and fundamentally different form of international commercial activity has developed, and this has greatly increased worldwide economic and political interdependence. Rather than merely buying resources from and selling goods to foreign nations, multinational firms now make direct investments in fully integrated operations, from extraction of raw materials, through the manufacturing process, to distribution to consumers throughout the world. Today, multinational corporate networks control a large and growing share of the world's technological, marketing, and productive resources.

Companies, both U.S. and foreign, go "global" for seven primary reasons:

1. *To seek production efficiency.* As competition increases in their domestic marketplace, and as demand increases in other markets, companies often reassess where it is best to produce their products. Depending on the nature of the

production process, the availability of labor with the requisite skills, and the adequacy of transportation infrastructure, companies that operate in high-cost countries have strong incentives to shift production to lower-cost regions. For example, GE has production and assembly plants in Mexico, South Korea, and Singapore, and even Japanese manufacturers have started to shift some of their production to lower-cost countries in the Pacific Rim and the Americas. BMW, in response to high production costs in Germany, built assembly plants in the United States, among other countries. These examples illustrate how companies strive to remain competitive by locating manufacturing facilities wherever in the world they can produce and transport their products to meet the demand in their major markets at the lowest total unit landed costs.

2. *To avoid political, trade, and regulatory hurdles.* Governments sometimes impose tariffs, quotas, and other restrictions on imported goods and services. They often do so to raise revenue, protect domestic industries, and pursue various political and economic policy objectives. To circumvent these government hurdles, firms often develop production facilities abroad. For instance, the primary reason Japanese auto companies moved production to the United States was to get around U.S. import quotas. Now, Honda, Nissan, Toyota, Mazda, and Mitsubishi are all assembling vehicles in the United States. This was also the situation with India in the 1970s when it was following a development strategy to compete domestically with imported products. One of the factors that prompted U.S. pharmaceutical maker SmithKline and Britain's Beecham to merge was that they wanted to avoid licensing and regulatory delays in their largest markets, western Europe and the United States. GlaxoSmithKline (the result of a 2000 merger between Glaxo Wellcome and SmithKline Beecham) now identifies itself as an inside player in both Europe and the United States.

3. *To broaden their markets.* After a company's home market matures and competition becomes more intense, growth opportunities are often better in foreign markets. According to Vernon's product life-cycle theory, a firm first produces in its home market, where it can better develop its product and satisfy local customers.[2] This attracts competitors, but when the home market is expanding rapidly, new customers provide the sales growth desired. However, as the home market matures, and the growth of total demand slows, competition becomes more intense. At the same time, demand for the product develops abroad, and this creates conditions favoring production in foreign countries both to satisfy foreign demand and to cut production and transportation costs so that the company can remain competitive. Thus, such homegrown firms as IBM, Coca-Cola, and McDonald's are aggressively expanding into overseas markets, and foreign firms such as Sony and Toshiba now dominate the U.S. consumer electronics market. Also, as products become more complex, and development becomes more expensive, it is necessary to sell more units to cover overhead costs, so larger markets are critical.

4. *To seek raw materials and new technology.* Supplies of many raw materials that are important for industrial societies are geographically dispersed, so companies must go where the materials are found, no matter how challenging it may be to operate in some of the locations. For example, major deposits of oil are located on the northern coast of Alaska, in Siberia, and in the deserts of the Middle East, all of which present unique challenges. This is why many U.S. oil companies, such as ExxonMobil, have major production facilities around the world to ensure access to the basic input resources needed to sustain the companies' primary business line. Because ExxonMobil has refineries,

[2] Raymond Vernon, "International Investment and International Trade in the Product Cycle," *Quarterly Journal of Economics* Vol. 80 (1966), pp. 190–207.

Vertically Integrated Investment
Occurs when a firm undertakes an investment to secure its input supply at stable prices.

distribution facilities, and oil production fields, this type of investment is referred to as a **vertically integrated investment,** whereby the firm undertakes an investment to secure its supply of inputs at stable prices.

5. *To protect the secrecy of their processes and products.* Firms often possess special intangible assets such as brand names, technological and marketing know-how, managerial expertise, and superior research and development (R&D) capabilities among others. Unfortunately, property rights in intangible assets are often difficult to protect, particularly in foreign markets. Firms sometimes invest abroad rather than license local foreign firms in order to protect the secrecy of their production process, distribution system, or the product itself. Once a firm's formula or production process is revealed to other local firms, they may then more easily develop similar products or processes, which will hurt firm sales. For example, to protect their formula, Coke builds bottling plants and distribution networks in foreign markets but imports the concentrate or syrup required to make the product from the United States. In the 1960s, Coke faced strong pressure from the Indian government to reveal its formula in order to continue its operations in India. Rather than reveal its formula, Coke withdrew its operations from India until the foreign investment climate improved.

6. *To diversify.* By establishing worldwide production facilities and markets, firms can cushion the effect of adverse economic trends in any single country. For example, General Motors softened the blow of poor sales in the United States during a recent recession with strong sales by its European subsidiaries. Also, oil companies were able to weather the recent disruption in Venezuelan oil production by increasing production in Mexico and elsewhere in the world. In general, geographic diversification of inputs and outputs works because the economic fluctuations or political vagaries of different countries are not perfectly correlated. Therefore, companies investing overseas can benefit from diversification in the same way that individuals benefit from investing in a broad portfolio of stocks. However, because individual shareholders can diversify their investments internationally on their own, it makes less sense for firms to undertake foreign investments solely for diversification purposes. Note, though, that in countries that place constraints on foreign stock ownership or that do not have internationally traded companies, corporate diversification might make sense because then companies can do something that shareholders cannot duplicate easily in their individual portfolios.

7. *To retain customers.* If a company goes abroad and establishes production or distribution operations, it will need inputs and services at these new locations. If it can obtain what it needs from a single supplier that also operates in the same set of countries, then managing the relationship is much easier, and it is likely that economies of scale and other synergies will be obtained. Therefore, from the perspective of the supplier of inputs or services, it makes good business sense to follow customers abroad to retain the business. Large U.S. banks, such as Citibank and Chase, initially expanded abroad to supply banking services to their long-time customers, although they quickly capitalized on their global network to develop new customer relationships. The same history is also true for accounting, law, and advertising firms and other similar service providers.

Over the past 10 to 15 years, there has been an increasing amount of investment in the United States by foreign corporations, and in foreign nations by U.S. corporations. This trend is shown in Figure 19-1, and it is important because of its implications for eroding the traditional doctrine of independence and self-reliance that has been a hallmark of U.S. policy. Just as U.S. corporations with extensive overseas operations are said to use their economic power to exert substantial

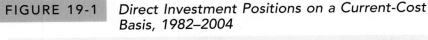

FIGURE 19-1 *Direct Investment Positions on a Current-Cost Basis, 1982–2004*

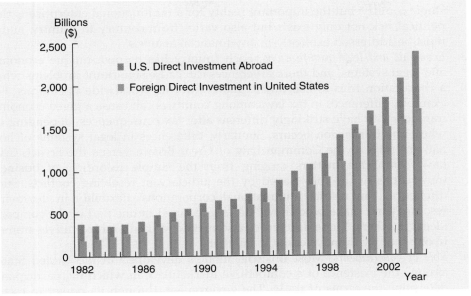

Sources: Elena L. Nguyen, "The International Investment Position of the United States at Yearend 2002," *Survey of Current Business*, July 2003, pp. 12–21; Patricia E. Abaroa, "The International Investment Position of the United States at Yearend 2003," *Survey of Current Business*, July 2004, pp. 30–39; and Bureau of Economic Analysis, "U.S. Net International Investment Position at Yearend 2004," *BEA News*, June 30, 2005.

economic and political influence over host governments in many parts of the world, it is feared that foreign corporations are gaining similar sway over U.S. policy. These developments suggest an increasing degree of mutual influence and interdependence among business enterprises and nations, to which the United States is not immune.

What is a multinational corporation?

Why do companies "go global"?

19-2 MULTINATIONAL VERSUS DOMESTIC FINANCIAL MANAGEMENT

In theory, the concepts and procedures discussed in the first 18 chapters are valid for both domestic and multinational operations. However, some additional factors need to be considered when firms operate globally. Five of these factors are listed here:

1. *Different currency denominations.* Cash flows in various parts of a multinational corporate system will be denominated in different currencies. Hence, an analysis of exchange rates must be included in all financial analyses.
2. *Political risk.* Nations are free to place constraints on the transfer or use of corporate resources, and they can change regulations and tax rules at any

time. At one extreme, they can even expropriate assets within their boundaries. Therefore, political risk can take on many subtle to more extreme forms. Of course, political risk is also present for companies operating in a single country, but the important reality for a multinational enterprise is that political risk not only exists but also varies from country to country, and it must be addressed explicitly in any financial analysis.

3. *Economic and legal ramifications.* Each country has its own unique economic and legal systems, and these differences can cause significant problems when a corporation tries to coordinate and control its worldwide operations. For example, differences in tax laws among countries can cause a given economic transaction to have strikingly different after-tax consequences, depending on where the transaction occurs. Similarly, differences in legal systems of host nations, such as the Common Law of Great Britain versus the French Civil Law, complicate matters ranging from the simple recording of business transactions to the role played by the judiciary in resolving conflicts. Such differences can restrict multinational corporations' flexibility in deploying resources and make procedures that are required in one part of the company illegal in others. These differences also make it difficult for executives trained in one country to move easily to another.

4. *Role of governments.* Most financial models developed in the United States assume the existence of a competitive marketplace in which the participants determine the terms of trade. The government, through its power to establish basic ground rules, is involved in the process, but other than taxes, its role is minimal. Thus, the market provides the primary barometer of success, and it gives the best clues about what must be done to remain competitive. This view of the process is reasonably correct for the United States and western Europe, but it does not accurately describe the situation in the rest of the world. Although market imperfections can complicate the decision process, they can also be valuable to the extent that they can be overcome by one firm but still serve as barriers to entry by competitors. Frequently, the terms under which companies compete, the actions that must be taken or avoided, and the terms of trade on various transactions are determined not in the marketplace but by direct negotiation between host governments and multinational enterprises. This is essentially a political process, and it must be treated as such. Thus, our traditional financial models have to be recast to include political and other noneconomic aspects of the decision. The ultimate outcome of such negotiations can provide access to additional profitable opportunities for the firm.

5. *Language and cultural differences.* The ability to communicate is critical in all business transactions. In this regard, U.S. citizens are often at a disadvantage because they are generally fluent only in English, while European and Japanese businesspeople are usually fluent in several languages, including English, hence they can operate in U.S. markets more easily than Americans can operate in their countries. At the same time, even within geographic regions that are considered relatively homogenous, different countries have unique cultural heritages that shape values and influence the conduct of business. Multinational corporations find that matters such as defining the appropriate goals of the firm, attitudes toward risk, decision processes, performance evaluation and compensation system design, interactions with employees, and the ability to curtail unprofitable operations vary dramatically from one country to the next.

These five factors complicate financial management, and they increase the risks faced by multinational firms. However, the prospects for high returns and other factors make it worthwhile for firms to accept these risks and learn how to manage them.

Identify and briefly discuss five major factors that complicate financial management in multinational firms.

19-3 THE INTERNATIONAL MONETARY SYSTEM

Every nation has a monetary system and a monetary authority. In the United States, the Federal Reserve is our monetary authority, and its task is to hold down inflation while promoting economic growth and raising our national standard of living. Moreover, if countries are to trade with one another, we must have some sort of system designed to facilitate payments between nations. The **international monetary system** is the framework within which exchange rates are determined. Because exchange rates are a function of the supply and demand for various national currencies, the international monetary system is also the blueprint for international trade and capital flows. Thus, the international monetary system ties together global currency, money, capital, real estate, commodity, and real asset markets into a network of institutions and instruments, regulated by intergovernmental agreements, and driven by each country's unique political and economic objectives.[3]

International Monetary System
The framework within which exchange rates are determined. It is the blueprint for international trade and capital flows.

19-3a International Monetary Terminology

When discussing the international monetary system, it is useful to introduce some important concepts and terminology:

1. An **exchange rate** is the price of one country's currency in terms of another currency. For example, on Monday, July 25, 2005, one U.S. dollar would buy 0.5724 British pound, 0.8286 euro, 1.2186 Canadian dollars, or 8.1097 Chinese yuan.

2. A *spot exchange rate* is the quoted price for a unit of foreign currency to be delivered "on the spot," or within a very short period of time. The rate quoted above, £0.5724/$, is a spot rate as of the close of business on July 25, 2005.

3. A *forward exchange rate* is the quoted price for a unit of foreign currency to be delivered at a specified date in the future. If today were July 25, 2005, and we wanted to know how many pounds we could expect to receive for our dollars on January 25, 2006, we would look at the six-month forward rate, which was £0.5740/$. Note that a *forward exchange contract* on July 25 would lock in this exchange rate, but no currency would change hands until January 25, 2006. The spot rate on January 25 might be quite different from £0.5740, in which case we would have a profit or a loss on the forward purchase.

4. A *fixed exchange rate* for a currency is set by the government and allowed to fluctuate only slightly (if at all) around the desired rate, called the *par value*. For example, Belize has fixed the exchange rate for the Belizean dollar at BZD 2.00/$1, and it has maintained this fixed rate for the past few years.

Exchange Rate
The number of units of a given currency that can be purchased for one unit of another currency.

*For a listing of world currencies, currency symbols, and their regimes, go to the University of British Columbia Sauder School of Business Pacific Exchange Rate Service Web site, **http:// fx.sauder.ubc.ca/ currency_table.html**.*

---

[3] For a comprehensive history of the international monetary system and details of how it has evolved, consult one of the many economics books on the subject, including Robert Carbaugh, *International Economics* (Mason, OH: Thomson/South-Western, 2004); Mordechai Kreinin, *International Economics: A Policy Approach*, 9th edition (Mason, OH: Thomson/South-Western, 2002); and Joseph P. Daniels and David D. Van Hoose, *International Monetary and Financial Economics*, 2nd edition (Mason, OH: Thomson/South-Western, 2002).

5. A *floating* or *flexible exchange rate* is one that is not regulated by the government, so supply and demand in the market determine the currency's value. The U.S. dollar and the euro are examples of free-floating currencies. Note, though, that central banks do from time to time intervene in the market to nudge exchange rates up or down, even though they basically float.

6. *Devaluation* or *revaluation of a currency* is the technical term referring to the decrease or increase in the par value of a currency whose value is fixed. This decision is made by the government, usually without warning. For example, on July 21, 2005, the Chinese government suddenly announced that it was revaluing the yuan to make it 2.1 percent stronger against the U.S. dollar. Even though it was widely believed that the yuan was significantly undervalued, this revaluation caught many by surprise since the exchange rate had been pegged at a fixed rate of CNY 8.2781/$ for nearly a decade.

7. *Depreciation* or *appreciation of a currency* refers to a decrease or increase in the foreign exchange value of a floating currency. These changes are caused by market forces rather than by governments.

8. A *soft* or *weak currency* is one that is expected to depreciate against most other currencies or else is being artificially maintained at an unrealistically high fixed rate by the government through open market purchases. A *hard* or *strong currency* is expected to appreciate against most other currencies or else is being artificially maintained by the government at an unrealistically low fixed rate. The revaluation of the Chinese yuan suggests that it is a strong currency.

19-3b Current Monetary Arrangements

At the most basic level, we can divide currency regimes into two broad groups: floating rates and fixed rates. Within the two regimes, there are graduations among subregimes in terms of how rigidly they adhere to the basic positions. Looking first at the floating-rate category, the two main subgroups are as follows:

Freely-Floating Regime
Occurs when the exchange rate is determined by supply and demand for the currency.

1. *Freely floating.* Here the exchange rate is determined by the supply and demand for the currency. Under a **freely-floating regime,** governments may occasionally intervene in the market to buy or sell their currency to stabilize fluctuations, but they do not attempt to alter the absolute level of the rate. This policy exists at one end of the continuum of exchange rate regimes. For example, the currencies of Australia, Brazil, and the Philippines are allowed to float.

Managed-Float Regime
Occurs when there is significant government intervention to control the exchange rate via manipulation of the currency's supply and demand.

2. *Managed floating.* Here there is significant government intervention to manage the exchange rate by manipulating the currency's supply and demand. The government rarely reveals its target exchange rate levels if it uses a **managed-float regime** because this would make it too easy for currency speculators to profit. For example, the governments of Colombia, Israel, and Poland manage their respective currency's float.

Most developed countries follow either a freely-floating or a managed-float regime. A few developing countries do as well, often reluctantly and as a result of a market that forces them to abandon a fixed-rate regime.

Types of fixed-exchange-rate regimes include the following:

1. *No local currency.* The most extreme position is for the country to have no local currency of its own. The country either uses another country's currency as its legal tender (such as the U.S. dollar in the Panama Canal Zone, Ecuador, and the Turks and Caicos Islands) or else belongs to a group of

countries that share a common currency (such as the euro). With this arrangement, the local government surrenders economic regulation.

2. *Currency board arrangement.* Under a variation of the first subregime, a country technically has its own currency but commits to exchange it for a specified foreign money unit at a fixed exchange rate. This requires it to impose domestic currency restrictions unless it has the foreign currency reserves to cover requested exchanges. This is called a **currency board arrangement**. Argentina had a currency board arrangement before its crisis of January 2002, when it was forced to devalue the peso and default on its debt.

3. *Fixed peg arrangement.* In a **fixed peg arrangement** the country locks, or "pegs," its currency to another currency or basket of currencies at a fixed exchange rate. It allows the currency to vary only slightly from its desired rate, and if the currency moves outside the specified limits (often set at ±1 percent of the target rate), it intervenes to force the currency back within the limits. An example is China, where the yuan is no longer just pegged to the U.S. dollar but rather to a basket of currencies. The Chinese government is keeping the currencies making up the basket secret, but the U.S. dollar will likely remain the most important. For right now (July 2005), China will limit the yuan's move each day to ±0.3 percent against the dollar. It's unclear whether it will move every day or how much it will move over time. Additional examples include Bhutan's ngultrum, which is pegged to the Indian rupee; the Falkland Islands' pound, which is pegged to the British pound; and Barbados's dollar, which is pegged to the U.S. dollar.

Other variations have been used, and new ones are developed from time to time. A majority of the world's countries employ some sort of fixed-exchange-rate arrangement. So, while the most important currencies (as measured by volume of transactions) are allowed to float, and the international monetary system is often called a floating regime, most currencies are actually fixed in some manner.

What is an international monetary system?

What is the difference between spot and forward exchange rates?

What is the difference between floating- and fixed-exchange rates?

Differentiate between devaluation/revaluation of a currency and depreciation/appreciation of a currency.

What is meant by a soft or weak currency? A hard or strong currency?

What are the two broad categories of the various currency regimes? What are the subgroups of these two broad categories?

19-4 FOREIGN EXCHANGE RATE QUOTATIONS

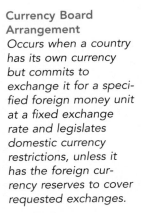

Foreign exchange rate quotations can be found in *The Wall Street Journal* and other leading print publications and Web sites. Exchange rates are given in two different ways. As shown in Table 19-1, which is an excerpt from *The Wall Street Journal*, in Column 1, they are quoted as "USD equivalent" and in Column 2 as "Currency per USD." For example, one Canadian dollar is worth (or can be exchanged for) 0.8206 U.S. dollar, or one U.S. dollar could buy 1.2186 Canadian dollars.

Currency Board Arrangement
Occurs when a country has its own currency but commits to exchange it for a specified foreign money unit at a fixed exchange rate and legislates domestic currency restrictions, unless it has the foreign currency reserves to cover requested exchanges.

Fixed Peg Arrangement
Occurs when a country locks its currency to a specific currency or basket of currencies at a fixed exchange rate. The exchange rate is allowed to vary only within ±1 percent of the target rate.

For up-to-date currency quotations on the Web, visit two popular sites: **www.bloomberg.com/ markets/currencies/fxc .html** *or* **finance.yahoo .com/currency.**

| TABLE 19-1 | *Sample Exchange Rates: Monday, July 25, 2005* |

	Direct Quotation: U.S. Dollars Required to Buy One Unit of Foreign Currency (1)	Indirect Quotation: Number of Units of Foreign Currency per U.S. Dollar (2)
Brazilian real	$0.4025	2.4845
British pound	1.7471	0.5724
Canadian dollar	0.8206	1.2186
Denmark krone	0.1618	6.1805
Euro	1.2069	0.8286
Hungarian forint	0.004918	203.33
Israeli shekel	0.2207	4.5310
Japanese yen	0.008974	111.43
Mexican peso	0.0931	10.7400
South African rand	0.1507	6.6357
Swedish krona	0.1281	7.8064
Swiss franc	0.7725	1.2945
Venezuelan bolivar	0.000466	2145.92

Note: Column 2 equals 1.0 divided by Column 1. However, rounding differences do occur.

Source: Adapted from *The Wall Street Journal*, July 26, 2005, p. C12.

Note that if the foreign exchange markets are in equilibrium, which is usually the case for the major traded currencies, then the two quotations must be reciprocals of one another as shown below for the Canadian dollar.

$$\text{Canadian dollar: } 1/1.2186 = 0.8206$$
$$1/0.8206 = 1.2186$$

19-4a Cross Rates

All of the exchange rates given in Table 19-1 are relative to the U.S. dollar. Suppose, though, that a German executive is flying to Tokyo on business. The exchange rate of interest is not euros or yen per dollar—rather, he or she wants to know how many yen can be purchased with euros. This is called a **cross rate,** and it can be calculated from the following data in Column 2 of Table 19-1:

Cross Rate
The exchange rate between any two currencies.

	Spot Rate
Euro	€0.8286/$1
Yen	¥111.43/$1

Because the quotations have the same denominator—one U.S. dollar—we can calculate the cross rate between these (and other) currencies by using the Column 2 quotations. For our German national, the cross rates are found as

$$\text{Euro/yen exchange rate} = \frac{\text{Euro/\$}}{\text{Yen/\$}}$$

and when we cancel the dollar signs, we are left with the number of euros 1 yen would cost.

$$€0.8286/¥111.43 = €0.007436/¥$$

	Dollar	Euro	Pound	SFranc	Peso	Yen	CdnDlr
TABLE 19-2 — *Key Currency Cross Rates*							
Canada	1.2186	1.4708	2.1291	0.9414	0.11347	0.01094	—
Japan	111.43	134.49	194.68	86.082	10.376	—	91.442
Mexico	10.7400	12.9621	18.764	8.2966	—	0.09638	8.8132
Switzerland	1.2945	1.5623	2.2616	—	0.12053	0.01162	1.0623
United Kingdom	0.57240	0.6908	—	0.4422	0.05329	0.00514	0.46969
Euro	0.82860	—	1.4476	0.64007	0.07715	0.00744	0.67992
United States	—	1.2069	1.7471	0.77250	0.09311	0.00897	0.82060

Source: Adapted from "Key Currency Cross Rates," *The Wall Street Journal*, July 26, 2005, p. C12.

Alternatively, we could find the number of yen 1 euro would buy:

$$\text{Yen/euro exchange rate} = \frac{\text{Yen/\$}}{\text{Euro/\$}}$$

$$¥111.43/€0.8286 = ¥134.48/€$$

Note that these two cross rates are reciprocals of one another.

Financial publications such as *The Wall Street Journal* and Web sites such as the Bloomberg and Yahoo sites provide tables of key currency cross rates. Table 19-2 gives the one published in *The Wall Street Journal* on July 26, 2005. Notice that there may be slight rounding differences when you calculate cross rates due to the rounding of individual quotations. Currency traders carry quotations out to 12 decimal places.

To facilitate worldwide currency trading through electronic media, the interbank foreign exchange market has adopted a system under which all quotations are given in European (Column 2) terms with a few exceptions. The exceptions—the euro, British pound, Australian dollar, and New Zealand dollar—are quoted in American terms (Column 1). Because of this convention, traders throughout the world see similar quotations on their computer screens, making it easy for them (and their computers) to compare rates quoted in different markets and to earn arbitrage profits if differences exist.

19-4b Interbank Foreign Currency Quotations

The quotations from *The Wall Street Journal* given in Tables 19-1 and 19-2 are sufficient for many purposes. For other purposes, however, additional terminology and conventions are useful. There are two ways to state the exchange rate between two currencies, either in **American** or **European terms.** Accordingly, we need to designate one of the currencies as the "home" currency and the other as the "foreign" currency. This designation is arbitrary. The *home* currency price of one unit of the *foreign* currency is called a **direct quotation.** Thus, to a person who considers the United States to be "home," American terms represent a direct quotation. On the other hand, the *foreign* currency price of one unit of the *home* currency is called an **indirect quotation.** European terms represent indirect quotations to people in the United States. Note that if the perspective changes and the "home" currency is no longer the U.S. dollar, then the designations of direct and indirect change. For the remainder of this chapter, we will assume that the United States is the "home" country, unless specifically stated otherwise.

American Terms
The foreign exchange rate quotation that represents the number of American dollars that can be bought with one unit of local currency.

European Terms
The foreign exchange rate quotation that represents the units of local currency that can be bought with one U.S. dollar. "European" is intended as a generic term that applies globally.

Direct Quotation
The home currency price of one unit of the foreign currency.

Indirect Quotation
The foreign currency price of one unit of the home currency.

Explain the difference between direct and indirect quotations.

What is a cross rate?

Assume that today 1 Canadian dollar is worth 0.75 U.S. dollar. How many Canadian dollars would you receive for 1 U.S. dollar? (1.333)

Assume that 1 U.S. dollar can either be exchanged for 105 Japanese yen or for 0.80 euro. What is the Euro/yen exchange rate? (€0.007619/¥)

Updated currency spot and forward rates (from 1 to 12 months) are provided by the Bank of Montreal Financial Group's Economic Research and Analysis at http://www .bmo.com/economic/ regular/fxrates.html.

19-5 TRADING IN FOREIGN EXCHANGE

Importers, exporters, tourists, and governments buy and sell currencies in the foreign exchange market. For example, when a U.S. trader imports automobiles from Japan, payment will probably be made in Japanese yen. The importer buys yen (through its bank) in the foreign exchange market, much as one buys common stocks on the New York Stock Exchange or pork bellies on the Chicago Mercantile Exchange. However, whereas stock and commodity exchanges have organized trading floors, the foreign exchange market consists of a network of brokers and banks based in New York, London, Tokyo, and other financial centers. Most buy and sell orders are conducted by computer and telephone.[4]

19-5a Spot Rates and Forward Rates

Spot Rate
The effective exchange rate of a foreign currency for delivery on (approximately) the current day.

Forward Exchange Rate
An agreed-upon price at which two currencies will be exchanged at some future date.

The exchange rates shown earlier in Tables 19-1 and 19-2 are known as **spot rates,** which means the rate paid for delivery of the currency "on the spot" or, in reality, no more than two days after the day of the trade. For most of the world's major currencies, it is also possible to buy (or sell) currencies for delivery at some agreed-upon future date, usually 30, 90, or 180 days from the day the transaction is negotiated. This rate is known as the **forward exchange rate.**

For example, suppose a U.S. firm must pay 500 million yen to a Japanese firm in 30 days, and the current spot rate is 111.43 yen per dollar. Unless spot rates change, the U.S. firm will pay the Japanese firm the equivalent of $4.487 million (500 million yen divided by 111.43 yen per dollar) in 30 days. But if the spot rate falls to 100 yen per dollar, for example, the U.S. firm will have to pay the equivalent of $5 million. The treasurer of the U.S. firm can avoid this risk by entering into a 30-day forward exchange contract. This contract promises delivery of yen to the U.S. firm in 30 days at a guaranteed price of 111.09 yen per dollar. No cash changes hands at the time the treasurer signs the forward contract, although the U.S. firm might have to put some collateral down as a guarantee against default. Because the firm can use an interest-bearing instrument for the collateral, though, this requirement is not costly. The counterparty to the forward contract must deliver the yen to the U.S. firm in 30 days, and the U.S. firm is obligated to purchase the 500 million yen at the previously agreed-upon rate of 111.09 yen per dollar. Therefore, the treasurer of the U.S. firm is able to lock in a payment equivalent to $4.501 million, no matter what happens to spot rates. This technique, which is called "hedging," was discussed in Chapter 18.

---

[4] For a more detailed explanation of exchange rate determination and operations of the foreign exchange market, see Roy L. Crum, Eugene F. Brigham, and Joel F. Houston, *Fundamentals of International Finance* (Mason, OH: Thomson/South-Western, 2005).

TABLE 19-3 *Selected Spot and Forward Exchange Rates (Number of Units of Foreign Currency per U.S. Dollar)*

| | Spot Rate | FORWARD RATES | | | Forward Rate at a Premium or Discount |
		30 Days	90 Days	180 Days	
British pound	0.5724	0.5730	0.5737	0.5740	Discount
Canadian dollar	1.2186	1.2177	1.2158	1.2120	Premium
Japanese yen	111.43	111.09	110.41	109.28	Premium
Swiss franc	1.2945	1.2913	1.2850	1.2740	Premium

Notes:
a. These are representative quotes as provided by a sample of New York banks. Forward rates for other currencies and for other lengths of time can often be negotiated.
b. When it takes more units of a foreign currency to buy one dollar in the future, the value of the foreign currency is less in the forward market than in the spot market, hence the forward rate is at a discount to the spot rate. Likewise, when it takes less units of a foreign currency to buy one dollar in the future, the value of the foreign currency is more in the forward market than in the spot market, hence the forward rate is at a premium to the spot rate.

Source: Adapted from *The Wall Street Journal*, July 26, 2005, p. C12.

Forward rates for 30-, 90-, and 180-day delivery, along with the current spot rates for some commonly traded currencies, are given in Table 19-3. If we can obtain *more* of the foreign currency for a dollar in the forward than in the spot market, the forward currency is less valuable than the spot currency, and the forward currency is said to be selling at a **discount.** Conversely, if we can obtain less of the foreign currency for a dollar in the forward than in the spot market, the forward currency is more valuable than the spot currency, and the forward currency is said to be selling at a **premium.** Thus, because a dollar would buy *fewer* Canadian dollars, yen, and Swiss francs in the forward than in the spot market, the forward Canadian dollars, yen, and Swiss francs are selling at a premium. On the other hand, a dollar would buy more pounds in the forward than in the spot market, so the forward pounds are selling at a discount.

> **Discount on Forward Rate**
> *The situation when the spot rate is less than the forward rate.*
>
> **Premium on Forward Rate**
> *The situation when the spot rate is greater than the forward rate.*

Explain what it means for a forward currency to sell at a discount and at a premium.

Suppose a U.S. firm must pay 200 million Swiss francs to a Swiss firm in 90 days. Briefly explain how the firm would use forward exchange rates to "lock in" the price of the payable due in 90 days.

19-6 INTEREST RATE PARITY

Market forces determine whether a currency sells at a forward premium or discount, and the general relationship between spot and forward exchange rates is specified by a concept called "interest rate parity."

Interest rate parity holds that investors should earn the same return on security investments in all countries after adjusting for risk. It recognizes that when you invest in a country other than your home country, you are affected by two forces—returns on the investment itself and changes in the exchange rate. It

> **Interest Rate Parity**
> *Specifies that investors should expect to earn the same return in all countries after adjusting for risk.*

follows that your overall return will be higher than the investment's stated return if the currency in which your investment is denominated appreciates relative to your home currency. Likewise, your overall return will be lower if the foreign currency you receive declines in value.

The relationship between spot and forward exchange rates and interest rates, which is known as interest rate parity, is expressed in the following equation:

$$\frac{\text{Forward exchange rate}}{\text{Spot exchange rate}} = \frac{(1 + r_h)}{(1 + r_f)}$$

Here both the forward and spot rates are expressed in terms of the amount of home currency received per unit of foreign currency, and r_h and r_f are the periodic interest rates in the home country and the foreign country, respectively. If this relationship does not hold, then currency traders will buy and sell currencies—that is, engage in *arbitrage*—until it does hold.

To illustrate interest rate parity, consider the case of a U.S. investor who can buy default-free 90-day Japanese bonds that promise a 4 percent nominal return. The 90-day interest rate, r_f, is $4\%/4 = 1\%$ because 90 days is one-fourth of a 360-day year. Assume also that the spot exchange rate is $0.008974, which means that you can exchange 0.008974 dollar for 1 yen, or 111.43 yen per dollar. Finally, assume that the 90-day forward exchange rate is $0.009057, which means that you can exchange 1 yen for 0.009057 dollar, or receive 110.41 yen per dollar exchanged, 90 days from now.

The U.S. investor can receive a 4 percent annualized return denominated in yen, but if he or she ultimately wants to consume goods in the United States, those yen must be converted to dollars. The dollar return on the investment depends, therefore, on what happens to exchange rates over the next three months. However, the investor can lock in the dollar return by selling the foreign currency in the forward market. For example, the investor could simultaneously

- Convert $1,000 to 111,430 yen in the spot market.
- Invest the 111,430 yen in 90-day Japanese bonds that have a 4 percent annualized return or a 1 percent quarterly return, hence will pay (111,430)(1.01) = 112,544.30 yen in 90 days.
- Agree today to exchange these 112,544.30 yen 90 days from now at the 90-day forward exchange rate of 110.41 yen per dollar, or for a total of $1,019.33.

This investment, therefore, has an expected 90-day return of $19.33/$1,000 = 1.933%, which translates into a nominal return of 4(1.933%) = 7.73%. In this case, 4 percent of the expected 7.73 percent return is coming from the bond itself, and 3.73 percent arises because the market believes the yen will strengthen relative to the dollar. Note that by locking in the forward rate today, the investor has eliminated any exchange rate risk. And, because the Japanese bond is assumed to be default-free, the investor is assured of earning a 7.73 percent dollar return.

Interest rate parity implies that an investment in the United States with the same risk as a Japanese bond should have an annual return of 7.73 percent. Solving for r_h in the parity equation, we indeed find that the predicted annual interest rate in the United States is 7.73 percent.

Interest rate parity shows why a particular currency might be at a forward premium or discount. Note that a currency is at a forward premium whenever domestic interest rates are higher than foreign interest rates. Discounts prevail if domestic interest rates are lower than foreign interest rates. If these conditions do not hold, then arbitrage will soon force interest rates back to parity.

What is interest rate parity?

Assume interest rate parity holds. When a currency trades at a forward premium, what does that imply about domestic rates relative to foreign interest rates? When a currency trades at a forward discount?

Assume that 90-day U.S. securities have a 3.5 percent annualized interest rate, whereas 90-day Canadian securities have a 4 percent annualized interest rate. In the spot market, 1 U.S. dollar can be exchanged for 1.4 Canadian dollars. If interest rate parity holds, what is the 90-day forward exchange rate between U.S. and Canadian dollars? ($0.7134/C$ or C$1.40173/$)

On the basis of your answer to the previous question, is the Canadian dollar selling at a premium or discount on the forward rate? (Discount)

19-7 PURCHASING POWER PARITY

We have discussed exchange rates in some detail, and we have considered the relationship between spot and forward exchange rates. However, we have not yet addressed the fundamental question, What determines the spot level of exchange rates in each country? While exchange rates are influenced by a multitude of factors that are difficult to predict, particularly on a day-to-day basis, over the long run market forces work to ensure that similar goods sell for similar prices in different countries after taking exchange rates into account. This relationship is known as "purchasing power parity."

Purchasing power parity (PPP), sometimes referred to as the *law of one price*, implies that the level of exchange rates adjusts so as to cause identical goods to cost the same amount in different countries. For example, if a pair of tennis shoes costs $150 in the United States and 100 pounds in Britain, PPP implies that the exchange rate be $1.50 per pound. Consumers could purchase the shoes in Britain for 100 pounds, or they could exchange their 100 pounds for $150 and then purchase the same shoes in the United States at the same effective cost, assuming no transactions or transportation costs. The equation for purchasing power parity is shown here:

> **Purchasing Power Parity (PPP)**
> *The relationship in which the same products cost roughly the same amount in different countries after taking into account the exchange rate.*

$$P_h = (P_f)(\text{Spot rate})$$

or

$$\text{Spot rate} = \frac{P_h}{P_f}$$

Here

> P_h = the price of the good in the home country ($150, assuming the United States is the home country).
> P_f = the price of the good in the foreign country (100 pounds).

Note that the spot market exchange rate is expressed as the number of units of home currency that can be exchanged for one unit of foreign currency ($1.50 per pound).

PPP assumes that market forces will eliminate situations in which the same product sells at a different price overseas. For example, if the shoes cost $140 in the United States, importers/exporters could purchase them in the United States for $140, sell them for 100 pounds in Britain, exchange the 100 pounds for $150 in the foreign exchange market, and earn a profit of $10 on every pair of shoes.

Ultimately, this trading activity would increase the demand for shoes in the United States and thus raise P_h, increase the supply of shoes in Britain and thus reduce P_f, and increase the demand for dollars in the foreign exchange market and thus reduce the spot rate. Each of these actions works to restore PPP.

Note that PPP assumes that there are no transportation or transactions costs, or import restrictions, all of which limit the ability to ship goods between countries. In many cases, these assumptions are incorrect, which explains why PPP is often violated. An additional complication, when empirically testing to see whether PPP holds, is that products in different countries are rarely identical. Frequently, there are real or perceived differences in quality, which can lead to price differences in different countries.

Still, the concepts of interest rate and purchasing power parity are critically important to those engaged in international activities. Companies and investors must anticipate changes in interest rates, inflation, and exchange rates, and they often try to hedge the risks of adverse movements in these factors. The parity relationships are extremely useful when anticipating future conditions.

What is purchasing power parity?

A television set sells for $1,000 U.S. dollars. In the spot market, $1 = 110 Japanese yen. If purchasing power parity holds, what should be the price (in yen) of the same television set in Japan? (¥110,000)

Price differences in "similar" products in different countries often exist. What can explain these differences?

19-8 INFLATION, INTEREST RATES, AND EXCHANGE RATES

Relative inflation rates, or the rates of inflation in foreign countries compared with that in the home country, have many implications for multinational financial decisions. Obviously, relative inflation rates will greatly influence future production costs at home and abroad. Equally important, inflation has a dominant influence on relative interest rates and exchange rates. Both of these factors influence the methods chosen by multinational corporations for financing their foreign investments, and both have an important effect on the profitability of foreign investments.

The currencies of countries with higher inflation rates than that of the United States by definition *depreciate* over time against the dollar. Countries where this has occurred include Mexico and all the South American nations. On the other hand, the currencies of Canada, Switzerland, and Japan, which have had less inflation than the United States, have *appreciated* against the dollar. *In fact, a foreign currency will, on average, depreciate or appreciate at a percentage rate approximately equal to the amount by which its inflation rate exceeds or is less than our own.*

Relative inflation rates also affect interest rates. The interest rate in any country is largely determined by its inflation rate. Therefore, countries currently experiencing higher inflation rates than the United States also tend to have higher interest rates. The reverse is true for countries with lower inflation rates.

It is tempting for a multinational corporation to borrow in countries with the lowest interest rates. However, this is not always a good strategy. Suppose, for example, that interest rates in Switzerland are lower than those in the United States because of Switzerland's lower inflation rate. A U.S. multinational firm could therefore save interest by borrowing in Switzerland. However, because of relative inflation rates, the Swiss franc will probably appreciate in the future, causing the dollar cost of annual interest and principal payments on Swiss debt to rise over time. Thus, *the lower interest rate could be more than offset by losses from currency appreciation.* Similarly, multinational corporations should not necessarily avoid borrowing in a country such as Brazil, where interest rates have been very high, because future depreciation of the Brazilian real could make such borrowing relatively inexpensive.

What effects do relative inflation rates have on relative interest rates?

What happens over time to the currencies of countries with higher inflation rates than that of the United States? To those with lower inflation rates?

Why might a multinational corporation decide to borrow in a country such as Brazil, where interest rates are high, rather than in a country like Switzerland, where interest rates are low?

19-9 INTERNATIONAL MONEY AND CAPITAL MARKETS

One way for U.S. citizens to invest in world markets is to buy the stocks of U.S. multinational corporations that invest directly in foreign countries. Another way is to purchase foreign securities—stocks, bonds, or money market instruments issued by foreign companies. Security investments are known as *portfolio investments,* and they are distinguished from *direct investments* in physical assets by U.S. corporations.

From World War II through the 1960s, the U.S. capital markets dominated world markets. Today, however, the value of U.S. securities represents less than one-fourth the value of all securities. Given this situation, it is important for both corporate managers and investors to have an understanding of international markets. Moreover, these markets often offer better opportunities for raising or investing capital than are available domestically.

19-9a International Credit Markets

There are three major types of credit markets in the international marketplace that mirror equivalent U.S. markets in many ways. Floating-rate bank loans, called **eurocredits**, are tied to a standard rate known by the acronym LIBOR, which stands for *London Inter Bank Offer Rate.* LIBOR is the interest rate offered by the largest and strongest London-based banks on large deposits. In July 2005, the three-month LIBOR rate was 3.6 percent. Eurocredits tend to be issued for a fixed term with no early repayment. The oldest example of a eurocredit is a **eurodollar** deposit, which is U.S. dollars deposited in a bank outside the United States. Today, eurocredits exist for most major trading currencies.

The eurobond market is the medium- to long-term international market for both fixed- and floating-rate debt. It is almost as old as the eurodollar market and is a natural extension of it. A **eurobond** is an international bond underwritten by an international bank syndicate and sold to investors in countries other than the one in whose money unit the bond is denominated. Thus, U.S. dollar–denominated eurobonds cannot be sold in the United States, sterling eurobonds cannot be sold in the United Kingdom, and yen eurobonds cannot be sold in Japan. This is a true international debt instrument and is usually issued in bearer form, which means that the owner's identity is not registered and known; to receive the interest payments the owner must clip a coupon and present it for payment at one of the designated payor banks. Most eurobonds are

Eurocredits
Floating-rate bank loans, available in most major trading currencies, that are tied to LIBOR.

Eurodollar
A U.S. dollar deposited in a bank outside the United States.

Eurobond
An international bond underwritten by an international syndicate of banks and sold to investors in countries other than the one in whose money unit the bond is denominated.

Hungry for a Big Mac?
Go to China!

Purchasing power parity (PPP) implies that the same product will sell for the same price in every country after adjusting for current exchange rates. One problem when testing to see if PPP holds is that it assumes that goods consumed in different countries are of the same quality. For example, if you find that a product is more expensive in Switzerland than it is in Canada, one explanation is that PPP fails to hold, but another explanation is that the product sold in Switzerland is of a higher quality and therefore deserves a higher price.

One way to test for PPP is to find goods that have the same quality worldwide. With this in mind, *The Economist* magazine occasionally compares the prices of a well-known good whose quality is the same in 118 different countries: the McDonald's Big Mac hamburger.

The tables shown in Panels A and B on the next page provide information collected during 2005. The Panel A table gives the price of a Big Mac in each country's local currency and the actual dollar exchange rate when these data were collected. In Panel B, the first numeric column calculates the price of the Big Mac in terms of the U.S. dollar—this is obtained by dividing the local price by the actual exchange rate at that time. For example, a Big Mac costs 6.30 Swiss francs in Zurich, which is shown in Panel A. Given an exchange rate of 1.25 Swiss francs per dollar (as shown in Panel A), this implies that the dollar price of a Big Mac is 6.30 Swiss francs/1.25 Swiss francs per dollar ≈ $5.05, shown in Panel B.

The second numeric column in Panel B backs out the implied exchange rate that would hold under PPP. This is obtained by dividing the price of the Big Mac in each local currency by its U.S. price. For example, as shown in Panel A, a Big Mac costs 41.92 rubles in Russia and $3.06 in the United States. If PPP holds, the exchange rate should be 13.7 rubles per dollar (41.92 rubles/$3.06), which is shown in Panel B.

Comparing the implied exchange rate (shown in Panel B) to the actual exchange rate (shown in Panel A), we see the extent to which the local currency is under- or overvalued relative to the dollar. Given that

the actual exchange rate at the time was 28.33 rubles per dollar, this implies that the ruble was 52 percent undervalued, which is shown in the last column of Panel B.

The evidence suggests that strict PPP does not hold, but recent research suggests that the Big Mac test may shed some insights about where exchange rates are headed. The average price of a Big Mac within the European Monetary Union (EMU) is 2.91 euros. This implies that the euro's PPP is $1.05, so at its current rate of $1.23 the euro is overvalued by 17 percent.

England, Sweden, Switzerland, and Denmark—four European countries that are not part of the EMU—have currencies that are significantly overvalued against the dollar. The British pound is overvalued by 12 percent, the Swedish krona is overvalued by 36 percent, the Swiss franc is overvalued by 65 percent, and the Danish krone is overvalued by 50 percent. In contrast, the Japanese yen is the most undervalued rich-world currency—by 23 percent.

According to the Big Mac Index, the U.S. dollar is no longer overvalued against the euro. However, the dollar may decline in value because of the increasing difficulty in financing the U.S. government's huge current account deficit. In addition, the index indicates that the Japanese yen is likely to see a large gain and the British pound will continue to fall against the euro. Moreover, this index suggests that the Chinese yuan was significantly undervalued relative to the U.S. dollar. Indeed, a month after this index was published, the Chinese government did announce a 2.1 percent revaluation of the yuan.

One last benefit of the Big Mac test is that it tells us the cheapest places to find a Big Mac. According to the data, if you are looking for a Big Mac, head to China, and avoid Switzerland. In other words, the Chinese yuan is the most undervalued currency and the Swiss franc is the most overvalued.

Sources: Adapted from "Fast Food and Strong Currencies," *The Economist*, Vol. 375 (June 11, 2005), pp. 70–72; and Li Lian Ong, "Burgernomics: The Economics of the Big Mac Standard," *Journal of International Money and Finance*, Vol. 16, no. 6 (1997), pp. 867–878.

PANEL A

	Big Mac Prices in Local Currency[b]	Actual Dollar Exchange Rate, 4/05[b]
United States[a]	$3.06	—
Argentina	Peso4.74	2.89
Australia	A$3.24	1.30
Brazil	Real5.91	2.47
Britain	£1.88	1.83[e]
Canada	C$3.27	1.24
Chile	Peso1,499.40	592.65
China	Yuan10.50	8.26
Czech Republic	Koruna56.30	24.48
Denmark	DKr27.75	6.06
Egypt	Pound9.00	5.80
Euro area	€2.91	1.23[g]
Hong Kong	HK$12.00	7.79
Hungary	Forint529.38	203.61
Indonesia	Rupiah14,599.26	9,542.00
Japan	¥250.00	106.84
Malaysia	M$5.26	3.81
Mexico	Peso28.00	10.85
New Zealand	NZ4.44	1.40
Peru	NewSol9.00	3.26
Philippines	Peso79.87	54.33
Poland	Zloty6.49	3.31
Russia	Rouble41.92	28.33
Singapore	S$3.61	1.66
South Africa	Rand13.95	6.64
South Korea	Won2,500.02	1,004.02
Sweden	SKr30.91	7.41
Switzerland	SFr6.30	1.25
Taiwan	NT$74.97	31.11
Thailand	Baht59.98	40.52
Turkey	Lira4.01	1.37
Venezuela	Bolivar5,599.80	2,629.01

PANEL B

	Big Mac Prices in Dollars[c]	Implied PPP of the Dollar[d]	Under (−) Over (+) Valuation against the Dollar, %
United States[a]	$3.06	—	—
Argentina	1.64	1.55	−46
Australia	2.50	1.06	−18
Brazil	2.39	1.93	−22
Britain	3.44	1.63[e]	12
Canada	2.63	1.07	−14
Chile	2.53	490	−17
China	1.27	3.43	−59
Czech Republic	2.30	18.4	−25
Denmark	4.58	9.07	50
Egypt	1.55	2.94	−49
Euro area	3.58[f]	1.05[g]	17
Hong Kong	1.54	3.92	−50
Hungary	2.60	173	−15
Indonesia	1.53	4,771	−50
Japan	2.34	81.7	−23
Malaysia	1.38	1.72	−55
Mexico	2.58	9.15	−16
New Zealand	3.17	1.45	4
Peru	2.76	2.94	−10
Philippines	1.47	26.1	−52
Poland	1.96	2.12	−36
Russia	1.48	13.7	−52
Singapore	2.17	1.18	−29
South Africa	2.10	4.56	−31
South Korea	2.49	817	−19
Sweden	4.17	10.1	36
Switzerland	5.05	2.06	65
Taiwan	2.41	24.5	−21
Thailand	1.48	19.6	−52
Turkey	2.92	1.31	−5
Venezuela	2.13	1,830	−30

Notes:
[a] Average of New York, Chicago, San Francisco, and Atlanta.
[b] Calculated from data provided in article.
[c] At current exchange rate.
[d] Purchasing power parity: Local price divided by price in the United States.
[e] Dollars per pound.
[f] Weighted average of member countries.
[g] Dollars per euro.

Sources: McDonald's; and "Fast Food and Strong Currencies," *The Economist*, Vol. 375 (June 11, 2005), pp. 70–72.

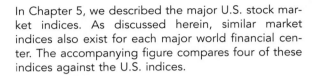

Stock Market Indices Around the World

In Chapter 5, we described the major U.S. stock market indices. As discussed herein, similar market indices also exist for each major world financial center. The accompanying figure compares four of these indices against the U.S. indices.

Hong Kong
In Hong Kong, the primary stock index is the Hang Seng. Created by HSI Services Limited, the Hang Seng index reflects the performance of the Hong Kong stock market. It is composed of 33 domestic stocks (accounting for about 70 percent of the market's capitalization), which are divided into four subindices: Commerce and Industry, Finance, Utilities, and Properties.

Germany
The major indicator of the German stock market, the XETRA DAX, is comprised of 30 German blue chip stocks. These stocks are all listed on the Frankfurt exchange, and they are representative of the industrial structure of the German economy.

Great Britain
The FT-SE 100 Index (pronounced "footsie") is the most widely followed indicator of equity investments in Great Britain. It is a value-weighted index composed of the 100 largest companies on the London Stock Exchange whose value is calculated every minute of trading.

Japan
In Japan, the principal barometer of stock performance is the Nikkei 225 Index. The index's value,

which is calculated every minute throughout daily trading, consists of a collection of highly liquid equity issues thought to be representative of the Japanese economy.

Chile
The Santiago Stock Exchange has three main share indices: the General Stock Price Index (IGPA), the Selective Stock Price Index (IPSA), and the INTER-10 Index. The IPSA, which reflects the price variations of the most active stocks, is composed of 40 of the most actively traded stocks on the exchange.

India
Of the 22 stock exchanges in India, the Bombay Stock Exchange (BSE) is the largest, with more than 6,000 listed stocks and approximately two-thirds of the country's total trading volume. Established in 1875, the exchange is also the oldest in Asia. Its yardstick is the BSE Sensex, an index of 30 publicly traded Indian stocks that account for one-fifth of the BSE's market capitalization.

Spain
In Spain, the IBEX 35 is the official index for measuring equity market performance for continuously traded stocks. This index is composed of the 35 most actively traded securities on the Joint Stock Exchange System (comprising the four Spanish stock exchanges).

Foreign Bond
A type of international bond issued in the domestic capital market of the country in whose currency the bond is denominated, and underwritten by investment banks from the same country.

not rated by one of the rating agencies such as S&P or Moody's, although an increasing number of them are starting to be rated. Eurobonds can be issued with either a fixed coupon rate or a floating rate depending on the preferences of the issuer, and they have medium- or long-term maturities.

Another type of international bond is a **foreign bond.** A foreign bond is issued in the domestic capital market of the country in whose currency the bond is denominated and is underwritten by investment banks from the same country. The only thing foreign about a foreign bond is the nationality of the borrower. For instance, Canadian companies often issue U.S. dollar–denominated foreign bonds in New York to fund their U.S. operations. Foreign bonds issued in the United States are sometimes called "Yankee bonds." Similarly, "bulldogs" are foreign bonds issued in London, and "samurai bonds" are foreign bonds issued in Tokyo. Foreign bonds can be either fixed or floating and have the same maturities as the purely domestic bonds with which they must compete for funding.

Selected International Stock Indices—Compound Returns Since January 1995

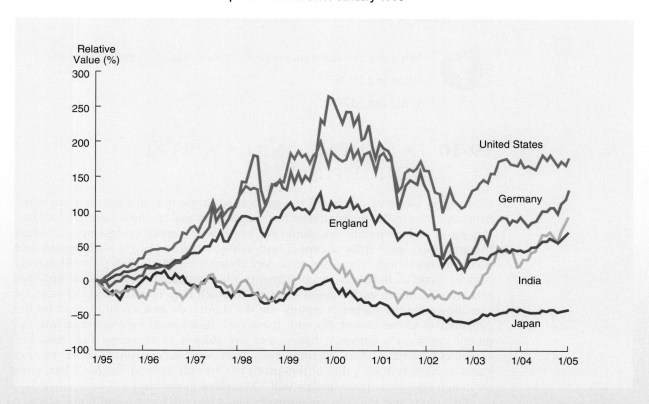

Source: Adapted from Yahoo Finance historical quotes obtained from the Web site at **http://finance.yahoo.com**.

19-9b International Stock Markets

New issues of stock are sold in international markets for a variety of reasons. For example, a non-U.S. firm might sell an equity issue in the United States because it can tap a much larger source of capital than in its home country. Also, a U.S. firm might tap a foreign market because it wants to create an equity market presence to accompany its operations in that country. Large multinational companies also occasionally issue new stock simultaneously in multiple countries. For example, Alcan Aluminum, a Canadian company, recently issued new stock in Canada, Europe, and the United States simultaneously, using different underwriting syndicates in each market.

In addition to new issues, outstanding stocks of large multinational companies are increasingly being listed on multiple international exchanges. For example, Coca-Cola's stock is traded on six stock exchanges in the United

States, four stock exchanges in Switzerland, and the Frankfurt stock exchange in Germany. Some 500 foreign stocks are listed in the United States—one example is Royal Dutch Petroleum, which is listed on the NYSE. U.S. investors can also invest in foreign companies through **American Depository Receipts (ADRs),** which are certificates representing ownership of foreign stock held in trust. About 1,700 ADRs are now available in the United States, with most of them traded on the over-the-counter (OTC) market. However, more and more ADRs are being listed on the New York Stock Exchange, including England's British Airways, Japan's Honda Motors, and Italy's Fiat Group.

American Depository Receipts (ADRs)
Certificates represent-ing ownership of foreign stock held in trust.

What are the three major types of international credit markets?

What is LIBOR?

What are ADRs?

19-10 INTERNATIONAL CAPITAL BUDGETING

Up to now, we have discussed the general environment in which multinational firms operate. In the remainder of the chapter, we will see how international factors affect key corporate decisions. We begin with capital budgeting. Although the same basic principles of capital budgeting analysis apply to both foreign and domestic operations, there are some key differences. First, cash flow estimation is more complex for overseas investments. Most multinational firms set up separate subsidiaries in each foreign country in which they operate, and the relevant cash flows for the parent company are the dividends and royalties paid by the subsidiaries to the parent. Second, these cash flows must be converted into the parent company's currency, hence they are subject to exchange rate risk. For example, General Motors' German subsidiary may make a profit of 100 million euros in 2005, but the value of this profit to GM will depend on the dollar/euro exchange rate: How many *dollars* will 100 million euros buy?

Dividends and royalties are normally taxed by both foreign and home-country governments. Furthermore, a foreign government may restrict the amount of the cash that may be **repatriated** to the parent company. For example, some governments place a ceiling, stated as a percentage of the company's net worth, on the amount of cash dividends that a subsidiary can pay to its parent. Such restrictions are normally intended to force multinational firms to reinvest earnings in the foreign country, although restrictions are sometimes imposed to prevent large currency outflows, which might disrupt the exchange rate.

Repatriation of Earnings
The process of sending cash flows from a for-eign subsidiary back to the parent company.

Whatever the host country's motivation for blocking repatriation of profits, the result is that the parent corporation cannot use cash flows blocked in the foreign country to pay dividends to its shareholders or to invest elsewhere in the business. Hence, from the perspective of the parent organization, *the cash flows relevant for foreign investment analysis are the cash flows that the subsidiary is actually expected to send back to the parent.* The present value of those cash flows is found by applying an appropriate discount rate, and this present value is then compared with the parent's required investment to determine the project's NPV.

In addition to the complexities of the cash flow analysis, *the cost of capital may be different for a foreign project than for an equivalent domestic project, because foreign projects may be more or less risky.* A higher risk could arise from two primary sources—(1) exchange rate risk and (2) political risk. A lower risk might result from international diversification.

Exchange rate risk relates to the value of the basic cash flows in the parent company's home currency. The foreign currency cash flows to be turned over to the parent must be converted into U.S. dollars by translating them at expected future exchange rates. An analysis should be conducted to ascertain the effects of exchange rate variations, and, on the basis of this analysis, an exchange rate risk premium should be added to the domestic cost of capital to reflect this risk. It is sometimes possible to hedge against exchange rate fluctuations, but it may not be possible to hedge completely, especially on long-term projects. If hedging is used, the costs of doing so must be subtracted from the project's cash flows.

Political risk refers to potential actions by a host government that would reduce the value of a company's investment. It includes at one extreme the expropriation without compensation of the subsidiary's assets, but it also includes less drastic actions that reduce the value of the parent firm's investment in the foreign subsidiary, including higher taxes, tighter repatriation or currency controls, and restrictions on prices charged. The risk of expropriation is small in traditionally friendly and stable countries such as Great Britain or Switzerland. However, in Latin America, Africa, the Far East, and eastern Europe, the risk may be substantial. Past expropriations include those of ITT and Anaconda Copper in Chile, Gulf Oil in Bolivia, Occidental Petroleum in Libya, and the assets of many companies in Iraq, Iran, and Cuba.

Note that companies can take several steps to reduce the potential loss from expropriation: (1) finance the subsidiary with local capital, (2) structure operations so that the subsidiary has value only as a part of the integrated corporate system, and (3) obtain insurance against economic losses due to expropriation from a source such as the Overseas Private Investment Corporation (OPIC). In the latter case, insurance premiums would have to be added to the project's cost.

Several organizations rate the country risk, or the risk associated with investing in a particular country. These ratings are based on the country's social, political, and economic environment, or its **business climate.**

Perhaps surprisingly, many of these types of studies suggest that the United States does not have the lowest level of country risk. This is particularly significant because even though people in the United States often assume that our bonds have no country risk, others do not agree. Foreign investors are concerned about how changes in U.S. policies (say, tax and Federal Reserve policies) might affect their investments. To the extent that these perceptions about U.S. country risk influence investors' willingness to hold U.S. securities, they will have an effect on U.S. interest rates.

Exchange Rate Risk
The risk that relates to what the basic cash flows will be worth in the parent company's home currency.

Political Risk
Potential actions by a host government that would reduce the value of a company's investment.

Business Climate
Refers to a country's social, political, and economic environment.

SELF TEST

List some key differences in capital budgeting as applied to foreign versus domestic operations.

What are the relevant cash flows for an international investment—the cash flows produced by the subsidiary in the country where it operates or the cash flows in dollars that it sends to its parent company?

Why might the cost of capital for a foreign project differ from that of an equivalent domestic project? Could it be lower?

What adjustments might be made to the domestic cost of capital for a foreign investment due to exchange rate risk, political risk, and country risk?

19-11 INTERNATIONAL CAPITAL STRUCTURES

Companies' capital structures vary among countries. For example, the Organization for Economic Cooperation and Development (OECD) recently reported that, on average, Japanese firms use 85 percent debt to total assets (in book value terms), German firms use 64 percent, and U.S. firms use 55 percent. One problem, however, when interpreting these numbers is that different countries often use very different accounting conventions with regard to (1) reporting assets on a historical- versus a replacement-cost basis, (2) the treatment of leased assets, (3) pension plan funding, and (4) capitalizing versus expensing R&D costs. These differences make it difficult to compare capital structures.

A study by Raghuram Rajan and Luigi Zingales of the University of Chicago attempts to control for differences in accounting practices. In their study, Rajan and Zingales used a database that covers fewer firms than the OECD but that provides a more complete breakdown of balance sheet data. They concluded that differences in accounting practices can explain much of the cross-country variation in capital structures.

Rajan and Zingales's results are summarized in Table 19-4. There are a number of different ways to measure capital structure. One measure is the average ratio of total liabilities to total assets—this is similar to the measure used by the OECD, and it is reported in Column 1. Based on this measure, German and Japanese firms appear to be more highly levered than U.S. firms. However, if you look at Column 2, where capital structure is measured by interest-bearing debt to total assets, it appears that German firms use less leverage than U.S. and Japanese firms. What explains this difference? Rajan and Zingales argue that much of this difference is explained by the way German firms account for pension liabilities. German firms generally include all pension liabilities (and their offsetting assets) on the balance sheet, whereas firms in other countries (including the United States) generally "net out" pension assets and liabilities on their balance sheets. To see the importance of this difference, consider a firm with $10 million in liabilities (not including pension liabilities) and $20 million in assets (not including pension assets). Assume that the firm has $10 million in pension liabilities that are fully funded by $10 million in pension assets. Therefore, net pension liabilities are zero. If this firm were in the United States, it would report a ratio of total liabilities to total assets equal to 50 percent ($10 million/$20 million). By contrast, if this firm operated in Germany, both its pension assets and liabilities would be reported on the balance sheet. The firm would have $20 million in liabilities and $30 million in assets—or a 67 percent ($20 million/$30 million) ratio of total liabilities to total assets. Total debt is the sum of short-term debt and long-term debt and excludes other liabilities including pension liabilities. Therefore, the measure of total debt to total assets provides a more comparable measure of leverage across different countries.

Rajan and Zingales also make a variety of adjustments that attempt to control for other differences in accounting practices. The effects of these adjustments are reported in Columns 3 and 4. Overall, the evidence suggests that companies in Germany and the United Kingdom tend to have less leverage, whereas firms in Canada appear to have more leverage, relative to firms in the United States, France, Italy, and Japan. This conclusion is supported by data in the final column, which shows the average times-interest-earned ratio for firms in a number of different countries. Recall from Chapter 4 that the TIE ratio is the ratio of operating income (EBIT) to interest expense. This measure indicates how much cash the firm has available to service its interest expense. In general,

TABLE 19-4					
Median Capital Structures among Large Industrialized Countries (Measured in Terms of Book Value)					
Country	Total Liabilities to Total Assets (Unadjusted for Accounting Differences) (1)	Debt to Total Assets (Unadjusted for Accounting Differences) (2)	Total Liabilities to Total Assets (Adjusted for Accounting Differences) (3)	Debt to Total Assets (Adjusted for Accounting Differences) (4)	Times Interest Earned (TIE) Ratio (5)
Canada	56%	32%	48%	32%	1.55×
France	71	25	69	18	2.64
Germany	73	16	50	11	3.20
Italy	70	27	68	21	1.81
Japan	69	35	62	21	2.46
United Kingdom	54	18	47	10	4.79
United States	58	27	52	25	2.41
Mean	64%	26%	57%	20%	2.69×
Standard deviation	8%	7%	10%	8%	1.07×

Source: Raghuram Rajan and Luigi Zingales, "What Do We Know about Capital Structure? Some Evidence from International Data," *Journal of Finance*, Vol. 50, no. 5 (December 1995), pp.1421–1460. Used with permission.

firms with more leverage have a lower times-interest-earned ratio. The data indicate that this ratio is highest in the United Kingdom and Germany and lowest in Canada.

Do international differences in financial leverage exist? Explain.

19-12 MULTINATIONAL WORKING CAPITAL MANAGEMENT

19-12a Cash Management

The goals of cash management in a multinational corporation are similar to those in a purely domestic corporation: (1) to speed up collections, slow down disbursements, and thus maximize net float; (2) to shift cash as rapidly as possible from those parts of the business where it is not needed to those parts where it is needed; and (3) to maximize the risk-adjusted, after-tax rate of return on temporary cash balances. Multinational companies use the same general procedures for achieving these goals as domestic firms, but because of longer distances and more serious mail delays, such devices as lockbox systems and electronic funds transfers are especially important.

Although multinational and domestic corporations have the same objectives and use similar procedures, multinational corporations face a far more complex task. As noted earlier in our discussion of political risk, foreign governments often place restrictions on transfers of funds out of the country, so although IBM can transfer money from its Salt Lake City office to its New York concentration bank just by pressing a few buttons, a similar transfer from its Buenos Aires office is far more complex. Buenos Aires funds are denominated in pesos (Argentina's equivalent of the dollar), so the pesos must be converted to dollars before the transfer. If there is a shortage of dollars in Argentina, or if the Argentinean government wants to conserve dollars to purchase strategic materials, then conversion, hence the transfer, may be blocked. Even if no dollar shortage exists in Argentina, the government may still restrict funds outflows if those funds represent profits or depreciation rather than payments for purchased materials or equipment, because many countries, especially those that are less developed, want profits reinvested in the country in order to stimulate economic growth.

Once it has been determined what funds can be transferred, the next task is to get those funds to locations where they will earn the highest returns. Whereas domestic corporations tend to think in terms of domestic securities, multinationals are more likely to be aware of investment opportunities all around the world. Most multinational corporations use one or more global concentration banks, located in money centers such as London, New York, Tokyo, Zurich, or Singapore, and their staffs in those cities, working with international bankers, know of and are able to take advantage of the best rates available anywhere in the world.

19-12b Credit Management

Like most other aspects of finance, credit management in the multinational corporation is similar to but more complex than that in a purely domestic business. First, granting credit is more risky in an international context because, in addition to the normal risks of default, the multinational corporation must also worry about exchange rate fluctuations between the time a sale is made and the time a receivable is collected. For example, if IBM sold a computer to a Japanese customer for 90 million yen when the exchange rate was 90 yen to the dollar, IBM would receive 90,000,000/90 = $1,000,000 for the computer. However, if it sold the computer on terms of net/6 months, and if the yen fell against the dollar so that one dollar would now buy 112.5 yen, IBM would end up realizing only 90,000,000/112.5 = $800,000 when it collected the receivable. Hedging can reduce this type of risk, but at a cost.

Offering credit is generally more important for multinational corporations than for purely domestic firms for two reasons. First, much U.S. trade is with poorer, less-developed nations, where granting credit is generally a necessary condition for doing business. Second, and in large part as a result of the first point, developed nations whose economic health depends on exports often help their manufacturing firms compete internationally by granting credit to foreign countries. In Japan, for example, the major manufacturing firms have direct ownership ties with large "trading companies" engaged in international trade, as well as with giant commercial banks. In addition, a government agency, the Ministry of International Trade and Industry (MITI), helps Japanese firms identify potential export markets and also helps potential customers arrange credit for purchases from Japanese firms. In effect, the huge Japanese trade surpluses are used to finance Japanese exports, thus helping to perpetuate their favorable trade balance. The United States has attempted to counter with the Export-Import Bank, which is funded by Congress, but the fact that the United States has a large balance of payments deficit is clear evidence that we have been less successful than others in world markets in recent years.

The huge debt that countries such as Korea and Thailand owe U.S. and other international banks is well known, and this situation illustrates how credit policy (by banks in this case) can go astray. The banks face a particularly sticky problem with these loans, because if a sovereign nation defaults, the banks cannot lay claim to the assets of the country as they could if a corporate customer defaulted. Note too that although the banks' loans to foreign governments often get most of the headlines, many U.S. multinational corporations are also in trouble as a result of granting credit to business customers in the same countries where bank loans to governments are on shaky ground.

By pointing out the risks in granting credit internationally, we are not suggesting that such credit is bad. Quite the contrary, for the potential gains from international operations far outweigh the risks, at least for companies (and banks) that have the necessary expertise.

19-12c Inventory Management

As with most other aspects of finance, inventory management in a multinational setting is similar to but more complex than for a purely domestic firm. First, there is the matter of the physical location of inventories. For example, where should ExxonMobil keep its stockpiles of crude oil and refined products? It has refineries and marketing centers located worldwide, and one alternative is to keep items concentrated in a few strategic spots from which they can then be shipped as needs arise. Such a strategy might minimize the total amount of inventories needed and thus might minimize the investment in inventories. Note, though, that consideration will have to be given to potential delays in getting goods from central storage locations to user locations all around the world. Both working stocks and safety stocks would have to be maintained at each user location, as well as at the strategic storage centers. Problems like the Iraqi occupation of Kuwait and the subsequent trade embargo, which brought with it the potential for a shutdown of production of about 25 percent of the world's oil supply, complicate matters further.

Exchange rates also influence inventory policy. If a local currency, say, the Danish krone, were expected to rise in value against the dollar, a U.S. company operating in Denmark would want to increase stocks of local products before the rise in the krone, and vice versa if the krone were expected to fall.

Another factor that must be considered is the possibility of import or export quotas or tariffs. For example, Apple Computer Company was buying certain memory chips from Japanese suppliers at a bargain price. Then U.S. chipmakers accused the Japanese of dumping chips in the U.S. market at prices below cost, so they sought to force the Japanese to raise prices.[5] That led Apple to increase

---

[5] The term "dumping" warrants explanation, because the practice is so potentially important in international markets. Suppose Japanese chipmakers have excess capacity. A particular chip has a variable cost of $25, and its "fully allocated cost," which is the $25 plus total fixed cost per unit of output, is $40. Now suppose the Japanese firm can sell chips in the United States at $35 per unit, but if it charges $40, it will not make any sales because U.S. chipmakers sell them for $35.50. If the Japanese firm sells at $35, it will cover variable cost plus make a contribution to fixed overhead, so selling at $35 makes sense. Continuing, if the Japanese firm can sell in Japan at $40, but U.S. firms are excluded from Japanese markets by import duties or other barriers, the Japanese will have a huge advantage over U.S. manufacturers. This practice of selling goods at lower prices in foreign markets than at home is called "dumping." U.S. firms are required by antitrust laws to offer the same price to all customers and, therefore, cannot engage in dumping.

its chip inventory. Then computer sales slacked off, and Apple ended up with an oversupply of obsolete computer chips. As a result, Apple's profits were hurt and its stock price fell, demonstrating once more the importance of careful inventory management. As mentioned earlier, another danger in certain countries is the threat of expropriation. If that threat is large, inventory holdings will be minimized, and goods will be brought in only as needed. Similarly, if the operation involves extraction of raw materials such as oil or bauxite, processing plants may be moved offshore rather than located close to the production site.

Taxes have two effects on multinational inventory management. First, countries often impose property taxes on assets, including inventories, and when this is done, the tax is based on holdings as of a specific date, say, January 1 or March 1. Such rules make it advantageous for a multinational firm (1) to schedule production so that inventories are low on the assessment date, and (2) if assessment dates vary among countries in a region, to hold safety stocks in different countries at different times during the year.

Finally, multinational firms may consider the possibility of at-sea storage. Oil, chemical, grain, and other companies that deal in a bulk commodity that must be stored in some type of tank can often buy tankers at a cost not much greater—or perhaps even less, considering land cost—than land-based facilities. Loaded tankers can then be kept at sea or at anchor in some strategic location. This eliminates the danger of expropriation, minimizes the property tax problem, and maximizes flexibility with regard to shipping to areas where needs are greatest or prices highest.

This discussion has only scratched the surface of inventory management in the multinational corporation—the task is much more complex than for a purely domestic firm. However, the greater the degree of complexity, the greater the rewards from superior performance, so if you want challenge along with potentially high rewards, look to the international arena.

What are some factors that make cash management especially complicated in a multinational corporation?

Why is granting credit especially risky in an international context?

Why is inventory management especially important for a multinational firm?

Tying It All Together

Over the past two decades, the global economy has become increasingly integrated, and more and more companies generate more and more of their profits from overseas operations. In many respects, the concepts developed in the first 18 chapters still apply to multinational firms. However, multinational companies have more opportunities but also face different risks than do companies that operate only in their home market. The chapter discussed many of the key trends affecting the global markets today, and it described the most important differences between multinational and domestic financial management.

SELF-TEST QUESTIONS AND PROBLEMS
(Solutions Appear in Appendix A)

ST-1   **Key terms** Define each of the following terms:
   a.   Multinational corporation
   b.   Vertically integrated investment
   c.   International monetary system
   d.   Exchange rate
   e.   Freely-floating regime; managed-float regime
   f.   Currency board arrangement
   g.   Fixed peg arrangement
   h.   Cross rate
   i.   American terms; European terms
   j.   Direct quotation; indirect quotation
   k.   Spot rate; forward exchange rate
   l.   Discount on forward rate; premium on forward rate
   m. Interest rate parity; purchasing power parity
   n.   Eurocredits; eurodollar
   o.   Eurobond; foreign bond
   p.   American Depository Receipts (ADRs)
   q.   Repatriation of earnings; exchange rate risk; political risk; business climate

ST-2   **Cross rates** Suppose the exchange rate between U.S. dollars and EMU euros is €1.1215 = $1.00, and the exchange rate between the U.S. dollar and the Canadian dollar is $1.00 = C$1.5291. What is the cross rate of euros to Canadian dollars?

QUESTIONS

19-1   Why do U.S. corporations build manufacturing plants abroad when they could build them at home?

19-2   If the euro depreciates against the U.S. dollar, can a dollar buy more or fewer euros as a result?

19-3   If the United States imports more goods from abroad than it exports, foreigners will tend to have a surplus of U.S. dollars. What will this do to the value of the dollar with respect to foreign currencies? What is the corresponding effect on foreign investments in the United States?

19-4   Should firms require higher rates of return on foreign projects than on identical projects located at home? Explain.

19-5   Does interest rate parity imply that interest rates are the same in all countries?

19-6   Why might purchasing power parity fail to hold?

19-7   What is a eurodollar? If a French citizen deposits $10,000 in Chase Manhattan Bank in New York, have eurodollars been created? What if the deposit is made in Barclay's Bank in London? Chase Manhattan's Paris branch? Does the existence of the eurodollar market make the Federal Reserve's job of controlling U.S. interest rates easier or more difficult? Explain.

PROBLEMS

19-1 **Exchange rate** If British pounds sell for $1.50 (U.S.) per pound, what should dollars sell for in pounds per dollar?

19-2 **Cross rates** A currency trader observes that in the spot exchange market, 1 U.S. dollar can be exchanged for 4.0828 Israeli shekels or for 111.23 Japanese yen. What is the cross-exchange rate between the yen and the shekel; that is, how many yen would you receive for every shekel exchanged?

19-3 **Interest rate parity** Six-month T-bills have a nominal rate of 7 percent, while default-free Japanese bonds that mature in 6 months have a nominal rate of 5.5 percent. In the spot exchange market, 1 yen equals $0.009. If interest rate parity holds, what is the 6-month forward exchange rate?

19-4 **Purchasing power parity** A television set costs $500 in the United States. The same set costs 725 euros. If purchasing power parity holds, what is the spot exchange rate between the euro and the dollar?

19-5 **Exchange rates** Table 19-1 lists foreign exchange rates for July 25, 2005. On that day, how many dollars would be required to purchase 1,000 units of each of the following: British pounds, Canadian dollars, EMU euros, Japanese yen, Mexican pesos, and Swedish kronas?

19-6 **Exchange rates** Look up the 6 currencies in Problem 19-5 in the foreign exchange section of a current issue of *The Wall Street Journal*.
   a. What is the current exchange rate for changing dollars into 1,000 units of pounds, Canadian dollars, euros, yen, Mexican pesos, and Swedish kronas?
   b. What is the percentage gain or loss between the July 25, 2005, exchange rate and the current exchange rate for each of the currencies in part a?

19-7 **Currency appreciation** Suppose that 1 Danish krone could be purchased in the foreign exchange market for 14 U.S. cents today. If the krone appreciated 10 percent tomorrow against the dollar, how many krones would a dollar buy tomorrow?

19-8 **Cross rates** Suppose the exchange rate between the U.S. dollar and the Swedish krona was 10 krona = $1.00, and the exchange rate between the dollar and the British pound was £1 = $1.50. What was the exchange rate between Swedish kronas and pounds?

19-9 **Cross rates** Look up the 3 currencies in Problem 19-8 in the foreign exchange section of a current issue of *The Wall Street Journal*. What is the current exchange rate between Swedish kronas and pounds?

19-10 **Interest rate parity** Assume that interest rate parity holds. In both the spot market and the 90-day forward market 1 Japanese yen = 0.0086 dollar. And 90-day risk-free securities yield 4.6 percent in Japan. What is the yield on 90-day risk-free securities in the United States?

19-11 **Purchasing power parity** In the spot market 7.8 Mexican pesos can be exchanged for 1 U.S. dollar. A compact disc costs $15 in the United States. If purchasing power parity (PPP) holds, what should be the price of the same disc in Mexico?

19-12 **Interest rate parity** Assume that interest rate parity holds and that 90-day risk-free securities yield 5 percent in the United States and 5.3 percent in Britain. In the spot market 1 pound = 1.65 dollars.
   a. Is the 90-day forward rate trading at a premium or discount relative to the spot rate?
   b. What is the 90-day forward rate?

19-13 **Spot and forward rates** Chamberlain Canadian Imports has agreed to purchase 15,000 cases of Canadian beer for 4 million Canadian dollars at today's spot rate. The firm's financial manager, James Churchill, has noted the following current spot and forward rates:

	U.S. Dollar/Canadian Dollar	Canadian Dollar/U.S. Dollar
Spot	0.6930	1.4430
30-day forward	0.6935	1.4420
90-day forward	0.6944	1.4401
180-day forward	0.6957	1.4374

On the same day, Churchill agrees to purchase 15,000 more cases of beer in 3 months at the same price of 4 million Canadian dollars.

   a.   What is the price of the beer, in U.S. dollars, if it is purchased at today's spot rate?

   b.   What is the cost, in U.S. dollars, of the second 15,000 cases if payment is made in 90 days and the spot rate at that time equals today's 90-day forward rate?

   c.   If the exchange rate for the Canadian dollar is 1.20 to $1 in 90 days, how much will Churchill have to pay for the beer (in U.S. dollars)?

19-14   **Exchange gains and losses** You are the vice president of International InfoXchange, headquartered in Chicago, Illinois. All shareholders of the firm live in the United States. Earlier this month, you obtained a loan of 5 million Canadian dollars from a bank in Toronto to finance the construction of a new plant in Montreal. At the time the loan was received, the exchange rate was 75 U.S. cents to the Canadian dollar. By the end of the month, it has unexpectedly dropped to 70 cents. Has your company made a gain or loss as a result, and by how much?

19-15   **Results of exchange rate changes** Early in September 1983, it took 245 Japanese yen to equal $1. Nearly 22 years later, in July 2005 that exchange rate had fallen to 111 yen to $1. Assume the price of a Japanese-manufactured automobile was $9,000 in September 1983 and that its price changes were in direct relation to exchange rates.

   a.   Has the price, in dollars, of the automobile increased or decreased during the 22-year period because of changes in the exchange rate?

   b.   What would the dollar price of the automobile be in July 2005, again assuming that the car's price changes only with exchange rates?

19-16   **Foreign investment analysis** After all foreign and U.S. taxes, a U.S. corporation expects to receive 3 pounds of dividends per share from a British subsidiary this year. The exchange rate at the end of the year is expected to be $1.60 per pound, and the pound is expected to depreciate 5 percent against the dollar each year for an indefinite period. The dividend (in pounds) is expected to grow at 10 percent a year indefinitely. The parent U.S. corporation owns 10 million shares of the subsidiary. What is the present value in dollars of its equity ownership of the subsidiary? Assume a cost of equity capital of 15 percent for the subsidiary.

19-17   **Foreign capital budgeting** Solitaire Machinery is a Swiss multinational manufacturing company. Currently, Solitaire's financial planners are considering undertaking a 1-year project in the United States. The project's expected dollar-denominated cash flows consist of an initial investment of $1,000 and a cash inflow the following year of $1,200. Solitaire estimates that its risk-adjusted cost of capital is 14 percent. Currently, 1 U.S. dollar will buy 1.62 Swiss francs. In addition, 1-year risk-free securities in the United States are yielding 7.25 percent, while similar securities in Switzerland are yielding 4.5 percent.

   a.   If this project were instead undertaken by a similar U.S.-based company with the same risk-adjusted cost of capital, what would be the net present value and rate of return generated by this project?

   b.   What is the expected forward exchange rate 1 year from now?

   c.   If Solitaire undertakes the project, what is the net present value and rate of return of the project for Solitaire?

COMPREHENSIVE/SPREADSHEET PROBLEM

19-18   **Multinational financial management** Yohe Telecommunications is a multinational corporation that produces and distributes telecommunications technology. Although its corporate headquarters are located in Maitland, Florida, Yohe usually must buy its raw materials in several different foreign countries using several different foreign currencies. The matter is further complicated because Yohe usually sells its products in other foreign countries. One product in particular, the SY-20 radio transmitter, draws its principal components, Component X, Component Y, and Component Z, from Switzerland, France, and England, respectively. Specifically, Component X costs 165 Swiss francs, Component Y costs 20 euros, and Component Z costs 105 British pounds. The largest market for the SY-20 is in Japan, where it sells for 38,000 Japanese yen. Naturally, Yohe is intimately concerned with economic conditions that could adversely affect dollar exchange rates. You will find Tables 19-1, 19-2, and 19-3 useful for this problem.

a. How much, in dollars, does it cost for Yohe to produce the SY-20? What is the dollar sale price of the SY-20?

b. What is the dollar profit that Yohe makes on the sale of the SY-20? What is the percentage profit?

c. If the U.S. dollar were to weaken by 10 percent against all foreign currencies, what would be the dollar profit for the SY-20?

d. If the U.S. dollar were to weaken by 10 percent only against the Japanese yen and remained constant relative to all other foreign currencies, what would be the dollar and percentage profits for the SY-20?

e. Using the 180-day forward exchange information from Table 19-3, calculate the return on 1-year securities in Switzerland, if the rate of return on 1-year securities in the U.S. is 4.9 percent.

f. Assuming that purchasing power parity (PPP) holds, what would be the sale price of the SY-20 if it were sold in England rather than Japan?

Integrated Case

Citrus Products Inc.

19-19   **Multinational financial management** Citrus Products Inc. is a medium-sized producer of citrus juice drinks with groves in Indian River County, Florida. Until now, the company has confined its operations and sales to the United States, but its CEO, George Gaynor, wants to expand into the Pacific Rim. The first step would be to set up sales subsidiaries in Japan and Australia, then to set up a production plant in Japan, and, finally, to distribute the product throughout the Pacific Rim. The firm's financial manager, Ruth Schmidt, is enthusiastic about the plan, but she is worried about the implications of the foreign expansion on the firm's financial management process. She has asked you, the firm's most recently hired financial analyst, to develop a 1-hour tutorial package that explains the basics of multinational financial management. The tutorial will be presented at the next board of directors meeting. To get you started, Schmidt has supplied you with the following list of questions.

a. What is a multinational corporation? Why do firms expand into other countries?

b. What are the 5 major factors that distinguish multinational financial management from financial management as practiced by a purely domestic firm?

c. Consider the following illustrative exchange rates:

	U.S. Dollars Required to Buy One Unit of Foreign Currency
Japanese yen	0.009
Australian dollar	0.650

(1) Are these currency prices direct quotations or indirect quotations?

(2) Calculate the indirect quotations for yen and Australian dollars.

(3) What is a cross rate? Calculate the two cross rates between yen and Australian dollars.

(4) Assume Citrus Products can produce a liter of orange juice and ship it to Japan for $1.75. If the firm wants a 50 percent markup on the product, what should the orange juice sell for in Japan?

(5) Now, assume Citrus Products begins producing the same liter of orange juice in Japan. The product costs 250 yen to produce and ship to Australia, where it can be sold for 6 Australian dollars. What is the U.S. dollar profit on the sale?

(6) What is exchange rate risk?

d. Briefly describe the current international monetary system. What are the different types of exchange rate systems?
e. What is the difference between spot rates and forward rates? When is the forward rate at a premium to the spot rate? At a discount?
f. What is interest rate parity? Currently, you can exchange 1 yen for 0.0095 U.S. dollar in the 30-day forward market, and the risk-free rate on 30-day securities is 4 percent in both Japan and the United States. Does interest rate parity hold? If not, which securities offer the highest expected return?
g. What is purchasing power parity (PPP)? If grapefruit juice costs $2.00 a liter in the United States and purchasing power parity holds, what should be the price of grapefruit juice in Australia?
h. What effect does relative inflation have on interest rates and exchange rates?
i. (1) Briefly explain the three major types of international credit markets.
   (2) Briefly explain how ADRs work.
j. To what extent do average capital structures vary across different countries?
k. What is the effect of multinational operations on each of the following financial management topics?
   (1) Cash management.
   (2) Capital budgeting decisions.
   (3) Credit management.
   (4) Inventory management.

cyberproblem

Please go to the ThomsonNOW Web site to access the Cyberproblems.

C H A P T E R

20

HYBRID FINANCING: PREFERRED STOCK, LEASING, WARRANTS, AND CONVERTIBLES

Taking a Wild Ride with Amazon's Convertible Debt

Amazon.com

The use of convertible securities—generally bonds or preferred stocks that can be exchanged for common stock of the issuing corporation—has soared during the last decade. In recent years there have been instances where the capital raised through convertible securities has exceeded the amount of capital raised through common stock.

Why do companies use convertibles so heavily? To answer this question, recognize that convertibles virtually always have coupon rates that are lower than would be required on straight, nonconvertible bonds or preferred stocks. Therefore, if a company raises $100 million by issuing convertible bonds, its interest expense is lower than if it financed with nonconvertible debt. But why would investors be willing to buy convertibles, given their lower cash payments? The answer lies in the conversion feature—if the price of the issuer's stock rises, the holder of the convertible can exchange it for stock and realize a capital gain. So, convertibles hold down the cash costs of financing by giving investors an opportunity for capital gains. A convertible bond's value is tied to the price of the stock into which it is convertible, whereas a nonconvertible bond's price is based on its fixed-income payments. Therefore, convertibles' prices rise and fall much more than regular bonds' prices; hence, convertibles are relatively risky. A 1999 article in *Forbes* estimated that if a company's common stock increases in value, the returns on its convertibles also rise, but by only 70 percent of the stock's percentage increase. However, if the stock declines, the convertible will decline by only 50 percent of the stock's decline. Thus, while convertibles are more risky than straight bonds, they are less risky than stock.

To illustrate all this, consider Amazon.com. In early 1999 Amazon issued $1.25 billion of 10-year convertible bonds. Amazon's bonds were issued at a par value of $1,000 and a 4.75 percent coupon rate. The bonds also had a conversion price of $78.0275, which meant that investors who purchased the bonds could at any time convert their bond to roughly 12.8 shares of Amazon common stock. Consequently, because they can be converted to Amazon common stock, changes in the stock price will have a profound effect on the convertibles' value.

During 1999 Amazon's convertibles took their holders on a wild ride. During the first four months Amazon's stock rose about 70 percent, to more than $100 per share, causing its convertibles to rise by 50 percent, to $1,500. During the next four months, the stock lost more than 60 percent of its value. This caused the convertibles' price to drop to $750. Three months later Amazon's stock had rebounded, and its convertibles were once again trading above $1,500, only to decline sharply one month later. By year-end 1999, the convertibles were about back to their $1,000 issue price.

In the two subsequent years, Amazon, like most other "tech" companies, witnessed a sharp decline in its stock price—Amazon dropped from its 1999 high of more than $100 to a low of $5.51 in 2001, or by about 95 percent. The convertibles also declined, but only to $376, or by about 75 percent, bad but not as bad as the stock. The convertibles held up better for two reasons. First, they paid $47.50 per year interest, whereas the common paid nothing, and second, if Amazon was forced into bankruptcy, which was a real possibility in 2001, the convertibles would have a claim on their $1,000 par value ahead of stockholders' claims. After the 2001 trough, Amazon's fortunes improved. Rumors of impending bankruptcy were dispelled, and by mid-2005, the stock stood around $46 a share, and the convertibles were once again trading around par.

Amazon's experience with convertibles is not unusual. The convertible bonds rose in price with the common, but not as rapidly, and the bonds also declined with the stock, but again the losses were less pronounced. Thus, convertibles offer investors a bit of protection against losses, but also opportunities for capital gains. Not surprisingly, convertibles are used by companies, whose futures are highly uncertain, to attract investors who are not willing to bear the risks inherent in their common stocks.

When you finish this chapter, you should have a good understanding of what convertibles are, how they are valued, and why a firm might choose to issue a convertible bond rather than either straight debt or common stock.

Source: John Gorham, "Chicken Little Stocks," *Forbes*, December 27, 1999, p. 200.

Putting Things In Perspective

In previous chapters we examined common stocks and the various types of long-term debt. In this chapter, we examine four other types of long-term capital: (1) *preferred stock*, which is a hybrid security that represents a cross between debt and common equity; (2) *leasing*, which is used by financial managers as an alternative to borrowing to finance fixed assets; (3) *warrants*, which are derivative securities issued by firms to facilitate the issuance of some other type of security; and (4) *convertibles*, which combine the features of debt (or preferred stock) and warrants.

20-1 PREFERRED STOCK

Preferred stock is a hybrid—it is similar to bonds in some respects and to common stock in other ways. Accountants classify perpetual preferred stock as equity, hence show it on the balance sheet as an equity account. However, from a finance perspective preferred stock lies somewhere between debt and common equity—it imposes a fixed charge and thus increases the firm's financial leverage, yet omitting the preferred dividend does not force a company into bankruptcy. We first describe the basic features of preferred, after which we discuss other types of preferred stock and the advantages and disadvantages of preferred stock.

20-1a Basic Features

Preferred stock has a par (or liquidating) value, often either $25 or $100. The dividend is stated as either a percentage of par, as so many dollars per share, or both ways. For example, several years ago Klondike Paper Company sold 150,000 shares of $100 par value perpetual preferred stock for a total of $15 million. This preferred had a stated annual dividend of $12 per share, so the preferred dividend yield was $12/$100 = 0.12, or 12 percent, at the time of issue. The dividend was set when the stock was issued; it will not be changed in the future. Therefore, if the required rate of return on preferred, r_p, changes from 12 percent after the issue date—as it did—then the market price of the preferred stock will increase or decrease. Currently, r_p for Klondike Paper's preferred is 9 percent, and the price of the preferred has risen from $100 to $12/0.09 = $133.33.

> **Cumulative**
> *A protective feature on preferred stock that requires preferred dividends previously not paid to be paid before any common dividends can be paid.*

> **Arrearages**
> *Unpaid preferred dividends.*

If the preferred dividend is not earned, the company does not have to pay it. However, most preferred issues are **cumulative,** meaning that the cumulative total of all unpaid preferred dividends must be paid before dividends can be paid on the common stock. Unpaid preferred dividends are called **arrearages.** Dividends in arrears do not earn interest; thus, arrearages do not grow in a compound interest sense—they only grow from additional nonpayments of the preferred dividend. Also, many preferred stocks accrue arrearages for only a limited number of years, say, three years, meaning that the cumulative feature ceases after three years. However, the dividends in arrears continue in force until they are paid.

Preferred stock normally has no voting rights. However, most preferred issues stipulate that the preferred stockholders can elect a minority of the directors—say, 3 out of 10—if the preferred dividend is passed (omitted). Jersey Central Power & Light, one of the companies that owned a share of the Three Mile Island (TMI) nuclear plant, had preferred stock outstanding that could elect a *majority* of the directors if the preferred dividend was passed for four successive quarters. Jersey Central kept paying its preferred dividends even during the dark days following the TMI accident. Had the preferred not been entitled to elect a majority of the directors, the dividend would probably have been passed.

Although nonpayment of preferred dividends will not bankrupt a company, corporations issue preferred with every intention of paying the dividend. Even if passing the dividend does not give the preferred stockholders control of the company, failure to pay a preferred dividend precludes payment of common dividends. In addition, passing the dividend makes it difficult to raise capital by selling bonds, and virtually impossible to sell more preferred or common stock. However, having preferred stock outstanding does give a firm the chance to overcome its difficulties—if bonds had been used instead of preferred stock, Jersey Central would have been in danger of being forced into bankruptcy before it could straighten out its problems. *Thus, from the viewpoint of the issuing corporation, preferred stock is less risky than bonds.*

However, for investors preferred stock is riskier than bonds: (1) Preferred stockholders' claims are subordinated to those of bondholders in the event of liquidation, and (2) bondholders are more likely to continue receiving income during hard times than are preferred stockholders. Accordingly, investors require a higher after-tax rate of return on a given firm's preferred stock than on its bonds. However, because 70 percent of preferred dividends is exempt from corporate taxes, preferred stock is attractive to corporate investors. In recent years, high-grade preferred stock, on average, has sold on a lower pre-tax yield basis than have high-grade bonds. As an example, Bear Sterns preferred G stock recently had a market yield of about 5.4 percent, whereas its bonds provided a yield of 5.9 percent, or 0.5 percentage point *more* than its preferred. The tax treatment accounted for this differential; the *after-tax yield* to corporate investors was greater on the preferred stock than on the bonds.[1]

About half of all preferred stock issued in recent years has been convertible into common stock. For example, on July 31, 2002, Corning Incorporated issued $500 million of mandatory convertible preferred stock with a 7 percent annual dividend rate. The issue is mandatorily convertible into between approximately 254 million and 313 million shares. Convertibles are discussed at length in Section 20.4.

Some preferred stocks are similar to perpetual bonds in that they have no maturity date, but most new issues now have specified maturities. For example, many preferred shares have a sinking fund provision that calls for the retirement of 2 percent of the issue each year, meaning that the issue will "mature" in a maximum of 50 years. Also, many preferred issues are callable by the issuing corporation, which can also limit the life of the preferred.[2]

Nonconvertible preferred stock is virtually all owned by corporations, which can take advantage of the 70 percent dividend exclusion to obtain a higher after-tax yield on preferred stock than on bonds. Individuals should not own preferred stocks (except convertible preferreds)—they can obtain higher yields on safer bonds, so it is not logical for them to hold preferreds. As a result of this ownership pattern, the volume of preferred stock financing is geared to the supply of money in the hands of corporate investors. When the supply of such money is plentiful, the prices of preferred stocks are bid up, their yields fall, and investment bankers suggest that companies that need financing consider issuing preferred stock.

For issuers, preferred stock has a tax *disadvantage* relative to debt—interest expense is deductible, but preferred dividends are not. Still, firms with low tax rates may have an incentive to issue preferred stock that can be bought by corporate investors with high tax rates, who can take advantage of the 70 percent dividend exclusion. If a firm has a lower tax rate than potential corporate buyers, the firm might be better off issuing preferred stock than debt. The key here is that the tax advantage to a high-tax-rate corporation is greater than the tax disadvantage to a low-tax-rate issuer. To illustrate, assume that risk differentials between debt and preferred would require an issuer to set the interest rate on new debt at 10 percent and the dividend yield on new preferred at 12 percent in a no-tax world. However, when taxes are considered, a corporate buyer with a high tax rate, say, 40 percent, might be willing to buy the preferred stock if it has an 8

---

[1] The after-tax yield on a 5.9 percent bond to a corporate investor in the 35 percent marginal tax rate bracket is 5.9%(1 − T) = 5.9%(0.65) = 3.84%. The after-tax yield on a 5.4 percent preferred stock is 5.4%(1 − Effective T) = 5.4%[1 − (0.30)(0.35)] = 5.4%(0.895) = 4.83%. Also, note that tax law prohibits firms from issuing debt and then using the proceeds to purchase another firm's preferred or common stock. If debt is used for stock purchases, then the 70 percent dividend exclusion is voided. This provision is designed to prevent a firm from engaging in "tax arbitrage," using tax-deductible debt to purchase largely tax-exempt preferred stock.

[2] Prior to the late 1970s, virtually all preferred stock was perpetual, and almost no issues had sinking funds or call provisions. Then, insurance company regulators, worried about the unrealized losses the companies had been incurring on preferred holdings as a result of rising interest rates, put into effect some regulatory changes that essentially mandated that insurance companies buy only limited-life preferreds. From that time on, virtually no new preferred has been perpetual. This example illustrates the way securities change as a result of changes in the economic environment.

percent before-tax yield. This would produce an 8%(1 − Effective T) = 8%[1 − 0.30(0.40)] = 7.04% after-tax return on the preferred versus 10%(1 − 0.40) = 6.0% on the debt. If the issuer has a low tax rate, say, 10 percent, its after-tax costs would be 10%(1 − T) = 10%(0.90) = 9% on the bonds and 8 percent on the preferred. Thus, the security with lower risk to the issuer, preferred stock, also has a lower cost. Such situations can make preferred stock a logical financing choice.[3]

20-1b Other Types of Preferred Stock

In addition to the "plain vanilla" variety of preferred stocks, several variations are also used. Two of these, floating rate and market auction preferred, are discussed in the following sections.

Adjustable Rate Preferred Stock

Adjustable Rate Preferred Stocks (ARPs)
Preferred stocks whose dividends are tied to the rate on Treasury securities.

Instead of paying fixed dividends, **adjustable rate preferred stocks (ARPs)** have their dividends tied to the rate on Treasury securities. The ARPs, which are issued mainly by utilities and large commercial banks, were touted as nearly perfect short-term corporate investments because (1) only 30 percent of the dividends are taxable to corporations, and (2) the floating-rate feature was supposed to keep the issue trading at near par. The new security proved to be so popular as a short-term investment for firms with idle cash that mutual funds designed just to invest in them sprouted like weeds (shares of the funds, in turn, were purchased by corporations). However, the ARPs still had some price volatility due to (1) changes in the riskiness of the issues (some big banks that had issued ARPs, such as Continental Illinois, ran into serious loan default problems) and (2) fluctuations in Treasury yields between dividend rate adjustments dates. Thus, the ARPs had too much price instability to be held in the liquid asset portfolios of many corporate investors.

Market Auction Preferred Stock

Market Auction (Money Market) Preferred
A low-risk, largely tax-exempt, seven-week-maturity security that can be sold between auction dates at close to par.

In 1984, investment bankers introduced **money market,** or **market auction, preferred.** Here the underwriter conducts an auction on the issue every seven weeks (to get the 70 percent exclusion from taxable income, buyers must hold the stock at least 46 days). Holders who want to sell their shares can put them up for auction at par value. Buyers then submit bids in the form of the yields they are willing to accept over the next seven-week period. The yield set on the issue for the coming period is the lowest yield sufficient to sell all the shares being offered at that auction. The buyers pay the sellers the par value; hence, holders are virtually assured that their shares can be sold at par. The issuer then must pay a dividend rate over the next seven-week period as determined by the auction. From the holder's standpoint, market auction preferred is a low-risk, largely tax-exempt, seven-week-maturity security that can be sold between auction dates at close to par. However, if there are not enough buyers to match the sellers (in spite of the high yield), then the auction can fail, which has occurred on occasion.

20-1c Advantages and Disadvantages of Preferred Stock

There are both advantages and disadvantages to financing with preferred stock. Here are the major advantages from the issuers' standpoint:

---

[3] For a more rigorous treatment of the tax hypothesis of preferred stock, see Iraj Fooladi and Gordon S. Roberts, "On Preferred Stock," *Journal of Financial Research*, Winter 1986, pp. 319–324. For an example of an empirical test of the hypothesis, see Arthur L. Houston, Jr., and Carol Olson Houston, "Financing with Preferred Stock," *Financial Management*, Autumn 1990, pp. 42–54.

1. In contrast to bonds, the obligation to pay preferred dividends is not contractual, and passing a preferred dividend cannot force a firm into bankruptcy.
2. By issuing preferred stock, the firm avoids the dilution of common equity that occurs when common stock is sold.
3. Because preferred stock sometimes has no maturity, and because preferred sinking fund payments, if present, are typically spread over a long period, preferred issues reduce the cash flow drain from repayment of principal that occurs with debt issues.

There are two major disadvantages:

1. Preferred stock dividends are not deductible to the issuer, hence the after-tax cost of preferred is typically higher than the after-tax cost of debt. However, the tax advantage of preferreds to corporate purchasers lowers its pre-tax cost and thus its effective cost.
2. Although preferred dividends can be passed, investors expect them to be paid, and firms intend to pay the dividends if conditions permit. Thus, preferred dividends are considered to be a fixed cost. Therefore, their use, like that of debt, increases financial risk and thus the cost of common equity.

Should preferred stock be considered as equity or debt? Explain.

Who are the major purchasers of nonconvertible preferred stock? Why?

Briefly explain the mechanics of adjustable rate and market auction preferred stock.

What are the advantages and disadvantages of preferred stock to the issuer?

20-2 LEASING

Firms generally own fixed assets and report them on their balance sheets, but it is the *use* of buildings and equipment that is important, not their ownership per se. One way of obtaining the use of assets is to buy them, but an alternative is to lease them. Prior to the 1950s, leasing was generally associated with real estate—land and buildings. Today, however, it is possible to lease virtually any kind of fixed asset.[4]

20-2a Types of Leases

Leasing takes three different forms: (1) *sale-and-leaseback* arrangements, (2) *operating leases*, and (3) straight *financial*, or *capital, leases*.

Sale and Leaseback

Under a **sale and leaseback,** a firm that owns land, buildings, or equipment sells the property and simultaneously executes an agreement to lease the property back for a specified period under specific terms. The purchaser could be an insurance company, a commercial bank, a specialized leasing company, or even an individual investor. The sale-and-leaseback plan is an alternative to taking out a mortgage loan.

Sale and Leaseback
An arrangement whereby a firm sells land, buildings, or equipment and simultaneously leases the property back for a specified period under specific terms.

---

[4] For a detailed treatment of leasing, see James S. Schallheim, *Lease or Buy? Principles for Sound Decision Making* (Boston: Harvard Business School Press, 1994).

Funny-Named Preferred-Like Securities

Wall Street's "financial engineers" are constantly trying to develop new securities with appeal to issuers and investors. One such new security is a special type of preferred stock created by Goldman Sachs in the mid-1990s. These securities trade under a variety of colorful names, including MIPS (modified income preferred securities), QUIPS (quarterly income preferred securities), and QUIDS (quarterly income debt securities). The corporation that wants to raise capital (the "parent") establishes a trust, which issues fixed-dividend preferred stock. The parent then issues bonds (or debt of some type) to the trust, and the trust pays for the bonds with the cash raised from the sale of preferred. At that point, the parent has the cash it needs, the trust holds debt issued by the parent, and the investing public holds preferred stock issued by the trust. The parent then makes interest payments to the trust, and the trust uses that income to make the preferred

dividend payments. Because the parent company has issued debt, its interest payments are tax deductible.

If the dividends could be excluded from taxable income by corporate investors, this preferred would really be a great deal—the issuer could deduct the interest, corporate investors could exclude most of the dividends, and the IRS would be the loser. The corporate parent does get to deduct the interest paid to the trust, but IRS regulations do not allow the dividends on these securities to be excluded.

Because there is only one deduction, why are these new securities attractive? The answer is as follows: (1) The parent company gets to take the deduction, thus its cost of funds from the preferred is $r_p(1 - T)$, just as it would be if it used debt. (2) The parent generates a tax savings, and it can thus afford to pay a relatively high rate on trust-related preferred; that is, it can pass on some of its tax savings to investors to

---

Lessee
The party that uses, rather than the one who owns, the leased property.

Lessor
The owner of the leased property.

The firm that is selling the property, or the **lessee,** immediately receives the purchase price put up by the buyer, or the **lessor.**[5] At the same time, the seller-lessee firm retains the use of the property just as if it had borrowed and mortgaged the property to secure the loan. Note that under a mortgage loan arrangement, the financial institution would normally receive a series of equal payments just sufficient to amortize the loan while providing a specified rate of return to the lender on the outstanding balance. Under a sale-and-leaseback arrangement, the lease payments are set up in exactly the same way; the payments are set so as to return the purchase price to the investor-lessor while providing a specified rate of return on the lessor's outstanding investment.

Operating Leases

Operating Lease
A lease under which the lessor maintains and finances the property; also called a service lease.

Operating leases, sometimes called *service leases,* provide for both *financing* and *maintenance.* IBM is one of the pioneers of the operating lease contract, and computers and office copying machines, together with automobiles and trucks, are the primary types of equipment involved. Ordinarily, these leases call for the lessor to maintain and service the leased equipment, and the cost of providing maintenance is built into the lease payments.

Another important characteristic of operating leases is the fact that they are frequently *not fully amortized*; in other words, the payments required under the lease contract are not sufficient to recover the full cost of the equipment. However, the lease contract is written for a period considerably shorter than the expected economic life of the leased equipment, and the lessor expects to recover all investment costs through subsequent renewal payments, through subsequent leases to other lessees, or by selling the leased equipment.

---

[5] The term *lessee* is pronounced "less-ee," not "lease-ee," and *lessor* is pronounced "less-or."

induce them to buy the new securities. (3) The primary purchasers of the preferred are low-tax-bracket individuals and tax-exempt institutions such as pension funds. For such purchasers, not being able to exclude the dividend from taxable income is not important. (4) Due to the differential tax rates, the arrangement results in a net tax savings. Competition in capital markets results in a sharing of the savings between investors and corporations.

A 1999 *SmartMoney Online* article argued that these hybrid securities are a good deal for individual investors for the reason set forth above and also because they are sold in small increments—often as small as $25. However, these securities are relatively complex, which increases their risk and makes them hard to value.

If this isn't confusing enough, recent tax law changes have made things even more complicated.

As we discussed in our chapter on dividends, in 2003 Congress passed legislation that reduced the individual tax rates on dividends. It turns out that these lower tax rates do not apply to these types of preferred securities where the issuing company is allowed to deduct the interest paid to the trusts. As a result, some analysts speculate that some companies may once again start issuing more traditional preferred securities.

Sources: Kerry Capell, "High Yields, Low Cost, Funny Names," *BusinessWeek*, September 9, 1996, p. 122; Leslie Haggin, "SmartMoney Online: MIPS, QUIDS, and QUIPS," *SmartMoney Interactive*, April 6, 1999; Kathleen Pender, "Taxing Dividends on Preferred Stock Quite a Mind-Bender," *The San Francisco Chronicle*, June 1, 2003, p. I1; and Jane J. Kim, "Getting Personal: Tax Law May Create New Preferred Stocks," Dow Jones *Newswires*, August 6, 2003.

A final feature of operating leases is that they frequently contain a *cancellation clause*, which gives the lessee the right to cancel the lease before the expiration of the basic agreement. This is an important consideration for the lessee, for it means that the equipment can be returned if it is rendered obsolete by technological developments or if it is no longer needed because of a decline in the lessee's business.

Financial, or Capital, Leases

Financial leases, sometimes called *capital leases,* are differentiated from operating leases in three respects: (1) they do *not* provide for maintenance services, (2) they are *not* cancelable, and (3) they *are* fully amortized (that is, the lessor receives rental payments that are equal to the full price of the leased equipment plus a return on the investment). In a typical financial lease arrangement, the firm that will use the equipment (the lessee) selects the specific items it requires and negotiates the price and delivery terms with the manufacturer. The user firm then negotiates terms with a leasing company and, once the lease terms are set, arranges to have the lessor buy the equipment from the manufacturer or the distributor. When the equipment is purchased, the user firm simultaneously executes the lease agreement.

Financial leases are similar to sale-and-leaseback arrangements, the major difference being that the leased equipment is new and the lessor buys it from a manufacturer or a distributor instead of from the user-lessee. A sale and leaseback may thus be thought of as a special type of financial lease, and both sale and leasebacks and financial leases are analyzed in the same manner.[6]

Financial Lease
A lease that does not provide for maintenance services, is not cancelable, and is fully amortized over its life; also called a capital lease.

---

[6] For a lease transaction to qualify as a lease for *tax purposes,* and thus for the lessee to be able to deduct the lease payments, the life of the lease must not exceed 80 percent of the expected life of the asset, and the lessee cannot be permitted to buy the asset at a nominal value. These conditions are IRS requirements, and they should not be confused with the FASB requirements discussed later in the chapter concerning the capitalization of leases. It is important to consult lawyers and accountants to ascertain whether or not a prospective lease meets current IRS regulations.

20-2b Financial Statement Effects

Lease payments are shown as operating expenses on a firm's income statement, but under certain conditions, neither the leased assets nor the liabilities under the lease contract appear on the firm's balance sheet. For this reason, leasing is often called **off balance sheet financing.** This point is illustrated in Table 20-1 by the balance sheets of two hypothetical firms, B (for Buy) and L (for Lease). Initially, the balance sheets of both firms are identical, and both have debt ratios of 50 percent. Each firm then decides to acquire fixed assets that cost $100. Firm B borrows $100 to make the purchase, so both an asset and a liability are recorded on its balance sheet, and its debt ratio is increased to 75 percent. Firm L leases the equipment, so its balance sheet is unchanged. The lease may call for fixed charges as high as or even higher than those on the loan, and the obligations assumed under the lease may be equally or more dangerous from the standpoint of financial safety, but the firm's debt ratio remains at 50 percent.

To correct this problem, the Financial Accounting Standards Board issued **FASB #13,** which requires that for an unqualified audit report, firms that enter into financial (or capital) leases must restate their balance sheets to report (1) leased assets as fixed assets and (2) the present value of future lease payments as a liability. This process is called *capitalizing the lease,* and its net effect is to cause Firms B and L to have similar balance sheets, both of which will resemble the one shown for Firm B after the asset increase.[7]

The logic behind FASB #13 is as follows. If a firm signs a lease contract, its obligation to make lease payments is just as binding as if it had signed a loan agreement. The failure to make lease payments can bankrupt a firm just as surely as can the failure to make principal and interest payments on a loan. Therefore, for all intents and purposes, a financial lease is identical to a loan.[8]

Off Balance Sheet Financing
Financing in which the assets and liabilities involved do not appear on the firm's balance sheet.

FASB #13
The statement of the Financial Accounting Standards Board that details the conditions and procedures for capitalizing leases.

TABLE 20-1	*Balance Sheet Effects of Leasing*

BEFORE ASSET INCREASE

Firms B and L

Current assets	$ 50	Debt	$ 50
Fixed assets	50	Equity	50
Total	$100		$100

Debt ratio: 50%

AFTER ASSET INCREASE

Firm B, Which Borrows and Buys

Current assets	$ 50	Debt	$150
Fixed assets	150	Equity	50
Total	$200		$200

Debt ratio: 75%

Firm L, Which Leases

Current assets	$ 50	Debt	$ 50
Fixed assets	50	Equity	50
Total	$100		$100

Debt ratio: 50%

---

[7] FASB #13, "Accounting for Leases," November 1976, spells out in detail the conditions under which leases must be capitalized, and the procedures for doing so. Also, see Schallheim, *Lease or Buy?*, Chapter 4, for more on the accounting treatment of leases. The FASB has recently added leasing to the scope of its Fair Value Measurement project, and a final statement had not yet been issued at the time we were writing this chapter (August 2005).

[8] There are, however, certain legal differences between loans and leases. In a bankruptcy liquidation, the lessor is entitled to take possession of the leased asset, and, if the value of the asset is less than the required payments under the lease, the lessor can enter a claim (as a general creditor) for one year's lease payments. In a bankruptcy reorganization, the lessor receives the asset plus three year's lease payments, if needed, to bring the value of the asset up to the remaining investment in the lease. Under a secured loan arrangement, on the other hand, the lender has a security interest in the asset, meaning that if it is sold, the lender will receive the proceeds, and the full unsatisfied portion of the lender's claim will be treated as a general creditor obligation (see Web Appendix 7B). It is not possible to state as a general rule whether a supplier of capital is in a stronger position as a secured creditor or as a lessor. Since one position is usually regarded as being about as good as the other at the time the financial arrangements are being made, a lease is about as risky as a secured term loan from both the lessor-lender's and the lessee-borrower's viewpoints.

This being the case, when a firm signs a lease agreement, it has, in effect, raised its "true" debt ratio and thereby has changed its "true" capital structure. Accordingly, if the firm had previously established a target capital structure, and if there is no reason to think that the optimal capital structure has changed, then using lease financing requires additional equity just as does debt financing.

If a disclosure of the lease in the Table 20-1 example were not made, then investors could be deceived into thinking that Firm L's financial position is stronger than it actually is. Even if the lease were disclosed in a footnote, investors might not fully recognize its impact and might not see that Firms B and L are in essentially the same financial position. If this were the case, Firm L would have increased its true amount of debt through a lease arrangement, but its required return on debt, r_d, its required return on equity, r_s, and consequently its weighted average cost of capital, would not have increased as much as those of Firm B, which borrowed directly. Thus, investors would be willing to accept a lower return from Firm L because they would mistakenly view it as being in a stronger financial position than Firm B. These benefits of leasing would accrue to stockholders at the expense of new investors, who were, in effect, being deceived by the fact that the firm's balance sheet did not fully reflect its true liability situation. This is why FASB #13 was issued.

A lease must be classified as a capital lease, and hence be capitalized and shown directly on the balance sheet, if any one of the following conditions exists:

1. Under the terms of the lease, ownership of the property is effectively transferred from the lessor to the lessee.
2. The lessee can purchase the property or renew the lease at less than a fair market price when the lease expires.
3. The lease runs for a period equal to or greater than 75 percent of the asset's life.
4. The present value of the lease payments is equal to or greater than 90 percent of the initial value of the asset.[9]

These rules, together with strong footnote disclosures for operating leases, are sufficient to ensure that no one will be fooled by lease financing. Thus, leases are recognized to be essentially the same as debt, and they have the same effects as debt on the firm's required rate of return. Therefore, leasing will not generally permit a firm to use more financial leverage than could be obtained with conventional debt.

20-2c Evaluation by the Lessee

Any prospective lease must be evaluated by both the lessee and the lessor. The lessee must determine whether leasing an asset will be less costly than buying it, and the lessor must decide whether or not the lease will provide a reasonable rate of return. Since our focus in this book is primarily on financial management as opposed to investments, we restrict our analysis to that conducted by the lessee.[10]

---

[9] The discount rate used to calculate the present value of the lease payments must be the lower of (1) the rate used by the lessor to establish the lease payments or (2) the interest rate that the lessee would have paid for new debt with a maturity equal to that of the lease.

[10] The lessee is typically offered a set of lease terms by the lessor, which is generally a bank, a finance company such as General Electric Capital (the largest U.S. lessor), or some other institutional lender. The lessee can accept or reject the lease, or shop around for a better deal. In this chapter, we take the lease terms as given for purposes of our analysis. See Chapter 18 of Eugene F. Brigham and Phillip R. Daves, *Intermediate Financial Management*, 8th ed. (Mason, OH: Thomson/South-Western, 2004), for a discussion of lease analysis from the lessor's standpoint, including a discussion of how a potential lessee can use such an analysis in bargaining for better terms.

In the typical case, the events leading to a lease arrangement follow the sequence described in the following list. We should note that a great deal of theoretical literature exists about the correct way to evaluate lease-versus-purchase decisions, and some very complex decision models have been developed to aid in the analysis. The analysis given here, however, leads to the correct decision in every case we have ever encountered.

1. The firm decides to acquire a particular building or piece of equipment. This decision is based on regular capital budgeting procedures, and the decision to acquire the asset is a "done deal" before the lease analysis begins. Therefore, in a lease analysis we are concerned simply with whether to finance the machine by a lease or by a loan.
2. Once the firm has decided to acquire the asset, the next question is how to finance it. Well-run businesses do not have excess cash lying around, so new assets must be financed in some manner.
3. Funds to purchase the asset could be obtained by borrowing, by retaining earnings, or by issuing new stock. Alternatively, the asset could be leased. Because of the FASB #13 capitalization/disclosure provision for leases, a lease would have the same capital structure effect as a loan.

As indicated earlier, a lease is comparable to a loan in the sense that the firm is required to make a specified series of payments, and a failure to make these payments can result in bankruptcy. Thus, it is most appropriate to compare the cost of leasing with that of debt financing.[11] The lease-versus-borrow-and-purchase analysis is illustrated with data on the Mitchell Electronics Company. The following conditions are assumed:

1. Mitchell plans to acquire equipment with a five-year life that has a cost of $10,000,000, delivered and installed.
2. Mitchell can borrow the required $10 million, using a 10 percent loan to be amortized over five years. Therefore, the loan will call for payments of $2,637,974.81 per year, found with a financial calculator as follows: input N = 5, I/YR = 10, PV = −10000000, and FV = 0, and then press PMT to find the payment, $2,637,974.81.
3. Alternatively, Mitchell can lease the equipment for five years at a rental charge of $2,800,000 per year, payable at the end of the year. The lessor will own the asset at the expiration of the lease.[12] The lease payment schedule is established by the potential lessor, and Mitchell can accept it, reject it, or negotiate.
4. The equipment will definitely be used for five years, at which time its estimated net salvage value will be $715,000. Mitchell plans to continue using the equipment beyond Year 5, so (a) if it purchases the equipment, the company will keep it, and (b) if it leases the equipment, the company will exercise an option to buy it at its estimated salvage value, $715,000.
5. The lease contract stipulates that the lessor will maintain the equipment. However, if Mitchell borrows and buys, it will have to bear the cost of maintenance. This service will be performed by the equipment manufacturer at a fixed contract rate of $500,000 per year, payable at year-end.

---

[11] The analysis should compare the cost of leasing to the cost of debt financing *regardless* of how the asset is actually financed. The asset may actually be purchased with available cash if it is not leased, but because leasing is a substitute for debt financing, a comparison between the two is still appropriate.

[12] Lease payments can occur at the beginning of the year or at the end of the year. In this example, we assume end-of-year payments, but we demonstrate beginning-of-year payments in Self-Test Problem ST-2.

6. The equipment falls in the MACRS 5-year class life, and Mitchell's effective federal-plus-state tax rate is 40 percent. Also, the depreciable basis is the original cost of $10,000,000. The MACRS depreciation rates are 20, 32, 19, 12, 11, and 6 percent.

NPV Analysis

Table 20-2 shows the cash flows that would be incurred each year under the two financing plans. The table is set up to produce two time lines of cash flows, one for owning as shown on Line 5 and one for leasing as shown on Line 10. All cash flows occur at the end of the year.

TABLE 20-2   *Mitchell Electronics Company: NPV Lease Analysis (Thousands of Dollars)*

				YEAR		
	0	**1**	**2**	**3**	**4**	**5**
I. COST OF OWNING						
1. Net purchase price	($10,000)					
2. Maintenance cost		($ 500)	($ 500)	($ 500)	($ 500)	($ 500)
3. Tax savings from maintenance		200	200	200	200	200
4. Tax savings from depreciation		800	1,280	760	480	440
5. Net cash flow	($10,000)	$ 500	$ 980	$ 460	$ 180	$ 140
6. PV cost of owning at 6%	($ 8,023)					
II. COST OF LEASING						
7. Lease payment		($2,800)	($2,800)	($2,800)	($2,800)	($2,800)
8. Tax savings from lease payment		1,120	1,120	1,120	1,120	1,120
9. Cost to exercise option						(715)
10. Net cash flow	$ 0	($1,680)	($1,680)	($1,680)	($1,680)	($2,395)
11. PV cost of owning at 6%	($ 7,611)					
III. COST COMPARISON						

12. Net advantage to leasing = NAL
    = PV cost of owning − PV cost of leasing
    = $8,023 − $7,611 = $412 = $412,000

Note: A line-by-line explanation of the table follows:

1. If Mitchell buys the equipment, it will have to spend $10,000,000 at t = 0.
2. If the equipment is owned, Mitchell must pay $500,000 at the end of each year for maintenance.
3. The $500,000 maintenance expense is tax deductible, so it will produce an annual tax savings of (Tax rate)(Maintenance expense) = 0.4($500,000) = $200,000.
4. If Mitchell buys the equipment, it can depreciate it for tax purposes and thus lower taxable income and taxes. The tax savings in each year is equal to (Tax rate)(Depreciation expense) = 0.4(Depreciation expense). As shown in Appendix 12A, the MACRS rates for 5-year property are 20, 32, 19, 12, and 11 percent in Years 1–5, respectively. To illustrate the calculation of the depreciation tax savings, consider Year 2. The depreciation expense is 0.32($10,000,000) = $3,200,000, and the tax savings is 0.4($3,200,000) = $1,280,000.
5. The net cash flows associated with owning are found by summing Lines 1 through 4.
6. The PV (in thousands) of the Line 5 cash flows, when discounted at 6 percent, is −$8,023.
7. The annual end-of-year lease payment is $2,800,000.
8. Because the lease payment is tax deductible, a tax savings of (Tax rate)(Lease payment) = 0.4($2,800,000) = $1,120,000 results.
9. Because Mitchell plans to continue to use the equipment after the lease expires, it must exercise the purchase option for $715,000 at the end of Year 5 if it leases.
10. The net cash flows associated with leasing are found by summing Lines 7 through 9.
11. The PV (in thousands) of the Line 10 cash flows, when discounted at 6 percent, is −$7,611.
12. The net advantage to leasing is merely the difference between the PV cost of owning (in thousands) and the PV cost of leasing (in thousands) = $8,023 − $7,611 = $412. Since the NAL is positive, leasing is favored over borrowing and buying.

The top section of the table (Lines 1 through 6) is devoted to the cost of owning (borrowing and buying). Lines 1 through 4 show the individual cash flow items. Line 5 is a time line that summarizes the annual net cash flows that Mitchell will incur if it finances the equipment with a loan. The present values of these cash flows are summed to find the *present value of the cost of owning*, which is shown on Line 6 in the Year 0 column. (Note that with a financial calculator, we would input the cash flows as shown on Line 5 into the cash flow register, input the interest rate, $I/YR = 6$, and then press the NPV key to obtain the PV of owning the equipment.)

Section II of the table calculates the present value cost of leasing. The lease payments are $2,800,000 per year; this rate, which in this example (but not in all cases) includes maintenance, was established by the prospective lessor and then offered to Mitchell Electronics. If Mitchell accepts the lease, the full $2,800,000 will be a deductible expense, so the tax savings is (Tax rate)(Lease payment) = (0.4)($2,800,000) = $1,120,000. These amounts are shown on Lines 7 and 8.

Line 9 in the lease section shows the $715,000 that Mitchell expects to pay in Year 5 to purchase the equipment. We include this amount as a cost of leasing because Mitchell will almost certainly want to continue the operation and thus will be forced to purchase the equipment from the lessor. If we had assumed that the operation would not be continued, then no entry would have appeared on this line. However, in that case, we would have included the $715,000, minus applicable taxes, as a Year 5 inflow in the cost of owning analysis, because if the asset were purchased originally, it would be sold after five years. Line 10 shows the net cash flows associated with leasing for each year, and Line 11 shows the PV cost of leasing. (As indicated earlier in the cost of owning analysis, using a financial calculator, we would input the cash flows as shown on Line 10 into the cash flow register, input the interest rate, $I/YR = 6$, and then press the NPV key to obtain the PV cost of leasing the equipment.)

The rate used to discount the cash flows is a critical issue. In Chapter 8, we saw that the riskier a cash flow, the higher the discount rate used to find its present value. This same principle was observed in capital budgeting, and it also applies in lease analysis. Just how risky are the cash flows under consideration here? Most of them are relatively certain, at least when compared with the types of cash flow estimates that were developed in capital budgeting. For example, the maintenance payments are set by contract, as is the lease payment schedule. The depreciation expenses are also established by law and are not subject to change. The tax savings are somewhat uncertain because tax rates may change, although tax rates do not change very often. The residual value is the least certain of the cash flows, but even here the $715,000 cost is set, and Mitchell's management is fairly confident that it will want to acquire the property.

Since the cash flows under both the lease and the borrow-and-purchase alternatives are all reasonably certain, they should be discounted at a relatively low rate. Most analysts recommend that the company's cost of debt be used, and this rate seems reasonable in our example. Further, since all the cash flows are on an after-tax basis, *the after-tax cost of debt, which is 6 percent, should be used.* Accordingly, in Table 20-2, we used a 6 percent discount rate to obtain the present values of the costs of owning and leasing. The financing method that results in the smaller present value of costs is the one that should be selected. The example shown in Table 20-2 indicates that leasing has a net advantage over buying: the present value of the cost of leasing is $412,000 less than that of buying. Therefore, it is to Mitchell's advantage to lease.

20-2d Factors That Affect Leasing Decisions

The basic method of analysis set forth in Table 20-2 is sufficient to handle most situations. However, two factors warrant additional comments.

Estimated Residual Value

It is important to note that the lessor will own the property upon the expiration of the lease. The estimated end-of-lease value of the property is called the **residual value.** Superficially, it would appear that if residual values are expected to be large, owning would have an advantage over leasing. However, if expected residual values are large—as they may be under inflation for certain types of equipment as well as if real property is involved—then competition among leasing companies will force leasing rates down to the point where potential residual values will be fully recognized in the lease contract rates. Thus, the existence of large residual values on equipment is not likely to bias the decision against leasing.

Residual Value
The value of leased property at the end of the lease term.

Increase Credit Availability

As noted earlier, leasing is sometimes said to have an advantage for firms that are seeking the maximum degree of financial leverage. First, it is sometimes argued that a firm can obtain more money, and for a longer period, under a lease arrangement than under a loan secured by the asset. Second, because some leases do not appear on the balance sheet, lease financing has been said to give the firm a stronger appearance in a superficial credit analysis, thus permitting it to use more leverage than it could if it did not lease. There may be some truth to these claims for smaller firms. However, now that larger firms are required to capitalize major leases and to report them on their balance sheets, this point is of questionable validity.

Define each of these terms: (1) sale-and-leaseback arrangements, (2) operating leases, and (3) financial, or capital, leases.

What is off balance sheet financing, what is FASB #13, and how are the two related?

List the sequence of events, for the lessee, leading to a lease arrangement.

Why is it appropriate to compare the cost of lease financing with that of debt financing? Why does the comparison not depend on how the asset will actually be financed if it is not leased?

20-3 WARRANTS

A **warrant** is a certificate issued by a company that gives the holder the right to buy a stated number of shares of the company's stock at a specified price for some specified length of time. Generally, warrants are distributed with debt, and they are used to induce investors to buy long-term debt with a lower coupon rate than would otherwise be required. For example, when Infomatics Corporation, a rapidly growing high-tech company, wanted to sell $50 million of 20-year bonds in 2005, the company's investment bankers informed the financial vice president that the bonds would be difficult to sell, and that a coupon rate of 10 percent would be required. However, as an alternative the bankers suggested that investors might be willing to buy the bonds with a coupon rate of only 8 percent if the company would offer 20 warrants with each $1,000 bond, each warrant entitling the holder to buy one share of common stock at an exercise price of $22 per share. The stock was selling for $20 per share at the time, and the warrants would expire in the year 2015 if they had not been exercised previously.

Warrant
A long-term option to buy a stated number of shares of common stock at a specified price.

Why would investors be willing to buy Infomatics' bonds at a yield of only 8 percent in a 10 percent market just because warrants were also offered as part of the package? It is because the warrants are long-term *call options* that have value because holders can buy the firm's common stock at the exercise price regardless of how high the market price climbs. This option offsets the low interest rate on the bonds and makes the package of low-yield bonds plus warrants attractive to investors. (See Chapter 18 for a more complete discussion of options.)

20-3a Initial Market Price of a Bond with Warrants

The Infomatics bonds, if they had been issued as straight debt, would have carried a 10 percent interest rate. However, with warrants attached, the bonds were sold to yield 8 percent. Someone buying the bonds at their $1,000 initial offering price would thus be receiving a package consisting of an 8 percent, 20-year bond plus 20 warrants. Since the going interest rate on bonds as risky as those of Infomatics was 10 percent, we can find the straight-debt value of the bonds, assuming an annual coupon for ease of illustration, as follows:

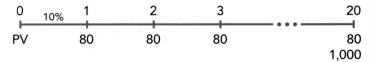

Using a financial calculator, input $N = 20$, $I/YR = 10$, $PMT = 80$, and $FV = 1000$. Then, press the PV key to obtain the bond's value, $829.73, or approximately $830. Thus, a person buying the bonds in the initial underwriting would pay $1,000 and receive in exchange a straight bond worth about $830 plus 20 warrants presumably worth about $1,000 − $830 = $170:

$$\begin{array}{ccccc} \text{Price paid for} \\ \text{bond with warrants} \end{array} = \begin{array}{c} \text{Straight-debt} \\ \text{value of bond} \end{array} + \begin{array}{c} \text{Value of} \\ \text{warrants} \end{array} \qquad \textbf{(20-1)}$$

$$\$1,000 \qquad = \qquad \$830 \quad + \quad \$170$$

Investors receive 20 warrants with each bond, so each warrant has an implied value of $170/20 = $8.50.

The key issue in setting the terms of a bond with warrants is valuing the warrants. The straight-debt value can be estimated quite accurately, as was done above. However, it is more difficult to estimate the value of the warrants. The Black-Scholes Option Pricing Model (OPM), which we discussed in Chapter 18, can be used to find the value of a call option. There is a temptation to use this model to find the value of a warrant, since call options are similar to warrants in many respects: Both give the investor the right to buy a share of stock at a fixed exercise price on or before the expiration date. However, there is a major difference between call options and warrants: When call options are exercised, the stock provided to the optionholder comes from the secondary market, but when warrants are exercised, the stock provided to the warrant holders are newly issued shares. This means that the exercise of warrants dilutes the value of the original equity, which could cause the value of the original warrant to differ from the value of a similar call option. Therefore, investment bankers cannot use the Black-Scholes model to determine the value of warrants.

It is extremely important to assign the correct value to the warrants. If, when the issue is originally priced, the value assigned to the warrants is greater than their true market value, then the coupon rate on the bonds will be set too low, and it will be impossible to sell the bond-with-warrants package at its par value. In this case, Infomatics will not be able to raise the full $50 million that it needs to fund its growth.

Conversely, if the value of the warrants is underestimated, then the coupon rate will be set too high. This means that the true value of the bonds with warrants will be greater than the issue price. Suppose this happens, and the true value of the bonds with warrants is $60 million. Investors will eagerly buy all of the bonds with warrants at the issue price, and Infomatics will receive the full $50 million that it needs. But this is not good news for the existing shareholders.

To see this, think of the total value of Infomatics as being analogous to a pie. The size of the pie is equal to the present value of all the future cash flows expected to be generated by Infomatics' operations and investments. Pieces of the pie belong to different groups of investors, such as debtholders and holders of bonds with warrants. Shareholders come last and get the remaining piece of the pie, after the other investors have received their fair share.

At the time of the bond offering, Infomatics had 10 million shares of common stock outstanding and no other debt or preferred stock. The stock price was $20 per share, so the total market value of Infomatics was 10 million × $20 = $200 million. The offering itself will raise $50 million in cash, which will subsequently be invested in projects. Therefore, immediately after the offering the total value of Infomatics is $250 million ($200 million in stock plus $50 million in cash).[13] If investors in the bonds with warrants pay only $50 million for a piece of pie that is worth $60 million, then the piece of pie remaining for the original shareholders is only worth $190 million ($250 million − $60 million). The result is a $10 million transfer of wealth from the original shareholders to the investors in the bonds with warrants. Therefore, it is extremely important for Infomatics to correctly estimate the value of the warrants at the time the bonds with warrants are issued.

20-3b Use of Warrants in Financing

Warrants generally are used by small, rapidly growing firms as "sweeteners" when they sell debt or preferred stock. Such firms frequently are regarded by investors as being highly risky, so their bonds can be sold only at extremely high coupon rates and with very restrictive indenture provisions. To avoid this, firms such as Infomatics often offer warrants along with the bonds. However, some years ago, AT&T raised $1.57 billion by selling bonds with warrants. This was the largest financing of any type ever undertaken by a business firm, and it marked the first use ever of warrants by a large, strong corporation.[14]

Getting warrants along with bonds enables investors to share in the company's growth, assuming it does in fact grow and prosper. Therefore, investors are willing to accept a lower interest rate and less restrictive indenture provisions. A bond with warrants has some characteristics of debt and some characteristics of equity. It is a hybrid security that provides the financial manager with an opportunity to expand the firm's mix of securities and thus to appeal to a broader group of investors.

---

[13] We assume that the average expected net present value of these projects is zero. If NPV > 0, then the total value of Infomatics will be greater than $250 million. In this case, there will be little change in the price of the bonds, since bondholders receive the fixed coupon payment no matter how well the company does. However, the stock price and the value of the warrants will increase, since the total value of the company has increased without a commensurate increase in the value committed to the bondholders. The reverse would occur if NPV < 0.

[14] It is interesting to note that before the AT&T issue, the New York Stock Exchange's stated policy was that warrants could not be listed because they were "speculative" instruments rather than "investment" securities. When AT&T issued warrants, however, the Exchange changed its policy, agreeing to list warrants that met certain requirements. Many other warrants have since been listed.

It is also interesting to note that, prior to the sale, AT&T's treasury staff, working with Morgan Stanley analysts, estimated the value of the warrants as a part of the underwriting decision. The package was supposed to sell for a total price in the neighborhood of $1,000. The bond value could be determined accurately, so the trick was to estimate the equilibrium value of the warrant under different possible exercise prices and years to expiration, and then to use an exercise price and life that would cause Bond value + Warrant value = $1,000. Using a warrant pricing model, the AT&T/Morgan Stanley analysts set terms that caused the warrant to sell on the open market at a price that was only 35¢ off from the estimated price.

Detachable Warrant
A warrant that can be detached from a bond and traded independently of it.

Virtually all warrants today are **detachable.** Thus, after a bond with attached warrants is sold, the warrants can be detached and traded separately from the bond. Further, even after the warrants have been exercised, the bond (with its low coupon rate) remains outstanding.

The exercise price on warrants is generally set some 20 to 30 percent above the market price of the stock on the date the bond is issued. If the firm grows and prospers, and if its stock price rises above the exercise price at which shares may be purchased, warrant holders could exercise their warrants and buy stock at the stated price. However, without some incentive, warrants would never be exercised prior to maturity—their value in the open market would be greater than their value if exercised, so holders would sell warrants rather than exercise them. There are three conditions that encourage holders to exercise their warrants: (1) Warrant holders will surely exercise and buy stock if the warrants are about to expire and the market price of the stock is above the exercise price. (2) Warrant holders will exercise voluntarily if the company raises the dividend on the common stock by a sufficient amount. No dividend is earned on the warrant, so it provides no current income. However, if the common stock pays a high dividend, it provides an attractive dividend yield but limits price growth. This induces warrant holders to exercise their option to buy the stock. (3) Warrants sometimes have **stepped-up exercise prices,** which prod owners into exercising them. For example, Williamson Scientific Company has warrants outstanding with an exercise price of $25 until December 31, 2009, at which time the exercise price rises to $30. If the price of the common stock is over $25 just before December 31, 2009, many warrant holders will exercise their options before the stepped-up price takes effect and the value of the warrants falls.

Stepped-Up Exercise Price
An exercise price that is specified to rise if a warrant is exercised after a designated date.

Another desirable feature of warrants is that they generally bring in funds only if funds are needed. If the company grows, it will probably need new equity capital. At the same time, growth will cause the price of the stock to rise and the warrants to be exercised, hence the firm will obtain additional cash. If the company is not successful, and it cannot profitably employ additional money, the price of its stock will probably not rise sufficiently to induce exercise of the warrants.

20-3c Wealth Effects and Dilution Due to Warrants

Assume that the value of Infomatics' operations and investments, which is $250 million immediately after issuing the bonds with warrants, is expected to grow, and does grow, at 9 percent per year. When the warrants are due to expire in 10 years, the total value of Infomatics will be $250(1.09)^{10} = 591.841 million. How is this value allocated among the original stockholders, the bondholders, and the warrant holders? The bonds will have 10 years remaining until maturity, with a fixed coupon payment of $80. If the expected market interest rate is still 10 percent, then:

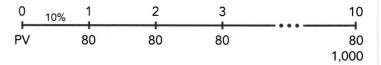

Using a financial calculator, input N = 10, I/YR = 10, PMT = 80, and FV = 1000. Press the PV key to obtain the bond's value, $877.11. The total value of all of the bonds is 50,000($877.11) = $43.856 million.

The value remaining for the original stockholders and the warrant holders is equal to the remaining value of the firm, after deducting the value due to the bondholders. This remaining value is $591.841 − $43.856 = $547.985 million. If there had been no warrants, then the original stockholders would have been entitled to all of this remaining value. Recall that there are 10 million shares of stock, so the price per share would be $547.985/10 = $54.80. Suppose the company has a basic earning power of 13.5 percent (recall that BEP = EBIT/Total Assets) and total assets of $591.841 million.[15] This means that EBIT is 0.135($591.841) = $79.899 million; interest payments are $4 million ($80 coupon payment per bond × 50,000 bonds); and earnings before taxes are $79.899 − $4 = $75.899 million. With a tax rate of 40 percent, after-tax earnings are equal to $75.899(1 − 0.4) = $45.539 million, and earnings per share are $45.539/10 = $4.55. Therefore, if Infomatics had no warrants, the stock price would be $54.80 per share, and the earnings per share would be $4.55.

But Infomatics *does* have warrants, and with the stock price over $50 the warrant holders surely will choose to exercise their warrants. Infomatics will receive $22 million when the 1 million warrants are exercised at a price of $22 per warrant. This makes the total value $613.841 million (the $591.841 million total value of the firm plus the $22 million raised by the exercise of the warrants). The total value remaining for stockholders is now $569.985 million ($613.841 million less the $43.856 million allocated to bondholders). There are now 11 million shares of stock (the original 10 million plus the new 1 million due to the exercise of the warrants), so the stock price is $569.985/11 = $51.82 per share. Note that this is lower than the $54.80 price per share that Infomatics would have had if there had been no warrants. In other words, the warrants have diluted the value of the stock.

A similar dilution occurs with earnings per share. After exercise, the asset base would increase from $591.841 million to $613.841 million, with the additional $22 million coming from the purchase of 1 million shares of stock at $22 per share. If the new funds have the same basic earning power as the existing funds, then the new EBIT would be 0.135($613.841) = $82.869 million. Interest payments would still be $4 million, so earnings before taxes would be $82.869 − $4 = $78.869 million, and after-tax earnings will be $78.869(1 − 0.4) = $47.321 million. With 10 + 1 = 11 million shares now outstanding, EPS would be $47.321/11 = $4.30, down from $4.55. Therefore, exercising the warrants would dilute EPS.

Has this wealth transfer harmed the original shareholders? The answer is yes and no. Yes, because the original shareholders clearly are worse off than they would have been if there had been no warrants. However, if there had been no warrants attached to the bonds, then the bonds would have had a 10 percent coupon rate instead of the 8 percent coupon rate. Also, if the value of the company had not increased as expected, then it might not have been profitable for the warrant holders to exercise their warrants. In other words, the original shareholders were willing to trade off the potential dilution for the lower coupon rate. In this example, the original stockholders and the investors in the bonds with warrants got what they expected. Therefore, the answer is no, the wealth transfer at the time of exercise did not harm the original shareholders, because they expected an eventual transfer and were fairly compensated by the lower coupon payments.

Note too that investors would recognize the situation, so the actual wealth transfer would occur gradually over time, not in a fell swoop when the warrants were exercised. First, EPS would have been reported on a diluted basis over the years, and on that basis, there would be no decline whatever in EPS. (We discuss this in a later section of this chapter.) Also, investors would know what was happening, so the stock price, over time, would reflect the likely future dilution, so it too would be stable when the warrants were exercised. So, whereas our calculations show the effects of the warrants, those effects would actually be reflected in EPS and the stock price on a gradual basis over time.

---

[15] In this case, the total market value equals the book value of assets, but the same calculations would follow even if market and book values were not equal.

20-3d The Component Cost of Bonds with Warrants

When Infomatics issued its debt with warrants, the firm received $50 million, or $1,000 for each bond. Simultaneously, the company assumed an obligation to pay $80 interest for 20 years plus $1,000 at the end of 20 years. The pre-tax cost of the money would have been 10 percent if no warrants had been attached, but each Infomatics bond had 20 warrants, each of which entitles its holder to buy one share of Infomatics stock for $22. What is the percentage cost of the $50 million? As we shall see, the cost is well above the 8 percent coupon rate on the bonds.

As we demonstrated earlier, when the warrants expire 10 years from now, the expected stock price is $51.82. The company would then have to issue one share of stock worth $51.82 for each warrant exercised and, in return, Infomatics would receive the exercise price, $22. Thus, a purchaser of the bonds, if he or she holds the complete package, would realize a profit in Year 10 of $51.82 − $22 = $29.82 for each common share issued. Since each bond has 20 warrants attached, and each warrant entitles the holder to buy one share of common stock, investors would have a gain of 20($29.82) = $596.40 per bond at the end of Year 10. Here is a time line of the cash flow stream to an investor:

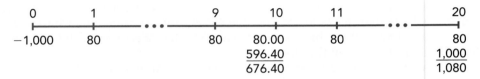

The IRR of this stream is 10.7 percent, which is the investor's overall pre-tax rate of return on the issue. This return is 70 basis points higher than the return on straight debt. This reflects the fact that the issue is riskier to investors than a straight-debt issue because some of the return is expected to come in the form of stock price appreciation, and that part of the return is relatively risky.

The expected rate of return to investors is the before-tax cost to the company—this was true of common stocks, straight bonds, and preferred stocks, and it is also true of bonds sold with warrants.

20-3e Problems with Warrant Issues

Although warrants are bought by investors with the expectation of receiving a total return commensurate with the overall riskiness of the package of securities being purchased, things do not always work out as expected. For example, in 1989 Sony paid $3.4 billion for Columbia Pictures, a U.S. movie studio. To help finance the deal, in 1990 Sony sold $470 million of four-year bonds with warrants at an incredibly low 0.3 percent coupon interest rate. The rate was so low because the warrants, which also had a maturity of four years, allowed investors to purchase Sony stock at 7,670 yen per share, only 2.5 percent above the share price at the time the bonds with warrants were issued.

Investors snapped up the issue, and many of the warrants were "peeled off" and sold separately on the open market. The warrant buyers obviously believed that Sony's stock would climb well above the exercise price. From Sony's point of view, the bond-with-warrants package provided a very low-cost "bridge loan" (the bonds) that would be replaced with equity financing when the warrants were exercised, presumably in four years when the bonds became due. This very low cost capital encouraged Japanese firms to acquire foreign companies and to invest huge amounts in new plant and equipment.

However, the willingness of investors to buy Japanese warrants suffered a severe blow when the Japanese stock market fell by 40 percent. By 1994, when the warrants expired, Sony's stock sold for only 5,950 yen versus the 7,670 yen exercise price, so the warrants were not exercised. Thus, Sony's planned infusion of equity capital never materialized, and it had to refinance the four-year bond issue at much higher rates.

Both Sony and its investors lost on the deal. The investors lost because they did not get the return they expected on the issue. Sony lost because it had to alter its financing plans because the warrants were not exercised. In spite of presumably good planning by both the company and investors, this bond-with-warrants issue, and many like it, did not work out as anticipated.

What is a warrant?

Describe how a new bond issue with warrants is valued.

How are warrants used in corporate financing?

The use of warrants lowers the coupon rate on the corresponding debt issue. Does this mean that the component cost of a debt-plus-warrants package is less than the cost of straight debt? Explain.

A company recently issued bonds with attached warrants. The bond-plus-warrants package sells at a price equal to its $1,000 face value. The bonds mature in 10 years and have a 6 percent annual coupon. The company also has 10-year straight debt (with no warrants attached) outstanding. The straight debt has a yield to maturity of 8 percent. What is the straight-debt value of the bonds? What is the value of the warrants? ($865.80; $134.20)

20-4 CONVERTIBLES

Convertible securities are bonds or preferred stocks that, under specified terms and conditions, can be exchanged for (that is, converted into) common stock at the option of the holder. Unlike the exercise of warrants, which brings in additional funds to the firm, conversion does not provide capital: debt (or preferred stock) is simply replaced on the balance sheet by common stock. Of course, reducing the debt or preferred stock will improve the firm's financial strength and make it easier to raise additional capital, but that requires a separate action.

> **Convertible Security**
> A security, usually a bond or preferred stock, that is exchangeable at the option of the holder for the common stock of the issuing firm.

20-4a Conversion Ratio and Conversion Price

One of the most important provisions of a convertible security is the **conversion ratio, CR**, defined as the number of shares of stock a bondholder will receive upon conversion. Related to the conversion ratio is the **conversion price, P_c**, which is the effective price investors pay for the common stock when conversion occurs. The relationship between the conversion ratio and the conversion price can be illustrated by the Silicon Valley Software Company's convertible debentures issued at their $1,000 par value in August 2005. At any time prior to maturity on August 15, 2025, a debenture holder can exchange a bond for 20 shares of common stock; therefore, the conversion ratio, CR, is 20. The bond cost purchasers $1,000, the par value, when it was issued. Dividing the $1,000 par value by the 20 shares received gives a conversion price of $50 a share.

> **Conversion Ratio, CR**
> The number of shares of common stock that are obtained by converting a convertible bond or share of convertible preferred stock.

> **Conversion Price, P_c**
> The effective price paid for common stock obtained by converting a convertible security.

$$\text{Conversion price} = P_c = \frac{\text{Par value of bond given up}}{\text{Shares received}} \quad \textbf{(20-2)}$$

$$= \frac{\$1,000}{CR} = \frac{\$1,000}{20} = \$50$$

Conversely, by solving for CR, we obtain the conversion ratio.

$$\text{Conversion ratio} = \text{CR} = \frac{\$1{,}000}{P_c} \qquad\qquad \textbf{(20-3)}$$

$$= \frac{\$1{,}000}{\$50} = 20 \text{ shares}$$

Once CR is set, the value of P_c is established, and vice versa.

Like a warrant's exercise price, the conversion price is typically set at from 20 to 30 percent above the prevailing market price of the common stock at the time the convertible issue is sold. Exactly how the conversion price is established can best be understood after examining some of the reasons firms use convertibles.

Generally, the conversion price and conversion ratio are fixed for the life of the bond, although sometimes a stepped-up conversion price is used. For example, the 2005 convertible debentures for Breedon Industries are convertible into 12.5 shares until 2015; into 11.76 shares from 2015 until 2025; and into 11.11 shares from 2025 until maturity in 2035. The conversion price thus starts at $80, rises to $85, and then goes to $90. Breedon's convertibles, like most, have a 10-year call protection period.

Another factor that may cause a change in the conversion price and ratio is a standard feature of almost all convertibles—the clause protecting the convertible against dilution from stock splits, stock dividends, and the sale of common stock at prices below the conversion price. The typical provision states that if common stock is sold at a price below the conversion price, then the conversion price must be lowered (and the conversion ratio raised) to the price at which the new stock was issued. Also, if the stock is split, or if a stock dividend is declared, the conversion price must be lowered by the percentage amount of the stock dividend or split. For example, if Breedon Industries were to have a two-for-one stock split during the first 10 years of its convertible's life, the conversion ratio would automatically be adjusted from 12.5 to 25, and the conversion price lowered from $80 to $40. If this protection were not contained in the contract, a company could completely thwart conversion by the use of stock splits and stock dividends. Warrants are similarly protected against dilution.

The standard protection against dilution from selling new stock at prices below the conversion price can, however, get a company into trouble. For example, assume that Breedon's stock was selling for $65 per share at the time the convertible was issued. Further, suppose the market went sour, and Breedon's stock price dropped to $50 per share. If Breedon needed new equity to support operations, a new common stock sale would require the company to lower the conversion price on the convertible debentures from $80 to $50. That would raise the value of the convertibles and, in effect, transfer wealth from current shareholders to the convertible holders. This transfer would, de facto, amount to an additional flotation cost on the new common stock issue. Potential problems such as this must be kept in mind by firms considering the use of convertibles or bonds with warrants.

20-4b The Component Cost of Convertibles

In the spring of 2005, Silicon Valley Software was evaluating the use of the convertible bond issue described earlier. The issue would consist of 20-year convertible bonds that would sell at a price of $1,000 per bond; this $1,000 would also be the bond's par (and maturity) value. The bonds would pay a 10 percent annual coupon interest rate, or $100 per year. Each bond would be convertible into 20 shares of stock, so the conversion price would be $1,000/20 = $50. The stock was expected to pay a dividend of $2.80 during the coming year, and it sold at $35 per share. Further, the stock price was expected to grow at a constant rate of 8 percent per year. Therefore, $r_s = \hat{r}_s = D_1/P_0 + g = \$2.80/\$35 + 8\% = 8\% + 8\% = 16\%$. If the bonds were not made convertible, they would have to offer a yield of 13 percent, given their riskiness and the general level of interest rates. The convertible bonds would not be callable for 10 years, after which they could be called at a price of $1,050, with this price declining by $5 per year thereafter. If, after 10 years, the conversion value exceeds the call price by at least 20 percent, management would probably call the bonds.

Figure 20-1 shows the expectations of both an average investor and the company.[16]

1. The horizontal line at M = $1,000 represents the par (and maturity) value. Also, $1,000 is the price at which the bond is initially offered to the public.
2. The bond is protected against call for 10 years. It is initially callable at a price of $1,050, and the call price declines thereafter by $5 per year. Thus, the call price is represented by the solid section of the line V_0M''.
3. Since the convertible has a 10 percent coupon rate, and since the yield on a nonconvertible bond of similar risk was stated to be 13 percent, the expected "straight-bond" value of the convertible, B_t, must be less than par. At the time of issue, assuming an annual coupon, B_0 is $789:

$$\begin{matrix} \text{Pure-debt value} \\ \text{at time of issue} \end{matrix} = B_0 = \sum_{t=1}^{N} \frac{\text{Coupon interest}}{(1 + r_d)^t} + \frac{\text{Maturity value}}{(1 + r_d)^N} \qquad \textbf{(20-4)}$$

$$= \sum_{t=1}^{20} \frac{\$100}{(1.13)^t} + \frac{\$1,000}{(1.13)^{20}} = \$789$$

Note, however, that the bond's straight-debt value must be $1,000 just prior to maturity, so the straight-debt value rises over time. B_t follows the line B_0M'' in the graph.

4. The bond's initial **conversion value, C_t,** or the value of the stock the investor would receive if the bonds were converted at t = 0, is $700. The bond's conversion value is $P_t(CR)$, so at t = 0, Conversion value = $P_0(CR)$ = $35(20 shares) = $700. Since the stock price is expected to grow at an 8 percent rate, the conversion value should rise over time. For example, in Year 5 it should be $P_5(CR) = \$35(1.08)^5(20) = \$1,029$. The expected conversion value over time is given by the line C_t in Figure 20-1.
5. The actual market price of the bond can never fall below the higher of its straight-debt value or its conversion value. If the market price dropped below the straight-bond value, those who wanted bonds would recognize the bargain and buy the convertible as a bond. Similarly, if the market price dropped below the conversion value, people would buy the convertibles, exercise them to get stock, and then sell the stock at a profit. Therefore, the higher

Conversion Value, C_t
The value of common stock obtained by converting a convertible security.

---

[16] For a more complete discussion of how the terms of a convertible offering are determined, see M. Wayne Marr and G. Rodney Thompson, "The Pricing of New Convertible Bond Issues," *Financial Management*, Summer 1984, pp. 31–37.

FIGURE 20-1   *Silicon Valley Software: Convertible Bond Model*

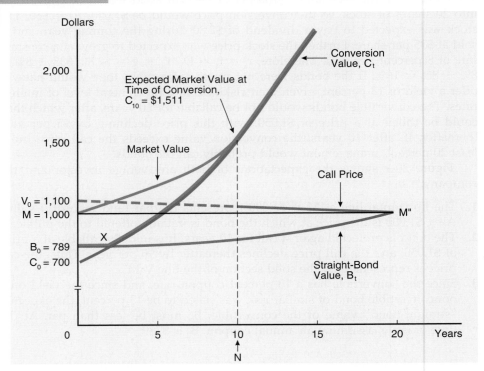

Year	Pure-Bond Value, B_t	Conversion Value, C_t	Maturity Value, M	Market Value	Floor Value	Premium
0	$ 789	$ 700	$1,000	$1,000	$ 789	$211
1	792	756	1,000	1,023	792	231
2	795	816	1,000	1,071	816	255
3	798	882	1,000	1,147	882	265
4	802	952	1,000	1,192	952	240
5	806	1,029	1,000	1,241	1,029	212
6	811	1,111	1,000	1,293	1,111	182
7	816	1,200	1,000	1,344	1,200	144
8	822	1,296	1,000	1,398	1,296	102
9	829	1,399	1,000	1,453	1,399	54
10	837	1,511	1,000	1,511	1,511	0
11	846	1,632	1,000	1,632	1,632	0
.	.	.	.	.	.	.
.	.	.	.	.	.	.
.	.	.	.	.	.	.
20	1,000	3,263	1,000	3,263	3,263	0

of the bond value and conversion value curves in the graph represents a *floor price* for the bond. In Figure 20-1, the floor price is represented by the thicker shaded line $B_0 X C_t$.

6. The bond's market value will typically exceed its floor value. It will exceed the straight-bond value because the option to convert is worth something—a 10 percent bond with conversion possibilities is worth more than a 10 percent bond without this option. The convertible's price will also exceed its conversion value because holding the convertible is equivalent to holding a call option, and, prior to expiration, the option's true value is higher than its

expiration (or conversion) value. Without using a sophisticated pricing model, we cannot say exactly where the market value line will lie, but as a rule it will be at or above the floor set by the straight-bond and conversion value lines.

7. At some point, the market value line will touch the conversion value line. This convergence will occur for two reasons. First, the stock should pay higher and higher dividends as the years go by, but the interest payments on the convertible are fixed. For example, Silicon's convertibles would pay $100 in interest annually, while the dividends on the 20 shares received upon conversion would initially be 20($2.80) = $56. However, at an 8 percent growth rate, the dividends after ten years would be up to $120.90, while the interest would still be $100. Thus, at some point, rising dividends could be expected to push against the fixed interest payments, causing the premium to disappear and investors to convert voluntarily. Second, once the bond becomes callable, its market value cannot exceed the higher of the conversion value and the call price without exposing investors to the danger of a call. For example, suppose that 10 years after issue (when the bonds were callable), the market value of the bond was $1,600, the conversion value was $1,500, and the call price was $1,050. If the company called the bonds the day after you bought 10 bonds for $16,000, you would be forced to convert into stock worth only $15,000, so you would suffer a loss of $100 per bond, or $1,000, in one day. Recognizing this danger, you and other investors would simply not pay a premium over the higher of the call price or the conversion value once the bond becomes callable. Therefore, in Figure 20-1, we assume that the market value line hits the conversion value line in Year 10, when the bond becomes callable.

8. Let N represent the year when investors expect conversion to occur, either voluntarily because of rising dividends or because the company calls the convertibles to strengthen its balance sheet by substituting equity for debt. In our example, we assume that N = 10, the first call date.

9. Since N = 10, the expected market value at Year 10 is $35(1.08)^{10}(20) = $1,511$. An investor can find the expected rate of return on the convertible bond, r_c, by finding the IRR of the following cash flow stream:

The solution is r_c = IRR = 12.8%.

10. The return on a convertible is expected to come partly from interest income and partly from capital gains; in this case, the total expected return is 12.8 percent, with 10 percent representing interest income and 2.8 percent representing the expected capital gain. The interest component is relatively assured, while the capital gain component is more risky. Therefore, a convertible's expected return is more risky than that of a straight bond. This leads us to conclude that r_c should be larger than the cost of straight debt, r_d. Thus, it would seem that the expected rate of return on Silicon's convertibles, r_c, should lie between its cost of straight debt, r_d = 13%, and its cost of common stock, r_s = 16%.

11. Investment bankers use the type of model described here, plus a knowledge of the market, to set the terms on convertibles (the conversion ratio, coupon interest rate, and years of call protection) such that the security will just

"clear the market" at its $1,000 offering price. In our example, the required conditions do not hold—the calculated rate of return on the convertible is only 12.8 percent, which is less than the 13 percent cost of straight debt. Therefore, the terms on the bond must be made more attractive to investors. Silicon Valley Software would have to increase the coupon interest rate on the convertible above 10 percent, raise the conversion ratio above 20 (and thereby lower the conversion price from $50 to a level closer to the current $35 market price of the stock), lengthen the call-protected period, or use a combination of these three such that the expected return on the convertible ends up between 13 and 16 percent.[17]

20-4c Use of Convertibles in Financing

Convertibles have two important advantages from the issuer's standpoint: (1) Convertibles, like bonds with warrants, offer a company the chance to sell debt with a low interest rate in exchange for a chance to participate in the company's success if it does well. (2) In a sense, convertibles provide a way to sell common stock at prices higher than those currently prevailing. Some companies actually want to sell common stock, not debt, but feel that the price of their stock is temporarily depressed. Management may know, for example, that earnings are depressed because of startup costs associated with a new project, but they expect earnings to rise sharply during the next year or so, pulling the price of the stock up with them. Thus, if the company sold stock now, it would be giving up more shares than necessary to raise a given amount of capital. However, if it set the conversion price 20 to 30 percent above the present market price of the stock, then 20 to 30 percent fewer shares would be given up when the bonds were converted than if stock were sold directly at the current time. Note, however, that management is counting on the stock's price to rise above the conversion price to make the bonds attractive in conversion. If earnings do not rise and pull the stock price up, hence conversion does not occur, then the company will be saddled with debt in the face of low earnings, which could be disastrous.

How can the company be sure that conversion will occur if the price of the stock rises above the conversion price? Typically, convertibles contain a call provision that enables the issuing firm to force holders to convert. Suppose the conversion price is $50, the conversion ratio is 20, the market price of the common stock has risen to $60, and the call price on a convertible bond is $1,050. If the company calls the bond, bondholders can either convert into common stock with a market value of 20($60) = $1,200 or allow the company to redeem the bond for $1,050. Naturally, bondholders prefer $1,200 to $1,050, so conversion would occur. The call provision gives the company a way to force conversion, provided the market price of the stock is greater than the conversion price. Note, however, that most convertibles have a fairly long period of call protection—10 years is typical. Therefore, if the company wants to be able to force conversion fairly early, then it will have to set a short call-protection period. This will, in turn, require that it set a higher coupon rate or a lower conversion price.

From the standpoint of the issuer, convertibles have three important disadvantages: (1) Although the use of a convertible bond may give the company the opportunity to sell stock at a price higher than the price at which it could be sold currently, if the stock greatly increases in price, the firm would probably find that it would have been better off if it had used straight debt in spite of its

---

[17] In this discussion, we ignore the tax advantages to investors associated with capital gains. In some situations, tax effects could result in r_c being less than r_d.

higher cost and then later sold common stock and refunded the debt. (2) Convertibles typically have a low coupon interest rate, and the advantage of this low-cost debt will be lost when conversion occurs. (3) If the company truly wants to raise equity capital, and if the price of the stock does not rise sufficiently after the bond is issued, then the company will be stuck with debt.

20-4d Convertibles and Conflicts of Interest

A potential conflict of interest between bondholders and stockholders is asset substitution. Stockholders have an "option-related" incentive to take on projects with high upside potential even though they increase the risk of the firm. When such an action is taken, there is potential for a wealth transfer between bondholders and stockholders. However, when convertible debt is issued, actions that increase the risk of the company may also increase the value of the convertible debt. Thus, some of the gains to shareholders from taking on high-risk projects have to be shared with convertible bondholders. This sharing of benefits reduces conflicts of interest between bondholders and stockholders. The same general logic applies to convertible preferred and to warrants.

What is a conversion ratio? A conversion price? A straight-bond value?

What is meant by a convertible's floor value?

What are the advantages and disadvantages of convertibles to issuers? To investors?

How do convertibles reduce possible conflicts of interest between bondholders and stockholders?

A convertible bond has a par value of $1,000 and a conversion price of $40. The stock currently trades for $30 a share. What are the bond's conversion value and conversion ratio at t = 0? [CR = 25; P_0(CR) = $30 × $25 = $750]

20-5 A FINAL COMPARISON OF WARRANTS AND CONVERTIBLES

Convertible debt can be thought of as straight debt with nondetachable warrants. Thus, at first blush, it might appear that debt with warrants and convertible debt are more or less interchangeable. However, a closer look reveals one major and several minor differences between these two securities.[18] First, as we discussed previously, the exercise of warrants brings in new equity capital, while the conversion of convertibles results only in an accounting transfer.

A second difference involves flexibility. Most convertible issues contain a call provision that allows the issuer either to refund the debt or to force conversion, depending on the relationship between the conversion value and call price. However, most warrants are not callable, so firms generally must wait until maturity for the warrants to generate new equity capital. Generally, maturities also differ between warrants and convertibles. Warrants typically have much

---

[18] For a more detailed comparison of warrants and convertibles, see Michael S. Long and Stephen F. Sefcik, "Participation Financing: A Comparison of the Characteristics of Convertible Debt and Straight Bonds Issued in Conjunction with Warrants," *Financial Management*, Autumn 1990, pp. 23–34.

shorter maturities than convertibles, and warrants typically expire before their accompanying debt matures. Further, warrants provide for fewer future common shares than do convertibles because with convertibles all of the debt is converted to common whereas debt remains outstanding when warrants are exercised. Together, these facts suggest that debt-plus-warrant issuers are actually more interested in selling debt than in selling equity.

In general, firms that issue debt with warrants are smaller and riskier than those that issue convertibles. One possible rationale for the use of option securities, especially the use of debt with warrants by small firms, is the difficulty investors have assessing the risk of small companies. If a startup with a new, untested product seeks debt financing, it is very difficult for potential lenders to judge the risk of the venture, hence it is difficult to set a fair interest rate. Under these circumstances, many potential investors will be reluctant to invest, making it necessary to set very high interest rates to attract debt capital. By issuing debt with warrants, investors obtain a package that offers upside potential to offset the risks of loss.

Finally, there is a significant difference in issuance costs between debt with warrants and convertible debt. Bonds with warrants typically require issuance costs that are about 1.2 percent more than the flotation costs for convertibles. In general, bond-with-warrant financings have underwriting fees that closely reflect the weighted average of the fees associated with debt and equity issues, while underwriting costs for convertibles are substantially lower.

What are some differences between debt-with-warrant financing and convertible debt?

Explain how bonds with warrants might help small, risky firms sell debt securities.

20-6 REPORTING EARNINGS WHEN WARRANTS OR CONVERTIBLES ARE OUTSTANDING[19]

If warrants or convertibles are outstanding, a firm could theoretically report earnings per share in one of three ways:

1. *Basic EPS*, where earnings available to common stockholders are divided by the average number of shares actually outstanding during the period.
2. *Primary EPS*, where earnings available are divided by the average number of shares that would have been outstanding if warrants and convertibles "likely to be converted in the near future" had actually been exercised or converted. In calculating primary EPS, earnings are first adjusted by "backing out" the interest on the convertibles, after which the adjusted earnings are divided by the adjusted number of shares. Accountants have a formula that basically compares the conversion or exercise price with the actual market value of the

---

[19] As part of the FASB's short-term convergence project with the IASB, to improve financial reporting in the U.S. while concurrently eliminating individual differences between U.S. GAAP and international financial reporting standards, the FASB expects to issue a final statement in the first quarter of 2006 that will make additional changes to FASB #128 (issued in February 1997), which is discussed in this section.

stock to determine the likelihood of conversion when deciding on the need to use this adjustment procedure.

3. *Diluted EPS*, which is similar to primary EPS except that *all* warrants and convertibles are assumed to be exercised or converted, regardless of the likelihood of exercise or conversion.

Under SEC rules, firms are required to report both basic and diluted EPS. For firms with large amounts of option securities outstanding, there can be a substantial difference between the basic and diluted EPS figures. For financial statement purposes, firms reported diluted EPS until 1997, when the Financial Accounting Standards Board (FASB) changed to basic EPS. According to FASB, the change was made to give investors a simpler picture of a company's underlying performance. Also, the change makes it easier for investors to compare the performance of U.S. firms with their foreign counterparts, which tend to use basic EPS.

What are the three possible methods for reporting EPS when warrants and convertibles are outstanding?

Which methods are most used in practice?

Why should investors be concerned about a firm's outstanding warrants and convertibles?

Tying It All Together

While common stock and long-term debt provide most of the capital used by corporations, companies also use several forms of "hybrid securities." The hybrids include preferred stock, leasing, convertibles, and warrants, and they generally have some characteristics of debt and some of equity. We discussed the pros and cons of the hybrids from the standpoints of both issuers and investors, how to determine when to use them, and the factors that affect their values. The basic rationale for these securities, and the procedures used to evaluate them, are based on concepts developed in earlier chapters.

SELF-TEST QUESTIONS AND PROBLEMS
(Solutions Appear in Appendix A)

ST-1   **Key terms** Define each of the following terms:
     a.   Cumulative dividends; adjustable rate preferred stock
     b.   Arrearages; market auction preferred
     c.   Lessee; lessor
     d.   Sale and leaseback; operating lease; financial lease
     e.   Off balance sheet financing; FASB #13
     f.   Residual value
     g.   Warrant; detachable warrant; stepped-up exercise price

h.   Convertible security; conversion ratio, CR; conversion price, P_c; conversion value, C_t
i.   Basic EPS; primary EPS; diluted EPS

ST-2   **Lease analysis** The Olsen Company has decided to acquire a new truck. One alternative is to lease the truck on a 4-year contract for a lease payment of $10,000 per year, with payments to be made at the beginning of each year. The lease would include maintenance. Alternatively, Olsen could purchase the truck outright for $40,000, financing with a bank loan for the net purchase price, amortized over a 4-year period at an interest rate of 10 percent per year, payments to be made at the end of each year. Under the borrow-to-purchase arrangement, Olsen would have to maintain the truck at a cost of $1,000 per year, payable at year-end. The truck falls into the MACRS 3-year class. The applicable MACRS depreciation rates are 33, 45, 15, and 7 percent. It has a salvage value of $10,000, which is the expected market value after 4 years, at which time Olsen plans to replace the truck irrespective of whether it leases or buys. Olsen has a federal-plus-state tax rate of 40 percent.

a.   What is Olsen's PV cost of leasing?
b.   What is Olsen's PV cost of owning? Should the truck be leased or purchased?
c.   The appropriate discount rate for use in Olsen's analysis is the firm's after-tax cost of debt. Why?
d.   The salvage value is the least certain cash flow in the analysis. How might Olsen incorporate the higher riskiness of this cash flow into the analysis?

QUESTIONS

20-1   For purposes of measuring a firm's leverage, should preferred stock be classified as debt or equity? Does it matter if the classification is being made (a) by the firm's management, (b) by creditors, or (c) by equity investors?

20-2   You are told that one corporation just issued $100 million of preferred stock and another purchased $100 million of preferred stock as an investment. You are also told that one firm has an effective tax rate of 20 percent, whereas the other is in the 35 percent bracket. Which firm is more likely to have bought the preferred? Explain.

20-3   A company's bonds are often found to have a higher yield than its preferred stock, even though the bonds are considered to be less risky than the preferred to an investor. What causes this yield differential?

20-4   Why would a company choose to issue floating-rate as opposed to fixed-rate preferred stock?

20-5   Distinguish between operating leases and financial leases. Would a firm be more likely to finance a fleet of trucks or a manufacturing plant with an operating lease?

20-6   One alleged advantage of leasing voiced in the past was that it kept liabilities off the balance sheet, thus making it possible for a firm to obtain more leverage than it otherwise could have. This raised the question of whether or not both the lease obligation and the asset involved should be capitalized and shown on the balance sheet. Discuss the pros and cons of capitalizing leases and related assets.

20-7   Suppose there were no IRS restrictions on what constitutes a valid lease. Explain in a manner that a legislator might understand why some restrictions should be imposed.

20-8   Suppose Congress changed the tax laws in a way that (a) permitted equipment to be depreciated over a shorter period, (b) lowered corporate tax rates, and (c) reinstated the investment tax credit. Discuss how each of these changes would affect the relative use of leasing versus conventional debt in the U.S. economy.

20-9   What effect does the expected growth rate of a firm's stock price (subsequent to issue) have on its ability to raise additional funds through (a) convertibles and (b) warrants?

20-10   a.   How would a firm's decision to pay out a higher percentage of its earnings as dividends affect each of the following?
(1) The value of its long-term warrants.
(2) The likelihood that its convertible bonds will be converted.
(3) The likelihood that its warrants will be exercised.
b.   If you owned the warrants or convertibles of a company, would you be pleased or displeased if it raised its payout rate from 20 to 80 percent? Why?

20-11 Evaluate the following statement: "Issuing convertible securities represents a means by which a firm can sell common stock at a price above the existing market price."

20-12 Suppose a company simultaneously issues $50 million of convertible bonds with a coupon rate of 9 percent and $50 million of pure bonds with a coupon rate of 12 percent. Both bonds have the same maturity. Does the fact that the convertible issue has the lower coupon rate suggest that it is less risky than the pure bond? Would you regard the cost of capital as being lower on the convertible than on the pure bond? Explain. (Hint: Although it might appear at first glance that the convertible's cost of capital is lower, this is not necessarily the case because the interest rate on the convertible understates its cost. Think about this.)

PROBLEMS

**Easy
Problems 1–3**

20-1 **Leasing** Connors Construction needs a piece of equipment that can either be leased or purchased. The equipment costs $100. One option is to borrow $100 from the local bank and use the money to buy the equipment. The other option is to lease the equipment. If Connors chooses to lease the equipment, it *would not* capitalize the lease on the balance sheet. Below is the company's balance sheet *prior* to the purchase or leasing of the equipment:

Current assets	$300	Debt	$400
Fixed assets	500	Equity	400
Total assets	$800	Total liabilities and equity	$800

What would be the company's debt ratio if it chose to purchase the equipment? What would be the company's debt ratio if it chose to lease the equipment? Would the company's financial risk be different depending on whether the equipment was leased or purchased?

20-2 **Warrants** Gregg Company recently issued two types of bonds. The first issue consisted of 20-year straight (no warrants attached) bonds with an 8 percent annual coupon. The second issue consisted of 20-year bonds with a 6 percent annual coupon with warrants attached. Both bonds were issued at par ($1,000). What is the value of the warrants that were attached to the second issue?

20-3 **Convertibles** Petersen Securities recently issued convertible bonds with a $1,000 par value. The bonds have a conversion price of $40 a share. What is the bonds' conversion ratio, CR?

**Intermediate
Problems 4–7**

20-4 **Balance sheet effects of leasing** Two textile companies, McDaniel-Edwards Manufacturing and Jordan-Hocking Mills, began operations with identical balance sheets. A year later, both required additional manufacturing capacity at a cost of $200,000. McDaniel-Edwards obtained a 5-year, $200,000 loan at an 8 percent interest rate from its bank. Jordan-Hocking, on the other hand, decided to lease the required $200,000 capacity from National Leasing for 5 years; an 8 percent return was built into the lease. The balance sheet for each company, before the asset increases, is as follows:

		Debt	$200,000
		Equity	200,000
Total assets	$400,000	Total liabilities and equity	$400,000

a. Show the balance sheet of each firm after the asset increase, and calculate each firm's new debt ratio. (Assume Jordan-Hocking's lease is kept off the balance sheet.)
b. Show how Jordan-Hocking's balance sheet would have looked immediately after the financing if it had capitalized the lease.
c. Would the rate of return (1) on assets and (2) on equity be affected by the choice of financing? How?

20-5 **Lease versus buy** Morris-Meyer Mining Company must install $1.5 million of new machinery in its Nevada mine. It can obtain a bank loan for 100 percent of the required amount. Alternatively, a Nevada investment banking firm that represents a group of investors believes that it can arrange for a lease financing plan. Assume that the following facts apply:

(1) The equipment falls in the MACRS 3-year class. The applicable MACRS rates are 33, 45, 15, and 7 percent.

(2) Estimated maintenance expenses are $75,000 per year.

(3) Morris-Meyer's federal-plus-state tax rate is 40 percent.

(4) If the money is borrowed, the bank loan will be at a rate of 15 percent, amortized in 4 equal installments to be paid at the end of each year.

(5) The tentative lease terms call for end-of-year payments of $400,000 per year for 4 years.

(6) Under the proposed lease terms, the lessee must pay for insurance, property taxes, and maintenance.

(7) Morris-Meyer must use the equipment if it is to continue in business, so it will almost certainly want to acquire the property at the end of the lease. If it does, then under the lease terms, it can purchase the machinery at its fair market value at that time. The best estimate of this market value is the $250,000 salvage value, but it could be much higher or lower under certain circumstances.

To assist management in making the proper lease-versus-buy decision, you are asked to answer the following questions.

a. Assuming that the lease can be arranged, should Morris-Meyer lease, or should it borrow and buy the equipment? Explain.

b. Consider the $250,000 estimated salvage value. Is it appropriate to discount it at the same rate as the other cash flows? What about the other cash flows—are they all equally risky? (Hint: Riskier cash flows are normally discounted at higher rates, but when the cash flows are *costs* rather than *inflows*, the normal procedure must be reversed.)

20-6 **Warrants** Pogue Industries Inc. has warrants outstanding that permit its holders to purchase 1 share of stock per warrant at a price of $21. (Refer to Chapter 18 for parts a, b, and c.)

a. Calculate the exercise value of Pogue's warrants if the common stock sells at each of the following prices: $18, $21, $25, and $70.

b. At what approximate price do you think the warrants would actually sell under each condition indicated in part a? What premium is implied in your price? Your answer will be a guess, but your prices and premiums should bear reasonable relationships to each other.

c. How would each of the following factors affect your estimates of the warrants' prices and premiums in part b?

(1) The life of the warrant is lengthened.

(2) The expected variability (σ_p) in the stock's price decreases.

(3) The expected growth rate in the stock's EPS increases.

(4) The company announces the following change in dividend policy: whereas it formerly paid no dividends, henceforth it will pay out *all* earnings as dividends.

d. Assume Pogue's stock now sells for $18 per share. The company wants to sell some 20-year, annual interest, $1,000 par value bonds. Each bond will have 50 warrants, each exercisable into 1 share of stock at an exercise price of $21. Pogue's pure bonds yield 10 percent. Regardless of your answer to part b, assume that the warrants will have a market value of $1.50 when the stock sells at $18. What annual coupon interest rate and annual dollar coupon must the company set on the bonds with warrants if they are to clear the market? Round to the nearest dollar or percentage point.

20-7 **Convertibles** The Hadaway Company was planning to finance an expansion in the summer of 2005 with a convertible security. They considered a convertible debenture but feared the burden of fixed interest charges if the common stock did not rise enough to make conversion attractive. They decided on an issue of convertible preferred stock, which would pay a dividend of $1.05 per share.

The common stock was selling for $21 a share at the time. Management projected earnings for 2005 at $1.50 a share and expected a future growth rate of 10 percent a year in 2006 and beyond. It was agreed by the investment bankers and management that the common stock would continue to sell at 14 times earnings, the current price/earnings ratio.

a. What conversion price should be set by the issuer? The conversion rate will be 1.0; that is, each share of convertible preferred can be converted into 1 share of common. Therefore, the convertible's par value (as well as the issue price) will be equal to the conversion price, which, in turn, will be determined as a percentage over the current market price of the common. Your answer will be a guess, but make it a reasonable one.

b. Should the preferred stock include a call provision? Why or why not?

Challenging Problems 8–10

20-8 **Lease analysis** As part of its overall plant modernization and cost reduction program, the management of Tanner-Woods Textile Mills has decided to install a new automated weaving loom. In the capital budgeting analysis of this equipment, the IRR of the project was found to be 20 percent versus a project required return of 12 percent.

The loom has an invoice price of $250,000, including delivery and installation charges. The funds needed could be borrowed from the bank through a 4-year amortized loan at a 10 percent interest rate, with payments to be made at the end of each year. In the event that the loom is purchased, the manufacturer will contract to maintain and service it for a fee of $20,000 per year paid at the end of each year. The loom falls in the MACRS 5-year class, and Tanner-Woods's marginal federal-plus-state tax rate is 40 percent. The applicable MACRS rates are 20, 32, 19, 12, 11, and 6 percent.

United Automation Inc., maker of the loom, has offered to lease the loom to Tanner-Woods for $70,000 upon delivery and installation (at t = 0) plus 4 additional annual lease payments of $70,000 to be made at the end of Years 1 through 4. (Note that there are 5 lease payments in total.) The lease agreement includes maintenance and servicing. Actually, the loom has an expected life of 8 years, at which time its expected salvage value is zero; however, after 4 years, its market value is expected to equal its book value of $42,500. Tanner-Woods plans to build an entirely new plant in 4 years, so it has no interest in either leasing or owning the proposed loom for more than that period.

a. Should the loom be leased or purchased?
b. The salvage value is clearly the most uncertain cash flow in the analysis. Assume that the appropriate salvage value pre-tax discount rate is 15 percent. What would be the effect of a salvage value risk adjustment on the decision?
c. The original analysis assumed that Tanner-Woods would not need the loom after 4 years. Now assume that the firm will continue to use it after the lease expires. Thus, if it leased, Tanner-Woods would have to buy the asset after 4 years at the then existing market value, which is assumed to equal the book value. What effect would this requirement have on the basic analysis? (No numerical analysis is required; just verbalize.)

20-9 **Financing alternatives** The Howe Computer Company has grown rapidly during the past 5 years. Recently, its commercial bank urged the company to consider increasing its permanent financing. Its bank loan under a line of credit has risen to $150,000, carrying a 10 percent interest rate, and Howe has been 30 to 60 days late in paying trade creditors.

Discussions with an investment banker have resulted in the decision to raise $250,000 at this time. Investment bankers have assured Howe that the following alternatives are feasible (flotation costs will be ignored):

- *Alternative 1:* Sell common stock at $10 per share.
- *Alternative 2:* Sell convertible bonds at a 10 percent coupon, convertible into 80 shares of common stock for each $1,000 bond (that is, the conversion price is $12.50 per share).
- *Alternative 3:* Sell debentures with a 10 percent coupon; each $1,000 bond will have 80 warrants to buy 1 share of common stock at $12.50.

Keith Howe, the president, owns 80 percent of Howe's common stock and wishes to maintain control of the company; 50,000 shares are outstanding. The following are summaries of Howe's latest financial statements:

Balance Sheet

		Current liabilities	$200,000
		Common stock, $1 par	50,000
		Retained earnings	25,000
Total assets	$275,000	Total liabilities and equity	$275,000

Income Statement

Sales	$550,000
All costs except interest	495,000
EBIT	$ 55,000
Interest	15,000
EBT	$ 40,000
Taxes (40%)	16,000
Net income	$ 24,000
Shares outstanding	50,000
Earnings per share	$0.48
Price/earnings ratio	18×
Market price of stock	$8.64

a. Show the new balance sheet under each alternative. For Alternatives 2 and 3, show the balance sheet after conversion of the debentures or exercise of the warrants. Assume that $150,000 of the funds raised will be used to pay off the bank loan and the rest to increase total assets.

b. Show Howe's control position under each alternative, assuming that he does not purchase additional shares.

c. What is the effect on earnings per share of each alternative if it is assumed that earnings before interest and taxes will be 20 percent of total assets?

d. What will be the debt ratio under each alternative?

e. Which of the three alternatives would you recommend to Howe, and why?

20-10 Convertibles O'Brien Computers Inc. needs to raise $35 million to begin producing a new microcomputer. O'Brien's straight, nonconvertible debentures currently yield 12 percent. Its stock sells for $38 per share, the last dividend was $2.46, and the expected growth rate is a constant 8 percent. Investment bankers have tentatively proposed that O'Brien raise the $35 million by issuing convertible debentures. These convertibles would have a $1,000 par value, carry an annual coupon rate of 10 percent, have a 20-year maturity, and be convertible into 20 shares of stock. The bonds would be noncallable for 5 years, after which they would be callable at a price of $1,075; this call price would decline by $5 per year in Year 6 and each year thereafter. Management has called convertibles in the past (and presumably will call them again in the future), once they were eligible for call, as soon as their conversion value was about 20 percent above their par value (not their call price).

a. Draw an accurate graph similar to Figure 20-1 representing the expectations set forth in the problem.

b. Suppose the previously outlined projects work out on schedule for 2 years, but then O'Brien begins to experience extremely strong competition from Japanese firms. As a result, O'Brien's expected growth rate drops from 8 percent to zero. Assume that the dividend at the time of the drop is $2.87. The company's credit strength is not impaired, and its value of r_s is also unchanged. What would happen (1) to the stock price and (2) to the convertible bond's price? Be as precise as you can.

COMPREHENSIVE/SPREADSHEET PROBLEMS

20-11 Lease analysis Use the spreadsheet model to rework parts a and b of Problem 20-8. Then, answer the following question.

c. Accepting that the corporate WACC should be used equally to discount all anticipated cash flows, at what cost of capital would the firm be indifferent between leasing and buying?

20-12 Warrants Storm Software wants to issue $100 million in new capital to fund new opportunities. If Storm were to raise the $100 million of new capital in a straight-debt 20-year bond offering, Storm would have to offer an annual coupon rate of 12 percent. However, Storm's advisors have suggested a 20-year bond offering with warrants. According to the advisors, Storm could issue 9 percent annual coupon-bearing debt with 20 warrants per $1,000 face value bond. Storm has 10 million shares of stock outstanding at a current price of $25. The warrants can be exercised in 10 years (on December 31, 2015) at an exercise price of $30. Each warrant entitles its holder to buy 1 share of Storm Software stock. After issuing the bonds with warrants, Storm's operations and investments are expected to grow at a constant rate of 10 percent per year.

a. If investors pay $1,000 for each bond, what is the value of each warrant attached to the bond issue?

b. What is the expected total value of Storm Software in 10 years?

c. If there were no warrants, what would be Storm's price per share in 10 years? What would be the price with the warrants?

d. What is the component cost of these bonds with warrants? What is the premium associated with the warrants?

Integrated Case

Fish & Chips, Inc., Part I

20-13 **Lease analysis** Martha Millon, financial manager for Fish & Chips Inc., has been asked to perform a lease-versus-buy analysis on a new computer system. The computer costs $1,200,000, and, if it is purchased, Fish & Chips could obtain a term loan for the full amount at a 10 percent cost. The loan would be amortized over the 4-year life of the computer, with payments made at the end of each year. The computer is classified as special purpose, and hence it falls into the MACRS 3-year class. The applicable MACRS rates are 33, 45, 15, and 7 percent. If the computer is purchased, a maintenance contract must be obtained at a cost of $25,000, payable at the beginning of each year.

After 4 years, the computer will be sold, and Millon's best estimate of its residual value at that time is $125,000. Because technology is changing rapidly, however, the residual value is very uncertain.

As an alternative, National Leasing is willing to write a 4-year lease on the computer, including maintenance, for payments of $340,000 at the beginning of each year. Fish & Chips' marginal federal-plus-state tax rate is 40 percent. Help Millon conduct her analysis by answering the following questions.

a. (1) Why is leasing sometimes referred to as "off balance sheet" financing?
    (2) What is the difference between a capital lease and an operating lease?
    (3) What effect does leasing have on a firm's capital structure?
b. (1) What is Fish & Chips' present value cost of owning the computer? (Hint: Set up a table whose bottom line is a "time line" that shows the net cash flows over the period t = 0 to t = 4, and then find the PV of these net cash flows, or the PV cost of owning.)
    (2) Explain the rationale for the discount rate you used to find the PV.
c. (1) What is Fish & Chips' present value cost of leasing the computer? (Hint: Again, construct a time line.)
    (2) What is the net advantage to leasing? Does your analysis indicate that the firm should buy or lease the computer? Explain.
d. Now assume that Millon believes the computer's residual value could be as low as $0 or as high as $250,000, but she stands by $125,000 as her expected value. She concludes that the residual value is riskier than the other cash flows in the analysis, and she wants to incorporate this differential risk into her analysis. Describe how this could be accomplished. What effect would it have on the lease decision?
e. Millon knows that her firm has been considering moving its headquarters to a new location for some time, and she is concerned that these plans may come to fruition prior to the expiration of the lease. If the move occurs, the company would obtain completely new computers, and hence Millon would like to include a cancellation clause in the lease contract. What effect would a cancellation clause have on the riskiness of the lease?

Fish & Chips, Inc., Part II

20-14 **Preferred stock, warrants, and convertibles** Martha Millon, financial manager of Fish & Chips Inc., is facing a dilemma. The firm was founded 5 years ago to develop a new fast-food concept, and although Fish & Chips has done well, the firm's founder and chairman believes that an industry shake-out is imminent. To survive, the firm must capture market share now, and this requires a large infusion of new capital.

Because the stock price may rise rapidly, Millon does not want to issue new common stock. On the other hand, interest rates are currently very high by historical standards, and, with the firm's B rating, the interest payments on a new debt issue would be too much to handle if sales took a downturn. Thus, Millon has narrowed her choice to bonds with warrants or convertible bonds. She has asked you to help in the decision process by answering the following questions.

a. How does preferred stock differ from common equity and debt?
b. What is floating-rate preferred?
c. How can a knowledge of call options provide an understanding of warrants and convertibles?
d. One of Millon's alternatives is to issue a bond with warrants attached. Fish & Chips' current stock price is $10, and its cost of 20-year, annual coupon debt without warrants is estimated by its investment bankers to be 12 percent. The bankers suggest attaching 50 warrants to each bond, with each warrant having an exercise price of $12.50. It is estimated that each warrant, when detached and traded separately, will have a value of $1.50.

    (1) What coupon rate should be set on the bond with warrants if the total package is to sell for $1,000?

(2) Suppose the bonds are issued and the warrants immediately trade for $2.50 each. What does this imply about the terms of the issue? Did the company "win" or "lose"?

(3) When would you expect the warrants to be exercised?

(4) Will the warrants bring in additional capital when exercised? If so, how much and what type of capital?

(5) Because warrants lower the cost of the accompanying debt, shouldn't all debt be issued with warrants? What is the expected cost of the bond with warrants if the warrants are expected to be exercised in 5 years, when Fish & Chips' stock price is expected to be $17.50? How would you expect the cost of the bond with warrants to compare with the cost of straight debt? With the cost of common stock?

e. As an alternative to the bond with warrants, Millon is considering convertible bonds. The firm's investment bankers estimate that Fish & Chips could sell a 20-year, 10 percent annual coupon, callable convertible bond for its $1,000 par value, whereas a straight-debt issue would require a 12 percent coupon. Fish & Chips' current stock price is $10, its last dividend was $0.74, and the dividend is expected to grow at a constant rate of 8 percent. The convertible could be converted into 80 shares of Fish & Chips stock at the owner's option.

(1) What conversion price, P_c, is implied in the convertible's terms?

(2) What is the straight-debt value of the convertible? What is the implied value of the convertibility feature?

(3) What is the formula for the bond's conversion value in any year? Its value at Year 0? At Year 10?

(4) What is meant by the term "floor value" of a convertible? What is the convertible's expected floor value in Year 0? In Year 10?

(5) Assume that Fish & Chips intends to force conversion by calling the bond when its conversion value is 20 percent above its par value, or at 1.2($1,000) = $1,200. When is the issue expected to be called? Answer to the closest year.

(6) What is the expected cost of the convertible to Fish & Chips? Does this cost appear consistent with the riskiness of the issue? Assume conversion in Year 5 at a conversion value of $1,200.

f. Millon believes that the costs of both the bond with warrants and the convertible bond are essentially equal, so her decision must be based on other factors. What are some of the factors that she should consider in making her decision?

cyberproblem

Please go to the ThomsonNOW Web site to access the Cyberproblems.

© MIKE SIMONS/GETTY IMAGES INC.

MERGERS AND ACQUISITIONS

Procter & Gamble Acquires Gillette

Over the past several years a series of large mergers have reshaped the corporate landscape. Recent events suggest that this trend is showing no signs of slowing down. Within the first three months of 2005, plans for four major mergers were announced: Procter & Gamble's $55 billion bid for Gillette, SBC Communications' $14.7 billion acquisition of AT&T Corp., Federated Department Store's $10.5 billion acquisition of May Department Store, and Verizon's $7.5 billion revised bid for MCI Inc.

Combining consumer products giants Procter & Gamble (P&G) and Gillette immediately produced several winners. When the deal was announced, Gillette's shareholders saw the value of their stock rise by more than 17 percent. One particular winner was Gillette's largest shareholder, Warren Buffett, who owned roughly 96 million shares. Other winners include Gillette's senior executives, who saw the values of their stock and stock options increase, and the investment banks that helped put the deal together. (Estimates suggest that Goldman Sachs, Merrill Lynch, and UBS each received $30 million from the transaction.)

What remains to be seen is whether the deal makes sense for P&G's shareholders. While many have applauded the deal, others suggest that P&G will have to work hard to justify the price it paid for Gillette. Moreover, as we point out in this chapter, the track record for acquiring firms in large deals has not always been that good.

In an article written for *The Wall Street Journal*, shortly after the P&G–Gillette announced deal, David Hardin and Sam Rovit discuss the potential pitfalls of large acquisitions, and they estimate that only 3 out of 10 large deals between 1995 and 2001 created meaningful benefits for the acquiring firm's shareholders. Hardin and Rovit (who are Bain & Company partners and co-authors of a recent book entitled *Mastering the Merger: Four Critical Decisions That Make or Break a Deal*) argue that there are five major criteria that determine whether a merger is successful:

1. *Is management successful in deal making?* They argue that experienced acquirers tend to do better than firms that make infrequent acquisitions.

Procter & Gamble

2. *Will the acquisition strengthen the buyer's core?* Here they argue that companies tend to do better when they acquire companies that operate in businesses they understand.

3. *Did management do its homework?* Successful acquirers take the time to do the necessary due diligence.

4. *Is the company addressing merger integration issues up front?* Hardin and Rovit point out that deals can often unravel because there isn't a clear plan for how the two management teams are going to be integrated following the acquisition.

5. *Is the executive team prepared for the unexpected?* History shows that nothing turns out the way it was planned. Successful acquirers anticipate the unexpected and are able to adapt well to changing circumstances.

The early indications are that the P&G–Gillette merger has the potential to be quite successful, but we will have to wait and see if the deal provides long-term value to P&G shareholders.

Sources: Nikhil Deogun, Charles Forelle, Dennis K. Berman, and Emily Nelson, "Razor's Edge: P&G to Buy Gillette for $54 Billion—Deal Joins Iconic Giants of Consumer Products; 21 Billion-Dollar Brands—A Green Light for Takeovers," *The Wall Street Journal*, January 28, 2005, p. A1; A. G. Lafley and Patricia Sellers, " 'It Was a No-Brainer' That's What Procter & Gamble's A. G. Lafley Says of His Decision to Buy Gillette. Here's Why He Thinks So—and How the Deal Came About," *Fortune*, February 21, 2005, p. 96; Shawn Tully, "The Urge to Merge With the Tally of High-Priced Mergers Growing by the Day, One Can't Help but Ask: Did We Learn Nothing from the Crash?" *Fortune*, February 21, 2005, p. 21; David Hardin and Sam Rovit, "Five Ways to Spot a Good Deal," *The Wall Street Journal*, March 29, 2005, p. B2; Dennis K. Berman, "Stock Market Quarterly Review: Wave of Megamergers Keeps Rolling On—Big Companies Look to Deals for Spurring Profit Growth; Private Equity's Brief Pause," *The Wall Street Journal*, April 1, 2005, p. C13; and Robert Barker, "P&G's $57 Billion Bargain," *BusinessWeek*, July 25, 2005, p. 26.

Putting Things In Perspective

Most corporate growth occurs by internal expansion, which takes place when a firm's existing divisions grow through normal capital budgeting activities. However, the most dramatic examples of growth, and often the largest increases in firms' stock prices, result from mergers, the first topic covered in this chapter. *Leveraged buyouts*, or *LBOs*, occur when a firm's stock is acquired by a small group of investors rather than by another operating company. Because LBOs are similar to mergers in many respects, they are also covered in this chapter. Conditions change over time, causing firms to sell off, or *divest*, major divisions to other firms that can better utilize the divested assets. We also discuss divestitures in the chapter. We leave the discussion of the *holding company* form of organization, wherein one corporation owns the stock of one or more other companies, for Web Appendix 21A.

21-1 RATIONALE FOR MERGERS

Many reasons have been proposed by financial managers and theorists to account for the high level of U.S. merger activity. The primary motives behind corporate **mergers** are presented in this section.[1]

21-1a Synergy

The primary motivation for most mergers is to increase the value of the combined enterprise. If Companies A and B merge to form Company C, and if C's value exceeds that of A and B taken separately, then **synergy** is said to exist. Such a merger should be beneficial to both A's and B's stockholders.[2] Synergistic effects can arise from four sources: (1) *operating economies*, which result from economies of scale in management, marketing, production, or distribution; (2) *financial economies*, including lower transactions costs and better coverage by security analysts; (3) *differential efficiency*, which implies that the management of one firm is more efficient and that the weaker firm's assets will be more productive after the merger; and (4) *increased market power* due to reduced competition. Operating and financial economies are socially desirable, as are mergers that increase managerial efficiency, but mergers that reduce competition are socially undesirable and often illegal.[3]

21-1b Tax Considerations

Tax considerations have stimulated a number of mergers. For example, a profitable firm in the highest tax bracket could acquire a firm with large accumulated tax losses. These losses could then be turned into immediate tax savings rather than carried forward and used in the future.[4] Also, mergers can serve as a way of minimizing taxes when disposing of excess cash. For example, if a firm has a shortage of internal investment opportunities compared with its free cash flow, it could (1) pay an extra dividend, (2) invest in marketable securities, (3) repurchase its own stock, or (4) purchase another firm. If it pays an extra dividend, its stockholders would have to pay immediate taxes on the distribution. Marketable securities often provide a good temporary parking place for money, but they generally earn a rate of return less than that required by stockholders. A stock repurchase might result in a capital gain for the remaining stockholders. However, using surplus cash to acquire another firm would avoid all these problems, and this has motivated a number of mergers.

Merger
The combination of two firms to form a single firm.

Synergy
The condition wherein the whole is greater than the sum of its parts; in a synergistic merger, the post-merger value exceeds the sum of the separate companies' pre-merger values.

---

[1] As we use the term, *merger* means any combination that forms one economic unit from two or more previous ones. For legal purposes, there are distinctions among the various ways these combinations can occur, but our focus is on the fundamental economic and financial aspects of mergers.

[2] If synergy exists, then the whole is greater than the sum of the parts. Synergy is also called the "2 plus 2 equals 5 effect." The distribution of the synergistic gain between A's and B's stockholders is determined by negotiation. This point is discussed later in the chapter.

[3] In the 1880s and 1890s, many mergers occurred in the United States, and some of them were obviously directed toward gaining market power rather than increasing efficiency. As a result, Congress passed a series of acts designed to ensure that mergers are not used as a method of reducing competition. The principal acts include the Sherman Act (1890), the Clayton Act (1914), and the Celler Act (1950). These acts make it illegal for firms to combine if the combination tends to lessen competition. The acts are enforced by the antitrust division of the Justice Department and by the Federal Trade Commission.

[4] Mergers undertaken only to use accumulated tax losses would probably be challenged by the IRS. In recent years Congress has made it increasingly difficult for firms to pass along tax savings after mergers.

21-1c Purchase of Assets below Their Replacement Cost

Sometimes a firm will be touted as an acquisition candidate because the cost of replacing its assets is considerably higher than its market value. For example, in the early 1980s oil companies could acquire reserves cheaper by buying other oil companies than by doing exploratory drilling. Thus, Chevron acquired Gulf Oil to augment its reserves. Similarly, in the 1980s several steel company executives stated that it was cheaper to buy an existing steel company than to construct a new mill. For example, LTV (the fourth largest steel company) acquired Republic Steel (the sixth largest) to create the second largest firm in the industry.

21-1d Diversification

Managers often cite diversification as a reason for mergers. They contend that diversification helps stabilize a firm's earnings and thus benefits its owners. Stabilization of earnings is certainly beneficial to employees, suppliers, and customers, but its value is less certain from the standpoint of stockholders. Why should Firm A acquire Firm B to stabilize earnings when stockholders can simply buy the stock of both firms? Indeed, research of U.S. firms suggests that in most cases diversification does not increase the firm's value. To the contrary, many studies find that diversified firms are worth significantly less than the sum of their individual parts.[5]

Of course, if you were the owner-manager of a closely held firm, it might be nearly impossible to sell part of your stock to diversify. Also, selling your stock would probably lead to a large capital gains tax. So, a diversification merger might be the best way to achieve personal diversification.

21-1e Managers' Personal Incentives

Financial economists like to think that business decisions are based only on economic considerations, especially maximization of firms' values. However, many business decisions are based more on managers' personal motivations than on economic analyses. Business leaders like power, and more power is attached to running a larger corporation than a smaller one. Obviously, no executive would admit that his or her ego was the primary reason behind a merger, but egos do play a prominent role in many mergers.

It has also been observed that executive salaries are highly correlated with company size—the bigger the company, the higher the salaries of its top officers. This too could play a role in corporate acquisition programs.

Personal considerations deter as well as motivate mergers. After most takeovers, some managers of the acquired companies lose their jobs, or at least their autonomy. Therefore, managers who own less than 51 percent of their firms' stock look to devices that will lessen the chances of a takeover. Mergers can serve as such a device. For example, several years ago Paramount made a bid to acquire Time Inc. Time's managers received a lot of criticism when they rejected Paramount's bid and chose instead to enter into a heavily debt-financed merger with Warner Brothers that enabled them to retain power. Such **defensive mergers** are hard to defend on economic grounds. The managers involved invariably argue that synergy, not a desire to protect their own jobs, motivated the acquisition, but observers suspect that many mergers were designed more to benefit managers than stockholders.

Defensive Merger
A merger designed to make a company less vulnerable to a takeover.

---

[5] See, for example, Philip Berger and Eli Ofek, "Diversification's Effect on Firm Value," *Journal of Financial Economics*, Vol. 37 (1995), pp. 37–65; and Larry Lang and René Stulz, "Tobin's Q, Corporate Diversification, and Firm Performance," *Journal of Political Economy*, Vol. 102 (1994), pp. 1248–1280.

21-1f Breakup Value

Firms can be valued by book value, economic value, or replacement value. Recently, takeover specialists have begun to recognize breakup value as another basis for valuation. Analysts estimate a company's breakup value, which is the value of the individual parts of the firm if they were sold off separately. If this value is higher than the firm's current market value, then a takeover specialist could acquire the firm at or even above its current market value, sell it off in pieces, and earn a substantial profit.

Define *synergy*. Is synergy a valid rationale for mergers? Describe several situations that might produce synergistic gains.

Give two examples of how tax considerations can motivate mergers.

Suppose your firm could purchase another firm for only half of its replacement value. Would that be a sufficient justification for the acquisition?

Discuss the pros and cons of diversification as a rationale for mergers.

What is breakup value?

21-2 TYPES OF MERGERS

Economists classify mergers into four types: (1) horizontal, (2) vertical, (3) congeneric, and (4) conglomerate. A **horizontal merger** occurs when one firm combines with another in its same line of business—the NationsBank/BankAmerica merger is an example. An example of a **vertical merger** would be a steel producer's acquisition of one of its own suppliers, such as an iron or coal mining firm, or an oil producer's acquisition of a petrochemical firm that uses oil as a raw material. Congeneric means "allied in nature or action," hence a **congeneric merger** involves related enterprises but not producers of the same product (horizontal) or firms in a producer-supplier relationship (vertical). The Citicorp/Travelers merger is an example. A **conglomerate merger** occurs when unrelated enterprises combine, as illustrated by Mobil Oil's acquisition of Montgomery Ward.

Operating economies (and also anticompetitive effects) are at least partially dependent on the type of merger involved. Vertical and horizontal mergers generally provide the greatest synergistic operating benefits, but they are also the ones most likely to be attacked by the Department of Justice as anticompetitive. In any event, it is useful to think of these economic classifications when analyzing prospective mergers.

> **Horizontal Merger**
> *A combination of two firms that produce the same type of good or service.*
>
> **Vertical Merger**
> *A merger between a firm and one of its suppliers or customers.*
>
> **Congeneric Merger**
> *A merger of firms in the same general industry, but for which no customer or supplier relationship exists.*
>
> **Conglomerate Merger**
> *A merger of companies in totally different industries.*

What are the four economic types of mergers?

21-3 LEVEL OF MERGER ACTIVITY

Five major "merger waves" have occurred in the United States. The first was in the late 1800s, when consolidations occurred in the oil, steel, tobacco, and other basic industries. The second was in the 1920s, when the stock market boom helped financial promoters consolidate firms in a number of industries, including utilities, communications, and autos. The third was in the 1960s, when conglomerate mergers were the rage. The fourth occurred in the 1980s, when LBO firms and others began using junk bonds to finance all manner of acquisitions. The fifth, which involves strategic alliances designed to enable firms to compete better in the global economy, is in progress today.

As can be seen from Table 21-1, which lists some of the more recent larger mergers, some huge mergers have occurred in recent years.[6] In addition, there have been a number of high-profile global mergers recently, including the mergers of Daimler-Benz and Chrysler, Deutschebank and Bankers Trust, and British Petroleum and Amoco. In general, these mergers have been significantly different from those of the 1980s. Most 1980s mergers were financial transactions in which buyers sought companies that were selling at less than their true values as a result of incompetent or sluggish management. If a target company could be managed better, if redundant assets could be sold, and if operating and administrative costs could be cut, profits and stock prices would rise. On the other hand, most of the mergers have been strategic in nature—companies are merging to gain economies of scale or scope and thus to be better able to compete in the world economy. Indeed, many recent mergers have involved companies in the financial, defense, media, computer, telecommunications, and health care industries, all of which are experiencing structural changes and intense competition.

Recently, there has also been an increase in cross-border mergers. Many of these mergers have been motivated by large shifts in the value of the world's

TABLE 21-1	*A Sample of Large Mergers Announced in Recent Years*		

Buyer	Target	Announcement Date	Value (Billions, U.S. $)
America Online	Time Warner	January 10, 2000	$160.0
Vodafone AirTouch	Mannesmann	November 14, 1999	148.6
Pfizer	Warner-Lambert	November 4, 1999	90.0
Exxon	Mobil	December 1, 1998	85.2
Bell Atlantic	GTE	July 28, 1998	85.0
SBC Communications	Ameritech	May 11, 1998	80.6
Vodafone	AirTouch	January 18, 1999	74.4
Royal Dutch Petroleum	Shell Trans. & Trading	October 28, 2004	74.3
British Petroleum	Amoco	August 11, 1998	61.7
AT&T	MediaOne Group	May 6, 1999	61.0
Sanofi-Synthelabo	Aventis	January 26, 2004	60.2
Pfizer	Pharmacia Corporation	July 15, 2002	60.0
JP Morgan Chase	Bank One	January 14, 2004	58.8
Procter & Gamble	Gillette	January 28, 2005	55.0
Comcast	AT&T Broadband	July 8, 2001	47.0

Source: Adapted from recent "Year-End Review" articles from *The Wall Street Journal.*

---

[6] For detailed reviews of the 1980s merger wave, see Andrei Shleifer and Robert W. Vishny, "The Takeover Wave of the 1980s," *Journal of Applied Corporate Finance*, Fall 1991, pp. 49–56; Edmund Faltermayer, "The Deal Decade: Verdict on the '80s," *Fortune*, August 26, 1991, pp. 58–70; and "The Best and Worst Deals of the '80s: What We Learned from All Those Mergers, Acquisitions, and Takeovers," *BusinessWeek*, January 15, 1990, pp. 52–57.

leading currencies. For example, in the early 1990s, the dollar was weak relative to the yen and the mark. The decline in the dollar made it easier for Japanese and German acquirers to buy U.S. corporations.

What five major "merger waves" have occurred in the United States?

What are some reasons for the current wave?

21-4 HOSTILE VERSUS FRIENDLY TAKEOVERS

In the vast majority of merger situations, one firm (generally the larger of the two) simply decides to buy another company, negotiates a price with the management of the target firm, and then acquires the target company. Occasionally, the acquired firm will initiate the action, but it is much more common for a firm to seek acquisitions than to seek to be acquired.[7] Following convention, we call a company that seeks to acquire another firm the **acquiring company** and the one that it seeks to acquire the **target company.**

Once an acquiring company has identified a possible target, it must (1) establish a suitable price, or range of prices, and (2) tentatively set the terms of payment—will it offer cash, its own common stock, bonds, or some combination? Next, the acquiring firm's managers must decide how to approach the target company's managers. If the acquiring firm has reason to believe that the target's management will approve the merger, then it will simply propose a merger and try to work out some suitable terms. If an agreement is reached, then the two management groups will issue statements to their stockholders indicating that they approve the merger, and the target firm's management will recommend to its stockholders that they agree to the merger. Generally, the stockholders are asked to *tender* (or send in) their shares to a designated financial institution, along with a signed power of attorney that transfers ownership of the shares to the acquiring firm. The target firm's stockholders then receive the specified payment, either common stock of the acquiring company (in which case the target company's stockholders become stockholders of the acquiring company), cash, bonds, or some mix of cash and securities. This is a **friendly merger.**

Often, however, the target company's management resists the merger. Perhaps they feel that the price offered is too low, or perhaps they simply want to keep their jobs. In either case, the acquiring firm's offer is said to be *hostile* rather than friendly, and the acquiring firm must make a direct appeal to the target firm's stockholders. In a **hostile merger,** the acquiring company will again make a **tender offer,** and again it will ask the stockholders of the target firm to tender their shares in exchange for the offered price. This time, though, the target firm's managers will urge stockholders not to tender their shares, generally stating that the price offered (cash, bonds, or stocks in the acquiring firm) is too low.

While most mergers are friendly, recently there have been a number of interesting cases in which high-profile firms have attempted hostile takeovers. For example, Warner-Lambert tried to fight off a hostile bid by Pfizer; however, the

Acquiring Company
A company that seeks to acquire another firm.

Target Company
A firm that another company seeks to acquire.

Friendly Merger
A merger whose terms are approved by the managements of both companies.

Hostile Merger
A merger in which the target firm's management resists acquisition.

Tender Offer
The offer of one firm to buy the stock of another by going directly to the stockholders, frequently (but not always) over the opposition of the target company's management.

---

[7] However, if a firm is in financial difficulty, if its managers are elderly and do not think that suitable replacements are on hand, or if it needs the support (often the capital) of a larger company, then it may seek to be acquired. Thus, when a number of Texas, Ohio, and Maryland financial institutions were in trouble in the 1980s, they lobbied to get their state legislatures to pass laws that would make it easier for them to be acquired. Out-of-state banks then moved in to help salvage the situation and minimize depositor losses.

merger was completed in 2000. Looking overseas, Olivetti successfully conducted a hostile takeover of Telecom Italia, and in another telecommunications merger Britain's Vodafone AirTouch made a hostile bid for its German rival, Mannesmann AG, which was successful.

 What's the difference between a hostile and a friendly merger?

21-5 MERGER REGULATION

Proxy Fight
An attempt to gain control of a firm by soliciting stockholders to vote for a new management team.

Prior to the mid-1960s, friendly acquisitions generally took place as simple exchange-of-stock mergers, and a **proxy fight** was the primary weapon used in hostile control battles. However, in the mid-1960s corporate raiders began to operate differently. First, it took a long time to mount a proxy fight—raiders had to first request a list of the target company's stockholders, be refused, and then get a court order forcing management to turn over the list. During that time, the target's management could think through and then implement a strategy to fend off the raider. As a result, management won most proxy fights.

Then raiders began saying to themselves, "If we could bring the decision to a head quickly, before management can take countermeasures, that would greatly increase our probability of success." That led the raiders to turn from proxy fights to tender offers, which had a much shorter response time. For example, the stockholders of a company whose stock was selling for $20 might be offered $27 per share and be given two weeks to accept. The raider, meanwhile, would have accumulated a substantial block of the shares in open market purchases, and additional shares might have been purchased by institutional friends of the raider who promised to tender their shares in exchange for the tip that a raid was to occur.

Faced with a well-planned raid, managements were generally overwhelmed. The stock might actually be worth more than the offered price, but management simply did not have time to get this message across to stockholders or to find a competing bidder. This situation seemed unfair, so Congress passed the Williams Act in 1968. This law had two main objectives: (1) to regulate the way acquiring firms can structure takeover offers and (2) to force acquiring firms to disclose more information about their offers. Basically, Congress wanted to put target managements in a better position to defend against hostile offers. Additionally, Congress believed that shareholders needed easier access to information about tender offers—including information on any securities that might be offered in lieu of cash—in order to make rational tender-versus-don't-tender decisions.

The Williams Act placed the following four restrictions on acquiring firms:

1. Acquirers must disclose their current holdings and future intentions within 10 days of amassing at least 5 percent of a company's stock.
2. Acquirers must disclose the source of the funds to be used in the acquisition.
3. The target firm's shareholders must be allowed at least 20 days to tender their shares; that is, the offer must be "open" for at least 20 days.
4. If the acquiring firm increases the offer price during the 20-day open period, all shareholders who tendered prior to the new offer must receive the higher price.

In total, these restrictions were intended to reduce the acquiring firm's ability to surprise management and to stampede target shareholders into accepting an inadequate offer. Prior to the Williams Act, offers were generally made on a first-come, first-served basis, and they were often accompanied by an implicit threat to lower the bid price after 50 percent of the shares were in hand. The legislation also gave the target more time to mount a defense, and it gave rival bidders and *white knights* a chance to enter the fray and thus help a target's stockholders obtain a better price.

Many states have also passed laws designed to protect firms in their states from hostile takeovers. At first, these laws focused on disclosure requirements, but by the late 1970s several states had enacted takeover statutes so restrictive that they virtually precluded hostile takeovers. In 1979, MITE Corporation, a Delaware firm, made a hostile tender offer for Chicago Rivet and Machine Co., a publicly held Illinois corporation. Chicago Rivet sought protection under the Illinois Business Takeover Act. The constitutionality of the Illinois act was contested, and the U.S. Supreme Court found the law unconstitutional. The court ruled that the market for securities is a national market, and even though the issuing firm was incorporated in Illinois, the state of Illinois could not regulate interstate securities transactions.

The Illinois decision effectively eliminated the first generation of state merger regulations. However, the states kept trying to protect their state-headquartered companies, and in 1987 the U.S. Supreme Court upheld an Indiana law that radically changed the rules of the takeover game. Specifically, the Indiana law first defined "control shares" as enough shares to give an investor 20 percent of the vote. It went on to state that when an investor buys control shares, those shares can be voted only after approval by a majority of "disinterested shareholders," defined as those who are neither officers nor inside directors of the company, nor associates of the raider. The law also gives the buyer of control shares the right to insist that a shareholders' meeting be called within 50 days to decide whether the shares may be voted. The Indiana law dealt a major blow to raiders, mainly because it slows down the action. Delaware (the state in which most large companies are incorporated) later passed a similar bill, as did New York and a number of other important states.

The new state laws also have some features that protect target stockholders from their own managers. Included are limits on the use of golden parachutes, onerous debt-financing plans, and some types of takeover defenses. Since these laws do not regulate tender offers per se, but rather govern the practices of firms in the state, they have withstood all legal challenges to date.

Is there a need to regulate mergers? Explain.

Do the states play a role in merger regulation, or is it all done at the national level? Explain.

21-6 MERGER ANALYSIS

In theory, merger analysis is quite simple. The acquiring firm simply performs an analysis to value the target company and then determines whether the target can be bought at that value or, preferably, for less than the estimated value. The target company, on the other hand, should accept the offer if the price exceeds either its value if it continued to operate independently or the price it can receive from some other bidder. Theory aside, however, some difficult issues are involved. In this section, we first discuss valuing the target firm, which is the initial step in a merger analysis. Then we discuss setting the bid price and post-merger control.

21-6a Valuing the Target Firm

Several methodologies are used to value target firms, but we will confine our discussion to the two most common: (1) the discounted cash flow approach and (2) the market multiple method. However, regardless of the valuation methodology, it is crucial to recognize two facts. First, the target company typically will not continue to operate as a separate entity but will become part of the acquiring firm's portfolio of assets. Therefore, changes in operations will affect the value of the business and must be considered in the analysis. Second, the goal of merger valuation is to value the target firm's equity, because a firm is acquired from its owners, not from its creditors. Thus, although we use the phrase "valuing the firm," our focus is on the value of the equity rather than on total value.

Discounted Cash Flow Analysis

The discounted cash flow (DCF) approach to valuing a business involves the application of capital budgeting procedures to an entire firm rather than to a single project. To apply this method, two key items are needed: (1) pro forma statements that forecast the incremental free cash flows expected to result from the merger and (2) a discount rate, or cost of capital, to apply to these projected cash flows.

Pro Forma Cash Flow Statements Obtaining accurate post-merger cash flow forecasts is by far the most important task in the DCF approach. In a pure **financial merger**, in which no synergies are expected, the incremental post-merger cash flows are simply the expected cash flows of the target firm. In an **operating merger**, where the two firms' operations are to be integrated, forecasting future cash flows is more difficult.

Table 21-2 shows the projected cash flow statements for Apex Corporation, which is being considered as a target by Hightech, a large conglomerate. The projected data are for the post-merger period, and all synergistic effects have been included. Apex currently uses 50 percent debt, and if it were acquired, Hightech would keep the debt ratio at 50 percent. Both Hightech and Apex have a 40 percent marginal federal-plus-state tax rate.

Lines 1 through 4 of the table show the operating information that Hightech expects for the Apex subsidiary if the merger takes place, and Line 5 contains the earnings before interest and taxes (EBIT) for each year. Unlike a typical capital budgeting analysis, a merger analysis usually does incorporate interest expense into the cash flow forecast, as shown on Line 6. This is done for three reasons: (1) Acquiring firms often assume the debt of the target firm, so old debt at different coupon rates is often part of the deal; (2) the acquisition is often financed partially by debt; and (3) if the subsidiary is to grow in the future, new debt will have to be issued over time to support the expansion. Thus, debt associated with a merger is typically more complex than the single issue of new debt associated with a normal capital project, and the easiest way to properly account for the complexities of merger debt is to specifically include each year's expected interest expense in the cash flow forecast. Therefore, we are using what is called the **equity residual method** to value the target firm. Here the estimated net cash flows are a residual that belongs solely to the acquiring firm's shareholders. Therefore, they should be discounted at the cost of equity. This is in contrast to the corporate value model of Chapter 9, where the free cash flows (which belong to all investors, not just shareholders) are discounted at the WACC. Both methods lead to the same estimate of equity value.

Line 7 contains the earnings before taxes (EBT), and Line 8 gives taxes based on Hightech's 40 percent marginal rate. Line 9 lists each year's net income, and depreciation is added back on Line 10 to obtain each year's cash flow as shown

Financial Merger
A merger in which the firms involved will not be operated as a single unit and from which no operating economies are expected.

Operating Merger
A merger in which operations of the firms involved are integrated in hope of achieving synergistic benefits.

Equity Residual Method
A method used to value a target firm using net cash flows that are a residual and belong solely to the acquiring firm's shareholders.

TABLE 21-2	Projected Post-Merger Cash Flow Statements for the Apex Subsidiary as of December 31 (Millions of Dollars)				
	2006	**2007**	**2008**	**2009**	**2010**
1. Net sales	$105.0	$126.0	$151.0	$174.0	$191.0
2. Cost of goods sold	75.0	89.0	106.0	122.0	132.0
3. Selling and administrative expenses	10.0	12.0	13.0	15.0	16.0
4. Depreciation	8.0	8.0	9.0	9.0	10.0
5. EBIT	$ 12.0	$ 17.0	$ 23.0	$ 28.0	$ 33.0
6. Interest[a]	8.0	9.0	10.0	11.0	11.0
7. EBT	$ 4.0	$ 8.0	$ 13.0	$ 17.0	$ 22.0
8. Taxes (40%)[b]	1.6	3.2	5.2	6.8	8.8
9. Net income	$ 2.4	$ 4.8	$ 7.8	$ 10.2	$ 13.2
10. Plus depreciation	8.0	8.0	9.0	9.0	10.0
11. Cash flow	$ 10.4	$ 12.8	$ 16.8	$ 19.2	$ 23.2
12. Less retentions needed for growth[c]	4.0	4.0	7.0	9.0	12.0
13. Plus terminal value[d]					127.8
14. Net cash flow to Hightech[e]	$ 6.4	$ 8.8	$ 9.8	$ 10.2	$139.0

Notes:

[a] Interest payments are estimates based on Apex's existing debt, plus additional debt required to finance growth.

[b] Hightech will file a consolidated tax return after the merger. Thus, the taxes shown here are the full corporate taxes attributable to Apex's operations: there will be no additional taxes on any cash flows passed from Apex to Hightech.

[c] Some of the cash flows generated by the Apex subsidiary after the merger must be retained to finance asset replacements and growth, while some will be transferred to Hightech to pay dividends on its stock or for redeployment within the corporation. These retentions are net of any additional debt used to help finance growth.

[d] Apex's available cash flows are expected to grow at a constant 5 percent rate after 2010. The value of all post-2010 cash flows as of December 31, 2010, is estimated by use of the constant growth model to be $127.8 million.

$$V_{2010} = \frac{CF_{2011}}{r_s - g} = \frac{(23.2 - \$12.0)(1.05)}{0.142 - 0.05} = \$127.8 \text{ million}$$

In the next section, we discuss the estimated 14.2 percent cost of equity. The $127.8 million is the PV at the end of 2010 of the stream of cash flows for Year 2011 and thereafter.

[e] These are the net cash flows projected to be available to Hightech by virtue of the acquisition. The cash flows could be used for dividend payments to Hightech's stockholders, to finance asset expansion in Hightech's other divisions and subsidiaries, and so on.

on Line 11. Because some of Apex's assets will wear out or become obsolete, and because Hightech plans to expand the Apex subsidiary should the acquisition occur, some equity funds must be retained and reinvested in the business. These retentions, which are not available for transfer to the parent, are shown on Line 12. Finally, we have projected only five years of cash flows, but Hightech would likely operate the Apex subsidiary for many years—in theory, forever. Therefore, we applied the constant growth model to the 2010 cash flow to estimate the value of all cash flows beyond 2010. (See Note d to Table 21-2.) This "terminal value" represents Apex's projected value at the end of 2010, and it is shown on Line 13.

The net cash flows shown on Line 14 would be available to Hightech's stockholders, and they are the basis of the valuation.[8] Of course, the post-merger

---

[8] We purposely kept the cash flows relatively simple to help focus on key issues. In an actual merger valuation, the cash flows would be much more complex, normally including such items as additional capital furnished by the acquiring firm, tax loss carry-forwards, tax effects of plant and equipment valuation adjustments, and cash flows from the sale of some of the subsidiary's assets.

cash flows are extremely difficult to estimate, and in a complete merger valuation, just as in a complete capital budgeting analysis, sensitivity, scenario, and simulation analyses should be conducted. Indeed, in a friendly merger the acquiring firm would send a team consisting of literally dozens of accountants, engineers, and so forth, to the target firm's headquarters. They would go over its books, estimate required maintenance expenditures, set values on assets such as real estate and petroleum reserves, and the like. Such an investigation, which is called *due diligence*, is an essential part of any merger analysis.

Estimating the Discount Rate The bottom-line net cash flows shown on Line 14 are after interest and taxes, hence they represent equity. Therefore, they should be discounted at the cost of equity rather than at the overall cost of capital. Further, the discount rate used should reflect the risk of the cash flows in the table. The most appropriate discount rate is Apex's cost of equity, not that of either Hightech or the consolidated post-merger firm.

Although we will not illustrate it here, Hightech could perform a risk analysis on the Table 21-2 cash flows just as it does on any set of capital budgeting flows. Sensitivity analysis, scenario analysis, and/or Monte Carlo simulation could be used to give Hightech's management a feel for the risks involved with the acquisition. Apex is a publicly traded company, so we can assess directly its market risk. Apex's market-determined pre-merger beta was 1.63. Because the merger would not change Apex's capital structure or tax rate, its post-merger beta would remain at 1.63. However, if Apex's capital structure had changed, then the Hamada equation (which was discussed in Chapter 14) could have been used to determine the firm's new beta corresponding to its changed capital structure.

We use the Security Market Line to estimate Apex's post-merger cost of equity. If the risk-free rate is 6 percent and the market risk premium is 5 percent, then Apex's cost of equity, r_s, after the merger with Hightech, would be about 14.2 percent.[9]

$$r_s = r_{RF} + (RP_M)b = 6\% + (5\%)1.63 = 14.15\% \approx 14.2\%$$

Valuing the Cash Flows The current value of Apex's stock to Hightech is the present value of the cash flows expected from Apex, discounted at 14.2 percent (in millions of dollars):

$$V_{2005} = \frac{\$6.4}{(1.142)^1} + \frac{\$8.8}{(1.142)^2} + \frac{\$9.8}{(1.142)^3} + \frac{\$10.2}{(1.142)^4} + \frac{\$139.0}{(1.142)^5} \approx \$96.5$$

Thus, the value of Apex's stock to Hightech is $96.5 million.

Note that in a merger analysis, the value of the target consists of the target's pre-merger value plus any value created by operating or financial synergies. In this example, we held the target's capital structure and tax rate constant. There-

---

[9] In this example, we used the Capital Asset Pricing Model to estimate Apex's cost of equity, and thus we assumed that investors require a premium for market risk only. We could have also conducted a corporate risk analysis, in which the relevant risk would be the contribution of Apex's cash flows to the total risk of the post-merger firm.

In actual merger situations among large firms, companies almost always hire an investment banker to help develop valuation estimates. For example, when General Electric acquired Utah International, GE hired Morgan Stanley to determine Utah's value. We discussed the valuation process with the Morgan Stanley analyst in charge of the appraisal, and he confirmed that they applied all of the standard procedures discussed in this chapter. Note, though, that merger analysis, like the analysis of any other complex issue, requires judgment, and people's judgments differ as to how much weight to give to different methods in any given situation.

fore, the only synergies were operating synergies, and these effects were incorporated into the forecasted cash flows. If there had been financial synergies, the analysis would have to be modified to reflect this added value. For example, if Apex had been operating with only 30 percent debt, and if Hightech could lower Apex's overall cost of capital by increasing the debt ratio to 50 percent, then Apex's merger value would have exceeded the $96.5 million calculated above.

Market Multiple Analysis

The second method of valuing a target company is **market multiple analysis,** which applies a market-determined multiple to net income, earnings per share, sales, book value, or, for businesses such as cable TV or cellular telephone systems, the number of subscribers. While the DCF method applies valuation concepts in a precise manner, focusing on expected cash flows, market multiple analysis is more judgmental. To illustrate the concept, note that Apex's forecasted net income is $2.4 million in 2006, and it rises to $13.2 million in 2010, for an average of $7.7 million over the five-year forecast period. The average P/E ratio for publicly traded companies similar to Apex is 12.5.

To estimate Apex's value using the market P/E multiple approach, simply multiply its $7.7 million average net income by the market multiple of 12.5 to obtain the value of $7.7(12.5) = $96.25 million. This is the equity, or ownership, value of the firm. Note that we used the average net income over the next five years to value Apex. The market P/E multiple of 12.5 is based on the current year's income of comparable companies, but Apex's current income does not reflect synergistic effects or managerial changes that will be made. By averaging future net income, we are attempting to capture the value added by Hightech to Apex's operations.

Note that measures other than net income can be used in the market multiple approach. For example, another commonly used measure is *earnings before interest, taxes, depreciation, and amortization (EBITDA)*. The procedure would be identical to that just described, except that the market multiple would be price divided by EBITDA rather than earnings per share, and this multiple would be multiplied by Apex's EBITDA.

As noted, in some businesses such as cable TV and cellular telephone, an important element in the valuation process is the number of customers a company has. The acquirer has an idea of the cost required to obtain a new customer and the average cash flow per customer. Managed care companies such as HMOs have applied similar logic in acquisitions, basing their valuations on the number of people insured.

21-6b Setting the Bid Price

Using the DCF valuation results, $96.5 million is the most Hightech could pay for Apex—if it pays more, then Hightech's own value will be diluted. On the other hand, if Hightech can acquire Apex for less than $96.5 million, Hightech's stockholders will gain value. Therefore, Hightech will bid something less than $96.5 million when it makes an offer for Apex.

Figure 21-1 graphs the merger situation. The $96.5 million is shown as a point on the horizontal axis, and it is the maximum price that Hightech can afford to pay. If Hightech pays less, say, $86.5 million, then its stockholders will gain $10 million from the merger, while if it pays more, its stockholders will lose. What we have, then, is a 45-degree line that cuts the X-axis at $96.5 million, and that line shows how much Hightech's stockholders can expect to gain or lose at different acquisition prices.

Market Multiple Analysis
A method of valuing a target company that applies a market-determined multiple to net income, earnings per share, sales, book value, and so forth.

*A video clip entitled "T. Boone Pickens on White Knights," which discusses mergers and takeovers, is available at Ohio State University's Web site at **http://www.cob.ohio-state.edu/~fin/clips.htm**. The clip requires a QuickTime video player for either Windows or Macintosh machines (which you download for free over the Internet at **http://www.apple.com/quicktime/**). One caveat is that the video clip is in excess of 5 MB in size and should therefore only be accessed with a rapid Internet connection.*

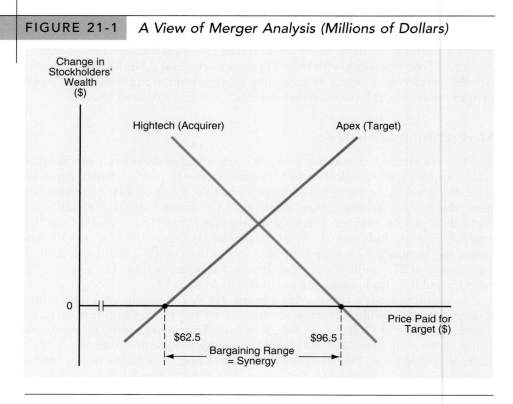

FIGURE 21-1 *A View of Merger Analysis (Millions of Dollars)*

Now consider the target company, Apex. It has 10 million shares of stock that sell for $6.25, so its value as an independent operating company is presumably $62.5 million. [In making this statement, we assume (1) that the company is being operated as well as possible by its present management and (2) that the $6.25 market price per share does not include a "speculative merger premium" in addition to the PV of its operating cash flows.] If Apex is acquired at a price greater than $62.5 million, its stockholders will gain value, while they will lose value at any lower price. Thus, we can draw another 45-degree line, this one with an upward slope, to show how the merger price affects Apex's stockholders.

The difference between $62.5 and $96.5 million, or $34 million, represents synergistic benefits expected from the merger. Here are some points to note:

1. If there were no synergistic benefits, the maximum bid would be equal to the current value of the target company. The greater the synergistic gains, the greater the gap between the target's current price and the maximum the acquiring company could pay.
2. The greater the synergistic gains, the more likely a merger is to be consummated.
3. The issue of how to divide the synergistic benefits is critically important. Obviously, both parties will want to get as much as possible. In our example, if Apex's management knew the maximum price that Hightech could pay, it would argue for a price close to $96.5 million. Hightech, on the other hand, would try to get Apex at a price as close to $62.5 million as possible.
4. Where, within the $62.5 to $96.5 million range, will the actual price be set? The answer depends on a number of factors, including whether Hightech

More Than Just Financial Statements

When corporations merge, they combine more than just their financial statements. Mergers bring together two organizations with different histories and corporate cultures. Deals that look good on paper can fail if the individuals involved are unwilling or unable to work together to generate the potential synergies. Consequently, when analyzing a potential merger, it is important to determine whether the two companies are compatible.

Many deals fall apart because, during the "due diligence" phase, synergistic benefits are revealed to be less than was originally anticipated, so there is little economic rationale for the merger. Other negotiations break off because the two parties cannot agree on the price to be paid for the acquired firm's stock. In addition, merger talks often collapse because of "social issues." These social issues include both the "chemistry" of the companies and their personnel and such basic issues as these: What will be the name of the combined company? Where will headquarters be located? And, most important: Who will run the combined company? Robert Kindler, a partner at Cravath, Swaine & Moore, a prominent New York law firm that specializes in mergers, summarizes

the importance of these issues as follows: "Even transactions that make absolute economic sense don't happen unless the social issues work."

Investment bankers, lawyers, and other professionals state that mergers tend to be most successful if there is a clear and well-arranged plan spelling out who will run the company. This issue is straightforward if one firm is clearly dominant and is acquiring the other. However, in cases where there is "a merger of equals," senior personnel issues often become sticky. This situation is made considerably easier if one of the chief executives is at or near the retirement age.

Some analysts believe that social issues often play too large a role, derailing mergers that should take place. In other cases where a merger occurs, concerns about social issues preclude managers from undertaking the necessary changes—like laying off redundant staff—for the deal to benefit shareholders.

Source: "In Many Merger Deals, Ego and Pride Play Big Roles in Which Way Talks Go," *The Wall Street Journal,* August 22, 1996, p. C1. Reprinted by permission of *The Wall Street Journal,* Copyright © 2002 Dow Jones & Company, Inc. All Rights Reserved Worldwide.

offers to pay with cash or securities, the negotiating skills of the two management teams, and, most importantly, the bargaining positions of the two parties as determined by fundamental economic conditions. To illustrate the latter point, suppose there are many companies similar to Apex that Hightech could acquire, but no company other than Hightech that could gain synergies by acquiring Apex. In this case, Hightech would probably make a relatively low, take-it-or-leave-it offer, and Apex would probably take it because some gain is better than none. On the other hand, if Apex has some unique technology or other asset that many companies want, then once Hightech announces its offer, others will probably make competing bids, and the final price will probably be close to or even above $96.5 million. A price above $96.5 million would presumably be paid by some other company that had a better synergistic fit or, perhaps, whose management was more optimistic about Apex's cash flow potential. In Figure 21-1, this situation would be represented by a line parallel to that for Hightech but shifted to the right of the Hightech line.

5. Hightech would, of course, want to keep its maximum bid secret, and it would plan its bidding strategy carefully and consistently with the situation. If it thought that other bidders would emerge, or that Apex's management

might resist in order to preserve their jobs, it might make a high "preemptive" bid in hopes of scaring off competing bids and/or management resistance. On the other hand, it might make a low-ball bid in hopes of "stealing" the company.

We will have more to say about these points in the sections that follow, and you should keep Figure 21-1 in mind as you go through the rest of the chapter.

21-6c Post-Merger Control

The employment/control situation is often of vital interest in a merger analysis. First, consider the situation in which a small, owner-managed firm sells out to a larger concern. The owner-manager may be anxious to retain a high-status position, and he or she may also have developed a camaraderie with the employees and thus be concerned about their retention after the merger. If so, these points would be stressed during the merger negotiations.[10] When a publicly owned firm that is not owned by its managers is merged into another company, the acquired firm's managers will be worried about their post-merger positions. If the acquiring firm agrees to retain the old management, then management may be willing to support the merger and to recommend its acceptance to the stockholders. If the old management is to be removed, then it will probably resist the merger.[11]

What is the difference between an operating merger and a financial merger?

Describe the way post-merger cash flows are estimated in a DCF analysis.

What is the basis for the discount rate in a DCF analysis? Describe how this rate might be estimated.

Describe the market multiple approach.

What are some factors that acquiring firms consider when they set a bid price?

How do control issues affect mergers?

---

[10] The acquiring firm may also be concerned about this point, especially if the target firm's management is quite good. Indeed, a condition of the merger may be that the management team agree to stay on for a period such as five years after the merger. In this case, the price paid may be contingent on the acquired firm's performance subsequent to the merger. For example, when International Holdings acquired Walker Products, the price paid was an immediate 100,000 shares of International Holdings stock worth $63 per share plus an additional 30,000 shares each year for the next three years, provided Walker Products earned at least $1 million during each of these years. Since Walker's managers owned the stock and would receive the bonus, they had a strong incentive to stay on and help the firm meet its targets.

Finally, if the managers of the target company are highly competent but do not wish to remain on after the merger, the acquiring firm may build into the merger contract a noncompete agreement with the old management. Typically, the acquired firm's principal officers must agree not to affiliate with a new business that is competitive with the one they sold for a specified period, say, five years. Such agreements are especially important with service-oriented businesses.

[11] Managements of firms that are thought to be attractive merger candidates often arrange *golden parachutes* for themselves. Golden parachutes are extremely lucrative retirement plans that take effect if a merger is consummated. Thus, when Bendix Corp. was acquired by Allied Automotive, Bill Agee, Bendix's chairman, "pulled the ripcord of his golden parachute" and walked away with $4 million. If a golden parachute is large enough, it can also function as a poison pill—for example, where the president of a firm worth $10 million would have to be paid $8 million if the firm is acquired, this will prevent a takeover. Stockholders are increasingly resisting such arrangements, but some still exist.

What is the value of XYZ Corporation to JKL Enterprises, assuming the following facts? XYZ's post-merger cash flows in Years 1–3 are estimated to be $7 million, $10 million, and $12 million. In addition, its terminal value in Year 3 is $318 million. The firm's cost of equity is 10 percent and its growth rate is 6 percent. ($262.56 million)

21-7 FINANCIAL REPORTING FOR MERGERS

Although a detailed discussion of financial reporting is best left to financial accounting courses, the accounting implications of mergers cannot be ignored. Currently, mergers are handled using **purchase accounting**.[12] Keep in mind, however, that all larger companies are required to keep two sets of books. The first is for the IRS, and it reflects the tax treatment of mergers as described in the previous section. The second is for financial reporting, and it reflects the treatment described below. *The rules for financial reporting differ from those for the IRS.*[13]

> **Purchase Accounting**
> *A method of accounting for a merger as a purchase. In this method, the acquiring firm is assumed to have "bought" the acquired company in much the same way it would buy any capital asset.*

21-7a Purchase Accounting

Table 21-3 illustrates purchase accounting. Here Firm A is assumed to have "bought" Firm B in much the same way it would buy any capital asset, paying for it with cash, debt, or stock of the acquiring company. If the price paid is exactly equal to the acquired firm's *net asset value*, which is defined as its total assets minus its liabilities, then the consolidated balance sheet will be the same as if the two statements were merged. Normally, though, there is an important difference. If the price paid exceeds the net asset value, then asset values will be increased to reflect the price actually paid, whereas if the price paid is less than the net asset value, then assets must be written down when preparing the consolidated balance sheet.

Note that Firm B's net asset value is $30, which is also its reported common equity value. This $30 book value could be equal to the market value (which is determined by investors based on the firm's earning power), but book value could also be more or less than the market value. Three situations are considered in Table 21-3. First, in Column 3 we assume that Firm A gives cash or stock worth $20 for Firm B. Thus, B's assets as reported on its balance sheet were overvalued, and A pays less than B's net asset value. The overvaluation could be in either fixed or current assets; an appraisal would be made but we assume that it is fixed assets that are overvalued. Accordingly, we reduce B's fixed assets and also its common equity by $10 before constructing the consolidated balance sheet shown in Column 3. Next, in Column 4, we assume that A pays exactly the net asset value for B. In this case, the financial statements are simply combined.

Finally, in Column 5 we assume that A pays more than the net asset value for B: $50 is paid for $30 of net assets. This excess is assumed to be partly attributable to undervalued assets (land, buildings, machinery, and inventories), so to reflect this undervaluation, current and fixed assets are each increased by $5. In addition, we assume that $10 of the $20 excess of market value over book value is due to a superior sales organization, or some other intangible factor, and we post this excess as **goodwill.** B's common equity is increased by $20, the sum of

> **Goodwill**
> *Refers to the excess paid for a firm above the appraised value of the physical and intangible assets purchased.*

---

[12] In 2001, the Financial Accounting Standards Board (FASB) issued Statement 141, which eliminated the use of pooling accounting.

[13] For additional information, refer to Eugene F. Brigham and Phillip R. Daves, *Intermediate Financial Management*, 8th edition (Mason, OH: Thomson/South-Western, 2004), Chapter 25.

TABLE 21-3	*Accounting for Mergers: A Acquires B*

	Firm A (1)	Firm B (2)	POST-MERGER: FIRM A		
			$20 Paid[a] (3)	$30 Paid[a] (4)	$50 Paid[a] (5)
Current assets	$ 50	$25	$ 75	$ 75	$ 80[c]
Fixed assets	50	25	65[b]	75	80[c]
Goodwill[d]	0	0	0	0	10[d]
Total assets	$100	$50	$140	$150	$170
Debt	$ 40	$20	$ 60	$ 60	$ 60
Equity	60	30	80[e]	90	110[f]
Total claims	$100	$50	$140	$150	$170

Notes:

[a] The price paid is the *net asset value,* that is, total assets minus debt.

[b] Here we assume that Firm B's fixed assets are written down from $25 to $15 before constructing the consolidated balance sheet.

[c] Here we assume that Firm B's current and fixed assets are both increased to $30.

[d] *Goodwill* refers to the excess paid for a firm above the appraised value of the physical assets purchased. Goodwill represents payment both for intangibles such as patents and for "organization value" such as that associated with having an effective sales force. Beginning in 2001, purchased goodwill such as this could not be amortized for financial statement reporting purposes.

[e] Firm B's common equity is reduced by $10 prior to consolidation to reflect the fixed assets write-off.

[f] Firm B's equity is increased to $50 to reflect the above-book purchase price.

the increases in current and fixed assets plus goodwill, and this markup is also reflected in A's post-merger equity account.[14]

21-7b Income Statement Effects

A merger can have a significant effect on reported profits. If asset values are increased, as they often are under a purchase, this must be reflected in higher depreciation charges (and also in a higher cost of goods sold if inventories are written up). This, in turn, will further reduce reported profits. Prior to 2001, goodwill was also amortized over its expected life. Now, however, goodwill is subject to an "annual impairment test." If the fair market value of the goodwill has declined over the year, then the amount of the decline must be charged to earnings. If not, then there is no charge, but gains in goodwill cannot be added to earnings.

Table 21-4 illustrates the income statement effects of the write-up of current and fixed assets. We assume that A purchased B for $50, creating $10 of goodwill and $10 of higher physical assets value. As Column 3 indicates, the assets markups cause reported profits to be lower than the sum of the individual companies' reported profits.

The asset markup is also reflected in earnings per share. In our hypothetical merger, we assume that nine shares exist in the consolidated firm. (Six of these shares went to A's stockholders, and three to B's.) The merged company's EPS is $2.33 while the individual companies' EPS is $2.40.

What is purchase accounting for mergers?

What is goodwill? What effect does goodwill have on the firm's balance sheet? On its income statement?

---

[14] This example assumes that additional debt was not issued to help finance the acquisition. If the acquisition were totally debt financed, the postmerger balance sheet would show increases in the debt account rather than increases in the equity account. If it were financed by a mix of debt and equity, both accounts would be changed.

Tempest in a Teapot?

In 2001, amid a flurry of warnings and lobbying, the Financial Accounting Standards Board (FASB) in its Statement 141 eliminated the use of pooling for merger accounting, requiring that purchase accounting be used instead. Because the change would otherwise have required that all purchased goodwill be amortized, and reported earnings reduced, the FASB also issued Statement 142, which eliminated the regular amortization of purchased goodwill, replacing it with an "impairment test." The impairment test requires that companies evaluate annually their purchased goodwill and write it down if its value has declined. This impairment test resulted in Time Warner's unprecedented 2002 write-down of $54 billion of goodwill associated with the AOL merger.

So what exactly is the effect of the change? First and foremost, the change does nothing to the firm's actual cash flows. Purchased goodwill may still be amortized for federal income tax purposes, so the change does not affect the actual taxes a company pays, nor does it affect the company's operating cash flows. However, it does affect the earnings that companies report to their shareholders. Firms that used to have large goodwill charges from past acquisitions saw their reported earnings increase, because they no longer have to amortize the remaining goodwill. Firms whose acquisitions have fared badly, such as Time Warner, must make large write-downs. Executives facing an earnings boost hoped, while executives facing a write-down feared, that investors would not see through these accounting changes. However, evidence suggests that investors realize that a company's assets have deteriorated long before the write-down actually occurs, and they build this information into the price of the stock. For example, Time Warner's announcement of its $54 billion charge in January 2002 resulted in only a blip in its stock price at that time, even though the write-down totaled more than a third of its market value. The market recognized the decline in value months earlier, and by the time of the announcement Time Warner had already lost more than $100 billion in market value.

TABLE 21-4   *Income Statements Effects*

	PRE-MERGER		POST-MERGER
	Firm A (1)	Firm B (2)	Merged (3)
Sales	$100.0	$50.0	$150.0
Operating costs	72.0	36.0	109.0[a]
Operating income	$ 28.0	$14.0	$ 41.0[a]
Interest (10%)	4.0	2.0	6.0
Taxable income	$ 24.0	$12.0	$ 35.0
Taxes (40%)	9.6	4.8	14.0
Net income	$ 14.4	$ 7.2	$ 21.0
EPS[b]	$ 2.40	$ 2.40	$ 2.33

Notes:
[a] Operating costs are $1 higher than they otherwise would be to reflect the higher reported costs (depreciation and cost of goods sold) caused by the physical assets markups at the time of purchase.
[b] Firm A had six shares and Firm B had three shares before the merger. A gives one of its shares for each of Bs, so A has nine shares after the merger.

21-8 THE ROLE OF INVESTMENT BANKERS

Investment bankers are involved with mergers in a number of ways: (1) they help arrange mergers, (2) they help target companies develop and implement defensive tactics, (3) they help value target companies, (4) they help finance mergers, and (5) they invest in the stocks of potential merger candidates. These merger-related activities have been quite profitable. For example, Thomson Financial estimated that financial advisors received more than $13 billion in fees from worldwide merger activity generated during just the first half of 2005. No wonder investment banking houses are able to make top offers to finance graduates!

21-8a Arranging Mergers

The major investment banking firms have merger and acquisition groups that operate within their corporate finance departments. (Corporate finance departments offer advice, as opposed to underwriting or brokerage services, to business firms.) Members of these groups identify firms with excess cash that might want to buy other firms, companies that might be willing to be bought, and firms that might, for a number of reasons, be attractive to others. Also, if an oil company, for instance, decided to expand into coal mining, then it might enlist the aid of an investment banker to help it acquire a coal company. Similarly, dissident stockholders of firms with poor track records might work with investment bankers to oust management by helping to arrange a merger. Investment bankers are reported to have offered packages of financing to corporate raiders, where the package includes both designing the securities to be used in the tender offer, plus lining up people and firms who will buy the target firm's stock now, and then tender it once the final offer is made.

Investment bankers have occasionally taken illegal actions in the merger arena. For example, they are reported to have parked stock—purchasing it for a raider under a guaranteed buy-back agreement—to help the raider de facto accumulate more than 5 percent of the target's stock without disclosing the position. People have gone to jail for this.

21-8b Developing Defensive Tactics

Target firms that do not want to be acquired generally enlist the help of an investment banking firm, along with a law firm that specializes in mergers. Defenses include such tactics as (1) changing the by-laws so that only one-third of the directors are elected each year and/or so that a 75 percent approval (a *supermajority*) versus a simple majority is required to approve a merger; (2) trying to convince the target firm's stockholders that the price being offered is too low; (3) raising antitrust issues in the hope that the Justice Department will intervene; (4) repurchasing stock in the open market in an effort to push the price above that being offered by the potential acquirer; (5) getting a **white knight** who is acceptable to the target firm's management to compete with the potential acquirer; (6) getting a **white squire** who is friendly to current management to buy enough of the target firm's shares to block the merger; and (7) taking a *poison pill*, as described next.

Poison pills—which occasionally really do amount to committing economic suicide to avoid a takeover—are such tactics as borrowing on terms that require immediate repayment of all loans if the firm is acquired, selling off at bargain prices the assets that originally made the firm a desirable target, granting such lucrative **golden parachutes** to their executives that the cash drain from these payments would render the merger infeasible, and planning defensive mergers which would leave the firm with new assets of questionable value and a huge

White Knight
A company that is acceptable to the management of a firm under threat of a hostile takeover and that will compete with the potential acquirer.

White Squire
An individual or company who is friendly to current management and will buy enough of the target firm's shares to block a hostile takeover.

Poison Pill
An action that will seriously hurt a company if it is acquired by another.

Golden Parachutes
Large payments made to the managers of a target firm if it is acquired.

debt load. Currently, the most popular poison pill is for a company to give its stockholders stock purchase rights that allow them to buy at half-price the stock of an acquiring firm, should the firm be acquired. The blatant use of poison pills is constrained by directors' awareness that excessive use could trigger personal suits by stockholders against directors who voted for them, and, perhaps in the near future, by laws that would further limit management's use of pills. Still, investment bankers and antitakeover lawyers are busy thinking up new poison pill formulas, and others are just as busy trying to come up with antidotes.[15]

Another takeover defense that is being used is the employee stock ownership plan (ESOP). ESOPs are designed to give lower-level employees an ownership stake in the firm, and current tax laws provide generous incentives for companies to establish such plans and fund them with the firm's common stock.

21-8c Establishing a Fair Value

If a friendly merger is being worked out between two firms' managements, it is important to document that the agreed-upon price is a fair one; otherwise, the stockholders of either company may sue to block the merger. Therefore, in most large mergers each side will hire an investment banking firm to evaluate the target company and to help establish the fair price. For example, General Electric employed Morgan Stanley to determine a fair price for Utah International, as did Royal Dutch to help establish the price it paid for Shell Oil. Even if the merger is not friendly, investment bankers may still be asked to help establish a price. If a surprise tender offer is to be made, the acquiring firm will want to know the lowest price at which it might be able to acquire the stock, while the target firm may seek help in "proving" that the price being offered is too low.[16]

21-8d Financing Mergers

Many mergers are financed with the acquiring company's excess cash. However, if the acquiring company has no excess cash, it will require a source of funds. Perhaps the single most important factor behind the 1980s merger wave was the development of junk bonds for use in financing acquisitions.

Drexel Burnham Lambert was the primary developer of *junk bonds*, defined as bonds rated below investment grade (BBB/Baa). Prior to Drexel's actions, it was almost impossible to sell low-grade bonds to raise new capital. Drexel then pioneered a procedure under which a target firm's situation would be appraised very closely, and a cash flow projection similar to that in Table 21-2 (but much more detailed) would be developed.

To be successful in the mergers and acquisitions (M&A) business, an investment banker must be able to offer a financing package to clients, whether they are acquirers who need capital to take over companies or target companies trying

---

[15] It has become extremely difficult and expensive for companies to buy "directors' insurance," which protects the board from such contingencies as stockholders' suits, and even when insurance is available it often does not pay for losses if the directors have not exercised due caution and judgment. This exposure is making directors extremely leery of actions that might trigger stockholder suits.

[16] Such investigations must obviously be done in secret, for if someone knew that Company A was thinking of offering, say, $50 per share for Company T, which was currently selling at $35 per share, then huge profits could be made. One of the biggest scandals to hit Wall Street was the disclosure that Ivan Boesky was buying information from Dennis Levine, a senior member of the investment banking house of Drexel Burnham Lambert, about target companies that Drexel was analyzing for others. Purchases based on such insider information would, of course, raise the prices of the stocks and thus force Drexel's clients to pay more than they otherwise would have had to pay. Levine and Boesky, among others, went to jail for their improper use of insider information.

to finance stock repurchase plans or other defenses against takeovers. Drexel was the leading player in the merger financing game during the 1980s, but since Drexel's bankruptcy Goldman Sachs, Merrill Lynch, UBS, Morgan Stanley, and others are all vying for the title.

21-8e Arbitrage Operations

Arbitrage
The simultaneous buying and selling of the same commodity or security in two different markets at different prices, and pocketing a risk-free return.

Arbitrage generally means simultaneously buying and selling the same commodity or security in two different markets at different prices, and pocketing a risk-free return. However, the major brokerage houses, as well as some wealthy private investors, are engaged in a different type of arbitrage called *risk arbitrage*. The *arbitrageurs*, or "arbs," speculate in the stocks of companies that are likely takeover targets. Vast amounts of capital are required to speculate in a large number of securities and thus reduce risk, and also to make money on narrow spreads. However, the large investment bankers have the wherewithal to play the game. To be successful, arbs need to be able to sniff out likely targets, assess the probability of offers reaching fruition, and move in and out of the market quickly and with low transactions costs.

What are some defensive tactics that firms can use to resist hostile takeovers?

What role did junk bonds play in the merger wave of the 1980s?

What is the difference between pure arbitrage and risk arbitrage?

21-9 DO MERGERS CREATE VALUE? THE EMPIRICAL EVIDENCE

All the recent merger activity has raised two questions: (1) Do corporate acquisitions create value? (2) If so, how is the value shared between the parties?

Most researchers agree that takeovers increase the wealth of the shareholders of target firms, for otherwise they would not agree to the offer. However, there is a debate as to whether mergers benefit the acquiring firm's shareholders. In particular, managements of acquiring firms may be motivated by factors other than shareholder wealth maximization. For example, they may want to merge merely to increase the size of the corporations they manage, because increased size usually brings larger salaries plus job security, perquisites, power, and prestige.

The validity of the competing views on who gains from corporate acquisitions can be tested by examining the stock price changes that occur around the time of a merger or takeover announcement. Changes in the stock prices of the acquiring and target firms represent market participants' beliefs about the value created by the merger, and about how that value will be divided between the target and acquiring firms' shareholders. So, examining a large sample of stock price movements can shed light on the issue of who gains from mergers.

We cannot simply examine stock prices around merger announcement dates, because other factors influence stock prices. For example, if a merger was announced on a day when the entire market advanced, the fact that the target firm's price rose would not necessarily signify that the merger was expected to create value. Hence, studies examine *abnormal returns* associated with merger announcements, where abnormal returns are defined as that part of a stock price change caused by factors other than changes in the general stock market.

The Track Record of Recent Large Mergers

Academics have long known that acquiring firm's shareholders rarely reap the benefits of mergers. However, this important information never seemed to make it up to the offices of corporate America's decision makers; the 1990s saw bad deal after bad deal, with no apparent learning on the part of acquisitive executives. *BusinessWeek* published an analysis of 302 large mergers from 1995 to 2001, and it found that 61 percent of them led to losses by the acquiring firms' shareholders. Indeed, those losing shareholders' returns during the first post-merger year averaged 25 percentage points less than the returns on other companies in their industry. The average returns for all the merging companies, both winners and losers, were 4.3 percent below industry averages and 9.2 percent below the S&P 500. The article cited four common mistakes:

1. The acquiring firms often overpaid. Generally, the acquirers gave away all of the synergies from the mergers to the acquired firms' shareholders, and then some.

2. Management overestimated the synergies (cost savings and revenue gains) that would result from the merger.

3. Management took too long to integrate operations between the merged companies. This irritated customers and employees alike, and it postponed any gains from the integration.

4. Some companies cut costs too deeply, at the expense of maintaining sales and production infrastructures.

The worst performance came from companies that paid for their acquisitions with stock. The best performance, albeit a paltry 0.3 percent better than industry averages, came from companies that used cash for their acquisitions. On the bright side, the shareholders of the companies that were acquired fared quite well, earning on average 19.3 percent more than their industry peers, and all of those gains came in the two weeks surrounding the merger announcement.

Source: David Henry, "Mergers: Why Most Big Deals Don't Pay Off," *BusinessWeek*, October 14, 2002, pp. 60–70.

Many studies have examined both acquiring and target firms' stock price responses to mergers and tender offers.[17] Jointly, these studies have covered nearly every acquisition involving publicly traded firms from the early 1960s to the present, and they are remarkably consistent in their results: On average, the stock prices of target firms increase by about 30 percent in hostile tender offers, while in friendly mergers the average increase is about 20 percent. However, for both hostile and friendly deals, the stock prices of acquiring firms, on average, remain constant. However, as the accompanying box entitled "The Track Record of Recent Large Mergers" suggests, abnormal returns vary considerably among mergers, and it is not unusual for acquiring firms to see their stock prices fall when mergers are announced. On balance, the evidence indicates (1) that acquisitions do create value, but (2) that shareholders of target firms reap virtually all the benefits.

In hindsight, these results are not too surprising. First, target firm's shareholders can always say no, so they are in the driver's seat. Second, takeovers are a competitive game, so if one potential acquiring firm does not offer full value for a potential target, then another firm will generally jump in with a higher bid. Finally, managements of acquiring firms might well be willing to give up all the value created by the merger, because the merger would enhance the acquiring managers' personal positions without harming their shareholders.

---

[17] For an excellent summary of the effects of mergers on value, see Michael C. Jensen and Richard S. Ruback, "The Market for Corporate Control: The Scientific Evidence," *Journal of Financial Economics*, April 1983, pp. 5–50.

It has also been argued that acquisitions may increase shareholder wealth at the expense of bondholders—in particular, concern has been expressed that leveraged buyouts dilute the claims of bondholders. Specific instances can be cited in which bonds were downgraded and bondholders did suffer losses, sometimes quite large ones, as a direct result of an acquisition. However, most studies find no evidence to support the contention that bondholders, on average, lose in corporate acquisitions.

Explain how researchers can study the effects of mergers on shareholder wealth.

Do mergers create value? If so, who profits from this value?

Do the research results discussed in this section seem logical? Explain.

21-10 CORPORATE ALLIANCES

Corporate, or Strategic, Alliance
A cooperative deal that stops short of a merger.

Mergers are one way for two companies to join forces, but many companies are striking cooperative deals, called **corporate, or strategic, alliances,** which stop far short of merging. Whereas mergers combine all of the assets of the firms involved, as well as their ownership and managerial expertise, alliances allow firms to create combinations that focus on specific business lines that offer the most potential synergies. These alliances take many forms, from simple marketing agreements to joint ownership of worldwide operations.

Joint Venture
A corporate alliance in which two or more independent companies combine their resources to achieve a specific, limited objective.

One form of corporate alliance is the **joint venture,** in which parts of companies are joined to achieve specific, limited objectives.[18] A joint venture is controlled by a management team consisting of representatives of the two (or more) parent companies. Joint ventures have been used often by U.S., Japanese, and European firms to share technology and/or marketing expertise. For example, Whirlpool announced a joint venture with the Dutch electronics giant Philips to produce appliances under Philips's brand names in five European countries. By joining with their foreign counterparts, U.S. firms are attempting to gain a stronger foothold in Europe. Although alliances are new to some firms, they are established practices to others. For example, Corning Glass now obtains more than half of its profits from 23 joint ventures, two-thirds of them with foreign companies representing almost all of Europe, as well as Japan, China, South Korea, and Australia.

What is the difference between a merger and a corporate alliance?

What is a joint venture? Give some reasons joint ventures may be advantageous to the parties involved.

21-11 LEVERAGED BUYOUTS

Leveraged Buyout (LBO)
A situation in which a small group of investors (which usually includes the firm's managers) borrows heavily to buy all the shares of a company.

In a **leveraged buyout (LBO)** a small group of investors, which usually includes current management, acquires a firm in a transaction financed largely by debt. The debt is serviced with funds generated by the acquired company's operations and, often, by the sale of some of its assets. Sometimes, the acquiring group

---

[18] Cross-licensing, consortia, joint bidding, and franchising are still other ways for firms to combine resources. For more information on joint ventures, see Sanford V. Berg, Jerome Duncan, and Phillip Friedman, *Joint Venture Strategies and Corporate Innovation* (Cambridge, MA: Oelgeschlager, Gunn and Hain, 1982).

plans to run the acquired company for a number of years, boost its sales and profits, and then take it public again as a stronger company. In other instances, the LBO firm plans to sell off divisions to other firms that can gain synergies. In either case, the acquiring group expects to make a substantial profit from the LBO, but the inherent risks are great due to the heavy use of financial leverage. To illustrate the profit potential, Kohlberg Kravis Roberts & Company (KKR), a leading LBO specialist firm, averaged a spectacular 50 percent annual return on its LBO investments during the 1980s. However, strong stock prices for target firms have dampened the returns on LBO investments, so recent activity has been slower than in its heyday of the 1980s.

What is an LBO?

What actions do companies typically take to meet the large debt burdens resulting from LBOs?

21-12 DIVESTITURES

Although corporations do more buying than selling of productive facilities, a good bit of selling does occur. In this section, we briefly discuss the major types of divestitures, after which we present some recent examples and rationales for divestitures.

21-12a Types of Divestitures

There are four types of **divestitures**: (1) sale of an operating unit to another firm, (2) setting up the business to be divested as a separate corporation and then "spinning it off" to the divesting firm's stockholders, (3) following the steps for a spin-off but selling only some of the shares, and (4) outright liquidation of assets.

Sale to another firm generally involves the sale of an entire division or unit, usually for cash but sometimes for stock of the acquiring firm. In a **spin-off**, the firm's existing stockholders are given new stock representing separate ownership rights in the division that was divested. The division establishes its own board of directors and officers, and it becomes a separate company. The stockholders end up owning shares of two firms instead of one, but no cash has been transferred. In a **carve-out**, a minority interest in a corporate subsidiary is sold to new shareholders, so the parent gains new equity financing yet retains control. Finally, in a **liquidation** the assets of a division are sold off piecemeal, rather than as an operating entity. To illustrate the different types of divestitures, we present in the next section some high-profit examples that have occurred over the past several years.

21-12b Divestiture Illustrations

1. Pepsi spun off its fast-food business, which included Pizza Hut, Taco Bell, and Kentucky Fried Chicken. The spun-off businesses now operate under the name Tricon Global Restaurants. Pepsi originally acquired the chains because it wanted to increase the distribution channels for its soft drinks. Over time, however, Pepsi began to realize that the soft-drink and restaurant businesses were quite different, and synergies between them were less than anticipated. The spin-off is part of Pepsi's attempt to once again focus on its core business. However, Pepsi will try to maintain these distribution channels by signing long-term contracts that ensure that Pepsi products will be sold exclusively in each of the three spun-off chains.

Divestiture
The sale of some of a company's operating assets.

Spin-Off
A divestiture in which the stock of a subsidiary is given to the parent company's stockholders.

Carve-Out
A minority interest in a corporate subsidiary is sold to new shareholders, so the parent gains new equity financing yet retains control.

Liquidation
Occurs when the assets of a division are sold off piecemeal, rather than as an operating entity.

GLOBAL PERSPECTIVES

Governments Are Divesting State-Owned Businesses to Spur Economic Efficiency

In many countries governments have traditionally owned or controlled a number of key businesses. When Margaret Thatcher became prime minister of Britain in 1979, she set out to reverse this trend, and soon her officials were devising methods for the government to divest state-owned enterprises. Thatcher coined the term "privatization" to describe the process of transferring productive operations and assets from the public sector to the private sector.

The privatization momentum picked up in the early and mid-1980s, expanding to other countries including France, Germany, Japan, and Singapore. Privatization accelerated further as the communist countries and authoritarian regimes across Eastern Europe, Asia, and Latin America shifted toward market-based economies.

Telecommunications, electric power, and airlines are examples of industries that have undergone extensive privatization throughout the world. These industries are vitally important to the economic infrastructure of every nation, and for this reason governments have historically been heavily involved in owning and regulating them within their national borders. Gener-

ally, the government-owned enterprise was granted monopoly power to supply the service in question and was subsidized in an effort to hold down costs to consumers. However, economists have long argued that government operations are inherently less efficient than are enterprises that are subject to competitive pressures and whose managers are guided by the profit motive. Thus, in recent years there have been numerous privatizations in these important industries, and as governments have sold their interests, competition has led to lower costs and improved service.

In Western Europe, privatizations in the telecommunications industry have been given an extra push by a European Union plan that opened markets to competition. Because most European telecoms were government owned, the resulting privatizations brought to market tens of billions of dollars of telecom stock. Globally, governments have raised hundreds of billions of dollars through privatizations.

The results are not all in, but it is clear that the removal of bureaucrats and politicians from the control of key enterprises often results in increased economic efficiency and a higher standard of living.

2. United Airlines sold its Hilton International Hotels subsidiary to Ladbroke Group PLC of Britain for $1.1 billion and also sold its Hertz rental car unit and its Westin hotel group. The sales culminated a disastrous strategic move by United to build a full-service travel empire. The failed strategy resulted in the firing of Richard J. Ferris, the company's chairman. The move into nonairline travel-related businesses had been viewed by many analysts as a mistake, because there were few synergies to be gained. Further, analysts feared that United's managers, preoccupied by running hotels and rental car companies, would not maintain the company's focus in the highly competitive airline industry. The funds raised by the divestitures were paid out to United's shareholders as a special dividend.

3. General Motors (GM) spun off its Electronic Data Systems (EDS) subsidiary. EDS, a computer services company founded in 1962 by Ross Perot, prospered as an independent company until it was acquired by GM in 1984. The rationale for the acquisition was that EDS's expertise would help GM both operate better in the information age and build cars that encompassed leading-edge computer technology. However, the spread of desktop computers and the movement of companies to downsize their internal computer staffs caused EDS's non-GM business to soar. Ownership by GM hampered EDS's ability to strike alliances and, in some cases, to enter into business agreements. The best way for EDS to compete in its industry was as an independent, hence it was spun off.

4. AT&T was broken up in 1983 to settle a Justice Department antitrust suit filed in the 1970s.[19] For almost 100 years AT&T had operated as a holding company that owned Western Electric (its manufacturing subsidiary), Bell Labs (its research arm), a huge long-distance network that was operated as a division of the parent company, and 22 Bell operating companies, such as Pacific Telephone, New York Telephone, Southern Bell, and Southwestern Bell. In 1984, AT&T was reorganized into eight separate companies—a slimmed-down AT&T, which kept Western Electric, Bell Labs, and the long-distance operations, plus seven new regional telephone holding companies that were created from the 22 old operating telephone companies. The stock of the seven new telephone companies was then spun off to the old AT&T's stockholders. A person who held 100 shares of old AT&T stock owned, after the divestiture, 100 shares of the "new" AT&T plus 10 shares of each of the seven new operating companies. These 170 shares were backed by the same assets that had previously backed 100 shares of old AT&T common.

   The AT&T divestiture resulted from a suit by the Justice Department, which wanted to divide the Bell System into a regulated monopoly segment (the seven regional telephone companies) and a manufacturing/long-distance segment that would be exposed to competition. The breakup was designed to strengthen competition and thus speed up technological change in those parts of the telecommunications industry that are not natural monopolies. Ironically, in 2005 SBC Communications, which can trace its roots back to the original Bell Telephone Co., announced plans to acquire AT&T for $16 billion. The merger is expected to take place in early 2006 and to result in a premier global communications company.

5. Some years ago, Woolworth liquidated all of its 336 Woolco discount stores. This made the company, which had had sales of $7.2 billion before the liquidation, 30 percent smaller. Woolco had posted operating losses of $19 million the year before the liquidation, and its losses in the latest six months had climbed to an alarming $21 million. Woolworth's CEO, Edward F. Gibbons, was quoted as saying, "How many losses can you take?" Woolco's problems necessitated a write-off of $325 million, but management believed it was better to go ahead and "bite the bullet" rather than let the losing stores bleed the company to death.

6. As a result of some imprudent loans to oil companies and to developing nations, Continental Illinois, one of the largest U.S. bank holding companies at the time, was threatened with bankruptcy. Continental then sold off several profitable divisions, such as its leasing and credit card operations, to raise funds to cover bad-loan losses. In effect, Continental sold assets in order to stay alive. Ultimately, Continental was bailed out by the Federal Deposit Insurance Corporation and the Federal Reserve, which arranged a $7.5 billion rescue package and provided a blanket guarantee for all of Continental's $40 billion of deposits, which kept deposits in excess of $100,000 from fleeing the bank because of their uninsured status.

As the preceding examples illustrate, the reasons for divestitures vary widely. Sometimes the market feels more comfortable when firms "stick to their knitting"; the Pepsi and United Airlines divestitures are examples. Other companies need cash either to finance expansion in their primary business lines or to reduce a large debt burden, and divestitures can be used to raise this cash;

---

[19] Another forced divestiture involved Du Pont and General Motors. In 1921, GM was in serious financial trouble, and Du Pont supplied capital in exchange for 23 percent of the stock. In the 1950s, the Justice Department won an antitrust suit that required Du Pont to spin off (to Du Pont's stockholders) its GM stock.

Continental Bank illustrates this point. The divestitures also show that running a business is a dynamic process—conditions change, corporate strategies change in response, and as a result firms alter their asset portfolios by acquisitions and/or divestitures. Some divestitures, such as Woolworth's liquidation of its Woolco stores, are to unload losing assets that would otherwise drag the company down. The AT&T example is one of the many instances in which a divestiture is the result of an antitrust settlement. The GM spin-off illustrates a situation in which parts of the business can operate more efficiently alone than together.

What are some reasons companies divest assets?

What are four major motives for divestitures?

Tying It All Together

This chapter included discussions of mergers, divestitures, and LBOs. The majority of the discussion in this chapter was on mergers. We discussed the rationale for mergers, different types of mergers, the level of merger activity, merger regulation, and merger analysis. We showed how to use two different approaches to value the target firm: discounted cash flow and market multiple analyses. We also explained how the acquiring firm can structure its takeover bid, the accounting treatment of mergers, and investment bankers' roles in arranging and financing mergers. In addition, we discussed two cooperative arrangements that fall short of mergers: corporate, or strategic, alliances and joint ventures.

SELF-TEST QUESTIONS AND PROBLEMS
(Solutions Appear in Appendix A)

ST-1 **Key terms** Define each of the following terms:
- a.   Synergy; merger
- b.   Horizontal merger; vertical merger; congeneric merger; conglomerate merger
- c.   Friendly merger; hostile merger; defensive merger; tender offer; target company; breakup value; acquiring company
- d.   Operating merger; financial merger; equity residual method; market multiple analysis
- e.   White knight; white squire; poison pill; golden parachute; proxy fight
- f.   Joint venture; corporate alliance
- g.   Divestiture; spin-off; leveraged buyout (LBO); carve-out; liquidation
- h.   Arbitrage
- i.   Goodwill; purchase method

ST-2 **Merger value** Pizza Place, a national pizza chain, is considering purchasing a smaller chain, Western Mountain Pizza. Pizza Place's analysts project that the merger will result in incremental net cash flows of $1.5 million in Year 1, $2 million in Year 2, $3 million in Year 3, and $5 million in Year 4. In addition, Western's Year 4 cash flows are expected to grow at a constant rate of 5 percent after Year 4. Assume all cash flows occur at the end of the year. The acquisition would be made immediately, if it were undertaken. Western's post-merger beta is estimated to be 1.5, and its post-merger tax rate would be 40 percent.

The risk-free rate is 6 percent, and the market risk premium is 4 percent. What is the value of Western Mountain Pizza to Pizza Place?

QUESTIONS

21-1 Four economic classifications of mergers are (1) horizontal, (2) vertical, (3) conglomerate, and (4) congeneric. Explain the significance of these terms in merger analysis with regard to (a) the likelihood of governmental intervention and (b) possibilities for operating synergy.

21-2 Firm A wants to acquire Firm B. Firm B's management agrees that the merger is a good idea. Might a tender offer be used?

21-3 Distinguish between operating mergers and financial mergers.

21-4 In the spring of 1984, Disney Productions' stock was selling for about $3.125 per share (all prices have been adjusted for 4-for-1 splits in 1986 and 1992). Then Saul Steinberg, a New York financier, began acquiring it, and after he had 12 percent, he announced a tender offer for another 37 percent of the stock—which would bring his holdings up to 49 percent—at a price of $4.22 per share. Disney's management then announced plans to buy Gibson Greeting Cards and Arvida Corporation, paying for them with stock. It also lined up bank credit and (according to Steinberg) was prepared to borrow up to $2 billion and use the funds to repurchase shares at a higher price than Steinberg was offering. All of these efforts were designed to keep Steinberg from taking control. In June, Disney's management agreed to pay Steinberg $4.84 per share, which gave him a gain of about $60 million on a 2-month investment of about $26.5 million.

When Disney's buyback of Steinberg's shares was announced, the stock price fell almost instantly from $4.25 to $2.875. Many Disney stockholders were irate, and they sued to block the buyout. Also, the Disney affair added fuel to the fire in a congressional committee that was holding hearings on proposed legislation that would (1) prohibit someone from acquiring more than 10 percent of a firm's stock without making a tender offer for all the remaining shares, (2) prohibit poison pill tactics such as those Disney's management had used to fight off Steinberg, (3) prohibit buybacks such as the deal eventually offered to Steinberg (greenmail) unless there was an approving vote by stockholders, and (4) prohibit (or substantially curtail) the use of golden parachutes (the one thing Disney's management did not try).

Set forth the arguments for and against this type of legislation. What provisions, if any, should it contain? Also, look up Disney's current stock price to see how its stockholders have actually fared. Note that Disney's stock was split 3-for-1 in July 1998.

21-5 Two large, publicly owned firms are contemplating a merger. No operating synergy is expected. However, since returns on the 2 firms are not perfectly positively correlated, the standard deviation of earnings would be reduced for the combined corporation. One group of consultants argues that this risk reduction is sufficient grounds for the merger. Another group thinks this type of risk reduction is irrelevant because stockholders can themselves hold the stock of both companies and thus gain the risk-reduction benefits without all the hassles and expenses of the merger. Whose position is correct? Explain.

PROBLEMS

The following information is required to work Problems 21-1, 21-2, and 21-3.

Harrison Corporation is interested in acquiring Van Buren Corporation. Assume that the risk-free rate of interest is 5 percent and the market risk premium is 6 percent.

Easy Problems 1–3

21-1 **Valuation** Van Buren currently expects to pay a year-end dividend of $2.00 a share ($D_1 = 2.00). Van Buren's dividend is expected to grow at a constant rate of 5 percent a year, and its beta is 0.9. What is the current price of Van Buren's stock?

21-2 **Merger valuation** Harrison estimates that if it acquires Van Buren, the year-end dividend will remain at $2.00 a share, but synergies will enable the dividend to grow at a constant rate of 7 percent a year (instead of the current 5 percent). Harrison also plans to increase the debt ratio of what would be its Van Buren subsidiary—the effect of this would be to raise Van Buren's beta to 1.1. What is the per-share value of Van Buren to Harrison Corporation?

21-3 **Merger bid** On the basis of your answers to Problems 21-1 and 21-2, if Harrison were to acquire Van Buren, what would be the range of possible prices that it could bid for each share of Van Buren common stock?

Intermediate
Problems 4–5

21-4 **Merger analysis** Apilado Appliance Corporation is considering a merger with the Vaccaro Vacuum Company. Vaccaro is a publicly traded company, and its current beta is 1.30. Vaccaro has been barely profitable, so it has paid an average of only 20 percent in taxes during the last several years. In addition, it uses little debt, having a debt ratio of just 25 percent.

    If the acquisition were made, Apilado would operate Vaccaro as a separate, wholly owned subsidiary. Apilado would pay taxes on a consolidated basis, and the tax rate would therefore increase to 35 percent. Apilado also would increase the debt capitalization in the Vaccaro subsidiary to 40 percent of assets, which would increase its beta to 1.47. Apilado's acquisition department estimates that Vaccaro, if acquired, would produce the following net cash flows to Apilado's shareholders (in millions of dollars):

Year	Net Cash Flows
1	$1.30
2	1.50
3	1.75
4	2.00
5 and beyond	Constant growth at 6%

These cash flows include all acquisition effects. Apilado's cost of equity is 14 percent, its beta is 1.0, and its cost of debt is 10 percent. The risk-free rate is 8 percent.

a. What discount rate should be used to discount the estimated cash flows? (Hint: Use Apilado's r_s to determine the market risk premium.)
b. What is the dollar value of Vaccaro to Apilado?
c. Vaccaro has 1.2 million common shares outstanding. What is the maximum price per share that Apilado should offer for Vaccaro? If the tender offer is accepted at this price, what will happen to Apilado's stock price?

21-5 **Capital budgeting analysis** The Stanley Stationery Shoppe wishes to acquire The Carlson Card Gallery for $400,000. Stanley expects the merger to provide incremental earnings of about $64,000 a year for 10 years. Ken Stanley has calculated the marginal cost of capital for this investment to be 10 percent. Conduct a capital budgeting analysis for Stanley to determine whether or not he should purchase The Carlson Card Gallery.

Challenging
Problem

21-6 **Merger analysis** TransWorld Communications Inc., a large telecommunications company, is evaluating the possible acquisition of Georgia Cable Company (GCC), a regional cable company. TransWorld's analysts project the following post-merger data for GCC (in thousands of dollars):

		2006	2007	2008	2009
Net sales		$450	$518	$555	$600
Selling and administrative expense		45	53	60	68
Interest		18	21	24	27
Tax rate after merger	35%				
Cost of goods sold as a percent of sales	65%				
Beta after merger	1.50				
Risk-free rate	8%				
Market risk premium	4%				
Terminal growth rate of cash flow available to TransWorld	7%				

If the acquisition is made, it will occur on January 1, 2006. All cash flows shown in the income statements are assumed to occur at the end of the year. GCC currently has a capital structure of 40 percent debt, but TransWorld would increase that to 50 percent if the acquisition were made. GCC, if independent, would pay taxes at 20 percent, but its income would be taxed at 35 percent if it were consolidated. GCC's current market-determined beta is 1.40, and its investment bankers think that its beta would rise to 1.50

if the debt ratio were increased to 50 percent. The cost of goods sold is expected to be 65 percent of sales, but it could vary somewhat. Depreciation-generated funds would be used to replace worn-out equipment, so they would not be available to TransWorld's shareholders. The risk-free rate is 8 percent, and the market risk premium is 4 percent.

a. What is the appropriate discount rate for valuing the acquisition?
b. What is the terminal value? What is the value of GCC to TransWorld?

COMPREHENSIVE/SPREADSHEET PROBLEM

21-7 **Merger analysis** Use the spreadsheet model to rework Problem 21-6, and then answer the following question:

c. Suppose GCC has 120,000 shares outstanding. What is the maximum per-share price TransWorld should offer for GCC?

Integrated Case

Smitty's Home Repair Company

21-8 **Merger analysis** Smitty's Home Repair Company, a regional hardware chain that specializes in "do-it-yourself" materials and equipment rentals, is cash rich because of several consecutive good years. One of the alternative uses for the excess funds is an acquisition. Linda Wade, Smitty's treasurer and your boss, has been asked to place a value on a potential target, Hill's Hardware, a small chain that operates in an adjacent state, and she has enlisted your help.

The table below indicates Wade's estimates of Hill's earnings potential if it came under Smitty's management (in millions of dollars). The interest expense listed here includes the interest (1) on Hill's existing debt, (2) on new debt that Smitty's would issue to help finance the acquisition, and (3) on new debt expected to be issued over time to help finance expansion within the new "H division," the code name given to the target firm. The retentions represent earnings that will be reinvested within the H division to help finance its growth.

Hill's Hardware currently uses 40 percent debt financing, and it pays federal-plus-state taxes at a 30 percent rate. Security analysts estimate Hill's beta to be 1.2. If the acquisition were to take place, Smitty's would increase Hill's debt ratio to 50 percent, which would increase its beta to 1.3. Further, because Smitty's is highly profitable, taxes on the consolidated firm would be 40 percent. Wade realizes that Hill's Hardware also generates depreciation cash flows, but she believes that these funds would have to be reinvested within the division to replace worn-out equipment.

Wade estimates the risk-free rate to be 9 percent and the market risk premium to be 4 percent. She also estimates that net cash flows after 2009 will grow at a constant rate of 6 percent. Smitty's management is new to the merger game, so Wade has been asked to answer some basic questions about mergers as well as to perform the merger analysis. To structure the task, Wade has developed the following questions, which you must answer and then defend to Smitty's board.

a. Several reasons have been proposed to justify mergers. Among the more prominent are (1) tax considerations, (2) risk reduction, (3) control, (4) purchase of assets at below-replacement cost, and (5) synergy. In general, which of the reasons are economically justifiable? Which are not? Which fit the situation at hand? Explain.
b. Briefly describe the differences between a hostile merger and a friendly merger.
c. Use the data developed in the table to construct the H division's cash flow statements for 2006 through 2009. Why is interest expense deducted in merger cash flow statements, whereas it is not normally deducted in a capital budgeting cash flow analysis? Why are earnings retentions deducted in the cash flow statement?

	2006	2007	2008	2009
Net sales	$60.0	$90.0	$112.5	$127.5
Cost of goods sold (60%)	36.0	54.0	67.5	76.5
Selling/administrative expense	4.5	6.0	7.5	9.0
Interest expense	3.0	4.5	4.5	6.0
Necessary retained earnings	0.0	7.5	6.0	4.5

d. Conceptually, what is the appropriate discount rate to apply to the cash flows developed in part c? What is your actual estimate of this discount rate?
e. What is the estimated terminal value of the acquisition; that is, what is the estimated value of the H division's cash flows beyond 2009? What is Hill's value to Smitty's? Suppose another firm were evaluating Hill's as an acquisition candidate. Would they obtain the same value? Explain.
f. Assume that Hill's has 10 million shares outstanding. These shares are traded relatively infrequently, but the last trade, made several weeks ago, was at a price of $9 per share. Should Smitty's make an offer for Hill's? If so, how much should it offer per share?
g. What merger-related activities are undertaken by investment bankers?

cyberproblem

Please go to the ThomsonNOW Web site to access the Cyberproblems.

Solutions to Self-Test Questions and Problems

Note: Except for Chapter 1, we do not show an answer for ST-1 problems because they are verbal rather than quantitative in nature.

CHAPTER 1

ST-1 Refer to the marginal glossary definitions or relevant chapter sections to check your responses.

CHAPTER 2

ST-2 a.

```
1/1/06   8%   1/1/07        1/1/08        1/1/09
  |------------|-------------|-------------|
-1,000                                    FV=?
```

$1,000 is being compounded for 3 years, so your balance on January 1, 2009, is $1,259.71:

$$FV_N = PV(1 + I)^N = \$1,000(1 + 0.08)^3 = \$1,259.71$$

Alternatively, using a financial calculator, input N = 3, I/YR = 8, PV = −1000, PMT = 0, and FV = ? Solve for FV = $1,259.71.

b.

```
1/1/06   2%   1/1/07        1/1/08        1/1/09
  |--|--|--|--|--|--|--|--|--|--|--|--|
-1,000                                    FV=?
```

$$FV_N = PV\left(1 + \frac{I_{NOM}}{M}\right)^{NM} = FV_{12} = \$1,000(1.02)^{12} = \$1,268.24$$

Alternatively, using a financial calculator, input N = 12, I/YR = 2, PV = −1000, PMT = 0, and FV = ? Solve for FV = $1,268.24.

c.

```
1/1/06   8%   1/1/07        1/1/08        1/1/09
  |------------|-------------|-------------|
          -333.333     -333.333     -333.333
                                      FV=?
```

Using a financial calculator, input N = 3, I/YR = 8, PV = 0, PMT = −333.333, and FV = ? Solve for FV = $1,082.13.

d.

```
1/1/06   8%   1/1/07        1/1/08        1/1/09
  |------------|-------------|-------------|
 -333.333   -333.333     -333.333     FV=?
```

Using a financial calculator in begin mode, input N = 3, I/YR = 8, PV = 0, PMT = −333.333, and FV = ? Solve for FV = $1,168.70.

e.

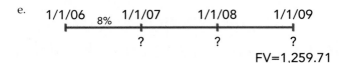

Using a financial calculator, input N = 3, I/YR = 8, PV = 0, FV = 1259.71, and PMT = ? Solve for PMT = −$388.03. Therefore, you would have to make 3 payments of $388.03 each beginning on January 1, 2007.

ST-3 a. Set up a time line like the one in the preceding problem:

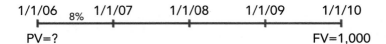

Note that your deposit will grow for 4 years at 8 percent. The deposit on January 1, 2006, is the PV, and the FV is $1,000. Using a financial calculator, input N = 4, I/YR = 8, PMT = 0, FV = 1000, and PV = ? Solve for PV = −$735.03.

$$PV = \frac{FV_N}{(1 + I)^N} = \frac{\$1,000}{(1.08)^4} = \$735.03$$

b.

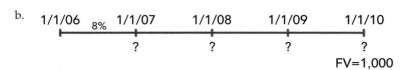

Here we are dealing with a 4-year annuity whose first payment occurs 1 year from today, on 1/1/07, and whose future value must equal $1,000. You should modify the time line to help visualize the situation. Using a financial calculator, input N = 4, I/YR = 8, PV = 0, FV = 1000, and PMT = ? Solve for PMT = −$221.92.

c. This problem can be approached in several ways. Perhaps the simplest is to ask this question: "If I received $750 on 1/1/07 and deposited it to earn 8 percent, would I have the required $1,000 on 1/1/10?" The answer is no.

1/1/06 8% 1/1/07   1/1/08   1/1/09   1/1/10

          −750   FV=?

$$FV_3 = \$750(1.08)(1.08)(1.08) = \$944.78$$

This indicates that you should let your father make the payments of $221.92 rather than accept the lump sum of $750.

You could also compare the $750 with the PV of the payments as shown here:

1/1/06 8% 1/1/07   1/1/08   1/1/09   1/1/10

          −221.92   −221.92   −221.92   −221.92
          PV=?

Using a financial calculator, input N = 4, I/YR = 8, PMT = −221.92, FV = 0, and PV = ? Solve for PV = $735.03.

This is less than the $750 lump sum offer, so your initial reaction might be to accept the lump sum of $750. However, this would be a mistake. The problem is that when you found the $735.03 PV of the annuity, you were finding the value of the annuity *today*, on January 1, 2006. You were comparing $735.03 today with the lump sum of $750 one year from now. This is, of course, invalid. What you should have done was take the $735.03, recognize that this is the PV of an annuity as of January 1, 2006, multiply $735.03 by 1.08 to get $793.83, and compare $793.83 with the lump sum of $750. You would then take your father's offer to make the payments of $221.92 rather than take the lump sum on January 1, 2007.

d.

1/1/06	I=?	1/1/07	1/1/08	1/1/09	1/1/10
	−750				1,000

Using a financial calculator, input N = 3, PV = −750, PMT = 0, FV = 1000, and I/YR = ? Solve for I/YR = 10.0642%.

e.

1/1/06	I=?	1/1/07	1/1/08	1/1/09	1/1/10
		−200	−200	−200	−200
					FV=1,000

Using a financial calculator, input N = 4, PV = 0, PMT = −200, FV = 1000, and I/YR = ? Solve for I/YR = 15.09%.

You might be able to find a borrower willing to offer you a 15 percent interest rate, but there would be some risk involved—he or she might not actually pay you your $1,000!

f.

1/1/06	4%	1/1/07	1/1/08	1/1/09	1/1/10
	−400	? ?	? ?	? ?	
					FV=1,000

Find the future value of the original $400 deposit:

$$FV_6 = PV(1.04)^6 = \$400(1.2653) = \$506.13$$

This means that on January 1, 2010, you need an additional sum of $493.87:

$$\$1,000.00 - \$506.13 = \$493.87$$

This will be accumulated by making 6 equal payments that earn 8 percent compounded semiannually, or 4 percent each 6 months. Using a financial calculator, input N = 6, I/YR = 4, PV = 0, FV = 493.87, and PMT = ? Solve for PMT = −$74.46.

Alternatively, input N = 6, I/YR = 4, PV = −400, FV = 1000, and PMT = ? Solve for PMT = −$74.46.

g. Effective annual rate $= \left(1 + \dfrac{I_{NOM}}{M}\right)^M - 1.0$

$$= \left(1 + \dfrac{0.08}{2}\right)^2 - 1 = (1.04)^2 - 1$$

$$= 1.0816 - 1 = 0.0816 = 8.16\%$$

$$APR = I_{PER} \times M$$

$$= 0.04 \times 2 = 0.08 = 8\%$$

ST-4 Bank A's effective annual rate is 8.24 percent:

$$\text{Effective annual rate} = \left(1 + \dfrac{0.08}{4}\right)^4 - 1.0$$

$$= (1.02)^4 - 1 = 1.0824 - 1$$

$$= 0.0824 = 8.24\%$$

Now Bank B must have the same effective annual rate:

$$\left(1 + \dfrac{I_{NOM}}{12}\right)^{12} - 1.0 = 0.0824$$

$$\left(1 + \dfrac{I_{NOM}}{12}\right)^{12} = 1.0824$$

$$1 + \frac{I_{NOM}}{12} = (1.0824)^{1/12}$$

$$1 + \frac{I_{NOM}}{12} = 1.00662$$

$$\frac{I_{NOM}}{12} = 0.00662$$

$$I_{NOM} = 0.07944 = 7.94\%$$

Thus, the two banks have different quoted rates—Bank A's quoted rate is 8 percent, while Bank B's quoted rate is 7.94 percent; however, both banks have the same effective annual rate of 8.24 percent. The difference in their quoted rates is due to the difference in compounding frequency.

CHAPTER 3

ST-2   a.

EBIT	$5,000,000
Interest	1,000,000
EBT	$4,000,000
Taxes (40%)	1,600,000
Net income	$2,400,000

b.   NCF = NI + DEP and AMORT
  = $2,400,000 + $1,000,000 = $3,400,000

c.   NOPAT = EBIT(1 − T)
    = $5,000,000(0.6)
    = $3,000,000

d.   OCF = NOPAT + DEP and AMORT
   = EBIT(1 − T) + DEP and AMORT
   = $5,000,000(0.6) + $1,000,000
   = $4,000,000

e.   NOWC = Current assets − Non-interest-bearing current liabilities
    = $14,000,000 − $4,000,000
    = $10,000,000

f.   Operating capital$_{BOY}$ = $24,000,000

Operating capital$_{EOY}$ = NOWC + Net fixed assets
         = $10,000,000 + $15,000,000
         = $25,000,000

Δ in Operating capital = $25,000,000 − $24,000,000
         = $1,000,000

Note that the investment in operating capital must include depreciation so the investment is calculated as follows:

Investment in operating capital = $1,000,000 + $1,000,000
            = $2,000,000

FCF = Operating cash flow − Investment in operating capital
   = $4,000,000 − $2,000,000
   = $2,000,000

g.   Retained earnings at the end of the year can be calculated as follows:

Balance of retained earnings$_{BOY}$	$4,500,000
Add: Net income*	2,400,000
Less: Common dividends	1,200,000
Balance of retained earnings$_{EOY}$	$5,700,000

*Net income was calculated in part a.

CHAPTER 4

ST-2 Billingsworth paid $2 in dividends and retained $2 per share. Because total retained earnings rose by $12 million, there must be 6 million shares outstanding. With a book value of $40 per share, total common equity must be $40(6 million) = $240 million. Since Billingsworth has $120 million of debt, its debt ratio must be 33.3 percent:

$$\frac{\text{Debt}}{\text{Assets}} = \frac{\text{Debt}}{\text{Debt} + \text{Equity}} = \frac{\$120 \text{ million}}{\$120 \text{ million} + \$240 \text{ million}}$$

$$= 0.333 = 33.3\%$$

ST-3 a. In answering questions such as this, always begin by writing down the relevant definitional equations, then start filling in numbers. Note that the extra zeros indicating millions have been deleted in the calculations below.

(1) $\text{DSO} = \dfrac{\text{Accounts receivable}}{\text{Sales}/365}$

$40.55 = \dfrac{\text{A/R}}{\text{Sales}/365}$

$\text{A/R} = 40.55(\$2.7397) = \$111.1 \text{ million}$

(2) $\text{Current ratio} = \dfrac{\text{Current assets}}{\text{Current liabilities}} = 3.0$

$= \dfrac{\text{Current assets}}{\$105.5} = 3.0$

$\text{Current assets} = 3.0(\$105.5) = \$316.5 \text{ million}$

(3) $\text{Total assets} = \text{Current assets} + \text{Fixed assets}$

$= \$316.5 + \$283.5 = \$600 \text{ million}$

(4) $\text{ROA} = \text{Profit margin} \times \text{Total assets turnover}$

$= \dfrac{\text{Net income}}{\text{Sales}} \times \dfrac{\text{Sales}}{\text{Total assets}}$

$= \dfrac{\$50}{\$1,000} \times \dfrac{\$1,000}{\$600}$

$= 0.05 \times 1.667 = 0.083333 = 8.3333\%$

(5) $\text{ROE} = \text{ROA} \times \dfrac{\text{Assets}}{\text{Equity}}$

$12.0\% = 8.3333\% \times \dfrac{\$600}{\text{Equity}}$

$\text{Equity} = \dfrac{(8.3333\%)(\$600)}{12.0\%}$

$= \$416.67 \text{ million}$

(6) $\text{Current assets} = \text{Cash and equivalents} + \text{Accounts receivable} + \text{Inventories}$

$\$316.5 = \$100.0 + \$111.1 + \text{Inventories}$

$\text{Inventories} = \$105.4 \text{ million}$

$\text{Quick ratio} = \dfrac{\text{Current assets} - \text{Inventories}}{\text{Current liabilities}}$

$= \dfrac{\$316.5 - \$105.4}{\$105.5} = 2.00$

(7) Total assets = Total claims = $600 million

Current liabilities + Long-term debt + Equity = $600 million

$105.5 + Long-term debt + $416.67 = $600 million

Long-term debt = $600 − $105.5 − $416.67 = $77.83 million

Note: We could have found equity as follows:

$$\text{ROE} = \frac{\text{Net income}}{\text{Equity}}$$

$$12.0\% = \frac{\$50}{\text{Equity}}$$

$$\text{Equity} = \$50/0.12$$

$$= \$416.67 \text{ million}$$

Then we could have gone on to find long-term debt.

b. Kaiser's average sales per day were $1,000/365 = $2.74 million. Its DSO was 40.55, so A/R = 40.55($2.74) = $111.1 million. Its new DSO of 30.4 would cause A/R = 30.4($2.74) = $83.3 million. The reduction in receivables would be $111.1 − $83.3 = $27.8 million, which would equal the amount of cash generated.

(1) New equity = Old equity − Stock bought back

$$= \$416.7 - \$27.8$$

$$= \$388.9 \text{ million}$$

Thus,

$$\text{New ROE} = \frac{\text{Net income}}{\text{New equity}}$$

$$= \frac{\$50}{\$388.9}$$

$$= 12.86\% \text{ (versus old ROE of 12.0\%)}$$

(2)

$$\text{New ROA} = \frac{\text{Net income}}{\text{Total assets} - \text{Reduction in A/R}}$$

$$= \frac{\$50}{\$600 - \$27.8}$$

$$= 8.74\% \text{ (versus old ROA of 8.33\%)}$$

(3) The old debt is the same as the new debt:

$$\text{Debt} = \text{Total claims} - \text{Equity}$$

$$= \$600 - \$416.7 = \$183.3 \text{ million}$$

New total assets = Old total assets − Reduction in A/R

$$= \$600 - \$27.8$$

$$= \$572.2 \text{ million}$$

Therefore,

$$\frac{\text{Debt}}{\text{Old total assets}} = \frac{\$183.3}{\$600} = 30.6\%$$

while

$$\frac{\text{New debt}}{\text{New total assets}} = \frac{\$183.3}{\$572.2} = 32.0\%$$

CHAPTER 6

ST-2 a. Average inflation over 4 years = $(2\% + 2\% + 2\% + 4\%)/4 = 2.5\%$

      b. $T_4 = r_{RF} + MRP_4$

            $= r^* + IP_4 + MRP_4$

            $= 3\% + 2.5\% + (0.1)3\%$

            $= 5.8\%$

      c. $C_{4,\,BBB} = r^* + IP_4 + MRP_4 + DRP + LP$

                $= 3\% + 2.5\% + 0.3\% + 1.3\% + 0.5\%$

                $= 7.6\%$

      d. $T_8 = r^* + IP_8 + MRP_8$

            $= 3\% + (3 \times 2\% + 5 \times 4\%)/8 + 0.7\%$

            $= 3\% + 3.25\% + 0.7\%$

            $= 6.95\%$

      e. $C_{8,\,BBB} = r^* + IP_8 + MRP_8 + DRP + LP$

                $= 3\% + 3.25\% + 0.7\% + 1.3\% + 0.5\%$

                $= 8.75\%$

      f. $T_9 = r^* + IP_9 + MRP_9$

         $7.3\% = 3\% + IP_9 + 0.8\%$

           $IP_9 = 3.5\%$

        $3.5\% = (3 \times 2\% + 5 \times 4\% + X)/9$

       $31.5\% = 6\% + 20\% + X$

         $5.5\% = X$

           X = Inflation in Year 9 = 5.5%

ST-3 $T_1 = 6\%$; $T_2 = 6.2\%$; $T_3 = 6.3\%$; $MRP = 0$

      a. Yield of 1-year security, 1 year from now is calculated as follows:

$$2 \times 6.2\% = 6\% + X$$

$$12.4\% = 6\% + X$$

$$6.4\% = X$$

      b. Yield of 1-year security, 2 years from now is calculated as follows:

$$3 \times 6.3\% = 2 \times 6.2\% + X$$

$$18.9\% = 12.4\% + X$$

$$6.5\% = X$$

      c. Yield of 2-year security, 1 year from now is calculated as follows:

$$3 \times 6.3\% = 6\% + 2X$$

$$18.9\% = 6\% + 2X$$

$$12.9\% = 2X$$

$$6.45\% = X$$

CHAPTER 7

ST-2   a.   Pennington's bonds were sold at par; therefore, the original YTM equaled the coupon rate of 12 percent.

b. $$V_B = \sum_{t=1}^{50} \frac{\$120/2}{\left(1 + \frac{0.10}{2}\right)^t} + \frac{\$1,000}{\left(1 + \frac{0.10}{2}\right)^{50}}$$

With a financial calculator, input the following: N = 50, I/YR = 5, PMT = 60, FV = 1000, and PV = ? Solve for PV = \$1,182.56.

c.   Current yield = Annual coupon payment/Price

$$= \$120/\$1,182.56$$

$$= 0.1015 = 10.15\%$$

Capital gains yield = Total yield – Current yield

$$= 10\% - 10.15\% = -0.15\%$$

Total return = 10%

d.   With a financial calculator, input the following: N = 13, PV = −916.42, PMT = 60, FV = 1000, and $r_d/2$ = I/YR = ? Calculator solution = $r_d/2$ = 7.00%; therefore, r_d = YTM = 14.00%.

Current yield = \$120/\$916.42 = 13.09%

Capital gains yield = 14% – 13.09% = 0.91%

e.   The following time line illustrates the years to maturity of the bond:

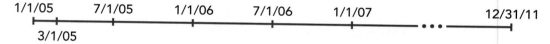

Thus, on March 1, 2005, there were $13\frac{2}{3}$ periods left before the bond matured. Bond traders actually use the following procedure to determine the price of the bond:

(1) Find the price of the bond on the next coupon date, July 1, 2005. Using a financial calculator, input N = 13, I/YR = 7.75, PMT = 60, FV = 1000, and PV = ? Solve for PV = \$859.76.

(2) Add the coupon, \$60, to the bond price to get the total value, TV, of the bond on the next interest payment date: TV = \$859.76 + \$60.00 = \$919.76.

(3) Discount this total value back to the purchase date (March 1, 2005): Using a financial calculator, input N = 4/6, I/YR = 7.75, PMT = 0, FV = 919.76, and PV = ? Solve for PV = \$875.11.

(4) Therefore, you would have written a check for \$875.11 to complete the transaction. Of this amount, $(\frac{1}{3})(\$60)$ = \$20 would represent accrued interest and \$855.11 would represent the bond's basic value. This breakdown would affect both your taxes and those of the seller.

(5) This problem could be solved *very* easily using a spreadsheet or a financial calculator with a bond valuation function, such as the HP-12C or the HP-17BII. This is explained in the calculator manual under the heading "Bond Calculations."

ST-3   a.   (1) \$100,000,000/10 = \$10,000,000 per year, or \$5 million each 6 months. Because the \$5 million will be used to retire bonds immediately, no interest will be earned on it.

(2) VDC will purchase bonds on the open market if they're selling at less than par. So, the sinking fund payment will be less than \$5,000,000 each period.

b.   The debt service requirements will decline. As the amount of bonds outstanding declines, so will the interest requirements (amounts given in millions of dollars). If the bonds are called at par, the total bond service payments are calculated as follows:

Semiannual Payment Period	Sinking Fund Payment	Outstanding Bonds on Which Interest Is Paid	Interest Payment[a]	Total Bond Service
(1)	(2)	(3)	(4)	(2) + (4) = (5)
1	$5	$100	$6.0	$11.0
2	5	95	5.7	10.7
3	5	90	5.4	10.4
.	.	.	.	.
.	.	.	.	.
.	.	.	.	.
20	5	5	0.3	5.3

[a] Interest is calculated as (0.5)(0.12)(Column 3); for example: Interest in Period 2 = (0.5)(0.12)($95) = $5.7.

The company's total cash bond service requirement will be $21.7 million per year for the first year. For both options, interest will decline by 0.12($10,000,000) = $1,200,000 per year for the remaining years. The total debt service requirement for the open market purchases cannot be precisely determined, but the amounts would be less than what's shown in Column 5 of the table above.

c. Here we have a 10-year, 7 percent annuity whose compound value is $100 million, and we are seeking the annual payment, PMT. The solution can be obtained with a financial calculator. Input N = 10, I/YR = 7, PV = 0, and FV = 100000000, and press the PMT key to obtain $7,237,750. This amount is not known with certainty as interest rates over time will change, so the amount could be higher (if interest rates fall) or lower (if interest rates rise).

d. Annual debt service costs will be $100,000,000(0.12) + $7,237,750 = $19,237,750.

e. If interest rates rose, causing the bond's price to fall, the company would use open market purchases. This would reduce its debt service requirements.

CHAPTER 8

ST-2   a.   The average rate of return for each stock is calculated simply by averaging the returns over the 5-year period. The average return for Stock A is

$$r_{\text{Avg A}} = (-24.25\% + 18.50\% + 38.67\% + 14.33\% + 39.13\%)/5$$

$$= 17.28\%$$

The average return for Stock B is

$$r_{\text{Avg B}} = (5.50\% + 26.73\% + 48.25\% + -4.50\% + 43.86\%)/5$$

$$= 23.97\%$$

The realized rate of return on a portfolio made up of Stock A and Stock B would be calculated by finding the average return in each year as r_A(% of Stock A) + r_B(% of Stock B) and then averaging these annual returns:

Year	Portfolio AB's Return, r_{AB}
2001	(9.38%)
2002	22.62
2003	43.46
2004	4.92
2005	41.50
	r_{Avg} = 20.62%

b.   The standard deviation of returns is estimated, using Equation 8-3a, as follows:

$$\text{Estimated } \sigma = S = \sqrt{\frac{\sum_{t=1}^{N}(\bar{r}_t - \bar{r}_{\text{Avg}})^2}{N-1}} \tag{8-3a}$$

For Stock A, the estimated σ is 25.84 percent:

$$\sigma_A = \sqrt{\frac{(-24.25\% - 17.25\%)^2 + (18.50\% - 17.28\%)^2 + (38.67\% - 17.28\%)^2 + (14.33\% - 17.28\%)^2 + (39.13\% - 17.28\%)^2}{5 - 1}}$$

$$= 25.84\%$$

The standard deviations of returns for Stock B and for the portfolio are similarly determined, and they are as follows:

	Stock A	Stock B	Portfolio AB
Standard deviation	25.84%	23.15%	22.96%

c. Because the risk reduction from diversification is small (σ_{AB} falls only to 22.96 percent), the most likely value of the correlation coefficient is 0.8. If the correlation coefficient were −0.8 the risk reduction would be much larger. In fact, the correlation coefficient between Stocks A and B is 0.76.

d. If more randomly selected stocks were added to a portfolio, σ_p would decline to somewhere in the vicinity of 20 percent; see Figure 8-8. σ_p would remain constant only if the correlation coefficient were +1.0, which is most unlikely. σ_p would decline to zero only if the correlation coefficient, ρ, were equal to zero and a large number of stocks were added to the portfolio, or if the proper proportions were held in a two-stock portfolio with $\rho = -1.0$.

ST-3 a. $b = (0.6)(0.70) + (0.25)(0.90) + (0.1)(1.30) + (0.05)(1.50)$

$= 0.42 + 0.225 + 0.13 + 0.075 = 0.85$

b. $r_{RF} = 6\%$; $RP_M = 5\%$; $b = 0.85$

$r = 6\% + (5\%)(0.85)$

$= 10.25\%$

c. $b_N = (0.5)(0.70) + (0.25)(0.90) + (0.1)(1.30) + (0.15)(1.50)$

$= 0.35 + 0.225 + 0.13 + 0.225$

$= 0.93$

$r = 6\% + (5\%)(0.93)$

$= 10.65\%$

CHAPTER 9

ST-2 a. This is not necessarily true. Because G plows back two-thirds of its earnings, its growth rate should exceed that of D, but D pays higher dividends ($3 versus $1). We cannot say which stock should have the higher price.

b. Again, we just do not know which price would be higher.

c. This is false. The changes in r_d and r_s would have a greater effect on G; its price would decline more.

d. The total expected return for D is $\hat{r}_D = D_1/P_0 + g = 12\% + 0\% = 12\%$. The total expected return for G will have $D_1/P_0 < 12\%$ and $g > 0\%$, but $\hat{r}_G$ should be neither greater nor smaller than D's total expected return, 12 percent, because the two stocks are stated to be equally risky.

e. We have eliminated a, b, c, and d, so e should be correct. On the basis of the available information, D and G should sell at about the same price, $25; thus, $\hat{r}_s = 12\%$ for both D and G. G's current dividend yield is $1/$25 = 4\%$. Therefore, $g = 12\% - 4\% = 8\%$.

ST-3 The first step is to solve for g, the unknown variable, in the constant growth equation. Since D_1 is unknown but D_0 is known, substitute $D_0(1 + g)$ as follows:

$$\hat{P}_0 = P_0 = \frac{D_1}{r_s - g} = \frac{D_0(1 + g)}{r_s - g}$$

$$\$36 = \frac{\$2.40(1 + g)}{0.12 - g}$$

Solving for g, we find the growth rate to be 5 percent:

$$\$4.32 - \$36g = \$2.40 + \$2.40g$$

$$\$38.4g = \$1.92$$

$$g = 0.05 = 5\%$$

The next step is to use the growth rate to project the stock price 5 years hence:

$$\hat{P}_5 = \frac{D_0(1 + g)^6}{r_s - g}$$

$$= \frac{\$2.40(1.05)^6}{0.12 - 0.05}$$

$$= \$45.95$$

(Alternatively, $\hat{P}_5 = \$36(1.05)^5 = \$45.95$)

Therefore, the firm's expected stock price 5 years from now, $\hat{P}_5$, is $45.95.

ST-4　a.　(1) Calculate the PV of the dividends paid during the supernormal growth period:

$$D_1 = \$1.1500(1.15) = \$1.3225$$

$$D_2 = \$1.3225(1.15) = \$1.5209$$

$$D_3 = \$1.5209(1.13) = \$1.7186$$

$$PV\ D = \frac{\$1.3225}{1.12} + \frac{\$1.5209}{(1.12)^2} + \frac{\$1.7186}{(1.12)^3}$$

$$= \$1.1808 + \$1.2125 + \$1.2233$$

$$= \$3.6166 \approx \$3.62$$

(2) Find the PV of the firm's stock price at the end of Year 3:

$$\hat{P}_3 = \frac{D_4}{r_s - g} = \frac{D_3(1 + g)}{r_s - g}$$

$$= \frac{\$1.7186(1.06)}{0.12 - 0.06}$$

$$= \$30.36$$

$$PV\ \hat{P}_3 = \frac{\$30.36}{(1.12)^3} = \$21.61$$

(3) Sum the two components to find the value of the stock today:

$$\hat{P}_0 = \$3.62 + \$21.61 = \$25.23$$

Alternatively, the cash flows can be placed on a time line as follows:

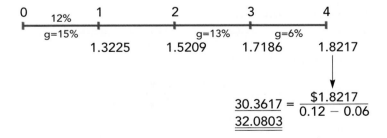

Enter the cash flows into the cash flow register and I/YR = 12, and press the NPV key to obtain $P_0 = \$25.23$.

b. $$\hat{P}_1 = \frac{\$1.5209}{1.12} + \frac{\$1.7186}{(1.12)^2} + \frac{\$30.36}{(1.12)^2}$$

$$= \$1.3579 + \$1.3701 + \$24.2028$$

$$= \$26.9308 \approx \$26.93$$

(Calculator solution: $26.93)

$$\hat{P}_2 = \frac{\$1.7186}{1.12} + \frac{\$30.36}{1.12}$$

$$= \$1.5345 + \$27.1071$$

$$= \$28.6416 \approx \$28.64$$

(Calculator solution: $28.64)

c.

Year	Dividend Yield	+	Capital Gains Yield	=	Total Return
1	$\frac{\$1.3225}{\$25.23} \approx 5.24\%$		$\frac{\$26.93 - \$25.23}{\$25.23} \approx 6.74\%$		$\approx 12\%$
2	$\frac{\$1.5209}{\$26.93} \approx 5.65\%$		$\frac{\$28.64 - \$26.93}{\$26.93} \approx 6.35\%$		$\approx 12\%$
3	$\frac{\$1.7186}{\$28.64} \approx 6.00\%$		$\frac{\$30.36 - \$28.64}{\$28.64} \approx 6.00\%$		$\approx 12\%$

CHAPTER 10

ST-2 a. Component costs are as follows:

Common: $r_s = \dfrac{D_1}{P_0} + g = \dfrac{D_0(1 + g)}{P_0} + g$

$$= \frac{\$3.60(1.09)}{\$54} + 0.09$$

$$= 0.0727 + 0.09 = 16.27\%$$

Preferred: $r_p = \dfrac{\text{Preferred dividend}}{P_p} = \dfrac{\$11}{\$95} = 11.58\%$

Debt at $r_d = 12\%$: $r_d(1 - T) = 12\%(0.6) = 7.20\%$

b. WACC calculation:

$$\text{WACC} = w_d r_d(1 - T) + w_p r_p + w_c r_s$$

$$= 0.25(7.2\%) + 0.15(11.58\%) + 0.60(16.27\%) = 13.30\%$$

c. LEI should accept Projects A, B, C, and D. It should reject Project E because its rate of return does not exceed the WACC of funds needed to finance it.

CHAPTER 11

ST-2 a. *Net present value (NPV):*

$$\text{NPV}_X = -\$10,000 + \frac{\$6,500}{(1.12)^1} + \frac{\$3,000}{(1.12)^2} + \frac{\$3,000}{(1.12)^3} + \frac{\$1,000}{(1.12)^4} = \$966.01$$

$$\text{NPV}_Y = -\$10,000 + \frac{\$3,500}{(1.12)^1} + \frac{\$3,500}{(1.12)^2} + \frac{\$3,500}{(1.12)^3} + \frac{\$3,500}{(1.12)^4} = \$630.72$$

Alternatively, using a financial calculator, input the cash flows into the cash flow register, enter I/YR = 12, and then press the NPV key to obtain $\text{NPV}_X = \$966.01$ and $\text{NPV}_Y = \$630.72$.

Internal rate of return (IRR):
To solve for each project's IRR, find the discount rates that equate each NPV to zero:

$$IRR_X = 18.0\%$$

$$IRR_Y = 15.0\%$$

Modified internal rate of return (MIRR):
To obtain each project's MIRR, begin by finding each project's terminal value (TV) of cash inflows:

$$TV_X = \$6,500(1.12)^3 + \$3,000(1.12)^2 + \$3,000(1.12)^1 + \$1,000 = \$17,255.23$$

$$TV_Y = \$3,500(1.12)^3 + \$3,500(1.12)^2 + \$3,500(1.12)^1 + \$3,500 = \$16,727.65$$

Now, each project's MIRR is the discount rate that equates the PV of the TV to each project's cost, $10,000:

$$MIRR_X = 14.61\%$$

$$MIRR_Y = 13.73\%$$

Payback:
To determine the payback, construct the cumulative cash flows for each project:

CUMULATIVE CASH FLOWS

Year	Project X	Project Y
0	($10,000)	($10,000)
1	(3,500)	(6,500)
2	(500)	(3,000)
3	2,500	500
4	3,500	4,000

$$Payback_X = 2 + \frac{\$500}{\$3,000} = 2.17 \text{ years}$$

$$Payback_Y = 2 + \frac{\$3,000}{\$3,500} = 2.86 \text{ years}$$

Discounted payback:
To determine the discounted payback, construct the cumulative discounted cash flows at the firm's WACC of 12 percent for each project:

Project X

	Years 0	1	2	3	4
Cash flow	−10,000	6,500	3,000	3,000	1,000
Discounted cash flow	−10,000	5,803.57	2,391.58	2,135.34	635.52
Cumulative discounted cash flow	−10,000	−4,196.43	−1,804.85	+330.49	+966.01

$$\text{Discounted Payback}_X = 2 + \$1,804.85/\$2,135.34 = 2.85 \text{ years}$$

Project Y

	Years 0	1	2	3	4
Cash flow	−10,000	3,500	3,500	3,500	3,500
Discounted cash flow	−10,000	3,125.00	2,790.18	2,491.23	2,224.31
Cumulative discounted cash flow	−10,000	−6,875.00	−4,084.82	−1,593.59	+630.72

$$\text{Discounted Payback}_Y = 3 + \$1,593.59/\$2,224.31 = 3.72 \text{ years}$$

b.   The following table summarizes the project rankings by each method:

	Project That Ranks Higher
NPV	X
IRR	X
MIRR	X
Payback	X
Discounted payback	X

Note that all methods rank Project X over Project Y. In addition, both projects are acceptable under the NPV, IRR, and MIRR criteria. Thus, both projects should be accepted if they are independent.

c. In this case, we would choose the project with the higher NPV at r = 12%, or Project X.

d. To determine the effects of changing the cost of capital, plot the NPV profiles of each project. The crossover rate occurs at about 6 to 7 percent (6.2 percent). See the accompanying graph.

If the firm's cost of capital is less than 6.2 percent, a conflict exists because NPV_Y > NPV_X, but IRR_X > IRR_Y. Therefore, if r were 5 percent, a conflict would exist. Note, however, that when r = 5.0%, $MIRR_X$ = 10.64% and $MIRR_Y$ = 10.83%; hence, the modified IRR ranks the projects correctly, even if r is to the left of the crossover point.

e. The basic cause of the conflict is differing reinvestment rate assumptions between NPV and IRR. NPV assumes that cash flows can be reinvested at the cost of capital, while IRR assumes reinvestment at the (generally) higher IRR. The high reinvestment rate assumption under IRR makes early cash flows especially valuable, and hence short-term projects look better under IRR.

NPV Profiles for Projects X and Y

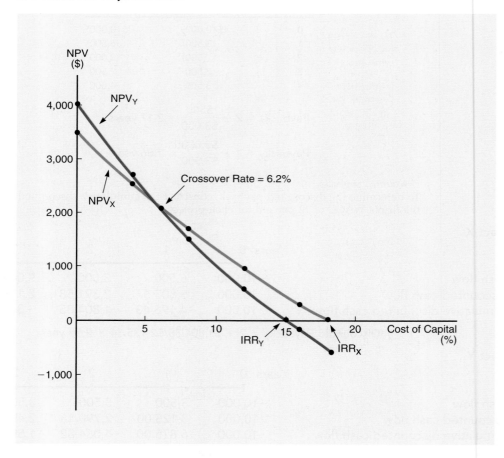

Cost of Capital	NPV_X	NPV_Y
0%	$3,500	$4,000
4	2,545	2,705
8	1,707	1,592
12	966	631
16	307	(206)
18	5	(585)

CHAPTER 12

ST-2   a.   Estimated investment requirements:

Price	($55,000)
Installation	(10,000)
Change in net operating working capital	(2,000)
Total investment	($67,000)

b.   Depreciation schedule:
Equipment cost = $65,000; MACRS 3-year class

	YEARS		
	1	**2**	**3**
MACRS depreciation rates	33%	45%	15%
Equipment depreciation expense	$21,450	$29,250	$9,750

Note that the remaining book value of the equipment at the end of the project's life is $0.07 \times \$65,000 = \$4,550$.

c.   Terminal cash flow:

Salvage value	$10,000
Tax on salvage value[a]	(2,180)
Net operating working capital recovery	2,000
Termination cash flow	$ 9,820

[a] Sales price	$10,000
Less book value	4,550
Taxable income	$ 5,450
Tax at 40%	$ 2,180

Book value = Depreciable basis − Accumulated depreciation
= $65,000 − $60,450 = $4,550

d.   Net operating cash flows:

	Year 1	Year 2	Year 3
Revenues (4,000 × $50)	$200,000	$200,000	$200,000
Variable costs (70%)	140,000	140,000	140,000
Fixed costs	30,000	30,000	30,000
Depreciation	21,450	29,250	9,750
EBIT	$ 8,550	$ 750	$ 20,250
Taxes (40%)	3,420	300	8,100
NOPAT	$ 5,130	$ 450	$ 12,150
Add back: Depreciation	21,450	29,250	9,750
Operating cash flow	$ 26,580	$ 29,700	$ 21,900

e.   Project cash flows:

	0	1	2	3
	11%			
Operating cash flows	−67,000	26,580	29,700	21,900
Terminal cash flow				9,820
Project cash flows	−67,000	26,580	29,700	31,720

f.   From the time line shown in part e, the project's NPV can be calculated as follows:

$$\text{NPV} = -\$67,000 + \$26,580/(1.11)^1 + \$29,700/(1.11)^2 + \$31,720/(1.11)^3$$

$$= \$4,245$$

Alternatively, using a financial calculator, you would enter the following data: $CF_0 = -67000$; $CF_1 = 26580$; $CF_2 = 29700$; $CF_3 = 31720$; I/YR = 11; and then solve for NPV = $4,245.
   Since the NPV is positive, the project should be accepted.

g.   Project analysis if unit sales turned out to be 20 percent below forecast:
Initial projection = 4,000 units; however, if unit sales turn out to be only 80 percent of forecast then unit sales = 3,200.

	Year 0	Year 1	Year 2	Year 3
Equipment purchase	-$65,000			
Change in NOWC	-2,000			
Revenues (3,200 × $50)		$160,000	$160,000	$160,000
Variable costs (70%)		112,000	112,000	112,000
Fixed costs		30,000	30,000	30,000
Depreciation		21,450	29,250	9,750
EBIT		-$ 3,450	-$ 11,250	$ 8,250
Taxes (40%)		-1,380	-4,500	3,300
NOPAT		-$ 2,070	-$ 6,750	$ 4,950
Add back: Depreciation		21,450	29,250	9,750
Operating cash flow	-$67,000	$ 19,380	$ 22,500	$ 14,700
Terminal cash flow				9,820
Project cash flows	-$67,000	$ 19,380	$ 22,500	$ 24,520

Project NPV:

```
  0         1         2         3
  |---11%---|---------|---------|
-67,000   19,380    22,500    24,520
```

NPV = -$67,000 + $19,380/(1.11)^1 + $22,500/(1.11)^2 + $24,520/(1.11)^3
    = -$13,350

Alternatively, using a financial calculator, you would enter the following data: CF_0 = -67000; CF_1 = 19380; CF_2 = 22500; CF_3 = 24520; I/YR = 11; and then solve for NPV = -$13,350.

Since the NPV is negative, the project should not be accepted. If unit sales were 20 percent below the forecasted level, the project would no longer be accepted.

h. *Best-case scenario:* Unit sales = 4,800, Variable cost % = 65%.

	Year 0	Year 1	Year 2	Year 3
Equipment purchase	-$65,000			
Change in NOWC	-2,000			
Revenues (4,800 × $50)		$240,000	$240,000	$240,000
Variable costs (65%)		156,000	156,000	156,000
Fixed costs		30,000	30,000	30,000
Depreciation		21,450	29,250	9,750
EBIT		$ 32,550	$ 24,750	$ 44,250
Taxes (40%)		13,020	9,900	17,700
NOPAT		$ 19,530	$ 14,850	$ 26,550
Add back: Depreciation		21,450	29,250	9,750
Operating cash flows	-$67,000	$ 40,980	$ 44,100	$ 36,300
Terminal cash flow				9,820
Project cash flows	-$67,000	$ 40,980	$ 44,100	$ 46,120

Project NPV:

```
  0         1         2         3
  |---11%---|---------|---------|
-67,000   40,980    44,100    46,120
```

NPV = -$67,000 + $40,980/(1.11)^1 + $44,100/(1.11)^2 + $46,120/(1.11)^3
    = $39,434

Alternatively, using a financial calculator, you would enter the following data: CF_0 = -67000; CF_1 = 40980; CF_2 = 44100; CF_3 = 46120; I/YR = 11; and then solve for NPV = $39,434.

Base-case scenario: The NPV was calculated in part f as $4,245.

Worst-case scenario: Unit sales = 3,200; Variable cost % = 75%.

	Year 0	Year 1	Year 2	Year 3
Equipment purchase	−$65,000			
Change in NOWC	−2,000			
Revenues (3,200 × $50)		$160,000	$160,000	$160,000
Variable costs (75%)		120,000	120,000	120,000
Fixed costs		30,000	30,000	30,000
Depreciation		21,450	29,250	9,750
EBIT		−$ 11,450	−$ 19,250	$ 250
Taxes (40%)		−4,580	−7,700	100
NOPAT		−$ 6,870	−$ 11,550	$ 150
Add back: Depreciation		21,450	29,250	9,750
Operating cash flows	−$67,000	$ 14,580	$ 17,700	$ 9,900
Terminal cash flow				9,820
Project cash flows	−$67,000	$ 14,580	$ 17,700	$ 19,720

Project NPV:

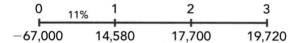

$$NPV = -\$67,000 + \$14,580/(1.11)^1 + \$17,700/(1.11)^2 + \$19,720/(1.11)^3$$
$$= -\$25,080$$

Alternatively, using a financial calculator, you would enter the following data: $CF_0 = -67000$; $CF_1 = 14580$; $CF_2 = 17700$; $CF_3 = 19720$; $I/YR = 11$; and then solve for NPV = −$25,080.

Scenario	Probability	NPV
Best case	25%	$39,434
Base case	50	4,245
Worst case	25	−25,080
	Expected NPV =	$ 5,711

$$\sigma_{NPV} = [0.25[\$39,434 - \$5,711]^2 + 0.50[\$4,245 - \$5,711]^2 + 0.25[-\$25,080 - \$5,711]^2]^{1/2}$$
$$\sigma_{NPV} = [\$284,310,182 + \$1,074,578 + \$237,021,420]^{1/2}$$
$$\sigma_{NPV} = \$22,856$$
$$CV_{NPV} = \$22,856/\$5,711 = 4.0$$

i. The project's CV = 4.0, which is significantly larger than the firm's typical project CV. So, the WACC for this project should be adjusted upward, 11% + 3% = 14%.

To calculate the expected NPV, standard deviation, and coefficient of variation you would recalculate each scenario's NPV by discounting the project cash flows by 14 percent rather than 11 percent.

Best-case scenario:

```
   0       14%    1        2        3
   +--------------+--------+--------+
 −67,000       40,980   44,100   46,120
```

$$NPV = -\$67,000 + \$40,980/(1.14)^1 + \$44,100/(1.14)^2 + \$46,120/(1.14)^3$$
$$= \$34,011$$

Alternatively, using a financial calculator, you would enter the following data: $CF_0 = -67000$; $CF_1 = 40980$; $CF_2 = 44100$; $CF_3 = 46120$; $I/YR = 14$; and then solve for NPV = $34,011.

Base-case scenario:

```
   0       14%    1        2        3
   +--------------+--------+--------+
 −67,000       26,580   29,700   31,720
```

$$NPV = -\$67,000 + \$26,580/(1.14)^1 + \$29,700/(1.14)^2 + \$31,720/(1.14)^3$$
$$= \$579$$

Alternatively, using a financial calculator, you would enter the following data: $CF_0 = -67000$; $CF_1 = 26580$; $CF_2 = 29700$; $CF_3 = 31720$; $I/YR = 14$; and then solve for NPV = $579.

Worst-case scenario:

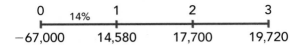

```
0        14%   1          2          3
├─────────────┼──────────┼──────────┤
-67,000      14,580     17,700     19,720
```

NPV = -$67,000 + $14,580/(1.14)^1 + $17,700/(1.14)^2 + $19,720/(1.14)^3
    = -$27,281

Alternatively, using a financial calculator, you would enter the following data: $CF_0 = -67000$; $CF_1 = 14580$; $CF_2 = 17700$; $CF_3 = 19720$; $I/YR = 14$; and then solve for NPV = -$27,281.

Scenario	Probability	NPV
Best case	25%	$34,011
Base case	50	579
Worst case	25	-27,281
	Expected NPV =	$ 1,972

$\sigma_{NPV} = [0.25[\$34,011 - \$1,972]^2 + 0.50[\$579 - \$1,972]^2 + 0.25[-\$27,281 - \$1,972]^2]^{1/2}$
$\sigma_{NPV} = [\$256,624,380 + \$970,225 + \$213,934,502]^{1/2}$
$\sigma_{NPV} = \$21,715$
$CV_{NPV} = \$21,715/\$1,972 = 11.0$

The expected NPV of the project is still positive so the project would still be accepted.

CHAPTER 13

ST-2   a.   No abandonment considered; WACC = 12%.

Years	0	1	2	3	NPV
25%	-25,000	18,000	18,000	18,000	$18,233
50	-25,000	12,000	12,000	12,000	3,822
25	-25,000	-8,000	-8,000	-8,000	-44,215
				Expected NPV =	-$ 4,585

b.   Abandonment considered; WACC = 12 percent.

Years	0	1	2	3	NPV
25%	-25,000	18,000	18,000	18,000	$18,233
50	-25,000	12,000	12,000	12,000	3,822
25	-25,000	-8,000			
		Abandon project	15,000	0	-20,185
				Expected NPV =	$ 1,423

c.   Value of the abandonment option:

NPV with abandonment	$1,423
NPV without abandonment	(4,585)
Value of abandonment option	$6,008

ST-3   a.   Machine W:

```
0       10%    1          2
├─────────────┼──────────┤
-500,000    300,000    300,000
```

$$NPV_W = -\$500,000 + \frac{\$300,000}{(1.10)^1} + \frac{\$300,000}{(1.10)^2}$$

$$= \$20,661.16$$

Machine WW:

```
0          1          2          3          4
|-----10%--+----------+----------+----------|
-500,000   165,000    165,000    165,000    165,000
```

$$NPV_{WW} = -\$500,000 + \frac{\$165,000}{(1.10)^1} + \frac{\$165,000}{(1.10)^2} + \frac{\$165,000}{(1.10)^3} + \frac{\$165,000}{(1.10)^4}$$

$$= \$23,027.80.$$

Since the projects are independent and both have positive NPVs, both projects should be accepted.

b. Since the projects are mutually exclusive, only one project can be accepted. Therefore, Machine WW has the higher NPV and should be chosen.

c(1). Machine W's NPV needs to be recalculated under the assumption that it is repeated in Year 2.

Replacement chain analysis:

Machine W:

```
0          1          2          3          4
|-----10%--+----------+----------+----------|
-500,000   300,000    300,000    300,000    300,000
                     -500,000
                     -200,000
```

$$NPV_W = -\$500,000 + \frac{\$300,000}{(1.10)^1} + \frac{-\$200,000}{(1.10)^2} + \frac{\$300,000}{(1.10)^3} + \frac{\$300,000}{(1.10)^4}$$

$$= NPV_W = \$37,736.49$$

Machine WW:

$NPV_{WW} = \$23,027.80$ (NPV remains the same since it's calculated over a 4-year life.)

Since the projects are mutually exclusive but repeatable, Machine W should be chosen because its 4-year NPV is higher than Machine WW's.

c(2). *Equivalent annual annuity analysis:*

Machine W:
Using a financial calculator, enter the following data: N = 2; I/YR = 10; PV = −20661.16; FV = 0; and then solve for EAA_W = PMT = $11,904.76.

Machine WW:
Using a financial calculator, enter the following data: N = 4; I/YR = 10; PV = −23027.80; FV = 0; and then solve for EAA_{WW} = PMT = $7,264.60.
    The equivalent annual annuity analysis arrives at the same decision as the replacement chain method. EAA_W = $11,904.76 and EAA_{WW} = $7,264.60; therefore, Machine W should be chosen if the projects are mutually exclusive and can be repeated indefinitely.

d. Yes. If the two projects can be repeated indefinitely over time but the cash flows are expected to change, then the replacement chain analysis can be used. The analysis would be similar to what was done in part c(1) except that the repeated cash flows would not be identical to the original cash flows.

CHAPTER 14

ST-2 a. The following information is given in the problem:

$$
\begin{aligned}
Q &= \text{Units of output (sales)} = 5,000 \\
P &= \text{Average sales price per unit of output} = \$100 \\
F &= \text{Fixed operating costs} = \$200,000 \\
V &= \text{Variable costs per unit} = \$50 \\
EBIT &= \text{Operating income} = \$50,000 \\
\text{Total assets} &= \$500,000 \\
\text{Common equity} &= \$500,000
\end{aligned}
$$

(1) Determine the new EBIT level if the change is made:

$$\text{New EBIT} = P_2(Q_2) - F_2 - V_2(Q_2)$$
$$\text{New EBIT} = \$95(7,000) - \$250,000 - \$40(7,000)$$
$$= \$135,000$$

(2) Determine the incremental EBIT:

$$\Delta\text{EBIT} = \$135,000 - \$50,000 = \$85,000$$

(3) Estimate the approximate rate of return on the new investment:

$$\Delta\text{ROA} = \frac{\Delta\text{EBIT}}{\text{Investment}} = \frac{\$85,000}{\$400,000} = 21.25\%$$

Since the ROA exceeds Olinde's average cost of capital, this analysis suggests that the firm should go ahead and make the investment.

b. The change would increase the breakeven point. Still, with a lower sales price, it might be easier to achieve the higher new breakeven volume.

$$\text{Old: } Q_{BE} = \frac{F}{P - V} = \frac{\$200,000}{\$100 - \$50} = 4,000 \text{ units}$$

$$\text{New: } Q_{BE} = \frac{F}{P_2 - V_2} = \frac{\$250,000}{\$95 - \$40} = 4,545 \text{ units}$$

c. The incremental ROA is

$$\text{ROA} = \frac{\Delta\text{Profit}}{\Delta\text{Sales}} \times \frac{\Delta\text{Sales}}{\Delta\text{Assets}}$$

Using debt financing, the incremental profit associated with the investment is equal to the incremental profit found in part a minus the interest expense incurred as a result of the investment:

$$\Delta\text{Profit} = \text{New profit} - \text{Old profit} - \text{Interest}$$
$$= \$135,000 - \$50,000 - 0.10(\$400,000)$$
$$= \$45,000$$

The incremental sales is calculated as:

$$\Delta\text{Sales} = P_2Q_2 - P_1Q_1$$
$$= \$95(7,000) - \$100(5,000)$$
$$= \$665,000 - \$500,000$$
$$= \$165,000$$

$$\text{ROA} = \frac{\$45,000}{\$165,000} \times \frac{\$165,000}{\$400,000} = 11.25\%$$

The return on the new equity investment still exceeds the average cost of capital, so the firm should make the investment.

ST-3 a.

EBIT	$4,000,000
Interest ($2,000,000 × 0.10)	200,000
Earnings before taxes (EBT)	$3,800,000
Taxes (35%)	1,330,000
Net income	$2,470,000

$$\text{EPS} = \$2,470,000/600,000 = \$4.12$$

$$P_0 = \$4.12/0.15 = \$27.47$$

b. Equity $= 600,000 \times \$10 = \$6,000,000$

Debt $= \$2,000,000$

Total capital $= \$8,000,000$

$$\text{WACC} = w_d r_d(1 - T) + w_c r_s$$
$$= (2/8)(10\%)(1 - 0.35) + (6/8)(15\%)$$
$$= 1.63\% + 11.25\%$$
$$= 12.88\%$$

c.

EBIT	$4,000,000
Interest ($10,000,000 × 0.12)	1,200,000
Earnings before taxes (EBT)	$2,800,000
Taxes (35%)	980,000
Net income	$1,820,000

Shares bought and retired:

$$\Delta N = \Delta Debt/P_0 = \$8,000,000/\$27.47 = 291,227$$

New outstanding shares:

$$N_1 = N_0 - \Delta N = 600,000 - 291,227 = 308,773$$

New EPS:

$$EPS = \$1,820,000/308,773 = \$5.89$$

New price per share:

$$P_0 = \$5.89/0.17 = \$34.65 \text{ versus } \$27.47$$

Therefore, Gentry should change its capital structure.

d. In this case, the company's net income would be higher by $(0.12 - 0.10)(\$2,000,000)$ $(1 - 0.35) = \$26,000$ because its interest charges would be lower. The new price would be

$$P_0 = \frac{(\$1,820,000 + \$26,000)/308,773}{0.17} = \$35.17$$

In the first case, in which debt had to be refunded, the bondholders were compensated for the increased risk of the higher debt position. In the second case, the old bondholders were not compensated; their 10 percent coupon perpetual bonds would now be worth

$$\$100/0.12 = \$833.33$$

or $1,666,667 in total, down from the old $2 million, or a loss of $333,333. The stockholders would have a gain of

$$(\$35.17 - \$34.65)(308,773) = \$160,562$$

This gain would, of course, be at the expense of the old bondholders. (There is no reason to think that bondholders' losses would exactly offset stockholders' gains.)

e.

$$TIE = \frac{EBIT}{I}$$

$$\text{Original TIE} = \frac{\$4,000,000}{\$200,000} = 20 \text{ times}$$

$$\text{New TIE} = \frac{\$4,000,000}{\$1,200,000} = 3.33 \text{ times}$$

CHAPTER 15

ST-2   a.

Projected net income	$2,000,000
Less projected capital investments	800,000
Available residual	$1,200,000
Shares outstanding	200,000

$$DPS = \$1,200,000/200,000 \text{ shares} = \$6 = D_1$$

b. EPS = $2,000,000/200,000 shares = $10
Payout ratio = DPS/EPS = $6/$10 = 60% or
Total dividends/NI = $1,200,000/$2,000,000 = 60%

c. Currently, $P_0 = \dfrac{D_1}{r_s - g} = \dfrac{\$6}{0.14 - 0.05} = \dfrac{\$6}{0.09} = \$66.67$

Under the former circumstances, D_1 would be based on a 20 percent payout on $10 EPS, or $2. With r_s = 14% and g = 12%, we solve for P_0:

$$P_0 = \frac{D_1}{r_s - g} = \frac{\$2}{0.14 - 0.12} = \frac{\$2}{0.02} = \$100$$

Although CMC has suffered a severe setback, its existing assets will continue to provide a good income stream. More of these earnings should now be passed on to the shareholders, as the slowed internal growth has reduced the need for funds. However, the net result is a 33 percent decrease in the value of the shares.

d. If the payout ratio were continued at 20 percent, even after internal investment opportunities had declined, the price of the stock would drop to $2/(0.14 − 0.06) = $25 rather than to $66.67. Thus, an increase in the dividend payout is consistent with maximizing shareholder wealth.

Because of the diminishing nature of profitable investment opportunities, the greater the firm's level of investment, the lower the average ROE. Thus, the more money CMC retains and invests, the lower its average ROE will be. We can determine the average ROE under different conditions as follows:

Old situation (with founder active and a 20 percent payout):

$$g = (1.0 - \text{Payout ratio})(\text{Average ROE})$$

$$12\% = (1.0 - 0.2)(\text{Average ROE})$$

$$\text{Average ROE} = 12\%/0.8 = 15\% > r_s = 14\%$$

Note that the *average* ROE is 15 percent, whereas the *marginal* ROE is presumably equal to 14 percent.

New situation (with founder retired and a 60 percent payout):

$$g = 6\% = (1.0 - 0.6)(\text{ROE})$$

$$\text{ROE} = 6\%/0.4 = 15\% > r_s = 14\%$$

This suggests that the new payout is appropriate and that the firm is taking on investments down to the point at which marginal returns are equal to the cost of capital. Note that if the 20 percent payout was maintained, the *average* ROE would be only 7.5 percent, which would imply a marginal ROE far below the 14 percent cost of capital.

CHAPTER 16

ST-2 **The Calgary Company: Alternative Balance Sheets**

	Restricted (40%)	Moderate (50%)	Relaxed (60%)
Current assets	$1,200,000	$1,500,000	$1,800,000
Fixed assets	600,000	600,000	600,000
Total assets	$1,800,000	$2,100,000	$2,400,000
Debt	$ 900,000	$1,050,000	$1,200,000
Equity	900,000	1,050,000	1,200,000
Total liabilities and equity	$1,800,000	$2,100,000	$2,400,000

The Calgary Company: Alternative Income Statements

	Restricted	Moderate	Relaxed
Sales	$3,000,000	$3,000,000	$3,000,000
EBIT	$ 450,000	$ 450,000	$ 450,000
Interest (10%)	90,000	105,000	120,000
Earnings before taxes	$ 360,000	$ 345,000	$ 330,000
Taxes (40%)	144,000	138,000	132,000
Net income	$ 216,000	$ 207,000	$ 198,000
ROE	24.0%	19.7%	16.5%

ST-3   a. and b.

Income Statements for Year Ended December 31, 2005 (Thousands of Dollars)

	VANDERHEIDEN PRESS		HERRENHOUSE PUBLISHING	
	a	b	a	b
EBIT	$ 30,000	$ 30,000	$ 30,000	$ 30,000
Interest	12,400	14,400	10,600	18,600
Taxable income	$ 17,600	$ 15,600	$ 19,400	$ 11,400
Taxes (40%)	7,040	6,240	7,760	4,560
Net income	$ 10,560	$ 9,360	$ 11,640	$ 6,840
Equity	$100,000	$100,000	$100,000	$100,000
Return on equity	10.56%	9.36%	11.64%	6.84%

The Vanderheiden Press has a higher ROE when short-term interest rates are high, whereas Herrenhouse Publishing does better when rates are lower.

c.   Herrenhouse's position is riskier. First, its profits and return on equity are much more volatile than Vanderheiden's. Second, Herrenhouse must renew its large short-term loan every year, and if the renewal comes up at a time when money is very tight, when its business is depressed, or both, then Herrenhouse could be denied credit, which could put it out of business.

CHAPTER 17

ST-2   To solve this problem, we will define ΔS as the change in sales and g as the growth rate in sales, and then we use the three following equations:

$$\Delta S = S_0 g$$

$$S_1 = S_0(1 + g)$$

$$AFN = (A^*/S_0)(\Delta S) - (L^*/S_0)(\Delta S) - MS_1(RR)$$

Set AFN = 0, substitute in known values for A^*/S_0, L^*/S_0, M, RR, and S_0, and then solve for g:

$$0 = 1.6(\$100g) - 0.4(\$100g) - 0.10[\$100(1 + g)](0.55)$$
$$0 = \$160g - \$40g - 0.055(\$100 + \$100g)$$
$$0 = \$160g - \$40g - \$5.5 - \$5.5g$$
$$\$114.5g = \$5.5$$
$$g = \$5.5/\$114.5 = 0.048 = 4.8\%$$
$$= \text{Maximum growth rate without external financing}$$

ST-3   Assets consist of cash, marketable securities, receivables, inventories, and fixed assets. Therefore, we can break the A^*/S_0 ratio into its components—cash/sales, inventories/sales, and so forth. Then,

$$\frac{A^*}{S_0} = \frac{A^* - \text{Inventories}}{S_0} + \frac{\text{Inventories}}{S_0} = 1.6$$

We know that the inventory turnover ratio is sales/inventories = 3 times, so inventories/sales = 1/3 = 0.3333. Further, if the inventory turnover ratio can be increased to 4 times, then the inventory/sales ratio will fall to 1/4 = 0.25, a difference of 0.3333 − 0.2500 = 0.0833. This, in turn, causes the A^*/S_0 ratio to fall from A^*/S_0 = 1.6 to A^*/S_0 = 1.6 − 0.0833 = 1.5167.

This change has two effects: First, it changes the AFN equation, and second, it means that Weatherford currently has excessive inventories. Because it is costly to hold excess inventories, Weatherford will want to reduce its inventory holdings by not replacing inventories until the excess amounts have been used. We can account for this by setting up the revised AFN equation (using the new A^*/S_0 ratio), estimating the funds that will be needed next year if no excess inventories are currently on hand, and then subtracting out the excess inventories that are currently on hand:

Present conditions:

$$\frac{\text{Sales}}{\text{Inventories}} = \frac{\$100}{\text{Inventories}} = 3$$

so

$$\text{Inventories} = \$100/3 = \$33.3 \text{ million at present}$$

New conditions:

$$\frac{\text{Sales}}{\text{Inventories}} = \frac{\$100}{\text{Inventories}} = 4$$

so

$$\text{New level of inventories} = \$100/4 = \$25 \text{ million}$$

Therefore,

$$\text{Excess inventories} = \$33.3 - \$25 = \$8.3 \text{ million}$$

Forecast of funds needed next year:

$$\Delta S \text{ in first year} = 0.2(\$100 \text{ million}) = \$20 \text{ million}$$

$$\text{AFN} = 1.5167(\$20) - 0.4(\$20) - 0.1(0.55)(\$120) - \$8.3$$

$$= \$30.3 - \$8 - \$6.6 - \$8.3$$

$$= \$7.4 \text{ million}$$

CHAPTER 18

ST-2 $V = P[N(d_1)] - Xe^{-r_{RF}t} [N(d_2)]$

   $= [\$33(0.63369)] - [\$33(0.95123)(0.55155)]$

   $= \$20.91 - \$17.31$

   $= \$3.60$

CHAPTER 19

ST-2 $\dfrac{\text{Euro}}{\text{C\$}} = \dfrac{\text{Euros}}{\text{US\$}} \times \dfrac{\text{US\$}}{\text{C\$}}$

   $= \dfrac{1.1215}{\$1} \times \dfrac{\$1}{1.5291} = \dfrac{1.1215}{1.5291} = 0.7334$ euro per Canadian dollar

CHAPTER 20

ST-2 a. *Cost of leasing:*

	BEGINNING OF YEAR			
	0	1	2	3
Lease payment (AT)[a]	($ 6,000)	($6,000)	($6,000)	($6,000)
Total PV cost of leasing =	($22,038)			

[a]After-tax payment = $10,000(1 − T) = $10,000(0.6) = $6,000

Using a financial calculator, input the following data after switching your calculator to "BEG" mode: N = 4, I/YR = 6, PMT = 6000, and FV = 0. Then press the PV key to arrive at the answer of ($22,038). Now, switch your calculator back to "END" mode. Note that the interest rate used is the after-tax cost of debt, 10% (1 − T) = 6%.

b. *Cost of owning:*

Depreciable basis = $40,000

Here are the cash flows under the borrow-and-buy alternative:

	END OF YEAR				
	0	1	2	3	4
1. Depreciation schedule					
(a) Depreciable basis		$40,000	$40,000	$40,000	$40,000
(b) Allowance		0.33	0.45	0.15	0.07
(c) Depreciation		13,200	18,000	6,000	2,800
2. Cash flows					
(d) Net purchase price	($40,000)				
(e) Depreciation tax savings		5,280[a]	7,200	2,400	1,120
(f) Maintenance (AT)		(600)	(600)	(600)	(600)
(g) Salvage value (AT)					6,000
(h) Total cash flows	($40,000)	$ 4,680	$ 6,600	$ 1,800	$ 6,520

Total PV cost of owning = ($23,035)

[a]Depreciation(T) = $13,200(0.40) = $5,280
Input the cash flows for the individual years into the cash flow register and enter I/YR = 6, then press the NPV key to arrive at the answer of ($23,035). Because the present value of the cost of leasing is less than that of owning, the truck should be leased: $23,035 − $22,038 = $997, net advantage to leasing.

c. The discount rate is based on the cost of debt because most cash flows are fixed by contract and, consequently, are relatively certain. Thus, the lease cash flows have about the same risk as the firm's debt. Also, leasing is considered to be a substitute for debt. We use an after-tax cost rate because the cash flows are stated net of taxes.

d. The firm could increase the discount rate on the salvage value cash flow. This would increase the PV cost of owning and make leasing even more advantageous.

CHAPTER 21

ST-2 Time line numbers are in millions of dollars:

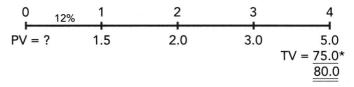

$$r_s = 6\% + 4\%(1.5)$$

$$= 12\%$$

$$*\text{Terminal CF} = \frac{\$5(1.05)}{0.12 - 0.5} = \$75.00$$

To solve this problem, use your financial calculator to enter the following input data: $CF_0 = 0$; $CF_1 = 1.5$; $CF_2 = 2.0$; $CF_3 = 3.0$; $CF_4 = 80$; and $I/YR = 12$. Then, solve for NPV = \$55.91 million.

Answers to Selected End-of-Chapter Problems

We present here some intermediate steps and final answers to selected end-of-chapter problems. Please note that your answer may differ slightly from ours due to rounding differences. Also, although we hope not, some of the problems may have more than one correct solution, depending on what assumptions are made in working the problem. Finally, many of the problems involve some verbal discussion as well as numerical calculations; this verbal material is not presented here.

2-2 PV = $1,292.10.
2-4 N = 11.01 years.
2-6 FVA_5 = $1,725.22; $FVA_{5\ Due}$ = $1,845.99.
2-8 PMT = $444.89; EAR = 12.6825%.
2-10 a. $895.42.
     b. $1,552.92.
     c. $279.20.
     d. $499.99; $867.13.
2-12 a. 7%.
     b. 7%.
     c. 9%.
     d. 15%.
2-14 a. $6,374.97.
     d(1). $7,012.47.
2-16 $PV_{7\%}$ = $1,428.57; $PV_{14\%}$ = $714.29.
2-18 a. Stream A: $1,251.25.
2-20 Contract 2; PV = $10,717,847.14.
2-22 a. $802.43.
     c. $984.88.
2-24 a. $279.20.
     b. $276.84.
     c. $443.72.
2-26 $17,290.89; $19,734.26.
2-28 I_{NOM} = 7.8771%.
2-30 a. E = 63.74 yrs.; K = 41.04 yrs.
     b. $35,825.33.
2-32 $496.11.
2-34 a. PMT = $10,052.87.
     b. Yr 3: Int/Pymt = 9.09%;
        Princ/Pymt = 90.91%.
2-36 a. $5,308.12.
     b. $4,877.09.
2-38 $309,015.
2-40 $9,385.

3-2 $2,500,000.
3-4 $20,000,000.
3-6 $89,100,000.
3-8 NI = $450,000; NCF = $650,000;
    OCF = $650,000.

3-10 a. $2,400,000,000.
     b. $4,500,000,000.
     c. $5,400,000,000.
     d. $1,100,000,000.
3-12 a. $592 million.
     b. RE_{04} = $1,374 million.
     c. $1,600 million.
     d. $15 million.
     e. $620 million.
3-14 a. $2,400,000.
     b. NI = 0; NCF = $3,000,000.
     c. NI = $1,350,000; NCF = $2,100,000.

4-2 D/A = 58.33%.
4-4 M/B = 4.2667.
4-6 ROE = 8%.
4-8 15.31%.
4-10 NI/S = 2%; D/A = 40%.
4-12 TIE = 2.25.
4-14 ROE = 23.1%.
4-16 7.2%.
4-18 6.0.
4-20 $405,682.
4-22 A/P = $90,000; Inv = $90,000; FA = $138,000.
4-24 a. TIE = 11; EBITDA coverage = 9.46;
        Profit margin = 3.40%; ROE = 8.57%.

6-2 2.25%.
6-4 1.5%.
6-6 21.8%.
6-8 8.5%.
6-10 6.0%.
6-12 0.35%.
6-14 a. r_1 in Year 2 = 6%.
     b. I_1 = 2%; I_2 = 5%.
6-16 14%.
6-18 a. r_1 = 9.20%; r_5 = 7.20%.

7-2 a. 7.11%.
    b. 7.22%.
    c. $988.46.
7-4 YTM = 6.62%; YTC = 6.49%;
    most likely yield = 6.49%.
7-6 a. C_0 = $1,012.79; Z_0 = $693.04;
       C_1 = $1,010.02; Z_1 = $759.57;
       C_2 = $1,006.98; Z_2 = $832.49;
       C_3 = $1,003.65; Z_3 = $912.41;
       C_4 = $1,000.00; Z_4 = $1,000.00.

7-8 15.03%.
7-10 a. YTM = 9.69%.
     b. CY = 8.875%; CGY = 0.816%.
7-12 a. YTM = 8%; YTC = 6.1%.
7-14 10.78%.
7-16 $987.87.
7-18 8.88%.
7-20 a. 8.35%.
     b. 8.13%.

8-2 $b_p = 1.12$.
8-4 $r_M = 11\%$; $r = 12.2\%$.
8-6 a. $\hat{r}_Y = 14\%$.
     b. $\sigma_X = 12.20\%$.
8-8 $b = 1.33$.
8-10 4.2%.
8-12 $r_M - r_{RF} = 4.375\%$.
8-14 $b_N = 1.16$.
8-16 $r_p = 11.75\%$.
8-18 a. $0.5 million.
     d(2). 15%.
8-20 a. $r_A = 11.30\%$.
     c. $\sigma_A = 20.8\%$; $\sigma_p = 20.1\%$.

9-2 $\hat{P}_0 = \$6.25$.
9-4 b. $37.80.
     c. $34.09.
9-6 $r_p = 8.33\%$.
9-8 a. $125.
     b. $83.33.
9-10 $23.75.
9-12 a(1). $9.50.
     a(2). $13.33.
     a(3). $21.00.
     a(4). $44.00.
     b(1). Undefined.
     b(2). −$48.00, which is nonsense.
9-14 $\hat{P}_3 = \$27.32$.
9-16 $P_0 = \$19.89$.
9-18 6.25%.
9-20 a. $P_0 = \$54.11$; $D_1/P_0 = 3.55\%$;
     CGY = 6.45%.
9-22 $35.00.
9-24 a. $2.01; $2.31; $2.66; $3.06; $3.52.
     b. $P_0 = \$39.43$.
     c. $D_1/P_{0\ 2006} = 5.10\%$; $CGY_{2006} = 6.9\%$;
     $D_1/P_{0\ 2011} = 7.00\%$; $CGY_{2011} = 5\%$.

10-2 $r_p = 8\%$.
10-4 $r_s = 15\%$; $r_e = 16.11\%$.
10-6 a. $r_s = 16.3\%$.
     b. $r_s = 15.4\%$.
     c. $r_s = 16\%$.
     d. $r_{s\ AVG} = 15.9\%$.
10-8 $r_s = 16.51\%$; WACC = 12.79%.
10-10 WACC = 11.4%.

10-12 a. $r_s = 14.40\%$.
     b. WACC = 10.62%.
     c. Project A.
10-14 11.94%.
10-16 a. $g = 8\%$.
     b. $D_1 = \$2.81$.
     c. $r_s = 15.81\%$.
10-18 a. $r_d = 7\%$; $r_p = 10.20\%$; $r_s = 15.72\%$.
     b. WACC = 13.86%.
     c. Projects 1 and 2 will be accepted.
10-20 a. $r_d(1 - T) = 5.4\%$; $r_s = 14.6\%$.
     b. WACC = 10.92%.

11-2 IRR = 16%.
11-4 4.34 years.
11-6 a. 5%: $NPV_A = \$3.52$; $NPV_B = \$2.87$.
     10%: $NPV_A = \$0.58$; $NPV_B = \$1.04$.
     15%: $NPV_A = -\$1.91$; $NPV_B = -\$0.55$.
     b. $IRR_A = 11.10\%$; $IRR_B = 13.18\%$.
     c. 5%: Choose A; 10%: Choose B; 15%: Do not
     choose either one.
11-8 a. Without mitigation: NPV = $12.10 million;
     With mitigation: NPV = $5.70 million.
11-10 Project A; $NPV_A = \$30.16$.
11-12 $IRR_L = 11.74\%$.
11-14 a. HCC; PV of costs = −$805,009.87.
     c. HCC; PV of costs = −$767,607.75.
     LCC; PV of costs = −$686,627.14.
11-16 a. $NPV_A = \$14,486,808$; $NPV_B = \$11,156,893$;
     $IRR_A = 15.03\%$; $IRR_B = 22.26\%$.
     b. Crossover rate ≈ 12%.
11-18 a. No; $PV_{Old} = -\$89,910.08$; $PV_{New} = -\$94,611.45$.
     b. $2,470.80.
     c. 22.94%.
11-20 $10,239.20.
11-22 $250.01.

12-2 a. $2,600,000.
12-4 b. Accelerated method; $12,781.64.
12-6 a. −$178,000.
     b. $52,440; $60,600; $40,200.
     c. $48,760.
     d. NPV = −$19,549; Do not purchase.
12-8 a. Expected $CF_A = \$6,750$;
     Expected $CF_B = \$7,650$; $CV_A = 0.0703$.
     b. $NPV_A = \$10,036$; $NPV_B = \$11,624$.
12-10 a. NPV = $37,035.13.
     b. NPV = +20%: $77,975.63;
     −20%: NPV = −$3,905.37.
     c. E(NPV) = $34,800.21;
     $\sigma_{NPV} = \$35,967.84$;
     CV = 1.03.

13-2 a. Project B; $NPV_B = \$2,679.46$.
     b. Project A; $NPV_A = \$3,773.65$.
     c. Project A; $EAA_A = \$1,190.48$.

13-4   A; EAA_A = \$1,407.85.
13-6 NPV_A = \$9.93 million.
13-8 EAA_Y = \$7,433.12.
13-10   No, NPV_3 = \$1,307.29.
13-12   a.   NPV = \$4.6795 million.
       b.   No, NPV = \$3.2083 million.
       c.   0.

14-2   30% debt and 70% equity.
14-4 b_U = 1.0435.
14-6   a(1). −\$60,000.
       b. Q_{BE} = 14,000.
14-8 r_s = 17%.
14-10   a. FC_A = \$80,000; V_A = \$4.80/unit;
          P_A = \$8.00/unit.
14-12   a. EPS_{Old} = \$2.04; New: EPS_D = \$4.74;
          EPS_S = \$3.27.
       b.   339,750 units.
       c. $Q_{New, Debt}$ = 272,250 units.

15-2 P_0 = \$60.
15-4 D_0 = \$3.44.
15-6   Payout = 31.39%.
15-8   a.   12%.
       b.   18%.
       c.   6%; 18%.
       d.   6%.
       e.   28,800 new shares; \$0.13 per share.

16-2   73 days; 30 days; \$1,178,082.
16-4   a.   83 days.
       b.   \$356,250.
       c.   4.87×.
16-6   a.   32 days.
       b.   \$288,000.
       c.   \$45,000.
       d(1). 30.
       d(2). \$378,000.
16-8   a. ROE_T = 11.75%; ROE_M = 10.80%;
          ROE_R = 9.16%.
16-10   a.   October loan = \$22,800.

17-2   AFN = \$610,000.
17-4   a.   \$133.50 million.
       b.   39.06%.
17-6   \$67 million; 5.01.
17-8   a.   \$480,000.
       b.   \$18,750.
17-10   \$34.338 million; 34.97 ≈ 35 days.
17-12   a.   \$2,500,000,000.
       b.   24%.
       c.   \$24,000,000.
17-14   a.   33%.
       b.   AFN = \$2,549.

18-2   \$27.00; \$37.00.
18-4   \$1.82.
18-6   b.   Futures = +\$4,180,346; Bond = −\$2,203,701;
          Net = \$1,976,645.

19-2   27.2436 yen per shekel.
19-4   1 euro = \$0.68966 or \$1 = 1.45 euros.
19-8   15 kronas per pound.
19-10 $r_{NOM-U.S.}$ = 4.6%.
19-12   b.   \$1.6488.
19-14   +\$250,000.
19-16   \$468,837,209.

20-2   \$196.36.
20-4   a. D/A_{J-H} = 50%; D/A_{M-E} = 67%.
20-6   a.   EV = −\$3; EV = \$0; EV = \$4; EV = \$49.
       d.   9%; \$90.
20-8   a.   PV cost of owning = −\$185,112;
          PV cost of leasing = −\$187,534;
          Purchase loom.

21-2 P_0 = \$43.48.
21-4   a.   16.8%.
       b.   V = \$14.93 million.
21-6   a.   14%.
       b.   TV = \$1,143.4; V = \$877.2.

C APPENDIX

Selected Equations and Data

CHAPTER 2

$$FV_N = PV(1 + I)^N$$

$$PV = \frac{FV_N}{(1 + I)^N}$$

$$FVA_N = PMT\left[\frac{(1 + I)^N - 1}{I}\right]$$

$$FVA_{Due} = FVA_{Ordinary}(1 + I)$$

$$PVA_N = PMT\left[\frac{1 - \dfrac{1}{(1 + I)^N}}{I}\right]$$

$$PVA_{N\,Due} = PVA_{Ordinary}(1 + I)$$

$$PV \text{ of a perpetuity} = \frac{PMT}{I}$$

$$PV_{Uneven\ stream} = \sum_{t=1}^{N} \frac{CF_t}{(1 + I)^t}$$

$$I_{PER} = \frac{I}{M}$$

$$APR = (I_{PER})M$$

$$\text{Number of periods} = NM$$

$$EFF\% = \left(1 + \frac{I_{NOM}}{M}\right)^M - 1.0$$

CHAPTER 3

EBIT = Sales revenues − Operating costs

Net cash flow = Net income + Depreciation and amortization

$$\frac{\text{Net operating}}{\text{working capital}} = \frac{\text{All current assets}}{\text{required in operations}} - \frac{\text{All non-interest-bearing}}{\text{current liabilities}}$$

$$\begin{matrix}\text{Net operating}\\\text{working}\\\text{capital}\end{matrix} = \left(\begin{matrix}\text{Cash}\\\text{and cash}\\\text{equivalents}\end{matrix} + \begin{matrix}\text{Accounts}\\\text{receivable}\end{matrix} + \text{Inventories}\right) - \left(\begin{matrix}\text{Accounts}\\\text{payable}\end{matrix} + \text{Accruals}\right)$$

Total operating capital = Net operating working capital + Net fixed assets

NOPAT = EBIT(1 − Tax rate)

Operating cash flow = NOPAT + Depreciation and amortization

$$FCF = \left[EBIT(1 - T) + \begin{matrix}\text{Depreciation and}\\\text{amortization}\end{matrix}\right] - \left[\begin{matrix}\text{Capital}\\\text{expenditures}\end{matrix} + \begin{matrix}\Delta\text{Net operating}\\\text{working capital}\end{matrix}\right]$$

Free cash flow = Operating cash flow − Investment in operating capital

MVA = Market value of stock − Equity capital supplied by shareholders

= [(Shares outstanding)(Stock price)] − Total common equity

EVA = NOPAT − Annual dollar cost of capital

$$= (EBIT)(1 - T) - \left(\begin{array}{c} \text{Total investor-supplied} \\ \text{operating capital} \end{array} \times \begin{array}{c} \text{After-tax percentage} \\ \text{cost of capital} \end{array} \right)$$

CHAPTER 4

$$\text{Current ratio} = \frac{\text{Current assets}}{\text{Current liabilities}}$$

$$\text{Quick, or acid test, ratio} = \frac{\text{Current assets} - \text{Inventories}}{\text{Current liabilities}}$$

$$\text{Inventory turnover ratio} = \frac{\text{Sales}}{\text{Inventories}}$$

$$\text{DSO} = \text{Days sales outstanding} = \frac{\text{Receivables}}{\text{Average sales per day}} = \frac{\text{Receivables}}{\text{Annual sales/365}}$$

$$\text{Fixed assets turnover ratio} = \frac{\text{Sales}}{\text{Net fixed assets}}$$

$$\text{Total assets turnover ratio} = \frac{\text{Sales}}{\text{Total assets}}$$

$$\text{Debt ratio} = \frac{\text{Total debt}}{\text{Total assets}}$$

$$\text{D/A} = \frac{\text{D/E}}{1 + \text{D/E}}$$

$$\text{Debt ratio} = 1 - \frac{1}{\text{Equity multiplier}}$$

$$\text{D/E} = \frac{\text{D/A}}{1 - \text{D/A}}$$

$$\text{Times-interest-earned (TIE) ratio} = \frac{\text{EBIT}}{\text{Interest charges}}$$

$$\text{EBITDA coverage ratio} = \frac{\text{EBITDA} + \text{Lease payments}}{\text{Interest} + \text{Principal payments} + \text{Lease payments}}$$

$$\text{Profit margin on sales} = \frac{\text{Net income}}{\text{Sales}}$$

$$\text{Return on total assets (ROA)} = \frac{\text{Net income}}{\text{Total assets}}$$

$$\text{Basic earning power (BEP) ratio} = \frac{\text{EBIT}}{\text{Total assets}}$$

ROA = Profit margin × Total assets turnover

$$\text{ROA} = \frac{\text{Net income}}{\text{Sales}} \times \frac{\text{Sales}}{\text{Total assets}}$$

$$\text{Return on common equity (ROE)} = \frac{\text{Net income}}{\text{Common equity}}$$

$$\text{ROE} = \text{ROA} \times \text{Equity multiplier}$$

$$= \text{Profit margin} \times \text{Total assets turnover} \times \text{Equity multiplier}$$

$$= \frac{\text{Net income}}{\text{Sales}} \times \frac{\text{Sales}}{\text{Total assets}} \times \frac{\text{Total assets}}{\text{Common equity}}$$

$$\text{Return on investors' capital} = \frac{\text{Net income} + \text{Interest}}{\text{Debt} + \text{Equity}}$$

$$\text{Price/earnings (P/E) ratio} = \frac{\text{Price per share}}{\text{Earnings per share}}$$

$$\text{Price/cash flow ratio} = \frac{\text{Price per share}}{\text{Cash flow per share}}$$

$$\text{Book value per share} = \frac{\text{Common equity}}{\text{Shares outstanding}}$$

$$\text{Market/book (M/B) ratio} = \frac{\text{Market price per share}}{\text{Book value per share}}$$

$$\text{EVA} = \text{Net income} - \left(\text{Equity capital} \times \% \text{ Cost of equity capital} \right)$$

$$\text{EVA} = \text{Equity capital} \times (\text{ROE} - \% \text{ Cost of equity capital})$$

CHAPTER 6

$$r = r^* + \text{IP} + \text{DRP} + \text{LP} + \text{MRP}$$

$$r_{RF} = r^* + \text{IP}$$

Considering cross term, $r_{RF} = r^* + I + (r^* \times I)$. Assume no cross term, unless specified.

$$r = r_{RF} + \text{DRP} + \text{LP} + \text{MRP}$$

$$\text{IP}_N = \frac{I_1 + I_2 + \cdots + I_N}{N}$$

CHAPTER 7

$$V_B = \sum_{t=1}^{N} \frac{\text{INT}}{(1 + r_d)^t} + \frac{M}{(1 + r_d)^N}$$

$$\text{Price of callable bond} = \sum_{t=1}^{N} \frac{\text{INT}}{(1 + r_d)^t} + \frac{\text{Call price}}{(1 + r_d)^N}$$

$$\text{Current yield} = \frac{\text{Annual interest}}{\text{Bond's current price}}$$

$$V_B = \sum_{t=1}^{2N} \frac{\text{INT}/2}{(1 + r_d/2)^t} + \frac{M}{(1 + r_d/2)^{2N}}$$

CHAPTER 8

Expected rate of return $= \hat{r} = \sum_{i=1}^{N} P_i r_i$

Variance $= \sigma^2 = \sum_{i=1}^{N} (r_i - \hat{r})^2 P_i$

Standard deviation $= \sigma = \sqrt{\sum_{i=1}^{N} (r_i - \hat{r})^2 P_i}$

Estimated $\sigma = S = \sqrt{\dfrac{\sum_{t=1}^{N} (\bar{r}_t - \bar{r}_{Avg})^2}{N - 1}}$

$CV = \dfrac{\sigma}{\hat{r}}$

$\hat{r}_p = \sum_{i=1}^{N} w_i \hat{r}_i$

$\sigma_p = \sqrt{\sum_{j=1}^{N} (r_{pj} - \hat{r}_p)^2 P_j}$

$b_p = \sum_{i=1}^{N} w_i b_i$

$RP_i = (r_M - r_{RF})b_i = (RP_M)b_i$

$SML = r_i = r_{RF} + (r_M - r_{RF})b_i$

CHAPTER 9

$\hat{P}_0 = \text{PV of expected future dividends} = \sum_{t=1}^{\infty} \dfrac{D_t}{(1 + r_s)^t}$

$\hat{P}_0 = \dfrac{D_0(1 + g)}{r_s - g} = \dfrac{D_1}{r_s - g}$

$\hat{r}_s = \dfrac{D_1}{P_0} + g$

Capital gains yield $= \dfrac{\hat{P}_1 - P_0}{P_0}$

Dividend yield $= \dfrac{D_1}{P_0}$

For a constant growth stock, $\hat{P}_N = P_0(1 + g)^N$

For a zero growth stock, $\hat{P}_0 = \dfrac{D}{r_s}$

Horizon value $= \hat{P}_N = \dfrac{D_{N+1}}{r_s - g}$

$V_{Company} = \dfrac{FCF_1}{(1 + WACC)^1} + \dfrac{FCF_2}{(1 + WACC)^2} + \cdots + \dfrac{FCF_\infty}{(1 + WACC)^\infty}$

Terminal value $= V_{Company\ at\ t=N} = \dfrac{FCF_{N+1}}{WACC - g_{FCF}}$

$$V_p = \frac{D_p}{r_p}$$

$$\hat{r}_p = \frac{D_p}{V_p}$$

CHAPTER 10

After-tax component cost of debt $= r_d(1 - T)$

Component cost of preferred stock $= r_p = \dfrac{D_p}{P_p}$

$r_s = \hat{r}_s = r_{RF} + RP = D_1/P_0 + g$

$r_s = $ Bond yield + Risk premium

$r_e = \dfrac{D_1}{P_0(1 - F)} + g$

$g = $ (Retention rate)(ROE) $= $ (1.0 − Payout rate)(ROE)

$RE_{Breakpoint} = \dfrac{\text{Addition to retained earnings}}{\text{Equity fraction}}$

$WACC = w_d r_d(1 - T) + w_p r_p + w_c r_s$

CHAPTER 11

$$NPV = CF_0 + \frac{CF_1}{(1 + r)^1} + \frac{CF_2}{(1 + r)^2} + \cdots + \frac{CF_N}{(1 + r)^N}$$

$$= \sum_{t=0}^{N} \frac{CF_t}{(1 + r)^t}$$

$$IRR: \sum_{t=0}^{N} \frac{CF_t}{(1 + IRR)^t} = 0$$

MIRR: PV costs = PV terminal value

$$\sum_{t=0}^{N} \frac{COF}{(1 + r)^t} = \frac{\displaystyle\sum_{t=0}^{N} CIF_t(1 + r)^{N-t}}{(1 + MIRR)^N}$$

$$PV\ costs = \frac{TV}{(1 + MIRR)^N}$$

$$Payback = \text{Number of years prior to full recovery} + \frac{\text{Unrecovered cost at start of full recovery year}}{\text{Cash flow during full recovery year}}$$

CHAPTER 14

$EBIT = PQ - VQ - F$

$$Q_{BE} = \frac{F}{P - V}$$

$$EPS = \frac{(S - FC - VC - I)(1 - T)}{\text{Shares outstanding}} = \frac{(EBIT - I)(1 - T)}{\text{Shares outstanding}}$$

$$b_L = b_U[1 + (1 - T)(D/E)]$$

$$b_U = b_L/[1 + (1 - T)(D/E)]$$

$$r_s = r_{RF} + \text{Premium for business risk} + \text{Premium for financial risk}$$

CHAPTER 15

$$\text{Dividends} = \text{Net income} - [(\text{Target equity ratio})(\text{Total capital budget})]$$

CHAPTER 16

$$\begin{matrix} \text{Inventory} \\ \text{conversion} \\ \text{period} \end{matrix} + \begin{matrix} \text{Average} \\ \text{collection} \\ \text{period} \end{matrix} - \begin{matrix} \text{Payables} \\ \text{deferral} \\ \text{period} \end{matrix} = \begin{matrix} \text{Cash} \\ \text{conversion} \\ \text{cycle} \end{matrix}$$

$$\text{Inventory conversion period} = \frac{\text{Inventory}}{\text{Cost of goods sold}/365}$$

$$\text{Average collection period} = DSO = \frac{\text{Receivables}}{\text{Sales}/365}$$

$$\text{Payables deferral period} = \frac{\text{Payables}}{\text{Cost of goods sold}/365}$$

$$\text{Accounts receivable} = \text{Credit sales per day} \times \text{Length of collection period}$$

$$ADS = \frac{(\text{Units sold})(\text{Sales price})}{365} = \frac{\text{Annual sales}}{365}$$

$$\text{Receivables} = (ADS)(DSO)$$

$$\text{Nominal annual cost of trade credit} = \frac{\text{Discount \%}}{100 - \text{Discount \%}} \times \frac{365}{\text{Days credit is outstanding} - \text{Discount period}}$$

$$\text{Simple interest rate per day} = \frac{\text{Nominal rate}}{\text{Days in year}}$$

$$\text{Simple interest charge for period} = (\text{Days in period})(\text{Rate per day})(\text{Amount of loan})$$

$$\text{Approximate annual rate}_{\text{Add-on}} = \frac{\text{Interest paid}}{(\text{Amount received})/2}$$

$$APR = (\text{Periods per year})(\text{Rate per period})$$

$$\text{Effective annual rate}_{\text{Add-on}} = (1 + r_d)^N - 1.0$$

CHAPTER 17

$$AFN = \begin{matrix} \text{Required} \\ \text{asset} \\ \text{increase} \end{matrix} - \begin{matrix} \text{Spontaneous} \\ \text{liability} \\ \text{increase} \end{matrix} - \begin{matrix} \text{Increase in} \\ \text{retained} \\ \text{earnings} \end{matrix}$$

$$= (A^*/S_0)\Delta S - (L^*/S_0)\Delta S - MS_1(RR)$$

Full capacity sales $= \dfrac{\text{Actual sales}}{\text{Percentage of capacity at which fixed assets were operated}}$

Target FA/Sales ratio $= \dfrac{\text{Actual fixed assets}}{\text{Full capacity sales}}$

Required level of FA $=$ (Target FA/Sales ratio)(Projected sales)

CHAPTER 18

Exercise value $=$ Current price of stock $-$ Strike price

$$V = P[N(d_1)] - Xe^{-r_{RF}t}[N(d_2)]$$

$$d_1 = \frac{\ln(P/X) + [r_{RF} + (\sigma^2/2)]t}{\sigma\sqrt{t}}$$

$$d_2 = d_1 - \sigma\sqrt{t}$$

Values of the Areas under the Standard Normal Distribution Function

z	0.00	0.01	0.02	0.03	0.04	0.05	0.06	0.07	0.08	0.09
0.0	.0000	.0040	.0080	.0120	.0160	.0199	.0239	.0279	.0319	.0359
0.1	.0398	.0438	.0478	.0517	.0557	.0596	.0636	.0675	.0714	.0753
0.2	.0793	.0832	.0871	.0910	.0948	.0987	.1026	.1064	.1103	.1141
0.3	.1179	.1217	.1255	.1293	.1331	.1368	.1406	.1443	.1480	.1517
0.4	.1554	.1591	.1628	.1664	.1700	.1736	.1772	.1808	.1844	.1879
0.5	.1915	.1950	.1985	.2019	.2054	.2088	.2123	.2157	.2190	.2224
0.6	.2257	.2291	.2324	.2357	.2389	.2422	.2454	.2486	.2517	.2549
0.7	.2580	.2611	.2642	.2673	.2704	.2734	.2764	.2794	.2823	.2852
0.8	.2881	.2910	.2939	.2967	.2995	.3023	.3051	.3078	.3106	.3133
0.9	.3159	.3186	.3212	.3238	.3264	.3289	.3315	.3340	.3365	.3389
1.0	.3413	.3438	.3461	.3485	.3508	.3531	.3554	.3577	.3599	.3621
1.1	.3643	.3665	.3686	.3708	.3729	.3749	.3770	.3790	.3810	.3830
1.2	.3849	.3869	.3888	.3907	.3925	.3944	.3962	.3980	.3997	.4015
1.3	.4032	.4049	.4066	.4082	.4099	.4115	.4131	.4147	.4162	.4177
1.4	.4192	.4207	.4222	.4236	.4251	.4265	.4279	.4292	.4306	.4319
1.5	.4332	.4345	.4357	.4370	.4382	.4394	.4406	.4418	.4429	.4441
1.6	.4452	.4463	.4474	.4484	.4495	.4505	.4515	.4525	.4535	.4545
1.7	.4554	.4564	4573	.4582	.4591	.4599	.4608	.4616	.4625	.4633
1.8	.4641	.4649	.4656	.4664	.4671	.4678	.4686	.4693	.4699	.4706
1.9	.4713	.4719	.4726	.4732	.4738	.4744	.4750	.4756	.4761	.4767
2.0	.4773	.4778	.4783	.4788	.4793	.4798	.4803	.4808	.4812	.4817
2.1	.4821	.4826	.4830	.4834	.4838	.4842	.4846	.4850	.4854	.4857
2.2	.4861	.4864	.4868	.4871	.4875	.4878	.4881	.4884	.4887	.4890
2.3	.4893	.4896	.4898	.4901	.4904	.4906	.4909	.4911	.4913	.4916
2.4	.4918	.4920	.4922	.4925	.4927	.4929	.4931	.4932	.4934	.4936
2.5	.4938	.4940	.4941	.4943	.4945	.4946	.4948	.4949	.4951	.4952
2.6	.4953	.4955	.4956	.4957	.4959	.4960	.4961	.4962	.4963	.4964
2.7	.4965	.4966	.4967	.4968	.4969	.4970	.4971	.4972	.4973	.4974
2.8	.4974	.4975	.4976	.4977	.4977	.4978	.4979	.4979	.4980	.4981
2.9	.4981	.4982	.4982	.4982	.4984	.4984	.4985	.4985	.4986	.4986
3.0	.4987	.4987	.4987	.4988	.4988	.4989	.4989	.4989	.4990	.4990

CHAPTER 19

$$\frac{\text{Forward exchange rate}}{\text{Spot exchange rate}} = \frac{1 + r_h}{1 + r_f}$$

$$P_h = (P_f)(\text{Spot rate})$$

$$\text{Spot rate} = \frac{P_h}{P_f}$$

CHAPTER 20

Price paid for bond with warrants = Straight-debt value of bond + Value of warrants

$$\text{Conversion price} = P_c = \frac{\text{Par value of bond given up}}{\text{Shares received}}$$

$$\text{Conversion ratio} = CR = \frac{\text{Par value of bond given up}}{P_c}$$

INDEX

FREQUENTLY USED SYMBOLS/ABBREVIATIONS

ACP	Average collection period
ADR	American depository receipt
APR	Annual percentage rate
A/R	Accounts receivable
b	Beta coefficient, a measure of an asset's riskiness
b_L	Levered beta
b_U	Unlevered beta
BEP	Basic earning power
BVPS	Book value per share
CAPM	Capital Asset Pricing Model
CCC	Cash conversion cycle
CF	Cash flow; CF_t is the cash flow in Period t
CFPS	Cash flow per share
CR	Conversion ratio
CV	Coefficient of variation
D_p	Dividend of preferred stock
D_t	Dividend in Period t
DCF	Discounted cash flow
D/E	Debt-to-equity ratio
DPS	Dividends per share
DRIP	Dividend reinvestment plan
DRP	Default risk premium
DSO	Days sales outstanding
EAR	Effective annual rate, EFF%
EBIT	Earnings before interest and taxes; net operating income
EBITDA	Earnings before interest, taxes, depreciation, and amortization
EPS	Earnings per share
EVA	Economic value added
F	(1) Fixed operating costs
	(2) Flotation cost
FCF	Free cash flow
FV_N	Future value for Year N
FVA_N	Future value of an annuity for N years
g	Growth rate in earnings, dividends, and stock prices
I	Interest rate; also referred to as r
I/YR	Interest rate key on some calculators
INT	Interest payment in dollars
IP	Inflation premium
IPO	Initial public offering
IRR	Internal rate of return
LP	Liquidity premium
M	Maturity value of a bond
M/B	Market-to-book ratio
MIRR	Modified internal rate of return
MRP	Maturity risk premium
MVA	Market value added
N	Calculator key denoting number of periods
$N(d_i)$	Represents area under a standard normal distribution function
NOPAT	Net operating profit after taxes
NOWC	Net operating working capital
NPV	Net present value
P	(1) Price of a share of stock in Period t; P_0 = price of the stock today
	(2) Sales price per unit of product sold

P_c	Conversion price
P_f	Price of good in foreign country
P_h	Price of good in home country
P/E	Price/earnings ratio
PMT	Payment of an annuity
PPP	Purchasing power parity
PV	Present value
PVA_N	Present value of an annuity for N years
Q	Quantity produced or sold
Q_{BE}	Breakeven quantity
r	(1) A percentage discount rate, or cost of capital; also referred to as I
	(2) Nominal risk-adjusted required rate of return
$\bar{r}$	"r bar," historic, or realized, rate of return
$\hat{r}$	"r hat," an expected rate of return
r*	Real risk-free rate of return
r_d	Before-tax cost of debt
r_e	Cost of new common stock (outside equity)
r_f	Interest rate in foreign country
r_h	Interest rate in home country
r_i	Required return for an individual firm or security
r_M	Return for "the market," or an "average" stock
r_{NOM}	Nominal rate of interest; also referred to as I_{NOM}
r_p	(1) Cost of preferred stock
	(2) Portfolio's return
r_{PER}	Periodic rate of return
r_{RF}	Rate of return on a risk-free security
r_s	(1) Cost of retained earnings
	(2) Required return on common stock
ρ	Correlation coefficient; also denoted as R when using historical data
ROA	Return on assets
ROE	Return on equity
RP	Risk premium
RP_M	Market risk premium
RR	Retention rate
S	(1) Sales
	(2) Estimated standard deviation for sample data
SML	Security Market Line
Σ	Summation sign
σ	Standard deviation
σ^2	Variance
t	Time period
T	Marginal income tax rate
TV_N	A stock's horizon, or terminal, value
TIE	Times interest earned
V	Variable cost per unit
V_B	Bond value
V_p	Value of preferred stock
VC	Total variable costs
WACC	Weighted averaged cost of capital
X	Exercise price of option
YTC	Yield to call
YTM	Yield to maturity